A HISTORY *of the*
FAR EAST
in MODERN TIMES

HAROLD M. VINACKE

University of Cincinnati

SIXTH EDITION

New York: Appleton-Century-Crofts, Inc.

A HISTORY *of the*
FAR EAST
in MODERN TIMES

PREFACE TO THE SIXTH EDITION

BEFORE World War II the term "Far East" was applied primarily to China, Japan, Korea, and the Russian territories east of Lake Baikal rather than to all of the countries of eastern Asia. This restricted geographical use of the term was originally in mind in establishing the framework for this *History of the Far East in Modern Times.* Usage both established and sanctioned the restriction of the area, but there were additional reasons for accepting it. With the exception of Siam (now Thailand), the countries of southeastern Asia, as well as India, had fallen under European control. Consequently their history had been largely that of colonies of the several European countries rather than that of independent or semi-independent peoples. Thus the history of India had been of great importance, but from the standpoint of relationship it seemed more logical to bring its consideration within that of the history of the British imperial system than to tie it in with that of China and Japan. Except for the importation of Buddhism shortly after the Christian era, those countries, as well as southeastern Asia, had not been affected by India until England's control of that country brought about an indirect relationship. Similarly the Philippines, Indo-China, and the Netherlands East Indies were important in the Far East, but as appanages of the United States, France or Holland, which countries controlled their development, rather than directly in terms of that development. This condition began to change before World War II, and the tendency was accelerated in the 1940's, but the full consequences of the change are only now appearing. In addition to the implications of colonialism, none of the Oriental countries (with the exception of India) save China and Japan had separate cultures of great development; and none, up to the very recent past, had seriously affected the course of international relations and of world history. Consequently, since restriction of scope in both time and space was necessary in a single-volume treatment, it seemed, in the first editions of this work, entirely justified to restrict by acceptance of the customary terminology.

The modern period is dated from the time of the movement to bring China, and subsequently Japan and Korea, into an enlarged contact with the world. Thus "modern" is defined in terms of the Far East rather than of Europe. Institutional changes commenced after that time, even though there were significant internal movements antedating the application of foreign pressure. The Chinese and Japanese political, economic, and social systems had continued virtually unchanged for more than two hundred years before the establishment of treaty relations with Western nations.

v

A new order began to evolve after the negotiation of the first treaties. It is this which distinguishes the modern from the pre-modern period.

In this volume it would have been out of place, even if it had been possible, to enter into a comprehensive and detailed description of the institutions and cultures of pre-modern China, Japan, and Korea. All that could be attempted was to lay a foundation sufficient (1) to be built upon by making use of the reading lists appended to Chapters I and IV, and (2) to make possible the tracing of the changes which have taken place in the modern period. Since, until recently, these changes have been largely political and economic, there has been relatively more consideration of political and economic development than of social and cultural. As recent tendencies toward social, intellectual, and artistic change become more than tendencies, and as their significance becomes more fully revealed, the historical emphasis naturally shifts from the politico-economic to the cultural realm.

It must be recognized that the most important single conditioning factor in the development of the Far East in modern times has been the impact of the West. In order to withstand the pressure of the Powers the countries of the Orient which were free to do so had at once to attack the problems related to their political and economic modernization. The larger cultural background of political and economic life was more gradually adapted to the new world; and just as the foreign impact led to an over-emphasis on political development, so the rivalries of the Powers assumed a larger relative importance in the Orient than was the case in the Occident. For that reason, more space has been given to international relations in this volume than would otherwise have appeared justified. The history of the Far East, from the standpoint of movement, has been more largely political and diplomatic than it would have been if the Far Eastern countries had taken their place in the modern world at an earlier time or in a more normal and natural manner.

Thus the logic of events has determined the general treatment of the subject. The plan of the book has been similarly fixed. The streams of modern Japanese and Chinese history ran in separate channels until the struggle over Korea caused them to converge. After 1895 they continued to diverge somewhat, but never as widely as in the previous years. The attempt was made in the first, as in subsequent, editions of this work to follow these natural lines of development. Sometimes the two streams flow together, and at other times they have separated; but most of the time the two main channels have been fed by waters from Europe and America, from Korea and Siberia, and now from the colonial area.

In successive editions there has been some reorganization of materials where either the author or interested readers have felt that reorganization within the general plan would enhance the usability of the book. The attempt has been made to correct errors both of fact and of interpretation, as they have been revealed by reviewers, by readers, or by consultation of new literature on various aspects of the subject. In the latter connection, it should be pointed out here that there has been a consistent attempt with each revision to include new titles in the chapter references, for it must be recognized that much of the scholarly work on the Far East has been done during the past three decades. Thus for the improvement of this text through successive revision I am deeply indebted to monograph writers as well as to those who have been so good as to call attention to needed corrections or changes.

Beyond this, the successive revisions have enlarged the historical picture from the standpoint of time by bringing the treatment to date. Thus, in this sixth edition, there has been considerable enlargement of the text, as well as revision of the materials in the fifth edition, so as to include World War II and postwar developments to the end of 1958. The nature of those developments, furthermore, required the enlargement of the original plan to provide for more extensive treatment of the countries of Southeast Asia, Indonesia, and the Philippines. The displacement of the National Government of the Republic of China by the People's Government of the People's Republic in mainland China necessitated the addition of a new chapter on Communist China in this revision. Developments in Korea are also treated in a new chapter, as is post-occupation Japan.

While, as stated above, I have drawn on the studies of others and have had the benefit of advice of successive editors, as well as users of the book as a text, and of informed readers, the responsibility for any errors of omission or commission remains mine.

H. M. V.

Cincinnati, Ohio

CONTENTS

CHAPTER **V**

JAPAN IN TRANSITION: 1868–1894

CHAPTER **VI**

THE CONTEST FOR KOREA

CHAPTER **VII**

CUTTING THE CHINESE MELON

CHAPTER **VIII**

THE RUSSO-JAPANESE WAR

CONTENTS

CHAPTER IX

FINANCIAL IMPERIALISM IN CHINA

CHAPTER X

REFORM AND REVOLUTION IN CHINA

CHAPTER XI

THE PHANTOM REPUBLIC: 1912–1926

CHAPTER XII

THE PROGRESS OF CHINA: ECONOMIC AND SOCIAL:
1900–1931

CHAPTER XIII

THE PROGRESS OF CHINA: INTELLECTUAL AND CULTURAL

CHAPTER XIV

THE PROGRESS OF JAPAN: INTELLECTUAL, SOCIAL, AND CULTURAL

CHAPTER XV

THE POLITICAL AND ECONOMIC PROGRESS OF JAPAN: 1895–1931

CHAPTER XX

THE NATIONALIST REVOLUTION

CHAPTER XXI

THE EAST AND THE WEST: 1830–1930

CHAPTER XXII

JAPAN IN MANCHURIA

CHAPTER XXXI

SOUTHEASTERN ASIA

CHAPTER XXXII

THE PHILIPPINES AND INDONESIA

CONTENTS

A HISTORY *of the*

FAR EAST

in MODERN TIMES

CHAPTER I

CHINA UNDER THE MANCHUS

1. THE COUNTRY AND ITS RESOURCES

THE modern history of the Far Eastern countries begins with the drawing of those states from their long-continued seclusion into contact with the Occidental world. This history has been shaped in large part by outside forces, the operation of which in each case has resulted in a modification of ancient cultures and long-established and firmly-rooted institutions. If these changes and the historical developments attending them are to be understood, the general condition of society at the beginning of the modern period must be appreciated. Consequently the attempt must be made to describe pre-modern China in its many-sided life as a necessary preliminary to the tracing of the pattern of its history since 1842.

At the time of the opening of the East to intercourse with the West the Chinese Empire consisted of: (1) China proper, comprising the eighteen provinces; (2) Manchuria, now divided into three provinces; (3) such dependencies as Tibet, Mongolia, and Sinkiang, with which close supervisory relations were maintained; and (4) nominally vassal states such as Korea and Annam. Excluding the vassal states, but including the dependencies, China had a total area of 4,277,170 square miles of compact territory—an area exceeding that of the United States, including Alaska, Hawaii and Puerto Rico, by 705,947 square miles. We may place the region geographically, and to some extent climatically, by observing that it extends, from north to south, from the extremes presented by Vancouver, B. C., on the north and Mexico City on the south. Thus it falls largely in the north temperate zone, with variations ranging from the tropical to the extremely cold regions.

This made possible a well diversified agricultural life, with the staple crops including rice, cotton, sugar, tea, wheat, barley, millet, and other cereals. Because of this varied productivity the Chinese were able not only to provide themselves with food, but also to develop an industrial activity sufficient to supply their limited needs for clothing, implements, and ornaments. It made possible the development of as extensive a trade as the limited means of communication permitted.

Add to this the richness in the sub-soil or mineral wealth, and at once the explanation of the self-sufficiency of China begins to appear. Coal and iron, copper, tin, lead, antimony, and silver—all are found in the country and in pre-modern times they were sufficiently worked to supply the primitive needs of the people. Economically, then, the Empire was sufficient unto itself, and hence was regarded with some envy by early European travelers and traders. At no time before the modern period did the Chinese look abroad to supply their real needs, whereas other peoples have always, if intermittently, been interested in establishing trade contacts with China. This interest has unquestionably led to an over-estimate of the natural resources of the country, but with all due allowance for exaggeration it represents an appreciation of a reality—that of a basically richly-endowed country.

The diversity in agricultural production not only was made possible by a wide variation in climate, but indicates as great a range of physical features as that presented by the United States. Over against the desert and pasture lands of northwestern China and Mongolia may be set the fertile loess plains of the north, watered and often inundated by the Yellow River —"China's Sorrow." South of the Yellow River lies the broad central area drained by the Yangtse River, the greatest waterway of China and one of the greatest in the world. Still farther south lies the basin of the West River and its confluents. These three river basins represent as many natural geographical regions, each one distinct, with its own contributions to make to the life of the Chinese people, and yet each presenting many features of similarity to the others. The most important of these similarities is the great fertility of the soil from north to south.

The monotony of the plains is relieved by mountain ranges, which rise ever higher to the west and the southwest until they reach the Himalayan system. There are four main chains of mountains—the Tien Shan, the Kwanlun, the Hingan, and the Himalayan—which serve, as do the river systems, to distinguish different geographical areas. They further serve the life of the country by furnishing much of its mineral wealth. But where the rivers facilitate communication and intercourse, the mountain ranges obstruct them, making Szechuan province virtually an empire within China, cutting it off from constant and effective contact with the rest of the country, and retarding relations with, and control of, the other southwestern provinces. On the other hand, the western chain of mountains has served as a barrier between China and the regions to the west.

<h3 style="text-align:center">2. THE PEOPLE</h3>

In 1842 not only was China one of the largest political-geographic areas in the world, but it was also one of the greatest population units. Only estimates of population are available, due to faulty methods of census-taking, but that for 1812—362,467,182—may be accepted as fairly accurate.[1]

---

[1] WILLIAMS, S. W., *Middle Kingdom*, vol. I, p. 263.

Because of the pressure of population the people on the whole were poor, and the standard of living, judged by modern Western standards, was low —although for the masses it was not materially lower than the standard in seventeenth- and eighteenth-century Europe.

The people now known collectively as the Chinese undoubtedly consist of a blending of the various stocks which came into the country from Central Asia originally and from the northwest subsequently. The first migrants seem to have settled in the Yellow River valley, pushing the aboriginal inhabitants farther south. They and, in turn, their successors were driven southwards by succeeding waves of migration. After these movements of peoples stopped, the blending process began, or proceeded further toward completion. At the present time remnants of the original inhabitants, such as the Miao people, may be found in southwestern China; others, driven southeast, found their way into Indo-China, Siam, and Malaysia. Physical differences between the southern and northern Chinese are still clearly perceptible, preserved partly because of climatic differences and partly because of imperfect assimilation of stocks, due to the pushing of one group out by another rather than to the overlaying of one by another. At the time of the Manchu conquest the cultural assimilation had proceeded further than the physical.

3. PRE-MODERN SOCIETY

Both theoretically and actually the people were divided into five divisions or occupational groups. Highest in the social scale were the scholars or literati, from whom the officials were selected. Next came the farmers, numerically by far the largest group and the most important for the maintenance of life in a self-sufficient state. The artisans ranked third, with the merchants and traders fourth, while at the bottom of the social scale were the servants and the soldiers. There is a Chinese proverb to the effect that "good iron is not used for nails, nor are soldiers made of good men."

Partly because the road to official position and preferment lay through learning, but also because of the general esteem in which learning was held, the scholars constituted the highest class in Chinese society. All of the sages urged respect for the learned, whose success reflected glory upon the entire community. Furthermore, the road of the scholar was rough and toilsome. The difficulties encountered caused a high mortality among those seeking degrees, and this of course enhanced the prestige of the successful.

The emphasis on learning did not, however, lead to the establishment of "schools" as we understand this term in the West, nor did it result in a progressive broadening of knowledge. In fact, education came to constitute one of the greatest barriers to enlightenment in the Empire. This was due in large part to the exclusive emphasis laid upon reproducing the ideas and sayings of the Ancients, but also to the educational objective, which was preparation for the examinations.[2] These were set entirely on the basis of the Classics, and candidates knew that their time would be wasted if they devoted it to study outside of the literature on which the examinations were based.

The educational system produced stability through its emphasis on the past, and consequently it amply served the ends of a stable society conscious of having perfected its culture. It had the merit, as far as the examination system was honestly applied, of attracting men of ability to the public service, in so far as a purely reproductive training developed, and the examinations revealed, a talent fitted for the performance of public duties. It produced persevering scholars of a high refinement according to the standards of the time. But in spite of its good features, and notwithstanding its utility in preserving and perpetuating the best elements of a developed social life, the fact must be emphasized that it did not adequately serve a society which had to adapt itself to new ideas and practices.

The prestige attached to membership in the class of scholars caused many to aspire to it—or caused their families to aspire for them. Often one member of a family would be devoted to learning, as in other countries one child might be consecrated to the church. Such a fortunate individual would be supported by the family, or sometimes by the village, if he were a promising student and his family could not afford to give him an education. At the age of seven or eight he would attend the village school, an institution maintained by those who had children to be educated; and while his brothers worked or played, he would pore over his books from early to late. His task was to learn by rote the various books set before him, beginning usually with the "Trimetrical Classic," followed by such an elementary book as the "Thousand Character Classic." From these he proceeded to the "Four Books"—the Confucian Analects, the Great Learning, the Doctrine of the Mean, and the works of Mencius. These were followed by the Poetical Classic, the Book of History, the Book of Changes, and the Spring and Autumn Annals. All of these the pupil was expected gradually to memorize, with imperfect understanding and with little or no explanation of their meaning. Further learning consisted of a mastery of the innumerable commentaries on the Classics. At the same time the embryo scholar began to learn to form characters as a necessary antecedent to his entrance upon the next stage of his education. This consisted of mastering the art of essay-writing, preliminary to undergoing examination for the lowest degree.

Once in three or twice in five years an examiner came to the province from Peking. Prior to his arrival qualifying examinations were held in the

2 The system of civil service examinations dates from the Han dynasty (B.C. 206–A.D. 214), but it was not firmly established in its modern form until the T'ang dynasty (618–906).

several districts of the province for the purpose of selecting the candidates to appear for the provincial examinations. Five hundred or more would be found competing in the district examination. On the first day three themes would be announced for treatment, two in the form of a classical essay and one in the poetical form. Starting at daylight, few candidates finished before three or four o'clock in the afternoon; some might not finish until midnight; and the slowest, if permitted, might write until the next morning. After an interval of one or two days for considering the results, the examination would be continued, with perhaps half of the original number of contestants. There were in all four separate sittings in this district examination, with some of the candidates eliminated after each sitting.

The next competition, limited to candidates successful in the district examinations, took place in the prefectural city. The contestants came from all of the districts in the prefecture and numbered into the thousands. The examination procedure was similar to that followed in the district city, although the standards of achievement were higher and the essay subjects were more difficult. Success in the prefectural examination was rewarded by the granting of a degree—the Hsiu Ts'ai or Bachelor's Degree.

The holders of this degree were entitled to compete in the provincial examinations for the next higher award—the degree of Chü-Jén. Those who achieved it might receive an appointment to office or compete in the metropolitan examinations for the third degree, the Chin Shih. The highest degree of all (the Hanlin) was rather an office, as it admitted to the Imperial Academy and to a salary.

This education might entitle the student to an official appointment, provided he was successful in the examinations, but it failed to prepare him to grapple satisfactorily with the complex problems of modern life. Failing in the examinations, or finding himself among the large number of those qualified for official position in excess of the offices to be filled, the scholar could support himself in only two ways—by teaching or by doing clerical work. In spite of the respect for learning, the emoluments of the teacher were small. Furthermore, for each school there were always several applicants, whom the patrons could play against one another with a view to lowering the teaching cost.

Thus the life of even the successful scholar was not free from anxiety unless he gained admission to officialdom. And in order to secure office, in spite of the theory, it was usually necessary to have either influence or wealth, for those controlling the appointments expected a reward for favors extended. Consequently there were large numbers among the literati who had a very precarious economic existence in spite of the prestige which they enjoyed. In a material way, the scholar might derive only a meager livelihood from teaching. Among his privileges, however, was a standing at the magistrate's yamen not enjoyed by the common man, and in case he was an offender against the law he might not be beaten with the bamboo.

Among people who emphasized learning as did the Chinese, it seems strange, on first thought, that scientific knowledge failed to develop, or that large professional classes should not have existed; but such indeed was the case. Medical practice was largely quackery, because knowledge was not gained from experiment; the legal profession, as such, had no existence; engineering and mechanical knowledge had been left in an undeveloped condition after a promising start. The fêng shui,[3] for example, had more to do with the location and construction of buildings than did an analysis of the problems confronted. This state of arrested development in all branches of learning, it must be reiterated, was due fundamentally to an educational system (1) established on the basis of an acceptance of the teachings of the past as embodying the wisdom of all times, and (2) motivated by a desire to prepare for examinations set for the purpose of selecting officials whose primary qualifications were considered to be the ability to write essays well and to reproduce the maxims of the philosophers. It was also due to the lack of contact with other societies which had undergone as great an advancement as China. Out of such contact and the resultant comparisons of ideas and practices would have come a stimulus to development which was lacking. This was, perhaps, as fundamental a reason for the arrested development as was the educational emphasis. Certainly both need to be considered in seeking an explanation of it.

About eighty per cent of the people of China were engaged in agriculture. They did not live on farms, as the agricultural population of the United States does, but in villages, which sometimes consisted of only a few houses, sometimes of several hundred. With so large a population engaged in tilling the soil it was inevitable that in some parts of the country one village would seem to begin almost where another left off. To an American the peculiarity of the Chinese landscape lay in the fact that no houses were to be seen outside the villages.

Since so large a part of the population lived in villages, it will be well to consider briefly the make-up and life of the village community. Because the villages were usually named after one or two families, the limited number of surnames meant a multiplication of Chang, Wang, Li, and other chuang or villages. But sometimes the name came from a temple, if the village contained one at a comparatively early time, or from the distance to the seat of the district magistrate. Often a nickname was given

---

[3] The doctrine of "wind and water." "The earth and air are supposed to be filled with good and evil influences, and these must be taken into consideration before the site of any building is chosen, or any grave is located, or a city begun." K. S. LATOURETTE, *The Development of China*, p. 124.

the village, which came to be known by it, both unofficially and officially, rather than by the original name.[4]

The life of the village was centered in the temple, whether ancestral or Buddhistic, although there was no influential priestly class to guide and admonish the people. The temple grounds, or the area adjacent to them, usually provided the place for the weekly or bi-weekly market to which the people brought their surplus produce to exchange for the goods of the itinerant traders who moved from one market to another. They also provided space for the theatrical entertainments which were the primary source of amusement for the people. And they furnished neutral territory on which the "peace-talkers" could meet to compose the innumerable disputes which arose between the individual inhabitants, or the members of families.

Socially China was organized on the basis of the family rather than the individual. To this rule the village was naturally no exception. The Chinese family, furthermore, consisted of much more than husband, wife, and children. The young man brought his wife to the home of his parents, whose parents might also be living. Thus within the same establishment might be found a great-grandfather, grandfathers, fathers and their sons, all under the control of the oldest male, or, in case the great-grandmother or grandmother outlived her husband, under her authority. A man thirty, forty, or even fifty years old was not the master of his household merely by reason of his age.

Where this patriarchal conception of the family existed it might be expected that particular emphasis would be laid on its perpetuation and on relationships within the family. Since this was so, the individual was not free to marry or remain single as he chose, but his marriage was arranged for him at an early age to ensure a continuation of the group; and one of his primary duties was to have sons to carry on the family name. Since the family could be perpetuated only through male children, girls were at a discount and boys at a premium. The birth of a son was an occasion of great rejoicing, while the coming of a daughter passed virtually unnoticed where it was not actually lamented. This difference was further emphasized by the fact that girls on marriage severed their connection with their own families and merged their fortunes with that of the husband. Thus not only could they not perpetuate the family, but their labor and service were early lost to it. The only advantage to be gained by affording them educational or other opportunities lay in the possibility of increasing the chances of making a favorable alliance and thus strengthening the family.

One may see the prevalence of this view of the family in the grounds

[4] See SMITH, A. H., *Village Life in China,* ch. 3, for a discussion of village nomenclature.

recognized for divorce. A man might be freed from his wife for any one of the following reasons: barrenness, lasciviousness, disregard of her husband's parents, talkativeness, thievish propensities, envious and suspicious temper, and inveterate infirmity. This, however, was possible only if the wife had parents to whom she might be returned; in case she had not yet mourned for her husband's parents during the customary period; or if she had not passed from a state of poverty to one of riches with him. On the other hand, the only recourse of the wife, except in very extreme cases, lay in the pressure which the family from which she came might exert to protect her interests. Thus divorce in fact was a rare occurrence.

The development of ancestor-worship gave added importance to bearing sons and providing for their marriage. A father who had no heir would have no offerings laid before his tablet after his death, and for the same reason he would fail in his duty to his father and his father's father. Thus religious practice grew out of the emphasis on the family and, in turn, added to the emphasis.

Concubinage also grew out of, and was justified by, the obligation to continue the family line. In case of barrenness or failure of the wife to give birth to a son, the husband, if well-to-do, might take one or more "secondary wives" or concubines. They had a status inferior to that of the wife, both legally and in authority within the home. Their children were considered as the children of the wife, from the standpoint of obedience and also from that of mourning in case of death.

Within the family great importance naturally was attached to filial obedience, but the relations of husband and wife, of brother to brother, and of brother and sister, were all regulated under the direction and subject to the authority of the head of the house. This should have led to harmony and household quiet, but perhaps because of the monotony of life, and in part because of the lack of privacy due to the number of persons living within the family compound, dissension was frequently rife. If the quarrel became noticeable it might easily attract the neighbors, on the theory that what was anybody's business became everybody's business; for the family life itself was not lived in the privacy which is accepted as natural in the West.

Inter-family relations within the village were adjusted, as the common affairs were carried on, through the medium of a Council of Elders under the direction of a village headman. This council was never formally selected at one time, but might consist of the heads of households, or of a few persons generally recognized as capable of carrying on village business. The practice differed from one section of the country to another. Often difficulties were adjusted through the efforts of those who may be described as "peace-talkers"—individuals who were drawn in or who took it upon themselves to find a basis of agreement between the parties to a particular controversy. Usually they were rewarded for their services by a feast.

The land outside the village was held in individual ownership by the villagers. As a result of continued subdivision among the sons after the death of the father or on his retirement, holdings were small and often scattered. Consequently many mouths had to be filled from the production of what, to an American farmer, would seem a totally inadequate allotment of land. Hence the Chinese farmer was led to extremely skillful intensive farming, and even with primitive implements he was able to get a large return from the soil. This, however, demanded unceasing toil on the part of all and the practice of numberless small economies in farming. Since the soil had been worked by so many preceding generations it had continually to be restored. All waste and refuse was carefully collected and prepared for use as fertilizing material. Modern science in the West is just beginning to give the farmer knowledge of soil treatment which the Chinese had gained from the experience of their ancestors.

But with all of his skill the Chinese farmer gained only a bare subsistence from his small holding of land. Most of the farmers lived from year to year, able to make ends meet, to buy seed and replace implements, to provide for weddings and funerals, and to help support the village theatricals and take part in an occasional feast, but unable to lay by sufficient reserves to banish the specter of want. If crops failed because of drought or flood, or if the returns were under the normal, there was no way of meeting the emergency. Famine conditions would ensue, with all of their attendant horrors—subsistence on roots and herbs; the break-up of families, the daughters being sold into slavery; and for many, actual starvation.

Even in normally good years there would be some who could not make ends meet and who might have to be cared for by the more fortunate members of the family, if such there were. Sometimes they were able to tide themselves over by gleaning from the fields after their neighbors had harvested, and if opportunity afforded they might pilfer before the harvest. This possibility led each farmer to watch his crops day and night during the growing season and until they had been stored after the harvest. Often the entire village united to hire watchers, or the inhabitants took turns in standing guard. The apprehended thief was liable to harsh treatment at the hands of the villagers.

Thus, in spite of the natural fertility of the soil and the skill of the farmer, and in spite of the natural resources of China, the Chinese farming population lived a precarious life. To a great extent the intense struggle for existence resulted from the size of the population, together with the constant tendency toward increase because of the premium on birth. It was a struggle for the necessities of life and not for its luxuries. Mud-walled and thatched-roofed houses, unheated and unadorned; cotton clothing, padded for winter; a subsistence allowance of food; and a round of unceasing labor—were what the majority of the people had to look forward to and what they looked back upon.

And yet the life of the people was not hopeless, nor was it altogether devoid of interest. Occasional theatrical entertainments relieved the monotony of toil. Every pretext for a feast was seized upon—eating being one of the chief sources of enjoyment. And gambling opportunities were eagerly sought, even though loss meant actual suffering.

The artisan class ranked next to the farmers. Since industry was in the handicrafts stage, there was no industrial class divided sharply into two groups—the employers, or capitalists, and the workers—as there is in most Western countries today. All work was done in a small establishment which served as the home as well as the shop. Often the shop opened on the street, so that the passer-by could see the men at work. The establishment consisted of the master, journeymen, and apprentices. A long term of apprenticeship, usually seven years, had to be served before the aspirant was admitted to the craft as a workman or as a master. As the number of apprentices to each journeyman in the shop was limited by the craft rules, there was little danger of an excessive supply of workmen or of an overexpansion of the industry. After serving his apprenticeship the individual might remain in the shop, receiving pay for his work instead of the maintenance given him as an apprentice; he mght find employment in some other shop; or he might go into business for himself. Usually, however, he continued to work, at least for a time, in the same shop.

The larger undertakings were often operated on the basis of a partnership of two or more men, but the corporate or joint-stock form of organization was unknown. The partners were jointly and severally responsible for the obligations of the firm and for the fulfillment of its engagements. And this was reënforced by the prevailing system of family responsibility for its members. It has become almost proverbial that the word of a Chinese is as good as his bond, which indicates that individual business standards were comparatively high. It must be recognized, however, that the social organization, with its system of family responsibility, and the close economic organization, helped to establish and perpetuate these high standards.

The entire craft was organized into a guild, to which all but apprentices might belong and which all were expected to support. The guild organization consisted of a president, an executive committee elected at the annual meeting, and a secretary, who was invariably one of the literati and a degree-holder, and the real administrator of the guild affairs.

The guild controlled prices, fixed quality, and determined wages within the craft to the extent that the minimum price and minimum wages were

decided upon in its annual meetings and minimum standards were established. The minimum might be, but seldom was, raised at the discretion
of the master. This control had the effect of preventing unfair competition
and thus helped to stabilize the industry, just as did the limitation of the
number of apprentices who might be received.

Fully as important a work was that of adjusting disputes between guild
members, between masters and workmen, and between the guild and other
industries. Rarely was there appeal from the decisions of the guild arbitration committee to the magistrate, for he almost invariably found it expedient to accept the committee's award. The only other recourse was to withdraw from the organization rather than accept its penalties, but this extreme step was seldom or never taken because it put the individual at the
mercy of his competitors. They were free to entice his workmen away from
him; they could throw innumerable petty obstacles in his way; and the
whole craft and others from whom he obtained his supplies might use their
collective power to drive him out of business.

The settlement of trade disputes and inter-craft difficulties through guild
intervention was no more important an activity than that of serving as
the connecting link between the magistrate and the crafts. While the industry ruled itself, as has been suggested, its members sometimes came into
the magistrate's yamen over actions affecting the public peace which he
could not overlook or leave for decision by the guild. In that case the
organization stood behind the individual, aiding him in his defense. The
guild secretary, as a degree-holder, had access to the magistrate on terms
enabling him to prevent too arbitrary action. He could also inform the
magistrate as to local feeling in the matter and thus prevent him from
taking action likely to cause trouble. Thus the individual as a guild member had in his dealing with officials a support which it would have been
difficult to replace from any other source. This economic group solidarity
was just as marked a feature of the life of China as was the social solidarity
represented by the family.

The magistrate, in turn, found it expedient to consult with the guild
before imposing any new taxes or increasing customary levies, or before
taking any other action affecting the craft. If he did not reach agreement
with its officers in advance he was merely courting trouble in case his action aroused opposition. He might find trade stopped and production
brought to an end. On occasion a mob could easily be raised which would
storm the yamen, loot his premises, and even threaten his life. Consequently
the successful magistrate kept on good terms with the guild officers, aiding
them, when necessary, in the enforcement of guild rules and penalties,
and working with and through them in the performance of the duties of
his office.

Many of the guilds had their own halls for meetings and for social purposes, and some of the wealthier and more important ones maintained large establishments. Here feasts and theatrical entertainments for the members were held. A poorer organization might rent the hall of another guild for its meetings and entertainments; for it must be emphasized that the guild served as a social as well as an economic organization. Its benevolent activities were also important, although perhaps not so much emphasized in the case of the craft guilds as in that of the provincial or trade guilds.

The traders and merchants were organized in much the same way as the artisans. The dealer in local products, of course, was also an artisan, and sold over the counter in the front of his establishment the goods produced in the rear. But where traders took the specialized production of the locality to other parts of the Empire they felt the need for membership in some sort of organization. This took the form of the provincial club, or guild, composed of men from different economic groups but from the same geographical area. Thus the Fukien or Shantung men in Tientsin, Peking, or Shanghai, whether they were officials or traders, would be found organized in their club. The advantage of this organization can be appreciated when one calls to mind the wide variation in dialect, amounting in some cases to a difference in the spoken language, and the important differences in custom and manner of living from district to district and from province to province. For in the north the Cantonese was really a foreigner, unable to make himself readily understood and without understanding the customs of the region. More important to him, he was likely to find himself receiving the treatment accorded to foreigners in a strange land. Under these circumstances it was not strange that he should come into association with others in similar circumstances and through union erect a buffer between himself and the community. This organization also stood him in good stead in his dealings with the officials, who might have treated him with scant courtesy as an individual, but who did not dare to deal in summary fashion with an organization.

Thus we find the entire economic life of the country organized and largely self-controlled—the farmers in the village, the artisans, merchants, and traders in the guild. The range of the guild organization is indicated by enumeration of a few of them: the spinners' and weavers' guilds in various parts of the Empire; the bankers' guild, also a provincial organization, since the bankers came from Shansi province; the silk guild; the piece-goods guild; the goldbeaters' guild; the wheelbarrow guild; the organizations maintained by the beggars and the thieves; and the provincial clubs found in every sizable city.

By implication, since there were traders, there must have been trade. This, in turn, implies means of communication. Internal trade in premodern China, however, existed in spite of poor means of communication rather than because of highly-developed and well-maintained arteries of commerce. Goods could be transported from one coastal place to another, but only with risk, since the average small Chinese junk was not well fitted to withstand violent storms or long voyages. Some of the rivers afforded admirable arteries for the shipping of goods from far inland to the sea. Thus the Yangtse River, navigable for over sixteen hundred miles from its mouth, together with its tributaries, made trade possible throughout the great central basin. The West River served the south in the same way, and the Peiho and Yellow Rivers facilitated east and west communication in the north so far as they were navigable. The system of waterways was further artificially expanded by means of canals, the greatest of these being the Grand Canal, running from Peking in the north to Hangchow, south of the Yangtse, thus affording a north-and-south waterway. In central and southern China, particularly in the eastern provinces, there were many smaller canals which helped in the moving of goods from one region to another. Unfortunately many of these, including some sections of the Grand Canal, had been so neglected during the last part of the Manchu period that they were little used.

Beyond the places served by waterways, communication and transportation were more difficult. Of good roads there were none, for such as had been constructed for Imperial military and courier purposes had been allowed to fall into disrepair. The camel was used as a medium of transportation in the north, together with the donkey-cart, but the load had to be carried or pulled along paths which had become mere ruts, often sunk many feet below the level of the surrounding country, and during part of the year absolutely impassable. In the central and southern provinces even the pretense of roads had disappeared. Their place was taken by narrow foot-paths between the paddy fields. On the northern plain and in central China the wheelbarrow was in common use for the transportation of goods and sometimes for the conveyance of people. The wheel was placed in the center and goods were loaded high on either side. It was sometimes propelled by pullers as well as pushers, and in this way a considerable load could be carried. For short distances, in the south, goods were moved by human carriers, the load being suspended on either end of a pole balanced on the shoulder.

Given such primitive means of conveyance, it is remarkable that there should have been as much internal trade as was carried on. And it is not surprising that the movement of peoples was reduced to a minimum—the principal exception being officials who were forced to move from province to province. This difficulty of travel was fully as effective as the family tie in keeping people at home and consequently in preserving a spirit of provincialism and localism.

For while we have been speaking of China and the Chinese we must not forget that there was almost as much variety within the Empire as there was in nineteenth-century Europe. The differences in spoken language and the lack of uniformity of custom and tradition have already been mentioned. This diversity extended to food, beyond certain large staples, and particularly to the preparation of food, and to the minutiæ of every-day life. The people, prior to the coming of the Europeans to China, thought of themselves in terms of the locality, and, at the maximum, of the province. Thus an individual would first of all place himself, in terms of his village, as a man from the village of the Wang family (Wang chuang-jên). His problems were local in character, to be settled to the local advantage, even though the consequences of his decisions were felt elsewhere. While it was possible for him to coöperate readily with his fellow-villagers or townsmen, it was almost impossible to bring him into coöperation with outside groups. Flood-prevention measures along the Yellow River, for example, would be taken coöperatively in the region locally affected, often with disastrous consequences to other villages. But inter-village coöperation in the solution of such a common problem was rare. Each village took care of its own interests, and expected others to do likewise.

4. CULTURAL LIFE

The common bonds of union which make it permissible to think of China as an entity lay in the larger cultural life and in the political organization. To offset the variety of the spoken was the unity of the written language. A Cantonese might not be able to talk to a northerner, but he could communicate with him in writing. The written language, non-alphabetical, consisting of many distinct characters each representing a particular thing or concept, had been used to develop and preserve a common literature and a broad community of ideas, ideals, and culture. The Confucian code, with its emphasis on the family relationship, and the doctrines of other great philosophers were uniformly taught and accepted throughout the Empire. Buddhism was not a local cult but was diffused throughout the state, not as a foreign religion, but as one which was essentially Chinese as a result of long modification of an originally foreign system. The southerner could feel at home in the Taoist temple north of the Yangtse. And all of the common people were united in their superstitious belief in good and evil spirits. That certain days were propitious for beginning journeys, marrying and burying; that demons might be exorcised; that evil spirits always moved straight ahead; that the spirits of the air had an effect on the destinies of men—these were national and not local beliefs, although there were emphases and variations due to peculiar local conditions. Deities might be given local names, but their characteristics were the same and the methods employed to hoodwink them were similar throughout the Empire.

It was this superstition, rather than any real religious bent, which had corrupted Buddhism from the originally subtle doctrines received from India into a system of propitiatory acts undertaken occasionally under stress of adverse circumstances. It was this which had overlaid the teachings attributed to the Old Philosopher (Lao Tzu) with all sorts of debased ceremonies and rites, so that the original doctrines relating to the Tao or Way, leading to the living of correct and virtuous lives, had been lost to sight and certainly to practice.

Even Confucianism had been altered. Although Confucius refrained from pronouncements as to God and an after-life, and attempted to focus attention on right living, he himself had not escaped from deification and his philosophical system had been changed into a religious one. Yet Confucianism had been corrupted less than Buddhism or Taoism, for the elements of worship in it had been accepted much more perfunctorily than had the teachings with respect to living in this world. His exhortations to obedience, to filial piety and right conduct toward one's neighbors, were thoroughly inculcated into the thinking and living of the people. The unfortunate consequences of Confucianism came from the over-emphasis on the past. The Great Teacher did not profess to create a system, but only to restate and systematize the moral experience of the past. He thus emphasized adherence to former practice rather than experiment and innovation. To get back to the ideal life rather than to go forward to it, was his exhortation. The long acceptance of the Confucian view was a reflection of a highly stable society, which it was possible to maintain because of the relative absence of contact with the non-Chinese world after the Manchu conquest in 1644.

5. THE POLITICAL SYSTEM

In addition to this cultural unity there was a political unity in the China opened to limited foreign intercourse in 1842. The Empire was, it is true, divided into provinces, each of which constituted a political as well as an administrative subdivision of the state. And although the provincial officials were all appointed by the Emperor, they were allowed so much discretion in carrying out the Imperial commands that they were in reality semi-independent rulers. This was necessary because of the poor means of communication and the variety of local problems and customs. Nevertheless, the allegiance of the officials was to Peking; they were moved freely from post to post throughout the Empire; there was a common obligation to preserve peace and good order in the provinces, and to transmit funds for the support of the central government; and appeals from the decisions of provincial officers went to Peking.

The provinces were subdivided into prefectures (fu), which, in turn, were combined for administrative purposes into circuits (tao). In the eighteen provinces there were about one hundred eighty-four prefectures and ninety-five circuits. Each prefecture consisted of several districts (hsien), of which there were all together fourteen hundred and seventy. The district was the political and administrative unit, although it usually consisted of several villages.

Surrounded by tributary states, and enjoying little of that contact with the European world which might have developed national feeling, China tended toward internal variation rather than toward national unity. Loyalty was contracted to the locality or expanded at the most to the province. Until the impact of the West had afforded a new basis for comparison and differentiation, what went on in other localities or beyond the province was the concern only of the people immediately affected. The historical consequences of this localism were fully revealed in the years following the opening of China. But the importance of the territorial decentralization of the country must be emphasized at this point in order to focus attention on an explanation of later happenings in the Empire.

Similarly it is necessary to turn attention to the actual political organization of pre-modern China, both at Peking and in the provinces, in order to lay the foundations for an understanding of the history of modern China and of the Far East as affected by that of China.

An informed writer describes the political system of the Chinese Empire as an "autocracy superimposed on a democracy." From one point of view the justification for this characterization is exhibited in the theory of political relationships in the Empire. The Emperor theoretically exercised the powers of an autocrat. He was the supreme lawmaker of the state; the executive and administrative functions were exercised under his direction and control; and he was the fountain of justice. In other words, the people, including the officials, were accustomed to a complete concentration of power in the hands of one individual. In a very real, even though theoretical, sense he governed by "divine right," for his responsibility was not to any body representative of the people as a whole or of important groups in the state. Heaven bestowed upon him a "mandate" to rule, and until that mandate was withdrawn there was no authority to which he could be held accountable for his acts. Practically, to be sure, he was expected to act responsibly in accordance with advice tendered by members of the Censorate and other high-ranking official bodies. The Emperor did, consequently, act under a limited sense of responsibility. In return for the autocratic power conferred on him by Heaven he assumed a definite responsibility for the maintenance of peace, order, and comparative prosperity within the Empire. Thus if famine became widespread, the condition was held to be a result of some failure on the part of the Emperor. Famine, of course, would produce brigandage, and the gathering together of large bodies of armed men might easily result in rebellion against the

Imperial authority. A successful rebellion would bring the dynasty to an end, and consequently would indicate that the "mandate of Heaven" had been withdrawn. Obviously it was to the real interest of the Emperor to make certain, so far as he could, through such organs as the Censorate, that the condition of the people was good. As a matter of fact, the end of many of the dynasties in Chinese history had come as a direct result of some such process as that just described, whether the new rulers came from within the country or subjugated it from without. It should be said, however, that, coupled with hard times, the hand of authority would have to be relaxed throughout the country in order that a rebellion might be carried to a successful conclusion. The forcible overthrow of the Manchus in 1911, then, was not a new method of getting rid of a dynasty. The right of rebellion was given explicit recognition in Chinese political theory, and China has always been known as a country of rebellions.

A few quotations from the Confucian Classics may serve to illustrate the theory back of the old Chinese political institutions. "Heaven hears as the people hear. Heaven sees as the people see." Again: "In a political state the people are the most important, institutions come next, the monarch is the least important of all." This conception of the importance of the people, enforced by the theory and practice of rebellion, gave China a very workable theory of "divine right" indeed, from the complete operation of which would result a well-ordered state.

But there were other restrictions and limitations on the absolute power of the Emperor. He was restricted in the exercise of his supremacy by the Imperial House Laws and by the edicts of his predecessors. While he was not absolutely bound by them, they constituted a valuable guide for his conduct, both personally and in the government of the realm. Furthermore, he was decidedly limited by custom and tradition. While he had the power to issue orders contrary to custom, yet it is never possible to change a custom by a law, and nowhere is this more true than in China where it is impossible to over-estimate the force of tradition.

In a country of personal rule the first autocrats may personally exercise their authority to a large extent; but by degrees, as the dynasty continues, the rulers tend to concern themselves less and less with affairs of state, leaving the real power in the hands of their advisers. When the ruler confines himself to his palace or his capital, it becomes more and more necessary for him to rely upon the advice of others in formulating the policy of the state, thus transferring the real power to those who can gain and retain his confidence, often mere servitors in the palace. In any case the autocrat must rely upon others to carry out his commands. This reliance still further modifies his actual power.

In formulating his will the Emperor of China was assisted by two bodies, the Grand Secretariat and the Grand Council. The former, after 1729, had become a Court of Archives and was of little importance in the actual government. The Grand Council, on the other hand, was a very important advisory body. It usually consisted of six members, all of whom held other high offices in the central government, usually the presidency of one of the administrative boards.

It was through the administrative boards that the actual administration of the Empire, so far as Peking had any relation to it, was carried on. They were six in number until administrative reforms introduced after 1901 increased the number to eleven. The original six were: Civil Appointments, concerned primarily with the disposal of the patronage; Revenue, under the direction of which the contributions from the provinces were received and assigned to the various services; Rites, concerned with the regulation of ceremonial, a very important function at an Oriental court; War, superintending such of the military and naval establishment as was not under provincial control, or otherwise provided for; Punishments, corresponding somewhat to the Department of Justice in this country; and Works, entrusted with the superintendence of the public buildings, highways, and other public property.

One of the organs of the central government deserving of more than incidental mention was the Censorate, which has been well described as the "eyes and ears" of the Emperor. There were twenty-four Censors in Peking and fifty-six in the provinces, the Viceroys and Governors of the provinces being honorary members. The function of the Censor was to criticize, and this function he exercised freely, though not always without bias. No one in the entire official system, from the highest, the Emperor, to the lowest, the district magistrate, was immune from this criticism. As late as the last quarter of the past century one of these critics sent in a memorial to the Empress-Dowager, then the ruler of China, severely censuring her conduct in not making suitable provision for an heir to carry on the worship of the late Emperor, at the same time committing suicide in order to lend weight to his criticism as well as to avoid the displeasure of the Empress-Dowager. The provincial censors were, in a sense, spies sent out to report on the conduct of the officials in the provinces in order that the Emperor might be kept informed of their acts, rewarding those who were faithful and punishing those who were lax in the performance of their duties or who might be suspected of disloyalty. This was one of the means by which the Imperial Government was able to maintain its control over the provincial officials.

It has already been pointed out that the provinces were semi-autonomous units in the Empire. While the general policy was established in Peking, it had to be carried into effect in the provinces, where it was modified as local customs and conditions, or the sympathy of the higher provincial officials with the policy, determined. A good example of this is to be found in the development of the Boxer movement. When the Empress-Dowager finally determined to support the Boxers, secret orders were sent out to the provinces to drive all foreigners into the sea. While in some few provinces attempts were made to carry out this command, in others it was totally disregarded, and, in violation of the Imperial orders, the foreigners were protected to the extent of the ability of the officials. When the Boxer movement collapsed, these men, among them Yüan Shih-k'ai and Chang Chih-tung, were honored for their superior understanding of the strength of the Powers instead of being punished for their disobedience to the Imperial orders. But while in this instance the exercise of discretion justified itself, it must be recognized that here was an element of serious weakness whenever it was desirable to secure complete uniformity in the administration of a policy.

At the head of the province stood the Viceroy or Governor. Most of the provinces were grouped into viceroyalties. The exceptions were Shantung, Shansi, and Honan, which were headed by only a Governor. In two cases, Chihli and Szechuan provinces, the single province constituted a viceroyalty, and over it no Governor was placed. One viceroyalty was made up of three provinces (Kiangsu, Anhui, and Kiangsi), and each of the other five were formed by a combination of two provinces.

The Viceroy, unless he assumed the functions of the Governor of one of the provinces in addition to his viceregal duties, as in Kansu, Chihli, and Szechuan provinces, was a kind of superior colleague to the Governor, having a general power of supervision of the provinces within his jurisdiction. Both officials bore the same general relationship to the viceroyalty or the province as the Emperor bore to China. They were held responsible to him for the condition of the province and for the transmission of the provincial contributions to Peking. In the accomplishment of these limited ends they were allowed a wide choice of means, so that theoretically they exercised absolute authority in the area over which they had control. However, it should be borne in mind that in the exercise of this power they were subject to the same general limitations as the Emperor, i.e., custom and tradition in the province, and the necessity of maintaining peace and order, and comparative prosperity. They were naturally forced to act under a greater feeling of immediate responsibility also, since they were accountable directly to the central government. At the same time they were limited in their authority by the presence of other officers in the provincial system who were appointed and acted directly under central government supervision. These officers served as a check on the Governor and on one another. Finally, the high provincial officials were supreme only to the extent to which the prefect and the district magistrate accepted their commands and faithfully carried them into effect.

Among the other important provincial officials was the Treasurer. "He is the nominal head of the civil service in each province, in whose name all patronage is dispensed, even when directly bestowed by the Governor, and is treasurer of the provincial exchequer, in this capacity providing the Imperial Government with a check on his nominal superior, the Governor." [5] Others were the Judge, with supervision of the criminal law, and appellate jurisdiction in criminal cases; the Salt Comptroller, "in control of the manufacture, movement and sale of salt," a government monopoly; and the Grain Intendant, controlling the collection of the grain tribute. These officials constituted the general provincial official system.

Each circuit was presided over by an official called the Tao-tai, with special administrative functions, and the prefecture was supervised by the Prefect, together with his deputies.

At the bottom of the official ladder we come to the Hsien, or district magistrate, the real administrative officer in the Empire, and in many respects the most important official in the entire system. His functions were many and diverse, and a complete enumeration of them is impossible here. The general position of the magistrate in the official system, and in his relation to the people, is indicated by the title sometimes given him— "the father and mother official." Some of his more important duties may be indicated. He was the police magistrate and decided ordinary police cases. He was court of first instance in all civil and criminal cases. He was also coroner, prosecuting attorney, sheriff, jail warden, the agent of the Imperial Government in the collection of the land tax and grain tribute, registrar of the land, famine commissioner for his district, and the local representative of the Board of Works and the provincial treasurer in the custody of official buildings. Aside from his manifold duties, the magistrate was important because he was the only official within the cognizance of the great majority of the people—the connecting link between them and the political system of the country. This fact has considerable importance in view of the later attempts to establish a national system of representative government.

The provincial system during Imperial days has been described in some detail because it furnished the real foundation on which the Republic had to be built. And out of it grew the post-revolutionary condition of military rule in China—a rule based upon control of the province which was gradually extended to Peking.[6]

All of the members of the official hierarchy were appointed by the Emperor, acting either directly or upon the recommendation of one of the higher officials. In making his choice the Emperor was supposed to appoint from among those who had qualified in the examinations held at regular intervals throughout the country. Thus one who wanted to enter into the

[5] MORSE, H. B., *Trade and Administration of China*, p. 51.
[6] As indicated more fully in chapter XI, pp. 227–232.

civil service would start with the local examination, pass from there to the prefectural and provincial examinations, and, if again successful, perhaps go up to Peking to compete in the metropolitan examinations. Anyone, with certain exceptions, such as soldiers and members of certain occupational groups, was eligible to compete. However, success did not ensure appointment to office, or promotion after appointment, for in order to get ahead it was necessary to have a friend at court or among the higher officials, or, in the latter years of the Manchu rule, to gratify the cupidity of one or more of those with influence. In fact, there existed a regular system of traffic in office which radiated from the Palace. While the eunuchs were not supposed, under the Imperial House Laws, to concern themselves with public affairs, under the Empress-Dowager the real power had come to reside in the hands of the chief eunuch. This condition was partly responsible for the political decay which set in during the last half-century of Manchu rule.

In spite of this fact the examination system did mean that officialdom was largely recruited from among those with a satisfactory education according to the standards of the time. Unfortunately administrative capacity was not tested at all in examinations, nor knowledge of the problems of government, since the educational system was built on the Confucian Classics, and the abilities stressed in the examinations were those relating to essay-writing on classical subjects. So long, however, as the duties of the administrator were nominal rather than real, and demanded the attribute of common sense rather than a technical training in administration, the system gave satisfactory results.

All officials were appointed, according to the general rule, for three years, with the possibility of one reappointment before transfer to another post. This was not an absolute rule, however, for some officials were retained in the more important posts for much longer periods. A notable example of this deviation from the general practice was the maintenance of Li Hung-chang in the Tientsin viceroyalty for twenty-four years. But a rule that was never departed from was that no official, whether governor or district magistrate, should be appointed to his native place. There was good reason for both of these rules, especially the latter. If a wise and capable administrator were appointed to the governorship of his native province, for example, and left in the one post over a long period of time, he would be able to establish himself in a position of independence of the Imperial Government. This would be possible because as a successful fellow-provincial he would initially have a local following which would be strengthened and extended because his family life would be deep-rooted in the province. By appointing him to a province where he was unfamiliar with the local customs, and by transferring him to a new environment frequently, the central authorities prevented the development of a sense of independence and the possibility of an attempt to detach the province from the Empire. This danger was, of course, greater in the provinces most remote from Peking. These two practices help to account for the maintenance of the Imperial rule in spite of the large discretionary power vested in the officials.

Another practice which serves to explain the continuance of the Imperial rule was that of balancing the various cliques or factions in dispensing patronage. In the first place, in the central government care was taken, in the making of appointments, to strike a balance between the Manchus and the Chinese, and this practice continued until near the end of the last century, when the Manchus began to predominate. In the second place, during the same period the two major factions, known because of the province of their leaders as the Chihli and Anhui men, were played against each other in order that neither should gain the supremacy to the disadvantage of the Manchus. After 1895 a third group, the Cantonese, who had always been discriminated against in official life, came into prominence by supporting the Emperor in his attempt to reform the government.[7] With the failure of the reform movement many of them were driven into exile, so that the Cantonese became identified with the revolutionary propaganda. This partly explains the leadership of the south in the uprising of 1911. This balancing of the various groups against one another was followed in distributing provincial posts as well as those of the central government.

Before we turn from the official to the extra-official system of government, the relationship between the various officials in the hierarchy should be explained more fully. The Emperor, as has been pointed out, was responsible for the government of the entire country. But he exercised his responsibility by the appointment of the Governor or Viceroy, holding him to account for the government of the viceroyalty or province. The Governor held the Prefect responsible for the condition of the prefecture, and he passed the responsibility on to the magistrates of the several districts in his jurisdiction. The magistrate, in his turn, held the headmen of the villages responsible for those under their direction. However, in spite of this complete devolution of responsibility, no one was able to plead the negligence of those inferior to him as an excuse for the non-fulfillment of his own duties.

This delegation of responsibility is well illustrated by the specimen proclamation given by Parker: "The magistrate has had the honor to receive instructions from the prefect, who cites the instructions of the Tao-tai, moved by the Treasurer and the Judge, recipients of the commands of their Excellencies the Viceroy and Governor, acting at the instance of the Foreign Board, who have been honored with his Majesty's commands."

Still another feature of Chinese political life remains to be noted. None of the officials received salaries large enough to enable them to support

[7] The reform movement is discussed infra. ch. VII. sec. 8.

their establishments adequately, or to provide for their own future. The official salary of the magistrate is given by Morse as ranging from 100 to 300 taels per annum, and the pay of the higher officials, while proportionately greater, was equally inadequate. This salary was supplemented by an allowance "for the encouragement of integrity among officials" amounting to several times the salary. But even with this allowance the official was decidedly underpaid. The natural result was that all added to their salaries by whatever means came to hand. The system of financial administration in the Empire enabled the officials to "squeeze" (i.e., graft) more than enough to recompense themselves for the meagerness of their official doles.

The Imperial government did not tax the individual directly, but apportioned its needed income among the provinces according to their ability to contribute. Thus the Governor would be notified that his province would be expected to send in a given amount to the Imperial Treasury. If this contribution was paid, the central government had no further interest in the methods of finance of the province. Since the Imperial expenses were not great, normally the province could pay more, from the established sources of revenue, than was actually requested by the Board of Revenue. Consequently the practice early developed for the Governor to add to the contribution demanded a sum large enough to enable him to maintain properly his official establishment, consisting of a large number of necessary officers who were entirely unprovided for in the official system, and whom he was expected to pay out of his own purse. This increased sum he would divide among the various prefectures. If the requested amounts were duly paid, his responsibility ended, and he, in turn, made no attempt to see that the amount paid in to the provincial treasury was that actually collected. The Prefect then took the liberty of adding to the sum assessed on him an amount which would enable him to take care of his own needs. This further increased sum was then distributed among the districts for actual collection under the direction of the magistrate. Since he had to account, not for the amount actually collected, but only for that sum for which the district was assessed, he in turn fixed the taxes to be collected from the individual according to the amount which he thought could be collected without undue friction. The balance he retained for his own needs.

It is immediately apparent that there would be a wide discrepancy between the revenue collected from the villagers and the sum actually delivered to the Imperial Treasury. The fact of this divergence was well known and these successive accretions were considered to be entirely right and proper. It would seem, however, that under this system, as in that of "farming" the taxes resorted to in the Turkish Empire, the burden on the individual would soon become intolerable. This would have been the case had it not been for the fact that there was a natural disinclination on the part of the individual to pay more than his ancestors had paid, and, in the annual struggle between the tax collector and the farmer or villager, the force of custom was on the latter's side. In a society where custom was the determinant in all disputes, the interests of the individual were fairly well protected. The sources of direct revenue were fixed and immutable, and the levy on those sources could not go far above the customary rate without provoking disturbance. Since undue disturbance would reflect on the governing ability of the magistrate, his normal tendency would be not to exceed the figure marked by the individual as the point of open resistance. As a matter of fact, taxes were not unduly burdensome at the time of the opening of China.

The same system of finance marked the collection of the customs duties and the administration of the salt monopoly, Peking losing and the individual official decidedly gaining. Some of the most lucrative posts in the Empire were those connected even indirectly with the foreign trade at Canton. The payments to secure these posts were correspondingly heavy, but the officials usually managed to amass more than a competency before being transferred. There was no regular schedule of charges upon the importation of goods into, or their exportation from, the Empire, and the foreign traders were taxed all that the traffic would bear. Much of what was received went into the pockets of the officials.[8]

Throughout, then, there was what may be described as corruption in the financial administration, justified in part by the small salaries paid, but having its effect in the lowering of the public integrity of the officials.

So long as the Imperial government needed only a nominal and fairly constant revenue, the system just described proved to be workable. But with the added demands on the treasury of the central government due to the imposition of foreign indemnities, the necessity for more extensive armaments, and the cessation of contributions from provinces devastated by famine or rebellion, it became necessary either to increase the levy on the existing sources of revenue and develop new sources, or to bring to Peking a greater proportion of the amounts actually collected. Increase in the levy, however, as in the case of the tax on land, could not go beyond a certain point without provoking resistance to the tax collector. New resources could not be developed rapidly enough to meet the expanding needs, because of the force of customary modes of procedure, although substantial revenue was derived from the likin, a transit tax developed after the middle of the last century; and the greatest source of expansion of income for a state, the foreign customs, early became fixed by treaty at a low point. The third

[8] This was true only up to the time of the first treaties, when a regular system of charges was provided. Corruption disappeared from their collection and transmission to Peking when the foreign customs service was organized with an inspectional staff largely made up of foreigners.

alternative proved impossible as a solution, owing to the unwillingness of the officials to abate their own needs and demands. Consequently the financial problem became one of increasing difficulty during the last period of Manchu rule.

Thus far we have described a highly centralized administrative system in a decentralized territorial system, the main feature of which was autocracy with some important democratic modifications. The soundness of the characterization of political China as an autocracy superimposed on a democracy has not yet, however, been fully demonstrated, since we have not called attention to the democratic features of the system. These are to be found in the village, family, and guild systems which have already been described. The official system stopped where the real control of the lives of the people began—below the district magistrate. The people paid taxes and in return expected the government to maintain peace and order. From the standpoint of law this meant that the officials made and administered the criminal law. Commercial law was established and enforced through the guild organizations, and trade disputes were usually settled out of court. Even the taxes were often not collected by the magistrate, but were returned to him by the village headman, who was selected by the village rather than by the magistrate.[9] As has been indicated,[10] the village largely controlled itself through its Council of Elders, and the family, the real unit in the country, served as an agency of control to a much greater extent than in Occidental states.

It thus becomes clear that the real life of China, both social and economic, was carried on without the direction of the officers of government, and yet with a high degree of organization. The people were self-controlled in virtually all of their activities. With the provincial and craft guilds and the village and family organizations, it was possible to get along with a government that exercised the minimum of actual power. The official system was grafted on to the family and guild systems, and was supported by the people for the reasons already mentioned. It is in this extra-political system of government that the democratic element in the Chinese state was to be found, and largely from it, as the conservator of local custom, that the autocratic features of the official system were modified. But the fact is worthy of note that it was not democracy in the political sense.

The account of how these features of Chinese life were modified will be found to be part of the history of modern China, dating from the attempt on the part of the states of the West to establish political relations with the Chinese Empire.

[9] Subject, however, to his confirmation. In some parts of the country it would seem that the magistrate suggested the headman. But this was rather the exception than the rule.
[10] Supra, pp. 10–11.

REFERENCES FOR FURTHER STUDY

J. T. Addison, *Chinese Ancestor Worship* (1925); a good brief treatment of a most important subject. Capt. F. Brinkley, *China, Its History, Arts and Literature,* 4 vols. (1902) (Oriental Series, vols. 9–12), vol. 10, ch. 1–4. Chang Chung-li, *The Chinese Gentry* (1955). H. G. Creel, *Confucius, The Man and the Myth* (1949). George B. Cressey, *China's Geographic Foundations* (1934); a standard text, surveying the land and the people. Wolfram Eberhard, *A History of China,* transl. by E. W. Dickes (1950). J. K. Fairbank, *The United States and China* (1948), ch. 1–6; a penetrating analysis of the weaknesses of traditional China as they have been perpetuated and revealed in modern China. H. A. Giles, *Civilization in China* (1911); an interesting popular account. Marcel Granet, *Chinese Civilization* (1930); a penetrating analysis and synthesis of the civilization of ancient China. H. C. Hinton, *The Grain Tribute System of China, 1845–1911* (1956). Lewis Hodous, *Folkways in China* (1929), Arthur W. Hummel, *Eminent Chinese of the Ch'ing Period* (1943–44), 2 vols. F. H. King, *Farmers of Forty Centuries* (1911); a careful description of the system of agriculture. K. S. Latourette, *Development of China* (1917), ch. 1–4; a good account of early history and pre-modern culture; a more complete and detailed historical treatment and institutional analysis may be found in K. S. Latourette, *A Short History of China,* 2 vols. (1934). Y. K. Liang and L. K. Tao, *Village and Town Life in China* (1915); an excellent study, although not as comprehensive as Smith. Thomas T. Meadows, *The Chinese and Their Rebellions* (Stanford, Academic Reprints, 1953). Franz Michael, *Origin of Manchu Rule in China* (1942); frontier and bureaucracy as interacting forces in the Chinese Empire. H. B. Morse, *Trade and Administration of China* (1920); excellent for reference purposes. H. B. Morse, *Gilds of China* (1909); a good brief description of their organization and functions. E. H. Pritchard, *Anglo-Chinese Relations during the 17th and 18th Centuries* (1929). L. Richard, *Comprehensive Geography of the Chinese Empire,* transl. by M. Kennelly (1908); still worth consulting. A. H. Smith, *Village Life in China* (1899); an excellent study of the various aspects of life in the village. E. D. Thomas, *Chinese Political Thought* (1927); an excellent study of the political theory of the formative Chou period. Yu-yue Tsu, *Spirit of Chinese Philanthropy,* in Columbia University Studies, vol. 50, pt. 1 (1912); a suggestive study of one phase of Chinese life. E. T. C. Werner, *China of the Chinese* (1919); an excellent brief historical and descriptive account of economic, social, religious, and political institutions. Richard Wilhelm, *A Short History of Chinese Civilization* (1929); should be consulted. E. T. Williams, *China, Yesterday and Today* (1923); valuable for Chinese economic and social life and institutions. S. Wells Williams, *The Middle Kingdom,* 2 vols. (1882); a monumental work covering all phases of Chinese life. Karl A. Wittfogel and Feng Chia-sheng, *History of Chinese Society, Liao* (1949); a detailed study of Chinese society during the period 907–1125. K. C. Wu, *Ancient Chinese Political Theories* (1928); summarizes the theories of the principal philosophers from the Chou dynasty through Mencius and Hsuantze.

CHAPTER II

THE OPENING OF CHINA

I. EARLY RELATIONS WITH THE WEST

FROM the middle of the eighteenth century until 1842 the Chinese Empire was closed to foreigners except for peep-holes at Canton and Macao. Before 1757 the Chinese government had passively permitted rather than actively encouraged the entrance of foreigners into the country. The Portuguese were the first Westerners to reach China by sea in modern times. After the first visit of Portuguese ships in 1516, other Europeans began to come in search of trade. The Spanish arrived in 1575, the Dutch in 1604, the English in 1637, and the Americans in 1784. At the same time that the south of China was being visited by the vessels of those states, Russia was reaching out territorially toward the Pacific.[1] By 1689 the establishment of a common frontier with China necessitated an agreement regulating trade across it and arranging for control of the peoples moving back and forth, and China made her first modern treaty in that year (Treaty of Nerchinsk). This treaty also gave the Russians the right to send a mission to Peking and consequently placed them on a different footing in China than other foreigners.

In harmony with a long tradition of hospitable treatment of strangers, no serious obstacles were placed in the way of foreign traders. Nevertheless there must have been some doubt from the first as to the proper policy to be pursued toward them, for news of Portuguese activities in India and Malaysia, of the occupation of the Philippines by the Spanish, and of Dutch and English aggressions, must have reached Peking. That these tales were not exaggerated was revealed by the behavior of the first arrivals in China. The Portuguese showed themselves to be more interested in loot than in legitimate trade, and were soon restricted to contact at Macao. The Spanish were early warned off and made no real attempts to establish trade relations. The Dutch tried to establish themselves first in the Pescadores and then in Formosa, where they remained for a time. And the Chinese were prejudiced against the English both by the Portuguese, who gave them a bad name in the hope of keeping them from trade, and by the brusque conduct of the English themselves. All of these things gave the foreigners a poor start, and their chances were not bettered by the tendency of one group to fight another.

[1] For a discussion of the early Russian movement eastward, infra, ch. XVIII, sec. 2.

At the same time the reigning dynasty was being threatened from the north by the Manchus, and rebellion was rife south of the Great Wall. Consequently it is not strange that the Ming rulers began to fear the complications presented by the coming of the Westerners, whose behavior was so often alarming. After the Manchus gained control of the country they, by edict in 1685, permitted foreigners to trade at all the coast ports, but in their turn, perhaps in part because of their experiences in attempting to control the traders, they finally decided to restrict access to the country. In 1757 trade was definitely confined to the southernmost port, Canton.

Just as commercial relations came to be restricted, so the Chinese government, after favorably receiving Christian emissaries from the West, gradually became less friendly to them and finally prohibited Christian propaganda. The first period of Roman Catholic missionary activity in China extends from the thirteenth to the sixteenth century. The second and more fruitful period, beginning after the middle of the sixteenth century with the establishment of Matteo Ricci in the country, deserves a few words of comment. The first missionaries were Jesuits, who established themselves firmly in the country by largely adapting their religious views to the practices and prejudices of the Chinese, coming as philosophers and men of science rather than as priests. By 1601 Ricci was able to establish himself at Peking, where he and his associates and successors won favor at court and made converts among the higher officials. Many conversions took place in the provinces also as a result of Jesuit labors. After the Jesuits, the Franciscans and Dominicans found a footing in China in spite of some opposition from the Jesuits.

After the Catholic missionaries had secured a firm hold no serious obstacles were placed in their way until there developed a rivalry among the various orders. This rivalry, which also infected the converts, was made more significant politically by reason of the fact that some of the priests had been drawn into public positions, both at Peking and in the provinces, and by the tendency of others to assert a lay as well as a spiritual authority over their flocks. Consequently fear was expressed that missionary zeal might give rise to serious internal disturbance.

Even more serious in its consequences was a controversy which arose as to the legitimacy of the continuance of ancestor-worship by native Christians, together with a controversy over a suitable Chinese term for the Christian concept of God. Appeal was taken both to the Emperor of China and to Rome, and, as their conclusions ultimately differed, question was raised as to the effect on the Chinese state of the propagation of a faith which led its believers to recognize as supreme a distant and external authority. "The disputes between the various orders of missionaries and the resistance of some converts to the Emperor's commands respecting the ancestral rites, together with the representations of his own officers upon the tendency of the new religion to undermine his own authority, gradually opened his eyes to the true character of the propagandists." [2] Consequently, in 1724 an edict was issued prohibiting the propagation of the "religion of the Lord of Heaven."

Some of the missionaries were permitted to remain at Peking for a time in scientific capacities. Some others, after they had been ordered out, secreted themselves at various places in the provinces and continued the work. Their presence, together with that of native Christians, led intermittently to persecutions, which, however, did not result in the extermination of the faith. "In 1820 an estimate gives six bishops, two coadjutors, twenty-three foreign missionaries, eighty native priests, and 215,000 converts." [3]

Thus a survey of the first two centuries of Occidental contact with China reveals the fact that it was experience and experiment rather than innate hostility to foreigners which resulted in the closing of the Empire. A few missionaries remained *sub-rosa,* and Christianity itself was not wholly eliminated, it is true; but Catholic missions did not begin to regain their former importance until steps were taken to lift the ban (1844). The trader was also barred from the Empire except for the limited access permitted through Canton and Macao, a restriction which continued until 1842. The sole relations permitted through those places were commercial, the only contact being with Chinese merchants. Portugal, Holland, and England all attempted to establish direct political relations with Peking by sending embassies to the capital, but each attempt resulted in failure. The ambassadors were invariably treated as tribute-bearers, and they were expected to perform the kowtow (the nine prostrations) before the Emperor or his picture, which the English invariably refused to do, and which the Dutch did without avail. After exhortations to obedience and good conduct the foreign missions were informed that the Emperor saw no reason to change established procedures.

2. THE CANTON TRADE

While the trade was carried on at Canton the foreign merchants were not permitted to reside there throughout the year. During the summer months, or from the end of one trading season to the beginning of the next, the traders retired to Macao, which was in the nature of a Portuguese leasehold, although Chinese jurisdiction was maintained. When they returned to Canton they were forced to leave their wives and children, if they had any, at Macao. This served to emphasize the temporary and precarious nature of their stay.

[2] WILLIAMS, S. WELLS, *Middle Kingdom,* vol. II, p. 303.
[3] Ibid., p. 307.

The conditions of trade were determined exclusively by the Chinese and, so far as charges were concerned, were variable, fixed by the operation of the principle that levies should be as heavy as the traffic would bear. Only a small part of the income reached Peking, the balance being pocketed by the collectors and the officials from the magistrate to the viceroy. Tonnage, export and import duties, together with a variety of service charges, all contributed to swell the total.

In order to milk the trade effectively the Chinese set up a monopoly organization through which alone it could be carried on. In 1702 an individual known as the "Emperor's merchant" [4] was appointed as the sole agent with whom the foreigners might deal. This system proved unsatisfactory and was replaced fifty years later by that of "security merchants" organized into what came to be known as the Co-hong, the guild of Chinese merchants engaged in foreign trade. Formally abolished in 1771, the Co-hong was revived in 1782 and continued until 1842. This revival did not destroy the monopoly system, but merely modified it by increasing the number of Chinese firms entitled to participate in the trade first to twelve and then to thirteen. Each foreign trader had to be "secured" by one of the Hong merchants. This meant that he could buy and sell only through him, buying at the minimum the Hong merchant would consider and selling at his maximum. On his side the "security merchant" took care of all payments to the officials, relieving the foreigner of the task of meeting the innumerable petty exactions which burdened the trade. These of course were figured in as part of the price finally agreed upon.

The Co-hong was the buffer between the foreign community and the Chinese official world. The thirteen merchants were the sole medium of communication between the factories and the viceroy, governor, and magistrate. Letters, even though carrying complaints of the conduct of Hong merchants, could be transmitted only through them, and in the form of petitions. After some time it was agreed that petitions might be transmitted direct, but there was no assurance that this regulation would be invariably observed. Furthermore, other Chinese could participate in the trade only through members of the Co-hong. Thus the control both of exports and imports lay in their hands, subject to official interference; and official interference was rare so long as each official, from the highest to the lowest, received his "squeeze." As good business men the "security merchants" conducted the trade with a view to securing the maximum of return, and so adjusted prices and exactions as not to make it unprofitable for the foreigners. These realized such large profits, in spite of the monopoly control, that they were ready to endure almost any inconvenience to keep the

[4] After the Co-Hong was instituted, the most important official under the Governor was the Hoppo, from the Board of Revenue (Hu Pu), to which he was responsible essentially as commissioner of the customs at Canton.

trade open. It was this desire, well realized by the Chinese, which gave them the upper hand in their dealings with the foreign community.

The members of this community lived, while at Canton, in a restricted area just outside the city walls. They had their residences over their warehouses and offices in buildings called "factories," from the name "factor" given to the permanent representative of the foreign firm. The establishment, in addition to foreign clerks and other assistants, consisted of a compradore, a trusted Chinese who served as the buffer between the foreigner and his "security merchant," linguists, and servants. Since the foreign trader had not learned the language or studied the business needs of the country, and could not buy its products directly himself, he had to have a Chinese whom he could trust to look after the Chinese end of the business. From the standpoint of their personal needs and comforts the foreigners were dependent on the good will of the Chinese. It was only by connivance, and not of right, that Chinese servants were permitted to serve them. Their food and water came to them from the Chinese city, and their recreation and pleasure grounds were restricted. Judging by Chinese regulations and proclamations, Europeans were considered to be of a lower order of moral being than the natives and were so treated. It must be remembered, however, that these proclamations were issued by officials who knew the traders either not at all or only at second-hand. With the Hong merchants and others with whom they came in close contact the Europeans were often on the friendliest terms. And it must also be remembered, when one is considering the tone of the proclamations, that not all of the traders were representative of the best elements in the countries from which they came.

Before the middle of the eighteenth century the English had outstripped all of their competitors in the Canton trade. After the East India Company established its factory at Canton in 1715, the bulk of the trade was under its control, due to its monopoly of the English trade. Other Englishmen were permitted to participate only under license of the company, and then only partially. The company was represented at Canton by superintendents who were to a large extent the spokesmen for the entire body of foreign merchants. Since these superintendents had a larger control over their countrymen than other foreign representatives, and since the English formed the largest group, the Chinese tended to deal with them and to hold them responsible for the conduct of the trade on the foreign side.

After 1789 the Americans rapidly assumed a position second only to that of the English. By 1832 there were seven well-established firms and twenty Americans regularly coming to Canton. These firms served as brokers for almost the entire American trade, disposing of goods brought in and securing outward cargoes. The Americans, it should be noted, came to China as individuals, and while they gained from that fact a freedom in trade denied to their English competitors, they lost by not having behind them a powerful organization such as the British East India Company. They were served, it is true, by a merchant-consul, but with the Chinese he had little more standing than any of his fellow-merchants. "The consul was merely a merchant whose only compensation was the fees of the office, the dignity of the position, and such information as to the business transactions of his competitors as would become available to him because of his access to official reports." [5] While the position was actively sought, this was not because the consul had any real authority over his fellow-traders. Unable to unite them in the pursuit of any common policy except by consent, he could not deal with the Chinese as the authoritative spokesman of a well-organized group. Thus what the Americans gained through release from the discipline of a controlling company, they lost in their relations with the Chinese.

One of the peculiarities of the early trade was that it was largely one-sided. The Chinese did not desire European products, while the Europeans were willing to make the long voyages and take the grave risks necessary to secure Chinese goods. The Chinese consequently came to believe that the peoples of Europe were dependent on China for their well-being. This is clearly indicated in the references made by Commissioner Lin, as late as 1839, to the foreign inability to do without China's "tea and rhubarb."

For this reason there developed among the Chinese a feeling of strength in dealing with the traders. Stoppage of the trade merely affected Chinese pocket-books, while there was a feeling that it not only did that to the European traders but injured the well-being of their countrymen as well. They came, therefore, to look upon a threat to stop the trade as a very effective weapon to be used in controlling the foreign merchant. The trade was permitted as a privilege and not as a matter of right—a privilege to be withheld at the discretion of the Chinese authorities. Thus the fact that relations between the outer world and China were solely on a commercial basis, that the traders seemed willing to accept almost any conditions laid down by China in order to keep the port of Canton open to trade, and that the trade was granted as a privilege rather than conceded as a right, developed in the Cantonese an undue sense of the inferiority of the foreigner, and bred in him an arrogance which finally reacted to his own disadvantage.

While at first the trade was entirely one-sided, Chinese products being paid for in specie or bullion, an exchange of commodities was gradually built up. In return for tea, silks, nankeen cloth, and other Chinese products, the English and Americans brought to the Empire ginseng, for which there was an existent market, furs, from both the eastern and northwestern American coasts and from the sealing trade, sandalwood, some cotton goods, increasing in amount in the first quarter of the nineteenth century,

[5] DENNETT, T., *Americans in Eastern Asia*, p. 63.

rice, and other commodities. An enumeration of the imports indicates that the trade was triangular rather than direct. The traders had to exchange their own products in various places for the goods to be used in the China trade. The Americans especially had to acquire not only goods but specie to supplement them; for it was only after opium began to figure largely in the imports that specie was no longer needed to settle a balance adverse to the foreigners.

The demand for opium grew until by 1830 the balance of trade had become unfavorable to the Empire, the value of the opium imported alone exceeding that of all of the commodities exported. Most of the opium came from India, some from Persia, and, toward the last, some Turkish opium was imported by the Americans. All of the nationalities represented at Canton, but not all of the traders, participated in the traffic, although here as in the general trade the English occupied a leading position, the carrying, however, being left to the "country" ships. The larger British responsibility was due not so much to their bringing opium to China as to the official encouragement of cultivation in India, to the official control of sales in India for export, and to the interest in the trade as a source of revenue for the Indian government.

This great increase in importation [6] was indicative of an increasing number of users. It may be pointed out here that opium smoking was not a natural vice of the Chinese, but one that had been introduced into the country. The drug had been known for its medicinal properties long before it began to be used for its narcotic effect. Its use in the pipe, first mixed with tobacco, itself brought to China by foreigners, and then unmixed, seems to have been introduced from Formosa following the temporary Dutch occupation of that island in 1624. After its introduction opium smoking rapidly became a common practice and soon attained the proportions of a national vice. Many of the officials and the gentry, together with people from all classes who could afford it, became addicts.

Objections to its use on both moral and hygienic grounds were raised from an early time. Edicts in 1729 and 1800 fulminated against the practice, and that of 1800 prohibited opium importation. In spite of the prohibition, however, the trade in the foreign product increased to the extent of dominating the import trade, although both the Co-hong and the British East India Company ceased to engage in it. Officials were ordered to bring it to an end, but they found it too profitable as a source of "squeeze" to regard the edicts as anything more than an excuse for taxing the traffic much more heavily than would have been possible if it had not been illicit. After 1820, under orders from Peking, the trade was driven away from

---

[6] The average importation from 1800 to 1811 was 4016 chests; 1811–1821, 4494 chests (I, MORSE, *International Relations*, p. 176); 1821–1828, 9708 chests; 1828–1835, 18,712 chests (I, MORSE, p. 182).

Canton for a time, but this only resulted in the traders' going up the coast to dispose of their cargo. It further resulted in such a loss of "squeeze" to the officials at Canton that they winked at the trade and permitted the traders to establish themselves in receiving ships at Lintin. Not until 1838 was an honest attempt made to enforce the prohibition, and it was out of this attempt that the conflict grew which resulted in war and the treaty of Nanking.

The foreign responsibility for the fostering of opium smoking by the Chinese cannot be overlooked, nor should it be minimized. But the inability of the Imperial government to control the evil must not be forgotten, or the reasons for it. The institution of "squeeze" was largely responsible for the failure to enforce the prohibition against importation. The decentralized system of administration—the discretion left to officials in carrying out Imperial commands—made it impossible to check consumption except by limiting the supply. And the foreign supply was augmented from a rapidly increasing home production in the south-central and western provinces. This production had to be brought to an end if the use of opium was to be restricted. But the crop was very profitable because of the demand for it throughout the Empire, and production was certain to increase unless the officials took severe action against the producers. The official could either carry out the commands of the Emperor or could charge heavily for immunity. He usually chose to do the latter. This production, it should be noted, had an important consequence other than that of adding to the supply of opium available to the smoker: it withdrew land from cereal growing and thus tended to interfere with the food supply in some sections of the country. This consequence as well as the other should be borne in mind as one of economic importance.

Another economic factor at work grew out of the foreign trade in opium and served to emphasize the social objections to it. As the opium imports increased, the specie of the Empire was drawn to Canton and was exported in settlement of an adverse trade balance. The ultimate possible effects of this on the monetary system and the economic life of China were soon perceived by some of the higher officials and brought to the attention of the Emperor in memorials and petitions. Some looked upon it as an added argument for prohibition, while others advocated legalization of the trade as the easiest means of controlling it. For a time, just before the final attempt to enforce the prohibitory edicts, it appeared certain that the advocates of legalization and restriction would carry the day at Peking, but on the eve of success the Emperor determined on the enforcement of the established policy. The prospect of change, felt at Canton to be a certainty, made the action finally taken seem to the foreigners more drastic than it actually was.

While the traders engaged in the traffic without regard to nationality, it may be pointed out that some of them were in sympathy with the prohibition policy. The social objection had its weight with a few of them, and some of the American and English traders saw in the enlarged importation of opium a decided handicap to the development of a more legitimate import trade. Even then many of them were as much interested in exploiting China as a market as in drawing supplies from her. Importation of opium unquestionably interfered with the development of a market for foreign goods, both because of the ease with which it could be handled, and because of the impossibility of China's paying in specie both for opium and for other imports. Thus there was a conflict of interest as to opium among the foreigners toward the end of this pre-modern period of intercourse.

3. ANGLO-CHINESE RELATIONS (1834–1840)

Opium, however, was the occasion, and not the cause, of the war between the British and the Chinese. In order to understand this, for a moment we must turn our attention back to the conditions of trade at Canton. For a long time independent British merchants had been agitating in favor of ending the East India Company's monopoly at Canton. They wanted to join in the trade competition as freely as the nationals of other Powers, particularly the Americans. This agitation, coupled with the situation in India, finally (1834) moved the British government to abolish the monopoly. But its abolition forced the government to devise something to take its place for the purpose of supervising and promoting British interests in the Far East. It also presented to the Chinese in a new form the problem of controlling the traders. The Imperial government had tried to extend the principle of responsibility to foreigners by holding the British superintendent largely responsible for them, dealing with them through him. Both sides, therefore, desired to see some officer appointed to take over the duties formerly performed by the agents of the company. The Chinese, however, were more than satisfied with a commercial agent empowered to deal with the Chinese merchants.

The English, on the other hand, decided to appoint superintendents who should represent the British government rather than a commercial company. These superintendents were to exercise the powers that had been vested in the agents of the East India Company, and to that extent the desires of the Chinese were complied with. But Lord Palmerston went a step farther and directed Lord Napier, who was appointed (1834) as the chief among three superintendents of trade, to "announce your arrival at Canton by letter to the Viceroy." Bearing in mind the fact that the former agents had dealt with a commercial agent or group of merchants, and only through them with the regular provincial officials, and that they represented a commercial company, and not a sovereign nation, the reader will perceive what a great change this instruction to communicate only with the Viceroy, the highest official of the province, would inevitably work.

The Chinese could see no reason for change in a method of communication which was working to their entire satisfaction. Even if the Viceroy had been willing to deal with the English representative, which he was not, it would not have been on terms satisfactory to one who felt that he represented one of the great states of the world. The Viceroy would have dealt with him, not as the direct representative of England, but as a commercial agent, and consequently as one inferior to himself in rank. Since Lord Napier was prepared to insist on treatment in accordance with his position as the representative of a state equal in every respect to China, his appointment and subsequent arrival at Canton opened the whole question of the establishment of the states of the Western world in China on a footing of equality.

The conception of the equality of states was entirely foreign to China, as well it might be. She had lived her own life so long, apart from contact with all states except those which were inferior to herself in size, power, and civilization, that she conceived herself as the one civilized state, surrounded by others which were in a more or less highly developed condition of barbarism. It was this conception which caused China to call herself the "Middle Kingdom." All attempts that had been made before this time to establish relations on a footing of equality had failed because of this attitude, and such a feeling of superiority, ingrained through the centuries of isolation, could not be immediately overcome. As a matter of fact, it took force, and the subjection of the Empire to repeated humiliation, before the Imperial government could be brought to an understanding of its true position in the world.

The fact that the British were the first to apply force to China is readily understandable. They were the chief traders at Canton and had always had a semi-governmental backing in their trade. When the East India Company was brought to an end it was only natural that its position should be officially taken by the government. The Americans, the next largest group of traders, had always been less restricted by governmental supervision. American contacts continued to be non-diplomatic and non-political, and the merchants were desirous of having them continue so lest the trade should be disturbed and they should lose the slight hold which they, with the other traders, had gained at Canton. They were interested, immediately, in peace at any price; and even after the partial opening of the country, American interest and policy were directed toward peace. The Americans continued their trade after the British traders had been forced to withdraw from Canton, and, in fact, their presence there proved to be an advantage to the English traders, as through the Americans they were able to discharge their cargoes in spite of their own government's embargo.

But the British insistence on the establishment of official intercourse and on enlarged trade opportunities was dictated by more than the ending of the East India Company's monopoly. Indeed that act was an expression of a larger interest. This was in the development of markets and the opening-up of new supplies of raw materials throughout the non-European world. Other states developed the same interest later than England, and, with the interest, used much the same means to satisfy it. The Commercial Revolution brought in its train the discovery of America as the result of the European desire for commerce with the Orient. And the Industrial Revolution, with its consequent development of trade on account of the demand that it brought for raw materials and for markets, made it certain that the industrialized nations of Europe would not permit any profitable center of trade to remain unexploited because of a desire on the part of its government or people to remain aloof from the current of world affairs. If other states had become industrialized before Great Britain, they would have played the leading rôle in forcing intercourse with the West on the countries of the East. If China had not been opened by the application of British force in 1840–1842, she would have had other assaults to withstand, all of them motivated by an insistence on the establishment of interstate relations according to the basic principles of the international law developed in Europe.

Lord Napier,[7] arriving at Macao in July, 1834, was placed in a most unfortunate position by his instructions and the construction he placed on part of them. He was to announce his arrival at Canton as the representative of England, and not the agent of a commercial company, directly to the Viceroy. His interpretation of his instructions forbade his using the Hong merchants as the medium of communication and forced him to regard himself as the guardian of the honor of his sovereign and his country. And yet he bore the same title as the representatives of the British East India Company and his duties were similar to theirs. Furthermore, he was instructed not to run counter to Chinese prejudices, to behave in a conciliatory and circumspect manner, and to seek to maintain a friendly understanding with the Chinese so as not to endanger the trade. Under the existing conditions it was impossible for him to carry out from the beginning, as he tried to do, the part of his instructions which referred to his position, without offending Chinese prejudices, stirring up trouble, and endangering trade relations at Canton. Trouble began when he proceeded to Canton

---

[7] Lord Napier was actually first among three appointed as superintendents of the trade. Since the lead was his throughout, his name is used as if he alone were the English representative.

without bothering to notify the Chinese and obtain a permit. After his arrival he tried to communicate directly with the Viceroy. This led to a series of abortive negotiations, Napier trying to live up to his instructions, and the Chinese attempting to preserve the old practices. The Chinese view of the general principles governing their intercourse with the foreigner was given by the Viceroy as follows: [8]

The object of the said barbarian headman (Lord Napier) in coming to Canton is for commercial business. The Celestial Empire appoints officials-civilian to rule the people, military to intimidate the wicked; but the petty affairs of commerce are to be directed by the merchants themselves. The officials are not concerned with such matters. In the trade of the said barbarians, if there are any changes to be made in regulations, in all cases the Hong merchants are to consult together, and make a joint statement to the superintendent of customs and to my office, and they will then be informed officially whether the proposals are to be allowed or disallowed. . . .

The great ministers of the Celestial Empire are not permitted to have private intercourse by letters with outside barbarians. If the said barbarian headman throws in letters, I, the Viceroy, will not at all receive or look at them. With regard to the barbarian factory of the company, without the walls of the city, it is the place of temporary residence for barbarians coming to Canton to trade. They are permitted to eat, sleep, buy and sell in the factories. They are not permitted to go out and ramble about. All these points are decided by fixed and certain laws and statutes, which will not bear to be confusedly transgressed.

To sum up the whole matter: the nation has its laws; it is so everywhere. Even England has its laws; how much more the Celestial Empire! How flaming bright are its great laws and ordinances! More terrible than the awful thunderbolt! . . .

It is clear that, so long as the Chinese officials acted on such views, any attempt to shift from a commercial basis to even a semi-political one was foredoomed to failure. All of Lord Napier's endeavors to open direct intercourse with the Viceroy proved unavailing, and his very presence at Canton constituted an embarrassment to the traders, who preferred the old conditions, no matter how unsatisfactory, to an endangering of the trade. Consequently, being unable to accomplish his mission as he interpreted it, and becoming ill, Lord Napier finally retired to Macao, where he died. The victory in the first contest rested wholly with the Chinese, who continued to dictate the terms of contact at Canton. Their confidence in their ability to deal with the foreigners as they chose was strengthened by the retirement of the English representative. They drew the natural conclusion that he had withdrawn because of the Viceroy's orders, supported by the stoppage of the English trade and the proclamation of non-intercourse.

Lord Napier's place was taken by Mr. L. V. Davis, who shortly gave way to Sir George B. Robinson, both of whom had been Lord Napier's associates. They were succeeded by Captain Eliot as Chief Superintend-

[8] MORSE, H. B., *International Relations*, vol. I, pp. 126–127.

ent. For the next few years no serious attempts were made to open direct intercourse with China through official channels. The matter was suspended, however, and not abandoned. During this period of quiet the trade was supervised by the British superintendent from Macao.

The whole question of the regulation of the trade was again opened in 1838, when the Emperor appointed a special commissioner to deal with the opium question, giving him instructions and authority to enforce the prohibitory edicts. The commissioner, Lin Tse-hsü, assumed the offensive from the time of his arrival [9] at Canton. After a brief study of the situation he decided to compel the foreigners to enforce the prohibition edicts for him. Thus he demanded that they give up all of the opium in their possession, and give bond not to engage in the traffic. To force compliance with his demand he threatened a complete stoppage of the trade. The English finally complied partially with the demand for the opium, that on the American ships being surrendered through them at the same time; but they refused to give the required bond not to engage in the traffic in the future. Consequently all intercourse with the factories was brought to an end, including the furnishing of food, water, and personal service. The British merchants finally withdrew under the direction of the superintendent of the trade, and established themselves at Hongkong. The Americans accepted a modified form of the bond, and trade was re-opened with them. After a time the English traders began to discharge their cargoes through the Americans, so that they did not suffer greatly as a result of their withdrawal.

Out of this controversy over the method of enforcing the prohibitory edicts, together with other difficulties, active hostilities developed.[10] These were confined at first to Canton and its vicinity, but later operations were carried farther up the coast, and war was finally brought to an end only after British vessels had proceeded a short distance up the Yangtse, cutting the eastern part of the Empire in two, thus making Peking realize the gravity of the conflict as it had not done so long as hostilities were confined to Canton.

4. CAUSES AND RESULTS OF THE ANGLO-CHINESE WAR

From the Chinese point of view the sole question at issue was that of the importation of opium, so that their case, they felt, rested on high moral grounds. This view of the struggle was also taken, in the main, in the United States, where the traditional hostility to England still existed. At this time, and for several years afterwards, the Americans viewed Great

[9] March 10, 1839.

[10] The initial hostilities occurred in November, 1839. It was not, however, until June, 1840, that a British force sufficient for the undertaking of offensive operations had been assembled.

Britain's every move in China as an expression of an aggressive policy. There were many who regarded the treaty of peace, with its cession of Hongkong, as the initial step toward the dismemberment of China. This conception of an aggressive England, determined to force opium on China, helped to shape American policy from 1842 until the period of the second advance. Public opinion in the United States was thus greatly and adversely excited by an address which John Quincy Adams made before the Massachusetts Historical Society, in which he said:

> The fundamental principle of the Chinese Empire is anti-commercial . . . It admits no obligation to hold commercial intercourse with others. It utterly denies the equality of other nations with itself, and even their independence. . . .
> This is the truth, and, I apprehend, the only question at issue between the governments and nations of Great Britain and China. It is a general, but I believe altogether mistaken opinion that the quarrel is merely for certain chests of opium imported by British merchants into China, and is a mere incident to the dispute; but no more the cause of war than the throwing overboard of the tea in the Boston harbor was the cause of the North American revolution. [11]

From the English standpoint Adams' statement was correct. The opium question was decidedly subordinate to the broader question of the establishment of political relations with the Empire, as a result of which sounder commercial relations might be developed. For it must be remembered that commercial relations were unsatisfactory because of the restriction of the trade to the one port, Canton, and the additional restriction that only a selected group of merchants, the Co-hong, might be dealt with. Furthermore, as a consequence of the credit nature of many of the transactions between foreign and Chinese merchants, considerable sums were due British traders. These amounts the Hong merchants were unable to raise, and the claims were advanced by the British government as another reason for hostilities.

Questions of jurisdiction were also involved in existing relations at Canton and served to maintain the British determination to bring about their readjustment. As early as 1784 a jurisdictional issue had been raised when a Chinese had been accidentally killed by the firing of a salute by a gunner of the English vessel, the *Lady Hughes*. Under pressure, he was handed over to the Chinese authorities and was condemned to death by strangulation. This led to an attempt, in connection with the unsuccessful Macartney mission (1793), to secure extraterritorial rights for Englishmen. Similar cases subsequently arose in which occasionally the foreigners successfully challenged Chinese assertions of jurisdiction, and sometimes, as in the *Terranova* case (1821), when the Americans were involved, they failed to do so. The handling of criminal cases by the Chinese authorities,

---

[11] Quoted in DENNETT, *Americans in Eastern Asia*, p. 107.

applying Chinese law, had thus aroused considerable dissatisfaction among both the English and the Americans.[12]

Military operations began with the blockading of Canton by the British, who, however, immediately moved northwards as the instructions of Admiral George Elliot and Captain Elliott, the plenipotentiaries, prescribed. Their orders were to deliver into official hands, for transmission to Peking, a letter from Lord Palmerston concerning the questions at issue. Tinghai, on the island of Chusan, was taken on July 6, 1840. The British thereupon attempted to send the letter from Amoy and Ningpo, but they were unsuccessful. Then the fleet moved directly to the Peiho, where communications were finally opened with the Viceroy of Chihli province. After some delay it was decided to transfer the negotiations back to Canton, the seat of the trouble.

At Canton negotiations were begun which promised some success; but they were eventually broken off, and hostilities were resumed. In 1841 the British temporarily occupied Canton, but the forces were soon withdrawn on the payment of $6,000,000, which the Chinese regarded as settlement for the opium surrendered to Commissioner Lin, but which the British seem to have considered as a payment on account of the expenses of the war. The restoration of Canton to Chinese control led to a resumption of trade, although hostilities were continued in the north. Amoy, Tinghai, Chinhai, and Ningpo were all occupied, and from Ningpo an advance was begun toward Chinkiang and Nanking.

The whole course of the war revealed one of the great weaknesses of China, from which she continued to suffer for many years. The Chinese Empire as an entity did not engage in war with Great Britain, but only parts of the country participated in the hostilities, and then only when directly attacked. Until Peking itself became conscious of the dangers resulting from war, it was impossible to reach a satisfactory settlement of the terms of intercourse. If the British had pressed the issue at Tientsin in 1840, instead of allowing themselves to be deflected to the south, the difficulties of the succeeding years might have been avoided.

Peace negotiations were entered upon after the country had been divided by the British movement up the Yangtse River to Nanking, which cut the line of communications from the north to the south. The terms of peace were contained in the treaty of Nanking, signed August 29, 1842. China ceded Hongkong to Great Britain. She also agreed to pay an indemnity of $21,000,000, $6,000,000 being in compensation for the opium actually seized at Canton, $3,000,000 for settlement of debts due the British merchants from the Hong merchants, and $12,000,000 to cover the expenses of the expedition. Five ports—Canton, Amoy, Foochow, Ningpo, and Shanghai—were to be opened to trade, with the right of residence for the

[12] Costin, W. C., *Great Britain and China, 1833–1860* (1936), pp. 4–7.

foreign merchants conceded, and with the right to appoint at each port consuls empowered to treat with the local officials. The monopoly of the trade given to certain designated Chinese merchants was to be done away with, and a uniform and moderate tariff on imports and exports was to be imposed, the regulations to be drawn up later. It was understood that the duties fixed at this time should not be increased later except by mutual agreement. This schedule of duties was promulgated by the Emperor in the form of a "Declaration" issued on June 26, 1843. From then until 1930 China was unable of her own will to determine the rates of her import and export duties. So far as the collection of the duties was concerned, however, the British consuls assumed, under the treaty, the duty of seeing "that the just dues and other dues of the Chinese Government, as here-inafter provided for, are duly discharged by Her Britannic Majesty's subjects." The British representative, Sir H. Pottinger, also offered to coöperate in the suppression of smuggling.[13]

It will have been noticed that the treaty of Nanking was silent concerning what was, from the Chinese point of view, the chief issue of the war. Nothing was said about the opium trade, although the Chinese were forced to make compensation for the opium actually seized. The English negotiator did, informally, express his conviction that China would do well to legalize the importation of the drug and then regulate its admission. This suggestion, which had been made earlier by some of the advisers to the Emperor, was not acceptable to the Chinese representatives, and since England would not undertake to enforce China's prohibition for her, although insisting that no protection or support would be given to Englishmen engaged in the traffic, the treaty was silent concerning the trade.

5. THE ESTABLISHMENT OF TREATY RELATIONS

The burden of partially forcing open the door to China fell upon England. Other nations, however, immediately prepared to take advantage of the new situation thus presented. The American, Commodore Kearny, on October 8 (thus shortly after the signature of the Treaty of Nanking) called attention to the interests of the United States and expressed the hope to the Viceroy at Canton, Kekung, that Americans might be accorded most-favored-nation treatment. The possibility that other foreigners than the English might seek a new status had apparently already occurred to the Nanking Viceroy Kiying, who negotiated the English treaty. In a memorial which reached Peking on January 19th, 1843, he reported: "In August, while I was negotiating with English (at Nanking), I already thought of the possibility of all barbarians demanding the same privileges (as the English). I then made inquiries of the English and their reply

[13] DENNETT, p. 165; I, MORSE, pp. 320–321.

was that if the trade of the other maritime nations should still be confined to Canton, they (the English) will not proffer demands on the behalf of the others, but that if the Great Emperor should permit the others to resort to Fukien, Chekiang, and Kiangsu for trade, the English would not be small-minded about it; that they would not mind if the ships of other nations frequented Hongkong." The initial reaction of the Imperial Government, however, was adverse to the granting of the additional privileges to others than the English. In the light of arguments presented by the Imperial Commissioners, Ilipoo and Kiying, after their arrival at Canton, in favor of giving the same status to the nationals of all states (as had been the case in pre-treaty days at Canton) the decision was taken by the Imperial Government to generalize the benefits of the treaty of Nanking. Thus the "open door" principle of "most-favored-nation" treatment requested by Commodore Kearny was accepted by China from the first. But its acceptance "was due primarily to the ideas and actions of two Chinese (or rather two Manchu) statesmen, Ilipoo and Kiying, who, however, only continued the Chinese tradition of the eighteenth century. The attitude of Great Britain, as declared by Sir Henry Pottinger at Nanking, made the Chinese statesmen feel free to carry out their policy of equality. The diplomacy of Commodore Lawrence Kearny put the question of America's claim for equality on the agenda of the Chinese Government so that it was taken up and decided at that particular time, so soon after the Treaty of Nanking. And Caleb Cushing simply put the previous developments into a treaty." [14]

While war between England and China was still in progress a movement was set on foot in the United States which led to the appointment of the first American minister to China. Mr. Caleb Cushing, selected by President Tyler for the delicate task of negotiating the first treaty between the two countries, arrived off the port of Macao on February 24, 1844. He was instructed to negotiate with the Chinese officials only on terms of complete equality, to make clear to the Chinese that the United States had no aggressive aims, to make a treaty similar to the British treaty of Nanking, but with fuller terms if possible, and to attempt to reach Peking and place a letter from the President in the hands of the Emperor or, failing in that, in the hands of some high official of the central government. While he did not reach Peking, he did, after some delay,[15] succeed in the negotiation of a treaty. This followed the general lines of the British treaty, but enlarged

[14] T. F. TSIANG, *The Extension of Equal Privileges to Other Nations than the British after the Treaty of Nanking, Chinese Social and Political Science Review*, vol. 15, p. 443. The previous quotation is from the same article, p. 428. The article (pp. 422–444), based on Chinese sources, is a careful review of the question. For a somewhat different conclusion see the article by THOMAS KEARNEY, *The Tsiang Documents*, C.S. & P.S.R., vol. 16, pp. 75–109.

[15] Mainly due to the determination of the Chinese officials to carry out their instructions to prevent them "at all costs" from going to Peking.

upon its provisions in several respects, the most important addition being a clear and explicit statement of the principle of extraterritoriality. Article XXI of the treaty of 1844 provided:

Subjects of China who may be guilty of any criminal act towards citizens of the United States shall be arrested and punished by the Chinese authorities according to the laws of China, and citizens of the United States who may commit any crime in China shall be subject to be tried and punished only by the Consul or other public functionary of the United States thereto authorized according to the laws of the United States; and in order to secure the prevention of all controversy and disaffection, justice shall be equitably and impartially administered on both sides.

This provision, which related only to criminal cases, was extended to civil cases as well by Articles XXIV and XXV. Consequently, two of the limitations on China's sovereignty (i.e., loss of tariff and judicial autonomy), which the Chinese were long desirous of having removed, date from the earliest English and American treaties respectively.[16]

France followed the United States in the negotiation of a treaty. The French treaty contained much the same matter as the other two, but the French envoy, although not through treaty provision, carried the movement toward opening China a short step further by persuading the Chinese commissioner to memorialize the Throne to permit Roman Catholic missionaries to build churches in the treaty ports, and to grant toleration there to native as well as foreign Christians. The Emperor accepted the suggestion and extended this limited toleration later to Protestant missionaries as well.

The latter had been attempting to establish themselves in the country since 1807, when the Rev. Robert Morrison, sent out by the London Missionary Society, reached Canton. Because of the restricted opportunities at Canton the work had not been greatly extended by 1844. More attention, in fact, was paid to Chinese in the Malay Archipelago than in China proper. However, the Protestant missionary community had enlarged somewhat and a few converts had been won. But the real importance of the Protestant missionary at this time and for the next several years lay in his linguistic rather than in his evangelical work. The commercial and political agents had to rely on him to a large extent for making translations and serving

[16] The English negotiators understood extraterritoriality to be enjoyed by their nationals under the Treaty of Nanking, although it was not expressly stipulated for, and Orders in Council providing for its exercise were soon issued. The detailed provisions in the American treaty were insisted upon as an offset to the advantage gained by Great Britain through the cession of Hongkong. In any case the deficiencies in Chinese administration of justice in cases involving foreigners had been so forcibly brought home to the Americans at the time of the Terranova case (1821) that some protection to foreign life was felt to be absolutely necessary.

For a good brief discussion of extraterritoriality in China from 1844 to the present time, see WILLOUGHBY, W. W., *Foreign Rights and Interests in China*, ch. II. For text of the treaty of 1844, see MALLOY, vol. 1, pp. 196–210.

as interpreter, and in this way individual missionaries often came to exert considerable influence. Furthermore, these pioneers in the field, beginning with Morrison, prepared dictionaries to serve their successors, and began the task of translating Western works into Chinese and Chinese works into English, in the former case beginning with religious tracts and gradually including important non-religious works. In this, as in the medical field, where they had also begun work, they initiated what as time went on became a most important contribution to Chinese development as well as to that of the West. Their position became somewhat more tolerable after 1844, as did that of the Catholic missionaries, and the possibilities of their work enlarged as fuller toleration was provided for by treaty in 1858.

The treaty of Nanking, the supplementary treaty of the Bogue, and the succeeding American and French treaties inserted the opening wedge for the development of direct intercourse between the outside world and China, but they left much to be accomplished—for it took other blows, driving the wedge in more and more deeply, before China was actually opened.

This entering wedge was the provision for the opening of the five ports to trade, and for the right to carry on the trade freely without the interposition of a Chinese monopoly. But while this concession had been made by China, under the coercion of British arms, the difficulties in the way of making the concession effective were immediately revealed. In the first place, the Peking government did not thereby abate its feeling of superiority to the outside world. It yielded to the pressure applied, but as soon as the pressure was relaxed it tacitly and openly encouraged those who desired to see the former conditions restored. It yielded in negotiation but tried to recover the lost ground by procrastination in making effective the provisions of the treaties. In the second place, even if the central government had made every effort to live up to its newly assumed obligations, which it did not do, it would have been difficult for it to enforce them in the face of local opposition because of the large measure of autonomy enjoyed by the provinces and the localities under the Chinese system of government.

At some places no difficulty was encountered in the opening of the port, in providing adequately for the residence of foreigners, and in making the necessary arrangements for trade. At Shanghai, for example, the relations between the foreigners and the local authorities were comparatively amicable from the very beginning. Ground was set aside for foreign residents and every effort was made to facilitate trade. The arrangements for residence made at Shanghai mark the beginning of the system of concessions, or foreign residential districts, at the treaty ports. The original British settlement, into which American traders came, and in which an American consulate was established, became in time, through American insistence, an international settlement. The French insisted on a separate area. From that time to the present the international settlement has been maintained and further extended, with a separate concession beside it for the French. The foreign communities soon came to administer these areas as separate municipalities.

At Amoy and Ningpo the foreigners had little difficulty in establishing their position under the treaties, although at Amoy the participation of foreigners in the coolie traffic proved a source of friction, particularly as they attempted to shield natives working for them in it by invoking the extraterritorial system in their behalf. At Foochow the establishment of amicable relations proved more difficult, partly because a profitable trade was slower to develop.

But it was at Canton that the chief obstacles were encountered. At the other ports there was an interest in breaking down the monopoly of the trade which had formerly been enjoyed by the Cantonese, while at Canton there was an established tradition of superiority and of dictation, together with a more recently engendered popular hostility to foreigners, which made it difficult for the local populace and officialdom to accept the new conditions. Relations were fairly satisfactory as long as the Manchu Kiying, one of China's plenipotentiaries at Nanking, remained as the Imperial commissioner, for he tried to carry out at least the letter of the treaties; but after his removal not only acute friction but actual strife developed.

The officials tried so to regulate the contacts between Hongkong and the mainland as to strangle the Hongkong settlement. They denied the right of residence at Canton or tried to delay its realization.[17] They would not permit direct official intercourse on terms of equality; they attempted to keep the trade in the hands of an enlarged monopoly of Chinese merchants; and they refused to acquiesce in the extraterritorial provisions of the treaties. On the whole the foreigners and their representatives were conciliatory in their conduct, but individuals on occasion behaved so as to re-arouse Chinese hostility, and the representatives continued to press their claims for a complete fulfillment of treaty provisions.

6. TREATY REVISION

Furthermore, the passage of time revealed defects in the operation of the treaties which the foreigners were anxious to see removed. The American treaty provided for revision at the end of a twelve-year period, and the other Powers could claim a similar right by virtue of the "most-favored-nation" clause in their treaties. The need for revision was urged unsuccessfully by successive American commissioners, who could not even secure an interview with Yeh, the Chinese commissioner at Canton, with whom

[17] It should be noted, however, that the treaties in the Chinese text did not specify the right of residence *within* the *walled city*, which is what the foreigners insisted upon at Canton, so that technically the Chinese action was not in violation of the treaties.

alone they were permitted to discuss the question. English attempts proved equally fruitless. This question, together with the unsatisfactory relations existing at Canton, finally led to what many believed to be the only satisfactory method of dealing with China—negotiation supported by force.

The crisis was actually produced by a conflict over jurisdiction at Canton known as the *Lorcha Arrow* case. The *Lorcha Arrow* was a Chinese-owned but Hongkong-registered [18] vessel, carrying an English master and flying the English flag. While lying in the river she was boarded by Chinese acting under the Viceroy's orders and twelve of her crew were removed. The British demanded their return, a demand which the Chinese at first refused and later complied with in an unsatisfactory manner. The dispute continued until it finally led to hostilities at Canton in 1856, and to occupation of the city in 1857. It appeared that the English had become involved in a war with China again, but as a matter of fact the trouble was entirely localized until the foreigners decided again to move north and press the issue of treaty revision at Tientsin. The English remained on as good terms as usual with the Chinese officials and merchants at the other treaty ports, a condition which was reversed when hostilities were suspended and trade was resumed at Canton while the British and French were advancing on Peking.

All four of the states having important contacts with China—England, France, Russia, and the United States—were interested in establishing more satisfactory terms of intercourse. England's policy, conciliatory since 1842, had come after 1856 to be that of forwarding negotiations by the show and application of force, a reversion to the program of 1840–1842. France, as an unimportant trading Power, had indicated that her particular interest in China was that of protecting the Roman Catholic missions for which her envoy had secured a measure of toleration. At the time of the Canton trouble in 1856–1857 the French had a grievance against the Chinese government on account of the "judicial" murder of the Abbé Chapdelaine. He, as was a common missionary habit, had penetrated into the interior and, while favorably received at first, had been seized and finally put to death at the direction of a Chinese magistrate. Efforts to obtain reparation having failed, the French joined the English in the second bombardment and the occupation of Canton. This coöperation [19] was continued when a joint expedition, supporting Lord Elgin and Baron Gros, the British and French plenipotentiaries, was sent north in 1858.

Russian and American ministers accompanied the Anglo-French expe-

[18] Her registry had expired at the time of the trouble, but this entered into the case only as a subsequent justification for the Chinese action as it was unknown to them at the time. Furthermore she was on her way to Hongkong where her license would have been renewed.

[19] England and France had joined together at this same time in action against Russia (the Crimean war). Thus, in a sense, their coöperation was a projection into the Far East of a temporary European collaboration

dition, but did not participate in its hostile activities because of their explicit instructions to avoid warlike measures. For the policy of the United States continued to be that of peaceful negotiation. Her representatives in China had repeatedly advocated the threat of force to advance American interests, and at this time proposals were made in Washington by the British ambassador for a triple alliance of Great Britain, France, and the United States directed against China. But in spite of the fact that all attempts to negotiate with the Imperial government without a show of force had been unsuccessful from 1854 to 1858, the United States adhered to its earlier policy. Minister Reed, while instructed to coöperate in all peaceful measures, was also instructed not to join in any hostile demonstrations against China. The Russians were equally enjoined to a peaceful procedure. As a matter of fact, they were applying pressure in the north by their steady advance to the Pacific. This made possible a change in the territorial status on the north when the treaty of Aigun (1858) was negotiated by Count Muraviev, named Amurski for his achievements. He secured a delimitation of the frontier by which Russian title to the territories north of the Argun and the Amur to its mouth was recognized, while title to the area between the Ussuri and the sea was left for subsequent determination. All that remained for Count Putiatin, who accompanied the Anglo-French expedition, to accomplish was to secure what was for Russia the less important right to trade with China by sea, and treatment within China equivalent to that accorded to other foreigners.

England and France, therefore, moved north to Tientsin in force, followed by the American and Russian negotiators, thus dividing the Western states into two groups, since the American and Russian representatives early established close and harmonious relations. It was at Tientsin that new treaties were made (1858) to replace the first agreements. In addition to preserving the gains already made, the treaties provided for the opening to trade of eleven new ports, including several on the Yangtse River, for navigation of the river to Hankow, and for the residence in Peking of diplomatic representatives. The advantages gained by any one nation, under the operation of the most-favored-nation clause in the other treaties, accrued to the other states. Provision was also made for revision, largely in the foreign interest, of the tariff schedules, which became fixed at a levy of five per cent *ad valorem* on the basis of the prevailing prices. In this revision a duty was put on the importation of opium, thus legalizing and regulating the traffic. It is interesting to note that the opium question was taken up at this time and that legalization of its importation was secured at the urgent request of the American minister. This constituted a reversal of the earlier American position with respect to the trade in the drug. The American treaty also contained a stipulation for toleration for missionaries and converts without specification of the place where they might live and work, thus for the first time putting their position on a treaty basis. The British treaty contained a similar provision, while that of France stipulated, in addition, for protection for missionaries in the interior. It may be added here that the French convention of Peking (1860) went still further in that it required the Chinese government to proclaim throughout the Empire that missionary activities were permitted and that those who indiscriminately arrested Christians would be punished, and to agree that all real estate confiscated when the Catholics were expelled from China would be paid for. In 1865 the Imperial government also assented to provisions surreptitiously inserted in the Chinese text of the convention of 1860 granting the right to missionaries to purchase land and erect buildings thereon in all parts of the Empire.[20]

The other treaties, completed before the English had finished their negotiations, differed from that signed by Lord Elgin in some other details, but principally in that they provided for embassies to Peking rather than for the establishment of permanent missions. But all were put upon an equal basis through the operation of the most-favored-nation principle. While the Americans and Russians were successful in negotiating treaties without a show of force, their experiences with the Chinese, complying so far as possible with all the demands made on them, demonstrated conclusively that the treaties of 1842–1844 would not have been revised if it had not been for the pressure applied jointly by England and France. The British envoy, who had been the most insistent on the right of residence at Peking, was asked to request his government not to insist on an immediate effect being given to the right. Also the attempt was made to secure an exchange of ratifications of the treaty, not at Peking, as provided for by its terms, but at Canton or Shanghai. When this effort proved unavailing the attempt was made to effect the exchange at Tientsin. Finally the English, together with their French allies, again resorted to force and moved directly against Peking. Attempts to obstruct their advance proved unsuccessful. Peking was finally occupied, the Manchu court fleeing north to Jehol, and the summer Palace at Peking was destroyed as a measure of retaliation for mistreatment of some prisoners by the Chinese. This was the last forcible step necessary in the process of causing the Chinese grudgingly to admit the foreigner to intercourse on terms of equality.

During the advance on Peking and while the allies, in occupation of the capital, were negotiating with Prince Kung as the representative of the Imperial government, the Russians consistently posed as the friends of China. When peace was made they secured compensation for their friendship in the form of a cession of the region between the Ussuri and the Pacific to Russia, thus completing the westward movement of that Empire and bringing her into territorial contact with Korea as well as China,

---

[20] DENNETT, TYLER, *Americans in Eastern Asia*, pp. 561–563.

and giving her an interest in the islands off the northeastern coast of Asia.[21]

The occupation of Peking and the acceptance of the treaties of 1858 did not cause the Chinese people and the Imperial government to revise their opinion of the foreigner or of the inherent superiority of China. They had given way under pressure and they had conceded only what had been presented to them as the irreducible minimum in the foreigner's demands. Where force had not been applied they had not voluntarily made any concessions. If after 1860 the Imperial government had accepted in good faith the new relationships established, if China had made a more extensive effort to acquaint herself with the conditions of the outside world, and had attempted to make use of the opportunities presented to strengthen herself by borrowing more than she did from the material civilization of the West, and if she had not attempted again to neutralize the advance made by the Powers, the history of the next sixty years might have been very different. But she did few of these things. Instead of accommodating herself fully and freely to the new world and the new conditions, she kept her eyes fixed on the glorious past, attempting to modernize for the most part only the defense forces of the Empire. Instead of treating with the newly-established envoys of the Powers on terms of complete equality,[22] she persisted in small slights that reacted only to her own disadvantage. That the Chinese attitude, except in a few individual instances, was not fundamentally changed was due in part to the circumstances under which China's relations to the West were defined and fixed—circumstances which were certainly not conducive to a free and full acceptance of the new contacts. It was also due in part to the attitude and actions of the Powers after 1860. But whatever the reason for her attitude, the fact remains that China stood to lose more than anyone else as a result of the failure freely to accept the new order, forced on her though it was.[23]

REFERENCES FOR FURTHER STUDY

M. J. BAU, *Foreign Relations of China* (1921), ch. 1; a brief account of the opening of the country from the Chinese point of view. CAPT. F. BRINKLEY, *China, Its History, Arts and Literature,* 4 vols. (1902) (Oriental Series, vol. 9–12), vol. 11. MAURICE COLLIS, *Foreign Mud* (1946). W. C. COSTIN, *Great Britain and China, 1833–1860* (1936). T. DENNETT, *Americans in Eastern Asia* (1922), ch. 1–18; written largely from American sources; serves

[21] For a more detailed account of this Russian move to the Pacific see ch. XVIII. sec. 1, 2.

[22] Representatives of the Powers were established in Peking after 1860, but they were denied direct access to the Emperor. A Board of Foreign Affairs (Tsungli Yamen) was established in 1861, not as an independent board, but rather as a group of men representative of the other branches of administration. This board was not designed to promote the interests of China in her contacts with the outside world, but to confine those contacts within the narrowest possible limits.

[23] On the extent of change by 1894 see, infra, ch. III, sec. 7.

as a corrective to MORSE, *International Relations,* vol. 1; both are of great importance to the student; excellent bibliography of sources. R. K. DOUGLAS, *China* (1907), ch. 8–9–10. H. H. GOWEN and J. W. HALL, *An Outline History of China* (1926), ch. 16–22; internal history from the Manchu conquest to and including the first war with England. ELDON GRIFFIN, *Clippers and Consuls: American Consular and Commercial Relations with East Asia—1845–1860* (1938). A. E. HAKE, *The Story of Chinese Gordon* (1884). HARRY HUSSEY, *Venerable Ancestor, the Life and Times of Tz'u Hsi, 1835–1908* (1949). THOMAS KEARNEY, *The Tsiang Documents: Elipoo, Keying, Pottinger, and Kearney and the Most Favored Nation and Open Door Policy in China in 1842–1844: An American Viewpoint,* Chinese Social and Political Science Review, vol. 16, pp. 75–109. G. W. KEETON, *The Development of Extraterritoriality in China,* 2 vols. (1928), vol. 1, ch. 1–4. V. K. W. KOO, *Status of Aliens in China,* in Columbia University Studies, vol. 50, pt. 2 (1912), ch. 1–9; an account of one phase of the early foreign relations, from the Chinese point of view. K. S. LATOURETTE, *History of the Early Relations between the United States and China, 1784–1844* (1917); an excellent study of the question. K. S. LATOURETTE, *The Chinese: Their History and Culture* (1934), ch. 9, 10; a standard work. K. S. LATOURETTE, *A History of Christian Missions in China* (1929), ch. 1–14; the most valuable work on the subject. LI CHIEN-NUNG, *The Political History of China, 1840–1928;* good translation of standard nationalist text. H. F. MACNAIR, *Modern Chinese History, Selected Readings* (1913), ch. 1–5. H. B. MORSE, *International Relations of the Chinese Empire,* vol. 1 (1910); an excellent volume, written from materials in the Chinese Repository and from British sources; needs to be used with DENNETT, *Americans in Eastern Asia.* H. B. MORSE, *The Chronicles of the East India Company Trading to China, 1636–1834* (1926). L. OLIPHANT, *Narrative of Earl of Elgin's Mission to China and Japan in the Years 1857, '58 '59,* 2 vols. (1860). E. H. PARKER, *China, Her History, Commerce and Diplomacy* (1901), ch. 5; a good brief treatment. E. H. PARKER, *Chinese Account of the Opium War* (1881); very interesting although brief. E. H. PRITCHARD, *Anglo-Chinese Relations during the Seventeenth and Eighteenth Centuries* (1929). A. J. SARGENT, *Anglo-Chinese Commerce and Diplomacy* (1907), ch. 1–5; an excellent study, containing bibliography of source materials. SSU-YÜ TENG, *Chang Hsi and the Treaty of Nanking, 1842* (1944). SSU-YÜ TENG, *New Light on the History of the Taiping Rebellion* (1950). T. F. TSIANG, *The Extension of Equal Commercial Privileges to Other Nations than the British after the Treaty of Nanking,* Chinese Social and Political Science Review, vol. 15, pp. 432–444.

CHAPTER III

THE FOREIGN IMPACT: 1860–1894

1. CONDITIONS ANTECEDENT TO REBELLION

THE end of a dynasty in the Celestial Empire has always been marked by an extended period of internal turmoil. The hand of the Imperial authority has relaxed its hold. Officials have become venal and uninterested in the welfare of the people. The basic tax on land has come to be evaded by the rich gentry, with the connivance of the officials. The tax burden, in consequence, has fallen more and more heavily on the lesser peasants. Surtaxes, commutation charges, and "costs of collection" charges of various sorts have begun to be imposed and to increase in amounts. Tenantry has increased on account of the inability of the "small families" to hold their land in the face of these increasing charges. As the burden has increased, to the profit of the provincial officials, in the main, rather than of the Imperial government, the economic and social causes of unrest have been accentuated.[1] The weakening of the central authority has, consequently, permitted banditry to increase on land and piracy on the water. Frequently the condition of unrest has been aggravated by flood or drought, or both, additionally upsetting the economy of the country and stimulating organized robbery as a means of livelihood. Secret societies with antidynastic aims have sprung up and multiplied. And sometimes there has been an attack from the outside too strong for a decadent rule to withstand. The dynasty has thereupon fallen because the "mandate of Heaven" has been withdrawn—the evidence of it being the inability of the Emperor to preserve the domestic tranquillity, to protect the people against excessive exploitation, and to safeguard the country from external attack.

2. FOREIGN RELATIONS

All of these conditions, normally antecedent to a change in rule, were present in nineteenth-century China, although the foreign foes of the Manchu Emperor came from distant countries rather than from just across the frontier. By the middle of the century the foreigners had successfully broken down the first barriers. They had established their representatives

[1] For exposition of this factor during the Manchu period see an illuminating article by WANG YÜ-CH'ÜAN, *The Rise of the Land Tax and the Fall of Dynasties in Chinese History*, Pacific Affairs, vol. 9, pp. 201–220.

in Peking, forced cessions of territory (Hongkong to England and the territory to the north to Russia), and penetrated the Empire beyond Canton for trade and missionary purposes under conditions removing their peoples from the effective control of the Imperial authorities. They had waged two successful wars against the Empire and had occupied the capital, driving the Emperor into temporary exile. They had not, it is true, attempted to take over the government of the country, but had allowed the Emperor to resume his sway.

As a matter of fact, the foreigners seemed to assume that the establishment of their legations at Peking, the opening of ports and the consequent enlargement of trade, and the securing of toleration for the missionary, would result in the removal of the psychological as well as the material barriers to free intercourse. What they found was that their presence was still resented, that they had continually to struggle to maintain their newly-won privileges, and that the government and the people alike remained hostile or indifferent to suggestions of further change.

From 1842 to 1860 the European Powers had been forced to deal with the local officials at each place where a foothold had been secured in order to obtain a definition of their rights and position under the treaties. The only official competent to discuss matters of general importance, such as treaty revision, was the one farthest removed from Peking—the Canton Viceroy. Until the movement on Peking, pressure had been applied on local governments when and where it was needed. It was hoped and expected that the establishment of the right of residence at Peking would result in contact with the center of power, so that pressure on the localities would become unnecessary.

In applying this local pressure one state had taken the lead, but the advantages won by it had become common property, and no state had attempted to secure special privileges by pursuing an independent policy. With the possible exception of Russia, the Western Powers had a common aim—that of ending the period of seclusion. From 1860 to about 1875 the representatives of the West at Peking continued to think and act largely in terms of the common interest—the basis of their policy being the wider opening of the breach in the wall of seclusion, but not the destruction of China. Mr. Anson Burlingame, the American representative at Peking from 1861 to 1867, who was largely responsible for the establishment of the coöperative policy in a specific and practical form, gave it a very clear and fair statement.[2]

The policy upon which we are agreed is briefly this: that while we claim our treaty right to buy and sell, and hire, in the treaty ports, subject, in respect to our rights of property and person, to the jurisdiction of our own govern-

[2] Diplomatic Correspondence, 1864, pp. 859 ff. Quoted in full by DENNETT, T., *Americans in Eastern Asia*, pp. 375-376.

ments, we will not ask for, nor take concessions of, territory in the treaty ports, or in any way interfere with the jurisdiction of the Chinese government over its own people, nor ever menace the territorial integrity of the Chinese Empire. That we will not take part in the internal struggles in China, beyond what is necessary to maintain our treaty rights. That the latter we will unitedly sustain against all who may violate them. To this end we are now clear in the policy of defending the treaty ports against the Taipings, or rebels; but in such a way as not to make war upon that considerable body of the Chinese people, by following them into the interior of their country.

This policy gradually gave way to one of separate action to secure redress of grievances, or new privileges, so that after 1875 there was not the unity of purpose among the Powers, founded upon a willingness to respect the integrity of China, that the earlier period had produced.

The outstanding diplomatic question at Peking after 1860 was that of securing audience with the Emperor. For almost the entire period under review the foreign representatives were forced to deal exclusively with the members of the Tsungli Yamen, a board organized in 1861 to deal with the problems of foreign affairs. This board gradually assumed the appearance of an Imperial Cabinet because of the great importance of its decisions, for it was in connection with treaty enforcement that the central government was forced slowly to a greater measure of interference in the administration of affairs in the provinces, dropping its hortatory rôle and assuming more of a mandatory rule. The members of the Tsungli Yamen long stood as buffers between the Emperor and the foreign ministers, doing all in their power to prevent the latter from securing the reception to which they felt that they were entitled and which would have helped to establish relations on a more tolerable basis.

A plausible pretext for delay in the granting of an audience existed in the fact that the Emperor was a minor, and the government was conducted in his name by a regency. When the Emperor attained his majority, in 1873, the audience question was pressed upon the Tsungli Yamen. Since there was no further excuse for postponement, the Emperor expressed his willingness to receive the diplomatic corps. But when the audience was granted it took place in the hall where tributary missions were customarily received, and was, consequently, considered no concession by the Chinese. The only gain made lay in the fact that for the first time the kowtow, or nine prostrations, was dispensed with. It was only in 1893, thirty years after the right of residence had been conceded, that voluntary and gracious provision was made for the reception of the foreign representatives on fitting terms and under proper conditions. It is true that another regency intervened (1875-1889) between the original reception and the final attainment of the goal, but the fact remains that the minority of the Emperor was taken advantage of by the Manchu government to prevent the establishment of intercourse on a basis satisfactory to Europe and usual among members of the European society of nations.

Before China could be considered to have emerged from her seclusion it was also necessary for her to reciprocate the establishment of legations at Peking by sending representatives abroad. This it was to her advantage to do in order that she might present her views on Chinese questions direct to the heads of foreign governments. She did not act, however, until 1877, when the first Chinese envoy to England presented his credentials. Prior to 1877, however, some indications of an intention to treat with the foreigner on his own ground were given. When Sir Robert Hart, head of the Chinese Maritime Customs, returned to Europe on leave in 1866, he took with him an official delegate appointed by the Chinese government. But this delegate "was not commissioned as an envoy, but was charged to investigate and report on what he should see." [3] Nothing came of this move, for the envoy gave no favorable impression to Europe of Chinese civilization, and in return found nothing favorable to report.

In 1867, again on Sir Robert Hart's recommendation, the Chinese government asked Mr. Anson Burlingame, the retiring American minister to Peking, to head a mission to the West. Mr. Burlingame had taken a leading part in bringing about a coöperation of the Powers based upon the preservation of the integrity and the maintenance of the sovereignty of China. The coöperation was largely personal, however, and had partially broken down even before Mr. Burlingame's departure from Peking. He was interested in his new appointment largely because of a desire to establish the policy on a governmental rather than a personal basis. The mission proceeded first to the United States, where it was received enthusiastically by the people and cordially by the government, which was glad to reëndorse its former policy authoritatively in articles supplementary to the Tientsin treaty. It was also well received in England. The French government was less cordial, while Bismarck was rather noncommittal in his exchange of views with Mr. Burlingame. Upon the death of the head of the mission in St. Petersburg, the Chinese members returned home.

Mr. Burlingame was eminently fitted to arouse interest in the Chinese in foreign lands. His oratorical gifts, however, led him into an overstatement of the actual readiness of the Chinese to advance along Western lines. For that reason he did perhaps as much harm as good. Those familiar with the attitude of the Chinese government as well as that of its officials, must have been amazed to read that China "tells you she is ready to take upon her ancient civilization the graft of your civilization. She tells you she is ready to take back her own inventions, with all their developments. She tells you that she is willing to trade with you, to buy of you, to sell

[3] II, Morse, H. B., *International Relations of Chinese Empire*, p. 187.

to you, to help you strike off the shackles from trade. She invites your merchants, she invites your missionaries. She tells the latter to plant the shining cross on every hill and in every valley. For she is hospitable to fair argument." [4]

3. CHINESE EMIGRATION

The Burlingame treaty with the United States, in addition to giving more formal statement to the policy of respect for the integrity and sovereignty of China, had importance because it gave to Chinese laborers a treaty right to enter the United States and to receive as fair treatment as that accorded to the citizens or subjects of the most-favored-nation. This treatment was promised just at the time when agitation in California against the Chinese laborer was beginning. The number resident there had increased from about 25,000 in 1852 to 50,000 in 1867, and by 1882 there were 132,000 Chinese on the Pacific coast, drawn or brought there by the demand for cheap labor. At first they were well, even eagerly, received, but as their numbers increased they became more and more unpopular. Legislation discriminating against them was enacted, and popular hostility was shown by active ill-treatment accorded both by individuals and by mob action. The legislation ran counter to the provisions of the Burlingame treaty, and the treatment of the Chinese laborers certainly conflicted with its guarantees. The agitation finally extended to Congress and resulted in the passage of a measure limiting to fifteen the number of Chinese immigrants who might be brought in any one vessel. The bill was vetoed by the President, who sent a commission to China to secure revision of the immigration clauses of the treaty as a preliminary to the enactment of restrictive legislation. The best that could be secured was a revision giving the right to "regulate, limit or suspend," but not to prohibit, the entrance of Chinese. Those already in the country were to receive most-favored-nation treatment.

Congress immediately (1882) enacted a restrictive measure suspending the immigration of Chinese laborers for ten years, but the ill-treatment of Chinese on the Pacific coast continued, giving the Chinese minister one occasion after another to demand redress from the American government. Furthermore, while the Imperial government was not particularly solicitous as to the welfare of its subjects abroad, it was not strengthened in its regard for foreigners or in its regard for treaties by the action of the United States and the treatment accorded to Chinese resident in California. It was unfortunate that the immigration question should have become acute so soon after the Chinese representative had secured for the Chinese a treaty right of entrance and good treatment.

[4] Quoted by DENNETT, p. 385.

A more serious and perplexing question than that of emigration to the United States and to British possessions was presented in the sending of Chinese laborers to Cuba, Peru, and other places. While Chinese had long been prohibited by Imperial law from emigrating, some had gone to seek their fortunes overseas at a comparatively early time. At first this emigration was individual and free, as it continued to be to the United States. But after the middle of the last century, as the demand for cheap Chinese labor increased, the contract-labor system developed, and with it grave abuses. Coolies were procured against their will or by false representations; they were packed like sardines on the foreign coolie-carrying vessels, and they found themselves in a condition worse than slavery upon arrival at their destination. Conditions grew so bad that the Chinese government was finally forced to act. France, England, and the United States were willing to coöperate with the Imperial government to break up the traffic, but most of the contract laborers were being dispatched from under Portuguese jurisdiction at Macao. By 1875 the "conscience" of the Western Powers was fully awakened and strong in its condemnation of Portugal for conniving with the traffickers at the point of departure, and of Spain and Peru because of conditions at the destination. The British government in 1874 made representations on the subject to the government of Portugal, and in 1875 the authorities at Macao were instructed to forbid the emigration of Chinese under contract as well as all free migration from that place. While this did not immediately end contract migration, it did mark the beginning of the end. Meanwhile Spain had been led, as had Peru, to abate the intolerable condition of the laborers already under their respective jurisdictions.

A result of the Burlingame treaty more beneficial to China than its immigration clauses was the fact that it prevented the carrying through of a revision of the Tientsin treaties under the direction of the British traders, who were agitating for the complete opening of China to trade. This would have tremendously complicated the problems of the Chinese government, and, because of the extraterritorial status of foreigners, would have been most unwise at that time. Unquestionably one of the motives of the Imperial government in authorizing the Burlingame mission was to forestall such a revision, or any revision at all. Mr. Burlingame, as a matter of fact, seems to have exceeded his authority in negotiating the Washington articles, judging by the reception of the treaty by the Tsungli Yamen and the hesitancy of that body in recommending its ratification. Another important effect of the Burlingame mission was the action of the British and Prussian governments. They declared as their policy for the future that "unfriendly pressure should not be applied inconsistent with the independence and safety of China." The American treaty provided for freedom from interference in the development of China. The Powers, on the whole, followed this policy, which superseded the former policy of coercing local officials, in the development of their interest in China during the succeeding years. Moral pressure on Peking to secure treaty enforcement was substituted for physical pressure on the provinces.

4. ATTITUDE TOWARD FOREIGNERS

Individual relations with the Chinese were not more harmonious, as a rule, than official relations. As foreigners spread more widely through the country, and particularly as missionaries went into the interior away from the treaty ports, distrust and hostility showed itself in anti-Christian riots resulting in loss of life and property. One of the worst of these demonstrations took place at Tientsin, where a mob destroyed the Catholic orphanage and cathedral. This was typical of incidents in other parts of the country. After establishing the orphanage and a hospital the sisters found that few children were brought to them voluntarily. Consequently they offered a premium for each child brought in. They also seem to have offered inducements to have children in the last stages of illness brought to them for the purpose of being baptized *in articulo mortis*. Because of this there were large numbers of burials from the orphanage.

These were verifiable facts; and on this substructure of fact, the credulous Chinese built up a superstructure of their own fancy-incitement to kidnapping, mystic rights of baptism, extraction of eyes and hearts, and other horrors, all working them into a frenzy of fear and hatred.[5]

An epidemic which visited the orphanage in the early summer of 1870 and caused the death of between thirty and forty children brought on a crisis.

A massacre may or may not have been premeditated and impending, but it was now inevitable. A half-century of racial antipathy; a decade of national hatred; the gathering growth of anti-Christian feeling, based partly on religious bigotry, partly on superstition, partly on credulity; all these were brought to a common focus, and the growing disorder culminated in three hours of murder, arson and plunder.[6]

Such factors as these made for popular hostility in this case and in others, but one must remember that many of the officials and members of the educated classes disliked the foreigner and all of his works. Instead of investigating and restraining, or protesting to the consuls on the basis of the facts found, local officials in many cases stimulated the people to action which under the circumstances could have but one result—further humiliations

[5] II, MORSE, p. 242.
[6] Ibid., p. 248.

for their country. The magistrate at Tientsin, for example, made no apparent effort to allay the hostility of the people, but rather encouraged it.

On the other hand, one can understand and partly justify the Chinese attitude when one considers the arrogance of many foreigners, including some of the consuls. This arrogance was based on their privileges and on the assumption that the Chinese were pagans, which they seemed to think justified any sort of treatment of the common people. Then there was the attempt of some missionaries, more especially the Roman Catholics, to throw the mantle of their protection around their converts in their dealings both with the people and with the officials. Finally, the Chinese naturally, if unjustifiably, blamed the foreigners because men were thrown out of work by the introduction of steamboats on the rivers and on account of other Western innovations.

The Tientsin massacre was a blow directly aimed at France, since she asserted a protectorate over Roman Catholic interests in China and since the mission itself was French, having been established as a result of the French occupation of territory in Tientsin in 1858–1860. For that reason she served drastic demands on China and required immediate acceptance of them. Because of the outbreak of the war with Prussia she was unable to enforce her demands, and finally accepted satisfaction in the form of punishment of those guilty and the dispatch of a mission of apology to France. Since this outbreak was, in another sense, simply an exaggerated expression of the general Chinese hostility to foreign missionary activities, the Powers acted unitedly in demanding satisfaction for anti-missionary outbreaks and adequate security for the future. A united front was maintained in spite of the outbreak of the Franco-Prussian War.

Another illustration of hostility to foreigners is to be found in the Margary case. Desirous of opening up a route for trade with southwestern China by way of Upper Burma, Great Britain dispatched an expedition of investigation from that region in 1876. In order to facilitate its penetration of Yunnan province, passports were secured from the government of China. Mr. Margary, a young member of the British consular service, was sent from Peking to join the expedition at the frontier of Yunnan. He encountered no difficulty on his way down, but when the expedition had progressed a short distance into Yunnan rumors reached Colonel Brown (the commander) and Mr. Margary that trouble was brewing. The latter, with a party of Chinese, went ahead to investigate the situation, and he, with five of his companions, was set upon and killed. The entire expedition was then forced to retire.

The British minister at Peking, Sir Thomas Wade, received word of the occurrence some weeks later by way of the India Office in London. He immediately remonstrated with the Chinese government, demanding full

satisfaction for the outrage and including in his demands extraneous matter such as adjustment of the audience question, and, in fact, a satisfactory
settlement of all questions at issue between the two governments. To his
demand for an investigation of the murder, in which a British officer should
participate, the Chinese soon agreed. But it was necessary for him to leave
Peking, taking the legation staff with him, before the Chinese government
would consider his other demands. Finally Li Hung-chang, Viceroy of
Chihli province, was appointed to negotiate a settlement. This settlement
was reached at Chefoo on September 13, 1876. The first section of the
Chefoo convention provided satisfaction for the murder of Mr. Margary;
the second, for a betterment of the conditions of official intercourse; and
the third, for an extension of the trade, including the opening of several new
ports. Ten years later came the loss of China's claim to suzerainty over Upper
Burma.

5. POLICIES AND INTERESTS OF THE POWERS

It might have been thought, in view of the attitude of the Manchu
government and of the Chinese people toward Europeans, that the Powers
would have continued to stand solidly together in the protection of their
interests. So long as the diplomatic corps presented a united front to the
Tsungli Yamen the Chinese government could not afford to refuse redress
for grievances flowing from the non-observance of treaty stipulations, etc.;
but when England, France, and Russia began to put the advancement of
their own special interests ahead of the collective good it weakened the
common cause by enabling the Chinese to play one Power against another.
It also gave good grounds for the belief that it was not the desire to bring
China into the family of nations so as to promote mutually advantageous
relationships which was motivating the foreign states.

From 1844 to about 1875, and especially after 1850, England, France, and
the United States, as has already been pointed out, coöperated in the advance on China with a view to breaking down the walls she had erected
around herself. Russia worked in harmony with the others on some occasions, but did not hesitate to advance her own interests at the expense of
all concerned when that appeared possible. And, if we exclude the cession
of Hongkong, which was made a free port, and of the Kowloon territory
opposite to it, it was Russia, as early as 1860, which initiated the process of
trimming off the edges of the Empire. After the cession of the right bank of
the Amur and the territory east of the Ussuri in 1860, no further territorial
advance was made for several years, except as the establishment of concessions in the various treaty ports resulted in the limitation of the territorial
integrity of China. The next loss was that just noted—namely the ultimate
surrender of a claim to suzerainty over Upper Burma. And in 1881 the
Chinese finally gave way before the Japanese assertion of the right to con-

trol over the Loochoo Islands, a claim definitely maintained after 1875. It was as a result of that claim that war almost came between the two countries in 1874. Some Loochuans, who had been shipwrecked on Formosa, were killed by the aborigines. The Japanese demanded that China act to punish the guilty, and when the Peking government disclaimed responsibility the Japanese sent an expedition to Formosa (1874). A rupture was averted at that time, China allowing Japan to secure her own satisfaction. She refused, however, to acquiesce in the Japanese government's assertion of suzerainty over the Loochoo Islands until 1881.

A more important move on the outlying dependencies of China produced a crisis in 1884–1885, when as a result of war with France the Manchus lost their nominal control of Annam and Tonking. While Annam had its own king and government, it had paid tribute to China regularly since the fifteenth century and intermittently from the period of the Han dynasty. The earliest French interest in the kingdom was manifested at the beginning of the nineteenth century, but no advance toward establishing a territorial footing there was made until the middle of the century. Murders of missionaries which occurred between 1843 and 1851 invited several naval expeditions to secure redress, and finally brought about a joint intervention by France and Spain in 1858. The peace made in 1862, after over three years of warfare, gave Spain a share of the indemnity of four million dollars demanded, but conceded to France, in addition to her part of the indemnity, three provinces in Cochin-China and a promise that the king of Annam would never cede any part of his kingdom to any other Power. A treaty with Cambodia established a French protectorate there at the same time. The advance was continued in 1867, when Annam was forced to cede the three western provinces of Cochin-China to France.

The real French interest, however, was in gaining a position from which trade with the southwestern provinces of China could be developed. The natural approach was by way of the Red River in Tongking. A pretext for intervention in that province was presented in 1874 when permission was denied a Frenchman to trade with Yunnan through the use of the Red River route. Gains made through the medium of a "filibustering expedition" were subsequently given up, only to be regained in a different form through the exertion of diplomatic pressure on the Annamese government. Full sovereignty over Cochin-China, right of trade through Tongking to Yunnan, toleration and privileges for Roman Catholic missionaries, and an extraterritorial status for all foreigners, were all conceded in return for protection from foreign aggression and internal disturbance and a remission of indemnities.

During this time the Chinese government had not failed to protest against the steady French advance, but it had not been in a position to do more. From 1874 to 1881 the Annamese, on their side, sought in various ways to reaffirm the Chinese connection, and in 1881 the Chinese minister at Paris explicitly reasserted the Chinese claim to suzerainty. Chinese irregular troops were drawn into Tongking, and they not only guarded the Yunnan frontier but blocked the Red River route. In 1883 a credit was voted by the French Chamber to send an expedition to Annam and Tongking, with the result that a French protectorate was established over the entire country, foreign affairs being brought completely under French control, and Tongking being placed under a French Resident. Because of this move war broke out between China and France in 1884, when the French forces in Tongking came into collision with Chinese troops.

After hostilities had begun, however, diplomacy was again resorted to, and on May 11, 1884, the Li-Fournier convention was signed. By it the French agreed to respect and protect the southern boundaries of China, while the Imperial government waived its claim to suzerainty over the disputed territories and sanctioned freedom of trade between Tongking and the southwestern provinces. Because of a misunderstanding over the time of evacuation of the Chinese troops from Tongking, hostilities again broke out and continued in a desultory fashion until 1885. The military operations reflected no great credit on either belligerent and proved entirely inconclusive. Eventually a new agreement embodying the terms of the Li-Fournier convention was drawn up at Paris, through the intermediation of Sir Robert Hart, head of the Chinese Imperial Maritime Customs, and was accepted by both France and China. Another step had been taken toward the restriction of the Chinese Empire to the boundaries of China proper.

6. INTERNAL POLITICAL CONDITIONS

It would seem that with the problems presented by the foreign impact the Celestial Empire was confronted with a sufficiently dangerous and perplexing situation. But the picture of the years 1842–1894 would not be complete, nor would it be possible to gain an adequate understanding of later developments, if the internal situation were passed over in silence. The foreign impact was one, but not by any means the sole, indication that Heaven had withdrawn its favor from the Manchus, for internal conditions during the nineteenth century were very bad.

The Emperor Tao Kuang, who "ascended the dragon" in 1850, succeeded to the Throne in 1820. He it was who was forced to consent to depart from the customary policy of seclusion. While that was the most significant event of his reign, it was not the only one that was unfortunate from the Chinese standpoint. A serious drought occurred in 1832, which year also saw an outbreak among the aborigines of three provinces. This uprising had been preceded by one in Formosa and another in Hainan. While all were put down, it was not without some difficulty, and they indicated a measure of dissatisfaction with the Imperial rule.

Tao Kuang was succeeded by one of his seven sons, who took the reign title of Hsien Feng. The father, while not a man of great ability, had devoted himself to the affairs of state, and he had earnestly, even if unsuccessfully, sought to check the growing corruption and indifference to the public welfare of the officials. Hsien Feng was not only an incapable man, but he was also unwilling to devote his time and his attention to public affairs. He was much more interested in the pleasures of the Palace and in the night life of the capital than in statecraft. Consequently there was not the strong and capable direction of affairs which was needed at a most critical time in the history of the Empire.

Hsien Feng died in exile at Jehol in 1860 at the time of the allied occupation of Peking, leaving an infant heir to the throne. As a result of a Palace revolution the Empress-mother, Tzu Hsi, and the Empress-consort, Tzu An, together with the Imperial Prince Kung, were able to establish themselves as regents during the minority of the Emperor, known by the reign title of T'ung Chih. T'ung Chih died (1875) shortly after attaining his majority in 1873, without leaving an heir, and Tzu Hsi, an able and ambitious woman, succeeded in having another infant chosen as his successor. This necessitated the revival of the regency, which was continued for another period of years, Kuang Hsü (the successor to T'ung Chih) attaining his majority only in 1887. Thus for a period of thirty years the titular rulers of China were children, and the actual ruler was a woman. While Tzu Hsi is one of the remarkable women of history, her previous training and experience had by no means fitted her to lead China to a solution of the numberless difficulties in managing internal affairs and in dealing with the foreign impact. While she had some able official advisers—Prince Kung and Wen Siang in the Tsungli Yamen and as members of her Council of State, Li Hung-chang in the Tientsin viceroyalty, in whose hands the control of foreign affairs came more and more to reside, Tsêng Kuo-fan, Tso Tsung-tang and then Chang Chih-tung in the central provinces—Tzu Hsi allowed the Palace eunuchs to interfere in affairs of state, notably in the making of appointments. This led to an even higher development of the practice of traffic in office, and to a diversion of public funds to uses other than those intended. It also meant the substitution of unofficial and irresponsible advisers for the responsible officials in Peking. Her rule was further marked by an extension of the number of Manchus, as compared with Chinese, in the public services, which ultimately aroused dissatisfaction. The policy of divide and rule was, however, successfully invoked by the Old Buddha, as Tzu Hsi came to be called, so far as distribution of spoils among the Chinese cliques and factions was concerned. But the existence of factions, in Peking as well as in the provinces, prevented a whole-hearted and unified grappling with the difficulties of the times.

Among these internal difficulties the most significant was the T'ai P'ing rebellion. The movement, in its political aspects, grew out of small beginnings of a religious character. The original societies formed were "Associations for Worshiping God" (Shang Ti Hui). Since the worship of Shang Ti was a recognized and peculiar function of the Emperor, it was not long until this worship came to be interdicted, although at first the ultimate political aims of the leader of the movement were not set forth by him or appreciated either by the officials or by the majority of the members of the "Associations." The leader of the movement was a native of Kwangtung province named Hung Hsiu-ch'üan, who was a scholar by profession and ambition. Hung appeared at Canton at least three times to compete in the provincial examinations and was always unsuccessful, although he had shown great promise in his studies. Following his last appearance he fell seriously ill, being in a trance part of the time. While in this state he had visions which became intelligible to him only as he began to read in a pamphlet, "Good Words to Exhort the Age," which he had received from a Chinese preacher at Canton. His visions, thus interpreted, led him to attempt to found a new religion which had mixed up in it many elements of Christianity, notably an antipathy to idolatry. The Christian elements in his belief were increased as a result of his contacts with a Baptist missionary at Canton, Mr. Issachar Roberts. After winning a few converts nearer home he moved with them into Kwangsi province, where he continued to teach, preach, and have visions. His following increased rapidly, especially after his societies were put under the Imperial ban. Finally, as a result of persecution, and in obedience to his visions, Hung proclaimed himself as the "Heavenly King," and declared his intention of founding a new rule, to be known as the "Perfect Peace" (T'ai P'ing) dynasty. He then began to move north, swelling his following continually, but leaving behind him a trail of blood and ruin. Finally the T'ai P'ing hordes (called by the Chinese the "long-haired rebels" because of their manner of wearing their hair) reached Nanking, where the "Heavenly King" stopped. A band of his followers moved on northwards and reached the environs of Tientsin, but they were soon forced to return to the Yangtse valley. This marked the high tide of the movement.

Because of the supposedly Christian foundation of the T'ai P'ing belief there was considerable agitation among the Protestant missionaries, as also among many traders, to force recognition and foreign support of the rebels. The Catholics in China, on the other hand, were opposed to recognition because the religion supposedly contained Protestant elements. For some time the British representative inclined toward recognition of the rebels and active intervention against the Manchus, in the hope that the rebels would be more sympathetic toward foreign intercourse. The American official policy, on the other hand, looked rather toward support of the Imperial government. By 1859, because of successful treaty revision and by reason of a more accurate understanding of the true character of the T'ai P'ing rule, the British accepted the American position and the foreigners united in the endeavor to strengthen the Manchus without officially intervening in the struggle.

Lack of space prevents a more detailed discussion of the rebellion, but attention should be called to some of its significant implications. Such a widespread revolt, continuing from as early as 1851 to 1864, was possible only because of the weakness of the government. The regular military establishment initially showed its inability to maintain the civil authority. If the T'ai P'ing leaders had been able to replace the tottering Manchus with something of more promise, the Dynasty might then have been ended. But since the movement developed no constructive leadership, because some of the men of greatest ability early lost their lives, and because the more fanatical and less able leaders thereafter dominated Hung, it eventually collapsed because of its own weakness.

There were two factors other than its own deficient leadership, however, which brought about the overthrow of the T'ai P'ing movement. One was the gradual creation by Tsêng Kuo-fan, an able Imperial official, of a new militia force of fighting qualities superior to those of the regular armies. Persistently keeping his armies in the field against the superior forces of the T'ai P'ings in spite of inadequate financial support, Tsêng was able gradually to clear the central Yangtse provinces of the rebels and ultimately to besiege and capture their capital, Nanking. In the process he forced the rebels toward the sea, where the second factor became operative. This was the foreign aid which was finally given to the Imperial authorities.

First, financed by the merchants of Shanghai, an American, Frederick T. Ward, came into the Chinese service. Against initial opposition of the British authorities at Shanghai, he organized a force capable of recapturing some of the towns which the rebels had occupied. Ward's force was virtually a band of freebooters who were rewarded with the loot or ransom of towns captured from the rebels. In spite of its character it was remarkably successful against the imperfectly armed and trained T'ai P'ings until Ward's death in 1862. By that time its value had become so apparent that the Chinese officially decided to continue it. The English authorities at Shanghai were thereupon asked to nominate a successor to Ward.[7] Having concluded that the foreign interest lay in upholding the Manchu authority,

---

[7] Another American, Burgovine, was placed in command of the force after the death of Ward. But he developed ambitions inconsistent with his position as a subordinate officer of the Chinese government, so that he could not be continued in a position of command. It was after his failure that Captain Gordon was nominated by the British.

they nominated Captain Gordon of their own forces to take command. He rapidly restored discipline to Ward's force, which had become demoralized after his death, and made it again the "Ever-Victorious Army." Its victories strengthened the Imperialists' morale, and this, together with the new effectiveness gained through the military reorganization undertaken by Tsêng Kuo-fan and, under his direction, by another able new official, Li Hung-chang, enabled the Chinese to succeed more rapidly on their own account, so that by 1864 the rebellion had been brought to an end.

But while the rebellion was not successful, it left its imprint on the country for many years. Devastation and destruction had marked its progress, many of the richest provinces of the Empire having been laid waste. It resulted in a partial or total stoppage of revenue from many of the greatest revenue producing areas in the country for a period of years, and prevented the collection of normal revenues from the devastated regions for a much longer time than the actual duration of rebel control. It threw many people into a condition of poverty, which, as is usual in China, resulted in an increase of brigandage, and made it difficult for the orderly processes of administration to be revived. And, above all else, it revealed the inability of the Imperial Government to carry out its primary duty of preserving peace and order in the country. Such a rebellion, even when unsuccessful, is usually the harbinger of the end of a dynasty. And it is not going too far from the facts to say that the successful revolt against the Manchus in 1911 was begun in the middle of the preceding century.

Again, this loss of revenue came at a time when the government was assuming increased burdens in order to pay foreign indemnities and for the sake of securing armaments of the new sort that had been brought to the notice of the Chinese with the foreign impact. Deprived for a time of some of the accustomed sources of income, and burdened with increased expenses, the government either had to find new sources or put a heavier burden on those available and in use. Since the sources of revenue had been fixed by the custom of many generations, the latter expedient had to be resorted to. This naturally led to complaint and dissatisfaction which came to a head just when the foreign Powers were making their advance on the Empire after 1895. It was for that reason diverted, for a short time, from the Manchus and directed against foreigners.

Two by-products of the rebellion of future importance remain to be noted. As the Imperial administration became disorganized or ineffective, no authority remained at Shanghai for the collection of the customs. A foreign service was organized for temporary purposes, and this was later taken over by the Chinese government as one of its own administrative services. An Englishman, Mr. Lay, was first put at the head of the customs. He was shortly succeeded by another Englishman, Sir Robert Hart. While the personnel of the service was foreign, its members were agents of the

Imperial government and not of foreign states. Due largely to the administrative ability of Sir Robert Hart, and to his honesty and devotion to the interests of his employers, the foreign-administered Chinese Maritime Customs continued to the 1920's, with the modifications in its control later made necessary by the attitude of the states of Europe.

The second by-product of the rebellion was the introduction of the likin tax as a temporary means of producing revenue. This is an internal transit tax imposed at various points within a province as well as at provincial boundaries.[8] Being extremely flexible and a good revenue producer, it was continued until abolished in 1931. Unlike the institution of the foreign customs, the development of the likin tax has been a grave disadvantage to the development of modern China, as it constitutes a serious hindrance to the movement of goods within the country and, for that reason, to the development of trade.

The suppression of the T'ai P'ing rebellion did not restore peace and prosperity to the country. In addition to numerous smaller uprisings, and to widespread brigandage with which the officials seemed unable to cope, there occurred two other major uprisings. Both of these were expressions of Mohammedan discontent with their treatment by the Chinese officials. Occurring as they did at widely separated places, the one in Yunnan province and the other in the northwest, they were indicative of a widespread dissatisfaction. Although neither attained the proportions of the T'ai P'ing movement, they resulted in the devastation of parts of the country left untouched by that rebellion and consequently added materially to the embarrassment of the Manchus. In addition to its internal consequences, the rebellion in the northwest resulted in a temporary loss to China of the district of Ili, which was seized by Russia, ostensibly for the purpose of holding it safe for China. After the rebellion was crushed the Chinese asked for its return, and, after some evasion, all but a small part of the territory was given up by Russia.

Before the country had time to recover from the effects of these rebellions it was visited (1876) by floods in the southern and south-central provinces and by drought in the provinces north of the Yangtse, the drought being accompanied by a plague of locusts. "The floods visited five provinces; the locusts devastated parts of three; and the drought destroyed crops and lives in the whole or parts of nine."[9] The drought continued during the years 1876–1878, and resulted in great suffering because of its duration.

---

[8] " 'Likin' was, in its original and strict meaning, a charge levied on goods in transit, calculated on the value of the goods, at the rate of one or more thousandths. But in a broad sense and in popular usage the term 'likin' " came to be "employed to designate collectively a broad category of taxes levied in various amounts and under a variety of names upon internal trade." STANLEY K. HORNBECK, *China Today: Political*, p. 460; quoted as note 5 in H. S. QUIGLEY AND G. H. BLAKESLEE, *The Far East*, p. 124.

[9] II, MORSE, p. 308.

Many millions of lives were lost, and in addition the revenue system of the Empire was gravely affected, both because of direct loss of revenue and because of the necessity for devoting funds to relief of the people in the provinces affected. This loss, coupled with that due to the T'ai P'ing rebellion, seriously weakened the ability of the Manchus to preserve their power internally and to protect the country against assaults from the outside.

7. BEGINNING OF CHANGE

We cannot leave, without further comment, this picture of a China devastated by rebellion, flood, and drought, with weak and incompetent Manchu rulers most of whom had become interested more in their own pleasures than in the solution of the problems confronting the state over which they had been called to rule, harassed by the problems of foreign intercourse, and unwilling to accept the new conditions of life in the modern world. We must go on to make certain explanations and to record some tentative experiments in the introduction of new ideas and practices.

It has been intimated rather strongly that China, both the government and the people, failed to live up to the treaty obligations assumed under the pressure of foreign force. The fact that the concessions were not made voluntarily, but under compulsion, serves to explain much of their unwillingness to give effect, except so far as they were compelled to do so, to the provisions of the treaties. Most other peoples would have acted in exactly the same way under the same circumstances. And it must be borne in mind, in estimating China's actions and her policy, that she had back of her a long tradition of superiority to other nations, and of dictation of the terms of intercourse with the outside world. Such a tradition could not be broken down in a day. Furthermore, the mere fact of foreign military successes did not cause the Chinese to lose their feeling of superiority. Many times in the past foreign arms had been successful against them, but in the long run the Chinese race had proved invincible. This latter consideration helps to explain the unreadiness of the Chinese to recognize the superiority of the material civilization of the West, and the dangers to their own civilization and life developing from the foreign impact.

We must also bear in mind, when considering the good or bad faith of the Imperial government in giving effect to its obligations, that Peking might command, but that it lay within the discretion of the provincial authorities to execute the command according to circumstances and conditions in the province. In the United States a somewhat similar condition obtains because of the federal system of government. Washington may enter into treaty engagements in perfectly good faith, and yet find extreme difficulty in carrying certain of its agreements into effect uniformly throughout the country. Protection may be promised to Italians, Japanese, or Chinese within our borders, but that protection must be afforded by the local authorities. We have had our own difficulties due to mob action in places as widely separated as New Orleans and San Francisco. The Peking government, to an even greater extent, and with much more justification, might have urged its system of government as an explanation of its inability to afford uniform and adequate protection to foreign lives and property in all parts of China. The truth is that even if the Imperial government had attempted to carry out its engagements in perfectly good faith, it would have found it extremely difficult to do so uniformly throughout the country. Unfortunately for China, her system of government, and her territorial decentralization, was not sufficiently familiar to Europe, and, even if it had been, the powerful states of the West would not have allowed it to be urged in justification of non-fulfillment of treaty obligations. And of course there was not that good faith on the part of the central government which might conceivably have inclined the foreign representatives to leniency. Peking shielded the official who was responsible for failure to protect the foreigner, instead of being the first to suggest his punishment. Censure came from the Imperial authority only under compulsion.

In further explanation of some of the difficulties that arose between Europe and China it may be pointed out that individual foreigners were not too careful to keep within their treaty rights. Missionaries and traders often went into parts of the country where their presence was certain to be misconstrued and resented. When trouble arose they were given the support of their respective governments without regard to local conditions, and the Chinese government was expected to afford them absolute security even though it was without power to ensure it. The extraterritorial system, giving immunity from the operation of Chinese law, also caused complications, often rising out of foreign arrogance, and in these cases the tendency was to conclude, without regard to the facts in the case, that the Chinese were in the wrong.

It may also be pointed out that the Western governments themselves, while insisting on fulfillment by China of her obligations to the letter, did not always trouble to keep within the letter and spirit of the treaties. Attention has already been called to the controversy over the right of residence at Canton, the British insisting on residential areas being set apart for foreign use within the walled city although the treaties did not provide explicitly for this, and to the American attitude toward the immigration clauses of the Burlingame treaty. Another example of the foreign attitude is to be found in the assertion, at Shanghai and other open ports, of a governmental right in the concessions that was expressly repudiated by the treaties, which carefully reserved Chinese sovereignty over the residential areas.

When we turn to the positive advances made by China, and to the better side of her relations with the foreigners, the educational work of the missionaries comes first to mind. In addition to their interest in evangelization, the missionaries early realized that China offered a vast field for applied Christianity which would have to be exploited before the peoples could be Christianized on any large scale. Dictionaries had to be compiled and the language learned before any effective evangelical work could be undertaken. This knowledge of the language came to be of great service in the establishment of contacts with the officials and the people. The missionary supplemented and advanced the work of the diplomat, and helped to make possible wider commercial contacts. After they had gained a familiarity with the Chinese language, the missionaries began the work of translating foreign books into the Chinese, and in this they by no means limited themselves to religious literature. Thus educated Chinese at the treaty ports began to gain a better knowledge of the world. Then mission schools were established and through them many Chinese were introduced to the learning of the West more directly than by means of the translated works. All of this began to awaken an interest in non-Chinese societies which could not help but bear fruit.

In 1872 the first Chinese educational mission was sent abroad. A group of thirty boys was taken to the United States under the supervision of Yung Wing, a Yale trained Chinese. This was made possible by the action of one of the more enlightened of the Viceroys, Li Hung-chang, who had come to see that China could strengthen herself by becoming familiar with the ideas and the devices of the West. The mission was recalled shortly, in 1881, but meanwhile one hundred and twenty boys had some direct contact with the West. This educational mission served to mark a beginning in the breakdown of the intellectual isolation of the Chinese.

Even before this a school for interpreters, with some foreign teachers, had been established in Peking. In 1865 this school became Tungwen College, with a scientific department added to the language school, and with additions to the foreign staff. Sir Robert Hart, Inspector-General of the Imperial Maritime Customs, and a trusted adviser to the Chinese government, was a moving spirit in the establishment of the college, setting aside funds for its maintenance from the customs collection, and (in 1869) securing the appointment of Mr. W. A. P. Martin, an American missionary, as its president. The establishment of Tungwen College, accepting as it did only students with a good Chinese education, was certainly a long step for the Empire to take at that time.

The exploits of Gordon's "Ever-Victorious Army" in the struggle against the T'ai P'ing movement aroused an interest in foreign engines of warfare, with the result that the Chinese took tentative steps toward reorganizing the army and building up a navy. Vessels were purchased from England and other states and they were for a time put under foreign direction. Unfortunately nothing came of this first venture, and the circumstances were such as to prejudice the Chinese against foreign aid and direction. Consequently the fleet actually built up by 1894 had its efficiency impaired because it was kept under exclusive Chinese direction. Furthermore, both the army and the navy offered opportunities for "squeeze" that the officials could not disregard. It thus happened that, while on paper China built up a well-equipped fighting force, when it actually took the field its supplies were deficient or non-existent and the force itself was poorly trained.

The foreign impact began to make itself felt gradually in the economic as well as in the governmental life of China. In 1876 a railway was opened from Shanghai to Wusung. This was only a small project, and even so it was unsuccessful. Owing to the opposition of the official and literate classes it was repurchased by the Chinese in 1877 and the rails were torn up and transported to Formosa, where, together with the other equipment of the road, they were allowed to disintegrate. But in 1881 the Tongshan railway was opened, largely because of the interest in the project of Li Hung-chang, the Viceroy of Chihli province. This was the beginning of a new development which continued slowly until after 1894 but thereafter went on with constantly accelerated momentum. The important thing is, after all, the beginning. In 1882 another venture in the field of communications was made when a telegraph line from Shanghai to Tientsin was opened. In the same decade with these beginnings came the promise of industrial development. The Kaiping mines were opened by Li Hung-chang in 1878, and it was this enterprise which led to the building of the Tongshan railway. The year 1873 saw the organization of the first Chinese steam navigation company, the China Merchants. In this also Li Hung-chang was the prime mover. A little later, in 1890, Chang Chih-tung opened the Han Yang Iron Works, destined to develop into the largest enterprise of its kind in China proper.

These indications of a willingness to change must not be over-emphasized. They were only indications, and the initiative came from a very small group of officials and gentry. Li Hung-chang in the north and Chang Chih-tung in the Yangtse region were the moving spirits among the officials. But officialdom as a whole remained as conservative and as untouched by the foreign influence as before. The introduction of Western learning met with firm opposition from most of the literati, and, of course, by 1894 the "new thought" had not even commenced to penetrate to the masses. It had begun to be realized that China was weak and, for that reason, in danger. This realization did not, however, bring with it a recognition of the necessity for making institutional changes for the purpose of strengthening the country in the face of the foreign impact. The Western influence did not make itself felt at all in the realm of economic and social organization, and it did not modify Chinese cultural life to any appreciable extent. Political organization and practices were slightly adjusted to meet the need for diplomatic intercourse, and a tentative movement toward centralization to meet the demand for uniform treaty application was inaugurated. But there failed to appear the rapid movement toward reorganization and change which was so marked in Japan during the same years.

One more observation may conclude this chapter. It had been shown that China was unable to defend herself against the military power of the nations of the West; she was weakened by internal strife and by widespread famine conditions, and she offered plenty of excuses for aggressive action by the Powers. In view of these facts it may be wondered why the Powers did not move on her as they had on India, and as France had on Annam and Tongking, and Great Britain on Burma. The explanation lies (1) in the wholesome respect that they had for the potential power of the Chinese Empire, (2) in the fear that existed lest the "sleeping dragon" should be too rudely awakened and should turn and rend the disturbers of its peace, and (3) in the restraints imposed by the coöperative policy. It was realized that China herself had not been touched—that the Empire had not been stirred to united action in its own defense—and it was felt that a united opposition to aggression would be successful. Furthermore, a move to bring China out of her isolation could be more easily justified than an attempt to absorb or divide her. Coupled with this was the fear lest one Power's gain should be another's loss, a possibility which restrained all the Powers. It remained for an Asiatic state to reveal the actual helplessness of the Chinese Empire and to lessen the respect felt for its potential power.

By way of summary it may be said that by 1894 the process of opening China to foreign intercourse had been begun; that in the development of that process China had been brought under two important treaty restrictions—the imposition of a conventional tariff and the establishment of the extraterritorial system by treaty; that the Chinese Maritime Customs had become a foreign organized and administered service of the Chinese government; that China had lost several of the outlying dependencies over which her control was more nominal than real, but that the territories administered from Peking, or directly supervised by the Imperial government, had not been touched by the foreign impact; that in spite of several military defeats, and the establishment of relations with the states of the West on a footing of equality, the Chinese had not lost their sense of superiority to the "outer barbarians"; that the process of internal disorganization had set in, but had been temporarily checked; and, finally, that some small and tentative attempts had been made to introduce Western ideas and practices, but that there was no widespread interest in them, and no general recognition of the desirability of institutional reform or reorganization.

REFERENCES FOR FURTHER STUDY

SIR RUTHERFORD ALCOCK, *Journey of Augustus Raymond Margary, from Shanghai to Bhamo, and Back to Manwyne* (1876), based on Margary's journal. M. J. BAU, *Foreign Relations of China* (1921), ch. 2; an outline sketch of the period by a Chinese student. J. O. P. BLAND, *Li Hung-chang* (1917), the least unsatisfactory biography of that Chinese statesman. J. O. P. BLAND and E. BACKHOUSE, *China under the Empress-Dowager* (1914), ch. 1–9; an interesting account of court life and politics, and of the ruler of the country. CHIANG SIANG-TSEH, *The Nien Rebellion* (1954). P. H. CLYDE, *United States Policy Toward China, Diplomatic and Public Documents, 1839–1939* (1940); a useful collection to use in connection with this and subsequent chapters. MARY R. COOLIDGE, *Chinese Immigration* (1909), esp. part II, *Restriction and Exclusion.* H. CORDIER, *Histoire générale de la Chine et ses relations avec les Pays Etrangers,* 4 vols. (1920); vol. 4 comprehends the years from 1820–1912. W. C. COSTIN, *Great Britain and China, 1833–1860* (1936). T. DENNETT, *Americans in Eastern Asia* (1922), ch. 9–12, 15–18, 20, 22, 28–30; authoritative treatment of American diplomacy during the period. PRINCESS DER LING, *Two Years in the Forbidden City* (1912); entertaining account of court life. PRINCESS DER LING, *The Old Buddha* (1929); interesting biography of the Empress-Dowager. W. S. HAIL, *Tsêng Kuo-fan and the Taiping Rebellion* (1927); the best study of the movement. A. E. HAKE, *Events in Taeping Rebellion* (1891); General Gordon's account. G. W. KEETON, *The Development of Extraterritoriality in China,* 2 vols. (1928), vol. 1, ch. 5–8, vol. 2, appendices. E. KIERNAN, *British Diplomacy in China, 1880–1885* (1939). K. S. LATOURETTE, *A History of Christian Missions in China* (1929), ch. 15–21. LIN-LI (pseud.), *Ti-Ping-Tien-Kwoh; the History of the Ti-Ping Revolution,* 2 vols. (1866); an interesting account by a friend of the rebels; needs to be used with care. H. F. MACNAIR, *Modern Chinese History, Selected Readings* (1923), ch. 6–11. W. A. P. MARTIN, *A Cycle of Cathay* (1896), esp. ch. 9–25; observations of an early missionary who served his own and the Chinese government. W. H. MEDHURST, *Foreigner in Far Cathay* (1872). A. MITCHIE, *The Englishman in China,* 2 vols. (1900); a valuable study of China (1842–1890) centered on career of Sir Rutherford Alcock. H. B. MORSE, *International Relations of the Chinese Empire* (1918), vol. 2; an authoritative treatment of the subject. CYRUS H. PEAKE, *Nationalism and Education in Modern China* (1932), ch. 1; discusses modern education and its aims as marked out from 1860 to 1895. NATHAN A. PELCOVITS, *Old China Hands and the Foreign Office* (1948); an interesting study of British China policy. S. A. ROBERTS, *History of French Colonial Policy,* 2 vols. (1929), vol. 2, ch. 11. A. J. SARGENT, *Anglo-Chinese Commerce and Diplomacy* (1907), ch. 5–10; a careful study in a limited field. EARL SWISHER, *China's Management of the American Barbarians* (1951). WANG YÜ-CH'ÜAN, *The Rise of Land Tax and the Fall of Dynasties in Chinese History,* Pacific Affairs, vol. 9, pp. 201–220; an illuminating article. E. T. WILLIAMS, *China, Yesterday and Today* (1923), ch. 18–19. S. WELLS WILLIAMS, *The Middle Kingdom,* 2 vols. (1882), vol. 2, ch. 24, 26; the T'ai P'ing rebellion and a brief review of events after 1860; two chapters from a monumental work. YUNG WING, *My Life in China and America* (1909). MARY C. WRIGHT, *The Last Stand of Chinese Conservatism, 1862–1874* (1957). C. K. WU, *The International Aspect of the Missionary Movement in China* (1930).

CHAPTER IV

THE OPENING OF JAPAN

1. SIGNIFICANCE OF 1894 IN FAR EASTERN HISTORY

THE intricacies in the modern pattern of Far Eastern history began to appear after the year 1894. It was a war between China and her then small neighbor, Japan, which revealed the complete helplessness of China and encouraged the Powers of Europe to believe that she might shortly fall to pieces and be partitioned among them. At the same time an Oriental people was seen to be fully capable of adapting to its own use the material and mechanical elements of Western civilization. By 1894 Japan had completed the period of probation that preceded her complete admission to the modern society of nations. The years from 1853, when Perry arrived in Yokohama Bay, to the end of the Sino-Japanese War witnessed what is usually called the "transformation" of Japan. During this time her political institutions were gradually shaped into the form which endured with but slight modifications until after 1937, and the broad outlines of her modern economic and social institutions became clear. At the same time some indications were given of what her future policies would be as opportunity was afforded for their development.

The rise of Japan as a modern Power in such a short period of years and the military achievements of the Japanese in the subsequent war against Russia were not the result, in any real sense, of the occidentalizing of Japan —of any revolutionary transformation of the life of the country. Rather her achievements were made possible because the events and changes of the years following her opening worked a gradual transition from the old order to the new. Modern Japan is the logical outgrowth of pre-Restoration Japan. This being true, it is obvious that only through an adequate understanding of the old Japan can the new Japan be properly appreciated.

2. THE LAND AND PEOPLE

Territorially, pre-Restoration Japan consisted of the largest group of the chain of islands extending from Kamchatka in the north through Formosa in the south. Saghalin was known to the Japanese, but not occupied or actively governed by them; and this was also true of the Kurile Islands, which lie outside Saghalin and serve as stepping-stones from Yezo (Hokkaido) to Kamchatka. Since tribute had intermittently been sent to Japan by the Loochoo islanders, an historical claim to suzerainty over those islands existed, but it was weakened by a similarly founded Chinese claim. The Loochoo group served as connections between Japan and Formosa, which was definitely under the supervision of China.

A glance at the map serves to indicate clearly the position of Japan with respect to the Asiatic mainland. Only a narrow strait separates her from the Korean promontory, which is the natural Japanese point of entrance to the continent. Even here there is a stepping-stone furnished by the island of Tsushima. This geographical relationship gives a clue to the early as well as the later continental interests of Japan. Through Korea, and perhaps through Saghalin, came some of the racial elements which in combination with others from the south form the modern Japanese. Through Korea as well as more directly from China came much of the old Japanese culture. Religious ideas, art, literature, many of the crafts—all were affected by the proximity of Korea. The greatest pre-modern threat to the independence of Japan developed when the Mongols extended their power over Korea as well as China; and the only extensive early external movements of Japan were directed toward Korea, with China, at one time, as the ultimate objective.

Mingled with the continental there is undoubtedly a Malayan strain in the Japanese blood, carried to the Japanese archipelago probably on the "Black Current," which washes the southern and eastern shores of the country. These outsiders gradually forced the Ainu peoples, the aboriginal inhabitants, to the northernmost island, Hokkaido.

This Black Current serves Japan in another way, for it moderates the climate on the south and east in much the same way as the Gulf Stream affects that of the southeastern United States. Unfortunately it cannot serve the entire country because of its extremely mountainous character, which is largely a consequence of the volcanic origin of the land. The numerous mountain ranges serve also to break the territory up into small valleys, which were largely cut off from one another in the days of primitive means of communication. This had important political consequences in the pre-modern history of the country.

The lack of navigable rivers also affected the development of Japan. There are many small, turbulent streams, but none of great length or of any importance from the standpoint of trade or industry. This handicap to development was, however, partially neutralized by the elongated character of the main islands, which, together with the multitude of small islands and the numerous good harbors, made possible a coastwise trade comprehending the entire area.

Turning our attention from the geographic environment to the people, we find that prior to the seventh century Japan was inhabited by a number of groups organized on a patriarchal basis. While there was an Emperor who was nominally the ruler of these groups, practically he was merely one, the strongest, of the patriarchal chiefs. As the strength of his clan increased or declined, his control was strengthened or weakened. The strongest tendency, under such conditions, was toward decentralization.

To remedy this condition by counteracting the tendencies toward decentralization a reform (the Taikwa) in the system was attempted in 645 A.D. This reform took the direction of the introduction and adaptation to Japanese conditions of the Chinese administrative system. Japanese society was divided, broadly, into two classes—the governing and the governed. The governing classes constituted an appointive civil bureaucracy made up of the high civil officials. Membership in this bureaucracy included, in the provinces, district as well as provincial governors and numerous local officials. Between the eighth and twelfth centuries, originally appointive offices became hereditary, thus establishing government on a class basis. This hereditary civil bureaucracy was supported by grants of rice lands to be held during the tenure of office of the official. At the same time the remainder of the rice lands was divided among the supporting or governed classes, subject in theory to periodic redistribution. Tribute was levied on the rice lands, except those held by the bureaucracy, which were exempt.

Since it was only the rice lands which were so distributed, the other lands were subject to preëmption by those who could make use of and hold them. As a result great estates gradually were built up either by members of the bureaucracy or by others. Because taxes were assessed only on the rice lands, the burden imposed on the holders became heavier as the expenses of the government increased. Even without such increase some of the people found it unprofitable to remain in possession of the lands assigned to them. They may be described, perhaps, as the marginal producers—those who could not make a living and at the same time pay their contributions. These people either offered to give up their lands to members of the governing classes on condition of being allowed to remain in possession, or they merely vacated them, allowing them to be preëmpted by officers of the state. When these lands came under the control of the bureaucrats, they, in turn, were exempt from taxation. This meant that the remaining rice lands had to pay greater contributions to make up the deficit, which, in turn, created another group who could not till their lands profitably—the new marginal producers. As this process went on, coupled as it was with the carving-out of estates from the undistributed lands, a class of territorial magnates with comparatively great resources came into being. At the same time the resources of the central establishment were steadily decreasing, and as a result the territorial nobility became more powerful than the Emperor and the central government.

Another consequence of this process was the gradual creation of a military class. In order to maintain themselves, men who deserted the land offered their personal services to those who were building up landed estates. The landed gentry, as the acquisitive instinct became developed, found it expedient to maintain large establishments, in the first place in order to defend what they had, and in the second place in order to acquire more land by force. The necessity for defense, again, was two-fold: strife developed among the possessors of land—between the different clan groups; and the territorial magnates had to ensure themselves against dispossession by the central authority.

In this feudal organization which developed out of the attempt to establish an imported centralized system of administration on the basis of the early purely patriarchal society, there gradually evolved two distinct groups in the governing class—a civil bureaucracy and a military nobility. The former finally came to control only the Emperor and the central administration, while the latter was provincial or territorial. As the resources of the central government declined, the governors sent out to supervise the provinces lost in effective control except as they were supported by the military power, which soon came to constitute the only real authority outside the capital. By the end of the twelfth century this transfer of governing power had been completed, and with it had come decentralization on a feudal instead of a patriarchal basis. From the thirteenth to the end of the sixteenth century the internal history of Japan was characterized by a succession of attempts to unite the country under the direction of the strongest of the feudal lords, who also sought to control the Imperial establishment. After 1192 the Emperor became a puppet in the hands of one after another of the Daimyō, or feudal chiefs. He was never displaced as Emperor, but was forced to invest the successful Daimyō with the office and title abbreviated to Shōgun or, in full, "barbarian-quelling-generalissimo." From this time the government of Japan was military in character.

The rule through the Shōgunate of one clan succeeded that of another until at last a man reached eminence as Shōgun who was able to consolidate and continue his power by other than military means. Hideyoshi, one of the great figures in the military annals of Japan, died at the end of the sixteenth century in the midst of his unsuccessful attempts to subdue Korea and the Empire of China, and the reins of power fell into the hands of Iyeyasu, one of his supporters. The latter was created Shōgun by the Emperor in 1603. He was the first in the long line of Tokugawa Shōguns who ruled Japan from that time until the restoration of the Emperor in 1867. This unprecedentedly long rule, of over 250 years, by the one clan was possible only because of the development of a system of administration by which the continued power of the Tokugawa could be ensured against the weakness of rulers less capable than Iyeyasu and his immediate successors. The administrative system evolved during the seventeenth century was, with some small changes, that found by the Europeans in 1853.

3. THE PRE-RESTORATION POLITICAL SYSTEM

At the head of the state stood the Emperor. Theoretically he was both its temporal and its spiritual ruler, but, as has been pointed out, since the twelfth century he had "reigned without governing." He lived in seclusion and obscurity at Kyoto, surrounded by the court nobility (Kuge). It was this very obscurity which had preserved since antiquity the succession in the one line of rulers—that and the practices of concubinage and adoption which between them ensured an heir to the throne.

The actual power was in the hands of the Shōgun, or rather of the institution, the Shōgunate. The Shōgun always sought and received his investiture from the Emperor, preserving the fiction of ruling in his name. The Tokugawa, when they came to power in 1603, divided the territory of those who opposed them among their own followers and supporters. Such of the territorial nobles as acknowledged their overlordship were allowed to remain in control of their lands, but the more powerful among them were separated from one another by the interposition of estates or dominions governed directly by members of the Tokugawa clan or their vassals. This helped to secure the Shōgun against rebellion. Furthermore, the Daimyō (feudal lords) were compelled to live part of each year at Yedo, the seat of government of the Shōgun, and to leave their immediate families there throughout the entire year as hostages for their good behavior and continued loyalty. The Daimyō were in practice divided into two groups: (1) the hereditary vassals (Fudai), i.e., those who had throughout their struggle for power supported the Tokugawa; and (2) the "Outer Lords" (Tōzama), who were in control of approximately half of Japan. The Outer Lords were prohibited from entering into alliances. In addition to this, the principle of "divide and rule" was invoked by the Shōgun to keep the powerful clans from conspiring to overthrow his power. Traditional clan hostilities, the legacies of the years of inter-clan warfare, were kept alive, so that while many of the clans at heart were opposed to the continuance of the Tokugawa rule, they were too hostile to one another to combine against it, even though the Outer Lords had not been prohibited from entering into alliances.

But the Tokugawa Shōguns themselves did not personally rule the country after the death of Iyeyasu, Hidetada, and Iyemitsu, the first three of the family to gain the position. If the Emperor was merely a figurehead, the Shōgun was not in a position of much greater personal authority. His powers were put in commission, as one might call it, and he was more often than not a puppet in the hands of his Upper and Lower Councils. They, in turn, were in reality controlled by subordinate office-holders. Professor Gubbins describes the actual condition of affairs as follows: [1]

[1] *Progress of Japan*, p. 21.

What for want of a better name may be termed the figurehead system of government is noticeable throughout the whole course of Japanese history and is the natural outcome of Japanese social and political ideas. Real and nominal power are rarely seen combined either socially or politically. The family, which is the unit of society, and not, as with us, the individual, is nominally controlled by the individual who is its head. But practically the latter is in most cases a figurehead, the real power being vested in the group of relatives who form the family council.

As has been said, this condition of affairs extended to the Shōgunate and Imperial Court as well as to the control of the smaller family groups.

Next to the Shōgun in theoretical importance came the territorial nobility, the Daimyō. They ruled over the several Daimyates, or territorial subdivisions of Japan, as feudal lords. In reality they were the heads of clans. Their position and power were supported by the samurai, the warrior class of old Japan. But here again we find the figurehead system of government, since "with one or two notable exceptions, the Daimyō did not administer their fiefs. The administration of these was entrusted to a group of retainers, known as karo, who held office hereditarily in their respective clans." [2] Thus the actual administration of affairs, at the time of the arrival of Commodore Perry in Japan, had passed into the hands of a group of men who may be called the "business samurai" of the various clans.

The samurai, as has been said, made up the fighting class of the country. As warriors, occasionally called upon to defend the country itself as well as the interests of their chiefs, they were supported in idleness, except when fighting was in order, by the remainder of the inhabitants. They constituted a very real privileged group by 1853, since the Tokugawa clan, after consolidating its power, had brought both internal and external peace to Japan and had thus rendered unnecessary dependence on the peculiar abilities and training of the samurai.

At the outset of the Tokugawa period Japan had what might be called a "rice" economy. Income of the Daimyō and samurai as well as of other classes was measured in rice rather than in its money equivalent. "Wealth was measured in terms of rice, because it was the most important medium of exchange as well as the staple foodstuff." [3] As the governing class (and a leisure class during times of peace), the Daimyō and samurai had to be supported out of the product of the labor of the peasants. Although there were such sayings as "A farmer is worth two samurai and three beggars are worth four townsmen," the fact was that "these were mere vestiges of ancient practice, and in reality the peasant was regarded, and was treated, as a machine to produce rice for the samurai to swallow. Statesmen thought highly of agriculture, but not of agriculturalists." [4]

[2] Gubbins, op. cit.
[3] G. B. SANSOM, *Japan: A Cultural History* (1931), p. 455.
[4] Ibid., p. 457.

During the period of peace and stability organized by the Tokugawa Shōgunate, however, a money economy began to replace that in which rice was the medium of exchange and the measure of wealth. "As metal money permeated the economic life of the people, rice lost its function as a medium of exchange, until by the end of the 17th century it was completely disregarded." [5] Concurrently with this, under Tokugawa auspices town life came to be of great importance. To support the rather luxurious manner of life developed in the towns and cities such as Yedo, Sakai, Kyoto, Osaka, and Nagasaki, as well as to meet the heavy demands of the Shōgunate for income for such purposes as castle and temple building, rice income had to be translated into money income. This transition gave a new importance to the merchants and other "service" classes in the towns, who rapidly increased in wealth, and consequently in power, even though their theoretical social status remained below that of the farmers as well as the samurai. To meet the demands on them, the upper classes began to live in excess of their rice income, which fluctuated due to speculation by the "rice brokers" and due to natural causes. In consequence they fell into debt to the merchants, pledging their income in certain cases several years in advance. Making use of this indebtedness, the merchant families were enabled to advance their social status by such devices as having their sons adopted into samurai families and by marriage. Thus class lines became more blurred than the sharp lines of Tokugawa regulations would indicate. As early as 1700 the merchants "were already one of the strongest and most enterprising elements in the state, and the military caste was slowly losing its influence." [6] But it was the interpenetration of the merchant and samurai classes as much as the supplanting of the one by the other which had ultimate importance in causing "a slow but irresistible revolution, culminating in the breakdown of feudal government and the resumption of intercourse with foreign countries after more than two hundred years of seclusion. What opened the doors was not a summons from without but an explosion from within." [7]

4. JAPANESE SOCIETY AND CULTURE

The culture and social arrangements of old Japan present many interesting similarities and contrasts to those of pre-modern China. At the beginning of the modern period each had its own peculiar culture. That of Japan had been tremendously influenced from the continent, but it was by no means a mere importation. Buddhism, for example, was imported into both countries, and into Japan at second hand. But each adapted the Indian system to its own uses, so that the Japanese cults differed widely from the

[5] SANSOM, op. cit., p. 460, quoting M. TAKIZAWA, *The Penetration of Money Economy in Japan* (1927).
[6] Ibid., p. 462.
[7] Ibid., p. 460.

Buddhism of the Celestial Empire. Brought into Japan at an early time, it partly absorbed, partly displaced, and in part left untouched the native Shintoism (the Way of the Gods). In turn Buddhism was in part displaced, among the upper classes, by the Confucian philosophers, the study of whose works was revived and encouraged by the Tokugawa Shōguns. The rulers, however, were also patrons of Buddhism, building and endowing some of the most elaborate temples and establishments in the region around and north of Yedo (Tokyo). And Buddhism maintained its supremacy among the common people unchallenged by Confucianism. Neither of these importations served to bring the Japanese under the cultural dominance of China.

In China, as has been pointed out, learning was elevated above all things; the literati constituted a distinct class, and indeed the highest in the country; and officialdom was recruited from this class. In Japan learning was also respected, but it had to share the supremacy with skill in arms. During the centuries before the establishment of peace and order by reason of the long-continued Tokugawa supremacy, the Buddhist priesthood was the custodian of knowledge. From the seventeenth to the middle of the nineteenth century, however, with the cessation of internal warfare, the samurai became students as well as men-at-arms, and the class became the learned one. A knowledge of the Confucian classics became as much a part of the samurai equipment as a knowledge of sword-play. This situation presents a decidedly interesting contrast with that in China, where the learned were the least martial of men.

Both societies emphasized politeness and ceremony in every-day life, particularly among the upper classes. Here perhaps the Japanese went farther than the Chinese, developing elaborate rituals for what to the Westerner are matters of daily routine. The several forms of the tea ceremony are among the better known illustrations of this phase of Japanese life.

In both empires the farmer class in theory ranked next to the top in point of social importance. Rice and sericulture were the most highly developed rural activities in Japan, although barley and wheat were raised on the uplands and often as a second crop after rice; and a variety of vegetables was grown. The tea plant also occupied a most important place in the Japanese economy.

Farms in Japan were necessarily small, as they were in most parts of China, and cultivation was very intensive; not even the Chinese excelled the Japanese as intensive farmers. Necessity had also taught the Japanese, as it had their continental neighbors, to make use of all of their waste in replenishment of the soil.

An important staple of Japanese diet, even as important as rice, was fish.

The juncture of the warm Black Current with the cold Kamchatka current off the coast of Japan provided excellent fishing grounds. Thus fishing came to be one of the major occupations of the working population.

Next to the farmers stood the artisans, in which group might also be included the artists, who were really the best and most self-respecting artisans. Industry was organized into guilds in Japan as in other countries at the same stage of development, but the Japanese guilds did not develop the power that the Chinese guilds had, nor did they elevate the standards of workmanship and produce honesty in trade as they were able to do in China. Individuals had high standards and did superlative work in the more artistic lines, but they were the artists of old Japan rather than the ordinary craft-workers, and they were unable to impress their standards of excellence on their fellows. They were held in high respect as individuals, but the group of which they were a part was held in relatively low esteem. As for traders,[8] they were lowest, except for a few groups of virtual outcasts, in the social scale. This rating, emphasizing the military art and possession of learning, and assigning to a low level the industrial and commercial classes, has an important bearing on the development of modern Japan. The samurai had standards of conduct and were held to their observance; the mercantile community failed to develop its own standards. Consequently modern Japanese business had to pass through a period of world-wide disrepute while attempting to evolve a code of business ethics, but the conduct of military and naval men, and to a less extent of officials, has compared very favorably with that of corresponding groups throughout the world.

This summary view of society in pre-modern Japan would not be complete without reference to the prevailing esthetic tone. Lower and upper classes alike were lovers of beauty—a love created or enhanced by their environment. Ceremonial in the ordinary life of the upper classes was refined to the point of estheticism, as has been pointed out. Much money and labor were devoted to the construction and maintenance of ornate and beautiful shrines and temples in picturesque surroundings, Nikko, Nara, and Kyoto being perhaps the best known examples. The most important festivals were devoted to celebration of the seasonal beauties of nature— the people going considerable distances to observe the cherry and plum trees, and the chrysanthemum, in blossom. The people were greatly interested in gardens, frequently attempting to reproduce natural scenes in miniature on even the smallest plots, and often achieving the most remarkable effects. This estheticism could not help but have an important influence on the character of the Japanese people, on their industry, and on their manner of life. Industrially it revealed itself, for example, in the cloisonné, lacquer, and damascene wares.

It is also necessary, in concluding this summary, to make reference to

---

[8] But, supra, p. 82, for a brief discussion of the change in actual status of the merchant class.

and to emphasize the attempts made by the Tokugawa administration to supervise and regulate the daily life of the people of all classes. Its legislation was based upon the careful maintenance of class distinctions, establishing different rights and responsibilities for the members of the different social classes. Perhaps the word legislation is not the proper term to use since the conduct of citizens was supposed to be based upon ethical principles rather than legal norms. But the application in detail of ethical principles was made for the people by state authorities. Thus offenses of a criminal nature were described in what may be thought of as laws, but the offenses, and the prescribed punishment for their commission, were different for the various classes. Similarly, details of dress, of manners, and of behavior in general were to a considerable extent regulated in terms of social status. The direction of such legislation was toward making as rigid and unchangeable as possible the existing system.

5. EARLY FOREIGN INTERCOURSE

While during almost the entire period of the Tokugawa Shōgunate Japan had lived apart from the outside world, the people had been in contact with foreigners during pre-Tokugawa days. During the sixteenth century foreign traders and missionaries were permitted, and even encouraged, to come to the country. Chinese, Portuguese, Spanish, English, and Dutch vessels anchored in Japanese ports, and Japanese vessels went to foreign Asiatic ports. The Jesuits, the Dominicans, and the Franciscans converted the people to Christianity in large numbers, and even some of the feudal lords accepted the new faith. But the time was not ripe then for the perfecting of this intercourse. The conduct of the foreigners themselves, and the condition of the European world, made it seem advisable and necessary for the Japanese narrowly to limit their contacts. Instead of all working together to develop trade relations, the European traders, as in other places, tried to restrict the trade each to his own state. The Dutch warned the Japanese against having anything to do with the Spanish and English, and they in turn worked against the Dutch interests. It was not perceived that the interests of the individual states in the long run were identical. The consequence was that distrust of almost all foreigners developed in the minds of the rulers of Japan. This distrust was strengthened by tales of Spanish activities in the Philippines, of Portuguese behavior on the China coast, of British and French actions in India, and of Dutch exploits in the East Indies. It was further augmented by what must have appeared to the Japanese as the fratricidal strife among the foreigners—the Dutch and the English fighting the Spanish, and then falling-to against each other, sometimes in Japanese waters.

Even these conditions might not have been sufficient to bring about the closing of Japan to foreign intercourse, had it not been for the attitude and activities of the Roman Catholic missionaries. The Christian communities, as they increased in number, tended to withdraw themselves more and more from the effective control of the central government. The possibility of a double allegiance was apparent, appeal being taken to the Pope as against the ruler of Japan. The fear of the development of an *imperium in imperio,* coupled with the growing distrust, brought forth in the seventeenth century a proscription of Christianity and persecution of the Christians as well as the edicts closing Japan to general foreign intercourse. Japanese were prohibited from venturing abroad or from building vessels in which they could engage in foreign trade. Only the construction of craft suitable for the coastwise trade was permitted.

As in the case of China, this cutting-off of intercourse with the outside world was not absolute. The Dutch, partly because for some time they were not suspected of being aggressive in propagating their faith, and partly because their character was believed to be non-warlike, were permitted a limited commercial intercourse through the port of Nagasaki, with the right to maintain a factory on the little island of Deshima in that harbor; but to preserve this privilege they were forced to submit to many humiliations. And the Chinese carried on a less restricted trade than did the Dutch.

6. INTERNAL CONDITIONS DURING TOKUGAWA SHŌGUNATE

As a result of seclusion, for more than two hundred years the Japanese were undisturbed by foreign wars or the rumors of war that seem to be bred by contact between states. With this went internal peace. As this peace continued during the years, the hand of the Shōgun by degrees relaxed its firm grip on the country. A machine had been created which ran on its own momentum, or rather on the momentum given it by the first and the third Shōguns, but it gradually slowed up in its operation. If new problems, either external or internal, had been presented, its functioning might have been disturbed. But the other clans singly could not dispute the Tokugawa power, the possibility of coöperation against the Shōgun had been reduced to the minimum, and the time had not come when Europeans insisted on their right to trade with the Japanese or to make treaties with their government.

The cessation of internal war, however, caused the Shōgun to turn his attention more and more to the pleasures of the Palace, with a consequent lessening of interest in maintaining the military strength and efficiency of his immediate following. On the other hand, the arts of war remained the primary concern of the Daimyō. As the military power of the Tokugawa declined, the strength of the more powerful of the other clans increased. The inauguration of the period of peace did not lessen the martial ardor of the samurai, but their tastes had to be satisfied in petty quarreling and warlike games instead of in actual organized combat. As the relative power of the secretly dissatisfied clans increased, their reluctance to accept the dictates of the Tokugawa also naturally increased in proportion to their feeling of strength. For a long time they were impotent in the face of the system, but as the system decayed the autonomy of the provinces increased. By 1853 this relaxation of the hand of authority had gone so far that there were good prospects for a successful revolt against the Shōgun if several of the clans could combine and if a good reason for revolt could be found.

The Shōguns themselves provided the excuse. In lieu of war they had to find other interests for the turbulent samurai. This they did by encouraging the development of learning and of every cultural pursuit. The consequent revival of learning took the students at first to the Chinese classics and then to the Japanese past, and this study revealed the extent of the inroads made on the original Japanese culture by the Chinese influence. A revival of the old religion, Shinto, was undertaken. This recalled to mind the Emperor as the spiritual head of the nation and brought to him increased respect. At the same time with the Shinto revival came a development of historical studies, and in 1715 a monumental history of Japan was completed. This work revealed clearly that in actual fact the Shōgun had usurped powers which had originally been exercised by the Emperor. This point of view was further developed in a history of the Shōgunate which was completed in 1827. Thus reverence for the institution, the Shōgunate, was lessened, since it was shown to be misplaced. Scholars began to ask why the Emperor should remain in obscurity at Kyoto—why the Shōgunate should be maintained. The entire revival of Japanese learning had the natural effect of stimulating two sentiments: that of nationality, and that of loyalty to the Emperor, "of direct descent from the Gods."

The system of ideas which had come into vogue by the time of the opening of Japan to foreign intercourse, consequently, was essentially nationalistic and imperialistic. The feudal clan system of government, with its centralization under the Shōgunate, was being seriously questioned by some of the anti-Chinese philosophical schools. It was also being repudiated by such men as Yoshida Shoin, who refused to acquiesce in the existing passport system for travel within Japan, insisting on his right, as a Japanese, to travel freely within the country.

Students were coming into contact with foreign learning as well as reviving knowledge of the medieval Japan during this time of increased interest in things of the mind. The Yedo government kept itself somewhat informed as to external conditions through reports required of the Dutch when they made the required periodic visits to Yedo. These were made annually until after 1790, and thereafter at intervals of four years. The importation and study of foreign books (except by official interpreters) and unauthorized contact with the foreigners were strictly prohibited, however, until after 1720. The prohibition had been occasionally disregarded, so that through the Dutch at Deshima there had always been some inflow of foreign knowledge, especially of anatomy and medicine. After 1720, however, the introduction and dissemination of western learning were naturally more rapid and extensive. Through the prohibitions of internal movement, except with permission of the Shōgunal government, the attempt was made to prevent too wide a contact with the Dutch and the new learning. But, even among the retainers of the Outer Lords, medical, military, geographical, and other scientific books from the West came, through translation, to be studied. Consequently some of the people in the Western clans, as well as at Yedo, were to some extent prepared for the changes in policy made necessary after the Americans, followed by other foreigners, demanded a wider intercourse with Japan.

The "Land of the Rising Sun," it must be recognized, then, was not in the calm and placid state in 1853 that is sometimes indicated. The condition at the time of Commodore Perry's arrival is summarized by Professor Gubbins as follows: [9]

He found a highly organized community excelling in arts, industries and agriculture, wedded to ceremonial, and permeated by Chinese ideas, with a gift for imitation happily controlled by assimilative genius, and independence of character, and enjoying a system of government very cumbrous, and obscure, and quite unique of its kind. The central authority was nominally vested in a shadowy personage in Yedo, whose exact relationship to a still more shadowy personage in Kioto it was not easy to determine. There was a feudal system under which the daimios ruled their own territories, or under Shogunate supervision, those of their neighbors, certain localities, including what were known as the Shoguns' dominions, being reserved for the direct administration of the Yedo government, and the central authority was exercised by means of Councils of State, and of a vast assemblage of executive and judicial officers. This central authority was weak, and growing weaker, an uneasy feeling was abroad, and the first signs of the troubles which culminated in the downfall of the Shogunate were beginning to show themselves. Clan jealousies and feudal restrictions hindered national progress in many directions, there was much distress and discontent, and the currency of the country was in a state of great confusion. Foreign intercourse was confined to the Chinese and Dutch traders visiting Nagasaki, and, when it was not Chinese, Dutch was the medium of intercourse with the outside world.

7. THE COMING OF COMMODORE PERRY

The opening of Japan was quite as inevitable as the attempt to break down China's isolation. In the movement that culminated in the opening of Japan the development of better means of communication and the desire for trade were supplemented by the need of mariners, especially those

[9] Op. cit., pp. 38-39.

engaged in the whaling and fur-sealing industry in the north Pacific, for places into which they could safely put to take on provisions and to repair damages. Not infrequently vessels were driven ashore by storms off the coast of Japan. Sometimes the survivors were killed and sometimes they were sent out through the Dutch at Nagasaki. But in every case the Japanese steadfastly refused to allow foreign vessels to put into their harbors, and compelled those that were driven in immediately to depart. Sometimes Japanese were blown out to sea in their small coasting craft, and no favorable interest was manifested in the foreign vessels which picked them up and tried to return them to their homeland.

The position of the Japanese islands in relation to the Chinese coast also made it inconvenient to have her refuse to establish relations of any kind with foreign states. The Americans, in particular, if they were to develop direct communications with China from the Pacific ports by means of steam-propelled vessels, needed coaling stations or ports of call *en route*. Formosa was thought of for this purpose, but since the American policy did not include territorial aggrandizement, it seemed more desirable to secure coaling rights in Japan. Thus there were very definite reasons for the interest shown after 1825 in the opening of the islands.

The Perry expedition was not the first modern manifestation of the interest of foreign governments in the condition of affairs in Japan. Russian interest had been shown during the last decade of the eighteenth and the first part of the nineteenth century. This interest arose from the geographical proximity of the two countries, which jointly occupied the island of Saghalin, with Russia also claiming the Kurile Islands. In 1792 a Russian expedition landed on Hokkaido with the ostensible mission of returning a party of shipwrecked Japanese sailors, but with the real purpose of establishing relations with the Japanese government. Both this expedition and a second, sent shortly afterwards (1804) were unsuccessful.

The English, in their turn, made several attempts to open the country. They used various pretexts, such as the need for supplies and the making of surveys, to explain their expeditions. But again their real mission was the opening of the country, and they, like the Russians, were unsuccessful. The activities in which they engaged during the years 1833–1860 in China, attempting to force open the door to that country, however, prevented the English from concentrating their attention on Japan.

The several earlier attempts made by the United States to establish relations with Japan, dictated largely by the treatment of distressed American whalers in Japanese waters, were somewhat half-hearted, and hence entirely unsuccessful. But finally the Washington government decided to make a determined effort, and engaged in extensive preparations preliminary to the sending of an expedition. The Dutch government, and the other European governments, were notified (1849) of the American intention, and the Dutch were asked to furnish such advice and aid as might make the expedition successful. Presents illustrative of many features of Western civilization were prepared. The objects of the Perry expedition were stated in the instructions to be: 1) protection for our shipwrecked sailors; 2) the opening of the ports for the entry of vessels to refit and obtain coal; and 3) the opening of ports for trade.

Commodore Perry sailed from Norfolk on November 24, 1852, and his expedition steamed into Yokohama Bay on July 3, 1853, disregarding all signals to stop until a suitable anchorage had been reached off the little fishing village of Uraga. The appearance of the steam vessels, a new sight to the Japanese, caused great consternation. And the excitement in Yedo, when the news reached the Shōgun's capital, was no less than that in the village. "The popular commotion in Yedo at the news of a 'foreign invasion,'" says a native writer, "was beyond description. The whole city was in an uproar. In all directions were seen mothers flying with children in their arms, and men with mothers on their backs. Rumors of an immediate action, exaggerated each time they were communicated from mouth to mouth, added horror to the horror-stricken. The tramp of war-horses, the clatter of armed warriors, the noise of carts, the parade of firemen, the incessant tolling of bells, the shrieks of women, the cries of children, dinning all the streets of a city of more than a million souls, made confusion worse confounded." [10]

In the Perry expedition, as in most American actions in the Far East during the nineteenth century, a distinction must be made between the policies of the American government and those of its agents. Perry's instructions were eminently pacific. Given force, he was to use it only in the last resort and for self-protection. He was to obtain all he could by pacific measures, and he was to emphasize first, the friendliness of the United States to Japan; second, the separation of church and state in the United States, in order to remove the fear that might exist lest the power of the state should be used to force Christianity on the Japanese; and third, the desire of the United States to see peace preserved in the Pacific. But the position taken by the American government was that "no friendship can long exist between them unless Japan should change her policy and cease to act towards the people of the United States as if they were her enemies." [11] Furthermore:

If such arguments did not secure any relaxation of the policy of exclusion, or even any assurance of humane treatment for seamen, Perry was instructed to "change his tone, and to inform them in the most unequivocal terms that it is the determination of this government to insist that hereafter all citizens or

[10] Quoted by Foster, J. W., *American Diplomacy in the Orient*, pp. 151–152.
[11] Quoted by Dennett, T., *Americans in Eastern Asia*, pp. 263–264.

vessels of the United States that may be wrecked on their coasts or driven by stress of weather into their harbors shall, so long as they are compelled to remain there, be treated with humanity; and that if any acts of cruelty should hereafter be practiced upon citizens of this country, whether by the government or the inhabitants of Japan, they will be severely chastised.[12]

During the voyage Perry had marked out for himself the course he intended to follow in his dealings with the Japanese, and to this plan of action he rigidly adhered. He had determined "to demand as a right, not solicit as a favor, those acts of courtesy due from one civilized nation to another; to disregard the acts and threats of the authorities, if in the least respect in conflict with the dignity of the American flag; to practice a little of Japanese diplomacy by allowing no one on board the ships except officers having business, and they only on the flagship; and by personally conferring with no one except an official of the highest rank in the Empire." [13]

Adherence to this program accounts in a large measure for the success of the Perry mission. If the Japanese had been successful in their attempts to remove the negotiations to Nagasaki; if Perry had been content to treat with subordinate officials instead of holding himself aloof until suitable officers had been sent to confer with him; and if he had not realized when and to what extent to modify his position, the opening of Japan would have been postponed. After being accorded a fitting reception and delivering the President's letter for transmission to the Emperor, Perry acceded to the Japanese request for time to consider the proposals of the American government. He stated that he would be back the next spring for an answer, and refused to go to Nagasaki to receive his answer through the Dutch or the Chinese. He then withdrew to the China coast.

Owing to the fact that a Russian fleet visited Nagasaki shortly after his departure from Yokohama Bay and that squadrons of other nations, notably the French, were available for service in Japanese waters, Commodore Perry returned to Japan at an earlier time than he had originally contemplated. He was fearful lest he should be forestalled by the Russians and the French if he delayed longer than February, 1854. Upon his return to Yokohama he steamed farther up the bay than on his first visit before dropping his anchors. He was well received this time, and after a period of negotiation succeeded in making a treaty along the lines of his instructions. Two ports in addition to Nagasaki were to be opened to foreign vessels for the purpose of coaling, provisioning, and refitting; the right to appoint a consul to reside at Shimoda was accorded; it was agreed that protection should be afforded to shipwrecked sailors; and "most-favored-nation" treatment was promised. The Perry treaty was the entering wedge,

12 DENNETT, op. cit., p. 264.
13 FOSTER, p. 152.

and advantage was taken of the success of his mission by other Powers, England negotiating a similar treaty in 1854, Russia in 1855, and Holland during the years 1855–1857.

8. ESTABLISHMENT OF RELATIONS WITH THE WEST

Commodore Perry inserted the wedge, but it remained for another American, Townsend Harris, to establish relations on a firmer foundation. Perry deserves to be remembered for his tact and skill, but it must not be forgotten that his undertaking was supported by force. Mr. Harris, appointed in 1856 as the first American consul to Japan, had no such support. He came to a new land and took up his residence among a people entirely unaccustomed to the foreigner and hostile to him. His position among them was one of complete isolation. The foreign community of a few years later was entirely non-existent. Unable to speak the language of the people among whom he lived and with whom he had to deal, he yet was able finally to overcome their hostility and to inspire their officials with some confidence in his honesty of intention and in his judgment. Further than this, he was able to lead them to see the advisability of still further broadening their contact with the outside world. All of this he accomplished within a period of two years, without the use or the threat of force except as he intentionally played on the fear of the Japanese government that England or Russia would send armed expeditions to compel the signing of treaties or to conquer the islands. He was able to reënforce the argument by pointing to the expedition to Tientsin in 1858 and to the consequent presence of foreign forces in Eastern waters. He had little difficulty in showing the Japanese officials that the position of their country would be better under a treaty negotiated with him voluntarily than under one dictated under the shadow of British, French, or Russian guns.

The second step in the opening of Japan came in 1858 with the signing of the treaty of that year. Commodore Perry had secured the elementary privileges of intercourse. Consul Harris regularized the contacts and intercourse of Japan with the outside world. The treaty of 1858 resulted in the establishment of regular diplomatic and consular relations with Japan; it brought about the opening of four additional ports; it made possible the carrying on of trade at the ports opened, instead of restricting their use to the refitting of foreign vessels; and by it the United States offered its "good offices" to Japan in case of trouble with other states. All of these were distinct gains and could have resulted only in good for Japan as well as for Europe and America. Three other features of the treaty were not so advantageous to Japan. Following the precedent set in the China treaties of the same general period, the Harris treaty established a tariff on goods imported into and exported from Japan, and thus it deprived her for the time, as was the case in China, of the right to regulate her trade relations through her own legislation, and reduced her future income at the same time. The duties agreed upon, it should be noted, gave distinct advantages to American as compared with European trade. This was remedied in subsequent treaties when England, France, and Holland secured a lowering of their duties to the American level. This, however, was of distinct disadvantage to Japan, as it reduced her income from foreign trade. In the second place, the treaty provided, against the better judgment of Mr. Harris, for the establishment of the extraterritorial system. And, in the third place, the treaty stipulated for the introduction and free exchange of foreign coins in the country, and for a right of exportation of Japanese coins. This provision led to considerable speculation in exchange, drained specie from the islands, and proved seriously embarrassing to the Japanese. It can be truly said that Mr. Harris acted in good faith in advising Japanese officials to permit the insertion of these provisions in the treaty; and it may have been to the temporary interest of Japan to have been under these restrictions at the outset. But after the reorganization of the country had been undertaken she undeniably suffered from and was humiliated by these provisions, and her outlook was colored by them.

9. INTERNAL EFFECTS OF ENDING OF SECLUSION

When Perry knocked so loudly at the door that the Japanese government could not refuse to hear, a very difficult problem was presented to the Shōgun. As has already been pointed out, his power had been gradually weakening, and the position of the Emperor had been strengthened by a recognition of the fact that he was the rightful ruler of the country. The policy of seclusion had been initiated by the Tokugawa, but it had become a national policy through its long continuance, and it was, contrary to precedent, given Imperial sanction, in the first years of his rule, by the Emperor reigning at the time of the Perry mission. The Emperor Komei, shortly after 1846, the year of his accession to the throne, instructed the Shōgun that the traditional policy of seclusion had to be maintained. While this action was unprecedented, it was directly in line with the tendency toward the restoration of power to the Emperor. Because of that tendency it demanded the careful consideration of the Yedo government. When the question of foreign intercourse could not be evaded, the Shōgun submitted it to the advice of a council of the feudal chiefs. All but a small minority declared themselves in favor of maintaining the traditional policy. So far as their advice was given in good faith, it was determined by a lack of knowledge of the forces to be contended against and of the impossibility of successful resistance. With a larger knowledge of the actual conditions, both internal and external, the Shōgun and his council at Yedo were forced to side with the minority, and the decision was made to comply with the demands of the foreigners. On the one hand, the government had to reckon with the possible and probable invasion of the country, and with the inability of Japan successfully to resist such an invasion. On the other hand, it faced the certainty that it was giving a powerful weapon to the opponents of the Shōgunate if the treaties were signed. What appeared to be the lesser of the two evils was chosen.

The opening of the country revealed immediately the weakness of the dual system of government. Perry and other foreign representatives thought that they were dealing with the Emperor—with the titular as well as the real ruler of Japan—when they negotiated treaties with the government of the Shōgun. Later, when troublesome questions arose, they hesitated to recognize the plea of the Shōgun that he must refer the matter to Kyoto before he could make a decision, thinking it an indication of bad faith and of double dealing on his part. And each reference to Kyoto revealed more clearly to the Japanese themselves that the Shōgun was in reality exercising powers which belonged to the Emperor. The very fact that for the first time in generations matters of importance were referred to the Emperor indicated a recognition of weakness on the part of the Shōgun. If he had acted decisively, as an Iyeyasu might have done, and made his own decisions without consulting the Emperor, simply notifying him of them, the Shōgunate might have been saved. Or if he had been able to make the Emperor see the problem as he saw it, so that the Imperial decision would have been in harmony with the action which had to be taken, the events of the years after 1858 might have been differently shaped.

But the Shōgun, doubting his ability to control the country with a strong hand, felt compelled to strengthen his position by invoking the Imperial authority on the question of foreign relations. Unfortunately for him, the court at Kyoto was under the influence of the western clan leaders, and particularly the leaders of Satsuma and Choshu. These clans had long been jealous of the supremacy of the Tokugawa, and they used their influence with the Emperor to embarrass the Shōgun. Hostile to the foreigner as they undoubtedly were, the western clans were more interested in using the issue of foreign relations to weaken the Shōgunate than in determining upon the action which would result in the greatest good for Japan. Consequently, during the early period of intercourse, the Emperor insisted upon maintaining the policy of seclusion, and the Shōgun, although he solicited advice from the Emperor, was forced to go counter to the Imperial commands under the constant and unrelaxed pressure of the Powers. As they came to realize the exact relationship of the Shōgun to the Emperor, the Powers began to demand that the Emperor himself ratify the treaties. This demand, however, was not pressed until ten years after the first treaty had been made.

Meanwhile several incidents occurred which had an effect both on foreign relations and on internal politics. The western clans, and all of those who were not self-interested in the maintenance of the Shōgunate, were hostile to the foreigners. There was division even within the Tokugawa clan, first over the question of the succession to the position of Shōgun, and second over the advisability of departing from the policy of seclusion. Under the pressure of all these forces the Yedo government alternately blew hot and cold. It promised the Emperor that the foreigners should be driven out as soon as adequate preparations could be made, and it kept assuring the foreign representatives, who were at last (1859) installed at Yedo, that it would observe the treaties as soon as it could quiet the populace. Hostility to the foreigners was shown in Yedo as well as in other parts of the country.

In 1862 an incident occurred which brought matters to a head so far as the Satsuma clan was concerned. The Lord of Satsuma was proceeding with his retainers from Yedo to his own dominions. On the road they were traversing an Englishman named Richardson and three companions were riding. Ignorant of the custom of the country which gave the right of way to such elevated personages as the Prince of Satsuma, they affronted his followers by refusing to draw out of the road until the procession had passed. The consequence was that Mr. Richardson lost his life. The British government immediately demanded satisfaction for the affair, and when the Shōgun proved unwilling, or rather unable, to afford it, a British squadron bombarded Kagoshima, the Satsuma capital. This revealed to that clan the inferiority of Japanese arms and helped to bring about a reversal of its general attitude toward foreigners. Another effect was to bring home the military weakness of the Shōgun, a weakness which made it impossible for his government either to chastise its own vassal or to protect him from the foreigner.

The other great western clan, Choshu, was brought to terms by similar means. Under the pressure of the anti-foreign party, and of the court, the Shōgun had finally issued a secret order for the expulsion of the foreigners. Before the time set for action the Lord of Choshu ordered his retainers (1863) to close the Inland Sea to foreign vessels by firing on all that attempted to pass through the straits of Shimonoseki. An American vessel was the first fired upon. The Americans effected immediate reprisal, sending a war vessel to bombard the town. Other merchant vessels were fired upon, however, and a joint expedition was finally decided upon.[14] The British, French, Dutch, and Americans contributed vessels to make up the expedition sent in 1864. It was completely successful in bringing home to Choshu the superior power of the foreigners.

14 By the time the plans for the expedition had matured, its real purpose had changed from that of enforcing treaty rights to that of striking a blow in support of the Shōgun. See TREAT, P. J., *Early Relations*, ch. 10.

With this demonstration, and the weakening of the anti-foreign attitude of his chief supporters in which it resulted, the Emperor began to waver in his own demand that the Shōgun restore the old condition of isolation. By this time the foreigners fully realized the weakness of their position in the country so long as it had not received the stamp of Imperial approval, for successive incidents had brought home to them the dual nature of the Japanese government. Consequently, in 1866 the British minister, Sir Harry Parkes, offered to remit part of the fine which had been imposed on Choshu by the allied Powers if the Emperor would ratify the treaties. This assent was given finally, and the third step in the opening of Japan had been taken.

Meanwhile the internal situation was gradually shaping itself. The country was in a turmoil, and internal disintegration, with the passing of the old order, appeared to be a possibility. Choshu had been intriguing to get control of the person of the Emperor in order to justify a regency under its control—a new Shōgunate. This attempt was unsuccessful. The order from Kyoto that the Shōgun should punish Choshu for its action resulted in the assembling of large bodies of men and in the sending of an expedition, but complete success did not result. Some of the wiser heads in the clans were making attempts to bring about a union for the purpose of overthrowing the Shōgun. Shortly after this union had been effected two new faces appeared. The old anti-foreign Emperor died in February of 1867, and was succeeded by one who was not so hampered by the traditions and hostilities of the past. Mutsuhito took as his reign title Meiji ("enlightened rule"), and as his policy the reorientation of Japanese life with respect to the outside world. During the previous year the Shōgun had died and his successor was also prepared to further the progress of the nation by opening it fully to foreign intercourse.

The accession of a new Emperor provided a logical opportunity for the western clans to realize their object and bring the Shōgunate to an end. Consequently, in the fall of 1867 a memorial, concurred in by Satsuma, Choshu, Tosa, and Hizen, the powerful western clans, was sent to the new Shōgun requesting that the actual power be restored to the Emperor. The dangers inherent in the dual system of government at a time when pressure was being constantly exerted against Japan from the outside were emphasized in the memorial. The new Shōgun was not much inclined to cling to an office which carried with it so much care and anxiety, and he responded to the memorial by abdicating his position.

This brought the Shōgunate to an end, but it did not end the troubles connected therewith. A restoration of power to the Emperor should have put all of the clans on an equal footing before the Throne. Appointments to office should have been equally distributed, and favors should have been impartially bestowed. This was certainly the expectation of the Shōgun, for otherwise he would scarcely have resigned his power without a fight to secure the future interest of his clan. But this was not the idea of the western clans. Their intention may have been purely patriotic and disinterested, but their actions fail to justify such a conclusion. Offices were monopolized by the western clansmen, and the Tokugawa were pushed into the background. The situation was similar to that existing in the United States when a party which had been long in power goes out of control. The newcomers are favor-hungry, and naturally expect and demand a reward for their long patience. Two hundred and fifty years had passed since the Tokugawa had begun its monopoly, and the newcomers were determined to make good the opportunity offered them, in their turn, to secure exclusive control.

Judging from all indications the real intention of those back of the "Restoration of Meiji" was not to set up a personal rule by the Emperor in place of the rule of the Shōgun. Rather it was to replace the Tokugawa as "advisers" to the Emperor. When this was perceived by the followers of the ex-Shōgun they took up arms in defense of their interests. This uprising was easily put down by the new régime, and by 1869 all opposition had come to an end. The "Restoration" had been effected and the four western clans were in complete control.

REFERENCES FOR FURTHER STUDY

SIR RUTHERFORD ALCOCK, *The Capital of the Tycoon,* 2 vols. (1863); a narrative of three years' residence in Japan. CAPT. F. BRINKLEY, *History of the Japanese People* (1915); excellent for the early history of Japan. DELMER M. BROWN, *Money Economy in Medieval Japan* (1951). B. H. CHAMBERLAIN, *Things Japanese* (1905); short reliable sketches on all topics from abacus to zoology. GEORGE B. CRESSEY, *Asia's Lands and Peoples* (1944); a standard text in human geography, ch. 10–14 deal with Japan. TYLER DENNETT, *Americans in Eastern Asia* (1922), ch. 13, 14, 19; excellent accounts of American policy. J. W. FOSTER, *American Diplomacy in the Orient* (1903), ch. 5, 6; good general discussion of the Perry expedition and the work of Townsend Harris. W. E. GRIFFIS, *The Mikado's Empire,* 2 vols. (1876), esp. book 21; personal experiences, observations, and studies in Japan, 1870–1874; later editions. W. E. GRIFFIS, *Townsend Harris, First American Envoy in Japan* (1895); contains his journal, together with a biographical sketch. J. H. GUBBINS, *Progress of Japan* (1911); an invaluable study of the internal politics of Japan, 1853–1871. J. H. GUBBINS, *Making of Modern Japan* (1922); ch. 1–7 covers same period as *Progress of Japan.* JOHN A. HARRISON, *Japan's Northern Frontier* (1953). EIJIRO HONJO, *The Social and Economic History of Japan* (1935); worth consulting. BARON KIKUCHI DAIROKU, *The Introduction of Western Learning into Japan,* in The Book of the Opening of Rice Institute, vol. 3, pp. 681–725; an excellent survey of the introduction of Western learning through the Dutch before the Restoration. G. W. KNOX, *Japanese Life in Town and Country* (1905); title indicates its scope, within which it is good. GEORGE A. LENSEN, *Russia's Japan Expedition of 1852–1855* (1955). GEORGE A. LENSEN, *The Russo-Japanese Frontier* (1954). J. M. MAKI, *Japanese Militarism. Its Cause and Its Cure* (1944), ch. 2, 3, 5; a penetrating analysis of the development of authoritarianism in Japan. W. W. McLaren, *Political History of Japan during the Meiji Era* (1916), ch. 1; an excellent summary of the internal conditions out of which the Restoration was precipitated. James Murdock, *History of Japan,* vol. 1 (1910); from the origins to the arrival of the Portuguese; vol. 2 (1903), from 1592 to 1651; vol. 3 (1926), the Tokugawa epoch; the most comprehensive and careful work in English on the pre-modern period. David Murray, *Japan* (1894); good for early history of Japan; not so detailed and comprehensive as Brinkley. E. Herbert Norman, *Andō Shōeki and the Anatomy of Japanese Feudalism,* transl. Asiatic Society of Japan, 3rd series, vol. 2 (December, 1949). Count Shigenobu Okuma (ed.), *Fifty Years of Modern Japan,* 2 vols. (1909); contains chapters on pre-Restoration conditions. Edwin O. Reischauer, *Japan, Past and Present* (1946), ch. 1–8; a good summary of pre-Restoration history. G. B. Sansom, *Japan—A Cultural History* (1931), part 7; a careful and informed study. G. B. Sansom, *The Western World and Japan* (1950); a valuable study. Sir Ernest Satow, *A Diplomat in Japan* (1921); gives an interesting view of pre-Restoration conditions in Japan. R. L. Stevenson, *Familiar Studies of Men and Books, Yoshida Torajiro (Shoin)* (1895); an enthusiastic literary study of a great pre-Restoration figure. A shorter sketch is in vol. 15, *Encyclopedia of the Social Sciences,* p. 514. The *Encyclopedia* also contains short studies of other important Japanese leaders. Takekoshi Yosaburo, *The Economic Aspects of the Civilization of Japan* (1930); a standard but somewhat difficult work. M. Takizawa, *The Penetration of Money Economy in Japan* (1927); well worth consulting. P. J. Treat, *Early Diplomatic Relations between the United States and Japan, 1853–1865* (1917); a careful survey. P. J. Treat, *Diplomatic Relations between the United States and Japan, 1853–1895* (1932), ch. 1–11; a reproduction, with additional documentation and minor modifications of the materials in *Early Diplomatic Relations.* It is the standard study of the topic. Chitoshi Yanaga, *Japan Since Perry* (1949), ch. 1–2.

CHAPTER V

JAPAN IN TRANSITION: 1868–1894

I. THE RESTORATION OF MEIJI

THE restoration of the Emperor to power as a result of the resignation of the Shōgun did not mark a sharp break with the past. The feudal régime was left intact. The ideal back of the Restoration movement had been a return to past practices and institutions as much as a reorganization of the country on the basis of new ideas imported from Europe; and those who brought about the return of temporal power to the Emperor considered that the movement meant that they should exercise the power in place of the Tokugawa. The great break had been made by the Shōgun and his advisers when the policy of isolation was given up, and by the Emperor Meiji and the western clan leaders when foreigners were admitted to Kyoto and the anti-foreign policy was reversed. Foreign policy had been changed radically, but internal conditions had to be shaped, and the new order had to be developed out of the past as the result of a slow transitional process. This transition, in many important respects, is still evident. Striking beginnings, however, were made during the twenty years following the Restoration of Meiji. It is with these beginnings that this chapter is concerned.

The resignation of the Shōgun left the western clans free to carry out their plan of substituting their authority for that of the Tokugawa, or more accurately, to replace that clan as the chief advisers to the Emperor in the exercise of his powers. The attempt of the Tokugawa to regain a position of equality was ended when the superior power of the new group was revealed as a result of the crushing of the Tokugawa rebellion. But a system had to be devised to replace the Shōgunate if the new régime was to maintain itself over a long period of time. The Shōgun had resigned as a result of a temporary alliance of several of the clans, and this alliance had to be maintained or else replaced by something more permanent.

While the new régime was clearly built on the foundations of the past, its construction was just as clearly influenced by the ideas of the West as they came to be more fully appreciated. The chief Western contribution was the idea of a deliberative assembly as a part of the machinery of government. The attempt to work out this idea in the Japanese system by successive adaptations can be perceived in the several changes made during the years of political experimentation. This, in turn, was part of the transitional process, to the description of which attention must now be turned.

It is not necessary to consider the several steps in the organization and reorganization of the new system from 1869 to 1889 except in a summary way. From the beginning the new Emperor allowed himself to be guided by his councillors from the four clans making up the Satcho-Hito combination, i.e. Satsuma, Choshu, Hizen, and Tosa.[1] Under their direction a central organization was created in which use could be made of both the court and the territorial nobility. The leaders worked mostly behind the scenes, exercising the real power, but allowing the more prominent offices to be held by others.

The Emperor and the Kuge [writes Dr. McGovern] had been eagerly looking forward to their restoration to power, determined to enjoy their long-lost privileges to the fullest possible extent. The Daimyō or feudal lords who had brought about the change considered that they had no less a right to the fruits of office, and since both parties were no less incompetent than powerful, it followed that both sections had to be appeased by high-sounding names, and yet so placed that they could not interfere with the policy of the Samurai Bureaucrats who were to remain the real masters of the State.[2]

This was accomplished by making provision for three offices in the central government. The first office, that of Supreme Head (Sosai), was awarded to a Prince of the Blood. The second office, made up of Councillors of the First Class (Gijo), consisted of members drawn half from the ranks of the court nobility (Kuge) and half from the Daimyō of the leading clans. This body was intended to be partly deliberative and partly administrative. The third office, the Councillors of the Second Class (Sanyo), was made up of five Kuge and fifteen samurai. Both of these offices were subordinate to the Sosai. The most prominent of the Restoration figures attached themselves to the office of the Supreme Head in subordinate positions, but from the beginning they exercised the real power. This organization was changed in the same year (1868) in which it had been established. The authority of these three "offices" was transferred to a body called the Daijokwan, or Deliberative Assembly, which consisted of two houses. The upper house, or Council of State, was made up of the former Gijo and Sanyo, and the lower house, or Assembly, of the representatives of the feudal class. The real power lay in the hands of the Council of State, the members of the Assembly deliberating only on matters sent to them by it. In addition, provision was made for two chief ministers of state and their subordinates, who served as the medium of communication between the

---

[1] A leading spirit in this combination was Kido, a Choshu man. Others were Saigo, Okubo (Satsuma samurai), Itagaki (Tosa), Ito (Choshu), and Okuma (Hizen). Prince Iwakura, representing the court nobility, also played a leading rôle in Restoration and post-Restoration days.

[2] McGovern, Modern Japan, p. 46.

Daijokwan and the court. This organization had the two-fold advantage of concentrating power in one body, and of satisfying the promise in the Imperial oath of 1868 that advice should be taken in administering public affairs.[3]

2. THE FEUDAL SYSTEM ENDED

The new régime, working through the Daijokwan, was confronted by many important and difficult problems. The most urgent need was that of establishing its authority throughout the country. This brought it squarely against the whole problem of feudalism. No effective centralization of authority could be made so long as the feudal lords stood between the Imperial Government and the individual.

After the overthrow of the Tokugawa the direct administration of their estates was assumed by the central government. Otherwise the feudal régime remained untouched. The first step looking toward an effective concentration of authority was taken, however, in 1868 when provision was made for the appointment of an Imperial official in every fief. But this did not amount to an extension of the Imperial authority into the fief, for the original clan rulers were left in control. It merely served to accustom them to the presence of the central authority. In 1869 the second step looking toward the abolition of the feudal order was taken. Kido, Saigo, and other leaders of the western clans, having reached an agreement as to the necessity for strengthening the central government, persuaded the Lords of Satsuma, Choshu, Hizen, and Tosa to hand over their registers of land and of people to the Emperor, thus restoring his power over their territories. This put those clans openly behind the policy of centralization and enabled the government, a few months later, to take the next logical step of ordering the other clans to return their registers. At the same time the announcement was made that the feudal lords would be retained as governors of their respective domains. In 1871 an Imperial rescript was issued formally abolishing feudalism.

It is not usually so easy to disestablish a privileged class, and a sort of super-patriotism has been ascribed to the Japanese nobility in consequence of the easy relinquishment of its privileges to the nation. Certainly it was a patriotic and laudable thing for the feudal lords to do, but it cannot be wholly ascribed to patriotism. The brains of the government, both central and provincial, were of the samurai class rather than of the nobility. The Daimyō had long been rulers only in name in their fiefs. It was these samurai who, seeing, as a result of the abolition of feudalism, a larger field in which their talents might be displayed, persuaded the four powerful

---

[3] This oath and the so-called "constitution" of 1868 will be dealt with in connection with the constitutional movement.

western Daimyō voluntarily to surrender their positions as territorial magnates. Their persuasion was rendered more effective by their recognition of
the real necessity for the abolition of feudalism and for the concentration
of authority if Japan was to maintain herself in the face of the foreign impact. In other words, self-interest and the national good suggested the
same move. The other clans had no alternative but to comply with the demand of the government, supported as it was by the military strength of
the four most powerful clans.

Furthermore, the interests of the Daimyō were amply protected in the
settlements made at the time of the abolition of their privileges. The settlement made with the Daimyō and samurai was in the nature of an enormous
pension scheme. The Daimyō were guaranteed one-tenth and the samurai
one-half of their nominal revenues.[4] Since the nominal revenue of the
Daimyō was usually very much greater than his real income, this scheme
worked to his decided advantage. He no longer had to maintain the provincial administration out of his own purse, but was free to use for his
own purposes the entire sum paid him by the government. Neither did his
income any longer vary with the production and price of rice.

While the settlement was advantageous to the Daimyō, the samurai did
not fare so well under the application of the same principle. Their nominal
and real incomes were more nearly identical than were those of the
Daimyō, and were none too large for their adequate maintenance. Cutting
this income in two worked an undoubted hardship on many of them. It is
true that the settlement left them free to add to their incomes, but a class
maintained in idleness for so many generations found it hard immediately
to engage successfully in gainful pursuits. And not only was their income
reduced materially by the abolition of feudalism, but special privileges,
such as wearing the two swords, which had served to distinguish them
from the rest of the populace, were also taken away from them. Thus from
the first there was dissatisfaction among the samurai class, but they could
do nothing for the time except grumble. They had been brought up in a
tradition of loyalty to their lords, so that revolt appeared to be out of the
question against a decree acquiesced in by the Daimyō and bearing the now
sacred signature of the Emperor. Furthermore, their confidence in the
rightfulness of their privileged position had been seriously undermined
during the years between the Restoration and the abolition of feudalism.
This bewildered state of mind had been created by a change in the public
attitude. "The general public, in so far as it took any interest in politics, by
a series of inspired articles which appeared in the limited newspaper press

---

[4] McLaren, *Political History of Japan*, ch. 3. McLaren indicates that the Daimyō also received one-half of their nominal revenues, as does Norman, *Japan's Emergence as a Modern
State*, p. 94. One-tenth, however, seems to be the correct percentage.

of the time had been instructed to regard the samurai as a parasitic class 'eating the bread of idleness,' " [5] and the public attitude could not help but affect the samurai.

In the last analysis, however, the success of the abolition rested upon the power of the government with its conscript army, recruited from all classes and equipped with modern weapons, supported as it was by the four strongest clans, to crush any opposition to its decree.

This plan, by which the nobility and the samurai were made pensioners of the state, hereditarily in some cases, and during life in others, imposed an extraordinary financial burden on the government, and one that it was not at all prepared to assume. As a matter of fact, ordinary expenses had been increasing rapidly, more rapidly than the income of the government, which had to meet the increased expenditure out of heavier direct taxation of the people, since Japan was prevented by treaty from adding to her revenues by increased customs charges. An attempt was made to secure a revision of the treaties in 1871, but the foreign Powers proved to be unwilling to modify the advantageous commercial position thus secured to them. Consequently, out of an inflexible revenue system the government was hard pressed to find the funds necessary for its maintenance. When to its increasing ordinary expenditures there was added the extraordinary burden of the pensions, its problem became so much greater that it soon appeared to be hopeless of solution.

Finally, in 1873, Count Okuma, who had become Finance Minister, resorted to a necessary expedient to save the situation. Upon his recommendation it was decided to commute the pensions. First of all, an optional scheme was tried, applying only to samurai with pensions amounting to 100 *koku,* or less, of rice. It was announced in 1873 "that the Government would be willing to commute the pensions on the basis of the market price of rice after the next harvest for a single payment, half in cash and half in Government bonds bearing 8 per cent interest. . . . The commutation was to be made at the rate of six years purchase for hereditary pensions and four years purchase for life incomes." [6] In 1876 this optional plan of commutation in a modified form was made compulsory.[7] In its compulsory form it worked real hardship on the samurai and caused great dissatisfaction among them. It was, of course, nothing but a scheme for the partial repudiation of the original settlement, and as such it was unjust. But it served to relieve the financial pressure, and, in spite of the hardship it worked on individuals, from the standpoint of the interest of Japan it must be considered a necessary expedient.

[5] McLaren, op. cit., p. 77.
[6] Ibid., ch. 3.
[7] See Norman, *Japan's Emergence as a Modern State,* pp. 94–96, for details.

3. DIVISION IN THE BUREAUCRACY

Another problem confronting the government was of a very different nature, although it also related to the question of general policy. Shortly after the Restoration there appeared a line of cleavage among the supporters of that movement. One element in the revival preceding the Restoration had been the preaching of the doctrine of expansion under Imperial direction. This had served to arouse the latent chauvinism of a large element among the samurai. The whole pre-Restoration propaganda had been intensely nationalistic, and, under the circumstances, it is not strange that the expression of national patriotism took the direction of advocacy of Imperial expansion. At any rate, among the clique left in control after the accession of the Emperor to power, there was a group, called by Dr. McGovern the "Military Bureaucrats," which advocated the unification and the strengthening of the state by means of foreign wars. Of this group Dr. McGovern writes:

> . . . the Military Bureaucrats were what might be called the Reactionaries, those who regarded the Restoration as a reversion to the past, who looked with suspicion towards ideas imported from the Occident, who regretted the downfall of feudalism, were uninterested in social reform, and looked forward eagerly to Japan's expansion on the Continent of Asia, who desired Korea, Manchuria, and a large portion of China and Siberia. They pandered to the intensely chauvinistic spirit of the nation, and were somewhat impatient of the respect paid to treaties contracted with the Western Powers. This was the prevailing spirit of the large majority of the Daimyō and Samurai, and in the oligarchy was chiefly represented by Saigo Takamori, Goto, Soyejima, and Eto.
>
> The second party, or the Civil Bureaucrats, were those in favor of reconstruction or reform, the introduction of the culture, the efficiency, and the methods of the West. They were opposed to militarism and imperialistic expansion. They desired to foster education, industry and commerce, to codify the laws and to inspire scientific research. . . . This section, which constituted the core of the new Government, and was the party which guided the ship of State through all the troublous waters of the early days, had for its leaders Kido, Okubo and later Ito.[8]

The first real clash, on principle, between these two groups in the government came after 1871. In that year some of the inhabitants of the Loochoo Islands were wrecked on the southern coast of Formosa, and were killed by the Formosan savages. The Loochoo peoples had long been considered tributary by both Japan and China. Japan immediately asserted them to be under her protection and demanded from China satisfaction for the murder. This China refused to give on the ground that both parties were under her jurisdiction. When Japan continued to insist, the Chinese government

[8] McGovern, W. M., *Modern Japan*, p. 61. But the opposition of the second group to expansion, it should be noted, was on account of the need for prior reorganization and not because they rejected it as ultimately undesirable. Infra, ch. VI.

shifted its position, claiming that it had no effective control over the inhabitants of southern Formosa, thus virtually inviting Japan to redress her own grievance. The military party in Japan loudly demanded war on China, a clamor increased in volume because of the attitude of Korea, tacitly encouraged by China, toward Japan. The military group urged the immediate necessity of a Korean expedition. And as the leaders of the "peace and internal progress" party were abroad at the time, the war party had the upper hand in the government. A conflict might have been precipitated if the Emperor had not insisted that no decision be reached until the return from abroad of the mission headed by Prince Iwakura and made up of such of the great leaders as Kido and Okubo. Upon their return a sharp struggle within the bureaucracy took place, with the result that the peace party triumphed, but at the expense of the maintenance of the coalition. This division of counsel, coupled with the general unrest incident to the introduction of reforms on a large scale, led to numerous riots and small uprisings. In order to restore quiet the government eventually compromised with the chauvinists to the extent of authorizing a punitive expedition against Formosa, without declaring war on China. This, it may be noted, was following the precedent set by Europe and the United States when action had been taken against Choshu and Satsuma under somewhat similar circumstances. It was also following more directly in the footsteps of the United States, which had sent an expedition to Formosa to secure redress for a similar outrage. The compromise restored temporary harmony in the government at Tokyo, but it had the unfortunate consequence of losing for it the services of Kido, who resigned rather than accept the policy.

The victory of the peace advocates, somewhat qualified though it was by the later decision on the punitive expedition, enabled the government to carry its program of internal reorganization and reform toward completion. But before turning back to a consideration of that program we may note another incident in the foreign field. Shortly after the Formosan trouble had arisen, another external source of friction developed, this time in Korea. At the time of the accession of Mutsuhito to the Throne the Korean government was notified of the change and invited to resume its allegiance to Japan. This invitation to vassalage was declined, and in 1875 a Korean fort fired upon a Japanese war vessel which was making surveys in Korean waters. This revived the military party in Japan, and war was averted only through the acceptance by the Korean government of a treaty of amity and commerce.

This, however, did not fully satisfy the Japanese military party, which had hoped for a war of conquest against the neighboring kingdom. The consequence was that another grievance was added to the list of samurai complaints. The announcement of the compulsory commutation policy of the government brought matters to a crisis. Saigo Takamori, who had also resigned from the government after the triumph of the peace party in 1872, put himself at the head of the dissatisfied Satsuma samurai in 1877 and they rose in arms against the government. The expressed attitude of the revolting samurai reveals clearly the feudal conception of the whole Restoration movement. It was urged in justification of the uprising that it was necessary again to resort to force in order to restore power to the Emperor. A careful distinction was made between the Emperor and his government, the samurai holding the view that the Imperial powers were being usurped by the government and denied to the Emperor himself, just as had been done during the Shōgunate. In essence, however, what they were really fighting for was the right to displace those who were advising the Emperor in order themselves to become his advisers. The samurai forces proved to be unable to make any great headway against the national conscript army sent against them, and, with the collapse of the rebellion, the theoretical distinction between the Emperor and the government was overthrown, not to be revived again until after 1930. This success of the government forces also marked the final collapse of the feudal system, and it ensured the advocates of peaceful development complete opportunity to carry their plans into effect.

The revolting samurai were right in their belief that the Restoration had not meant the resumption by the Emperor of personal power, for this had never been intended by the leaders in the movement, and it would not have been feasible if it had been part of their plan. On the other hand, the Restoration had not brought political power to the people as a whole or to a large upper class. That had not been intended either by the leaders. What had resulted had been the assumption of power by a small group of leaders from the four clans, as already described. Most of the subordinate positions, also, were filled from these clans. This small controlling group steadily narrowed as a result of such differences of view as that between the Military and Civil Bureaucrats. From the standpoint of the personal exercise of power by the Emperor conditions had not been materially changed by the overthrow of the Shōgun.

But those who had concentrated all power in their own hands, and who felt that it must remain narrowly concentrated if the unity necessary to the reorganization of the country and its preservation from the foreign Powers was to be maintained, soon encountered a new force—the idea imported from the West of popular participation in government—which had to be reckoned with more and more as time went on. In the bureaucracy itself there developed a third group, differing from those designated as the Military and the Civil Bureaucrats, which may be called the Radical group.

The Radicals were those who were opposed to the cliquishness of the bureaucracy, and who for various reasons favored the calling of a Diet, to be elected on a popular basis, to which the Ministers of State were to be responsible. Unlike the Radical parties of Europe, which are on the whole tinged with pacifism, the Radicals of Japan sought to increase their popularity with the people by advocating a policy of aggrandizement. This phase of political opinion was represented by Itagaki, and later by Okuma.[9]

Itagaki was one of the original group which had brought about the Restoration, but he was driven into opposition, together with Saigo, at the time of the Formosan trouble. His opposition, however, took a very different form from that of most of the samurai. In 1874 he organized an association for the study of political science. Immediately thereafter, in the same year, he and his associates memorialized the Throne asking for the establishment of a representative assembly. From this time on the agitation, which was partly due to a real desire for representative government, continued and grew in importance. The memorialists based their petition on the promise made by the Emperor in 1868 to govern according to the wishes of the nation.

This promise was made in the first article of the so-called Constitution of 1868. The article, generally known as the Charter Oath, reads as follows:

The practice of discussion and debate shall be universally adopted and all measures shall be decided by public argument. High and low shall be of one mind and social order shall thereby be perfectly maintained. It is necessary that the civil and military power be concentrated in a single whole, the rights of all classes be assured, and the national mind be completely satisfied. The uncivilized customs of former times shall be broken through, and the impartiality and justice displayed in the working of nature shall be adopted as a basis of action. Intellect and learning shall be sought for throughout the world in order to establish the foundations of the Empire.

That which was in the mind of the government when it drew up and promulgated this part of the Constitution of 1868 was something very different from what had been demanded by Itagaki in 1874. Undoubtedly the conception of that time was that the feudal nobility should be worked into the scheme of things by means of the establishment of the National Deliberative Assembly. No one would have attempted to maintain that this was an assembly representative of the nation, but through it the feudal governing classes were given an opportunity to express themselves. That it was not intended to do more than this, is indicated by the memorial sent in by Kido upon his return with the Iwakura mission from abroad in 1872. In this memorial he advocated as an entirely new proposal the establishment of representative government. Since he was one of the leading figures in the government at the time when the Constitution of 1868 was promulgated, it must be that he thought something else was meant by the provisions of the Charter Oath.

Nevertheless, the position of the government in 1874, with the break-

9 McGovern, op. cit.

down of the Satcho-Hito combination, was so weak that an endeavor was made to placate the protestant elements. This was arranged in the Osaka compromise, by which a Senate (Genro-in) and a separate Court of Justice were to be established to meet the outcry against the high centralization of power that had been effected, and an Assembly of Prefectural Governors was to be made part of the machinery of government so that the opinion of the people might be obtained. Itagaki and Saigo agreed to come back into the governing oligarchy, the latter being partially satisfied by the agreement on the Formosan expedition, the former by the reorganization of the government. Kido, however, remained lost to the government. Saigo and Itagaki were not satisfied with the manner in which this compromise was carried into effect, and they also soon left the government. The former, as has been noted, shortly took up arms in defense of the samurai interest, while the latter returned to the agitation for a representative assembly, since a Council of Governors, all of them appointed by the central government, could not be considered in any real sense an assembly representative of the people. The agitation was so far successful as to call forth another concession in 1878, when provincial assemblies were constituted to aid the governor and the local authorities in administering the duties of their offices.

These concessions, if such they may be called, served merely to add fuel to the fire. In 1881 the society for the study of political science changed its character and became a party definitely organized to promote the cause of constitutional and representative government in Japan. Other societies for the study of political questions had been formed after 1874 and some of these merged with Itagaki's association to form the Jiyuto or Liberal Party. Itagaki became the leader of the party, which was organized as a central association with local divisions.

4. THE CONSTITUTIONAL MOVEMENT

In 1881 Count Okuma, another of the Bureaucrats, came to support the constitutional movement. He had been Finance Minister at the time the commutation of the pensions had been effected and had continued in that position until 1881 when he resigned, ostensibly to protest against the sale to a private company, for a song, of the extensive government development in the northern island of Hokkaido, work which had been undertaken as a stimulus to colonization. The colonization scheme had been a failure, and, after pouring great sums of money into the island, government officials proposed to withdraw and give over the profitable government properties to private interests. Okuma from his position as Finance Minister knew of the proposed deal and denounced it to a huge mass meeting of the people of Tokyo. At the same time he voiced a demand for a representative assembly. Instead, however, of uniting his influence with that of Itagaki and thus concentrating opposition to the government in the one party or group, he proceeded to organize the second political party in Japan, the Rikken Kaishinto or Progressive Party (1882). This illustrates a constant tendency in party development in Japan: the fact that different leaders held essentially the same principles did not serve to unite them in one party, but each leader brought a group of his own followers into a separate organization. Both Itagaki and Okuma were nominally interested in the attainment of the same ends, but one party could not contain the two personalities.

Following Okuma's withdrawal from the government, an Imperial rescript was issued, in 1881, promising a parliament for 1890 and ordering all agitation for an earlier convocation to cease. This action may be interpreted in two ways. It may be considered as forced by the party agitation and particularly by Count Okuma's somewhat spectacular action, or it may be construed as being the next considered step in the reorganization movement, which merely happened to coincide with the other event. During the two decades following the Restoration the government seemed to pursue alternately a policy of advance and one of restraint. Thus it may be considered to have had in mind the taking of certain steps, regardless of public opinion, but only as the time for them appeared to be ripe. Each advance needed consolidation, which was possible only if agitation for further change were restricted. This alternation is certainly evident. But it might be construed as a policy of making only such concessions as were demanded, and then trying by coercion to stop there. Whichever interpretation is correct, the issuance of the rescript of 1881 was followed by strict repression of anti-governmental agitation. Steps had already been taken to circumscribe the activities of the Radicals. As early as 1875 the government promulgated a drastic press law; it undertook strict supervision of public and party meetings; and in 1883, in consequence of a growing disorder and unrest in the country which the parties were accused of fomenting, it ordered them to disband their organizations. The Jiyuto complied in 1884 by formally dissolving, and the Progressive Party came to a natural end because of its inability to maintain its local organizations.

Quite properly the leaders of Japan felt that it would be unwise to inaugurate constitutional government in a country just out of the feudal condition without careful study and some preparation. Consequently, after it was committed to the advance by the rescript of 1881, it took preliminary steps to carry out the promise at the appointed time. Count (then Mr.) Ito, who had succeeded Kido and his successor, Okubo, as the real directive force in the government, went abroad in 1882 to study Western constitutional systems. He had a definite idea of what must be accomplished with the introduction of constitutionalism into Japan: (1) the constitution must be the gift of the sovereign and must amply safeguard his powers and dignity; (2) it must make provision for a retention of power by those who had seen Japan through the critical period of the abolition of feudalism; and (3) it must meet the demand for a representative assembly. Obviously there was no great need for him to study in any great detail the republican system of the United States or that of France. Neither could the government of England serve as his model, for the English constitution was the result of a long evolution, and was designed to safeguard the people in their rights and privileges rather than to buttress the position of the monarch. But in Prussia Ito found a system of government embodying the ideas and the needs of the Japanese governing clique, and it was the Prussian constitution and government which served as the model for Japan. It is not meant to imply that Ito copied the Prussian constitution, but merely that he found in that country what appeared to be the solution of the problem of continuing the general system evolved after the Restoration and incorporating in it a representative assembly.

Count Ito returned from abroad in 1883 and immediately set about the construction of the constitution. By order of the Emperor he was transferred to the Household Department. A bureau for the study of constitutional and administrative reforms was established in connection with that department, and the framing of the constitution was undertaken by the bureau under Ito's direction, and in "absolute secrecy." When work on the constitution had gone far enough, a Privy Council was established (1888) as a part of the governmental machinery. Ito assumed the presidency of the Privy Council, which then undertook the task of revising the constitution. After it had been ratified by that body, it was promulgated by the Emperor. Thus it can be seen that there was no consultation of the party leaders in the framing of the instrument, but that it was largely the work of Ito, revised under his supervision by the other leaders in the oligarchy.

Meanwhile other steps had been taken to pave the way for the establishment of constitutional government. In 1884 the nobility was reconstructed; five orders were created, and five hundred patents of nobility issued. In establishing these orders the Prussian model again was followed, the ranks established being Prince, Marquis, Count, Viscount, and Baron. This step was taken in order to make due provision for the upper house which was provided for in the constitution. Then in 1885 the executive system was remodeled by the establishment of a Cabinet to replace the Council of State which had been the governing body almost since the Restoration.

5. THE CONSTITUTION OF 1889

The constitution was actually promulgated in 1889. Those who were in control and who knew of its nature must have realized that it would not meet with the approval of the party leaders, for they ordered all newspapers to refrain from unfavorable criticism of it for a time (on the pretext that an opportunity should be afforded for its careful examination), and the known radical papers were suppressed.

The new constitution [10] was built upon a combination of the Restoration idea that the Emperor was the source of all power and the dispenser of all favors and the feudal idea that the real power was exercised for the Emperor by others, either agents or agencies. The first chapter was devoted to the position and powers of the Emperor, "sacred and inviolable." He was characterized as "the head of the Empire, combining in himself the rights of sovereignty, and exercises them according to the provisions of the present constitution." He determined the organization of the several administrative services, appointing to and removing from both civil and military office, and fixing the salaries of officers, both civil and military. He exercised the supreme command of the army and navy, determined the organization and peace standing of the army and navy, declared war, made peace, and concluded treaties. All laws were to be made by the Emperor with the consent of the Imperial Diet, and after that consent had been given in the form of legislation the law had to receive the Imperial sanction and promulgation before becoming effective. This sanction and promulgation did not have to be, and were not, given as a matter of course. Furthermore, a very wide ordinance power was retained by the Emperor, although "no ordinance shall in any way alter any of the existing laws."

In exercising these powers, however, the Emperor acted through two constitutional advisory bodies, the Council of Ministers and the Privy Council, both of them established before the promulgation of the constitution. Chapter 4 of the constitution was devoted to these two bodies. While seventeen articles were necessary to describe the powers and position of the Emperor, only two were required for the Council of Ministers (Cabinet) and the Privy Council, since their position had already been fixed by Imperial ordinance. Both bodies were composed of Imperial appointees, and, under the constitution, the responsibility of the Cabinet (according to the interpretation of Ito) was solely to the Emperor.

Thus far we have been describing those features of the government, as provided in the constitution, which were merely projections of the political and administrative system which had been evolved after the Restoration— an Emperor exercising his powers through a bureaucracy. Later an extra-constitutional feature more strongly suggestive of the feudal age was added in the form of that unique body, unknown to the constitution or laws of the Empire, known as the Elder Statesmen (Genro). This group, made up of the men leading the nation during the transition period, came to possess great power. It deliberated on questions of war and peace and all great questions of policy, and advised the Emperor on the choice of men

[10] The translation used here is found in WILLOUGHBY AND ROGERS, *An Introduction to the Study of Government*, Appendix.

for Cabinet position. In all of these matters it came to have the determining voice.

The new feature of the constitutional system was the representative assembly, the Diet. Its powers, functions, and relations to the other parts of the system were set forth in the third chapter of the constitution. The Japanese Diet was to be made up of two houses: the Upper House, consisting of Peers sitting either by right or by election from their class, and of Imperial nominees; the Lower House, consisting of members elected by the qualified voters. The details concerning the composition and choice of members of the two houses are to be found in Imperial ordinances supplementary to the general provisions of the constitution. All laws, to be effective, had to receive the assent of the Diet, the two chambers acting separately. Full control over the meetings of the Diet was vested in the Emperor. He could summon it in regular and special session, prorogue it within certain limits of time, and dissolve the House of Representatives, which brought about a prorogation of the Upper House. However, the Diet had to be convoked every year for a three months' session. Its principal function was to deliberate on matters submitted to it, giving or withholding its assent, although bills might originate in either house.

The section on finance (Chapter 6) is one of the most instructive and interesting in the document. The control of the purse was carefully withdrawn from the House of Representatives, which, however, had to give its assent before the budget proposals became effective. The tax system of the country had been evolved before the constitution came into being, and so the provision was made merely that the Diet must assent before new taxes were imposed or the old ones modified. Further than this, an independent source of revenue was provided the government in administrative fees and other revenues having the nature of compensation, since these were expressly exempt from the scrutiny of the Diet. Concerning expenditure article 67 provided: "The expenditures already fixed and based upon the powers belonging to the Emperor by the Constitution (such as salaries), and such expenditures as may have arisen by the effect of law, or that relate to the legal obligations of the government, shall neither be rejected nor reduced by the Imperial Diet, without the concurrence of the government"; and article 68: "In order to meet special requirements, the government may ask the consent of the Imperial Diet to a certain amount as a continuing expenditure fund, for a previously fixed number of years." Also the next article provided for a reserve fund for contingent expenses, and, finally, article 71 provided that the budget of the current year should be continued in case the Diet failed to enact the budget presented to it by the government. Thus the sole power of the Diet was to prevent increases in expenditure.[11]

[11] Prince Ito's view of the budget is sufficiently interesting and instructive to deserve quotation. It was that "a budget is simply a sort of gauge to be observed by the administrative officials

The constitution contained three other chapters. One related to the judicial power (Chapter 5); the second chapter set forth the rights and duties of subjects, which were of the usual sort, but it should be noted that all rights of subjects were qualified by their guarantee "subject to law"; and the last chapter (7) contained supplementary rules, the most important having reference to the amendment of the constitution, which was reserved to Imperial initiative.

6. GOVERNMENT UNDER THE CONSTITUTION

The new system came into full operation in 1890 with the convocation of the first Diet. Immediately the future line of division became apparent. The parties controlled the House of Representatives, while the Cabinet was controlled by the clan leaders. It soon became evident that the Diet had been given sufficient power to enable it to obstruct but not to control, and no provision, save resort to the Imperial rescript, had been made for a composition of differences between the two branches of the government. The clan leaders either had to control the Diet or govern in spite of its obstruction. The only alternative was one that had never been contemplated, the recognition of Cabinet responsibility to the House of Representatives. The bureaucrats had one weapon which they frequently used in the struggle for control—they could dissolve the House and then attempt to influence the electorate to return members favorable to the government. But uniformly during the first four years of government under the constitution the Cabinet was confronted by a House removed from its effective control. During these four years three ministries were formed, under Yamagata (December 24, 1889), Matsukata (May 6, 1891), and, finally (August 8, 1892), Ito, the framer of the constitution. And during the same period the Diet was twice dissolved, in 1891 and again in 1893. The struggle invariably centered around the budget. Over it ministries fell and Diets were dissolved. Ito, in order to bring temporary harmony, was forced to ask for an Imperial rescript ordering the Diet to give way to the government, and finally he resorted to the questionable expedient of a foreign war to rally the parties to the support of his government.

7. FOREIGN RELATIONS

But before turning to the war of 1894–1895 between China and Japan it seems advisable to survey very briefly certain non-political changes in

for a current year. . . . It is to be borne in mind that a deficit rather than a surplus is, in fact, to be expected from a budget that has been accurately prepared. If the Ministers of State are not required, merely because they have not been settled in the budget, to make outlays that are unnecessary, neither are they forbidden by the constitution to make outlays exceeding the appropriations or not provided for in the budget, that may be necessary on account of unavoidable circumstances." STEAD, *Japan by the Japanese*, p. 57.

Japan.[12] Among these are the relations of Japan with the European Powers; her expansion during the period under review; and the economic, social, and military reorganization undertaken.

It will be remembered that the treaties negotiated by Japan in 1858 and thereafter left her with serious restrictions on her judicial and fiscal autonomy. All of her European contacts and many of her internal decisions between 1870 and 1894 were conditioned by this fact. The Iwakura mission was sent abroad in 1871 in order to secure a modification of the treaties. When the mission returned it reported not merely its lack of success but the long preparation that must be undertaken by Japan before she could hope to regain her freedom of action. Before judicial autonomy could be regained it would be necessary to reorganize her administration of justice so as to afford adequate protection to foreigners under a legal system which conformed to European ideas rather than to the feudal and patriarchal traditions of the Japanese. Before Japan could secure the right to impose her own customs charges the European nations would have to be assured that they would have free access to the country for purposes of trade, and that customs charges would not be fixed with a view to a return to the earlier condition of restricted intercourse. Consequently the several features of the internal reforms, both political and judicial, which were actually carried to completion by 1894, were made necessary by the desire to secure a revision of the treaties, if for no other reason. In addition to the political reorganization just described, the Japanese began the work of building up civil and criminal codes, and of elaborating a judicial system along European lines. By 1890 the new codes had received the sanction of the Emperor and the new judicial system had come into being. In the main the codes and the judiciary were modeled upon those of France and Prussia, legal advisers from both countries having assisted in their preparation.

Meanwhile, as the work of reform had proceeded, several attempts had been made to secure a revision of the treaties. The American Minister, Mr. Bingham, interested himself in revision in the years from 1874 to 1878. In 1878 revision of portions of the American commercial treaty was agreed upon, but did not become effective because of the failure of other states to accept similar changes. The next move came in 1882 when the Japanese Foreign Minister entered upon negotiations at Tokyo with the Powers. As a preliminary move an organized effort was made to introduce European dress and pastimes with a view to showing the West that Japan was occidentalizing her life. Just as agreement on revision appeared to be in view the negotiations were brought to an end by a popular agitation against the establishment of "Mixed Courts" as part of the agreement. The foreign Powers, in order to protect the supposed interests of their nationals, had demanded that courts composed of Japanese and foreign jurists should hear

[12] As pointed out in chapter IV.

disputes to which foreigners were parties. This was a concession in which Japanese public opinion would not acquiesce. The next attempt was made by Count Okuma in 1888. This time, instead of negotiating collectively with the treaty Powers, he undertook to secure a revision of the treaties one at a time. He was able to carry through a revision of the treaty with Mexico, which had few interests to protect, and with the United States, although the latter revision was to become effective only after similar treaties had been negotiated with the other Powers. But the other states demanded concessions, as before, and again the mob prevented action. Success was finally attained in 1894, when England, the foremost among the trading Powers, agreed to a revision of her treaty, to become effective in 1899.[13] The "humiliation" of the "Mixed Court" was waived by England so that public opinion in Japan was satisfied, even though the revision was not to become effective at once and was made contingent on the successful operation of the judicial system. The United States agreed also to revision of its treaties, following the English leadership but at the same time fulfilling its own policy, which had looked toward revision at an earlier period. The other states also revised their treaties in the course of the next three years.

Before 1894 Japan had begun to round out her frontiers. The Formosan affair, already referred to, had resulted in the relinquishment by China of her claim to suzerainty over the Loochoo Islands. In 1875, as a result of negotiations with Russia, Japan gave up her claim to the southern half of Sakhalin in return for a recognition of her title to the northern Kurile Islands. This was done under compulsion, as Japan had as good a claim to both as any other Power. In 1876 she extended her Empire to include the Bonin Islands.

8. SOCIAL AND ECONOMIC DEVELOPMENT

Paralleling the political developments and diplomatic achievements of the decades following the Restoration, were significant economic, social, and military changes. In fact, in the economic field in particular, there were effected the beginnings of a real transformation rather than a mere reorganization. Before tracing the changes made, however, we should call attention to a few important features of the transformation movement. In the first place, one should note the lead taken by the government, for otherwise one would receive a wrong impression of what went on. In the second place, the deliberate and systematic way in which changes were made is significant. And in the third place, it is of interest to note the extent to which the needs of Japan as construed by the government were elevated over the interests of individuals or groups.

[13] This time negotiations were transferred from Tokyo to London in order to eliminate the influence of the Tokyo mob.

Even before the Restoration, when foreign travel was forbidden, individuals had begun to go abroad to investigate at first hand Western ideas, institutions, and methods. After the Restoration the obstacles in the way of foreign travel were removed and students were sent to Europe and America. Furthermore, as the work of reorganization was actively undertaken, commissions were sent to the West to investigate special phases of European life. And until foreign-trained Japanese advisers were available, foreigners were drawn into the service of the government in various advisory capacities. Experiments were freely made and errors revealed by experiment were as freely corrected.

In no field of activity was the spirit of new Japan more clearly revealed than in education. As early as 1872 the Japanese adopted the principle of compulsory elementary education and made a start in the establishment of a system of public schools. In the development of the system three distinct foreign influences showed themselves. The American system of primary and secondary education was introduced in a modified form; the French university organization was adopted; and the German emphasis on vocational education was reproduced.

Beginning at the age of six, both boys and girls were required to attend school for four (later increased to six) years. During these years they were taught the usual elementary subjects, with as much emphasis on character development as on mental training. Loyalty to the Emperor and devotion to the state were also carefully inculcated through the studies in the elementary as well as the higher schools. Elementary education was extended over eight years, divided into two parts of four years each. Secondary or middle schools were designed to give special training to those who would go no farther, and to prepare students for entrance to the university. To train the large numbers of teachers required for the elementary schools, normal schools were established. Then, as the need arose, a number of special schools such as commercial institutes were organized.

The education of girls differed but little from that of boys in the first years of school, except for an emphasis on the qualities of the home-maker. This emphasis became stronger in the later years, intellectual training being subordinated to it, and until 1902 no provision was made by the state for university training for women. The provision made for girls in the public school system from the first, however, is significant of a changing point of view.

It is also significant that public education should have been so earnestly and comprehensively introduced into Japan from the beginning of the new era. The activity in this particular has kept Japan technically abreast of the most advanced Western nations and has been partly responsible for her unusually rapid economic progress. Naturally, many mistakes were made, school laws had to be altered several times, and much of the training was superficial. But with all of its deficiencies the system must be considered remarkably good when the newness of the problem and the immensity of the task are considered, and when the other problems demanding simultaneous solution are recalled.

The development of journalism in Japan may be noted at this point as naturally as at any other. Education was under government control, although there were numerous private schools, the establishment of which was encouraged rather than discouraged. But the many newspapers and magazines which came into existence owed less than nothing to government aid. Since almost all of them which were interested in politics were opposed to the government and were extremely critical of it, they had a precarious existence. Suspension of papers was common, the fines imposed on them were large, and jail sentences for their editors became extremely numerous. In spite of these handicaps the number of daily papers increased, and toward the end of the period under review some of them had attained a sound financial basis. Magazines of a non-political nature found it easier to establish themselves, and every realm of interest was represented in their company. There was even a Japanese "Ladies' Home Journal."

The new rulers of Japan also undertook military reorganization. A nation with a strong military tradition would naturally not underestimate the necessity of modernizing the military establishment. As has been pointed out,[14] some of the clans had imported Western arms before the Restoration, and some study had been made of military tactics by the Dutch scholars. At first the new Imperial Government had to rely on troops furnished by the western clans. Immediately, however, it began the organization of an independent force. Universal service was introduced and the army nationalized in 1873, and this non-samurai disciplined force showed its mettle in putting down the Satsuma samurai rebellion. Not only did the government introduce universal military service. eliminating feudal and class ideas, but the army was equipped with modern weapons and trained at first under French and, after 1885 under German direction. Steps were also taken, so far as the national finance permitted, to build up a navy. Here there was nothing upon which to build, except perhaps a national aptitude, for the Japanese had been restricted for generations to the use of small vessels in their home waters. Again they chose the best foreign aid, going to England for officers to advise them on naval matters, and securing from the British the vessels which they could not build in their own newly-established shipyards.

Perhaps it is not so remarkable that the leaders of modern Japan, in view of their national traditions, should have interested themselves in education and in military reorganization. But it is remarkable that they should have seen clearly the need for systematic economic development.

[14] In chapter IV, pp. 87-88.

As part of the political program may be considered the establishment of a postal system to replace the former courier service, and the introduction of the telegraph (1868) for governmental and then for commercial use. And while improved transportation facilities were of use to commerce and industry, the railroad was also important as a unifying and nationalizing agency. The first railroad, eighteen miles in length, was opened to traffic in 1872. Railroad construction was undertaken almost exclusively by the government until after about 1887, when private enterprise was definitely encouraged. By 1894 there were 2,118 miles of road constructed and in operation. This enterprise unquestionably aided in the development of commerce, just as it helped to bring the peoples of the different clans into more intimate contact with one another.

But it is more difficult to explain, except in terms of sound foresight, the changed attitude toward what had been the lowest class above the *pariah*. The end of feudalism resulted in a fusion of all classes of commoners, and the policy of the government was to direct the energies of the samurai and former nobles into commercial and industrial undertakings by insisting on their respectability. Where the government led it was expected that the people would follow. The government not only built railways, but it went into the shipping business, at first as a stockholder in various companies, and then by subsidy. It took the initiative in forming exchanges of various sorts, including one to end the European control of foreign trade. It fostered the textile industry in several ways: the product of the Japanese loom was presented to the world at several international expositions; model factories, with modern machinery, were established under government auspices; internal exhibitions were held to popularize the native product; and permanent commercial museums were established in various centers. A study of various types of raw cotton was made, with the result that Japanese cotton was rejected as inferior and foreign cotton was imported on a large scale. The formation of new trade associations to replace the old guilds was encouraged. This is merely exemplary of what was done in the development of all kinds of industry. It should be said, however, that the real expansion of Japanese industry dates from the end of the war with China. It has taken a long time to build up business standards, both of excellence of goods and honesty in representing them to the purchaser, for, as has been pointed out, such standards were not developed in old Japan, where sharp practice was the rule rather than the exception in business.

Another important task confronting the government after 1868 was that of currency reform. Gold and silver were both used as media of exchange, and in addition both the Shōgun's government and the several Daimyō had issued currency. The relation between gold and silver coins, furthermore, was such that it was possible for foreigners to import their silver, exchange it for Japanese silver, as guaranteed in the treaty of 1858 and subsequent agreements, use the Japanese silver to exchange for gold, and profitably export the gold. As a result gold was drained from the country. The only solution here was treaty revision, and control of exchange. Again, in 1868 the government had insufficient revenue to meet its needs, even after the taxation system had been revised, and this led to the issue of large amounts of inconvertible paper. The problem was further complicated by reason of the non-existence of adequate banking facilities.

The first step in the solution of the currency and banking problem was taken in 1872 when, upon Ito's recommendation, regulations for national banks on the American plan were promulgated, these banks being given the power to issue inconvertible notes. The First National Bank was established in 1873, two families being ordered to participate in financing it. At first the development was slow, and in 1876 there were only four banks. In that year regulations were revised, permitting the conversion of notes into currency, with the result that development was accelerated. By 1879 there were in existence 151 National Banks with deposits of almost twelve million yen. This expansion led to further increases in the issue of inconvertible notes, which was also one result of the increased expenditure made necessary by the Satsuma rebellion. This currency expansion led to higher prices and to considerable distress among the people. The problem of redemption of the paper money was considered by successive Finance Ministers during the late 'seventies and the early 'eighties. And finally, after 1885, provision for redemption was made and a convertible currency was established. The country continued, however, on a silver basis until after 1896, when the payment of the Chinese indemnity made possible a change to the gold standard.

Meanwhile the defects in the system of National Banks led to the establishment, in 1882, of a central institution, the Bank of Japan, as the chief fiscal agency of the government. After the establishment of the Parliament bills were introduced at successive sessions providing for the ending of the National Banks as such through their transformation into private institutions. This provision was finally made in 1896. After the establishment of the Bank of Japan, and as the purposes of the government were not served by the National Banks, separate institutions for special purposes were organized. The first was the Yokohama Specie Bank, established in 1887, for the purpose of financing foreign trade and controlling the foreign exchange business. Subsequently, after the war with China, the Hypothec Bank and forty-six industrial and agricultural banks were established, and as time went on other special banks, such as the Bank of Formosa and the Hokkaido Colonization Bank, came into existence. Thus, gradually, by a trial and error method, a satisfactory financial and banking system was evolved as part of the process of bringing into being a new Japan.

Even a brief summary of the transitional period in Japan would not be complete without reference to the effects of the Restoration and of post-Restoration policy on the peasants. The first effect was the establishment of private right in the land cultivated. Thus the Meiji period began with widespread peasant proprietorship. Certificates of ownership of land (chiken) were issued in 1872. In the same year the ban against the sale of land was removed. These steps, together with that of valuation of the land on the basis of capitalization of its average rice yield at the average value of rice during a five-year period, were taken preliminary to the introduction of a land tax in place of the feudal payments in kind. The new land tax was introduced in 1873 as the basis of the state revenue system. From that time the peasant owners had to pay, in money, a fixed amount proportioned to the assessed value of the land regardless of fluctuations in the yield or in the price of the crop. This amounted to from twenty-five to thirty per cent of his crop. Since it had to be paid in money, "the peasant was forced to sell his rice as soon as it was harvested, and thus exposed to all the dangers arising from price fluctuations which did not affect to the same extent the position of the large landlords who could store rice in granaries." [15] The peasant also immediately faced additional burdens since the common lands, to which no one could lay claim to title, became state lands of which the peasant lost the use. Thus he had to supply himself with fuel. He began to have to purchase artificial fertilizers and, with the breakdown of the household production of cotton and other goods under the pressure of the lower-priced imported cottons and of national industry, he faced a new money outlay for clothing.

Under the new system, which involved production for the market instead of a comparatively self-sufficient village economy, peasants who could not meet the new costs began to sell some or all of their holdings. Thus tenantry increased. "From 1883 to 1890, 367,744 agricultural producers suffered forced sales for arrears in the payment of the land tax. Among these, 77 per cent failed to pay their land tax because of poverty." [16] By 1892 39.99 per cent of the total cultivated area in Japan was worked by tenants. Some of the peasants, of course, were tenants with respect to part of their holdings only since they sold and then worked for the new owners only the land necessary to enable them to meet their monetary charges. As tenants they paid their rent in kind, it being fixed in terms of a proportion of the crop, as all charges had been fixed during the feudal period. This was a factor in preventing the consolidation of agricultural lands for cultivation since it was more profitable to the landlord, who, because of the excessive population, which had not been, and could not yet be, drawn from the land into urban industry, could secure high returns as rent from

[15] NORMAN, *Japan's Emergence as a Modern State*, pp. 143–144.
[16] Ibid., p. 144

numerous small tenants. Thus the capitalist system in agriculture failed to displace completely the feudal during the transitional period.

There is not space to describe the systematic efforts to improve agricultural production, to colonize the Hokkaido, to reconstruct local government, and to accomplish the manifold other tasks which were undertaken. Nor is it possible to paint the darker side of the picture, for there was a dark as well as a bright side. There were comparatively few major scandals, but there were few exceptions to the rule that men in high office created large fortunes for themselves. As the new parliamentary system went into effect there was widespread buying and selling of votes. And it must be recognized that the nation as a whole lagged behind its leaders. There were no national propulsions toward change, and there was much latent dissatisfaction with the creators of new Japan.

But with full recognition of all deficiencies it may truly be said that:

By 1894 the crisis of the transition period had passed. The government had been completely reorganized and a constitution had been given several years of trial. An army and navy had been built up after approved Western models. A modern school system was in successful operation. Tariff and judicial autonomy were on the point of being granted. Industry and commerce were given promise of vigorous life. The reorganization was not complete and its fruits were only beginning to be seen, but in the main the shock caused by internal adaptation to the modern world was over. From 1894 on, the reorganized Japan was to expand and take her place as an equal and increasingly important member in the family of nations.[17]

REFERENCES FOR FURTHER STUDY

HUGH BORTON (ed.), *Japan* (1951); chapters on various aspects of Japanese culture. DELMAR M. BROWN, *Nationalism in Japan, an Introductory Historical Analysis* (1955). J. H. GUBBINS, *Making of Modern Japan* (1922), ch. 7–21; one of the best accounts of the period. SIDNEY L. GULICK, *Evolution of the Japanese* (1903); a psychological and social study. S. K. HORNBECK, *Contemporary Politics in the Far East* (1916), ch. 8–9; an excellent analysis of the constitutional system and discussion of the parties. HIROBUMI ITO, *Commentaries on the Constitution of the Empire of Japan* (1931). T. IYENAGA, *Constitutional Development of Japan, 1853–1881* (1891), Johns Hopkins Studies, vol. 9. N. KITAZAWA, *The Government of Japan* (1929), ch. 1–4. K. S. LATOURETTE, *Development of Japan* (1916), ch. 8–9; a good brief treatment of the transition period. EMIL LEDERER, *Japan in Transition* (1938); a useful study. W. M. McGOVERN, *Modern Japan: Its Political, Military and Industrial Organization* (1920); a valuable study of the topics indicated; very readable. W. W. McLAREN (ed.), *Japanese Government Documents, Transactions Asiatic Society of Japan*, vol. 42, part 1; an invaluable collection of source materials; other volumes of the transactions contain valuable studies of various aspects both of the old and the new Japan. W. W. McLAREN, *Political History of Japan During the Meiji Era* (1916), ch. 2–9; an excellent treatment of the period 1867–1894. E. S. MORSE, *Japan*

[17] LATOURETTE, *Development of Japan*, p. 163.

Day by Day; 1877–79, 1882–83 (1917). E. H. NORMAN, *Japan's Emergence as a Modern State* (1940); an exceptionally illuminating study of the last three decades of the nineteenth century. E. H. NORMAN, *Soldier and Peasant in Japan: the Origins of Conscription* (1943). COUNT S. OKUMA (ed.), *Fifty Years of Modern Japan,* 2 vols. (1909); a valuable reference work; a wide range of topics treated by well-known Japanese; the constitution of Japan is printed as Appendix A. P. R. PORTER, *Japan, the Rise of a Modern Power* (1918). HAROLD S. QUIGLEY, *Japanese Government and Politics* (1932), esp. ch. 1–3, appendices 1–9; an excellent text on the subject as government and politics had developed to 1932. EDWIN O. REISCHAUER, *Japan, Past and Present* (1946), ch. 9, 10; a sympathetic summary of post-Restoration history. ALFRED STEAD (ed.), *Japan by the Japanese* (1904); a survey by its highest authorities. BARON KENCHO SUYEMATSU, *Fantasy of Far Japan* (1905), esp. Appendix 4; sketches of Ito, Yamagata, and other leaders. P. J. TREAT, *Japan and the United States* (1921), ch. 1–7; a description sympathetic to Japan. P. J. TREAT, *Diplomatic Relations between the United States and Japan,* 2 vols. (1932); vol. 1, ch. 12–22, vol. 2, ch. 23–41; a detailed chronological treatment based upon an examination of all the American archival and much other source material. G. E. UYEHARA, *Political Development of Japan, 1867–1909* (1910); a valuable study of constitutional development. CHITOSHI YANAGA, *Japan Since Perry* (1949), ch. 3–13; a careful study.

Encyclopedia of the Social Sciences; for brief biographical sketches of leading Japanese statesmen.

CHAPTER VI

THE CONTEST FOR KOREA

I. PRE-MODERN RELATIONS OF CHINA AND JAPAN WITH KOREA

THE historical relations of Japan and China all center in Korea, and it was in and over Korea that they first came into serious conflict in the modern period of their history. From this conflict developed consequences of grave significance, not only for the parties immediately concerned, but for the entire world. The earlier struggles over Korea had involved only the immediate participants, but, with the coming of Europeans to the Far East, changes in the relative position of the Celestial Empire developed European consequences. This was particularly true because of the gradual Russian territorial expansion to the borders of the Chinese Empire and the Korean Kingdom. Back of Russia lay the other Powers with interests which were inevitably affected by any changes involving that territorial giant.

The pre-modern relations of Korea with her neighbors can be sketched in a few words. Her geographical position explains much of her history. Marked off from Manchuria only by the Yalu River as a natural frontier, and stretching almost due south from Manchuria toward Japan, with only a narrow strait separating her from the Japanese islands, Korea inevitably found that the threads of her history were inextricably interwoven with those of her two immediate neighbors. When the hordes of Genghis and Kublai Khan swept over China from Mongolia through the Manchurian gateway, Korea had been in contact with China for more than twelve centuries. It was only natural that the Mongol invasion should make its approach to Japan through Korea, first subjecting the latter kingdom as a preparation for the attempted conquest of the former. From that time, as well as before, Korea paid tribute to China and her kings received their investiture from Peking, although this relationship of suzerain and vassal was disturbed temporarily during the sixteenth century by invasion and conquest from another direction.

Then Japan, in her turn, had visions of empire, and, under the great commander Hideyoshi, attempted to establish herself on the Asiatic continent. China was her objective, just as Japan had been the objective of the Mongol rulers of China. And again, as a preliminary step to operations against China, the Japanese found it necessary first to subjugate the Koreans. In spite of the resistance of Korea, later aided by China, the kingdom was overrun by the Japanese. But, just as the sea had saved Japan from the earlier attempted invasion of her shores, so it prevented Hideyoshi from carrying his operations farther than Korea. The Korean fleet, well commanded at first, was able so to obstruct the transportation of troops and supplies that his armies could not maintain themselves. Upon his death the expedition was given up. Shortly thereafter, as has been pointed out,[1] the Tokugawa clan established itself in power in Japan and intercourse with the outside world was cut off. This brought to an end, for a time, the contact of Japan with China through Korea. The only permanent result of the invasion was the maintenance of a colony of Japanese at Fusan, just across the channel from Shimonoseki, and a devastation of Korea from which she never fully recovered and which left the people with a feeling of hatred and fear for the Japanese.

Shortly after the evacuation of Korea by the Japanese armies the Manchus established themselves in China. From Peking they reasserted successfully the former Chinese suzerainty over Korea, and the relationship then re-established was formally continued until after the war with Japan in 1894–1895.

So far as the non-Chinese world was concerned, Korea, after the invasion of the Japanese, became the most secluded of the Far Eastern nations. For a time its government sent tributary missions to Japan as well as to China, but these were gradually discontinued as Japan retired into herself. The Japanese colony at Fusan remained, but it was virtually cut off from contact with the homeland. There were no other contacts. The Chinese kept the door ajar at Canton and the Japanese did likewise at Nagasaki, but there were no openings except for the Chinese into Korea. She well deserved the name, the "Hermit Kingdom."

As she was the most closely sealed, so Korea was the last of the Far Eastern countries to be opened to general foreign intercourse. This was, of course, partly due to her relative unimportance and to her geographical position, which did not bring the Western nations into contact with her until they had knocked successively at the doors of China and Japan; but it was also due, in part, to the fact that she had so cut herself off from the outside world that very little was known of her. It was not until thirty years after the first treaties had been negotiated with China and twenty years after the Perry expedition to Japan that the first treaty was made with the government of Korea, and then it was not a Western but an Eastern state which penetrated behind the Korean barriers.

2. THE OPENING OF KOREA

France was the first to try to force open the door into Korea. In 1866, after French Catholic missionaries who had been carrying on their activities in

[1] Chapter IV.

that country in secret had been murdered, together with some of the native priests and converts, the French government sent a naval expedition to secure redress for the murders.[2] The expedition was able to force a landing on the coast, but the Korean government refused to enter upon any negotiations. Since the French admiral did not dare, with the force at his disposal, to move into the interior even the short distance to the capital, he was compelled finally, in the face of the resistance of the Koreans and the refusal of the government to negotiate, to depart without having fulfilled his mission. That nothing was done subsequently to advance French interests in the peninsula may be explained by a desire to concentrate efforts on expansion on the southern borders of China. It was in 1867 that three provinces of Cochin-China were occupied.

In the same year (1866) an American vessel, the *Surprise,* was wrecked on the Korean coast. The American sailors, however, did not fare as badly as had the French priests, being well treated while in the country and finally being sent out by way of Manchuria. But another American vessel, the *General Sherman,* was not so fortunate. While she was stranded in a Korean river, some of her crew became involved in a brawl on shore. They were rescued, but the vessel itself was set upon and destroyed. Eight of the crew were killed and the remainder made prisoners. Some years later (1871) an American expedition was sent to ascertain the facts in the case and to restore any of the prisoners still living. As in the case of the French expedition, little trouble was found in effecting a landing after the forts at Kianghwa had been destroyed. But again the Korean government refused to open negotiations, and the expedition had to withdraw without having accomplished its mission of establishing some sort of contact with Korea.

Four years later a Japanese vessel was fired upon while cruising in Korean waters. Immediately, only local retaliatory action was taken, although the incident aroused great popular excitement in Japan, where the samurai were already restless and getting out of hand. They had wanted war in 1872 at the time of the Formosan difficulty and had not been altogether satisfied with the mere sending of a punitive expedition to Formosa. Consequently, when what they regarded as a legitimate *casus belli* was presented in and after 1875, the cry for war arose again even more strongly. Before taking action, however, the Japanese government instituted negotiations with China.

By the time of this incident Japan and China had themselves entered into treaty relations. A treaty was negotiated in 1871, following Japanese overtures in 1870, but ratifications were only exchanged in 1873. This treaty

---

[2] After first sounding out the Chinese government to determine its attitude. The Tsungli Yamen "simply expressed the hope to Bellonet (the French Admiral) that France should proceed with peaceful investigation and negotiation." T. F. Tsiang, *Sino-Japanese Relations, 1870-1894,* Chinese Social and Political Science Review, vol. 17, pp. 53-54.

differed from those in force between both China and Japan, on the one side, and the Western Powers, on the other, in that: (1) China refused to introduce the most-favored-nation principle; (2) extraterritoriality was provided for reciprocally, but in a modified form; and (3) although reciprocal rights of trade were granted along the lines of the other treaties, Japanese were not granted the right of travel in the interior since China feared a considerable movement toward herself of Japanese adventurers.

There was one provision only of this treaty which had any relevance with respect to the Korean question. Article I provided for mutual non-aggression against each other's territorial possessions. At the time of the negotiations Li Hung-chang had begun to be seriously concerned over the status of some of the outlying territories. The Formosan question, together with that of the status of the Loochoo Islands, immediately aroused this concern. But even then he apparently had in mind the possibility of difficulties over the status of Korea. This he thought was safeguarded, so far as Japan was concerned, by this provision for mutual non-aggression, since the characters used for the English phrase territorial possessions meant "states and lands. Li, in his preliminary report to the Court on August 31st (1871), explained that the phrase was intended to cover Korea and such like states." [3]

After the incident of 1875 the Japanese government sent a mission to Peking to negotiate with the Imperial government and one to Korea, supported by force, to maintain the demand for reparation and for a treaty. The result of the negotiations at Peking was that China suggested to Korea a change of policy and the negotiation of a treaty. Whether it was this suggestion or the Japanese show of force which was responsible for it, Korea was made aware of the ever-pressing forces from the outside which had broken down stronger barriers to intercourse than she could hope to erect, and thus gave way. A treaty of amity and commerce between Korea and Japan was consequently signed on February 26, 1876. This treaty, as had the Sino-Japanese treaty, included a modified form of extraterritoriality, as well as other provisions which were in the Japanese treaties with Western states, to which Japan was even then making vigorous objections as they applied to herself. The most significant clause of the treaty, however, was the declaration in the first article that "Korea, being an independent state, enjoys the same sovereign rights as Japan." The Tsungli Yamen, when it received a copy of the treaty, "made no comment on it, though it contained a clause recognizing Korean's [sic] independence by Japan. The Yamen, assured of Korea's loyalty, did not recognize the implications of the clause." [4]

At the time when this treaty was signed there was a mutually respected,

[3] Tsiang, op. cit., p. 11.
[4] Op. cit., p. 61.

even though nominal, historical bond between China and Korea. The relationship (of suzerain and vassal) "was alien then to the Western juridical system." [5] It is described by another Chinese scholar as follows. "In law and ceremony the subjection (of Korea to China) was even abject. Korean kings received their investiture from Peking; every year tribute missions were sent. On the accession and death of a Chinese Emperor, Korea must send representatives to attend the ceremonies. When the Emperor sent an agent to Korea, the King himself kowtowed to him. In case of internal trouble or foreign invasion in the vassal state, the suzerain was obliged to send aid. *Otherwise, Korea was left entirely to itself. . . .* China with her tributary states formed a family as it were, with China as the big brother and the tributaries as the younger brothers." [6] It was on account of the traditional attitude of non-interference in internal affairs that the Chinese government felt that it was appropriate to allow Korea to make her own arrangements with other states except as she was directly attacked. But it was this attitude of non-interference that caused Japan and other states to deny the reality of China's suzerainty. Given Korean loyalty, there was no reason for the exercise, by China, of the powers of interference implicit in her position as suzerain until other states developed an interest and built up interests in Korea. But even with full Korean loyalty, it was essential to the preservation of the Chinese position, as against third states, either that the traditional conception should be defined in agreement or that it should be modified to the extent of the assumption of responsibility for the behavior of the Korean government as it affected the interests of third states. This was only fully realized after 1885.

Thus it proved to be a grave mistake from her standpoint for China to allow Japan to undertake to secure for herself redress for the wrong done by firing on her vessel. The same mistake had been made repeatedly in other places because of failure to perceive the full consequences of non-action, and always with unfortunate consequences from the standpoint of preserving China's authority as suzerain. The policy initially followed led to equally disastrous results for her in Korea. In spite of repeated attempts to repair the initial blunder by a reassertion of her authority and its actual enlargement, China gradually found Korea slipping from her grasp as had Upper Burma and what has since come to be known as French Indo-China. The mistake had been made by China. It was left for Japan to take full advantage of it. This she did by insisting that Korea virtually repudiate the bond by declaring herself an independent state with full sovereign rights. Korea, as well as China, soon saw the error, but neither was able to rectify it.

---

[5] T. C. LIN, *Li Hung-chang: His Korean Policies, 1870–1885,* Chinese Social and Political Science Review, vol. 19, p. 203. Professor Lin finds its closest analogue in recent times in the relation of the British Dominions to the Crown.

[6] TSIANG, op. cit., pp. 53–54. The italics are mine.

The success of the Japanese in establishing relations with Korea led to a renewal of the American effort to negotiate a treaty. At the same time China had begun to feel that it would be desirable to neutralize the Japanese influence at Seoul by a widening of Korea's external contacts. As early as 1879 "Li Hung-chang gave the considered advice to a high Korean official that 'as poison must be met by antidote,' the only way to combat Japanese intrigue was to conclude treaties with Western powers." [7] China's interest in the matter was definitely aroused, when, in 1880, the American Commodore Shufeldt attempted to get in touch with the Korean government by invoking the aid of Japan. Viceroy Li thereupon invited Commodore Shufeldt to visit him at Tientsin. Since his response from the Japanese had been unsatisfactory, he accepted the invitation and also Li Hung-chang's offer of his good offices in opening up relations with Korea. A treaty was finally negotiated at Tientsin in 1882, the Chinese Viceroy serving as the intermediary. England, Germany, Italy, Russia, and France also entered into treaty relations with Korea in the succeeding four years.

These treaties all followed the Japanese precedent, recognizing the government of Korea as that of a fully sovereign state.

However, the European powers evaded a settlement of the question of independence by commissioning their envoy at Peking to be also their representative, under various titles, at Seoul; but the United States, influenced by the waiving of responsibility at Peking, followed Japan in commissioning to Korea a minister plenipotentiary, independent of the legations at Peking and Tokyo, a procedure which was highly gratifying to Japan.[8]

Furthermore, when China attempted to regain ground thus lost by demanding that the Korean envoy sent to Washington in 1887 should communicate with the American government through the Chinese legation, the Secretary of State insisted on dealing with him directly as the representative of an independent state. The American treaty itself varied from those with the other Western states in that it contained a provision similar to that in the Harris treaty, offering the good offices of the United States, in case they should be needed, to compose disputes between Korea and other Powers. On this provision the Koreans came to rely as a last resort when the struggle for possession of the country entered upon its final phases, but they failed to understand that both parties to a dispute must accept the offer of "good offices," or action taken would constitute intervention. This was not made clear to Korea, China, or Japan.

---

[7] Morse, *International Relations,* vol. 3, p. 9.

[8] Morse, op. cit., p. 9. Commodore Shufeldt had, however, in an exchange of letters with Li, stated that he had secured the assistance of China in negotiating the treaty because Korea was her dependency, and he transmitted to Washington a letter from the Korean king in which he affirmed this dependency. These letters, unfortunately for China, had no official value. For a discussion of the whole question see Dennett, pp. 454–464, also Tsiang, op. cit., pp. 68–70. Li Hung-chang's purpose in bringing Korea to negotiate these treaties, as Tsiang shows, was to neutralize Japanese influence by introducing that of the Western stat\

3. INTERNAL CONDITIONS IN KOREA

The Korea opened to foreign intercourse was in such a deplorable condition that it invited rather than repelled foreign interference. The reigning dynasty, the House of Yi, had been established more than five centuries before the opening of the country. The first ruler made certain notable improvements, including a clean sweep of the incompetent, corrupt, and Buddhist dominated officialdom. A phonetic alphabet had been evolved, although it proved to be impossible to introduce it among the men in place of the Chinese system of writing, and it was finally relegated to exclusive use by the women. Movable metal type was cast. "Art, literature, science, economics, agriculture and every form of human activity felt the impulse, and before long the former degraded condition of the people was transformed." [9]

Unfortunately the founder of the dynasty was succeeded by weaker rulers. And during the sixteenth century factionalism, which came to be the bane of Korea, developed. This division into factions weakened the initial resistance of the Koreans to the Japanese invaders at the end of the century, but factionalism might have been replaced by a more unified spirit if they had been repulsed without Chinese aid. However, although the Japanese hosts were ultimately withdrawn, even while the second attempt at conquest was going on, the party spirit was revived and was never thereafter displaced.

Korea had never fully recovered from the devastation of the country by the Japanese. But internal conditions more than the terrible loss of life and destruction of property explain the lack of recuperative ability. More and more after the sixteenth century the country became divided into two groups, the exploited people and the exploiting court and officialdom. The nobles and officials, in turn, may be broadly divided into those in power and those out of favor and struggling to get into power. Constant intrigue, supported by assassination, marked this struggle. No man's life or property was safe, no matter how high his rank, except as he was able to cling to public office. And, among the masses, there was no incentive to improvement. If a man were a successful farmer or merchant and had begun to accumulate a surplus, he was certain to have his property taken from him by the tax-gatherer or by means of an enforced loan to a noble or an official. Consequently a premium was put on living up to one's income, or on concealing the fact of prosperity by living as though impoverished. Certainly thrift and improvement were not encouraged. The people lived in mud hovels, under extremely unsanitary conditions. They put their surplus on their backs or in their stomachs, or kept it in careful concealment. There was wealth in the country, as was evidenced by the ability of the Koreans

[9] HULBERT, *Passing of Korea*, p. 93.

to undertake enterprises demanding considerable capital when it became safe to admit its possession; but the appearance of the country could only lead to an impression of great poverty.

There was a careful gradation of rank. Privileges, such as the use of the donkey or the chair, were apportioned according to position in the social scale. Among the ruling class there was considerable extravagance and ostentation in living. And always rank and power were shown by a disregard for the personal rights of the people.

However, just as in China, there was one relief from actions and ex-actions of officials when they became intolerable. Local riots were common as means of redress. If the people rose against an official and drove him out, the government promptly replaced him, seldom attempting to keep a particular official in place against an active expression of popular hostility. However, the new appointee would only be sufficiently regardful of the desires of the people to prevent rioting, so that, while the worst actions were punished, uprisings did not serve to secure good government. On the whole the people acquiesced passively in the system, since they could find no substitute for it.

From the standpoint of her social institutions Korea was organized on the basis of the family, with the concomitant of ancestor-worship. There was a premium put on male children, as in other Oriental countries, and the position of women was low, when judged in comparison with either Japan or China. While at one time Buddhism had been very strong, after the fifteenth century it had been largely displaced by Confucianism, which, however, had not been highly developed. So far as the people had any religion, it was demonism, which had permeated and degraded Korean Buddhism where it had not displaced it.

Most of the people were farmers, cultivating, in the main, rice, which, together with fish, constituted the staple in the diet. Millet and other cereals and some varieties of vegetables were grown in addition to rice. Trade was carried on mainly by wandering peddlers, and there was only a limited and extremely primitive industry. The very flourishing ceramic industry of an earlier time had been destroyed when the Korean artists and artisans had been transplanted to Japan with the withdrawal of the invaders at the end of the sixteenth century. The industry in Korea never recovered from the blow thus struck. It proved profitable to Japan, however, for it laid the foundations for the development of the well-known Satsuma ware.

4. THE STRUGGLE FOR CONTROL OF KOREA

It was this impoverished, misgoverned, faction-disturbed country, so long a hermit kingdom, which was destined to bring its two more powerful neighbors to blows. Even in that event factionalism played an important part. Just as the Western states were beginning to manifest an interest in the "Land of the Morning Calm," in 1863 the ruler died without issue. As a result a twelve-year-old boy ascended the throne, his father, best known as the Taiwunkun, becoming the Regent. One of the first acts of the Regent was to marry his son to his wife's niece, a member of the Min family, hoping in that way to consolidate and perpetuate his own power. The King was a weak character, easily influenced by those about him, and his father, a man of very strong will, would have continued to dominate him if the Queen had not chosen to assert herself. After the King had attained his majority a bitter struggle commenced between the Min faction, led by the Queen, and the Yi family, consisting of the blood relatives of the King and headed by the Taiwunkun. It was fundamentally a struggle for power, and it was only the chance of the foreign impact which led to a division over the question of foreign policy. The Queen's faction became the party of progress, advocating the opening of the country, and the ascendancy she gained over the King helped to bring about the reversal of the anti-foreign policy of the Regent, the making of the treaty of 1876 with Japan, and the establishment of a Japanese legation at Seoul.

But in 1881 there came a famine with resulting hard times for all. The agents of the Regent busily worked to undermine the Queen, whispering that the hard times were caused by the opening of the country to foreigners, and that they would continue until the former seclusion had been restored. The people in the capital became inflamed and riots occurred. Finally a mob moved on the palace to murder the Queen. After invading the palace grounds they were turned in the direction of the Japanese legation. The minister and his suite, together with the civilian Japanese who had been fortunate enough to reach the legation safely, cut their way through the mob, worked their way out of the city, and finally reached the sea. Some three weeks later the Japanese minister returned to Seoul with a strong military escort and demanded suitable reparation for the outrage. His demands for "the punishment of the murderers, the honorable burial of the Japanese dead, and indemnity of 400,000 *yen*, and further privileges of trade for the Japanese" [10] were conceded by the Korean government.

At the same time China asserted her right of interference as the sovereign power and virtually kidnapped the Regent, who was responsible for the entire affair. He was taken to China, where he was kept a prisoner for some years. By this time China's policy had changed; she suggested the ratification of the American treaty, and inaugurated a more positive Korean policy.

This did not end the difficulty, but it did serve to inaugurate a new phase of the old struggle between China and Japan. In 1883 the Tientsin Viceroy, Li Hung-chang, in whose hands the Emperor of China had placed Korean affairs, sent Yüan Shih-k'ai (later President of the Chinese Republic) to

[10] McKENZIE, *Korea's Fight for Freedom,* pp. 26–27.

Korea as the representative of the suzerain power. From this time China attempted to assert herself more and more in Korean affairs and to bind that country ever more closely to herself. One method used for promoting a closer relationship was to bring into a partial union the Chinese and the Korean maritime customs. Li nominated a foreigner to serve as adviser to the Korean government, and one of his first moves was to organize a Korean customs service with himself at the head. Later, upon his removal, an attempt was made to promote a union of the two services by appointing an inspector from the Chinese service as head of the Korean customs. It was expected that he would take his direction from Sir R. Hart and would look after the interests of China. At the same time the Imperial Resident at Seoul, Yüan Shih-k'ai, asserted his precedence over other foreign envoys at all court functions, and kept in intimate touch with the Korean government in all of its affairs. And, finally, one result of the invasion of the Japanese legation in 1882 was the decided strengthening of the Chinese influence at the court, even though the Japanese were successful in pressing on the King their demand for reparation.

On the other hand, if the Chinese influence was strong the Japanese endeavor to undermine that influence was constant. The former struggle for power between the Yi and the Min factions changed its character slightly after 1882, becoming a contest between two groups, one of which desired to modernize the country after the fashion of the changes made in Japan, while the other represented the old order and desired to see as few changes as possible made. The latter group, headed by the Queen, who had lost her desire for change, controlled the government and was supported by the Chinese Resident. The Progressives looked to the Japanese legation for counsel and active aid.

In 1884 the struggle came to its inevitable conclusion—an attempt by the "outs" to gain control by murdering the leaders of the opposition—the usual way in Korea. The Progressives worked out their plans carefully, probably in consultation with the Japanese minister. The plan was to arrange a dinner to celebrate the inauguration of a new postal service. During the course of the dinner a fire was to be reported at the Palace. This would give an opportunity to strike down the reactionary ministers as they rushed out of the banqueting hall. All went according to plan up to a certain point. The cry of fire was raised, and one of the ministers rushed out and was attacked. He was able to get back into the hall, however, and give the alarm. The conspirators then rushed to the Palace and persuaded the King and the Queen to come with them for safety. They were surrounded by Japanese and Koreans in the employ of the Progressives. Under compulsion the King reorganized the government and issued a number of edicts looking toward the transformation of Korea, on paper, into a modern state.

At this stage of the affair the Chinese took a hand.

The Chinese Resident, Yüan Shih-k'ai, with the Chinese guard stationed there since 1882, proceeded to the palace to protect the King, but found it occupied by the Japanese envoy and Japanese troops. The Chinese troops opened fire on the Japanese, and a general commotion followed, in which the civil inhabitants of Seoul joined. The Japanese then fought their way out of the city and down to Chemulpo, where they were received on a Japanese steamer. China was then in the midst of the Tongking trouble, and could not oppose Japan, whose special ambassador, Count Inouye Kaoru, supported by a strong naval force, obtained full reparation by a convention signed on January 9th, 1885. By this Korea agreed to apologize and punish the rioters; to pay $30,000 indemnity; and to construct barracks for the Japanese legation guard.[11]

All of this the Korean government had to concede in spite of the fact that Japan had fomented the trouble by her intrigue with the Progressives, to whom she had promised and given active support up to the time of the Chinese intervention.

The trouble between China and France over Tongking was settled in 1885, and China was free to turn her attention to her interests in Korea. She was not, however, in a position to embark on a war against Japan, even though a faction at the Court and among the officials underrated the strength of the Japanese and overrated that of China. Neither did the Japanese want war over the question, since the peace party was still in control of the government and had not yet carried to completion its work of political reorganization. Both countries wanted time before they entered upon a final struggle for control in Korea. Thus it was possible for them to agree upon a *modus vivendi,* which was embodied in a convention drawn up at Tientsin by the two most eminent statesmen of their respective countries, Viceroy Li Hung-chang for China and Count Ito for Japan. By this convention both parties agreed to withdraw their troops from Korea within four months; Korea was to be left free and encouraged to re-organize her army under foreign direction, which should be neither Japanese nor Chinese; and, in case it should become necessary for either party to send troops to Korea in the future, previous notice in writing of its intention to do so was to be given, and the troops thus sent were to be withdrawn as soon as the trouble causing their dispatch had been settled.

This convention cannot but be considered as a partial diplomatic victory for Japan, since it limited the freedom of China to take action which was perfectly within her right if she was to be regarded as the suzerain power, and consequently it advanced the Japanese contention that Korea was an independent state. The end and aim of Japanese policy since the negotiation of the treaty of 1876 had been to establish this contention, and it was the independence policy of the Progressives which led to their receiving Japa-

---

[11] MORSE, op. cit., p. 11. According to Tsiang (op. cit., pp. 80–81) the chief Chinese representative at this time was Chen Hsu-tang, Yüan Shih-k'ai having the post of quartermaster to General Wu Ch'ao-yu, in command of the Chinese troops. Yüan became Resident in 1885.

nese support. They desired to throw off the Chinese connection because they considered it an obstacle to reform, but they failed to perceive that Japan's ultimate aim was not a really independent Korea, strong and able to protect herself, but a state independent of external control because of the aid and support given it by Japan, for which aid the Japanese might demand a *quid pro quo* in the form of rights of supervision.

Although the Tientsin convention strengthened Japan's contention on paper, in reality the Chinese, for two reasons, were stronger at Seoul after this "oriental general election" of 1884 than they had been before. In the first place, the progressive group was eliminated from the Court, some of the leaders being killed by the mob and some of them, including the chief conspirator, Kim Ok-kuin, escaping to Japan, where they were given asylum. In the second place, the part the Japanese had played in the affair had aroused the latent popular hostility to them. This showed itself by the placing of more reliance on the Chinese.

The provision in the Tientsin convention for the reorganization of the Korean army under foreign direction had already been carried into effect by the employment of Russian officers, who were introduced into Korea at the suggestion of the foreign adviser, Mr. von Mollendorf. He made the suggestion in 1884 ostensibly in order to offset the growing power of Japan. But, in return for lending Korea officers to train her army, Russia was to receive the use of Port Lazareff for her navy. This gave her a comparatively ice-free naval base.

Japan saw in it (the granting to Russia of the use of this port) a threat directly across the Sea of Japan; to China it appeared to endanger the independent existence of Korea, and therefore China's suzerainty over the kingdom; and England had to face a disturbance of the Asiatic equilibrium in favor of her principal rival in Asia, while at the same time France was still occupying the Pescadores, and relations between China and Japan were strained.[12]

To restore the balance, England occupied Port Hamilton, "an anchorage in a group of islets off the southern coast of Korea, strategically placed to watch the movements of Russia, Japan, and China, as they might effect Korea." China and Japan, both fearful of the Russian menace, composed their differences temporarily, and China demanded that the agreement with Russia be cancelled. Mr. von Mollendorf, who had advised it, was dismissed from the Korean service and an American took his place. All who were appointed to advisory position in Korea thereafter, or who were put at the head of the Korean customs, which was made more and more an independent but subsidiary branch of the Chinese customs, were advised to remember that "in all that concerns Korea, the one point to start from is that Korea *is* China's tributary, and that China *will not only* fight any-

[12] Morse, op. cit., p. 12.

body rather than give up her suzerainty, but will be forced to absorb Korea if troublesome scheming goes on there." [13] The Chinese Resident, Yüan Shih-k'ai, probably under instructions from Li Hung-chang, also took every opportunity to assert China's superior position.

As a result of the Chinese activity there rapidly developed friction between Yüan and the American who had been installed at Seoul as adviser to the Korean ministry of foreign affairs. The latter, Mr. Denny, who had never been in the service of China, felt that it was his first duty to advance the movement toward Korean independence. This led ultimately to such friction with Yüan Shih-k'ai that one of them had to go. Mr. Denny agreed to withdraw (1889) on certain conditions, one of which was the recall of Yüan. These were agreed to, but the recall of the Resident was postponed on account of the growing friction with Japan.

During the five years, from 1889 to 1894 [writes Mr. H. B. Morse], Russian plans were in abeyance, the Platonic support given by America to Korean independence was no longer in evidence, and China and Japan were left face to face at the Court of Seoul. The party of content, those who supported the existing administration, who desired to maintain the Chinese connection, who wished to keep things as they were, found their support at the Chinese Residency; the party of discontent, the "Young Korea" party who demanded reform, those who leaned toward Japan as a country which had modernized her outward form, and away from China and her antiquated system, all these found support at the Japanese legation. All the forms of oriental intrigue were adopted —demonstrations, denunciations, palace cabals, assassinations of ministers, revolts in the provinces—but in none was any proof ever obtainable of the agency of the side which would be benefitted. Plotting and counterplotting, charge and counter-charge, advice and counter-advice, all were poured into the ears of the distracted puppet king, until nothing was left but the final arbitrament of war.[14]

5. THE CAUSES OF THE CHINO-JAPANESE WAR (1894–1895)

The immediate cause of the war which broke out in 1894 was the growth of rebellion in Korea and the inability of the Korean government to maintain its authority against the rebels. The Tong-haks, a sect which had sprung up in Korea in 1859 and which was founded on a combination of elements of the three Oriental religions—Confucianism, Taoism, and Buddhism—petitioned in 1883 for a reversal of the decree which had branded their leader as a sorcerer and heretic, and for tolerance of the sect.

There was a decided anti-foreign feeling among the Tong-haks, as was evidenced by statements of their leaders, and by placards denouncing foreign ideas which were put on some of the American mission buildings in Seoul. Partly because of the anti-foreign spirit in the movement the government declined to receive the petition. Following this there were constant reports of unrest in some of the provinces, and eventually there

[13] Sir R. Hart to Mr. Merrill, May 29, 1880. Cited, MORSE, p. 16.
[14] Ibid., p. 18.

came an open outbreak. The government seemed unable to cope with it, and finally requested the aid of the suzerain power to put it down. This aid had already been offered by the Chinese Resident, and had even been urged on the government. "The Viceroy, Li Hung-chang, only sent these troops after long hesitation, the Chinese resident at Seoul having first requested his interference about a month ago. He insisted on an express request from the King of Korea, so that the responsibility for the movement should rest on him." [15] About fifteen hundred troops were sent to Asan from Weihaiwei, and *after* [16] this action had been taken the Japanese were notified, and were informed that the troops would be withdrawn as soon as the occasion for their presence in Korea had passed.

The Japanese countered by sending large detachments of troops to Seoul by way of Chemulpo. By the time the Chinese troops had reached Korea the revolt had been put down by the Korean army, and the need for their services had passed. China, however, refused to withdraw her force until Japan had recalled hers from the country. The government of Korea began negotiations with both countries to bring about the evacuation of the kingdom, but during the course of the negotiations both sides augmented rather than reduced their forces. Japan proposed to China that the two countries should unite in pressing reform on the Korean government. China refused to act with Japan in the matter, taking the attitude that both should withdraw and allow Korea freedom of action in determining upon reform. Japan, in turn, refused to consider the Chinese proposal for simultaneous withdrawal as a preliminary to reform proposals, even though it was supported by the diplomatic and consular body at Seoul. Japanese opinion had been aroused by China's sending troops to Korea as to a tributary state, which was the phrase used in the notification. And it had already been aroused by the murder at Shanghai of the Korean arch-rebel, Kim Ok-kuin, and the action of the Chinese government in sending the body in state to Korea, where it was beheaded and quartered, the parts of the body being exhibited throughout the country as a reminder of the fate which befell traitors. Japan seemed determined on war, and the continued maintenance of the troops of the two countries in Korea could not but eventuate in war. Each side, however, wanted to evade the responsibility for the commencement of hostilities. The overt act was finally committed when Japanese war vessels fired upon the Chinese troop-ship, the Kowshing,[17] which was bringing reënforcements to the force at Chemulpo. This brought the period of negotiation to an end.

[15] Mr. Denby to Mr. Gresham, *Foreign Relations of the United States,* 1894, appendix 1 (no. 12), p. 20.

[16] The Tientsin convention provided for *previous* notice. Li Hung-chang claimed to have been informed that notice had been sent from Peking before the troops were dispatched.

[17] The fact that the Kowshing was a British chartered steamer and was flying the British flag caused considerable discussion of Japan's action.

Before tracing the course of the war, and considering its results, we must attempt to discover why Japan wanted war, if such was really the case, since the answer to this question may shed some light on subsequent Japanese policy in eastern Asia. The statement is sometimes made that all of Japan's wars in the modern period of her history have been defensive, but it is hard to see how the war with China can be so considered. It arose, to be sure, over Korea, the "dagger pointed at the heart of Japan." A foreign Power actually in control of Korea, if aggressively inclined, would be able to threaten seriously the integrity and the peace of Japan. But China was not actively in control of the kingdom; her position as suzerain had long been nominal rather than real, and had not been utilized to enable her to dictate the internal arrangements of the Korean state. She began to interfere actively in Korean affairs only when even this nominal relationship was threatened by Japanese policy. This policy was directed from the beginning toward the detachment of Korea from the Chinese connection, apparently, from the Chinese point of view, in order to replace it with a Japanese connection which, in turn, would be detrimental to China's interest.

But while China's nominal control of Korea cannot be considered immediately to have menaced the safety of Japan, there is more substance to the Japanese argument that internal conditions in Korea made her a "nuisance" and, for that reason, a danger to the bordering states. The chronic condition of unrest in the provinces and of turmoil at the court could not but arouse the displeasure of a neighbor trying to keep her own house in good order. Furthermore this state of unrest in Korea directly invited continual interference from the outside by stronger Powers than Japan and China.

Russian expansion to the Pacific had already brought her into contact with Japan in such a way as to awaken the Japanese government to the danger of allowing Russia to establish herself as close to the Japanese islands as Korea. In 1884 Russia had revealed her interest in that country by undertaking a reform of the Korean army. The request for the use of Port Lazareff indicated the Russian objective. Thus in order to forestall Russia it was necessary for Japan to establish herself securely in the peninsula. But China, prior to the war with Japan, was also mistrustful of Russia. One way of meeting any threat to Korea from the north would have been to strengthen the Chinese connection rather than to break it down.[18] Russia and Japan, if the Japanese policy of establishing Korean independence proved successful, would meet at Seoul on terms of equality in the struggle for control, whereas the Chinese position had long been accepted. Of course China might ultimately develop aggressive tendencies,

[18] Except as it may be considered that China was herself so weak and backward that she would be unable to defend either Korea or herself from external aggression.

as she had in the distant past, and thus prove as much of a menace to Japan as Russia, and fear of the future may have determined Japan to secure her interest by her own action. There were two ways of doing this: (1) the Japanese government could establish the independence of Korea and then insist on a reorganization of the country and such modernization of its political system as would enable Korea to maintain her independence by herself and remove the excuse for foreign intervention on the ground of bad internal conditions; or (2) it could, after breaking down the connection with China, establish Japanese control over the peninsula. From the beginning Japan insisted on the necessity for reform, and gave her active support to the reform party; but after both China and Russia had been eliminated from the country, Japan actually proceeded to carry out the second policy. Whether she had this in mind from the beginning, it is impossible to say; but it is possible to establish the fact that much of the disorder in Korea during the years after 1876 was the result of Japanese, countered by Chinese, intrigue. And it was this disorder which Japan used as the excuse for her interest in Korean affairs.

Another possible reason for Japan's interest in Korea was economic. The kingdom produced a considerable amount of rice, but its export was forbidden since it furnished the most important item in the diet of the people. A dominant Japan could use Korea for the purpose of enlarging the food supply of the Japanese people. As a matter of fact, in 1894 the Korean government had been persuaded by Japan to suspend the decree forbidding the export of rice, and Japanese agents had purchased every cattie of it that could be secured, much to the dissatisfaction of the Korean people, who had to pay higher prices. Further than this, the Japanese had developed shipping and trade interests in Korea very rapidly, controlling forty per cent of the imports in 1894, and an even larger proportion of the shipping. Thus there was presented a valuable market, still largely undeveloped, which the Japanese undoubtedly desired to control. And they had absorbed the European doctrine that political ascendency in a country must be secured as a preliminary to the establishment of a safe economic position. This, again, may represent a point of view toward the continent which gained a hearing later than 1894, or it may have had an important bearing on Japanese policy at that time. At any rate it deserves consideration in any estimate of the causes of the Japanese determination to fight for Korea.

In evaluating Japanese policy after the opening of Korea we must bear in mind also that the doctrine of continental expansion had been preached as part of the pre-Restoration program. One of the most active leaders in the campaign which ultimately undermined the Shōgunate was Yoshida-shoin, who was an expansionist of the first water. His school harked back to the sixteenth century and the Hideyoshi campaign against Korea and

China, and urged the overthrow of the Shōgunate and a concentration of power in the Emperor as a preliminary step to the establishment of Japanese power on the continent through the conquest of Korea. Among those who sat at his feet were Prince Yamagata and Count (later Prince) Ito, the former one of the organizers of the modern Japanese army, and the latter the father of the Japanese constitutional system. Count Ito, it is true, had been one of the leaders of the peace party in Japan during the transition period, but this did not mean that he had forgotten the teaching of Yoshida. It meant that he believed it necessary for Japan to strengthen herself at home before undertaking any continental adventures. That he believed Japan sufficiently transformed by 1894 to develop a strong continental policy, is perhaps open to question. He was firmly seated in power so long as the peace party remained in control, and for that reason he might have wished to avoid the war, had it not been for the new forces which appeared in Japanese politics with the promulgation of the constitution.

But the years 1890–1894 revealed the inability of the oligarchy to control Japan effectively in the face of the opposition of the political parties in the Diet. Prince Yamagata, leader of the war party, tried and failed, and after the Matsukata ministry had resigned, Ito himself had undertaken to run the governmental machine. In order to carry on he was forced to resort to the Imperial Rescript, and yet that only temporarily ended the opposition of the Diet to his government. It was necessary for him to acknowledge that the system he had provided could not function in the face of the development of the political party, and that the oligarchy must retire into the background, entrusting power to the parties, a solution which would not be accepted by the other clan leaders; or he had to ask for a revision of the constitution such as would enable the government to be carried on without the Diet; or, finally, he had to find some method of overcoming the opposition of the parties to his government. In those circumstances the most feasible method of rallying the nation to the support of the government was to resort to a foreign war.

The opportunity was presented by the action of China in refusing to join Japan in urging reform on the Korean government. The people were ready and clamoring for war. There was only one drawback—war meant that the Civil Bureaucrats would be pushed into the background, at least temporarily, and that the power of the Military Bureaucrats would be enhanced. The former had to gamble on their ability to restore themselves to power after the war had been brought to a conclusion. Count Ito took this chance rather than face the certainty of seeing his constitutional structure broken down by the assaults of the parties. The Sino-Japanese War was caused by the condition of Japanese politics, coupled with the centuries-old interest of Japan in Korea as the gateway to continental expansion, supplemented by a national fear lest Korea should come under the control of some strong foreign Power, and by a budding interest in control of the resources of the peninsula and in Korea as a market.

China, on her side, accepted the possibility of war and by her actions transformed a possibility into a certainty. There were several reasons for her attitude. Fundamentally her whole policy after 1876 was directed toward correcting the mistake made when she allowed Japan to redress her own grievances against Korea and to negotiate a treaty on the basis of independence. This error was not repaired as a result of the introduction of the Western Powers into the kingdom on the same basis. England by her subsequent actions sought to strengthen China as the suzerain, but the policy of the United States supported that of Japan. Consequently China sought to revive her pretensions by continued interference in Korean affairs, an interference which was welcomed by the conservative party. Her actions were certain to result in conflict with Japan if that state carried into effect its program. To the extent that China opposed Japanese policies in order to maintain her claim to suzerainty, she must accept responsibility for the conflict of 1894-1895.

Aside from the Korean policy, Chinese action may also be explained in terms of internal politics. There was an anti-Li party at Peking which sought to weaken his influence by attacking his Korean policy as weak. This clique was willing as early as 1884-1885 to resort to war if thereby his dominance might be weakened. Many of its members were ultra-conservative and consequently anti-foreign. They believed China to be strong and thought it possible to restore Manchu prestige by a successful war against Japan, which they considered weak. Li Hung-chang himself was supposed to have strengthened China's army and so he was not in the best position, even if he believed it, to proclaim China's weakness and inability to sustain a foreign war, especially against a Power considered in every way inferior. Thus his position at Court depended upon putting up a bold front to Japan. He had evaded the issue with the Chinese war party in 1884-1885 by counselling patience until his army reorganization had been carried to completion, and until the Tongking trouble had been ended. These excuses for postponement did not exist ten years later. Thus we see that, while Japan was determined on war, China was not in a position to go to the limit in the search for a peace formula.

6. THE COURSE OF THE WAR

It seemed presumptuous for Japan to challenge the Celestial Empire to combat—a case of the giant and the dwarf, if size of territory and population and greatness of resources are considered. To superficial observers it seemed that such a war could have but one outcome, an overwhelming defeat for Japan. The American minister at Peking in a despatch to the State Department summarized the general attitude well: "The army of Japan upon a war footing is only 120,000, men, while the Viceroy Li alone has 50,000 foreign drilled troops armed with modern arms, and of fine discipline and efficiency. Besides these there are many thousand foreign-drilled troops in other parts of the Empire, and a practically inexhaustible supply of the old fashioned native soldiery." [19]

To say that the course of the war surprised all but the informed few, is to put it mildly. China did have an inexhaustible supply of men, but she had no modern army worthy of the name, and her navy, on paper greatly superior to that of Japan, proved entirely unable to cope with the Japanese navy. Japan had thoroughly reorganized and modernized her fighting services, from the standpoint of both training and equipment. Nothing less than the best that she could get had satisfied her. China, on the other hand, had reorganized part of her military establishment, but had been satisfied with inferior instruction and equipment, the difference in cost between old and discarded weapons and the newer types of armament going to line the pockets of officials and their friends, from Li Hung-chang down. Consequently the greater resources of China proved to be more than neutralized by the superior training of the Japanese and the better weapons with which they were supplied. The difference in training was especially noticeable in the leadership of the Japanese forces on both land and sea. They were masters of modern tactics and strategy. China was further handicapped by the feeling south of the Yangtse River that the war was the private affair of Li Hung-chang, or, at the most, of the north. The southern Chinese navy refused to participate in the struggle, and the governors whose territories were unaffected failed fully to support the Imperial cause. The reasons for this attitude have already been referred to. The consequence at this time was that the war was carried on largely between Japan and the followers of Li Hung-chang.

The lessons of their own earlier conflicts with Korea and China had not been lost on the Japanese. Before sending troops into Korea in large numbers, the navy went into action in order to secure the line of communications with the home base. The Chinese fleet was defeated off the mouth of the Yalu, and again, toward the end of the war, at Weihaiwei, where it had put in for refuge.

After control of the seas had been established, Japanese troops began to pour in large numbers into Korea, where they quickly made themselves master. The King was forced to issue a number of edicts changing the entire governmental system, and modernizing, on paper, the economic and social life of Korea almost overnight. From Korea the Japanese forces

[19] Mr. Denby to Mr. Gresham, *Foreign Relations of the United States*, 1894, appendix 1, no. 17 (p. 24).

pushed on into Manchuria, driving the Chinese forces before them. When they were on the point of invading China proper, the Manchu government indicated its desire to open negotiations for peace. Overtures were made at first through the United States, which had been entrusted with the care of the interests of each belligerent in the other country. Before Japan would consent to begin conversations, China was forced to sue directly for peace through the American minister, her first intimations having been of a willingness to accept the good offices of the United States. Japan delayed the opening of negotiations as long as possible in order that the Chinese fleet at Weihaiwei might first be disposed of, and so that Formosa might be occupied by the force sent to effect its conquest. The government consequently declined to treat with the first Chinese mission, taking exception to the credentials given the negotiators, and insisting that an official be appointed of sufficiently high rank to ensure the acceptance by the Manchu court of any engagements he might make without reference of details back to Peking.

7. THE TREATY OF SHIMONOSEKI

Brought to a proper humility by the disaster of the war, the Emperor finally appointed Li Hung-chang, restored to his dignities,[20] to negotiate the peace. Shortly after negotiations had been begun at Shimonoseki an attempt was made on his life by a Japanese fanatic. This delayed negotiations, but resulted in advantage for China, as Japan modified her peace demands in order to show her regret for the injury to China's foremost statesman. The terms finally agreed upon at Shimonoseki and embodied in the treaty of peace were as follows: China recognized definitely the full and complete independence and autonomy of Korea; she was forced to "cede to Japan in perpetuity and full sovereignty" (a) that part of Manchuria lying east of the river Liao (Liaotung) and south of a line from the junction of the rivers Anping and Yalu, by Fenghwang-cheng and Haicheng, to Yingkow, (b) Formosa, and (c) the Pescadores group; an idemnity of 200,000,000 taels was to be paid by China, and Weihaiwei was to be occupied by the Japanese until this indemnity had been paid, and until a satisfactory treaty of commerce was signed and ratified; [21] and, finally, four new ports were to be opened to foreign trade,—Shasi and Chungking on the Yangtse River, and Soochow and Hangchow on the

[20] After the first disaster of the war he was deprived of the Peacock Feather and the Yellow Jacket, and removed from his post at Tientsin, although he was forced to continue his direction of the war.

[21] This treaty was concluded July 21, 1896. It advanced the Japanese position in China to that of equality of privilege with the Western states. In addition China conceded to Japan the right to engage in industry in the treaty ports. Under the most-favored-nation clause this new right was generalized. It had most important consequences.

Grand Canal—and the direct waterways leading to them were to be opened to traffic.

Of these conditions, the cession of Formosa and of the Pescadores group and the recognition of Korean independence merely carried a step further the process already described of trimming off the fringes of the Empire, and China had already been accustomed to the assumption of indemnities and to the opening of ports under pressure. But the cession of the Liaotung peninsula threatened Manchuria, the home of the ruling family, and brought a foreign Power very close to Peking itself. Consequently this demand must have greatly alarmed the Chinese government, and might have brought it to the point of continuing the war, if it had not received some assurances of support which would neutralize the fact of the cession.

That there might come European intervention, if the turn of the conflict should seem to invite it, had been apparent from the outset. Japan's success and her presence on the continent would tend to upset the power equilibrium *vis-à-vis* China. The advance actually made had the effect of throwing Japan into the pathway of Russian expansion. Furthermore, England had come to base her policy on the preservation of the territorial integrity of China. In fact, from the first, Japan had been fearful of British intervention in favor of China. This danger of intervention the American government had called to the attention of the Japanese in the following words: "If the struggle continues without check to Japan's military operations on land and sea, it is not improbable that the powers having interests in that quarter may demand a settlement not favorable to Japan's future security and well-being." [22]

In the interests of other states lay the Chinese assurance that the Empire would be saved from the imposition of too harsh terms. Li Hung-chang may not have had definite promises of foreign support and intervention, but he undoubtedly had good reason to believe that Russia, for one, would not acquiesce in the establishment of Japan on the mainland in such a position as to prevent or limit Russian expansion. The one provision of the treaty of Shimonoseki which would have this effect was that ceding to Japan the Liaotung promontory. To this provision there came objection even before the exchange of ratifications of the treaty. Russia, joined by France, her European ally, and also by Germany, presented a demand to Japan that the Liaotung territory be restored to China. The reason given for the demand was that the proximity of the territory to Peking made its possession by any Power other than China a perpetual threat to the Chinese capital. In the face of superior and overwhelming force Japan gave way, receiving in lieu of the territory an additional indemnity of 30,000,000 taels.

The Russian action did not greatly surprise Japanese statesmen, nor did the support given to Russia by France, her ally in Europe; but the Japanese

[22] Quoted by DENNETT, p. 499.

were unable to understand and for some time refused to forget the support given to Russia at this time by Germany. It was clear that Russia stood to lose by the entrenchment of Japan so close to Peking, since Russia and Japan were not, and, by the nature of their respective interests and policies in the Far East at that time, could not be expected to be, on friendly terms. But Germany had no territorial interests in eastern Asia, and it seemed like a gratuitous insult for her to aid in depriving Japan of a part of the fruits of her victory. It could be explained at that time only by a desire on the part of Germany to cultivate Russia by supporting her in the Far East in order to advance German interests in Europe.

On the other hand, the Japanese were pleasantly surprised by the attitude of Great Britain throughout the war and at the time of the intervention. As the struggle progressed the British position came close to being sympathetic to the Japanese, and the British government, although it advised Japan to accede to the demand of the three intervening Powers, did not itself raise any objection to the terms of the treaty. The British attitude at the time, together with the increased good will shown by the revision of the Japanese treaty in 1894, seemed to indicate a change in the Far Eastern policy of the British Empire.

In spite of the intervention, however, the final effect of the war was to demonstrate beyond all doubt the weakness of China. Her victory strengthened Japan immeasurably in the eyes of the world. It changed the course of development in the Far East, as a consequence of the revelation of the weakness of China and of the strength of Japan. It gave to Japan far more than she had hoped to obtain at the outset—Formosa and the Pescadores, in addition to the recognition by China of the complete independence of Korea. The Japanese war party was disappointed in that the Empire was not extended to include continental territory, but that dream was not given up because of the temporary set-back resulting from the Three-Powers' intervention.

REFERENCES FOR FURTHER STUDY

H. M. Allen, *Things Korean* (1908); sketches and anecdotes by a missionary diplomatist. G. A. Ballard, *Influence of the Sea on the Political History of Japan* (1921), ch. 5–6. I. B. Bishop, *Korea and Her Neighbors* (1897); the impressions of a traveler in Korea, giving interesting pictures of the condition of the country and the life of the people. A. J. Brown, *Mastery of the Far East* (1919), ch. (1–6) 7. P. H. Clyde, *International Rivalries in Manchuria* (1926), ch. 1–2. T. Dennett, *Americans in Eastern Asia* (1922), ch. 23–26; the best account of American policy toward Korea. *Foreign Relations of the United States* (1894), Appendix 1 (House Doc. 1894–1895, v. 2); excellent as source of information concerning the crisis of 1894. John Foreman (pseud. Vladimir), *China-Japan War* (1905); primarily concerned with military and naval events; contains appendices worth consulting. J. W. Foster, *American Diplomacy in the Orient* (1903), ch. 9. W. E. Griffis, *Korea the Hermit Nation* (1882);

7th edition (1904). J. H. GUBBINS, *Making of Modern Japan* (1922), ch. 22–23. H. B. HULBERT, *Passing of Korea* (1906), ch. 1–9 (espec. ch. 8–9); valuable as study of Korea by one familiar with the country and people. H. B. HULBERT, *History of Korea*, 2 vols. (1905); a standard work; written mainly from Korean sources. T. C. LIN, *Li Hung-Chang: His Korean Policies, 1870–1885*, Chinese Social and Political Science Review, vol. 19, pp. 202–233; a valuable article based largely on Chinese sources. J. H. LONGFORD, *Story of Korea* (1911); a readable book by a well-known author who was sympathetic to Japan. J. V. A. MAC-MURRAY, *Treaties and Conventions with and Concerning China* (1921); vol. 1 for treaty of Shimonoseki. F. A. McKENZIE, *Korea's Fight for Freedom* (1920). ch. 1–3; an account very sympathetic to Korea. H. F. MacNAIR, *Modern Chinese History, Selected Readings* (1923), ch. 12. W. W. McLAREN, *Political History of Japan* (1916), ch. 10; interprets the Japanese position in terms of internal politics. H. B. MORSE, *International Relations of the Chinese Empire*, vol. 3 (1918), ch. 1–2; a good account of the struggle for Korea, emphasizing the Chinese point of view. R. T. POLLARD, *American Relations with Korea, 1882–1895*, Chinese Social and Political Science Review, vol. 16, no. 3, pp. 425–471. P. J. TREAT, *Diplomatic Relations between the United States and Japan, 1853–1895*, 2 vols. (1932), vol. 2, ch. 42–44; excellent on the relationship of the United States to the belligerents; presents a view of Sino-Japanese relations sympathetic to Japan and thus one worth comparison with the above account. T. F. TSIANG, *Sino-Japanese Relations, 1870–1894*, Chinese Social and Political Science Review, vol. 17, pp. 1–106; an important and valuable account documented from Chinese records. L. H. UNDERWOOD, *Fifteen Years Among the Top-Knots* (1904); a woman missionary's observations in and impressions of Korea.

CHAPTER VII

CUTTING THE CHINESE MELON

1. CONSEQUENCES OF WAR OF 1894-1895

THE Sino-Japanese War marked a reversal in the relative positions of China and Japan in the Far East. Before the war the Western nations had respected the potential if not the actual power of China, and had patronized Japan. After 1895 but scant respect was paid to the Chinese Empire, which had shown itself not only weak in a military sense, but lacking in that national consciousness which rallies a people behind its government in the face of the foreign foe. One effect of the spirit of localism, made glaringly apparent during the course of the war, was the lack of ability, or even desire, to concentrate the entire strength of the nation against the Japanese. Further than this, the lack of integrity of many of the high officials, as well as their inefficiency in the face of modern conditions, was completely revealed. The stock of Japan, on the other hand, took a sudden rise. Her army and navy received nothing but the highest praise from foreign critics, and it was conceded that they made Japan a factor which could not be disregarded in the future politics of the Far East. The war marked the reception of Japan as an adult member of the society of nations. No longer could the West dictate the terms of its intercourse with her. Even if the treaties with Japan had not been modified prior to the outbreak of hostilities, they would have had to be revised in her favor after the signature of the treaty of Shimonoseki.

Nevertheless the war, successful though it was from the Japanese standpoint, did not leave Japan a primary force in the Far East. The Great Powers were led to respect her but not to concede her a determining voice in continental politics. She was taught her place for the time being by the Three-Powers intervention in favor of China.

2. RUSSIA MOVES SOUTH

The period from 1895 to 1902 was one of Russian domination. China had a wholesome respect for the power of her great neighbor—a respect which had been not a little tinged with fear as Russia had pressed in from the west and down from the north. But any conception that Chinese officials may have had of Russia as the state to be dreaded was changed for a few years after the war with Japan. Russia had taken the lead in averting the danger and humiliation that would have come from the establishment of Japan in Manchuria and close to Peking, and she further intimated that she would stand between China and future encroachments on the part of the Japanese. Consequently Russian influence became predominant at Peking. This influence was strengthened by the support given Russian policy by the French minister. Incidentally France herself benefited materially by the alliance with Russia, since it gave her diplomats a standing at the Tsungli Yamen which otherwise they would not have had. Germany, the third party in the intervention, had a claim on the gratitude of the Chinese government, and, by working partly with Russia and in part with British financiers, she was able in due course to reap the reward for her action.

With the enhancement of Russian influence at Peking, however, that of Great Britain declined. Almost single-handed England had opened China to foreign intercourse. From 1860 until 1895 the British minister had taken the lead in all movements designed to make that intercourse more satisfactory and profitable to the states of the West.[1] England was still the greatest trading Power in 1895 and for some time thereafter, and yet her political influence during the critical period from 1895 to 1901 was less than it had ever been. This was partly due to her preoccupation in other parts of the world, but it was also due to her inability to obtain support from any other legation and to the negative character of her policy. France and Russia were working together to promote their interests, and China's most prominent statesman had swung over to the Russian side. Germany was desirous of strengthening her position, which could best be done by utilizing first Russia and then England, but not by taking a permanent stand with the latter. And the United States was too preoccupied with Cuban developments and too little interested in the Far East in 1895 to develop a positive plan of action.

Shortly after the signature of the treaty of Shimonoseki Russia moved to strengthen her new position as the protector of China. Partly from considerations of internal politics and partly because of its friendly relations with Russia, the Manchu government sent Li Hung-chang to St. Petersburg to represent China at the ceremonies of May, 1896, attendant upon the coronation of the Czar. Count Witte, the eminent Russian statesman, urged upon the Chinese plenipotentiary, during his stay in the Russian capital, the negotiation of a treaty of alliance.[2] He pointed out that the danger to China had been averted only for the time, that Russia was desirous of giving China effective aid in case her territory should again be menaced, and that it was advisable for China to give Russia the right and the means to aid her effectively in time of need. His argument convinced

---

[1] Except during the period of service at the legation of the United States of Mr. Burlingame, when the leadership passed for a time to the Americans.

[2] See *Memoirs*, ch. IV, for detailed account.

Li Hung-chang so completely that before he left St. Petersburg a secret treaty of alliance was initialed.[3] The alliance was directed specifically against Japan, the High Contracting Parties agreeing to support each other reciprocally, making war and peace in common, in the event of Japanese aggression in eastern Asia, whether against Russian or Chinese territory. In time of war China agreed to allow Russia freely to use her harbors and other facilities. This guarantee of protection for China against a possible Japanese attack was given by Russia in return for the right to project the Trans-Siberian Railroad across northern Manchuria directly to Vladivostok.

Pursuant to the terms of a supplementary convention, Russia chartered a private corporation known as the Russo-Chinese Bank, to which China entrusted the financing of the Manchurian section (called the Chinese Eastern Railway) of the Trans-Siberian. This bank became the chief instrument for the Russian penetration of Manchuria. As described in its charter, it was to be an agency for "the collection of duties in the Empire of China, and the transactions relating to the State treasury of the respective place, the coinage, with the authorization of the Chinese government, of the country's money, the payment of interest on loans, concluded by the Chinese Government, the acquisition of concessions for the construction of railways within the boundaries of China, and the establishment of telegraph lines." [4] Thus although organized and controlled under Russian law, the Russo-Chinese Bank was to serve as the fiscal agent of the Chinese government in addition to undertaking the work of financing railroads and other projects in Manchuria. The first railroad concession falling to its lot was one for the construction of the Chinese Eastern. For this purpose it organized a construction company which had the right to construct and operate the road and to control properties, such as quarries, necessary to its construction. In addition, the company had administrative rights in the railway zone. The concession was to run for eighty years from the time of the completion of the road, when it was to revert to China without payment. China reserved to herself, however, the right to redeem the road at the end of a period of thirty-six years, "but the terms of the redemption were so burdensome that it was highly improbable that the Chinese government would ever attempt to effect the redemption. It was calculated that should the Chinese government wish to redeem the road at the beginning of the 37th year, it would have to pay the corporation, according to the terms of the concession, a sum not less than 700 million rubles." [5]

The terms of this concession were extremely favorable to Russia, but the right to build the Siberian railroad to Vladivostok across northern

---

[3] It has also been charged that Li Hung-chang's venality explained his action in entering into the agreement.

[4] WILLOUGHBY, *Foreign Rights and Interests in China*, pp. 296–297.

[5] WITTE, *Memoirs*, p. 95.

Manchuria would have been advantageous under almost any conditions. It not only gave a direct route, cutting off the wide detour which would have been necessary had the road been completed entirely in Russian territory, but it also introduced Russian economic influence into northern Manchuria.[6] The entire railroad project seems to have been economic in its origin—part of Count Witte's statesmanlike plans for the industrial development of Russia. The Siberian railroad justified his expectations from the outset. Peasants began to settle the country on either side as the road was constructed section by section, and trade developed with the settlement of the territory. That Manchuria might be similarly developed under Russian direction and to her economic advantage, was far from improbable. And Russia would gain as much from the development as if it had come in her own territory. Of course, in addition to the economic motive back of the Trans-Siberian Railroad there was the strategical. The railroad would serve to unify the Russian territories more effectively than was possible in any other way. But, so far as Manchuria was concerned, Alexander III, the initiator of the project, and Count Witte, had in mind an economic penetration rather than a territorial gain for the Russian Empire.

3. THE GERMAN ADVANCE

The so-called "battle of the concessions," however, was initially inaugurated by France in 1895, but it was vigorously taken up and carried on by Germany and Russia. Germany had determined to insist on adequate recognition by China of her aid in securing the retrocession of the Liaotung peninsula. In the spring of 1897 she intimated to the other Powers her desire to secure a coaling and naval station on the coast of China, and began to make surveys with a view to fixing upon a suitable port. However, before acting, it was necessary to find a suitable pretext. This was afforded by the murder of two German priests in Shantung province. Within a period of two weeks after the murder the German government had served demands on the Tsungli Yamen, including: 1) a ninety-nine year lease of Tsingtao and an area comprehending the entire bay of Kiaochow; 2) the sole right of railway construction and the exploitation of the coal mines of Shantung province; and 3) the payment of an indemnity and the expenses of the naval expedition which had occupied Tsingtao prior to the serving of the demands.

These demands were substantially accepted by the Chinese government and embodied in the agreement of March 6, 1898. The area surrounding Kiaochow Bay was leased, provisionally, for a period of ninety-nine years

---

[6] Art. 10 of the Chinese Eastern agreement provided that goods imported into or exported from China or Russia overland via the railway should pay according to the treaty tariff, with a deduction of one-third from the tariff rates. It was expected that this would stimulate trade.

to Germany. The Emperor of China, while retaining title to the territory, agreed not to exercise his sovereign rights therein for the period of the lease. Germany, on her side, reserved the right to restore the territory to China at any time and to secure, as compensation, a station at some other point on the coast. The territory was never to be sublet to any other Power. Instead of exclusive railroad and mining rights in the province, specific concessions for the building of roads and the opening and operation of mines were given to Germany.[7]

4. THE "BATTLE OF THE CONCESSIONS"

The granting of these demands meant a serious disturbance of the balance of power in the Far East in favor of one state. Consequently all the others moved immediately to secure their separate interests. Russia occupied Port Arthur and demanded a lease of the tip of the Liaotung promontory (the Kwantung area), including Port Arthur and Talienwan, for a period of twenty-five years; an extension of the concessions of the Russo-Chinese Bank to include a projection southward to Port Arthur of the Chinese Eastern Railroad; and mining rights in southern Manchuria.

This led England to request the lease of Weihaiwei for the period of the Russian occupation of Port Arthur. She also demanded from China: 1) a declaration that she would not alienate to any Power the provinces bordering on the Yangtse River; 2) a promise that an English subject should hold the post of Inspector-General of the Maritime Customs so long as British trade supremacy was maintained in China; and 3) an extension of the lease of the territory on the mainland opposite Hongkong.

France had already, in 1895, secured a statement from China that she would not alienate to any other Power the island of Hainan. She had also gained a concession in the matter of customs charges on goods entering China from the French dependencies in the south;[8] a priority in the exploitation of the mines of Yunnan, Kwangsi, and Kwangtung provinces; and permission to extend the Annam railway into Chinese territory. In 1897–1898 she further advanced her interests (1) by securing a non-alienation agreement covering the provinces bordering on Tongking; (2) by demanding and receiving definite concessions for the building of railroads in Yunnan province; (3) by the gaining of a lease for ninety-nine years of Kwangchou Bay; and (4) by securing from China a promise that whenever a separate postal service was established the Imperial Government would be "willing to take account of the recommendations of the French Government in respect to the selection of the Staff." Japan, in her turn,

---

[7] China agreed, however, to call upon Germany first in case she needed foreign money for the development of Shantung province, and to purchase materials from Germany, provided, in both cases, that Germany's terms were as favorable as could be obtained elsewhere.

[8] The regular maritime customs charges were to be reduced by four-tenths.

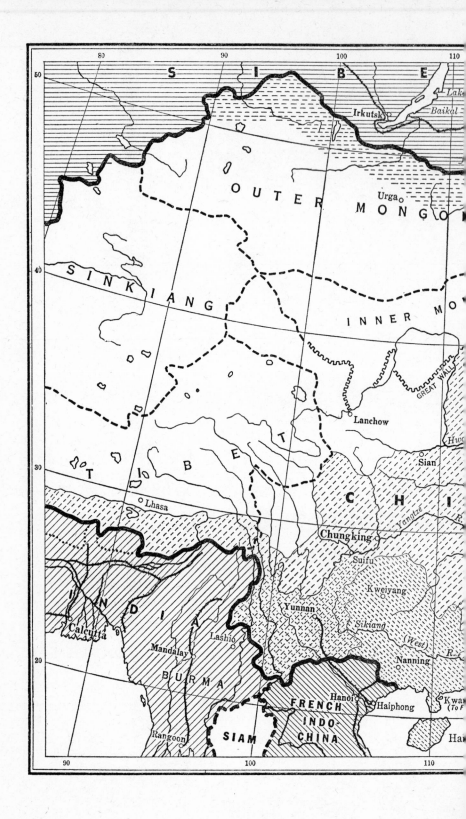

120 130 140 150 50

Sakhalin

Amur

I A N

Khabarovsk

Aigun

Tsitsihar

M A N C H U R I A

Harbin

Hakodate

Kirin

From Russia to
Japan, 1905

Vladivostok

Mukden

40

Chinchow

S E A   O F

J A P A N

Peking

Port Arthur
To Russia 1898
To Japan 1905

K O R E A
To Japan 1910

Seoul

Tokyo

Weihaiwei
To Britain 1898
To China 1922

Yokohama

Tsinan

Tsingtao
To Germany 1898
To Japan 1920
To China 1922

Fusan

Kobe

Osaka

30

Nagasaki

anking

Shanghai

E A S T

Hangchow

C H I N A

Nanchang

S E A

P A C I F I C

O C E A N

CHINA
IN 1922

Foochow

Amoy

Taiwan
(Formosa)

Boundary of Chinese Republic, 1922

Railways

| British Possessions | British Spheres of Interest | 20 |

kong

French   "   French   "   "   "

German   "   German   "   "   "

Russian   "   Russian   "   "   "

Japanese   "   Japanese "   "   "

Scale of Miles
0   100   200   300   400   500

PHILIPPINE
ISLANDS

120 130

asked for an agreement from China not to alienate to any other 'Power Fukien province, which lies opposite Formosa. All of these demands were acceded to by the Chinese government, but when Italy requested a lease of Sanmen Bay it screwed up its courage to the sticking point and refused to grant it. This brought the "concession grabbing" to an end for the time being.

5. SPHERES OF INTEREST

So quickly had these developments come and so little resistance had the Imperial Government been able to make, that the end of the Chinese Empire apparently might come at any time. The first step looking toward the partition of such a state as China is likely to be the marking out of the country into spheres of special interest, and these several agreements between the Powers and China resulted in the application of that term to various parts of the Empire. Thus Manchuria was said to be Russia's sphere of interest, Shantung the sphere of Germany, etc. The term, "sphere of interest," as applied to China, carried primarily an economic significance.

Its essential element [says Overlach] [9] is a negative one; namely, the term expresses the principle that no other power except the one in whose favor the "sphere of interest" exists shall be permitted to acquire concessions or to exert any control or influence whatsoever—not to speak about military occupation—at the same time giving the privileged power a monopoly of the right to seek concessions. This privilege, however, does by no means entitle its holder to any positive exercise of influence within the sphere which would change the sphere of interest to a sphere of influence. For the latter term, which has never been used officially, as far as China is concerned, suggests a certain degree of authority or control, either financial or political, exercised by a foreign power within a certain territory.

The great danger to a country such as China is the possibility that, as a result of the development of exclusive interests in one section by any one state, there should be found an excuse for the establishment of a measure of control, either political or financial, thus translating the "sphere of interest" into a "sphere of influence." After the latter is established, it is likely to be but a short step to the assertion of a "protectorate" by the gradual enlargement of the powers of control. The logical conclusion of the development of the "sphere" conception is, through the gradual introduction of political control, complete absorption of the territory concerned into the empire of the state first asserting therein its priority of economic interest. That this would have been the ultimate fate of China, had not the development of "spheres of interest" been checked at an early stage, cannot be doubted.

The assertion of claims to "spheres of interest" in China was commonly

[9] OVERLACH, *Foreign Financial Control in China*, p. 5.

based on a series of less inclusive concessions, which have just been described. First we have the leasehold on the coast, giving a presumptive claim to the hinterland in the event of the actual partition of China. When a Power secured a leasehold, however, it also secured, as a rule, certain economic concessions in the region, either in the hinterland of a leased area or in a specified region in which no lease had been demanded. These concessions, as has been pointed out, consisted of rights to finance the construction of, and to construct, railroads with materials furnished from the state of the concessionaire, and in some cases to operate the railroad after its completion; and of the right to exploit the mineral wealth of the region. And in the third place, we have the non-alienation agreements regarding various sections. These also were usually joined with economic concessions granted in the provinces which the Chinese government promised not to alienate to any other Power.

All of this was accomplished by agreement between China and the European state concerned in each case. It still remained for the latter to make good its claim to a "sphere of interest" against the other Powers. This produced the fourth type of agreement and the real establishment of a "sphere." The first three did not prevent China from making other agreements, if she could, giving to third parties specific concessions in the area marked off as a "sphere." In fact it was to her interest to do so in order to make clear her title to the territory. Consequently each one of the Powers proceeded to secure from the others the fullest possible recognition of its exclusive interest in the area claimed by it for exploitation.

In pursuance of the Siam Convention of 1896, France and Great Britain had agreed to share any special privileges that either secured in Yunnan and Szechuan provinces. In 1898, however, France asserted her superiority of interest in the provinces bordering on Tongking, including Yunnan, when she secured a non-alienation agreement from China respecting them. She also gained for her nationals then, and by an earlier agreement, the right to construct railways in Yunnan. Great Britain quietly acquiesced in this change in status, seeking compensation in the Yangtse valley. Thus there was a tacit recognition given to the French claim to a "sphere of interest" in Yunnan, Kwangsi, and Kweichow provinces. Kwangtung also fell within the group of provinces which China agreed not to alienate, but owing to the British ownership of Hongkong, and the extension of her interest in eastern Kwangtung by the lease of the Kowloon territory, Kwangtung province may be considered as divided, only the western part of the province falling within the French sphere. Szechuan may also be considered as a field for joint exploitation. Since Great Britain was the only other Power with an interest in southwestern China, with British recognition of the priority of her claim France may be considered to have safeguarded herself from encroachment on her sphere.

The chief international interest lies in the agreement reached between Great Britain, on the one hand, and Russia and Germany, on the other, concerning the Yangtse valley, Shantung, and Manchuria. When Great Britain demanded the lease of Weihaiwei, on the northern coast of Shantung province, she was careful to assure the German government that she had no intention of encroaching on the German preserve in that province so far as the seeking of economic concessions was concerned. In 1898 a further understanding as to railroad concessions in China was reached directly between English and German financiers. This agreement defined the British sphere of interest so as to include roughly all of the provinces drained by the Yangtse River and its tributaries, with certain exceptions giving Shantung railroads the right of connection with the Yangtse lines. Shansi province, subject to a reserved right of connection, also went to the British. The German sphere was defined to include the Yellow River valley, including specifically Shantung province, subject to certain rights of connection. Each agreed not to compete for concessions in the other's sphere.

Russian-British differences were composed by the Scott-Mouravieff agreement (1899), by which Great Britain agreed not to go north of the Great Wall in search of railroad concessions, while Russia agreed, for her part, to respect the British sphere in the Yangtse valley.

6. ATTITUDE AND INTEREST OF THE UNITED STATES

These agreements would have left China helpless if the Powers making them had observed them in good faith, and if all the Powers had been similarly committed to respect these claims to "spheres of interest." But the United States had not taken part in the scramble of 1897–1898, although she was just reawakening to the importance of questions of foreign politics. Intermittently the United States had manifested an active interest in the Far East. At the time of the opening of China she was the second trading Power at the port of Canton. Her share in the opening of Japan has already been described.[10] After the American Civil War, however, the active interest of the United States in the outside world, including the Far East, was greatly lessened as attention came to be concentrated on domestic development. But during the years 1865–1898 the American nation went through a transformation, emerging an industrial rather than primarily an agricultural state. By the 'nineties this industrial progress had gone so far that many Americans felt that foreign markets were needed to absorb the excess production of industry, and capital had been accumulated, it was felt by many, beyond the ability of the home field to absorb it. Joined with this purely economic interest in the outside world, there came an added interest in international relations due to the war with Spain. That war left

[10] Chapter IV. pp. 88–93.

the United States with the Philippines as a territorial stake in the Far East, making her an Asiatic Power. All of this produced an interest in the question of China beyond that which would normally have been manifested. This interest necessitated a positive reaction to the new situation.

When the "battle of the concessions" began, and during its course, the United States was engaged in the war with Spain and could take no direct action. Taking stock of the situation as it had developed up to 1899 from the American standpoint, it would seem obvious that three alternatives were presented to the government of the United States: it might recognize the advances made by the Powers in China and do nothing, allowing the spheres of interest to ripen in the natural way into protectorates, with the consequent ultimate exclusion of American trade from China; it might enter into the competition and try to stake out a sphere for American exploitation; or it might try to safeguard American commercial interests within the spheres of the Powers. Given the widespread belief in the United States that it would be necessary for American industry and capital to go abroad, the first alternative was impossible of acceptance, since China seemed to offer one of the greatest potential markets and fields for investment in the world. The second alternative was equally unacceptable. The American policy in the Far East had been fixed traditionally as non-exclusive. In none of its dealings with Far Eastern states had the government of the United States sought to secure exclusive privileges for itself or for its nationals. It had always demanded "most-favored-nation" treatment for itself, and had been willing to see any advantages it secured extended equally to all trading powers. It was willing to compete, but the terms of competition had to be equal and non-discriminatory. This had been true of its relations with Latin America as well as in the Far East. Consequently, for the United States to attempt to get a slice of the "Chinese melon" would have been for it to make a violent departure from its past policy. The departure would have been even more marked if adopted in China than if adopted elsewhere, because after 1842 the government of the United States had almost uniformly urged the necessity of maintaining the territorial integrity of China. For a long time it had been fearful lest England should add materially to her colonial territory at the expense of the Celestial Empire and had scrutinized carefully and critically every move the English made in the Far East. Later, when Burlingame was minister, he, and through him the United States, took the lead in establishing a policy of coöperation founded upon a common recognition of the need for strengthening and preserving China as a state.

The third alternative remained, but it had to be given some concrete expression. The general lines to be followed were clear. The broad interest of the United States continued to be the preservation of China from territorial disintegration. But a series of moves had already been made in the opposite direction, and it would take more than wordy protests to restore to the Chinese Empire control of the territory lost through the leasehold agreements, and to persuade the European states to relinquish the economic privileges secured at the same time. If there had been the will to act, this might have been accomplished by a union of forces on the part of the trading states, England, Germany, the United States, and possibly Japan. But Germany had played a prominent rôle in the scramble for concessions, and so had England, by the time the American government awakened to the necessity for action. England did semi-officially express the desire for coöperation, but on the basis of joint control by the coöperating Powers of the Chinese army and of the finances of the country. Such a coöperation was not acceptable to the United States, so that Secretary Hay was compelled to formulate a policy independently. This policy was outlined in the famous "Open Door" circular.

7. THE POLICY OF THE "OPEN DOOR"

On September 6, 1899, notes were sent for transmission to the governments of England, France, Italy, Germany, Russia, and Japan, asking each to give "formal assurances and lend its coöperation in securing like assurances from other interested Powers, that each, within its respective sphere of whatever influence: First. Will in no way interfere with any treaty port or any vested interest within any so-called 'sphere of interest' or leased territory it may have in China. Second. That the Chinese treaty tariff of the time being shall apply to all merchandise landed or shipped to all such ports as are within said 'sphere of interest' (unless they be 'free ports'), no matter to what nationality it may belong, and that duties so leviable shall be collected by the Chinese government. Third. That it will levy no higher harbor dues on vessels of another nationality frequenting any port in such 'sphere' than shall be levied on vessels of its own nationality, and no higher railroad charges over lines built, controlled, or operated within its 'sphere' than shall be levied on similar merchandise belonging to its own nationals transported over equal distances." [11] Thus the policy of the United States was to accept the existing status, including the claims of the several states to spheres of interest, and the establishment of the leaseholds, and to secure a definition of the attitude of each within its sphere so as to ensure therein complete equality of commercial opportunity for the citizens of the United States. The "open door" policy was one of commercial self-interest, and as actually formulated and expressed it was not in any direct way founded upon the desire to preserve the independence and the integrity of China. It accepted the sphere of interest conception and might be construed to accept also the logical end of the development of the conception, annexation of Chinese

[11] V, MOORE's *Digest of International Law*, 535. (Taken from note to German government.)

territory, provided American trading rights in the annexed region were fully safeguarded.

The two conceptions,—that of "spheres of interest" and of the "open door" or equality of commercial opportunity,—are, however, fundamentally inconsistent and incompatible. The chief purpose of the establishment of a sphere of interest is to secure, as far as possible, exclusive rights to obtain concessions for the building of railroads, the opening of mines, and the industrial exploitation of the region marked out.[12] Furthermore, as the sphere of interest merges gradually into a sphere of influence, or into a protectorate, the state gaining political control almost invariably uses its control or influence to monopolize the economic development of the area so far as it can with profit to itself. In other words, the "open door" policy, if it is maintained, works a limitation and modification of the sphere conception and ultimately demands its own extension to include the preservation of the independence and the territorial and administrative integrity of such a country as China, in order to preserve equality of commercial opportunity.

Two Powers were primarily interested in safeguarding China as a whole as a market for their goods and as a field for the investment of their capital. The interest of the United States lay in the future, as her actual trade interests in China were not so great in 1899 as to demand strong action for their preservation. On the other hand, British commercial interests were actual rather than potential, immediate rather than lying in the future. These interests were not confined to one part of the Empire, but had been developed in the north and the south as well as in the central part of the country. Consequently Great Britain stood to lose more by a restriction of her trade to one part of the Chinese Empire than she stood to gain by a recognition of the priority of her interest even in such a vast region as that comprised in her sphere. This the British traders in China clearly recognized. The British government, however, let the opportunity for an effective protest against the staking out of "spheres" pass and then tried to protect itself by demanding compensation. The South African trouble, coming to a crisis just when it did, the trouble with France over Egyptian affairs, culminating in Fashoda, and the desire to conciliate the German government, all played a part in weakening the British resistance to the China policy of the several continental European states at this time.

But when the American government took the stand it did, the British,[13]

[12] To this should be added the desire to establish a claim to the territory in case of a possible partition of China among the Powers.

[13] There was an indirect British influence in the formulation of the Hay circular through Mr. Hippesley, an English subject who was an officer of the Chinese Maritime Customs Service. For an account of the formulation of the doctrine see GRISWOLD, *The Far Eastern Policy of the United States*, ch. 2. His conclusions as to the British influence on American policy, however, seem somewhat exaggerated.

recognizing in the Hay proposals a revival of their own China policy of the years 1860–1885, gladly gave the promises requested, stipulating, however, that their promises be considered to be conditional on similar promises being made by the other Powers.[14] The German government had already indicated its intention of allowing the Chinese tariff to govern the importation of goods into its leasehold, negotiating to that end with the Inspector-General of the Imperial Maritime Customs service. It gave freely the other pledges requested. France, Italy, and Japan also gave full assent to the Hay proposals.

Russia, however, while couching her reply in terms that enabled Secretary Hay to consider it an acceptance, did not give as unequivocal pledges as did the other governments. Preliminary steps had already been taken to incorporate Talienwan into the Russian customs union, and Port Arthur had been closed to the vessels of countries other than China and Russia, and was rapidly being turned into a strongly fortified naval base. Thus, while Russia took steps to make Talienwan a free port so far as its being opened to trade was concerned, she merely promised that if "at some future time that port, although remaining free itself, should be separated by customs limits from other portions of the territory in question, the customs duties would be levied, in the zone subject to the tariff, upon all foreign merchandise without distinction as to nationality."[15] "Foreign" meant non-Russian, so that the statement cannot be construed as other than an equivocation. Furthermore, nothing was said in the Russian reply as to the Russian attitude or policy with regard to railroad rates and the other matters mentioned in the Hay circular.

The acceptance of the Hay principles by the Powers temporarily checked the movement toward the partition of China at the first stage of its development. The reaction of the Chinese government and people toward this foreign aggression, however, brought the question of the extinction of Chinese national life again to the front. The lesson of the Sino-Japanese War and the years immediately following was, fundamentally, that China must so reorganize herself that she could successfully defend herself against attacks from the outside. The government's policy in the past had been to rely for the defense of the country upon the lack of harmony of interest among the European Powers. Russia's aggressive tendencies, for example, would be held in check, it was thought, by Great Britain. One Power could be so played off against another as to safeguard China. This "balance of power" theory, however, broke down in the face of the revelation of China's weakness, and of the bringing into play of the sphere conception. A Russian alliance, it is true, was accepted to secure China against Japan. But the

[14] This condition was also put by the other Powers on their acceptance of Secretary Hay's proposals.
[15] V. Moore's *Digest*, 545.

German demand for a leasehold, and the acquiescence of the other states in the advance she made, changed the situation materially. The Russian alliance did not cover European aggression, and China found no one to give her active support in the face of the German threat. The "balance of power" idea was invoked, certainly, but to the entire disadvantage of China, since each Power demanded compensation for gains made by the others in order that the "balance" should be preserved. Ultimately the action of a foreign state, the United States, did bring some external support to China, but only after the active contestants had stopped to take stock of the situation.

8. THE "HUNDRED DAYS" OF REFORM

These successive shocks, coupled with the gradual infiltration of new ideas, produced a reform party and gave it its brief moment on the metropolitan stage. Almost all of the advocates of reform came from the Yangtse and southern provinces. The individual reformer who came to be best known outside of China was Dr. Sun Yat-sen, a revolutionary Cantonese whose father has been represented to have been a Christian convert, and who was himself a Christian who had been educated along Western lines at foreign institutions in Hawaii and Hongkong. Dr. Sun led a revolutionary attempt against Canton in 1895, which was unsuccessful. As a result of it he had to flee the country with a price on his head. A more important figure in the early reform movement, however, was K'ang Yu-wei, known at the time as the "modern sage." He also was from Kwangtung province, but he differed from Dr. Sun in that he was not a revolutionary but advocated the gradual establishment of a constitutional monarchy and immediate reform of the existing machinery of government. Among the officials two stood out prominently as interested in reform. These were the Yangtse Viceroys, Chang Chih-tung and Liu Kun-yi. The former attracted much attention to the need for reorganization by his book "Learn," [16] which committed him definitely, for the time, to the cause of reform. Many of the younger officials, both Manchu and Chinese, also sympathized with the advocates of change, at least until they perceived that reform could come only at the expense of the privileges of the official and literate classes.

The reform party, Cantonese in its leadership and principal support, would not have been able to inaugurate its program when it did, however, if it had not been for conditions at the Imperial Court. The Emperor, Kuang Hsü, had attained his majority some years before, and the "Old Buddha" had retired to the Summer Palace. But the change in control was more nominal than real. Most of the important officials looked to her in her retirement for direction, and she did not hesitate to interfere in affairs of state when she felt moved to do so. The most important faction at Court,

[16] Translated as *China's Only Hope*.

the so-called "northern party," did not conceal its belief that she should resume the Regency. The other, or southern, party, headed by the Emperor's Grand Tutor, seemed to its leaders to be losing ground in 1898. For some years this group had been moving away from the Empress-Dowager and toward support of the Emperor. Its Peking leaders were not reformers, but they were gradually forced into support of the reform movement as part of the struggle to maintain themselves in the contest for power at the Court.

The Emperor himself showed leanings toward reform after the war with Japan. He then revealed an interest in Western ideas, institutions, and practices which indicated that he would not be difficult to convert if once brought into direct contact with the leaders of the party of change. This was not accomplished until June, 1898, when K'ang Yu-wei was introduced to the Emperor by his tutor, Weng Tung-ho, who was probably led to take this step because of the death of Prince Kung, his strongest supporter in the clientele of the Empress-Dowager. Prince Kung was a leading Manchu statesman of moderate views, who served for many years as a "balance wheel" at Peking, restraining both the Empress and the Emperor from following extreme counsels.

The Emperor came under the dominance of K'ang Yu-wei immediately and embarked at once on a program of reform under his direction. During the summer of 1898 a number of edicts [17] were issued making changes in the educational and examination systems, establishing a translation bureau, abolishing numerous sinecures, promoting reorganization of the military forces, and undertaking numerous other reforms.

From the first there was serious opposition to the activities of the Emperor. As time went on the opposition became more intense, and finally the Empress-Dowager was moved to intervene. The reformers had feared this possibility, and they now urged the Emperor to safeguard himself and the cause by moving against the old Buddha. Toward the last he was persuaded to act. Yüan Shih-k'ai, former Chinese Resident at Seoul and later President of the Chinese Republic, who was supposed to be sympathetic to reform, was called into the councils of the reformers. He was appointed as Viceroy of Chihli province, and was instructed to proceed to Tientsin, put himself at the head of the troops there, march on the Summer Palace, and seize the Empress-Dowager. Instead, he united forces with the Manchu Viceroy Jung Lu, his "sworn" brother, who was a relative and a devoted supporter of Tzu Hsi. Under her orders he seized the Emperor, who was kept in confinement until his death ten years later. This brought the first attempt at reform to an end. K'ang Yu-wei escaped from Peking and took up his residence in Japan, whence he carried on a campaign for the introduction of constitutional monarchy into China. Many of his followers also escaped, but others were captured and killed. The entire period of reform

[17] List of edicts given by MORSE, vol. III, pp. 137–139.

extended over just one hundred days. Its failure threw control into the hands of the conservatives and paved the way for a fundamentally different reaction to the situation.

The reform movement was a reaction against the ineffectiveness of Manchu rule in the face of the changed conditions of life and the active aggressions of the Powers. Discontent had been manifested almost from the beginning of the century. It was especially pronounced during its third quarter, when only their own ineptitude and foreign support of the Imperial government prevented the T'ai P'ing leaders from overturning the dynasty. Rioting, piracy, brigandage—all of these were present on a wide scale in the last half of the century. The government had suffered defeat at the hands of foreign states in 1842, 1858–1860, and 1884–1885. Finally it proved unable to preserve its dominions even against invasion by the Japanese. Many of the officials were corrupt or incompetent or both; funds which should have been used for national defense had been diverted to private uses and court pleasures; offices were bought and sold, the traffic leading direct to the Chief Eunuch and through him to the Empress-Dowager. The indictment of the Manchus as rulers, and of their officials, was severe and deserved, and the swelling tide of discontent should have been directed against them. But the actions of the foreigners from 1869 to 1899 redirected popular hostility. The first internal reaction to the "cutting of the Chinese melon" was the attempt to strengthen the power of China to resist external encroachments by reorganization and reform on Western lines. This movement failed, as has been pointed out, by reason of the internal conditions that had made it possible. When the conservatives came back into control they had only one solution to present—a restoration of the former condition of isolation. "Get rid of the foreigners and all difficulties will have been overcome," became their slogan. It is easy to see, when the events of the years 1840–1899 are recalled, why they were able to divert attention from the shortcomings of the rulers by stimulating anti-foreignism.

9. THE BOXER MOVEMENT

As a matter of fact, they had only to take advantage of an already marked popular feeling. The year 1899 saw anti-foreign outbreaks in all parts of the country. The previous actions of the Powers would serve fully to explain these outbreaks, but it may be well to examine the causes of friction more closely to see why they became as much anti-Christian as anti-foreign. The obvious explanation would be that the foreigners called themselves Christians and that the missionary work in the interior emphasized this relationship. But the initial outbreaks were caused by and directed against native Christians even more than foreigners. Thus one explanation of the growth of hostility is to be found in the status and conduct of the convert and in the missionary's position with respect to him and to the non-Christian. The converts were considered renegades who sought foreign aid and a privileged status by embracing Christianity. They not only practiced strange rites, which in itself aroused occasional antagonism, but, of much more importance, they abandoned some of the ways of the past, and showed insufficient respect for the teachings of the sages. This was considered a direct consequence of their acceptance of foreign teachings. Of still more practical importance, they often refused to help defray the expenses connected with village entertainments and festivals, putting the refusal on the ground that the festivals were pagan and offensive to their new belief. Since these celebrations were community affairs, and since they constituted one of the few forms of relief from the general monotony of village life, it is not surprising that any opposition to them created friction. Furthermore the withdrawal of support by some increased the financial burden for the others. In addition to this, it may be suspected that in his contact with his fellows the convert on occasion assumed an attitude of superior morality on account of his new faith. Where this was the case it could not help but be offensive to those who felt no inferiority attaching to them for clinging to the old and tried beliefs.

Added to these causes of friction was the popular belief, still strong in 1900 in the interior parts of the country, that the Christian indulged in strange orgies and inhuman practices, such as plucking out the eyes of children. The fact that such charges were found baseless wherever investigated did not detract from their force in arousing hostility to Christians.

But perhaps as serious as any cause of trouble was the fact that the Roman Catholic priests often, and Protestant missionaries sometimes, intervened in litigation in behalf of their converts, seeking to throw the mantle of the special position of the foreigner around them. The priests went a step further and demanded magisterial honors in their intercourse with officials. This added to the hostility of many officials and aroused that of others, causing them to connive at persecution of converts and attacks on missionaries.

Thus it is easy to explain the outbreaks of 1899–1900 in terms of the private as well as the public relations of Christians, both native and foreign, and the Chinese. Join to this the aggressions of the Powers and the fear thereby engendered of the partition of China, and the development of anti-foreignism is readily understandable. Of course the movement of the Powers on China was checked in 1899, but as the attempt was made in that year and in 1900 to put into effect concessions secured earlier, the consequences of the events of 1897–1898 were driven more fully home to the people.

The initial unrest showed itself first in the provinces, although the situation in Peking became so serious in 1899 that the legation guards were augmented for a time. Chinese friends told the foreigners openly that there was a concerted move on foot to eliminate them and their influence from the country. They refused to heed the warnings, however, regarding such action as inconceivable. Protests of course were addressed to the Tsungli Yamen against occurrences in the various parts of the country. But no serious attention was paid to the storm clouds which were gathering until May, 1900, when a stronger force than before was brought to Peking to guard the legations.

The anti-foreign movement gained greatest headway in Shantung province. Report after report came to the legations in Peking of outrages committed by organized groups, of which the strongest and best known was the "Society of Harmonious Fists" or Boxers. Boxerism spread from Shantung to Chihli province, and early in 1900 members of the society began to practice their rites in Peking. From their first appearance they had strong support at the Court, as also among the officials in the provinces, but it was not until the siege of the legations had commenced that the Court finally threw its official support to the side of Boxerism. The formal relation of the government to the inception of the movement has never been fully established, but that it was committed to Boxerism in its final stages is perfectly clear.

As the Boxers assumed more control in Peking the legations were put in what may be described as a state of semi-siege, communication with the outside being largely cut off. In consequence of this the attempt was made to bring in an additional force for the protection of foreigners. While Admiral Seymour's column was on the road from Tientsin the decision was made by the commanders of the foreign squadrons which had been sent to north China, the Americans alone dissenting, to force the road to Tientsin. The Taku forts were consequently bombarded. This precipitated in fact a state of war between the foreign governments and China and had much to do with bringing the Imperial troops and the Court into open cooperation with the Boxer forces. It was largely responsible, for that reason, for the failure of the Seymour expedition to reach Peking. It also reacted to the disadvantage of those in the legations, since the semi-siege conditions were thereafter transformed into a fully organized attack on the legations.

The siege of the legations continued from June to August, 1900, when an allied expeditionary force relieved the beleaguered foreigners. This produced the collapse of Boxerism throughout the country. The officials of the Yangtse region and the southern provinces had refused to participate in the movement and had kept down manifestations of anti-foreignism in the face of Court orders to "drive the foreigners into the sea," so that it was only the north over which the allied expedition had to gain control. Consequently the uprising of 1900 cannot be considered a truly national movement.

10. THE CONSEQUENCES OF BOXERISM

When the allied troops approached Peking the Court fled from the capital, as it had in 1860 under similar circumstances, and the foreigners were left in control. The question of the future of China was thus raised again in an acute form. There seemed to be presented to the foreign Powers three possible alternative policies. They might complete the partition of China along the lines indicated in the years after the war with Japan; they might establish a new dynasty with international support; or they might bring the Manchus back to Peking and support them in an attempt to reorganize, modernize, and strengthen the government.

The United States took the lead in persuading the other states to accept the third alternative, thus adding eleven unearned years to the life of the dynasty. In the midst of the siege of the Legations, Secretary of State John Hay, in a circular letter to our representatives abroad, declared that: "the policy of the United States is to seek a solution which may bring about permanent safety and peace to China, preserve Chinese territorial and administrative entity, protect all rights guaranteed to friendly powers by treaty and international law, and safeguard for the world the principle of equal and impartial trade with the Chinese Empire." [18] He also declared for coöperative action by the Powers to reach a settlement with the Chinese government. This declaration of policy was a complete reversion to that established in 1857 and given formal expression in the coöperative policy of Anson Burlingame. The American principles were finally accepted by the other states, which proceeded, after the relief of the legations, to formulate their demands on the Chinese government in common, although not in entire harmony. It was this lack of harmony, rather than the unwillingness of the Chinese to reach a settlement, which protracted the negotiations into the summer of 1901, when the Boxer protocol was finally signed and the trouble officially brought to an end.

The net results to China of her attempt to get rid of foreigners were: 1) the acceptance of an indemnity charge of 450,000,000 taels, secured on the Maritime Customs and the Salt Gabelle, which seriously complicated her financial problems; 2) the raising of the customs charges to an effective five per cent, solely in order that she might be able to meet the indemnity payments, and a further change of the duties from a partially *ad valorem* to a completely specific basis; 3) the punishment by death or in other ways of some of her officials; 4) the permanent quartering of foreign troops in her capital as legation guards, and the foreign policing of the area from Peking to the sea; 5) the establishment of a Foreign Office to replace the Tsungli Yamen, and a revision, in the foreign interest, of the ceremonial to be used

[18] V, Moore's *Digest*, p. 482.

in case of audiences with the Emperor; 6) the suspension of the examinations for five years in all cities where anti-foreign outbreaks had occurred; and 7) the prohibition of the importation of arms for two years, extended by two-year periods if and as long as the foreigners desired. These were among the formal terms of settlement.

From the point of view of future development the collapse of this conservative reaction to the movement of the Powers on China had the further important consequences of inaugurating an era of conservative reform in the endeavor to strengthen China and preserve the dynasty, and of producing a significant redirection of the European impact on the Celestial Empire.

REFERENCES FOR FURTHER STUDY

LORD C. BERESFORD, *Break-up of China* (1899); presents a semi-official view of British policy and attitude, J. O. P. BLAND AND E. BACKHOUSE, *China under the Empress-Dowager* (1914), ch. 10–17; an account from Chinese sources of the Reform and Boxer movements. CHANG CHIH-TUNG, *China's Only Hope* (1900), transl. by S. I. Woodbridge; a plea for reform by one of the ablest of the Viceroys. P. H. CLEMENTS, *The Boxer Rebellion, a Political and Diplomatic Review,* in Columbia University Studies, vol. LXVI, No. 3; a good study of the diplomatic aspects of the movement (1915). P. H. CLYDE, *International Rivalries in Manchuria* (1926), ch. 3–4; a thorough diplomatic study. TYLER DENNETT, *Americans in Eastern Asia* (1922), ch. 32–33; the best account of American policy. *Foreign Relations for 1901,* and appendix, *Affairs in China,* give the Conger and Rockhill correspondence, and contain much valuable material on the Boxer movement and the negotiations for settlement. A. W. GRISWOLD, *The Far Eastern Policy of the United States* (1938), ch. 1; the most recent study based in part on unpublished American documents. SIR ROBERT HART, *These from the Land of Sinim* (1901); comments on Boxerism, its causes and possible solutions by the well-informed head of the Imperial Maritime Customs. S. K. HORNBECK, *Contemporary Politics in the Far East* (1916), ch. 12–13; contains an excellent summary and interpretation of the scramble for concessions and the open door policy. HU SHIH, *K'ang Yu-wei,* in Encyc. of the Social Sciences, vol. 8, p. 537. P. JOSEPH, *Foreign Diplomacy in China, 1894–1900* (1928); a careful treatment based on an examination of the diplomatic documents published since the war. J. V. A. MACMURRAY, *Treaties and Conventions with and Concerning China* (1921), pp. 35–200; for texts of agreements. H. F. MACNAIR, *Modern Chinese History, Selected Readings* (1923), ch. 13. R. S. McCORDOCK, *British Far Eastern Policy, 1894–1900,* New York (1931); a careful study. J. B. MOORE, *Digest of International Law,* vol. 5, pp. 533–552, for "open door" negotiations and agreements; 476–529 for American position during Boxer uprising and negotiations. H. B. MORSE, *International Relations of the Chinese Empire,* vol. 3 (1918), ch. 5–14; excellent treatment of the movement of the Powers on China, the 1898 reform movement, the Boxer uprising and the settlement. T. W. OVERLACH, *Foreign Financial Control in China* (1919); a valuable analysis of the establishment of the spheres of interest. P. S. REINSCH, *World Politics* (1900), part II, ch. 2–4; an interesting study of the movement on China in relation to world politics. A. J. SARGENT, *Anglo-Chinese Commerce and Diplomacy* (1907), ch. 9, 11. G. N. STEIGER, *China and the Occident: the Origin and Development of the Boxer Movement* (1927); the best and most comprehensive account. CH'UN-LIU T'AN, *The Boxer Catastrophe* (1955). W. W. WILLOUGHBY, *Foreign Rights and Interests in China,* 2 vols. (1927); a careful analysis and authoritative treatment. COUNT SERGE WITTE, *Memoirs* (1921), ch. 4; a Russian account of the negotiation of the treaty of alliance and the railway concessions. EN TSUNG YEN, *The Open Door Policy* (1923); from the point of view of a Chinese student of the question.

CHAPTER VIII

THE RUSSO-JAPANESE WAR

I. RUSSIA AND JAPAN NATURAL ANTAGONISTS

TEN years after the outbreak of hostilities between China and Japan, the latter found itself engaged in war with a much more powerful antagonist. Japan's success, instead of leaving her supreme in Korea, had the effect of substituting for the decaying Chinese Empire in the struggle for control at Seoul a far more dangerous opponent. Russian influence was re-introduced into Korean affairs immediately after the signature of the treaty of Shimonoseki, and Japan found herself forced to share the position of dictator to the Korean government with that ever-expanding Power. Furthermore, the aftermath of the war, the struggle for concessions in China, had resulted in the establishment of a claimed sphere of interest for Russia in Manchuria, and the leasing of a port and the building of a strong naval base in the Liaotung peninsula, so located as to enable Russia to threaten both Peking and Seoul. This Russian advance was of such a nature as seriously to alarm Japan, causing her inevitably to become the primary opponent of Russia in the Far East.

It is to this developing conflict of interest that we now turn our attention. As indicated, it involved two separate regions—Korea and Manchuria—and it will be best to treat the problems centering in these two areas separately. It will be most convenient, and will furnish the clearest approach to the problem, if we consider first of all the interests of Japan and Russia in Korea and Manchuria; then trace the development of Russian interests and policy in Manchuria in some detail and indicate the various steps taken by the Powers to check her move southward from Siberia; and finally turn our attention to the struggle of Japan to maintain herself in Korea.

2. THE STATUS OF MANCHURIA IN 1900

It will be of advantage, however, preliminary to this, to consider the status of Manchuria in the Chinese Empire before it became a center of international interest. Situated in the northeastern part of China, although cut off from the eighteen provinces of China proper by the Great Wall, Manchuria includes a total area of 365,000 square miles, lying within the parallels of 39° and 53° 30′ north. The climate is very cold in winter and hot in the summer, becoming ever more rigorous as one moves northwards. In spite of the severe climate, however, most parts of the region are very productive. The principal crop in 1895 was the soya bean, large quantities of which were exported south into China. It was only after 1890 that Japan began to import Manchurian beans, the bean being used for food purposes, the oil for sauces, and the cake for fertilizer. From that time she became an increasingly important market for it. In addition Manchuria produces millet, kaoliang, wheat, and other cereals. By 1900 it was already evident that the country could be looked to as a great granary for the future. In addition to its agricultural productivity Manchuria possesses tremendous wealth in timber and is rich in minerals, including coal, iron, and gold. Such a domain was well worth a struggle to gain or to retain.

From the point of view of politics and government Manchuria differed from Korea in that it was an integral part of the Chinese Empire, governed directly from Peking. Furthermore, since the ruling dynasty in China had come from there, the territory had a peculiar interest for it. Because of this interest the Manchu policy had long been to keep their Chinese subjects out of the region north of the Great Wall. But by 1900 this policy had broken down and settlers from Shantung and Chihli provinces had populated the land so extensively that the Manchus were decidedly in the minority. It is to these Chinese immigrants that credit must be given for the economic development of the country.

From every point of view, then,—legal title to the territory, predominance of population, and credit for economic development—Manchuria was as much a part of China as any of the eighteen provinces. Russia, in other words, was seeking, after 1895, to detach part of the Chinese Empire, and Japan was playing the game of China so far as she was interested merely in checking Russian aggression.

The region which aroused so much interest after 1900 was divided into three parts for governmental purposes. In the south was Fengtien province, including, prior to 1898, the Kwantung, or Liaotung, promontory. This was the most thickly settled and the most highly developed part of Manchuria, and had been brought under the usual Chinese civil administration. To the north lay Kirin province, less settled and kept under the Manchu military régime; and still further north lay the almost totally undeveloped province of Heilungkiang. The movement of population was naturally from the south northwards and was, no less naturally, a gradual one. It was, however, a Chinese movement, as no Russian settlers had come down from the north, across the Russian frontier, except as they were brought in to serve the railway or as soldiers. This remained true even to the time of the outbreak of war with Japan.

3. RUSSIA IN MANCHURIA

The Russian interest in Manchuria and Korea must be considered, therefore, as political and strategic rather than economic. Prior to the occupation of Port Arthur and Dalny (Talienwan), there was, to be sure, an economic motive underlying the Russian advance. Russian policy during the years from 1896 to 1899 was designed to facilitate the completion of the Trans-Siberian Railroad by securing a right of way across northern Manchuria, and to bring about a peaceful economic penetration of China. Back of this economic penetration, however, there was a political motive. Russia had no great trading or financial interests urging that the government secure privileges for them. But the government was interested in the building of railroads and the furtherance of other Russian interests in Manchuria and China in the hope that ultimately, upon the disintegration of the Chinese Empire, or even without its complete disintegration, large sections might be brought into the Russian state as a result of a previous economic attachment to it.

After the scramble for concessions began, however, the idea of peaceful penetration gave way before the prospect of an immediate partition of China among the Powers. Instead of living up to its expressed intention [1] of protecting China, the Russian government acquired Chinese territory—by lease only, it is true—and instead of utilizing her new territory for commercial purposes she proceeded to make of Port Arthur the strongest naval base in the East, closing it altogether to commerce, although leaving Dalny a commercial port. From this time Russian policy in Manchuria became more and more one of direct aggression, marked by the attempt to assume governmental functions. That this was not altogether to the liking of some of the Russian statesmen is revealed by Count Witte in his Memoirs. But he also shows that political expansion was behind the several Russian moves on the Manchurian chess-board. Russia wanted the Liaotung peninsula in order that she might have a warm-water port for the use of her fleet; she built railroads in Manchuria with the domination of that area in view; and after 1900 she tried in every possible way to detach Manchuria from the control of Peking. In short, her policy was one of deliberate aggression on a state to which she was united by a mutually defensive alliance.

If the Russian interest in Manchuria was, at least in its origin, partly economic, in Korea her policy was entirely political. She had no trading interests there worth mentioning and no territorial contact with Korea except that at the southern end of the maritime province. Furthermore, she had no goods for which a market was necessary and no surplus capital demanding an outlet under the national protection. Any moves Russia made to establish herself in Korea must be considered as signs of an aggressive intention, and of an aggression in no way necessitated by the economic needs of the Russian Empire.

---

[1] The obligation had only been assumed to protect China against Japan, but China was justified in assuming at least that Russia herself would not try to seize her territories.

4. THE JAPANESE INTEREST

While the primary interest of Russia was in Manchuria, that of Japan was in Korea. In that country she had built up substantial commercial and financial interests. And, as has been pointed out,[2] she had a natural self-protective interest in preventing Korea from falling into the hands of any other Power, especially such a strong and naturally expansive state as Russia. The comparison of Korea with a dagger pointed at the heart of Japan had real significance when the hand holding the dagger threatened to be that of Russia.

The Japanese economic interest in Manchuria was, prior to 1905, potential rather than actual. The Japanese had begun to import the principal Manchurian product, the soya bean, and far-sighted Japanese statesmen undoubtedly appreciated the future possibility of drawing raw materials, as well as an enlarged supply of foodstuffs, from Manchuria. But at the beginning of the twentieth century the food problem in Japan had not become acute and industrial development was just commencing. This development had been stimulated by the war with China and still further advanced by the indemnity payment secured as one of the conditions of peace. In the four years following 1900 Japan certainly began to show signs of change from an agricultural to an industrial base, but it was particularly after the war with Russia that the tendency became marked. Thus Manchuria was not an area in which Japan had existing economic interests of any importance. Her potential interest, however, would help to explain the Japanese attitude toward the development of Russia's exclusive policy.

It is also necessary to guard against reading into the Japanese policy in 1904 the interest (which developed later) in Manchuria as a colonizing area in which a surplus population might be settled. Both economic interest and the need of an outlet for her surplus population may perhaps be accepted in partial explanation of Japan's policy after 1905, but they did not greatly influence it during the development of the conflict with Russia.

There were two much more fundamental reasons for Japanese action up to 1905. As early as 1895 the Japanese government had shown a desire to expand territorially on the Asiatic mainland when it had demanded the cession of the Liaotung peninsula. This indicates an aggressive tendency, which was restrained only temporarily by the Three-Powers' intervention. Japan wanted a foothold in Manchuria just as much as Russia did and possibly for the same reason—empire building. But since she could not hold it she was content to accept the *status quo*. The establishment of Russia in Manchuria, however, disturbed that status and at the same time threatened Japanese security. Every advance made by Russia brought her into

[2] Supra, pp. 137–138.

closer contact with Korea and, through Korea, with Japan. Aggressive Russia on the Korean border and at Port Arthur menaced Japan indirectly through a threat to her position in Korea and directly because of her closer proximity. Consequently, while Japan could afford to forego Manchuria, which she would have liked to possess herself, rather than embark on an expensive war for its control, she would fight rather than see a strong European Power entrenched therein, unless at the same time her position in Korea was fortified. In pursuance of this policy she showed a willingness to compromise with Russia, in order to avoid war, if Russia would recognize her supremacy in Korea; this compromise Russia rejected. It must be observed, therefore, that it was the Russian advance toward the south which made war with Japan inevitable, even though it is true that Japan had an ultimate interest in Manchuria similar to that of Russia.

5. RUSSIAN POLICY IN AND AFTER 1900

The interests of Russia in Manchuria in 1900, at the time of the Boxer uprising, may be briefly summarized, since they have already been partially described. As a reward for her leadership in the intervention which had restored the Liaotung peninsula to China, Russia had been granted the right to construct the Trans-Siberian Railroad across northern Manchuria from the Chinese village of Manchuli to Vladivostok. By a later convention she had been given, in addition, the right to drop a branch of this line southwards from Harbin to Port Arthur. China's participation in the construction and operation of these roads was limited to the investment of five million taels in the Russo-Chinese Bank, which was brought into being in 1896 under a Russian charter to finance the construction of the railroad, and to the appointment of the president of the railroad company. The duty of the president was to supervise the operations of both the bank and the company to see that they did not overstep the bounds of their authority under the concession agreements.

The Russo-Chinese Bank was purely a Russian concern so far as its incorporation and control were concerned. In addition to financing the various projects conceded to it by the Chinese government, it was empowered to bring into being a corporation for the construction of the railroads and for their operation after completion. The company building and operating the Manchurian section of the Trans-Siberian Railroad was known as the Chinese Eastern Railway Company, and that for the building of the southern projection as the Manchurian Railway Company. Both were controlled and directed by the Russian government as Russian concerns. The money for the financing of the roads was found by the bank, not in Russia, which was borrowing largely abroad for her own needs, but in France. The investor was protected in his rights by a Russian government guarantee instead of by a mortgage on the railroad properties. The other functions of the bank have already been sufficiently described.[3] China was placed under an obligation, by the terms of the several agreements, to protect the railroad properties, but the company had the right to acquire lands necessary for their construction and effective operation, and had "the absolute and exclusive right of administration of these lands."

In addition to these railroad rights in Manchuria, Russia had the lease in the Liaotung peninsula which has been mentioned. This she had demanded even though she had previously pointed out (at the time of its acquisition by Japan) that the control of this territory by a foreign Power constituted a direct threat to Peking and could not be tolerated. Giving back the territory to China was hard for Japan, but having Russia step into her shoes so soon afterwards created a dangerous situation for her. This was especially true since that Power began immediately to fortify Port Arthur so strongly as to signify an intention of remaining there for a longer period than the twenty-five years of the leasehold. A commercial port under Russian control in the Liaotung peninsula was bad, but a strong naval base was infinitely worse.

It was particularly after 1900, however, that Russia displayed her true intentions in Manchuria. At the time of the Boxer trouble in China unrest developed in Manchuria. Brigands became even more active than usual. The same anti-foreign spirit developed that showed itself in the south, and the Boxers themselves put in an appearance. Consequently Russia took steps to protect her interests by throwing troops into Manchuria to guard the railroad. While the Powers were sending their expedition to relieve the Peking legations, in which expedition Russia took part, Russian troops were spreading out over Manchuria from the railroad zone as a center. The Chinese authority was supplanted for the time by the Russian military command. The other Powers were informed that the Russian occupation was only temporary, since it was made necessary by the inability of the Chinese government to control the Boxers and brigands, and that the troops would be withdrawn and Chinese control restored as soon as protection could be afforded to foreign, i.e., Russian, interests.

In November of 1900 [4] an agreement was reached between the Russian commander and the Chinese Viceroy (Tsêng-Alexieff Convention) by which the southern province (Fengtien) was to be restored to the Chinese civil administration on condition that the Chinese soldiers should be disarmed and disbanded, that all munitions of war should be given up to the Russians, and that all fortifications not in the control of Russia should be demolished. Russian troops were to be withdrawn, however, only when the pacification of the province, in the opinion of the Russian government, had

[3] Supra, p. 148.
[4] Although apparently it was not signed until January 30, 1901.

been completed. Law and order were to be maintained by the local police, with Russian aid if necessary. It is obvious that pacification could not be successfully brought about by a local police when order had not been maintained by the police and the military in combination, and that the forced disarming of the Chinese troops meant continual unrest in the province. This would give Russia the necessary excuse for its continued occupation. This convention was not concluded with the Imperial government but with a local official, and it was never ratified. But its publication caused a stir abroad. This led to a second denial by Russia that she had any aggressive designs in Manchuria. In this denial, however, the Russian government insisted that before it could evacuate Manchuria it would have to receive effective guarantees from China against a renewal of the disorder which had led to the intervention.

Negotiations for the evacuation of Manchuria continued during 1901 and 1902, Russia always conditioning her withdrawal on the acceptance of terms by China which would strengthen Russian political influence there and would make inevitable a second intervention and permanent occupation.

Meanwhile there had been other indications of Russian policy. The Boxer outbreak reached Peking in June of 1900. By August the Powers had relieved the legations, and, since the court had fled to Sianfu, had assumed complete control in north China. This presented an extremely favorable opportunity for the extinction of China by completing the process of division of the Empire among the Powers along the lines marked out in 1898. The United States, however, immediately announced its continued adherence to the policy of the "open door." It further declared its belief that the Powers should open negotiations with the Chinese government on the basis of the maintenance of the independence and territorial and administrative integrity of the Empire. During the negotiations which followed the suppression of the Boxer uprising the United States consistently maintained this attitude, protesting against the Russian occupation of Manchuria, and against the acceptance by China of such conditions of evacuation as those contained in the Tsêng-Alexieff agreement. This protest was reaffirmed from time to time after the signature of the Boxer protocol when later Russian demands made protest necessary.

The Russian policy in Manchuria also led Great Britain and Germany to draw together in alarm at the threat from the north. In 1900 they reached an agreement, to which they invited the adherence of the other Powers. By this they were committed to maintain the *status quo* territorially in China, without seeking to take advantage in their own interest of the disorganization of the Empire; to work for the opening of the entire Empire to the trade of all nations; and to concert the necessary measures for the protection of their interests in case any one state attempted to change the *status quo* in its own interest. The effectiveness of this agreement in checking the

Russian advance in Manchuria was decidely lessened, however, by the construction put upon it by Germany, restricting its scope to include only the eighteen provinces. The agreement, none the less, may be regarded as having been of importance for China. It was, of course, not altruism which prompted this action, but rather a recognition by the trading Powers that their interests demanded the preservation of China, and the fear felt by all that an attempt at partition would result in a grave international crisis.

For Russia conditions after the Boxer uprising offered an exceptional opportunity to fish in troubled waters. Following precedent, she attempted to promote her interests at the expense of China by posing as a friend. After seizing the railroad from Shanhaikwan to Tientsin against the protests of the Americans and the British, she proceeded to insist upon the evacuation of North China by the allied troops before the signature of the peace agreement between China and the Powers. She withdrew her legation to Tientsin, and she urged the return of the Chinese Court to Peking, and absolute non-interference by the Powers in the internal affairs of the Chinese Empire. Naturally she made, so far as this policy was concerned, a distinction between China and Manchuria, insisting that the Manchurian settlement must be the concern solely of herself and China.[5] It may be seen that her intention was to secure herself in Manchuria and strengthen her footing at the Court by appearing otherwise as China's defender against the other Powers. This time, however, she was not as successful as she had been in 1860, when she had secured the Primorsk as a reward for mediating between China and the Anglo-French occupiers of Peking. The Chinese were coming to recognize Russian friendship as a dangerous thing to encourage. And when peace was actually made it was found that Russia had not allowed her consideration for China to go to the length of preventing her from receiving the lion's share of the indemnity of 450,000,000 taels.

After the Boxer uprising had been put down in North China, it soon became apparent that Russia had no intention of retiring from Manchuria except on her own terms. She professed one policy to the maritime Powers, the United States, England, and Japan, who repeatedly protested against the continued presence of her troops north of the Great Wall, but continued steadily to press her terms on Peking. What she desired to do was to present the protesting states with the accomplished fact of an agreement with the Imperial government of China. This she expected to accomplish by insisting that Manchuria was a subject for negotiation only between the Powers concerned—herself and China—and then after securing an agreement to her demands she intended to insist that China as an independent state had the right to make any agreements she liked. She felt confident that no Power would be sufficiently interested or would have the power to make an issue of the matter. That this interpretation of her policy is

[5] A distinction subsequently made and insisted upon also by the Japanese government.

correct is shown by Count Lamsdorff's reply to Secretary Hay's protest against Russia's demand on China for exclusive privileges in Manchuria. Lamsdorff stated that "negotiations carried on between two entirely independent states are not subject to be submitted to the approval of other Powers." China, however, under pressure from, and with the assurance of the support of, England, Japan, and the United States, refused to accept the successive conditions laid down during 1901 by Russia for the evacuation of Manchuria.

6. THE ANGLO-JAPANESE AGREEMENT OF 1902

Then in 1902 an event took place which had an immediate effect on Russian policy and ultimate consequences of great significance. This event was the signature of the Anglo-Japanese agreement. Conversations looking to the conclusion of an agreement respecting their interests and policy in the Far East were begun at London early in 1901. The initial suggestion that negotiations be undertaken came from Germany rather than from either Japan or Great Britain, and was for the making of an alliance among the three Powers. The exact reason for the German proposal is not clear, but she had been coöperating with England financially in the years after 1895, and had entered into an agreement with her in 1900 to protect the *status quo* in China. Consequently it would seem that there was at Berlin a recognition of the similarity of German and British interest in the Far East. Furthermore, after 1900 there was an influential group in Germany interested in bringing about a *rapprochement* with England. But the constant shifting of German policy at this time is indicated by her insistence on restricting the scope of the 1900 agreement to exclude Manchuria from its guarantees. She showed indications of wanting to coöperate with England, but not to the point of antagonizing Russia. And English and Japanese interests could be protected only by adopting a strong attitude toward Russia's Manchurian policies. Thus while Germany, for whatever reason, made the suggestion, the negotiations for an alliance were carried to completion with little attempt to draw her into them.

In Japan, after the war of 1894–1895 with China, there were two conceptions of the proper policy to be pursued. One group thought that the best way for Japan to protect herself against the Russian advance was to enter into an alliance with Russia, reaching an agreement with her as to their respective interests in the Far East. The other party inclined toward an alliance with England as the most logical and desirable step to be taken. Among the believers in the desirability of an alliance with England was Count Hayashi, the Japanese minister at the Court of St. James. After the suggestion had been made by the German Ambassador that an agreement might be reached so far as England was concerned, Count Hayashi asked permission from his government to commence informal conversations with the British Foreign Office. These informal discussions eventually were changed into official negotiations, and were carried to a successful conclusion by the end of January, 1902.

The making of an alliance with one of the strongest of the Western states marks a milestone in the development of Japan as an Asiatic Power. It was the first treaty of alliance in modern times between an Occidental and Oriental state in which the two parties were on a footing of equality. More conclusively than any other accomplishment it marked the recognition of Japan and her elevation to a high seat at the Asiatic council board. More immediately important for Japan, however, was the fact that the alliance made it possible to take the necessary steps to protect her interests against Russia. In 1895 she had been forced to recede from the continent at the dictation of the Czar's ministers. In 1904 she would have had to give way again if it had not been for the protection afforded by British support.

That Japan should have wanted an alliance is readily appreciated; but why England should have departed from her policy of refusing to make permanent alliances by entering into an agreement with an Oriental state, is not at first glance obvious. Her interests were menaced by the Russian advance, which could have no other effect ultimately than to lessen the British trade opportunities in Manchuria. But she had recognized the superiority of Russian interest there by the Scott-Muravieff Convention of 1899 in return for a recognition of her position in the Yangtse provinces. It must be recognized, however, that her participation in the scramble for concessions was a departure from her former China policy.[6] That departure was made necessary by the preoccupation in Africa, both in the north and the south, which made it impossible for her to assert herself in the Far East in opposition to the other Powers. Her African difficulties had been largely brought to an end by 1902, however, so that she was free to turn her attention again to China. And between 1899 and 1902 had come the Boxer rebellion, and the Russian move southward which, if allowed to become an accomplished fact, would make Russia dominant at Peking. Furthermore, Russia had not respected the spirit of the agreement of 1899. Belgian capital, well known to represent Russia and France, and actively supported by Russo-French diplomacy, had secured a concession for the construction of a road from Peking to Hankow in the heart of the Yangtse region. This projected Russian influence so far southward that it caused British diplomacy immediately to become apprehensive concerning India. It also brought Russia and France close to union of their respective spheres of interest. Such a union would have meant the end of the Chinese Empire,

[6] Except, of course, for the early acquisition of Hongkong. Her participation was, of course, consistent with her general Asiatic and imperial activities.

since both Powers had political rather than strictly economic aims in their respective spheres. These developments had caused Downing Street to return to its original China policy.

But in order to make that policy effective a combination of forces was required. First of all, England tried Germany, but found that she was not willing to antagonize Russia.[7] France was an ally of Russia, and was herself interested in the further development of the sphere of interest conception. The United States and England had similar interests, but those of the United States were potential, and she was already showing that she could not be relied upon to do more than protest against changes in the *status quo*. Further than this, she would not have been willing to tie herself to any Power even to accomplish her own ends. This attitude she carried to the extent of refusing to participate in joint protests against the Russian policy, although she did send identic notes on several occasions. Japan alone was left. And the interest of Japan in checking Russia was even greater than that of England. Consequently, after considerable hesitation, Great Britain broke from her isolation and signed an agreement which put her behind Japan in case the latter became involved in war with the Russian Empire.

The preamble of the Anglo-Japanese agreement stated the general policy of the High Contracting Parties to be the maintenance of the *status quo* and of general peace in the Far East through the preservation of the independence and territorial integrity of China and Korea. In the first article recognition was given to the fact that the British interest was primarily in China, while Japan, in addition to her interest in China, was peculiarly interested in Korea, these interests in both cases, however, being non-aggressive in character. Each recognized the right of the other to take the steps necessary to the protection of its interests. If, in the defense of its interests, one of the parties to the agreement became engaged in war with another Power, the other would maintain a strict neutrality, and would use its best endeavor to prevent the other belligerent nation from securing support. In case any other Power should join the enemy of one of the members of the alliance, the other agreed to come immediately to its ally's assistance, making war and peace in common with it. The alliance was to run for five years, and, if not denounced at the end of that time, was to continue for a period of one year beyond the time of its denunciation. Thus the agreement meant that Japanese and English diplomacy would work hand in hand at Peking to check Russia, failing in which Japan would oppose her in the field while England prevented Russia from securing active support from any other Power.

Russia and France replied to the challenge by announcing that, while

---

[7] Furthermore, Anglo-German relations in Europe were becoming strained, and England was the only Power in Europe without assured support. The Anglo-Japanese alliance was a significant play on the world stage as well as on the Far Eastern stage.

they were in sympathy with the purpose of the Anglo-Japanese agreement —the preservation of the independence and the integrity of China and Korea—they had agreed to extend the scope of their alliance to cover the Far East. France, however, seems to have let it be known that she would actively support Russia in case war broke out only if the peace were disturbed in Europe.

But in spite of this tacit acceptance of the challenge, Russia immediately modified her policy in Manchuria by accepting the proposals made by China for the evacuation of her territory. These proposals, as finally embodied in the Manchurian Convention of 1902, provided for a complete evacuation of Manchuria within eighteen months, south Manchuria to be evacuated at the end of six months, central Manchuria at the end of twelve months, and the entire territory to be restored to China's control at the end of the period. Some conditions, relating to the method of withdrawal and to the protection by China of Russia's interests, were attached to the agreement to leave, but the joker in it lay in the proviso that Russia would withdraw "provided that no disturbances arise and that the actions of other Powers furnish no obstacle." So long as the Russian troops remained, the prevention of disorder was sure to be difficult, and Russia might easily so construe the actions of other Powers as to give an excuse for the nonfulfillment of the engagement.

As a matter of fact, Russia herself acted in such a way as to justify charges of lack of good faith in the fulfillment of her obligation. Southwestern Manchuria was duly evacuated, but the troops, instead of being withdrawn from Manchuria, were merely concentrated in other parts of the province. Barracks were constructed along the railroad to make provision for them, and Russian action indicated that use would be made of them as railroad guards. In other words, Russia indicated that she would fulfill her engagements only so far as she was compelled to do so by an unremitting pressure strong enough to prevent her from defying it. This pressure had to be supplied by other Powers than China, as the Imperial government could not enforce the terms of the agreement against her northern neighbor.

7. THE KOREAN QUESTION

Besides this indication of bad faith in Manchuria, Russian action in Korea and particularly on the Korean border was becoming alarming. In order to understand this, we must turn to the second field of conflict of Russian and Japanese interest.

During the war with China, and for a short period following that struggle, Japanese interests were in the ascendency at Seoul. During this time the Japanese acted as masters in the Korean kingdom, and they used their mastery to transform Korea, on paper and overnight, from a misgoverned

Oriental despotism into a modern state. Because of the resistance this policy encountered from the Queen and her adherents, the Japanese were led to instigate, and actively participate in, a midnight attack on the Palace, with the result that the Queen, as the focal point of opposition to their policy, was murdered.

This action aroused the Koreans, but they were unable to retaliate immediately. In 1896, however, an uprising occurred on the northern frontier which caused the sending of troops out of the capital city. At the same time a detachment of Russian marines arrived in Seoul from Chemulpo. On the day following the arrival of the Russians the King of Korea fled in disguise from the Palace to the Russian legation, where he was received and given asylum. For a short period the government was directed from the Russian legation. Japanese ascendency, after an eminently successful war, was replaced by that of Russia. She had her own policy to blame, of course, but Russian control was no less distasteful for that reason. In the summer of 1896 Japan abandoned her claim to supremacy in Korea and made an agreement (the Yamagata-Lobanoff Protocol) with Russia by which the two parties were put upon a footing of equality in the kingdom. Both parties agreed: (1) that, withdrawing their forces from the peninsula, they should allow Korea, so far as possible, to police her own territory; and (2) that they should unite in pressing financial reforms on the Korean government, and that, if it needed foreign money to carry out the indispensable reforms, the two governments should "of a common accord render their support to Korea." During the time of her ascendency, however, Russia had secured for herself two concessions, a valuable timber concession on the Yalu River which became of great importance later, and a mining concession on the Tumen River.

Before the ink was fairly dry on the Yamagata-Lobanoff Protocol Russia began to violate its terms. Instead of allowing Korea to reorganize her army unaided, Russia introduced into the kingdom advisers to aid in its organization along Russian lines. She also attempted to obtain control of Korean finance.

As a result of her policy a reaction against Russia set in in Korea, and this brought with it a strengthening of the Japanese position. In the face of the apparent bad faith of Russia, Japan instituted new negotiations with her. Made more conciliatory by her policy in Manchuria, and by the lease she had secured from China in the Liaotung peninsula, which could not but be objectionable to the Japanese, the Russian government agreed, in 1898, to a redefinition of its position in Korea. Recognizing the sovereignty and independence of Korea, each contestant for power agreed not to assist Korea in the reorganization of her army and her finances without having reached a previous agreement with the other party, and the Russian government agreed not to impede the development of Japanese commercial and industrial interests in Korea. This convention (the Nishi-Rosen Convention) remained as the formal basis of Russian and Japanese policy in Korea from 1898 to the outbreak of war.

But while this agreement had been reached, it did not settle the Korean question. Russia remained intermittently active there, pressing demands for concessions on the government and trying to secure a port for her use. Japan worked feverishly to strengthen her position and to check the successive moves made by Russia, and in both aims she was largely successful. The Japanese population increased by leaps and bounds, trade developed enormously, and large sums of money were invested in the Korean railways and other utility enterprises. The only serious competitors to the Japanese were the Americans, and even this competition did not seriously check the establishment of Japan, by 1904, in a dominant economic position. Five years from the signature of the Nishi-Rosen Convention found the Japanese Foreign Minister able to say with truth: "Japan possesses paramount political as well as commercial interests and influence in Korea, which, having regard to her own security, she cannot consent to surrender to or share with any Power." [8]

8. FUSION OF KOREAN WITH MANCHURIAN QUESTION

This position of predominance had been achieved by the time when, in 1902–1903, the Manchurian and Korean questions became fused. Among other expedients resorted to by Russia to dispose of her troops in Manchuria without withdrawing them to Siberia was that of sending them into the Yalu River region as woodcutters to make use of the timber-cutting concession gained in 1896. This concession, by its terms, had lapsed, since Russia had made no attempt to develop it during the five-year period specified in the agreement. This did not, however, prevent her from insisting on its revival. Her insistence was the firmer because the Czar himself had become interested in it, and since he had been persuaded that no effective opposition could be made by Japan.

Japan's Korean and Chinese policies had been kept distinct up to this point. Her policy had been to defend her interests in Korea by her own independent action, and to coöperate with other Powers in Chinese affairs. Now she recognized that she must reach some sort of agreement with Russia which would take both regions into consideration. In 1903 the Japanese minister at St. Petersburg was instructed to ask the Russian government to enter upon discussions with a view to a complete definition of the eastern interests of the two states. Russia agreeing, Japan submitted a series of proposals as a basis for discussion. These proposals may be summarized as follows: (1) that both countries agree to respect the inde-

[8] ASAKAWA, *Russo-Japanese Conflict*, p. 298.

pendence and territorial integrity of China and Korea, and to maintain the "open door" principle in those countries; (2) that Russia recognize Japan's special interests in Korea, and concede her right (a) to develop those interests further, and (b) to give advice to the Korean government in the interest of reform. In return, Japan would recognize Russia's special railway interests in Manchuria and concede her the same right of future development within the limitations of the first stipulation. The Russian counter-proposals provided: (1) for a mutual agreement to respect the independence and integrity of Korea, omitting the similar Japanese proposal as to China; (2) for a Russian recognition of Japan's superior interests in Korea, and of her right to assist in reforming the civil administration; (3) for an engagement by Russia not to interfere with the development and protection of Japanese commercial and industrial interests in the kingdom; (4) for a mutual agreement not to fortify on the coasts of Korea so as to menace freedom of navigation in the Straits of Korea, or to use any Korean territory for strategical purposes; (5) for the erection of the portion of Korea north of the thirty-ninth parallel into a neutral zone; and (6) for "recognition by Japan of Manchuria and its littoral as in all respects outside her sphere of interest." In other words, Japan was to allow Russia a free hand in China and Manchuria, while Russia was to allow Japan to develop only industrial and commercial interests in Korea, a development which Russia had previously shown herself powerless to prevent.

The final Japanese proposals conceded a little to the Russian position, mainly by making the limitations on her action in Korea applicable to Russia in Manchuria, and by recognizing not merely the Russian railway interests in Manchuria but also all of that territory as outside Japan's sphere of interest. Russia, however, refused to recede from her original position until too late. Japan severed diplomatic relations, and the war began in February, 1904.

9. THE RUSSO-JAPANESE WAR

It would be interesting, if space permitted, to dwell on some of the many interesting features of the war. Here was a war fought entirely on the territory of states not parties to the struggle. This made necessary some sort of agreement as to the exact status of Korea and China. The position of the former was easily defined. Japan occupied the peninsula immediately upon her declaration of war, and secured a treaty of alliance from the Korean king. The United States, however, took the lead in the endeavor to protect China by securing the agreement of the belligerents to localize hostilities to Manchuria. If Russian policy had been different from 1896 to 1904, she might easily have averted some of the naval disasters of the war by drawing China in under the terms of their alliance, and making use of her port and other naval facilities. The alliance must be considered to have lapsed, however, as a result of the systematic aggression of the one "ally" on the other. Consequently, under the pressure of foreign opinion, both parties agreed to respect the neutrality of China outside of Manchuria. Each accused the other of violating its pledges from time to time, but on the whole Chinese territory was respected.

Throughout the last stages of negotiation the autocratic Czar of All the Russias apparently assumed that the decision for war or peace rested with him alone—that the Japanese would accept whatever concessions he chose to make rather than resort to war. This feeling, coupled with faulty advices as to the state of Japan's military and naval power, help to explain the fact that Russia resorted to actions which could only result in war and yet made no adequate military preparations for that eventuality.

But beyond this, a satisfactory explanation of the entire Russian policy requires a recognition of the internal conflict at St. Petersburg. Three programs were competing for the favor of the Czar. The Minister of Finance had one program—that of peaceful penetration of Manchuria and China by means of the railway and of capital—which has already been outlined together with the steps taken to put it into effect after 1895. After 1898 appeared the group, identified in view with and represented by the adventurer Bezobrazov, who urged a program of economic activities supported by force. And finally there was the military-naval group, the members of which were interested in securing a Korean port and in gaining military control of Manchuria. The third group was primarily responsible for the throwing of such large bodies of troops into Manchuria in 1900 and for the seizure of the Peking-Mukden railway north of Tientsin. Of course the interests built up in furtherance of Count Witte's program gave the necessary excuse for military intervention. The navalists were also responsible for the contradictions between diplomatic professions and military and political actions (1900–1902), the responsible ministers often being uninformed concerning actions of the military commanders in the Far East which belied their professions, and certainly being unable to control them.

After 1902 the Bezobrazov group, which had been intermittently active since 1898, became dominant in the councils of the Czar, their ascendency being signalized by the dropping of Count Witte from the ministry. Their program involved a combination of pressure with extensive economic adventures, such as the use of the Yalu timber concession. It was this intensification of economic activities both in Manchuria and in Korea, coupled with the indications of bad faith in fulfillment of the Manchurian Convention of 1902, and the dilatoriness of Russia in responding to the Japanese proposals for a definition of interests in Korea and Manchuria, which so alarmed the Japanese government that it took the decision as to peace or war out of the hands of the Czar.

It would also be interesting to dwell on the attitude of the Western states toward the two belligerents. Here only a bare summary may be made. England, of course, was committed to "keeping the ring" for Japan, financing her and generally acting as a "benevolent" neutral. Had it not been for the Anglo-Japanese agreement, and an early intimation from President Roosevelt that the United States would not tolerate intervention, Japan would almost certainly have faced a continental European intervention in support of Russia. As it was, both France and Germany went as far as they dared, without an open departure from neutrality, in support of Russia—France because of the alliance, although she was not at all pleased to see Russia exhausting herself in the Far East and thus weakening her position in Europe, and Germany because she had been steadily encouraging the Russian move eastwards. American bankers supported the external credit of Japan. The people of the United States were entirely sympathetic to the Japanese, as was also President Roosevelt, although neutrality was carefully maintained.

At first sight the war appeared to be between two entirely unmatched antagonists, another case of the giant and the dwarf. But the dwarf again was prepared and the giant was not. Japan had begun to concentrate on naval development immediately after the peace of Shimonoseki, using part of the Chinese indemnity for that purpose, while still not neglecting her army. Consequently, she had a well-trained army and an efficient navy to meet the forces of Russia, more formidable on paper, but poorly led and ill-disciplined. Again Japan began by naval operations to secure her communications. Then she commenced to push the Russian armies back from one position to another until, with the fall of Port Arthur after a long siege and the display of heroism on both sides, and the defeat of Russia at the Yalu and again in the battle of Mukden, Manchuria had been cleared of the Russian invader as far north as Mukden.

10. THE TREATY OF PORTSMOUTH

The war had been a series of uninterrupted successes for Japan, but it had involved great loss of life and a very heavy drain on the national treasury. Furthermore, she had not begun to touch Russia, not even having driven her back on to her own territory, and not having been able to destroy her armies. When President Roosevelt, at the request of Japan, offered his "good offices" to the belligerents in the spring of 1905, the Japanese government, recognizing its inability to continue the struggle much longer, but without giving evidence to its opponent of its weakness, consented to enter upon peace negotiations with the Russians. The Russian government, on the other hand, was desirous of continuing the struggle until it had regained the ground lost, but it was not in a position, because of internal conditions and also on account of its financial weakness, to refuse to go into conference with the Japanese. Accordingly Viscount Komura met Count Witte at Portsmouth in the summer of 1905. The Russians hoped that the Japanese, flushed with victory, would make demands which could reasonably be refused on grounds that would make the opinion of the world more favorable toward Russia and would rally the Russian people to the support of the government in a continuation of the war.

On the face of it that was just what the Japanese did. They demanded: 1) the recognition of the supremacy of Japan in Korea—a recognition which they had already secured from England in the revision of the Anglo-Japanese alliance effected toward the end of the war; 2) the transfer to Japan of the Russian interests, including the leasehold and the railroad, in south Manchuria; 3) the surrender to Japan of all Russian war vessels interned in neutral ports during the war and the limitation of Russia's Far Eastern naval force; 4) an indemnity to cover the cost of the war; 5) the grant to Japanese subjects of fishing rights off the coast of Siberia; and 6) the cession of Saghalin to Japan. In her counter proposals Russia accepted some of these demands, but refused absolutely to consider the limitation of her navy, the demand for an indemnity, and the cession of Saghalin. Continued negotiations failed to bring the two parties to an agreement in spite of the pressure which President Roosevelt exerted on both sides. Finally they came together in what was expected by the Russians to be the last meeting of the conference. At that meeting Russia offered to cede half of Saghalin to Japan in lieu of an indemnity, expecting that the Japanese plenipotentiaries would refuse, since Japanese public opinion seemed to be insistent on the latter. To the surprise of Count Witte, the Japanese delegation announced that it was instructed to waive the demand for an indemnity and that the Russian offer would be accepted. Nothing remained for Count Witte to do but to sign the articles, to his own personal satisfaction, but to the dissatisfaction of his government.

The Portsmouth Treaty, signed on September 5, 1905, provided: (1) For recnition of Japan's "paramount political, military and economic interests" in Korea; (2) For transfer of the rights of Russia in the Liaotung peninsula to Japan; (3) That the southern section of the Manchurian railway be ceded to Japan; (4) That the portion of Saghalin south of the 50th parallel be ceded to Japan; (5) That Russia and Japan should withdraw their troops from Manchuria but retain railway guards; (6) That neither Japan nor Russia should obstruct "any general measures common to all countries which China may take for the development of the commerce and industry of Manchuria"; (7) That railways in Manchuria be exploited purely for commercial and industrial, and in no way for strategical purposes—except in the Liaotung peninsula.[9]

Thus the war resulted in a second advance of the Japanese position in the Far East. This time Japan gained the position on the mainland, once se-

[9] HORNBECK, *Contemporary Politics in the Far East*, pp. 253–254.

cured and then lost, which had been the goal of her policy in the sixteenth century. And she secured far more than her responsible statesmen thought possible at the time of the outbreak of the war. Taking up arms to defend herself against the menace of a strong and aggressive Power, she had effectively displaced that Power, leaving Russia, as the result of her activity, only a foothold in northern Manchuria. Supported during the negotiations preceding the war, and during the struggle, by her alliance with a strong Occidental state, she had carried through an advantageous revision of that alliance. Entering upon a contest to prevent the domination of Korea by Russia, she so effectually disposed of her second opponent in that land that she was able to throw her protection over the kingdom merely as a preliminary step in the direction of its annexation. Since she had attained and gone beyond her objectives, the war must be considered, from that point of view, a complete success for Japan. The question remained as to what use she would make of her new position.

REFERENCES FOR FURTHER STUDY

K. Adachi, *Manchuria* (1925), ch. 1–5; a description of Manchuria, of its early history, and of the Russian advance; a book to be used with care. K. Asakawa, *Russo-Japanese Conflict* (1904); a full and scholarly treatment, but emphasizing the Japanese side of the case. G. A. Ballard, *Influence of the Sea on the Political History of Japan* (1921), ch. 7, 8, 9. Paul H. Clements, *Boxer Rebellion* (1915), in Columbia University Studies, vol. LXVI, no. 3; account of the Manchurian and diplomatic aspects of the movement. P. H. Clyde, *International Rivalries in Manchuria* (1926), ch. 4–7. T. Dennett, *Roosevelt and the Russo-Japanese War* (1925); the most complete and authoritative treatment of the subject; good also for discussion of the attitude of the European Powers. E. J. Dillon, *Eclipse of Russia* (1918), ch. 15; an account of Russian policy by one who had the confidence of Count Witte. A. W. Griswold, *The Far Eastern Policy of the United States* (1938). J. H. Gubbins, *Making of Modern Japan* (1922), ch. 24, 25, 26; a good brief treatment by a competent student. A. S. Hershey, *International Law and Diplomacy of the Russo-Japanese War* (1905), esp. ch. 1 and 13. S. K. Hornbeck, *Contemporary Politics in the Far East* (1916), ch. 14; a brief, impartial summary of the conflict over Manchuria. A. Hosie, *Manchuria, Its People, Resources and Recent History* (1904); the best account of its kind up to the time of publication; still worth consulting. S. A. Korff, *Russia's Foreign Relations during the Last Half Century* (1922), ch. 3–4. W. W. McLaren, *Political History of Japan* (1916), ch. 12; especially valuable for discussion of Japanese politics and internal conditions during the period of the conflict and its genesis. W. L. Langer, *The Origin of the Russo-Japanese War,* article published in *Europaische Gespräche,* Hamburg, 1926; English original privately circulated; a most careful analysis; particularly good for an analysis of the elements entering into and motivating Russian policy; valuable bibliographical data in footnotes. H. F. MacNair, *Modern Chinese History, Selected Readings* (1923), ch. 14. J. V. A. MacMurray, *Treaties and Conventions with and Concerning China* (1921); texts of agreements and other documents. J. B. Moore, *Digest of International Law,* vol. 5; pp. 476–529. A. M. POOLEY (ed.), *Secret Memoirs of County Tadasu Hayashi* (1915); a valuable discussion, by one of the participants, of the nego- tiations of the Anglo-Japanese Alliance, and of the basis of Japan's foreign policy during and after 1895. B. L. SIMPSON (PUTNAM WEALE), *Manchu and Muscovite* (1904); an interesting description of conditions in Manchuria dur- ing the Russian occupation. SOUTH MANCHURIA R. R. Co., *Manchuria, Land of Opportunities* (1922), ch. 1–2; geography, history, government and nat- ural resources. CHITOSHI YANAGA, *Japan since Perry* (1949), ch. 19–21. W. W. WILLOUGHBY, *Foreign Rights and Interests in China,* 2 vols. (1927), vol. 1, ch. 6, 15, 16; a good analysis of Russian interests and policy in Manchuria and Mongolia. COUNT SERGE WITTE, *Memoirs* (1921), ch. 5, 6.

CHAPTER IX

FINANCIAL IMPERIALISM IN CHINA

I. METHODS OF CONQUEST OF CHINA

IN HER earlier contacts with other peoples and states China had repeatedly been conquered by military means. But the Chinese had then proceeded to conquer the victor by assimilating him—by causing him to accept the culture of China, both in its political and in its economic and social manifestations. This was possible for two principal reasons: 1) because the invaders were invariably not so highly developed as the Chinese, except in the art of warfare; and 2) because, in the process, the invaders came in person to establish themselves in the Celestial Empire, so that peoples met peoples and the stronger and more highly developed impressed their standards on those of a lower civilization.

In the modern period the conquest of China has proceeded by very different means. True, force was either actually present or close in the background as Europe advanced into the East; but European peoples did not come to China in great numbers, nor did their governments attempt to gain physical control of China proper. Nevertheless a very real conquest of China was undertaken after 1900. The agencies of control were less tangible than armies, thus more insidious and, ultimately, more to be feared. To the Chinese, the process was that of being gradually enfolded in the invisible tentacles of an octopus—European finance. The foreign customs were pledged as security for the Boxer indemnity and for other charges; provincial revenues were hypothecated; the salt tax was reorganized and brought under foreign administration because pledged as security for loans made to the government by foreign capital; the arteries of communication —the railway trunk lines—were built with borrowed money, and were subject to varying degrees of foreign control during the period of the loans. These were some of the concrete manifestations of the growing foreign financial control of China which might ultimately have meant the extinction of the state.

It is the purpose of this chapter to examine briefly the establishment of this control through finance—financial imperialism. The field of inquiry is thus narrower and more definite than an investigation of the economic interests of the European states and the United States in China. Financial imperialism is but a phase of the larger economic imperialism, but in China, prior to 1914, it was politically the most important phase.

2. EARLY WESTERN INTEREST IN CHINA

It has already been made clear that the chief early interest of the Western nations in the opening of the Chinese Empire was a commercial one. England, as the chief trading state, took the lead in breaking down the barriers to commercial intercourse. As a rule the rights and privileges demanded for foreigners were those considered necessary in order to enable them to carry on their trade more profitably, with perhaps a secondary interest in the missionary and his work. How far this was true of the attitude of any given Power, depended on whether its interest was purely economic or commercial or chiefly political or territorial. Toward the end of the nineteenth century the Powers showed an interest in the development of exclusive positions in parts of the Empire, and this interest, though given an economic expression, was largely political in its nature. But throughout the modern period of their intercourse with the Far Eastern countries, profit for the Western states lay at the back of the development of policy. As Overlach truly says: [1] "This, then, is the point of extreme significance, namely: that the bottom idea of all treaty stipulations and agreements as to intercourse, customs, extraterritoriality, spheres of interest, railway concessions and control was not the welfare of the people of China, but the profit and ease of doing business by the people of the west."

It is impossible to assign these prescribed conditions of intercourse as the sole, or even the most important, causes of expansion of the trade sought by Europe, except as the treaties did broaden access to the country by the opening of new ports and by somewhat ensuring the trade against the operation of hostile local opinion. But whatever the causes, foreign trade increased greatly after the ratification of the Tientsin treaties, and that without developing serious fear of foreign control of China. The total imports increased from 69,329,741 taels in 1867 to 447,100,791 taels in 1905. Exports expanded less rapidly, but still substantially, from 57,895,713 taels in 1867 to 227,888,197 taels in 1905.[2] The import figures are especially interesting as indicating the growth of a larger market for Western manufactured goods. It was the opium traffic which had turned the trade balance against China at the time when the country was opened by treaty. In 1867 opium still accounted for forty-six per cent of the total imports, while in 1905 the percentage had been decreased to seven and a half. This represented only a slightly decreased actual importation. The failure of the opium trade to expand was largely due to an increase in domestic production rather than to a change in the moral attitude of the traders. It had, however, come to be recognized that the traffic did retard the development of legitimate

---

[1] *Foreign Financial Control in China*, p. 272.
[2] Morse, *Trade and Administration of China*, 312–327. The chart opposite p. 297 is worth consulting.

trade by exhausting the purchasing power of the Chinese. Importation of cotton manufactures, including yarn, increased from 21 to 40 per cent of the total imports, metals from 2 to 10 per cent, and sundries from 20 to 40 per cent from 1867 to 1905, while woolens fell from 10 to 1 per cent. Turning to exports we find a similar change, although perhaps one not so striking. Tea accounted for 59 per cent of the exports in 1867, silk and its products for 34 per cent, and sundries for 7 per cent. In 1905 tea had declined to 11 per cent of the total, while silk and sundries accounted for 31 and 58 per cent respectively. The same year found China with an adverse trade balance of slightly over 219,000,000 taels, due to an increased use of Western products disproportionate to the enlarged demand for Chinese commodities. Indian and Japanese competition, together with that of Ceylon, decreased the market for Chinese teas; Japanese and European competition made inroads on the silk market; and while new commodities, listed as sundries, appeared in the trade, the demand for them was not great enough to restore the balance which remained steadily against China.

During this period, since the Powers were primarily interested, as has been pointed out, in the development of trade, the traders had considerable influence in the shaping of policies. The governments of England and the United States, for example, were under a constant pressure and criticism from the China traders, who almost uniformly wished to proceed faster and farther than their governments. But while policy was influenced it was not controlled by the traders, nor was trade used unduly to develop and advance purely political aims. The diplomat did, however, in China as elsewhere, come to be more and more involved in the pressing of claims of an economic character and to be less and less concerned with purely legal and political relations. And as financial, or investment, interests began to appear, particularly after 1895, the union of finance and diplomacy became very close, with sometimes the one taking the lead and sometimes the other. This fact makes necessary a preliminary examination of the relationship with a view to ascertaining its justification as well as its essential nature, before we attempt to trace the growth of foreign financial interests in China.

3. RELATIONSHIP BETWEEN FINANCE AND DIPLOMACY

True diplomacy may be defined roughly as the art of maintaining relations of friendship and understanding between two states, and of promoting the legitimate interests of the one in the other. In the advancement of these interests, if friendship is to be maintained and understanding to be developed, a careful distinction must be made between illegitimate and proper interests. By a proper interest should be understood one the promotion of which will result in mutual advantage.

Trade, if developed on the basis of reciprocity, is entirely legitimate and necessary, and diplomatic agents can and should attempt to secure the right to buy and to sell by showing the advantage of extended relations. They should be alert to safeguard trade interests against discrimination in favor of others. Again, a country such as China may be in need of foreign capital for its development, and the foreign representative should consider it to be part of his duty to ensure the capital of his state a complete equality of consideration for investment, and should see to it, as far as possible, that the interests of investors from his country are properly safeguarded.

But when the diplomatic agent begins to exert pressure on the government of a politically backward country such as China to secure a monopoly of trade or investment privileges for the nationals of his state, or when he brings pressure to bear to force conditions of trade which are wholly disadvantageous to the backward state, or when he seeks to coerce that state into borrowing on terms less advantageous than could be secured elsewhere, it must be considered that he is over-stepping his true position. In the long run such activities do not advance the real interests of either state.

Furthermore, when the lead is taken by diplomacy in securing privileges which are not being requested by the traders, or, more particularly, by finance, then there is justification for thinking that there is a motive behind the act which is political in its character and not purely economic.[3] In other words, when there is a proper relationship established between business and diplomacy, the latter should be used to advance the legitimate interests of the former rather than to bring them into being in order to utilize them for its own ends.

If this point of view is correct, then the diplomatic activity of the several Powers represented at Peking should have been closely proportioned either to their trading or investment interests in China or to pressure exerted by national trade and finance on the government to secure its aid in the establishment and development of commercial and financial undertakings. Otherwise it is fair to assume a political motive back of diplomatic action.

When we look to trade we find that, prior to 1905, it was not considered necessary to keep separate record of the commerce of the states of continental Europe, except Russia, with the Chinese Empire. In the customs reports they were grouped together as a trading unit. The greatest trading Power in 1900 was Great Britain. Japan came second, both as to imports and exports, with the United States third. Russian trade amounted to about half that of the United States, while that of Germany and France, together with all of the other states of continental Europe, in total of imports and exports, was very little greater than that of the United States. In 1896 the trade of these several states with China was considerably less, the activities

---

[3] Of course diplomacy may and should turn the attention of national trading and financial institutions to a field hitherto neglected by them, and take the lead in that way. What is meant is the practice of extorting concessions for its nationals which they are not in a position to use.

of the years from 1896 to 1900 having brought a slight proportional increase.

When we turn to their diplomatic activity, however, there is a different story to tell. The most active Power at Peking was Russia, supported by France. The least active in pressing its claims on the Chinese government was the United States. And it was not the desire to promote trade relations which was the most marked feature of the pressure on China during those years and immediately after 1900. The reason for this is, perhaps, the fact that political ends could not be so readily advanced by the promotion of trade. Consequently it is to finance that we must turn to estimate the position and the policy of the Powers.

Beyond this, however, in determining the relationship between finance and diplomacy, it is necessary to try to ascertain whether the latter was merely making use of the former, or the reverse, if we are to gain an adequate understanding of the international situation. Too often, in the case of countries such as China, diplomatic pressure has been exerted to introduce national finance into the country. It is hoped then to utilize it in order to afford a pretext for later intervention on the ground of the necessity for protection of the initial investment. As a result of this intervention further privileges have been secured, whether or not they could be utilized, and thus a broader ground has been laid for intervention. Perhaps as a result of an intervention some measure of political supervision, especially of finance and of the protective services, might result. In other words, the ultimate aim of this apparently peaceful economic penetration of a backward country may have been consistently political rather than economic. And where the initiative has come from government rather than from finance, there is more likely to be a political motive involved than when the initiative has come from finance.

4. SPECIAL CHARACTERISTICS OF CHINA'S FINANCIAL PROBLEM

Before proceeding further we must observe certain special characteristics of the financial problem in China. In the first place, China was for a long time almost completely dependent on foreign capital for her development and for meeting the increases in her governmental expenditure which necessarily arose from the imposition of indemnity payments. For developmental purposes there was no domestic money market, not because there was no available capital in China, but because of lack of confidence in the government as an agency for the construction of railroads and the opening of mines—the two great fields for the use of capital. There was also a lack of familiarity with and confidence in the stock company as a form of organization capable of drawing into one set of hands large amounts of capital. To meet increased public expenditure there was an inflexible revenue system, and one not easily changed, since it was founded on immemorial custom. Taxes on land and the production of salt could produce greater revenue only by an increase in the rate, which, of course, would meet with serious popular resistance. Furthermore, whereas modern states find the foreign customs the chief flexible source of income, China, because the rates were fixed by treaty, could not, until after 1930, meet her new needs by an increase in the foreign customs levies. Finally, it was impossible to produce increased revenues by a reorganization of the collection of the existing taxes, because of official interest in the possibility of "squeeze." Consequently, in spite of the fact that per capita taxes in China were comparatively small, the Empire had to depend on the foreign money market to take care of its immediate governmental needs, and to provide for the great developmental undertakings such as the construction of railways.

In the second place, as will be readily appreciated, if the obligations of the Chinese government are carefully examined, it is almost impossible, because of the intimate relationship between foreign finance and diplomacy, to distinguish between China's public and private obligations as they existed prior to the World War.[4]

In the third place, it must be noted that special national financial institutions usually secured the exclusive support of their governments in seeking concessions and in other ways securing the right to aid in the financing of China.

Thus Japanese loans have been made, for the most part, through the Yokohama Specie Bank . . . and a syndicate consisting of the Bank of Taiwan, the Bank of Chosen, and the Industrial Bank of Japan. . . . British financial interests have operated through the Hongkong and Shanghai Banking Corporation, and the British and Chinese Corporation, formed, in 1908, by the Hongkong and Shanghai Banking Corporation and the trading firm of Jardine, Matheson and Company. German financial interests have operated in China through the Deutsch-Asiatische Bank. Russian financial interests have employed as their agency the Banque Russo-Asiatique, earlier known as the Banque Russo-Chinoise. France has used the Banque de l'Indo-Chine, and, in association with it, the Credit Lyonnais, the Comptoir National d'Escompte de Paris, and other banks. Belgium has used the Société Belge d'Etudes de Chemins Fer en Chine. American interests, for the most part, have acted through a banking group (originally constituted by J. P. Morgan and Company, Kuhn, Loeb and Company, the First National Bank of New York, and the National City Bank of New York), the International Banking Corporation, and Lee, Higginson and Co.[5]

Thus, in some cases (as the Crisp Loan) [6] it has been impossible for responsible financial concerns to participate in the financing of China because they could not secure the support of their governments, since such support had already been promised exclusively to other institutions or groups. This has

[4] MacMurray, Treaties, etc., vol. 1, pp. xiv–xv.
[5] Willoughby, Foreign Rights and Interests in China, pp. 485–486.
[6] Infra, p. 235.

had the effect of restricting China's access, on competitive terms, to the loan markets of the world.

5. FINANCIAL ACTIVITIES OF POWERS (1895–1908)

With this introduction it is possible to turn to the financial activities of the Powers after 1895. A survey of these activities may be conveniently divided into two periods, the first extending from 1895 to 1908, a time of intense competition among the several Powers; and the second including the years following 1908, when the Powers showed an increasing realization of the dangers of an unrestricted competition, and, as a result of this appreciation, tended to coöperate in the development and economic and financial exploitation of China.

Prior to the war with Japan, China had no appreciable foreign debt. The war, however, resulted in her agreement to pay an indemnity of 230,000,000 taels. Immediately Russia came to her aid, as she had in the matter of the cession of the Liaotung promontory, and offered the Imperial government a loan out of which to meet the first payments on the indemnity. This loan of four hundred million francs, while made by Russia and France jointly, was almost entirely subscribed in France. It was secured on the Maritime Customs receipts, and by a Russian government guarantee. Russia had no money to lend, but was willing to guarantee the loan because of the effect it would have on her position at Peking.

The British immediately pressed on the Chinese government a loan to meet the second instalment of the indemnity, to the amount of sixteen million pounds.[7] This was an Anglo-German loan and marks the beginning of coöperation of English and German finance in Chinese affairs. In 1898, when the final installment was due, the Anglo-German financiers were forced to compete with the Russians and French, both groups strongly urging their claims to consideration on the Chinese government. The former were successful, although offering less advantageous terms, because of the strong pressure brought to bear on China from the British legation. No government guarantee, however, was involved in the Anglo-German loans, which must be considered as more nearly financial in their ends than the Russo-French loan. It was, nevertheless, the desire to combat the Russian influence which caused the British government to insist that her financiers should have the privilege of helping China out of the difficulties created by the war with Japan. It has already been seen that both groups reaped an abundant reward for their benevolence when it came to the scramble for economic privileges in the Empire during and after 1898.

The next great public debt fastened on China resulted from the failure of the Boxer movement, the indemnity imposed amounting to 450,000,000

---

[7] Also secured by the Maritime Customs and certain provincial likin. They had, however, made earlier loans for war-financing purposes.

taels. The security taken for this charge was: the unpledged balance of the Maritime Customs, increased by the raising of the tariff charges to an effective five per cent; the revenues from the native customs administered in the open ports by the Maritime Customs service; and the revenues from the Salt Gabelle. The Maritime Customs were taken as security for these early debts primarily because it was a service efficiently organized and administered under foreign supervision.

It was not until 1911 that China was again forced to borrow for governmental purposes. But with the (uncompleted) currency loan of that year and the reorganization loan of 1913, following the revolution of 1911, she began increasingly to seek funds abroad for general administrative purposes. Consideration of these loans, however, will be postponed for the present, since they fall within the second period, that of international coöperation.

While governmental loans were important, the principal field for foreign finance lay in securing and utilizing railway concessions. It was through railway construction that the Powers hoped effectively to penetrate and develop the areas claimed as spheres of interest, and it is in the control provisions of the various loan agreements that the policy and intention of the several European states is most clearly revealed. So far as the primary interest of a state was purely financial and economic, the control provisions in its railway contracts were designed merely to afford ample security to the bondholders. Where, on the other hand, the interest was partly or wholly political, more extensive control was demanded. These control provisions, whether of the one sort or the other, were five in number. They involved: 1) supervision of construction of the road; 2) a national priority in the purchase of materials; 3) audit, or other supervision of expenditure; 4) actual operation of the road during the life of the loan; and 5) administration of the railway zone and police rights therein. In some cases the roads themselves were pledged as security for the loan, whether with or without the above-mentioned control provisions. In other cases the loan was secured by a general Imperial government guarantee, and by the pledging of certain revenues for the repayment of the loan together with the interest on it.

As examples of roads which provided for control of operation for strategical or other political purposes, may be mentioned the Russian and Japanese lines in Manchuria, the German Tsingtao-Tsinanfu line in Shantung province, and the French system in Yunnan and Kwangsi provinces. The several loan agreements for these systems contain all five of the provisions described above. They were contructed, and for some years operated, under the supervision of the foreign governments concerned rather than by the government of China. The nature of the transaction in each case warrants the conclusion that the foreign government was interested in the loan for its own purposes rather than on behalf of national finance. In other words, the loans were not made primarily as good investments, nor were the roads constructed for the sake of the advantage derived from the sale of materials to be used in building them or because of the profits that would be made out of their operation. In some cases it was apparent that the roads would not be immediately or even for a long time profitable, and the railway tariffs were not fixed with a view to profit but were established for political reasons.[8] Furthermore, the above-mentioned governments, in addition to specific concessions, sought continually to secure a general monopoly of construction in their respective spheres, with a view to determining the course of development of those areas. In consequence of this China was for some years greatly handicapped in the development of her communications along national lines.

As examples of roads the control provisions concerning which, although extensive, were designed primarily to afford security to the investor, may be mentioned the Peking-Mukden, the Shanghai-Nanking, and the Peking-Hankow railways. In each of these cases the security for the loan was the railway properties, which, upon default, might be taken over and administered in the interest of the bondholders. They differed from the French, Russian, and Japanese lines chiefly in that the construction and supervision of the operation of the roads lay in the hands of corporations which were not under the direct control of foreign governments and which were not in a position, under their agreements, to shape the policies of the railways along non-commercial lines. The roads themselves were the properties of the Chinese government rather than of foreign governments.

The groundwork for the construction of these railways was laid in the years from 1898 to 1900, and the concessions obtained were, on the whole, in the respective spheres of interest of the Powers. Consequently they served to emphasize the division of China into spheres. Each Power sought to strengthen itself in its sphere by keeping out the others, either by direct agreement, or by pressure exerted at Peking to prevent the granting of concessions to nationals of other states. We have already referred [9] to the agreements reached between Great Britain, on the one hand, and France, Russia, and Germany, on the other, providing for a mutual respect for each other's priority of interest in a specified region. These agreements were, on the whole, lived up to by both England and Germany. Russia, however, as has been indicated, tried indirectly to force her way into the British sphere by utilizing Belgian capital, and France tried to project her influence northwards into the Yangtse provinces.

American interests secured only one concession for the construction of part of the rail system of China during this early period, and this one American capitalists failed to utilize. An Anglo-American syndicate, headed

---

[8] This was true of the French, Russian, and Japanese systems.

[9] Supra, pp. 151–153.

by Senator Brice, sought in competition with the Belgian interests for the right to construct the road from Peking to Hankow. When China granted the concession to the Belgian interests she compensated the Americans by a concession for the line south from Hankow to Canton. In this way it was hoped to introduce a disinterested influence into the construction of her main north-and-south artery. But, although the concession agreement provided specifically that control in the enterprise should not be allowed to pass from American hands, Belgian interests did gain control through purchases in the open market, and in 1903 the concession was cancelled, although control had been regained through the activity of J. P. Morgan and Company.

After this failure American interest next manifested itself in Manchuria, which, even after the Russo-Japanese War, continued to be the international storm center.

At the conclusion of the war with Russia the statesmen of Japan were undecided as to their future policy in Manchuria. When Mr. Harriman, the American railroad magnate, approached the Japanese government with a proposal to lease the South Manchurian and operate it as part of a projected round-the-world system, a preliminary understanding was reached which was embodied in the Ito-Harriman agreement. But when Count Komura, the chief Japanese plenipotentiary, returned from Portsmouth, he strongly opposed any Japanese withdrawal from Manchuria. As a result of the opposition which developed, the agreement was not carried into effect, the cancellation being put on the ground that the road did not become the property of Japan until after China's consent to the transfer from Russia had been obtained.

Then Japan embarked on a systematic development of her newly acquired holdings. First of all, she undertook negotiations with the Chinese government to secure its acquiescence in the transference of the Russian rights and interests to Japan. This agreement was embodied in the Komura (Peking) treaty of December 22, 1905. But in the unpublished minutes of the Peking Conference it was recorded that China should grant no concessions to foreign capital for construction of railways paralleling or competitive with the South Manchurian. As it was later interpreted and used, this alleged secret agreement denied the right of foreign (non-Japanese) capital to enter South Manchuria for the purpose of financing railway construction, giving Japan a virtual monopoly there. In addition to this the Japanese used their control of rail communications to advance their business interests at the expense of other foreigners doing business in Manchuria. The commercial port, Dairen, was for some time closed to all but Japanese goods and vessels. From Dairen the goods were carried on the Japanese-controlled railway to points in the interior, although the railway was supposedly being used at the time only for the evacuation of troops and for other military purposes. In this way Japan attempted to establish a market for her goods before admitting her foreign competitors. Furthermore, rebates on the railroad were given to Japanese goods; the Japanese demanded exemption from the operation of the Chinese consumption taxes; and, in general, they indulged in many of the practices which they had objected to and protested against in the Russian action in Manchuria prior to the war and in the German action in Shantung, on the ground that such practices constituted a violation of the doctrine of the Open Door. From the administrative side Japan balanced an efficient administration by continued encroachments on and offenses against the Chinese position outside of the railway zone, and in the zone she made herself supreme so far as China was concerned.

Japan's use of her position and rights in Manchuria made some of the Chinese officials desirous of introducing non-Japanese capital north of the Great Wall in order to emphasize the fact of Chinese sovereignty. Consequently in 1907 an agreement was reached between the Manchurian Viceroy and Mr. Willard Straight, the American Consul-General at Mukden, for the financing of a Manchurian Bank with American capital. This bank was to serve as the fiscal agent of the Manchurian government, and was to participate in financing railway construction. The panic of 1907 in the United States, however, prevented even consideration of this project. Later in the year British capitalists were interested in, and secured a concession for, the construction of a railway from Hsinmintun to Fakumen. Japanese opposition to this concession developed immediately, based on its violation of the terms of the annexes to the Komura treaty. The British legation was unwilling to support its nationals in ventures north of the Great Wall in the face of Japanese opposition, and the project was not carried through. In 1908, however, negotiations were begun again between the Chinese government and Anglo-American financiers for the financing of a line from Chinchow to Aigun. This concession was pushed by the American government after the election of Taft to the presidency, and after the admission of American bankers to the Hukuang railway project had been secured. The Chinchow-Aigun agreement was secretly ratified by the Imperial Government of China on January 20, 1910.

6. THE KNOX NEUTRALIZATION PROPOSALS

Before securing the Imperial ratification of this concession-agreement the State Department made a move looking toward the clarification of the whole situation in Manchuria, when Secretary Knox made his famous proposal for the neutralization of the railroads in Manchuria. These proposals, it was felt, were justified for two reasons. In the first place, the Chinchow-Aigun concession, which had been initialed October 4, 1909, had given

American interests a tangible basis in Manchuria, so that the United States was not coming forward entirely as a disinterested outsider. She had something to give up in return for concessions from the other interested Powers. This was the real justification for pushing the Chinchow-Aigun negotiations. In the second place, Mr. Harriman had revived his round-the-world transportation project in 1909, just before his death, because of an intimation from Russia that the Czar's government would be willing to consider the lease or sale of the Chinese Eastern Railway. It was well known, on the other hand, that the Japanese government was in considerable financial straits, and it was felt that Japan might be willing to dispose of her South Manchurian holdings if Japanese interests were not thereby sacrificed. Consequently the Knox proposals were not so ill-advised as has sometimes been represented.

The methods employed to secure assent to them were, on the other hand, open to severe criticism. In the first place, the intimation from Russia should have been followed up and a promise to sell the Chinese Eastern secured. This would have made it possible to bring a more effective pressure to bear on Japan to induce her to internationalize the control of the South Manchurian. It might also have prevented Russia from opposing the American policy because of the offense to her pride due to the fact that it was apparently assumed that she would assent to a policy which had Anglo-American support. It would have been more expedient to have approached England only after negotiations had been instituted with Russia and then with Japan. In any case, when England did not respond warmly to the American proposals, other support should have been sought before proceeding further, except as it may be assumed that the American government was more interested in focusing attention on the real Manchurian aims and intentions of the Powers than in successfully carrying out its own plans.

Briefly, the proposal was that an international syndicate should be formed to make a large loan to China so that she might buy out the Russian and Japanese interests, and that the Manchurian railways should be neutralized and internationally administered during the period of the loan. In sounding out the British attitude toward the proposal Secretary Knox suggested that if the British government was not willing to support the larger project, it might at least join the United States in supporting diplomatically the Chinchow-Aigun scheme, in the development of which other Powers might be given a share.

The British reply was disappointing in that it intimated that the British government felt that the time was inopportune for the making of such far-reaching proposals,[10] and in that it suggested that the Japanese be invited to participate in the Chinchow-Aigun concession because of their peculiar interest in Manchuria. Thus instead of supporting the American position

[10] Until after all details of the Hukuang loan had been settled.

that Manchuria was a proper field for the activities of non-Japanese finance, the British government accepted the Japanese contention that South Manchuria was an exclusive Japanese preserve so far as investment rights and railroad development were concerned.

The Japanese and Russian governments finally gave a categorical refusal to consider the American proposals, the wording of their answers being so similar as to indicate a prior agreement. It is interesting to note that the refusal of both countries was put, in part, on political and strategical grounds, indicating that the two governments construed their interests in Manchuria to be political and not purely commercial and financial. In opposing the Chinchow-Aigun concession both Japan and Russia produced secret agreements with the Chinese government by which it agreed not to undertake railway developments in Manchuria without first consulting Russia if north Manchuria was affected, or Japan if the projects involved the territory south of Changchun. In the face of the open Russian opposition and the Japanese expression of a willingness to participate on entirely unacceptable terms, the Chinchow-Aigun concession was allowed to lapse.

The total effect of the Knox activity is summarized by Mr. Millard in the following terms: [11] 1) The right of China to decide upon the course of railway development within her territory was denied by foreign nations. 2) Certain foreign nations declared that their strategical and political interests must be considered as paramount in planning a railway system within China's territory. 3) Certain foreign nations asserted the right to decide who would finance, construct, and operate railways within China's territory and to veto arrangements in regard to these matters which China wishes to carry out. To these may be added two other effects; 1) Great Britain reversed her policy, returning to the sphere of interest conception and partially repudiating the principle of the Open Door, of equal opportunity in its enlarged conception. 2) Japan and Russia drew together in defense of their exclusive and preferential interests in the Manchurian provinces. In 1907 they had entered into a political convention in which each agreed to respect the Manchurian rights of the other so far as they were not inconsistent with the principle of equal opportunity, and they recognized in general the independence and territorial integrity of China and the Open Door principle and agreed to sustain and defend them. But in 1910 Russia and Japan entered into both a public and a secret convention defining their respective spheres in Manchuria, agreeing not to interfere with each other in developing their positions within their spheres, and stipulating for concerted action in case their special interests in Manchuria were threatened. The 1910 conventions contain no acceptance of the principle either of equal opportunity or of the integrity of China.

[11] MILLARD. *Our Eastern Question*, p. 25.

7. INTERNATIONAL COÖPERATION IN FINANCE

In a sense this Knox proposal for the neutralization of the Manchurian railways was but a part of a general movement toward financial coöperation in China. The British objection to a discussion of the internationalizing of the Manchurian lines rested partly on the fact that the Powers were then engaged in working out arrangements for coöperating in the building of railways in western and southern China. Finance was rapidly finding out the difficulties of competition for concessions, and governments apparently were beginning to realize that there was room for all in the financing of the great trunk lines of China. They were coming to perceive that competition had the effect of playing into the hands of China by securing her more favorable terms in the making of loans than could otherwise have been obtained.

Thus when a road was projected from Tientsin to the Yangtse River, England and Germany competed for the right to finance it. Both nations had a claim to participation, because the road penetrated their respective spheres of interest. The Germans proved agreeable to the granting of more favorable terms to China than the British (who insisted on the usual financial control provisions), but British diplomacy was stronger at Peking than that of Germany. Furthermore, the hands of both parties were tied by their agreement to respect each other's spheres. Finally, since both recognized the desirability of constructing the road, an agreement with the Chinese government was signed January 13, 1908, by which they shared in the undertaking. The Germans gained the right to construct the section from Tientsin to the southern border of Shantung province, while the British were to complete the road to its juncture, at Pukow, with the (British) Shanghai-Nanking railway. The competition, however, had resulted in China's securing the elimination of many of the usual control provisions. The road itself was not made the security for the loan, certain provincial revenues being pledged as the security. Consequently the road would not have to be administered in the interest of the bondholders. In fact, the construction and operation of the road was to be in the hands of China herself, although she agreed to appoint British and German engineers for their respective sections. Furthermore, there was no provision made for supervision of expenditure of the loan funds.

Tientsin-Pukow terms came to be synonymous with terms favorable to China for railway loans. Many foreigners, however, were skeptical as to the advisability of this weakening of the control provisions of the loan, and were particularly dubious about eliminating the right to supervise expenditure. And it must be admitted that this skepticism was somewhat justified by the event. It proved to be necessary to float a supplementary loan to complete the road, owing to the high cost of construction under Chinese control, for there was much squandering of funds.

For some years prior to 1908 there had been intermittently discussed the project of constructing a road south from Hankow to Canton, and westwards from Hankow into the great province of Szechuan. These discussions were renewed in 1908–1909, primarily in order to reach an agreement as to the measure of control which should be insisted upon, in the light of the Tientsin-Pukow experience, in the making of future loans. France and England, and, still earlier, the United States and England, had been interested in these two roads. In 1908 Germany also turned her attention toward them, and it was as a result of her activity that British, French, and German financiers and government officials undertook conversations in the hope of finding a basis for coöperation in the undertaking by reconciling their respective claims. Just when they had reached an agreement among themselves and with Chang Chih-tung, the Viceroy in charge of railway affairs in the area involved, the American government interfered in the interest of American finance. When diplomatic action at Peking failed to achieve any results, President Taft took the unusual step of cabling the Regent, requesting that Americans be admitted to participation. The basis for this request was the old concession of 1898–1903. After the intervention of President Taft, an American group was allowed to participate and the Four Powers Banking Group came into being. In order to show its real desire to extend the operation of the coöperative principle the American government at this time invited the other three Powers to join it in making a loan for currency reform in China, a project in which the United States had been given an exclusive interest. However, work on the railway project and the issuance of the currency loan were both retarded by the revolutionary developments of the year 1911 and thereafter.

8. EFFECTS OF REVOLUTION AND EUROPEAN WAR

The revolution brought with it new financial problems for the Chinese government, and as a result it began to look to foreign sources for funds for general administrative purposes. On account of its immediately pressing needs and because of the large sums ultimately required, the Chinese government turned to the international syndicate for advances. It also began to negotiate with the syndicate for a comprehensive loan to be devoted to reorganization and reconstruction purposes, giving the syndicate, in return for its advances for immediate needs, an option on the comprehensive loan. When the new Republican government began to negotiate for this loan it found that the syndicate (extended to include Japan and Russia because of the political character of the loan contemplated) insisted on adequate provision for control of the revenues to be pledged as security.

In consequence the government tried to secure the necessary funds outside of the Six Power Group, but was unable to do so as the several national groups had the exclusive support of their respective governments. Finally, in 1913, agreement was reached on the Salt Gabelle as the security for the loan, and provision was made for its reorganization under foreign supervision.

The outbreak of war in Europe in 1914 interfered with an extension of the financial operations of the first consortium. The American group had withdrawn from participation in the reorganization loan because the State Department under the direction of President Wilson refused to pledge its support to the members of the group, taking the stand that "the conditions of the loan seem to us to touch very nearly the administrative independence of China itself, and this Administration does not feel that it ought, even by implication, to be a party to these conditions." [12] After the outbreak of war German interests became inactive. And finally consortium advances on the loan came almost entirely from Japan. Additional loans for governmental purposes, as they became necessary, were also made by Japanese agencies acting independently, and, on a small scale, by American interests. Thus group action gave way to separate action until the revival and reorganization of the consortium at Paris, this time as the result of American initiative. [13]

The same reversion appeared in the railroad field. Contracts made after 1912 provided for the construction of over six thousand miles of road with foreign funds. A little less than a third of this mileage was granted to British financial institutions, the terms providing, among other conditions, for the employment of a British engineer-in-chief, chief accountant, and traffic manager, and for the pledging of the road as security for the loan. The Russians and Japanese [14] extended their railway interests in Manchuria, north and south, on the usual terms. The German contracts in Shantung for the Kaomi-Yihsien and Tsinan-Shuntefu roads (1913) were transferred to Japan and later by her to the second consortium. The French were awarded concessions of almost two thousand miles carrying them northwards through Szechuan, Shansi, and Shensi provinces to an ultimate connection with the Peking-Kalgan road. Except for the northwestern extension of French interests, all of these concessions fell within the claimed spheres of interest of the respective Powers. When an American concern, the Siems-Carey Company, secured contracts for fifteen hundred miles of construction in 1916, it found the old sphere conception fully revived.

[12] From President Wilson's announcement, reproduced in WILLOUGHBY, *Foreign Rights and Interests*, p. 501.

[13] It seems advisable to postpone further discussion of the financial problem in China after the Revolution to succeeding chapters, since it can be most easily followed in connection with the discussion of the evolution of the political system after 1911.

[14] Japanese interests are more fully discussed in chapter XVI.

This made it a problem for the Chinese government to mark out the lines for American construction so as to meet the objections raised by the several interested Powers.

Due to the war-time and post-war financial conditions, little was done until after 1930 toward completing these lines. The contracts served principally as barriers to the undertaking of work by others than the concessionaires, and to that extent hindered rather than helped the development of an adequate system of rail communications in China. By 1925 there was upwards of seven thousand miles of line in operation. This must be considered a good total in view of the general obstacles to construction, and it must, on the whole, be recognized that China was materially benefited by the enlargement and improvement of her means of communication in spite of the introduction of foreign influence with the many problems and dangers presented by it. The dangers have been pointed out, and some of the problems may be stated very briefly. The conditions under which loans were granted were so different, and the provisions for the supervision of construction so varied, that a non-uniform gauge resulted. Some of the roads had the standard gauge, the Russian roads used the five-foot gauge, and the French roads the meter gauge. This prevented a satisfactory utilization of rolling stock and stood in the way of the administration of the roads as a unit. Then there was the very serious problem presented by the variety of administrations, with the Chinese Ministry of Communications unable to control all of the roads effectively. These and other administrative problems arising out of the conditions of financing and constructing the Chinese system were attacked and partially solved by the institution of "conferences," which sought to work out coöperatively a uniform system of operation. Representatives of the non-government as well as the government lines participated in these conferences. In spite of the handicaps presented by the political disorganization of the years 1916–1926, and the interference of the military with the normal operation of the railways, their financial condition steadily improved with their more extensive use.

So far as equipment and general maintenance were concerned, however, military interference and internal turmoil resulted in deterioration, which naturally affected the foreign investment. They also resulted during this period in the suspension of payment of both interest and principal on a number of the loan accounts.

9. CHINA'S ATTITUDE TOWARD AND INTEREST IN RAILWAY CONSTRUCTION

Before concluding this discussion of financial imperialism in China it is proper to consider the general effect of the activities of the Powers on Chinese opinion. First of all, we must remember that China was totally unable initially to finance the construction of railways, the opening of mines, and the general industrial and political reorganization of the country. This fact necessarily modified the Chinese attitude from time to time as it was brought home to the educated classes. With this modification in mind, however, it may be said that the attitude of the Chinese people was determined by their fear of foreign financial control of their country.

During the years immediately after the war with Japan the Chinese little realized the significance of the process of economic penetration which was being provided for by the agreements entered into from 1896 to 1900. The use made of the Manchurian railway by the Russians, however, wakened many of the officials to the danger to the state inhering in the foreign-controlled railway. Consequently there came a period when the Chinese were unwilling to accept foreign loans. The concentration of attention on the developing conflict between Japan and Russia over Korea and Manchuria also led to the cessation of loans.

After the Russo-Japanese War the Chinese wakened still more fully to the gravity of the situation. The war promoted the movement toward internal reform, one phase of which was the attempt to develop a national system of communications. Immediately before and after the conflict in Manchuria the attempt was made to construct provincial railways out of locally subscribed funds. This, in the long run, would have had the effect of retarding the unification of the country, and the more capable of the Imperial officials soon perceived this fact. The perception of the possibility and the necessity for unification of the country by means of the construction of railways under the control and direction of Peking led to the elaboration of a program of railway nationalization. The consortium program of the Powers fitted in perfectly with this policy as it provided Peking with the necessary funds for the construction of the great trunk lines, from which feeders could be thrown out gradually as opportunity offered.

Provincial opinion, however, had to be considered, and the gentry in the provinces were afraid of the gradual development of an international control of China through control of a centralized system of communications. Furthermore, the provinces had to be considered so far as they had invested in local railway undertakings. Their natural tendency, too, was to fight centralization unless they stood to profit by it. It was from this direction that part of the opposition which was connected with the revolutionary movement of 1911, such as the insurrection in Szechuan province, came.

Fear of foreign financial control, the natural centrifugal tendency in the country, and the interest of the gentry in securing favorable terms for themselves in giving up to the central government their provincial railway investments—all conspired to make more difficult of execution the policy of centralization determined upon in 1907–1909.

REFERENCES FOR FURTHER STUDY

J. O. P. Bland, *Recent Events and Present Policies in China* (1912). Grover Clark, *Economic Rivalries in China* (1932). F. V. Field, *American Participation in the China Consortiums* (1931), ch. 1–5, R. R. Gibson, *Forces Mining and Undermining China* (1914). A. W. Griswold, *The Far Eastern Policy of the United States* (1938), ch. 3–5; a recent carefully documented study of American policy. S. K. Hornbeck, *Contemporary Politics in the Far East* (1916), ch. 15. F. H. Huang, *Public Debts in China* (1919), in Columbia University Studies, vol. LXXXV, no. 2. P. H. Kent, *Railway Enterprise in China* (1907). J. V. A. MacMurray, *Treaties and Agreements,* 2 vols. (1921). J. V. A. MacMurray, *Problems of Foreign Capital in China,* in *Foreign Affairs,* April, 1925. T. F. F. Millard, *Our Eastern Question* (1916), ch. 1. H. B. Morse, *International Relations* (1918), vol. 3. E. B. Price, *The Russo-Japanese Treaties of 1907–1916 Concerning Manchuria and Mongolia* (1933); an important study. John G. Reid, *The Manchu Abdication and the Powers, 1908–1912* (1935); a careful diplomatic study of railway politics in relation to the revolution. W. W. Willoughby, *Foreign Rights and Interests in China,* 2 vols. (1927), vol. 2, ch. 39–42. S. Wagel, *Finance in China* (1914), ch. 2.

CHAPTER X

REFORM AND REVOLUTION IN CHINA

I. CONDITIONS UNDER WHICH REFORM WAS UNDERTAKEN

THE internal history of China during the decade following the signature of the Boxer Protocol presents two patterns which are distinct and yet closely interwoven. The first is that of reform and the second that of revolution. And through both runs the thread of international relations. Since the narrative will be clearer if the two patterns are kept distinct, we shall attempt first to trace the development of the Manchu reform program up to the outbreak of the revolution in October of 1911, and after that has been done we shall try to picture the larger background of the revolution. It will then be possible to consider the revolution and the history of the eventful years following the abdication of the Manchu Emperor.

To preserve the sequence, a brief recapitulation may well be undertaken at this point. In the first chapter a summary description of the political organization of China was given. Two of its features, it will be remembered, were the decentralized territorial system resulting from the high development of provincial and local autonomy, and the inflexible revenue system which could not be readily adapted to meet the new burdens on the state resulting from unsuccessful war and from the attempted introduction of such Western inventions as the steam engine. Succeeding chapters indicated the reaction of China to the contact with the West, particularly her failure to strengthen her political system, her military organization, and her economic life so as to enable her to protect herself against those who, because of her weakness and economic backwardness, became her despoilers. Such limited reorganization as had been attempted had been only partially successful because of the innate conservatism and feeling of superiority of the officials and the gentry, and, so far as it related to military and naval reform, had been largely neutralized by the widespread system of "squeeze." As a direct consequence of her weakness and the unwillingness of her officials to recognize the changed conditions, China lost most of her dependencies, suffered repeated defeats, both military and diplomatic, the most humiliating being that administered by Japan, and was finally threatened with partition along the lines marked out in 1897–1898. This could not help but engender dissatisfaction with the reigning dynasty. Furthermore, it has been pointed out that the foreign impact synchronized with bad internal conditions, partly the result of famine, piracy and brigandage, and widespread rebellion. For these internal conditions, as well as for external aggression, the dynasty was held responsible. Consequently by 1900 it was presented with the alternatives of reform or elimination, because of its inability to fulfill its obligations to the country. We have briefly described the attempt at reform, as it was made rather impulsively in 1898, and the overthrow of the reformers, as well as the successful attempt to divert the discontented elements into the channel of anti-foreignism. The failure of Boxerism made almost inevitable a renewal, in a more conservative way, of the attempt to preserve the dynasty by reform of the governmental system.

That this attempt was to be made was clearly indicated in an edict issued in 1901 by the Empress-Dowager from Sianfu, whence the Court had fled as the foreign expeditionary force approached Peking. Parts of the edict deserve quotation as predicating the course of events of the next few years.[1] "Looking at the matter broadly, we may observe that any system which has lasted too long is in danger of becoming stereotyped, and things which are obsolete should be modified. The essential need which confronts us is at all costs to strengthen Our Empire, and to improve the condition of our subjects. . . . The Empress-Dowager has now decided that we should correct our short-comings by adopting the best methods and systems which obtain in foreign countries, basing our future conduct on a wise recognition of past errors." In order to placate those who had objected to the K'ang Yu-wei reforms, the edict then pointed out that the objects of the Empress-Dowager were fundamentally different from those of the 1898 reformers. "Their main object is not reform but a revolution against the Manchu Dynasty," while the Old Buddha's object was to preserve the dynasty. Furthermore she intimated that she was not interested in making radical changes, but in reality was merely aiming at removing evil growths from the age-old system. "The teachings handed down to us by our Sacred Ancestors are really the same as those upon which the wealth and power of European countries have been based, but China has hitherto failed to realize this, and has been content to acquire the rudiments of European languages or technicalities while changing nothing of her ancient habits of inefficiency and deep-rooted corruption." The whole edict was primarily devoted to the important work of convincing the conservative officials that it would be safe to inaugurate a program of change under the supervision of the Empress-Dowager, although a similar program proposed by the Emperor had been properly condemned as revolutionary.

Upon the return of the Court to Peking the reform era was inaugurated and an opportunity was afforded for judgment as to the sincerity of the Empress-Dowager. It is obvious that changes could be made only with

[1] The following excerpts are taken from the translation given by BLAND AND BACKHOUSE, China under the Empress-Dowager, pp. 419–424.

the coöperation of the officials of the metropolitan area and the provinces, and two of these stood out as honest supporters of progress. Yüan Shih-k'ai, who had served as Chinese Resident at Seoul from 1885 until 1895, and who had thereafter been Judicial Commissioner of the Metropolitan province, Junior Vice-President of the Board of Works, and Governor of Shantung during the Boxer uprising, was appointed Viceroy of Chihli province at the end of 1901, when he was also made Junior Guardian of the Heir Apparent. It was under his direction that many of the changes in the central administration were carried out. He also showed his interest in army reorganization. Another leading advocate of reform was Chang Chih-tung, who as the Hukuang Viceroy dominated reform in the provinces up to the time of his death in 1909. While Yüan was primarily interested in political and military reorganization, Chang would seem to have been principally concerned with the strengthening of the economic foundations of the state.

2. THE FIRST PERIOD OF REFORM

The first concrete interest was manifested in military reform. Until after 1895 China had no real modern national army, her military forces consisting of the Banner troops, and of the Green Flag or provincial troops.[2] The latter were in reality provincial constabulary and were organized and controlled by the provincial officials. After 1895 an attempt at reorganization was made but without permanent effect. In 1901 an Imperial edict again ordered reorganization, which was begun in Chihli province by reason of the interest of Yüan Shih-k'ai. Between 1903 and 1906 he created a model force of six divisions. Four of these were transferred in 1906 to the then established Ministry of War, and a plan was projected for the formation of a National Army of thirty-six divisions. In 1907 it was ordered that this program should be completed by 1912. The real advance in program came as a direct result of the interest created by the war between Russia and Japan. By 1911 progress had been made in this part of the reform program, and it will be interesting subsequently to note how the partial formation of a modern army affected the fortunes of the Manchus.

A second and more fundamental reform was inaugurated in theory in 1905, when by edict the age-old examination system was abolished. This struck a blow at the heart of the old order, for it forecast the end of the dominance of the classical tradition and the putting of a premium on knowledge of Western subjects. It meant immediately a paper rather than a real change, but it was no less significant for that reason. Previously permission had been given to Imperial Clansmen and Nobles to send their children abroad for education. These successive acts, coupled with the

[2] Li Hung-chang was supposed to have a modern force under his direction, but it could not be considered as constituting a modern or national army.

action of the United States in returning a portion of the Boxer indemnity and the decision to use it for educational purposes, and with the successes of Japan in the war with Russia, gave a tremendous impetus to the interest in foreign study and led many to go abroad for that purpose. The consequences of this movement will be indicated when we attempt to picture the background of the revolution.

Among other changes predicated or actually undertaken were a removal of the ban on intermarriage of Manchus and Chinese; an attempt at the abolition of official sinecures; some reorganization in the central administrative system, mainly by changing the names of various offices, consolidating agencies and redistributing functions; and the active encouragement of railroad building, the undertaking of mining operations with Chinese capital, and the construction of arsenals.[3]

After the outbreak of war between Russia and Japan, which was fought almost entirely on Chinese territory, the reform movement was accelerated and, moreover, took on the character of real institutional change. The victory of a reconstructed Oriental state over a powerful Occidental antagonist created active and widespread interest in reform as the earlier defeats of China had not done. A reference to the reform edicts of 1898 [4] will indicate how closely the changes proposed from 1901–1905 paralleled the earlier program, and will consequently serve to show how little growth there had been in appreciation of the necessity for fundamental reconstruction of the political system. After 1905 the movement began to look toward the ultimate introduction of constitutional government into China. And there began also a conscious effort to centralize authority—to break down the autonomy of the provinces by means of the establishment of a national system of rail communications, which would ultimately make possible a more effective supervision over them. It must be here pointed out, however, that the policy of railway centralization was adopted only after several years had been given over to an attempt to finance and construct railways by and in the provinces with local funds. This question of railway policy acquired major importance as the revolutionary movement developed, and will be discussed more fully later.[5]

3. THE CONSTITUTIONAL MOVEMENT

The idea of constitutionalism as a panacea for the ills of the state was, in large part, an importation from Japan. Prior to 1890 that country had been considered weak, and the Japanese had been looked down upon as an inferior people. Then suddenly China had been forced to revise her impression of her neighbor. First Japan showed herself to be stronger than

[3] Social and general economic changes of this period are discussed in chapter XII.
[4] Supra, pp. 158–160.
[5] Infra, pp. 218–220.

China, and then she successfully challenged the great European Power, Russia. The chief secret of the newly acquired strength of Japan was felt to be her introduction of Western methods of government. And, since it was after the establishment of the Japanese constitution that the strength of the Island Empire was first revealed, the belief was natural enough. Furthermore, all the great European states except Russia, as the edict accepting the report of a commission sent abroad in 1905 to study Western forms of government pointed out, had constitutions. And Russia had just been defeated by the first Asiatic state to establish a constitutional system. The conclusion seemed to be perfectly obvious.

The report of the commission also indicated to the Empress-Dowager that the Japanese had found it possible to continue, through constitutional forms, the old absolutist system of government. There was no reason apparent to her why the same result might not be achieved in China. Thus she said: "As for ourselves, it is necessary at present to make a careful investigation into the matter, and prepare ourselves to imitate this government by constitution, in which the supreme control must be in the hands of the Throne, while the interests of the masses shall be given to the elect, advanced to such position by the suffrage of the masses." [6]

It is certainly questionable whether the autocratic Tzu Hsi would have even contemplated seriously the establishment of a constitutional system if she had thought that it would introduce any real limitation on her own power, or that it would affect the Manchu supremacy. But to recognize that fact is not to impugn the motives of the Court and the reform party among the officials. The constitution itself, it was their honest belief, was what would serve to strengthen China, just as it had Japan, even though the old system really functioned under and through the new forms. Their knowledge of Western systems of government was slight, and their understanding of the tendencies in political development after the principle of popular participation has been admitted was just as limited. So there may well have been honesty of intention in the attempt to establish a constitutional form of government in China while maintaining the autocracy. It was only in and after 1910, when the ultimate end of the movement began to be made apparent, that the Manchus laid themselves open to the charge of insincerity and double-dealing.

Had it not been for the revolutionary year 1911, the great year for modern China might have been 1908, for it was then that the government took the first steps toward the establishment of a constitutional régime. The Throne promulgated the "principles" of the constitution, announced a definite program of gradual progress, leading up to the calling of the National Parliament within nine years, and sanctioned regulations governing the provincial assemblies which were to be called into being within a year.

[6] *China Year Book*, 1912, p. 353.

It is only necessary here to note the point of view expressed through the "Principles of the Constitution." It was identical with that originally expressed by the Empress-Dowager. A quotation from the edict accepting the "Principles" will serve to illustrate it. The foreign nations which "have established their constitutions under influences from above have first determined the ultimate authority of the Court, and thereafter there has been granted to the people the advantage of inquiring about the affairs of government. . . . In most of the nations in which the constitution has been granted from above the origin of all powers is in the Court. The Parliament must grow out of the constitution, not the constitution out of Parliament. The government of China is to be constitutional by imperial decree."[7] Consequently the primary emphasis was laid on securing the powers of the Throne in order to ensure that "the Ta Ts'ing Dynasty shall rule over the Ta Ts'ing Empire for ever and ever, and be honored through all ages." This was not a very good start, it must be recognized, toward convincing the country of the sincerity of Manchu professions, but it was, nevertheless, a distinct step in advance.

The setting-up of a program of gradual reform extending over a nine-year period was an indication of wisdom rather than of bad faith. It revealed a perception of the fact that China was not prepared for a representative system of government and that the foundations should be carefully laid before the superstructure was erected. Of course it could also be interpreted in another way—as providing a breathing space for the Manchus, during which they could revivify their rule. During the period each year was to witness certain changes such as the introduction of local self-government, law reform, census-taking, police reorganization, the extension of the educational system so as gradually to reduce illiteracy, the introduction of a budget and auditing system, and the issue of constitutional laws, imperial house laws, and parliamentary laws. The whole program was to culminate in the establishment of a parliament and the organization of a privy council and a cabinet in the ninth year. Certainly all of these reforms were necessary and, if carried out in good faith, would have served as foundations for the new régime. However, because of the confusion of the years after 1908, coupled perhaps with a lack of real interest in reform, many steps in the program were taken only on paper.

A third important advance, promised in 1907 and incorporated in the program of 1908, related to the establishment of provincial assemblies as a preliminary step to the convocation of a National Assembly. This promise was actually carried out when the former were convened in October of 1909. The members were selected by electoral colleges composed of representatives chosen by a carefully restricted electorate, and the powers and functions of the assembly were limited with equal care. The regulations

[7] *"Amer. For. Rel.,"* 1908, incl. 1 in no. 1005, p. 192.

governing them stated that "it must not be forgotten that all deliberative bodies are restricted in their functions to debate. They have absolutely no executive powers." [8] And in the main they could only debate propositions submitted to them by the Viceroy or Governor. The intention obviously was to create agencies for the ascertainment of public opinion rather than governing bodies. As such they would have served to indicate the sincerity of the rulers while not unduly interfering with them. Unfortunately for the Manchus, however, the assemblies immediately began to give voice to provincial grievances, serving as focal points for the expression of unrest and dissatisfaction. They united in pressing for a shortening of the period of preparation before the establishment of a parliament; they expressed dissatisfaction with the Imperial government's railway policy; and they asserted themselves in the actual development of provincial policy, many times in opposition to the Governor or Viceroy. Their activities outside the range of their legal functions were so noteworthy that it may be said that in some of the provinces they were in a fair way to establish themselves in a controlling position. After the outbreak of the revolution they served in some cases as an agency of direction. On the whole they facilitated the revolutionary development instead of helping to retard it.

In yet another direction the year 1908 was of outstanding importance, for within a short interval of time both the Emperor and the Empress-Dowager died. The death of Kuang Hsü was not especially significant, but the death of the Empress-Dowager at almost the same time removed from the helm the strong hand of the truly remarkable woman who had ruled China since 1860. When the Emperor died the Old Buddha, not anticipating her own early end, provided for the accession of another minor to the Throne, with Prince Ch'un named as the nominal Regent. Her death left him in a position of real rather than nominal authority.[9] The Regent was a well-meaning man, but had not sufficient knowledge or strength to cope with an increasingly difficult and complex situation. Nor was there at Peking any man of sufficient wisdom and ability to deal with it. The one strong man of progressive tendencies who might have saved the Manchus was sent into retirement in 1908 in fulfillment of a last request of the Emperor. Yüan Shih-k'ai had incurred the undying enmity of Kuang Hsü as a result of his participation in the coup d'état of 1898. In consequence of this the Emperor demanded, on his death bed, Yüan Shih-k'ai's life. Moreover, Yüan Shih-k'ai had the strong man's usual quota of active enemies at court, and the death of Tzu Hsi removed his principal supporter. Prince Ch'un did not feel free to accomplish his death, but he did give him leave to go into retirement. "He has now, however, been seized with a disease in the

[8] From translation of regulations given *"Amer. For. Rel.,"* 1908, incl. in no. 989.

[9] Which, however, he had to share with the widow of Kuang Hsü, the new Empress-Dowager.

feet which makes it difficult for him to move about and thus renders him unfit for the performance of his duties. We therefore Decree that as a mark of compassion he shall forthwith vacate his posts and retire to his native place for the purpose of treating his complaint." [10] With him went out of public life many of the able officials with whom he had surrounded himself.

Thus simultaneously the two principal figures of strength at Peking were lost to the government, and with their passing a question was automatically raised as to the future of reform. This question was answered in an edict of November 25, 1909. "We will reverently obey the edict issued on the first day of the eighth moon last year." Reform was to be continued but without a strong central direction, and, in the result, in such a manner as to justify the belief that only constantly applied pressure would avail to secure the realization of the 1908 program.

The new régime continued the issuance of proclamations instituting, by edict and in most cases on paper only, changes in the system of local government and enlarging educational opportunities. There was, however, a tendency then, as also later under the Republic, to consider the reform accomplished with the publication of the edict. And so far as the central government assumed a merely hortatory rôle, it laid itself open to the charge of lack of sincerity. On the other hand, since many of the changes could be inaugurated only with the coöperation of provincial officials, the Peking government may deserve only part of the blame.

One major change which passed beyond the paper stage, the establishment of provincial assemblies, has already been noted. Another was the convocation of the National Assembly in October, 1910. This body was so constituted as entirely to warrant the belief that it would be essentially conservative, seeing "eye to eye" with the government. One-half of its membership was selected by Imperial appointment and the other half was elected by the provincial assemblies. Since the members of the latter were chosen indirectly on the basis of a carefully restricted electorate, the provincial representatives should have been little less conservative than the Imperial nominees. But actually the history of the National Assembly resembled that of the provincial bodies. It asserted itself from the beginning in opposition to the government. It took up and pressed the case for an earlier promulgation of the constitution than was contemplated in the nine-year program, securing a promise of the shortening of the period of preparation to five years, with the establishment of a parliament in 1913. It attacked the policy of the government in financial matters and on questions of administration, and was prevented from impeaching the Council of State only because of concessions on the point at issue. It demanded, in the spring of 1911, the creation of a responsible cabinet and forced an acceptance of the principle before its adjournment. All of its activities

[10] KENT, *Passing of the Manchus*, p. 43.

indicated its intention of keeping the government in the path of reform, and even of modifying and enlarging the reform program. These intentions, it may be noted, were indicated before the outbreak of rebellion in the Yangtse provinces, and there is therefore reason to believe that the Chinese autocracy would have been transformed gradually into a constitutional monarchy had it not been for the revolution. Developments in the fall of 1911, however, were so entirely controlled by the condition of revolution that they must be treated in connection with it. Consequently it now becomes necessary to estimate the causes of the revolution as a preliminary step to the consideration of its events.

4. UNDERLYING CAUSES OF REVOLUTION

Underlying every movement of the kind in China there has been the population problem, growing out of too great a pressure of peoples on the means of subsistence. "A nation which implicitly believes, and unanimously acts on the belief, that a man's first duty in life is to provide as many male heirs as possible for the comfort of himself and of his ancestors, inevitably condemns vast masses of its people to the lowest depths of poverty, and condemns the body politic to regularly recurring cataclysms." [11] The cycle begins with an equipoise of population and food supply. Given normal conditions of production, the number of people rapidly increases. As the equilibrium is upset some are inevitably condemned to starvation or to outlawry. Since the number of brigands and pirates increases with population expansion, the public peace becomes increasingly disturbed as part of the survival struggle. If the government is strong and efficient, many of the brigands are caught and killed, and the ultimate trouble is postponed. However, normal conditions give way to abnormal because of flood or drought. A large number die of starvation or become outlaws. If outlawry is controlled by the strong hand of authority and there are many deaths, the equilibrium may be partially restored and rebellion averted. If authority is weak there may ensue more or less widespread rebellion, and out of the resulting conflict there may come a restoration of the equilibrium. In either case the solution is only a temporary one.

It has already been pointed out that the Manchu authority had been steadily growing weaker during the nineteenth century. The T'ai P'ing rebellion was in part put down with foreign aid. But its destructiveness to human life temporarily checked population expansion, as did the two Mohammedan rebellions and numerous smaller uprisings. It was only a check, however, even though supplemented by famines such as that of 1878, which, it was estimated, took over nine million lives. All of these crises were tided over, partly because most of them were localized. The

[11] BLAND, *Recent Events and Present Policies in China*, p. 14.

increase in population went on in spite of them, and with it the usual increase in unrest and discontent. In 1910–1911 normal conditions of production were again disturbed by floods in the central provinces "the worst in
forty years . . . millions of people were made homeless and the ruin of
their crops in the two former Provinces (Anhui and Kiangsu) for the
third time in five years, added the horrors of famine and pestilence. The
Provinces of Shantung, Chekiang, Kiangsi and Hupeh also suffered, some
from floods, and some from droughts, so that in the seven provinces affected a total of 600,000 families or 3,000,000 people, were actually starving
and dying. . . . Discontent in such circumstances is easily swollen into a
rage of rebellion." [12] It may be pointed out also that the foreign-introduced
idea of the sanctity of human life led to more energetic famine-relief measures than would have been taken in pre-modern days. Consequently people
avoided starvation, but their lives were not subsequently put on a normal
basis. Thus many more were preserved to serve purposes of rebellion than
would usually have been the case.

This pressure of population might have been relieved by other means
than starvation or the violent deaths incident to rebellion. The surplus
people of the eighteen provinces might, for example, have migrated to the
less densely populated parts of the Empire or to foreign countries. One
serious impediment to migration, however, lay in the necessity of keeping
up the worship at the ancestral tombs,—for "it is the duty of every man to
sacrifice at stated intervals at his ancestral tombs and to be buried, in due
season, with his fathers. Thus the great bulk of the population has for
centuries been rigidly localized." [13] Another thing which, until after 1900,
localized the population was the difficulty of movement from place to
place. In spite of these impediments, however, population had begun to
move into Manchuria from Chihli and especially from Shantung provinces.
Many who moved northwards in the spring returned home after the harvest, but increasingly large proportions remained to find homes and found
families in Manchuria. Nothing probably accounts for this movement to
a greater extent than the building of the Peking-Mukden and the other
Manchurian railways. This improvement in communications had not extended very far into the northwest, another colonization area, at the time
of the revolution, and as a result there had not been so extensive a movement into the other dependencies, although there had been a slight migration to them from neighboring provinces.

In the same way some of the overflow from the southern provinces, notably Kwangtung, had begun to seek an outlet overseas. The Cantonese

---

[12] BROWN, *The Chinese Revolution*, pp. 3–4. It is interesting to note the coincidence of the
famine and active revolutionary areas.

[13] BLAND, op. cit., p. 15.

were more venturesome by disposition than their fellows north of the Yangtse and they had been longer in contact with the outside world, a contact which tended gradually to draw them outside of the homeland. Reference has already been made to the coming of the Chinese laborer to the Pacific coast of the United States, and to the coolie traffic at Macao. The latter was broken up and the United States closed its doors to the Chinese by the exclusion acts of the 1880's and 1890's. The total number of immigrants to the United States between 1830 and 1911 was slightly over 300,000, a few over a thousand having entered in 1911. Denied admission to the United States, the Chinese turned to Hawaii, the Philippines, the Malay archipelago—Singapore, the Federated Malay States, etc.—and Canada. Immigration to Hawaii was soon prohibited and the exclusion acts were extended to the Philippines in 1902. Canada enacted a $500 head tax on entering Chinese in 1903, which served to restrict immigration there. Singapore and the Federated Malay States by 1911 had received about 1,300,000 Chinese, but all in all the number of overseas Chinese at that time must have totaled well under two and a half million. This was a drop in the bucket so far as taking care of the surplus population in even Kwangtung was concerned. It did help out in another way, however. The Chinese abroad were able to send comparatively large remittances home and thus added to the resources of their families. The revolution was aided materially by the wealth of the overseas Chinese also, for they subscribed most liberally to the cause.

It is clear, however, that neither by colonization nor by emigration was the problem being solved, any more than it was by famine and rebellion, for the total population is estimated to have increased from over 377 millions to over 430 millions between 1885 and 1911. Thus by the latter year the pressure on the food supply had become acute enough, coupled with the famine conditions of 1910–1911, to furnish the material for a widespread revolt.

Another economic factor was finance. Expenses had been steadily mounting after 1900 because of new expenditures made necessary by the reorganization program. These included the paying and equipping of the model army, the construction of railways, and the establishment of new educational institutions. The payments on the loans to meet the Japanese war indemnity had to be made, as did the much heavier payments on the Boxer indemnity. These absorbed virtually the entire revenue from the customs and from some other revenue services, thus withdrawing them from use in meeting the general expenses. Consequently the tax levies became increasingly heavy and new charges had to be made. This substantially increased the volume of discontent and dissatisfaction with the dynasty.

5. INFLUENCE OF THE REVOLUTIONARY GROUPS

This economic unrest created a receptive state of mind for the message of those who were true revolutionaries rather than discontented subjects. There had been a revolutionary party among the Chinese since before the expulsion of the reformers in 1898. The reform and revolutionary elements were largely concentrated in Tokyo and they maintained distinct programs. The reformers, headed by K'ang Yu-wei and his leading disciple Liang Ch'i-ch'ao, preached the doctrine of constitutional monarchy, which, as the constitutional movement developed under the Manchus after 1905, made them merely advanced advocates of the theoretical Manchu program. Their activities during the first decade of the century, however, undoubtedly helped to bring into existence the sentiment for constitutional reform which expressed itself through the provincial and national assemblies and acted as a strong propulsive force on the Manchus. The revolutionaries were led by Dr. Sun Yat-sen and had frankly anti-dynastic aims. They were definitely organized by 1905, when they took the name of the T'ung Meng Hui (Alliance Society), were responsible for sporadic outbreaks in 1906, 1907, and 1910, and took the initiative in transforming the outbreak of 1911 into a revolution.

For a time the revolutionary ranks were largely recruited from among the overseas Chinese, among whom Dr. Sun traveled extensively, preaching the doctrines of the society. But after 1905 the field in China was more intensively cultivated. Converts were made among those who had been or were affiliated with one or more of the several secret societies which had a perennial existence south of the Yangtse. Effort was concentrated on the new model army, whence recruits to the anti-Manchu, or at least the reform, cause were enlisted in comparatively large numbers, especially in the divisions which were centered at Hankow and Nanking. Not so much progress was made among the northern soldiery.

A third center of revolutionary propaganda was among the new student class. After 1900, and particularly after 1905, large numbers went abroad to study. Some went to America and Europe with the expectation of devoting several years to a mastery of Western learning. But many more went to Japan, where, in many instances, they fell into the clutches of those who promised to conduct them along the royal road to Western learning, preparing them in the new subjects in a few weeks. Since their sole object was to equip themselves for government position in the shortest possible time, many of the Chinese students preferred to work in these mushroom schools which were organized "for Chinese only," rather than to spend several years in the regular Japanese institutions, where there was not room for all of them in any case. And since they could secure diplomas by the payment of fees they had time to spare, in the use of which they were often brought into contact with the exiled revolutionists. Upon their return to China they usually found that there were no governmental positions open to them, in spite of the possession of foreign diplomas. Thus they were furnished with a grievance against the government, and were very susceptible to the continued revolutionary propaganda. While their learning was, at the best, superficial, the fact of their foreign experience gave them a certain position which made them effective centers from which revolutionary doctrines might be spread. Thus, in addition to the exiled leaders in the revolutionary movement, a native local leadership was gradually built up. While some of the returned students undoubtedly had a thorough grounding in the new learning, many more of them had only a phrase book knowledge of republicanism and all of the things which were so soon to become of real importance. The significance of Young China thus lay not so much in its enlightenment as in its discontent with the political *status quo.*

The relation of the student to the revolution would not be completely revealed without mention of the influence of the mission schools, which were even more materially adding to the ranks of Young China by sending out their graduates year by year. It is not to reflect on their standards to say that many of their graduates were dissatisfied with their prospects and that they were ready converts to the cause of revolution without having more than a surface or book knowledge of the problems connected with the successful operation of a representative system of government. But the fact is significant that the student class, with its peculiar position in China, was sufficiently imbued with new ideas by 1911 to swing into the revolutionary movement with almost its full force. It is also significant that many of the radicals in the first assemblies set up during and after the revolution had been either graduated from or had spent time in study in the mission schools. Likewise noteworthy is the fact that, as the government attempted to put its new educational program into effect after 1905, it was forced to turn to the mission schools and the returned student group for its teachers. Thus their zone of influence was appreciably widened as a direct result of the Manchu reform activity.

6. IMMEDIATE CAUSES OF REBELLION

We may note, in passing, the importance of improved communications, through the extension of the postal, the telegraph, and the railroad systems, in facilitating the spread of revolutionary doctrines and the making of revolutionary plans. We may also call attention to the rapid growth of a vernacular press, which was concerned principally with discussion of reforms, and which openly, although cautiously, followed the lead of the revolutionary and reform papers published in Tokyo and brought clandestinely into China. The most radical papers were distributed from the foreign concessions in such places as Shanghai and were consequently not under the control of the Chinese government.

These were among the more fundamental factors which produced revolution rather than abortive rebellion on a restricted scale. A more direct and immediate cause, as well as the actual occasion, for rebellion was an outgrowth of the Peking government's railroad policy during the years from 1909 to 1911. As a reaction to the concession-grabbing period there came, following a distinct lull, a pronounced movement looking toward railroad construction on a provincial rather than a national basis, with a financing of enterprises with Chinese rather than foreign funds. The fundamental question was that of centralization as against decentralization. But the advocates of a decentralized system did not have to defend it on its essential merits, for the problem was complicated by the fear of foreign control through the financing of a national system. The demand for provincial control was the central feature of a "Rights Recovery" movement which developed after 1905. One of the leading advocates of the enlargement of China's railway system was the Hukuang Viceroy, Chang Chih-tung, but he perceived the dangers in the concessions policy and advised that control should be vested in the provinces. Thus it was largely because of his insistence that the Hankow-Canton trunk line was turned over to the provinces concerned for construction and that the same policy was followed with respect to the Hankow-Szechuan road. The Chêkiang railroad bureau was also able to prevent the construction of the Shanghai-Hang-chow-Ningpo railway as a national enterprise, although the Peking government was compelled to borrow the money for it from the British and Chinese Corporation in fulfillment of a promise made in 1898.

By 1909 not only the central government but Chang Chih-tung as well had come to perceive the unwisdom of the policy. In the first place, the large sums necessary could not be found in the provinces. In the second place, the money actually collected tended to disappear without an equivalent part of the railway program being realized, for there was much diversion of funds to other uses, and "squeeze" was prevalent. Consequently, if the vitally necessary trunk lines were to be built, the central government would have to take them in hand again. And in the third place, the relation of communications to the strengthening of the authority of Peking became clearer to those in power. The death of Chang Chih-tung in 1909, before the new policy could be put into effect, was unfortunate as he had the confidence of the provinces, whereas the man appointed as President of the Board of Communications did not. Before his death, however, preliminary negotiations for foreign financing and supervision of construction of the Hukuang railways had been concluded.

Sheng Hsüan-huai was appointed President of the Board of Communications early in 1911 and the policy of centralization was actively put into effect. As the first step, negotiations with the Four Power Banking Group for a large loan for the construction of the Hankow-Canton and Hankow-Szechuan railways were carried to completion. At the same time a $10,000,-000 loan for currency reform and for industrial development in Manchuria was negotiated. As a preliminary step to the realization of the purposes of the railway loan it was necessary to reach an agreement with the provincial interests affected. The conclusion of the loan agreement had been followed by protests from the provinces through which the roads would pass and by riots in some places, so that it was necessary for Peking to go as far as possible in placating the gentry in the provinces. The solution adopted for Kwangtung, Hunan, and Hupeh provinces was to exchange interest-bearing government bonds for the railway shares to their full value, except in Kwangtung, where the shares were at a discount of over fifty per cent. There interest-bearing bonds were to be issued to sixty per cent and non-interest-bearing bonds for the remaining forty per cent of the shares. "In view of the complicated nature of the situation, and of the fact that each one of the railway companies was virtually bankrupt, the government proposals appeared to be not only reasonable but generous." [14] For the Szechu-anese, however, the government proposed redemption only of the sums actually expended for railway purposes rather than the amount subscribed or collected by special tax levies. Fourteen million taels had been subscribed. Of this sum, half was supposed to be available for subscription to government bonds, industrial needs in the province or return to the shareholders. Almost half of the remaining seven million taels had been lost in the Shanghai rubber boom through the speculations of one of the managers.[15] The government consequently proposed to give bonds to the holders of securities in the Szechuan enterprise to the amount of about four million taels. Protest was immediately made against this settlement by means of memorials presented to the Throne through the Viceroy. The protest stage was succeeded by one of passive resistance. "Shops were closed, employees struck, students refused to attend the schools and colleges, payment of taxes was refused." [16] The arrest of some of the leaders in the movement of opposition led to an attack on the Viceroy's Yamen and to active resistance. This was in September, 1911. Instead of using all available force to put down the uprising the Imperial government resorted to a policy of "pacification," which, while it might ultimately have been successful, was too slow a process for the times. This policy may have resulted both from a feeling of weakness and from the recognition that the Szechuanese were not alone in their opposition to the policy of centralization. Furthermore, the government may have been influenced by the distrust of Sheng Hsüan-

[14] KENT, op. cit., p. 58.
[15] Ibid., p. 59.
[16] Ibid., p. 60.

huai, who, though a man of great ability, had a somewhat unsavory financial reputation as a result of his management of the China Merchants Steam Navigation Company and of some of his previous posts held under the adroit Li Hung-chang. It was felt that it was somewhat inconsistent for him to suggest penalizing the gentry of Szechuan because of peculation and misuse of funds by the managers of their enterprise.

7. THE REVOLUTION OF 1911

The revolt in Szechuan was not anti-dynastic in motive, and so the revolution is not dated from its outbreak but from the aftermath of an accidental bomb explosion which took place in Hankow on October 10, 1911, while the attempt at pacification was going on in the great western province. Upon investigating the place where the explosion occurred, the police found it to be the headquarters of a revolutionary group engaged at the time in the making of bombs, and they secured lists containing the names of local revolutionaries. This led to the arrest and execution of several members of the group. As a result of this and of the fear of further action, the troops at Wuchang, just across the Yangtse, broke out in revolt, forcing their commander, Colonel Li Yuan-hung, to assume the leadership. He himself had not previously been won over to the revolutionary cause, but after accepting the command he proved to be one of the most trustworthy of the republican leaders. After some fighting the Wuchang troops, augmented by recruits from the countryside, gained control of Hankow and Hanyang as well as Wuchang, thus establishing themselves in the largest center in central China.

The flame of revolt spread rapidly up and down the Yangtse and to the south. In the north, Shantung province declared its independence for a time, although soon returning to the Imperial fold, and there was disaffection in parts of Chihli, principally among the troops. However, the northern Imperial forces on the whole remained loyal and the situation was kept well in hand north of the Yangtse River, except in Shensi province. The entire movement had the appearance of a series of spontaneous independent revolts rather than of a well-planned and coördinated revolution. This is partially accounted for by the revolutionary strategy which was, apparently, to try out the revolutionary sentiment at various centers, trusting that ultimately the flame would spread. Thus there had been an earlier outbreak at Canton which had been put down without spreading. It is also to be explained by the fact that the adherents of revolution had necessarily been brought together into local rather than national groups and had been forced to lay their plans on a local basis. And it is also claimed that plans had been made for a concerted effort at a later date so that, when the discovery came at Hankow, the action taken, although necessary, was premature so far as the plans of the other groups were concerned. However this may be, the fact remains that there was no common direction of the revolution until at a comparatively late time. The original leadership was centered at Wuchang, although it had no effective control over activities elsewhere. Finally steps were taken to coördinate the movement by requesting the "independent" provinces to send delegates to Wuchang to serve as a revolutionary council, and a pact was subscribed to which served as the basis of the instrument later adopted at Nanking as the provisional constitution of the Republic.

Meanwhile the revolt had reached Shanghai, where a "Military Government" was set up. This government immediately asserted the right to speak for the entire revolution. Wu T'ing-fang, formerly minister to the United States, assumed the position of Minister for Foreign Affairs and issued a manifesto setting forth the aims of the revolution and appealing for foreign sympathy. This group also demanded that the Powers preserve neutrality, threatening not to recognize the validity of loans made to the Imperial government in the event of its overthrow. The pretensions of the Shanghai government soon brought it into conflict with that at Wuchang, especially over the control of peace negotiations with the Imperial government when the stage of negotiation was reached, and it was only the self-effacing character of Li Yuan-hung, who allowed the direction to pass to the Shanghai group, which prevented a break in the revolutionary ranks. One reason for their assertiveness undoubtedly was the fact that they were determined to ensure control of the new régime by Cantonese, for the leaders at Shanghai were from Canton while those at Wuchang were from the central provinces.

At this point it is necessary to turn our attention back to Peking. The story of reform was left with the adjournment of the National Assembly in the spring of 1911. The Assembly reconvened on October 22, ten days after the Wuchang outbreak. Its first act was to secure the dismissal of Sheng Hsüan-huai, thus taking its stand with the provinces on the question of railway centralization. It then opened an attack on the government because of its failure to constitute a real Cabinet, as it had promised to do before the summer. The promise had been carried out merely by changing the name of the Grand Council to that of Cabinet. The Assembly formulated three fundamental demands for the acceptance of the government. These were that a capable and virtuous person be immediately appointed to organize a responsible Cabinet, from which members of the Imperial Family should be explicitly excluded; that an amnesty should be proclaimed for all political offenders, including the exiled reformers of 1898; and that a constitution should be framed only after consultation with the assembly. Added weight was given to these demands by reason of the spread of the rebellion and by a refusal of troops stationed at Lanchou, on the Peking-

Mukden railroad, to entrain for the south until they had been accepted. They were all three accepted in a series of edicts issued on October 30. A new set of "Constitutional Principles" was drawn up by the Assembly and received the Imperial approval November 3. Briefly, they created a constitutional monarchy of a very limited sort, the Emperor being assigned much the same position as that enjoyed by the English king. Thus, by the beginning of November, the Manchus, under the double pressure of the assembly of their own creation and of the anti-dynastic revolution, had agreed to give up the substance of power in the endeavor to retain the Imperial title.

While making these concessions the Regent had also taken steps to put down the rebellion by other means. The first step in that direction was the recall of Yüan Shih-k'ai to office. This was done only after it had become apparent that no one else was strong enough to deal with the revolution. He was recalled on October 14, but on the plea of a continuation of his old trouble, which he had been sent home to cure, and of other ailments, he declined to return to official life until October 27. Negotiations during this interval resulted in acceptance of his terms, which amounted to conferring the powers of a dictator on him. In addition to being made the Hukuang Viceroy he was given supreme command of the army and navy and, on November 8, he was elected Premier by the National Assembly.

His primary object was apparently to secure a settlement which would retain the monarch while depriving him of all power. There has always been doubt as to his desire to preserve the Manchu dynasty, but the available evidence seems to indicate that he was loyal to the Emperor so far as the latter was willing, in good faith, to accept the status of a constitutional ruler. Certainly he did not believe then, or later, in the feasibility of a republic for China. To bring the rulers to an acceptance of the status he had in mind, it was necessary that the rebellion should continue to make some headway. On the other hand, it was necessary to bring the revolutionaries to an acceptance of the same status by a manifestation of the Imperial strength. Only by accepting some such hypothesis as this is it possible to explain the failure of the Imperial troops to follow up advantages which they won in the fighting around Hankow.

From the military standpoint it is only necessary to say that the Imperial troops on several occasions demonstrated their superiority of leadership, of training, and of equipment, over the revolutionary army led by Li Yuan-hung, joined shortly by Huang Hsing, one of the original revolutionaries. When Yüan made up his mind to fight, his troops gained one success after another, and yet they were never allowed to push forward to a decisive victory. The other place where active organized fighting took place was at Nanking. There an old-school commander named Chang Hsun assumed control and remained faithful to the Manchus after the revolutionists refused to buy his support because his terms were too high. Nanking was defended for some time, but finally was occupied by the republican forces and was made the temporary southern capital.

8. NEGOTIATIONS FOR PEACE

While Yüan Shih-k'ai had been directing hostilities at Hankow he had also been attempting to open negotiations with Li Yuan-hung. As a result of Imperial successes the latter consented to discuss terms of settlement at the end of November. The Shanghai government, however, insisted that the conditions of peace must be negotiated with it. Yüan at first refused to deal with it, but finally consented since General Li accepted it as entitled to speak for the republican forces. T'ang Shao-yi, an American educated Cantonese who had been Yüan Shih-k'ai's ablest lieutenant before 1908, was appointed as the Imperial delegate to confer with Dr. Wu T'ing-fang, another Cantonese, who was the Minister for Foreign Affairs of the Shanghai government.

Before the negotiations were brought to a conclusion delegates from the rebellious provinces, mainly self-selected, although some were chosen by the provincial assemblies and some were appointed by the military governors of the provinces so controlled, had met at Nanking and assumed the supreme direction of the revolution. Li Yuan-hung had taken the initial steps to bring this council into being and it was completed as to membership, and its meeting place changed to Nanking, at the instigation of the Shanghai government. After meeting it elected Dr. Sun Yat-sen, who had just returned to China, as the provisional President. It was with this government that peace negotiations were finally concluded.

Space precludes a detailed consideration of the negotiations. It may be said, however, that the republicans included as their primary demand an end of the monarchy and the acceptance of the Republic. They did suggest the submission of the question of the form of government to a National Convention, but when the Imperial government agreed to this the two sides failed to unite on a method of bringing such a convention into being and the project failed. The republicans then returned to their original position. The Imperial delegate seems to have accepted immediately the suggestions of the southern representative as to the advisability of ending the Manchu monarchy and to have thereby disqualified himself to represent the northern interest. Later he became a leader of the southern party.

As negotiations continued, the necessity for a settlement became increasingly apparent to both sides. Both the imperialists and the republicans were weak financially. The Peking treasury was empty, and it had been necessary for Yüan to force the Regent to contribute from the Household treasure to pay the troops. And Nanking had no treasury and no treasure. Both were prevented from financing themselves from foreign sources by reason of the financial neutrality agreed to by the Powers. If peace had not come, however, it is possible that the loan embargo might have been lifted in Yüan's favor, since the foreign representatives looked upon him as the strong man capable of preventing a possible eventual chaos. The republicans were financed at first through the generous subscriptions made to the cause by overseas Chinese, and out of such provincial revenues as were at their command. They also received some funds from non-official Japanese sources, and were able to negotiate a few loans on the security of some semi-public enterprises such as the Hanyehp'ing iron and coal corporation. But all of these sources of income had been largely exhausted by the end of the year. Consequently acute financial embarrassment rather than the strength of either side ultimately forced a settlement.

Yüan Shih-k'ai began the last stage of the negotiations by attempting to secure good terms for the Manchus, who were gradually brought to an acceptance of the necessity for abdication, and to strengthen his personal position. About the middle of January Dr. Sun Yat-sen, seemingly on his own initiative, telegraphed Premier Yüan, offering him the presidency if he would accept the Republic and consequently the necessity for abdication. The Manchus countered by elevating him to the rank of Marquis. He did not openly accept the former offer, but he did decline, four times, the Manchu tender.

9. THE SETTLEMENT

The final terms of settlement were agreed to and the abdication edicts issued on February 12, 1912.[17] The dynasty abdicated in consideration of: (1) a good financial settlement; (2) the promise of security for members of their race, and of the Imperial Household; and (3) provision for the upkeep of the Imperial tombs. By the terms of one of the edicts the Emperor transferred power to Yüan Shih-k'ai, rather than to the southern government, thus putting him in a strong position in the eyes of the common people. The exact words of the edict, in translation, were: "Let Yüan Shih-k'ai organize with full powers a provisional republican government, and confer with the Republican Army as to methods of union, thus assuring peace to the people and tranquility to the Empire, and forming the one Great Republic of China by the union as heretofore of the five peoples, namely, Manchus, Chinese, Mongols, Mohammedans, and Tibetans, together with their territory in its integrity." Dr. Sun, for the Nanking Government, responded to this part of the edict that "the Republican Government cannot be organized by any authority conferred by the Ch'ing Emperor. The exercise of such pretentious power must surely lead to serious trouble." Yüan, however, assured Dr. Sun that he did not intend to take advantage

[17] See *China Year Book*, 1913, pp. 481–484, for translation of the abdication edicts.

of the wording of the edicts, and the Republicans accepted his assurances. The wording was not changed and the "serious trouble" which Dr. Sun foresaw came in due course.

The negotiations with the "Republican Army" were completed by the resignation of Dr. Sun Yat-sen from the provisional presidency, followed by the election by the Nanking Assembly, upon his advice, of Yüan Shih-k'ai as the first provisional President of the Republic of reunited China. This action was a compromise pure and simple, since the southerners did not trust the new President and had justifiable doubts as to the sincerity of his action in accepting the Republic. Since they were not prepared to fight to secure his elimination, however, it was a necessary compromise. A consideration of its consequences will be a central feature of the next chapter.

A long chapter of Chinese history was thus closed with the abdication of the Manchu rulers and the formal ending of the Ta Ch'ing dynasty. They had wielded the vermilion pencil since 1644 and had contributed much brilliance as well as several shadows to the history of China. While the Republican picture of systematic Manchu misrule was far from accurate, it must be recognized that the dynasty had clearly exhausted the "mandate of Heaven" and had been preserved in power for over a half century by the lack of an adequate and acceptable alternative to their rule. Whether the Republic presented a satisfactory alternative time alone could show, and it would be deeds and not manifestos which would count.

REFERENCES FOR FURTHER STUDY

J. O. P. BLAND, *Recent Events and Present Policies in China* (1912), ch. 1–9. A. J. BROWN, *Chinese Revolution* (1912). M. E. CAMERON, *The Reform Movement in China, 1898–1912* (1931); the most recent study of the movement. JAMES CANTLIE and C. S. JONES, *Sun Yat Sen and the Awakening of China* (1912). Not a very critical study. FERNAND FARJENEL, *Through the Chinese Revolution* (1916), transl. from the French by Dr. Margaret Vivian; experiences and observations of the author in both the revolutionary provinces and the north; suggestive and informative. F. V. FIELD, *American Participation in the China Consortiums* (1931), ch. 6–8. H. A. GILES, *China and the Manchus* (1912). H. H. GOWEN and J. W. HALL, *An Outline History of China* (1926), ch. 26–30. A. N. HOLCOMBE, *The Chinese Revolution* (1930), ch. 1–4; a penetrating analysis of the nature of the "scholastic" empire and its implications for the revolution. S. K. HORNBECK, *Contemporary Politics in the Far East* (1916), ch. 1, and biographical notes, pp. 405–412. FRANKLIN W. HOUN, *Central Government of China, 1912–1926* (1957); an institutional study. LEONARD HSU, *Sun Yat-sen* (1933); a good sympathetic treatment. R. F. JOHNSTON, *Twilight in the Forbidden City* (1934); gives a view of the abdication from within the Manchu Court. P. H. KENT, *Passing of the Manchus* (1912). L. LAWTON, *Empires of the Far East*, 2 vols. (1912), vol. 2, book 3. P. M. A. LINEBARGER, *Sun Yat-sen and the Chinese Republic* (1925); better than CANTLIE and JONES. H. F. MACNAIR, *Modern Chinese History, Selected Readings* (1923), ch. 15. FREDERICK McCORMICK, *Flowery Republic* (1913); an account of the Revolution to the abdication of the Manchus. RALPH L. POWELL, *The Rise of Chinese Military Power, 1895–1912* (1955); a penetrating study. JOHN G. REID, *The Manchu Abdication and the Powers, 1908–1912* (1935); a thorough study. T'ANG LEANG-LI, *The Inner History of the Chinese Revolution* (1930), ch. 1–7; an instructive account by a convinced supporter of Dr. Sun Yat-sen. Y. H. TSENG, *Modern Chinese Legal and Political Philosophy* (1930); ch. 2–5. H. M. VINACKE, *Modern Constitutional Development in China* (1920), ch. 2–5.

CHAPTER XI

THE PHANTOM REPUBLIC: 1912–1926

I. INTERNAL CONDITIONS IN 1912 REVIEWED

A BRIEF review of internal conditions at the time of the inauguration of the republican form of government will serve as the best introduction to what may properly be called the era of military dominance. In fact although not in theory, this period included the years (1912–1916) of the ascendency of Yüan Shih-k'ai. In both theory and fact the decade from 1916 to 1926, frequently referred to as the period of the Tuchunate, would have to be included. During that decade all but a bare pretense at the maintenance of a central government had ceased, and authority had come to be exercised by the military leaders in the provinces. Since control of troops established the right to exercise authority, our review of internal conditions may best be started with the genesis and development of this military rule. Then we can consider the internal and external factors which initially operated to obscure its existence or to modify its operation. Finally, we can attempt to appraise its consequences.

It will be remembered that under Manchu rule the provincial establishment had consisted of a viceroy or governor, a treasurer, a judge, a salt comptroller, and a grain intendant, together with their deputies and assistants.[1] This officialdom, civil rather than military in nature, was kept under the control of the central government on account of (1) the method of selection and promotion of officials, (2) the rule of appointment which kept the higher officials away from their home provinces, and (3) the tenure of particular appointments. Division of authority also served to preserve loyalty to the central government. Subordinate officials were under the supervision of their superiors, and all officials were under the eye of the members of the censorate. An additional safeguard for the Manchu authority was erected in the form of the military governors who commanded the Banner and Green Standard troops. These troops, used to garrison the country in the interest of the Manchu conquerors, may be thought of as the pre-modern Chinese equivalent of a national army. Experience during the nineteenth century showed that they had become negligible as a fighting force, but they had, nevertheless, continued to serve the Manchu purpose of balancing the Chinese civil hierarchy against a corresponding military officialdom. Thus they not only supported the civil

---

[1] See chapter I, sec. 5, for a review of the political system.

authority in the province but at the same time helped to keep it loyal to Peking.

In addition to this force, kept under the direction of a separate Manchu military officialdom, militia forces were created from time to time as there was need for additional troops to preserve order by keeping down brigandage or preventing rebellion. These militia forces, essentially a provincial constabulary, were organized by and were under the direction of the Viceroy or the civil Governor. As the new national army came to be organized, such parts of it as had not yet, by the time of the revolution, been transferred to the control of the Board of War acted under the authority of the provincial officialdom. All of these troops were paid out of the provincial treasury. As a consequence, the allegiance of the soldier was to the Governor, who paid and kept him, rather than to the state.

The new national army, referred to above, had been in process of creation for some years, first under the direction of Li Hung-chang and then of Yüan Shih-k'ai. It had not, however, become truly national by 1911, existing mainly in the northern and central provinces, as was indicated in the name which came to be attached to it—the Peiyang (northern-ocean region) army. Since this army was organized by Yüan Shih-k'ai, its officers were subsequently found to be loyal to him rather than to the state.

As a result of the constitutional movement under the Manchus, provincial assemblies were provided for as part of the governmental machinery. They were actually opened in most of the provinces in 1909. These assemblies were retained as part of the provincial system after the revolution, with the exception of the period of personal rule by Yüan Shih-k'ai. Then they were temporarily abolished, to be later restored for a time with the reëstablishment of parliamentary government.

When the revolution broke out in 1911, in some cases the regular provincial officials proclaimed their allegiance to the republican cause and thus retained control of the province. In other cases the provincial assembly took control, ousted the Imperial officials, and selected the head for the province from among the gentry, or from among the natives of the province who had been in the Imperial service but who had declared for the revolution. This reconstitution of the government took place, during the course of the revolution, only in the provinces south of the Yangtse. In the main, the officials who successfully established themselves in control of the southern provinces were those whose authority was supported by troops who were responsive to their personal leadership. The limits within which they at first acted were, of course, either nominally or actually set by the purposes of the revolutionary leadership.

In the provinces loyal to the Dynasty the revolution merely affected the transfer to Yüan Shih-k'ai of the allegiance of the governors. This allegiance Yüan was given both personally and in his position as the legal successor to the Manchus. But in these provinces, as well as in those to the south, military power came to be the sole basis of authority, after the revolution as well as during its course. Yüan ruled and the authority of the central government was maintained after the establishment of the Republic because he could lead and effectively coördinate the activities of the military-civil authorities in the provinces.

As has been pointed out, the Governor had control of the troops even before 1911. In the course of the uprising the number of men under arms increased very greatly in all parts of the country. The recruits for both the Imperial and the Revolutionary armies came mostly from those living on the economic margin of existence, and from those living as brigands—men who went into the military service because of the guarantee of pay and the certainty of food and clothing. The pay was not always forthcoming, but as long as the commander retained control of the territory, the subsistence was more certain. The more troops a man had the larger the district which he could control successfully, and thus the more important the political figure he could cut. Many armed bands sprang up within the province, their leaders rendering nominal allegiance to the legal or self-constituted provincial authorities but establishing themselves in control of prefectures or districts. They supported themselves by force, and maintained themselves by collecting taxes over the smaller area or by requisitioning the people for supplies. Part of the taxes might be turned over to the provincial leader, after the expenses of the local régime had been defrayed, but very little went beyond the province.

2. MEANING OF THE REVOLUTION

When Yüan Shih-k'ai became President, he undertook to restore peace and order in the country. But he did not have the means to disband these practically independent troops in the face of the opposition of their leaders. Neither did he have the financial resources with which to buy them off and make up the arrears of pay due their soldiers, without which it would have been impossible to persuade them to return to civil life. Furthermore, it would have been a dangerous undertaking to disband them without making some temporary provision for their support. To do so would have meant that they would become brigands and thus be even more of a menace to the country than they were as soldiers. The consequence was that the President legalized the position in the province of many of their commanders by giving them official rank as Governor, expecting to carry out a gradual demobilization of troops as conditions returned to the normal. Under the circumstances the only limitation on the power of the Tutuh, or Military Governor, lay in such public opinion as could make itself heard directly, or indirectly through the assembly where such a body was in existence, and in the requirement of the central government that a measure of peace and order should be maintained in the province. In addition to the military governorship, certain other offices were created to make provision for the support of such men as Chang Hsun, the Imperial commander at Nanking when that city was captured by the revolutionists. General Chang retired up the Tientsin-Pukow railroad from Nanking and established his headquarters at Hsüchow in southern Shantung province. Since he was too powerful to be antagonized, and, further, gave assistance to Yüan by serving as a perpetual threat to the parliamentarians, he was given an office to retain his allegiance. The President's desire to control strategic locations within provinces whose military governors were not fully trusted provided another reason for complicating the system. Thus Shanghai was separated from Kiangsu province under a Defense Commissioner who was controlled directly from Peking.

In the spring of 1913, with a view to the ultimate restoration of civil government, Yüan Shih-k'ai undertook in a few of the provinces to replace the Tutuh with a Civil Administrator. The paying off of troops was one of the declared purposes of the Reorganization Loan negotiated in 1913 with the Five Power Banking Group. Some of the funds were used for this purpose, commanders being paid at the rate of fifty dollars per head of their soldiery. However, Yüan soon found other uses both for the money and for the men. After the President had made himself the dictator, he retained the Military Governor as head of the province but changed the title from Tutuh to Chiang-chün, the former Manchu Banner title for General. On the whole he restored the historic Manchu system of provincial administration, even abolishing the assemblies created just before the Republic was established. In order to strengthen his own position during this period he attempted to entice to Peking men of whose allegiance he was doubtful. By getting them away from their provinces and their troops, he was able effectively to deprive them of political influence. This was accomplished in the case of Li Yuan-hung, the Vice President, and others of prominence. This maneuver and its result reveal clearly the military basis of authority during the Yüan period.

Under these circumstances only one thing could have prevented the enthronement of military power within the Republic and thus the destruction of republicanism. If there had been a powerful middle class to support it, which there was not, or if the idea of republicanism had been widely and deeply implanted in the masses, the goal of the leaders of the 1911 revolution might have been attained without a new revolution. This was not the case, however, and the parliamentary leaders of the new régime had to contend against Yüan Shih-k'ai unsupported by either middle-class or mass loyalties either to themselves as individuals or to the idea of self-government through representative institutions.

So far as the masses were concerned, to the extent that they ideologically participated in the revolution and supported it, it was essentially an anti-Manchu and anti-dynastic revolt. The slogan coming from the southern secret societies was "down with the Manchus, up with the Mings." The alien dynasty had been overthrown, but the alternative for a "Ming" (i.e., a Chinese) dynasty was the foreign-born conception of a Republic. Experience revealed that the idea and ideals of republicanism had not been driven into the thinking of the masses. Republicanism had yet to be naturalized. Thus the people, so far as they were directly touched by the fact of revolution, were left in a condition of uncertainty as to its meaning. To the extent that economic forces had made the revolution possible, it soon became clear that the mere change in the form of the state did not alter those economic conditions or the restlessness growing out of them. Good harvests alone could serve that purpose. Nor did the victory of republicanism solve the problem presented by an unduly expansive population. Nevertheless, the change to a republic did have certain effects on the people. The conventional grooves of allegiance and loyalty were disturbed, for the masses were asked to render obedience to a régime which was more or less of an abstraction, rather than to an individual concretely personifying the state, except as that personification was made in the person of the President, in whose favor the Manchu ruler had actually abdicated. It remained to be seen what effect this would have on their willingness to obey their new officers or, more abstractly, on their acceptance of presidential as against parliamentary authority.

Furthermore, the shibboleths of the revolution had been translated for the masses into the conception that republicanism meant an end to tax levies and to every repression of the individual. This interpretation had been strengthened by the action of the Shanghai government in declaring a remission of taxes, as well as by the relaxation of control incident to revolution. This point of view complicated the problems of restoring order and of financing the new régime. Again, in the active revolutionary area, the overthrow of the dynasty was construed as a decided victory for the principle of provincial autonomy, and yet, just as centralization had been forced on the Manchus, so it was a necessity for the Republic. This meant that the new rulers in the end would encounter the same hostility as had the Manchus.

When the decisive struggle for control of the Republic began, however, with Yüan and the parliamentarians as the antagonists, the balance of advantage rested with the former. He had the support of the military in the north; he found access to funds through the Consortium; and the principle of autonomy accepted in the south worked in his behalf rather than in that of its parliamentary advocates. The parliamentarians were rapidly divorced from their followers in the south and were supported only by the power of words and an ill-understood idea. The understanding of the masses could not be sought as a basis of support because it was not considered that government was their business. Officials had always ruled, and the people had not been educated to the idea of change in that respect. Thus there came into rapid play the traditional view that government and the business of life were divorced. The people turned to their own affairs and left political controversy to those who made it their business. Deprived of real support from the mass constituency, the new politician faced the task of controlling a bureaucracy, personified by the President, which maintained its control over the country through military power.

3. THE NEW GOVERNMENT

The structural chart of the new plan of government was presented in the Nanking Provisional Constitution. This was the first in a series of republican attempts to define and limit the powers of government, or at least to state the competency of the several organs of government and fix their relationship to one another. Drawn up by the revolutionary party in council at Nanking in 1912, the first provisional constitution was clearly designed to establish parliamentary supremacy over the President. To accomplish this the French plan of government, with some minor modifications, was introduced. Thus provision was made for a cabinet, responsible to a bicameral legislature [2] rather than to the President, which was to exercise the executive power, controlling the President through the requirement of countersignature of every presidential act. In addition it was provided that financial arrangements, treaties, and administrative regulations had to receive the assent of the legislature to be valid.

It is, of course, possible that the new instrument of government was drawn up without reference to the compromise by which Sun Yat-sen withdrew from the presidency in favor of Yüan Shih-k'ai. The fact remains, however, that the revolutionary leaders, and the south in general, distrusted Yüan and accepted him as President only because of (1) his control of the northern soldiery, (2) his recognized administrative ability, and (3) his standing with the Western governments. This mistrust immediately found justification when the new President, after having agreed as part of the settlement to the transfer of the capital from Peking to Nanking, found an excuse in an opportune mutiny of troops in Peking to stay at that place, where he was duly inaugurated on March 10, 1912. This was also the date of promulgation of the provisional constitution. The necessity that Yüan found to remain in Peking compelled the Nanking Council to move north, from the center of its strength to the

---

[2] The Nanking Council exercised the legislative function until the elections in 1913 which brought into being the Senate and the House of Representatives.

center of that of the President. Thus Yüan Shih-k'ai won the first contest of
strength, and in the process indicated the difficulty which would be found
in controlling him through paper agreements. Consequently it may be
concluded that it was because of their distrust of the new President that
the Nanking Council attempted constitutionally to put the presidential
powers into commission. The only drawbacks to this plan proved to be
very important ones: (1) the ability which Yüan showed to evade the
limitations put upon him as head of the executive; (2) where evasion
proved impossible, his failure to recognize their validity, in which refusal
he was tacitly encouraged by the diplomatic corps; and (3) the inexperience
and the resulting incompetence of the Council and, after it, of the Assembly.

4. PROBLEMS OF GOVERNMENT

The two major problems immediately confronting the newly established
Republic were (1) the reconstruction of the old governmental and administrative machinery both at Peking and in the provinces so that civil
might replace military control, and (2) the finding of ways and means of
financing itself.

Yüan Shih-k'ai had declared his attitude toward the provincial administrations even before his election as provisional President. On February 13,
1912, he announced the continuation in office of those who actually held
position, whether they had gained power as the agents of the Imperial
government or of the revolution, and he ordered them to carry on as usual.
The mandate then issued announced in no uncertain terms that the new
régime accepted as its primary obligation the restoration of peace and the
preservation of order. The continuance in official position of those who
held power gave them more of a legal title to rule and brought them under
the theoretical supervision of Peking. From another standpoint it meant,
roughly speaking, that the President had men in high position in the
northern provinces who were loyal to him rather than to the Republic,
while in the southern provinces many of the officials were supporters of
the republican principle and of the radical party which disputed Yüan's
supremacy at Peking. It was at the capital rather than in the provinces
that the immediate contest for control was carried on.

In the construction of the new central government the first step, after
the inauguration of Yüan as the provisional President, was the constitution of a cabinet, since it was understood that the Nanking Council would
serve as the legislature until election laws could be enacted and elections
to the Senate and the House of Representatives held. A tug-of-war developed between Peking and Nanking over the personnel of the Cabinet.
The Premier chosen, T'ang Shao-yi, was satisfactory to both sides since,
although he had been one of Yüan's protégés in Imperial days, he had

decided to throw in his lot with the T'ung Meng Hui (Sun Yat-sen's revolutionary society). Compromise dictated the other choices made, with the balance of advantage resting with the President. His man, Tuan Chi-jui, was confirmed as the Minister of War, a key position, while the Finance Minister selected was not the first choice of the Council, and thus was more acceptable to the President. These, under the existing circumstances, were the important ministries. With the legalization of the position of the provincial officials, the adoption of a provisional constitution, the organization of a cabinet, and the transfer of the legislature from Nanking to Peking, the provisional republican government may be considered to have been fairly well established.

Turning now to the second major problem confronting the republican government, that of finance, we find one much more difficult of solution. As has already been pointed out,[3] the national treasury was empty, and it would take time and the restoration of order in the provinces before tax collections could be expected to approach the normal. Consequently the President faced the necessity of borrowing to meet immediate administrative needs and to finance the disbandment of the swollen military forces as well as to effect a general administrative reorganization. The way was prepared for this when the Powers, after the Emperor had abdicated, intimated that the ban on loans had been lifted. Negotiations were immediately instituted with the members of the Six Powers Banking Group (the Consortium) for a large administrative loan. The group had been expanded to include Russia and Japan, although they were borrowing rather than lending nations, and England and France had to agree to help them float their respective shares of the loan. The reason for their inclusion was political, and was due to the fact that (1) the loan proceeds were to be used for general governmental purposes, and (2) the loan was to be secured by the pledging of parts of the revenue system of the Republic. They were also included as a means of reënforcing the financial monopoly of the group.

To meet the most pressing needs, the group bankers agreed to make monthly advances in February and March, in return for which the President gave them on March 7 a "firm option" on the comprehensive loan of $125,000,000 for reorganization purposes, provided their terms were as favorable as could be obtained elsewhere.

In spite of this undertaking, and only six days after it had been entered into, the government concluded an agreement for a loan of £10,000,000 with an Anglo-Belgian syndicate. The International Loan Group, charging bad faith, immediately suspended negotiations with the Premier, who, however, secured the ratification of the Belgian loan agreement by the Nanking Council at the same time that he was seeking to persuade it to

[8] Pp. 223–224.

accept the President's Cabinet nominations. Upon his return to Peking, however, the Premier found that he would have to resume negotiations with the Six Powers Group, as he could not find the sums needed elsewhere. Consequently he was compelled to accede to the demand that the Belgian agreement be canceled except with respect to the advances already made. A subsequent attempt to secure funds outside the group failed when the governments concerned brought pressure to bear on the London financier, C. Birch Crisp, who had ventured, despite the Consortium, to make a loan agreement with the Chinese government, and forced him to cancel his agreement. Thus by reason of its own financial necessity and its inability to secure funds elsewhere because of the virtual monopoly of support given by England, France, Germany, the United States, Japan, and Russia to the financial institutions included in the Group, the Chinese government was finally compelled to accept the terms offered by the international syndicate in spite of the internal opposition which developed.

This opposition, centering in the legislative body, was based upon the demand of the bankers for reorganization, under foreign direction, of the Salt Gabelle, which was to serve as the principal security for the loan, and that for supervision of expenditure of the loan funds. These conditions, unobjectionable in themselves in view of past experience with Chinese officialdom in financial matters, were opposed as driving in still further the wedge of foreign financial control. It was pointed out that they were as objectionable as any suggested during Imperial days and that the new, enlightened, and republican régime did not deserve the treatment justly meted out to the corrupt and backward Manchus. This position was also taken by President Wilson, who withdrew official and exclusive governmental support from the American bankers immediately after he came to office in 1913, partly on the ground of the monopoly character of the groups, and partly because the loan conditions unduly impaired the administrative integrity of China. Thus American participation in the international financing of China, insisted upon by President Taft as a method of making effective the American policy of the Open Door and that of the integrity of China, was terminated for the time by President Wilson for substantially the same reason. The loan contract consequently was entered into with a Five Powers Group.

The negotiations between China and the Group were completed by the end of 1912, and the agreement received the assent of the Council. Since much was made of this later, it may be well to point out here that at the time many of the T'ung Meng Hui members were away campaigning for election to the new Parliament, and that the measure was put through a rump legislature largely by bribery. Furthermore, after China had assented to the terms of the contract, the Powers fell into a dispute over the apportionment of adviserships among the participating states. Thus it was not until the spring of 1913, as the new Parliament was convening, that the agreement was put into its final form and duly signed.

5. YÜAN SHIH-K'AI VS. PARLIAMENT

The new elected Assembly was a much more difficult body for the President to deal with than the Council which sat in Peking during 1912. The members of the latter had been divided into many groups, three of which were of importance, but none of which had an absolute control of the legislature. One group was, on the whole, conservative, and consequently it generally supported the President. A second was representative of the more radical elements of the south. And the third, holding the balance of power, had no definite point of view in parliamentary matters. This situation was of advantage to the President since, by playing off one group against another, and by occasionally using money to convert the third element to his point of view, he was generally able to find enough votes to get his policies adopted. It was thus that he was able to secure assent to the loan agreement.

This must not be taken to imply, however, that Peking was placid during the life of the Council, for quite the contrary was the case. In addition to controversy between the President and the Council, for example, a conflict between the President and the Premier developed, the latter seeking to make the Cabinet rather than the President the real executive. In this, as in the controversy over the location of the capital and that over the loan agreement, the President emerged victorious, finally establishing a non-party cabinet with the T'ung Meng Hui excluded from participation.

The antagonism between the radical party and the President was further increased when, in July and August, 1912, two prominent revolutionaries were seized and shot, the charges against them being preferred by Vice-President Li Yuan-hung.[4] The Council, refused proofs of their guilt, threatened to impeach the government but was unable to carry out the threat since the conservative members absented themselves, preventing action since there was no quorum. Subsequent attempts to impeach were similarly prevented, but the fact that they were made indicates the lack of harmony at Peking, and the outcome of each trial points to the strength of the President.

The Parliament which met in 1913 presented a much more difficult problem since it was controlled in both branches by the radical party. The T'ung Meng Hui had reorganized in August, 1912, amalgamating with several other factions to form the Kuomintang (nationalist-democratic party) in order to carry on the contest against the President more effectively. Consequently Yüan Shih-k'ai had to face a united and much more formidable

[4] Elevated to that position by the Nanking Council at the time when it elected Yüan to the presidency. He was also acting concurrently as the Hukuang Viceroy.

opposition than before. Of the method of election of members of the Assembly it is only necessary to say that it was fixed by election laws passed by the Council in August; that the members of the Senate were chosen indirectly, either by the provincial assembly or by electoral colleges, six being selected by an electoral college of overseas Chinese; and that the House of Representatives consisted of members chosen theoretically by direct vote of the people but actually indirectly, with every eight million people being entitled to one representative, but with every province, regardless of population, having at least ten.[5]

In spite of its reorganization and of its success in the elections the Kuomintang lost in its first opposition to presidential policy. It protested vehemently against the signature of the Reorganization Loan Agreement before it had been submitted to and had received the assent of Parliament. Yüan Shih-k'ai, however, maintained that the constitutional requirement had been observed since it had been accepted by the Council; and the diplomatic body, when directly appealed to, took the position that it was empowered to deal with China only through the President. Consequently the agreement was signed by the representatives of the financial groups.

This action strengthened the position of the President in two ways. In the first place, it gave him the moral support of the Powers. It indicated clearly that they preferred to deal with the "strong man" capable of affording security for an investment rather than to strengthen the cause of parliamentary government by insisting upon the observance of the constitutional provision by which all loan agreements had to receive the assent of the Assembly before becoming effective. In the second place, the President was strengthened by being furnished with the financial resources necessary to consolidate his power. The major portion of the loan, it is true, was devoted to paying off existing foreign obligations—returning the funds already advanced, and making up arrears in payment of interest and principal on the Boxer indemnity—but the remainder was available for use by Yüan Shih-k'ai.

Strengthened by the loan, the President proceeded to the task of consolidating his power. Parliament continually struggled against this, opposing all suggestions, whether good or bad, emanating from the President's office. By doing this, instead of attempting to develop a constructive program of its own, the Assembly gained the name of a purely obstructive body, active only in interfering with the President, who was attempting to restore peace and order in the country. In spite of this opposition at Peking, Yüan Shih-k'ai gradually gained the upper hand in the provinces. He used every possible means to assert and consolidate his authority: gradually displacing troops and commanders in central and southern China with those faithful to himself; maintaining agents everywhere to keep him in-

[5] For a detailed analysis see VINACKE, *Modern Constitutional Development in China* (1922), pp. 141–147.

formed of conditions and sentiment throughout the country; and even resorting, according to his opponents, to assassination for political purposes. The murder at Shanghai in March, 1913, of Sung Chiao-jen, one of the Kuomintang leaders, was the first in a series of acts of violence for which he was held responsible.

Unable to make any headway against the President in Peking, the opposition again became revolutionary and violent. However, the "Summer Revolution" of 1913, an uprising in the Yangtse valley, merely served to exhibit the weakness of the opposition and the strength of the President. Yüan's troops suppressed the rebels with remarkable ease. Pressing his advantage, the President sent additional troops to strategic centers, drove some of the opposition leaders out of the country, and finally ordered the dissolution of the Kuomintang itself on the ground that participation of some of its leaders in the revolt proved it to be a treasonable organization.

Before this was accomplished, and with it the virtual dissolution of the Parliament, the legislature completed part of the permanent constitution on which it had been at work since its convocation. This endeavor to frame a permanent instrument of government to replace the Nanking (provisional) constitution was one undertaking of a constructive character which must be set down to the credit of the Parliament. If it had concentrated its efforts so as to complete it within a few months, it might have justified itself in the eyes of the country. As it was, it paid only intermittent attention to the work of constitution-drafting until after the end of the rebellion. Then, seeing the hand-writing on the wall, the Assembly hurried to complete the document. It was being framed by a large committee of members selected by each House. This committee met, interestingly enough, at the Temple of Heaven to engage in the work of laying the permanent foundations for the republican structure. Even here the executive-legislative antagonism revealed itself in the refusal of the committee to allow the President to influence its work, not even consenting to hear his views as to the needed governmental machinery.

Yüan, however, was interested in consolidating his position through election as permanent President. Consequently he urged, bribed, and cajoled the Assembly into passing the section of the constitutional draft dealing with the presidential office in advance of completion of the entire instrument. Then, under the double pretext of celebrating the anniversary of the revolution and of securing recognition from the Powers,[6] he carried through his election as permanent President. He was duly inaugurated on October 10, 1913, thus further strengthening his position in the eyes of the people.

The constitution-drafting committee passed the entire draft of the per-

[6] The United States alone among the Great Powers had recognized the Republic. England had withheld recognition pending settlement of the Tibetan question.

manent constitution on October 26, 1913, but before it could be formally
accepted by Parliament, that body had ceased to exist. Protests against the
terms of the draft were made by officials, possibly at the suggestion of the
President, and these, together with the implication of Kuomintang leaders
in the "Summer Revolution," were used by Yüan Shih-k'ai to justify his
next moves. On November 4, 1913, with the concurrence of his Cabinet,
he ordered the dissolution of the Kuomintang as a seditious organization.
This automatically brought about the dissolution of the Parliament for
lack of a quorum, and, while never formally dissolved, it was indefinitely
suspended by a presidential mandate issued on January 10, 1914. This step
virtually ended the parliamentary régime in China, although the fiction
of its existence was carefully preserved by the President for a year. The
suspended Parliament, in fact, came back to Peking for a short time after
the death of Yüan Shih-k'ai.

The people, it may be noted, showed their complete indifference to the
change in government by raising no objection to the dissolution. The idea
that the Republic, and with it representative government, was founded
upon an active popular desire and interest was shown to be nothing more
than a theory developed for revolutionary purposes. Of course some explanation in justification of the popular attitude may be made, but it is not
entirely complimentary to the Assembly. Put in a strong position by a constitution of its own making, that body had shown itself to be obstructive
rather than constructive, and it was more than suspected of corruption.
It had developed no plan of reorganization of its own to substitute for
that of the President to which it objected. Yüan, on the other hand, had
been active in the development of a program looking toward the reëstablishment of order. Further than this, many argued that he had a legal
right to effect changes in the governmental system as long as he maintained
China as a republic, for he had been commissioned by the Manchus to
organize a republican form of government for the country.

In defense of the Parliament the fact may be noted that it was controlled
by inexperienced young men, intolerant of the old régime and its officers
by reason of their training. They needed time in which to temper their
ideas and to evolve satisfactory methods of parliamentary action. Yüan
Shih-k'ai made no greater allowance for their impulsiveness and inexperience than they made for his effort to keep the administrative machinery
running. The intolerance of inexperienced reformers was met by the
intolerance of the tried administrator for the projects of the untried. Furthermore, the attitude of the so-called democratic states from the very
beginning constituted a hindrance to the establishment of a satisfactory
parliamentary régime. It is strangely true that the democratic governments
of the West have been suspicious of democratic experiments in regions
where their nationals have built up property interests, and that they have

invariably sought a strong man with whom to deal. The 'slap in the face" administered to the parliamentarians early in 1913 had much to do with the failure of the Parliament to maintain itself.

6. PRESIDENTIAL DICTATORSHIP

After the dissolution of the Assembly, Yüan Shih-k'ai proceeded to work out his own conception of a republican régime, one adapted to a country accustomed to personal rule and with a population of a low degree of literacy.

The first step toward establishing the new régime was taken in January, immediately after the suspension of the Parliament, when a hand-picked Political Council was constituted. Under its advice the President then brought into being a Constitutional Council, which met for the first time March 18, 1914. Its chief function was to revise the Nanking constitution so as to give a constitutional status to the new order. This it did by framing what came to be known as the Constitutional Compact, China's second republican provisional constitution. Under the Compact all power was concentrated in the hands of the President, who was to be elected for a ten-year period, with the right to extend his own term of office if he saw fit, or virtually to name his own successor.[7] The Cabinet was replaced by a Secretary of State, appointed by and responsible to the President, as were all heads of departments or boards. The legislature was given merely advisory powers,[8] and a Council of State was to serve as the only advisory body until the creation of the Li Fa Yuan (legislative assembly). It was thereafter to have the sole right to recommend constitutional changes. A reference to the "constitutional principles" of the Empress Dowager will serve to show the similarity of the President's ideas to those accepted in the earlier period of constitutional development. On the whole his system embodied also the ideas of Dr. Frank Goodnow, an American who was one of his foreign advisers. The latter suggested that China was ready only for a dictatorship, tempered by the existence of an advisory body which should be constituted largely by appointment and which should represent group interests rather than individuals. These views coincided with the President's conceptions as well as his interest. Thus during the early part of 1914 it became clear that China had reverted to the status of about 1909 as far as her political life was concerned, and that the attempt would be made to develop from that point, if any evolution occurred. The chief difference was that she had a dictatorial President rather than a weak Emperor, and consequently it was probable that her evolution would be even slower than might have been expected under the Manchus.

[7] This was provided for in the interesting Presidential Election Law.

[8] This was the only part of the proposed organization which was never brought into existence.

Under the Constitutional Compact the President proceeded to govern as the dictatorial "strong man" whom China was assumed to need. He ruthlessly removed his political opponents where he was able to reach them. Those who, while outwardly friendly, were strong enough conceivably to oppose him, in case matters were pushed to the extreme, were concentrated in Peking, where he could closely supervise their actions. In spite of the paper developments toward a modified constitutionalism, China was governed during all of 1914 by terrorist methods. Spies were everywhere, and no man dared to express his thoughts freely; the press was muzzled, and political assassinations became even more common. And yet it must be recognized that the people, on the whole, were not greatly dissatisfied. Order was being gradually restored and with it a more normal life, even though by essentially military means and at the expense of failure to restore the old standards of civil administration through a caste of scholars. The sort of personal rule thus instituted was something to which the people were accustomed. The reëmphasis which Yüan laid on the Confucian morality, and the resumption of worship at the Altar of Heaven, furnished a link between past experience and the new order. And the Republic, with a fiction of representative government, was preserved. It was only the political "outs" and those who were revolutionaries from principle who were dissatisfied. The masses had no concern with forms of government and methods of political action so long as they could sow and reap, and thus provide for the needs of their ancestors and for their own needs as prospective ancestors. The revolution had disturbed some of them temporarily with its ideas of liberty, freedom from taxation, queue cutting, the end of footbinding, and, in general, modernization of the country. But, even so, the villagers had been very little disturbed. The new ideas had gained a real foothold only in the vicinity of the treaty ports. China, as represented by the villages, acquiesced readily enough in the régime set up by Yüan Shih-k'ai, the holder of the Imperial mandate to institute a republic, and the properly elected President. Thus by the end of 1914 the President seemed to be securely entrenched in control and, if he had been content with the substance of power, he might well have continued to rule for some time as the dictator within constitutional forms.

7. FOREIGN RELATIONS

But there were foreign foes as well as domestic opponents to reckon with. Shortly after the founding of the Republic, trouble had developed in Mongolia and an independent Mongol government had been proclaimed. There had been growing dissatisfaction with Chinese rule for some time. This was a result of (1) the encroachments of Chinese settlers and (2) the attempt to extend the governmental system of China proper to parts of Mongolia, an attempt which threatened the rule of the Mongol nobility. There seems also to have developed a nationalist movement which helped to strengthen the other separatist tendencies. Added to all of this was an active Russian intrigue against the Chinese rulers, Russia's interest being in checking the northward movement of the Chinese. It is not possible here to do more than note the consequences of this state of affairs. On December 1, 1911, the Chinese authorities were forced to withdraw from Mongolia, and an independent government was instituted at Urga. During 1912 China attempted, with partial success in Inner Mongolia, to reëstablish her authority. But in November Russia recognized the Urga government and concluded an agreement with it. Negotiations subsequently ensued between Russia and China and between Mongolia and China to secure a definition of the position of the area. China and Russia, without the participation of the Government of Outer Mongolia, concluded a convention on November 15, 1913, by which the autonomy but not the independence of Outer Mongolia was recognized, China continuing as the suzerain. On June 7, 1915, a tripartite agreement was reached by which Outer Mongolia accepted the terms of the Sino-Russian Convention. Under the circumstances this agreement was a diplomatic victory for Yüan Shih-k'ai, but it was only a partial one since it signalized, in conjunction with the 1913 agreement, the formal recognition of a Russian interest in Mongolian affairs.

At the same time Tibet revolted against the authority of China. The Chinese garrison at Lhasa revolted at the time of the revolution, the outbreak being marked by such excesses that the Tibetans rose and drove the Chinese out of the country. They later celebrated their triumph, on January 11, 1913, by concluding, as an independent people, an agreement with the Mongolian government. After the establishment of the republican régime at Peking, steps were taken to restore Chinese authority in Tibet, but the British protested against any effort, by military means, to reëstablish China's control. This led to fruitless negotiations during 1913 and to a tripartite conference in 1914 out of which came an agreement providing for (1) the complete autonomy of Tibet proper, (2) the right of China to maintain a Resident at Lhasa with a suitable guard, and (3) a semi-autonomous zone in eastern Tibet in which China would occupy a stronger position.[9] This agreement, however, was never ratified, and the end of the Yüan régime came before any solution had been found. Thus British action with respect to Tibet had the same embarrassing consequences for the Republic as Russian intrigue had in Mongolia.

But the most serious situation developed out of Japan's participation in World War I.[10] In the first place, the Japanese advance on Tsingtao

[9] *China Year Book*, 1916, p. 606.
[10] See chapter XVI, sec. 4.

put China as a neutral power in an anomalous position. A partially satisfactory way out was found in the proclamation of a war zone and the attempt to restrict Japanese military movements to this zone. At the beginning of 1915, since all reason for hostilities had ended, the zone was declared abolished. Following this action on the part of China, and using it as a pretext, Japan served the much discussed Twenty-one Demands on the President. These need not be discussed at this point,[11] but the internal consequences of Japan's action must be pointed out in order to make the tale of the Yüan Shih-k'ai period complete. The demands, when they became known, aroused a widespread hostility to Japan, and developed a united support of the President in his resistance to Japanese pressure. This support was manifested through the organization of national societies, the collection of funds for the defense of the country by widespread popular subscription, and the expression of loyalty on the part of leaders who had been in opposition to Yüan Shih-k'ai. All of this was assumed by the President to indicate his personal strength in the country, although it was, fundamentally, an expression of an incipient nationalism, awakened by the most dangerous single attack yet launched on the independence and the integrity of China.

8. THE MONARCHY MOVEMENT

During the course of the negotiations it seems to have been intimated to Yüan that Japan would be sympathetic to the reëstablishment of the monarchy, provided the aspirant to the Imperial position was favorably inclined toward her. To indicate this he should give concrete evidence of his favor by granting the Japanese request, embodied in the demands, for a dominant position in the country. It is well known that the leading Japanese statesmen had never looked with favor on the Republic and had hopes of its early demise. It is true that the 1911 and 1913 revolutionists had received aid and support from unofficial Japanese sources, but this was not indicative of an interest in the radical cause so much as of an interest in the creation of disorder in China. However, while not hostile to the monarchical principle, Japan not only distrusted Yüan Shih-k'ai but also feared him, because he seemed capable of restoring China to her natural position of strength, and because he had been in opposition to Japan's continental program since his Korean days. Consequently it was not considered to Japan's interest to see Yüan Shih-k'ai become the permanent ruler unless and until he became more sympathetic to her. When the monarchical suggestion was made, it was thus a bid for Yüan's support. This he refused to give, even in exchange for such a *quid pro quo*. But he apparently considered that the expressions of opinion in his favor in

[11] They are discussed in chapter XVI, sec. 5–6.

China as the defender of the country were such as to make it an opportune time for him to attempt to establish himself as the founder of a new dynasty.

Thus during the spring and summer of 1915 an active propaganda in favor of restoration of monarchy was undertaken by men close to the President. Much of the propaganda was based upon a memorandum prepared by a former legal adviser to the President, Dr. Frank J. Goodnow, who was visiting Peking. This memorandum represented an expression of an opinion, of an academic sort, as to the proper form of government for China. Dr. Goodnow expressed the view that "the monarchical system is better suited to China than the Republican system. For if China's independence is to be maintained, the government should be constitutional, and in consideration of China's conditions as well as her relations with other powers, it will be easier to form a constitutional government by adopting a monarchy than a Republic." [12] Three conditions must be met, however, the writer went on to point out, before such a change should be made. First, adequate provision for the succession should be made; second, it must be certain that the people would acquiesce in the change and that the Powers would not oppose it; and, third, definite provision must be made for the progressive development of constitutionalism in China.

When opposition began to develop, it established its theoretical position on a counter-argument prepared by the noted Chinese scholar, Liang Ch'i-ch'ao.[13] He had been one of the 1898 reformers, had stood for constitutional monarchy up to the organization of the Republic, and had supported the President in the overthrow of Parliament and the establishment of the dictatorship. Consequently he could not be accused of undue radicalism. His argument ran that the time for unsettling the country by a change in the form of the state had passed; that the Republic should be accepted as a fact; and that every effort should be bent toward a reorganization of the government so as to restore peace and order and give an effective administration. Furthermore, as he pointed out, Yüan Shih-k'ai had been given a term of office long enough to enable him to accomplish this task, and if ten years were not sufficient, his term could be extended for another ten-year period.

However, the President had already taken the decision to reëstablish the monarchy, although his determination was disguised, for form's sake, so that it might appear that he was being compelled by the pressure of opinion. Thus, not only did the Council of State have to memorialize three times on the subject to overcome his apparent reluctance to overturn the Republic before he would consent, but even then his consent was made conditional

---

[12] *National Review* (China), August 28, 1915.
[13] For translation of this pamphlet see B. L. Putnam Weale, *The Fight for the Republic in China*, ch. X.

on approval of the change being registered through a "Convention of Citizen's Representatives." Such approval was actually given almost unanimously by bodies constituted for the purpose and made fully aware of the need for a favorable decision.

This consultation of the opinion of the nation was necessary, as a matter of fact, for more than form's sake. On October 28, 1915, Great Britain and Russia united with Japan, at the latter's suggestion, in tendering advice against making the change. The United States refused to add its voice on the ground that only China was concerned with the form of her government. The foreign opposition was put upon the ground that it was unwise to disturb the existing equilibrium and to stir up trouble when the international situation was so unsettled. A further protest was voiced in November, this time Italy and France joining with the other three in making it.

By the time of the second protest Yüan was able to point to the affirmative vote of the Convention as indicative of popular approval of the change. Furthermore, he was sufficiently convinced of his ability to control any opposition which might develop to give assurances to the Powers that there would be no serious trouble. No further action was taken by the Powers, although Japan indicated that information at her disposal led to the belief that the southern provinces would not passively acquiesce in the reëstablishment of monarchy. The next few months revealed that Japan was better informed as to the possibility of opposition than was the Emperor-elect.

While plans for the coronation were being perfected, revolt did break out in the extreme southwest. On December 23 a memorial against the change and a demand for the cancellation of the monarchy was sent to Peking from Yunnan province. When this demand was not complied with, the standard of revolt was openly raised. In spite of every effort put forth by the government—and it may be noted that it was almost uniformly successful from the military standpoint—the revolt spread until province after province had declared its independence of Peking. The revolutionists at first demanded the cancellation of the monarchy, the restoration of the Nanking Constitution as the basic law, and the reconstitution of the 1913 Assembly.

In the face of this opposition and of defection in the ranks of his own followers in the northern provinces, Yüan Shih-k'ai weakened to the extent of declaring that he would give up the idea of restoring the monarchy. He sought to save his "face" by declaring that he had been misled in his belief that it was the wish of the country that he should ascend the Dragon Throne. This indication of weakness emboldened the republicans to extend their demands to include the complete elimination of Yüan from Chinese politics. This, for a time, he refused to consider, although he further temporized by reviving the Cabinet and ostensibly transferring the executive power to it and by handing over control of the military establishment to the Minister of War. Ultimately, however, he was forced to give in and consent to retire from office. Just when agreement was imminent, the controversy was settled unexpectedly by the death, on June 6, 1916, of the President. Thus the period of the first reaction against true republicanism came to an end with the elimination of the "strong man" who had been looked to by so many as the only person capable of bringing stability to China. Nevertheless, while the Republic remained, republicanism as a form of government had yet to establish itself in China.

9. THE REVIVAL OF THE REPUBLIC

The status, as of the beginning of 1913, which was restored after Yüan Shih-k'ai's death, was maintained precariously for less than a year. The military leaders in the provinces had been held under the control of the central government only because of the personal authority exercised over them by Yüan. Soon after his death they began to indicate a determination to accept the direction of Peking only to the extent that Peking acted in accordance with their views and only if the central government did not attempt to interfere with their separate prerogatives in the provinces. For a time they accepted the Premier, Tuan Chi-jui, as the successor, within their ranks, to Yüan Shih-k'ai. But they made it clear that their loyalty to him depended on his respecting and protecting their interests. He, in turn, derived his position in the central government from Yüan and was accepted by the Parliament, when it was restored to Peking, for the same reason that Yüan had been accepted initially by the revolutionary leaders of 1911, i.e., because of the support that he had among the military. The new President, by succession from the vice-presidency, Li Yuan-hung, although a military man, had come into prominence through participation in the 1911 revolution. He accepted the point of view embodied in the revived Nanking constitution with respect to parliamentary supremacy. But, it will be recalled, that constitution vested the executive power in the Cabinet and not the President. Consequently the new turn of the wheel presented a Premier, as head of the executive, who was in the tradition of Yüan Shih-k'ai and who soon came into conflict with the Parliament.

The causes of conflict were much the same as when Yüan had been President. There were differences of opinion over the proper steps to be taken to solve the financial problem. This involved the making of loans and the reorganization of the revenue system. Tuan, as had Yüan Shih-k'ai, made his arrangements without consultation with the Assembly and then asked it to approve what had already been undertaken. Controversy developed over appointments to office. The Assembly resorted to heckling of Cabinet representatives, frequently merely in the hope of embarrassing the government. In this and other respects the obstructionist tendencies of 1912–1913 reappeared, and partly for the same reason, i.e., the inability of the parliamentarians to exert an effective control over the conduct of the government. Finally, as was to be expected under these conditions, the interest of the members in their work declined to the extent that adjournments for lack of a quorum became common. Furthermore many of the sessions of the legislature were marked by extreme disorder, several of them ending in free-for-all fights.

Just as during the Yüan period, the major constructive endeavor of the Parliament was its attempt to complete the permanent constitution. Taking the earlier draft as the basis for discussion, the Conference on the Constitution, composed of the two chambers sitting at the Temple of Heaven as a constituent assembly, again proceeded slowly to work out an instrument of government which should establish parliamentary supremacy, going even further in that direction than in the draft which Yüan had found objectionable. Again, before the task had been carried to completion, the Parliament was driven out of Peking. This ended parliamentary constitutionalism in fact even though the pretense of parliamentary government was maintained for a time and was revived intermittently in connection with the contests for control at Peking which marked the period of provincial military ascendency. Even the completion and promulgation of a "permanent" constitution in 1923 did not have, nor was it in fact designed to have, the effect of reëstablishing parliamentary government.

The immediate issue which brought about the overthrow of the parliamentary Republic, however, was not an outgrowth of differences of opinion over the constitution, although a number of constitutional questions became involved. The issue was the effect in domestic politics of the question of China's participation in World War I.[14] That question was raised with the sending of a note of protest to Germany on February 9, 1917, against her declared policy of engaging in unrestricted submarine warfare. A month later diplomatic relations were severed since no satisfactory reply to the protest had been made. During this period the Premier, Tuan Chi-jui, had been engaged in negotiations with the Allied representatives at Peking over the conditions of Chinese participation so that he might show material advantages which China would gain through a declaration of war on Germany. Before the Powers had acceded to his terms, he gave Parliament to understand that he was assured of concessions with respect to the Boxer indemnity payments and other matters if only war was declared, while assuring the diplomatic representatives that war would be declared before he had overcome opposition to his war policy. Thus he stood to lose "face" domestically if he did not secure formally concessions which he could only receive if and after China declared war, and he stood to

14 On China's participation in the war see infra, chapter XVII.

lose "face" with the Powers if war was not declared in advance of their formal commitment. In order to divert attention from his negotiations with the diplomats and to manufacture sentiment in favor of his war policy, he finally resorted to the expedient of calling some of the military governors into conference. "From the time this Conference met the question of war became more a matter of internal politics than of foreign policy. The Military Governors assembled in Peking late in April and the attention of the country was immediately centered upon their activities." [15] From this time also dates the ascendency of the northern military party in Peking politics and with it the ascendency of the provincial warlords.

The immediate result of this and other pressures [16] applied to Parliament by Tuan Chi-jui to secure passage of his war bill was his dismissal as Premier by the President upon the demand of Parliament. He refused to acquiesce, and in his refusal he was supported by the military governors, who, in turn, demanded the dissolution of Parliament. In order to enforce their demand on a reluctant President, they launched a "punitive expedition" against Peking, assertedly to enforce respect for the constitution. For a time a stalemate was produced because President Li stood firm in his refusal to accede to the demand of the military governors that Tuan be reinstated and Parliament be dismissed. The deadlock was broken when the former invited the most notorious of the members of the provincial military junta, Chang Hsun, to come to Peking as mediator. His mediation took the form of reiteration of the demands of his colleagues and then of an attempt on July 1, 1916, to restore the Manchus to the throne. He found, however, that the other military governors were opposed to monarchy as well as to parliamentary republicanism. Thus the restoration lasted only three weeks, and it was those who were marching on Peking to overthrow Parliament who brought the monarchy to this abrupt end.

10. MILITARY ASCENDENCY

From this time until, almost a decade later, the revolution was recommenced in its nationalist phase, the political life of China was marked by incessant confusion. It could only represent confusion since there was an unending struggle for power between individuals, each seeking to serve his own purposes. The pattern was laid in the provinces in the form described at the beginning of this chapter. The more powerful of the provincial militarists, however, constantly struggled not merely to enlarge their territorial domains within the country but also to establish themselves in a position of dominance over the fiction of a central government, which, throughout, continued to exist at Peking. To accomplish either or both

[15] H. M. VINACKE, *Modern Constitutional Development in China*, p. 238.

[16] Including bribery, entertainment of parliamentarians, and a mob demonstration staged before the Parliament building.

purposes, alliances were made. These led to counter-alliances and to intrigue for the purpose of detaching elements of strength from the opposition
forces.

There were two principal reasons for the interest shown in controlling
Peking even though the central government, as such, had little or no actual
authority in the country. The first was that those who controlled the capital
had control of such national administrative machinery as continued to exist
and had a basis for claiming the allegiance of the country. The second,
and possibly more important, reason was that internationally the Peking
government continued to be dealt with by the foreign governments as if
it were the government of China. Thus it could assert a claim to any surpluses from the customs collections, after loan and indemnity charges defrayed from the customs had been met. The same was true of the internationally supervised Salt Gabelle. And foreign loans could be contracted,
if at all, most advantageously through the medium of the "government"
of China.

On the whole it is a warranted conclusion that the primary interest of
the Tuchuns and Super-tuchuns, as these military rulers were called, was
in gaining power as a means to the end of personal enrichment. Thus,
with only occasional exceptions, they ruthlessly exploited the territories
under their control, frequently collecting the taxes for years in advance.
Sometimes they compelled the peasants to cultivate the poppy rather than
food crops so that they might confiscate the proceeds from the illegal production of opium. And in every fashion they sought to profit as largely as
possible from what usually was a short tenure of office. What was true in
the provinces was also true at Peking, although there certain forms had to
be observed in order to impress the outside world, a safeguard unnecessary
in relation to the Chinese community.

At the outset there were two main factions in the group of northern
military leaders. This division dated back to Imperial days and was partly
the result of application of the old principle of division in order to rule.
After the death of Yüan Shih-k'ai, who had been the unifying agency,
one faction revolved around Fêng Kuo-chang, the Hukuang Viceroy in
1916, who became the Vice-President when Li Yüan-hung succeeded Yüan
as President. The other was under the leadership of Tuan Chi-jui. The
year from the time when the Manchu restoration was unsuccessfully attempted until the autumn of 1918 was taken up with a struggle for supremacy between Fêng, who had become President in succession to Li,
and Tuan Chi-jui, who resumed the premiership. In this contest the
Tuan faction was victorious, signalizing its victory with the election of
Hsü Shih-chang, an old-time official, to the presidential office when Fêng
Kuo-chang's term expired in October, 1918.

In order to ensure its success in the election, the Tuan faction organized itself into a society or club, the Anfu Club, which had as its ostensible purpose the carrying on of propaganda among the members of a newly elected Parliament in favor of Hsü Shih-chang for the presidency. After it had attained its object, the Anfu Club continued in existence for the purpose of promoting collectively the individual interests of its members. These interests related to the monopolizing of public office, largely for the purpose of lining the pockets of the Anfuites. To line their pockets they had to have access to some source of supply outside of the country. This source they found in Japan, whose financiers made loan after loan to the Peking government, either secured on various public services, in return for valuable concessions of various sorts, or without security. These loans were called the Nishihara loans and subsequently provided a fruitful source of controversy between China and Japan. Because of them the people of China came to consider the Anfu government as pro-Japanese and as engaged in selling the country out to Japan.

This Anfu control in the north continued until 1920, when the clique was driven out of Peking by a combination of the forces of the Manchurian warlord, Chang Tso-lin, and those of Tsao Kun, the leader, in succession to Fêng Kuo-chang, of the other faction in the Peiyang military element. Although the Anfuites were actually driven out of Peking by the forces of General Wu Pei-fu, a division commander under Tsao Kun, he was not able to control the new régime since he had been acting in the name of his superior. It soon became clear that such preponderance of power as existed at Peking rested with Chang Tso-lin rather than with Tsao Kun. Consequently the years 1920–1922 were devoted to preparation for a struggle to eliminate Chang from control. The issue was joined in 1922 with the result that Wu Pei-fu, whose power was based upon the central Yangtse provinces, in concert with his subordinate ally, General Fêng Yu-hsiang, succeeded in driving Chang Tso-lin back into Manchuria. They were not able to do more than that, however, because of Chang's strength and his special position in relation to Japan in Manchuria. Chang Tso-lin thereupon declared the "independence" of Manchuria. This did not mean, in the conception of the politics of the time in China, that his intention was to erect a new state but merely that he denied the authority of the Peking government until such time as he could exert some measure of control over it.

Between 1922 and 1924, when the Wu Pei-fu supporters were in control of Peking, the actual authority of the Peking government extended little beyond the walls of the city. Chang was ruling Manchuria, and each warlord, either standing by himself or organized within a hierarchy, ruled his own districts or province, engaging from time to time in wars with his neighbors with a view to displacing them and adding their domains to his own. And all of the time, under the surface, the lines were reforming for another and "final" struggle for mastery in the country. China, it seemed, was still waiting for the "strong man" to emerge, capable of bringing all of the other militarists under the effective authority of a central government. The effect of the various maneuvers which had been going on was revealed in 1924 when Wu Pei-fu was driven out of Peking because of the defection of his first lieutenant, Fêng Yu-hsiang, then known as the Christian General. The latter seized Peking, which had been left in his charge while Wu was attempting to meet an attack launched from Manchuria by Chang Tso-lin and from the southeast by remnants of the Anfu Club, supported to the best of his ability by Dr. Sun Yat-sen. Wu thereupon retired to his own provinces in the central Yangtse region, and the Peking government was reconstituted by the Chang-Fêng-Tuan coalition before Sun Yat-sen was able to reach Tientsin to attempt, through conference, to shape it along lines satisfactory to himself. Sun died in Peking soon after. Chang Tso-lin was thereafter able to maintain his hold in North China, although precariously, until driven out by the nationalist armies in 1928. His position was precarious because he had to face attacks from Fêng Yu-hsiang, who turned against him just as he had previously turned against Wu Pei-fu, and also from the latter. Thus he was constantly threatened with the possibility of attack from the northwest and from the central Yangtse area. Fêng actually drove him back into Manchuria in 1925, having weakened his position by securing the support of one of Chang's Manchurian generals. Chang was able, however, to put down this Manchurian rebellion against his authority and to maintain himself in Manchuria with the aid of Japan. And he was able to reënter North China through alliance with Wu Pei-fu. Just as Wu, however, was entering upon what it was hoped would be a final and decisive struggle against Fêng Yu-hsiang, he had to turn south, in 1926, to meet the attack of the nationalist armies as they reached the Yangtse in the first stage of the northern expedition, with their avowed purpose of eliminating the warlords.

Attention thus far has been centered on the struggle among the northern militarists. At this point it need only be said that a similar situation existed in the southern provinces. After 1917 the Kuomintang-dominated Parliament attempted to establish itself, first at Shanghai and then at Canton, and sought to maintain a parliamentary régime in the south while attempting to reconquer the north. The southern republican government, however, was in the same situation from the outset as the Peking government. It had only the authority which its military supporters were willing to concede to it, thus existing largely on their sufferance. After the overthrow of the Anfu Club, Sun Yat-sen entered into an alliance with its members, but he was never able independently to affect the situation either in the north or in the south. He was intermittently in a position of nominal authority at Canton, but only so long as his presence served the purposes of either the Kwangtung or the Kwangsi militarists, whichever group happened to be in control. Thus the period of the Tuchunate saw the same disintegration of both the civil and a central authority in the southern provinces as in the northern. China as a unified political entity disappeared during the years from 1917 to 1926, provincialism or, at the widest, regionalism seeming to represent the possibility of the future until the revivified Kuomintang, with its own revolutionary military force, recaptured the idea of national unity when it resumed the revolution in 1926, the year after the death of Sun Yat-sen.

REFERENCES FOR FURTHER STUDY

J. O. P. BLAND, *China, Japan and Korea* (1921), ch. 4–6. S. G. CHENG, *Modern China, A Political Study* (1919). *China Weekly Review* contains weekly summaries of events, together with good special articles and editorial comment. H. H. GOWEN and J. W. HALL, *Outline History of China* (1926), ch. 31–36. J. W. HALL, *In the Land of the Laughing Buddha* (1924); an excellent account of the methods of carrying on civil war in China. S. K. HORNBECK, *Contemporary Politics in the Far East* (1916); well worth consulting. FRANKLIN W. HOUN, *Central Government of China, 1912–1928* (1957); an excellent institutional study. H. F. MacNAIR, *Modern Chinese History, Selected Readings* (1916), ch. 3–6; contains much interesting material. H. F. MacNAIR, *China in Revolution* (1931), ch. 1–4; an excellent summary, with much acute observation. P. S. REINSCH, *American Diplomat in China* (1922), ch. 1, 2, 4, 5, 15, 16, 22–25, 31, 32; especially interesting because of the position of the author. T. E. LA FARGUE, *China and the World War* (1937); one of the best accounts of the subject. E. A. SELLE, *Donald of China* (1948); account of Chinese politics, 1911–1941, as told to author by a foreign participant. T'ANG LEANG-LI, *Inner History of the Chinese Revolution* (1930), ch. 8–9; written from the point of view of the left wing of the Kuomintang. *Times* (New York) *Current History Magazine*, monthly summary of events in China and Japan. H. M. VINACKE, *Modern Constitutional Development in China* (1920), ch. 6–11. S. WAGEL, *Finance in China* (1914), ch. 3. B. L. PUTNAM WEALE, *Fight for the Republic in China* (1917), ch. 1–15; not altogether unbiased, but contains interesting material and is worth using. H. G. W. WOODHEAD (ed.), *China Year Book* (1912), pp. xi–xxxii; (1913), ch. 21; (1916), ch. 21; (1924), ch. 29, *Defense,* for account of the Tuchun system and of military operations in 1923; ch. 33, *Chinese Politics, 1924–1925;* ch. 23, *China's Constitutions and Election Laws,* complete including text of constitution of 1923; ch. 36, *Political Parties;* ch. 37, for details of operations in 1924–1925.

CHAPTER XII

THE PROGRESS OF CHINA: ECONOMIC AND SOCIAL: 1900–1931

1. POLITICAL STABILITY NOT AN ABSOLUTE PREREQUISITE TO PROGRESS

For the Westerner, political stability is the absolute prerequisite of material progress, so intimately is government related to the economic life of the state. Consequently he finds it difficult to understand why the condition of political turmoil in China attending the revolution did not produce a corresponding economic chaos. The explanation, which is extremely simple, has already been indicated. It lies in the fact that the economic life of the country had been lived apart from governmental interference or direction, together with the localized character of the Chinese economy. The change in these particulars has been of recent development, and it had been carried such a short distance by 1931 that political instability did not prevent economic progress from being made. The relaxation of the hand of authority, with the resulting increase in brigandage and piracy, and the incessant turmoil due to civil war, undoubtedly retarded the normal economic development of the country. This was so particularly because civil war made difficult the undertaking of vitally necessary developmental functions by government after the necessity had been perceived. But changes in the economic life of the country occurred in spite of political disorganization to an extent impossible in an economic entity such as the Western state had become. During this period it was in the non-political fields that the significant changes took place which must be appreciated if contemporary China is to be understood. As far as possible their consideration has been postponed so that they might be given unified treatment at this point in the survey of the evolution of modern China. These changes came about so gradually that it was only after the World War that they began to become vitally important. But in estimating their significance we must bear constantly in mind the fact that in many cases, even by 1931, they really constituted beginnings or tendencies rather than completed movements. This both increases their interest and makes more difficult their adequate treatment.

2. FOREIGN TRADE

An important indication of the economic progress of China since 1900 is to be found in the expansion of the import and export trade and in the change in the character of both imports and exports.

Although treaties of trade and commerce were consummated between China and Western nations during the years 1842 and 1843 and as a result certain designated ports were formally opened to foreign trade, yet it was not until the last decade of the nineteenth century that the Chinese themselves exhibited an interest in intercourse with the outside world. China's geographical isolation, its huge continental proportions, its tendency to wall itself off from the outside world, the self-sufficient nature of its society, its racial homogeneity, the uniqueness of its civilization and its lack of adequate internal communications, all militated against an expeditious development of contact with the outside world.[1]

Thus it took half a century for China to manifest a real trade interest, although there was gradual expansion of trade during the nineteenth century. This growth was almost inevitable as the points of contact were increased. In 1842 five ports were opened to trade. With each successive application of pressure by the Powers new ports, known as Treaty Ports, were opened to foreigners and foreign trade. After a time the Chinese government opened a few ports of its own free will. The number of treaty ports opened by 1931 numbered sixty-nine, and there were eleven places voluntarily opened to trade and foreign residence. The trade naturally increased with this enlargement of the points of contact under the stimulus of foreign interest.

After 1900, as China committed herself more fully and freely to foreign intercourse, the foreign trade grew more rapidly. The value of imports increased between 1900 and 1910 from over 211,000,000 to almost 463,000,000 Haikwan taels. During the same period exports increased from almost 159,000,000 to just under 381,000,000 taels. The effect of the revolution, but more particularly of the European War, was to check the import trade and, after 1914, to expand the export trade. But in both cases the post-war years, which were also those of greatest political unsettlement in China, were marked by rapid expansion. The year 1930 saw a net importation valued at 1,309,755,742 Haikwan taels and an exportation valued at 894,843,594 taels.[2] Thus in a period of thirty years the foreign trade values increased over three hundred fifty per cent. While these values must be discounted because of a change in price levels and on account of fluctuations in exchange, still they represent an advance which becomes little short of remarkable when the abnormal internal and world conditions are taken into account.

Of much more significance than their increase in value, however, was the change in the character of the imports and exports. Considering the former first, an analysis of the trade warrants acceptance of the statement that "the old order—China importing opium, cottons, and a few sundries

---

[1] Arnold, *China's Post-War Trade*, in Annals of American Academy, November, 1925, p. 82.
[2] This is a decrease from the high export levels of the three previous years, but an increase over 1926

—has been completely swept away, and, although the country is looked to as a large supplier of foodstuffs to the Western world, it is no less an importer on a large scale." [3]

It was opium which first turned the trade balance against China, although its importation was not legalized until 1858. In 1882 it accounted for over thirty-four per cent of the imports. In 1902 importation of other goods had so much increased that only eleven per cent of the total imports was opium. Then in 1906, as part of the reform program, China reverted to her earlier attitude toward the drug, and an Imperial edict ordered that opium smoking should be brought to an end by 1917. At the same time an attempt was made to reach an agreement with England lessening importation from India. This resulted in an understanding with the Indian government by which the export from India to China was to be reduced ten per cent per annum for a period of three years (1908–1911).[4] A new agreement reached on May 8, 1911, "provided for the complete extinction by the end of 1917 of the export of opium from India to China, and of the Chinese production of opium. It also provided that Indian opium, meanwhile, should be barred 'from any province in China which can establish by clear evidence that it has effectively suppressed the cutivation and import of native opium.' " [5]

With this agreement as a stimulus, progress was made toward curtailment of domestic production, although the revolution caused a temporary set-back—by reason of disturbed conditions, however, and not because of any change in policy. In spite of China's failure to live up to the 1911 agreement, the Indian government announced that after 1913 no further sales for the Chinese market would be permitted. It was also excluded officially by 1915, on the ground of the ending of cultivation, from fifteen provinces of China. All of this must be distinctly set down on the side of progress, particularly the progress made toward the lessening, province by province, of internal production.

Unfortunately, after 1915 a different story must be told. As military government established itself in one province after another, and as the authority of Peking declined, cultivation was resumed. By 1923 the only provinces free from the poppy were those so located that it was more profitable to rely on imports from neighboring provinces than to furnish their own supplies. The military must be held responsible for this because in some cases the Tuchun forced cultivation, and in others encouraged it in order to augment his resources. A notable exception was Shansi, where, under Governor Yen Hsi-shan, an active campaign to suppress both cultivation and smoking was carried on successfully, except as conditions in neighbor-

[3] *China Year Book* (1924), p. 671.
[4] On condition that native production should be reduced in the same ratio.
[5] *China Year Book* (1924), p. 552.

ing provinces prevented the attainment of complete suppression. Elsewhere smoking went on openly, with the officials reaping a profit from it as well as from the cultivation. There was some decline in cultivation in 1924–1925, due rather to previous over-production than to any change of attitude on the part of officials. Thus China became by far the largest producer of opium in the world. As against the two million pounds produced in India in 1924 China produced over twenty-five millions. This meant that it was on China herself, rather than on England, that pressure had to be put to reduce production as a means of restricting consumption.

In this same connection must be noted the increased use by Chinese of other narcotics, such as morphia, during this period. Here the supply came from abroad, and, since it was smuggled, it is difficult to estimate its quantity and source. Such seizures as were made by the customs authorities, however, indicated that the smuggling was done mostly by Japanese and Germans. It was brought in mainly through the ports in leased territory and through Shanghai. Because of its cheapness and the ease of using it, the morphine pills bade fair to displace the opium pipe among the poorer classes.

Returning to the general question of foreign trade, we find that in 1902 cotton goods and sundries accounted for seventy-two per cent of the imports; and food products, kerosene, and metals for seventeen per cent. In 1910 cotton yarn and cotton goods represented twenty-six per cent of the total imports; rice seven per cent; metals and machinery eight per cent; kerosene five per cent; sugar four and a half per cent; railway materials three per cent; marine products two per cent; cigarettes and tobacco two per cent; coal two per cent; dyes one and a half per cent; matches one per cent; woolen goods one per cent; and other goods of various sorts thirty-seven per cent. By 1930 importation of raw cotton had increased from less than one per cent of the total in 1910 to ten per cent, which meant an increase in value from 4,500,000 to 132,266,000 Haikwan taels. The cotton goods imported in 1930 had increased in value, but represented only 10.7 per cent of the total import trade as against thirteen per cent in 1910. And cotton yarn had substantially fallen both in value and in proportion.[6]

Without making a more extensive analysis of the import trade, we may fairly say that it revealed a continual broadening of the demand for foreign goods, and that it showed a most interesting change in the character of the demand. The value of machinery imported had increased from nine to seventy-eight million taels—from two to six per cent of the import totals. This indicated a change in internal production from hand to machine work. To put it another way, it meant that the industrial revolution had reached China. The increased importation of raw cotton and the decrease

[6] These figures are drawn from a table presented by JULEAN ARNOLD, op. cit., p. 84, and from GROVER CLARK, *Economic Rivalries in China* (1932), p. 111.

in importation, both in value and in proportion, of cotton yarn revealed the same change. China had begun to manufacture to supply her own needs in cotton goods. This conclusion is not invalidated by the increased value of cotton goods brought into the country because the Chinese were not yet able to supply their own expanding needs, nor had weaving by modern means been undertaken as extensively as spinning. Since we shall have to return to this question in another connection, we may temporarily postpone the drawing of final conclusions.

Referring to another import commodity, kerosene, it may be pointed out that it represented an important change affecting the lives of the people by affording them better lighting at night in places where electric lighting had not been introduced. The development, during World War I, of new markets for China's vegetable oils was partly responsible for the increased demand for kerosene, as was also the increased wealth due to war trade, which made possible a wider replacement of vegetable oils by kerosene for illuminating purposes. But whatever the reason for the change, the improvement in lighting in the homes had significance in the development of the new China. A similar modernization of life is revealed in the importation of matches. The value of match importation had decreased by 1923, but this was due to the fact that China was supplying her own needs in the face of an enlarged demand, rather than to a lessening of the demand. Other changes in the life of the people were shown in the fourfold increase in importation of paper, largely due to the establishment and increase in the number of newspapers; in the introduction of motor cars; and in the importation of photographic, printing, and lithographing materials, telephone and telegraph supplies, and scientific instruments. These and other importations meant that the Chinese, from the material standpoint, were beginning gradually to change their manner of living.

In the same way, an analysis of the trade reveals a much wider range of commodities exported. The most notable change, perhaps, was the relative decline in exportation of tea, which represented almost forty-eight per cent of the export trade in 1882, ten per cent in 1902, and less than three per cent in 1930. This was to be explained by the inroads made on the Chinese overseas market by Japanese and Indian teas, by the failure of the Chinese to improve their output, and, for a time after 1917, by the temporary decline in the Russian demand due to conditions in Russia. Silk, the other great staple of export, had also shown a relative decline in terms of the total trade, although one not at all comparable to the decline in tea exportation. Another interesting development was the export of soya beans, bean-cake, and bean-oil, which was negligible in 1900, was eight per cent of the total in 1910, and had increased to 20.7 per cent of the 1930 total, becoming the outstanding export. In value this meant one hundred and eighty-five million taels. The rise of the soya bean to its present position in the trade paralleled the settlement and the development of Manchuria under the stimulation of the Japanese South Manchurian railway.

Exports were almost entirely <u>raw materials and foodstuffs</u>, except for certain manufactures peculiar to China such as silk piece-goods, carpets, embroideries and laces, hair nets, and a few other items. And yet we find listed among the exports egg products, a new and growing industrial commodity, nankeens, and even cotton yarn. These were indications, small to be sure, that China might soon be found competing with the Western states and Japan in their own markets. The increased variety of China's exports was indicated in the fact that in 1910 only thirty-three products were sufficiently important to be listed among the exports, while in 1930 there were over fifty separate types of export, each valued at more than a million taels.

It must of course be admitted that foreign trade, as such, played a relatively small part in the Chinese economy. But it deserves consideration both for itself and because of the indications it gives of changes going on within China during the first decades of the present century.

3. CHANGES IN AGRICULTURAL LIFE

These changes may be even better gauged by examining the internal productive processes and internal trade. As to the latter, it is impossible to present reliable and comprehensive figures showing its extent at the time under consideration. But where goods had to be moved on waterways by junk and flat-bottomed boats pushed and pulled by man power, and on land had to be carried on the camel and the donkey-cart or by the wheel-barrow, it is clear that trade on more than a local basis would be greatly restricted. The use of steam vessels along the coast and on the great navigable rivers, together with the building of roads and the construction of railways, assuredly greatly expanded internal trade, an expansion limited, of course, by the extent to which these innovations had been made. But even the small beginnings which had been made tended to break down economic provincialism and localism, and to create national markets. Thus it is fair to infer that internal trade had grown even more largely than foreign trade since 1900.

The agricultural population constituted in 1931, just as it did in 1842, the largest occupational group in China. Outwardly the village peoples engaged in farming had been the least affected in their lives and economic activities by the contact with the West. This would naturally be the case, since they lived in places where there was very little contact with the foreigner, and where they were largely shut off from the new currents. In the interior villages the ground was prepared in the same way that it had been generations earlier. The primitive plow, drawn perhaps by a donkey and bullock jointly, was used, and primitive methods of harvesting and threshing were employed. The farming implements and machinery of the West either had been rejected or had never been heard of. There had been little introduction of mechanical devices for labor-saving purposes.

While this was and for some time will be the case, there are certain explanations of it other than ignorance or unwillingness to change. In the first place, the farm machinery which has been so highly developed in the United States is not adapted to the needs of Chinese agriculture. It is all designed for extensive cultivation with the minimum use of human labor. Where individual land holdings are small and scattered, as they are in China, the farm machines such as a tractor or a gang plow cannot be readily used, and are uneconomical for the individual farmer. They could be introduced successfully only by an agreement to disregard boundary-lines in plowing. The Chinese farmer, who was an individualist, could be led only gradually to agree to this as he might be shown a positive advantage which he would secure from it. In the second place, Western tools and machines were so expensive that the Chinese could not afford to buy them even though he could see that they would ultimately pay for themselves. The chief advantage urged for them was that they replace labor, enabling one man to do the work of several. But this was not an advantage in China, where labor was too abundant. As long as the man-power available for agriculture was not decreased, labor-saving agricultural devices would make little appeal. On the contrary, they aroused opposition because they meant starvation for the people displaced. If industry should draw off enough men from the farms, or if an extensive emigration overseas or to Manchuria and Mongolia should take place, or if both in combination should happen, so that there would exist an acute labor shortage in agricultural regions, then Western farm implements might make an appeal, if it could be shown how they could be used effectively under Chinese conditions and if the farmers could finance their purchase.

But while there has been little change in the use of implements, there had been significant changes in the agricultural economy. In the first place, the improvement of communications had had its effect on the peasant population. For the first time it was beginning to be possible to produce primarily for sale rather than for use or for purely local exchange. This change could be fully realized, and its consequences manifested, only with the completion of a modern transportation system. But even as far as it had been carried by 1931 it resulted in the beginnings of agricultural specialization. Instead of the farmer directly attempting to supply his major wants and those of his family, which is bound to be uneconomical, he could grow the products best adapted to the soil and climate of the locality, and sell in an ever-widening market, supplying his needs by purchase with the pro-

ceeds derived from the sale of his crops. Thus one could see, in the light
of recent developments and also on the basis of experience in other countries, the end of the uneconomical, relatively self-sufficient family or village
in China. This was further indicated in the fact that the factory could
supply clothing and shoes, for example, more cheaply than could home
labor.

This should not, however, be taken to mean that there was no exchange
of goods in nineteenth-century China, or that the family or village was
completely self-sufficient. The farmer did not make all of his own tools, for
example, nor did he produce everything necessary to his well-being. The
existence of market towns, and the development of a town artisan class
and of a measure of specialized production in the handicrafts, indicated
that there was inter-change of goods. Much of this was local, but some exchange took place over a comparatively wide area. The change indicated in
the preceding paragraph was in the direction of enlarging this exchange
and of increasing specialization to the point of making the farmer ultimately dependent on the town for the satisfaction of his wants. This would
have the consequence of forcing him to produce primarily, rather than
secondarily, for the market, whereas formerly production was primarily
for use.

The increasing cultivation of crops which must be sold in a comparatively wide market afforded another indication of this change in agricultural China. The staple crop of Manchuria, for example, had come to be
the soya bean. In Chihli and Kiangsu provinces, the two largest areas, and
in Shansi and elsewhere on a smaller scale, cotton was being grown in
such quantities that China had become the third largest producer in the
world. Again, tobacco was being grown in marketable quantities in almost
every province. Some of it was undoubtedly produced for home and local
consumption, but more and more was being grown for the general domestic market, since the making of cigars and cigarettes had become an
important home industry. The increased cultivation of the poppy during
the period of military rule has already been referred to, and it must be
recognized that opium was produced for the market rather than for the use
of the cultivator. Other examples might be given, but enough has been
said to indicate the tendency. It is clear that the farmer who devotes himself to the production of a staple such as tobacco or cotton comes to depend
on others for his own foodstuffs, and that others consequently find a larger
market for their products. Thus the movement toward specialization is
carried a step further. The general movement may also lead to importation of agricultural products if the staple is widely enough cultivated to
restrict food-producing areas. Thus cotton, either raw or manufactured,
began to enter the list of exports, and rice and grains the list of increased

imports. As will be pointed out later,[7] the development of domestic industry was a substantial factor in producing this change in cultivation.

These three decades also witnessed a conscious movement to improve the
raw products. The government was partly responsible for attempts at improvement, both directly, and indirectly through the government schools.
Furthermore, private efforts, both individual and collective, were made in
the same direction.

It has been demonstrated that China can grow American cotton of good
quality and long staple. It has also been demonstrated that the native cotton,
which is of short fibre . . . , can also by the process of selection be greatly improved. . . . Chinese interested in the cotton industry are taking steps to improve the quality and quantity of the raw material, and arrangements have
been made for the retention by these interests of an American cotton expert
to work in conjunction with the Department of Agriculture of the University
of Nanking.[8]

Steps were also taken to weed out diseased silk worms, to bring about
more scientific care of the cocoon, and to prepare the raw silk in a way
better suited to the requirements of foreign high-speed looms. These efforts
must continue if China is to regain her former dominant position in the
silk trade. The same thing is true of tea-growing. The Chinese were beginning to study the needs of the foreign market, and as a result were
attempting to improve cultivation and to undertake more careful selection
and grading.

It was in those fields of production which were related to industry or
to foreign trade that the Chinese were making the most conscious efforts
toward improvement. But in other fields there were indications of change
which will be more marked as time goes on. The agricultural departments
of some of the schools and colleges experimented with a view to finding
products which might profitably be introduced. It was also discovered that
the Chinese farmer often saved the poorest part of his crop for seed purposes, and he was introduced to the idea that instead he should reserve the
best part of the crop for future sowing. From this it will be a short step to
specialization in the production of seeds. This will undoubtedly increase
the yield wherever it is done, and thus ultimately improve the condition
of the farmer. Scientific rotation of crops was also being urged, which would
help to reduce the cost and the labor of fertilization. It is not without significance that in 1910 the amount of artificial fertilizer imported was entirely negligible, while in 1923 it was valued at four million Haikwan taels,
ranking twenty-fifth on the list of imports.

It cannot be seriously argued that the standard of living of the Chinese

[7] Sec. 4 of this chapter.
[8] ARNOLD, *Commercial Handbook of China* (1919), vol. II, p. 322.

farmer had been notably elevated by 1931. In certain sections, due to drought and flood, and the consequent famine conditions, which reached their high-water mark in the great famine of 1921, living conditions became distinctly worse than usual. But with normal conditions restored, there were indications that the standard had been slightly elevated. This was indicated in the great growth in tobacco consumption and in increased importation of other luxuries, in the use of artificial fertilizers, in the amount of third-class travel on the railways, and in numerous other ways. It was so slight, however, as far as the masses were concerned, as to deserve no more than mention. In many sections, particularly those affected by flood or draught—Chihli province, for example—the majority of the farmers continued not only to be poor but even to live below the poverty-line.[9]

Another aspect of rural life which deserves consideration is rural industry. Spinning and weaving, particularly, had long been part of the rural economy. In order to live it was necessary for all members of the household to contribute something to its maintenance. And because of the inadequate communications the villagers had to produce everything possible for themselves. Since almost all of the men in the village were farmers, each household was also an industrial establishment, just as it was in the American frontier community. The materials for clothing either were produced on the land as part of the farming operations or were procured by exchange. But in either case they were usually transformed by home labor, particularly that of the women and children. Furthermore, where possible the attempt was made to eke out the family income by production for exchange or sale. Thus industry, outside the trading centers, and except for a limited specialized production, was diffused throughout the numberless villages of the country.

This continued to be true in spite of the move toward the establishment of the machine economy with its factory system. But even here a change might be perceived. In the cotton growing areas of Chihli and Kiangsu provinces, for example, the home industry continued, but the jobber or small capitalist was making himself more and more a dominant factor. Sometimes he furnished the tools such as the spindle and the loom, besides supplying the raw cotton or the yarn to the farmer. He then collected the yarn or cloth and sent it to the market. The rural household received a return only for the work done. In other cases the spindle or the loom, almost invariably of the primitive and familiar kind, belonged to the family, the dealer supplying materials and marketing the product. New type machines, more complicated than the old and with a much greater output per labor unit, were being introduced in some cases, but only gradually where they were used in the home. The improved machines were more usually oper-

---

[9] See *Chinese Rural Economy*, by J. B. TAYLOR, in Chinese Social and Political Science Review, vol. VIII, nos. 1 and 2. He fixes the poverty-line at an annual income of $150 or under.

ated under the supervision of the dealer in a semi-factory system. Here in the textile industry was shown the transitional stage from the old to the new order. The same change was going on in silk spinning and weaving, in paper-making, and in other household industries.

As illustrating what is happening to rural industry outside textiles, we may mention the paper industry of Ch'ien-an. Owing to the suitability of the water of a stream near the city and the existence of a supply of white earth, paper has long been made in the villages nearby. The paper shops of the old kind consisted of seven workers. Five of these prepare the raw materials (the paper is made from the mulberry) and dry the paper; one makes the paper and the head man finishes or smooths it. The owner of the plant usually has more than one such shop. He keeps the books and sees to the marketing beside supplying the capital. . . .

One of these small capitalists proved to be an enterprising man. In 1914 he went to Korea and Japan to study paper making in those countries and in 1916 started a "Korean paper mill." This was so successful that the next year he added another and in 1919 purchased some quite elaborate machinery. By this time others had become interested and a number of mills were started. These are of two types, a smaller with thirty workers each and a larger with over fifty workers. The latter use water power and have an output ten times greater than the former. In 1920 there were four of these Korean mills. They are usually owned by a group of partners. 1920 was very successful and 200% profit was made by some. This led to over-expansion, thirty-one mills operating in 1921. The large output however seriously reduced prices (from $32.00 to $9.50) and the following year only twenty mills continued to operate.[10]

Here we have an example of the first steps in putting on a factory basis an industry which had been attached to the rural household. In the case of the household industry of whatever kind, it occupied the time of the farmer and his household particularly during the winter and early spring, and served as a side-line to farming operations. As machinery is introduced, and with it the factory system, industry cannot be treated as incidental to farming, but has to recruit its own independent labor supply. In China, as elsewhere, the worker tends to leave the farm, thus lightening the pressure on the soil, or women and children are used, and the new industry, in a different way to be sure, continues to afford a supplementary income to the rural household, just as did the old. In either case such changes as that described were almost imperceptibly working a revolution in the rural economy.

4. INDUSTRIAL DEVELOPMENT

Even in the towns and cities of the nineteenth-century China, industry was in the handicrafts or cottage stage. With few exceptions production was for a strictly local market. The shop and the factory were the same.

[10] Op. cit., pp. 244–245.

The instruments of production were simple tools rather than elaborate and costly machines. All, or most, of the processes of an industry were carried on under one roof and by the same people, there being little subdivision of labor and industrial specialization. There was no problem of capital and labor, for instead of the employer and the wage worker we find the artisan, become the proprietor, assisted by the journeyman and the apprentice. All engaged in the same trade were united in the craft guild, which controlled prices, quality, wages, and the terms of apprenticeship, and fixed the number of apprentices in proportion to journeymen.

The old conditions persisted to such an extent that by 1931 most of China's industrial output continued to be produced in the home or small shop and with the same organization. But at the same time it must be recognized that the general movement was in the direction of placing industry on a modern basis. Thus while the hand loom persisted in both the cotton and silk industries, the modern machine loom had been introduced, together with the power spindle. In 1930 there were over four hundred fifty modern silk filatures and weaving mills, one hundred twenty-seven cotton mills, and sixteen woolen mills. The active cotton spindles numbered over three million. In addition to this, there were over forty albumen factories, more than forty canneries, thirty-four iron and steel works, fifty-three dockyard, ship-building, and engineering works, one hundred twenty-nine flour mills, upward of a hundred oil mills and bean-cake factories, two hundred seventy-four electric light and power works, twenty paper mills, and other modern undertakings too numerous to list. It must be re-emphasized that these establishments used modern machinery, and that in addition there was the transitional movement going on through the medium of the small capitalist, which has been mentioned. This will undoubtedly result eventually in large additions to the factory and machine economy.[11]

In comparison with the United States or even Japan, it must be admitted, the new economy was, even by 1931, merely in embryo in China, or at the most at a decidedly infantile stage. Nevertheless, when it is remembered that there had come virtually no change in methods of production before 1900, and when one recalls the difficulties of transportation and communications, together with the size of the country and the rigidity of its organized life, these beginnings assume a greater relative importance. Among the obstacles to industrialization which had to be overcome, in addition to those just mentioned, were such attitudes of the Chinese people as tended to make them hostile to innovation; the self-sufficiency of the Chinese economic system; the relative lack of standing of the commercial and industrial classes; the chaotic currency system, and its instability due to fluctuations

[11] The number of establishments doubled in some classes and quadrupled in others between 1922 and 1931.

in the price of silver; the foreign control of the tariff, which made it impossible for protection to be afforded to an infant industry; and the lack of free capital for investment, or, on account of governmental and political conditions, fear of the loss of any such large investment as the installation of machinery required.[12]

Two elements contributed to the development of the new industry. The first that naturally comes to mind is the influence of the West after China had come to accept more freely the new order of things. The second is to be found in the building of railroads and the establishment of steamship lines. It is unnecessary to dwell further on the improvement of communications except to point out that the large-scale production of the machine and factory system is based upon a national rather than a local market, and that the enlarged market is created as transportation facilities are improved. Thus industry was stimulated even more than agriculture by the building of railroads. For the sake of both branches of the national economy China, of course, needed much more mileage of railroads and highways than had been built by 1931.

Most of the Chinese enterprises of the modern sort which had been successful were individually financed, were family affairs, or were organized as partnerships, with two or several members. The joint-stock form of organization was only occasionally used with complete success. This was partly because legal regulation and control had not been effectively established. But even more it was due to the lack of a highly developed sense of corporate honesty, the same defect which had long manifested itself in government. Funds collected by stock subscription were often used for individual purposes, such as speculation unrelated to the business of the corporation, and thus were frequently dissipated. The distrust consequently engendered among possible investors retarded the development of larger enterprises than those coming within the means of, at the most, three or four individuals of wealth. It will undoubtedly take time for the proverbial honesty of the Chinese to be completely extended to the joint-stock undertaking. In the long run this may prove to be a good thing, however, if it leads to a multiplication of smaller industrial enterprises of a modern sort. These can be better controlled and will permit a better adaptation of the old organization to new needs than would otherwise be possible.

While the joint-stock enterprise was only gradually making its way by 1931, what is perhaps its necessary forerunner, or at least is related to it and to factory production—a modern banking system—was coming rapidly into existence. Here also the old and new were found side by side. The Shansi bankers still did a limited business in central China, and the old-

[12] For a discussion of these and other obstacles to industrialization see ORCHARD, *Contrasts in the Progress of Industrialization in China and Japan,* Political Science Quarterly, vol. 52, pp. 18–50.

style exchange shops remained. But after the revolution a large number of modern banks of the Western kind came into being. Many of these became organized in a National Banker's Association, which included: the Bank of China, which was the fiscal agency of the central government, and which had branches throughout the country; the Bank of Communications, which was similarly related to the Ministry of Communications; numerous provincial banks; and such institutions as the Chêkiang Industrial Bank, the Bank of the Salt Industry, the Ningpo Commercial Bank, and many others. The modern bank played and must continue to play an important rôle in promoting industrial development in China. Further than this, the government had shown a dependency on the modern banks in floating its internal loans and in tiding itself over financial crises at Peking and then at Nanking. The government banks not infrequently showed unsound tendencies in financing, particularly in their currency issues; but this was largely due to their governmental connection and to the exigencies of domestic politics, rather than to a failure of the bank managers to appreciate the principles of sound finance. The power of organized Chinese finance was illustrated on at least one occasion when the National Banker's Association was able to dictate the conditions of a loan to the government.

5. EFFECT OF INDUSTRIAL DEVELOPMENT ON GUILD SYSTEM

It is unnecessary here to recapitulate the description of nineteenth-century industrial organization, in and through the guild, which was given in the first chapter. It is, however, necessary to examine briefly the effects of the introduction of machine methods and factory production on the guild system.

In the first place, it must be recognized that much of the strength of the craft guild as a price-fixing and quality-establishing agency was due to the fact that production was local and found an outlet in local or provincial markets which the guild members monopolized. The local organization, which comprehended all who were engaged in a particular type of production in a restricted area, could control its members in these two matters. This control was further strengthened because all the processes of the industry were carried on in the one establishment, specialization being the exception rather than the rule. In other words, the organism was simple and it was integrated in the shop. The proprietors, controlling all of the steps in the manufacture of a particular commodity, were able to meet and establish standards and prices by agreement. Inter-guild agreements were necessary only in exceptional cases.

But with the broadening of the market as rail and steam communications developed, the craft guild lost the ability to control it. Where Shanghai and Tientsin goods competed in central China, for example, neither the

Shanghai nor the Tientsin guild could control the competition. Further-more, the division of industrial production into more and more separate processes, each carried on in an independent establishment, weakened the authority of the guild, which was able to exercise control over merely a part of the enterprise of production. The industrial organism becomes so complex under modern conditions of specialized production that the es-sentially simple guild organization loses its usefulness. Therefore the con-clusion is inevitable that modern industry, as it established itself in China, weakened the guild organization and would ultimately bring it to an end unless it found a basis of adaptation to the new order.

In still another particular the new industry has weakened the position of the guild. Under the old conditions of production it was possible to regulate the number of workers in a given industry, since a long apprentice-ship was required to produce the trained artisan. By fixing the number of apprentices in a shop, the guild could limit the number of journeymen, and it could also control the number of establishments and prevent undue ex-pansion of production. Furthermore, as the labor supply was restricted, the individual who underpaid his workmen, according to the minimum stand-ard set up by the guild, could not readily replace them.

In the new industry the necessity for a long apprenticeship disappeared, since the mastery of one process and of the operation of a machine could be readily gained. Thus the labor supply was immeasurably increased and dependence on the guild correspondingly lessened.

Again, under the old order, the master had been a workman himself before he became the proprietor, and he lived as master in intimate contact with his workmen, who were usually few in number. Consequently there was an intimacy of relationship which made it difficult to differentiate clearly the employer from the workman. This also made it possible for master and man to be united in the one organization, as they were in the guild. Since the affairs of the shop were known to the workers almost as well as to the proprietor, the problem of fixing wages was simplified. The whole relationship was normally not that of employer and employee, in the modern Occidental sense, but that of fellow-workers.

Here again the new order produced, or at least inaugurated, a change which became increasingly important as the industrial plant became larger. In China, just as elsewhere, the factory system impersonalized industry. It produced an industrial wage-worker who was no longer in intimate con-tact with the artisan proprietor, and who was not himself an artisan. The result was that the proprietor, who was an industrial capitalist rather than a former workman, did not find himself at home in an organization which included the wage-worker, nor did the latter find that the old organization served his purpose.

By 1931, in the places where modern industry had developed, the guild took on the character of an employers' association, and the workers were developing their organization in the labor union. The latter remained in an embryonic stage, except in such places as Shanghai, Canton, and Hongkong. The 1925 strikes in all three places demonstrated the power and effectiveness of action of organized Chinese labor. The organization for other than nationalist purposes, however, had to be built on national rather than local lines for it to be effective in purely industrial disputes.

The guild as an employers' or trade association may serve a useful purpose or it may give way to some other organization. By 1931 there had come into being Chinese chambers of commerce, which were modeled on the foreign chambers of such cities as Shanghai and Tientsin, which, in turn found their prototypes in those of English and American cities. The Chinese chamber of commerce was essentially an inter-guild organization, although it numbered individual enterprises as well as guilds in its membership. It served a distinctly useful purpose in integrating the increasingly complex business community. Here it served modern industry much as the guild itself served the craft in pre-modern times. It was by perpetuation of the guild as an employers' association, and by the establishment of chambers of commerce on the basis of the guild, that adaptation was by 1931 taking place.

An original development, rather than a purely imitative one, was to be found in one of the functions of the chambers of commerce as set forth in the law providing for their organization. They might legally serve as a court, acting through one of their committees, to settle industrial disputes where the parties in controversy were not members of the same guild, and to bring to an end conflicts between employers and employees over wages. This latter form of activity, however, leads to trouble unless the workers are given active representation. If local unions had been given representation as workers' guilds, this defect would have been remedied and the field of usefulness of the chamber of commerce court have been enlarged.

It should be noted in this connection that the chamber of commerce court did not supplant, but rather supplemented, the guild as an arbitral agency. Disputes between members of the guild were still subject to its adjudication, while disputes between those who were members of different guilds were arbitrated through the more inclusive organization. The craft guild might ultimately adjust itself to the new conditions by broadening into an organization of the related crafts. The beginnings of this development could be perceived in the attempt to establish such an organization as the Lu-Pan Industrial Union in Peking, with the intention of drawing together into one unit all of those (masters) connected with the building trades. This would not interfere at all with the extension of the chamber of commerce idea, as the chamber could continue to find a reason for existence as an integrating agency for the business community.

The keynote of Chinese life had been adjustment, and the utility of co-operation, rather than competition, had been fully accepted. Through the adaptation of the guild system to the new conditions there might have been successfully devised a new mechanism of adjustment which would have enabled modern China to escape some of the evils inherent in the industrial system which was being imported from the Western world. The greatest obstacle to be overcome did not lie in the realm of competition for markets, but in the field of labor relations, since the problem of keeping employer and employee on good terms had not yet been solved. The process of adaptation, however, was interrupted after 1931 under the impact of both domestic and foreign relations developments.

6. LABOR ORGANIZATION AND PROBLEMS

Organization of labor had not been unknown in the past, but it was temporary in character and was usually designed to effect some immediate end through collective action. Even so it proved on numerous occasions to be tremendously effective if the end aimed at could be quickly reached. Permanent organization was unnecessary under normal conditions, because the workers were entitled to, and did, participate in the guild meetings. Consequently it was only after 1918 that permanent labor organizations of the Western variety were formed. Such an organization was formed at Shanghai in 1919 and was called "The Union for the Improvement of Chinese Labor." The main purpose, however, was announced to be mutual benefit and protection, rather than defense against employers. This union was designed on a national basis, with the intention of establishing branches in other places. Many similar organizations were launched in Shanghai, Canton, Tientsin, and other industrial cities. It is difficult to distinguish those which had a political origin and objectives from those which had objectives such as are professed by labor unions in Western countries, but it is beyond question that the latter began to find a firm footing in the country. And although they were initially established primarily for mutual benefit and improvement purposes, they were directed more and more toward the objective of increasing wages and lessening the hours of work. Strikes for such purposes were numerous in the decade 1921–1931, although again it was difficult clearly to distinguish the political from the non-political strike. A Peking vernacular paper listed strikes from September to December, 1922, to the total of forty-one. Seventy and nine-tenths per cent, it says, were for increased wages; twelve and two-tenths per cent were in opposition to the foreman; twelve and two-tenths per cent were sympathetic strikes; and four and seven-tenths per cent were for the right to organize a union.[13] It may be noted that the formation of unions was

[13] *China Year Book* (1924), p. 658. Also J. B. CONDLIFFE, *China Today: Economic*, pp. 105–110.

neither prohibited nor authorized by national law in China until after the establishment of the nationalist government. A trade union Act was passed in October, 1929, which established the right of organization subject to a number of definite restrictions.

The remarkable thing was not the number of strikes after 1920 but rather the fact that there were not more of them. The constantly increasing cost of living had created a serious situation both for the factory workers and for the much larger number engaged in the handicrafts and trades. A careful study of prices, wages, and standards of living in Peking [14] showed that prices in that city had been steadily mounting since 1900 in the various dietary staples and in clothing such as was worn by the workers. There had been variations and fluctuations, but the constant trend had been upwards. This rise had been especially marked after 1920. The problem of living had also been complicated by the copper exchange, which in its turn had been increasing. This was due to a continual enlargement of the supply of coins and to their debasement. Again, the worst conditions had developed after 1920, with the result that wages had begun to be paid in silver instead of copper. During the years after 1900 guild action had brought about several wage increases, but the real wage of the workman was lower in 1924 than it was in either 1900 or 1913, the years taken as the bases of comparison. "The gilds have a minimum standard of living which they attempt to maintain. If conditions give the workers a temporary increase in their standard of living the gild does not attempt to help them maintain the increase. It will not try to raise wages until prices are such that real wages have reached the customary minimum." [15]

The rise of prices at Peking was probably fairly typical of the entire country. Prices at Canton, as a matter of fact, were reported to have reached an even higher level than at Peking. In the absence of similar detailed studies of other cities, it may be assumed that, so far as they were operative, the factors which produced price changes in one place had similar results elsewhere. These factors had not been political so much as economic. "The various political events, revolution, civil war, attempted restoration of the Emperor, have had but little effect on prices unless they have been accompanied by disturbances sufficiently severe to affect the harvest by destroying crops in the field, or to make transportation difficult by commandeering rolling stock and cutting communications." [16] Among the economic factors may be mentioned drought and flood over wide areas which affected production adversely, and population increases.

To better labor conditions, three methods appeared to be available.

[14] T. P. MENG, AND SIDNEY GAMBLE, *Prices, Wages and the Standard of Living in Peking, 1900–1924,* in special supplement to Chinese Social and Political Science Review, July, 1926.
[15] Ibid., p. 110.
[16] Ibid., p. 111.

First, industrial strife might develop, as it had in many Western countries, concessions in the form of ameliorative laws or betterment of conditions being extorted through pressure from below either on the government or on the employer. This seemed to be forecast from the organization of unions and a corresponding multiplication of strikes after 1920. Second, organizations such as the chamber of commerce court, with adequate labor representation, could prove a medium for the adjustment of difficulties. This would have better harmonized with the traditions and procedure of the past. Third, voluntary amelioration from the top, perhaps as a means of forestalling the application of pressure from below, might prove success-ful. This would accord with the more enlightened practice in Western countries.

Some employers were already developing the third procedure. Chang Ch'ien created a "model city" around his factories. The *Commercial Press* of Shanghai, until the destruction of its plant during the 1932 Sino-Japanese hostilities at Shanghai, provided school privileges for children, maintained a small hospital for its employees, gave its women employees a month off before and after confinement, and furnished an attractive resting place for its employees. Withal it was able to declare a fifty per cent dividend in 1922, and its shares appreciated almost one hundred per cent. The Han-yehp'ing Corporation similarly provided for its employees, as did Mr. Y. H. Moh, known familiarly as the "Cotton King" of China. This was all good as far as it went, but it was weakened by reason of the fact that it was done from the top down. Furthermore, the "model employer" left wages low, expecting that compensation in the form of gardens and rest rooms would take the place of higher pay. In general the movement suffered from the fact that it was done "on the best foreign lines," which had not served to prevent industrial strife in the West. And finally, these individual achievements served to obscure the fact that good working conditions were not the rule.

It must be recognized that most employers in China, as elsewhere at a similar or even more advanced stage of development, felt no interest in voluntarily improving the condition of workers by raising wages, lessening the hours of work, protecting women in industry, and refusing to make use of child labor. Wages were very low, and yet strikes were necessary to raise wages in such places as Shanghai in order partially to keep pace with the increase in the cost of living. Even among the more enlightened em-ployers there was no sentiment against the employment of women and children, and certainly there was little among the masses even of the industrialized workers, for the income from the labor of women and chil-dren appeared to be necessary to eke out the family income. Higher wages needed to be paid before there could come any pronounced demand from below for the safeguarding of women and children in industry. In this respect the enlightened employers were far in advance of the demands of labor. Government regulation was attempted (the Ministry of Agriculture and Commerce promulgated regulations governing such labor), but political stability was a prerequisite of effective governmental action.

Just how far legal regulation and control of industry would develop after 1931 was problematical. The old tradition was to allow the economic life of the country to control itself, subject to the interposition of the magistrate when the public peace was threatened. This tradition was continued, as has been pointed out, in the development of the chamber of commerce court. But the new point of view toward governmental functions, it could be expected, would continue to express itself, when political stability had been attained, through the development of some measure of legal regulation of industrial conditions.

7. EFFECT OF FOREIGN PARTICIPATION IN CHINESE INDUSTRY

In 1931, even if there had been political stability, the problem of regulation and control of the new industry would have been more difficult of solution than in most countries because of the extent of foreign participation in it. For example, thirty-four per cent of the modern cotton spinning plants were Japanese-owned or -controlled, and an additional three per cent were British-owned or -controlled, leaving sixty-four per cent to Chinese control. While the same proportions did not hold true for other industries, foreign participation in some industries being considerably less, and in others even greater, there was generally a substantial foreign interest in Chinese factory production. Inflation in Japan following the war, together with the efforts of the Japanese government to encourage investment in industrial undertakings in China, help to account for the striking movement of Japanese capital to China, and the cheapness of Chinese labor interested foreign capital in general in the establishment of factories in China. The problem of control arose from the fact that the foreigner was protected by the treaty system. It was further complicated by the establishment of many enterprises, some of them Chinese-financed, in the foreign residential areas, where they were largely removed from Chinese control.

It is readily apparent that the old idea of industrial self-control and regulation could not be maintained unless the entire industry was brought within the controlling organization, whether it was the craft guild or an industrial guild. Even government regulation could not be fairly introduced unless it could be extended over all engaged in the same type of production. For example, the native cotton industry could not establish regulation as to price, quality, wage and labor conditions, and make them effective, so long as the foreign mills in Shanghai were unregulated. Of course the reverse was also true. One difficulty encountered by the Shanghai Child

Labor Commission of 1924 in framing recommendations for the consideration of the Municipal Council lay in the existence of competitive industry
in the same industrial area which would not be affected by any regulation
so enacted. "It is obvious," reported the commission, "that any action
which might have the effect of raising the cost of production within the
settlement would not only be unfair to industries competing with those
outside, but would also be unwise from the more general point of view,
since it would tend to the subsidization outside the settlement of the very
evils which were being attacked within." [17] So long as the settlements remained under foreign jurisdiction, this anomalous condition would continue. Chinese regulation, whether in law or through the organization of
the native industry, could not extend over the foreign-controlled industry
located in the concessions, and regulation in the concessions would be
qualified in extent and operation, except as coöperative working arrangements were made between the two sets of authorities.

From this it may be argued, as the Chinese maintained for this and other
reasons, that the foreign concessions should have been restored to the control of China. This was part of the demand of the new nationalism. So far
as social legislation was concerned, however, this would probably not result in the immediate curtailment of the hours of labor for women and
children or in other safeguards for them in industry, for non-communist
and non-radical Chinese opinion on this point was not yet highly developed.

Another problem presented through the foreign-managed enterprise, no
matter where it was located, came from the fact that in all labor disputes
there was the possibility of race or national trouble developing. A strike in
a Japanese, British, or American mill, growing out of treatment of the
laborers by the foreman, or due to a controversy over wages, readily took
on the character of an anti-Japanese, anti-British, or anti-American movement, and led to an international difficulty. The 1924 strike of the Hongkong seamen, and that in the Japanese mills in Shanghai in 1925, served to
illustrate this ever-present possibility. The growth of nationalist sentiment
made the danger particularly acute. Any such diversion or enlargement of
issues was of course political and partly artificial in character. But it was
a factor which from 1920 to 1931 had to be seriously reckoned with.

These, then, were the significant economic changes which had been
taking place in the years from 1900 to 1931: (1) an expansion and change in
the character of the import and export trade; (2) some progress in agriculture, and, through improvement of communications, an enlargement of
the market for agricultural products; (3) the introduction of modern machine production, and the factory system in industry; and, as a result of
this, (4) changes in economic organization which were of great significance

[17] From the report of the Shanghai Child Labor Commission, published in full in *China
Year Book* (1924–1925), pp. 545–561.

for the future. Since 1931, when Japan renewed her continental expansion, marked changes have occurred in China's economic and social life.

REFERENCES FOR FURTHER STUDY

The Annals of the American Academy of Political and Social Science, vol. 152, November, 1930, *China,* espec. parts 2–3. JULEAN ARNOLD, *Commercial Handbook of China,* 2 vols. (1919); a compendium of information concerning China's economic life. JULEAN ARNOLD, *Agriculture in the Economic Life of the New China,* in Chinese Social and Political Science Review, vol. VII, no. 3, July, 1922. CHEN HAN-SENG, *Landlord and Peasant in China* (1936); one of the few studies of an important relationship. CHENG YU-K'UEI, *Foreign Trade and Industrial Development in China* (1956). C. C. CHU and T. C. BLAISDELL, *Study of the Rug Industry in Peking,* in Chinese Social and Political Science Review, Supplement, April, 1924. GROVER CLARK, *Economic Rivalries in China* (1932); a careful and convenient digest and summary of foreign interests. J. B. CONDLIFFE, *China Today: Economic* (1932); an excellent brief treatment of the subject. FEI HSIAO-TUNG, *Peasant Life in China* (1939); an interesting study. W. H. GALE and J. ARNOLD, *Labor and Industrial Conditions in China,* Trade Information Bulletin no. 75, U. S. Bureau of Foreign and Domestic Commerce (1922). SIDNEY GAMBLE, *Peking, a Social Survey* (1921); a most interesting and valuable study of the economic life of Peking. F. L. GOODNOW, *China, an Analysis* (1926), ch. 2, 5. GREAT BRITAIN, FOREIGN OFFICE, *Paper Respecting Labor Conditions in China,* China no. 1 (1925). R. B. HALL, *Chinese National Banks, from Their Founding to the Moratorium* (1921); a careful study of the question. STANLEY HIGH, *China's Place in the Sun* (1922), ch. 3. H. T. HODGKIN, *China in the Family of Nations* (1921), ch. 9. Hsü SHIH-CHANG, *China After the War* (1920); interesting because written by a President of China. W. C. JOHNSTONE, *The Shanghai Problem* (1937); an excellent legal and historical survey and analysis. MABEL PING-HUA LEE, *Economic History of China, with special reference to agriculture* (1921), espec. part 1, ch. 6; part 2, ch. 13; part 3, ch. 2. LIN TUNG-HAI, *The Labour Movement and Labour Legislation in China* (1933). H. F. MACNAIR, *The Chinese Abroad: Their Position and Protection* (1924). T. P. MENG and S. GAMBLE, *Prices, Wages and the Standard of Living in Peking, 1900–1924,* in Chinese Social and Political Science Review, Supplement, July, 1926. H. B. MORSE, *Trade and Administration of China* (1920); good for years before 1912. H. B. MORSE, *Gilds of China* (1900). JOHN E. ORCHARD, *Contrasts in the Progress of Industrialization in China and Japan,* Political Science Quarterly, vol. 52, pp. 18–50; the emphasis is on the reasons for the slower progress of China. P. S. REINSCH, *American Diplomat in China* (1922); contains interesting chapters dealing with personalities, commercial prospects, and some aspects of change prior to 1919. CHONG-SU SEE, *Foreign Trade of China* (1919). J. B. TAYLOR, *Study of Chinese Rural Economy,* in Chinese Social and Political Science Review, vol. VIII, nos. 1 and 2, January and April, 1924. M. T. Z. TYAU, *China Awakened* (1922), ch. 11–13. H. M. VINACKE, *Problems of Industrial Development in China* (1926), ch. 1, 6. YANG MOU-CH'UN, *A Chinese Village, Taitou, Shantung* (1945); a good study.

For current materials consult *Readers Guide* and indexes of Far Eastern journals and periodicals.

CHAPTER XIII

THE PROGRESS OF CHINA: INTELLECTUAL AND CULTURAL

I. POLITICAL REVOLUTION AND INTELLECTUAL RENAISSANCE

NORMALLY a fundamental change of ideas, if not a modification of a cultural heritage, precedes and makes possible a political upheaval which can be called a true revolution. But in China the intellectual revolution has paralleled the political and, to a degree, may be considered a consequence of it rather than its cause. As earlier pointed out, there had been an infiltration of new ideas during the late nineteenth century which prepared the way for the reform movement of 1898. In that attempted reform and also in the decade of reform before 1911 considerable emphasis had been laid on education along new lines. A serious blow had been struck at the old order of scholastic officialdom with the abolition of the examination system in 1905. Its modification had previously begun with the introduction of new subjects into the system of examinations. "The abolition of the examination system has proved to be a far more radical measure than even the most far-sighted officials of that time conceived it to be. It dealt the death-blow to Confucianism." [1] Beyond all of this, the new education began to introduce a shift in emphasis from the humanistic and historical (in which studies there had always been a considerable emphasis on what may be called the scientific attitude in distinction from the scientific method) to the scientific and technological. But "the period of Chinese scientific activity did not begin until the first years of the Republic. The older reformers had only introduced a book knowledge of the sciences, without fully understanding their intellectual significance, without adequate equipment for laboratory work, and without adequately trained leaders to organize the studies and researches." [2] Above all, the emphasis continued to be laid on scholarship as a means to the end of attaining official position, which militated against the educational order within China developing other than political emphases. To a large extent, consequently, the 1911 revolution was an anti-Manchu revolt, which assumed a republican character for lack of any other alternative to Manchu misrule, rather than an expression of a fundamental

[1] CYRUS H. PEAKE, *Nationalism and Education in Modern China*, p. 71.
[2] HU SHIH, *The Chinese Renaissance*, pp. 72–73.

change in the underlying philosophy of the peoples or even of those who became the new rulers of the country. There were notable exceptions to this among the leaders, but they were distinctly exceptions. "There being a premium on 'western learning,' they (the scholars 'left in the lurch' by the sudden abolition of the examination system) flocked in large numbers to Japan and, in smaller number, to western countries where they received a smattering knowledge of western ways and institutions. Upon their return to China they boldly attempted to apply their new knowledge with little understanding or adaptation to Chinese conditions." [3]

After 1911, however, there developed, slowly but surely, a new intellectual and cultural atmosphere which, by 1917, established the conditions for the renaissance which took place, outside the field of politics, in the next decade. This new development was as significant for the economic, social, and political future of China and her peoples, and of the world, as was any other single tendency in the Far East until after 1931. Consequently it is necessary to examine it, as closely as space permits, from the standpoint of its causes and its consequences, both immediate and remote, as a most important phase of the history of the Far East in modern times. While it was of major significance in the decade from 1920 to 1930, nevertheless it must be remembered that it had then affected largely only the educated class and that its full effects could be felt only as it penetrated the masses.

2. EDUCATIONAL DEVELOPMENT

Education was the primary cause of the change in Chinese ideas. Prior to 1898, and indeed before 1905, there was little attempt at public education in the country. The Empire's relationship to education had been largely restricted to the setting of the examinations, which have already been described, until their abolition in 1905. As long as the examinations were based upon the classics and the classical essay, the educational incentive was directly away from innovation and the propagation of new ideas. In other words, education was developed largely in terms of the learning of the past rather than primarily in relation to the present and the future. Furthermore, the result of education was a retentive memory rather than the abilities out of which develop creative thought. In addition to this, the intimate relationship between the "educated" class and officialdom created a vested interest in the maintenance of the old intellectual order. This served as a serious obstacle to educational change, since the acceptance of a new educational content would minimize the importance of the classically trained official. Consequently it was only slowly that even the more enlightened officials, those in closest contact

[3] PEAKE, op. cit., p. 71.

with foreigners, came to appreciate the importance of "Western learning."

Thus it was left to foreigners to begin the opening of the Chinese mind as the second and more important part of the process of "opening" China. Of the several foreign groups in China it was the missionary element which had a natural interest in education. The traders dealt with the Chinese through the compradore, made little effort to learn the language, and on the whole kept aloof from the Chinese world in which they found themselves. The business of the missionary, on the other hand, necessarily brought him into contact with the Chinese community so far as it would receive him. And he shortly found that it would receive him more readily if he offered services which were not directly evangelistic as a preliminary to the bringing of his religious message. Consequently a primary incentive for the establishment of schools, and also hospitals, lay in his desire to come into readier contact with the Chinese people than was possible when he limited himself to evangelistic work.

Another explanation, just as important, of the missionary interest in education was to be found in the desire to perform the same service for the Christian community that the church school performs in Western countries. The value of an educated constituency was certainly appreciated, particularly in view of the premium put on learning in China. Christian education on as wide a scale as possible was also necessary if the Christian ethical system was to displace or modify the Confucian. Furthermore, it was incumbent on the church to train a native leadership if its religious work was to be carried on successfully. This desire to train an adequate church leadership unquestionably explained much of the interest in education. The undertaking of medical education and the establishment of hospitals may be ascribed as much to a recognition of a great need as to the desire to establish contact with the people on a broader basis. The recognition of the social implications of the teachings of Christ would help to explain the willingness to serve the Chinese in these and many other ways. But the ultimate aim, naturally, was the evangelistic, and the attempted realization of this aim governed and colored, to a variable extent, the non-evangelistic phases of missionary work.

The missionary was also immediately and naturally forced into the work of dictionary making, language study, and translation as a preliminary to evangelization, for only as he was able to communicate directly with the Chinese, and as he could put his materials into a form which they could use, could he expect to accomplish his religious ends. At first his translation work took the form of the preparation of religious tracts. But again, in order to broaden the base of his approach, he was ultimately brought to translate secular literature. This work was distinctly educational in character, and led to the development of a more formal interest in education as a method of approach to the Chinese community.

Nevertheless, however much humanitarian and other interests may have prompted him, education was, for the missionary, a means to an end other than that of promoting an intellectual rebirth. The result of this was that those put in charge of schools were often selected primarily because of their interest in the spread of the gospel rather than because they had been trained as educators. They frequently emphasized the religious exercise in the school rather than the class room activity and consequently made, and for some time were qualified to make, no significant study of the educational problem in China. The schools were of the primary division until toward the end of the nineteenth century, and were often mere adjuncts to the mission.

The first higher schools established were Roman Catholic Seminaries. After the founding of St. John's University at Shanghai in 1879, however, Protestant mission schools of nominal collegiate rank multiplied rapidly. For some time they corresponded, in grade of work done, to the American high school, although they were called colleges or universities. Until after the 1911 revolution the same criticism could be made of these higher schools that has been made of missionary education in general—the teachers were missionaries first and educators second, so far as interest and training were concerned. Consequently the work done in the higher schools was open to serious criticism from the standpoint of the educationist. It would probably be fair to say that this continued to be true until after the end of the first decade of the present century. Schools—primary, middle and higher—multiplied, and from 1900 to 1910 the number of students increased, but methods and objectives remained approximately the same.

The method of instruction employed in the college was usually the lecture, combined where possible with the use of a text book. There was little laboratory science teaching and less use of the laboratory method. Consequently the emphasis in the mission school on the whole differed but little from that in the Chinese private school. The student continued to do memory work and was little stimulated to thoughtful examination of the world in which he lived. Western subjects were taught together with the Chinese classics, but they were unrelated to the experience of the student. He read and remembered and passed or failed in his examinations according to the retentiveness of his memory.

Public education in China dates from the end of the nineteenth century. Tungwen College had been established in 1865, it is true, but that did not mark the inauguration of a system of public schools. The first real Chinese university, Peiyang University, was founded by Li Hungchang in Tientsin in 1895. Two other universities, the Chiao-tung-pu

Nanyang and the Peking Universities, were established before 1900. Otherwise the sole public interest expressed was in the naval and military schools for the training of officers.

The beginning of a new day was heralded with the modification in the examination system and the establishment of a national school system proposed as part of the reform program of 1898. But the new era was only inaugurated with the abolition of the examination system in 1905, and the setting up of an elaborate educational program in 1908, as a basic part of the preparation for the introduction of constitutional government. Schools were built and many temples were transformed into schools for the teaching of Western learning. The multiplication of schools went further under the Republic, so that in 1931 there were about one hundred thirty thousand government schools of all grades, from the primary school to the university, enrolling approximately four and a quarter million students.

This expansion was so rapid that it was impossible to provide trained teachers for the modern schools. Consequently many who had only a smattering of Western knowledge were pressed into service. Many came from the mission schools, others were supplied from the stream of students who went to Japan to study after 1900, and some, particularly in the higher schools, had been trained in Europe and in the United States. As has already been pointed out, many of those who went to Japan to study were more interested in securing diplomas than in gaining knowledge. Those who studied in the Western countries lacked the background which alone could enable them to profit fully from their studies. And few of the students, trained either in or out of China during the first decade and a half of the nineteenth century, were primarily interested in the problem of education. Western learning was considered to be an open sesame to public office and was sought for that reason. Consequently it was usually the disappointed office-seeker who turned to teaching as a means of support, just as had been the case at an earlier time.

The ability of the foreign-trained Chinese to waken his country was conditioned by the degree of his own awakening. Increasing numbers who went abroad to study after about 1910 were prepared to study Western subjects in Western colleges and universities. They had some proficiency in the use of foreign languages, notably English, and they had been trained, partly by foreigners, in institutions of standing such as St. John's University and the American indemnity school, Tsinghua College. But, it must be repeated, they had too largely studied Western history, philosophy, political science, and other subjects as though they were American or English boys rather than as Chinese, interested in them in relation to Chinese life and the Chinese environment. This process usually was continued in the Western college which they attended. They knew

John Stuart Mill, but their teachers, who were in the main unfamiliar with China, did not, or were not able to, lead them to examine his ideas of government in relation to China. If they studied sociology, it was in relation to Western conditions and problems rather than to those of their own country. They tended to view China as if she were a Western country in direct ratio to the length of time they studied abroad. Upon their return they faced a serious problem of readjustment, which at first developed an extreme pessimism and only gradually led to a constructive criticism of Chinese society, based upon an attempt at gaining an intelligent understanding of its nature as contrasted with Western societies.

As time went on there came into being a more intelligent educational approach in the schools in China. The foreign teacher and the foreign-trained Chinese alike began to stress the understanding of some of the problems of life in China, and this called for a re-direction of the educational program. This was a result partly of the selection of teachers for mission schools because of some measure of training for the work rather than because of a "call" to save the heathen, and partly of a change in the class of studies pursued by Chinese abroad. Furthermore, normal schools were established as part of the governmental program, and teachers for the lower schools were given some training.

It is also important to note that after 1916 advanced students tended to emphasize preparation for private pursuits rather than training to secure public office. It was politics which engrossed the attention of scholars from 1898 until the time when it became increasingly apparent that the political revolution of 1911 had failed to transform China into an Occidental state of an advanced sort. It seems to have been only within the decade after 1915 that the truth came to be appreciated that fundamental change is dependent on social, economic, and intellectual change. Unfortunately this appreciation came only after the Western-trained Chinese found that the Republic, on the whole, left control in the hands of the old-style mandarin instead of effecting an overnight transfer of power to themselves. The point of view of the intellectuals after 1916 is fairly represented in the words of one of their number, who wrote:

In my humble opinion, politics is in such confusion that I am at a loss to know what to talk about. . . . As to fundamental salvation, I believe its beginning must be sought in the promotion of a new literature. In short, we must endeavor to bring Chinese thought into direct contact with the contemporary thought of the world, thereby to accelerate its radical awakening. And we must see to it that the basic ideals of the world thought must be related to the life of the average man.[4]

One result of the change in intellectual point of view was the introduction of vocational education and its acceptance as part of the educational

4 *China Year Book,* 1924, p. 643.

process. This in itself marked a distinct break with the age-old conception of education as a training of the mind (memory) and not a training of the hand. This same departure was marked in the higher technical schools, where a willingness to work with the hands in the laboratory and the field was gradually cultivated. In medical study the laboratory method was introduced, so that students had to learn partly by experimentation rather than wholly by listening to lectures, reading in books, and looking at pictures. Engineering students began to combine field work—application— with class room instruction. The recognition that one could work with his hands and still remain a scholar had a distinctly emancipating effect on the Chinese mind. The development of the experimental attitude of the scientist also encouraged a critical approach to literary and social studies.

3. THE PRESS AND THE INTELLECTUAL AWAKENING

Another influence, besides the school, in producing an intellectual awakening, was undoubtedly the press. It provided the vehicle for the expression of new ideas, and served as a medium of information concerning movements and events in the foreign as well as the Chinese world. There had long been foreign-language papers, mainly English, which served a useful purpose in carrying on discussions of happenings in China and elsewhere. There were substantial journals, such as the *Chinese Repository,* devoted to "things Chinese." But, after all, these foreign undertakings existed primarily for the information of foreigners and the expression of the Western point of view, rather than for the purpose of stimulating thought among the Chinese and affording it an outlet. It was in the native publications that China began both to evaluate and to express herself. The first Chinese newspaper was brought into existence in 1870. Two others were established before the war with Japan. After that war others appeared. The suppression of the Boxer movement, the inauguration of the Manchu reform program, and the growth of anti-Manchu sentiment were all instrumental in encouraging the founding of organs of opinion. But it was particularly after the revolution of 1911 that papers multiplied, until by 1931 every important town had its own newspaper. The improvement of communications widened the area of circulation of the more important papers and also made it possible for them to carry more than local news. Many, if not most, of the newspapers were mainly propaganda sheets, some of them foreign subsidized, and some of them personal organs of individuals or factions. But they all served the purpose of stimulating discussion and provoking thought about foreign relations and about domestic politics and problems.

In addition to the newspapers, and as a later development, there came into existence periodicals ranging from the woman's magazines to the literary and the scientific journals. These latter, especially, were significant as affording an outlet for the new thought of the student-teacher class. A good example of the scholarly journal was the *Chinese Social and Political Science Review*. Other magazines devoted especially to the expression of new ideas were the *New Youth,* founded in 1915 by the Dean of the Peking National University, which suspended publication in 1917 but was revived under the editorship of six university professors in 1918; the *Weekly Review,* also a Peking University publication, devoted mainly to politics; and the *New Tide* (later called *The Renaissance*), a publication sponsored by the students of Peking University. Other schools also established their publications, in which appeared stories, plays, essays, and serious articles of social interest.

Finally, we may mention, as an intellectual force, the increased movement of peoples. Railroads helped to create a more dynamic intellectual life by broadening the horizon of the thousands who traveled on them each year. The coolies who served behind the lines in France, and after the war returned to the villages of China with their tales of the outside world based on personal observation, helped to arouse the curiosity which the papers and magazines still further stimulated in trying to satisfy it.

4. THE LITERARY REVOLUTION

One expression of the new tide was the "literary revolution" which was systematically promoted in and after 1917. This was formally inaugurated by Dr. Hu Suh (Shih), an American-trained scholar and a member of the Faculty of Peking National University. At the beginning of 1917 he publicly announced his intention thereafter to write only in the spoken language, discarding altogether the old literary language as his medium of expression. The latter had long occupied the same position among Chinese scholars as that enjoyed by Latin among the scholastics of Europe at the time the national languages were coming to literary birth. The Wen Li, or Chinese classical language, had been "dead," except for its use by scholars, for a long time, but it had maintained its literary supremacy in spite of the fact that the mandarin dialects were not only widely spoken but had "produced a vast amount of literature, a literature more extensive and varied than any modern European language ever possessed at the time of its establishment as a national language." [5] This literature was in the novel form mainly, a form which had not been recognized and incorporated in the classical tradition. The maintenance of the authority of this Chinese "Latin" was due to the distinction which its mastery gave to the scholar. Even more, how-

[5] Hu Shih in *Chinese Social and Political Science Review,* vol. VI, p. 97. See also his penetrating lectures entitled *The Chinese Renaissance.*

ever, its position came from the fact that it was enforced "by the power of a long-united empire, and supported by a fairly extensive system of education where the sole aim of its students had been to win office, honor and recognition on the strength of their ability to read and write in the classical language." [6] Thus the abolition of the examination system and the collapse of the Empire were direct forerunners of the departure from the use of the classical language by scholars. In addition, it was necessary to overcome the inertia developed from a long-continued tradition. This could be done only by a frank and open recognition of the divorce of the classical language from the life of the nation, and of the possibility of using the vernacular for literary and scholarly purposes. This conscious defense of the vulgar tongue was supplied by Dr. Hu. Others were attracted to the support of his cause, though for a time there was considerable opposition to the new movement.

In 1920, the Ministry of Education issued an order to the effect that, beginning with the fall opening of the year, the national language should be taught in the first two grades of the primary school. In the course of a few years, all the grades in the primary schools will be using the living tongue in the place of the classical. This change has of necessity affected the middle and normal schools where the primary teachers are trained, and these higher schools are anticipating the coming change by voluntarily adopting texts in the vulgate. Most of the recent publications have been in the vulgate. The newspapers and periodicals have in most cases ceased to publish poems in the classical language, and "new poems" in spoken Chinese are taking their places. [7]

The significance of this loosing of the fetters of old literary forms is obvious. It indeed prepared the way for a revival of creative literary activity in a new and flexible medium. The break with tradition in this fundamental respect also helped to free the mind of educated Chinese and stimulated them to constructive rather than reproductive effort. The old classical tradition represented a literary refinement which had been carried to its ultimate conclusion generations ago. The departure opened the gate to a new literary life.

Of importance also was the language-simplification movement and its concomitant of mass education to reduce illiteracy. Spoken language unification was undertaken in 1913 by a conference which met under the auspices of the Ministry of Education. This conference worked out a phonetic alphabet of thirty-nine symbols or letters, the mastery of which enables a person to pronounce the characters in accordance with the official spoken language. This system was widely used in non-Mandarin speaking sections of China such as Shanghai and Canton. [8] Romanization systems were earlier

[6] Ibid., p. 97.
[7] Ibid., p. 99.
[8] PEAKE, op. cit., pp. 139 et seq. Also M. T. Z. TYAU, China Awakened, p. 11.

used as an actual substitute for the characters, however, in Protestant Christian circles.

Closely joined, in nationalistic objective, to this movement to unify the
system was the mass-education movement which was associated with the
name of its principal leader, Y. C. James Yen, and which was organized
through the National Popular Education Association. Mr. Yen and his
associates worked out a course of study based on 1300 characters. These
represented the characters in most common use in the vernacular. Their
mastery enabled the individual to "write simple business letters, keep accounts, and read simple newspapers intelligently." This, by demonstration,
could be accomplished in four and a half months with an application to
study of one and a half hours a day. The teachers volunteered their services.
They came from the regular teacher and student groups. The movement
spread rapidly and met with considerable interest and support among the
illiterate masses. The work was confined largely to the towns until taken
up with some adaptations by the communists.

5. INTELLECTUAL FERMENT

The transfer of the interest of Chinese intellectuals from the realm of
politics, after the establishment of military rule in the country, resulted in
an intellectual ferment of which the literary revolution was only one expression. The searchlight of criticism was directed toward all institutions
and practices, both Chinese and foreign, in an attempt to evaluate them
in terms of contemporary Chinese life and problems, and in the light also
of modern science and thought. The pragmatic test of social utility was generally applied. This showed the influence of John Dewey on that generation
of Young China, and was due to the number of Chinese who, while in
the United States, came into contact with him and his school of thought
This influence was strengthened when he was invited to China to lecture at
Peking University and throughout the country. Another strong influence
was that of Bertrand Russell, whose philosophy also captivated a group
among the intellectual leaders of the new China.

It must also be recognized that the World War and its aftermath helped
to stimulate a critical attitude of mind by lessening Chinese respect for the
foreign system which permitted organized slaughter on such a stupendous
scale, while theoretically accepting the Christian principle of peace. The
anti-German propaganda which reached China also served to provoke
thought about the Western world and its institutions. But above all the
Shantung award at the Paris Conference led to an outburst of feeling,
national and patriotic in character. From that moment dates the expression
of Chinese nationalism, a nationalism which became increasingly intensified after 1919.

6. THE STUDENT MOVEMENT

It was the students in Peking who voiced the first protest against the Paris decision when news of it reached China. They paraded to the legation quarter to ask the intercession of the American and other allied representatives. Denied admission to the legation quarter, they turned toward the homes of some of the Anfu Cabinet members, who were supposed to be tools in the hands of Japan. Tsao Ju-lin, Minister of Finance, was the most notorious of them. His house was partially wrecked, but he himself escaped and took refuge with the Japanese. The students then demanded the resignation of these ministers, and asked that the Chinese representatives at Paris be instructed to refuse to sign the peace treaty with Germany. Police measures were taken against the students, both in Peking and in other cities where student "unions" had been formed when the news from Peking arrived. The jails were filled, but the agitation did not cease. For every student imprisoned, several others appeared as agitators to stir up the people. The chambers of commerce and guilds joined the students, who went on strike, supplementing their propaganda work by proclaiming a boycott of Japanese goods. This boycott was maintained on a national scale for some months, and Japanese pressure on the Peking government for action against the merchants was unsuccessful in bringing it to an end. The power of the non-political classes was conclusively demonstrated, for the government was forced to give way. The treaty was not signed and the "traitors" were forced to resign.

However, the immediate accomplishments of the movement were not so important either as its ultimate implications or as the methods employed. Strikes among students for various reasons were a commonplace of school life. But for the students to go on the streets teaching and preaching to the masses concerning the wrongs done China in the present and the past, for them to organize demonstrations and to parade with banners proclaiming the national cause, and for them to suffer imprisonment willingly to carry conviction—these were new things which were soon to become common without losing their effectiveness. The boycott of foreign goods was not new. It had been used both during the nineteenth century and at the beginning of the twentieth. It had been used effectively at the time of the twenty-one demands. But its effectiveness as a national weapon was more conclusively demonstrated in 1919 than at any previous time. Beyond all this, the national character of the movement was in itself significant, for it indicated a perception of China as an entity, in striking contrast with, for example, the localism exhibited in 1895 and even in 1900.

The initial uprising, of course, subsided, although the voice of the student was heard from time to time between 1919 and 1925. But the educational aspects of the movement continued. Schools for the masses were conducted in an endeavor to reduce illiteracy, and to rouse the people to an appreciation of China's wrongs. These were supplemented by street-corner discussions led, or participated in, by students. Much criticism came to be voiced against mission schools as propagators of foreign ideas, and a distinct anti-Christian movement developed among the students. The West, generally, suffered as a result of the growing belief that Western countries would not voluntarily aid China to recover her ancient position in the world.

This feeling was only temporarily lessened as a result of the Washington Conference. Within a year Dr. Sun had inaugurated the collaboration with Soviet Russia and had begun the development and dissemination of the new Kuomintang ideology which was radical from the internal standpoint and anti-imperialistic from the standpoint of foreign relations. His movement attracted a large following from the student class whom the Soviet representatives had already begun to cultivate, having established sympathetic relations with the intellectual group represented by the national University at Peking. The Russians applauded their critical attitude of mind while "treaty-port" Westerners were inveighing against the new thought as immature, radical, and the result of Bolshevist propaganda. With the organization of the Chinese Communist Party and its admission into the Kuomintang, furthermore, a new stream of ideas began to flow through the southern part of the country, adding to the intellectual ferment as well as to the political confusion.

Student support of the Kuomintang as the anti-imperialist party was confirmed at the time of the Japanese mill strike in 1925 when, as a consequence of student parades in support of the strikers, the "incident" of May 30 occurred. Shanghai settlement police, commanded by an Englishman, fired on the parading students, killing some and wounding others. This led directly to the so-called Shameen massacre, when students at Canton were fired upon when parading in protest of the British action at Shanghai. The result was the revival of the boycott which had been instituted at the time of the Hongkong seamen's strike. Kuomintang support and direction of the boycott which grew out of student activities naturally strengthened the ties between the students and the Party. The British connection with the two incidents had the effect of diverting hostility from Japan to Great Britain, establishing the latter in the rôle of the imperialist enemy. This shift was made much more easily than it would have been a few years earlier by reason of the marked conciliatoriness of Japanese policy toward China during the years immediately after the Washington Conference. Anti-British sentiment was subsequently intensified by the Wanhsien incident in 1926, when a British gunboat fired on that Yangtse village as a punishment for the action of Chinese forces in firing on British merchant vessels. After the establishment of the Nanking government, however, anti-British sentiment abated as English policy clearly became that of conciliation of nationalist China, and as the nationalist movement became less radical. Until 1927 the unity maintained by the Powers at Peking helped to generalize this anti-British into an anti-foreign sentiment. Anti-foreignism, however, must also be explained in terms of the general anti-imperialist ideology of the Party. But it is obvious that this attitude of Chinese nationalists was not due to the desire to get rid of the foreigner and end intercourse with him. It represented rather a desire to get rid of the restrictions of the so-called "unequal treaties" so that China might assume a position of equality in the family of nations. Beyond this it represented a revulsion from the feeling that China could rely on the West for a solution of her international problems, and from the feeling that institutions, practices, and ideas were good because they were Western. Consequently, it served to strengthen the tide of critical discussion.

An added stimulus to critical thought was applied by Japan when she moved to sever Manchuria from China. The Chinese government relied for support on an essentially Western institution, the League of Nations, and on Western states acting through the League. But, in spite of the condemnation of Japan at Geneva, the Chinese found themselves immediately confronted with a loss of territory. The reaction in student circles was similar to that already noted, i.e., the development of the attitude that China must rely on herself, not on other states or on international institutions, for protection and to secure a redress of her grievances. Thus the Manchurian affair strengthened the intellectual reaction against imperialism; it added strength to the view, already widely expressed, that a primary emphasis must be placed on arms and on military training; and it confirmed the Chinese in their nationalism, weakening the position of those advocating internationalism. As Dr. Sun had previously put it, only a strong nation could afford to think internationally.

7. CHANGES IN FAMILY SYSTEM

The strongest evidence of conscious criticism of Chinese institutions was presented in the attack on, and the open repudiation of, the ancient clan-family system. Many factors had been at work to weaken the family system even before the young intellectuals began consciously to repudiate it. Among them may be noted, first, the enlarged movement of the people as the railway system had been extended. This made migration from the ancestral home easier and thus weakened the attachment to it. It also tended to break up the patriarchal family into smaller groups. The introduction of the Western industrial system had a similar effect by attracting workers from the villages into the towns and cities, where they were removed from the family authority, and were forced to set up separate establishments. The century of Christian propaganda, with its attack on ancestor-worship, concubinage, and other practices connected with the family system, was another factor. Yet another was the enlarged knowledge of the West, and an appreciation of some of the advantages presented by its emphasis on the individual, and by its single household system. This knowledge at least afforded an opportunity to evaluate the Chinese system on a comparative basis.

Another factor, which was both a cause and a consequence of the weakening of the family system, was the gradual emancipation of women. This commenced with the provision of girls' schools as part of the Republican educational program. Their education had been largely disregarded in Imperial days, as they could not take the examinations and in any case were considered to have no need of a classical education. Some of the mission schools, however, had made beginnings. After 1911 facilities were increasingly afforded for the higher, as well as the elementary, education of girls and women, both by the government and in mission and private schools. This resulted in taking girls out of the home and bringing them in contact with one another and with the world, and it postponed the marriage day among the educated classes. Furthermore, increasing numbers began to go abroad to study, which further postponed the day of marriage. The first girls to go abroad to study were sent to the United States in the 1880's. By 1931 there were over two hundred Chinese girls studying in American institutions of higher learning. Naturally, as this education proceeded, some women prepared themselves for occupations other than running a home. The chief attraction was into medicine and nursing, but some took a legal training, and others became journalists. Thus there was created, for the first time in the history of China, a class of economically independent unmarried women, a group which tended toward constant enlargement.

The girls in the schools took their place by the side of the boys in the 1919 student agitation, and in the subsequent student movement. This unprecedented performance produced no bad consequences, but it did suggest that women were likely to take a new initiative in China's life. Perhaps partly as a consequence of it, co-education was introduced into some of the colleges and universities, and was finally given a trial also in the lower schools.

The young men, particularly the American-educated students, had been gradually moving toward revolt against the marriage system of the country, which deprived them of a voice in the selection of their brides, although the first generations of returned students generally acquiesced in that as in other features of the old order. But finally the voice of the newly educated women was joined to that of the men in opposition to such an exercise of parental power. The result was that family arrangements began to be disregarded and the contracting parties began to make their own choices. Parental authority was further weakened by the refusal to take up abode in the family residence. In some cases, it must be admitted, the marriage ceremony was dispensed with, as a sign of complete emancipation. The pendulum was swinging from one extreme to another, although extremism would seem to have constituted the exception rather than the rule. On the whole, then, the effect of the education of women was to weaken the family system, though it had not been consciously directed toward that end.

Finally we come to the part played by conscious criticism of the system in terms of its utility. The reaction against parental or family selection of mates has just been mentioned. But that was an obvious and surface criticism of the system in only one of its aspects. It took historical studies to show that the clan-family status was one of arrested development, a stage through which other groups had evolved to the society founded on the individual. This realization made it possible for a few intellectuals consciously to repudiate the whole system as one unsuited to the China of the future. Some Chinese, though again a comparatively small number, perceived the deadening effect of life lived in terms of ancestral ways of acting and thinking, and in a society whose members had as their chief function the production of offspring to carry on the ancestral rites. It is interesting to note that birth-control advocates received a hearing in post-war China. Extremists went so far even as to attack ancestor-worship, which was the center and core of the system. It is only fair to note that, in the face of this conscious criticism, the family system found its strong defenders, some of them foreigners. The principal rational defense made of it was on the ground of its cohesive force. It was well pointed out that China had outlived her ancient neighbors, both far and near, largely because her life had been preserved through the clan-family. The lack of restraint of China's "younger generation" was pointed to as a symptom of disintegration and decay more serious than her political chaos. But without entering further into the argument it may merely be pointed out that both attack on, and defense of, a system long accepted without argument as sound was an indication that the old order was changing.

Before leaving the question of the family system, we must emphasize the fact that only a small number of Chinese had repudiated or questioned its soundness. The changing point of view was expressed by the younger generation of foreign-educated Chinese, and by well-to-do Chinese living in the cities, more particularly the places of foreign residence and trade. The village point of view, on the whole, was still the pre-modern one. The changes, however, although restricted to a small group, were significant because the attitude of that group ultimately determines that of the nation. What has been said, by way of caution, concerning the family system was also true of the rites connected with ancestor-worship. The masses still performed them, although the younger intellectuals attacked them. Ancestor-worship was being slowly undermined, but was far from having been destroyed.

The intellectual attack on ancestor-worship was indicative, from another point of view, of the purely rational and skeptical attitude of mind of many of the student class and their teachers. It was founded on a lack of belief in a spirit world and, consequently, a loss of faith in the efficacy of ancestral rites.

8. RELIGIOUS SKEPTICISM

This same skepticism led to an attack on religious belief in general, and was a root cause of anti-Christian sentiment, together with its foreign origin and support, and the feeling that it was an advance agent of Western imperialism. But Buddhism and Taoism, and the religious growths on Confucianism, came in for attack as well as Christianity.

The Confucian ethical system, apart from the elements of worship connected with it, was not so severely criticized, nor was a strong attempt made to uproot it. It remained fundamentally supported by whatever of soundness inhered in a moral system which had found acceptance for long ages, and by the authority of tradition, and respect for the Sage whose name had for so long been almost synonymous with that of China.

The post-war intellectual repudiation of Confucian worship did not seriously affect the masses of the people, although it may do so in time. The disappearance of the Empire carried with it the end of the worship of Heaven by the head of the state, except as it was temporarily revived by Yüan Shih-k'ai. The attempts to establish Confucianism as the national ethical system by constitutional enactment failed. Some of the official ceremonies in the provinces were discontinued. But the rites in honor of Confucius were largely maintained, conducted either by officials or by the Confucian societies which came into existence. Honors were also paid the Sage in many of the government schools. Consequently the masses were likely to cling to the elements of worship in Confucianism for some time to come, in spite of republican attempts to get rid of them.

The Confucian politico-ethical system was essentially concerned with the ordering of affairs in this world—with the relations of father and son, husband and wife, brother and brother, friend with friend, and ruler with people. These relations were formalized to a high degree by the Great Teacher and his successors, notably Mencius and Chu Tzu. The five cardinal virtues emphasized in the system were kindness, rectitude, decorum, wisdom, and sincerity. Confucius proclaimed, "What you do not like yourself do not extend to others"—the golden rule negatively stated. Neither Confucius himself nor his commentators claimed to do more than to formulate and systematize the wisdom of the Ancients. Consequently they continually pointed to the past as expressive of the highest type of life, thus inculcating a backward rather than a forward view. The emphasis on filial piety as the highest of all virtues led to the development of ancestor-worship, which supplied a quasi-religious authority for the backward look. It was these two features of Confucianism that were being consciously combatted by the skeptical intellectuals rather than the Confucian ethical system.

As a matter of fact, authority for their skeptical attitude was found in the very teachings of Confucius and Mencius. They took the position of the agnostic, so far as the conception of God and of life after death were concerned. Why trouble about the unknowable as long as there are the problems of this life to be solved? They did not repudiate the conception of God, but they did not develop it.

It is true that the official worship of Heaven by the Emperor was closely associated with Confucianism, but it merely represented the maintenance and development of an old ceremony. It is also true that worship both of Confucius and of lesser lights in the firmament, together with ancestors, established itself as part of the system, and that the Sage himself was canonized by Imperial order in 1907. But these elements represented growths on a politico-ethical system which, it was felt, could be pruned off, as had been the worship of Heaven, without impairing the validity of the system.

The other great indigenous philosophy—Taoism—long ago lost its philosophical character. As a religio-philosophical system it was essentially mystical and quietistic. It derives its name from its emphasis on Tao,—

. . . an impersonal Principle or Power, which, viewed in the absolute sense, is inscrutable, indefinable, and impossible to name. Viewed in the relative sense, it appears under many guises and in every part of the universe. It cannot be correctly translated as God. Indeed, in one obscure passage he says, "It appears to have been before God." Tao is, however, the source and support of all things. Calmly, without effort, and unceasingly, it works for good; and man by yielding himself to it, unresisting, unstriving may reach his highest well being. Suffering is the result of man's departure from the Tao state of pristine innocence and simplicity. It would be well to give up all study and the pursuit of knowledge, and return to the absolutely simple state of Tao. War, striving, suffering, would then all cease, and, floating along the placid river of time, the individual in due course would be absorbed in the ocean of Tao.[9]

This lofty mystical philosophy was too abstruse for the masses, and never gained the foothold among the educated that would enable it to displace Confucian philosophy. Consequently it early degenerated into a system of magic and superstition. The Taoist priests were "the prime leaders of magic and sorcery, which, as in other nations, is of prehistoric origin, and are the high priests of Animism. . . . They are open to any kind of engagement, whether exorcizing devils, releasing souls from hell, seeking the advice of the gods through divination or through a spiritualistic medium, organizing public processions to escort away with great *éclat* the demons of plague,

---

[9] SOOTHILL, *The Three Religions of China*. p. 49.

arranging theatrical performances to celebrate the 'birthdays' of the gods—indeed there is not a stroke of superstitious business in which they are not prepared to take a hand and turn a doubtful penny." [10]

This system, and that of the Fêng Shui, which was closely associated with it, held the common people, and many of the educated, in its grip. The latter, particularly, held back the introduction of the railway and other Western machines, since the superstitious feared their effects on the spirits of the air and water. Of course, many of the essentially hard-headed and reasonable Chinese professed disbelief in the whole régime of superstitious and magical practices even during the nineteenth century, but they seldom failed to avail themselves of the services of the priest in time of stress, on the off-chance that there might be something in it.

The breath of Western scientific education, however, began to clear away the mist of fear of the supernatural among the educated and partly educated. And skepticism as to the wonderfully developed spirit world of the Taoists was certain to spread as education was more widely diffused among the masses. As a matter of fact, the idols in many temples were destroyed or relegated to obscure corners after 1911, and the temple itself dedicated to Western learning. It will, however, be a long time before superstitious belief in demons and spirits is wholly eradicated. The introduction of modern medical science, the erection of high buildings, the construction of railways, the operation of machines, and the development of criticism were, however, all moving toward that end.

Buddhism, the third great religion of China, was also feeling the sweep of the twentieth-century tide. In its original form "Buddhism is founded upon the permanent impermanency of all things, an exaggerated estimate of suffering, and the extinction of self as the only way of escape. Neo-Buddhism, or Mahayanism, recognizes a Being who transcends the impermanent, and its objective is salvation to a permanent heaven through faith in, and invocation of, saviors." [11] It was the Mahayan form of Buddhism which had gained the strongest foothold in China. It was introduced into the country in the first century before Christ, but it made little progress for two and a half centuries, during which time no Chinese were permitted to become monks. After the interdiction was raised, it spread rapidly in spite of numerous persecutions due to the hostility of Confucian scholars to the new sect. Not making much headway among the scholars, it appealed particularly to the masses of the people. Even before its introduction into China, Buddhism had begun to lose its elevated character. This process was continued in China. The monks were usually ignorant and superstitious, incapable of appreciating the high moral teachings of the Buddha, even if they had known them. "As a so-called religion of the people it is

[10] Soothill, op. cit., p. 143.
[11] Ibid., p. 108.

hardly distinguishable from Taoism, whose deities it has had to borrow largely in order to popularize its own temples. Its hold on the people is restricted mainly to beliefs and ceremonies connected with death and burial." [12] On the other hand, Taoism had borrowed fully as much imagery from Buddhism as it had furnished it. And, in spite of its defects, Buddhism had had many good effects on China. "It has filled the land with beautiful pagodas. It has taught landscape gardening and encouraged sculpture and painting. Its symbols are common in all decorative art. The lion is seen at every palace gate; the umbrella is the emblem of imperial and magisterial authority; the rosary is, or was, a part of the ceremonial dress of every high official. The swastika, the net of metempsychosis, the wheel of the law— all these and many other symbols are woven into their fabrics, carved in their wood-work, and frescoed upon their ceilings." [13] Not all priests have been debased and ignorant, and at different periods Buddhism found many adherents among the educated gentry. But during the nineteenth century the dark side of the picture was certainly uppermost.

Consequently it began to meet the same criticism and rejection on rational grounds as did Taoism, although it still maintained itself among the masses. But, unlike Taoism, it began to show recuperative and reconstructive powers which could enable it to meet a large part of the criticism leveled against it and thus become again a vital power in Chinese life. Just as in Japan, Ceylon, and elsewhere, there was a strong reform movement in post-war Chinese Buddhism. It had made little headway by 1931, but this does not argue that it will not result in revivification of the religion. Partly it was taking a philosophical turn, motivated by a desire to return to the understanding and application of the teachings of the Buddha. This meant cutting through the superstitious growths and accumulations of the ages. Partly it was represented by a change of method and a revival of proselytizing. Here it was borrowing from the West. There developed a Buddhist missionary activity which was an attempt to meet Christianity on its own ground. Young Men's Buddhist societies were springing up, and social welfare work was being inaugurated. But on the whole, so far as China is concerned, it must be recognized that the revival was merely in its beginnings in 1931.

Christianity was being criticized severely also, and on several grounds. Its foreignizing influence was being attacked as part of the nationalist agitation. The fact that mission work had been so long foreign-financed and -controlled had made organized Christianity appear as an essentially alien thing. The extent to which the converts to Christianity drew apart from the normal village life, and failed to participate in many common village activities, centering their interests in and around the church or

[12] *China Year Book,* 1924, p. 614.
[13] WILLIAMS, *China Yesterday and Today,* p. 310.

mission, emphasized this point of view earlier in the present century. The relationship of this to the development of Boxerism has already been alluded to. But, more particularly after 1923, the educational work of the missions was criticized on the ground that it was essentially foreign in content, and unadapted to the needs of Chinese life. It was held to have a denationalizing effect at the time when China was dominated by the Western nationalist philosophy.

That these criticisms were at least partially valid was recognized in mission circles and among Chinese Christians. This led to two distinct but closely related movements. One was the development of an independent Chinese church, which was largely self-supporting and entirely self-controlling. Practically all Protestant missionaries looked to the ultimate transfer of the evangelistic side of the missionary activities to this native church, although there was difference of opinion concerning the rapidity with which it could be effected. It was hoped that thus the church could in time cease to be a mere adjunct to the mission, which had tended to dwarf it. As this happened, the foreign Christians would appear in China principally as advisers to the Chinese. In the second place, there was a movement toward giving control of the mission itself to the Chinese. This had already been done by the Y.M.C.A., and it appeared to be only a question of time until the several mission boards followed fully in the steps of the Christian Associations. When this was done, Christianity in China would be nationalized, as it has been in other countries. The Roman Catholics, whose ranks were substantially larger than those of the Protestants, seemed to be moving toward the establishment of a native hierarchy, and consequently toward minimizing foreign control of the church. But naturally, because of fundamental differences in organization, their procedure in meeting this type of criticism had to be quite different from that of the Protestants.

In the field of education, the Christian institutions had been studying the problem presented by criticisms which had been made. The result was an attempt to view the whole problem through Chinese as well as foreign eyes. An elaborate study of the question of Christian education in China was made in 1922 by a commission representing the mission boards and societies conducting work there. This commission had several Chinese members. The report made some severe criticisms of the educational work done in the past, and presented an elaborate program for the future. From this study, as well as from numerous other indications, it was clear that Christian educational work was undergoing revision to meet the criticisms which were being leveled against it.

The intellectuals, however, were attacking Christianity at a much more important point than its foreignism. They were examining it in the way they examined the more indigenous systems. And some of them reached the conclusion that the missionary was seeking to get the Chinese to discard one set of superstitions in favor of another set. Some of them were declared atheists; more were agnostics, and as such they were reproducing many of the arguments against Christianity which were heard in Western lands. The endeavor to meet their strictures, as well as the liberal theological training received by many of the missionaries, led to a split in the ranks of the workers in the field similar to that within the churches of the United States. Thus there came to be modernists in China, emphasizing the social message, and giving a liberal interpretation to the Bible, and there were fundamentalists who insisted that the primary function of the church was personal salvation. This cleavage disregarded denominational lines. In passing it may be noted that the Chinese had never understood denominationalism or appreciated the necessity of it, or of competitive Christianity. Consequently what bade fair to develop was an independent Chinese Christian church, with both a liberal and a conservative constituency, unless agnostic views became so widespread as virtually to eliminate Christianity. This latter seemed improbable. The chief ultimate result of the criticisms of the twenties would appear to be that of forcing those interested in Christianity, whether foreign or Chinese, to find some rational basis for the defense of their views.

9. CHINESE ARTS AND ARCHITECTURE

Another field in which new ideas had penetrated and Western influence had been felt, although but slightly by 1931, was that of art. There had been a high artistic development in pre-modern times, notably in painting. Many of the compositions dealt with nature, or with man in relation to nature. Others were concerned with religious subjects, showing the strong influence of both Buddhism and Taoism. Most stress was laid on the loftiness of the sentiment and on the tone rather than on the technical accuracy of the reproduction. A strong current of symbolism ran through the whole stream of Chinese art. Pictures were considered to be "voiceless poems," and they conformed more closely to the canons of poetry than to those of Western art. In its chosen field, and within its limitations, Chinese art was certainly as highly developed as that of Europe. The principal weaknesses, from the Western standpoint, lay in its lack of perspective and in its technical inaccuracy. Scientific knowledge will tend to remove the latter, particularly in the realm of portraiture, while study in the West, and of Western art, will aid in introducing the idea of perspective. On the whole, however, the contact with the West was not beneficial to Chinese art. What was gained in perspective and accuracy was more than compensated for in a loss of the best qualities of the native art. Western qualities are essentially complementary to Chinese qualities, but the attempt to combine the two resulted initially in a loss of the advantages of both.

The same thing was true in architecture. The old-style buildings were monotonous in their similarity, but they were distinctively Chinese. The principal distinguishing feature was the roof, with its upward-curved edges and its elaborate decorations. The introduction of "foreign-style" houses was for a time purely imitative, and produced buildings entirely without distinction except that resulting from a complete lack of harmony with their surroundings. Some attempts, partly by foreign architects, to work out a harmonious combination of Western and Chinese ideas were partially successful, indicating that the ultimate effect of the introduction of Western ideas may not be unproductive of good results.

The vogue of things distinctively Chinese in Europe and America in the post-war years prevented a blind imitation of the West, and consequently aided in the maintenance of Chinese art. For a time there was a serious danger that a complete swing from the old to the new would take place, instead of the development of a new art, distinctively Chinese because founded on the past, and yet new because modified in the light of contributions to knowledge from the West.

10. THE THEATER AND RECREATION

The Chinese theater was more beneficially affected by the stream of ideas imported from the Occident, although the improvement was noticeable mainly in what may be described as amateur circles. The art of the theater, so far as stage settings, or their lack, is concerned, was about at the point reached in Elizabethan England. No curtain was used, nor were stage sets prepared. The property man was placed on the stage in full view of the spectators, and he thus performed his functions publicly. Plays of a serious kind, usually historical dramas, were staged, and many broad farces were performed. In either case, the burden of creating an illusion rested solely on the actor and the audience, since the aids presented to a Western audience were lacking. But the acting in the professional theater was excellent, for there was present much natural ability to build on, and the actors had to undergo a rigorous training before being admitted to the stage.

The contribution that came from the West was on the mechanical side of play production, and in the development of dramatic subjects new to the Chinese theater. Furthermore, Western influence stimulated the presentation of a coherent drama, divided into acts, in place of the customary long series of short episodical plays. It was among the foreign-educated students, who were interested in the dramatic literature of the West, and in the Chinese middle schools and colleges, that an attempt was made to write and produce plays in the Western manner. That in itself was interesting, for the Chinese scholar of the past had regarded the theater as beneath his serious interest. Many of these plays produced in the schools were remarkably good when the difficulties of staging are remembered, and the acting was even better.

The motion picture, entirely a Western innovation, was introduced into the treaty ports, and to some extent outside them. This was a favorite form of entertainment offered, for example, by the Y.M.C.A. The pictures themselves were partly Occidental in content and on the whole tended to give the Chinese a rather distorted idea of Western life, especially as regarded the relations of the sexes. There were, after 1919, Chinese producing companies, and native production promised to become important. The broadening effect of some of the news, scenic, and educational pictures must be recognized, for the motion picture offered a wonderful opportunity to bring the material features of Western civilization before the eyes, and vicariously into the experience, of the Chinese people.

The contact with the West had in other respects changed the life of the Chinese, particularly the educated group, on its recreational side. The Confucian scholar, devoted to his studies, took no physical exercise of any kind, whether as a youth or as a man. The most he did was to take slow-paced, meditative walks. The foreigner brought with him his games and sports, which began to be taken over by the Chinese in the schools. Tennis, basketball, soccer, and track and field sports by 1920 attracted much interest and attention. The Y.M.C.A. played a major part in fostering athletic exercises in the schools, and the returned students also had their influence. Chinese field meets were held both locally and regionally, and Chinese athletes competed successfully with representatives from Japan and the Philippine Islands in the Far Eastern Olympics which were held for a time.

The significance of this change may be realized when the new activity is contrasted with that of the scholars who wondered why the barbarian foreigner did not have a servant do all of these things for him. The students of 1931 had been brought to an appreciation of the value of physical health which did not exist before the revolution. They had learned to appreciate the body as well as the mind, and were beginning to take care of it. By implication this meant also that a knowledge of hygiene was being given them, and with it some knowledge of sanitation. Ultimately it may mean a transformation of Chinese living conditions.

The interest in hygiene and sanitation was, of course, not solely due to the development of interest in sports. It was due even more to the spread of modern medical knowledge, as medical education was improved and modernized under Western influence. The two combined, however, were tending to produce a more vigorous student and scholar class, and to improve living conditions, though the latter almost imperceptibly.

It is true that all of the movements and changes noted had effected only the upper classes, and those living at, or in the vicinity of, the treaty ports, and that most of the people were still largely untouched by them. This led many foreigners to minimize their importance and significance. Not only that, but it caused some of them to criticize severely the student class because it alone appeared to be in ferment, and to be discarding the garments still worn by the nation. But it must be remembered that the students had always had a position of peculiar prestige and importance in China. As they have gone, the people have ultimately gone. For a long time they were the strongest conservative and anti-foreign influence in the Chinese state. After 1917 they had begun to move, and move rapidly. Many of their ideas were immature and crudely put, it may be conceded. They were ill-disciplined, as compared with their Confucian forebears, and were even a trifle over-assertive, in the strength of their new knowledge.

But the root of much of the criticism of them lay in the fact that they had begun to make logical application to their own lives and country of ideas brought to them from the West—such conceptions, for example, as nationalism and democracy. At the same time they had begun to view Western institutions, beliefs, and shibboleths critically. They had taken from the West the scientific method with its spirit of honest inquiry, and were beginning to make use of it.

What it would lead to, it was impossible to tell with certainty. In three decades it had led to intellectual ferment. Certainly, by 1931, China was no longer inert and static. It had entered upon a dynamic phase of intellectual and social life.

REFERENCES FOR FURTHER STUDY

Harold Balme, *China and Modern Medicine* (1921); a readable and informative study of the development of missionary medical work. Stephen Bushell, *Chinese Art,* 2 vols. (1904); a standard work. Chiang Monlin, *Tides from the West* (1947); autobiographical study of the transition from the old to the new. *China Educational Commission, Christian Education in China* (1922); a study well worth consulting; both descriptive and analytical. W. J. Cleenell, *Historical Development of Religion in China* (1917). John F. De Francis, *Nationalism and Language Reform in China* (1950). J. J. M. DeGroot, *Religion of the Chinese* (1910); an authoritative treatise. J. C. Ferguson, *Outlines of Chinese Art* (1919), an excellent brief treatment. H. A. Giles, *History of Chinese Literature* (1901); a standard account. H. A. Giles, *Confucianism and Its Rivals* (1915); excellent chronological treatment of development of Confucianism. Stanley High, *China's Place in the Sun* (1922); ch.

6–10; interesting account of the student movement. R. L. Hobson and Others, *Romance of Chinese Art* (1936). H. T. Hodgkin, *China in the Family of Nations* (1921), ch. 10; on the new thought movement. Lewis Hodous, *Buddhism and Buddhists in China* (1924); brief but suggestive, particularly as to new tendencies. Th. E. Hsiao, *History of Modern Education in China* (1935). Emile Hovelaque, *China* (1919), esp. book II, ch. 3–4; sympathetic interpretation of the religions of China and of her art. Hu Shih, *The Chinese Renaissance* (1933); an interesting study of the movement by one of its leaders. E. R. Hughes, *The Invasion of China by the Western World* (1937). A. W. Hummel, *The Autobiography of a Chinese Historian* (1931). Paul Hutchinson, *China's Real Revolution* (1924), esp. ch. 3–7. A. Jacovleff and Kiakien Tchou, *The Chinese Theatre* (1922); an interesting brief treatment. R. F. Johnston, *Confucianism under the Republic* (1935); instructive lectures on the subject. Olga Lang, *Chinese Family and Society* (1946). T. T. Lew and Others, *China Today, Through Chinese Eyes* (1922); an excellent discussion, by Chinese, of the literary and religious movements of the times. H. F. MacNair, *China's New Nationalism and Other Essays* (1925); suggestive essays on a variety of current questions. H. F. MacNair (ed.), *China* (1946); chapters on many aspects of Chinese culture. W. H. Mallory, *China, Land of Famine* (1926); best study of the famine problem. Hugo Munsterberg, *A Short History of Chinese Art* (1949). S. C. Nott, *Chinese Culture in the Arts* (1946). Cyrus H. Peake, *Nationalism and Education in Modern China* (1932); an excellent monograph on the subject. Cyrus H. Peake, *Some Aspects of the Introduction of Modern Science into China,* Isis, vol. 22, pp. 173–217. Arnold Silcock, *Introduction to Chinese Art and Its History* (1948). Rev. W. E. Soothill, *Three Religions of China* (1915); a most interesting description. C. G. Soulie, *History of Chinese Art from Ancient Time to the Present Day* (1931). M. Soyeshima and P. W. Kuo, *Oriental Interpretations of the Far Eastern Problem* (1925), part II, ch. 1; brief discussion of political, economic, and social tendencies in modern China. E. F. Tenollosa, *Epochs of Chinese and Japanese Art—An Outline History of East Asiatic Design* (1921). Mrs. W. R. Tredwell, *Chinese Art Motives Interpreted* (1915). M. T. Z. Tyau, *China Awakened* (1922), ch. 1–10; an optimistic account. T. C. Wang, *The Youth Movement in China* (1927). H. G. W. Woodhead (ed.), *China Year Book,* 1924, esp. ch. 10 (education), 22 (religions), 23 (Chinese renaissance), 24 (labor); 1925, ch. 34 (newspapers and periodicals). For materials in other years of issue, consult table of contents under same and other heads. A. E. Zucker, *Chinese Theatre* (1925); the most comprehensive treatment.

For periodical literature consult *Readers Guide*. See also files of *Chinese Social and Political Science Review* and *Pacific Affairs* for valuable articles.

CHAPTER XIV

THE PROGRESS OF JAPAN: INTELLECTUAL, SOCIAL, AND CULTURAL

BEFORE resuming the consideration of the political and economic progress of Japan, it will be well to paint in the larger background formed by changing ideas and social institutions. Since culturally Japan is still in a transitional state, this cannot be done in definitive terms. Some broad lines of development are quite clear, however, and a beginning may fairly be made with them.

I. RELIANCE ON LEADERSHIP

It is clear that Meiji Japan was what the group of able men who assumed power after the restoration sought to make her. They were interested in establishing a strong state—one capable of maintaining its independence in the face of Western aggressive tendencies, and of playing a dominating rôle in eastern Asia. To accomplish their purpose, they borrowed freely from the West those things which they felt would secure the material foundations of the state. First, they imported Western military and naval armament and methods. This was in line with the national military traditions, it is true, but it was also the result of an acute understanding, developed by experience and observation, of the basis of real independence in the modern world. They sensed the weakness of the agricultural state and consciously and purposefully promoted the development of modern industry, going to the West for their models and their machines. This led to the establishment of a modern banking and currency system, to the building of railways, and to the fostering of a merchant marine, both for coastwise and foreign trade purposes. It was not necessary for Western governments and capitalists to force these measures on Japan. The leaders of the country, after foreign intercourse had been accepted and the Restoration accomplished, went or sent abroad for instruction and information. They freely imported foreigners to teach them what they wanted to know, and they retained them as long as they felt a need for their instruction. It must be emphasized, however, that their interest in the West was largely material and almost entirely utilitarian. Consequently they failed to grasp the social implications of the industrial system of the West. As a matter of fact, with certain exceptions which will be noted, it was left to the West to bring to Japan such moral and philosophical conceptions as it had to offer to an

Eastern peoples, while Japan sought out for herself the mechanical and material benefits presented by the Occident.

In producing modern Japan the leaders of the state had certain materials to build with and certain foundations to build on. They had to deal with people accustomed to, and acquiescent in, leadership. The hierarchical series of loyalties developed with the feudal system was continued. The propaganda preceding the Restoration made it possible to concentrate the loyalty of the clan groups in the form of devotion to the Emperor, and through him to command support for the program of change and development which they inaugurated. The revival of Shinto as the national religion afforded an additional support for the new system which they sought to create. Furthermore, they did not have to build up a spirit of patriotism and of nationalism, as had to be done in China. The feudal loyalties were transferred to the Emperor. Loyalty to the Emperor was almost automatically transferred to the new state as Emperor and state were held to be organically unified.

2. CHANGES IN LIFE OF PEOPLE

This acceptance of leadership alone made it possible for Japan so rapidly to take on the appearance of a Westernized state. It was this which enabled the Japanese to change almost overnight from open hostility to foreigners to an outward acceptance of many of their ways. For the people followed the example set them and began to imitate the foreign world in many particulars. Here, again, they tended to interest themselves in the material things rather than in the ideas, and moral and cultural values, of the West. Western shoes began to replace somewhat the Japanese sandals and geta in the cities. Western clothes came to be worn in place of the kimono to an increasing extent. With coat and trousers or skirt was introduced Western furniture. Meat and milk found their way into the national diet, partly by reason of the introduction of meat into the diet of the military conscript. With meat came the knife and fork in addition to, or in place of, the chopstick. Electric lighting became almost as common as were Western clocks. But Western ideals of liberty, equality, and morality were not so freely drawn upon and diffused.

Part of this change may have been due to the vogue of things foreign during the first years after the Restoration. This vogue was started by the makers of modern Japan to serve national ends. But it was partly due to other causes. Foreign clothing, for example, proved less expensive than Japanese, particularly for the upper classes and for women and children. It was also better adapted to certain types of work. In other words, what was lost esthetically was compensated for in added utility. Even though foreign clothing was adopted for business purposes, however, the old costume was often worn at home, except where the house interior had been foreignized by the introduction of furniture. The adoption of a foreign-style uniform for the army and navy, which touched most of the young men, the requirement of a modified foreign dress, in the nature of a uniform, for school boys and girls, and the wearing of foreign clothing by those who had studied or been engaged in business abroad, all were factors in promoting a change in the national costume.

Foreign clothes are rather ill-adapted to the conventional method of sitting squatting on the floor. Consequently the change in dress resulted in the introduction of benches into the school room and of chairs, tables, and other Western furniture into the homes and places of business of those who made the change in costume. This change also resulted when the house itself was of Western style.

Again, while foreign clothing has certain advantages over the Japanese dress for outdoor wear in cold weather, it is not adapted to padding, and multiplication of garments to take the place of heat in the home. It was necessary, therefore, to introduce stoves in place of the charcoal brazier, which is useful only for warming the hands.

This is only one illustration of the way in which the habits and customs of the people begin to be modified. The greater freedom of movement which came with the building of railways and tramcar lines, both importations from the West, also had its effect in breaking down or modifying customary practices and established institutions. The importance of improved communications, however, except from the standpoint of facilitating trade, was not so great as it would ultimately be in China, because of the difference in size of the country, and because of the greater tendency to travel in old Japan than in nineteenth-century China. It tended, however, to uproot the population and make it more mobile, and consequently to weaken local control of the individual.

3. EDUCATION

Another importation from the West was the idea of a national school system and of compulsory education. Reference has already been made [1] to the establishment and extension of modern schools. At this point, however, the educational system should be reconsidered from the standpoint of its significance in the intellectual life of the nation. After the war of 1894–1895 with China the number of schools of all grades steadily increased. The period of compulsory school attendance was lengthened in 1908 from four to six years. The number of children actually in school, in proportion to those under an obligation to attend, increased with the extension of primary school facilities, until by 1922 there was just short of one hundred

[1] Supra, chapter V, sec. 8.

per cent attendance. This constituted, both absolutely and in comparison with the most advanced Western states, a remarkable quantitative record. It was the more remarkable when the actual period of time involved is considered. There were naturally defects in the system due to the rapidity of its development. It was not possible adequately to train the number of teachers required for the many elementary schools. The insufficiency of funds devoted to education, in view of the extensive program carried into effect, made for decided underpayment of teachers, and made it impossible to provide entirely satisfactory equipment, measured by the most advanced Western standards. The financing of the primary and secondary schools was entrusted partly to the local governments, the total expenditure for education out of the national treasury being in 1929 one and a half billion yen. To help finance the system all pupils, except paupers, paid a small fee, in addition to which the pupil purchased his own books. These, however, were supplied by the government rather than through commercial enterprise.

The elementary school curriculum "embraces instruction in Japanese history, geography, mathematics, science, drawing, singing, gymnastics, and sewing for girls, with manual training for boys; and during the last three years of the primary course agriculture, commerce and the English language may be added." [2] The hours of work in the schools were long, vacations were few, and pupils as well as teachers took the business of education seriously.

Only about half of those applying for admission to the secondary schools could be accommodated, and the proportion narrowed still further as higher institutions were reached. Thus it was only primary education which was put within the reach of every Japanese. This seriously restricted opportunity, as the desirable positions in the government service, in banks and commercial houses, and in teaching, were open only to those who had the coveted diplomas. The opportunity for middle and higher school education was offered, however, in privately maintained institutions which supplemented the government's activities. Many of the private schools were Christian, although some were secular, supported out of native endowments. All were kept under governmental supervision and had to conform to governmental requirements if their diplomas were to have practical value. They compared very favorably with the public institutions, and in some cases maintained even higher standards.

After this brief survey we may return to the original question of the effect of widespread education on the intellectual life of the people. Do we have in education a notable exception to the statement that modern Japan was interested more largely, even exclusively, in the material side of modern life, rather than in the realm of ideas and of moral and cultural values?

[2] BRYAN, *Japan from Within*, p. 197.

First of all it should be noted that the view was completely accepted that education should be for the purposes of the state rather than for the liberation of the individual. This attitude permeated and gave its character to the entire system, from primary school to university. The state, according to the accepted view, needed those who were steeped in loyalty to it and its established institutions. Consequently primary school instruction was concentrated on the development of an unquestioning loyalty. The instruction in Japanese ethics, for example, was in effect the cultivation of loyalty to the Emperor, of devotion to Japan, and of acceptance of the canons of authority. To this must be added, however, as an extension of the same idea, filial piety and obedience. The primary Japanese virtue was obedience, within the home and in the state. This emphasis developed unity of purpose on an authoritarian basis, but it prevented the growth of individuality of view, and the cultivation of a questioning attitude of mind.

All other subjects, within the limits of their content, were taught on the same basis. Since the text-books were prepared by the national Department of Education, there was little possibility of diversity of content in instruction throughout the country. The books were prepared with an emphasis on the Japanese nation which was clear and unmistakable.

In the second place, with the exception of singing and possibly drawing, the subjects not of a nationalistic character were utilitarian, and were designed to strengthen the material foundations of the state. This was natural and inevitable in the primary grades. Reading, writing, arithmetic, and geography certainly constitute the essential tools which must be put in the hands of the citizen. And the mastering of the tools was more difficult in Japan than in Western countries because of the nature of the language development, and of the literary heritage, which required knowledge of Chinese characters, since the Chinese classics were to be studied as part of the middle school curriculum. The effect of the type of study this demands is elsewhere mentioned, so that it need not be dwelt upon here.

It was, however, in the higher schools, including the universities, that the utilitarian character of education was most marked. The technical and commercial schools naturally had that character. Tokyo University comprised faculties of law, medicine, literature, science, engineering, and agriculture. With variations in the number of faculties, this typified the situation. An opportunity was afforded to secure the advanced preparation necessary to serve the state in the various professions and occupations, and thus, of course, to enable the individual to carve out a career for himself. Lawyers, doctors, engineers, trained agriculturalists, and administrators were necessary in modern Japanese society, as were bankers, machinists, and men trained in commercial and vocational lines. But outside of literature and the fine arts, there was no encouragement of study in what may be called the humanities—no stimulus to philosophical study, outside the native horizon, including that furnished in the Confucian heritage, or to investigation and study in the social sciences. Anything that might result in the introduction or development of what was called "dangerous thoughts," changing the political or social outlook of the students and of the people, was excluded, as far as possible, from the entire school system. Instruction and investigation in the natural and physical sciences and in applied economics was satisfactorily built up, with the result that Japanese schools produced able and well-trained men in those fields. But the scientific method of study of the state, and of social institutions, was not developed. Quite truly it was realized that that type of study and investigation would produce a less docile and more critical spirit, and perhaps might lead to the acceptance of the view that the state exists to serve the individual rather than to be served by him. Thus it may be said that education was not an effective agency for promoting an active intellectual life in Japan, except within the comparatively narrow limits fixed by the utilitarian point of view and by the fear of "dangerous thoughts."

4. STATUS OF WOMEN

A marked feature of the development of the first three decades of the twentieth century was the attention paid to the education of girls and women and to the development of new spheres of activity for them. Formerly woman's place was felt to be exclusively in the home,[3] and education, in the sense of intellectual training, was largely denied her. However, the elementary school was opened to both boys and girls, without segregation in separate institutions. For some time after the Restoration no governmental provision was made for higher education for women, although as early as 1871 five girls of varying ages were sent to America for training. It was understood that upon their return they would devote themselves to promoting education for their sex. The Christian mission workers first took up the task of providing facilities for advanced training for women, and they rendered a very valuable service. The government subsequently provided high schools for girls, and maintained normal and higher normal schools for training women teachers for the elementary schools. In the post-war years women were admitted as auditors at the lectures in the Imperial University at Tokyo. In addition to the Christian colleges for women, there was one privately maintained university, the Japanese Women's University, established in 1901.

While women were extensively engaged in teaching, and to some extent in medical practice, journalism, and other professional activities, it still remained true that the women of modern as of ancient Japan looked for-

---

[3] This statement, while generally true, needs to be qualified by recognition of the literary and entertainment activity of women in various eras of pre-modern times.

ward to marriage, and that at a comparatively early age. This complicated the problem for those interested in higher education, as frequently their students were compelled by their families to leave school before their work had been completed because a match satisfactory to the family had been arranged. There seemed, however, to be a tendency in Japan toward later marriages among the upper classes. Whether or not this was due in part to the extension of educational opportunities, it did make it possible for learning to be pursued a little farther before marriage than had previously been the case. Outside of the well-to-do classes it must be understood that women in Japan, both before and after marriage, were vital parts of the national economy. Since the larger part of the population was engaged in agriculture, it followed that Japanese girls and women in the rural districts helped with the rice cultivation, were the chief tenders of the silk worms, picked the tea, and did the spinning and weaving in the home. In the industrial world, it should be noted that sixty per cent of all factory workers were women, while eighty per cent of the operatives in cotton mills were women. Child labor in Japan, furthermore, meant primarily the labor of girls, for eighty per cent of the children employed were little girls.

Something is said elsewhere [4] about factory legislation and the need for it. At this point reference may well be made to the conditions under which the girls and women lived and worked. There were of course notable exceptions, but on the whole the conditions of industrial life were terrible. Here we have another illustration of the way in which the Japanese imported the material civilization of the West, its machines and devices of the most improved kind, without attempting an investigation of the methods which had begun to be developed of conserving human values.

The factory operatives were secured by systematic recruiting in the country districts. The advantages of life in the town were sufficiently vividly pictured to cause the girl willingly to leave the rural district. But the governing consideration was a money payment to her family, which often was barely able to eke out a living from the soil, and the prospect of what appeared to be a substantial addition to the family income, which would continue until marriage. Incidentally, the movement of women to the factories tended to promote later marriage among the poor more effectively than did education among the wealthy.

When the girl reached the factory, she was often housed in a closed compound, where the girls were locked up to prevent them from running away. They had no privacy, only mat space for sleeping being allotted to each one. Sometimes, where there was a day and a night shift, the bed was continually occupied. The hours were long, and fatigue interfered with normal recreation even when it was provided in suitable form. Due to the conditions under which they worked and slept, tuberculosis was rife among

[4] Chapter XV, sec. 6.

both men and women factory workers. Moral conditions were also bad. "A Japanese factory expert has affirmed that in some factories it is not uncommon for more than half the girls to lose their virtue in a year. The long hours leave the workers so weary that any sort of excitement is welcome, and consequently vicious pleasures and pastimes are encouraged and common. The most usual amusements are drinking, gambling and sensuality." [5] The consequence was that by reason of disease, desertion, and also because of approaching marriage, there was a labor turnover of about eighty per cent among the women operatives, and recruiting had to go on ceaselessly.

From the standpoint of health, as well as of industrial efficiency, the nation lost tremendously by the maintenance of these conditions. There is where the Japanese leaders failed most seriously, even on a purely utilitarian basis, in making importations from the West. They did not appreciate the social ideals or even the efficiency ideas which had begun to express themselves in the Occident. They saw the machine, but not the social implications of the machine economy. Consequently they made no systematic attempt to conserve the health of the nation by ensuring reasonably good living conditions for the future mothers who were engaged in industry. Christian employers often offered notable exceptions to the rule by attempting to look after their employees, and the Christian ideal of the sacredness of human life spread somewhat beyond the Christian community. But so materialistic had become the outlook of the Japanese industrial leaders that a satisfactory social program could be expected to be developed by them only when it was demonstrated that it was good business, and to the practical advantage of the nation, to give attention to the welfare of the women workers. They would, of course, be helped to gain this appreciation as labor organized to protect itself.

The statement that this large proportion of the girls in the factories lost their virtue does not constitute the moral indictment of the factory system that it would in many other countries. Premarital relations between the sexes were quite common in many of the rural districts, although the proportions would not seem to be nearly so great. And this did not serve as a bar to marriage for the girl, as to a large extent it does elsewhere.

The difference in moral code is further illustrated in the openness with which the trade of the prostitute was plied. It was carried on under governmental supervision as a recognized occupation, although not an honored one. It was estimated that there were not less than fifty thousand licensed prostitutes in the country. These women were kept in a condition of bondage, as otherwise it was difficult to hold them.

Most of them soon loathe the business, but are helpless, hopeless prisoners,— for the keepers who paid their parents a few score or hundreds of yen and loaded

[5] Bryan, op. cit., p. 139.

them with beautiful clothes, charge all these items to their account, so that they are under a heavy debt which must be paid before they can leave. This debt the laws of the land theoretically ignore but practically recognize, for the "keeper" keeps the books as well as the brothel, and the police and officials are often on his side.[6]

Aside from the official attitude, the principal support of the system lay in the poverty of the lower classes. "The girl goes to the brothel in obedience to her parents, who send her there to earn a living for herself and to help them out of special financial difficulties. Thus from first to last, so far as the girls, the parents, and the keepers are concerned, the question is economic."[7] Many of the prostitutes, it should be said, came from the former eta or pariah class.

To the number of licensed prostitutes, from the standpoint of morality, must be added the hotel and tea-house girls, for many of them were virtually in the same class. The Geisha, the class of entertainers, were also sometimes put in the same category. Their occupation, as that of the tea-house girls, might, and often did, lead to prostitution. But, occupationally, they were highly trained public entertainers.

As the economic condition of the lower classes was improved, the willingness of parents to see their children engaged in these occupations was certain to lessen, and to the extent to which the parental control weakened as a result of the introduction of the individualistic ideas of the West, the system was bound to weaken. Furthermore, partly as a result of the initial sensitiveness of Japanese to foreign opinion, there developed some condemnation of the open connection of the government with prostitution through the licensing system. This had the effect, not always of ending prostitution, but of pushing it more underground and out of the public view. Such a development might ultimately lead to the same reaction as is found in Western countries. Certainly prostitution was a less prominent feature of the Japan of 1931 than of 1921.

5. THE FAMILY SYSTEM

Due to the emphasis on material development, there occurred less change in the social than in the economic institutions of Japan. The family remained the basic unit of society, although the government dealt with the individual as it did not, by 1931, in modern China. Aside from ancestral worship, and from the Confucian emphasis on the family, and of the view of the nation as an enlarged family group, its principal support was to be found in the system of rural economy. "The family system, by which all is

[6] GULICK, Working Women of Japan, p. 105.
[7] Ibid.

subordinated to family, is convenient to farmers for it means increased labor and economy of living . . . generally speaking, the family system at one and the same time keeps young men from striking out in the world and compels their early marriage so that the helping hands to the family may be more numerous." [8] Industrial development had not broken down this point of view, because of the extent to which the labor of girls was used. This was another method of adding to the family income. Marriage in industrial centers, however, often resulted in the establishment of individual homes. The ultimate effect, furthermore, of the expansion of the industrial system will be to weaken the family system, as it promotes a movement from the village into the town.

But while the family system remained, certain modifications in it were made. In more advanced circles the marriage arrangements were not so exclusively in parental hands. The practice of "free" marriage was becoming more widespread each decade. By this was meant, sometimes, merely the right of an interview before the marriage arrangements were completed. In a more extreme form it carried with it a right of selection. Reference has already been made to the tendency to break up the household into its component parts with the drawing of the population into the cities. Under the influence of Western example, and also of teaching in the Christian schools and missions, the same thing was happening for other than economic reasons among the middle and upper classes. The tendency toward later marriages also had its effect on the family and indicated the weakening of family control.

6. ABOLITION OF CLASS DISTINCTIONS

One social change made after the Restoration was a redivision of society. Two distinct classes were recognized—the nobility, which was graded into various ascending ranks, and the commoners. Class distinction, as between groups of commoners, was legally brought to an end. This brought the samurai down and elevated the pariah classes such as the eta. Of course this did not prevent the establishment and perpetuation of distinctions due to occupation and wealth, but it did take away special privileges and particular disabilities. Thus the eta were no longer legally restricted to the performance of the most menial and unpleasant tasks. They were not required to live in separate villages. And the ban on marriage outside their group no longer existed. However, while for the samurai the change had immediate and real consequences, for the eta it was more nominal. They had so long regarded themselves, and been regarded, as pariahs that it will take several generations more before they can be merged in the general population if, indeed, that ever completely comes to pass.

[8] ROBERTSON-SCOTT. *Foundations of Japan,* p. 329.

7. NEW CLASS ALIGNMENTS

As the feudal class divisions were modified or ended, new ones began to arise. In another place [9] reference is made to the growth of a class of tenant farmers. This indicates that there was also a landlord class. Of course some farmers were part tenant and part owner, and many landlords were also farmers. But the general movement was in the direction of the two extremes—landlords who lived on rents paid them, and tenants who owned no land. This early produced friction and class antagonism. The Japanese landlord was prone to consider only the economic return and not to concern himself with the condition of his tenant. His point of view was generally that of the absentee landlord in other countries, even when he lived in the rural district. He usually received his rental in rice rather than money, which led to ill-feeling, since, when the crop yield was small and prices high in consequence, the landlord gained more than the tenant. He also gained rather than lost when the yield was good. On the other side, this method of payment led the tenant to try to pay his rent in the poorer part of his crop. Since he gave a large proportion of it to the landlord, he sometimes curtailed expenditure on fertilizer and other means of enlarging his production. Consequently the landlord had his grievances against the tenant. In many parts of the country the tenants were being driven steadily into debt, since their yearly necessary expenditure was greater than their income. This was also true, although not so extensively, of the small owner. Since interest rates were very high, a hopeless condition resulted.

One answer to the tenant's problem was found in a drift to the industrial city. This became so pronounced that the good tenant was at a premium, and both the landlords and the government were forced to consider ameliorative measures. The government helped by establishing land banks to make loans to the farmer at low interest rates. These came to be found in almost every prefecture. The landlord was forced to develop a sense of social responsibility. Some were more considerate in their demands; others helped to provide better manures for the paddys and fields; others sought, in coöperation with the government, to train the farmer to the improvement of his methods.

Rural coöperation developed somewhat, partly promoted by the landlord, but more largely independent of his direction. Paddy adjustment, among other things, showed the possibility of securing better results by coöperative action. There were all manner of rural or village societies for almost every conceivable purpose. Some were purely economic in character and end, but they ranged from societies to encourage the habit of early rising to agrarian coöperative institutions of a more usual sort. These societies were

[9] Chapter XV, sec. 9.

made up of all or part of the young men of the village. Many of them were valuable chiefly because they absorbed their surplus energies.

But withal it had to be recognized that class division and class feeling were on the increase in the rural districts.

Influenced by the labor movement, which developed in the industrial centers during and after the war, this depressed class (i.e., the tenants) has of late shown spirit. It has begun to assert its claims against landowners. At the end of 1920 there were as many as ninety associations of tenant farmers, and sixty of these had been started for the specific purpose of representing tenants' interests against landowners. Strikes of tenants began and continue. The end of this movement of a proverbially conservative class is not at all certain.[10]

It has been estimated that in the decade after 1920 the number of tenants' associations increased to four hundred, one-third of which were decidedly militant. It was the general rise in the cost of living after 1914, and especially during the post-war period, which produced this movement of protest.

In the industrial realm, also, class division developed as a consequence of the establishment of the factory system. The reasons for this need not be discussed here, since they are the ones which have produced the same division in other countries. In Japan, as elsewhere, the economic separation of the employer and worker grew ever more pronounced. Wages for the worker were low, hours were long and living conditions bad.

The movement toward organization of the workers is described in another connection.[11] Here, however, certain obstacles in the road of effective organization may be indicated. In the first place, unionism was associated in the public mind with socialism. Socialism embraced one set of the "dangerous ideas" which the government bent its efforts to keep out of the country, as being inimical to the public peace and welfare. Consequently unionism was branded as unpatriotic, a brand which served to keep many out of the organizations formed. In the second place, the enforcement of the "peace preservation law" made it difficult for union meetings to be held, or for other than benefit activities to be undertaken. In the third place, the proportion of women workers, as compared with men, handicapped effective organization and action. The woman was a temporary worker, pending marriage, and was in industry primarily to supplement the family income rather than as a self-supporting economic unit. Thus it was more difficult to interest her in organization. Her docility also had to be taken into account. Since so many workers were women, it was obviously difficult to organize the factory so as to bring effective pressure to bear on the employer. A fourth obstacle to the organization of labor could perhaps be found in the fact that modern industry tended to be diffused in many small factories rather than to be concentrated in a few large establishments.

[10] ROBERTSON-SCOTT, op. cit., p. 88.
[11] Chapter XV, sec. 7.

In a country where it was assumed that the initiative would come from above, where the people were indoctrinated with the claims of authority, and where the rights of the state were elevated at every point above those of the individual, it is not strange that the impetus toward the assertion of the rights of the masses came from the outside. The initial internal political liberalism lost its chief leader with the death of Itagaki. It was made futile, from the political standpoint, with the promulgation of the constitution, and with the establishment of the military bureaucracy in control of the state. Had it been allowed to develop, out of it might perhaps have come an economic and social liberalism. The early labor reform movement itself was handicapped because it was an Occidental importation, with the leaders dividing into an evolutionary or socialistic group, and a revolutionary or anarchistic group. The implication of a group of the radical leaders in a conspiracy against the Emperor in 1910, as a result of which some were executed and others imprisoned for life, was a fatal blow for the labor movement.

[It] became associated in the public mind with disloyalty and principles dangerous to the nation; which was just what its opponents desired for its overthrow. Suspicion of the labour movement has since continued, and, during the suspension of law and order during the recent earthquake in Japan, occasion was seized by rabid patriots to assassinate the leaders of socialism and labour. . . . All the authorities have to do, in order to destroy any new movement, is to brand it with the feared and hated name of socialism. . . . Labour unions are included in the regulations affecting socialism and anarchy, which is sufficient to give them the quietus. Nevertheless, there are many socialists still in Japan, some of them in labour circles, as well as among some young men of the middle class, but they can find no vent for expression.[12]

Some counter-currents, however, existed. There was, first, the fact that the working men and their children had had enough schooling to be able to read. Thus before censorship became complete and patriotic propaganda was instituted, they seemed certain to realize eventually that their lot was different in many respects from that of workers in the Occident, and to begin more strongly to insist upon recognition of their rights. In the second place, some employers and corporations, for example the Kanegafuchi Spinning Company, began to show an interest in the well-being of their employees. In other words, partly under the influence of Christian teaching, partly because of the force of Western example, and partly on account of a recognition of a sound business principle, a social responsibility seemed to be appearing. A third important influence until after 1931 was foreign opinion. Japanese sensitiveness to the opinions of others had been widely advertised. As the social backwardness of Japan was revealed to the Japanese representatives at labor conferences, and as there was increasing foreign

12 BRYAN. op. cit., p. 143.

criticism of conditions in Japan, the Japanese leaders tended to seek to remedy them, at least to the extent necessary to lessen the volume of criticism. Fourth, the broadening of the franchise gave the workers the possibility of political action which had been previously denied them. This gave an apparent assurance that legislation would cease to represent exclusively the point of view and conception of national economic interest of the industrial and commercial magnates. Thus, while "the Japanese capitalists as a class, are indifferent to labor interests and even labor questions, while the universities are more concerned with the economic than the human aspects of labor," [13] while the laborer had not yet fully awakened to his own backward condition and to the possibilities of redress, it was in 1931 possible to perceive an upward trend and to believe that it would be confirmed with the passage of time.

Two other forces had also operated to produce an intellectual and social outlook different from the conventional one, and these should be noted at this point. In the first place, the ending of World War I on the basis of Allied success, coupled with the emphasis, at least in propaganda, during the last year and a half of the war, on democracy and its concomitants, weakened the authoritarian point of view, and stimulated to active expression an already existent liberal movement. Politically, as is noted elsewhere, [14] this liberal movement resulted in a broadening of the franchise to the point of universal male suffrage. It also resulted in a distinct, if temporary, liberalization of both foreign and colonial policy. And, of even greater ultimate importance, it began to be appreciated among the intellectual and upper middle classes that the social thinking of Japan had not kept abreast of her material development. It is not going too far to say that in the period between 1918 and the overthrow of the Minseito government in 1931 the social ideas of the Japanese experienced more radical change—that there had been a greater liberalization of thought—than in the preceding three or four decades. Unfortunately, the undertaking of military adventures on the continent after September, 1931, which threw political control back into the hands of the military party, had the effect of bringing about a reaction in social thinking by a reassertion of the supreme importance of the state, and by a reëmphasis of traditional values. For the time, at least, liberalism in Japan again became impotent. At the same time, the exemplary force of Western ideals of social conduct was lost.

Another great influence in Japan, as in other countries, had been the Russian revolution. The government and the ruling classes were tremendously afraid of the new Russian ideas and of the effect of their introduction into Japan. Consequently every effort was made to keep them out of the country. Furthermore, a counter-current was maintained against

---

[13] *Ibid.*, p. 144.   [14] Chapter XV, sec. 4.

them to neutralize their effect, in case they should, in spite of all precautions, find their way into Japan. But the counter-current inevitably produced an interest in the current which it was designed to neutralize and minimize. Thus it was impossible to prevent Japanese thought from feeling the Russian influence to some extent. Coming just at a time when labor unrest, in both town and country, was beginning to manifest itself, a movement which was frankly based on the conception of control of the state by the workers, and which had world-wide repercussions, was certain to have some effect on the Japanese labor movement. That it did not have a greater effect was due to the abhorrence of "socialist" ideas as unpatriotic, an attitude which had been cultivated prior to the war. Thus two streams of ideas, the one from the capitalistic states of the West and the other from communist Russia, met in Japan to modify thinking about social relations after the end of World War I.

8. LITERATURE AND THE PRESS

In the realm of literature Japan felt the force of the Western impact almost as much as in the field of economic and social development. This is readily understandable since most of the old literary forms had developed under foreign (i.e., Chinese) influence. The great exception is to be found in poetry, the canons of which were and continued to be distinctly and distinctively Japanese. Its peculiar quality was produced by the use of alternate lines of five and seven syllables. The usual length was five lines, the first and third of five syllables, the second, fourth, and fifth of seven, giving a total of thirty-one syllables. This length was not invariable, a shorter form of seventeen syllables often being used, but the alternation of lines of five and seven syllables was compulsory. The poems composed under these restrictions were suggestive rather than fully expressive. They conveyed impressions rather than unfolding themes. Consequently Japanese poetry was essentially lyrical, the epic form being entirely foreign to its meter and spirit. The men and women of the Court and upper classes, in both ancient and modern times, engaged in the production of verse as one of their principal avocations. Poetry-writing competitions were frequent, and often the winner came from one of the lower classes, whose interest in poetry was also noteworthy. While Japanese poetic forms were virtually unaffected by the modern world, except for the work of Toson and a few others who broke through the restrictions as to length, the old forms were widely used to express new ideas and impressions. In this way, certainly, modern Japanese poetry felt the impact of the West without losing its distinctive Japanese flavor.

In fields of literature other than poetry, the production of pre-modern Japan was equally important. But it was so largely influenced from the continent that it was not as distinctively Japanese as the poetry. The earliest work extant is the Kojiki (Record of Ancient Matters), which is a saga of the beginnings of things and of the development of the Japanese nation. It was written in archaic Japanese. Almost immediately, however, it was displaced by the Nihongi (Chronicles of Japan), a work of similar content but written in the "classical" or quasi-Chinese language. This classical language, together with an imported Chinese literary canon, dominated Japan until a literary renaissance set in sometime after the firm establishment of order under the Tokugawa Shōguns. The Chinese influence continued, but there was a conscious attempt to break away from it. This was particularly marked in the field of historical writing and of religious investigation. There was also developed, under the Tokugawa, a wide variety of non-historical writings. Folk-tales and children's stories, moral discourses and novels, appeared in profusion.

With the Restoration, the interest in things Japanese ceased for a time, and attention was concentrated on Western literature, particularly the English. The years from 1868 to 1885 were not productive of literature. The Japanese gained a certain familiarity with the new world of letters through study, both at home and abroad, and through translation of Western books. But for obvious reasons the chief constructive interest of the nation was centered on political and economic reconstruction. This, together with the cult of the West, made literary production difficult if not impossible. The chief interest in Western literature was in that of England at first and subsequently in that of the continent.

In general the next two decades were dominated by romantic schools, one headed by Shoyo, a Shakespearean student, a second by Koyo, whose principal contributions to Japanese letters lay in the objectivity of his descriptions, and in his brilliant style, and a third by the idealist Rohan. The intensification of national feeling resulting from the war with China, together with the optimism resulting from the triumph of Japan over her large neighbor, set the tone for much of the literary output of the years from 1895 to 1904-1905. From the standpoint of style the decade 1895–1905 was significant because of the high level reached. During these years the predominant Western influence gradually changed from English to Russian.

Rapidly, after 1900, romanticism gave way to naturalism and realism. The displacement of English by continental literature was partly responsible for this change. The attitudes developed by scientific study, however, and the pessimism engendered by the sacrifices and losses of the Russo-Japanese War, also contributed materially to the changed point of view. To some extent, also, it may be accounted for as a natural swing from the extreme development of romanticism. In its earlier stages this naturalism was distinctly beneficial to Japanese letters, resulting in many notable contributions to the literature of the nation, and securing recognition for writers whose work, although noteworthy, had seemed destined to obscurity. But the movement, with its emphasis on subject, caused a decline in style and, with the passage of time, naturalism, with its free treatment of sex relations, resulted in decadence and sensualism.

About 1912 an independent stream, which had been running parallel with the current of naturalism, became the main stream. Idealism in literature had been preserved through the writings of Soseki Natsume, a student of the classical as well as of the Western learning. After 1912 idealism became stronger as a result of a reaction against the extreme tendencies of the naturalistic writers. This reaction was confirmed and redirected as one of the consequences of World War I. After the war, with the growth in importance of class struggles and alignments, Japanese literature was strongly affected by the problem of class adjustment.

It was in literary circles that the non-economic ideas and ideals of the West found their greatest hearing. And it was through literature, rather than the schools, that new ideas came into circulation in modern Japan.

While the drama was not as greatly affected as the novel by the three-quarters of a century of foreign intercourse, it did not entirely escape. Prior to the Restoration there were four forms of dramatic art. For the Court, the Daimyō, and the samurai, there was the Nō performance, a stately dance to singing, the themes being religious or martial. The costuming of the performers was extremely elaborate. Because of the somberness of the Nō dance, it became customary to insert a farce into the interludes. This was called the Kyōgen (Mad Words). For the common people, since they were excluded from the Nō performance, two other forms developed. The first was a dramatic ballad, given to the accompaniment of a musical instrument called the Samisen. Puppets were used in connection with the singing of the ballad. The themes were not light or laughter-provoking any more than was the Nō dance. Consequently, the Kabuki, or farce, came into existence, and with it arose the theater in the Western sense. By the end of the pre-Restoration period it had come to be a fixed custom, at first decreed by law, that women's parts should be played by men. The actors were invariably professionals, highly trained for their work. A revolving stage had come into use, together with other mechanical arrangements. The dramas themselves were either historical or domestic in theme.

After the Restoration the nobility began openly to patronize the plebeian theater, although they continued to interest themselves in the Nō representations. Women appeared on the stage. New theater devices were introduced. But so far as the professional stage was concerned, the dramatic art remained essentially Japanese. Some of Shakespeare's plays were translated and produced, as were those of a few continental European dramatists, but without marked success. There were some playwrights of reputation who found their models in the West, but their plays were produced more often by amateurs than by professional actors. They found a greater acceptance for their work in the periodicals than on the stage.

One of the most noteworthy developments in Japan was that of the press and of periodical literature. The newspaper is something entirely modern, and its real development was a matter of the first decades of the twentieth century. Some papers made their appearance shortly after the first treaties were signed, but the life of most was short. Only two existed in 1868. Others were established in 1871–1872, and as the agitation for a constitution commenced the papers multiplied. They were mostly organs of individuals who were opposed to the government. This led to the establishment of official journals. They were all interested in attack and counter-attack rather than in gathering and presenting the news of the day. Consequently they lost the support of their readers, who in time became disgusted with polemics. The result was that they were seldom sound enterprises from the financial standpoint. One of the notable exceptions was the *Jiji Shimpō,* which was founded in 1882. It, however was conducted as a politico-literary enterprise rather than as a purely commercial one, as were the other Tokyo papers. The newspaper considered purely as a business venture was first developed in Osaka. The Osaka *Asahi Shimbun* and the Osaka *Mainichi Shimbun* were brought into being, not to spread the ideas of the owners and editors, but to earn for them by gathering and selling the news. They were so successful that others were established for the same purpose. From that time, in spite of many handicaps, including government supervision, the number multiplied, until every town of any importance had its own paper, while there were more than fifty daily papers in Tokyo. To the nine hundred Japanese newspapers must be added several foreign-language papers, some of which were excellent journals.

Periodicals of all kinds, including religious publications, scientific journals, commercial, engineering, and financial weeklies and monthlies, women's and children's magazines, and comic papers came to be published in Japan.

All of these publications were kept under a more or less strict censorship, even before 1931, although the newspapers and political journals were the only ones seriously affected.

Warnings are issued by the censor as to what must not be mentioned, as occasion demands, and violation of the order is punished by fine. Every journal on its establishment must deposit (with the authorities) a sum varying from 2,000 yen downwards according to place and frequency of issue, and a fine is deducted from the deposit for every offense. When the deposit is thus exhausted it must be renewed. . . . The average number of summonses for violation of ban on news each year is about 250, and the number of issues forbidden sale or suspended is about 175. The same censorship is exercised over publication of books, the number thus prohibited annually being about five hundred out of a total publication of over 20,000 volumes, 37 of these prohibitions being in reference to books imported from abroad.[15]

The purpose of the censorship was to prevent the spread of "dangerous thought," or of information which it seemed undesirable, for various reasons, to have reach the people.

In spite of this control, it must be recognized that the press became increasingly powerful. If its case was reasonably good, a virtually unanimous press opposition could bring about the downfall of a government, or the modification of a policy, in Japan as in some other countries. The censorship was not maintained to prevent criticism of the Cabinet or of administrators, but to prevent the spread of ideas subversive of existing institutions.

9. JAPANESE ARTS AND CRAFTS

Japanese art, and the native crafts of an artistic character, did not show much positive advance in the period being reviewed and in some respects they suffered an actual decline. Painting and decorative work had been very highly developed prior to the Restoration. While they showed a strong Chinese influence, as did much of the culture of ancient Japan, in many respects the Japanese pupils surpassed their continental teachers. They excelled in line work, as did the Chinese, the reason being the development of fine brush work as part of the technique of good writing. The subjects treated were found in nature, and landscape work was especially good, although the draped figure was excellently portrayed. Nature was followed quite closely in landscape painting, except as far as perspective was concerned, and as far as the treatment was not purely imaginative. Old Japanese paintings and prints were designed to suggest the subject rather than to represent it in detail. This makes it impossible to compare the treatment fairly with that of European masters.

After the Restoration the attempt was made to introduce the methods and canons of Western art, a teacher being imported from Italy for that purpose in 1875. But European art encountered a long and honorable native tradition, and there was soon a swing back to the Japanese school. This was encouraged by the foreigners themselves, for the very good reason that the world would lose more than it could conceivably gain by an Europeanization of Japanese art. The Japanese public, furthermore, did not show itself interested in Western-style paintings to the extent of encouraging the few who completely made the break from the native tradition. Some of the younger painters attempted to draw upon the West. not by way of imitation, but by way of combination of the best elements in the two schools. Nothing especially noteworthy came from this move-

[15] BRYAN, op. cit., p. 247.

ment. Thus it may be said by way of summary: there was a strong conservative influence which strengthened the tendency toward maintenance of the ancient canons; there was a small group of painters who attempted to paint in the Western manner; and there was a middle group which sought to preserve the Japanese tradition, but which had studied in the West and sought to develop the ancient art by combining with it contributions to technique drawn from abroad.

Ancient Japan also excelled in metal work of all kinds. The bronze work ranged in size from such great statues of Buddha as those at Kamakura and Nara to small temple and house ornaments. The casting achievements of the large-scale work were only excelled by the exquisiteness of the small. The latter work was not all in bronze. The remarkable sword forging and sword ornamentation, as well as the netsuké, tiny carved ornaments for pipe-case and tobacco pouch, come to mind as examples of work done in other materials. Ivory and wood sculpture and carving were also highly developed. Buddhism and the military society both stimulated achievements in all of these lines.

Some of the modern work compared very favorably with that of the past. But the increasing demand for cheap ornamentation, both in Japan and in the West, and the time factor which began to enter into production, tended to commercialize the work, and resulted in a lessening of achievement. Much of the work done was decorative rather than artistic in the highest sense of the term.

The demand for quantities of Japanese porcelains and pottery in the West had a bad effect on the ceramic industry. The best pieces were produced for the domestic market and were fully equal to the standards of the past. The same was true of Japanese cloisonné. Much of the modern work was inferior. However, the work of some of the artists was not only equal but actually superior to the best of the past. "The use of silver, instead of copper, as a base, and the setting of designs on the surface in greater relief by the ishime process, indicates still more the recent progress of the art. Ando has successfully imitated the French process of translucent designs, and Ota is producing the red monochrome that is the ambition of all workers in this beautiful craft." [16] Lacquer and damascene work, embroidery, and weaving also were developed at least as highly in modern times as in the past. The reception accorded to native Japanese work in the West, together with the patronage of the Imperial Court and the nobility, served to promote the preservation and development of these and other native crafts. One modern influence, the commercial, tended to change the artist into a mere artisan, it is true, but the other influences aided in preserving the artist. Many of the examples which reached the European and American market were inferior, cheap

[16] Ibid., p. 215.

goods. They represented the commercial output. That which was absorbed in Japan, or only occasionally reached the West, represented the artistic achievement of the modern Japanese master.

The characteristic feature of private architecture in Japan was its extreme simplicity, together with its flimsiness of construction. In the towns the roof was of tile while in the rural districts it was thatched, except in the case of the wealthier farmers, who also used tile. The interior walls were sliding panels, which could be entirely removed if it was desired to combine two or more rooms into one. Public buildings such as Buddhist temples were, however, of marked elaborateness, not so much architecturally, perhaps, as in their decorative features. The style was Chinese, and it had been essentially unmodified in the Japanese environment. Shinto shrines represented the native architectural genius and the primitive simplicity of the people. They were enlargements of the primitive wooden huts of the early inhabitants. The distinctive feature was the torii under which the worshipper passed in approaching the shrine. It consisted of two upright trunks, the upper ends of which were mortised into two horizontal logs which projected beyond them on either side.

The temples and shrines were left architecturally unaffected by the contact with the West. Government buildings, on the other hand, began to be built in a Western or pseudo-Western style, which almost completely failed to harmonize with the surroundings. In the cities, foreign-style dwellings, stores, and manufacturing establishments were increasingly common. No style of building was evolved which offered the advantages of the foreign building and at the same time fitted altogether harmoniously into the Japanese scene.

10. RELIGIONS

One of the most prominent features of the Japanese landscape was the temple or shrine, from which it might be inferred that the people were very devout and intensely religious in their interests and outlook. Consequently this description cannot be concluded without a consideration of the status of religion in modern Japan.

The three organized religions were Shinto, the official cult, Buddhism, and Christianity. Confucianism did not exist as a distinct cult, although probably most non-Christian upper-class Japanese would have described themselves as Confucianists. The family system, and ancestor-worship, were of course indigenous, but the Confucian code of morals, emphasizing the filial virtues, reënforced and preserved the native system.

Shinto, "the way of the Gods," the original faith of the Japanese, was revived as part of the movement which culminated in the Restoration of Meiji. It was the officially favored religion, although the government professed not to regard it as a religion. In essence it was a system of ancestor-worship. Shinto deities and shrines alike were classified according to their official status. The national shrines, of which the Great Shrine at Ise must be placed first, were devoted to the worship of deities of the mythological age. Each village had its shrine, dedicated to a local hero or personage of meritorious deeds. Between the two were those dedicated to the memory of distinguished patriots. In addition, each household had its own shrine, before which it worshiped the family ancestors, for the spirits of all of the dead were kami, or "god-like" beings. The total number of shrines in 1933 was 111,037, of twelve grades. These were served by 15,586 priests. This represented a constant decrease in the number of shrines officially maintained and in active use, since the total number in 1908 was over 162,000. The number of priests remained about the same, the decrease being slight. There were thirteen officially recognized Shinto sects, and the total number of professed believers in 1933 was over seventeen million.[17]

The principal importance of Shintoism in modern times was nationalistic rather than religious. It was used to develop devotion to the Imperial House and to the state by cultivating an intense patriotism based upon the supposedly divine origin of the nation and of its rulers. With the spread of education its hold on the masses began to weaken, although it was principally among the more highly educated classes that an appreciation of its incongruities in the modern scientific world was felt. The rulers, however, felt that in this cult of patriotism they had an excellent means of preserving the political, economic, and social *status quo*. As a consequence the people were encouraged in their beliefs by those who possibly had themselves rejected them.

Buddhism was introduced into Japan from the continent in the sixth century. It established itself, after a struggle, by its customary compromise of admitting to its pantheon Shinto deities as Buddhist incarnations, and also by making concessions to the martial spirit of the Japanese. Its principal contribution to Japan was in its influence on the art, literature, and general culture of the country, rather than in the realm of moral development and individual conduct.

In 1933 there were twelve major Buddhist sects, with numerous sub-sects. Of these, three showed the most vitality and the most power of adaptation to modern conditions. These were the Zen, Nichirin, and Shin sects. This tendency toward division was one of the characteristic features of Japanese Buddhism. Including those of all sects, there were, in 1933, more than seventy-one thousand Buddhist temples, tended by more than fifty-five thousand priests. There were about forty-eight and one half mil-

[17] *Japan Year Book*, 1926, p. 187; 1940, p. 155; *Japan-Manchoukuo Year Book*, 1937, pp. 135–136.

lion adherents to Buddhism. Since, however, many Buddhists were also Shintoists, and vice versa, these figures are not of much absolute value in indicating the comparative strength of the two cults.

What seems as clear in the case of Buddhism as in that of Shintoism is that its hold on the people was more nominal than real. At the middle of the last century Buddhism was inert and stagnant. Its power came from the momentum acquired during previous ages and from the lack of alternative except that presented in Confucianism, which never found a footing among the masses. As in China, the Buddhist priest was related to death rather than to life. The disestablishment of Buddhism after the Restoration, and the competition of Christianity, served initially to weaken it, but later to restore to it a measure of its old vitality. The result was that Buddhist Young Men's Associations were organized, Sunday schools for children were established, and propaganda was undertaken in Formosa and elsewhere. Some of the priests began to interest themselves in the problems of their parishioners, and attempted to re-center the village life in the temple. But, on the whole, Japanese Buddhism did not develop an adequate moral code or any social program suited to the needs of modern society.

Christianity, as has been pointed out, was first introduced into Japan in the middle of the sixteenth century, but it was banned at the end of the century after it had begun to find a firm footing among the people. This early work was Roman Catholic. The Protestants were the first Christians to reënter the field after the re-opening of Japan to foreign intercourse. Both the Roman and the Orthodox churches, however, soon were also at work, the former representing mainly French Catholic, and the latter Russian, Christianity.

The evangelistic work made slow progress for a long time, and even by 1933 there were only about three hundred thousand converts, more than half of whom had been taken into the churches in the two previous decades. This seems slight progress to have been made in a period of over sixty years. On the other hand, the influence and importance of Christianity cannot be measured by the number of enrolled church members. Through the mission schools, the Y.M.C.A., the Y.W.C.A., the Salvation Army, and many other philanthropic enterprises, the Christian ideal was diffused among the people more widely than statistics can reveal.

The greatest obstacle to successful evangelistic work was the intense and narrow nationalism which regarded Christianity as alien and cosmopolitan, and consequently as something which would have a weakening effect on the state and on individual loyalty to it. Next to this the materialism of modern Japan was the principal handicap to the work of conversion. "Sectarianism in Christianity does not puzzle the Japanese much, as he is accustomed to it in Shinto and Buddhism," but he "considers the moral ideals of Christianity too elevated for the average man, especially in business and domestic life." [18]

The comparatively rapid increase in the number of converts from 1920 to 1933 may be explained in three ways. It may have been due to the fact that much spade work had to be done over an extended period of time before results could reasonably be expected. Thus after 1920 was the period of harvest. It might have represented a growing recognition of the necessity for elevating moral standards and developing a social program. Since the other cults offered little in the way of a moral or social code suited to the needs of the times, there may have been a movement toward Christianity. Or it might have been the result of the partial Japanization of the Christian churches, so that there was no longer fear of them as alien. Possibly all of these may serve to explain the acceleration of conversion.

The Japanese churches and other Christian institutions moved slowly toward self-control. Even in matters of finance dependence on foreigners steadily lessened, some of the churches reaching the point of financing themselves entirely from contributions of their Japanese members. In fact the Christian community did not increase proportionally as greatly as did the contributions to its support. This tendency toward independence was accelerated after 1924, since "a movement has recently appeared among Japanese Christian churches with the object of severing financial and other connections with the foreign mission boards, mostly British and American, and to take a free hand in their evangelistic work. This independence movment, it is significant to say, was voiced first immediately after the enforcement in 1924 of the new anti-Japanese immigration legislation in America, and has fast gained ground, meetings of influential Japanese Christians, exclusive of those of the Roman Catholic and Russian Orthodox churches, having been held in Tokyo to discuss the ways and means for carrying the movement to realization." [19]

This movement, it should be noted, was not directed against the missions, but was designed to render the church entirely independent of the foreign-supported mission. It should be added that this movement, generally speaking, had the support of the missionaries in Japan, just as did the similar movement in China. It was felt by many that Christianity could be much more effectively spread in Japan by Japanese through a purely Japanese institution. Through the spread of Christian ideals by means of the church a sounder social system might be developed than that which resulted from the modernization of the economic life of Japan. Thus the remedy may be introduced from the West for the evils developed partly as a result of Japanese material borrowings from the West.

[18] BRYAN, op. cit., p. 262.
[19] *Japan Year Book*, 1926.

In spite of the numerous cults and sects, however, and of many picturesquely placed and beautiful shrines and temples, it cannot be said that the Japanese are intensely religious people. On the whole, the effect of the emphasis on the material, the spread of modern scientific knowledge, and the bringing of people in large numbers into the cities to engage in factory work, had been distinctly to weaken traditional beliefs. This lack of faith was reported to be most noticeable among industrial workers. Certainly, by 1931, the hold of the national cult of Shinto had been weakened among them. This lessening of faith had been causing the political and industrial leaders a great deal of concern, for it presented them with the necessity of revivifying it or of replacing it, as a bond uniting the individual and the state, with something as useful and also in harmony with contemporary ideas and needs. This something was sought between 1931 and 1945 in the sedulous cultivation of support of the national state engaged in expansion as a defensive measure. Thus it was found essentially in a reëmphasis on the Shinto ideas. The ills of Japan were ascribed, as in pre-Restoration days, to foreign importations, and emphasis was put on the purification of the state through the subordination of private and class interests to the general interest, as defined in state terms by the military leaders as the most disinterested element in society. This new nationalism adversely affected all institutions and practices tinged with a foreign connection, as was Christianity.

REFERENCES FOR FURTHER STUDY

Sir Rutherford Alcock, *Art and Art Industries in Japan* (1878); a standard early account. W. G. Aston, *History of Japanese Literature* (1899); a careful study by a well-known student of things Japanese. Hugh Borton (ed.), *Japan* (1951); chapters by specialists on many aspects of Japanese culture. Faubion Bowers, *Japanese Theatre* (1952). J. Ingram Bryan, *Japan from Within* (1924); an informative study by an old resident. Otis Cary, *History of Christianity in Japan*, 2 vols. (1909); vol. 1 takes up the Roman Catholic and Orthodox missions, and vol. 2, the Protestant missions. B. H. Chamberlain, *Japanese Poetry* (1911); by a recognized authority. Charlotte B. De Forest, *The Woman and the Leaven in Japan* (1923); contains some interesting material, particularly on the Christian influence in education of women. Christopher Dresser, *Japan, Its Architecture, Art and Art Manufactures* (1882). John F. Embree, *Suye Mura* (1939); a study of a Japanese village. Earle Ernst, *The Kabuki Theatre* (1956). A. K. Faust, *Christianity as a Social Factor in Modern Japan* (1909). G. M. Fisher, *Creative Forces in Japan* (1923); emphasizes influence of Christianity. Sidney L. Gulick, *Working Women of Japan* (1915); a valuable study of that important part of the population. Tasuku Harada, *Faith of Japan* (1914). D. C. Holton, *The National Faith of Japan* (1938). D. C. Holton, *Modern Japan and Shinto Nationalism* (1943); the subtitle, "a study of present trends in Japanese religion," indicates its scope. Baron Hozumi, *Ancestor-Worship and Japanese Law* (1913). K. Kawabé, *Press and Politics in Japan* (1921); the best study of an important question. M. A. KEENLEYSIDE and A. F. THOMAS, *History of Japanese Education* (1935). STEPHEN KING-HALL, *Western Civilization and the Far East* (1924), ch. 12–14. INAZO NITOBE and OTHERS, *Western Influences in Modern Japan* (1931). P. S. REINSCH, *Intellectual and Political Currents in the Far East* (1911), ch. 7 (Intellectual Life in Japan). AUGUST K. REISCHER, *Studies in Japanese Buddhism* (1917). J. W. ROBERTSON-SCOTT, *Foundations of Japan* (1922); an excellent sociological study of rural Japan. ETSU (INAGAKI) SUGEMOTO, *A Daughter of the Samurai* (1925); gives an interesting picture of life in Japan after the Restoration. DAISETZ TEITARO SUZUKI, *Essays in Zen Buddhism* (first series, 1953). Y. TAKENOBU (ed.), *Japan Year Book*, yearly after 1906; esp. ch. 11–14, 16–21, in vol. for 1930. Y. TSURUMI, *Present Day Japan* (1926); devoted mostly to literature; should be consulted. Y. TSURUMI, *Difficulties and Hopes of Japan,* in Foreign Affairs, December, 1924. CHITOSHI YANAGA, *Japan Since Perry* (1949), ch. 14, 16. TAKATA YASUMA, *Conscription System in Japan* (1921).

Much material on the literature, art, religion, etc., of Japan may be found in the various volumes of *The Transactions of the Asiatic Society of Japan.* For periodical material, see *Readers Guide.*

CHAPTER XV

THE POLITICAL AND ECONOMIC PROGRESS OF JAPAN: 1895–1931

The consideration of the internal political history of Japan was interrupted at 1895 in order that the wars with China and Russia and their consequences might be fitted into the picture. It now becomes necessary to return to the point then reached, and outline internal developments after 1895, so that the international position and policies of Japan after 1905 may be adequately treated.

It will be remembered that the constitution was promulgated in 1889 and the new governmental system inaugurated in 1890. The new machinery was not designed to give control to the electorate, since the House of Representatives was denied the powers necessary to enable it to control the executive. Consequently the years from 1889 to 1894 were marked by a constant struggle between the clan leaders, entrenched in the Cabinet, and the parties, controlling the House of Representatives. The powers of the Diet proved extensive enough to enable the lower house to embarrass, but not to control, the government.

I. THE DEVELOPMENT OF PARTIES

The parties, led by Itagaki and Okuma, had been organized both as a means of carrying on the struggle against the control of the government by the Choshu and Satsuma clans and because of a desire to make the political system at least semi-popular in character. For a long time the parties were really personal followings of such men as Okuma and Itagaki, held together by the personality of the leader rather than by any common set of beliefs as to public policies. Both the Jiyuto (Liberal party), led by Count Itagaki, and the Kaishinto (Progressive party), organized by Count Okuma, professed to stand for the same things—the establishment of a constitution and of a representative system of government, with the abolition of clan control—and yet the two groups were unable to amalgamate until 1898, and then only temporarily, because they were factions organized around the personalities of two dominating individuals.

The establishment of the Diet afforded the party leaders a convenient center from which they could work toward the restriction of clan domination by the introduction of the principle of party control exerted through the representative branch of the government. From the first they indicated their intention to oppose a government which they could not control, in the hope that by such opposition they could force the acceptance of the principle that the Cabinet must be so constructed as to be able to secure a working majority in the House. By means of this systematic opposition, the House was able to bring about the downfall of successive ministries, but it was not able to determine their successors. The government, for its part, in its endeavor to break down the resistance of the forces opposed to it, resorted to successive dissolutions of the House. It also tried to control elections through manipulation of the election machinery. But no basis for compromise between the principles of party responsibility and non-responsible government could be found, since neither side was willing to give up its pretensions. Even Ito himself was unable to break down the opposition of the House, except by resort to the Imperial rescript. As a result of this situation, he utilized the Korean issue in 1894 as a means of rallying the nation to support of the government.

In this he was temporarily successful, but out of the war grew another conflict, this time within the oligarchy itself. From the time of the Restoration there had been two elements in the oligarchy with divergent views as to national policy. This divergence showed itself first in a definite way at the time of the Formosan difficulty, when the oligarchs split over the question of war or peace. The peace party, as has been related, gained the upper hand, which it retained until the time of the Sino-Japanese War. With that war the other party, led by Prince Yamagata, came into control, and from that time on, step by step, it pushed the Ito group into the background. Thus, while Ito brought party strife temporarily to an end by a resort to a foreign war, he raised a more formidable opposition to his dominance than that represented by the parties.

This militarist control was a logical outgrowth of the clan system of government. When the army was reorganized after the Restoration, and the navy brought into being, the two strongest of the clans monopolized the highest positions in those services. Satsuma went into the navy and Choshu into the army, which was organized on a national basis by Yamagata, a Choshu man. All of those in high rank, whether of his own clan or not, owed their positions to him and recognized him as their leader. Naturally both the army and navy men were interested in the development of their respective services. At first the army was considered to be more essential to the national protection and aggrandizement, and it consequently played the more important part in the struggles within the oligarchy.

Normally, the two protective services would be considered to exist for the purpose of giving effect to national policies as determined by the civilian branches of the government. Prince Yamagata, however, was a political as well as a military figure. He was consequently politically interested in the development of the army, and in its utilization for the carrying out of the dreams of the great pre-Restoration imperialist, Yoshida, whose pupil he had been. Adequate provision for this could not be made so long as the peace and internal progress faction in the oligarchy was in control of the policy-determining branches of the government. But in the midst of the war with China the Privy Council was persuaded to issue an ordinance providing that the Ministers of War and Marine must always be selected from high officers on the active list of the army and navy.[1] The consequence of this was that no Cabinet could be completed unless the Satsuma and Choshu military men, and this meant primarily Yamagata, were willing to support the Cabinet. Their support was usually conditioned on the willingness of the Cabinet to make adequate provision in its budget proposals for the expansion of the two forces, and thus on its acquiescence in a policy of expansion on the continent.

Ito was Premier in 1894, and the enthusiasm generated by the successful struggle against China, together with a virtual alliance with the Jiyuto, which was cemented by conferring the post of Minister of the Interior on Itagaki, enabled him to maintain himself for two years. He was succeeded by Count Matsukata (1896), in whose short-lived ministry Count Okuma was included "not as a leader of the Progressive Party, of course, but in order to separate him from his party." [2] Since this government was unable to control the Diet, Ito was again called upon to form a ministry.

By 1898 it had become clear that a severe struggle was going on within the oligarchy, as well as between the clan leaders and the parties. These two contests were merged when Ito suggested to the other clan leaders the formation of a government party, a proposal which was vetoed by Prince Yamagata. He, however, concurred in Ito's next proposal, which was that the party leaders should be invited to form a government since none of the clan leaders could command a majority in the House of Representatives. In retrospect, it appears that Yamagata's concurrence was dictated by his belief that a party government would be unsuccessful, and that in any case it could ultimately be controlled through the Ministries of War and Marine.

Consequently, in 1898, Okuma and Itagaki, who had amalgamated their following into a new party, the Kenseito, or Constitutional Party, were invited to form a government. This first so-called party government lasted only four months. From the first there was dissension between the two wings of the new party, principally over the distribution of the offices. The coalition had not been in existence long enough for the two elements to fuse, or to reach a completely satisfactory agreement as to program. The leaders were taken by surprise when invited to form a government, as it was probably intended that they should be, and the agreements reached

[1] This ordinance was modified in 1908 so that officers on the retired list might serve, but that did not deprive the army and navy of control. In any event the original provision was subsequently reinstituted.

[2] HORNBECK, Contemporary Politics in the Far East, p. 152.

were hastily concluded. The experiment proved premature, and left the clan leaders more securely entrenched in power than before.

After this demonstration of the futility of entrusting governing power to the parties, Prince (then Marquis) Yamagata consented to form a government which, while non-party from the standpoint of personnel, had a working arrangement with the Jiyuto. Thus the clan leaders were moving toward a recognition of the party while remaining unwilling to entrust it with power. This Yamagata ministry also represents the triumph of the military faction in the oligarchy.

It was clear that Ito was the only one strong enough to hope to oppose the entrenchment of the Yamagata faction in permanent control. He could do so, however, only provided he could find sources of strength outside the oligarchy. He frankly recognized this when, in 1900, he re-entered the arena as the organizer and recognized leader of a new party, which took the name Rikken Seiyukai (Constitutional Government Friend's Association). From the time of its organization it became the strongest single force in the Diet. At the same time the Progressive Party was reorganized, with Okuma still the leader, as the Kenseihonto. These developments left Yamagata without support in the Diet and forced him to retire from office. Ito, as his successor, found himself with adequate support in the House of Representatives, but confronted with the opposition of the House of Peers which, representative of the clan idea, resented the fact that Ito had gone over to the parties, and, under the direction of Yamagata, made war on him. Furthermore, Ito proved unsuccessful as a party leader. He alienated some of his supporters by his dictatorial methods, and others by his refusal to take care of his followers at the expense of the public services by allowing them to monopolize the offices. From this time it became apparent that the parties were more interested in the spoils of office than in controlling the government in the public interest.

In 1903 the leadership of the Seiyukai was turned over by Prince Ito to Prince Saionji, one of the Court nobility. The latter continued to serve as its leader until the end of the Meiji era. When the Ito ministry was overturned in 1901, a protégé of Prince Yamagata became Premier. The Elder Statesmen thereupon retired into the background, although continuing to dominate as the makers of ministries, since their advice was invariably sought, and followed, by the Emperor when it became necessary to select a new Premier, or to decide upon important departures in policy.

During the first decade of Japan's constitutional life the various parties had learned their lesson. They had found that opposition to the government deprived them of any share in the spoils of office, and they had learned that political activity was expensive, with its campaigns and canvassing, and its competitive buying of votes. Its expensiveness was decidedly enhanced by reason of the successive dissolutions, with the expenses of the election recurring not every four years, but sometimes every few months. Therefore, not being able to control the government and, consequently, to determine its constitution and the distribution of the spoils, the parties began to compete with one another for the privilege of an alliance with the government of the day in order that they might reap some of the rewards of political life and activity. This meant stagnation, as far as political progress was concerned, but it brought with it a comparative harmony in internal politics, which had been sadly lacking during the first decade after the promulgation of the constitution.

2. THE PARTIES AND THE GOVERNMENT—1901–1912

Count Katsura became Premier as the struggle against Russia reached its last peaceful stages. When the war broke out party strife again came to an end. This time, however, this merely meant that the opposition party ceased to oppose, for the Katsura government had enjoyed the support of the Seiyukai from the time of its organization. This condition continued to the death of the Emperor and the end of the Meiji era. Two men, Katsura and Saionji, alternated in the premiership from 1901 until 1912. Saionji, as the leader of the Seiyukai, was logically entitled to its support. It might, however, have been expected to oppose his rival, who was a bureaucrat opposed in principle to the parties. Nevertheless not logic but expediency prevailed, for Katsura enjoyed Seiyukai support equally with its leader. Nor was it always a loss of support in the Diet which caused one to retire in favor of the other. When one had enjoyed power for a considerable time the Diet was apt to become bored with his government. Furthermore, as the time for elections to the House of Representatives would approach, the interest of party members in support of the government would decline, its demands on it would become excessive, and then the Premier would retire. Still another and a more important factor in causing the resignation of the Premier was the difficulty of finding a solution for the financial problem. The end of the war with Russia left the nation saddled with a heavy debt, and with a mounting expenditure made necessary by the attempt to consolidate and extend the gains of the war and to promote internal development. Katsura retired in favor of Saionji in 1905, when peace approached, and left him to grapple with the financial problem. When Saionji failed to work it out, and as the people became increasingly restless under the heavy burden of taxation, Katsura resumed the helm in 1908, with a program of reform which failed to meet the situation. Saionji again tackled the problem in 1911, only to give way to Katsura in 1912. It may be noted here that the principal obstacle to a solution of the problem of balancing revenue and expenditure, and the thing which contributed most strongly to the overthrow of these several ministries, was the demand of the army, and particularly of the navy, for increased appropriations. An elaborate program of naval expansion, to be spread over a period of years, was proposed immediately after the war. Financial difficulties forced extension of the period, but the program remained, together with Prince Yamagata's insistence on its ultimate realization, to complicate the problem of finance.

3. RESUMPTION OF POLITICAL DEVELOPMENT

In 1912 [3] there began a new development which augured a renewal of the process of political evolution which had been checked by the long continued Seiyukai support of the government of the day. When Prince Katsura resigned in 1911 he announced the intention of retiring from the political arena. One explanation given at the time for his retirement was that he had grown restive under the dominance of Prince Yamagata, who remained as the power behind these alternating ministries. Furthermore, Yamagata had secured a post in the Imperial Household for him, and this automatically forced his withdrawal from politics. In 1912 the resignation of his successor precipitated a conflict among the Imperial advisers, as a result of which Katsura was enabled to emerge from his temporary obscurity and resume an active political life. His emergence carried with it a break with his former patron, Prince Yamagata, however, and led him to seek a new support, as had Ito before him, by the organization of a political party. Katsura's party, called the Doshikai, or Unionist Party, was recruited largely from the Kokuminto (Constitutional Nationalists), which name had been taken by the Progressives in 1910. The seceders were animated by the desire to participate in the spoils of office, long denied them as members of the party of opposition. The Kokuminto, with reduced strength, continued as an opposition party under the able leadership of Mr. Inagai. This raid on the Kokuminto netted for the new Doshikai only about seventy parliamentarians, and Katsura's attempt to add to this number from the ranks of the Seiyukai proved unsuccessful. Consequently, with no majority in the legislature, confronted with the opposition of the Seiyukai, unsupported by public opinion, and without substantial backing among the Elder Statesmen, the Katsura government fell. It carried with it Prince Saionji, however, for Katsura persuaded the Emperor to order Saionji to bring to an end his party's opposition to the Cabinet. This Saionji could not accomplish, and he therefore felt obliged to retire from politics, since he had been unable to carry the Emperor's will into effect.

The resignation of Katsura paved the way for another clan government, supported as in the past by the Seiyukai. Admiral Yamamoto, a Satsuma clansman, became Premier in 1913. The support of his Cabinet by the

[3] After the end of the Meiji era. The Emperor, Mutsuhito, died in 1912. His successor, Yoshihito, took the reign title of Taisho, meaning "Great Righteousness."

Seiyukai led to a revolt in the party which resulted in the formation of the Seiyu (Constitutionalists) Club, an organization consisting of the more idealistic members of the party. A naval scandal brought about the downfall of the Yamamoto government and, since none of the bureaucrats were able to form a cabinet, seemed to prepare the way for the introduction of party government.

Count Okuma, eighty years old, and "the man of all men in Japan who had consistently and indefatigably upheld and advanced the course of self-government," [4] accepted the premiership early in 1914. His program "emphasized economic reform, the eradication of corrupt practices, and the establishment of responsible government. Education should be fostered, peace maintained, productive enterprises advanced, and taxes reduced." [5] The Seiyukai refused to support Count Okuma's Cabinet, and he immediately dissolved the Diet and appealed to the country for support. For the first time since its formation, the Seiyukai found itself unable to command a majority in the House of Representatives. A new party formed by union of the Seiyu Club, the Doshikai, and a personal following of Count Okuma's, and taking the name of Kenseikai, became the majority party.

Since, with one exception to be noted later, the organization of the Kenseikai produced the last important change in the party system, at this point it will be well to describe briefly the major parties. After 1905, when the struggle to overthrow the clan system and to establish responsible government was given up for the time, a change in party objective became apparent. The tendency to struggle merely for participation in the spoils has already been referred to. But a more significant change was due to the development of modern industry, and the rise of a capitalist class whose interests needed to be protected. The Kokuminto early came to have a close relationship to the industrialists, a relationship which was taken over by the new Kenseikai after 1914. Consequently it stood for the reduction of the income and business tax, and in general for policies which would advance the interests of its constituents. In the field of foreign affairs, its policy was that of economic rather than territorial imperialism, as was well evidenced in the twenty-one demands served on China by Count Okuma's government. The Seiyukai had had much closer relations with the bureaucrats, and it participated in the benefits of their policy of expansion by force rather than by economic penetration, although after 1918 it also came to stand primarily for economic expansion. While not antagonistic to the industrial capitalists, its constituents were the large landowners and the commercial interests. Consequently, in the matter of taxation, it stood for the reduction of the land rather than the business tax. The Kokuminto, the weakest of the three, had a following in the industrial

[4] HORNBECK, op. cit., pp. 167–168.
[5] Ibid., p. 167.

centers. But as a party which had no hope of gaining the spoils of office, or of materially affecting public policy, "it can permit its principles to become slightly idealistic, and it talks about reducing the indirect taxes on consumption, which are paid by the non-voting masses." [6]

4. EFFECT OF THE WAR ON POLITICAL DEVELOPMENT

Count Okuma's pledges were never carried into effect. Before economic changes could be inaugurated or tax reduction considered, the European War broke out, and with Japanese participation, and subsequent develop ments, interest was shifted from internal conditions to foreign policy. This aspect of Okuma's ministry will be considered in another connection. Here it is sufficient to notice the fact that the most serious opposition which developed to his government was based on the claim that its foreign policy was not strong enough. It was overthrown in 1916, partly as a result of Prince Yamagata's opposition to its party character, as well as on account of its alleged failure to pursue a more vigorous continental policy.

Upon the recommendation of the Elder Statesmen, Count Terauchi, Yamagata's protégé, who had made his principal reputation as an iron-handed Governor-General of Korea, formed a non-party Cabinet supported in the Diet by the Seiyukai. He immediately dissolved the House and used the influence of officialdom against the Kenseikai candidates, with the result that it lost its control without, however, the Seiyukai securing an ab solute majority. Terauchi continued in control until 1918, when, due to the artificial raising of the cost of rice, there developed widespread dissatis faction, which found an outlet through riots in the industrial centers. Advantage was taken of this condition to procure the resignation of Count Terauchi.

He was succeeded by Mr. Hara, leader of the Seiyukai after the retirement of Prince Saionji, and the first commoner to assume the premiership. This elevation of a commoner was dictated by several considerations. In the first place, he was the recognized leader of a powerful party. In the second place, during 1917 and 1918 such great emphasis had been laid on the idea of democracy, as part of the war propaganda throughout the world, that it seemed fitting to show that Japan had accepted the new ideas. This was especially desirable because of the criticism which had been leveled against the militarism and clan government of Japan after 1914 in the Western world, and notably in the United States. And in the third place, there was no bureaucrat capable of forming a government.

The Diet was again dissolved in 1920 "on the avowed ground that he (Mr. Hara) considered it a public danger that the Kokuminto and the Kenseikai had introduced an universal suffrage bill into the Diet," [7] but in

[6] IWASAKI, *Working Forces in Japanese Politics*, p. 105.
[7] *Japan Year Book*, 1921–1922, p. 62.

reality to enable the Seiyukai to secure a stable majority. In this it was eminently successful, and consequently its power seemed secure for some time to come. Unfortunately Premier Hara was assassinated by a nationalist fanatic in 1921 while the Washington Conference was in session. His place was taken by Viscount Takahashi, who also succeeded to the leadership of the party. In 1922, however, there came a split in the Seiyukai over the Premier's policy of cabinet reconstruction. This resulted in the formation of a new party, the Seiyuhonto, and the overthrow of the government. The Elder Statesmen still living in 1922, Prince Saionji and Marquis Matsukata, dictated the choice of the new Premier. Admiral Kato, who had made a very favorable impression on the non-Japanese world as a member of the Japanese delegation at the Washington Conference, took office on a platform of complete fulfillment of the Washington agreements. While engaged in carrying out his pledges, Admiral Kato died on August 24, 1923. The great earthquake which came in September, 1923, and which resulted in such great losses, found Japan under a hastily formed transitional government headed by Admiral Yamamoto, which soon gave way to a more permanent non-party cabinet headed by Viscount Kiyouri. Thus for two years Japan was ruled by non-party governments, supported by the old government party but not founded on it.

It was not until after the elections of May, 1924, that a party government was again formed. In the elections the Kenseikai returned 151 members to the House, the Seiyuhonto 116, the Seiyukai 100, and the remainder were independents or members of unimportant factions. The leader of the Kenseikai, Viscount Kato, who had been the Foreign Minister in Count Okuma's 1914–1916 government, was invited to organize a Cabinet. He came into power on the basis of a coalition of the Kenseikai and the Seiyukai, produced out of the desire to overthrow the non-party Kiyouri Cabinet. With the attainment of the objective the coalition was disrupted and in 1925 the second Kato government, supported only by the Kenseikai, was formed. Kenseikai control lasted until 1927 when the government resigned because of Privy Council disapproval of its bill for the relief of the Bank of Taiwan. Baron Tanaka, a military man who had been made leader of the Seiyukai in the hope of strengthening it, was thereupon summoned to the premiership, holding his government together, in spite of the lack of a majority, until 1929.

When Tanaka finally resigned on account of growing dissatisfaction, he was succeeded by the head of the Minseito, a new party which had been formed in 1927 by an amalgamation of the Kenseikai and the Seiyuhonto. While the strongest single party in the house it did not have a majority at this time. This was secured, however, in the election of 1930 which gave the Minseito 273 seats to 174 for the Seiyukai. But in spite of its apparent strength the Minseito Cabinet was forced out of power at the end of 1931 because of dissatisfaction with its financial program and on account of the alleged weakness of its Manchurian policy following the Mukden incident of September 18, 1931. A Seiyukai ministry was then formed, headed by the veteran politician and former liberal Mr. Inukai, who had joined the party in 1925 and had succeeded Baron Tanaka as its President. Dissolution was resorted to in order to give the government a majority in the Diet, the general election of 1932 resulting in a return of 304 Seiyukai members as against 147 for the Minseito. The subsequent assassination of Premier Inukai brought about the institution of a non-party government supported by the Seiyukai but dominated by the Minister of War, General Araki.

This brief outline does not indicate that there had been much real political progress in Japan since 1895. The parties were largely opportunistic and followed individuals instead of developing competing programs designed to promote the general interest. Universal male suffrage was finally instituted in 1925, after a broadening of the franchise in 1900 and again in 1918–1919, but without any notable political consequences. Politics were, on the whole, conducted on a spoils basis, with the result that the parties and the Diet alike incurred a measure of popular opprobrium. Dissatisfaction with party government fitted in with a movement among the young men, especially in army circles, which looked toward the reëstablishment of bureaucratic government unhampered by parliamentary processes. It may also be noted that attempts were made to organize parties designed to speak for the proletarian and peasant interests, but without any great success.

5. ECONOMIC DEVELOPMENT

It had been in her economic life, however, that Japan had undergone the greatest changes since 1895. Here there had been much progress, if the development of a modern industrial system, the building-up of a great merchant marine, and a great expansion of foreign trade, may be considered indications of progress. Before the war with China, as has been pointed out in another connection,[8] there had been laid the foundations for the development of industry and commerce. Railways had been built; modern banks had been organized, and experimentation which finally led to the establishment of a satisfactory banking system was begun; the currency system had been reorganized and, shortly after the war, put on a gold basis; a modern postal system had been instituted; telegraphic and telephonic communication had been introduced; and a merchant marine, with the accompaniment of a ship-building industry, was in existence. Thus the basis for industrial development had been created. There had also taken place, largely under government auspices, some changes in the di-

[8] Chapter V, sec. 8.

rection of establishing a new industrial technique. But, on the whole, it may be said that it was only after 1895, and particularly after 1903, that Japan began to be transformed into an industrial nation, and that Osaka and other cities began to take on the appearance of, say, Birmingham or Fall River.

The wars in which modern Japan had been engaged before 1931 had had pronounced effects on her industrial progress. Each had resulted in an expansion of industry; each was followed by boom times, marked by much speculation, the temporary appearance of many new undertakings, and general over-expansion in industry; and each era of unlimited prosperity had been followed by a period of marked depression, carrying with it the collapse and disappearance of many of the unsubstantial prosperity-created undertakings. But the deflation of industry had invariably left Japan more distinctly industrialized than she had been before the war, and ready to begin a gradual progress on a more substantial basis.

A few figures will help us to visualize the economic development of Japan after 1895. Exports in 1885 were valued at slightly over 37 million yen, and imports at more than 29 million yen, making a total of 66.5 million yen. The war year (1894) saw this total increase to well over 230 million yen. The next war year (1904) found the total again increased to 690.5 million yen. The import trade of 1914 was valued at almost 596 million yen, while exports had increased to 991 millions. In 1919 the export total had risen to 2000 million yen, and the import total to slightly over 2000 million. The depression of 1920 and thereafter, together with similar conditions in Europe, immediately reduced the totals, which, however, by 1929 had surpassed those of 1919. Even when we make all necessary allowances for changes in price levels, and for fluctuations in exchange, these figures serve to indicate a tremendous expansion in trade.

An analysis of this trade reveals several significant facts. From 1882 to about 1894 there was an almost invariable excess of exports over imports, due largely to the fact that the Japanese people, agricultural in their interests, were still living the life of the past, and that need for Western commodities had not yet become strongly felt. After 1895, with but few variations, the excess lay on the side of imports—the so-called balance of trade remaining unfavorable to Japan until the outbreak of the European War, when the tables were again turned until after the end of that struggle. The depression followed the war, coupled with the return of her normal competitors to the trade arena, and the necessity for large imports to repair the damages of the great earthquake of 1923, again turned the balance against Japan.

A more significant conclusion that may be drawn from an analysis of the foreign trade is that its character gradually changed after 1895. Thus the imports came to be raw materials and partly finished commodities rather than finished manufactures, while the exports became finished or semi-finished industrial products. The nature and extent of the change as measured by the import and export trade are fairly represented by its distribution in 1919. Crude articles for food accounted for only 3.1 per cent of the exports but for 12 per cent of the imports; 4 per cent of the exports and 4.2 per cent of the imports were manufactured articles for food; raw materials other than food stuffs amounted to 5.2 per cent of the exports and 50.3 per cent of the imports; material for manufactures accounted for 43.2 per cent of the exports and 20 per cent of the total imports; and 43 per cent of the exports and only 12 per cent of the imports were finished goods. During the period of beginnings, from 1895 to the end of the Meiji era, when the balance of trade was consistently unfavorable, not only were many of the raw materials for industry imported, but machinery and industrial tools had to be purchased abroad, and the national industry was unable to meet the demand for manufactured goods. In the decade after 1914 all of that was changed, and Japan not only supplied most of her own industrial needs but also began to find a surplus for export.

Another way of illustrating this transformation of Japan into an industrial and capitalistic society is from the growth of the joint-stock form of enterprise. As late as 1905 there were only 83 joint-stock companies with a paid-up capital of a little over two million yen, as against 148 ordinary and limited partnerships with a paid-up capital of over 13 million yen; whereas in 1914 there were 198 joint-stock companies with a paid-up capital of almost 21 million yen, while the 293 partnerships had a capital of only six million yen.

Again, the number of machine looms in 1905 was only 19,040, as compared with almost 716,000 hand looms. By 1914 the number of machine looms had increased to almost 123,000, while there were less than 400,000 hand looms, indicating a substantial encroachment of the new on the old industry. This expansion was accelerated after 1914, and the expansion in that one industry may be taken as fairly typical of all others. The old, essentially esthetic, industries continued to exist by the side of the new large-scale production, but with a decreasing importance in the national economy. The tastes and habits of the Japanese, which disinclined them to the standardized product, undoubtedly helped to perpetuate the market for the goods of the hand-worker, but factory production rapidly developed an industrialized Japan.

It must be emphasized that the government took the initiative in the establishment of industries using modern machinery. Its interest was in releasing Japan from dependence on the West for the materials essential to every-day life, and in building up a substantial export trade. This led to an emphasis on utilitarian and large-scale production rather than the development of the esthetic and artistic native handicrafts. The new industry, consequently, paralleled that of the West. Without attempting an exhaustive enumeration, it may be pointed out that cotton and silk spinning and weaving, ship-building, match making, paper making, brewing and distilling, the manufacture of artificial fertilizers, and iron and steel works were among the more important modern industries. During and after the first World War there developed a chemical industry. In the modern industries the aim was standardization and large-scale production.

Electrical enterprise also became important in modern Japan. Electricity came to be used for lighting in all parts of the country, in addition to which it was used extensively in industry for motive power. The rapid-flowing streams were utilized to generate electricity, so that the current was cheap and power plentiful. No country has greater hydro-electrical possibilities than Japan. As it became fully developed, it partially compensated for the comparative inadequacy of her coal supply.

Prior to, and for a time after, the Russo-Japanese War the vogue of the West was so great in Japan that the native industries suffered an eclipse. At first they tried to adapt themselves by imitation and by acceptance of unfamiliar standards of artistry. The result was the creation of a hybrid which had no merit from the standpoint either of the West or of Japan. It was the foreigner who began to emphasize the esthetic values of the old Japanese handicrafts by his interest in them rather than in the Westernized product. Subsequently the Japanese themselves awakened to the possibilities of their native crafts, and Western influence came to be deprecated. This led to a revival of interest in essentially Japanese goods. The ceramic industry was one which had most strongly felt the Western influence but which soon began to revert to Japanese standards and patterns. The making of lacquer goods, of cloisonné, and of damascene ware was also rehabilitated in Japanese eyes. Silk production in the home, for the making of Japanese obi and other garments, without standardization of pattern, is another native enterprise which retained considerable importance. It must not be understood that these native industries ever disappeared or lost their economic importance, but only that they lost temporarily in popular esteem because they were non-Western, that they tried to lose their distinctive characteristics for a time, and that they then resumed their natural position.

6. EFFECTS OF INDUSTRIAL DEVELOPMENT

The introduction of the factory system into Japan strengthened the material foundations of the state, but it brought with it all of the evil conditions found in the industrial societies of the West. The industrial city, with its smoke-laden air and its crowded slums; the hordes of women and children driven from the home to work in the factory and the mine, instead of eking out the family income by working at home in a leisurely fashion at one of the handicrafts; the divorce of the workman from ownership of the tools of the trade; the submergence of the artisan in the wage-earner who performs one routine operation hour after hour; growing inequalities of wealth, without the maintenance, in the industrial centers, of the feudal-family tradition of mutual aid; the development of group and class antagonisms—all of these features of industrialism rapidly became characteristic of modern Japan.

These changes came so rapidly that no attempt was made, for a time, to grapple with the problems they created. As a matter of fact, the leaders, as well as the great majority of the enfranchised people, at first remained indifferent to them, and as a capitalist class developed it attained sufficient power, in union with the political parties, to prevent consideration of proposals for the amelioration of the condition of the workers. At the same time, the old nobility and the landed gentry felt no responsibility for conditions and consequently overlooked them. The first proposals for factory legislation were made in 1897, but it was not until 1911 that a measure was finally enacted, and not until 1916 that this measure was put into force. The law was significant because of the fact of its enactment rather than on account of the advanced character of its provisions. The act applied only to factories employing fifteen or more workers and to certain dangerous industries regardless of the number employed in the establishment. Employment of children under twelve was prohibited, subject to certain exceptions. The maximum number of hours of work for women and children under fifteen was fixed at twelve, but again subject to exceptions under which, in certain cases, a fourteen-hour employment was permissible. And two rest days a month were required. But, on the whole, the provisions of the law were based upon existing practice, and thus the minimum standards established were low and so many exceptions from the operation of the act were provided that its application was made almost farcical. The amendment of the act in 1923, effective in 1926, and a further amendment in 1929 finally brought within its control all factories using power-driven machinery. The amendments were also designed to make Japanese labor conditions, from the standpoint of hours of work, approximate more closely to the international standards accepted in the International Labor Convention of 1919.

A plentiful labor supply due to her expanding population, to the attraction of city life for the rural laborer, and to the constant recruiting of young women for industrial service, meant that wages were low in Japan until after 1914, and notably until 1918, when the tremendous overnight expansion of industry, with its boom times and its apparently unlimited demand for workers, brought about rapid wage increases. These, however, were virtually absorbed by the mounting cost of living, and by an increased consumption consequent on the new prosperity. And it was a question whether the new wage levels could be maintained after the war. The demand for raw and finished silk in the United States was one large factor in producing this post-war boom; another factor was the artificial maintenance of high prices in the cotton industry through agreements among the brokers. The boom collapsed in 1920, however, just as similar periods of prosperity, marked by speculation, over-expansion, and over-capitalization, following the wars with China and Russia, came to an end.

The immediate cause of the slump was the refusal of the Bank of Japan to continue to loan to private banks, and its further action in calling in all loans due and payable. But by 1920 the American demand for raw silk had been curtailed, shipping had suffered severe setbacks as a consequence of the end of the war monopoly of the Pacific carrying trade, and the China demand for Japanese cotton goods was lessened as a consequence of the boycott instituted when the decisions of the Paris Conference as to Shantung were made known in China. And, in any case, over-expansion ultimately brings its own penalties. This depression continued through the period of the Washington Conference, and one difficulty faced by the government was that of preventing further dislocation of industry as a result of the fulfillment of the pledges which made it impossible to carry out the already accepted program of capital ship construction. Partly to avoid throwing men in the shipyards out of work, a new program involving construction of cruisers was proposed. The repairing of the damage done by the great earthquake also quickened the stagnant industrial life.

It should be pointed out here that the problem of living had been greatly complicated for the people by reason of the heavy burden of taxation which they had to bear during the first three decades of the twentieth century. Public expenditure increased, from 1902 to 1914, from almost 300 million to about 550 million yen. After the entrance of Japan into the war, her expenditure mounted rapidly until the budget totals ran well over a billion yen. This was due in large part to her continental adventures, and to the expenditures made necessary by the military and naval program accepted in 1916 and revised in 1920, although general administrative expenditures also increased. During the same period, 1902–1914, the national debt increased from 500 million to 2500 million yen. The war with Russia was largely instrumental in bringing about this increase, but borrowings for railway development, after the railways were nationalized in 1906, and for the promotion of Japanese interests in Manchuria, materially helped to swell the total. This was further increased after 1914. As an offset to the latter, must be put the loans made by Japan to China from 1914–1918, many of which were political, and upon which payments both of interest and of principal were in arrears.

Every possible expedient was resorted to in order that these heavy charges might be carried. For example, the government instituted a tobacco, a camphor, and a salt monopoly for fiscal reasons, the first two following the war with China, the camphor monopoly also being designed to foster that industry in Formosa, and the third during the war with Russia. But nothing could avail to keep taxes from constant increase, so that, taking into account various luxury taxes, registration fees, and land, income, business, and inheritance taxes, the burden on the individual became very great. To these, of course, must be added the levies for local purposes. Thus, in the last analysis, it was not alone industrialization which made the poor grow poorer, even though that was responsible for the widening of the gap between the poor and the rich.

7. LABOR PROBLEMS

Before turning from this general question of economic conditions in modern Japan, we should say a word about the development of labor organizations. What amounted to a ban on the creation, or at least the effective utilization, of labor organizations was a clause in the "Peace Regulations" promulgated in 1900 which read: "Those who, with the object of causing a strike, seduce or incite others shall be sentenced to major imprisonment of one to six months with additional penalty of y 3 to 30." This virtually condemned labor organizations to serve merely as benevolent and social agencies. In spite of this, however, organization began shortly thereafter, although the various organizations changed so much from time to time that it was impossible to estimate their strength. In 1912 the Japanese Federation of Labor was established. After its reorganization in 1920 by Mr. Bunji Suzuki, it claimed an enrollment of about fifty thousand members, who, however, did not reach the point where they had sufficiently defined views to enable them to act unitedly. The position of this and other similar organizations was improved when the ban on them was partially lifted in 1919.

During the era of war and post-war prosperity, strikes multiplied in Japan, in spite of the lack of well-developed labor organizations. The principal reason for most of the strikes, several of which attained considerable dimensions, was an unsatisfactory wage scale. While the depression after 1920 lessened the amount of labor agitation, friction between capital and labor, in industry as well as in agriculture, subsequently increased, without satisfactory ameliorative measures being introduced. This was a factor in developing popular support for the Army program after 1931.

8. THE POPULATION PROBLEM

Industrial development made many Japanese wealthy, and undoubtedly added to the ability of the state to carry heavy financial burdens, since it added to the taxable wealth. That it did not more successfully raise the standard of living for the masses was due partly to the usual absorption of the largest share of the benefits by a comparatively small number of people; but fundamentally it was due to the great increase in population since the Restoration. Before 1867 the population had remained fairly stationary at about 30 millions. In 1913 the official estimate placed it at a little over 53 millions, and by 1920 it had increased to almost 56 millions. By 1931 it stood at around 70 millions. Better sanitary equipment and arrangements and modern medical methods conspired to reduce the death rate, while the birth rate underwent no decline. Thirty millions could be supported by the agriculture of pre-modern Japan only at a comparatively low standard of living. If the population had continued stationary, however, improvements in transportation and in agricultural methods, together with the cultivation of new lands and the more scientific utilization of the wealth in timber, would have materially aided in improving the living conditions of the people even though there had been no great development in industry. But the agricultural resources of Japan were not sufficient to take care of the great increase in population which had come after 1867, even when those resources were more fully and economically utilized than they were even by 1931, particularly if the island of Hokkaido is taken into account. Consequently, after 1905, when the industrial transformation really began on a large scale, the interest of Japan was increasingly manifested in securing the industrial foundations of the state. These interests, from one point of view lay in gaining control of adequate supplies of coal, iron, and petroleum, among the sub-soil products; in creating a source of supply of her own of raw cotton; and in enlarging her controlled supply of food products to take care of the needs of her industrial and commercial population, which obviously could not supply its own wants. Japan's continental Asiatic policy after 1905, and especially after 1914, indicated this changing interest, as will be subsequently revealed. [9]

From another point of view, the industrial state is actively interested in securing markets for its goods and, as far as possible, in establishing itself in those markets on a monopolistic or at least a preferential basis. While Japan held a satisfactory position in the West for her silks and teas, her textile industry was primarily interested, of necessity, in the China market, to which it sent its yarns as well as cotton piecegoods. Even before the war of 1914–1918 Japan had made remarkable gains in the China trade. After it she reached the point where her competition seriously threatened British trade supremacy. Her favorable location and the early growth of her production made it possible for Japan to become the dominant factor in continental markets, except as China and India industrialized. The antagonism resulting from Japan's foreign policy also jeopardized her trade position in China. Nevertheless, as one writer put it as early as 1912, "The

[9] See especially chapter XVI.

Western countries having given to Japan their industries will see the fruits of these industries passed on to China." [10]

Industry, then, enabled the Japanese to take care of their population expansion after 1905 without a lowering of the standard of living, but this expansion was so rapid that industrialization did not materially elevate the standard. It did, however, decidedly influence the development of Japan's foreign policy.

Another method of taking care of an expansive population is by means of colonization. While Korea and Formosa and a foothold in Manchuria were not acquired with a view to utilizing them as areas for colonization, an interest in Manchuria for such purposes might well be alleged, as it was repeatedly between 1915 and 1931. But the Japanese were not especially successful as colonizers. In Korea they were successful organizers and exploiters, but they did not settle there in any large numbers in spite of organized efforts in the direction of colonization; and, as a matter of fact, the comparatively large Korean population, in any case, had first claims on the land. Formosa might have taken care of Japanese settlers, but the pioneer nature of the work to be done there did not prove attractive to Japanese. There, as in Korea, they came as officials, as exploiters and as shopkeepers, but not as colonizers. The same thing was true of Manchuria, where the Chinese, rather than the Japanese, took possession of, and maintained themselves successfully on, the soil.

More Japanese agricultural laborers were attracted to Hawaii and continental America than to eastern regions, perhaps partly because the pioneer work had already been done. According to Japanese figures, by 1920 there were about 350,000 Japanese in China, including Manchuria and Hongkong; only about 18,000 in Singapore, the Malay Peninsula, Java, Sumatra, the Philippines, and other South Sea territories; 100,000 in Hawaii, constituting approximately half of the total population; about 90,000 in the United States, an underestimate according to some American figures; 14,-000 in Canada; 43,000 in Latin-America; and about 12,000 in Australasia. These emigrants contributed materially to the development of the regions to which they went in large numbers, but in North America and Australasia, as the number increased, the hostility which the Chinese settler had encountered earlier manifested itself and led to the enactment of exclusion measures, notably by the United States and Australia. These measures, together with others discriminating against Japanese already in this country, served to embitter the Japanese, as well as to close an outlet for Japan's surplus population. Since, however, this entered into her foreign policy rather than her internal arrangements, its more detailed consideration must be postponed to a later chapter.[11]

[10] LAWTON, *Empires of the Far East*, vol. 2, p. 926.
[11] Chapter XVI, sec. 3.

9. AGRICULTURAL LIFE

Thus far our discussion of the economic life of Japan has been concerned with industry. But that must not lead us to the conclusion that agriculture was of relatively little importance. The reverse is true, and because of its importance we can best conclude this chapter with a consideration of Japanese agriculture from the economic standpoint.

Agriculture in Japan has always been, and still is largely, synonymous with the cultivation of rice. Barley, wheat, and some legumes are grown, but rice is the staple both of cultivation and of diet. In 1919 there were 3,104,611 chō of land devoted to rice, and only 1,729,148 to barley and wheat. The production of rice, 60,818,000 koku, was much greater than the combined total production of wheat and barley. The rice grown was virtually all consumed at home, and was considered by the people to be much superior to that grown elsewhere and imported into the country.[12]

The holdings of land had always been small, and farming was very intensive. The average holding was only about two and one-half acres per family. Prior to the Restoration, the farmer held his land as a tenant of the samurai or Daimyō. Subsequently, with the abolition of feudalism, he was confirmed in the ownership of the land which he worked. From this basis of a land-owning peasantry the general movement, particularly in the last twenty-five years, had been toward an increase in tenantry. This was partly due to the attempts of the more prosperous and far-sighted farmers to increase the size of their holdings.

Some 34 per cent of the farmers are land-owners; about 40 per cent are owners and tenants; and about 28 per cent are tenants only. . . . But an unwholesome feature of recent years is that the number of landlords is decreasing, while the number of tenants is fast increasing. In 1919, for example, there were 30,500 fewer landlords and 25,163 more tenants than in 1914. . . . So that while many have lost their land, others have added field to field and become independent landlords, a class prone to be more parasitic in Japan than in Western countries. If the process continues it will very adversely affect the situation, for extension of tenancy always deprives the Japanese farmer of independence and incentive.[13]

In addition to this, the increase in tenantry maximized the consequences of friction between landlords and tenants. With a rise in the cost of living such as came after 1914, the tenant's problem of livelihood became more acute, and antagonism to the landlord developed. On the other hand, the landless man was more readily attracted into the factory town. This might be an advantage to industry, but it was not necessarily a good thing for the nation, and the competition with industry made it more difficult

[12] The largest export, that of 1917, was only 769,129 koku. Imports in the last fifteen years have varied from the 309,158 koku of 1916 to the 4,647,168 koku of 1918. J. W. ROBERTSON-SCOTT, *Foundations of Japan*, p. 388.

[13] BRYAN, *Japan from Within*, pp. 118-119.

for the landlord to secure and hold his tenants. While the tendency toward increased tenancy had to be deplored, the increase in the size of the holdings, together with consolidation and redistribution of individual properties, was of advantage in that it helped to increase productivity with the same application of energy. It also made possible, to a limited extent, the introduction of new methods and tools. The problem, then, was to eliminate the evils of the situation while making the most of its possibilities for good.

Every year additional land was brought under cultivation. From 1905 to 1934, the total cultivated land was increased from 5,382,378 to 6,037,645 chō. The percentage of cultivated to uncultivated land in 1909 was 14.6 per cent, while in 1934 it was 15 per cent. This must not be taken to mean that there were large areas which in the future could be brought under cultivation. It must be remembered that the islands are of volcanic origin, and are extensively broken up by mountain ranges and formations. The nature of the country, from the agricultural standpoint, is further indicated in the fact that there are fifty intermittently active volcanoes and about a thousand hot springs. Consequently the inhabitable and cultivable area will remain small in relation to the total area. As it was, the mountainsides were being farmed to an almost incredible extent. It was thus partly the character of the country which made certain the maintenance of comparatively small holdings of land.

While there was a slight increase in the area cultivated, there was a much greater increase in the yield, particularly of rice. The rice production in 1882 of 10,692,000 koku may be compared with that of 1913, 50,222,000, and of 1928, 60,303,000 koku.[14] This represented a seventy-five per cent increase of yield per chō or unit of land. During this same period the population increased only fifty-five per cent. The additional rice production, together with normal rice importations, indicated an increased per capita consumption and, consequently, a somewhat higher standard of living, notably among the upper classes. If, however, the population continued to increase as rapidly as in the past, it would not be many years before the increase in agricultural production would be outstripped by the growth of population. That would make Japan dependent on the outside world for her food supply, as she had by 1933 become for part of the raw materials for her industry.

This increased yield was partly due, as has just been noted, to an increase in the area under cultivation. More largely, however, it was the result of paddy adjustment, which made possible better irrigation; of more scientific manuring; of the use of improved implements; and of animal and mechanical power, where that was possible; of more careful seed selection

---

[14] This increase continued, with fluctuations until 1934, the largest production, that of 1933, being 70,829,117 koku. For figures see *Japan-Manchoukuo Year Book*, 1937, p. 366.

and a wider use of better seeds; of afforestation to prevent floods; and of the development of better rural loan facilities.

As was the case in other fields of development, the government played an important part in promoting agricultural progress. It established schools for the training of agriculturalists, and introduced agricultural studies in the curricula of the lower schools. It established and maintained experiment stations, which studied some of the technical problems of the farmer and made the results available to him, encouraging him, in turn, to experiment. It aided and fostered secondary rural production, such as sericulture and horticulture, though it did this, apparently, not so much because of an interest in rural development as because of a desire to promote industry and to create an export surplus. It sent lecturers on agricultural questions throughout the country. And it was instrumental in improving communications.

That more was not done was due to the lack of funds for these purposes. "I have been assured again and again by prefectural governors and agricultural experts—and in talking to a foreigner they would hardly be likely to exaggerate—that considered plans for the prevention of disastrous floods, for the breaking-up of new lands, for the provision of loans and for the development of public intelligence and well-being were hindered in their case by lack of money alone." [15] This lack of funds for development purposes, it may be noted, was due primarily to the excessive proportions of the national income which were devoted to the army and navy, and to the payments on the debt incurred as a result of successive wars. This, however, was true of other countries as well as Japan.

The principal secondary types of rural production were tea cultivation, sericulture, horticulture, tree and plant dwarfing and shaping, and animal husbandry. In some prefectures, tea cultivation and sericulture should perhaps be classed as primary rather than secondary pursuits, but for the country as a whole the former classification is sounder. Tea was grown throughout all but the northernmost prefectures, but the individual areas were small, and in most places the cultivation was carried on as a side line. Furthermore, the preparation of the tea for market in many instances was accomplished by hand rather than by machinery.

The importance of tea cultivation was indicated by the fact that in 1931 38,109 chō were devoted to it, and that there were 1,126,318 tea factories, including those attached to households. The total production in 1919 was valued at about 34 million yen, and tea to the value of about 18.5 million yen was exported every year. Most of the exported tea went to the United States and some to Canada. The exportation to the former country was decreasing—from 50,000 tons in 1918 to 23,000 in 1920. This was partly due

[15] ROBERTSON-SCOTT, *Foundations of Japan*, p. 370.

to increased consumption at home, but it was more adequately explained by the fact of an increased use of black teas by Americans.

The silkworm and cocoon production of Japan had an annual value of over 170 million yen. "One acre in every dozen in Japan produces mulberry leaves for feeding the silk-worms which two million farming families—more than a third of the farming families of the country—painstakingly rear." [16] These statements indicate the importance to the farmer of the production of raw silk. It lent itself admirably to service as a supplementary activity to crop farming, since the worm could be attended by girls and women, and since the rearing season was a restricted time in the spring and autumn.

Japanese silk exportation became twice that of China, her closest competitor, whom she passed in 1910. The production was three times that of Italy, and much greater than that of France. This was made possible by the abundance of mulberry leaves in Japan, which served to compensate for the atmospheric and climatic handicaps from which, in comparison with her competitors, she suffered. For a long time the bulk of the raw silk —seventy-five per cent—was exported, but as the number of factories increased, Japan steadily increased the proportion of the raw product transformed at home. This particular rural activity served as the foundation of a most important national industry.

As the domestic demand for raw silk increased, greater attention was paid to its production, with the consequence that in some regions the tendency was to make it a primary rather than a secondary activity. As supplementary to cultivation it was most important in adding to the income of the farmer, and thus in making him more prosperous. If he devoted himself to it exclusively, however, it might have directly contrary consequences, especially as he would become dependent on the condition of a world market, and on an industry in the control of which he could only indirectly share.

The income of many rural communities was further augmented from the fisheries. About a million and a half persons engaged in the fishing industry, and the *per capita* catch, in terms of the total population, averaged in annual value about seventy yen. This activity was among those encouraged by the government, which made scientific investigations, and stimulated the manufacture of marine products. It also interested itself in securing, or attempting to secure, fishing rights for Japanese along the coast and in the inland waters of Siberia. By 1933, deep-sea fishing as an industry had been transformed into at least a semi-capitalistic business.

The attempts to interest the farmer in stock-raising were comparatively unsuccessful outside of Hokkaido. There the government maintained a

[16] Ibid., p. 153.

stock farm, which was used to produce animals mainly for military uses. There was also some private stock-raising. But with an increase in the demand for dairy products and for meat, due to changes in the diet of the people, increased activity seemed to be imminent. Lack of adequate and suitable pasturage, however, will probably check the growth of animal husbandry before it assumes a great importance to the rural communities.

The contrary was the case with horticulture, and the growing of vegetables. The two combined yielded an annual production valued at two hundred million yen. Not only were the number and variety of fruit-bearing trees increased, but the fruit itself in some cases was much improved by experimentation.

By these and other activities supplementary to his fundamental rice and grain cultivation, the Japanese farmer added to his income and found it possible to live on his small allotment of land. Only to the extent to which these supplemental types of production were developed did he have more than a bare subsistence. The number of days of labor on the land averaged between 150 and 200, the latter a maximum estimate, for the year. Thus it is apparent that the farmer and the members of his household had surplus time which could be devoted to productive subsidiary pursuits without neglect of the main occupation or undue prolongation of the working day. What was necessary was to find the most profitable between-seasons occupations, and to encourage him to develop them even beyond the point reached up to 1933.

Before leaving the subject of agriculture a few words should be added concerning the development of Hokkaido. The rigorous climate of that island retarded its natural settlement and development by the Japanese, both because of their natural antipathy to the cold climate, and by reason of the fact that the manner of living in Japan did not teach the people how to meet the cold. The poor people who constituted the group naturally drawn out of the main islands, even though they had by knowledge, or adaptive ability, been equipped to deal with the changed conditions of life, did not have the capital to build houses with well-fitted and glassed windows and to equip them with suitable stoves. The nature of the country also required a break with traditional methods of cultivation. This militated against its rapid settlement. Again, "an undoubted hindrance to the colonization of Hokkaido has been scandals and land grabbing." Some of the scandals resulted in the overturning of governments. "Many of what the late Lord Salisbury called the 'best bits' are in the hands of big proprietors or proprietaries. Some large landowners no doubt show public spirit, but their class has contrived to keep farmers from getting access to a good deal of land which, because of its quality and nearness to practicable roads and the railway, might have been worked to the best advantage." [17] The re-

[17] ROBERTSON-SCOTT, op. cit., p. 359.

sult was that tenants, rather than freeholders, were sought and that many emigrants returned to their homes dissatisfied with their venture.

Much more might have been done to stimulate emigration to Hokkaido than was actually undertaken. The beginnings made during the last quarter of the nineteenth century were not progressively built upon, largely because of the increasingly heavy expenditure for other purposes after Japan became a World Power. More highways and railroads were needed. Capital needed to be made available on easy terms to prospective settlers, and the land policy needed to be so revised as to discourage landlordism.

It should not, however, be inferred that no progress took place in Hokkaido. A railway was built. Flour mills, breweries, beet-sugar factories, canning plants, and other enterprises sprang up. A university, begun as an agricultural college, played an important part in the life of the country. One might also mention stock raising for milk purposes and the establishment of enterprises for milk condensation. All of these represented developments begun at a comparatively early time.

There was room for much further development, as has been pointed out. In Hokkaido there was an area capable of absorbing a part of Japan's surplus population. So long, however, as the Japanese refused to emigrate to Hokkaido on any large scale, the non-Japanese world was certain to question the existence of an acute population problem. That the problem existed might be granted readily enough, but it might be a matter for question whether the right methods were being used for its solution.

For five years in succession Tokyo had cut down the Hokkaido budget. Necessary public work and schemes for development have been repeatedly stopped. At a time when the interests of Hokkaido demand more farmers and there is a general complaint of lack of labor, at a time when there are persistent pleas for overseas expansion, there are in Japan twice or thrice as many people applying for land in the island as are granted entry. [18]

Thus consideration of the agricultural aspects of the population problem, as well as its industrial aspects, brings us back to the question of foreign policy, which must be considered as a primary interest of modern Japan.

REFERENCES FOR FURTHER STUDY

G. H. BLAKESLEE (ed.), *Japan and Japanese-American Relations* (1912). E. W. CLEMENT, *Handbook of Modern Japan* (1905); by a competent student. K. W. COLEGROVE, *Militarism in Japan* (1936); an excellent brief study. *Department of Finance, Financial and Economic Annual,* yearly after 1900. W. R. CROCKER, *Japanese Population Problem* (1931). HONJO ELIJIRO, *Social and Economic History of Japan* (1935). J. H. GUBBINS, *Making of Modern Japan* (1922), ch. 9, 14, 18–20; by a leading authority. S. L. GULICK, *Evolution of the Japanese, Social and Psychic* (1903); an unusual approach. A. S. and SUSAN

[18] *Ibid.*, pp. 359–360.

HERSHEY, *Modern Japan, Social, Industrial, Political* (1919); contains much interesting material. A. E. HINDMARSH, *The Basis of Japanese Foreign Policy* (1936); a good analysis of the economic basis. NOBUTAKA IKE, *Beginnings of Political Democracy in Japan* (1950). ROYOICHI ISHÜ, *Population Pressure and Economic Life in Japan* (1936). U. IWASAKI, *Working Forces in Japanese Politics* (1921), in Columbia University Studies, vol. 97, no. 1; an important study. *Japanese Commission to the Louisiana Purchase Exposition, Japan in the Beginning of the Twentieth Century* (1904). N. KITAZAWA, *The Government of Japan* (1929). L. LAWTON, *Empires of the Far East,* 2 vols. (1912); vol. 1, books 4-5; well worth consulting; suggestive and informative. J. H. LONGFORD, *Japan* (1923), sec. A, ch. 15-19; sec. B, ch. 1-5; a book by an informed Englishman with a pronounced admiration for Japan. W. M. McGOVERN, *Modern Japan, Its Political, Military, and Industrial Organization* (1920); subtitle indicates its scope; one of the best brief studies. W. W. McLAREN, *Political History of Japan* (1916), ch. 11-15; the best single volume on political history of Meiji period. T. MIYAOKA, *Growth of Liberalism in Japan* (1918); two addresses on the subject. HAROLD G. MOULTON, *Japan, An Economic and Financial Appraisal* (1931); a very careful and authoritative study. COUNT S. OKUMA (ed.), *Fifty Years of Modern Japan,* 2 vols. (1909); chapters on the various topics written by recognized Japanese authorities. JOHN E. ORCHARD, *Japan's Economic Position, the Progress of Industrialization* (1930); an excellent treatment. R. P. PORTER, *Japan, the New World Power* (1915), ch. 7-37. HAROLD S. QUIGLEY, *Japanese Government and Politics* (1932); the most complete and best treatment of the subject. R. K. REISCHAUER, *Japan: Government and Politics* (1939); a penetrating study. ROBERT SCALIPINO, *Democracy and the Party Movement in Prewar Japan* (1953). CHITOSHI YANAGA, *Japan Since Perry* (1949), ch. 15, 16, 17, 22. TAKEKOSHI YOSABURO, *The Economic Aspects of the History of the Civilization of Japan* (1930), 3 vols.

CHAPTER XVI

THE ASSERTION OF JAPANESE HEGEMONY IN
THE FAR EAST: 1905–1918

A NEW level of Japanese power in eastern Asia had been reached in 1917–1918. The first World War had enabled Japan to change from a borrowing to a lending nation, from a state with a constantly adverse trade balance to one with a favorable balance; from a nation with inadequate gold reserves to one with a large gold surplus. It had also enabled her to give free play to any continental aspirations which she had, without fear of foreign interference. But it was because the necessary preliminary steps had been taken that Japan was able to utilize the opportunity presented to her by the war. It was because she had already introduced modern methods of production that she was able to enlarge her markets, and it was as a result of the earlier efforts to build up a merchant marine that Japanese shipping was able to monopolize the Pacific carrying trade. It was also because the spade-work had already been done that Japan was enabled to attain at least a temporary hegemony in the Far East.

I. JAPANESE DEPENDENCIES: FORMOSA AND KOREA

In order to complete the picture of Japan of World War I days, therefore, it is necessary to broaden the view from the Japanese State to the Japanese Empire. This involves, first, a consideration of the dependencies, Formosa and Korea; second, an estimation of Japanese activities and interests in Manchuria from 1905 to 1914; and third, an analysis of the China policy of the Japanese government from 1914 to 1918.

Space precludes an extensive consideration of Formosa, the southern outpost of the Empire. It had the advantage of commanding access to the waters and the coast of China north of Fukien province, and its possession enabled Japan to assert a special interest in that province. It was of interest to Japanese otherwise because it was acquired as a result of the country's first successful war in modern times, and also because it was a financial burden, for large sums had to be devoted to the subjugation of the aborigines in the uplands, a task which had not been completed by 1914. The numerous public works undertaken, such as highway and railroad building, harbor improvement, etc., together with the establishment of schools, added to the burden until the war period, when the administration became nearly self-supporting. From the economic standpoint the island furnished opium, salt, camphor, a little tobacco, all then controlled by government monopoly; tea, with sugar the largest item of export; fish and other marine products to the value of six and a half million yen; some coal and gold, and a little petroleum. The commerce of the island was mostly with Japan, China and the United States ranking a bad second and third in the trade. As has already been pointed out, Formosa did not attract Japanese settlers in large numbers, in spite of some efforts at colonization, for as late as 1925 there were only slightly over 187,000 Japanese in the island.

Korea, renamed Chosen after its annexation, deserves, as the major dependency of Japan, more extensive consideration. The changes in its status up to 1905 have previously been indicated.[1] The Chinese connection was finally broken off in 1895, from which time Russia and Japan struggled for supremacy. As one of the preliminaries to the final contest the first Anglo-Japanese agreement was negotiated in 1902. This was founded, among other things, on a recognition of the independence of Korea, with, however, a recognition as well of Japan's peculiar political as well as her commercial and industrial interests in the peninsula. The revised agreement of 1905 provided that "Japan, possessing paramount political, military, and economic interests in Korea, Great Britain recognizes the right of Japan to take such measures of guidance, control, and protection in Korea as she may deem proper and necessary to safeguard and advance these interests, provided always that such measures are not contrary to the principle of equal opportunities for the commerce and industry of all nations."[2] Following the war a protectorate was established, Prince Ito becoming the first Resident-General. This status was maintained until 1910, when a treaty of annexation was concluded between the Korean ruler and the Japanese Emperor, represented by General Terauchi, the Japanese Resident. Incorporation into the Japanese Empire, of course, ended for the time being the international personality of Korea. One consequence of the international acceptance of this change was the termination of foreign governmental intrigue in the country, although, from time to time, accusations were brought against American missionaries that they were preaching seditious doctrines in their schools, and as late as 1920 a British subject, resident at Antung, was arrested when in Korea "because he had long been a suspect as abettor and friend of the Korean independence agitators."[3] Internal turmoil, moreover, except for the independence movement, ceased.

In a brief estimation of the condition of Korea under Japanese rule, such

[1] Chapters VI and VIII.
[2] Article 3 from text as given in *Japan Year Book*, 1915, p. 570.
[3] *Japan Year Book*, 1921–1922, pp. 590–591.

as alone is possible here, it is difficult to do justice to the question. Certain things seem to be clear, however, and they may be stated in a summary way, leaving out of consideration more controverted matters. It is clear that the material condition of the country was greatly improved. As in Formosa, roads were improved and railroads built; harbors were improved; electric lighting, introduced into Seoul, was extended to other cities; lands were reclaimed and the agricultural system improved; better sanitary methods were introduced; a modern banking system was instituted; industry was promoted; and the export and import trade was expanded.

From the expansion of trade Japan naturally gained the greatest advantage. Of the exports in 1929 over three hundred million yen went to Japan, over thirty million to China, and smaller amounts to Asiatic Russia, the United States and others. Similarly, more than three hundred million yen of the imports came from Japan and seventy million from China, with the United States a poor third in the import trade. Thus almost ninety per cent of the total trade came to be with Japan.[4] In the internal development of the country the predominance of Japanese interest was even more marked. It was only in the gold mining industry that non-Japanese interests were able for a time to retain a foothold. This also was natural, although foreign capital would undoubtedly have participated more largely in the development of an independent Korea. But in the field of trade the Japanese predominance was due primarily to her need for Korean products and her ability to supply Korean needs, coupled with the natural advantage of geographical proximity; and only secondarily to a deliberate attempt to monopolize Korean trade.

It may also be pointed out that Japan gave Korea a far better government than the Koreans had shown any ability or desire to give themselves, even though that government was military in character and controlled from Tokyo. As a result of the agitation of 1919 the administration was reorganized in 1920, becoming somewhat more liberal in its national character. The reorganization provided for the abolition of certain notorious abuses, such as flogging and discrimination in salary between Japanese and Koreans holding the same rank, and moved a step toward the introduction of local self-government.

But it must also be noted that Japanese actions were motivated by the desire to make the area of greater value to Japan rather than by an interest in improving the condition of the Korean people. This is not to deny that the Koreans materially benefited by many of the improvements made. But, on the other side, it must be recognized that the forcible introduction of the Japanese language at the expense of the Korean; the suppression of the Korean literature and of Korean institutions; the expropriation and sale,

---

[4] The same relative position was maintained through the 1930's. See later editions of the *Japan Year Book*.

mostly to Japanese settlers, of a large part of the public lands which had been of common use to the people; the forced sale of much of the best privately owned property, with the consequent migration into Manchuria of the people whose lands had been taken; the repression of speech and suppression of Korean papers; and the exhibition of much actual brutality in dealing with the people—did not promote the free and full acceptance of Japanese overlordship. To this it may be added that the Koreans were not satisfied with the educational efforts of Japan. While there were 380 elementary schools solely for Japanese children, there were some four hundred for the Koreans, although the Japanese constituted less than two per cent of the total population. This seemed rather out of proportion. Furthermore, the schools for Koreans were designed primarily to make them good subjects of Japan, to which emphasis exception was taken. Even the mission and other private schools, to a number exceeding eight hundred, were brought under the regular administrative control, and were forbidden to engage in religious instruction.

The objections to Japanese rule, together with the 1918 world-wide enthusiasm for democracy and the principle of the self-determination of peoples, produced a serious revolt against the Japanese in Korea in 1919. This took the internal form of passive resistance and the external form of an appeal to the Paris Peace Conference, which, however, refused to take cognizance of the claims of the "Provisional Government of Korea" which was organized at Shanghai. The latter was dispersed by the authorities administering the French settlement, the internal Korean movement was ruthlessly suppressed, and Japanese prestige maintained. Many malcontents, however, were left on the Manchurian side of the border, in Siberia and elsewhere. The Japanese authorities dispersed the fugitives in Manchuria, after several raids on Chinese territory, and the independence movement, at least for the time, collapsed. It had, however, the good result, already noted, of modifying Japan's Korean policy.

2. JAPAN IN MANCHURIA

Turning our attention to the second great area of Japanese interest, Manchuria, we find the Japanese position not quite so clearly defined, and the policy of the Empire not so easy to treat fairly. There are several conflicting views as to Japan's activities in Manchuria from 1905 to 1914, and as many conclusions as to their justification. This divergence may be largely explained by the initial acceptance of basically different premises, which, without any attempt to elaborate them, may be briefly stated. The Japanese position, in essence, was that they made tremendous sacrifices in men and treasure to drive the Russians out of South Manchuria, and that by treaty they succeeded to a position there which justified them in regarding it as a "sphere of interest." They claimed that in the development of their interest in this sphere they made use only of such methods as the European states had employed in China and elsewhere, and they argued that until those methods were generally and universally repudiated they should not be condemned for utilizing them. They insisted that they were under only two limitations in their succession to the Russian position—that they would observe the Open Door principle, by which they understood the three propositions of Secretary Hay's Open Door circular of 1899, and that they would respect the independence and integrity of China. Those pledges they claimed, at least until 1931, to have observed, and consequently they maintained that the volume of criticism leveled against their Manchurian activities was totally unwarranted.[5]

The other position was founded on the major premise that Manchuria was an integral part of China, and that, consequently, Japanese activities must be estimated from the standpoint of their effect on the maintenance of Chinese control in its integrity, or at least on its preservation except so far as it had been explicitly weakened by the loss of the Kwantung promontory by lease, and by the granting of railway and appurtenant rights up to 1905. Any enlargement or strengthening of the Japanese position beyond that point was considered objectionable as militating against China's rights as well as the Chinese interest. The critics of Japanese policy also took their stand on the Open Door principle, and on the obligation to respect the independence and integrity of China, and found both of those undertakings violated by Japan from 1905 to 1914.[6]

In order to understand why the same facts led to charge and denial that Japan violated the Open Door principle and that of the maintenance of the independence and integrity of China, it will be well to analyze them briefly at this point. It must be recognized that the Japanese, together with the European governments, had formally accepted as embodying the Open Door doctrine only the original Hay propositions: (1) that there would be no interference with any treaty port or any vested interest within any leased territory or "sphere of interest"; (2) that the Chinese treaty tariff should be applied within a "sphere," and that the duties should be collected by the Chinese government; and (3) that railway and harbor charges should be non-discriminatory. Thus the doctrine subscribed to was founded on the sphere conception, and it was not concerned with the securing of equality of investment opportunities within a "sphere." The limited character of the doctrine came to be forgotten in the United States after 1900, when the principle became generalized as that of "equality of opportunity." The

[5] For an exposition of this point of view see the writings of KAWAKAMI, ADACHI, and others. It also underlies the analysis of the problem undertaken by CLYDE, in his study, *International Rivalries in Manchuria*.

[6] This point of view is notably revealed in the writings of such American publicists as Mr. T. F. F. Millard.

consequence was that Japanese policy was criticized on the basis of a broader conception than that accepted by the government of Japan. Even though recognizing the American conception as ultimately the sounder, we should admit the unfairness of criticizing Japanese policy as though Japan had agreed to be governed by it when she had not. This difference of construction must be constantly borne in mind in evaluating Japan's Manchurian activities from 1905 to 1914 in terms of the Open Door doctrine.

The question of the integrity of China needs a similar analysis. Japan's acceptance of this principle was to be found in the 1905 revision of the Anglo-Japanese agreement, in the Anglo-Japanese alliance of 1911, in the Franco-Japanese agreement of 1907, in the convention with Russia of 1907, and in the Root-Takahira notes of 1908. But the Japanese understood, apparently, that they were pledged to respect only the territorial integrity of China, which was, as a matter of fact, explicitly stated in the Russian convention. Thus they assumed that so long as they did not formally detach Manchuria from China they were living up to their agreement. The United States, however, as early as 1900 had come to realize that the administrative integrity of China must be maintained if her territorial integrity was to be preserved. In other words, the American position was that independence and integrity might be lost, even though both were formally and officially maintained, by continued encroachments on the administrative services, and that, furthermore, a curtailment of the right to decide the course of development within a portion of the state represented an impairment of its integrity and independence. Unfortunately, again, this broader and, from the Chinese standpoint, sounder conception of the principle was not officially elaborated and its acceptance secured by the Powers, including Japan. Instead, the old words and phrases reappeared, with no new definition, in the Root-Takahira notes, thus leaving ample room for legitimate difference of opinion, and also for subsequent misunderstanding. Also, in the same exchange of notes the American government agreed to help maintain the *status quo,* by which the Japanese understood, properly, the Manchurian status as it had been established by 1908.

With this introduction, we may now turn our attention more explicitly to a survey of the Manchurian interests of Japan as they were established from 1905 to 1914. A convenient starting point will be found in the economic realm. Economic development may be partially measured in terms of the total foreign trade which, in 1898, was valued at about forty million taels. By 1908 it had increased in value to almost one hundred million taels, in 1911 to almost one hundred eighty millions; and in 1920 this last figure had more than trebled. Even allowing for changes in price levels, this represented a tremendous expansion. In terms of internal production the soya bean cultivation, the production of kaoliang, millet, maize, wheat, barley, rice and all other staples was greatly expanded. All of this may be explained in part by the influx of Chinese settlers, but it was also due to the activities of the Japanese railway administration, and to the enlargement of the market consequent on the improvement of communications.

The South Manchurian Railway Company, it must be noted, engaged in manifold activities besides the usual one undertaken by a railway company. In addition to operation of the rail system in southern Manchuria, it exercised administrative functions in the railway zone, built and operated hospitals and schools in the zone, maintained research laboratories and experimental stations, controlled mining properties such as the Fushun and Yentai mines, operated steamship lines, was concerned with harbor improvement work at Dairen, maintained hotels, and operated electric plants at Dairen, Mukden, Changchun, and Antung. All of these activities, many of them governmental or semi-governmental in character, were designed to add to the prosperity of Manchuria, and consequently to increase its value to Japan.

Thus it may be inferred that the South Manchurian Railway Company was the principal agency through which Japan acted to develop her sphere of interest. The activities of the company, nevertheless, were those of the Japanese government, for it assumed, and retained, the position of the largest shareholder, fifty per cent of the original capital of 200 million yen having been subscribed by the Imperial government. When the share capital was increased to 440 million yen, the government continued to retain fifty per cent interest. Of this, 100 million yen represented the value of the original property turned over to the company by the government, and the balance represented the amount of London sterling debentures which it assumed. The development of the original properties was accomplished largely with British funds, the loans having been floated as government issues at a lower interest rate than could have been secured by a private concern. Thus British capital indirectly participated in the development of Manchuria, without, however, reaping the usual fruits of such development. As a matter of fact, the proceeds of loans made in Europe were expended for railway equipment in the United States rather than in the lending country. Since there was this close relationship between the company and the Imperial government, it must be recognized that in the last analysis the company's policies were the policies of the Japanese government and may be so considered.

Before leaving the question of Manchuria it is necessary to return to a consideration of the steps taken by Japan to consolidate her position there. It is clear that the country was materially developed after 1905. Did Japan alone benefit by this improvement? What were the effects of her activities on non-Japanese interests, including those of China?

The policy of Japan with respect to the development of rail communications has been discussed in a previous chapter.[7] Suffice it to say here that, after she had determined to operate the South Manchurian Railway, Japan claimed to have secured an agreement with China, when the Komura treaty was negotiated in 1905, that no railway would be built by China, without Japan's consent, which would parallel or compete with the South Manchurian. Supported by this agreement, she vetoed the Hsinmintun-Fakumen project, and with and through Russia prevented the Chinchow-Aigun concession from being utilized, as well as vetoing the larger neutralization project of Secretary Knox. As has been indicated, this did not constitute, from the Japanese standpoint, a violation of their Open Door pledge, since that did not cover equality of financial opportunity. It did, however, amount to the imposition of a restraint on China's freedom in determining the course of development in a part of the Empire, and consequently might well be considered as an impairment of her independence and administrative integrity. From the Japanese standpoint it did not serve to detach Manchuria from China and so was not considered a violation of their other pledge. Furthermore, the Manchu government had clearly agreed, it was asserted, not to do the things which it was attempting to do through these concessions, and so was accused of bad faith and double dealing. The only safe generalizations which can be made about railway politics in Manchuria from 1905 to 1914 are: (1) that Japan showed herself determined to maintain an exclusive position within her sphere, as did Russia to the north, and that she was consistently bent on consolidating that position by means of new agreements with China; (2) that China was not prepared to acquiesce freely in Japan's railway monopoly, but that she was helpless without adequate foreign backing, both financial and political; and (3) that the United States alone among the Powers was interested in destroying or disturbing the Japanese monopoly, but that she also needed support if she was to succeed, and that she could not find that support. Consequently the year 1914 found Japan securely in control of the railway field, but at the expense of arousing the distrust and hostility of interested Americans.

Commercially the Japanese had also entrenched themselves in Manchuria. During the period immediately following the war with Russia, and while the evacuation of troops was taking place, non-Japanese traders were denied access to the territory on the reasonable ground that military rule had not yet come to an end. But during this same time Japanese goods were brought in on the railroad supposed to be used solely for military purposes. The Japanese trader, as the first on the field, thus had an opportunity to establish himself before competition was possible. The Open Door principle, consequently, could not be considered to have come into application until after the summer of 1906. The pre-war Manchurian place of entry was the

---

[7] See chapter IX.

Chinese port of Newchwang. It was almost entirely displaced by the Japanese port of Dairen, partly because of the superior facilities for trade afforded at Dairen, but partly by reason of tariff discriminations against Newchwang on the part of the Japanese railway. This was not a violation of the Open Door principle, which had nothing to do with distinctions between places; but it did have the effect of militating against the American and British traders who had established themselves at the Chinese port of entry. The tariff schedules on the South Manchurian Railway did not discriminate in favor of the Japanese traders, but a system of rebates, which had the same result, was instituted, to be later given up, however, because of foreign criticism and complaint. The rebate system was replaced by one of subsidy, to which exception could not well be taken since it was frequently resorted to by other governments. Goods imported through Korea were given advantages in the Manchurian trade,[8] but since this advantage was open to all who chose to import in that way, it was claimed to be non-violative of the Open Door pledge. The Japanese who traded through Korea, however, were trading within their own tariff system, whereas foreigners were not; and this gave the former a decided advantage. In general, therefore, non-Japanese were not induced to import through Korea. Particularly in the early days, in case of freight congestion, foreign (non-Japanese) consignments were frequently delayed, while Japanese goods were transported expeditiously, and sometimes non-Japanese goods were even tampered with.[9] Foreign trademarks were also used by Japanese, but this was an indication of a low commercial morality rather than a violation of the Open Door principle, and it took place in Japan and in China proper as well as in the region north of the Wall. Finally, the Japanese tried to out-distance their foreign competitors by evasion of the payment of the Chinese production and consumption taxes, or by their commutation, which they were able to accomplish by reason of their political dominance. It must be recognized that Japan retreated to within the letter of her Open Door pledge when decidedly questionable practices were called to her attention, but that in many ways there were grounds for complaint on the score of unfairness of competitive methods, even though it be denied that these constituted violations of the original Open Door doctrine. Herein was to be found one reason for the Japanese-American friction over Manchuria.

From the administrative standpoint, it must be recognized that Japan stretched her powers very widely.

Japanese officialdom, from its base in the Leased Territory and through the consulates and the Railway Company, went on effectively consolidating and extending its influence. The result is that the Japanese authority has become prac-

---

[8] By agreement of May 29, 1913, they were to pay only two-thirds of the regular Chinese customs levies.

[9] Control of postal facilities was also used to embarrass the foreigner and aid the Japanese.

tically absolute, not alone in the Leased Territory and along the Railway Zone, but, indirectly, throughout all of Southeastern Manchuria; for, while the Chinese administration still functions, the Chinese officials submit to the exercise of a veto power by the Japanese which renders Japan for practical purposes the final authority in determining issues of importance.[10]

Furthermore, Japanese subjects penetrated the interior of the province illegally, since under the treaties they, together with other foreigners, were confined for residence to the treaty ports. This complicated the problem of administration for China, since the extraterritorial system extended to Manchuria. To control her nationals Japan instituted the "police box" system, thus asserting jurisdictional rights outside of the railway zone, and her position in the zone, whether deliberately or not, became distinctly embarrassing to the Chinese authorities.

By way of a summary statement, then, it may be said that by 1914 Manchuria had been developed greatly from the economic standpoint—a development from which primarily Japan profited, although certain indirect advantages, such as came from the purchase of railway materials and other commodities which Japan could not supply for herself, came to the United States. Japan's exclusive position within her sphere, so far as railway undertakings were concerned, had been established, with the acquiescence of England and the support of Russia. And her political position had been consolidated, without, however, violation of the territorial integrity of China. It had been revealed, furthermore, that England was prepared to support her ally in her attempts to consolidate her position in Manchuria in return for the benefits which accrued to her from the alliance, while the relations of the United States and Japan had become increasingly strained.

3. THE IMMIGRATION QUESTION

The growing friction between the United States and Japan had another cause, however, than that presented by the latter's Manchurian policy. The same years, between the war with Russia and the outbreak of the World War, were marked by the growth of sentiment on the Pacific Coast against the Japanese immigrant. This was, in a sense, merely a re-direction of the earlier hostility to the Chinese, when their numbers had materially increased, but it was now more serious because of the greater position of Japan in the world.

The Japanese began to come to the United States in large numbers only after 1900, when there were upwards of 24,000 in the country. By 1910 their number had increased to slightly over 72,000, and by 1920 to more than 110,-000. In proportion to the total population this was certainly not a threatening influx. But the concentration of the Japanese settlers in California and

10 HORNBECK, Contemporary Politics in the Far East, p. 262.

in other Pacific Coast states led to an exaggeration of the danger, an apprehension which was enhanced because the Japanese had settled on the land.

Without attempting to enter upon a detailed analysis of the question, it may be said that the same sort of action was taken which had marked the earlier anti-Chinese agitation. The primary demand of the Californians was for the enactment by the national Congress of an exclusion measure. In 1906 the San Francisco School Board, by resolution, barred Japanese children from attendance at public schools other than the one maintained for Orientals. Japan strongly protested and the President acted, securing the rescinding of the resolution on the understanding that he would take steps to end Japanese immigration. This led to the making of the Gentlemen's Agreement in 1907, an executive understanding with Japan by which her government agreed not to issue passports to Japanese laborers whose destination was the continental United States. It also voluntarily followed a similar policy with respect to emigrants to Hawaii and Mexico. This led to a gradual decline in the male Japanese population of the United States, as, during the fifteen years in which it was in force, less than 98,000 men entered, while over 120,000 departed. There was, however, an actual increase by immigration due to the fact that women married to Japanese were permitted to enter under the Gentlemen's Agreement.

While it must be admitted as a fact that Japan was scrupulous in the fulfillment of her obligations, the Gentlemen's Agreement did not satisfy the Californians, who continually pressed for exclusion by law. They pointed to the increase in the number of Japanese in the country and charged Japan with bad faith, alleging as an instance the granting of passports to the so-called "picture brides," women married at long distance. This was not an unusual custom for Japanese, but Californians claimed that it was encouraged to permit the entrance of child-bearers into the United States. As is usual in such cases, there was a great deal of misrepresentation of Japan by Californians to make a case for Congressional action.

Not satisfied with agitation for an exclusion measure, in 1913 the California legislature enacted a law under which the Japanese, as aliens ineligible to citizenship,[11] were granted the right to lease land only for three years, and to own land only for purposes specified by treaty, a clear discrimination against the Japanese. This action was extended and made even more drastic in 1920.

None of these acts could help but arouse antagonism to the United States in Japan. Protests were lodged officially against all of them, and they provoked widespread popular hostility. This feeling was further embittered when exclusion was finally provided for by law in the Immigration Act of 1924, which was aided in its passage by a statement of the Japanese ambassa-

[11] Finally decided by the Supreme Court in 1922. Takao Ozawa *v.* U. S.

dor, Mr. Hanahira, that "grave consequences" would follow from its enact·ment.

There are two aspects of the Japanese reaction to these successive acts which should be emphasized. The first is that they objected primarily to being singled out for discrimination, as though they were of a lower order than Europeans. Their protests were not directed against the policy of restriction, as was indicated when they willingly entered into the Gentlemen's Agreement. This was indicated by their acceptance, without particular bitterness, of the Australasian policy of exclusion by means of a dictation test, applied to all applicants for admission, even though it was administered so as to exclude Asiatics; and was further indicated by their self-limitation of emigration to Canada under an agreement similar to that made with President Roosevelt. This ground of objection, of course, applied not only to exclusion as finally accomplished by the United States, but to discriminatory legislation such as the California Land Laws and to the denial of the right of naturalization.

In the second place, the Japanese attitude toward exclusion from under-populated regions was like the attitude they took toward their expansion in Asia. They had, as has been already emphasized, a serious population problem. The surplus might, they argued, be taken care of by emigration, or by industrialization based upon control of continental resources and territories. The United States was most active in closing the door to the Japanese emigrant, and it was also the strongest, from 1905 to 1914, in its objections to Japanese imperialism, whether economic or territorial. Thus it was the primary obstacle after 1905 to the solution of Japan's pressing problem in either of the two satisfactory ways. Friction over Manchuria, in other words, was reënforced by emigration difficulties, and vice versa. This leads us back to a consideration of the policies of Japan in Eastern Asia, a consideration which had included only the years 1905–1914.

4. JAPAN ENTERS WORLD WAR I

With the outbreak of World War I in 1914 came what many Japanese described as the great opportunity for the Empire to establish itself more securely on the continent, and outside of Manchuria. The Far Eastern situation was necessarily very complicated and delicate because of the interwoven interests of the Powers in China. The Peking government, immediately upon the outbreak of hostilities in Europe, declared its neutrality. But the question of the status of such parts of China's territory as had been leased to foreign states was immediately raised. This question naturally centered around the German occupancy of Tsingtao. First of all, negotiations were undertaken between Germany and China with a view to the restoration of the German Leased Territory to the Republic. Under the terms of her agreement Germany had the right to give up her leasehold at Kiaochow at any time in return for a more suitable port elsewhere in China. Consequently the German government seems to have evinced its willingness to evacuate its position for the time, with a view to reëstablishing itself in the Orient after the war. At least it is alleged that this was one of the reasons why England opposed the reaching of an agreement between China and Germany concerning the leased territory.[12] Failing that, the Powers might have agreed not to utilize their bases in China for war purposes, thus extending China's declared neutrality over her entire territory. From the standpoint of the Far East, this would seem to have been the best solution. But before any agreement could be reached Japan so acted as to render further negotiations looking toward such an agreement impossible.

For the declared purpose of maintaining the general peace in the regions of eastern Asia and of India, Japan and Great Britain were united in a general treaty of alliance. By the first article of that treaty it was agreed that "whenever, in the opinion of either Great Britain or Japan, any of the rights and interests referred to in the preamble of this Agreement are in jeopardy, the two Governments will communicate with one another fully and frankly, and will consider in common the measures which should be taken to safeguard those menaced rights or interests." The second article continued that "if by reason of unprovoked attack or aggressive action, wherever arising, on the part of any Power or Powers, either High Contracting Party should be involved in war in defense of its territorial rights or special interests mentioned in the preamble of this Agreement, the other High Contracting Party will at once come to the assistance of its ally, and will conduct the war in common, and make peace in mutual agreement with it."

The outbreak of war in Europe in no way affected the territorial rights or the special interests of Japan, nor, so far as the initial appearance of the struggle was concerned, were the Far Eastern interests of England or her position in India so immediately threatened as to cause the alliance to become automatically operative to bring Japan to England's side. And in any case, since England was the member of the alliance which was involved in war, it would seem that the initiative in bringing Japan into the struggle should have come from her. In taking the initiative Britain apparently sought an explicitly limited Japanese participation, which did not interest the Japanese government. The Japanese at first based their participation on their obligations under the alliance, but they seem not to have felt their obligations so strongly after they had driven the Germans from their holdings in Shantung province, and from the islands in the Pacific north of the equator. At least one informed observer felt that Japan came into the war

[12] See WEALE, *Indiscreet Chronicle from the Pacific.*

in spite of, rather than because of, the desires of the British government. The American minister at Peking, Dr. Paul S. Reinsch, has the following to say of Japan's entrance into the war:

On August 8, 1914, Japanese war vessels appeared near Tsingtao. Japan suggested on August 10 that the British Government might call for the co-operation of Japan under the terms of the Alliance. In view of possible consequences the British Government hesitated to make the call; the British in China considered it important that independent action by Japan in that country should be precluded.

Acting on its own account on August 15, the Japanese Government sent the Shantung ultimatum to Germany. The British Government was then informed of the action taken.[13]

From this it appears either that Japan was moved by an unusually high sense of obligation, or else that she had certain ulterior motives in participating in the European War before it had become a world-wide struggle. From her later actions we may infer that the latter is the correct explanation of her move. In the ultimatum sent to Germany on August 15, 1914, she demanded that Germany turn over to Japan her leasehold interest in Shantung province, "with a view to the eventual restoration of the same to China," at a date not later than September 15, giving the German government a week in which to reply to the demand. When Germany made no reply to the note of "advice," the Japanese government declared war (August 23) and made preparations to drive the Germans from Tsingtao by armed force. In order to inform the rest of the world of Japan's intentions, the Premier, Count Okuma, cabled a message for publication in the United States in which he said: "Japan has no territorial ambition, and hopes to stand as the protector of peace in the Orient."

In moving on Tsingtao the Japanese landed their forces at a point about one hundred miles north of the port, moving toward their objective over Chinese territory, although that country had declared its neutrality in the struggle. After protesting, the Chinese government accepted the inevitable and tried to make as few breaches in its neutrality as possible. Since this was not the first time that their territory had been fought over by other nations when they were not a party to the struggle, the Chinese had precedent to guide them. They therefore resorted to the expedient adopted in 1904 at the suggestion of the United States, and delimited a "war zone," outside of which belligerent operations were not to be carried. This zone made ample provision for the Japanese plan of operations, but the latter immediately proceeded to disregard it by occupying the railway running into the interior of the province. This railway was, under the agreement of 1898 between China and Germany, a joint Chinese-German commercial enterprise of a private character, although it was operated under the supervision of the

[13] *American Diplomat in China*, p. 123. See also T. E. LA FARGUE, *China and the World War*, for a careful recent account of the Anglo-Japanese negotiations.

Tsingtao government. And, in the nature of the case, its occupation was not necessary to the success of the operations against the leased area, which was easily reduced by the Anglo-Japanese forces investing it.

After the fall of Tsingtao, on November 7, the Japanese proceeded in a systematic manner to establish themselves in Shantung province. They took over the German interests outside of the leased area as a matter of course, including the Tsinanfu-Tsingtao railway, the line southward from Kaomi, the mines developed by Germany in the fifteen years of her occupation, and the various public and private property rights of Germany throughout the province. Not stopping, however, with a mere succession to the German rights, title, and privileges, Japan added, or attempted to add, considerably to them. For example, although Chinese troops had always policed the railway zone, outside of the leased area, the Germans enjoying no such policing privileges as Japan and Russia had in Manchuria, the Japanese government took over the administration and policing of the railway area. These excessive rights were insisted upon even after the plea of military necessity could have no possible validity. The Japanese attitude was advertised in another particular. Under the German administration the Tsingtao customs service had been brought under the direct control of the Chinese Maritime Customs, with the limitation that the commissioner was a German, as were the members of the staff. But they were chosen from the regular service and worked under the general direction of its head, who, by the agreement of 1898, was a British subject. Also twenty per cent of the collections was turned over to the Tsingtao government for local purposes. After their occupation of the territory, the Japanese claimed the right to appoint a Japanese (not necessarily from the Chinese service) as Commissioner, with a full Japanese staff, similarly chosen. This, of course, would have removed the service at Tsingtao from the control of China, and, perhaps, would have resulted in the subtraction of the revenues from the general collection, although those revenues were hypothecated to meet the Boxer indemnity and other international charges. After protracted negotiations, however, Japan agreed to allow the German arrangements to continue, with the exception that Japanese were to replace Germans in the service at Tsingtao.

So far as the evacuation of the territory—"its restoration to China"—was concerned, the Japanese Foreign Minister, in reply to questions in the Diet, said that Japan was under no obligation to restore the leased area, as her pledge was made subject to Germany's handing it over to her without trouble. The sacrifice of Japanese men and the expenditure of Japanese money in the reduction of the port had created a new situation, which might have to resolve itself along different lines. What these new lines were to be was shortly indicated.

At the end of 1914, when German resistance in Shantung had been brought completely to an end and with it the need for the military zone, President Yüan Shih-k'ai informed the Japanese (January 7, 1915) that China's neutrality would again extend over all of the province of Shantung outside of the leased territory. The Japanese immediately protested against the ending of the military zone as an unfriendly act, seizing upon it as the excuse for the presentation to the Chinese government of far-reaching demands.

5. THE TWENTY-ONE DEMANDS

These demands, in five groups and twenty-one articles, were served on China on January 18, 1915, and were the subject of negotiation until well toward the end of May. They were presented directly to the President, in disregard of the Chinese Foreign Office, and he was enjoined to preserve a complete secrecy in regard to them prior to the conclusion of negotiations. News of the negotiations gradually filtered out to the foreign correspondents at Peking and through them to the outside world. As the veil of secrecy began to be lifted, the Japanese government was forced step by step toward an acknowledgment of the validity of the reports from Peking. At first it was denied absolutely "on high authority" at Tokyo that any "demands" had been served on China. When the fact of the demands was conclusively established, it was given out that they were comprised in eleven articles, the most innocuous being published. Finally it was admitted that there were twenty-one articles, but that Group Five had been submitted merely for the consideration of the Chinese government, and that it was not being pressed on it by Japan. These successive admissions came as the result of the publicity given to the Japanese action, which forced Japan either to acknowledge her plans or to give them up. There was indicated every desire to keep the foreign world in ignorance of what was going on at Peking until the Powers could be presented with a far-reaching change in the *status quo* in the Far East as an accomplished fact which, under the circumstances, they would have to accept.

In presenting and pressing its demands, the Japanese government attempted to bring a double pressure to bear on President Yüan. In the first place, there was continually emphasized the possibility of military action by Japan in case she was not conceded the position she coveted toward China. Secondly, it was intimated that there were alive, and concentrated in Japan, Chinese elements opposed to the personal rule established by Yüan in 1914, and it was hinted that these revolutionist elements might become very formidable if given active Japanese support in men and money, which support would be forthcoming if President Yüan were not complaisant. On the other hand, it was suggested that Japan would have no objection to the reëstablishment of monarchy in China, but on the contrary would be agreeable to it, if she could be assured of the friendly attitude of the monarch. This friendliness, it was hinted, might be exhibited by an acceptance of the demands. Thus the Japanese government threatened both the continued existence of China as a state and of Yüan Shih-k'ai as the ruler, while at the same time offering a bribe to the President in the form of support for his personal and family aggrandizement. There must have been, however, little hope in Japan that Yüan Shih-k'ai would accept her tutelage, as he had been a pronounced opponent of Japanese expansion since his days in Seoul as Chinese Resident.

As the negotiations proceeded, the Chinese insisted on separate discussions of the several items of the demands in the hope that, by making concession of the less objectionable, they might save themselves from acceptance of the more objectionable. It was also hoped that, if they protracted the negotiations by means of a detailed examination of the Japanese proposals, foreign opinion might be aroused and pressure be brought to bear on Japan so as to bring about a modification of her position. Finally the Japanese minister at Peking presented an ultimatum requiring acceptance of the demands, as they had been modified in the course of the negotiations, and excluding the notorious Group Five except as a possible subject for future negotiation. The conditions of this ultimatum, with a time limit for answer, and with the threat of force in case of non-compliance, were accepted by China, and the agreement thus reached was embodied in several treaties and a series of exchanges of notes.

"Japan," Yüan Shih-k'ai remarked to the American minister in 1914, "is going to take advantage of this war to get control of China." [14] When the demands are examined in detail, the conclusion is made inevitable that Japanese policy was clearly pointed in the direction that President Yüan feared it would take. As indicated by the demands—

there would be three centers from which Japanese influence would be exercised —Manchuria, Shantung, and Fukien. Manchuria was to be made more completely a reserved area for Japanese capital and colonization, but with administrative control wielded through advisers and through priority in the matter of loans. In Shantung, the interest formerly belonging to Germany was to be taken over and expanded. A priority of right in Fukien was demanded, both in investment and in development; this would effectively bar other nations and would assimilate this province to Manchuria. The northern sphere of Japan was to be expanded by including Inner Mongolia. From the Shantung sphere influence could be made to radiate to the interior by means of railway extensions to Honan and Shansi. Similarly, from the Fukien sphere, railway concessions would carry Japanese influence into the provinces of Kiangsi, Hupei, and Kwangtung. The Japanese interest already existing in the Hany'ehp'ing iron and coal enterprise, which was a mortgage with right to purchase pig iron at certain rates, was to be consolidated into a Japanese controlled company. Added to these was the significant demand that outsiders be denied the right to work any mines in the neighborhood of those owned by the Hany'ehp'ing Company without its consent; nor

[14] *American Diplomat in China*, p. 129.

were they to be permitted, lacking such consent, to carry out any undertaking that might directly or indirectly affect the interests of that company. This astonishing proposal sought to make the Japanese concern the arbiter of industrial enterprise in the middle Yangtze Valley.[15]

None of these proposals, if accepted by China, affected her formal independence, sovereignty, or integrity. But actually she would be brought under the sway of Japan in the manner most approved by modern imperialism.

On the other hand—

Group Five consisted of the sweeping demands which would have virtually deprived the Chinese Government of control over its own affairs. The employment of effective Japanese advisers in political, financial, and military affairs; the joint Chino-Japanese organization of the police forces in important places; the purchase from Japan of a fixed amount of munitions of war—50 per cent or more; and the establishment of Chino-Japanese jointly worked arsenals were embraced in these demands. The latter involved effective control over the armament and military organization of China.[16]

Group Five was eliminated from the demands, but in the final agreements was set aside for future consideration and not given up. Consequently it continued to hang over the heads of the Chinese as a potential threat.

Before turning from this important question it will be worth while to summarize the agreements actually reached between China and Japan under date of May 25, 1915. This can be most conveniently and simply done by geographical areas, beginning north of the Great Wall and working southwards.

6. THE 1915 TREATIES

The treaty respecting South Manchuria and Eastern Inner Mongolia provided: (1) that the lease of Port Arthur and Dalny, and of the terms of the South Manchurian and the Antung-Mukden railway agreements be extended to 99 years; (2) that Japanese subjects might reside and travel in South Manchuria, engage in business and manufacturing, and lease land outside of the treaty ports for trade or agricultural purposes; (3) that the Chinese government would give its permission to any joint Chinese-Japanese enterprises; (4) that Japanese subjects should be amenable to Chinese local law, but that the extraterritorial system, so far as the trial of offenders was concerned, should obtain; (5) that China should open to foreign trade and residence suitable places in Eastern Inner Mongolia; (6) that the Kirin-Changchun railway loan agreement should be revised in

---

[15] REINSCH, op. cit., p. 133.

[16] Ibid., p. 134. Thus Group V, apparently added to the demands as originally formulated by the capitalist-supported Okuma government because of Army insistence, expressed a political as distinguished from an economic imperialism.

favor of Japan. By separate notes China conceded: (1) that Japanese subjects should have the right to open mines in certain areas specified by the Japanese; (2) that if she sought foreign capital for railway construction in Manchuria in the future, application would be made first of all to Japan; and (3) that if she found it necessary to employ foreign financial, military, or police advisers in South Manchuria, they should be Japanese.

The Shantung treaty provided: (1) that China should give "full assent to all matters upon which the Japanese government may hereafter agree with the German government relating to the disposition of all rights, interests and concessions which Germany, by virtue of treaties or otherwise, possesses in relation to the Province of Shantung" (art. 1); (2) that Japanese capitalists should have the right to build the Chefoo-Weihsien railway, in case Germany abandoned the privilege of financing it; and (3) that additional places for foreign residence and trade should be opened by China herself in the province. In exchanges of notes, China agreed not to alienate any territory within the province or islands along the coast to any foreign Power on any pretext whatsoever. On her side, in a separate note, Japan indicated her intention of restoring the leased territory of Kiaochow Bay to China when she had received it from Germany, on condition that China open the whole of the bay as a commercial port, that she set aside an area to be designated by the Japanese government as a residential concession to be under the exclusive jurisdiction of Japan, and that an international settlement be provided for the residence of other foreigners if they desired it.

The demand of Japan with respect to the Hanyehp'ing Company was treated in an exchange of notes. The Chinese Minister for Foreign Affairs wrote:

> I have the honor to state that if in the future the Hanyehp'ing Company and the Japanese capitalists agree upon coöperation, the Chinese government, in view of the intimate relations subsisting between the Japanese capitalists and the said Company, will forthwith give its permission. The Chinese government further agrees not to confiscate the said Company, nor, without the consent of the Japanese capitalists, to convert it into a state enterprise, nor cause it to borrow and use foreign capital other than Japanese.

As to Fukien province, the Chinese government stated formally that it had given no permission to foreign nations to construct on its coast dockyards, coaling stations for military use, or naval bases, and that it had no intention of borrowing foreign capital for those purposes.

It is apparent at a glance that Japan's objectives on the continent had changed from the purely territorial to the economic. She had first urged, as justification of her policy, her need for room for expansion on the continent, so that by colonization she might take care of her excess population. From 1914 on, however, she did not demand control of territory for colonization purposes because all of her experiments in that direction had failed. It was not Japanese farmers who were to be found in Korea, Formosa, and South Manchuria, but shopkeepers, concession-hunters, and developers. This partly explains the change in her objective. To this fact must be added a change at home which tremendously affected the national development. The outbreak of the war gave a great stimulus to Japanese industry. Just as in the United States those industries relating to war supply were expanded in every direction, so in Japan the established undertakings, both in the field of munitions supply and in allied fields of production, and non-military production for the purpose of supplying markets temporarily vacated by Europe, were enormously expanded, and new enterprises sprang up over night. This industrial expansion strikingly called attention to Japan's reliance on foreign nations for certain of the essentials for an industrial life, such as coal and iron. It consequently caused Japanese statesmen to think of the war as giving them an opportunity to secure these essentials. Furthermore, a capitalist class had been developing in Japan as a result of her industrial development before but especially after the war with Russia, and this class became all-important during the World War. In order to secure support and to ensure their activities against interference on the part of the Diet, the industrial and commercial magnates had entered into a close alliance with some of the party leaders. And it happened that in 1914, after the failure of Katsura to organize and lead a party, an attempt which he made in 1913, and the fall of a navalist ministry headed by Yamamoto, Count Okuma was called upon to form a government, on the basis of party support in the Diet. It was this Okuma ministry, hailed as the first truly party government in the history of Japan, which, in the interests of its clients, the industrial capitalists, served the twenty-one demands on China. This may help to explain their basically economic character.

In China the effect of the serving of the demands was to rally all factions to support of the President. Large groups were in favor of resistance to the point of war, although China lacked the means of making any effective resistance. A fund, called the National Salvation Fund, was started and subscribed to by all classes, from the highest to the lowest, for the purpose of preparedness. The President undoubtedly withstood the Japanese pressure as far as he dared, and saved as much as possible out of the situation. But he did not dare resist to the point of provoking a declaration of war. Yet he was greatly encouraged by the spontaneous expression of opinion in support of his government, and, as has been pointed out,[17] was probably influenced by it to some considerable extent in undertaking the movement toward restoration of the monarchy. Indirectly, therefore, the demands had a considerable effect on the internal situation in China.

The Yüan Shih-k'ai government, having accepted the demands, was in no position to repudiate them. But after the overthrow of the President and

[17] Chapter XI.

the restoration to Peking of the Assembly, the central government, so far as it did not come under the control of Japan, as during the period of Anfu ascendancy, maintained that the agreements were invalid, first because they had been forced, and second, because they had not been assented to by Parliament. More will necessarily have to be said of the Chinese attitude in the next chapter, when we consider the effect of China's entrance into the war, and the succeeding Japanese advances in position may be considered at the same time. Here, however, it is necessary to point out that Japan did not stop because she had gained her new position, but continued to press on China, whenever occasion offered, some of the items that had not been conceded in 1915. Trouble was continually arising in Manchuria between Japanese and Chinese, and each incident was utilized by Japan to forward her interests. In many of these cases the Japanese were at fault, either wholly or in part, but that did not prevent them from pressing their claims on China. The most notorious of these incidents was that at Chengchiatûn, when trouble arose because a Japanese policeman took some of the products displayed by a Chinese vendor of merchandise and refused to pay for them. Troops of both sides were drawn by the trouble into a general affray, out of which the Japanese derived material for a claim on China, and again China had to make concessions.

Reference has been made to Japan's intimation to Yüan Shih-k'ai that trouble would arise for his government if he did not accede to the Japanese demands. In spite of the concessions made, this trouble actually came, although it was deferred until he attempted to make himself Emperor. Before the opposition to monarchy in China became active, Japan took the lead among the Powers in inquiring as to the ability of the Chinese government to repress the opponents of the movement. When Yüan replied that the nation was in favor of the restoration and that no trouble was to be apprehended, the Japanese minister said that his information led him to believe that Yüan was misinformed. As it proved, he was right and the President was wrong. Japan herself had something to do with the correctness of the information of her minister for, at the right moment, Chinese revolutionaries proceeded from Japan, where they had been harbored since 1913, to southwestern China and raised the standard of revolt. These men were supplied with funds from Japanese sources, and with military equipment which came from Japan. And from this time on, except for a short time after the Washington Conference, even if she had not done it previously, as is sometimes intimated, Japan consistently supported elements opposed to the government of the day in China, hoping, by fishing in China's troubled waters, to add to her already large catch.

7. THE 1917 SECRET TREATIES

But it was not enough for Japan to force China to concede her greater and greater rights while the Powers were engrossed in the European conflict. It was necessary for her to safeguard and consolidate her new position by agreement with those states with interests in the Far East. The United States was the only country in a position to protest effectively against the 1915 agreements, so far as they affected its treaty rights in China. It did make a formal diplomatic statement of its attitude, but went no further in the way of protest. In this statement, made to the government of China, the United States said that "it can not recognize any agreement or undertaking which has been entered into or which may be entered into between the Governments of China and Japan impairing the treaty rights of the United States and its citizens in China, or the international policy relative to China commonly known as the Open Door policy."

As the war in Europe proceeded it was marked by German successes, and it became more and more necessary for the Entente ranks to hold firm. During 1916 Japan apparently began to waver in her allegiance to her ally's cause. An aggressive press campaign against the maintenance of the Anglo-Japanese alliance was carried on, the press advancing the view that the alliance was one-sided and consequently unfair. Furthermore, the apparent invincibility of Germany was pointed out, and the desirability of a German-Japanese alliance to replace that with England was more than hinted. After the seed of discontent had been properly sown, the Japanese government demanded a *quid pro quo* for its continued adherence to the Allied side. This was given by England when she agreed to support the Japanese claims, at the peace table, to a reversion of the German rights in Shantung, and to the possession of the islands in the Pacific north of the equator taken from Germany. Japan, on her side, agreed to support the British claim to the islands to the south of the equator. France, at the same time, agreed to support the Japanese claims on condition that Japan would encourage the movement in China toward participation in the war on the Allied side. Italy entered into a similar agreement. All of these agreements, made in 1917 before the entrance of the United States into the war, were kept officially secret until the opening of the peace conference.

They were made the more necessary because of the outbreak of revolution in Russia in March, 1917, for Japan had attempted first of all to safeguard her position by agreement with the Czar's government. This agreement had been reached in the summer of 1916 when the two states entered into a firm alliance for the outward and published purpose of preserving the peace of the Far East, but, by secret protocols, with a view to delimiting their respective interests in Eastern Asia and coöperating in their maintenance against any attack whatsoever. In this delimitation of their interests, Russia recognized the changes made in the *status quo* by the Japanese 1915 Agreements with China, and accepted them as necessary of protection under the alliance, while Japan recognized as an accomplished fact the Russian advance into Outer Mongolia during the years 1912–1915. It is interesting to note that, whether intentionally or not, the alliance with Russia was to outlive the Anglo-Japanese alliance by one day.

8. THE LANSING-ISHII AGREEMENT

This left only the United States which had not recognized as an accomplished fact the establishment of Japanese hegemony on the continent. This recognition was delayed only until the war pressure began to be felt in this country. In November of 1917, in order to put at rest the rumors of antagonism between the United States and Japan by exhibiting their complete identity of policy and interest—rumors which the Secretary of State somewhat incorrectly ascribed to German propaganda—an exchange of notes took place between the United States and Japan, which constituted the so-called Lansing-Ishii Agreement. By this, the government of the United States recognized that Japan, because of geographical propinquity, had special interests in China. No attempt was made to itemize in detail these special interests, and consequently the Japanese considered, as did the Chinese, that it meant a recognition of the status of 1917, including the successive advances made since 1914. The note, it is true, went on to reaffirm the adherence of the two Powers to the classic formulas of the Open Door and the integrity of China. It later developed that the United States understood one thing and Japan another by this recognition of her special interests. This difference of interpretation was not unrecognized by the Japanese government, but, as was explained to the Russian ambassador at Tokyo, this fact was not considered prejudicial to Japanese interests, because it was felt that Japan would be in a position to enforce her own interpretation when the proper time came. In a secret protocol, however, Lansing sought to restrain Japan by getting her to agree not to ". . . take advantage of present conditions to seek special rights or privileges in China which would abridge the rights of citizens or subjects of other friendly states." [18]

Thus, by means of demands served on China, supplemented by the threat of interference in the internal political struggle in China, and by actual interference, Japan established her hegemony on the continent. Then, by successive agreements with Russia, England, France, Italy, and the United States, entered into largely because of war necessity, she safeguarded her supremacy against attacks from the outside world.

[18] A. W. GRISWOLD, *The Far Eastern Policy of the United States*, pp. 215–216.

REFERENCES FOR FURTHER STUDY

A. ADACHI, *Manchuria, a Survey* (1925); good for facts, but needs to be used with care where the facts are interpreted. *Annals of American Academy of Social and Political Science, Asiatic Immigration,* vol. 122, Nov., 1925, part 5. G. H. BLAKESLEE (ed.), *Japan and Japanese-American Relations* (1912), ch. 16–21. R. L. BUELL, *Japanese Immigration* (1924), World Peace Foundation pamphlets, vol. 7, nos. 5, 6; an excellent survey of the question in summary form. R. L. BUELL, *Washington Conference* (1922), ch. 1–4; critical of Japan. HENRY CHUNG, *Case of Korea* (1921); title indicates nature and scope. P. H. CLYDE, *International Rivalries in Manchuria* (1926), ch. 8–12; a careful study; extensive bibliography. A. L. P. DENNIS, *The Anglo-Japanese Alliance* (1923), ch. 1–3. GEORGE GLEASON, *What Shall I Think of Japan* (1921); friendly criticism of phases of Japan's continental policy. A. W. GRISWOLD, *The Far Eastern Policy of the United States* (1938), ch. 4–6; excellent as diplomatic history. J. H. GUBBINS, *Making of Modern Japan* (1922), ch. 27–28; brief discussion of questions of recent policy. *Government-General of Chosen, Annual Report* (1921–1922). A. S. AND SUSAN HERSHEY, *Modern Japan* (1919), ch. 14–19; a sympathetic treatment. KARL HONGKEE, *A Critical Evaluation of Modern Social Trends in Korea* (1938). S. K. HORNBECK, *Contemporary Politics in the Far East* (1916), ch. 15–18; particularly good for analysis of Japanese Manchurian policy, and for twenty-one demands. ALLEYNE IRELAND, *The New Korea* (1926); the most comprehensive treatment in a single volume. U. IWASAKI, *Working Forces in Japanese Politics* (1921), Columbia University Studies, vol. 97, ch. 13; on growth of power of industrialists and its effects on foreign policy. J. JONES, *Fall of Tsingtao* (1915); account of Japanese movement into Shantung province. YOUNGHILL KANG, *The Grass Roof* (1931); Life in Korea. K. K. KAWAKAMI, *American-Japanese Relations* (1912), ch. 1–17. K. K. KAWAKAMI, *Japan in World Politics* (1917); both are designed to present Japan in a favorable light. C. W. KENDALL, *Truth About Korea* (1919); as it seemed to Korean nationalists. T. E. LA FARGUE, *China and the World War* (1937), ch. 1–5; a careful study which throws light on Japanese policy as well as on China's position as affected by the World War. L. LAWTON, *Empires of the Far East,* 2 vols. (1912), vol. 2, bk. 6 (Korea); bk. 7 (Manchuria). LEE HOON-KOO, *Korean Immigrants in Manchuria* (1931). H. F. MACNAIR, *Modern Chinese History, Selected Readings* (1923), ch. 16, sec. 72–73. W. W. McLAREN, *Political History of Japan* (1916), ch. 11–15, esp. ch. 13. G. ONO, *War and Armament Expenditure of Japan* (1922); a careful study. R. P. PORTER, *Japan, the New World Power* (1915), ch. 38–47. P. S. REINSCH, *American Diplomat in China* (1922), ch. 21–26; Japan's war policy as it appeared to the American Minister at Peking. *South Manchurian Railway, Manchuria, Land of Opportunities* (1922); contains much interesting material on the country and its recent development. T. TAKEUCHI, *War and Diplomacy in the Japanese Empire* (1935); an important study. B. L. P. WEALE (pseud.), *Fight for the Republic in China* (1917), ch. 5–7; highly critical of Japan. HON. ICHIRO TOKUTOMI, *Japanese-American Relations* (1922); critical of the United States. CHITOSHI YANAGA, *Japan since Perry* (1949), ch. 22.

CHAPTER XVII

CHINA AND WORLD WAR I

I. THE CONSEQUENCES OF NEUTRALITY

CHINA declared war on the Central Powers in August, 1917, thereby ranging herself with the Allied Powers as a co-belligerent. From 1914 to 1917 she had maintained, to the best of her ability, her position of declared neutrality, which meant that the government had pursued a negative policy designed to keep the country free from entanglements. As a result of this negative policy had come the establishment of Japan in Shantung province, and the enlargement of her interests in other parts of the Chinese Republic.

Unquestionably, neutrality in a struggle which in no way affected her was the logical and proper policy for China to pursue. And yet, at an early period, she might have been brought into the war on the side of the Entente—not, however, because of any hostility to Germany, but from fear of Japan. Yüan Shih-k'ai intimated his readiness to undertake the reduction of Tsingtao in 1914, in order to prevent what actually took place, its occupation by Japan. Not only was he refused encouragement in the matter, but Japan actually vetoed Chinese action. The other Powers took their lead then, as later, from the Japanese because of their preoccupation in Europe. At a subsequent time President Yüan signified his willingness to depart from neutrality in favor of the Entente, without receiving a favorable reply to his suggestion.

It may be thought that China should have declared war on her own responsibility if it was believed that anything could be gained by so doing. But it must be remembered that the Powers had taught her to believe that she should show no initiative in foreign affairs, for, whenever she had gone ahead on her own responsibility, she had become involved in trouble. Another consideration must be kept in mind in regard to China's policy during the early years of the war. She had an empty treasury which was being supplied out of a foreign purse, and, after the American withdrawal from the International Banking Group, and subsequent indications of American unreliability as a source of supply for pressing governmental purposes, Japan furnished the funds for a large part of China's reorganization. The only advances on the part of the group after 1914 came necessarily through the Yokohama Specie Bank, representing the Japanese participants. Because of this dependence on foreign funds for reorganization purposes, the hesitancy of Peking in adopting any policy not endorsed by the foreign Powers is easily understood.

2. THE MOVEMENT TO END NEUTRALITY

By 1917, however, a very different situation had arisen. With the opening of that year there came the development of a positive American leadership in China which was productive of results while it lasted. A sketch has already been given of the movement of 1917 to bring China into the war under American guidance. February brought the request of the United States that other neutral states should join with her in a protest against the extended German submarine warfare on the ground that it violated accepted principles of international law and was an offense against humanity. The American minister at Peking urged that China should make use of this opportunity to develop a positive policy under the protection of the United States. Only in this way, it was maintained, could China gain admittance to the Peace Conference, and secure a voice in the settlement of the Far Eastern questions in which she had so vital an interest. Perhaps not realizing fully that such a protest could only be the first step in a series which would lead to a declaration of war, China despatched a dignified note to the German government, protesting in the name of International Law and humanity against the carrying on of an unrestricted submarine warfare. When a satisfactory answer was not received, as the next logical step China was brought face to face with the necessity of severing diplomatic relations with the Central Powers. If nothing else, the government stood to lose considerable "face" with the foreign and Chinese world alike if it failed to follow up its note of protest.

It was more clearly perceived that war might follow when the government came to contemplate breaking off relations with Germany than when the first step was taken. Consequently, some who had not opposed the first step hesitated over taking the second. The Premier, Tuan Chi-jui, who stood to lose more "face" than anyone else if nothing was done, favored going on. The President, however, was doubtful of the expediency of the new move. And it was still a question which, under the constitution, had the decisive voice in the matter, the President or the Cabinet. Before this question could be decided Tuan found it necessary to resign, retiring to his residence at Tientsin. This alarmed President Li, who felt that it would be impossible to reconstruct the Cabinet under any other leadership. Finally he was forced to give in on the war question in order to bring the Premier back to Peking. When the question of severing relations with Germany was presented to Parliament, the Premier was sustained by considerable majorities in both Houses.

Germany did not modify her policy as a result of the severance of relations with her by the United States, China, and the other states which followed the original American lead. Thus China was forced to consider the third step in the process, an actual declaration of war. As a preliminary to this, the Premier began negotiations in order to define the extent of China's participation, and secure tangible evidence of benefits to be derived from it. In return for a declaration of war, which the Entente Powers and the United States had come actively to desire, Tuan asked that they agree to the cancellation of the German and Austrian portions of the Boxer indemnity, and to the suspension of payments on the interest and principal of the Boxer indemnity due to the Allies; that foreign troops, maintained in China under the Boxer Protocol, should be withdrawn; and that the conventional tariff should be revised upwards. In return for this he was willing to promise to supply food stuffs, raw materials, and labor. The Allied ministers refused to give him any promises as to the action of their respective governments, and suggested that China declare war first and then negotiate for the concessions she wanted, intimating, however, that she would be well treated in the event of her adherence to their side in the struggle.

This was the attitude taken by many Chinese—that China should determine her policy independent of the attitude of the ministers, thus standing on her own feet in foreign affairs for the first time in many years. By so doing the government would make a decided break from the traditions of the past, from which only harm had come. In addition to this, a declaration of war could not but serve to make friends for China in the Entente camp; and the United States would be strengthened in her friendship for the Republic by the taking of a step in accordance with American advice. Thus the noted scholar, Liang Chi'ch'ao, after explaining his views in some detail, concluded: . . . "that whenever a policy is adopted we should carry out the complete scheme. If we should hesitate in the middle and become afraid to go ahead we will soon find ourselves in an embarrassing position. The Government and Parliament should therefore stir up courage and boldly make the decision and take the step." [1]

But the making of friends in such a manner involves also the making of enemies. This fact was brought home to the Chinese in many ways. It was pointed out to the government that Germany thus far had proven herself to be invincible in the war, and that it would be a great mistake for China to antagonize her. It would be better to play safe for the future, as in the past, by keeping on semi-friendly terms with the entire world.

This fear of German power is well illustrated in the exhortation of K'ang Yu-wei, another well-known scholar, and the leader in the early reform movement. He wrote as follows:

Which side will win the war? I shall not attempt to predict here. But it is undoubted that all the arms of Europe and the industrial and financial strength of the United States and Japan—have proved unavailing against Germany. On the other hand France has lost her Northern provinces, and Belgium, Serbia, and Rumania are blotted off the map. Should Germany be victorious, the whole

[1] Quoted by WEALE, *Fight for the Republic*, p. 332.

of Europe—not to speak of a weak country like China—would be in great peril of extinction. Should she be defeated, Germany still can—after the conclusion of peace—send a fleet to war against us. And as the Powers will be afraid of a second world war, who will come to our aid? Have we not seen the example of Korea? There is no such thing as an army of righteousness which will come to the assistance of weak nations. I cannot bear to think of hearing the angry voice of German guns along our coasts! [2]

Considering the matter from the standpoint of actions and policies of the belligerents, the opponents of a declaration of war could point out that China had no reason for hostility to Germany, except the ancient one of the seizure of Tsingtao in 1898. On the other hand, since 1914 she had been involved in a series of controversies with Japan, and had had a less important but still significant conflict with France, who had tried to extend the limits of her settlement in Tientsin against China's will (the Laohsikai affair), to say nothing of her difficulties with England and Russia over Tibet and Mongolia. Certainly the Entente Powers had not demonstrated to the Chinese a higher ideal of international action than had Germany.

On the other hand, there was a belief in the sincerity of the professions of the United States which led to a feeling of assurance that it would look after the interests of China if she became a belligerent, protecting her against her friends as well as her enemies. And, it must be recognized, the American declarations concerning the rights of small nations, and the necessity for waging war to end war by creating a more ideal international order, were peculiarly adapted to impress the Chinese scholar. But of even more importance in offsetting the argument against a declaration of war, so far as it was put in terms of external relations, was the fact that the United States and the Entente Powers were in a position enabling them immediately to aid the Chinese government, financially and otherwise, while Germany was not.

But there was also an internal argument against participation in the war. Many Chinese felt that it would be wrong for China to undertake a foreign war when she had not yet begun to solve her own pressing internal problems. Not a strong foreign policy, but internal consolidation and reorganization, would prove the best means of preserving the Republic. When one thinks of war he thinks in terms of armies, and when many Chinese thought of armies they thought of the possibility that a declaration of war would tend to strengthen the military party in China, and thus hold back indefinitely the realization of truly representative government.

This is what actually happened, although not directly as a result of participation in the war. Reference has already been made to the calling of a conference of the Tuchuns by the Premier, and to the subsequent happenings, such as the attempt to restore the Manchus, and the establishment of

[2] WEALE, p. 334.

the militarists in control at Peking. These developments grew out of the failure of the Premier to gain concessions from the Powers in advance of the declaration of war, for he had let Parliament know that he was carrying on negotiations, and that he confidently expected to be able to show concrete advantages to be gained by ending China's neutrality. When the negotiations were protracted, the people began to lose interest in the war question. In order to turn attention from their unsatisfactory state, while still keeping control of the situation in parliament and outside, the conference of the Tuchuns was called. From that time the war question fell into the background, and its place was taken by the much more interesting problem, to the Chinese, of the political effect of the consultation with the militarists.

After things had begun to settle down in the fall of 1917, with Tuan Chi-jui again in office as Premier, but with a new President, Fêng Kuo-chang, the war issue was revived. The declaration of a state of war with the Central Powers was actually issued on August 14, 1917. This step was necessary to demonstrate the sincerity of Tuan, to gain the support of the Powers for the new régime, and to put it in a favorable position to finance itself.

3. IMMEDIATE CONSEQUENCES OF PARTICIPATION IN THE WAR

This action had certain very desirable effects for China, and for the Entente as well. On the Chinese side, in the first place, after some negotiations, there was gained a substantial revision of the tariff—the charges being brought from an actual two and one-half per cent to an effective five per cent, which meant an increase of seven per cent over the valuations put on imports and exports in 1901. It should be noted that this was not a very great concession for the Powers to make to China, but rather was an act of elementary justice. She was entitled to this five per cent charge under the Boxer Protocol, but had been unable to get any revision of the treaties after 1901, as values changed, to give her the Customs revenues in percentages to which the Powers had then assented. In the second place, as a result first of her severance of diplomatic relations with the Central Powers in March, and then as a consequence of the declaration of war, China was enabled to resume control of the German and Austrian residential areas in the various treaty ports, such as Tientsin, where they had been granted exclusive concessions. Other German and Austrian public and private properties were assumed, or sequestered, pending adjustments following the war. In the third place, the Entente Powers agreed to a cancellation of the German and Austrian shares of the Boxer indemnity, and to a suspension of payments to the Allies for a five year period. This, together with the increase in revenue from the Customs, helped to relieve the financial situation. Finally, the Chinese thought that they had assured themselves of the right to a seat at the Peace Conference, whenever it should meet, on terms of complete equality with Japan.

The Allies, in turn, gained materially from Chinese participation. They had already been taking advantage of the Chinese labor supply, and the change of status materially facilitated the recruiting of laborers, their training, and their transportation to France. While China sent no armies to the West and did not take any great part in the Siberian operations of the Allies, yet she made a decided contribution to the war through her laborers used behind the lines in France. Their presence enabled many men to be released for military duty who would otherwise have been used in necessary but subsidiary services. Many favorable comments have been made on the value of the Chinese laborer to the Entente.

Again, China agreed to furnish the Allied and Associated Powers with primary materials. The available Chinese surplus, either in foodstuffs or raw materials, was small, but it might easily have been made much larger. This was particularly true of the industrial productivity of the Republic. China might have made a great contribution to the war by the supply of pig-iron and similar materials, if she had been able to finance an increased activity. Unfortunately she had no capital available for this purpose herself, and her allies in the war failed to furnish her with funds or the necessary credits for machinery and supplies. Here the fault lay particularly with the United States, which alone was in a position to take care of China's comparatively small needs. Financial support had been promised her by the American minister so far as he was able, without instructions, to commit his government. These promises were never made good, and, consequently, one effect of China's participation in the war was to throw her directly into the arms of Japan. The Japanese saw the advantage in financing China up to a certain point, and under advantageous conditions, while the Americans lacked their foresight. If Washington had read the future more clearly, there might easily have been a different aftermath to the war for China.

A third gain to the Allies from China's participation in the war, more important than those just mentioned, was the use of the German tonnage then interned in the ports of China. In 1917 the great cry was for ships, and more ships. The desire to get the use of these German vessels was, to a large extent, back of the eagerness of the Entente Powers to bring China into the war. And then German activities in the Far East were definitely brought to an end when China closed her doors to the Germans, driving out many, and interning the remainder for the period of the war. This was of more than immediate importance, particularly to England and Japan, for they had long felt German commercial competition in the Far East. It was well known that Germany was maintaining as many of her commercial contacts in China as possible, in order to resume her trading and financial operations there as soon as the war came to an end. This resumption was made much more difficult by the sequestration of German properties by China and by the internment of German and Austrian subjects.

4. POLITICAL EFFECTS OF CHINA'S ENTRANCE INTO THE WAR

The effects of the war on the Far East up to 1917 have been described in the preceding chapter. The political effects of China's participation during the remaining period before the Peace Conference can now be pointed out.

The initial step leading China into the war had been taken at the suggestion of the United States. At that time, and for some months thereafter, the Chinese attempted to model their conduct on that of their neighbor across the Pacific. This American leadership, if it had been continued and made effective, would have done much to break down the conception of Japanese hegemony on the continent which had been so carefully and systematically built up during the first three years of the war. To avoid this, after she had taken the steps necessary to safeguard her newly-won position through her alliance with Russia, and by means of the secret treaties of 1917 with England, France, and Italy, the Island Empire attempted to wrest the leadership in the move to bring China into the war from the United States. Thus the Japanese minister at Peking rather ostentatiously "advised" China to take the step which was already under contemplation. At the same time the Japanese newspapers in China continually emphasized the negligibility of the United States in the Far East, pointing out that in spite of repeated protestations of American sympathy for and interest in China, the government of the United States had consistently failed to do anything to protect her from the rapacity of the foreign Powers. A case in point was the American withdrawal from the first Consortium, on the ground that its terms for making the reorganization loan threatened the independence and the administrative integrity of China. Then the United States failed to finance the Republic on more favorable terms than those offered by the International Group, whose terms China was consequently forced to accept. On the other hand, it was pointed out that if China would only become more friendly to Japan, a nation of "doers" rather than of "sayers," she might expect to be helped out of her manifold difficulties. The Japanese also took advantage of every American slip in policy, such as the Lansing-Ishii Agreement, to bring home to the Chinese the apparent emptiness of American professions, and to emphasize the seeming fact that all of the Western nations recognized the primacy of Japan in the Far East. This policy was still further forwarded by the concentration of the authorities at Washington on the western phases of the struggle after the United States became an active participant. All other considerations were subordinated to that of winning the war in the West.

Thus, when China became disrupted in the spring and summer of 1917, prior to her declaration of war on Germany, the American government, in a note presented to the Chinese Foreign Office, declared that it was much more important that China should set her own house in order than that she should declare war on the Central Powers. The advice was not only well meant but it was sound. Yet it came strangely from the very government which, a few months earlier, had been urging China to get into the war. Japan took advantage of this note to protest vehemently, in the press of the country, against this foreign "interference" in the internal affairs of her neighbor. When nothing further was said about the matter by the United States, she was able to say to the Chinese that the Americans had recognized the right of Japan to determine the nature of the communications passed between Washington and Peking. It was considered by the Chinese to be but another indication of the recognition in the West of Japanese hegemony in eastern Asia.

When China, through the military government set up at Peking, had definitely committed herself to participation in the war, the Japanese set about reaping further advantages for themselves out of the new development. The failure of the United States to finance the Chinese government played directly into the hands of Japan, for she gladly undertook that task herself. Loan after loan was made to Tuan Chi-jui's government during 1918 and even after the end of the war in Europe. Sometimes security in the form of the pledging of provincial taxes was demanded; more often concessions of every sort, from the right to build railroads and open mines, to industrial undertakings, were made the *quid pro quo* for loans. Many of them were made under the terms of an agreement reached in 1918 for coöperative participation in the war. A War Participation Board was set up in Peking, for the ostensible purpose of working out plans for the rendering of military aid to the Allies, but for the real purpose of borrowing money from the Japanese for internal purposes, money which went to line the pockets of the officials. This period marked the height of Japanese power in China until after 1931. Under the direction of the War Participation Board, a military agreement was reached between the two countries in 1918, by the terms of which, briefly, they agreed to concert plans in common for war undertakings—the Japanese to furnish advisers for the Chinese army and navy, and to finance any activities undertaken; the Chinese, in turn, to furnish Japan with information as to their military resources, and to purchase war materials from her. The signature of the armistice agreement should have brought to an end the activities of the War Participation Board, but it was continued on the pretext of the necessity for protecting the two countries against the introduction of Bolshevism from the north. It was ended only with the overthrow of the Anfu clique, which was finally driven from Peking in the summer of 1920 by the armies of General Wu P'ei-fu.

But Japan's activities were not confined to Peking. She managed to put some of her eggs in other baskets, in order that they might be brought home the more safely. While Japanese money was flowing into the pockets of the Anfuites, some of it found its way into the coffers of the Canton government headed by Dr. Sun Yat-sen, and some of it was used to build up the power of Chang Tso-lin in Manchuria. Japan conceived her interest to demand the maintenance of the existing chaotic conditions in China, and she found that the easiest way to attain that end was to make it possible for all of the factions to be supplied, more or less well, with money and arms. To understand from this that every government in China was manipulated from Tokyo, of course, would be far from the truth. It was not necessary for Japan to direct their several activities to attain the end of the continuation of internal strife. All that was necessary was for her to provide, directly or indirectly, the sinews of war, and the real or fancied differences of interest between the various factions did the rest. Each faction thought, or professed to think, that only under its direction could China be reëstablished in her former honorable position in the world. Dr. Sun Yat-sen inveighed against the Anfu Club while it was in control at Peking, but that did not make him ready to coöperate with the government controlled by Ts'ao Kun and Chang Tso-lin, which succeeded it. On the contrary, he soon began to negotiate with the exiled Anfuites with a view to overthrowing the new régime with their help. And, when Chang Tso-lin was on the point of being driven out of Peking by Wu P'ei-fu, Dr. Sun was found to be in alliance with his former enemy, General Chang. All of this was made possible by a continued supply of Japanese money to the various factions, and by the furnishing of credits in Japan for the purchase of war materials.

5. THE LEGAL SITUATION AT TIME OF PARIS CONFERENCE

Before moving on to a consideration of the Peace Conference and the significance of its decisions in relation to the Far East, it may be well to summarize, from the legal standpoint, the situation as it had developed after 1914. The German holdings in Shantung province, as far as they were comprehended in the contract or lease of 1898, gave Germany no title to territory as owner, nor did Germany acquire sovereign rights in all or part of Shantung province. Sovereignty over the entire leased area was expressly reserved by China, the exercise of sovereignty being waived in favor of Germany for ninety-nine years. Legally Germany was merely an occupier, holding under the limitations of the lease contract. Consequently, all that could be acquired from Germany by any other Power was succession to her rights and privileges. But one of the limitations or conditions under which the leasehold was to continue was that it should not be transferred to any other Power by Germany. In other words, the maintenance of the lease was made dependent on its continuation in the hands of the original lessee.

Thus, without any other factors being considered, a transfer of the lease-hold by Germany to any other state, through the treaty of peace, should have brought with it the abrogation of the agreement.

Consequently the Japanese right of succession to Germany at Kiaochow Bay, because of her reduction of the territory by military means, was, at least, imperfect. When it is considered, further, that the original agreement was forced from China by Germany, it may be held that Japan was in the position of the receiver of stolen property. He does not have title to that property because he has taken it from the thief, but merely holds it until it can be restored to the original and rightful owner. So Japan may be con-sidered, after her operations in 1914, to have acquired Chinese property, which she held temporarily, pending its restoration to the original owner, or agreement as to its ultimate disposition. In other words, her title still remained to be established by agreement with China and not with Ger-many, who had no legal right to transfer the leasehold to any other Power, and consequently could not give a clear title to it.

The 1915 agreement with respect to Shantung, however, effected a funda-mental change in the situation. By the Shantung treaty, agreement was reached between China and Japan as to the ultimate disposition of this Chinese property. The government of the Republic recognized in advance any settlement which might be reached directly by negotiation between Japan and Germany, with the supplementary understanding that if Ger-many transferred her leasehold to Japan the latter would restore it to China on certain conditions. Furthermore, in 1918 the Chinese government sup-plemented its undertaking of 1915 by agreeing, in an exchange of notes, to an arrangement of the various questions in relation to Shantung. This agreement provided: (1) for joint working of the Kiaochow-Tsinan rail-way after its status had been finally established; (2) for the ending of Japa-nese civil administration outside of Tsingtao; (3) for a retirement of Japanese troops to Tsingtao, leaving the policing of the railway to Chinese troops; and (4) for the engagement of Japanese "for the headquarters of this police force, at the principal railway stations and at the police training school." The Japanese position was further strengthened by its recognition by Russia (the Czarist government) in 1916, and by England, France, and Italy in the 1917 secret treaties. It should be noted, however, that this recog-nition was not given because of the legality, under international law, of Japan's claims to the reversion of the German rights in Shantung, but from considerations of expediency.

China's participation in the war, in its turn, brought about certain legal conditions, and established certain legal relationships. In the first place, it brought to an end all treaty engagements between China and Germany which were in the nature of servitudes, or were inconsistent with the carry-ing on of war, or the making of peace. Thus, if China had declared war on

Germany in 1914, it would be clear that the 1898 agreements would have been brought to an end by that act, and that German extraterritorial rights in China would have ceased. These rights, resting on treaty provisions, could be restored only if directly revived, by mutual consent, in the peace settlement. In the second place, upon her declaration of war on Germany, all property of the German government in China reverted to that country for administration temporarily, or for confiscation immediately, depending upon the positive action of the Chinese government. Thus China would have reacquired her position as the exerciser of sovereignty in the leased territory. But China did not declare war until 1917, and at that time she had already agreed to abide by any decision reached by direct negotiation between Japan and Germany as to the disposition of the German interests. This agreement was not abrogated by China's entrance into the war, although the Chinese delegation at Paris maintained that their country's "entry into the War so vitally changed the situation contemplated in the treaty (of 1915) that, on the principle of *rebus sic stantibus,* it ceased to be applicable." [3]

6. THE PARIS CONFERENCE AND THE FAR EAST

When the Peace Conference met at Paris, in January, 1919, the Chinese factions united in sending a delegation to represent the interests of the country. The Chinese delegates presented to the conference a request for the direct restoration to China of the German leasehold and rights in Shantung province, and for the cancellation of the agreements relating to Shantung province made between Japan and China in 1915 and 1918. Their case was based upon several contentions. First of all, it was maintained that China's entrance into the war worked direct restitution to her of the German leased territory, in spite of the 1915 agreement to accept the result of direct negotiations between Japan and Germany. For, secondly, the Chinese delegates insisted that these agreements should be considered invalid in their totality, including the Shantung treaty. And, consequently, the 1918 agreements must be treated in the same way, since they rested for their validity on the agreements of 1915. The 1915 treaty, they maintained, should be considered invalid for two principal reasons: first, because it had been signed by the Chinese negotiators under threat of war, and, second, because it had never been ratified in the manner provided for by the Chinese constitution.

Before the Peace Conference convened, Japan had begun to lay her plans for the retention of the rights promised her by the Allies. Not much was said in the press discussions about the Japanese claims in Shantung. But

---

[3] Tyau, *China Awakened,* appendix B, p. 397. See also statement of Dr. John C. Ferguson before Foreign Relations Committee of Senate. Quoted by Willoughby, *Foreign Rights and Interests in China* (1st ed.), note, p. 392.

another issue was prepared to be presented to the delegates assembled at Paris. This was in the form of a demand for the recognition of the principle of racial equality. Apparently the Japanese people, if the press truly reflected their views, were much more interested in the establishment of that principle, one to which, on the surface, exception could hardly be justly taken by the nations fighting a war for democracy, than they were in the securing of material advantages out of the war. The principle, it need hardly be pointed out, had application particularly against the United States and the British Dominions, which had erected barriers against the free access of Asiatic peoples to their shores. It could have had no other significance, since in every other way the Japanese were on a footing of complete equality in their intercourse with the other members of the society of nations. To be sure, China and other Asiatic countries were not, but Japan had insisted upon the same special privileges in her intercourse with them that other states enjoyed, and had shown no indication of a willingness to give them up.

This part of her case was undoubtedly prepared by Japan to neutralize American opposition to her contentions with regard to Shantung province. It was well known that China was looking to the United States for support at Paris, and, in spite of the Lansing-Ishii Agreement, the government of Japan was fearful lest she should secure it.

The contentions of Japan may be summarized briefly. First, she demanded that her right of succession to the German holdings and rights in Shantung province, and in the north Pacific, should be recognized in the treaty of peace. She based her claims on her sacrifices of men and of treasure in the war, on the inter-Allied agreements, which she then produced for the first time officially, and on her willingness to restore Kiaochow to China by negotiation, after she had received it from Germany, and conditionally. Secondly, she asked for "acceptance of the principle of the equality of nations and the just treatment of their nationals."

The latter demand was rejected, largely as a result of the veto of President Wilson, put upon the ground that it referred to immigration and its restriction, and was consequently unacceptable to the United States. The Japanese were consequently in a strong position to press for the acceptance of their first contention, actually the more important to them. They had lived up to their obligations as an ally, not only clearing the Germans out of the Far East, but policing the Pacific and part of the route to Europe. This had meant a serious drain on the national treasury, in addition to involving the loss of life of Japanese subjects. Were they alone among the Allies to be cast aside and denied any share in the material fruits of victory? If so, then they would play a lone hand in the future and have nothing to do with the proposed League of Nations.

When the Japanese delegates began to intimate an intention of leaving

the conference, as the Italians had done over the Fiume question, the opposition of President Wilson weakened. And, with the loss of his support, the
Chinese lost their case at Paris, for the other Powers were definitely committed to Japan by their agreements made during the war. So, while Japan
failed to gain a recognition of racial equality, she did secure the reversion of
the German rights in the Far East which she had hoped for as the chief
result of her participation in the war for the purpose of "preserving the
peace of the Far East."

7. FAR EASTERN PROVISIONS OF TREATY OF VERSAILLES

By the terms of the peace, China was relieved of all responsibility for the
fulfillment of her obligations to Germany under the terms of the Boxer
Protocol; she regained control of the German concessions at Tientsin and
Hankow; she was confirmed in her possession of the public properties of
the German government in China, except those of a diplomatic and consular
character; she was relieved of all liability arising from the internment of
German nationals during the war, and from the seizure of the German
vessels interned in Chinese waters; and she secured the restitution of the
astronomical instruments taken from Peking at the time of the Boxer rebellion. Japan succeeded to the German position in Shantung acquired
under the agreements of 1898 and subsequent agreements, including
the leasehold of Kiaochow Bay and the economic rights enjoyed in the
province. This succession was conditioned by a verbal promise given to the
"Council of Three" that Japan would restore to China, by direct negotiation, all political rights in the province, retaining for herself only the economic rights and privileges.

It was this promise, coupled with the feeling that if only the League of
Nations could be established China would be able to secure ultimate justice,
which President Wilson used to justify his own participation in the award.
However, he failed completely to see that a restoration to China of her political rights in Shantung province, without the economic rights, would
leave China with the shadow and Japan with the substance.

This was the view of the Chinese people when the news of the award
reached them. It was also the view of their delegates at Paris. The latter
tried first of all to register their opposition to the award by signing the treaty
with a reservation as to the Shantung clauses, and, when they were denied
the right to sign with reservations, they refused to append their signatures
to the document. In this they were expressing the views of an aroused public opinion at home. The first reaction to the Shantung decision came in the
form of the student movement,[4] directed both against officials in the government who were suspected of being tools in the hands of Japan, and against

[4] On the student movement, see chapter XIII, sec. 6.

the Japanese in China. In the latter case their activities were largely confined to propaganda designed to show to the people the true state of affairs. But that it seriously affected the Japanese was shown by the pressure which the Imperial government brought to bear on Peking to compel the Chinese to put down the students by force. After the student protest had begun, it was sustained by the action of the merchants, who instituted a nation-wide boycott against the Japanese.[5] As a result of the pressure exerted by these two elements, Japan indicated a willingness to enter upon negotiations with China to carry out her promise with respect to Shantung. The Peking government, however, refused to consider such negotiations except on the basis of complete and unconditional restoration. This impasse continued until the meeting of the Conference at Washington.

8. REVIVAL OF THE CONSORTIUM

One other World War development was of sufficient importance to deserve notice. It was President Wilson who had refused the support of the American government when it was asked for by the American participants in the first International Banking Group. By November, 1917, however, he had reached the conclusion that there must be international coöperation in the financing of China, in order to prevent any one state from gaining financial control of the Republic. Consequently the State Department took the lead in the reorganization of the International Group, with the elimination of Germany and Russia, but the inclusion of the United States, making it again a Consortium of Four Powers. The idea back of the reorganization was the pooling of all agreements, past, present, and future, for the financing of the Chinese government, and for the development of communications and industry in China. After negotiations between the financial agents representative of the several countries concerned, agreement was reached as to the conditions of their activities, with one exception. The Japanese desired to exclude Manchuria and Eastern Inner Mongolia from the field of Consortium interest, in spite of the fact that those territories were an integral part of China, and that China was to be the field of interest of the Consortium. Under pressure, however, they receded from their position after they had been promised that nothing should be undertaken in those regions which would prejudice their interests therein.

The Consortium came into being again in 1920, but it found no scope for its activities, for the Chinese were hostile, fearing lest, under the guise of aiding China and developing her resources, the aim should be to establish an international financial control of the country. This fear was gradually allayed as the Chinese became convinced that the declared aims were also

[5] The effectiveness of the boycott is revealed by the fact that imports from Japan of cotton yarn declined, from May to September, from more than twelve to less than four thousand *piculs*. Other imports showed the same relative decline.

the true aims of the Consortium. But it nevertheless remained inactive, largely, perhaps, because of the internal turmoil in the Republic, but partly because of the lack of real interest on the part of some of its members in international as distinguished from national undertakings.

9. CONSEQUENCES OF CHINA'S REFUSAL TO ACCEPT TREATY

The refusal of the Chinese government and people to accept the Shantung provisions of the Treaty of Versailles, and, consequently, the non-signature of the treaty, meant that certain questions growing out of Japanese and Chinese participation in the war were left unsettled. The most difficult of these was that relating to the ultimate disposition of the German rights, titles, and interests in Shantung province. Since this delicate question was only settled in connection with the Washington Conference, its consideration may well be postponed to the chapter on the Conference.

Another series of questions related to the reëstablishment of normal treaty relations with Germany. The war between China and Germany was declared ended by presidential mandate of September 15, 1919, and German consular and diplomatic representation was renewed. Negotiations were then undertaken which resulted in the conclusion of an agreement on May 20, 1921, which was ratified by the Chinese President on June 28. The most important provisions of this agreement were those embodied in articles three and four, by which Germany permanently waived jurisdiction over her nationals in China, placing them entirely under the authority of China's law and her courts, and by which tariff autonomy, so far as German imports and exports were concerned, was conceded.

Since unusual interest attached to the abrogation of extraterritorial rights, the text of the third article of the treaty may be quoted.

The citizens of either Republic, residing in the territory of the other, shall in conformity with the laws and regulations of the country have the right to travel, to settle down, and to carry on commerce or industry in all places where the citizens of another nation are allowed to do so.

They are placed, both their persons and property, under the jurisdiction of the local courts; they shall respect the laws of the country wherein they reside. They shall not pay higher imposts, taxes or contributions than the nationals of the country.

In answer to certain questions raised by the German representative, the Chinese Foreign Minister, Dr. W. W. Yen, made the following statements in an appended note:

1) The Chinese government promises to give full protection to the peaceful undertakings of Germans in China, and agrees not to further sequestrate their properties except in accordance with the generally recognized principles of international law and the provisions of the laws of China; provided that the German Government will treat the Chinese residents in Germany in like manner.

2) . . . Law suits of Germans in China shall be tried in the modern courts, according to the modern codes, with the right of appeal, and in accordance with the regular legal procedure. During the period of litigation the assistance of German lawyers and interpreters who have been duly recognized by the court is permitted. 3) In regard to law suits in the Mixed Court, in which Germans are involved either as one or both of the parties, the Chinese Government will in the future try to find a solution so as to insure justice and fairness to all the parties concerned.[6]

A simultaneous German "Declaration" accepted the validity of Articles 128–134 of the Versailles treaty, bringing to an end the special privileges enjoyed by Germany in China prior to the war. Beyond this, the declarations provided the basis for the adjustment of war claims and those growing out of the sequestration by China of the property of Germans. By these provisions for the repeal of all the laws and regulations issued by China governing trading with Germany in war time, the way was opened for her reëntry as an active competitor in the China trade.

This preliminary commercial agreement, supplemented by another exchange of notes providing for the settlement of outstanding questions, terminated the war in its Far Eastern phase, except for the settlement of the questions at issue between the two "allies," China and Japan. The war, however, had temporarily complicated the politics of the Far East by reason of Allied intervention in the region north of China. This complication was the result of the collapse of Russia, and the establishment of the Bolshevists in control of the machinery of government. It remains, therefore, for the Siberian question to be considered, before we are in position fully to appraise the necessity for, and the results of, the Washington Conference.

REFERENCES FOR FURTHER STUDY

M. J. BAU, *Foreign Relations of China* (1921); a survey and study of the entire period by a competent Chinese student. CARNEGIE ENDOWMENT FOR INTERNATIONAL PEACE, *Treaties of Peace, 1919–1923*, vol. 1; for terms of treaties affecting China. FREDERICK V. FIELD, *American Participation in the China Consortiums*, 1931; ch. 9–11. RUSSELL H. FIFIELD, *Woodrow Wilson and the Far East* (1952). GREAT BRITAIN, FOREIGN OFFICE, *Correspondence Respecting the New Financial Consortium in China*, misc. no. 9 (1921). A. W. GRISWOLD, *The Far Eastern Policy of the United States* (1938), ch. 5–6; a completely documented study of American policy for the period covered. STANLEY HIGH, *China's Place in the Sun* (1922), ch. 7; good discussion of the student movement. T. E. LA FARGUE, *China and the World War* (1937), ch. 6–8; an excellent treatment of the subject. J. V. A. MacMURRAY, *Treaties and Conventions with and Concerning China*, 2 vols. (1921); see vol. 2 for text of agreements of the World War I period. H. F. MacNAIR, *Modern Chinese History, Selected Readings* (1923), ch. 17, sec. 74. T. F. MILLARD, *Democracy and the Eastern Question* (1919); critical of Japan. R. A. NOREM, *Kiaochow Leased Territory* (1936); a good legal

---

[6] From text as given, *China Year Book*, 1925, pp. 783–785.

treatment. P. S. REINSCH, *American Diplomat in China* (1922), ch. 24–27; gives point of view of and interpretation put on events by the American Minister. P. S. REINSCH, *Analysis of the Consortium Situation,* in Chinese Social and Political Science Review, vol. 7, no. 1, January, 1923. M. T. Z. TYAU, *China Awakened* (1922), ch. 16–18, appendix B; gives Chinese interpretation of international relations in Far East during World War I. B. L. PUTNAM WEALE (pseud.), *Fight for the Republic in China* (1917), ch. 15–16; documents in appendix. B. L. PUTNAM WEALE, *Truth About China and Japan* (1919); appendices especially worth consulting. W. R. WHEELER, *China and the World War* (1919); a good brief account of the subject. W. W. WILLOUGHBY, *Foreign Rights and Interests in China,* 2 vols. (1927), vol. 1, ch. 7–9, 12, 14. G. Z. WOOD, *Twenty-one Demands* (1921); analysis of demands and negotiations from Chinese point of view. H. G. W. WOODHEAD (ed.), *China Year Book,* issues of years 1916–1925, chapters on international events. CHITOSHI YANAGA, *Japan Since Perry* (1949), ch. 24–25.

CHAPTER XVIII

RUSSIA IN THE FAR EAST

I. AREA AND RESOURCES OF SIBERIA

No STUDY of the recent history of the Far East would be complete without more than incidental treatment of the development of Russian interests and an examination of Russian policy. Furthermore, developments during and after World War I made the Russian territorial position of almost equal interest, from the international standpoint, to that of Japan or China. But in order to understand these developments it is necessary to appreciate the position of Siberia in the Russian Empire prior to the revolution of 1917; to consider the character of its population; to estimate briefly its resources; and to understand its position, as a region of the Russian Empire, in the world movements of 1914–1917.

"Siberia," as Kropotkin points out,[1] "is not the frozen land buried in snow and peopled with exiles only, that it is imagined to be, even by many Russians. In its southern parts it is as rich in natural productions as are the southern parts of Canada, which it resembles so much in its physical aspects." It was in large part because of the circumstances of its acquisition and settlement that it came to mean, to many people, a land of total desolation.

At the time of the outbreak of World War I, Siberia, as an area in the Russian Empire, comprised over 4,800,000 square miles of territory, with a total population of somewhat over ten millions of people. This territory stretched from the Ural Mountains in the west to the Sea of Okhotsk in the east, and from Manchuria and Mongolia northwards to the Arctic Ocean. Large stretches of this area, it is true, were not inhabited, nor were they habitable for Europeans. Parts of it were suitable only for the raising of reindeer, and for fishing and hunting, many valuable fur-bearing animals being found. Another large section furnished vast timber tracts. Further to the south, Siberia contained fertile lands suitable for cultivation. In this area the climate is such that wheat and other cereals may be easily and profitably grown.

The entire region known as Siberia was divided, for governmental purposes, into ten governments and provinces. The most populous of these was the government of Tomsk with, in 1915, an estimated population of four million.

[1] *Memoirs of a Revolutionist*, p. 169.

2. ACQUISITION OF SIBERIA

This enormous territory was acquired by Russia in a piece-meal fashion, much as England, and later the United States, occupied the continental area of what is now the United States. As early as 1555 it is said that Russia received an annual tribute of one thousand sables from some of the tribes to the east of the Urals. But the actual conquest and occupation of the land dated from 1580, when Yermak, a Cossack brigand, having failed to keep out of trouble in European Russia, crossed the Urals with a small band of followers and took possession of the territory having as its seat of government a town called Sibir. From this place the name of the whole region was derived. The territory he occupied was offered to the Czar in return for a pardon for his past offenses. From this time on, for a century, the advance of Russia was slow but steady. In 1587 the town of Tobolsk was founded; the establishment of Yakutsk followed in 1632; Lake Baikal was reached in 1651, and the town of Irkutsk was founded; and the years 1655–1658 witnessed the conquest of the Buriat tribes living in the region around Lake Baikal, in spite of a strong resistance on their part. Prior to this time a rapid march was made across the frozen north, and the Sea of Okhotsk was reached in 1639, the whole northern region being added to the Russian Empire. Following this, an attempt was made to penetrate the regions east of Lake Baikal from farther to the south. Moving across northern Manchuria, Habarov sought the Amur, the great waterway of Eastern Siberia. Following along the Amur he came to the Ussuri River and attempted to occupy the region drained by it.

Up to this time the Russian advance had been opposed only by loosely-organized and weak tribes of semi-barbarians. But when the Amur and Ussuri regions were reached, the Russian advance was checked by the opposition of the Manchus, who had just established themselves in control of China. The attempt of the Manchus to drive the Russians out of northern Manchuria was eminently successful, the seal to their success being set in the treaty of Nerchinsk (August 27, 1689), the first treaty negotiated by China with a European state in the period of modern history. By it, the Russians agreed to withdraw from the region of the Amur. From 1689 until after the first quarter of the nineteenth century the Russian advance was halted.

But at the same time that the maritime nations of Europe were insisting on the opening of China to foreign intercourse on less restrictive conditions, the Russians again manifested an interest in the Amur territory. In 1846 an expedition was sent out to explore the river to its mouth. The report of this expedition was purposely made unfavorable, and Russian interest might not have been aroused in the East if it had not been for the work of one man, who bears to the second period of advance the relation that Yermak bears to the first. In 1847 Muraviev was appointed by the Czar to the position of Governor-General of Siberia. Under his direction a second expedition was sent to the mouth of the Amur. The report of this expedition was so favorable that Muraviev determined not to rest until Siberia had been extended until it had the river as its boundary to the south. In 1850, under his direction, the town of Nicolaievsk was founded at its mouth. But he realized that it would be difficult to substantiate Russia's claim to the territory on the basis of exploration and the establishment of one settlement, and he determined to colonize the entire region. In order to accomplish this, he was forced to rely on his own resources, as he could not get men and supplies from Russia. Consequently he asked for and received permission to raise an army from among the inhabitants of Siberia for the defense of the territory and for its settlement. He then proceeded to release convicts and enlist them in his force, and he added to their number from among the Cossacks. With them he began the settlement of the Amur and provided for its defense. De Castries Bay was occupied, Alexandrovsk was founded, and a claim was advanced to the island of Saghalin on the basis of exploration and occupation. All of this occupied the years from the time of Muraviev's appointment as Governor-General of Siberia until the outbreak of the Crimean War (1847-1856). At that time the problem was complicated by the appearance, off the mouth of the Amur, of an Anglo-French fleet. The initial attacks were repulsed, however, and, because of their preoccupation elsewhere, the English and the French made no further attempts to dispossess the Russians.

In 1858, while the Western Powers were attempting to secure a revision of the treaties with China, Muraviev sought to consolidate the Russian gains in the north by agreement with China. The result was the treaty of Aigun (1858), by which the Russo-Chinese boundary was fixed at the Amur River as far as the Ussuri River, from whence it was left undetermined. Count Putiatin, the Russian envoy to Peking in 1860, was able then to secure an additional agreement with China by which the territory east of the Ussuri was brought within the Russian Empire, and sanction was given to the Russian occupation of Peter the Great and Possiet Bays. This brought Russia to the Pacific and extended her territories south to the Korean border, giving her an excellent natural port at Vladivostok, although not satisfying her desire for an ice-free port on the Pacific.

It should be noted that this advance was largely the result of the foresight and labor of one man, Muraviev, and that it did not then represent the expression of a national policy of expansion to the east. As a matter of fact, Muraviev, from the beginning, had to combat the opposition of influential officials at St. Petersburg. This opposition was due, at first, to the desire to see Russia face ever westward, and then, in 1858-1860, to fear

lest the advance should embroil Russia with China. It was not until the
Court was presented with the accomplished fact in the form of the treaties
with China that Muraviev secured complete recognition for his services.
Then he was made a Count, with the full title Count Muraviev Amursky.

3. SETTLEMENT OF TERRITORY

The vast territory thus acquired over a period of three centuries was
settled at first very slowly and then, particularly after 1890, with increasing rapidity. Leaving out of consideration the native peoples such as the
Buriats, three distinct elements contributed to its settlement. The initial
occupation was largely the work of Cossacks. They spread out thinly over
the regions first acquired, thus holding them for Russia. The second element, brought into the country in comparatively large numbers after the
first quarter of the nineteenth century, was entirely different. From 1823
to 1887, no less than seven hundred thousand exiles were sent into Siberia from European Russia. Some of these were of the criminal classes,
but many of them were political prisoners, and men of a rather high type.
They were followed by their families and many of them settled permanently in the country. Among the political exiles may be mentioned
the Decembrists, following the failure of the revolutionary movement of
1825; Polish dissenters in and after 1863; and those who lent themselves
to the successive revolutionary movements up to the outbreak of the war
in 1914. This exile system, even for political offenders, was brought to an
end in 1914, but not before it had contributed materially to the upbuild-
ing of Siberia from the standpoint of population.

The third, and by far the most important, element consisted of peasant
emigrant settlers. This emigrant movement began after 1860, and was
given an impetus by the abolition of serfdom in European Russia. Thus
about two million emigrant settlers came into Siberia from 1860 to 1863.
About five hundred thousand more came in during the twenty-year
period following 1870. After that time, as rail communications were developed the tide of emigrants flowed much more strongly. The greatest
single contributing factor to the development of the country was undoubtedly the Trans-Siberian Railroad.

The first suggestion of a railway to the Pacific was made in 1858. In
1884 the Perm-Ekaterinburg-Tiumen Railroad, projected in 1875, was
carried to completion. In 1890 the Trans-Ural line was extended to Cheliabinsk, and, in 1891, the Trans-Siberian road was authorized by Imperial
Rescript. This railway development changed the entire character of the
Russian relationship to her Far Eastern provinces. As these successive
developments were carried to completion the country began to be more
fully settled, the emigrant following closely in the wake of the railway

pioneer. And this settlement, and the greater ease of communication, naturally attracted the attention of the Imperial government to the region east of Lake Baikal.

The railroad had been projected originally for economic reasons, but at the same time it was a sound move toward integrating the Empire. When the government came to undertake its construction, it was apparent that it would be a great saving if it could be built across northern Manchuria to Vladivostok; and the defeat of China in her war with Japan made it possible to secure the railway rights in Manchuria which have already been described.[2] The Manchurian section of the Trans-Siberian road was known as the Chinese Eastern Railway.

After 1896 the Russian government committed itself to a policy of open expansion in the Far East. This led it into the undertakings in Manchuria and Korea which brought it into conflict with Japan. But the policy was also expressed in the government's encouragement of the east-ward movement of the Russian peasant. This encouragement was made even more emphatic after the defeat of 1904–1905 in order to make sure that the territories actually incorporated in the Empire should be strongly Russian in their character and population. The Russian population of Siberia in 1904 was about 6,500,000. In 1906 over $1,300,000 was devoted to assisting emigration. This was increased in 1908 to ten million dollars, and in that year about half a million people settled in Siberia.

Siberia was not invaded by the Japanese armies in the course of the Russo-Japanese War, but many Russian troops passed through the territory on their way to the Manchurian battlefields. This revealed the nature of the country to many people who had gained no adequate conception of its possibilities prior to the war. In that way the conflict promoted the emigration movement, for many of the soldiers, upon their demobilization, returned for purposes of settlement on the land.

The treaty of Portsmouth had a more direct effect on Siberia, for it contained two clauses of extreme importance to its people. In the first place, Russia lost title to the southern half of the island of Saghalin, which she had gained in 1875 by exchange with Japan for her shadowy title to the Kurile Islands. In the second place, she was forced to grant to Japanese fishermen the right to fish in Siberian territorial waters. Another effect of the war was, through the loss to Russia of her port facilities in the Liaotung peninsula, the enhancement of the importance of Vladivostok, which she proceeded to make into a strongly fortified naval base.

By 1914, Siberia, in every sense, had become an integral part of the Russian Empire, ruled from St. Petersburg, and without any notable desire to break off from that rule. In many respects the status of the people of the country was higher than that of the peasants in European Russia.

[2] Chapter VII, sec. 2.

and their conditions of life were better. The smallness of the population and the abundance of land had made possible the development of larger holdings than was usual in Europe. The late development of the country, and the pioneer nature of the life there, had developed a pronounced spirit of individualism. This was enhanced by the fact that land was held in individual rather than in community ownership. Thus the ideas of the people, and their manner of life, were not dissimilar to those of the population of western Canada or the United States in the early days.

But while the people were Russian and the territory was an integral part of the Empire, they did desire a greater local autonomy in that Empire, although not expressing any great desire for independence. Many of them believed, quite correctly, that the development of the country would be retarded as long as purely local questions had to be decided after reference to an authority as distant as St. Petersburg. The desire for autonomy was expressed in 1905, at the time of the movement which resulted in the establishment of the first Duma. Then Siberians demanded local self-government, with Russian control restricted to matters of imperial interest. While they did not get what they wanted, the year 1905 did see a step in advance when the Zemstvo system was introduced.

During the early part of World War I, up to the time of the Russian Revolution, there was no indication of any great dissatisfaction in Siberia. The people responded to the demands made on them just as did the inhabitants of the other parts of the Empire. Their only peculiar relations to the war came through the use of their territories as areas for the confinement of German and Austrian prisoners of war, and because of the facilities they were able to afford, through Vladivostok and the Trans-Siberian Railway, as a port of entry and means of transportation for war material purchased in the United States and Japan.

Russia purchased large quantities of war materials in Japan, but finally she reached the end of her ability to pay for them. As a result she was forced to withdraw farther from Northern Manchuria. In part-payment for the munitions which she needed, and in order to persuade the Japanese to continue to supply her with materials of war, she transferred to Japan her railway properties from Changchun almost to Harbin, just falling short of giving Japan a long-coveted direct connection with the Trans-Siberian.

4. EFFECTS OF RUSSIAN REVOLUTION ON SIBERIA

The revolution which broke out in Russia in March, 1917, received the same sort of response in Siberia as in European Russia, but it developed different consequences. It was received with approval, and was hailed as the inauguration of a new era. Consequently there was no immediate attempt made to take advantage of it for the purpose of establishing a separate state. The first revolutionary governments were either heartily approved or passively accepted. But of course the upheaval brought with it a measure of uncertainty and of consequent instability. Immediately, the local government bodies, such as the Zemstvo, took over the direction of affairs. In addition, in many of the towns there were organized local committees (soviets) to supervise the officials, who were largely men put in office under the former régime, and to see to it that the interests of the people, and of the revolution, were safeguarded.

Naturally, a country settled as Siberia had been contained many radical and revolutionary individuals and groups. This number was increased immediately after the revolution by an influx of exiles who attempted to enter Russia by way of Vladivostok and the Trans-Siberian. Many of these people remained in Siberia.

In addition to establishing their own governments, thus realizing the decade-old demand for autonomy, the people sent representatives to the constituent assembly which was convened for the purpose of determining the form of government and framing an organic law for Russia.

With the overthrow of the constituent assembly, and the establishment of the Bolshevist group in control of European Russia, trouble in, and for, Siberia began. Among the workers in the towns there were many who sympathized with the Bolshevist communist program. But on the whole the peasants were, at first, non-communistic, although they were socialistic in their views. What the result would have been if they had been left to work out their problem unhindered, it is impossible to say, for they were worked upon from the outside and were, in some places, influenced by outsiders who came in following the first revolution. These outsiders were of two sorts: radicals who had been exiled under the Czarist régime; and conservatives who had fled from Russia at the time of the first outbreak of revolution or were driven into exile when the Bolshevists overthrew the Kerensky government. The first element, in coöperation with the Siberian radicals, was interested in establishing a communist state in the Far East. The second element sought the entire or partial restoration of the old régime.

5. FOREIGN INTERVENTION PROPOSED

Foreign intervention in Siberia did not come until 1918, and it was not seriously contemplated until the Russians, under the leadership of Lenin and Trotsky, withdrew from participation in the war. Immediately following the revolution, however, warships were sent to Vladivostok to follow developments. During this early period Rear-Admiral Knight, of the American Navy, tried to keep in touch with the various factions in the city, and, when dissension began to develop, suggested a plan by which they might be united with the aid and support of the Allied Powers. This plan was not acted upon by his government, and the situation in Siberia was permitted to develop until it began to appear possible that communism would find a firm hold there.

Early in 1918 official suggestions were made in favor of an allied intervention in Siberia. On March 14 Mr. Balfour, in the British House of Commons, urged that Japan be invited to intervene in order to prevent German domination of that country. It was alleged that large numbers of German and Austrian prisoners had been released and were working their way eastwards, and that Siberia would fall into their hands if steps were not taken to prevent it. This proposal, it may be noted, was for an exclusive intervention by the Japanese, rather than for an inter-allied move.

The early Japanese attitude toward intervention was expressed officially by Baron Goto, the Japanese Minister for Foreign Affairs, on May 1, 1918, when he said that "Japan must give encouragement, assistance and support to the work of reorganization" in Russia, and that she must continue to assume the burden of "preserving the peace in the Far East." His Government then, with the concurrence of Great Britain and France, proposed to the United States that Japanese troops should be sent to Vladivostok to protect the interests of the Allied states. When President Wilson expressed dissent as to the wisdom of this policy, the Japanese government assumed the attitude that it did not care to make any further overtures, but would wait until the Allies could agree among themselves as to the best course of action. However, because of an expressed fear as to the security of the supplies which had been concentrated at Vladivostok for transportation over the railway to the Russian front before the outbreak of the revolution, Japanese and British marines were landed at that city in April. Japan further prepared for eventualities when, on May 16, 1918, she signed an agreement with China, providing for coöperation in the defense of their interests to the north, and for the movement of troops over the Chinese Eastern railway.

It was not until the summer that the United States not only concurred in, but indeed proposed, active inter-allied intervention in Siberia. The reason for the change in the American attitude was stated to be the necessity for helping the Czecho-Slovaks to extricate themselves from a dangerous position which had been created by a change in the attitude of the Russian government toward them. This Czecho-Slovak force was made up of former subjects of the Austrian Empire who had either been captured by the Russians or had, at the earliest possible opportunity, deserted from the Austrian ranks and had been given asylum in Russia. When the Russian military collapse came, following the revolution, they indicated a desire to leave Russian soil and to secure transportation to

France in order to fight on the western front for the Allied cause. This desire was due to the hope and expectation that, out of the success of the Allies, would result the establishment of a Czech national state.

Soon after the assumption of power by the Bolshevists, the Czecho-Slovaks asked for permission to leave Russia. This permission was given them in February, and their withdrawal eastwards commenced. But in March the treaty of Brest-Litovsk between Germany and Russia was signed. Germany then proceeded to put pressure on the Russian government in order to secure a revocation of the permission given to the Czechs to withdraw. The Soviet government succumbed to this pressure, and in May the attempt was made to disarm the Czechs. Their response was immediate, taking the form of the occupation of territory from Cheliabinsk to Krasnoyarsk. They thus found themselves in occupation of what had become enemy territory, with no way of extricating themselves unless they could retain control of the Trans-Siberian Railway. Their main difficulties were supposed to come from Austrian and German prisoners of war, who, it was said, had been released and armed, but in fact it was their presence as an armed force in Russia which put them in danger.[3] It was this situation which caused the government of the United States to change its attitude toward intervention.

Preliminary to acting, the United States and Japan, the two principal parties, issued official declarations of their intentions. The American declaration first laid down the proposition that any general military intervention was unwise as having the effect, not of serving, but rather of using Russia, thus working an unjustifiable division of the Allied forces. It would also constitute an unwise diversion of attention from the western front. This was by way of reiteration of the original American attitude. The declaration then went on to state:

As the government of the United States sees the present circumstances, therefore, military action is admissible in Russia now only to render such protection and help as is possible to the Czecho-Slovaks against the armed Austrian and German prisoners who are attacking them, and to steady any efforts at self-government or self-defence in which the Russians may be willing to accept assistance. Whether from Vladivostok or from Murmansk and Archangel, the only present object for which American troops will be employed will be to guard military stores which may subsequently be needed by Russian forces and to render such aid as may be acceptable to the Russians in the organization of their own self-defence.[4]

[3] From the first, many people in the West looked to this force as a possible antidote to Bolshevism and urged that, instead of withdrawing, they be aided to assume control of Siberia. They refused to acquiesce in this plan for a time, but when attacked they defended themselves, and, as a result of this, found themselves involved in Siberian affairs. Their occupation of the country, coupled with the demand that they hold it for capitalism, led to their being viewed with suspicion by the Russians, and this it was, in reality, which made their situation dangerous, rather than the presence of armed Germans and Austrians in any numbers

[4] New York Times, Current History, vol. 8, pp. 466–467.

The American declaration carried with it an assurance that there would be no interference with the political sovereignty of Russia, no intervention in her internal affairs, and no impairment of her territorial integrity.

The Japanese government gave similar assurances as to the purpose of the intervention, and pledged itself not to interfere in the internal affairs of Russia, and to respect her territorial integrity. Both parties stated that they would withdraw their forces immediately upon the attainment of the limited objectives of the intervention.[5]

Small contingents were furnished by the European states to aid in making up the expeditionary force which was despatched to Vladivostok in pursuance of this agreement, and the United States and Japan agreed each to send seventy-five hundred soldiers. The American contingent actually consisted of about this number, but Japan sent troops out of all proportion to the importance of the intervention or its declared purposes, thus immediately justifying the fears of those who had felt that Japanese intervention in Siberia would be for some ulterior purpose. Estimates of the number of soldiers sent to Siberia by Japan range from a lower limit of about thirty thousand to a maximum of about ninety thousand.

This Siberian intervention was said to be necessary because of the danger to the Czecho-Slovaks from the German and Austrian prisoners who had been armed following the peace of Brest-Litovsk. As a matter of fact, however, it was fear of Bolshevism which, as much as anything else, brought about the intervention. To "steady Russian efforts at self-government" meant, so far at least as the Western Powers were concerned, giving aid and support to any faction in Siberia which would oppose the establishment of the Soviet rule. This was the Japanese attitude as well, although the Japanese policy seemed, subsequently, to have been dictated equally by a desire to fish in Siberian waters.

With a few exceptions the non-Japanese foreign troops remained at Vladivostok, although some small expeditions were sent into the interior along the railroad to facilitate the evacuation of the Czecho-Slovak troops. The Japanese, on the other hand, penetrated into the interior in force. Troops were landed at Nicolaievsk, at the mouth of the Amur; Habarovsk was occupied; Blagovensk and Alexievsk were captured, and were occupied in conjunction with American troops. Furthermore, a systematic advance along the Trans-Siberian Railway was begun. In all places, and on all occasions, the Japanese comported themselves as masters in the Siberian household, stirring up for themselves a legacy of distrust and ill-will.

[5] Ibid.

6. INTERNAL STRUGGLES

The people of Siberia, meanwhile, had begun the work of organization for themselves. In many places local soviets sprang up and took control of affairs. But, on the other hand, several attempts were made to establish non-Bolshevist governments. In spite of their pledges not to intervene in the internal politics of the region, these anti-Bolshevist governments were, one after the other, accorded support by one or another of the Allied Powers, with the Japanese systematically encouraging any of them which showed a willingness to deal with Japan on her own terms. It is not necessary to discuss these governments in any detail. General Horvath established an anti-Bolshevist government at Harbin, on Chinese soil, and he received Japanese support for a time. In spite of this support, or perhaps in part because of it, Horvath failed to gain a following in Siberia. His failure was also due to the fact that the Siberians were fearful of any cause which savored of reaction. After his collapse as a "savior" the Japanese turned elsewhere. In June, 1918, prior to the inter-Allied expedition, an attempt was made to establish an all-Siberian government at Omsk. This government was non-Bolshevistic. With it was later merged a government set up at Ufa. The consolidated government was brought under the control of a directory of five members, three of whom were socialistic in their affiliations. This directory appointed Admiral Kolchak as Minister of War. On November 17, 1918, by a *coup d'état,* he made himself the dictator of the Omsk government and declared his intention of driving the Bolshevists out of Siberia.

Because of his apparent strength, the Japanese then came to the support of Kolchak, although at the same time they were furnishing money and supplies to the Cossack Ataman Semenov, who had established himself at Chita. Since the aims of both Kolchak and Semenov were the same, the attempt was made to consolidate their strength, Semenov being brought under the nominal direction of the Kolchak government. However, he did not support it in good faith, and by his denial of support he contributed to its ultimate overthrow. The Kolchak government, however, passed from the scene, in its turn, because it over-reached itself in its attempt to clear the region east of the Urals of the Bolshevists. Its troops won some initial successes, principally during the period of the reorganization of the Red Army, but after that had been completed the Kolchak troops began to suffer reverses, and ultimately that move against Bolshevism went the way of the others.

After the defeat of Admiral Kolchak, the entire region between Lake Baikal and the Urals—western Siberia—declared itself in favor of sovietism and of incorporation into Soviet Russia. From this time it ceased to be seriously affected by the struggles in the eastern part of Siberia. The eastern region, however, had to go through an extended period of turmoil before it attained a measure of political stability. Semenov remained in Chita and profited by the defeat of his nominal superior through the addition of the remnants of Kolchak's troops to his own force. Outside of the region around Chita, which was ruled by Semenov by terrorist methods, extreme instability continued. Some territory was occupied by Japanese troops, or was controlled by Russian figureheads who were subsidized by Japan. Outside of these places there was little government.

Out of this condition of disintegration there were born bands of Partisans, a combination of Siberian patriots and freebooters, sometimes intermingled, and sometimes organized into separate bands. These Partisans gradually extended their control over eastern Siberia during 1919, and through them, ultimately, a semblance of order began to emerge. In the end even Semenov succumbed to them, and was driven out of Chita, which then became the center of a new government.

These Partisan bands were largely communist in complexion and were intent on establishing a communist régime in eastern Asia affiliated with the Moscow government. As they cleared the country westwards, however, they came into contact with a movement, largely initiated by one man, Krasnoschekoff, working eastwards under the direction of Moscow. Originally a communist, Krasnoschekoff had come to realize that Siberia could not be properly developed, at that stage of its progress, save through a capitalistic medium. He had also come to see that the Allied Powers would not readily sanction a communist state in the Far East. Consequently he undertook to persuade the Russian government of the advisability of erecting in eastern Siberia a democratic state as a buffer between it and Japan. He was successful in this, as in his subsequent attempt to convince the Partisans of the futility of their endeavor to establish communism in the region east of Lake Baikal. Out of his labors, with the sanction of Soviet Russia, there finally came into being the democratic state which took the name of the Far Eastern Republic of Siberia. But this new state did not include all of the Russian territory hitherto known as Siberia. In the first place, the region west of Lake Baikal elected to remain a part of Russia. Then, the former province of Kamchatka was reserved as Russian territory by the terms of an agreement with Moscow.[6] In the third place, the Japanese continued for some time in control of the Maritime Province, acting largely through Russian figurehead governments. And, in the fourth place, Saghalin which, north of the fiftieth parallel, had been part of the Russian Far East, was oc-

---

[6] This seems to have been done with a view to using it as a bait for American capital, the purpose of the Russian government being to grant concessions for its exploitation. It was said at the time that the Russian government hoped in this way further to embroil the United States and Japan.

cupied and held by the Japanese pending an adjustment of the Nicolaievsk difficulty.[7] Consequently the territory of the Far Eastern Republic extended only from the eastern side of Lake Baikal in a narrow strip eastwards to the Maritime Province. The Japanese commander expressed his gratification over its establishment, but Japan refused it recognition and tried to prevent its authority from being extended. By the end of 1920, however, the Vladivostok government had recognized the government established at Chita as the government of Siberia. As a result of negotiations with the other contending factions, and of the driving of Semenov out of the territory which had been under his control, it then became possible to proceed with the organization of a unified state.

Consequently provision was made, under the Kerensky election laws, for the choice of representatives to a constituent assembly. This body met for the first time on February 12, 1921, with a non-party peasant majority, and proceeded to frame a constitution for the newly established Republic. The constitution was adopted on April 17 and continued as the instrument of government until the Far Eastern Republic was formally incorporated into the Soviet Union on November 15, 1922.

For two years it struggled to secure recognition so that, through it, Russia might regain the voice in Far Eastern affairs that had been lost after 1917. Thus the Republic sent a delegation to Washington at the time of the Conference in the hope of being able to secure recognition and a right of participation, or at least of being able to present directly the Siberian point of view toward the continuation of the Japanese intervention. When this was denied one reason for continued existence of the Republic was lost. For a time, furthermore, it was thought that it would be possible for the Soviet government to negotiate more satisfactorily with Japan and with China through the medium of a non-communist state.

7. SOVIET RUSSIA AND JAPAN

Thus two conferences were held between Japanese representatives and those of the Far Eastern Republic, with Moscow represented only by an observer at the first, but with its representative playing an active part at the second. The first, held at Dairen, was intermittently in session from August, 1921 until April, 1922, thus extending over the period of the Washington Conference. No agreement on the questions at issue was reached because of the extremely objectionable nature of the Japanese proposals, and the refusal of the Japanese to modify them so as to make

---

[7] Several hundred Japanese, together with a large number of Russians, were killed at Nicolaievsk as a result of a conflict between the Japanese and Partisans. Part of the responsibility for the outbreak of trouble must be borne by the Japanese, who attempted to determine the type of government established there.

:hem more acceptable. The motive of the Japanese government in participating in the conference seems to have been to avoid a discussion of
Siberian questions at Washington on the ground that direct negotiations
between the immediately interested parties had already been instituted. In
this they were partially successful.

The second conference was convoked at Chang-chun in September,
1922. It broke down for quite different reasons. By that time influential
opinion in Japan had come to disapprove of the Siberian adventure because of its expensiveness and its apparent fruitlessness, as well as on account of the effect it had had on Japan's relations with other states. Consequently the government was more nearly ready to reach an agreement
than it had been the year before. It would not, however, accede to the
Russian demand for recognition and direct relations conducted on the
basis of full equality, nor was it willing to agree to evacuate Saghalin
without reparation for the Nicolaievsk massacre, although it was ready to
withdraw from Siberia. Consequently this second conference also failed.
In spite of the failure to reach an agreement, however, the Japanese withdrew their forces from the mainland and virtually brought the intervention to an end by November 1, 1922, almost two years after the withdrawal of the American troops in January, 1920. The end of 1922, then,
saw Siberia again an integral part of Russia, but with Saghalin still in the
possession of Japan and with other questions at issue between the two
countries which could only be settled by direct negotiations. These, in
turn, could only be instituted if Japan could be brought to the point of
recognition of the Soviet government.

This was accorded on January 20, 1925, after the hand of Japan had
been forced through the reaching of an agreement between China and
Russia, negotiations having intermittently been carried on during 1923
and 1924. The Convention signed at Peking by Japanese and Soviet
representatives on January 20, 1925, provided, in its first article, for the
establishment of regular diplomatic and consular relations. By Article
II the validity of the Portsmouth treaty was recognized by Russia, but
it was provided that all other treaties made from 1905 to 1917 should be
reëxamined at a subsequent conference. Article III safeguarded, for the
time, Japanese fishing rights off the coast of Siberia. Article IV set forth
the conditions upon which a later commercial treaty should be founded.
Article V stipulated against propaganda directed against the institutions
of either party by the other, and provided that neither signatory would
tolerate the presence in its territories "of organizations or groups pretending to be the government for any part of the territories of the other
party." Article VI contained an assurance of Russian willingness to grant
concessions to the Japanese "for the exploitation of minerals, forests, and
other natural resources." In protocols and annexes to this agreement, pro-

vision was made for the adjustment of questions of public properties and debts, for the evacuation of northern Saghalin by the Japanese troops, for the exploitation by Japanese concessionaires of fifty per cent of the oil fields of northern Saghalin, and for prospecting rights in additional areas for a period of years. Apology was also made by the Soviet authorities for the Nicolaievsk massacre of 1920, which had afforded the occasion for the occupation of the northern half of Saghalin.

It was with great hesitancy that Japan reëstablished treaty relations with Russia. No government had looked with greater fear or distrust on the Russian Revolution than had that of Japan. And certainly none showed a greater fear of such "dangerous ideas" as those embodied in the Soviet philosophy. It was only considerations of continental politics, and perhaps a feeling that possible subversive propaganda could be controlled more effectively if an agreement with Moscow was made, which produced a willingness to recognize and deal with the Soviet government.

8. SOVIET RUSSIA AND CHINA—1919-1933

Russian rights and interests in China as they existed at the time of the Russian Revolution may be grouped in two general classes. In the first place, Russia participated in and was a beneficiary of the general treaty system, giving to Russians the benefits of extraterritoriality, the customs régime, residential concessions in Chinese cities, a share in the Boxer indemnity payments, and the right to maintain a legation guard at Peking. In the second place, Russia had certain special rights in northern Manchuria, including the Chinese Eastern Railway as the most important. The Russian government had also indicated an interest in Mongolia, having encouraged and supported the Mongol independence movement of 1911. Chinese-Russian-Mongol relations, however, were established on the basis of the tripartite treaty of 1915, by which the autonomy of Mongolia under Chinese suzerainty had been established.

The immediate effect of the Bolshevist victory in Russia was to create an anomalous situation in China. The recognition which had been accorded to the March provisional Russian government was not extended to the Soviet government which succeeded that of Kerensky. China continued to recognize and deal with the Russian diplomatic and consular officers who were representatives of the former government, but who were expressly denied the right to speak for the new Soviet government. This recognition was continued until 1920.

In the interim, however, the Russian position in China had been steadily weakening. In the first place, since, under the circumstances, the Russian consular courts could not continue to function satisfactorily, the Chinese government terminated the extraterritorial rights of the Russians and resumed control of the Russian concessions. The Chinese Eastern Railway, similarly, passed from the control of the Russian government. At the time of the inter-Allied intervention the Chinese Eastern, which was then under the administration of a White Russian régime, and which Japan, with the connivance of the Anfu clique at Peking, was seeking to control, was brought under the control of an inter-Allied Board. This Board continued to supervise its operation until the Americans brought their share in the intervention to an end in 1920. Then, in the second place, since the agreement regarding inter-Allied supervision of the Siberian railway system provided that it should "cease to be operative upon withdrawal of the foreign military forces from Siberia," [8] China reasserted her interest in the Chinese Eastern Railway. On October 2, 1920, the Ministry of Communications reached an agreement with the Russo-Asiatic Bank by which, pending a final arrangement with a recognized Russian government, China assumed the supreme control and direction of the road. New arrangements were made for its administration as a purely commercial undertaking, and all governmental functions, including policing of the railway zone, were assumed by the Chinese government. This provisional status was maintained until a new arrangement was concluded with the Soviet government. And a third evidence of the weakening of the Russian position was afforded by the change effected in the status of Outer Mongolia. There the Chinese government pursued a strong policy during 1919 which was continued until the overthrow of the Anfu government. The terms of the 1915 Convention were violated by the introduction of Chinese troops into the territory and sufficient pressure was brought to bear on the Mongol authorities to compel them to ask to have their autonomy brought to an end.

At this time, however, when Russian power and influence in the Far East had reached the lowest point in three-quarters of a century, the Soviet government, perhaps because of its very weakness, marked out the lines of a policy toward China which subsequently enabled it to regain the influence formerly possessed by Tsarist Russia. In a declaration of policy made in 1919 and reiterated in 1920, all rights and interests gained by the Tsarist government at the expense of China's sovereignty and integrity, including extraterritoriality, were expressly renounced and the sympathy of the struggling Russian peoples for the oppressed Chinese was voiced. This declaration had little immediate effect, except as it may have encouraged the Chinese government to proceed to terminate extraterritoriality for the Russians by its own act, and to take over the administration of the Chinese Eastern Railway, it being perhaps inferred from this declaration of Soviet policy that no objection would be raised by Russia. The benevolence of Soviet professions did not, however, create any willingness on the

---

[8] Art. 5. For text see *Manchuria—Treaties and Agreements,* Carnegie Endowment for International Peace (1921), pp. 32–33.

part of Peking to recognize the Soviet government or to enter into negotiations looking toward recognition. One reason for this, unquestionably, was the pressure to prevent recognition brought to bear on the Peking government by the Western states. This pressure was doubly effective because, until after the Washington Conference, the Peking government looked to the capitalist world for aid and support, and for voluntary action in the direction of treaty revision. The pressure became much less effective after 1922, however, when the Washington Conference results came to be appraised by the Chinese, and as new sources of discord with the Powers appeared. Among these may be included: the Gold Franc dispute, the position taken by the diplomatic corps at the time of the Lincheng bandit case, and the controversy over the disposition of the Canton customs. Furthermore, Western prestige in China steadily declined after 1922 and Western methods of action came into disrepute.

Until after the Washington Conference, consequently, the Russians made no headway at Peking. Before the end of 1921, to be sure, they made no strong direct effort to reëstablish themselves, although indirectly the attempt was made, through emissaries of the Far Eastern Republic, to enter into relations with China. The mission headed by Ignatius Yourin was unofficially received in the face of Japanese protests at any dealings with the unrecognized Far Eastern Republic. M. Yourin was successful in stimulating the Peking government to terminate relations with the Russian Ambassador accredited by the old Russian régimes, and he consequently influenced policy in the direction of the termination of extraterritoriality, thus affecting adversely the interests of the large numbers of white Russians in China. But he failed to establish treaty relations between China and the Far Eastern Republic. A more important breach in the wall of non-intercourse had previously been made when the Chinese government ratified a commercial treaty which had been negotiated by the Tuchun of Sinkiang with the Tashkent Soviet. But this again only indirectly affected the relations of China with Moscow.

The real foundations were laid for the reëstablishment of diplomatic relations between China and Russia when that astute and informed diplomatist M. Joffe was sent to Peking in 1922. This instituted the period of direct negotiations, intermittently continued until they had been brought to a successful conclusion in 1924. The methods employed by Joffe and his successor, M. Leo Karakhan, were (1) to play upon the chord of Western capitalistic imperialism as contrasted with the non-imperialistic aims of the new Russia, which were set forth in the declarations of 1919–1920; (2) to play off Japan against China in negotiations with both; (3) to cultivate the Chinese intelligentsia, securing its support, and utilizing this support to bring pressure to bear on the Chinese government; and (4) to establish contact with Canton and use this as a lever with which to move Peking.

The influence of Soviet Russia on internal political developments in China will shortly be considered.[9] Here it needs to be stated, however, that this influence also worked toward promoting the interest of Russia in China and had a bearing on the reëstablishment of diplomatic relations.

Three serious obstacles to Sino-Russian accord had to be overcome by the Soviet representatives. The first was the general fear, in China as elsewhere, of communist propaganda subversive of the established order. This, however, was less important after 1922 than it had been before the Washington Conference. The second was the question of Mongolia. And the third was that of the future of the Chinese Eastern Railway.

The Mongolian question had entered upon a new phase in 1920–1921. As has been pointed out, the Chinese were able to end the autonomous régime, founded upon the tripartite Convention of 1915, in 1919. The Chinese officials, however, from the first defense commissioner, "Little Hsu" (Hsu Shu-tseng) down proceeded to rule with such a high hand that they succeeded rapidly in alienating the Mongols, who, in any case, had never been especially sympathetic to Chinese overlordship. Consequently it was with little difficulty that the White Russian General, Baron Ungern von Sternberg, was able to establish control of Outer Mongolia when the Semenov government at Chita found itself unable to maintain itself against the forces of the Far Eastern Republic. An independent Mongolia was proclaimed in 1920, with the Hutukhtu (the Living Buddha) at its head, but with the government actually dominated by the White Russians. Mongolia consequently became a suitable base from which attacks could be launched against the "Red" government in Siberia. This naturally invited a counterattack on the White Russian forces in Mongolia by Soviet troops as soon as the Russian military reorganization had been completed. Baron Ungern was driven out in 1921, and a Provisional Revolutionary Mongol People's Government was set up with the support of Soviet troops. Thus the independence of Mongolia was re-affirmed and the ground lost in the first years after the Russian Revolution had been more than regained. Not only did Soviet troops support this independent government but in addition Moscow entered into treaty relations with it. Since China claimed Mongolia as an integral part of the Chinese state it is evident that there was the necessity for some sort of adjustment here before the larger question of recognition of Russia could be dealt with.

The difficulty over the Chinese Eastern Railway arose because, while in 1919 the Chinese understood the Soviet declaration to have promised its return "to the Chinese people without demanding compensation of any kind," [10] by 1920 it was stipulated that a treaty should be made concerning

---

[9] Chapter XX, sec. 1–3.

[10] Text of the Declaration, in translation from the French translation, in *China Year Book,* 1924, pp. 868–870. As to whether the provision was actually in the Russian original of the

it, and from the time when M. Joffe reached Peking in 1922, the Russians manifested increasingly an interest in recapturing their administrative rights with respect to it.

From 1922 to 1924, then, negotiations continued intermittently over these questions and over that of the recognition of Russia before the reaching of a formal agreement, as the Soviet representatives desired. The convention then signed (May 31, 1924) provided, among other things, for the reëstablishment of normal diplomatic and consular relations. It made the necessary stipulations with respect to public property and treaties, and voided all the Tsarist treaties with and relating to China affecting her sovereign rights or interests,[11] together with similar Chinese treaties with respect to Russia. It provided for the withdrawal of Russian troops from Mongolia, and carried a stipulation against permitting propaganda against the established institutions in each country by the other. It provided for a later conference to work out the details of boundaries, use of waterways, etc., and to settle the question of the Chinese Eastern Railway, on the basis (1) of its recognition as a purely commercial undertaking, (2) of the maintenance of Chinese administrative authority, (3) of the right of China to redeem the road with Chinese funds, (4) of the provisional maintenance of the system of management of the road provided for in 1896, except so far as in conflict with the new agreement, and (5) for settlement of the whole question by China and Russia to the exclusion of third parties.[12] Finally, it effected a cancellation of the Russian share of the Boxer indemnity, with the understanding that it would be devoted to educational purposes.

The agreement as to the Chinese Eastern Railway could only be made effective by securing an acceptance of its terms by Chang Tso-lin, who had declared the independence of Manchuria in 1922. Advantage was taken of his political difficulties in 1924 to secure from him a separate and more detailed agreement on September 20, as to the conditions of operation and control of the road.[13]

This agreement with China, coupled with the one with Japan at the beginning of 1925, restored the Russian position in northern Manchuria.

Declaration, and for a full discussion of these questions see R. T. POLLARD, *China's Foreign Relations, 1917–1931* (1933). ch. 5, 6.

[11] This provision was extended in an annex to include similar Soviet treaties.

[12] This agreement, it should be noted, was protested as a departure from the principles accepted at the Washington Conference. The United States had set up the idea of a "moral trusteeship" for Russia, to be exercised pending the establishment of a "sane" and unified Russian state. In a conference Resolution this idea of trusteeship was applied to the Chinese Eastern Railway. The protests against the exclusion of third parties had no effect. Under this agreement, of course, the interests of the French bond-holders, of the Russo-Asiatic Bank, and of Americans having claims against the railway administration on account of supplies and equipment furnished during the period of inter-Allied control were not safeguarded at all.

[13] See *China Year Book*, 1925, pp. 797–800, for its text.

And, while the 1924 agreement incorporated a recognition of Outer Mongolia as an integral part of China, and provided for a withdrawal of the Soviet troops, it did not preclude the maintenance of a close relationship of an advisory character between the Mongol government and Moscow. Thus it did not in fact result in a restoration of Chinese control. Consequently the Russian position there was strengthened as compared with that established in 1915. When to this is added the fact of (1) the close advisory relationship to the Kuomintang which was instituted in 1924, (2) the maintenance of an Embassy at Peking through which an influence could be exerted in north China, and (3) the establishment of friendly relations with Fêng Yü-hsiang in the northwest, it must be recognized that the Soviet representatives had made a remarkable recovery of the ground which had been lost in the first years after the revolution of 1917.

Almost immediately, however, Russian influence in China proper was substantially lessened. As is elsewhere related,[14] the Kuomintang was purged of Communist-Russian influences in 1927, the Russian advisers being sent home. Simultaneously, Chang Tso-lin raided the Russian Embassy and adjacent buildings at Peking, and thereafter terminated relations with the Soviet government.

In Outer Mongolia, however, as has been stated, the Soviet maintained and consolidated its position in spite of its agreement with China. And in northern Manchuria, in spite of difficulties with the Mukden authorities, it maintained itself until the establishment of Manchukuo. Conflicts which arose with Japan over railway policies in Manchuria, over fishing rights in Siberian waters, and over the closing of the Vladivostok branch of the Bank of Chosen were all peacefully adjusted. On the other hand, the friction which developed between the Chinese and Russians over Manchurian questions resulted in an outbreak of hostilities in 1929.

Previous to this, in 1925-1926, the policies followed by Chang Tso-lin, culminating in the arrest of M. Ivanov, the Russian manager of the Chinese Eastern, had produced a serious crisis. Trouble was avoided only when Chang gave way in the face of strong Russian representations. After the assassination of Marshal Chang in 1928, further trouble developed on account of the attempt of the "Young Mongols," with Soviet support, to cut off the Barga district from Manchuria, erecting there an autonomous district. But it was after the Three Manchurian Provinces, under the rule of Chang Hsueh-liang, had accepted the control of the national government at Nanking that the most serious difficulty occurred. Having somewhat successfully put into effect the nationalist program of recovery of rights lost by treaty in China's relations with the Powers, it was decided to attempt to extend the program to include a recovery of the control of the Chinese Eastern Railway. In the late spring of 1929 the Russian con-

[14] Chapter XX, sec. 5.

sulates in northern Manchuria were raided and then closed. This action was followed by the arrest of Soviet consular officers and of a director of the Railway. Then, on July 10 and 11, the telephone and telegraph systems of the Chinese Eastern were taken over by the Chinese, Russian organizations of all kinds in Harbin and the railway zone were closed, the administration of the railway was taken over, and upwards of two hundred Russian members of the railway staff were arrested. These actions were justified on the score of Russian violation of the 1924 agreement, which the Russians also accused the Chinese of violating. The Russians retaliated by proceeding against Chinese within their jurisdiction.

At the outset the American government called the attention of the disputants to their obligations under the Kellogg Pact. Both disclaimed any intention of violating their obligations by a resort to war. Both also, at the beginning, fell back on the provision of the 1924 agreement making the settlement of the status of the Chinese Eastern a matter of sole concern to China and Russia, to the exclusion of third parties. Later China wished to introduce a third party influence but was unable to do so.

Ultimately the difference was adjusted as a result of the direction of military pressures by Russia against China, rather than on account of outside intervention. A preliminary agreement was signed on December 22, by the terms of which the *status quo ante* was restored. Thus the outbreak of difficulties between China and Japan in September, 1931, found the Russians still in control of the Chinese Eastern Railway, but without extensive influence in China proper, except as the Chinese communists were able to maintain contact with them.

REFERENCES FOR FURTHER STUDY

A. J. BEVERIDGE, *The Russian Advance* (1903). J. W. BOOKWALTER, *Siberia and Central Asia* (1899). A. BULLARD, *The Russian Pendulum* (1919), book II ch. 18–23; the views and analysis of a representative of the Committee on Public Information. VIOLET CONOLLY, *Soviet Trade from the Pacific to the Levant* (1935), ch. 1–5; a careful study of the subject. D. J. DALLIN, *Rise of Russia in Asia* (1949); useful especiallv for the Soviet period to 1933. GEOFFREY DRAGE, *Russian Affairs* (1904); good brief description of resources, people, etc. GEORGI GLEASON, *What Shall I Think of Japan?* (1921), ch. 3, and appendices. F. A. GOLDER, *Russian Expansion on the Pacific* (1914). Japan Chronicle, *Far East ern Republic, a Tour of Investigation* (Dec. 7 and 14, 1922, of weekly issue); good synopsis of existing conditions. P. A. KROPOTKIN, *Memoirs of a Revolutionist* (1899). OWEN LATTIMORE, *Political Conditions in Mongolia and Chinese Turkestan*, in *The Annals*, vol. 152, pp. 318–327. GEORGE A. LENSEN, *The Russo-Japanese Frontier* (1954). F. F. MOORE, *Siberia Today* (1919); observations and impressions of an officer in the American force sent to Siberia. JAMES W. MORLEY, *The Japanese Thrust into Siberia, 1918* (1957). F. NANSEN, *Through Siberia, the Land of the Future* (1914); observations of the writer during trip to open trade connection with the interior. HENRY NORMAN, *All the Russias* (1904), ch. 6–10. H. K. Norton, *Far Eastern Republic of Siberic* (1923); the best book on the subject. H. K. Norton, *International Aspects of the Chinese Eastern Railway,* in *The Annals,* vol. 152, pp. 308–317. Leo Pasvolsky, *Russia in the Far East* (1922). R. T. Pollard, *China's Foreign Relations, 1917–1931* (1933), ch. 5–6; a detailed treatment of Sino-Russian relations after 1917. M. P. Price, *Siberia* (1912). K. S. Weigh, *Russo-Chinese Diplomacy* (1928). G. F. Wright, *Asiatic Russia,* 2 vols. (1902); treats of geography and resources, the Russian occupation, and the political divisions. V. A. Yakhontoff, *Russia and the Soviet Union in the Far East* (1931); appendices contain important documents. V. A. Yakhontoff, *The Chinese Soviets* (1934).

For periodical literature dealing with Siberia and the Far Eastern Republic use *Readers Guide.*

CHAPTER XIX

THE WASHINGTON CONFERENCE AND AFTER

I. THE BACKGROUND OF THE CONFERENCE

THE Washington Conference originated out of a desire, in the interest of economy, to reduce naval armament. But since a navy is, or should be, a means of realizing the ends of national policy, it is clear that there is a close relationship between the existence of policies and interests which will lead to conflict, on the one hand, and the willingness to give up or reduce the means of putting policies into effect, or of protecting interests, on the other. So far as the United States was concerned, in 1921 the area of future conflict seemed to be the Far East. Japan seemed to be the potential opponent whose policies apparently conflicted with those of the United States. China, it appeared, might be the principal field of conflict, due to the weakness and disorganization of the Republic. Consequently it seemed necessary to seek a solution of the Far Eastern question if naval armament reduction was to be seriously considered. This explains the invitation issued to the Powers to confer on Pacific and Far Eastern questions, while simultaneously discussing questions of armament.

The modern history of the Far East serves as the background of the Washington Conference. This background, however, may be made clearer by a brief summary of the policies of Japan, the United States, and England.

The development of the Japanese position with respect to the continent of Asia has been discussed in some detail in the preceding pages. By 1921 Japan was in a position, strategically, to dominate the East. All of the sea approaches from the north to the south were controlled by her. In the north, the possession of half of the island of Saghalin and occupation of the remainder, and possession of the Kurile Islands, together with Hokkaido, gave her control of entry into the sea of Okhotsk; the Japan Sea was closed to the outside world by the Japanese control of Saghalin, Hokkaido, Japan proper, and Korea, reënforced by Japan's ownership of the island of Tsushima; possession of the Loochoo Islands and the Pescadores, running from the Japanese main islands south to Formosa, and of Formosa, enabled her to shut off the Yellow Sea. Thus she controlled all maritime access to China from Fukien province north, and all maritime access to Siberia. Further than this, her occupation of northern Saghalin gave her effective control of the mouth of the Amur River and thus of the great waterways of Siberia. From Korea and the Kwantung leased territory she controlled access to Manchuria. Her position north of the Great Wall and in Shantung province gave her the power to dominate Peking if she chose to exert it. The German railway rights in Shantung, coupled with the extension of them secured after 1914, gave the means of cutting off north China from the central part of the country. And working north from Fukien province, another Japanese sphere of interest, and south from Shantung, she could maintain an effective control of central China. Thus, from the military standpoint, Japan had gained a dominating position toward China, and had a great advantage over competitors for position who had to approach the continent from the eastern side and by sea.

In establishing this territorial position Japan had fought three successful wars at ten-year intervals, thus displacing China in Formosa and Korea, Russia in southern Saghalin and Manchuria, and Germany in Shantung. These territorial gains, it may be noted further, had been duplicated by economic advances. Korea became an exclusive field for Japanese exploitation; the Manchurian market was dominated by Japan, which asserted a virtual monopoly of investment rights there. Also, particularly in the field of railway financing, substantial interests had been built up in Shantung; the economic wedge was inserted in eastern Inner Mongolia in 1915; the attempt was being made in 1921 to secure a strong economic position in Siberia; and an important interest had been established in some of China's resources outside of Manchuria and Shantung.

After 1905 the principal opposition to Japan in her Asian ventures came from the United States. England, as an ally of Japan, and with a particular interest in her European relationships, was in no position to oppose the Japanese. Russian interest in the Far East lessened after Russia's defeat by Japan and the agreement with England in 1907. Thus the Czar's government rested satisfied with the preservation of its position in northern Manchuria and Outer Mongolia by agreement with Japan in 1907, 1910, and 1916. Consequently the United States, which, under Roosevelt, had looked upon Japan as the defender of the faith against Russia, and upon the Anglo-Japanese agreement as a beneficent instrument to preserve the peace in eastern Asia, became engaged in the thankless task of attempting to restrain Japan. America's opposition to her efforts to consolidate her position in Manchuria embittered Japan against the United States, and the failure of the policy of the United States enhanced its distrust of Japan. This estrangement was further emphasized by the immigration controversies.

The American interest in China, as has been revealed, antedated 1905 or even 1895. But the United States had shown no sustained interest in Far Eastern politics for three decades after the Civil War. From the beginning of treaty relations with China, Washington had demanded "most-favored-nation" commercial treatment, and had not asserted or attempted to gain for itself special rights except those accruing to it, together with all treaty Powers, by reason of the system of extraterritoriality, and through the treaty tariff system. Otherwise individuals had made American policy —when Seward was Secretary of State, for example, and during the Burlingame régime at Peking—with the consequence that interest and activity was intermittent. The same was true in the larger Pacific area, except for the sustained interest in the fortunes of Hawaii after the settlement of California and the Pacific Coast. And American policy even toward Hawaii veered from one extreme to another. Secretary Webster held that the independence of the islands should be respected by all, including the United States. Secretary Marcy stated that the United States would acquire the islands rather than see them controlled by any other country. Seward advocated a "strong" Pacific policy, preferring annexation to reciprocity. The policy then reverted to reciprocity, as embodied in the convention of 1875, and changed from that to the Blaine policy of 1881 of "drawing the ties of intimate relationship between us and the Hawaiian Islands so as to make them practically a part of the American system without derogation of their absolute independence." [1] The note sustained after 1850, however, was the assertion of American interest as against that of third parties.

But after 1895 American interest in the Pacific became intensified and the interest in China revived. The reasons for this were various, but all had a bearing on the subsequent Far Eastern activities of the United States. First may be noted the war with Spain and the simultaneous annexation of Hawaii, which advanced the frontier of the United States a considerable distance into the Pacific. Annexation had been actively agitated as early as 1893, following the establishment by revolution of the government headed by the American, Sanford B. Dole. A change of administration deferred ratification of the annexation treaty until after Cleveland passed from office, but a second treaty signed by President McKinley on June 16, 1897, was followed by annexation by joint resolution on July 7, 1898. It may be noted that Japan, whose peoples had begun to settle in Hawaii in considerable numbers, protested against this extension of the American position, but accepted the new status after the project had been carried to completion.

A more direct consequence of the war with Spain was the occupation of the Philippine Islands and the intermediate base at Guam. The former were eventually ceded to the United States by the treaty of peace, and the campaign of 1900, so far as the Philippines constituted an issue, established the intention to retain them at least until the peoples were ready to govern themselves. Here is not the place, even if space permitted, to embark on a discussion of the American Philippine policy. The history of the islands after their acquisition is part of the history of the United States. But the

[1] See I, MOORE's *Digest*, pp. 483–488, for American policy toward Hawaii. It may be here pointed out that it offers an interesting parallel to Japan's Manchurian policy.

retention of the Philippines had an important bearing on the Far Eastern policy of the United States which must be considered at this point. One reason urged for their acquisition and retention was that they would give the United States a tangible territorial footing in the Far East, thus entitling it to a voice in Far Eastern affairs. Another was that Manila would serve as a convenient base of approach to the China trade, enabling the United States to participate in it more largely and more effectively.

Just as the original American interest in China was due to her trade at Canton, so the revival of American interest was due to a feeling of need for overseas markets. Many were convinced by 1898 that the future prosperity of the United States was dependent on an enlarged participation in foreign trade, and on entering the competition for investment privileges in such regions as China. Both as a market and as a field for investment, China was conceded to be potentially the most promising uncontrolled backward state. This feeling, whether or not warranted by the facts, was enough to explain the interest in the Philippines as a stepping-stone to China, and in events in the Celestial Empire.

At the time when the United States was beginning again to look outward, economically and politically, the scramble for concessions was at its height in China, whose continued existence as a state, and consequently as a potential market, seemed to be threatened. The restatement, in the Hay notes, of the principle of equality of commercial opportunity was the American reaction to the situation. But the years from 1900 to 1904 revealed clearly that the United States had not a sufficiently vital interest herself to restrain Russia in Manchuria, and consequently to preserve the policy. This the American government left to Japan, sympathizing with and encouraging her, just as England was doing, and to almost the same extent. To the United States, Japan was fighting to preserve the Open Door and the integrity of China. Roosevelt was sufficiently a realist, however, to see that Japan herself, if unrestrained, might become a danger to American interests as a result of the elimination of Russia as a factor in Chinese politics. Consequently he hoped to see Russia and Japan serve as checks on each other's actions after 1905.

When Japan succeeded to Russian policy as well as to Russian interests in South Manchuria, and Russia failed to seek to restrain her, but rather agreed with her on their respective spheres, and to mutual support therein, it was necessary to devise some other plan of action to sustain American policy. This plan was the neutralization of the Manchurian railways, or at least the introduction of American and British capital into Manchuria. The proposals and actions of the years 1907-1910 indicate a Japanese-American conflict of interests and of policies. In this diplomatic conflict Japan was as victorious as she had been in her wars against China and Russia. But the fact of conflict of interest, together with the fact of Japanese victory, led to mutual antagonism and recrimination, which in turn had to be reckoned with in the policies of both countries. As has already been indicated, this hostility was confirmed and strengthened as a result of the unfair treatment of Japanese in the United States, and as a result of the movement toward exclusion. As early as 1911 there was talk of a possible war between the two countries.

This friction was not abated by reason of the actions of Japan following her entrance into the World War. Whereas before 1914 the Imperial Japanese government had been able to square its professions and its practices to the satisfaction of its supporters, justifying its Manchurian activities to a reasonable extent, its activities after 1914 could only be considered as frankly aggressive, and indicative of a desire to dominate China. Consequently, both in Japan, on account of American criticisms, official as well as unofficial, and in the United States, the situation was regarded as critical and highly explosive.

Thus when the Borah resolution, inviting the President to convoke a conference of the Powers to consider the reduction of naval expenditure by mutual agreement, passed the Senate (May 26, 1921) and the House (June 29), and the administration was moved to action, the scope of the conference was broadened to include a consideration of Far Eastern and Pacific questions. The impulse behind the Borah resolution was primarily the desire to reduce expenditure. But, as a practical proposition, it was apparent to the administration that armament reduction could not be undertaken successfully without a removal of some of the causes of international friction. At that time, so far as the United States was concerned, it has been seen that a primary source of discord was to be found in the condition of China, and in Japanese policy toward China and Siberia.

This proposal to make an adjustment in the Pacific meant that the interests of other states than the United States and Japan would have to be taken into account, and the interested parties consulted. One of the parties in interest was unquestionably China, and an invitation was necessarily extended to her government to send delegates, since the American government did not project a feast of the vultures with China furnishing the meal. We have already set forth China's position in detail, and we need only say that her aim was to recover ground lost during the years of her modern history.

Another state with an active interest in any attempted solution of the Far Eastern problem was Great Britain, including not only Imperial England but Canada and Australia as well. No adequate introduction to the Washington Conference could be made without a consideration of the part Great Britain has played in Eastern Asia. The conclusion of the war of 1840–1842, resulting in the Nanking treaty and the opening of China, left England with Hongkong, which rapidly became the most important commercial center in the Far East. No further territorial gains at China's expense were made by England until 1898, except that represented by the occupation of Upper Burma. Her interests were primarily commercial, although she played a leading political rôle at Peking after the right of legation had been established as a result of the war of 1858–1860. As the premier trading state, her policy ran parallel with that of the United States, as it was intermittently expressed from 1860 to 1895. This policy was to secure the progressive opening of China to trade on a "most-favored-nation" basis. Due to her interest in the protection of India, which has always been in the background of English Asiatic policy, she was opposed to any great weakening of China, particularly to the benefit of Russia.

An indication of a change in British policy, from support of China to support of Japan, was given when she not only did not lead in the movement to keep Japan off the mainland in 1895, but also refused to participate in the intervention which caused the retrocession of the Liaotung promontory. And when the movement on China began, after 1895, she participated in it to the extent of securing Weihaiwei and territory at Kowloon for herself, and demanding and receiving railroad concessions in the Yangtse valley, together with a non-alienation pledge as to that region, thus staking out a sphere of interest for herself. She reverted to her earlier China policy in accepting the Hay proposals of 1899, and in taking a stand in opposition to partition in 1900. As Russia threatened to establish too strong a position in Manchuria and North China, England, perceiving a threat to her trade, and to India as well, sought for support in attempting to check the Russian advance. Anglo-German agreement was tried and failed on account of the refusal of Germany to apply the principles of the Open Door and integrity of China to Manchuria. The United States insisted on playing a lone diplomatic hand. Thus England turned to Japan in the agreement of 1902. From that time England supported Japan faithfully, not only against Russia, but subsequently against the United States when American capital attempted, with government support, to invade Manchuria.

But the growth of American-Japanese antagonism caused much disquietude in England for several reasons. In the first place, there had been a growing friendliness between England and the United States, both expressed and promoted by the withdrawal of the former from the Caribbean in favor of the latter in and after 1902. This embryo friendship was threatened because of English support of Japan in Manchuria. In the second place, Englishmen were not wholly sympathetic to the idea of aiding Japan in case of war with the United States, as the revised agreement of 1905 would have obliged them to do, especially as English China traders and financiers of repute were as critical of Japan's Asiatic policy as were many Americans. And in the third place, so far as the immigration question entered into such a possible struggle, the Canadian and Australian policy and interests were identical with the American. The result was that the alliance of 1911 excluded from its operation any state with which either party had a general treaty of arbitration, such as had just been negotiated between England and the United States. The failure of the Senate to ratify the treaty, however, left matters as they had been before, until the so-called "Bryan Peace Commission" treaty was negotiated. This England construed as a general arbitration treaty in the sense of the alliance, without open Japanese objection. But whether Tokyo would have concurred in this construction in case of war, remains an open question.

War necessity forced England to acquiesce in the extension of Japanese power and influence after 1914, and to enter into the secret agreement of 1917. Loyalty to Japan, and respect for her word, caused her not to oppose Japan's claims at Paris. But it is not an over-statement to say that many Englishmen desired to see the alliance terminated because it constituted a handicap to the extension of British trade and financial interests in China, because it lent British passive support to the undue extension of Japanese influence in the Far East, and because it seriously prejudiced Anglo-American relations.

For these reasons, and because of Dominion, especially Canadian, pressure, the question of the Anglo-Japanese alliance was made a principal item on the agenda of the Imperial Conference convened at London in the summer of 1921. In the course of discussion of the alliance at that time it was made clear that it had not been terminated as inconsistent with the obligations of Great Britain under the League of Nations covenant, and that it did not lapse automatically at the end of the ten-year period of its duration, but could only be ended by affirmative action of either Japan or England. The latter naturally did not feel inclined to terminate it abruptly, or in such a manner as to appear arbitrarily to throw Japan over after having made use of her. Consequently it may be surmised that the American President's invitation was regarded as affording an opportunity to terminate the alliance as part of a general Far Eastern settlement.

Of the other Powers invited to participate in the Far Eastern phase of the Washington Conference not much need be said. France, as an Asiatic Power and one claiming a sphere of interest in China, with a leased area, and with a financial stake in the Republic, was naturally invited. Of her China policies it need only be said that they were not fundamentally dissimilar to those of Russia and Japan. Holland was invited by reason of her territorial possessions in the East rather than because she had been politically active there; and Portugal was recognized as a Far Eastern Power by reason of her possession of Macao, an unsavory reminder of her past glories. Finally, because of her financial interests, an invitation was also extended to Belgium.

There was one decidedly significant omission in the list of the elect, for

Russia was tendered no invitation, nor was the Far Eastern Republic included. At the time, perhaps, Russia was considered negligible in the East, although the reason she was not invited was rather the unwillingness of the American government to have any dealings with the unrecognized Soviet authorities, either directly or through the medium of the Far Eastern Republic of Siberia. This omission took away from the international character of the settlements arrived at, and, as has already been indicated, it did not prevent the reëmergence of Russia as a primary factor in the Far East.

There were two distinct phases of the work of the Washington Conference after its convocation on November 11, 1921. The first involved consideration of the problem of the limitation of naval armaments, while the second required a resolution of the conflicting interests of the Powers in the Pacific area. The second phase involved China, Siberia, and the mandated islands in the Pacific. With the first phase we are not concerned here except in its relation to the situation in the Far East. And we need consider the problems of the Pacific, and the solutions arrived at, only in so far as they had an effect on the Far East.

2. ARMS AGREEMENTS AND THEIR EFFECT ON THE FAR EAST

Consequently we may best begin to consider the work of the Conference by analyzing briefly the agreements made with respect to naval armament and the Pacific area. In this connection it is desirable first of all to call attention to the summary view given earlier in this chapter of Japan's position with respect to China and Siberia. At the same time her proximity to the Philippines from Formosa should be recalled to mind.

From the military and naval point of view, it is immediately apparent that effective military pressure could be brought to bear on Japan only by threatening her from the Pacific side, by an attack directed against the main islands of the Japanese archipelago and Formosa. Only in this way, furthermore, could China be aided against her, in case of need, by any Power other than Russia. Competent naval authorities held at that time that a successful war could be waged against Japan only by a Power with at least double her naval strength. Even then it would be necessary for that Power to conduct its operations from adequately fortified naval bases closer to Japan than, for example, Hawaii.

The bearing of these facts on the decisions as to naval armament reached at Washington is clear. The proposals of Secretary of State Hughes fixed the naval ratio, in terms of capital ships, at five for the United States, five for Great Britain, three for Japan, and one and seventy-five hundredths for France and Italy. This meant that neither the United States nor Great Britain could hope to attack Japan with any prospect of success. This conclusion is reënforced by an analysis of the agreement by which the *status quo* was to be maintained in fortification of islands in the Pacific, with certain exceptions. For the United States these exceptions were the islands "adjacent to the coast of the United States, Alaska and the Panama Canal zone, not including the Aleutian Islands, and the Hawaiian Islands." For Great Britain, exceptions were the islands west of the meridian of 110 degrees east longitude,[2] and "those adjacent to the coast of Canada, the Commonweath of Australia and its territories, and New Zealand." This meant that in case of war between the United States and Japan the former would have to conduct its operations from the Hawaiian Islands, since Guam had not been adequately equipped as a naval base, and could not be so equipped, and since the Philippine Islands were inadequately prepared to serve as a base of operations. With the 5–3 ratio of naval strength, a war conducted from the continental United States would be disastrous. Unless a combination of the United States and Great Britain should be directed against her, or unless Singapore should be made available as a base of operations, Japan was virtually guaranteed from attack from the outside for the period of the naval agreement. On the other hand, while Japan could not carry on a successful offensive war against the continental United States or Hawaii, she could readily occupy the Philippines, which were, consequently, potentially put in pawn to her.

Against a possible Anglo-American attack, Japan was protected by the Four Powers Pact, which constituted a pledge, by the Western Powers, of non-intervention in the Far East. Immune from attack from the West, Japan was secured in her continental interests because of her ability to dominate China and Siberia strategically from her well-chosen locations on the continent, since the Conference imposed no limitation on her right to construct submarines and aircraft, peculiarly suitable for use against the continent, and because of the failure of the Conference even to attempt to reach an agreement on the limitation of land armament. Thus it is clear that the Japanese won a substantial victory at Washington, unless they gave adequate compensation for this security by giving up some of their gains on the continent of Asia made during the past twenty-five years, or unless their government voluntarily modified its policy as a result of gaining immunity from attack. Without such a change of policy a fruitful source of discord would remain in spite of the labors of the delegates assembled at Washington.

3. THE NINE POWERS TREATY CONCERNING CHINA

The outstanding achievement of the Conference, so far as China and Siberia were concerned, was the Nine Powers Treaty concerning China. Siberia was dismissed with but scant attention. Briefly stated, the work of

---

[2] This exception gave Great Britain the right to fortify Singapore.

the Conference with respect to that great and undeveloped region was confined to the eliciting of a declaration from Japan that she intended to
evacuate Siberia whenever it was feasible to do so, and that she had no
aggressive intentions, and had never had any, with respect to it. The American delegation, through Secretary Hughes, while welcoming that declaration, pointed out that it had been made before, and that it was to be hoped
that Japan would live up to its terms more completely than she had observed
her past declarations.[3]

With respect to China it was quite different. Thirty of the thirty-one
sessions of the Far Eastern Committee were devoted to China and her
problems and claims. The attempt was first made to reach an agreement
on a definition of principles to be applied. At the request of the American
government, China prepared a statement of needs, from the standpoint of
general principles, and these were presented to the committee in the form
of ten points, or declarations of principle. They deserve to be quoted
textually: [4]

(1) *a*) The Powers engage to respect and observe the territorial integrity and
political and administrative independence of the Chinese Republic.

b) China upon her part is prepared to give an undertaking not to alienate or
lease any portion of her territory or littoral to any Power.

(2) China being in full accord with the principle of the so-called open door
or equal opportunity for the commerce and industry of all nations having treaty
relations with China, is prepared to accept and apply it in all parts of the Chinese
Republic without exception.

(3) With a view to strengthening mutual confidence and maintaining peace
in the Pacific and the Far East, the Powers agree not to conclude between themselves any treaty or agreement directly affecting China or the general peace in
these regions without previously notifying China and giving her an opportunity to participate.

(4) All special rights, privileges, immunities, or commitments, whatever their
character or contractual basis, claimed by any of the Powers in or relating to
China are to be declared, and all such or future claims not so made known are
to be deemed null and void. The rights, privileges, immunities, and commitments now known or to be declared are to be examined with a view to determining their scope and validity and, if valid, to harmonizing them with one another
and with the principles declared by this Conference.

(5) Immediately, or as soon as circumstances will permit, existing limitations
upon China's political, jurisdictional and administrative freedom of action are
to be removed.

(6) Reasonable, definite terms of duration are to be attached to China's
present commitments which are without time limits.

(7) In the interpretation of instruments granting special rights and privileges,
the well established principle of construction that such grants shall be strictly
construed in favor of the grantors, is to be observed.

[3] The Siberian question, both before and after the Washington Conference, is discussed,
supra, chapter XVIII, sec. 4–6.

[4] *Conference on Limitation of Armament,* Senate Document 126, p. 444; hereafter cited
as S. D. No. 126.

(8) China's rights as a neutral are to be fully respected in future wars to which she is not a party.

(9) Provision is to be made for the peaceful settlement of international disputes in the Pacific and the Far East.

(10) Provision is to be made for future conferences to be held from time to time for the discussion of international questions relative to the Pacific and the Far East as a basis for the determination of common policies of the Signatory Powers in relation thereto.

Instead of urging that these propositions, which it had asked China to advance, be discussed in detail, and supporting their adoption as far as possible, the American delegation almost immediately diverted attention from them by introducing a statement of principles to be applied to China in the form of a resolution presented by Mr. Elihu Root. This was: [5]

It is the firm intention of the Powers attending this conference.

(1) To respect the sovereignty, the independence, and the territorial and administrative integrity of China.

(2) To provide the fullest and most unembarrassed opportunity to China to develop and maintain for herself an effective and stable government, overcoming the difficulties incident to the change from the old and long continued Imperial form of government.

(3) To safeguard for the world so far as it is within our power, the principle of equal opportunity for the commerce and industry of all nations throughout the territory of China.

(4) To refrain from taking advantage of the present conditions in order to seek special rights or privileges which would abridge the rights of the subjects or citizens of friendly states, and from countenancing action inimical to the security of such states.

It will be seen immediately that the scope of the discussions was considerably limited when the Conference took the Root resolution, rather than China's Ten Points, as the basis for the formulation of the principles to be applied to the several phases of the Chinese question. Consequently the American delegation must accept a large measure of responsibility for the failure of the Conference to do much of a practical nature for China. One reason for this lay in American belief in the sanctity of vested interest, which made it dangerous to consider going further than the enunciation of general principles to be given future application, and not to be used to test the validity of existing rights and obligations. At any rate only general principles were to be found in the Nine Powers Treaty.

One of the greatest sources of trouble in China in the past, as has been pointed out, had been the tendency toward the building up, by the Powers, of exclusive interests in various parts of that country.

Attention has also been called to the logical conclusion of the application of the sphere conception, and to the broadening of the policy of the United States as it came to be fully appreciated that the maintenance of the Open

[5] S. D. No. 126, pp. 454–455.

Door demanded the preservation of China. The conflict of interpretation of the obligations assumed under the Open Door commitment has also been noted.[6] This difference of interpretation was clearly revealed at the Conference in the remarks of Baron Shidehara, one of the Japanese delegates, and in the statement made by Secretary Hughes. The former took the position that "it was then limited in its scope, both concerning its subject matter and the area of Chinese territory to which it applied; it simply provided, in substance, that none of the Powers having spheres of interest or leased territories in China should interfere with treaty ports or with vested rights or exercise any discrimination in the collection of customs duties or railroad or harbor charges." [7] The American Secretary of State, Charles E. Hughes, who was the head of the American delegation, in reply, reviewed the history of the doctrine at some length to show that the intent back of it had been fully appreciated by the Powers, and that its spirit, broader than the three propositions of the Hay circular, constituted the doctrine. The discussion, consequently, showed the necessity for greater precision of definition if future embarrassment was to be avoided.

A decided step in advance, then, was taken at the Conference when agreement was reached as to the scope of the policy. It was the enlarged American conception of it which was written into the Nine Powers Treaty in the form of a pledge: (1) to respect the sovereignty, the independence, and the territorial and administrative integrity of China; (2) to maintain and advance the principle of equality of commercial opportunity in China; and (3) not to take any action or support any action designed to create spheres of interest or to provide for the enjoyment of mutually exclusive opportunities in designated parts of Chinese territory.[8]

The sphere of interest conception and its antithesis, the Open Door principle, were brought definitely into opposition, and the former conception repudiated so far as the future acquisition of rights was concerned. The United States had long supported the broader Open Door principle almost unaided, but at the Conference England, through Lord Balfour, repeated a declaration previously made that spheres of interest were things of the past as far as England was concerned. This statement of policy was in addition to that made in the form of acceptance for future application of he principles embodied in the Nine Powers Treaty. If all of the states had been entirely sincere in their professions of policy made at Washington, or if effective penalties for action contrary to profession had been envisaged, less skepticism might have been expressed concerning the value of the Treaty. The justification for the expectation that the Treaty principles

---

[6] See chapter XVI, sec. 2; also chapter VII, sec. 7.

[7] S. D. No. 126, p. 630.

[8] See Treaty between Nine Powers relating to Principles and Policies, Art. 3 and 4, in S. D. No. 126, pp. 895–896.

would be observed lay in the belief that the two most powerful states signatory to it would find a substantial identity of interest in enforcing its observance. It remained to be seen, however, how far England and the United States would go in that direction in the event of its violation.

In addition to the Open Door definition and agreement, the Nine Powers Treaty contained an undertaking that the unfair discriminations made in tariffs and facilities on Chinese railroads in the past would not be resorted to in the future. The terms of the article implied that China had been an offender in that respect. This was far from the truth, for, as the Chinese delegation pointed out at the Conference, there was no case of discrimination that could be fairly charged against the Chinese railroad administration. The chief offenders had been some of the foreign states controlling various sections of the Chinese railways, and the provision was inserted because of their actions.

Finally, the treaty made provision for the respecting of China's rights as a neutral, in the event of a war in the future to which the Republic was not a party. China, on her side, agreed to observe the obligations of neutrality. Attention has already been called to the fact that one of the Allied Powers had violated China's neutrality at the same time that Germany was being so strongly condemned for her violation of the neutrality of Belgium. Not much was said at the time about Japan's action, but there can be no doubt that this provision of the Nine Powers Treaty was called forth by it, as well as by similar occurrences prior to World War I. The value of the agreement, like that of the other provisions of the treaty, could not become apparent until a test actually came.

That Japan made a concession in agreeing to the enlarged conception and definition of the Open Door principle cannot be denied; but that she lost anything of substantial value by it may be doubted. If the principles of the treaty had been applied to many foreign rights and interests built up in China in the past twenty-five years, those interests would have had to be declared null and void. The various leaseholds extorted from China during the years after the Sino-Japanese War would have had to be given up as in violation of her sovereignty and her administrative integrity; foreign post-offices would have had to be withdrawn from her territory; tariff autonomy would have had to be restored, together with judicial autonomy; foreign wireless stations would have had to be destroyed or turned over to China; agreements such as the Lansing-Ishii Agreement, the Anglo-Japanese Alliance, and the Twenty-one Demands would have had to be revised or annulled. It is in these things that a change of heart could have been indicated beyond all doubt.

The Lansing-Ishii Agreement, and the Anglo-Japanese Alliance were brought to an end; not, however, by the application of the principles of the Nine Powers Treaty, but by substituting for them the Four Powers Pact.

Japan refused to acquiesce in the discussion of the validity of the 1915 treaties and agreements. Rights already acquired were not tested by the "principles" at all, but were permitted to pass unchallenged, except by China. The principle upon which the Conference proceeded was that vested interests could not be interfered with, even when one set of interests or claims was in conflict with another. China was actually promised the restoration of only one leased territory, Weihaiwei, for which Great Britain had no further use, while France offered to discuss in the future the return of Kwangchow Bay, provided other Powers with leaseholds also did so. The Kiaochow leasehold was to be returned to China also, but, again, not as a result of the application of the principles of the treaty. The Conference adopted a resolution providing for the investigation of the judicial system of China, and for aid in its betterment, but extraterritoriality remained. Foreign post-offices were to be withdrawn from Chinese territory, except from the leased areas. Foreign radio stations were to be brought under the control of China except in the leased territories and the Manchurian railroad zone, and most of the Japanese stations were to be found in the excepted regions. Foreign troops were to be withdrawn from the territory of the Republic, whenever the representatives at Peking should find it expedient. Tariff autonomy was not restored to China, but some concessions were made which resulted in substantial additions to her revenue. With the exception of the minor concessions noted, the principles of the Nine Powers Treaty were not applied in such a way as to bring to an end rights and special privileges in conflict with them.[9]

And yet it may be said that China benefited in a negative fashion from the Washington Conference because she did not lose anything as a result of it. As Dr. W. W. Willoughby put it: [10]

Despite, then, the undeniable breakdown of the authority of the Central Government of China; despite the fact that it had been obliged to make default upon certain of its foreign debts; despite the fact that there was in the south of China a political party and political organization which denied, *in toto,* the legitimacy of the Peking Government itself, China came from the Conference not only without any new administrative or other limitations upon its autonomous powers, but with the formal and unqualified assurance that the Powers would not take any advantage of existing conditions to impose any new restraints upon her freedom of action.

In other words, China may be considered to have gained from the Conference because she did not lose more than had already been lost, and be-

---

[9] Another exception should also be noted, i.e., the resolution regarding existing commitments. This provided for the notification to the secretariat of the Conference, and the transmission to the Powers, of the terms of all agreements between foreign governments and China, and between nationals and China deemed to be still in force.

[10] *China at the Conference,* pp. 338–339.

cause the Powers did not take advantage of the internal situation to intervene to promote their own interests.

The question has already been raised as to how far it might be expected
that these agreements would be observed in good faith. The great defect
in the Open Door policy in the past had been the lack of machinery to
make it effective. The attempt was made at Washington to create this machinery by providing for the establishment of a Board of Reference, to
which appeal might be taken against any contract or agreement on the
ground of its being a departure from, and a violation of, the Open Door
principle. Such a board was to be established upon the recommendation
of the commission on tariff revision for which provision was made, but no
Power was obliged to accept this recommendation. Even if such a board
had been brought into being, however, it would have had only the power
of "investigation and report" and its report would not have had to be
accepted. Consequently, after the Conference the observance of the principle
depended entirely upon the good faith of parties which had not shown a
scrupulous regard for similar obligations in the past.

4. SETTLEMENT OF SHANTUNG QUESTION

The question which had, more than any other, turned the attention of
the American public to the Far East, was that relating to Shantung
province. Much of the opposition to the Versailles treaty in the Senate, and
in the country at large, had been ostensibly based upon the great injustice
done to China by the Paris award. Consequently the Washington Conference would not have been at all successful, in the mind of the American
people, if that moot question had not been settled. The Chinese wanted the
matter discussed by the whole Conference, but the Japanese demurred on
the ground that it was a matter of concern to only two members. In order to
get a settlement, the American delegation suggested a joint conference
between Japan and China, to be carried on simultaneously with the other
meeting and to be participated in by American and British "observers."
To this proposal the Chinese delegation was forced to consent, although
somewhat unwillingly, for to refuse would have been to appear obstructive,
and thus to lose its favorable position before the American public.

After prolonged discussion, and considerable disagreement as to details,
a settlement was finally reached. By its terms Japan agreed to restore the
entire leased territory to China, together with the public properties therein
formerly belonging to the German government. China was not required to
make compensation for these properties except where they had been added
to, or improved, by the Japanese during their occupancy, and then only to
the amount expended by Japan. Another limitation placed on China's succession was that the properties required for the Japanese consulate to be

established at Tsingtao, and those required for the use of the Japanese community for schools, shrines, etc., were to be retained by Japan.

All Japanese troops in the leased territory, or along the Tsingtao-Tsinan railway, were to be withdrawn as rapidly as possible, i.e., as the Chinese were prepared to take over the policing of the railway and of the port. They were all to be withdrawn within six months from the date of the signature of the agreement.

The Customs House at Tsingtao was to be made an integral part of the Chinese Maritime Customs, the agreement of 1915 between Japan and China respecting it ceasing to be effective.

The Tsingtao-Tsinan railway was to be returned to China upon the payment to Japan of the value of the railway and its properties as assessed by the German Reparations Commission, plus the amount expended by Japan on the railway during her occupancy and administration of it. This amount was to be fixed by a joint commission constituted by the two states. Payment was to be made by China in the form of treasury notes to be given to Japan, running for a period of fifteen years, although China was given the privilege of redeeming them at the end of five years.[11] During the period of redemption of the treasury notes Japanese interests were to be secured by the appointment by China of a Japanese to serve as traffic manager, and of another Japanese to serve jointly with a Chinese as chief accountant.

The extensions of the Shantung railways, which Japan had secured the right to finance, were to be undertaken by an international syndicate, unless China financed them herself.

Detailed arrangements for the application of the Shantung treaty were worked out in conferences held at Tokyo between representatives of China and Japan which extended from June 26, 1922, until December 5. The stipulated transfers, including the retrocession of the leased territory, were immediately thereafter completed, so that at the outset of 1923 that group of the 1915 treaties relating to Shantung province had been cancelled in fact as well as in theory. This removed a most important obstacle to the development of more friendly relations between the two countries. Substantial private Japanese interests, developed during the period of the occupation, remained, but under normal conditions this should not have adversely affected public relations. As is related elsewhere,[12] however, the necessity of affording protection to the lives and property of Japanese remaining in Shantung led the Tanaka government to throw troops into the province in 1927 and again in 1928, when the nationalist armies were moving north. A serious clash occurred in 1928 at Tsinan, and a new "Shantung question"

[11] It was stipulated that China should not secure the funds to redeem the treasury notes from any foreign source.

[12] Chapter XX, sec. 6.

was presented to complicate Sino-Japanese relations. Fortunately, it was possible to settle this question in March, 1929.

5. TREATY REVISION

After the Washington Conference the Powers were legally controlled in their future behavior toward China by the principles of the Nine Powers Treaty. But they were also protected by the established principles of the existing treaty-system. In addition, there were certain exceptional privileges which represented accretions on the general treaty-system or were based upon bilateral agreements. Since some of the Washington Conference agreements were concerned with this side of China's foreign relations, it will be convenient to summarize the effects of the Conference from this standpoint before turning to the independent initiatives undertaken by the Chinese governments with respect to treaty revision.

One of the privileges enjoyed by the Powers which rested, at best, only imperfectly on treaty provisions was that of the maintenance of armed forces on Chinese territory. Under the Boxer Protocol, the treaty states had the right to maintain legation guards in Peking and troops along the line of the railway from Peking to the sea. Furthermore some of the railway agreements were so interpreted as to authorize the maintenance of troops, as railway guards, in the railway zones. But beyond this, several states, in 1911 and thereafter, had introduced armed forces into various places in China where their nationals were concentrated for the purpose of protecting them and their interests. Naval forces were also to be found in Chinese waters, and particularly up the Yangtse River. One of the resolutions adopted at the Washington Conference, consequently, took cognizance of this situation to the extent of authorizing an investigation, the Powers declaring their intention of withdrawing such of their armed forces as were in China without treaty authorization whenever China could assure protection for the lives and property of foreigners. This time did not arrive during the period of concern with the Washington Conference agreements.

Another resolution provided for the withdrawal of foreign post offices maintained on Chinese territory, except in leased territories or where specifically provided for by treaty, subject to the requirement that an efficient Chinese postal service be maintained. This was duly accomplished, except for the maintenance of Japanese post offices within the South Manchurian Railway zone.

In regard to the qualification, perhaps a word should be said concerning postal arrangements in China, since the implication is that the Chinese government had not been maintaining effective postal facilities, and that therein lay the justification for the establishment of the foreign post offices. In pre-modern China the only agencies of communication of intelligence were the official courier system and the native posting houses, except, of course, for travelers who might carry letters from place to place. The courier system, in spite of its inefficiency and expensiveness, was continued until the establishment of the Republic when, in 1912–1913, the Chinese Post Office undertook the transmission of all government dispatches. Similarly, the native posting hongs were continued for some time after the establishment of a governmental postal system. They carried letters, parcels, bank drafts, and sycee, and they also engaged in trade. One agency did not serve the entire country but confined its activity to one or two provinces, or only to districts within the province. Their continuation was due to the strength of their organization; to the intimate relations which they sustained with the coast and river steamship companies; and to the fact that they were able to serve the postal authorities, prior to the extension of the postal system to the entire country, in remote districts and in inland provinces as collecting and distributing agencies. At the same time that they served the national Post, of course, they profited themselves by utilizing it for the carriage and delivery of the less profitable material entrusted to them. By 1922 their activities were restricted to small districts within which they could offer services impossible for the Post Office to establish.

The idea of a national postal system gained acceptance gradually and as a result of experiments conducted by the Maritime Customs service under the direction of Sir Robert Hart. By 1875 the Chinese government had become convinced of the desirability of extending its activities along this line, and it agreed to insert in the Chefoo Convention a clause undertaking to establish a postal system. Unfortunately this was not done and it was not until 1896 that the Chinese Post Office was formally established by Imperial decree. A parcel post system was introduced in 1898 and the money remittance system in 1897. In 1914 China formally adhered to the Universal Postal Convention, although the rules of the Union had always been observed. From 1896 the development of the system was rapid; one new office after another was opened until in 1922 the country was served as efficiently as the extension of the railway system permitted. Thus the number of offices and agencies increased from 2,096 in 1906 to 6,201 in 1911 and to 11,306 in 1922. Similarly, articles posted increased in number from 31,994,143 in 1906 to 426,363,616 in 1922, and parcels mailed from 400,126, in 1906 to 4,791,420 in 1922. Thus it must be recognized that at the time of the Washington Conference China had made very creditable progress in the introduction of modern postal facilities in the face of rather discouraging conditions. These were represented by the political turmoil and also by the necessity of competing, to a limited extent, with the foreign post offices which were discontinued after 1922.

Another problem, which may be considered collateral to those growing out of the treaty-system, was that represented by the leased territories.

While the leased territories were not directly dealt with at the Washington Conference, the effect of the repudiation of the sphere of interest conception was to direct attention to the leasehold as one of the bases for the establishment of a sphere. The German-Japanese lease at Kiaochow was terminated as part of the Shantung treaty. The French indicated a willingness to restore Kwangchou Bay to China if other Powers were willing to give up their leaseholds, and in any event to negotiate directly concerning its restoration. And England promised to enter into negotiations with a view to the restoration of Weihaiwei. Japan, however, indicated its intention of retaining its control of the Kwantung leased area, and England made no proffer with respect to the Kowloon territory. When it came to fulfillment of such pledges as were made at Washington, the French failed to enter into the promised negotiations. The English, on the other hand, entered into negotiations with China concerning the conditions of restoration of Weihaiwei in October, 1922, and a provisional agreement was initialed on May 31, 1923. This agreement proved to be unsatisfactory to the Peking government, however, and negotiations had to be resumed. An impasse was reached in 1924, and negotiations were dropped until 1930. An agreement satisfactory to both parties was finally reached on April 30, 1930.

But, perhaps, greatest interest attaches to the movement on the part of China to secure release from the two earliest restraints imposed upon her freedom of action—extraterritoriality and the treaty tariff arrangements. As to the first, it was promised at Washington that a commission would be appointed to investigate the administration of justice in China and make recommendations in regard to the extraterritorial system. This investigation was postponed until 1925, partly because of political conditions in the Republic, and at the request of the Chinese government. The commission first conducted its investigations at Peking into the actual and proposed changes in the legal system and the administration of justice, and then attempted to find out how far the local administration had been brought into harmony with modern ideas. Its work, particularly in the second phase, was interfered with because of the renewal of civil war and on account of the disturbed condition of the provinces. Its recommendations proposed certain steps to be taken by China before the Powers should relinquish control of their nationals; further suggested that, as the tests were partially satisfied, agreement should be reached as to the basis of progressive ending of the system; and proposed modifications in the operation of the system to make it function more efficiently and acceptably.[13]

In regard to the tariff the treaty entered into between the Nine Powers at Washington provided: (1) for immediate revision of the schedules in

[13] Text of the *Report* published by Department of State, Washington, 1927; Recommendations, pp. 107–109.

order to give China an actual return of five per cent on the value of the foreign trade; (2) for the meeting, within three months of the ratification of the treaty, of a special conference to consider the problem of the likin tax and its abolition, in return for which the special conference was authorized to provide for the levy of a general surtax of two and one-half per cent, and on certain articles of luxury of a surtax of not more than five per cent; and (3) for the acceptance of the principle of uniformity of levy on the land and maritime frontiers, in order that the trade of France in the south, and of Japan and Russia in the north, should not continue to enjoy advantages denied to the maritime traders.[14]

The immediate revision promised was duly accomplished, but the special conference was not convened until late in 1925 on account mainly of the failure of France to ratify the treaty. This was due to what is known as the gold franc controversy.[15] When it came to a resumption, in 1922, of payments on the French share of the Boxer indemnity, after the five-year war moratorium, the French insisted on payment in gold francs. The Chinese government insisted that it had the right to make payment in the depreciated paper franc. The controversy was not settled until April of 1925. After its settlement and the completion of ratification of the Nine Powers Customs Treaty, steps were taken to convene the special conference. When it met it was confronted with the demand of the Chinese delegation that tariff autonomy rather than merely revision upwards should be granted. This demand was accepted in principle, with the understanding that a Chinese national tariff was to go into effect on January 1, 1929, by which time China agreed to have abolished the likin system. The Powers regarded the one as dependent on the other, having joined them steadily, even when the limited question of revision was considered, since the signature of the Mackay treaty in 1902. The Chinese, however, considered that the Powers had accepted a commitment with respect to the customs régime which should be fulfilled without regard to their success in abolishing likin collections. But in any case, the conference was terminated without any official conclusion of agreements on account of the overturning of the Peking government during the civil war of 1925–1926. Subsequent negotiations were conducted on a separate basis from that established in the Washington agreement.

The next phase of the treaty revision movement was inaugurated in 1926. One avowed aim of the Kuomintang was to establish China's foreign relations on the basis of full equality. But it was the Peking government which took the first definite steps in that direction under the pressure of an empty treasury as well as that of articulate national opinion. Toward the end of 1926 Chang Tso-lin decreed the collection of the Washington sur-

---

[14] Text in *Senate Doc. No. 126*, pp. 897–901.

[15] For details see *China Year Book*, 1924, pp. 837–849. Also *China Year Book*, 1925, pp. 1296–1300.

taxes as from February 1, 1927, in spite of the fact that agreements authorizing their collection had not been made. Since Sir Francis Aglen, Inspector-
General of the Customs, refused to collect these unauthorized surtaxes he
was dismissed and Mr. A. H. F. Edwardes, also a British subject, was appointed acting Inspector-General. These actions were strongly objected to
by the diplomatic body at Peking but without avail.

Previous to this action, however, the significant move had been made
of indicating an intention of dealing with each of the treaty states separately
instead of negotiating with them collectively. Collective action had been
attempted at Paris and at Washington, and the question of treaty revision
had been raised by the Chinese delegation at the 1925 meeting of the Assembly of the League of Nations. The returns from these attempts to secure
international action had been disappointing, so that a new method of approach had to be sought, if results were to be obtained. The basis of the
new method was found in provisions of most of the treaties providing for
their revision at the expiration of ten-year periods at the request either of
one or of both parties. While these provisions contemplated partial revision
rather than termination of the instrument or the substitution of a new
agreement, the Chinese government at this time, and afterwards, insisted
that it would unilaterally terminate the particular treaty unless a new agreement, founded upon the principles of equality and reciprocity, were reached.
Thus it announced the terms on which it was willing to continue any treaty
in force instead of asking the foreign state to modify treaty provisions in a
satisfactory manner. This really represented a startling shift in attitude.

The first treaty approached in this way was that with Belgium, the re-
visory article of which quite clearly gave to Belgium alone the right to
propose modifications in the treaty. Notification of intention to revise the
treaty was given to the Belgian representative at Peking on April 16, 1926.
It was stated that the treaty would terminate in October, and that a new
agreement would have to be made to take its place. Belgium denied the
right of China to raise the question, but indicated a willingness to consider
limited revision. This in turn was unacceptable to China, and then Belgium
proposed to and did present the question to the Permanent Court of International Justice, under Article 36 of the Statute,[16] which both parties had
accepted. China denied that this was a justiciable question, and consequently one which could come before the Court except by agreement of
the parties, and the government proceeded to take steps looking toward
the assumption of jurisdiction over Belgians in the country, and to take
over the concession of Belgium in Tientsin. Before the Court had time to
act on the application of the Belgian government the latter decided to
negotiate a new treaty, at the same time agreeing in advance to China's
taking over the Tientsin concession. Negotiations were re-opened on Janu-

[16] Which established a unilateral right of instituting action.

ary 17, 1927, and the Chinese government announced suitable interim arrangements with respect to the protection of Belgian nationals: for their trial only in the modern law courts, and with respect to commerce. Thus, in dealing strongly with a small state, the Peking government had been able to establish a right to replace an unacceptable instrument with one more satisfactory to it in the face of the fact that its right to insist even upon limited revision was legally untenable. The same policy was followed by the Peking government as the ten-year period of French, Japanese, and Spanish treaties came to an end. Negotiations with all three governments were commenced during 1926–1927. It should be noted also that two new treaties, with Austria and Finland, were negotiated in 1925 and 1926 on a basis substantially of equality and reciprocity.

Before the negotiation of treaties to replace the Belgian, French, Japanese, and Spanish "unequal" treaties had been completed the northern government was displaced and the direction of foreign affairs was transferred to Nanking. This proved to be of advantage to the nationalists in continuing the negotiations and in inaugurating conversations with other states. It necessitated that the individual minister should come to Nanking, thus disrupting the unity of the diplomatic body for purposes of negotiation concerning the treaty rights which they, on the whole, possessed in common. After the Washington Conference the Powers had sought to follow a coöperative policy at Peking. This carried with it the maintenance of a united front in dealings with the Chinese government. This would have served a useful purpose to China if the principal immediate danger had been that of the pursuit by the treaty-states of separate national ends. From the standpoint of treaty revision, however, the coöperative policy was the reverse of useful to China, being of advantage only to the Powers. Before the unification of the country under the Nationalists, Peking had begun to breach the wall, as has been just pointed out. This made the task of the Nanking government easier of accomplishment. On the other hand, the Nationalists had already begun to make a similar breach in the united front of the Powers, and their agitation had facilitated the accomplishments of the Peking government in the field of foreign relations.

The rise of the nationalist movement in China, while it did not fundamentally change the conditions in contemplation of which the Washington Conference agreements and treaties had been concluded, introduced a new factor into the politics of the Far East. This factor was the assertion of a new independence of action by the Chinese government. To a limited extent this gave a new direction to China's foreign policies. Immediately, however, it only provided more vigorous movement toward the goals already in sight as a result of the Washington Conference, and of the activity subsequent to it of the Peking government. Nevertheless, to understand what occurred after 1928 in the field of foreign relations as well as in that of domestic politics in China, it is necessary to understand the rise and the program of nationalist China. We must, therefore, return at this point to the internal political evolution of China before beginning an examination of the breakdown of the Washington Conference system after 1931.

REFERENCES FOR FURTHER STUDY

M. J. Bau, *The Open Door Doctrine in Relation to China* (1923); an excellent analysis. R. L. Buell, *The Washington Conference* (1922); one of the most comprehensive early accounts of the Conference. H. C. Bywater, *Sea-power in the Pacific* (1921); the subtitle, "a study of the American-Japanese naval problem," indicates its scope. Carnegie Endowment for International Peace, *Treaties and Agreements with and Concerning China, 1919–1929.* Chinese Delegation, *Conversations Between the Chinese and Japanese Representatives in Regard to the Shantung Question* (1923); should be used with the *Précis* of the negotiations published by Japan (1922). A. L. P. Dennis, *The Anglo-Japanese Alliance* (1923), ch. 4, 5, and appendices. N. Golovin, *The Problem of the Pacific in the Twentieth Century* (1922); a suggestive analysis of the Pacific problem at the time of the Conference. A. W. Griswold, *The Far Eastern Policy of the United States* (1938), ch. 7–9. Y. Ichihashi, *The Washington Conference and After* (1928); an account by a careful Japanese student. F. C. Jones, *Shanghai and Tientsin* (1940). K. K. Kawakami, *Japan and the Pacific* (1922); a presentation of the Japanese point of view. A. M. Kotenev, *Shanghai, Its Mixed Court and Council* (1925). H. F. MacNair, *Modern Chinese History, Selected Readings* (1923), ch. 17, sec. 75, T. F. Millard, *The End of Extraterritoriality in China* (1931); an analysis of treaty revision by an American in the employ of China; valuable appendices. R. T. Pollard, *China's Foreign Relations, 1917–1931* (1933), ch. 7–12; a careful and valuable study. H. S. Quigley and G. H. Blakeslee, *The Far East, an International Survey* (1938), esp. ch. 10–13; an objective factual presentation of developments in the field of treaty revision. Sun Yat-sen, *The International Development of China* (1922). (China) Weekly Review, *Tariff Conference Issue*, Nov. 1, 1925; also articles and editorials during 1920–1931; much material may also be found in the Japan Chronicle (weekly ed.) during the same years. Senate Document no. 126, *Conference on the Limitation of Armaments* (1922), 67th Congress, 2nd session; contains the entire proceedings of the Conference, together with the texts of agreements. B. L. Putnam Weale (pseud.), *Indiscreet Chronicle from the Pacific* (1922); worth consulting, if used with other materials. W. W. Willoughby, *China at the Conference, a Report* (1922); the most authoritative discussion of the Conference as it affected China. H. G. W. Woodhead (ed.), *China Year Book, 1924*, ch. 28 (international issues); for treatment of post-Conference questions, including documents; appendix for Sino-Russian agreements; *1925*, ch. 17 (Chinese Customs Tariff), for treatment of that question; ch. 15 (Greater China), for questions relating to Mongolia, Manchuria, Tibet, and Chinese Turkestan; ch. 25 (Public Documents), for Russo-Japanese Convention of 1925, and the Mukden (Soviet and Manchuria) Agreement; pp. 925–936 for leased territories and colonies; appendix for Gold Franc case settlement. The table of contents of each annual volume gives a detailed guide to materials bearing on international relations as well as domestic developments. Chitoshi Yanaga, *Japan Since Perry* (1949), ch. 28–30.

CHAPTER XX

THE NATIONALIST REVOLUTION

THE first phase of the Chinese revolution, purely political in its mani-festations, accomplished the overturn of the Manchu Empire, but it did not attain its objective of the establishment of a parliamentary Republic. This phase was finished, in fact, although not in theory, with the failure of the "summer revolution" of 1913. To be sure, the parliamentary Republic was revived for a year, following the death of Yüan Shih-k'ai, but it could not maintain itself against the decentralizing militarist forces which definitively terminated it in 1917. All attempts to revive it in the face of the determi-nation of the provincial war-lords to rule were completely unsuccessful. The revolution, consequently, lost for a time its political character. From 1917 until 1924–1925, it began to plow the deeper soil presented in the eco-nomic, social, literary, and intellectual fields. This left politics to the military rulers, supported in the central government by those who may be described as professional politicians and career diplomatists, and to Dr. Sun Yat-sen and his small circle of followers.

I. THE KUOMINTANG—1912–1924

During the years between 1913 and 1924 the revolutionary party had become practically moribund. The secret revolutionary organization (the T'ung Meng Hui) which had been the instrument of the political revolu-tion of 1911 lost much of its revolutionary force when, after the revolution had been theoretically accomplished with the overthrow of the Manchus, it was reorganized as a non-secret political party including other groups than the T'ung Meng Hui. Because of this it was reconstructed as a secret revo-lutionary party after the failure of the rebellion of 1913, with all members required to take an oath of personal allegiance to Dr. Sun Yat-sen. This had the effect of restricting its membership since many of those who had been members of the T'ung Meng Hui refused to take the oath. There-after, the revolutionaries "were kept together solely by the personality of Dr. Sun Yat-sen; membership in the party became a matter of tradition; it merely meant that one had personal contact with Sun Yat-sen." [1] The weakening effects of this being perceived, the party was again reorganized after the capture of Kwangtung in 1920. The new National People's Party of China remained a secret society, but the personal oath was abolished,

[1] T'ANG LEANG-LI, *Inner History of the Chinese Revolution*, p. 139.

together with some other restrictions formerly imposed. This enlarged the membership, but it did not effectively energize the party since no provision was made for organization meetings for the coöperative development of a program. No relationship, furthermore, was established between party authority and political and military power. The party remained the instrument of the leader.

This party reconstruction did not enable Dr. Sun to maintain himself for long in power in Kwangtung. It did not serve to distinguish the southern government in any material respects from that at Peking since, as has been pointed out, the basis of such authority as Dr. Sun possessed was the support accorded him by provincial militarists. Conscious of this dependence, Dr. Sun sought to find a new basis of power by attempting another reorganization of the party along radically different lines.

The procedure followed in reorganizing the Kuomintang was suggested by Russian advisers who came to Canton in the autumn of 1923 at the invitation of Dr. Sun. The basis for collaboration with Soviet Russia had been laid at the beginning of the year when Dr. Sun had carried on extensive conversations at Shanghai with Mr. Joffe, the Soviet emissary to the Far Eastern countries. As a result a joint pronouncement [2] was issued in which Dr. Sun, with the concurrence of Mr. Joffe, stated that he did not feel that either communism or the soviet system could be introduced into China, whose problem was that of the attainment of unity and complete independence. In the solution of that problem Dr. Sun was assured of the support of Russia. The declaration then went on to reassure Dr. Sun as to Russian intentions with respect to the Chinese Eastern Railway and Outer Mongolia. This included a general reaffirmation of the principles of the Soviet Declaration of 1919, which established the Soviet policy as anti-imperialistic, as contrasted with the imperialism of the capitalistic states.

Michael Borodin was designated as the principal adviser to the southern government. From the time of his arrival at Canton in September, 1923, dates the vitalizing of the Kuomintang. The first objective was that of transforming it into a highly organized party of disciplined individuals, united by the acceptance of a common program of action instead of by only the personal tie of loyalty to Dr. Sun. The model for the reorganization was the Russian Communist Party. The steps taken to transform the party included a re-registration of the members of the old party. This resulted in the exclusion of many of those clinging to the ideology of 1911 and of those who were unwilling to accept the Russian orientation. The membership was increased, however, by permitting members of the Chinese Communist Party, as individuals, to register as members of the Kuomintang.

[2] The text of the Sun-Joffe Declaration is in the *China Year Book*, 1924, p. 863.

The base of the organization was established in local nuclei of registered party members, with control of activities to be exercised by the members meeting regularly every fortnight. This local meeting was also empowered to select an executive committee concerned with organization, discipline, and propaganda, and a supervisory committee, with the functions of auditing the accounts, maintaining a general control, and prosecuting against breaches of party rules and discipline. From this base the organization was pyramided through sub-district, district, and provincial organizations to the central organization, consisting of an annual National Congress, designed as the final authority on policy, and a Central Executive Committee and a Supervisory Committee to supervise and direct party affairs between the meetings of the Congress. In theory, power was to work from the bottom to the top of the pyramid, in contrast to the former practice of subordinating the party membership to Dr. Sun Yat-sen. The party constitution (Art. 21), however, designated Dr. Sun as the President of the Party during his lifetime. It was also provided (Art. 22) "that the members should follow the direction of the President and work for the advancement of the Party; (2) that the President should have the power to disapprove resolutions of the Party Congress, giving him the final control of policy; and (3) that his should be the decisive voice in the Central Executive Committee." Nevertheless, the provision for a Party Congress to meet regularly, and the establishment of the Central Executive Committee, had both the theoretical and the practical effect of broadening the basis of authority from that of the individual leader to the Party itself. The general chart of organization as approved by the first Party Congress on January 28, 1924, would seem to reflect the views of Borodin. The peculiar powers vested in Dr. Sun as President would seem to have resulted from the necessity of recognizing the fact that the Kuomintang had been for so long under his direction and control, and that "the reorganization was still in its transitional period, and was in need of the active guidance of Dr. Sun Yat-sen." [3]

This general scheme of organization proved sufficiently well adapted to the needs of the Party so that it was continued substantially unchanged after the party had gained control of the government. But the exigencies of the political situation prevented the holding of the contemplated annual Congresses. Thus only two were held between 1924, when the first was convoked, and 1931. The second was held in January, 1926, and the third

[3] T'ANG, *Inner History*, op. cit., p. 177. T'ang states that Sun proposed the abolition of the presidency, but that the committee appointed to report on the proposed party constitution overruled him. He also states that the draft of party organization was presented by Sun, implying, although not stating, that it was his work. On this, as well as on the question of Russian influence in the drafting of the Party Manifesto, the views of Chinese nationalist writers should be compared with the account given by L. FISCHER, *The Soviets in World Affairs*, 2 vols., vol. 2, pp. 636–640.

had to be postponed to March, 1929. This resulted in the national direction, from the Party standpoint, gravitating more completely than was originally contemplated into the hands of the Central Executive Committee.

The committee system of direction, on the other hand, in spite of its obvious defects, enabled those of divergent views and tendencies to be held somewhat together in at least a nominal common direction of affairs. Thus it served a useful purpose and justified its institution.

2. THE PARTY PRINCIPLES

The principles of the Kuomintang, which is to say the philosophy of the national revolution, were initially set forth in several important documents. These were: (1) the Party manifesto adopted by the Congress of 1924; (2) the series of lectures delivered by Dr. Sun Yat-sen in exposition of his principles, published as the San Min Chu I, or Three Principles of the People; and (3) the "Fundamentals of National Reconstruction," dated April 12, 1924. Reference should also be made to the "Will" [4] of Dr. Sun, drawn up just before his death on March 12, 1925.

The revolutionary philosophy can only be briefly summarized here in its broad outlines. It was based on Dr. Sun's "Three Principles of the People." The first of these principles was nationalism. Dr. Sun believed that the idea of a strong political unity must be established in the thinking of the Chinese people in place of the cultural unity which was the Chinese heritage. He compared China repeatedly, in his lectures, to a rope of sand. The particles were alike but the rope was not thereby made strong unless cement was used to bind the particles together. This cement was nationalism, which to Dr. Sun meant the transformation of the culture society into the political state by means of the development of authority. Thus, basically, the nationalism of Dr. Sun was not anti-foreignism but the transfer of traditional loyalties from the clan-family and the village to the state. Consequently, he emphasized nationalism in the sense of the development of national patriotism. But one way, probably the easiest, to develop patriotism is on the basis of hostility to those who threaten the integrity of the state. For that reason, if for no other, much emphasis was laid on the necessity of presenting a united national front against imperialism, which Dr. Sun found had reduced China to the status of a "hypocolony," a term he employed to describe a condition below that of the colony. But, it must be emphasized, he felt that anti-imperialism—which describes his position better than anti-foreignism—was not the whole of the principle of national-

---

[4] As to the drafting and authenticity of this document, see H. F. MacNair, *China in Revolution*, p. 79; T'ang, *Inner History*, pp. 193–197. The "Will" is important not so much because of its content as on account of its effect in crystallizing the nationalist thinking in terms of the documents enumerated in it.

ism. It might be immediately the most important, but ultimately the think- *Black Power* ing of the Chinese about themselves must be changed. That is, they must cultivate the ability to think, and thus to act, in terms of the state rather than of smaller groups. Furthermore, since China was composed of five races, the principle of equality of races must be given an internal as well as an external application.

The second principle was that of democracy, but a revised conception of democracy as contrasted with the thinking of 1911. By 1924 Dr. Sun had come to draw a clear distinction between government, which should be erected on an authoritarian basis, and control, at which place the sovereignty of the people should be exhibited. The devices of control which he proposed were election and recall of policy-determining officers, and the initiative and referendum. The system of government, controlled through these devices, should be instituted on the basis of the five-power constitution, adding to the organization of the functions of legislation, execution, and judgment, those of examination and censorship. The last two, it was felt, represented a return to past practices rather than an introduction of new conceptions. Government, in Dr. Sun's revised thinking, should be in the hands of superior men, but subject ultimately to control which would ensure the use of power in the interest of the masses.

Furthermore, it was recognized, as it had not been in 1911, that the people were not immediately ready to exercise their powers. Consequently, three distinct stages of progress toward democracy were envisaged. First, a period of military operations would be necessary when the military power would have to be dominant. Second, after military operations had been concluded, would come a period of political tutelage, during which the people would have to be trained in the use of their powers. This would have to be undertaken in the locality, with local popular control made effective, a step at a time, before national democracy could be introduced. Thus, development would be from the bottom up rather than from the top down. Given this method of approach, the period of tutelage could be inaugurated in any province or region whenever military operations had been successfully concluded, without waiting for success throughout the entire country. During the period of political tutelage the Party, rather than the people, would be in complete control of the machinery of government. Then, when the people had been prepared to exercise their powers on a national scale, the period of constitutional and democratic government could be safely and wisely inaugurated.

The third principle was that of the people's livelihood. It represented Dr. Sun's answer to the question of the use which should be made of power after it had been attained. Broadly characterized, his program was based upon a social rather than an economic interpretation of history. In the lectures on this principle Sun Yat-sen devoted considerable time to a critical analysis of the Marxian doctrine of materialism, reaching the conclusion that it, together with the conception of the class war, were inapplicable in and to China.[5] Since China was essentially an agricultural country, much attention was paid to the problem of livelihood of the peasant. In proposing lines of solution of this problem Dr. Sun's program was reminiscent of Henry George, involving an equalization of land-ownership by means of an appropriation by the state of value added to the land through social development. Beyond this, such indication as Dr. Sun gave in his lectures of the method of concrete application of the principle of livelihood would seem to justify classifying him as a radical bourgeois social reformer rather than a communist. The discussion of the principle was, however, general rather than particular so that it is difficult to deduce an actual realizable program from it. Because of its generality, furthermore, it was possible immediately to use it as the basis for holding together leaders of divergent social and economic aims and interests and ultimately for justifying attack on and defense of what came to be the communist program.

3. THE CONTEST FOR POWER AT CANTON—1924–1926

While these steps were being taken to reorganize and strengthen the Party, dissatisfaction was growing among the merchants of Canton and the gentry of Kwangtung province. Dr. Sun had returned to power in 1923 because of the support accorded him by Yunnan and Kwangsi militarists. Their interest was, however, not in good government but in enriching themselves by exploitation of the city and the province. Consequently their exactions were heavy. To defend themselves the merchants and gentry, apparently with Dr. Sun's approval, organized protective forces of a mercenary character which were called Merchants' Volunteer Corps. These bodies were organized locally to safeguard life and property against the military. But as the Party propaganda assumed a more and more radical character, and as it resulted in the organization of workers' and peasants' unions, the dissatisfaction of the gentry came to be with the Party rather than with its military supporters of the moment. The result was the organization of a movement to expel Dr. Sun from Canton by making use of the Merchants' Volunteer Corps, and by extending an invitation to Ch'en Chiung-ming to return to the city. When the clash came, in September and October, 1924, it was precipitated by the action of Dr. Sun in confiscating arms which were being imported for use of the merchants' forces. Consequently, it came before the latter were fully prepared to act,

---

[5] It may be noted in this connection that there is an inconsistency, from this standpoint, between the point of view expressed in the earlier lectures and that revealed in the uncompleted series dealing with the principle of livelihood. Dr. Sun's earlier views seem to have been modified after reading MAURICE WILLIAM's book, *The Social Interpretation of History*.

and the Kuomintang forces were completely victorious. Their victory was marked by considerable destruction of property, which did not enhance Dr. Sun's popularity at Canton.

Immediately thereafter, he left for the north. Since 1922 he had been in alliance with the Tuan Chi-jui faction in the north, and he sought to join with Tuan and Chang Tso-lin in overturning Wu P'ei-fu. However, without military forces at his disposal he was unable to contribute anything to the decision, which was actually determined in favor of the anti-Wu alliance on account of the defection of Fêng Yü-hsiang. In spite of his failure to launch a movement against Wu from the south Dr. Sun accepted an invitation to proceed to Peking to collaborate with Chang, Fêng and Tuan in the establishment of a government under which China could be united. He arrived at the northern capital in December, only to find that all of the important decisions had already been made, and on terms unacceptable to him. Already a sick man when he arrived, he died in Peking on March 12, 1925.

The death of Sun Yat-sen had two important but contradictory consequences. The first was that he was transformed overnight into the legendary hero and patron saint of the Kuomintang, and of nationalist China. All doubts as to his wisdom were laid at rest; his past mistakes and comparative political ineptitude were forgotten. From one who had been regarded by many as a visionary and by not a few as a chronic trouble-maker he came to be regarded as the fount of all wisdom. This, as well as the Russian influence and direction, had the effect of transforming the Kuomintang into a vital force in Chinese politics. Sunyatsenism was a much more vital force than Sun Yat-sen had ever been. His "Will" became the sacred canon of the Party, and his "Three Principles of the People" the nationalist bible.

But all of this did not prevent the second consequence from manifesting itself. His death opened the way for a conflict for leadership of the Party and made it possible for the leaders, as part of this conflict, to split on doctrinal grounds. This latter was possible because of the generality of expression of his views and the consequent room which was left for differences of interpretation over their correct application.

In the resulting struggle the balance of advantage rested with the left wing of the Party, supported by the communist members. They had the advantage of an initial control of the central machinery of the Party. The victory over the merchants and gentry of Kwangtung, who represented the right wing point of view, gave them the control of Canton. This position they maintained successfully against attacks in the spring of 1925 by the forces of Ch'en Chiung-ming and the Kwangsi and Yunnan militarists. And they were able to control the decisions of the Second Party Congress which was held in January, 1926. From the standpoint of the internal Party struggle, the most important of these decisions was that of continuing the

Russian connection. It was this, together with the admission of communists to Party membership, which represented the chief point of difference between the right and left wings of the Party leadership, as was indicated in the program drawn up by right wing leaders at the so-called Western Hills Conference. The refusal to consider their program at the second Party Congress ensured a continuation of the schism in the party.

The Russian orientation was also confirmed by reason of the difficulties with England which developed after the May 30 incident at Shanghai. Chinese students and others demonstrating in support of workmen on strike against Japanese mill-owners were fired upon by the police of the International Settlement, commanded by an Englishman. This aroused a storm of protest throughout the country and led to a similar demonstration at Canton. Again the demonstrators were fired upon by the British police, the result being the so-called Shakee-Shameen massacre. The immediate reaction to this was the institution of a boycott directed against Hongkong and against British trade in general.[6] The ultimate effect was to confirm the nationalists in the view that Dr. Sun's principle of nationalism meant exclusively anti-imperialism, and to establish this as the most important slogan of the Party. In the struggle against imperialism was presented a cause which could unite all elements of the Party. The inauguration of the struggle also served to strengthen the position of those who were supporters of the Russian relationship, since Russian policy was similarly announced to be that of anti-imperialism.

4. THE NORTHERN EXPEDITION

But a successful struggle against imperialism required the establishment of a broader base than was presented at Canton. This directed attention to another enemy, in opposition to which there was also a united front within the Party. This was northern militarism. The "northern expedition" had been the dream of Sun Yat-sen from 1917 until his death, and it was taken over as the objective of the Party. The decision was taken at the Party Congress of 1926 to launch the northern expedition immediately, but it was taken in the face of the opinion of the Russian advisers that the action should be postponed. However, because of the constant tendency toward factionalism at Canton, with the dangers to their own position inherent in it, as illustrated in the *coup d'état* of Chiang Kai-shek, directed against the left, in the spring of 1926, Borodin changed his mind and turned to advocacy of an attack on the northern militarists. The new point of view, also, was an outgrowth of the appreciation of the fact that a larger stage was needed on which to act against England and the other capitalist states.

[6] Which was continued for eighteen months.

The northern expedition was finally launched in the summer of 1926. The plan of attack, devised by the chief Russian military adviser, General Blücher, involved simultaneous movements north through Hunan and Kiangsi provinces, the immediate objective being Hankow. From Hankow it was planned to move down the Yangtse to Nanking and Shanghai. After Shanghai had been reached another northward movement could be inaugurated toward Peking along the lines of the Peking-Hankow and the Tientsin-Pukou railways. In the move to the Yangtse all of the armies were placed under the supreme command of General Chiang Kai-shek, who was also released for the period of military operations from the control of the supervisory organs of the Party. The armies operating through Kiangsi, however, were under his direct command rather than those moving on Hankow through Hunan.

By the time General Chiang had reached Nanchang, Hankow had been occupied by the forces striking directly at the center of the power of Wu P'ei-fu. This rapid elimination of one of the northern militarists had been made possible because of the tactics followed in the campaign. These involved an extensive propaganda among the peasants in advance of the military movement, and a similar propaganda among the opposing forces. The result was that the nationalist armies were augmented by additions from the peasantry and by defections from the ranks of Marshal Wu. Thus, while resistance was weakened, the ability to overcome it was constantly increased. Then, after the armies had advanced, the Party propagandists remained to organize the regions occupied and thus to consolidate the ground won. Since the propagandists were in many instances communist members of the Party and in the others were left wing extremists, the territories in Hunan traversed by the nationalist armies were given a radical and communist indoctrination.

After the drive north began, the government at Canton came to assume a more definitely communist character. Up to that time, while it had rested upon an alliance of the communists with the Kuomintang left, the emphasis had been laid upon the leadership of the left rather than that of the communists. This was clearly revealed when, as part of the truce that had been patched up after Chiang's anti-communist blow, executed in Borodin's absence and directed against the extremists, the communists had been denied the right to serve as heads of departments, in spite of the fact that Chiang had to make his peace with Borodin. This decision had been taken at a plenary session of the Central Executive Committee. But with Chiang away in command of the armies, and with Wang Ching-wei, the outstanding civilian leader of the left abroad, the restraining influences were removed. Consequently, the government which was removed to Hankow from Canton in November was dominated by the Russian advisers. Furthermore, its leaders were controlled somewhat by a desire to weaken the hitherto dominant position of Chiang within the councils of the Party, and a distinct anti-Chiang campaign developed.

Appreciating this, General Chiang sought to convoke a meeting of the Central Executive Committee at Nanchang, where he would be in a position to reassert his dominance. Instead it was convoked at Hankow, with Chiang abstaining from participation. The result was his removal from the positions of commander-in-chief and chairman of the Standing Committee, although he was continued as a member of the Central Executive Committee.

5. HANKOW AND NANKING

This was the prelude to the long-expected and often-deferred split in the Party, which, for a time, brought the struggle against the imperialists and the northern militarists to an end.[7] For a time even apparently anti-foreign movements, such as occurred when Nanking was occupied by communist nationalist troops, were designed fundamentally to produce internal rather than external consequences. When it was learned at Hankow that Chiang planned to occupy Nanking and to seize control of Shanghai, with a view to gaining the support of the wealthy bourgeois at the latter place, he was forestalled by the entrance into Nanking of nationalist troops, acting ostensibly under his orders, who immediately began to loot and destroy foreign property. The expectation was that this would embroil Chiang with the foreign Powers, who were already sufficiently alarmed over developments so that they were evacuating their nationals from the interior, sending additional contingents of troops to Shanghai, and erecting barricades there for the purpose of defending the International Settlement and the French concession.[8] Chiang, however, was able to avoid international difficulties for the time, although ultimately the government which he was largely instrumental in establishing at Nanking assumed responsibility for and reached an adjustment with the Powers concerning the Nanking affair.

Forestalled at Nanking, Chiang went directly to Shanghai, where he was able to secure the support of the bankers and merchants, of the old Kuomintang leaders who had withdrawn from participation in Party affairs because of dissatisfaction with the Russian orientation (the so-called Western Hills faction), and of the labor union leaders and members who had not succumbed to the left-communist propaganda. Consequently, he was able to gain control of the city without the employment of force, except

---

[7] Attempts to carry on the campaign were made by Hankow and Nanking, but with only temporary advantages won to compensate for reverses which were suffered.

[8] Their alarm was increased when the British concessions at Hankow and Kiukiang were taken over by the Hankow government. Eugene Ch'en's pronouncements as Hankow Foreign Minister were not designed to lessen foreign apprehensions.

as it was used after his establishment in power ruthlessly to crush out communism.

Some of the more moderate members of the Hankow government, disturbed by the extremist policies which were being inaugurated, joined Chiang at Shanghai after he had moved his base north from Nanchang. Others, and notably Wang Ching-wei, who were non-communist leaders of the left wing, attempted to reconcile Chiang with Hankow in order to avoid a disastrous rupture. These negotiations failing, Chiang was formally read out of the party by those in control at Hankow, while he established his seat of government at Nanking and invited the support of all who were opposed to communism and Russian domination. The moderate cause was strengthened when, in consequence of a raid by Chang Tso-lin on the Soviet headquarters at Peking, the Arcos raid in London, and the indiscretions of M. N. Roy, a communist agent attached to the Wuhan government, it was made clear that Russia was then more interested in using the Chinese revolution for her own purposes than in facilitating the attainment of the goal of the nationalist revolution in China. The left Kuomintang members were definitely alienated from the communists and brought into a rapprochement with the moderates, accepting the point of view that the Party must be purged of the communists, and that Borodin and the Russian advisers must be sent home. This, however, was not accomplished until the mid-summer of 1927, and it did not, even then, bring internal harmony sufficient to enable the campaign against the northern coalition to be prosecuted successfully. The Hankow leaders, supported as they were by the fact that they controlled the Central Executive Committee, asserted their supremacy in the Party as against Chiang Kai-shek and his supporters at Nanking. And in the struggle the other military leaders, such as the Kwangsi generals, and Fêng Yü-hsiang who had shifted from benevolent neutrality to active participation in the Party after the overthrow of Wu P'ei-fu, served as make-weights as between Nanking and Hankow.

The scales inclined first one way and then the other. Chiang Kai-shek, who had suffered reverses in the campaign he was carrying on against Sun Ch'uan-fang, and thus was weakened at Nanking, resigned his position in August and retired to Shanghai with the other Nanking leaders. The Wuhan leaders then decided to move the seat of government to Nanking. This was done in September, a basis of agreement with the Kwangsi generals who were in control there after Chiang's retirement having been found. This agreement was short-lived, however, and negotiations were begun with Chiang, after a period of retirement of the left wing leaders to Canton. By that time Chiang and Fêng Yü-hsiang had come into alliance. Consequently, by the end of 1927, Chiang Kai-shek had returned to power and a sufficiently united front had been instituted to enable the campaign against the northern militarists to be resumed. The situation then was that all of the country south of the Yangtse was nominally under the control of the reorganized Nanking Party government. The northwestern provinces and Honan were ruled by Fêng Yü-hsiang, who, however, accepted the direction of the Party. Yen Hsi-shan, the Governor of Shansi province, also had thrown in his lot with the nationalists. Consequently, only northern Anhui, Chihli, and Shantung provinces and the three Manchurian provinces remained under the control of the coalition headed by Chang Tso-lin.

6. CHINA UNIFIED BY THE NATIONALISTS

The military movement to unify China under the auspices of the nationalist Party was resumed in the early spring of 1928. Again the commander-in-chief was Chiang Kai-shek. And again the plan of campaign involved parallel movements north to the objective, Peking. And, just as in the movement north to the Yangtse, Chiang Kai-shek was held up so that the forces moving in the central part of the country were able to reach the objective ahead of him. This time, however, he was obstructed by the Japanese, who threw troops into Shantung along the line of the Tsingtao-Tsinan Railway for the purpose of protecting their interests. This had been done the year before when, after the establishment of the government at Nanking, Chiang had attempted to carry further the northward movement. At that time a clash had been averted. But this time one occurred between the revolutionary troops in control of Tsinan and the Japanese forces. The affair was localized so that its ultimate consequences were not serious. But it stirred up ill-will, and it prevented Chiang Kai-shek from participating in the actual driving of Chang Tso-lin from Peking.[9] This was accomplished in June, Chang retiring with his troops into Manchuria. Following the policy of keeping the area of their interests free from civil war, the Japanese prohibited the nationalist troops from following Chang to Mukden and thus extending their sway to include Manchuria. But that end was accomplished subsequently when Chang Hsueh-liang, the son and successor of Chang Tso-lin, who lost his life in consequence of a bomb explosion before reaching Mukden, hoisted the nationalist flag and voluntarily accepted the union of the Manchurian provinces with nationalist China.

With the capture of Peking it became possible to accomplish what Yüan Shih-k'ai had successfully prevented the 1911 revolutionists from doing i.e., to move the capital of united China from Peking to Nanking. To make even sharper the break with the past, the name of the pre-revolutionary capital was changed to Peip'ing.[10] With the removal of the government

[9] Yen Hsi-shan was instructed to take over the Peking-Tientsin area to forestall occupation by Fêng Yü-hsiang.

[10] The name was changed back to Peking after its occupation by Japanese troops in 1937.

offices to Nanking the only remaining indication of Peip'ing's former political supremacy was the legation quarter, the diplomats only gradually deciding to transfer their quarters to the new seat of government.

7. THE NATIONAL GOVERNMENT ESTABLISHED

The military period of the revolution having been completed, Chiang Kai-shek resigned his office as commander-in-chief and chairman of the military council, theoretically returning to the Party power which had been derived from it. Attention was then turned to the problem of reconstruction. The fifth plenary session of the Central Executive Committee, which was held in August, 1928, authorized the preparation of the Organic Law of the National Government. This was promulgated in October, and with it the country entered officially upon the second stage of the revolution, the period of political tutelage. During it, according to the plans of Dr. Sun, the control was to remain vested in the Party, to be exercised through the Party Congress, the Central Executive Committee, and its Standing Committee. Under the Organic Law, general supervision and direction of the organs of government was to be exercised by a Central Political Council, composed of the Central Executive Committee members and the members of the Central State Council. This established a direct personnel link between the Party and the government. From the governmental standpoint, the highest organ was to be the State Council, whose chairman was made the titular head of the state. Under it a scheme of governmental organization was introduced which embodied Dr. Sun's five-power conception of separate Yuan for the executive, legislative, judicial, examination and control functions.

A structure for the provincial governments was erected in a law of October 25, 1928, which was designed to unify the provincial establishments under the control of provincial councils. Their members, including the chairman, were to be designated by the National Government. Above the provincial councils, branch political councils were established at Canton, Hankow, Kaifeng, Taiyuan, Peking, and Mukden, which corresponded to the regional centers of influence competitive with Nanking.

The Organic Law, in substitution for a more formal constitution, continued in force as the basis of government until the adoption, on May 12, 1931, of a provisional constitution by a National People's Convention convoked for that purpose. The new constitution continued substantially the same scheme of organization as that provided for in the Organic Law, including the provision made for control of the government by the Kuomintang Central Executive Committee, but it substantially increased the powers of the Chairman of the State Council. It contained chapters, however, defining the territories of the state; determining citizenship, and the rights and duties of the people; concerning the application of the principle of the people's livelihood; on education; establishing a division of powers between the central and local governments; and providing for the establishment of local governments. Since the provisional constitution was adopted on the eve of the outbreak of trouble with Japan in Manchuria, and when a serious threat to stability was presented with the recrudescence of communism in south-central China, its ultimate importance was problematical. At any rate, it was the instrument under which government was to be conducted until the termination of the period of tutelage, supposedly in 1935.

8. DOMESTIC POLITICS—1929–1933

If China had been united in fact as well as in name after the overthrow of the northern militarists, and the acceptance of the authority of the Party by Chang Hsueh-liang on January 1, 1929, it would have been possible to move rapidly in the direction of national reconstruction. This movement was strongly retarded, however, on account of the fact that the government had constantly to struggle merely to preserve itself. The head of the government was Chiang Kai-shek, but he, and consequently the Nanking government which was immediately dominated by him, directly controlled only the provinces at the mouth of the Yangtse River. Elsewhere, the authority of the government was dependent upon a continuation of alliances with Fêng Yü-hsiang, Yen Hsi-shan, and the Kwangsi generals who were in control of the region centering at Hankow. Furthermore, while the drive against the communists had been immediately successful in breaking their power in south-central China, it had not resulted in their extinction. The movement was driven underground for the time, but propaganda continued, and a portion of the original nationalist armies retained its communistic complexion and kept alive resistance to the National government. From the doctrinal standpoint, also, the right wing of the Party was in control of the machinery of the Party and the possibility existed of a revival of the struggle between the right and the left. Immediately, the left group, which came to call itself reorganizationist, pursued essentially a policy of neutrality toward Nanking.

Consequently, it is not to be wondered at that the central government had to concentrate its energies on the task of maintaining itself. Fêng Yü-hsiang withdrew from personal collaboration with Chiang at Nanking before the termination of the sessions of the conference which was called in January, 1929, to plan the disbandment of the feudal military forces.[11] The leaders of the left denounced the Nanking leadership because of the decision which was taken with respect to the method of constitution of the

[11] This represented a direct attack on the major problem confronting every government since 1911. Agreement on a plan of regional disbandment was reached but not put into effect.

third Party Congress, which was summoned for March 15, 1929. This laid the basis for the subsequent raising of the standard of revolt at Canton. And a direct military struggle with the Kwangsi faction broke out in March. The Kwangsi generals were driven from Hankow by Chiang's troops, supported by those of Fêng Yü-hsiang, who responded to Nanking's call for action in the hope of adding to the territories under his control.

The decisive struggle between Chiang and Fêng, consequently, was postponed until 1930. In the interval each side attempted to weaken the other by charge and counter-charge, and by the traditional methods of Chinese military-diplomatic warfare. Both Chiang and Fêng maneuvered to secure the support of Yen Hsi-shan and of Chang Hsueh-liang. When the rupture came, Nanking faced a coalition of Yen and Fêng, but it was supported by the benevolent neutrality of Chang, which later was transformed into active support. In the result Yen was eliminated and Fêng was driven into his fastnesses in the northwest,[12] and their territories were brought under the control of Chang Hsueh-liang, who thus resumed the position in north China from which his father had been driven in 1928. The difference was that he professed allegiance to the Nanking government, dominated by Chiang Kai-shek, whereas his father had steadily opposed the nationalists. This position he maintained, under the Nanking government, until his power was broken in Manchuria by the Japanese, and until he was finally compelled to renounce his authority in North China on account of his failure to organize a successful resistance to Japan.

While this struggle for power had been going on in the north, the Nanking government had not found its authority uncontested south of the Yangtse. As has been stated, the reorganizationist leaders were dissatisfied with right wing control of the Central Executive Committee, and they did not like the growing concentration of power in the hands of Chiang Kai-shek. The situation at Nanking seemed to justify the conclusion that the result of the revolution had been to institute a new military control to replace the northern militarism. Consequently, the leftist leaders reverted to the tactics of Dr. Sun. They sought to gain and to maintain control of Canton, supporting General Chang Fa-kwei when he attempted to capture the city. When this attempt failed, they began negotiations with the anti-Chiang leaders in the north. Their first overtures were rejected, but when the Yen-Fêng coalition finally was formed and the standard of revolt raised, Wang Ching-wei and Ch'en Kung-po, the two outstanding reorganizationist leaders, accepted an invitation to collaborate in the establishment of a short-lived new government at Peip'ing. Subsequently a separate government was established at Canton, supported by the Kwangsi leaders who had previously been driven out of Hankow and pushed back to their

12 Where he remained inactive politically until 1933 when his voice was raised demanding continued opposition to Japan and denouncing the agreement on the terms of an armistice.

original sphere of control. The new government controlled Kwangtung and Kwangsi provinces only, but asserted itself to be the heir of the revolution, and it launched an expedition against Chiang and Nanking in the late summer of 1931. The difficulties with Japan led to a suspension of these hostilities, to negotiations, and finally to a reconstruction of authority at Nanking, with a virtual concentration of power in a committee of three composed of Chiang, Wang Ching-wei, and Hu Han-min. This alliance of the right and the left, with more than an inclination to the left, was short-lived. The next reconstruction restored the earlier supremacy of Chiang Kai-shek. But mid-summer of 1933 saw his government weakened in north China on account of the extension of Japanese operations, faced by a continuation of a separate régime at Canton, and in the midst of a struggle to overthrow the rising communist power in south-central China.

Chiang's policy of virtual non-resistance to the Japanese was largely determined by the desire to concentrate on the struggle against communism. In his belief that communism represented the outstanding menace Wang Ching-wei concurred. Other left wing leaders, however, wished to risk all in an attempt to resist Japan. Thus they were led to retire from collaboration with the Chiang-dominated régime.

9. THE COMMUNIST MOVEMENT

The revival of communist power to the point where it constituted a menace to the authority of Nanking was in part due to the fact that the energies, and especially the military power, of the government were diverted to the north after the initial anti-communist drive of 1927. This enabled the remaining communist forces gradually to strengthen themselves and to develop tactics of their own. The remnants of the communist military forces were driven into hiding in the mountainous regions of southern Kiangsi province. There they maintained themselves, with some difficulty at first. But as they gained the confidence of the peasantry and learned how to maintain themselves in conflict with the provincial military forces by adapting the mountainous terrain to their own purposes, they became more powerful and more aggressive. By 1930 they had become strong enough to undertake an offensive directed toward Changsha, which city they occupied but were unable to hold long because of foreign intervention in support of Nanking. Their military successes at this time were partly ascribable to the fact that Nanking was engrossed in the Yen-Fêng campaign.

After that campaign was ended, however, the Central Executive Committee called for "the complete extermination of the communist armies and the reoccupation of the sovietized areas." The attempt to carry out this direction was begun in December, 1931, and it was still being continued in

1933, four major campaigns having been carried on, up to that time, against the communist forces. While military successes had been gained, the communist armies had not yet been dislodged, nor had the communist influence been greatly lessened. In 1933, southeastern Kiangsi and western Fukien provinces were definitely organized under soviet governments, while the communist sphere of influence extended throughout Kiangsi and was marked in Hupeh provinces. In addition, smaller areas in Kwangtung and Hunan provinces to the south and Anhui to the north of the Yangtse River were subject to communist influences. The areas under communist control were agricultural rather than industrial, so that the development was toward peasant control rather than proletarian dictatorship. The communist policy had thus been directed toward the accomplishment of agrarian reforms. Large landed estates had been broken up and the land distributed. A banking system, together with coöperative credit societies, had been instituted. Cultivation of the poppy had been prohibited, so that land which had been forced out of food-crop production in order to enrich the military rulers of former days, had again become productive of food. Irrigation and flood-prevention work had been undertaken out of the revenues derived from public lands. And the tax system had been reformed, with a progressive land tax, bearing most heavily on *reforms* the well-to-do, replacing the old system of levies which had the effect of pauperizing the impoverished. On the industrial side, in the towns under soviet government, wages had been raised, just as they had been for agricultural laborers, hours had been shortened, and, in general, policies had been pursued designed to ameliorate the condition of the poorer classes.

The policies pursued by the communists in the areas under their control seemed to indicate the answer to the question raised by the spread of communism in the face of opposition to it by a government which had at its disposal much larger military forces and infinitely greater resources. The Nanking government had been so much engrossed with military operations and expenses resulting from them that it had been unable to make much headway in the endeavor to achieve the social and economic reforms regarded by Dr. Sun as a fundamental part of his program. Such reformative work as had been attempted, it was suggested by its critics, had been in the interest of the wealthier classes rather than of the impoverished masses. This had grown inevitably out of the right orientation of the party after 1927, and the deriving of its support from the wealthier merchant classes. After power had been attained by the party, it tended to lose its revolutionary character for that reason.

10. THE DOMESTIC ACHIEVEMENTS OF THE NATIONAL GOVERNMENT

It should not be inferred from this, however, that the Nanking government had no record of constructive achievement to its credit. Its greatest accomplishments, disregarding the loss of Manchuria, were in the field of foreign affairs, and these will be subsequently discussed. In the domestic field, however, it had faced the gigantic problem of public finance realistically and to some purpose. In the face of the aggravated expenditures for military purposes, both in the form of provision for amortization of debts contracted for those purposes and to maintain the armies in the field necessary to ensure its continued existence, provision had been made for the resumption of payments on the general public debt of the state, which Nanking inherited from the preceding Peking governments. And, in a world of unbalanced state budgets, China was enabled to announce the final balancing of its budget. These achievements must be credited largely to one man, T. V. Soong, who had been at the head of the Finance Ministry almost without interruption since the establishment of the Nanking government.[13] But his achievement was only possible because of the enlargement of income consequent on the attainment of customs autonomy; because of the gradual centralization of financial administration under the Nanking Ministry of Finance; and by following a course of the most rigid economy.[14] But, of course, a program of economy militated against the undertaking of other constructive work.

An advance was also made through the centralization of railway administration under the Ministry of Communications. This agency worked out extensive plans for railway construction to be undertaken as rapidly as circumstances permitted. It should also be noted that highways were constructed suitable to motor transport, thus enlarging the communication facilities of the country.

In the economic field, outside of communications, the work of the Nanking government perhaps fairly may be classed as exploratory. Extensive studies, aided by foreign commissions, were made of the currency problem, of education, of the problem of public health organization, of opium control, and of other problems of national reconstruction. In undertaking these studies, preparatory to action, a close relationship to the Secretariat of the League of Nations was established. Furthermore, legislation was enacted for the organization of labor unions, for the arbitration of labor disputes, and for the eight-hour day.

In the legal and judicial fields the process of constructing satisfactory codes of law and of procedure was carried further toward completion. Many new and modern courts were established in the areas under the control of Nanking, and progress was made with the establishment of modern prisons.

But all of this may be said to be the typical program of the capitalist state and did not directly move to meet the need for livelihood of the im-

[13] Having previously served Hankow in that capacity.
[14] It was also possible because he held the confidence of the Shanghai bankers.

poverished masses. This may also be said of many of the proposals for application of the principle of livelihood which were written into the provisional constitution. Consequently it enabled propaganda to be carried on successfully, denouncing the Nanking government as one substantially uninterested in the realization of Dr. Sun's third principle. This propaganda furthered the aims of the Chinese communists. No one had stated the position of the opposition, from this standpoint, more positively and clearly than Madame Sun Yat-sen did at the time of the break with the Russians in 1927, in 1929, and again in 1931. To her, and to those who thought in the same terms, the program of Nanking was one of social reform, and not one of revolution. Thus the underlying internal issue, in 1933, seemed to be clearly joined between those favoring the maintenance of the moderate, capitalist-supported government headed by Chiang Kai-shek, and those who were promoting what was essentially a peasant revolt. It did not follow that internal stability would be immediately attained with the triumph of Nanking over the communists, since there would still remain room for wide difference of opinion over the program of reform to be promoted. But the issue as between Nanking and Canton was much less fundamental than that between Nanking and communism.

But whatever the issue of that struggle, one conclusion quite clearly emerges from a study of political development in China since 1911. This is that there had been a constantly growing perception of the enlarged and more positive rôle which government has to play in a modern society. No longer was government, whether it be that of Canton or Nanking, or the Soviets, conceived of in terms of the performance of a negative and passive rôle, restricting public authority to the maintenance of peace and order and allowing the economic and social life of the country to be carried on without positive relationship of government to it. In this respect, nationalist China was not an innovator, but merely carried further the evolution which was begun with the establishment of intercourse with the West. The Kemmerer Commission on currency reform, for example, was established as the latest in a series of commissions and experts asked to propose solutions of the problem of bringing order out of the chaotic currency situation. Similarly the League Commission entrusted with a study of the problem of education reëxamined, for the National government, a phase of the national life which had previously been subjected to study. The significant thing, however, is that the successive governments of China began to attempt to relate government to these and other phases of the life of the country in a new way. To begin with, as this tendency began to manifest itself after 1900, the stimulus toward the revision of the rôle of government was applied by the Western States. But by 1933 it was China itself which was exhibiting an active interest in the transformation of the rôle of government from the negative to the positive. More and more definitely then it might be expected that government would interest itself in the development of communications, in the improvement of the condition of agriculture, in industrial undertakings and development, and in the direction of social relations. The only question in 1933 was whether the program of activity would be based upon the capitalist principle or on that of communism.

II. ACHIEVEMENTS IN THE FIELD OF FOREIGN RELATIONS

Similarly, achievements in the field of foreign relations were along lines already marked out. As pointed out in the previous chapter, the Peking government which was overthrown by the nationalists was at the time of its elimination engaged in negotiations looking toward revision of what the nationalists called the "unequal" treaties. But it was the Kuomintang which carried the process of revision toward completion. Its leaders singled out England as the principal target for their propaganda against imperialism, partly because England personified capitalistic imperialism to the Chinese, but in part because of the animosities which had been created by her position at Hongkong. The incidents connected with the seamen's strike at Hongkong and the boycott at Canton; the fact that it was an Englishman who commanded the Shanghai police when blood was shed in 1925; the fact that an Englishman, as head of the Maritime Customs service, refused to allow Canton a proportional share of the customs' surplus; the Wanhsien incident, when British gunboats shelled that village because Chinese troops fired on an English vessel—these and other things served to focus the attention of Chinese nationalists on England as the enemy. The fact that there were extenuating circumstances or reasonable explanations of specific British actions was not permitted to divert attention from the actions themselves. Imperialism is an abstraction the significance of which it is difficult for the mass-mind to grasp. The nationalist propagandist needed concrete acts undertaken by particular states to focus attention on as evidences of imperialism. These were at this time supplied him by the British.

The British government moved to placate the nationalists when, in December, 1926, it proposed to the interested Powers that they should establish a joint policy on a more liberal and advanced basis than that represented by the Washington Conference agreements. Among other things, the British memorandum proposed formal acquiescence in the immediate collection of the Washington Conference surtaxes; the acceptance of tariff autonomy whenever a national tariff law should have been constructed and be ready to be put into operation; and, while insisting on the observance of the treaties until they had been revised by agreement, that a willingness should be indicated to enter upon negotiations to satisfy Chinese national aspirations.

Hankow had fallen and a leftist-communist government had been established there before the Powers could act on the British proposals. Nevertheless, when the English concessions at Hankow and Kiukiang were taken over by the Hankow government, the British representative entered into negotiations with it, as the *de facto* authority in that area, concerning the conditions of restoration of those concessions to China. This started a movement of the Powers to negotiate with another than the Peking government, and prepared the way for the carrying on of separate negotiations with the several treaty Powers by the Nanking government both before and after the consolidation of the country under its authority in 1928.

As the Nanking government took over the problem of treaty revision it had a sound lead as to method in the above-mentioned activities of the Peking government. Previous negotiations, from the conferences of 1925 on, furthermore, had indicated that the Powers were readier to terminate the customs arrangements than they were to end the extraterritorial system. The British proposal of December, 1926, to the other states indicated this as did the acceptance in principle of customs autonomy at the Peking Conference of 1925, as contrasted with the recommendations of the commission on extraterritoriality. It was sound policy then for the Chinese Foreign Minister to concentrate attention first on the more readily obtainable. But before any negotiations could be instituted it was necessary to remove the obstacle resulting from the Nanking incident of 1927. The foreign representatives were naturally unwilling to enter into relations with the nationalist government (called after 1928 the National government) until reparation had been made for the unwarranted attack on foreigners and their property at the time of the entry of the nationalist armies into Nanking. The attack occurred on March 24 and identical notes were presented to the Foreign Minister and the head of the nationalist government by the United States, England, France, Italy, and Japan on April 11 demanding punishment of the guilty, apology from the Commander-in-chief, assurances that anti-foreign agitation and activity would not continue, and reparation for the personal and property damage done. When the moderates had gained the upper hand in the struggle with the Hankow faction the Nanking government indicated its readiness to reach a settlement. An exchange of notes with the government of the United States on April 2, 1928, cleared up the matter to the satisfaction of that government. The Chinese government accepted responsibility, while stating that the incident had resulted from communist activities, and it promised reparation for the damage which had been done; while the American Minister expressed regret that circumstances had compelled the use of force to safeguard the lives of Americans. The agreements reached with the other states were in substantially similar terms.

Following the settlement of the Nanking affair, the United States, on

July 25, entered into a treaty expressly abrogating all provisions of treaties in force between the two countries relating to customs, tonnage, and other charges, and conceding the principle of complete tariff autonomy, subject to the most favored nation principle, the treaty to become effective January 1, 1929, the date which had already been set for the application of a national tariff law. Similar treaties conceding tariff autonomy were concluded during 1928 with ten other states, including England, France, Belgium, Italy, and Germany. The date of application of the new tariff law was postponed from January 1 to February 1, by which time Japan, in advance of the conclusion of a treaty, agreed to respect it. Thus the long struggle to secure complete freedom to establish national customs charges, either in order to secure additional revenues, immediately the most important consideration, or to afford protection to China's infant industries, had been carried to a successful conclusion. After a similarly long resistance to revision, except as a *quid pro quo* in the form of abolition of likin was granted, the Powers gave way, although some of the treaties carried a provision that China would abolish likin as soon as possible.

This left only the extraterritorial provisions of the treaties to be abrogated. Here also some progress had been made before the assumption of power by the nationalists. The loss of extraterritorial rights to the Germans as a consequence of China's participation in the war and to the Russians as an aftermath of the Russian revolution have already been referred to. Comparative success in exercising jurisdiction over these Europeans had confirmed the Chinese in their belief that the system should be ended for the others. The new treaties negotiated by the Peking government with Austria, Finland, and Poland contained no provision for extraterritoriality. And the nationalists were just as determined as had been the Peking government to replace the old treaties, from this standpoint, with new ones as rapidly as they came up for revision in terms of the ten-year periods.

Consequently the treaties of 1928 with Belgium and Spain, of the ones previously denounced by the Peking government, stipulated for the assumption of jurisdiction over the nationals of those countries by January 1, 1930, provided the other treaty Powers had agreed to the same provision, or in any case when all of the Washington Conference states had accepted the abolition of extraterritoriality. Similar provisions were accepted by a number of other states during 1928 and 1929. But the Japanese treaty of 1929 made no such provision, and England, France, and the United States when they were approached in the matter in and after August, 1929, indicated sympathy with but an unwillingness to consider anything except a gradual abolition of the system. With a view to forcing the issue with the principal Powers the Central Political Council passed a Resolution on December 26, 1929, instructing the State Council to issue a mandate terminating extraterritorial rights for all foreigners still possessing them as from January 1, 1930. England, supported by the United States and Japan, replied to this action with the announcement that the government was not unwilling in principle to regard that as the date of commencement of the process of bringing the system to an end. Thereafter negotiations were continued during 1930, but without agreement being reached. Because of the pressure of internal politics, with a National People's Convention projected to adopt a constitution in the spring of 1931, the Chinese government promulgated regulations for the control of foreigners and for the assumption of jurisdiction over them, the regulations to go into effect on January 1, 1932. It was hoped that in the interim it would be possible to complete the process of treaty revision. Developments in Manchuria after September, 1931, however, together with the unsettled condition of the central Yangtse region, caused attention to be turned from the problem of revision of the treaties, and on December 29, 1931, the mandate providing for the enforcement of the regulations on January 1, 1932, was suspended for the time.

To complete this summary of the achievements of the National government between 1928 and 1933 reference must further be made to the status of the foreign residential areas and of the leased territories. It was only on October 1, 1930, that the British restored Weihaiwei to Chinese jurisdiction, the negotiations instituted after the Washington Conference suffering from frequent interruptions. Their satisfactory termination, to be sure, represented an indirect result of the Washington Conference and should be attributed to it rather than to nationalist ascendency in China, but it falls within the period of that ascendency. The restoration of the other leaseholds, which had not been promised at Washington, was not brought about within the period under review.

More positive advances were made, however, with respect to the concessions and settlements. The British followed their acceptance of a change in status for their concessions at Hankow and Kiukiang with agreements restoring to Chinese jurisdiction their concession at Chinkiang in 1929 and that at Amoy in 1930. The Belgian government took the same action with respect to its concession in Tientsin in 1931. This left thirteen concessions and settlements still in the hands of various foreign countries. Of these the most important, both to the Chinese and to the foreigners, was the International Settlement at Shanghai. In its growth it had come to include in its population well over a million Chinese in addition to the foreigners, who numbered approximately forty thousand. As a foreign residential area, the International Settlement was governed by a Municipal Council elected, until 1928, by the foreign rate payers, comprising less than a tenth of the total foreign population. The Settlement, adjoined by the French concession, merged into the Chinese city of some two and a quarter million inhabitants. Its location in relation to the greatest Chinese city, and as the entrepôt to the most important trade region of China, as well as the early concentration of industrial activity within its limits, had given it tremendous importance and was responsible for the genesis of a number of problems.

As the importance of the International Settlement came to be realized, the Chinese began to try to reestablish control over it. This demand was most vigorously made by the nationalists and, after its establishment, by the National government. Because of its importance to them the foreign governments and their nationals at Shanghai refused to consider the immediate rendition of the Settlement to Chinese control. It was agreed, on March 6, 1928, however, to give to the Chinese three representatives on the Municipal Council and to appoint six additional Chinese to serve on the administrative committees of the Settlement. In 1930 two additional seats on the Council were allotted to the Chinese.

This granting of representation did not end the Chinese agitation of the Shanghai question. Consequently the Municipal Council in 1929 asked Mr. Justice Richard Feetham of South Africa to make an extensive investigation of the questions at issue with a view to proposing practical methods of reform. His report, submitted in 1931, made recommendations which were adverse to the Chinese demand for immediate rendition of the Settlement. "The net result of the investigation, except for certain useful suggestions for reforms of a minor character, was a neatly organized compilation of facts and a carefully reasoned set of conclusions from legal and theoretical premises that were sound in themselves but had become outdated by the swift rise of Chinese national consciousness." [15] The fact of the report being authorized and made, however, as well as the fact of the granting of representation to Chinese, and other happenings, including the expressed willingness of the Settlement authorities to try to find a method of coöperation in applying Chinese national industrial legislation within the Settlement, all were evidential of the increasing prestige of the Chinese National government with the foreigners. Similar concessions had been sought in vain by its predecessors.

The treaty-situation, then, five years after the establishment of the National government at Nanking, was that tariff autonomy had been regained, and the movement toward the abrogation of the extraterritorial system had been carried many steps in advance. Ten states had definitely given up or lost extraterritorial rights for their nationals. Another group of states had been brought to agree to the abrogation of the system when the Washington Conference Powers agreed to its termination for their nationals. And England, Japan, and the United States were prepared to agree upon the gradual termination of their rights of extraterritoriality. One leased territory had been returned to China; a number of the resi-

[15] H. S. QUIGLEY AND G. H. BLAKESLEE, *The Far East, an International Survey*, p. 162.

dential concessions had been brought under Chinese administration; and the above mentioned readjustments had been made at Shanghai. All of these advances had been made in spite of the fact that the Nanking government was constantly struggling for its very existence against domestic enemies. It must be recognized, consequently, that its achievements in the field of foreign affairs were substantial. These achievements, to be sure, were partly made possible because of the conciliatory policies pursued by the Western states, and also by Japan as far as China proper was concerned. But these policies themselves were in part the result of the positive policies pursued by China as the Kuomintang assumed control of foreign affairs. At the same time considerable credit for the improvement of China's foreign relations must go to the Chinese diplomats, whether at Peking or at Nanking, who instituted and conducted with great skill the negotiations with the Western and Japanese representatives in and after 1926.

REFERENCES FOR FURTHER STUDY

T. A. BISSON, *The Nanking Government,* Foreign Policy Reports, vol. 5, No. 17. T. A. BISSON, *Reconstruction in China,* Foreign Policy Reports, vol. 5, No. 23. T. A. BISSON, *Ten Years of the Kuomintang,* Foreign Policy Reports, vol. 8, No. 25. T. A. BISSON, *The Communist Movement in China,* Foreign Policy Reports, vol. 9, No. 4. DOROTHY BORG, *American Policy and the Chinese Revolution, 1925–1928* (1947); a very useful study. H. O. CHAPMAN, *The Chinese Revolution, 1926–1927* (1928); the subtitle is "a record of the period under communist control as seen from the nationalist capital." LOUIS FISCHER, *The Soviets in World Affairs* (1930), 2 vols., vol. 2, ch. 23; a suggestive and important treatment of the Russian influence. A. N. HOLCOMBE, *The Chinese Revolution* (1930), ch. 5–10; a valuable analysis of the nationalist movement; contains appendices of important documents. LEONARD HSU, *Sun Yat-sen* (1933); a study of Dr. Sun's philosophy. HAROLD ISAACS, *The Tragedy of the Chinese Revolution* (rev. ed., reprinted 1951). MARIUS P. JANSEN, *The Japanese and Sun Yat-sen* (1954). W. C. JOHNSTONE, *The Shanghai Problem* (1937); a careful study. F. C. JONES, *Shanghai and Tientsin* (1940); an extensive assembly of data. V. K. WELLINGTON KOO, *Memoranda Presented to the Lytton Commission* (1932), 3 vols., Doc. no. 24; on communism in China. (JUDGE) P. M. A. LINEBARGER, *Sun Yat-sen and the Chinese Republic* (1925); an account by a friend of Sun Yat-sen. P. M. A. LINEBARGER, *The Political Doctrines of Sun Yat-sen* (1937); a careful exposition of the San Min Chu I. P. M. A. LINEBARGER, *Government in Republican China* (1938); essentially an ideological analysis of the problem of government. CHIH-PU LIU, *A Military History of Modern China, 1924–1949* (1956). H. F. MACNAIR, *China in Revolution* (1930), ch. 5–13; an excellent brief treatment. H. S. QUIGLEY and GEORGE H. BLAKESLEE, *The Far East, an International Survey* (1935), ch. 10–13; excellent on treaty revision and related questions. AGNES SMEDLEY, *The Red Army Marches* (1934); a sympathetic treatment of the Kiangsi Soviets. GEORGE E. SOKOLSKY, *The Tinder Box of Asia* (1932); a journalistic but penetrating study of nationalist China as well as of international relations. SUN YAT-SEN, *Memoirs of a Chinese Revolutionary* (1918). SUN YAT-SEN, *The International Development of China*

(1921), SUN YAT-SEN, *San Min Chu I* (1929); the lectures on the Three Principles of the People, translated by F. W. Price. T'ANG LEANG-LI, *The Inner History of the Chinese Revolution* (1930), ch. 10–15; a valuable study which must be used with some care as it is written distinctly from the standpoint of the Kuomintang left. A. J. TOYNBEE (ed.), *Survey of International Affairs* (1925), vol. 2, part 3; (1926) part 3; (1927); (1928). Also *Documents on International Affairs,* published annually from 1928. M. T. Z. TYAU, *Two Years of Nationalist China* (1930); a detailed description of the governmental system. ALLEN S. WHITING, *Soviet Policies in China, 1917–1924* (1953). C. MARTIN WILBUR and JULIE LIEN-YING How, *Documents on Communism, Nationalism and Soviet Advisers in China, 1918–1927* (1956); carefully edited volume. T. T. C. Woo, *The Kuomintang and the Future of the Chinese Revolution* (1928). C. C. Wu, *The Nationalist Program for China* (1929). C. F. Wu, *Chinese Government and Politics* (1934); a careful descriptive study. H. G. W. WOODHEAD (ed.), *The China Year Book,* issues (annual) from 1923 to 1931–1932; the chapters on the Kuomintang, the Chinese government, Defense, Army and Navy, etc., contain much detail not readily obtainable in other books.

The files of the *China Weekly Review,* and *North China Herald,* the *Chinese Social and Political Science Review,* and other periodicals should also be consulted.

CHAPTER XXI

THE EAST AND THE WEST: 1830–1930

Before turning to a consideration of the changes in the Far Eastern status which were effected after 1931, it will be worth while to review the relations of the Far Eastern states with those of the West, with special emphasis on the effect of the Western impact on the evolution of China and Japan. Thus it may be possible to discover the reasons for a growing tendency for the Far Eastern countries to attempt to throw off the leading-strings of the West and attempt to dissociate their politics from the politics of Europe.

I. INTEREST OF WEST IN THE EAST

The first thing to be remarked, as it is the most obvious, is the extent of Western dominance of the East. From Constantinople to Peking, European control had been wholly or partially established by 1914. In some places, as in India, Burma, and French Indo-China, this control was tangible because it was territorial and governmental. Elsewhere it was largely financial in character, as in the case of Persia, Turkey, and China. The control was none the less real because it was less tangible and concrete than the territorial and political.

The original motive bringing the West to the East was a desire to secure Eastern products such as tea, spices and silks. It was not until the nineteenth century that this original interest gave way to the desire to find a market for goods which were being increasingly manufactured in excess of the requirements of the European consumer. The interest of the West in tropical products, of course, continued during the nineteenth century, but it was distinctly secondary to the search for markets. With the development of the latter interest, consequent on the Industrial Revolution, Europeans began to move outward in larger numbers, and it became necessary to secure for them rights of residence so that they might carry on trade more comfortably, safely, and satisfactorily. Out of this need, coupled with the general trade interest, there developed in those Eastern countries which escaped control as colonies the extraterritorial system and the treaty tariff system. Those countries, in eastern Asia, were Siam, China, Korea, and Japan. In India, Burma, Indo-China, Borneo, Malaysia, and the Philippines, the control of foreigners rested with particular European Powers, and the extraterritorial and conventional tariff systems were unnecessary from the standpoint of the interests and needs of Europe.

The financial or investment interest became predominant only after the end of the nineteenth century. By that time Japan had emerged from her tutelage to Europe, and Siam, protected to an extent by reason of her position as a buffer state between French and British possessions, was reasonably stable, and was beginning to develop her economic and legal systems along Occidental lines. Korea was in the process of absorption by Japan. Consequently all three escaped from European financial control, while China did not.

Subsequently China entered upon a struggle to reëstablish her complete freedom of action. Furthermore, a reaction against Western dominance also exhibited itself strikingly in India and in the Philippine Islands. In passing, it may be noted that both China and Siam were long preserved as international entities partly at least because of the jealousies and the lack of community of interest of the Western Powers. England and France restrained one another in relation to Siam; Russia, England, France, the United States, Germany, and Japan had such differences of interest and jealousy of each other in China that China as an entity was preserved. But both the Chinese Empire and the Chinese Republic had been in the past, and the Republic in 1931 was, an international danger zone or storm center, whereas Japan had become a powerful member of the international community and, until her resignation from the League in 1933, a permanent member of the League Council, a significant recognition of her changed status. It is worth while at this point to summarize comparatively the reactions of Japan and China to the modern world as of 1931. Such a summary may properly be taken as a point of departure in appraising developments in the Far East in subsequent decades.

2. COMPARISON OF JAPANESE WITH CHINESE DEVELOPMENT

The first explanation of differences in initial reaction stems from geography. Japan is small in extent, whereas, in comparison, China is a vast territorial entity. Given the same primitive means of communication, it is apparent that a knowledge of the modern world could be much more rapidly diffused throughout Japan than would be possible in China. Closely joined to this is a similar contrast in the number of people who would have to be introduced to the modern world. The population of Japan, we may assume, was about thirty-three million in 1850, concentrated in a small territory; that of China, at the same time, was probably between three hundred fifty and four hundred millions, scattered over a wide area. Thus, purely quantitatively, the problem of diffusion of knowledge of the new world was many times greater in China than in Japan. Had both countries had railroads, steamships, radio, the telegraph, and the telephone, this difference would have been much less marked. But improved communications were part of the new order which was to be introduced, and consequently were not initially available for its introduction.

Second, pre-modern Japan at the start of the Western impact was already moving toward a new political order, which would restore power to the Emperor and unify the state under his authority rather than that of the Shōgun. The aim of the western clan leaders was not political devolution but close integration under their authority rather than that of the Tokugawa. This internal activity opened the way for the acceptance of new ideas so far as they were not incompatible with the ends of the leaders of the opposition to the Shōgunate. This view is not invalidated by the initial hostility of the western clans to foreign intercourse, since that was at least partially the product of expediency—of a willingness to use all available means to weaken the Tokugawa control. Furthermore, it must be recognized that before the first treaties were made Western ideas had begun to seep into the country from Nagasaki, and were being diffused through the Dutch school of learning.

The condition of Japan in this respect was markedly different from that of China. There were no new currents perceptible in pre-modern China. The Manchu rule was weakening, but due to its own ineffectiveness rather than to any virile opposition. The intellectual life of China was decidedly static rather than dynamic. The long intellectual inbreeding had fostered an intense conservatism which was nation-wide, and which permeated all classes. This was modified by no progressive intellectual movements, nor was the national conservatism stimulated by the periodic anti-dynastic revolts, for these were economic in origin and motivation.

Furthermore, the conditions of development of the cultures of Japan and China had an important bearing on their respective reactions to the new stream of ideas, institutions, and mechanical arrangements carried to them by Western traders, missionaries, and diplomatists. Chinese culture was almost wholly indigenous. Aside from the introduction of Buddhism, external contributions had been so slight as to be almost negligible. This immunity from outside influence had developed a feeling of innate cultural superiority which made it difficult for even the educated class to realize, much less to admit, the material and political backwardness of the Middle Kingdom in comparison with Europe. Japan, on the other hand, had imported many elements of her existing culture. She had modified the importation, and in some respects greatly improved on it, to be sure. But the thing to be remembered is that Japan had never been averse to recognizing her own cultural deficiencies, and remedying them by drawing upon others for what she lacked. Her arts and crafts, her religions, except Shinto, her administrative ideas, her philosophical systems, even her written language, were gifts from the continent or had been modified in the light of continental ideas. Thus there was no inherent repugnance to imitation or the borrowing of foreign ideas or practices which had value to Japan. The only change in the modern period was in the source from which contributions were drawn.

Another extremely important difference between the two countries, which made it possible for Japan to take on the garments of the West more rapidly than China, was the clearly recognized distinction between the governors and the governed. Since the trait of obedience to authority was highly developed in Japan, it was possible for the leaders, once they had determined on their course, to carry the people with them. Three points must be emphasized in this connection: (1) remarkably able leaders developed out of the pre-Restoration and post-Restoration struggle; (2) after they had effected the Restoration, thereby bringing the reins of power into their own hands, they freely accepted the Western contact, and determined to draw upon the West to strengthen Japan; and (3) the acceptance of the feudal obligation of obedience by the masses made it possible for the rulers to put their program into operation, as could not so readily have been done in a more individualistic society.

China, on the other hand, had no nationally accepted leadership capable of carrying into effect a program of reorganization and transformation of the state. The dynasty was alien, and could not be expected to command the support of the people as the Imperial House in Japan did after 1867. Such leaders as there were in nineteenth century China never fully admitted the weakness of the state, failed to perceive its real "backwardness" in the modern sense, and consequently were not led until after 1900 to set up an extensive program of change. Even if they had attempted to do what the rulers of Japan did, they would have encountered much more difficulty due to the greater individualism of the Chinese people. In China there was almost the reverse of the Japanese amenability to governmental direction. The governing class did not constitute a divinely ordained group set apart from the masses. The tradition of authority, in other words, was as lacking as was the existence of inherited loyalties of the kind so noticeable in Japan. Even though the educated group had not had an inherent consciousness of cultural superiority, it would have been difficult for it to move the people from accustomed grooves of thought and methods of action except by the slow process of education and by gradually demonstrating to the people the advantages of change.

From the political standpoint, furthermore, it was not a very great step from the old system of Japan to the creation of the legal-military society then known as a state. While the Japanese experienced difficulty in understanding and accepting the canons of democracy, the creation of an integrated political society was comparatively easy. But China was politically amorphous. As has been noted, it had an integrated administrative system, with the officials recruited by examination. But this organization functioned only slightly in relation to Chinese society. The conception of the omni-competent state was, consequently, more distinctly foreign to China than to Japan. The former was fundamentally more of a cultural than a political society, while the latter had more highly developed the functions of author-ity politically organized.

Finally, the most immediately impressive evidence of Western superiority to the East lay in its highly-developed engines of warfare. These demon-strated the superiority of the West readily enough to a warlike people such as the Japanese, and helped to pave the way for the introduction of the equally superior economic system of the West. This was natural in a feudal country where warriors were conceded such a privileged position as were the samurai. But it took a longer time for the Chinese to recognize the su-periority of the West on account of a demonstrated superiority of arma-ment. This also was natural in a country where the professional soldier was relegated to the lowest place in society. The bombardments of Kagoshima and of Shimonoseki were sufficient to open the eyes of the Japanese. A series of similar episodes on a much larger scale merely confirmed the Chinese in their view of the foreigner as a "barbarian." Since armament was the true test of superiority or of equality among states, the Japanese armed them-selves, demonstrated their military prowess, and left the ranks of "back-ward" nations. It was this demonstration, rather than the progressive mod-ernization of the country, although, of course, the two actually went hand in hand, which elevated Japan to a seat with the Powers.

The operation of all of the forces mentioned had served to retard the de-velopment of China in comparison with Japan. It was only a short fifteen years after the signature of the first treaty when Japan began her reorienta-tion in terms of the modern world. It took China approximately sixty years to change her outlook to the extent that Japan did in fifteen years. Then the Manchu rulers of the country tried to do what the Japanese did so success-fully after 1868 in the governmental field. They set up a program of political reform designed to bring into being a constitutional system through which absolutism could be continued. Their failure, where the Japanese had been successful, was partly due to the fact that they delayed too long; but in part it was due to some of these fundamental differences between China and Japan. Moreover, they did not attempt to put into effect an extensive pro-gram of economic change, except as they contemplated an enlargement of the railway system which had been initially forced on them, and as, at foreign suggestion, they contemplated currency reform.

With the inauguration of the Republic, however, China appeared to have gone further politically than Japan in meeting the new world on essentially Western terms. Both, to be sure, imported constitutionalism, adopting or projecting written instruments of government. China, however, began con-stitutional experimentation after 1911 with a view to the erection of political institutions on the foundation of the public will, whereas the Japanese constitution was designed to declare the channels through which the will of an hereditary and "divine right" ruler would find orderly expression. Thus the reorganization of Japan through the importation of Western political conceptions was not based upon any fundamentally different view than the indigenous one as to the source of authority. For that reason it must be concluded that the republican experiment in China carried that country much further from the traditional moorings than constitutionalism did Japan.

In this fact, also, may be found an important part of the explanation of the rapidity with which Japan stabilized her political life on the apparent basis of imported ideas, as contrasted with the slowness of the movement in China toward even comparative stability. The old institutional foundations and a considerable part of the superstructure were retained in Japan, some additions being made and a new coat of paint being applied. In contrast, China's movement had reached much more deeply back into the institutional life of the country. The break with the past was begun with the establishment of the Republic and the gradual acceptance, to be traced back in its beginnings before 1911, of the idea of government as a positive force in society. This accelerated a movement on a much wider front than that represented by the rejection of the Manchu dynasty and monarchy itself. It cannot be concluded that traditionalism gave way in China without a struggle. Quite the reverse was true, and it was this which forced a deeper probing than would probably have occurred if complete and immediate success had been attained by the new forces in 1911. It was lack of success in maintaining control of the government which they had been instrumental in establishing which forced Sun Yat-sen and his followers in the Kuomintang to continue their revolutionary course, until republicanism of the Western variety had been replaced by Sunyatsenism as the goal to be attained. The new program to some extent represented an attempt to effect a synthesis between the traditional and the new in the field of political organization and action. More definitely, however, it represented an attempt to chart a new course on the basis of the experiences of the post-Republican years. In both of these respects it revealed tentatively a desire to develop in terms of China rather than on the basis of acceptance as valid of Western ideas and experience. The new movement itself, however, was affected by the revolutionary currents in the Western world which were set in motion with the Russian revolution. The China of 1931 was, consequently, less free from the ideological influence of the West than it had been before the nationalist crusade got under way.

Political authority continued to rest in the hands of those who possessed military power, where it had come to reside after the first revolution. That in itself represented a change from the Manchu days of considerable sig-

nificance since it carried with it a modification of the old attitude toward
the military. For the dominance of the military over the civil authority,
which was traditional in Japan, and thus had in it an element of permanence, was recent in China, deriving from revolutionary conditions. Out
of the internal struggle for power, and as a result of the constant pressure
on the country, first of the Western states and then of Japan, the view of
the state itself as a power conception began working its way rapidly into
the thinking of the Chinese. But idealogically, even if established practically,
military power had not come to be accepted as the natural basis of authority.
Thus, in spite of the continuance of military rule, the accepted chart of
political evolution was derived from the traditional thinking, reënforced by
the pre-war Western view that the military power should be subordinated
to civil authority and act under its direction. It was not solely a cleavage
between the military and the civil elements that explained the confusion in
Chinese politics and the recurrent struggles between Canton, Nanking, and
other regions. Nor was it exclusively the rivalries of individual military
leaders. Part of the explanation must assuredly be sought in the differences
of opinion which existed under the surface as to the use to be made of
authority after it had been acquired, in terms of the class and sectional as
well as the individual beneficiaries of action.

Such deep cleavages as had arisen in China under the impact of new ideas
had never been permitted to find expression in Japan through the medium
of politics. Conflicts which might otherwise have developed had been resolved through the interposition of the Emperor. All classes of contestants
for power had been united in acceptance of the final authority of the Imperial House. Thus it had been possible to stabilize political authority and
prevent the new forces in economic life, for example, from exercising too
disruptive an influence.

An important difference, from the international as well as the domestic
point of view, therefore, between the China which had by 1931 virtually
succeeded in bringing to an end the nineteenth-century treaty-system and
the Japan which had successfully revised her "unequal" treaties in the last
decade of the nineteenth century, was legal and political. China was still
struggling to attain political unity and effective organization, as has already been suggested, while Japan in 1894 was highly organized. It was
still questionable how effectively China could extend full protection to
foreign lives and property throughout the Republic even by 1931. Japan had
a government capable of affording satisfactory protection to foreigners when
the treaty-yoke was thrown off. Japan had prepared and put into operation
modern law codes and was applying them through a modern judicial system. China had promulgated such codes and had established a number of
modern courts in various parts of the country to apply them. But the political confusion prevented the full application of the codes in all parts of

the country. The comparatively great size of the Republic, even with its reduced boundaries, also made it inevitable that some time would elapse before a sufficient number of modern courts of all grades would be established.

Consequently, while recognizing that progress had been made along these lines, it must be concluded that it was not the complete creation of a new legal and judicial order, nor even the attainment of the degree of political stability represented by that of Japan in 1894, which enabled China to make as much headway with treaty revision as had been made by 1931. It was rather because of (1) the pressure of assertive Chinese nationalism, and (2) the reluctance of the Powers to use sufficient force to maintain a position which was untenable in terms of their own ideology, that the old treaty-system had been so largely modified. Even though extraterritorial rights were still tentatively asserted by the United States, England, France, and Japan, it could be assumed that, if China continued to exist in the face of contemporary assaults on her integrity, she would soon be numbered among the fully sovereign members of the society of states. It is significant that, in spite of the restrictions of the treaties and the political turmoil, China had been a member of the League of Nations since its establishment and frequently, by election, a member of the Council.

3. FAR EASTERN ECONOMIC DEVELOPMENT

From the economic standpoint it took China ninety years, figuring from the period of the first treaties, to approximate the changes which were clearly apparent in Japan within fifty years. Some of these developments in China, even by 1931, were still mainly confined to a few centers and were in large part the result of foreign initiative. By the end of the fifty-year period Japan as a whole, in contrast, had begun to change, and Japanese rather than foreigners were the moving spirits in all kinds of new enterprises. The foreigner had largely been pushed into the background. Consequently the advance made by Japan in freeing herself from foreign influence over her economic life had been both relatively and absolutely greater than that which had been made by China. The same tendencies, to be sure, were showing themselves strikingly in the China of the years after 1928. Nevertheless the foreigner remained in 1931 as a more dominant economic factor in China than he had been in Japan after the Russo-Japanese war. And yet, although foreign participation in the economic life of China remained substantial—in absolute terms even increasing— it must be recognized that the conditions of that participation had commenced to change, just as they had already changed in the case of Japan. The advance made, while not so great, was nevertheless significant. Both countries, from the economic standpoint, had become aware of the modern world and were engaged in making the transition from their ancient régimes to a new order.

The trade figures and percentages have been given in part already, but for another purpose. As presented they do not by any means tell the whole story. The primary interest of the industrial states of the West in both China and Japan, as well as in similarly non-industrial countries, had become, by the end of the nineteenth century, a market interest. At first the search had been for Asiatic products, but this had been supplemented by the search for markets for the expanding output of the Western machines. As time went on, the machine itself became an article of export, and the East, under Western tutelage, began to supply itself with more and more of the goods previously imported from the Western countries. The number of spindles and power-looms in China and India began to increase, as had already been the case in Japan. The same thing happened in other fields of industrial production. Japan got the head-start over the other Far Eastern countries in this respect, just as England had developed ahead of other states in the Western world. But the process of self-supply had come, by 1931, to be well under way in the other countries mentioned. Of course in one respect all of this had the effect of changing the character of trade relationships rather than of lessening the economic power of the Western states. Western capital financed the development partly by direct loans to native industrialists to enable them to buy the Western machines. In part, and increasingly, Western industry itself moved to the Far Eastern area, establishing there its own plants for the manufacture of the goods for that market. To the extent that these things alone happened, the relationship of East and West was modified, certainly, but not fundamentally changed. The East still paid tribute, in a sense, to the West.

In yet another respect the industrialization of the Eastern countries may be considered to have changed the character of the trade without, up to the end of the period under review, fundamentally disturbing the balance between the two areas. Instead of marketing such finished goods as textiles, for example, the industrial states of the West marketed the machines and their parts which spun the yarn and wove the cloth. Markets contracted or were in process of contracting for one type of commodity, but that carried with it an inevitable expansion for others. The Far Eastern states had not developed heavy industries comparable to those of the Western states, and in that situation had been found a reorganized basis of exchanges. But aside from that, the third decade of the twentieth century terminated with China as well as Japan showing an increasing ability and also determination to supply herself with goods for which a demand had been created by the Western traders so that markets might be found for the industrial output of their countries. As this development of industry in the East continued, the old form of economic dependence was lost, since the Far Eastern countries were increasingly able to supply themselves instead of having to look to the West for the satisfaction of their economic needs.

Furthermore, as the capitalist economy established itself in Japan and China, the investment picture tended to change. In both countries, but up to 1931 more noticeably in Japan, there had been created the ability to supply internally the need for funds for investment and development purposes. Foreign investments for industrial purposes had continued, to be sure, as had foreign loans to some extent, but there had been an increasing reliance on a previously non-existent domestic money market to meet the needs of expanding industry and also those of government. The total foreign investment had increased from the 787.9 million American dollars of 1902 to 3,242.5 million in 1931, in the case of China, which had been the major field of economic as well as of political conflict. That represented a marked expansion and must be so recognized. But the fact remains that it had been paralleled by an even more marked participation of Chinese capital in domestic financing. Furthermore, the above total included the Japanese investments in China, including Manchuria. That investment, which had reached only the relatively negligible figure of one million dollars in 1902, increased materially during the first three decades of the twentieth century, and had reached a total of 1,136.9 million by 1931. This was 35.1 per cent of the total foreign investment in China. The bulk of this investment was in Manchuria, then the area of Japanese special interest. But the significance of the investment remains. Japan, a Far Eastern state, had become a capital-exporting state to that extent.

Another fact of even greater significance in measuring the new economic relationships was to be found in the invasion by Japan of the markets claimed by the Western states. It was not only raw or semi-finished goods from Japan which were appearing in increasing quantities in Western markets. That had long been so, and the Western states themselves had sought especially the raw materials for their own uses. But it was only in the 1920's that Japanese competition had made itself seriously felt in such finished products as textiles, electrical equipment, and other goods hitherto exclusively supplied by Western industry. This Japanese competition was most severely felt at the outset in other Asian countries: in India and Malaya, and in some parts of Africa, i.e., in non-European areas, but nevertheless in markets which the Western states had come to regard as their own. In addition, however, it was being increasingly felt in the home markets themselves. This reversal of the tide of trade is most significant of the changed relationships of the East and the West.

The method of trade had also begun to change by 1931, the change again revealing the development of a new relationship between the Far Eastern and the Western countries. In contrast with the time when the import and export trade of Japan and China had been handled by foreign houses, the new tendency was to dispense with the foreigner to an ever-increasing extent, thus further contracting the area of foreign economic influence or control. Japanese firms had begun to handle the sale of Japanese goods directly in the United States and other Western countries as well as in Siam, India, the Philippines, the Straits Settlements, and other Far Eastern colonies. In these latter cases they displaced Chinese businessmen rather than Westerners. The opportunity to do that really came with the institution of boycotts of the handling of Japanese goods in Chinese shops, the boycott being observed by over-seas Chinese as well as within the territories of the Republic. This forced the Japanese directly into the field of distribution if their exports were not to fall off. In Japan itself the import trade had come to be more and more completely taken out of the hands of the foreigners. The same thing was true of China, although on a lesser scale.

4. NATIONALISM IN THE FAR EAST

This change had only in part an economic motivation. More broadly, it resulted from the growing spirit of nationalism. Thus the elimination of foreign control of religious institutions founded and financed from the West; the closer supervision of foreign-established and financed educational institutions; and the nationalization of initially foreign philanthropic institutions had become the goal in China. It was a goal which had already been reached in Japan. A willingness remained to use the foreigner but not to be used by him.

This assertive nationalism, which showed itself in economic as well as in political relations, and in Japan as well as China, represented a legacy of the Western impact. The idea of the sovereign state, with its corollary of equality, was an importation into China, at least, from the West. The idea of the state as a national and homogeneous entity was a fundamental part of the stream of Western ideas which began to flow into the country, carried by missionaries, educators and diplomatists. Its reception was at first reluctant and defensive. In the twenties, however, it had been worked into the thinking of the country as having intellectual validity in its own right. In other words, Chinese nationalism at first represented a defensive reaction to the series of political, economic and financial aggressions which threatened the continued existence of the country. By 1931, however, there was nationalism in thought without regard to any specific acts or threatened acts of aggression. The tide turned during the years from 1925 to 1931 from defense of a threatened position to attack to recover lost "national" rights. But the whole movement, both defensive and aggressive, represented an introduction into China of an essentially foreign conception.

In contrast it may be pointed out that the Western nationalist philosophy of the state fitted perfectly into the ideology of pre-Restoration Japan. The words may have been new and imported but the conception itself was not. Thus it may be concluded that Japan was prepared in advance, in comparison with China, to move into the pre-war international society made up of national sovereign states.

On the other hand, by the time China had begun to accept the nationalist philosophy the Western world had made the tentative move away from it represented by establishment of the League of Nations. For a time the current swung from nationalism in its extreme manifestations toward internationalism. The new philosophy of internationalism and anti-militarism in international relations of the nineteen twenties, in its turn, found a readier and more complete acceptance in China than it did in Japan, which reproduced many of the contradictions in thought and behavior that showed themselves in the Western states. This difference must be explained, so far as China was concerned, on a double basis. First, the new tendencies harmonized with older currents of Chinese thought that had existed before the influence of the Western impact made itself felt. Older Chinese scholars, especially, felt more at home in the world of the new ideas than in that of the imported competitive nationalism. Adjustment of disputes through mutual accommodation of conflicting interests conformed more closely to the original Chinese pattern than did the ideology of conflict carried to its ultimate conclusion in war. Second, China, although large, was a weak and backward state in terms of national power. The new technique seemed to offer an opportunity of easier survival for such a state which was lacking in the pre-war world. Even in the years before 1914, however, the Chinese had sought preservation through international action in their behalf. They frequently sought, for example, to play off one Power or set of Powers against another, rather than to bring about the accumulation of sufficient power in their own hands to establish their own conception of justice. Given the difference in circumstance, it must be recognized that the method is not essentially dissimilar to that organized through the League system, which China, consequently, might be expected to accept. In the case of Japan, however, the reverse of these considerations was true. Internationalism rather than nationalism represented the foreign and imported conception, and thus the one which the country would find difficulty in rapidly assimilating.

It was thus natural that Japan should have rejected the newer internationalism in 1931, and reverted to the older methods of nationalism. It has come to be customary to explain her actions in and after that year in terms of economic pressures growing out of the population problem and her industrialization—themselves in a real sense the legacies of her intercourse with the West; but the full explanation goes deeper than that. It is true that Japan was one of the overpopulated states, and an under-privileged one from the standpoint of economic resources. It is also true that she had rights and interests in Manchuria which were being threatened on account of the Chinese policies which have previously been mentioned. But it is equally true that Japan made no effort to protect her legitimate interests by invoking the new international agencies before resorting to force in her own behalf. It is also true that, after they had been invoked by China, a settlement was proposed [1] that would have satisfied the original Japanese claims and her asserted needs, which settlement was rejected. The rejection was accompanied by the retirement of Japan from the League of Nations. The traditional methods of the expansionist national state were employed by Japan because the dominant thinking in that country was nationalist rather than internationalist.

In China, on the other hand, the initial reaction to the Japanese move in Manchuria was toward the West and toward international institutions. This may be accounted for in terms of recognition of the lack of resistive capacity of the country, measured in military power. Thus it was the reaction of the weak state in relation to a stronger one. But, again, the explanation must be broadened if it is to be a complete and satisfactory one. The non-resistive policy of the government at Nanking found a considerable measure of support among those who either were naturally inclined to accept as valid the ideas embodied in the League Covenant or who were accustomed to the earlier method of defense of the country represented by the playing-off of one set of interests against another. In either case there was presented a willingness to invoke the power of the West to preserve the *status quo* in the Far East. Thus while the Japanese action throughout was fundamentally based upon an unwillingness to accept Western intervention in the settlement of a Far Eastern question, the Chinese action represented a reference to the hitherto dominant Western states of this particular question for decision. The successful establishment of Manchukuo as an "independent" state, under the circumstances, had a double set of consequences. It forced China back upon the nationalist premise of national power as the determinative force in international relations through revealing the essential weakness of the new forces of internationalism as they were introduced from, and were based upon, Europe. At the same time it showed Japan that she could apparently proceed for almost the first time in the modern period in disregard of Europe.

5. FAR EASTERN POWER RELATIONSHIPS

The fact is that by 1931 the power-equation in the Far East had changed. Power is never an absolute conception which can be measured as such; that possessed by any one state is relative to that of others, and must be so estimated. Thus it could be true that the military and naval power of one

[1] By the Lytton Commission.

state might not have decreased within a fixed period of time, but if, within that period, the strength of another nation had materially increased, it would have to be concluded that the former had lost in power. With that in mind, it can readily be perceived that, so far as power-politics was concerned, the increased strength of Japan made others relatively weaker. In 1895 a threatened intervention of the European states had been sufficient to compel Japan to consent to the revision of the terms of the Treaty of Shimonoseki. At that time Japan was rated, at most, a third-class power. When, a decade later, Japan successfully engaged Russia in war, her power-rating relative to other states as well as Russia moved up several degrees. But that war and its successful outcome were possible only because of the assurance of support which the Anglo-Japanese Agreement gave to Japan, and also because of the friendly attitude of the United States. During the years from 1914 to 1918 the European states spent a large part of their power and much of their energy in war, while Japan preserved intact her military and naval power and her martial energies. At the same time she advanced her economic and political position on the continent of Asia. At the Washington Conference Japan's improved position was revealed in the naval ratio. The principle agreed upon in effect by the representatives of Great Britain, Japan, and the United States in determining this ratio was that each Power was to be rendered secure in its own area against the aggression of any single Naval Power. While the Conference agreements with respect to China represented for Japan a political recession, the naval ratio and the non-fortifications agreement thus left her in a predominant position in relation to the area of her Imperial interests. Thus, measured in terms of power, the Japanese Empire had been steadily moving forward relative to the European states. All of this meant a steady, not a sudden, loss to the West of the ability to control and direct Far Eastern developments. Thus the story of the rise to power of Japan is at the same time the story of the relative decline in power in the Far East of the Western states. Whereas, at the beginning of the twentieth century, Japan could pursue her Korean and Manchurian policies only with the support or the approval of Western states against other Western states, by 1931 only a concerted resistance of Western states would have been successful in bringing about the restraint of Japan.

One exception, possibly more apparent than real, may be noted to the generalization that Japan had been increasing in power relative to the Western states during the first three decades of the twentieth century. The United States provided this exception. Measured in naval power, the attainment of theoretical naval parity with Britain by the United States represented a greater advance for the latter than did the three-fifths ratio for Japan. The demonstration of the potentialities of military power possessed by the United States during the period of its participation in the war of

1914–1918 was similarly significant, as was also the realization of its tremendous economic and financial capacity. Consequently, on the face of it, World War I (American participation not having been exhaustive of its resources) left the United States in an even stronger position relative to other states, including Japan, than it did Japan relative to the European states. The Far Eastern policy decisions of the Washington Conference were indicative of the new American power of decision in Far Eastern politics. But to have a decisive voice in international politics it is necessary not merely to have actual or potential power but also to have the will to exercise it. This will seemed to be present in the United States at the time of the Washington Conference as it had not been before and as it seemed not to exist thereafter during the period under review.

A review of the preceding decades (1901–1931) serves to show that the United States had never been willing actively to exercise such power as it possessed in order to make effective its view of the proper policies to be pursued in Eastern Asia. It had defined policy in terms of the Open Door and the integrity of China, and it had secured at least a verbal acceptance of those policies as the basis of international relationships in China. But the actual support of policy when disregarded by particular states had invariably come from others. Thus it was Japan, not the United States, which prevented Russia from establishing permanent control of Manchuria, at the expense both of the Open Door and of the integrity of China, after the Boxer episode. The Portsmouth Treaty was received with approval by Roosevelt because he thought that Japan would be restrained by Russia, and Russia by Japan, since each was left with a position of its own to defend in Manchuria. When the reverse proved to be true and those whom Roosevelt had thought would remain in permanent opposition reached an agreement on their respective spheres and policies, the United States raised diplomatic objection to their actions but made no other use of its power to implement its policies. Thus Manchuria was closed to American capital as a field for investment in spite of attempts which were made to introduce it during the Taft administration. The American policies and protests were disregarded in part because of a realization that they would not proceed beyond the verbal. The attempt was made to draw England into action in support of a common interest in investment, but unsuccessfully since England was in alliance with Japan, and the United States was not willing to give England the same assurances of support which the latter had received from Japan.

One explanation of this lack of willingness of the United States to implement effectively, and by means of exercise of power, its Far Eastern policies was the relative unimportance of its material interests in that region in comparison with the stake elsewhere. The American investment in China had increased substantially in the first three decades of the twentieth century, but it had never been of major importance. The increase had been from 19.7 million dollars in 1902, to 49.3 million in 1914, to 196.8 million in 1931. But in 1902 the American percentage of the total foreign investment in China was only 2.5, as against 33 for Great Britain, 31.3 for Russia, 11.6 for France, and 20.9 for Germany. The American percentage of the total had increased by 1914 only slightly, to 3.1; and the 196.8 million dollar total of 1931 represented only 6.1 per cent of the substantially enlarged total foreign investment. By that time the Japanese proportion had risen from 0.1 in 1902 to 35.6 per cent, the amount being only slightly less than the total British investment. Thus it is clear that, measured by investment, the material interest in China, which may possibly be considered to be the basis for taking or refraining from the action necessary to implement policy, was never as great for the United States as for some other Powers. Another measure which serves to reënforce the above conclusion, not only for the United States but also for the European states, except Russia, is to be found in the relationship between the investment in China and the total foreign holdings of the country. "Contrary to popular assumption, foreign holdings in China are relatively unimportant when compared with the total foreign investment of the principal countries involved. Thus Professor Remer concluded that to the United States Chinese investments (including Manchurian) represent about 1.3 per cent of all foreign investments; to Germany 4.3 per cent; to France 4.8 per cent; and to Great Britain 5.9 per cent." [2] Consequently, if it is investment interest that determines the strength or weakness, from the power standpoint, of national policy, it is clear that there had been relatively little incentive to the United States to utilize effectively its power to establish its China policies. Its interests had always been potential rather than actual, and, while a state may act diplomatically in terms of the potential, it usually hesitates to use material means in defense of potential or of non-material interests.

As measured by trade, however, the United States had played an increasingly more important part in China than it had in the investment field. In values, its total trade with China had increased from 71.6 million Haikwan taels in 1912 to 210.3 million in 1920, 285.7 million in 1925, 364.3 million in 1930, and 441.5 million in 1931. In proportion to the total trade of China this represented an increase from 8.5 in 1912 to 18.8 per cent in 1931. This constant increase in the American proportion of the trade was due in part to the active search for foreign markets which went on in the period covered by the above figures; to the temporary withdrawal of the European states from the supply of the Far Eastern market during the war period, which gave both the United States and Japan an opportunity to establish

---

[2] *Economic Handbook of the Pacific Area*, edited by FREDERICK V. FIELD, 1934, p. 353. Other citations of figures in this chapter are from this volume. See also Professor C. F. REMER's painstaking study, *Foreign Investments in China* (1933).

themselves in the absence of intense competition; and to the ability of the United States to take the place in trade of countries against whom Chinese boycott measures were from time to time directed. But this increased participation in the China trade was merely part of a world expansion of American trade, and, in spite of the figures, it represented rather an insubstantial proportion of the American foreign trade total. Thus it was unimportant relative to the interest in trade in other regions.

This material interest in the Far East, represented by trade and investments, was not, of course, localized to China. The American trade with Japan had also shown a constant increase during the first three decades of the twentieth century. Thus in 1913 the trade of the United States with Japan was valued at 306 million yen, in 1920 at 1,438 million yen, in 1925 at 1,670 million yen, in 1930 at 940 million yen, and in 1931 at 761 million yen. During this period the American proportion of the total trade of Japan increased from 22.5 to 32.2 per cent. The high point, up to 1931, had been reached in 1929 when 35.9 per cent of Japan's total trade had been with the United States. Thus the totals of American trade with Japan were larger, by 1931, than they were with China. The same thing was true with respect to investment. Thus the United States Bureau of Foreign and Domestic Commerce estimated total American capital invested in Japan at the end of 1930 at approximately $444,639,000.

American relations with Japan, however, and the protection of existing or potential trade and investment interests in that country, did not present the peculiar problems, either directly or on account of the policies and activities of other states, that brought about the enunciation and compelled consideration of the problem of implementation of such distinct policies as those developed with respect to China. No peculiar rights or privileges were possessed in Japan after 1894 by the United States, or other Western states, which were threatened by reason of the policies or actions of the Japanese government and which thus had to be maintained against it or renounced under its pressure. And Japan had reached a position of strength sufficient not only to guard against Western rivalries for special privilege in the Empire but also to enable Japan to compete with the Western Powers for privilege in China. Thus the willingness or unwillingness of the United States to use its power to implement policy was important, so far as Japan was concerned, in relation to conflicts of policy with respect to other parts of the Far Eastern area than the Japanese Empire.

6. THE PHILIPPINES

In addition to considerations of trade and investment possibilities in China, and of sentiment centered around religious, philanthropic, and cultural interests and activities in that country, the inclusion of the Philippine Islands in the American empire compelled concern on the part of the United States with the politics of the Far Eastern area. It was with an eye to enlarged participation in the economic and political life of that area that the decision to demand the Philippines from Spain was taken. But the Philippine question produced immediate division of opinion within the United States, which substantially expressed itself along party lines. The Democratic Party declared itself to be anti-imperialist and thus in favor of Philippine independence. The Republican Party, in power when the Islands were acquired and for some time thereafter, came to promise ultimate independence, but subject to two conditions: ". . . independence was to be granted when the United States should deem the Filipinos capable of maintaining it; and it was to be granted if at that time the Filipinos were still convinced that they wanted it. There was never any wavering in the conviction of these Republican leaders that a permanent connection between the two peoples was wise and desirable. . . ." [3] In effect, however, Republican as well as Democratic policy established the premise of independence as the ultimate goal. Upon that basis there developed an independence movement in the Islands, with the support, in terms of the immediacy of its attainment, of those in the United States who considered themselves to be anti-imperialist in their views.

From the beginning Filipinos were associated with Americans in the government. Thus the Organic Act of 1902 made provision for an elective assembly, and, as quickly as they were considered to be prepared, Filipinos were introduced into the executive and administrative services in subordinate capacities. The more important positions, and thus effective control, remained practically as well as theoretically with the American officials, during periods of Republican ascendency. The first decisive advance toward the goal of the advocates of independence was made under the auspices of the Democrats with the enactment of the Jones Law in 1916. This law, and especially its administration under Governor-General Harrison, went a very considerable distance toward placing control of the government in the hands of the Filipinos. With the return to power of the Republicans after the election of 1920, however, steps were taken administratively to restore effective American control on the theory that so long as there was American responsibility there should be reserved adequate power to discharge that responsibility.

With the coming of the depression in the United States, toward the conclusion of the Hoover administration, political attitudes began to be modified in the light of new economic considerations. The advocates of independence on political and "moral" grounds found their cause being

[3] *Encyclopedia of the Social Sciences*, vol. 12, pp. 110–111.

advocated on economic grounds, in terms of American rather than Philippine interest, by the representatives of various farm interests in the country, by groups of processors, and by organized labor groups.

Three decades of American control, however, had resulted in the creation of very intimate relations between the economy of the United States and that of the Philippines. Especially after 1909, when virtually free trade relations between the Islands and the United States, and "closed door" relations between the Philippines and the non-American world had been inaugurated, the economic ties had been drawn closer and closer. This evolution is interestingly revealed in the trade figures. On the side of imports, the Philippines supplied an increasingly important market for American goods. "In 1899, the United States was sending to the Islands goods valued at $1,150,000. By 1908, the last year before free trade, sales had barely reached $5,000,000, but during the first full year of free trade this amount doubled, and by 1929, which was the peak year, it had reached the amazing figure of $92,592,959. As a result of the depression, American exports to the Philippines sank by 1933 to less than half of this amount, but during 1934 there was a slight recovery up to a total of $54,680,000." [4] The American market was of even greater importance to producers in the Philippines: 79 per cent in 1930, 87 per cent in 1933, and 84 per cent in 1934, of the total volume of Philippine exports going to the United States. While it might be concluded that the United States could get along without the Philippine market for its manufactured goods, the Islands had been brought into a condition of complete dependence on reasonably free access to the American market. This condition had been the direct result of American policy. Because of this economic inter-relationship it had come to be considered questionable whether the United States would ever fulfill its apparent promise to grant independence to the Islands, or whether it would actually be to the interest of the Filipino to be placed beyond the American customs frontier. The support for the fulfillment of that promise, up to 1930, lay in a point of view, essentially political, that the responsibility of the United States, sharing in the bearing of the "white man's burden," was to uplift the Filipino and train him in the art of self-government so that he could finally be entrusted with the responsibility of governing himself. Thus independence sentiment was founded upon concern for the welfare of the Filipino. To retire from the islands was conceived as an ultimate duty, an unusual act of self-abnegation, rather than as an action to be taken in the interest of the United States and its nationals.

The first concrete evidence of a shift in point of view from concern with the Filipino to concern with the interest of the American producer of competitive products came when, in connection with the enactment of the

[4] Grayson Kirk. *Philippine Independence*, 1936, p. 60.

Smoot-Hawley tariff measure, an amendment was offered providing for the "levy of import duties upon Philippine products." [5] Consideration of the amendment was postponed pending the holding of committee hearings on the question. Almost immediately the issue was changed from that of tariff legislation to that of independence, on the basis of a bill presented to the Senate committee by Senators Hawes and Cutting. Their measure provided for a transitional period of five years, during which tariff duties would be applied gradually in an ascending scale by the two governments, and finally for a vote, at the end of the period, by the Philippine peoples to determine whether or not they wanted political independence after experimentation with economic independence. Discussion of this measure continued during the years 1930–1933. From the economic-interest-group point of view, it was supported by spokesmen for the agricultural sections of the country and found its principal opposition among those speaking for the manufacturers, who were interested both in the Philippine market and in the supply of essential raw materials. To both sides were joined those who were principally concerned with the political implications of the proposed action. Thus the advocates of independence on grounds of economic interest were joined by those who believed in the right of the people to govern themselves. The opponents found support among those who held to the view that the Filipino was not yet ready for self-government and that the international consequences of independence would be unfortunate for the Filipino and also for other colonial Powers. This latter consideration was especially emphasized by the executive branch of the government.

The combination of those who wanted to protect themselves against asserted Philippine competition with the earlier advocates of independence, including the Philippine leaders themselves, resulted finally in the enactment of an independence measure, the Tydings-McDuffie Act, in March, 1934, after the Hare-Hawes-Cutting measure had been enacted over a veto by President Hoover in the last days of his administration. The latter measure provided for an immediate legislative vote in the Philippines. This, when taken, was adverse to the measure, not so much on account of opposition to independence as because of objection to some of the conditions of its attainment. Reconsideration in Congress resulted in the enactment of the Tydings-McDuffie measure.

This authorized the holding of a constitutional convention, after approval of independence either by the Philippine legislature or by a special convention called for that purpose. The constitution had to be drafted to conform to certain conditions defined in the Act, and it had to be approved

[5] KIRK, *op. cit.,* p. 103. Chapter 5 reviews and analyzes consideration of the question in Congress.

by the American President. The constitution was successfully drafted and
received Presidential approval so that the new Commonwealth government
was inaugurated before the end of 1935. The new régime was not that of
an independent state, the final severance of American control having been
postponed until the end of a ten-year period, during which economic relations were to be adjusted toward the realization of the status of complete
independence, and also arrangements were to be made which would enable the new state to sustain that position.

It must be noted at this point that these developments coincided in point
of time with the period of disturbance in Far Eastern relationships resulting from Japan's expansionist activities on the continent of Asia. If Philippine independence had been undertaken at a time of stability and international calm, it could have fairly been considered, as on the whole it was
in the United States, solely from the point of view of its effects domestically within either country and on their economic relationships. Under
existing circumstances, however, the decisions taken had just as great importance on account of the effects they had on political relationships in
the Far Eastern region. It is apparent that the decision to grant independence within the ten-year period served to introduce a new factor into the
Far Eastern equation since it would result in Philippine participation in the
politics of the region as an independent state rather than as a dependency
primarily affecting the policies of the United States. Essentially the question
immediately came down to the prospective ability of the people of the
Islands to sustain an orderly existence. If they could, they would afford
no justification to other governments to intervene for the purpose of protecting their interests and those of their nationals. They would need also to
be able to maintain their independence by their own efforts in the face of
possible attempts to destroy it; unless it could be assumed that after the
ten-year period the United States would continue to interest itself in the
Islands to the extent of affording them a protection from aggression which
they might not be able to give themselves. The conditions of establishment
of the Commonwealth government were such that during the ten-year
period there might develop more than a moral obligation of the United
States to preserve the independence which had been granted. Thus a right
of intervention to maintain conditions of internal peace and order was
reserved, as was the right to establish and maintain a base for naval
operations. Beyond that, the obligation was introduced to seek to provide a
permanently neutralized status for the Islands on the basis of international
agreement by the end of the ten-year period. Thus it could not be concluded even at the time that the establishment of the Philippine Commonwealth would bring about, either immediately or ultimately, a withdrawal
of the United States from a position of responsibility for the Islands. What

it did do immediately was to underscore a note of uncertainty as to the position of the United States in relation to the activities of other states.

The general direction in the policies of other states than Japan, and possibly Russia, in and after 1931 was toward stability. That is to say, England, France, and the Netherlands were no longer expansive. They, together with the United States, had reached the point of defense of an existing political position. That position, as has already been indicated, was already in process of modification in China under the pressure of Chinese nationalism. In that respect the year 1931 found the Western tide on the ebb rather than the flow. Change in the status of the Philippines and in American policy with respect to the Philippines would have little effect on the Western position in China. On the other hand, the developments in and with respect to China, whether domestic or international, might readily have significance with respect to the future of the Philippines and of other colonial territories in the Far East. This significance was, however, found after 1931 in relation to Japan's policies toward, and activities in, China, rather than in consequence of further expressions of Chinese nationalism. Thus it was in relation to Japan and to Japanese expansion, that Philippine independence presented a problem.

By 1931 the trade position of Japan in the Islands had come to be second only to that of the United States. This did not give it a very important place, with only 7.2 per cent of the total. But this subordinate position was undoubtedly due to the preferred status of the American traders growing out of the free trade arrangements between the United States and the Philippines. If the "open door" principle, as regards non-domestic producers, should be applied, the Islands offered the possibility of an expanding market for Japanese manufacturers. This expansion might well take place without any disturbance of the balance of political forces in the Far East unless it should be impeded either by the Philippine government or by the failure to maintain orderly processes of government, which would give a reason and an excuse for Japanese intervention. Furthermore, the balance of political forces might be disturbed if there should be inclusion of the Philippines within the charted area of Japanese expansion. This might result from a desire to control trade arrangements by bringing the Islands within the Japanese Empire, so as to introduce similar preferences for Japanese to those previously enjoyed by Americans.

Potentially, it must be recognized, the Philippines had then and still have an economic interest for Japan beyond that represented by their possibilities as a market. They are capable of sustaining a much increased population. Japanese would not meet the same lower-standard competition there that they had in Chosen, Manchuria, and China; thus they could maintain themselves more readily in competition with the native peoples. Some resources of the Islands are of a supplementary rather than a competitive type, and thus control of their exploitation would be advantageous. Even under American supervision, Japanese established themselves in virtual control of hemp production in the province of Davao. In addition to hemp, the iron reserves, chromite, lumber, and gold could be exploited profitably by Japan as desirable supplements to her own resources. Beyond the market and the exploitive interest, Manila had assumed great importance as a center of air communications for the southeastern Asiatic and Pacific areas, which would add to its economic significance for Japan as well as for other states.

Furthermore, a glance at the map will reveal the close proximity of the Philippines to the southern point of the then existing Japanese Empire in Formosa. Control of the Islands would help to complete the protective screen cutting off access to China by sea. It would also serve to put the then Japanese mandated islands in a new relationship with the rest of the Empire. But such expansion would also have served to bring the Japanese Empire into territorial proximity to the Dutch and British colonial possessions in southeastern Asia and the Pacific. The Dutch possessions would then have been the only barrier between Japan and Australia. Control of the Philippines, furthermore, would help to make the French position in Indo-China potentially untenable, especially if it should be coupled with Japanese control of the Island of Hainan and southeastern China. Thus, it must be concluded that any change in the status of the Philippines, especially if it offered the possibility of the replacement of the United States by another state as the colonial Power, would be of importance to the position of all the Western states with interests and possessions in the Far Eastern or Pacific areas. Under 1931–1940 conditions, involving expansion by Japan from the north to the south, the Philippines stood as a barrier to Japan rather than as a springboard from which the United States or other Western states might leap toward an extension of their interests northward into China. Thus, after 1931, their historic rôle in Far Eastern politics had come to be reversed.

7. THE BRITISH POSITION AND INTERESTS

Of the maritime Western states with territorial possessions in eastern Asia the United States was the only one which, in 1931, was even contemplating retirement from control of its possessions. England was, it is true, making slow progress toward the creation of dominion status for India under the constant pressure of Indian nationalism. The first distinct steps toward representative government were taken with the Morley-Minto reforms of the years 1907–1909. The magnificent response of India to the war needs of the Empire after 1914, coupled with the pressure for recognition on the part of Indian nationalists, brought about an official commitment of the British government, in 1917, to "the gradual development of self-governing institutions, with a view to the progressive realization of responsible government in India as an integral part of the British Empire." [6] This was followed in 1918 with the Montagu-Chelmsford report, and this by the enactment, in 1919, of a new Government of India Act. This Act introduced the system of dyarchy, under which certain fields of action in the provinces were reserved to the control of the Governor and his executive council, while others were transferred to the control of a ministry responsible to an elective provincial legislature. With respect to policy affecting the entire country, however, the Viceroy was left in control, although he was given an advisory council with elective as well as appointive members, and a legislative assembly with a majority of elective members.

By the time of this enactment, however, conditions of serious conflict had developed. Mahatma Gandhi assumed leadership of the nationalist movement, organized in the Congress party, introducing "civil disobedience" and passive resistance as the methods of opposition. In the face of this opposition the new plan was put into effect. One of its provisions was for another parliamentary commission, within ten years, to investigate the operation of the new system and make proposals for its improvement or modification in the light of experience. Two years before the expiry of the time limit the new commission, the Simon Commission, was duly constituted. Its composition was unfortunate in that it failed to include any Indian members, and consequently it met with no effective coöperation in India in making its investigations and formulating its recommendations. Its report was most elaborate, but its recommendations failed to meet with the approval of the Indian nationalists since it did not propose home rule or dominion status for India. It did recommend the abolition of the system of dyarchy and an extension of responsible government in the provinces but not in relation to the central government.

When the second Labor government came into office in 1929, the attempt was made to conciliate Indian opinion, offended as it had been by the nature and the findings of the Simon Commission, by the offer of a Roundtable Conference. The first Roundtable Conference failed to gain the participation of Mr. Gandhi and his followers because the British government refused to commit itself to propose a dominion constitution for India. Civil disobedience became the order of the day, and the pressure was sufficiently intense to bring about a further modification of British policy by the time of the second Roundtable Conference in 1931. This was also made possible

[6] Quoted by G. N. STEIGER in his *History of the Far East* (1936), p. 807, from statement of Mr. Montagu in the House of Commons. The Montagu-Chelmsford report recommended a "cautious yet appreciable surrender of power to the elected councils both central and provincial." *Encyc. of the Social Sciences*, vol. 7, p. 669.

because the Indian Princes, at the first Conference, proposed federation of their states with British India and thus indicated a possibility of action within a framework which the British felt would afford more adequate safeguards for their interests, which, as against the nationalists, were similar to those of the Princes and would be supported by them.

Three Roundtable Conferences in all were held before a new constitution was prepared for the consideration of Parliament. This plan, presented in a White paper in 1933, was finally enacted in 1935. It created a federal union for all of India. Within the federation the franchise was considerably extended, and provision was made for the limited introduction of responsible government at the center as well as in the provinces. Important subjects were, however, reserved from the control of the legislature. Consequently the full demand for dominion status was far from met, and pressure for it continued and found a new effectiveness with the outbreak of war again in 1939.

The nationalism in India which brought about this modification of the colonial relationship, while not originated from the Far East, was decidedly stimulated by developments in that area. The successes of nationalist Japan in maintaining independence of, and establishing equality with, the Western states, but especially the Japanese victories over Russia in the war of 1904–1905, had a definitely stimulative effect on Indian as well as on Chinese nationalism. But it cannot be said that there were any reverse currents. Developments in India along political lines had not, by the 1930's, affected the situation in the Far East.

On the economic side, however, the conclusion would have to be different. Paralleling the political movement was an economic one essentially directed toward the development of modern industry in India. Large aggregations of English capital had moved to India for purposes of direct investment during and after the last decades of the nineteenth century, while a native capitalism also had come into existence. This had not only produced a new relationship between India and England, but it had also created a local interest in protection when the Japanese textile industry began to reach out for new foreign markets after 1930. From the economic standpoint, consequently, Indian and British interests seemed to have converged as against Japan, even though politically the example of Japan stimulated the Indian nationalists' determination to win independence from England.

Except for Burma, developments similar to those in India or the Philippines were not in prospect for the other British territorial possessions in southeastern Asia. English control not only remained intact but was in process of being strengthened through the establishment of a strong naval and air base at Singapore. With no developed native threat to the British position as the colonial Power, even though there was no territorial expansionism left in British policy, there was an evident determination to retain the control established as a result of past expansionist activities in Malaysia. And, given the position of other Powers in that area, the only threat to the British position would be one presented if Japan should direct its expansion southward in Asia. In 1931, and for some time thereafter, there seemed to be no real possibility of such a development. The principal area of asserted Japanese interest was Manchuria and Inner Mongolia. In those regions the British interest was slight. South of the Wall stood China, under the control of nationalist leaders. Within China proper the British interest was much larger. The Japanese and British proportions of the total foreign investment in China were approximately the same in 1931. Japanese investment, however, was largely concentrated in Manchuria, while that of Britain was in China proper, her direct investment centering principally in the Shanghai area. In trade the British had lost the preëminent position enjoyed throughout the nineteenth century, having, if Hongkong is excluded, fallen behind both Japan and the United States. Nevertheless, the extent of both the British trade and investment interest in China was sufficient to make England an important influence in relation to China. She had taken a leading part in readjusting the foreign position to the demands of Chinese nationalism, and in the process had given evidence of a desire to conserve as much as possible of her traditional position in China. All of the indications in 1931 were, however, that her economic, as well as her political, position in China was defensive rather than expansive. But the defense was thought of in relation to Chinese nationalism, rather than the expansive nationalism of Japan, because of the concentration of Japan's interests in Manchuria.

From the territorial standpoint the outpost of Britain to the north in Asia was Hongkong, unless the British concession in Tientsin and the International Settlement in Shanghai are conceived of as territorial bases. And certainly there had been given, in 1931, no evidence of British intention to retire from Hongkong, or to consider a readjustment of the status there. Thus it stood as a first, even if a relatively weak, line of defense against a threat from the north to the British territorial position in Malaysia. It also gave a base for action in defense of the British interests in China. Its real value, from the defense standpoint, however, depended upon the status of China. But behind Hongkong stood Singapore, and between China or Japan and the British colonies, other than Hongkong, were, in the maritime belt, the Philippines, and, on the continent, French Indo-China. Thus the British position in North Borneo, Sarawak, Malaya, and the Straits Settlements would inevitably be affected by the status of the Philippines and Indo-China. This made American policy of considerable importance to the English government. It was also of more than casual importance to the

British Dominions in the Pacific, since the only barrier between the Philippines and Australasia is the chain of Islands constituting what were then the Netherlands Indies. If the Philippines proved unable to sustain their independence, and if they should, in consequence, come under the control of an expansive Power, the potential threat would be extended to Australia and New Zealand, bringing them more definitely into the system of power-relationships centering in the Far East.

8. THE NETHERLANDS INDIES

If a figure of speech may be borrowed from the Japanese, in relation to the Netherlands Indies the Philippines might be likened to a dagger pointed at the heart of the Dutch possessions—a dangerous weapon if, from the Dutch standpoint, in the wrong hands. It was sometimes forgotten that, in the broader area of the Western Pacific, Holland was a great colonial power with its dominions spread out over more than four degrees of latitude. This Island empire of 733,494 square miles, with more than sixty million inhabitants, lay between the British possessions in eastern Asia and the great Dominion of Australia. Sprawled out east and west, it is approached rather closely by the southernmost of the Philippine Islands, stretching down from the north to the south, and serving either as a link or as a barrier with respect to the Far East, depending upon political circumstance.

Since the return of their possessions by decision of the Congress of Vienna in 1815, there had been no serious threat of disturbance of the Dutch position in their eastern empire. This was due, in the first place, to their withdrawal from any active participation in European politics, and to their similar abstention from participation in world politics. In the second place, it had been the result of successful administration of their empire, so that no reason had been afforded to others to assert the need for action to preserve order. They had also been enabled to preserve a position which they lacked the power to maintain otherwise on account of the early focusing of the rivalries of the stronger European Powers on China. In other words, it was not Dutch power which kept the empire intact during the nineteenth century and the first three decades of the twentieth against other states seeking colonial dominion.

Neither, however, had it been the lack of value of the territories in question which had caused stronger states to leave Holland undisturbed in their possession. As a market they were important, the imports increasing from 175.5 million dollars in 1913 to a peak of 431 million in 1929. While the Netherlands supplied the largest proportion of the imports, the United States, Germany, England, and Japan shared in the competition, with the Japanese steadily moving toward the point of predominance, even over the Dutch, a position which had been attained by 1932. But the principal importance of the Netherlands Indies was to be found in their position as a source of supply of such commodities as sugar, coffee, tea, tobacco, and areca nuts, among agricultural products; of rubber, petroleum, tin, copra, coconut oil and palm oil, among its products of industrial importance. All of this made the Dutch colonies, and the conditions of their administration, of great interest to the industrial states, and, among them, to Japan.

The Dutch administration of their colonies was essentially economic rather than political or social in direction. That is, they did not concern themselves with the disturbance of native ways any more than was necessary for purposes of successful economic exploitation. Thus they ruled in part through the native princes, who were kept under the supervision of Residents, and in part directly. But even where the rule was direct, local affairs were administered under native headmen, and largely in accordance with native tradition. Thus, until after the first World War, they avoided many of the difficulties growing out of the importation and diffusion of Western ideas of nationalism and democracy. On the other side, the Dutch administrators, especially after the third quarter of the last century, showed regard for the material well-being of the peoples under their rule, bringing new lands under cultivation, extending production through irrigation, and establishing conditions of land tenure founded upon a perception of the interests and needs of the subject peoples. While their rule had been exploitative in character, a measure of concern had been shown for the welfare of the people.

The stability engendered by their rule, coupled with their non-participation in international politics, as has been stated, had been factors in enabling the Netherlands government, essentially without effective military and naval power, to maintain its empire. A third factor had been the preference of other states to see this rich domain in Dutch hands rather than in the hands of competitors for political as well as economic power. Thus it had become to the British interest to maintain Holland in possession as against, say, Japan or Germany. And, as has already been indicated, the position of the United States in the Philippines had been essentially protective of the Dutch position in their territories. But when stability disappeared from the Pacific and Far Eastern region with the pursuit of aggressive trade and territorial policies by the Japanese Empire after 1931, a new situation was shaped for the Dutch as well as for other Powers with interests in the region. Nevertheless, the immediate point of emphasis remained that they were no more prepared to withdraw voluntarily from their colonies than were the British, from whom they may be said to have taken their lead, from this standpoint, rather than from American policy in the Philippines.

9. FRANCE IN THE FAR EAST

The same conclusion is presented with respect to France, the third Western Power with an important territorial position in the Far East. French Indo-China, which comprised the colony of Cochin China and the protectorates of Cambodia, Annam, Tongking, and Laos, had an area of about 284,900 square miles and a population estimated in 1931 at 21,600,000. Thus, it was not only the largest and most populous of the French colonies but somewhat larger than the colonial state itself, and with half its total population. Its importance, moreover, was not so much due to its size in comparison either with France or with the other French colonies as it was to be found in its economic resources. Among its principal exports, besides such agricultural production as rice, pepper, cinnamon, tea, and other tropical products, were zinc and zinc ore, of which it was a principal source of supply, tin, coal, rubber, and copra. In 1931 almost half of the imports were from France, and a quarter of its exports were taken by the controlling country.

While only Cochin China was called a colony, the other parts of Indo-China being called protectorates, the entire region was, to all intents, under direct administration, since the Residents in the protectorates exercised as effective a power of direction as did the governor of Cochin China. The whole administration was in fact centralized under the authority of the Governor-general, whose seat of government was at Hanoi. After 1923 his supervisory authority had also been extended over the French islands in the south Pacific. In relation to the home government his responsibility was to the Minister of Colonies.

The movement in French policy, since the separation finally of Tongking from China in 1885, had been toward consolidation, centralization, and assimilation of France's territories in the Far East. In the protectorates, to be sure, the native régimes were preserved in the exercise of nominal governmental authority, and to some extent they were strengthened. Internal government was also based on respect for local custom and tradition where it did not come into conflict with the needs and interests of the colonial Power. Since the natives were affected to a greater extent, certainly, than the natives in the Dutch possessions by Western currents and ideas, partly because of the success of Siam in establishing and maintaining its independence, and partly because of its nearness to revolutionary China, the French had to reckon to an increasing extent with demands for the introduction of institutions of local self-government. These demands were met in part by the creation of an advisory council to the Governor-general, which, however, while locally composed, had only a small proportion of members representative of the masses of the native peoples. In part the demands were countered through the strengthening of native institutions. But in spite of these tendencies, the fact remains that the historic movement had been toward, rather than away from, the strengthening of the French position as the colonial Power.

From the position established in Tongking, France extended her view to the southeastern provinces of China. The leasehold at Kwangchouwan remained as evidence of the desire of France to maintain her position and her interests in China, as did also the French railway from Indo-China into Yunnan. Railway rights and economic priorities, the leased territory, and a non-alienation agreement with respect to the Island of Hainan, served to mark out a French sphere of interest in China as against other European states. The intention to develop and, if possible, extend her position within this sphere had not been disavowed by France at the Washington Conference nor in the decade following. Beyond this, the French remained in control of their Concessions at Tientsin and Shanghai; and they had an important investment interest in China, about equally divided between direct investments and holdings of government obligations. Their total business investment had increased from the 60 million dollars of 1914 to 95 million in 1931, while their holdings of government obligations had decreased between 1914 and 1931 from 111.4 million dollars to 97.4. To these totals, from the political standpoint, might be added the Belgian investment, which was considerably smaller, but still not unimportant. Thus, the French interest of a material character in China, while decreasing proportionately to that of some other states, remained substantial. The foundation of the French position, however, remained Indo-China. The French reaction to developments in the Far East would be determined not by their ultimate effects on the French interests in China, but by their significance for the French position in their colonial empire.

10. SUMMARY

By way of summary of the position of the West in relation to the East, in 1931, then, it may be said that Europe, through Russia, extended across the north of Asia to the Pacific, as far south as the Amur, and that European colonies stretched south from the frontiers of China and eastward across the Pacific from the twentieth degree of latitude south. Off the continent Japan stretched southward toward the Philippines, and had built up an important position on the continent, including Korea in her empire, asserting a predominant position in Manchuria, and having an increasingly important economic position, among the foreign states, within China. A question mark had been written after the Philippines in relation to their future status, with the American move toward withdrawal from the Islands; and that question carried with it questions of future policy for the Dutch, the British, and the French, who might have to concern themselves directly with the Philippines as an independent buffer state between their colonies and Japan. Nationalism was in process of unifying and modernizing China, and, as part of the process, was compelling readjustment to it of Western rights and interests in China. With each additional increment of strength gained through unification and internal consolidation, China bade fair to regain control of her own destinies, and at the end to emerge as the strongest single factor in the politics of the Far East. In moving toward that end China was supposedly protected by the Nine Powers Treaty of Washington, which guaranteed to her "the fullest and most unembarrassed opportunity," as far as other states were concerned, to work out of political turmoil into the stability which would give her strength, and possibly a dominant position. But just at that time new currents were started moving from Japan which changed the problem of politics for China, and for all other states with Far Eastern interests.

REFERENCES FOR FURTHER STUDY

KURT BLOCH, *German Interests and Policies in the Far East* (I. P. R. Inquiry Series, 1940). GROVER CLARK, *Economic Rivalries in China* (1932); contains many useful data. PAUL H. CLYDE, *Japan's Pacific Mandate* (1935); a useful study. COUNCIL ON FOREIGN RELATIONS, *Survey of American Foreign Relations,* annual volumes 1928–1931. T. E. ENNIS, *French Policy and Developments in Indo China* (1936); especially good on the administrative system. *Far Eastern Survey,* vol. 4–5; under that title continues the American Council, Institute of Pacific Relations, *Memoranda,* which constitute vol. 1–3. These fortnightly publications present factual materials dealing mainly with economic and social developments in the entire Pacific area. FREDERICK V. FIELD (ed.), *Economic Handbook of the Pacific* (1934); an indispensable book of reference. *Foreign Policy Reports,* vol. 6, Nos. 3–4; vol. 7, No. 7; vol. 9, No. 22; vol. 12, No. 19. E. M. GULL, *British Economic Interests in the Far East* (1943); careful survey from pre-treaty period to 1941. RALSTON HAYDEN, *The Philippines in Transition,* Foreign Affairs, vol. 14, No. 4, pp. 639–653. G. E. HUBBARD and D. BARING, *Eastern Industrialization and Its Effect on the West* (1935). (British Royal) INSTITUTE OF INTERNATIONAL AFFAIRS, *Survey of International Affairs,* annual after 1924; a most valuable series. INSTITUTE OF INTERNATIONAL AFFAIRS, *Documents on International Affairs* (1933, 1934); an exceedingly useful collection. GRAYSON L. KIRK, *Philippine Independence* (1936); an objective analysis of American-Philippine relations. K. P. LANDON, *Siam in Transition* (1940). E. LEDERER, *Japan in Transition* (1938), especially ch. 6–10; throws much light on the development of China and Japan by comparison and contrast. GEORGE A. MALCOLM, *The Commonwealth of the Philippines* (1936). I. F. G. MILNER, *New Zealand's Interests and Policies in the Far East* (I. P. R. Inquiry Series, 1940). WILLARD PRICE, *Japan in the Philippines,* Harper's Magazine, May, 1936, pp. 609–619. WILLARD PRICE, *Pacific Adventure* (1936); a travel and journalistic study of the mandated islands. C. F. REMER, *Foreign Investments in China* (1933); a most valuable study. JACK SHEPHERD, *Australia's Interests and Policies in the Far East* (I. P. R. Inquiry Series, 1940). AMRY VANDENBOSCH, *Dutch East Indies: Its Government, Problems and Politics* (1933). EDITH E. WARE, *Business and Politics in the Far East.*

CHAPTER XXII

JAPAN IN MANCHURIA

THE THREADS of change in the Far Eastern pattern down to 1931 have been traced in the preceding chapters. In that year a series of movements began which were of great significance for Manchuria, for Japan, for China, and for the Western states with Far Eastern interests. These movements must now be considered in terms of their immediate causes and their consequences. The emphasis initially will be placed on Manchuria and on Japan. The Manchurian crisis of 1931 had its local causation in the projection into China's three eastern provinces of the force of Chinese nationalism. Consequently it will be necessary to review and to evaluate the impact of nationalism on the position of Japan in Manchuria in order to understand the moves made by that country in and after 1931. But those moves also need to be related to the operation of domestic forces in Japan. This is particularly the case with reference to the consequences of the operation of the forces set in motion in 1931. Those consequences were important for Manchuria, but they were of even greater significance for Japan herself, and, through Japan, for China and for the Western world. Japanese policy in relation to Manchuria reacted back upon Japan, affecting her both economically and politically. Thus in terms both of the causes and of the effects of events in and after 1931 the explanation must first be sought in Japan.

I. JAPAN: INTERNAL CONDITIONS IN 1931

The Japan which began to re-shape the Far East to her own ends in and after 1931 had a population of almost 70 million people, living in Japan proper. The significance of that figure and the national strength it represents can be realized only when contrasted with those of the nation rediscovered by Commodore Perry in 1854—less than thirty millions, living a meager existence, economically still in the Middle Ages. The contrast is almost equally vivid if one considers the Japan of 1894, launching its first war of modern times—against China—and looked upon by the rest of the world as a weakling upstart. In the endeavor to adjust itself to the modern world and also to take care of this increased population Japan had, while not losing its fundamental agricultural basis, industrialized itself. It had also expanded territorially, but its expansion had not been of any real help in taking care of the annual rise in the population through resettlement,

This was revealed in the increase on the main islands, and in the fact that Chosen had attracted less than half a million Japanese; Taiwan and Karafuto less than a quarter of a million each; and the mandated islands, acquired at the end of World War I, under 20,000. Neither, on the whole, had its contact with the non-Asian world enabled the population problem to be solved by emigration beyond the limits of the Empire. This was in part due to the policy of exclusion generally followed in the Western world. That the Asian countries, including China and Manchuria, the Philippines and the Straits Settlements had not attracted the Japanese in any large numbers, is evidenced in the fact that less than a million Japanese had taken up residence outside of the Empire by 1935. Not even the establishment of Japanese control over under-settled Manchuria brought about more than a slight increase in migration. Attempts at colonization of the settlement type had almost invariably been a failure.

Thus it was industrialization that was responsible for such solution as there had been of the population problem. But, as an industrial state, Japan was lacking in resources. And industrialization carried with it a need for constantly expanding markets for Japanese goods. Both markets and access to resources, when they lie outside the state, are precarious, which means that the livelihood of the people dependent on industry is precarious. Consequently, out of industrialization came an economic re-direction of Japanese foreign policy, strengthening an earlier aspiration with the recognition of a new need.

The 1931–1941 expansionist moves, consequently, can only be understood in the light of industrialization, both from this standpoint, and from that of some of its effects on the economic, social, and political structure of Japan itself. Since the development of modern industry has already been considered, together with some of its social consequences, at this point all that need be attempted is the completion of the picture in terms of the more recent developments. This will, however, necessitate a certain amount of recapitulation.

Nineteenth-century Japan, it will be recalled, was a fairly unified and socially homogeneous country. The lines of division between the governed and the governing classes were not, at the same time, lines of cleavage. Within the governing classes, however, there had appeared cleavages which were in part between clans, but in part between those who had centered their interests in the military services and those who had undertaken the reorganization and management of the civil establishment. Thus one of the bases of internal divisions which showed themselves in and after 1931 defined itself at a comparatively early time. At a somewhat later time, although considerably before 1930, differences of opinion as to the direction of policy, both internal and external, arose between the army and navy leaders. This further cleavage in governing circles, however, was given point and its direction on account of other changes which had occurred.

As the economic transformation of Japan took place, a new type of important interest arose within the state. This was the capitalist interest produced, in contra-distinction to the landed interest, out of the industrialization previously referred to. The development of the new industry took place in close coöperation between the government, interested for its own reasons in promoting it, and the capitalists. Under these circumstances, and perhaps partly because of the rapidity of the development, the concentration of industrial power and control in a few sets of hands, which was a later stage of evolution in the industrial countries of the West, appeared at a relatively early stage in Japan. Thus the power of the army and navy groups and the civil bureaucrats, expressed through a comparatively few dominant leaders, began to be paralleled by the power of an equally small number of powerful industrial and financial leaders.

While the foundations of Japan's industrial organization in great family business combines, the Zaibatsu, were laid during the Meiji period, their superstructure appeared as a dominant feature of the Japanese economic and political landscape in the 1920's. As Professor W. W. Lockwood put it:[1]

Already dominant in the more modern sectors of the Japanese economy, they now extended their control indirectly over an increasing share of small-scale commerce and manufacturing. Through an intricate, pyramided structure of inter-corporate, personal, and political ties, the larger combines, notably Mitsui and Mitsubishi, developed into huge agglomerations of heterogeneous enterprise—trading, shipping, banking, insurance, real estate, mining, manufacturing, and colonial undertakings.

. . . This concentration of control had been facilitated from the beginning by close association with the military oligarchy and the civil bureaucracy. . . .

Probably no other modern industrial society organized on the basis of private property has offered a comparable display of the unrestrained power of bigness, employing all of the devices of monopolistic control. . . . As a group, in any case, the zaibatsu and their satellites dominated the more modern sector of the Japanese economy. With controls ramifying outwards from their nuclei of great financial, industrial, and trading concerns, they presented the most extreme contrast to the small-scale pattern of organization which persisted in agriculture and even in a large proportion of Japanese manufacturing and commerce.

The institution of the zaibatsu contributed greatly to the rapid accumulation of capital and modernization of technology which underlay Japan's industrial development.

On the other hand, if the concentration of control in Japanese industry and finance was progressive in these technical aspects, its social aspects were less admirable. It was one of the factors perpetuating inequalities of income and opportunity in modern Japan almost as wide as those of feudal times. It carried over into modern industry the tradition of hierarchical status and autho-

[1] Lockwood, *The Economic Development of Japan* (1954), pp. 59–60.

ritarian control which was inimical to political and social democracy. . . . And in politics the plutocratic alliance of the zaibatsu and the political parties contributed eventually to the defeat and discrediting of parliamentary government after 1930.

A few figures will help to fix the situation in mind. At the time of the first Sino-Japanese War "the total of nominal capital of companies amounted to 308 million yen. Since 1895, Japan's industrial capital has increased over a hundred times and her commercial capital more than fifty times; in 1929 the total capital was estimated at 13,790,758,000 yen. The bulk of the capital, 44.7 per cent, is now invested in manufacturing industries and mining; commerce and banking account for 42.7 per cent." [2] While there were to be found a large number of small enterprises, it is significant that over 65 per cent of Japanese capital was invested in 1.5 per cent of the total number of companies. These are 1929 figures, but the tendency they represent was accentuated rather than reversed after that time. It should be pointed out, further, that the ownership of these large companies was not so widely dispersed through the holding of shares as to invalidate the conclusion that industrial ownership, and thus economic power, was rather narrowly concentrated and might consequently be effectively brought into play.

To further indicate the nature of this side of Japanese development it is only necessary to make reference to the Sumitomo Company, capitalized at 150 million yen, controlling, through associated companies with a total capitalization of 180 million yen, such varied activities as a banking and trust business, electric wire and fertilizer manufacturing, copper and coal mining activities, warehousing, life insurance, and building; and further controlling collateral companies capitalized at an additional 49.5 million yen. Or there was the Mitsui Company, capitalized at 300 million yen, with associated and collateral companies with a further combined capitalization of over 800 million yen, carrying on an equally diversified program of business activity. A third industrial empire within the state, conforming to the pattern of the other two mentioned, was the Mitsubishi Company. These capitalists had their own interests to serve through the medium of the state, and, within limits, they possessed the power to compel consideration of their interests.

By the time this capitalist interest had begun to define itself as a distinctly significant one the political parties had also become important factors in Japanese life. During the first decade of operation of the constitutional system, as has been pointed out, the parties struggled to wrest control of the government from the hands of the civil and military bureaucrats by exercising the powers of obstruction which had been given to the Diet. Failing in their endeavor to establish the principle that the Cabinet should be

[2] I. L. O., *Industrial Labor in Japan*, Series and Reports, Series A, No. 37, p. 36.

constituted from the majority party in the House of Representatives, a *modus vivendi* was accepted under which the majority party supported the government in return for a share of the spoils of office. This arrangement continued from 1900 to 1912, during which the Seiyukai, which was the majority party, alternately supported the Saionji and Katsura governments. Subsequently a greater measure of party participation in and control over Cabinets, from the standpoint of personnel, developed. The first real party government, however, was not established until the Hara government of 1918. The assassination of Mr. Hara by a nationalist fanatic brought about a temporary reversion to the non-party principle in the formation of Cabinets, but the progression toward party government was resumed after the elections of 1924. From 1925, when the law providing for universal male suffrage first went into effect, to 1932, governments were constituted regularly on the basis of majority party support in the House of Representatives. Party government in the Western sense seemed to have been established in Japan.

During this period of movement toward party government the parties had become the instruments of the capitalists. The Seiyukai, originally concerned with the protection and the promotion of the interests of the land-owning class, allied itself with the Mitsui interests and became in part their spokesman. The Minseito had come into being through a coalition of the earlier parties which had been primarily concerned with the promotion of industrial interests, and was even more perceptibly the party of "big business." Thus party government after 1925 represented government in the interest of large-scale enterprise, in its turn controlled by concentrated capital or financial interests, modified, especially during periods of Seiyukai control, by an expression of concern for the land-owning class and especially the landlords.

The old bureaucracy, both civil and military, tracing its descent back to the feudal aristocracy, acted in alliance with, or under the direction of, the parties and shared in the material benefits that resulted from the alliance of the parties with the dominant capitalists. This was revealed from time to time in the out-cropping of "scandals" involving admirals and generals as well as distinguished party and business leaders. The earliest of these, denounced to serve his own purposes by Okuma in 1881, grew out of the attempt to promote the colonization of Hokkaido. Another example was afforded by the "naval scandals" of 1913, which brought about the downfall of the government headed by Admiral Yamamoto. A third example was the case involving the Finance Minister in the fraudulent sale of shares of certain rayon and steel works.

With the system of government existing in Japan this control of the Cabinet and Diet through the medium of the parties would not have had

such great importance if it had not been paralleled by an infiltration into
the Privy Council, the Chamber of Peers and the Imperial Household
Ministry. Even in these bodies the newer aristocracy of wealth established
its representatives or drew members of the hereditary aristocracy into its
ranks. The last of the Elder Statesmen, Prince Saionji, who had the function
of advising the Emperor in the selection of the Premier, had associations
with the Sumitomo interests.[3]

The general line of policy followed by the governments in power after
the Washington Conference was marked out by the dominant capitalist
interests. Industrial concentration was at first permitted and then, after
1929, actively promoted by the government. Monetary policy was determined in the interest of the industrialists. Tariffs and quotas were similarly
established. The rationalization of industry which was begun after the
financial crisis of 1927 strengthened the position of the industrialists at the
expense of the laboring class. The well-established subsidy system for industry was extended. Monopoly business, consequently, supported as it
was by the power of government, weathered the economic storms of the
1920's in good shape.

The reverse, however, was true in the case of other important elements
in the national economy. Shopkeepers and small business men were unable
to withstand the simultaneous shocks of the depression and the increased
concentration of industry. Not only were they finding themselves going
deeper and deeper into debt—the total standing at 2.5 billion yen in 1932—
but the banking agencies on which they depended for financing were themselves in trouble and unable to extend further credit in sufficient amounts.
Thus dissatisfaction with conditions which resulted partly from the operation of external causes and partly from internal developments arose among
this section of Japanese society.

Industrial laborers had also been adversely affected by conditions. Under
other circumstances their recourse might have been to effective unionization or to separate action through their own political parties. Political organization began to be attempted in and after 1925, but it did not immediately attain any great measure of success, partly because of internal divisions within the labor groups, partly because of the inability of industrial
and agricultural labor to find common ground on which to stand, but
mainly because of the tendency to regard proponents of labor organization
for political purposes as exponents of "dangerous thought" and to proceed
against them as enemies of the state. Unionization also had to overcome
somewhat the same type of difficulty. It was decidedly held back, as well,
by the paternalistic tradition in the country and by the problem presented
by the large proportion of women in industry, many of whom regarded

[3] On this, see *Foreign Policy Reports*, vol. 10, No. 25, p. 320, hereafter cited as *F. P. R.*

themselves as only temporarily employed. Nevertheless, by 1930, the number of unions had increased to 77, with a total membership of 350,000. As a political force, however, these unions were weakened by division into right, center, and left wing elements. Still, they did attempt to advance the economic interests of their members with some degree of success. But the measure of dissatisfaction with existing conditions was shown by an increase in the number and the intensity of strikes.

Unrest and dissatisfaction with existing conditions was, however, most marked in the agricultural villages. Although the base of the national economy was still agriculture in the 1930's, state policy was primarily directed toward the fostering of industry. The increase in tenant farming has already been referred to, as has the struggle between the landlords and the tenants' associations. This gives one measure of the existing agricultural unrest, as well as an indication of its cause. It also stemmed from the increasing burden of debt of both tenants and landlords that resulted from a steady fall in the prices of agricultural products after 1926. Thus the Bank of Japan reported that the index figure for three of Japan's most important agricultural products, rice, wheat, and raw silk, fell from 100 in 1926 to 45.5 at the low point in 1931. In this period the gross income of the Japanese farmers was cut almost in half, with a corresponding increase in indebtedness. Meanwhile taxes increased and prices of non-agriculural products, where they did not actually increase, did not fall to the same extent as agricultural prices.

These conditions produced a movement toward organization in agriculture beyond that represented by the tenants' leagues formed to act against the landlords. Coöperatives, which had a membership of 5.5 million in 1935, established themselves as a factor in Japanese life. But their political influence was less than their numbers would imply because of a continuation of the old feudal psychology, and also on account of the great respect for authority which still operated to restrain the expression of dissatisfaction. There was, however, sufficient expression of dissatisfaction through these channels and those of the labor organizations to indicate an approaching social crisis. New forces were stirring under the surface of Japanese life.

2. THE ARMY RESUMES THE LEADERSHIP

It took an old force, however, to bring about action based upon these dissatisfactions. This old force was the Army and, to a lesser extent, the Navy. These two services had long been dominated by the Choshu and Satsuma Clans respectively, especially the former. Their control had been exerted through the monopolization of the higher directive positions. But, after World War I, a new element began to work its way to the top. As death or resignation eliminated the older leaders their places were taken

by those, hitherto subordinated, who came from the originally less influential clans. Their connections were with the smaller land-owners and
the lower middle class elements in Japanese society. "Between 1920 and
1927, 30 per cent of the new officers came from families of small land-
owners, rich farmers and lower middle classes in urban areas, and this
percentage steadily increased. Their background led these young officers
to oppose the effects of monopoly capitalism, while their personal interests
led them to challenge the positions held in the army by the older conservative clan generals," [4] who were, however, already being displaced by those
who sympathized with the newer point of view. "By 1930 this middle group
of officers, including Generals Muto, Araki, Mazaki and Hayashi, began to
gain control of the Supreme War Council." [5]

From the standpoint of the background influence, it must be recognized
that it was confirmed and strengthened by reason of the fact that the conscript system constantly brought young men into the Army and Navy who
were recruited from the classes which had been most seriously affected
by economic conditions. They were, consequently, ripe for the propaganda
which began to be circulated attacking the alliance between government
and business, emphasizing the corruption in politics which had grown out
of this relationship, and weakening respect, already slight, for the parties
and those affiliated with them.

The fact that there was a personal interest back of this propaganda, and
back of the tolerance of "patriotic" societies, of a terroristic inclination so
far as their methods were concerned, which began to multiply, should not
be allowed to obscure the underlying motivation. This was a real concern
for the welfare of the state. The patriot could not help but feel that there
was something wrong in view of the implication of high-placed public
officials in "scandals," not all of which were brought into the light. The
advance to control of the younger element in the Army was also facilitated
by the implication in these affairs of the higher-placed officers, and by the
knowledge of their willingness to attach themselves to the industrialists for
their own gain. Thus there was a basis for a propaganda of a patriotic
and appealing sort.

The personal interest to which reference was made is to be found in the
decreasing emphasis put on the Army and Navy in the budgets of the years
after 1922. On the side of the naval expenditures, the Washington Conference agreements gave a legitimate excuse for non-expansion. This
limitation through international agreements was extended by means of
the London agreements of 1930, ratification of which by the Diet was
strongly opposed by the younger elements in the Navy. Both agreements

[4] *F. P. R.*, vol. 10, No. 25, p. 320.
[5] *Ibid.*

were entered into by party governments which were also responsible for the consequent reductions of appropriations.

✗   The same thing threatened to happen to military appropriations. Part of the program of the Minseito government involved balancing the budget without a resort to further loans. Naval expenditures had already been stabilized on the basis of international agreements. Internal conditions precluded a reduction of expenditure for relief and other internal civil purposes. Taxes were already high. The best opportunity for retrenchment was presented in the military budget. Reduction there could be further justified on account of the negotiations which were being conducted looking toward the general reduction of armament. These movements, in other words, pointed toward contraction of the defensive services. This would mean a limitation of opportunity for advancement on the part of those already in the Army or Navy, and thus handicap those ambitious to go forward in their chosen profession.

These motives of interest and of patriotism could be most readily fused in relation to foreign policy. From the nationalist standpoint a case could be made out satisfactorily against the "weak" foreign policy which had been pursued by the parties since the Washington Conference. From 1929–1931 strong pressure was brought to bear on the government to act positively in defense of Japanese interests in Manchuria, threatened by the policies of the Chinese nationalists. This gave a focal point for the anti-government propaganda which, inspired by the Army leaders, was circulated through the medium of the various "patriotic" societies. An indication of what was to come was given with the assassination by a "patriot" of Premier Hamaguchi in 1930. It began to be argued that Japan's economic dilemma might be resolved by the pursuit of a strong Manchurian policy. But, it was also argued, that could be accomplished only if control was resumed by the Army as the only disinterested, uncorrupted force in Japanese life. Under its auspices Manchuria might be exploited in the interest of the nation and not of a few capitalists. This argument, in turn, pointed the way to the conclusion that Japan itself would be better off if the Army returned to control, administering the state in the interest of the people instead of the politicians and their capitalist allies.

Thus the way was paved for the military usurpation of power in and after 1931. In a sense, of course, this was not usurpation. The power of decision rested finally and exclusively with the Emperor. The Ministers of War and Marine had a direct access to him as advisers which was not possessed by the other Ministers. His acceptance of their advice instead of that of the Cabinet was sufficient to give legal validity to what would otherwise have been revolutionary action. This was done at first, as far as actions taken on the continent were concerned, as an acceptance of the accomplished fact. Similarly, since the government was not in a position effectively to control the Army, marking out for it the lines of action to be taken and keeping it within those lines, both government and nation rallied in defense of what had already been done, while seeking to prevent further unauthorized action. Furthermore, the Army propaganda at home was immediately intensified and the terroristic "patriotic" societies made it dangerous for dissent to be expressed even by high-placed officers of government. Under the pressure of constant attack, both verbal and physical, the Minseito government weakened and finally fell. Its fall represented a victory for the Army policy of expansion in Manchuria and also an initial reaction of the Manchurian policy on Japanese domestic politics.

3. THE MANCHURIAN QUESTION REOPENED

The Washington Conference had seemed to put a period to the aggressive policy which had been pursued by Japan toward China after 1905, a policy which apparently had found its highest expression in the period 1915–1918. At Washington Japan not only had accepted the enlarged definition of the open door policy and agreed to apply it, but, together with the other interested states, had also specifically accepted the obligation to respect the independence and the territorial and administrative integrity of China. Previously Japan, as a signatory of the League Covenant, had accepted the obligation to respect and preserve as against external aggression the independence and integrity of member states, as well as to attempt to settle disputes by arbitration, conciliation, or court judgment before resort to war. The Nine Powers Treaty, from this standpoint, had the effect of applying specifically to China the principles of Article 10 of the Covenant, reënforcing the Covenant obligation as applicable to China. Also Japan, as one of the nine Powers, agreed not to take advantage of the existing political situation in China to advance her own interests when it was agreed to allow China the fullest and most unembarrassed opportunity to work out her own political solutions. Furthermore, the Shantung Treaty liquidated the Shantung question, and a possibility of future trouble seemed removed when the Japanese delegation at Washington withdrew as a subject of future negotiation the fifth group of the 1915 Demands.

All of this, together with the termination of the Anglo-Japanese Alliance and the Lansing-Ishii Agreement, seemed to indicate the inauguration of a new era in international relations in the Far East. The atmosphere within which the relations of Japan and the United States were conducted was certainly changed for the better until after the enactment of Japanese exclusion in 1924. And there seemed to be no reason why Sino-Japanese hostility should not be succeeded by Sino-Japanese friendship.

A qualification would have to be put on the last statement, however, in the interest of accuracy. It was made clear at Washington that Japan was determined to maintain her position in Manchuria, even though no attempt should be made to extend it, since she expressly refused to consider the abrogation of the 1915 treaties which extended the railway and appurtenant concessions and the period of the lease of the Kwantung territory to 99 years and gave to Japanese the right to acquire land by lease for agricultural purposes in Manchuria. In the insistence by Japan on the validity of the 1915 treaties while Chinese governments refused to regard them as in force lay the possibility of future trouble.

On the whole, with the exception of the years 1927–1929, when the Tanaka government was in power in Japan, the China policy of the Japanese government after the Washington Conference was one of conciliation. Thus the conclusion seemed warranted that the peace of the Far East would not soon be disturbed by Japan and that Sino-Japanese relations would be characterized by an increasing friendliness.

Support for this conclusion could be found in other than the concrete evidences given of the desire to promote friendly relations. It has been alleged, with justification, that Japanese imperialism was directly related to and was in a measure an outgrowth of the control exercised over the Japanese government by the Army and the Navy. But the tendency in Japanese politics after 1922, as already pointed out, had been toward the establishment of the political parties in control of the government and toward the more effective control of the Army and Navy by the Cabinet. A new balance of political forces seemed to be shaping.

Furthermore, the economic position of Japan, complicated by the postwar depression and the disaster of the earthquake of 1923, was not strong, so that foreign adventuring seemed to be out of the question. A correct reading of the economic necessities of the country led to the conclusion that the primary Japanese interest must be in markets. The two important foreign markets for Japanese goods were China and the United States, and their security seemed to depend on the pursuit of a conciliatory policy toward China. As the Japanese Foreign Minister, Baron Shidehara, put it in 1927: "It is . . . of the utmost importance for us to concentrate our attention and energy on the promotion of foreign trade, without unjust infringement upon the interests of any nation. It is not territory, but markets, that we have in view. It is not alliances, but economic solidarity, that we seek in our foreign relations." [6] A Japan thinking in terms of the China market rather than in terms of control of raw materials and mineral resources was bound to follow a policy of conciliation of the customer.

The Shidehara policy was revealed in the willingness to negotiate with China, without coercion, over the revision of the treaties. It was revealed

[6] Quoted in Foreign Policy Association, Information Service, vol. 6, no. 16, p. 281.

in the willingness to reach a reasonable settlement of the Nanking and Tsinan affairs, the latter of which resulted from the shift back to the old "strong" policy during the Tanaka period of control.

But that reversion in itself was significant of the strength of old attitudes. Furthermore, throughout the entire period, there was a constant tendency in Japan to distinguish the country's Manchurian from its Chinese policy. The interest in Manchuria was deep-rooted and was based upon an interest in resources rather than in markets. It remained a question as to whether, in case of necessity, the market would be sacrificed to the maintenance of the rights which had been acquired in Manchuria from Russia at considerable cost, and which had been carefully consolidated and extended after 1905.

At the risk of antagonizing the customers in China proper the nationalist armies had been prevented from following Chang Tso-lin into Manchuria in 1928, and his son and successor, Chang Hsüeh-liang, had been warned against accepting the authority of Nanking. Much earlier, in 1923, at the same risk, the Japanese government had responded unfavorably to the suggestion of the Peking government that since the original period of the lease of the Kwantung territory had expired negotiations should be instituted looking toward its restoration to China. The same response had been made to a request for the turning over to China of the Mukden-Antung Railway, the period of the fifteen-year concession having also been reached in 1923. In both cases the Japanese stand was taken on the validity of the 1915 treaties.

In other words, it had been made clear that the Japanese government was determined to maintain the rights acquired in Manchuria for the 99 year period, no matter what the effect of this determination should be on Sino-Japanese relations. The reason for this determination is to be found in the conception, which had become fixed in Japanese thinking, that Manchuria was economically indispensable not merely to the well-being, but even to the continued existence of Japan. This view was based upon the apparent need of control of the coal and iron and other resources of Manchuria by an industrialized Japan.

The policies pursued by China, however, tended to make precarious the Japanese position. The expression of the desire to recover lost rights was by no means restricted to the region south of the Great Wall. During the period of control by Chiang Tso-lin the relations of Japan with the Manchurian administration were on the whole satisfactory to Japan. But even during this period incidents occurred to mar the friendly relations of the two countries. They indicated that it was only a recognition of the superior power of Japan which prevented these incidents from developing into attempts to eliminate the Japanese influence. Chang Tso-lin's activities were directed rather toward the elimination of Russian influence in north-ern Manchuria than against Japan. And his attempts to make untenable the Russian position in 1926 were repeated by Chiang Hsüeh-liang, with the encouragement and support of Nanking, in 1928. It was not unreasonable for the Japanese to feel that the same policy would be followed in southern Manchuria as soon as the Chinese felt strong enough, and that success in dealing with Moscow would be an incitement to adopt the same tactics against Japan. This would explain the policy Japan pursued in 1929 of non-protest against the methods employed by Russia, including the use of force, to reëstablish administrative control of the Chinese Eastern Railway.

Furthermore, it must be recognized that the time factor worked to strengthen the Chinese position, and consequently to weaken that of Japan; unless, of course, the Chinese could be brought to accept and to apply in good faith the Manchurian treaties of 1915. In the first place, the numerical disparity between the Japanese and Chinese in Manchuria was constantly increasing. The Chinese population had been increasing rapidly during the decade from 1921 to 1931 by migration from the northern provinces of China proper, and especially from Shantung province. The movement into Manchuria had been stimulated by the civil wars in north China, and by recurrent famine conditions, but it would have unquestionably occurred, although perhaps on a restricted scale, in any event. The significant thing, however, from the point of view of the struggle for control of the region, was that the land itself was being literally taken over by the Chinese peasants, without a corresponding infiltration of Japanese settlers. Thus by 1930 the population figures stood at about 29 millions, only some 250,000 of whom were Japanese, with about 800,000 Koreans, and 100,000 Russians. The remainder, except for a small number of Manchus, Mongols, and other "native" peoples, were Chinese. Thus the longer the time which elapsed before the decisive struggle for control, the more difficult it would be for the Japanese to maintain themselves against the constantly enlarging Chinese population.

One factor which militated against the enlargement of the Japanese population was their inability to secure land for agricultural purposes. The attempt had been made to remedy this weakness in their position in 1915 by demanding the right to purchase land. In place of this, the Chinese had conceded the right to acquire land by lease. But the attempts which had been made to apply this agreement of 1915 had been, on the whole, un-successful due to impediments put by the Chinese authorities in the way of consummating leasing agreements. Constant friction resulted from the attempts made by Japan to overcome the reluctance of the Chinese to put into operation this provision. The lack of pioneering qualities of the Japanese farmer, however, together with his inability to compete successfully with Chinese and Korean farmers, also served to explain the fact that Chinese rather than Japanese, were taking possession of the region which Japan aspired to control.

The irony of the situation lay in the fact that the Japanese railway facilitated the movement of Chinese into Manchuria, and the efforts made through the South Manchurian Railway enterprises to improve the crop production of the region helped to attract Chinese to Manchuria as a land of plenty.

Another way in which time served to strengthen the Chinese position was that it enabled a program of railway construction to be carried through which, when completed, would have the effect of weakening the commercial value of the South Manchurian line and lessening its effectiveness as an instrument of economic penetration. For some time Japan had been successful in preventing the construction of railways in southern Manchuria by prohibiting the use of non-Japanese foreign capital for the purpose. The Japanese government alleged that China had agreed not to construct with foreign capital lines parallel to or competitive with the South Manchurian Railway.[7] In the period of Anfu control at Peking, however, Japanese funds had been made available for the construction of certain lines which it was to the interest of the South Manchurian Railway to have constructed in order to drain the produce of northern Manchuria out through Dairen rather than Vladivostok. Subsequently these loans were defaulted, the failure to make payment being justified by the Chinese on the ground of the political character of the loans. Since they, together with the other so-called Nishihara loans of 1917, were unsecured, the Japanese were left without any redress except that which might be afforded through a change of attitude on the part of the Chinese government.

Of even greater importance were the construction of a separate Chinese railway system in the region that was previously served exclusively by the South Manchurian Railway, and also the attempt to connect the Sino-Japanese railways with the Chinese rather than the Japanese system. That the Chinese efforts along the line of railway construction had not been unsuccessful is indicated in the fact that "by September, 1931, the Chinese had built unaided and were owning and operating railways with a total length of nearly a thousand kilometers. . . . During the two years preceding the outbreak of the present conflict, the Chinese attempted to operate these various lines as a great Chinese railway system and made efforts to route all freight, if possible, exclusively over the Chinese-operated lines, with a seaboard exit at the Chinese port of Yingkow (Newchwang)—potentially

[7] As to the existence and nature of this agreement see L. of N., Appeal of the Chinese Government, *Report of the Commission of Enquiry* (VII. Political 1932. VII. 12), pp. 44–45.

at Hulutao. As a result, the Chinese made through-traffic arrangements for all parts of their railway system and refused in important sections to make similar traffic agreements between their lines and the South Manchurian system. The Japanese claimed that this discrimination deprived the South Manchurian Railway of much freight from North Manchuria which would normally pass over at least a part of its line and would find an outlet at Dairen."[8] Thus the Chinese railway policy was designed ultimately to make less valuable and even untenable the Japanese position in Manchuria. These and related railway questions were productive of much friction between the two countries.

One of these related questions was that of the maintenance of railway guards in the South Manchurian Railway zone. The Chinese contested the Japanese interpretation of the provision in the South Manchurian Railway concession granting "the absolute and exclusive right of administration" of the zone as establishing a treaty right to maintain therein railway guards. But in any case, the mere presence of Japanese troops in the midst of the Chinese population of southern Manchuria was certain to be a constant source of friction.

The theoretical unification of China under the auspices of the Kuomintang did not serve to lessen the tension in Manchuria. The fact that the Japanese interposed a barrier of troops in Shantung which prevented the movement north of the armies of Chiang Kai-shek, and the resulting clash at Tsinanfu in 1928 revived the latent anti-Japanese feeling of the Chinese. When this was followed by the Japanese declaration, when Chang Tso-lin seemed to be threatened with defeat, that Japan's special interests in Manchuria made it necessary for her to maintain peace and order in the Three Eastern Provinces, Chinese antagonism was strengthened. And when, in pursuance of this policy the Japanese government notified the leading Chinese generals that the Nationalists might not complete the unification of the country by carrying the struggle against Chang Tso-lin into Manchuria, while allowing him, with his defeated troops, to retire north of the Great Wall,[9] the Nationalist government could only reply, as did also the still existent Peking government, that the application of this policy would be not only "an interference with Chinese domestic affairs, but also a flagrant violation of the principle of mutual respect for territorial sovereignty." Certainly, this clear and unequivocal expression of the sphere of interest conception could only provoke the resentment of those whose thinking was based upon the

---

[8] Lytton Commission, *Report, op. cit.,* pp. 47–48.

[9] The declaration stated that unless Chang retired peacefully from Peking, his troops would not be permitted to reënter Manchuria. But when he refused to retire and his troops retreated toward Manchuria they were permitted to enter but the Nationalists were not allowed to follow them.

premises of nationalism. It was equally certain that the conclusion would be drawn that complete national unity could be attained only as the special position of Japan in Manchuria was terminated.

When Chang Hsüeh-liang succeeded his father in control of the Three Eastern Provinces the region was brought under the authority of Nanking by voluntary agreement with the young Marshal, but in the face of the strong advice against union tendered by the Japanese government. Administrative autonomy was retained but the direction of foreign affairs and matters of national interest was transferred to Nanking. Thus, while previously the Japanese had been able to negotiate concerning Manchurian questions directly with the Mukden government, after the Nationalist banner was hoisted at Mukden the government insisted that all questions of foreign relations must be discussed through the Foreign Office of the National government. That government was less amenable to direct pressures than the Mukden government had been, and it was even less inclined toward a settlement of questions at issue, except on its own terms, than had been the government of Chang Tso-lin.

During this most difficult period, when nationalism in the sense of anti-imperialism was the point of emphasis in China, and when the Powers were being brought to a more conciliatory attitude than ever before, being put strictly on the defensive in their dealings with China, the Japanese government was headed by Baron Tanaka. His government reverted to the "strong" policy of pre-war days just when that could only intensify and embitter national sentiment in China. Unquestionably, the Tanaka policy, with its emphasis on the special position of Japan in Manchuria, strengthened the determination of Chinese nationalists to recover the "lost rights" in Manchuria as rapidly as possible.

Attention was temporarily diverted toward Russia in 1929, and a primary emphasis was also put on treaty revision. But when the national tariff was put into effect, and an advance had been made toward the recovery of jurisdictional rights, after 1929 more attention began to be paid to Japan in southern Manchuria. Thereafter antagonism steadily increased and "incidents" multiplied. Kuomintang organizers were sent into Manchuria to preach the doctrines of nationalism. "Such propaganda was bound to make a profound impression in Manchuria, where the reality of foreign interests, courts, police, guards or soldiers on Chinese soil, was apparent. Through the Nationalist school-books, party propaganda entered the schools. Associations such as the Liaoning Peoples' Foreign Policy Association made their appearance. They stimulated and intensified the nationalist sentiment and carried on an anti-Japanese agitation." [10]

[10] Lytton Commission, *Report, op. cit.,* p. 30.

As anti-Japanese feeling increased, and with it action directed against individual Japanese, so did, correspondingly, the Japanese determination strengthen to maintain the position which they regarded as essential to their economic well-being. Fuel was added to the flame in the summer of 1931 on account of the Wanpaoshan and Nakamura cases, which were directly contributory to the September outbreak. The first involved Koreans [11] who had leased from a Chinese company land which it had leased from the original Chinese owners. The original lease stipulated that its validity depended upon the approval of its terms by the district magistrate. This approval was not obtained before the signature of the second leasing agreement, the validity of which, however, was not made dependent on approval. The success of the Korean venture was dependent upon irrigation of the land. The Koreans immediately set about the construction of the necessary ditches and dam. This aroused the hostility of neighboring Chinese land-owners not parties to either lease agreement. After a period of negotiation the Chinese farmers drove the Koreans away. Japanese consular police came to the aid of the Koreans and took control of the area while the Koreans completed their work. The various encounters resulted in no casualties on either side, but sensational accounts were published both in Korea and Japan, with anti-Chinese riots occurring in Korea and Japan as a result. These aroused Chinese opinion, just as the accounts of the original series of incidents had inflamed opinion in Korea and Japan. Negotiations over the questions involved were instituted but agreement had not been finally reached by September, 1931.

The Nakamura case came as the culmination of the series of "incidents" which had embittered Chinese-Japanese feeling during 1930 and 1931. It was especially important in its effects on Japanese opinion because it involved an officer of the Japanese Army. Captain Nakamura was killed by Chinese soldiers "in an out-of-the-way region in Manchuria" in June, 1931. Although a Japanese military officer on active duty, on a mission under the orders of the Japanese Army, he represented himself to the Chinese authorities at Harbin, who examined his passport, to be an agricultural expert. Consequently his exact character and position were only subsequently revealed to the Chinese authorities. Nevertheless "the Japanese insisted that the killing of Captain Nakamura and his companions was unjustified and showed arrogant disrespect for the Japanese Army and nation; they asserted that the Chinese authorities in Manchuria delayed to institute official enquiries into the circumstances, were reluctant to assume responsibility for the occurrence, and were insincere in their claim that they were making every effort to ascertain the facts in

[11] The status of Koreans in Manchuria is discussed in the Lytton *Report, op. cit.,* pp. 55–63.

the case." [12] The Chinese asserted, on their side, that Captain Nakamura had been detained pending an examination of his passport, which he and all foreigners were required to carry during travel in the interior; that he was shot by a sentry while trying to escape; and that documents found on him proved that he was either a military spy or an officer on a special military mission. But regardless of the facts, his death had a tremendous effect in inflaming Japanese opinion, and it strengthened the feeling which had long been held in Army circles that a strong policy must be followed toward China if Japan was to maintain her position. Thus it prepared the way for the military reaction to the "incident" of September 18.

"By the end of August, 1931, therefore, Sino-Japanese relations over Manchuria were severely strained in consequence of the many controversies and incidents described in this chapter. [13] The claim that there were 300 cases outstanding between the two countries and that peaceful methods for settling each of them had been progressively exhausted by one of the parties cannot be substantiated. These so-called 'cases' were rather situations arising out of broader issues, which were rooted in fundamentally irreconcilable policies. Each side accused the other of having violated, unilaterally interpreted, or ignored the stipulations of the Sino-Japanese agreements. Each side had legitimate grievances against the other.

"In the course of September, public sentiment regarding the Chinese questions, with the Nakamura case as the focal point, became very strong. Time and again the opinion was expressed that the policy of leaving so many issues in Manchuria unsettled had caused the Chinese authorities to make light of Japan. Settlement of all pending issues, if necessary by force, became a popular slogan. Reference was freely made in the Press to a decision to resort to armed forces, to conferences between the Ministry of War, the General Staff and other authorities for the discussion of a plan with this object. . . ." [14]

It is only if the incident of September 18 is placed in relation to the constantly growing feeling in Japan and China, and especially in Manchuria, that subsequent developments can be understood. The incident was the destruction by bomb explosion of a portion of one of the rails of the South Manchurian line. The damage done was not serious in itself, but the consequences were far-reaching. The Japanese claimed that the bomb had been set by Chinese soldiers. This was denied by the Chinese. Whatever the facts with respect to and responsibility for the explosion, the result was the initial occupation of Mukden and its environs by Japanese

[12] Lytton Commission, *Report, op. cit.,* p. 64; the facts are completely summarized on pp. 63–66.

[13] Cf. the *Report.*

[14] *Report,* as cited, p. 66.

troops, and the gradual elimination of Chinese military and civil authority from Manchuria. This had been substantially accomplished by the end of 1931.

4. THE MANCHURIAN CRISIS

Meanwhile, the Chinese government had immediately appealed to the League of Nations, invoking Article 11 of the Covenant. The Council being in session, it was able without delay to begin a consideration of the problem. By September 30 it had reached an agreement on the terms of a Resolution, voted unanimously, including the disputants, which provided for the evacuation, as rapidly as circumstances permitted, of the limited area then under Japanese occupation. The qualification was accepted apparently because of the desire to avoid the appearance of putting undue pressure on Japan, and because the Japanese insisted that they could withdraw their troops only as assurance was given of protection of their properties against the activities of bandits, who had become more active as Chinese control had been weakened. However, when the Council reconvened in October, it was found that the Japanese occupation had been extended rather than restricted in accordance with the September agreement. At this time, although not by unanimous vote since Japan objected, a Resolution was adopted which reaffirmed the necessity of withdrawal of the Japanese forces within the railway zone, and set a time limit within which the movement should have been carried toward completion. When the Council reconvened at Paris in November it was confronted with the situation created by a further extension of the occupation, rather than by an attempt at fulfillment of the terms of the governing Resolution [15] of September 30, to say nothing of the more peremptory October Resolution. At the next session of the Council, on December 10, it was decided to establish a Commission of Inquiry to conduct an investigation on the spot into conditions in Manchuria and in China in so far as conditions there bore on the Manchurian dispute. At this time the Japanese agreed, pending the report of the Commission, not to aggravate further the situation by moving to eliminate the Chinese authority from Chinchow, which alone remained outside the field of Japanese control. Chinchow, however, was occupied by force of arms by January 3, 1932.

During this period of negotiation at Geneva the Japanese government had not only been extending the occupation, but it had shifted its diplomatic position. Having first agreed to withdraw its troops as rapidly as the unsettled condition in Manchuria permitted, it thereafter insisted that it would only withdraw after an agreement had been reached with the

---

[15] This first Resolution established the controlling principles because it had been voted unanimously.

Chinese government as to the principles to be applied to a settlement of the various questions at issue between the two countries. The Chinese insisted, however, on the withdrawal of the Japanese troops as the necessary antecedent to the institution of negotiations.

The Chinese reaction to the situation, other than that represented by the appeal to Geneva, was the institution, after the Wanpaoshan affair, of a boycott of Japanese goods. The effectiveness of this boycott is indicated in the fact that Japanese exports to China declined from the September, 1931, figure of yen 12,706,000 to the December, 1931, figure of yen 4,299,000. [16] The serious consequences to Japan of this loss of a primary market are readily apparent. In consequence, in January, 1932, Japanese warships were sent to Shanghai, rightly considered to be the center of the boycott organization, to attempt to break Chinese resistance. The institution of the boycott was declared, then and subsequently, by Japan to be an act of aggression directed by China against Japan, which could only have serious consequences from the standpoint of the preservation of peace between the two countries.

This attempt to break the boycott by force turned attention temporarily from Manchuria to Shanghai. The Chinese resistance which developed proved to be stronger than the Japanese could have anticipated, with the result that they became ever more deeply involved. Ultimately they were glad to attempt to liquidate the Shanghai affair by negotiations which were conducted under international auspices and supervision. An armistice agreement was finally reached, May 5, 1932, and the Japanese troops were withdrawn from Shanghai.

Meanwhile there had been certain other developments with respect to Manchuria. On January 7, 1932, the American Secretary of State, Mr. Stimson, announced it to be the policy of his government not to recognize gains made or changes accomplished as a result of the employment of methods proscribed under such international instruments as the Kellogg-Briand Pact for the renunciation of war as an instrument of national policy. This represented a distinct American initiative in contrast with the policy previously pursued of lending support to the efforts made at Geneva to settle the difficulty.

In March the entire dispute was transferred from the Council to the Assembly of the League. The Assembly constituted a Commission of Nineteen to follow developments. [17] It reaffirmed the validity of the Covenant principles and the Council Resolutions and took over the problem of consideration of the report of the Commission of Inquiry, which had been duly constituted and was then conducting its investigation in

[16] Figures given in GROVER CLARK, *Economic Rivalries in China*, p. 109.
[17] Immediately concerning itself with the situation at Shanghai.

the Far East. And it accepted the Stimson Doctrine of non-recognition for application by the League states with respect to violations of the Covenant.[18]

5. THE NEW STATE—MANCHUKUO

Another important development in the spring of 1932 had been maturing during the entire period of the Japanese occupation. This was the establishment of a new state, independent of China, which proclaimed its existence on February 18, 1932. Parallel to the driving out of the régime of Chiang Hsüeh-liang, stated to be a major Japanese objective, there had proceeded the organization of local government in the regions under Japanese control. These were finally coördinated into the new state, which called itself Manchukuo. Its territories were defined to include all of the Three Eastern Provinces of China and the province of Jehol. Control of the latter province, however, was not gained until the spring of 1933, at which time military operations were undertaken there and the Chinese forces and officials were driven out after an ineffective resistance to the advance of the Japanese armies.

On March 4, 1932, the deposed Emperor of China, known after the abdication in 1912 as Mr. Henry Pu Yi, accepted the headship of the new state, with the title of Regent. On March 9 an Organic Law was promulgated which, with a Guarantee Law of Civil Rights, provided the first constitution of Manchukuo. This Organic Law vested supreme executive authority in the Regent and provided for executive, legislative, judicial, and supervisory departments to act under his direction. The government thus created absorbed all of the powers exercised previously by the provincial governments and the central government of China, together with the control of the maritime customs and the salt gabelle, in this latter field infringing upon foreign administrative rights.

Japan recognized the new state on September 15, 1932. This recognition had the virtual effect of serving notice on the world that Japan would not accept any solution of the Manchurian question which involved even a partial restoration of the *status quo ante*. Fearing this consequence, an unsuccessful attempt had been made to keep the Japanese government from decisively committing itself to the preservation of the new state until after the (Lytton) Commission of Inquiry had presented its report to the League Assembly. The Report itself was signed at Peking on September 4, 1932. On all of the major points involved it found against Japan, but it made recommendations for settlement which if accepted would have strengthened rather than weakened the position of Japan in Manchuria as that position had existed in 1930. The report and the recom-

[18] The basis of action was also shifted from Article 11 of the Covenant to Article 15.

mendations, however, were unacceptable to the Japanese government. A short time after their adoption by the Assembly, on February 17, 1933, Japan formally gave notice of intention to withdraw from the League of Nations.

The effect of the events of the years 1931–1933 may be summarized at this point. China's authority had been definitely eliminated from Manchuria. The Chinese government had not, however, recognized this change as permanent through any treaty or other ratification. Not only did Manchukuo remain unrecognized by the Nanking government, but the governments of the United States and the states members of the League of Nations continued to follow the principle of non-recognition as defined by the American Secretary of State. Thus the permanence of status that results from recognition had not been attained.

But China was not the only state, other than Japan, which had vested rights and an important position in Manchuria. The Russian position in north Manchuria had been affected by the establishment of Manchukuo in somewhat the same fashion as had the Chinese. The new state extended its boundaries to include the territory previously explicitly recognized by Japan as the Russian sphere of interest, and it assumed the Chinese rights in the Chinese Eastern Railway. Constant friction marked the relations of Russia and Japan during the period of extension of the authority of the new government over the Russian sphere. Conflict was avoided, however, largely because of the determination of the Soviet government not to be drawn into an undeclared war with Japan. A continuing source of friction existed, however, in the Russian interest in the railway. This had to be eliminated, by sale of the Chinese Eastern, before friendly relations between Japan and Russia could be restored. Furthermore, the very fact of Japan's control of northern as well as southern Manchuria brought the two countries face to face over a common frontier. This in itself augured a period of friction until frontier arrangements could be perfected by agreement acceptable to both parties.

6. INTERNAL REACTIONS ON JAPAN OF THE MANCHURIAN ADVENTURE

From the standpoint of Japan herself the Manchurian adventure had important domestic consequences. It had been initiated by the Kwantung Army leaders, who had thereupon received the support of the Army High Command in Japan. The government, presented with the accomplished fact of military action in Manchuria, had been compelled to assume responsibility for the actions of those whom, because of the peculiar features of the Japanese governmental system, it could not effectively control. At the same time, the Minseito government sought to reconcile the actions taken with Japan's obligations under the Covenant of the

League and under treaty provisions. This brought it under attack from two sides and led, as already stated, to its fall in December, 1931. That did not, however, have the result, anticipated by the Army extremists, of establishing a government "purified" of the corruptive party elements. The new government was formed, under advice of Prince Saionji, the last remaining "elder statesman," by the veteran Seiyukai leader, Tsuyoshi Inukai. Thus it involved party succession, rather than the assumption of internal political power by the "disinterested" Army leaders. Consequently it meant the retention of the objectionable party system. The Seiyukai, however, had always been an advocate of a "stronger" foreign policy than had the Minseito and thus could be expected to give more vigorous support to the Manchurian policy of the Army leaders. For that reason their reaction to its establishment must be thought of in domestic terms rather than in those of foreign relations.

Elections for the Diet were held in February, 1932, and, since it controlled the election machinery, a Seiyukai majority was returned to replace that of the Minseito. The struggle to overthrow the party system of government was, therefore, resumed. Even before the elections, on February 9, Inouye, former Finance Minister, was assassinated. About a month later Baron Dan, head of the Mitsui interests, was shot. According to police findings, other assassinations of politicians, financiers, and industrialists were planned. Finally, on May 15, Premier Inukai himself was killed and other terroristic acts occurred. Although disowned by the Army heads, all of these acts were planned and executed by organizations made up of young military and naval officers, students, and peasants who had been inflamed by the intense propaganda campaign which had been directed against party government and the capitalists. Furthermore, the real Army attitude was revealed in the method of conduct of the trials of the assassins and in the sentences imposed upon them. They were treated as unfortunate "patriots" rather than murderers. Their trial was, in essence, a public arraignment of the Western Powers who were opposing Japanese expansion. Those found guilty of the assassinations were given such light sentences that their terms were substantially covered by the time spent in jail during the period between the commission of the offense and the conclusion of the trial.

This time a non-party Cabinet, headed by Admiral Saito as a compromise candidate, was established. Although non-party it did include three representatives of the Seiyukai and two from the Minseito, thus making it partially acceptable to them. This compromise government, containing as its two important figures General Araki, the militant Army leader, as War Minister and Korekiyo Takahashi as Finance Minister, endured only until 1934 when it was overturned on account of a financial scandal in which the Vice-Minister of Finance was implicated. Under the circumstances this seemed to indicate a tendency to return to the less "pure" political atmosphere of the preceding decade. It did not, however, bring about an immediate return to the conditions of intensified struggle of the period from 1930–1932, possibly because the new Army leaders had begun to realize some of the advantages of the old type of relationship. For that reason a new Cabinet was readily constituted under Admiral Okada. Its policy was announced to be one of moderation, but it was well known that the new Premier was an ardent advocate of a strong navy. It was this navalist government which denounced the Washington Naval Limitation Treaties.

Relative calm thus reigned in the internal politics of Japan until the beginning of 1936. The new leaders of the Army and Navy had apparently reverted to the same type of alliance with the capitalist and party forces as that which had existed for two decades after 1900, and to which they had previously been making such strong objections. However, the elections which were held on February 20, 1936, and which seemed to augur a return to earlier conditions, represented the last of the calm before a new storm. As a result of the elections the Minseito regained its position as the leading party in the Diet with 205 members. The Seiyukai representation was reduced to 174; the Showakai, a fascist party, returned 20; the Kokumindome 15; labor 18; independents 25; and others 9.

The return of the Minseito to control of the Diet probably had something to do with the resumption of assassination as a political method. The threat of such direct action had, however, been constantly present during the preceding years. There had been no revulsion of popular feeling against the earlier assassins. The Army leaders had only reluctantly undertaken their trial and punishment, and had imposed on them what must be considered to be light sentences, which had, in many cases, been almost immediately suspended. The organizations whose members had been responsible for the assassinations had not been broken up nor had similar organizations been discouraged. The military-fascist organizations which emphasized essentially terrorist methods had, in total, large and influential memberships. Thus, although during 1934 and 1935 "there were no assassinations of prominent politicians such as had marked the previous two years, there was ample evidence, if not of the government's subservience to irresponsible elements from without, at least of their powerlessness to curb illegitimate political activities." [19] Thus the military authorities, now in power, who had ridden back into control on the wave of propaganda and of terrorism, having sowed the wind had to face the whirlwind of renewed assassination only six days after the elections. Admiral Viscount

[19] *Survey of International Affairs,* 1934, p. 641.

Makato Saito, Lord Keeper of the Privy Seal, Viscount Takahashi, who had only returned to the Cabinet as Finance Minister a short time before, and General Jotaro Watanabe were all killed by young Army officers. Premier Admiral Okada escaped death only by concealment and because of a mistake in identity.

This time the Emperor and the Army High Command took the matter more seriously. The former, in his address to the Diet, took the unprecedented step of making direct reference to the incident in the following terms: "We regret the incident that occurred in Tokyo in February. We expect our faithful subjects, the government and the people, civil and military, to unite as one man to advance the nation's well-being." [20] The military leaders showed their change of attitude in the rapidity with which a high military court was constituted and with which it proceeded to try those accused of participation. Instead of protracting or deferring the trial until public opinion subsided so that there would be acquiescence in the usual light sentences which had become customary, the court handed down sentences of death, without appeal, for the seventeen leaders of the revolt on July 7. All were Army officers. In addition, under Imperial direction the Military Councils and High Command were reorganized. Since the Army had regained control of policy there was every evidence given of an intention to prevent the repetition of such occurrences.

The government, of course, had to be reconstituted. As a candidate satisfactory to the Army and Navy, and also to the parties, the non-party Foreign Minister, Koki Hirota, was elevated to the premiership on March 9, 1936. His appointment was favorably received both at home and abroad, but it could not be taken to mean any change in the balance of forces in Japan, unless possibly as between the Army and the Navy. In the construction of his government, furthermore, the Army showed its strength by refusing to furnish a War Minister except after its terms had been met. Thus the new government meant no change in policy.

7. INTERNAL EFFECTS OF ARMY RULE: 1933–1936

Having been in virtual control of internal and foreign policy for a period of four years, had the new rulers made any material improvements in the conditions to which they had objected?

From the economic standpoint it must be recognized that the balance remained about as it had been. Agricultural conditions had not been materially improved, as is evidenced in the increase of the farm-debt total from an estimated 4,000 million to 4,800 million yen in 1932 to approximately 6,000 million in 1936. This contrasts with 2,182 million yen total farm income. There had been some government aid extended to agriculture, but

[20] *New York Times,* May 6, 1936.

it took the form of totally inadequate appropriations for relief purposes, of tariffs on imported foodstuffs, and of attempts at the regulation of domestic agricultural prices. One bright spot, however, was the success of the Five Year Wheat Plan, which increased wheat production by 60 per cent after 1932, making Japan independent of foreign supplies of wheat, as it virtually was in other items of its food supply. The value to the farmer of the fostered increase in wheat production was not, however, so much in terms of the resulting national self-sufficiency as on account of the fact that wheat was raised by the rice farmer as a supplementary crop, thus effecting a similar increase in his income to that derived from sericulture. The decline in farm income after 1930 resulted in part from an over-production in 1933, when there was a bumper crop, followed by an exceptionally poor year in 1934. The operation of the government stabilization system prevented the farmer from benefiting from the higher prices of the 1933 crop excess which the shortage of the next year brought. Decline in income also resulted from the reduction of the American demand for raw silk, which was a consequence of the depression. The development of the rayon industry, both at home and abroad, also affected the silk market. Since sericulture was one of the important supplementary rural occupations, the drop in the demand for and value of silk had extremely unfortunate effects for the Japanese farmers.

The expansion of Japan into Manchuria did not have the predicted effects in relieving the plight of Japanese agriculture. None of the announced plans of the Army leaders for extensive colonization, for example, had been put into successful operation. But, while not realizing any perceptible advantages, agriculturalists had to bear a disproportionate share of the increased expenditure which the Manchurian expansion entailed. Military-naval expenditures increased from 442.8 million yen in 1930–1931 to 937.3 million in 1934–1935. Further increases were made in the budget for 1935–1936, and still another increase was demanded for 1936–1937. Not all of these were a direct consequence of the occupation of Manchuria. The demand for naval increases, for example, was a consequence of the termination of the Naval Limitation Agreements. Nevertheless, either directly or indirectly, the increases were a result of the new rôle which Japan was insisting on playing in the Far East.

The proportion of the taxes paid by the farmers is revealed in the following figures: "In the annual income group of 300 yen, peasant proprietors paid 35 per cent in taxes, while manufacturers paid 1.5 and traders 12.5. In the 500 yen group, landlords paid 51, peasant proprietors 31.5, manufacturers 18 and traders 14 approximately." [21] Thus the mounting burden of taxation, which was on the "debit" side of the "strong" foreign policy

21 *Far Eastern Survey*, vol. 5, No. 1, p. 4.

of the past several years, fell most heavily on the farmer, who reaped few of the benefits.

Industry, on the other hand, showed a marked improvement after 1931. This cannot, however, be wholly, or perhaps even largely, ascribed to the positive foreign policy which was being pursued. A number of factors began to operate at about the same time to bring about a trade boom which continued through 1935, although beginning to slow down in 1936. One of these factors, unquestionably, was the military operations on the continent. This brought with it increased expenditures for military equipment, thus stimulating the heavy industry of the country. Control of the policies of Manchukuo enabled Japan to dominate the market there of thirty million people, supplying 64 per cent of Manchukuoan imports in 1934 in contrast with 42 per cent in 1929. This represented an increased proportion of a larger total trade than that of 1929. Japanese capital had been flowing into Manchuria for purposes of development of agriculture, industry and communications. This was an even more important factor in the increase of Japan's trade than the ability to exercise political control, although it goes without saying that, in this case, the two were intimately related reciprocally as cause and effect. At any rate, the stimulation of Japanese industry as a result of the new situation in Manchuria cannot be denied or overlooked.

On the other hand, there had also been a marked expansion of Japanese trade elsewhere after 1932, and on another basis than that represented by capital exports. This has already been referred to as an indication of the reversal of the trade relations of the East and West, and as a continuation of an earlier trend. Here it needs only to be pointed out that this trade boom, which carried Japan into what had formerly been Western markets, had brought her exports, by the end of 1935 somewhat above the 1929 level, as measured in yen and substantially above it in volume, although materially below the 1929 gold value as measured in dollars. Imports had also increased both in yen value and in volume. But it is significant that the trade in 1935 showed a favorable balance for the first time since World War I. Of even greater significance, in terms of the internal economy, was the fact that the imports had substantially changed their character, being mainly raw or semi-finished commodities, while the exports had shifted, in balance, to manufactured goods. Thus textiles, rather than raw silk, bulked largest in the export trade of the new Japan. In 1935 the volume of her cotton textile exports was 40 per cent greater than that of Great Britain. Japan had assumed the leading position in the import of textiles into British India and China. She virtually monopolized the market in the Netherlands Indies, and furnished 64 per cent of the total cotton textile imports into the Philippines. Her exports to Central America increased 500 per cent and to

South America more than 300 per cent, between 1931 and 1933. This expanded trade was maintained until 1936, by which time restrictions had been imposed by the Latin-American countries because of the resulting adverse trade balances. In eastern Asia 1936 saw a decrease in exports from both Japan and Great Britain. This marked a movement toward the restoration of the earlier position since the Japanese decline was much greater than the British.

This sudden trade boom is to be explained in terms of the operation of several different factors. One of these was the low wages paid to Japanese labor, which, at least in the case of textiles, had not been compensated for by an equally low productivity of Japanese labor. Second, the rationalization of Japanese industry after 1927 tremendously increased its competitive efficiency. Third, the organization of industry, under government auspices, for foreign trade purposes, and the constant increase in governmental efforts to open up new or to expand old markets, aided the expansion. And, fourth, the depreciation of the yen, which followed the removal of the gold embargo when the Minseito government, which had imposed it, fell, gave Japan a substantial, even if a temporary, advantage in the search for foreign markets. The first, second, and fourth of these factors operated collectively to enable Japan to supply goods at lower cost and thus to penetrate and then capture markets which had previously been exploited by European states or the United States. This was accomplished in a world of depression and of safeguards thrown by each state around its own markets.

Internally, the effect of the boom was to create an appearance of activity, if not of prosperity, which was somewhat belied by the fact that agriculture, comprising roughly half of the population, was unaffected, and that it did not carry with it any increase in the proportion of the national income received by industrial labor. In the main, in terms of business, it was large-scale enterprise that participated in this industrial expansion and benefited from it.

Externally it had the not unnatural effect of producing antagonism on the part of those who found their markets being invaded by the Japanese. Considerable friction in Anglo-Japanese relations, growing out of commercial considerations, marked the years after 1932. Canada and Japan found themselves engaged also in a trade dispute, carried on by mutually retaliatory methods, which had been compromised rather than finally settled at the beginning of 1936. In order to keep up her markets Japan began to insist that Australia, from whom she was a large purchaser, should take increased amounts of Japanese goods. So 1936 found Japan and Australia engaged in negotiations, with Great Britain interested in their outcome, since increased Australian purchases from Japan would necessarily mean a restriction of the market for Britain. The United States joined the list of those feeling the pressure of Japanese trade expansion in 1935, with American businessmen protesting that Japanese goods were entering into competition in the home market as well as in the Philippines and other territories of interest to the United States. Thus this development of trade in the period under review accentuated the antagonism to Japan in the industrial states of the West which had been aroused by the Army policies on the continent of Asia. In estimating this antagonism, however, it must be realized that the search for markets was an inescapable corollary of the industrialization of Japan and the attempt to solve the population problem of that country by that means. It must also be recognized that the restrictive trade policies increasingly emphasized by the Western states and China stimulated the use by Japan of political means to safeguard its overseas economic interests.

8. JAPAN IN MANCHUKUO

The most marked changes resulting from the Manchurian crisis, actually the accentuation of earlier tendencies, were, however, made in the continental position of Japan. The establishment of Manchukuo as an "independent" but highly protected and strongly advised dependency of Japan has already been referred to as the first fruit of the ascendency of the Army. The position then won had to be consolidated thereafter.

Japan's control over Manchukuo was exhibited and exercised in several different ways. The General Affairs Board, the policy-determining agency within the Manchukuoan State Council, was dominated by Japanese officials. The key administrative positions under the heads of the ten administrative departments, who were non-Japanese, were all held by Japanese subjects. In the filling of subordinate civil service positions, also, the tendency was to increase rather than decrease the proportion of Japanese to Manchurians. At the end of 1936, "taking the administrative branches of the government as a whole, including the provincial offices, the tendency was to approximate a ratio of 40 per cent Manchurians to 60 per cent Japanese in the three upper grades of the Civil Service." [22] In the lowest grade there was an approximate equality in 1936 in contrast with the situation in 1933, when there were 1,547 "Manchurians" as against only 740 Japanese. These Japanese administrators were technically, of course, officers of the Manchukuoan and not of the Japanese government. Nevertheless they took their direction from and were expected to serve the purposes of the latter.

The direct authority of Japan was represented by: (1) the Governor of the Kwantung Leased Territory, who had civil jurisdiction in the territory, control of the police in the Territory and in the Railway Zone, and a meas-

[22] T. A. BISSON, *Japan in China*, p. 367.

ure of direction of the administration of the South Manchurian Railway; (2) the Commander-in-chief of the Kwantung Army; (3) the South Manchurian Railway, which conducted various enterprises of a civic character within the Railway Zone; and (4) the consular officers scattered through the country, exercising extra-territorial authority over Japanese subjects. In addition, an Ambassador was appointed to Hsinking, the new Manchukuoan capital, on October 1, 1932. In and after 1932, however, all of these various authorities, who sometimes came into conflict, were brought under one head: the Commander-in-chief of the Kwantung Army being appointed concurrently the Governor of the Leased Territory and the Ambassador to Manchukuo. This had the effect of extending the authority of the Japanese Army itself over the civil advisers and administrators and thus over the government of Manchukuo. Consequently, the complete monopoly of power which the military had sought, but had gained only in part, in Japan was actually acquired in Manchukuo.[23] This had important consequences in the development of the region.

The policy of the new state toward Japan and Japanese interests was defined in a Protocol of September 15, 1932. In this agreement all of the rights and interests claimed by Japan in Manchuria on the basis of treaties with China, including those of 1915 as well as all private and public contracts and concessions, were recognized. In return, Japan assumed responsibility for the defense of Manchukuo and for the maintenance of peace and order in the new state. This gave her an unquestioned right of military action within the state in addition to the general direction which her participation in civil administration gave her in the field of domestic and foreign policy. To all intents, it brought Manchukuo into the Japanese imperial system as a protectorate.

So far as non-Japanese rights and interests in Manchukuo were concerned, the new government, on March 14, 1932, defined its policy as follows in a note addressed to seventeen foreign states:

(1) to conduct its foreign relations according to principles of faith, harmony, justice, peace, and international law; (2) "to succeed to those obligations incurred by the Republic of China by virtue of treaty stipulations with foreign countries in the light of international laws and conventions and to discharge those obligations faithfully; (3) not only to respect the acquired rights of the peoples of foreign countries within the limits of the State of Manchuria, but to give full protection to 'their persons and properties'; (4) to invite 'the entry of the peoples of foreign nations into, and their residence in, Manchuria' and to accord equal and equitable treatment to all races; (5) to facilitate trade and commerce with foreign countries, in order to contribute to the development of

---

[23] The Ambassador, as such, acted under the direction of the Japanese Foreign Minister. In relation to Manchurian affairs, however, his home relationship was directly with the Premier. As Commander-in-chief, he was entitled to direct access to the Emperor. The general supervisory agency in Japan, after 1934, was the Manchuria Affairs Board.

world economy; (6) to observe the principle of the Open Door regarding the economic activities of the peoples of foreign nations within the state of Manchuria." [24]

Certainly no complaint could be made, by third parties, of the announced policy of the Manchukuoan government. There was, nevertheless, considerable fear expressed by foreign interests concerning their future under the new conditions on the score of a possible divergence of practice from profession. These fears were largely justified, although only in part because of the divergence of practice from the declared principles. The development of the country was undertaken by Japan to promote her own interests, and it was financed with Japanese capital. This inevitably resulted in an increase in the Japanese proportion of Manchukuo's foreign trade, especially on the import side. The methods which came to be employed to control the course of trade, however, were clearly out of harmony with the principles of relationship which had been proclaimed.

An illustration of this was given when, under a law of February 21, 1935, effective on April 10, an oil monopoly was established. The law provided for the establishment of the Manchuria Petroleum Company to handle the importation and refining of crude oil. This Company was capitalized at 5 million yen, 3 million being allotted to the government and the South Manchurian Railway Company and the remaining 2 million being divided among four Japanese oil companies. Foreign companies were not admitted to participation. They were, however, given the right to import under license, and, also under license, to engage in refining. An Oil Monopoly Bureau was constituted under the same law, and it was given complete control of the sale and distribution of petroleum products. The application of this law could only result in the driving out of the foreign companies which had been doing an extensive business in Manchuria, and some of which had built up elaborate sales organizations.

The Oil Monopoly became an immediate subject of diplomatic controversy, protests being addressed to Japan against it as violative of the treaty pledge to respect the principle of equality of trade opportunity. At first the Japanese attempted to dissociate themselves from responsibility on the ground that the action was taken by an independent state. The action was, however, defended on the ground of public policy, and thus as not violating the Open Door commitment. This commitment, in any case, it was pointed out, represented a voluntary unilateral declaration of policy on the part of Manchukuo rather than a treaty obligation as in the case of other states. And, in the course of the diplomatic discussion, it was implied that Manchukuo could not be expected to continue to extend the same

[24] From the note, as printed in *Fourth Report on Progress in Manchuria to 1934,* South Manchurian Railway Company, 1934, Appendix No. 5.

favors to non-recognizing states as were given to those recognizing it. In some respects the creation of the Monopoly presented the appearance of a venture partly planned with a view to bringing pressure to bear to break down the policy of non-recognition which was being followed by the Western states.

Concerning this, it may be stated that the policy enunciated by Secretary Stimson in January, 1932, for the United States, and taken over and applied by the League states, had been maintained in force following the failure to bring about a settlement of the Sino-Japanese dispute on the basis of the recommendations of the Lytton Commission. From the nature of its position Russia, not bound by the League decision on non-recognition but following that policy independently, had gone further in the direction of *de facto* recognition than any other state, having received consular representatives from Hsinking in Siberia, and having regularized the position of its own consular officers in Manchukuo. Negotiations preceding the sale to Manchukuo of the Chinese Eastern Railway had also been carried on with the representatives of that state as well as of Japan. Russia, however, made it clear that there was no intention, in any of these actions, of according *de jure* recognition. The other principally interested state, China, had not even gone this far toward *de facto* recognition. It had, however, consented to arrangements in 1934 under which through-traffic was resumed on the Peking-Mukden Railway, and mails originating in or destined for Manchukuo were handled. In both instances, however, the agreements carefully safeguarded the principle of non-recognition. Thus Manchukuo had its dependent relationship to Japan emphasized through its non-acceptance by the other members of the international community.

Aside from the institution of monopolies, such as that of oil, which had the effect of virtually pushing foreign companies out of Manchuria on "forced sale" terms, so far as their properties were concerned, the elimination of the Russian interest, represented by the Chinese Eastern Railway, from northern Manchuria was the most marked development within Manchukuo after 1933 affecting foreign interests. The immediate future of the C.E.R. was determined, in point of fact, with the Japanese military occupation of Manchuria in 1931-1932. It was thereafter only a question of the time and of the conditions of terminating the Russian rights and interest, unless the Soviet government was prepared to undertake an effective resistance to the extension of the Japanese-controlled state's boundary to the Amur. This Russia was not then, or later, prepared to undertake. Consequently the alternative was followed of trying to get as large a payment as possible for the road.

Since this was only one of a number of points of Russo-Japanese friction, however, the negotiations over the railway were frequently complicated by other considerations than that of price. After a period of suspension of negotiations on account of the arrest of Soviet railway officials in 1933, and in spite of the constant complication of Russo-Japanese relations on other issues, the negotiations which were resumed in 1934 were finally carried to a successful conclusion and the transfer of title was effected on March 23, 1935. China, the other party in interest, protested the transaction, but rather for the record than with any expectation of having her voice heard.

The elimination of Russia from Manchuria with the transfer of the Chinese Eastern Railway completed the movement begun in 1931 to preserve Japanese rights and interest. It was completed, however, on an expanded basis since, before 1931, Japan had recognized northern Manchuria to be beyond her sphere of interest. Thus a movement designed to establish Japan, against Chinese opposition, in southern Manchuria had rapidly grown beyond its original objectives. Had the end appeared, by 1934, to be the elimination of foreign, in the sense of non-Japanese, interests from all of Manchuria, the attainment of that end might have been expected to inaugurate a period of quiet in the Far East. But the reverse proved to be the case, even in Japanese-Russian relations. There were other sources of friction besides the question of ownership of the railway. And the particular difficulties were enlarged by a feeling of uncertainty as to the ultimate objectives of Japan.

As a general method of promoting more amicable relations the Russians after 1932 repeatedly proposed the conclusion of a non-aggression pact similar to the ones which they had been negotiating with the states on their western frontier. The first proposal along this line met with no response. Subsequently, however, the Japanese made it clear that in their opinion all pending questions should be settled prior to the consideration of such a pact. This attitude tended to strengthen the view held elsewhere that Japan's full objectives had not been attained.

Among the questions which disturbed Russo-Japanese relations during 1933 and, to a somewhat lesser extent, in 1934, were those of frontier relations, since the establishment of Manchukuo gave the two states in fact, if not in theory, a common frontier. Especially in 1933 there were repeated complaints on each side of armed incursions into the territory of the other. Questions of navigation rights on boundary rivers also arose to complicate relations until, in August, 1934, an agreement was reached to establish a joint technical commission to work out regulations for the use of waterways. The new regulations were approved and put into force after January, 1935. Thus another source of friction was at least abated if not entirely removed. As far as the other incidents were concerned, they increased or decreased with changes in other fields of policy and relationship.

The major cause of these incidents in the first years was the relative military weakness of Russia in the Far East, together with the perception of the fact that Russia's intentions at the moment were entirely pacific. This conclusion was, of course, drawn from Moscow's failure to take any strong steps to preserve its interests in northern Manchuria during the period of preliminary occupation. The result was to encourage Japanese military forces to continue to test the Russian position on the frontier.

The Russian reaction to Japanese expansion, after the initial gains had been made, however, took the form of intensive efforts to strengthen their military and economic position in their own territories. These efforts took two related forms. One was to speed up application of the Far Eastern provisions of the second Five Year Plan, emphasizing those aspects of it which would enable the region to supply itself in the event of the outbreak of war. The population was expanded through a system of state colonization so as to give a military reserve to draw upon. The agricultural productivity of the Far Eastern Territory was increased to the point of self-sufficiency in food supply. The output of coal was increased after 1933 from 240,000 to over 3 million tons. The oil production in northern Sakhalin was similarly expanded, and a good start was made in the development of industry. Much of this had been projected in the first Plan, of 1928, but the real progress made dated from 1933 and must be largely ascribed to the threat that Japanese expansion was felt to offer to the Russian territories in the Far East.

Another defensive measure was that of railway construction. The double-tracking of the Trans-Siberian Railway, contemplated since 1905, was finally undertaken and completed after 1933 to the Manchurian frontier, thus giving Russia more adequate facilities for the movement of troops and supplies in the event of war. To supplement the Amur Railway, highly vulnerable in the event of war with Japan because it runs throughout close to the frontier, a new railway was projected in 1934 from Lake Baikal to the Sea of Okhotsk, to be completed within two years.

The Russian position was further strengthened through the completion of an elaborate system of frontier defenses of the "pill-box" type, with strong military bases established at Pogranichnaya, Blagoveschensk, and Khabarovsk. The air force was increased, also, to the point where it represented a formidable offensive weapon as well as a strong defensive one. Finally, the military effectives of Russia in the Far East were greatly increased, the force being expanded until it was estimated to comprise more than 250,000 of her best troops.

This strengthening of the Russians from the military standpoint had the important effect of modifying the Japanese attitude of over-assertiveness along the northern frontier, and undoubtedly was a factor in reducing the number of frontier incidents which continued to disturb the friendly relations of the two states. But it also helped to strengthen the long-existing latent fear of Russia felt in Japan. What to the Russians was clearly a defensive development could be pictured to the Japanese as an ultimate threat to their position in Manchuria and, through Manchuria, to Japan. Thus, to reiterated expressions from Russia of a willingness and a desire to enter into a non-aggression pact, the Japanese replied by proposals for a demilitarized zone along the common frontier. This proposal the Soviet authorities refused to entertain since, in their view, their fortifications, suitably manned, were essential to the defense of their territories. Their position, behind their fortifications, was fixed and strong but it did not lend itself to attack.

Counter-developments in Manchukuo after 1933, on the other hand, were complained of by the Russians on the ground that they were pointed toward attack on Russian territories. Thus while Russian railways, both existing and planned, were mainly east-west lines across Russian territory, the new lines constructed or planned by the Japanese in Manchukuo led to the Siberian frontier, except for those directed toward the penetration of Mongolia and the development of rail communications with Jehol.[25] Thus, for war purposes, the Japanese communication system seemed to be developed for purposes of attack on Russian territory, giving a greater mobility to the Japanese forces operating to the north than Russian forces would have had operating to the south. The Russian plans were developed in terms of the static, while the Japanese gave all the appearance of the dynamic and expansive.

There were two further sources of possible conflict, one an old cause of friction, and the other and politically more important one related directly to the newer expansionist movement. The older one was the question of Japanese access to the Russian fisheries. This was especially important to Japan because of the fact that fish bulk large in the national diet. Japanese fishermen, in the absence of any agreement, had long been accustomed to resort to the northern coastal waters, coming to consider that they really had a right to fish in Russian territorial waters. As Russia became more definitely interested in her Far Eastern territories, the attempt was made to drive the Japanese out of the fishing grounds. Finally, after prolonged negotiations, a fisheries convention was signed in 1907, as stipulated in Article XI of the Portsmouth Treaty.

It defined the areas along the Far Eastern Coast where the Japanese might fish and those from which they were excluded, the conditions on which they might develop the fishing industry, i.e., build canning stations, depots, etc., on Russian territory, and established a system of annual auctions at Vladivostok where

---

[25] Some Russian new construction, however, was also directed toward Outer Mongolia from the Western side, as a study of a railway map will show.

the Japanese might bid on equal terms with Russian subjects for leases of these fishing grounds. This Convention remained in force until 1919, when it automatically lapsed through non-renewal. Practically speaking it is still the charter of Japanese rights in the Far Eastern fisheries, as the new Fisheries Convention signed by Japan with the Soviet Government in 1928 only modified certain details of the old text.[26]

Under these agreements the Japanese interests were not only protected but even expanded, partly because of lack of Russian interest in the exploitation of their reserved areas. After 1928, however, the Soviet government began to exhibit an increasing concern with the situation. By 1930

the fishing grounds in Russian hands had risen from 42 in 1928 to 313, when for the first time they exceeded the Japanese. From 1930, Soviet competition began to threaten the whole status of the carefully built up Japanese fishing industry. Owing to the high prices now demanded in roubles by the Soviet authorities for the fishing grounds (and the impossibility for the Japanese at this stage of further speculation in roubles to counter-balance the unfavorable official rouble-yen parity for Japan) Japanese fishing interests rapidly declined in extent and value from 1930 to 1933, while the backward Soviet industry made rapid progress.[27]

The Japanese sought to maintain their competitive position and pressed for a new agreement, which was concluded, as a supplementary understanding, in 1932. This, however, did not actually improve the position of Japan, although it did confirm the Japanese in certain of their asserted rights. Aside from the increased participation of Soviet government enterprises in the annual auctions, at the expense of Japan, greatest aggravation was produced by the question of the relationship of the rouble to the yen. While the rate was fixed at 32.5 sen per rouble in 1932, in 1934 the rate was raised to 75 sen. This rate was applied after the auctions when the Japanese attempted to pay at the old rate, and their bids were declared invalid by the Russians. After negotiation, however, it was decided to hold new auctions, and to apply the old rate for the time being. This agreement ran to 1936, and thereafter unless denounced by either party. As the time for extension or denunciation approached the Japanese government indicated a desire to conclude another supplementary agreement rather than to revise the entire Convention. The Russians, however, proposed the extension of the 1932 supplementary Agreement and subsequent discussion of possible revisions. An important national interest, involving not only those engaged in the fisheries but numerous collateral occupations, was involved, with the Japanese, in this instance, on the defensive.

As previously pointed out, the governmental and supervisory machinery

[26] VIOLET CONOLLY, *Soviet Trade from the Pacific to the Levant*, p. 34. Text of the 1907 Convention, appendix 3; text of the 1928 Convention, appendix 6.
[27] *Ibid.*, p. 38.

established by Japan in Manchukuo threw control of the course of internal development into the hands of the Kwantung Army leadership. It exercised this control, narrowly, to serve military and strategic purposes and, broadly, to prevent development and exploitation of Manchuria by capitalists in their own interests. It was apparently intended to develop Manchuria to the benefit of the Japanese people as a whole through the establishment of a system that might equally be called one of state capitalism or of state socialism. After a period of experimentation, during which considerable development took place on the basis of Japanese capital imported mainly through the South Manchurian Railway Company, an Industrial Control Law was enacted, on May 1, 1937. This law defined "nineteen key industries which are to be under the close supervision of the government as essential to the national defense and a sound national economy. As a sop to private enterprise, all other industrial activity is to be 'free' and uncontrolled. . . . The law has very simply labelled all the important industries as key industries, leaving little but the crumbs to 'free' enterprise."[28] It thus carried the initial Army policy to its logical conclusion. Before its enactment there had been pressure in Japan for a removal or lessening of the earlier restrictions on private investment in Manchukuo. Its enactment represented a decisive victory for the Army policy, and created the conditions for the realization of the aim of the Kwantung Army "to build up in Manchukuo an economic and military base which will be as self-sufficient as possible." Movement in this direction, it may be noted, was also movement toward the determination of policy in Manchukuo by the Kwantung Army, independent of the control and direction of Tokyo itself.

9. THE DEVELOPMENT OF MANCHUKUO

After the establishment of Manchukuo Japan's capital exports to it had risen annually from the investment of 97.2 million yen of 1932 to the 431.0 million yen invested in 1938.[29] These funds were used to build railways, and add otherwise to the communications system; to extend the facilities of the existing iron and coal enterprises; to start new exploitation; to modernize the cities, including the construction of a virtually new city at Hsinking to serve as the capital; and to develop public utilities. Thus Japanese capital was introduced into what was essentially an agricultural country to promote industrialization. The large amounts of capital imported had the effect of making Manchukuo the exclusive field for Japanese overseas investment, but put a very severe strain on Japan herself through draining off the major portion of the capital available for invest-

[28] *Far Eastern Survey*, vol. 6, No. 13, p. 148.
[29] G. C. ALLEN, *Japanese Industry, Its Recent Development and Present Condition*, pp. 94-95.

ment, without any prospect of immediate return because of the uses to which the investments were put.

One of the important achievements of Japan in Manchuria was the reform of the currency system. The Manchukuoan yuan was made the unit, and steps were taken to replace the various local currencies with that unit as well as to withdraw the Japanese banknotes which had been circulating in Manchukuo, thus unifying the currency system. The yuan was originally linked to the Chinese dollar as the silver currency, although from the outset it was in fact a managed currency, an embargo having been placed on the export of silver. In 1935 it was established at parity with the Japanese yen, and the beginning was made in the creation of the so-called yen bloc, with both currencies supported by the Japanese government.

A second major reform undertaken by Japan was the unification of the Manchurian railway system and its extension. The former Chinese government lines and the Chinese Eastern, after its purchase from Russia, were brought in 1935 under the management of the South Manchurian Railway Company and thus merged with the existing Japanese railways. This of course enhanced the importance of the South Manchurian Railway Company. Its importance was also increased since it was used as a principal medium for Japanese investment in Manchuria for development purposes. These investments took the form of extension of the railway network, resulting, in a four-year period (1932–1936), in a 40 per cent increase in mileage. The aim in the planning of new railways was primarily strategic, but the lines built were also useful "in the long campaign against banditry and, in addition, are valuable economically in opening new areas to settlement." Communications were further improved through the construction of new highways, on which bus lines were put into operation, and through the improvement of river navigation. "In addition, air routes operated by the Manchurian Aviation Company now link the principal cities in Manchukuo. The telephone and telegraph systems have been expanded by the Manchuria Telephone and Telegraph Co., which also controls radio broadcasting, with a powerful new station at Hsinking." [30]

10. MANCHURIA AS JAPAN'S ECONOMIC LIFE-LINE

Manchuria had been declared, in 1931 and previously, to be Japan's economic life-line. By this had been meant principally that its resources were essential, in their exploitation, to sustain Japanese industry and, through further industrialization, to enable Japan to maintain its expanding population. It was also thought of, in this same connection, as an area which might, under proper circumstances, afford an outlet by emigration for

[30] The quotations are from the *Far Eastern Survey*, vol. 5, No. 6, pp. 53–59. This article gives an excellent brief survey of "Four Years of Manchukuo."

Japan's population surplus. In both of these respects it proved immediately disappointing. On the basis of imported Japanese capital, it is true, industrial enterprise was expanded in Manchukuo. But, partly at any rate because of the desire of the Kwantung Army command to make Manchukuo self-sustaining in the event of war, the development which occurred was not supplementary to but was competitive with the industries of Japan. The production of pig iron was increased, as was the extraction of oil from shale at Fushun and the production of industrial salt and beancake. In this and other respects the raw materials supply of Japan was augmented through exploitation in Manchuria. But the production of coal, ammonium sulphate, and soda ash was directly competitive with Japanese industry. Thus it became clear that the development of Manchukuo, especially if continued along the lines planned by the Army leadership, would produce competition with Japanese industry in the home markets or reduce the market for Japanese goods in Manchuria. This helped to bring about the shift in Japanese interest from Manchuria to North China.

Nevertheless Japan's political control of Manchuria had the result of immediately enlarging her exports to the new state. Thus, while in 1932 Japan had an adverse balance of 26 million yen in her trade with Manchuria, in 1936 she sold to Manchukuo 270 million yuan more than she bought. This change was the result in part of a slight decline in Manchukuoan exports to Japan, but it resulted more largely from an expansion of imports from Japan due to her capital exports for development purposes. The expansion did not, consequently, improve the position of Japan's established export industries, such as textiles. It worked instead to accelerate a shift in emphasis in the economic life of Japan from light to heavy industry and in the process increased instead of lessened the dependence of the country on the non-Japanese world for raw materials of industrial importance. This shift in emphasis was, however, also due to the development of armament production within Japan which, in turn, was a natural result of the extended use of military power on the continent.

As far as colonization in Manchuria was concerned, during the years between the Mukden "incident" of 1931 and the outbreak of what the Japanese called the China "incident" in 1937, the results were meager. The Japanese population of Manchukuo more than doubled during this period, as is shown in the 1935 census figures of a total of 501,251. To this figure may be added 834,539 Korean and Formosan immigrants, bringing the total to 1,335,790. But the bulk of the Japanese came as officials, technical railway and industrial experts, and businessmen rather than as agricultural colonizers. This form of immigration did not serve to relieve the pressure of population in the agricultural villages of Japan. The latter was attempted through subsidized colonial projects, which became possible after the political obstacles to agricultural settlement raised by the Chinese had been removed in 1933. The first attempts at settlement were essentially military in character, being undertaken by armed reservists under the supervision of the Japanese Ministry of Overseas Affairs. Five such settlements had been established by the end of 1936, with a total population in May, 1937, of 4,245 persons, not an impressive total. In addition the South Manchurian Railway Company "settled ex-servicemen in protective villages along the railway lines," and there were some private or "free" settlers. At the end of 1937 "the population of these various unofficial colonies totalled 1,138 families and 2,150 persons. More than half of the farm immigrants were thus in the five official colonies." [31]

These ventures may be described as experiments to determine the feasibility of agricultural colonization. The conclusion having been reached that it was feasible, a twenty-year program of colonization was launched in 1937. This involved the settlement of a million families on the land in Manchuria within that period. The new project involved, in the main, group colonization, under government supervision and with direct government subsidization, although provision was also made for "free" settlement. Up to 1940, partly because of war conditions, the annual settlement contemplated in the plan had not taken place, only 1,500 of the 6,000 families, for example, which were to have been colonized in 1937 having been settled. Nevertheless sufficient progress was made to indicate the determination of the Japanese government to push forward colonization as rapidly as possible.

Experience had shown that if Manchuria was to serve Japan as a colonization area, both Korean and Chinese immigration would have to be controlled, since the voluntary movement into Manchuria had been from China, primarily, and Korea, secondarily, rather than from Japan. Even aside from political factors operative during the "pre-incident" years to prevent Japanese settlement, it had been made evident that, in free agricultural competition, Japanese settlers could not maintain themselves in the face of Chinese and Korean competition. In other words, the land had to be reserved for Japanese colonization if even subsidized settlement could be expected to be successful. Consequently Koreans were restricted to certain areas in eastern Manchuria for permanent settlement and, beyond that, were used to open up the land for Japanese settlement. Chinese immigration was restricted after the establishment of Manchukuo and, after 1935, was rigidly controlled so that only seasonal laborers on a quota basis, for service in construction, mining, and agricultural activities, were admitted to the country. Thus economic policy had been developed in this respect

[31] See *Japan's Strategic Settlements in Manchukuo*, *Far Eastern Survey*, vol. 8, No. 4.

with a view to the protection of Japanese rather than Manchukuoan interests.

11. THE MAINTENANCE OF PUBLIC ORDER

One of the primary measures of success in government is to be found in the ability which is shown to preserve peace and maintain order. This test the Japanese had applied to Chinese rule in Manchukuo as well as in China proper, finding Chinese rule inadequate. Banditry, and thus disturbance of the public order, had been a normal condition of life in Manchukuo under Chinese rule, and its suppression became a principal task of the Japanese-Manchukuoan régime instituted in 1932. The accomplishment of this task was rendered more than ordinarily difficult because of the failure of the population to give full and voluntary allegiance and support to the new government. Consequently, to the normal number of those who engaged in banditry as a "hard-time" occupation, supplementary to agriculture, there were added those who engaged in "banditry" as a form of guerrilla war against the new régime, pursuing essentially political rather than economic ends. It is, of course, impossible to make any statistical differentiation between the two elements, both of whom were equally classed by the Japanese as bandits. The first type, however, would increase or decrease in numbers with the rise and fall of economic conditions, particularly in agriculture. In bad times there would be a problem of suppression by force, regardless of the government, which would be greater in magnitude than in good times, when the reabsorption of the bandits into the peaceful community would take place without the extensive use of force for purposes of suppression. The second type could be eliminated only by force or by creating conditions of government satisfactory to the populace. Forcible suppression would be rendered easier or more difficult depending upon the support given to the guerrillas by the people of the countryside. This, in turn, would be determined by their satisfaction with the conditions both of government and of economics.

From the economic standpoint the problem of banditry was made more difficult of normal solution because of the condition of Manchurian agriculture during the first years of Japanese rule. Crop production fell off considerably during 1932 and 1934, with a resulting depression. The staple crop, which may be used to measure prosperity, was the soya bean. Soya bean prices fell after 1932 in spite of a decrease in production from 5,300,000 tons in 1930 to 3,350,000 tons in 1934. This was due to the closing of the Chinese market because of political reasons and to the decline in the world demand, especially that of Germany, a principal market for the crop.

The emphasis placed by Japan on non-agricultural developments prevented satisfactory steps being taken to alleviate the lot of the farmers. Crop diversification was fostered by the Manchukuoan government, and that, in long-run terms, especially if markets were developed for the new crops, would help to improve the position of the farmers. But, immediately, they did not share in the urban prosperity resulting from Japanese constructional activities. Nor could they expect immediately to have their condition improved as a result of the building of the new railways and highways in view of their essentially strategic planning. Thus the constructive steps which might have helped to reduce banditry through inducing agricultural prosperity were not taken. And there was not present in the Chinese population the voluntary acquiescence in the new political order, which severed Manchuria from China, which would have made "political banditry" i.e., the guerrilla warfare carried on by remnants of Chang Hsüeh-liang's forces remaining in Manchuria and others with an anti-Japanese bias—gradually lessen and ultimately disappear. Consequently military suppression had to be resorted to in the face of an immediate increase of banditry and an extension of disorder.

The *Japan-Manchukuo Year Book* for 1937 presents [32] a ten-page "Chronology of Bandit Suppression" by the Manchukuo Army covering the years from March, 1932, to March, 1935. This shows the extent of preoccupation of the Japanese with the problem as well as being designed to indicate success in the suppression of banditry. And yet, in the face of the official contention that success had been attained in bandit suppression, and thus in the pacification of the country, it was in 1936 that Army authorities began to institute the system of concentration of the population of the countryside in protected villages.

. . . outlying farm houses were burned to the ground, and in some districts the standing grain was fired. Around each of these villages the farmers were compelled to build high mud walls. The villagers themselves were registered, in order to control the entrance of outsiders; and the headman was made responsible, on pain of death, that no "bandit" received asylum in his village. Those villagers unable to produce their residence certificates were summarily executed; at times such executions occurred in some districts at the rate of ten a day. By the middle of 1937 well over 2,000 of these "protected villages" had been established; the total population in areas affected by this program was estimated to range between five and six millions. [33]

Such a drastic step as this would seem to indicate the extension of banditry, with the support of the countryside, rather than its virtual suppression through direct military activity such as had been undertaken during the first four years of Manchukuo. The same conclusion is indicated in the continued allotment of a large proportion of the state income to defense pur-

[32] Pp. 728–737.

[33] T. A. BISSON, *Japan in China*, pp. 392–405. The quotation is from p. 393.

poses, including under that head bandit suppression. Furthermore, it must be noted that the total Japanese military force in Manchuria (i.e., the Kwantung Army), as distinguished from the Manchukuoan Army, had been increased rather than decreased during the period from 1932 to 1937. This is to be explained primarily by the possibility of trouble with Russia as well as by the policy being followed toward China; but it is, secondarily, indicative of the fact that the new state, and the régime instituted within it, had to be constantly propped up with Japanese bayonets because of the lack of voluntary support given to it by the peoples of Manchuria. Thus one of the results of the Japanese occupation of Manchuria had not been, during the period of years under review, the establishment of a larger measure of peace and order than that which had existed under Chinese administration of the Three Eastern Provinces.

These debit items in the ledger of the Japanese occupation—i.e., agricultural distress and the failure to relieve the country of the bandit and also the necessity of supporting government by enlarged military power—cannot be attributed solely to Japanese policy especially in its positive expression. This was particularly the case with respect to economic conditions. Floods, as well as banditry and continued political instability due to insurgency, were responsible for crop deficiencies. World conditions, as has been suggested, reduced the market for the soya bean, the export staple of Manchuria, until it began to be restored, so far as Germany was concerned, with the conclusion of a tripartite barter agreement in 1936. Thus exports had attained the "pre-incident" level by 1938, being valued at 714.4 million Manchurian yuan. Exports remained, however, agricultural, the Japanese investment directed toward industrial development not creating any export industries. This capital investment by Japan, in fact, produced a somewhat different situation, from the export standpoint, than that existing before the occupation. Then Manchuria had generally enjoyed a favorable balance of trade. After 1932, and especially after agricultural recovery had set in after 1936, the balance was favorable beyond the Japan-Manchukuo bloc, but adverse in the relations of Japan and Manchukuo. This was due to the importation of capital goods from Japan for purposes of urbanization and industrialization, and also to a decrease in exportation to Japan until after the outbreak of the war with China in 1937. This latter was in face of the fact that Manchuria was supposed to be indispensable to Japan as a source of supply of raw materials.

12. SOCIAL AND CULTURAL RESULTS OF ESTABLISHMENT OF MANCHUKUO

One other aspect of policy must be considered in estimating the effects of establishment of the new régime on Manchuria and its people. This relates to social and cultural as distinguished from economic development.

It had long been recognized that one of the problems of development of China, including Manchuria, was that of control of the use of opium and its derivatives. The Chinese record in dealing with the problem had varied, depending upon the elements in control of the government at different periods. But the Japanese record in Manchuria during the period after 1931 was certainly no better that that of China in its worst periods. The agency of supervision and control was the Opium Monopoly Bureau. Its approach to the problem was apparently in terms of expansion of revenue rather than limitation of use of narcotic drugs. The acreage which might legally be devoted to opium cultivation was increased, and, by such means as reduction of the fee for smoking permits and relaxed control of the retailers, the use of opium and its derivatives was substantially increased.

The principle underlying the formulation of policy within Manchukuo was proclaimed to be that of Wang-tao, "the Kingly Way." It represented a conscious attempt to link the new order with those aspects of the Chinese classical system from which might be derived a moral support for authority. There was rejected, however, the Confucian corrective to rule by a bureaucracy designed to ensure that the rulers would in fact govern "benevolently" which was represented by the right of rebellion. The meaning practically put on the principle, making it a "golden mean between fascism and Bolshevism" and thus neither "nationalistic nor communistic," may best be found through consideration of the policies which were followed with respect to education.

The total expenditure on education, in comparison with the last years of Chinese control, was cut approximately in half. The allotments in the budget for education in the years after the occupation also showed decreases rather than increases, only 2.2 per cent of the estimated expenditure for 1937 having been for school maintenance purposes, as against 3.24 per cent in 1934–1935. This contrasts with about 40 per cent of total income devoted to military purposes. The peculiar problems connected with the establishment and consolidation of the new state might serve to explain the decrease in financial provision for the schools. Of possibly more significance from the point of view of the cultural implications of the new order was the exclusive preoccupation with elementary education and vocational training at the elementary level. The colleges and universities provided for under the Chinese system were eliminated. Ninety-five per cent of the schools were elementary, the remaining 5 per cent being middle and technical schools. Throughout the entire system the old textbooks, expressive of the ideas of the San Min Chu I, and thus of Chinese nationalism, were naturally eliminated. The substitute ideas, introduced through new texts, emphasized reverence for the Emperor, the benefits to be derived from close association with Japan, the Confucian conceptions of virtue, right conduct, propriety, and benevolence, "all of which tend toward submission and minimize self-assertion." The purpose of education was the development and crystallization of loyalty to the new régime. Thus it reproduced the emphasis which was to be found within the educational order in Japan itself. This emphasis, coupled with the failure to provide for higher education and the concentration on the vocational, together with the extension of the Japanese element in officialdom, indicated the aim "to prepare the great bulk of the Chinese population for a well defined position of subservience in their new national life, with the ruling places reserved to the Japanese and those few Chinese who emerge acceptably from a university education in Japan." [34] The Japanese did, it may be remarked, open an opportunity for higher education, but for a comparatively few selected to be trained in the Japanese universities.

The work of indoctrination in the schools at the elementary level was supported by control of the press and of news services, on the negative side of censorship, and by the positive activities of the Concordia Society, founded in 1932. This society had the function of carrying on patriotic publicity work designed to win support for the government and for Japan in Manchuria. In this respect its rôle was supplementary to that of the schools in bringing about voluntary acceptance of the new state of affairs, which brought Manchuria into the Japanese cultural pattern by severing its intellectual and sentimental attachment to China. This, judging by the constant attention which had to be paid to the problem, had not yet been accomplished by the time of outbreak of war between China and Japan.

REFERENCES FOR FURTHER STUDY

T. A. Bisson, *Japan in China* (1938), ch. 12; a suggestive summary treatment. *China Year Book*, 1931–1932, ch. 23, Japanese Invasion of Manchuria and the Shanghai Area. Department of State, *Foreign Relations of U. S., 1931,* vol. III (1946), 1932, vol. IV (1947) gives U. S. diplomatic correspondence on Manchurian crisis. (British Royal) Institute of International Relations, *Survey of International Affairs; Documents on International Affairs;* 1931–1936. *Japan-Manchoukuo Year Book,* annual since 1933. Owen Lattimore, *Manchuria, Cradle of Conflict* (1932); a suggestive study of social relationships in Manchuria. League of Nations, *Report of the* (Lytton) *Commission of Enquiry* (League Publications VII. Political 1932. VII. 12); gives a careful background survey as well as an authoritative treatment of the situation in Manchuria. For discussion of the Manchurian question at Geneva see League of Nations, *Official Journal;* other materials may be found in League publications by using the World Peace Foundation "Key" to League Publications. Mitsubishi Economic Research Bureau, *Japanese Industry, Present and Future* (1936); a valuable reference work R. K. Reischauer, *Conflicts Inside Japan,* Harpers Magazine, July, 1936, pp. 157–165; gives an interesting analysis

[34] Bisson, *op. cit.,* p. 374.

of the operative social forces. EDGAR SNOW, *Far Eastern Front* (1933). G. E. SOKOLSKY, *The Tinder Box of Asia* (1932); a penetrating study of Far Eastern politics with an emphasis on the Manchurian situation (ch. 5–11). SOUTH MANCHURIAN RAILWAY, *Fourth Report on Progress in Manchuria* (1934); the appendices especially will be found to be useful. See also other *Reports* in the annual series. H. L. STIMSON, *The Far Eastern Crisis* (1936); an account by the American Secretary of State at the time of the Manchurian crisis. FREDA UTLEY, *Japan's Feet of Clay* (1937); a careful analysis, emphasizing the weaknesses of the Japanese economy. C. WALTER YOUNG, *Japan's Jurisdictional and Legal Position in Manchuria,* 3 vols. (1931); vol. 1, *Japan's Special Position in Manchuria;* vol. 2, *The International Legal Status of the Kwantung Leased Territory;* vol. 3, *Japanese Jurisdiction in the South Manchurian Railway Areas.* These three volumes present an exhaustive analysis of the legal position at the time of the Manchurian crisis of 1931. C. WALTER YOUNG, *The International Relations of Manchuria* (1929). AMERICAN COUNCIL, INSTITUTE OF PACIFIC RELATIONS, *Far Eastern Survey,* vol. 4–9; an indispensable publication; consult index for articles on Japan, Manchukuo. Also files of *Amerasia; Asia; Contemporary Japan; Contemporary Manchuria, Pacific Affairs* and other periodicals. The ones mentioned are especially useful.

CHAPTER XXIII

OVERTURE TO WAR

1. JAPANESE PRESSURE IN NORTH CHINA: 1933-1935

THE YEARS between the formal establishment of Manchukuo and the outbreak of major hostilities between Japan and China in 1937 were as significant on account of the constant pressure of Japan on China as they were for the definition of the status of Manchukuo. The possibilities of effective pressure were enhanced because of domestic conditions in China, but those conditions were, in turn, materially affected by the state of China's relations with Japan. Thus the reader must bear in mind the fact of this interaction of foreign and domestic politics even though it will be necessary to separate the two for the sake of clarity of discussion. It will be most convenient to begin with the development and application of Japanese policy as it affected China, outside of the Three Eastern Provinces, after 1932.

By 1932 China's military and administrative authority had been eliminated from Manchuria with the occupation by Japanese troops of the border city of Chinchow. At no stage had any military resistance been offered to Japan, reliance having been placed on the guarantees of the League Covenant and other international instruments. At Shanghai, however, Chinese forces did put up a vigorous resistance when, in 1932, the Japanese used force in the endeavor to break the boycott which had been popularly instituted as a reaction to the situation in Manchuria. This seemed to indicate an intention to follow a stronger policy of defense of the eighteen provinces than of Manchuria.

The intention was put to the proof when, at the beginning of 1933, Shanhaikwan was attacked by the Japanese, preliminary to the launching of an attack on Jehol province. The young Marshal, Chang Hsüeh-liang, pacification commissioner of the Peip'ing area, and only that since he had been driven out of Manchuria, issued a joint statement with T. V. Soong announcing the intention to resist to the last man. In spite of this pronouncement, however, Jehol was conquered with a rapidity only to be explained by the collapse of Chinese resistance, the capital, Chengteh, being occupied on March 3 without fighting.

When the struggle was carried into North China, the Chinese troops held fast at the passes into Hopei province. The Japanese were more successful in their advance to the Luan River. Nevertheless they did not push their advance although it would have turned the Chinese flank. Instead, there followed a period of negotiation, prepared for by a reconstitution of the personnel of the Hopei [1] régime along lines favorable to Japan. These negotiations led to the conclusion of the Tangku truce agreement, which was signed May 25, 1933. Under its terms the entire Peip'ing-Tientsin area was to be demilitarized through a withdrawal of the Chinese army. Peace and order were to be maintained by a Chinese police force so constituted as not to contain any "armed units hostile to Japanese feelings." Japan, however, under the Boxer Protocol, had the right to maintain garrisons along the line of the railway from Peip'ing, through Tientsin to Shanhaikwan. Thus Japan was left in a position to apply effective pressure to the local governments in the region, and, under the fourth article of the agreement, to ensure that "peace preservation" forces would respond to Japanese direction as much as to that of local Chinese authorities. The only counter-pressure was that which could be supplied from Nanking. Although the agreement was carried out, there was constant criticism on the part of Japanese military officers of conditions in the Peip'ing-Tientsin region. Officials were accused of not fully coöperating with the Japanese; friction marked the relations of the Japanese with the Chinese inhabitants, with disorder occasionally resulting; and it was alleged that an anti-Japanese propaganda was kept up by the students and others with the connivance of some of the officials. The situation was not improved, from Japan's point of view, when personal adherents of Chiang Kai-shek were appointed to replace officials whose actions were objectionable to the Japanese. Neither was it improved by the inability of Japanese officers to bring Chiang to the point of discussion of the conditions of which the Japanese government disapproved. Under the surface, consequently, there went on a struggle—on the part of Japan to establish a régime of officials acceptable and amenable to her; on the part of Chiang and the Nanking government to maintain some measure of control of the northern provinces.

As far as North China was concerned, the maneuvering of the two years from June, 1933, to June, 1935, resulted in a substantial strengthening of the Japanese position. As marked out, the demilitarized zone gave Japan control of access to China from the north and thus enhanced the effective pressure of a threat of military action. The acceptance of the Japanese demand, at a conference held at Dairen in July, 1933, that irregulars who had aided in the Japanese invasion should be employed in "peace preservation" corps, gave Japan rather than China the effective control of the police in the demilitarized area. The other three demands[2] made at this conference were secretly accepted by the Chinese in November. It was this

---

[1] The name of Chihli province had been changed to Hopei by the National government.
[2] For the terms of the demands see T. A. BISSON, *Japan in China*, p. 48.

acceptance which led to the reopening of rail and postal communications between China and Manchuria, although under arrangements carefully made to avoid formal recognition of the loss of the Manchurian provinces by China. One of the conditions also made it possible for Japan to lease lands and residences in designated places for the use of Japanese troops. All of this represented a consolidation of the new Japanese position in a limited area in the north. Further steps in the same direction were not taken until after the opening months of 1935, since, during 1934, the major diplomatic effort was being made at Nanking rather than Peip'ing. These steps were taken partly because of continued friction in the north resulting from Chinese efforts to minimize the consequences of the concessions previously made and partly because of the desire of the Japanese military to extend rather than merely to consolidate their new position, at home as well as abroad. Under renewed Japanese pressure the Chinese officials again gave way, making the new concessions which were embodied in the Ho-Umetsu Agreement of July, 1935. While there was subsequent disagreement as to the extent of the concessions actually made, it is clear that the Chinese gave way to the Japanese demands: (1) for the removal of objectionable troops and officials, both military and civil; (2) for the virtual elimination of the Kuomintang organization from the area of Japanese interest; and (3) for vigorous action to bring to an end all anti-Japanese activities in that area.

2. JAPAN AND MONGOLIA

Meanwhile an equally vigorous offensive had been undertaken by Japan in Chahar and Suiyuan provinces, the two provinces of Inner Mongolia of immediate importance from the standpoint of Manchukuo and North China. This affected her relations with Russia as well as China. Both before and after the Washington Conference, Russia and Japan had been contesting the Chinese position, Japan having first definitely asserted an interest in Inner Mongolia in 1915, while Russia had centered its policy on Outer Mongolia, where a most interesting condition and set of relationships had been in process of development. It will be recalled that a movement among the Mongols toward independence of China began almost coincidentally with the establishment of the Chinese Republic. By 1933 in spite of its accepted status as a dependency of China, Outer Mongolia had become a separate region, with its own government and with intimate relations existing between the Mongol People's Republic and the Soviet Union. With Soviet "advisers" attached to each government office, the Mongolian army actually under Soviet command, and the Mongolian economy being integrated with that of the Soviet Union, "Outer Mongolia was the first component whose area and people became a part of the Soviet zone or sphere." [3]

Nevertheless the Mongolian "independence" movement was as much anti-Chinese as pro-Russian, representing a defensive reaction against the glacial movement of Chinese colonists into the Inner Mongolian grasslands, and the extension to Mongolia of the Chinese administrative system, forecast in its introduction into Inner Mongolia in 1928. Chinese penetration had gone furthest in Inner Mongolia. The tribesmen were either forced to move back with their herds as the colonists pushed in and began cultivation or they were impoverished. The perception of the ultimate end of this process helped to bring about the establishment of the Outer Mongolian autonomous régime which was given tripartite recognition until 1921–1922, when Russian "white" and then "red" influence helped to establish an "independent" government. The Soviet government in 1924, however, to improve its relations with China, accepted Chinese sovereignty over Outer and Inner Mongolia, with the status of the former being that of virtual autonomy. Power was taken from the hereditary princes and, under Comintern direction, an attempt was made to create "a non-capitalist and not-yet socialist economy." Feudal relations continued in Inner Mongolia, however, with Chinese support, so that it did not come into the orbit of the People's Republic, but more because of internal division than of external influence. Thus it was only Outer Mongolia which was within the Russian sphere when the Japanese army moved into Manchuria in and after 1931. Inner Mongolia remained as a buffer between Russia and China.

The Japanese had expressed an interest in Inner Mongolia when they served their Demands on China in 1915. But up to 1932–1933 they had not been overly successful in penetrating the region. When they established their control over Manchuria, however, they were brought into a position of territorial proximity to Mongolia. The addition of Jehol to Manchuria brought the frontier even closer. Manchukuo, when finally established, numbered approximately 2 million Mongols in its population, thus giving Japan control over a larger proportion of the Mongol "nation" than was contained in either Outer or Inner Mongolia. These were organized into a separate province in Manchukuo and were, at first, given quite liberal treatment, to the point almost of autonomy. This was apparently done in the double hope of winning the Manchukuoan Mongols to voluntary acceptance of their new status, and of using them as a magnet to attract the Inner Mongolian Princes and Bannermen to union with Manchukuo. It was also hoped that the enthronement of the last Manchu Emperor of China as Emperor of Manchukuo would serve to draw the other Mongols

[3] DAVID J. DALLIN, *Soviet Russia and the Far East*, p. 77.

into the new state, since the Dynasty had been the bond of union between Mongolia and China.

This outwardly liberal Japanese policy was shortly modified, since it did not immediately produce the desired results. But the Princes of Inner Mongolia, because of the possibility of their coming under Japanese influence, had an effective lever on Nanking. This enabled them, in 1934, to establish an autonomous régime for their region with Chinese approval, and to secure an agreement with China under which the process of colonization would be checked. This proved to be a sufficient immediate counter-pull to keep them from voluntarily throwing in their lot with the semi-autonomous Mongols of Manchukuo. The conclusion seemed to be reached that autonomy would be harder to keep in a relationship with strong Japan than in one with a weak and politically still remote China.

Thus in 1934 there was a triple division into the Mongols of the Hsingan province of Manchukuo, those of Inner Mongolia, still recognizing a relationship to China, and those of Outer Mongolia, looking to Russia for guidance and protection. It might well be repeated that the stabilized Republic of Outer Mongolia failed to draw Inner Mongolia into union with it partly because of the greater Chinese influence in the latter, but more fundamentally because of the attitude of the Princes seeking to maintain their power and feudal prerogatives.

The policy of attraction having failed, Japan began to apply pressure to the autonomous government of Inner Mongolia in 1935. A frontier dispute caused military action to be taken against Chahar in January, as a result of which a slice of the province was incorporated in Manchukuo. Another incident in June resulted in a further advance of the Japanese position through forcing the acceptance by China of the dissolution of all Kuomintang branches in Chahar, cessation of Chinese emigration to the eastern part of the province, removal of Chinese troops from Changpei, and the establishment of a demilitarized zone in eastern Chahar. Proposals were made at the same time to the head of the Inner Mongolian Council that the entire region should join itself to Manchukuo. In July the Japanese announced the appointment of military and civil advisers to the Chahar government, thus establishing Japanese political influence at Kalgan, the "most strategic position in the whole of Inner Mongolia."

This penetration of Inner Mongolia forecast the ultimate encirclement of Outer Mongolia on the east and to the southeast. Thus it brought Russia again into the foreground of relationships. The creation of Manchukuo had established a frontier between the Japanese-controlled state and the Russian, as well as a common frontier to the north along the Amur and its confluents. Already there had been frontier disputes between Manchukuo and Mongolia, inevitably so because of the largely undefined nature of the frontier. The first of these came in January, 1935. Each side claimed in this, as in subsequent incidents, that the clash occurred because the troops of the other were on the wrong side of the frontier. Partly successful attempts were made to settle these questions in a conference of representatives of Mongolia and Manchukuo. The conference which convened on June 3, 1935, was immediately deadlocked on account of the refusal of the Mongols to entertain the demand that more than the immediate frontier incidents should be considered. The Japanese-Manchurian desire was to agree upon conditions of opening Mongolia to trade and residence. This the Mongol authorities were not willing to consider, although agreeing to "the exchange of resident representatives." They specified, however, that the competence of the representatives should be restricted to the settlement of border disputes and that they should be stationed at prescribed points near the boundary. Manchukuo agreed to this, but on condition that the number of representatives and the places where they were to be stationed should be considered at a subsequent conference.

Negotiations were renewed in October but no agreement was reached because of insistence on the part of Japan that three representatives should be appointed for residence in the principal cities of each country. Threats failed to move the Mongolian representatives beyond an acceptance of the appointment of a purely frontier representative for each party.

These incidents, on both frontiers, were ascribed by the Japanese to the fact that neither frontier had been fully and definitely marked out. The Russians asserted that the Manchurian-Siberian frontier had been well defined by treaty and by accompanying maps. The Japanese, however, insisting on a new demarcation of boundaries, refused to accept such treaties and maps as a basis. As to the Manchurian-Mongolian boundary, there appears to have been no detailed delineation at any time. Custom and tradition had established it satisfactorily until Japan, bent on expansion, began to think in terms of strategic frontiers, with boundaries always well advanced from the customarily accepted lines. Until an agreement on frontiers had been reached, boundary disputes of at least a minor sort were certain to continue.

But what began as a series of minor incidents, with individual sentries and patrols sniping at each other, grew progressively as the border forces on both sides were increased. Each was apparently determined to test the other's mettle. Thus the minor incidents of 1934-1935 led up to major clashes in 1936. Such a major incident on the Mongol-Manchurian border February 8-10, 1936, when several hundred Japanese and Manchukuoan troops, using trucks, tanks and planes, penetrated some six miles into Mongolia, resulted in hostilities. In the encounter which followed the Japanese, definitely worsted, withdrew behind their own boundary. An even more dangerous climax was reached on the Manchukuoan-Siberian frontier when a Russian force of about 4,000, consisting of all arms, faced a mixed Japanese-Manchukuoan force of about 2,500 from March 25 to March 29, 1936. A little indiscretion on the part of either of the commanders would probably have committed the two countries to a war for which, obviously, neither side was ready. Each opponent found an answer to its question— it knew that the other would fight to preserve its boundary inviolate. In particular, Japan was forced to realize that the process of successive penetration and seizure, almost uniformly successful against China and Inner Mongolia, could not be utilized for the moment against Siberia, or Outer Mongolia backed by Russia. Once that fact was clear, the border incidents relapsed for a time into minor affairs.

In all of these negotiations, and in the resistance in general to Japanese pressure, Russia stood behind the government of Outer Mongolia. A Pact of Mutual Assistance, in essence a defensive alliance between Russia and Outer Mongolia, was announced by Moscow on March 31, 1936, and Stalin further definitely stated that an attack on Outer Mongolia by Manchukuo, supported by Japan, would be considered as an act of war on Russia itself. This defensive alliance checked Japanese and Manchukuoan border aggressions. At the same time it provided Japanese militarists with further arguments in their efforts to secure larger appropriations for military purposes. No other position could really have been taken by Russia since Japan's control of the territory would enable her readily to cut off and establish control of Siberia. It probably would not be very far from the facts to conclude that one Japanese interest in securing control of Outer Mongolia was strategic in relation to the Russian Far East. An additional reason for the attempt at penetration was the desire to establish a buffer territory between Russia, Inner Mongolia, and North China. It may be questioned, however, whether these interests were considered to be sufficiently important to warrant their being pressed to the point where war with Russia could not be avoided, unless there were assurance of support from one or more European states.

Such an assurance the military group in Japan felt had been initiated with the signature at Berlin on November 25, 1936, of the German-Japanese Anti-Comintern Pact. While directed, in its terms, against the activities of the Comintern rather than the Soviet Union, this agreement established working political relationships between Berlin and Tokyo of a friendly sort. It also gave Japan a basis of association with Italy, similarly committed subsequently against the Communist International. This collaboration of Japan with two strong European Powers on the basis of hostility to communism helped to immobilize the Soviet Union and to weaken the vigor of its opposition to Japan as that country enlarged its continental objectives after 1936. Immediately, on the other hand, it prejudiced the prospects of conclusion of a long-term fisheries convention, then under negotiation.

3. JAPAN DEFINES HER POLICY

Outer Mongolia being protected by Russia, the point of least effective resistance to Japan, as well as the area of maximum attraction after the occupation of Manchuria, continued to be Inner Mongolia and China. The general lines of Japanese policy began to be marked out during the period of pressure applied locally in the north, the initial development of which has already been summarized. These general definitions of policy were then summed up as the declaration of a Japanese "Monroe Doctrine" for eastern Asia. On the face of it, the Japanese "Monroe Doctrine" was designed to protect China against the imperialism of the Western states. The policies of those states, in the interest of peace, order, and stability, it was declared, must be satisfactory to Japan as the guardian of the peace in the Far East, and as the defender of the integrity of China against the assaults of Europe. Thus the spokesman of the Japanese Foreign Office declared, on April 18, 1934:

. . . . It goes without saying that Japan at all times is endeavoring to maintain and promote her friendly relations with foreign nations, but at the same time we consider it only natural that to keep peace and order in East Asia we must even act alone on our own responsibility, and it is our duty to perform it. At the same time there is no country but China which is in a position to share with Japan the responsibility for the maintenance of peace in East Asia.

Accordingly, unification of China, preservation of her territorial integrity as well as restoration of order in that country, are most ardently desired by Japan. History shows that these can be attained through no other means than awakening and voluntary efforts of China herself.

We oppose therefore, any attempt on the part of China to avail herself of the influence of any other country in order to resist Japan; we also oppose any action taken by China calculated to play one power against another. Any joint operations undertaken by foreign powers even in the name of technical or financial assistance at this particular moment after Manchurian and Shanghai incidents are bound to acquire political significance. Undertakings of such nature, if carried through to the end, must give rise to complications that might eventually necessitate discussion of problems like division of China and at the same time would have most serious repercussion upon Japan and East Asia.

Japan, therefore, must object to such undertakings as a matter of principle, although she will not find it necessary to interfere with any foreign country negotiating individually with China on questions of finance or trade as long as such negotiations benefit China and are not detrimental to peace in East Asia.

However, supplying China with war aeroplanes, building aerodromes in China, and detailing military and naval instructors or military advisers to China, or contracting a loan to provide funds for political uses, would obviously tend to alienate friendly relations between Japan, China, and other countries, and to disturb peace and order in Eastern Asia. Japan will oppose such projects. [4]

Statements to the same effect were also made during 1934 by the Japanese Foreign Minister, Mr. Hirota, who became the Premier in 1936; by the Japanese Ambassadors at Berlin and Washington and, in more qualified terms, in a note addressed to France, Great Britain, and the United States.

The external reaction to this spate of Japanese declarations and to the note took the general form of a reservation of rights under treaty, and especially under the Nine Powers Treaty of Washington. The Chinese government also issued a statement on April 19 affirming the interest of China in the maintenance of peace and justice. Among other things the statement declared that: "No State has a right to claim exclusive responsibility for maintaining peace in any part of the world. . . .

"No nation not harbouring ulterior motives against China need entertain any fears concerning her policy of national reconstruction." [5]

The pointed observation was made in a statement issued by the Chinese Legation in London that: "The surest guarantee of peace in the Far East is to be found not in the abstention from friendly and fruitful collaboration with China by the Western Powers, but in the abandonment by Japan of her policy of ruthless imperialism in Asia, and in a scrupulous respect by her of her treaty obligations." [6]

The reason for this war of words may be briefly summarized. First, it may be said to have been timed to coincide with the submission at Geneva of the Rajchman report on League assistance to China. League experts had been studying phases of the problem of reconstruction in China, at the request of the Nanking government, for some time. The Technical Agent of the Council, Dr. Rajchman, who presented this report recommending lines of future development of the League's work, had come to be considered in Japan as antagonistic to that country. The Japanese thus sought to make it clear in advance that they would oppose the acceptance of the recommendations of the report. Since they were no longer represented at Geneva in consequence of their withdrawal from the League, their point of view had to be made clear in advance, and in this particular way of warning the League off by declarations of policy. In this they were only partly successful since the report was accepted and referred to the Technical Organizations immediately concerned for further study.

Second, the Chinese had secured aid from Americans and others in their endeavor to build up an air force. "The Curtiss-Wright Company had . . . contracted to erect an aeroplane factory to be operated with the help of

[4] *Documents on International Affairs, 1934*, pp. 472–473.
[5] *Ibid.*, p. 473.
[6] *Ibid.*, p. 474.

American engineers." An aviation base had been established at Hangchow "with a school for military pilots attached," under the supervision of a retired Colonel of the United States Air Corps. And the United States had sold China a number of fighting planes. Furthermore, Sino-American and Sino-German corporations operated the two principal civil aviation lines in the country. An Italian Air Mission was maintained at General Chiang Kai-shek's headquarters out of the remitted portion of the Italian Boxer Indemnity, part of which had also been used to maintain an aviation center at Nanchang. And, in April, 1934, in addition, a German, General von Seeckt, former head of the Reichswehr, had been appointed as chief military adviser at Nanking. [7]

All of these developments were directed toward increasing the military power of China with foreign (i.e., non-Japanese) aid. Other internal developments in China, both political and economic, which will be considered shortly, were designed to have the same ultimate effect. As China became stronger, the ability of Japan to exert successful pressure either on local régimes responsive to the direction of Nanking or on the central government itself would correspondingly decrease. But the immediate prospect of China's creating sufficient power to resist Japan's expansion seemed to depend upon foreign aid. Therefore, in 1934, Japan declared herself to be in favor of strengthening China, but only by China's unaided efforts unless she were willing to accept Japanese aid.

These definitions represented the negative reaction to China's attempt to secure assistance from the Western Powers, either directly or through the League of Nations. The positive emphasis was made in the important definition of policy which came to be known as the Hirota "three point" policy. This was presented to the Chinese Ambassador to Japan on October 28, 1935, and was given full exposition by the Japanese Foreign Minister in a statement to the Diet on January 21, 1936. The first point "is concerned with the basic readjustment of Sino-Japanese relations, by which we aim to bring about the cessation by China of all unfriendly acts and measures, such as have been hitherto adopted." Second, "the rehabilitation of Sino-Japanese relations must necessarily be attended by the regularization of the relations between *Manchukuo* and *China*, because in North China particularly the interests of these two countries and Japan are directly and closely bound up. . . . We are convinced that as the first step to a complete and final readjustment of the relations between Japan, Manchukuo, and China, the Chinese Government should recognize Manchukuo, and the two countries should open diplomatic intercourse and

---

[7] The American Wheat Loan had also been objected to on the ground that the funds were used to purchase armament. The quotations in this paragraph are from *Survey of International Affairs*, 1934, pp. 247–249.

harmonize their interests." Third, "it is the desire of the Japanese Government to coöperate with China in various ways for the eradication of communism." [8]

4. AUTONOMY FOR NORTH CHINA

These three points had in them large implications. Immediately, however, they seemed designed mainly to establish the larger framework within which a new forward movement in North China could be placed. On the following day, October 29, the North China authorities were presented with five demands designed to bring about a further restriction of Kuomintang control in the northern provinces. While China partially met these local demands, the action did not go far enough or rapidly enough to meet the requirements of the Japanese military leaders. Consequently, early in November reports began to circulate of the existence of a popular desire to establish an autonomous régime in North China. These reports were clearly of Japanese inspiration and were the surface indications of activity undertaken to establish the basis for carrying into effect the "popular demand" just as had previously been done in Manchuria. The reports themselves took the form at first of declarations of an intention to use force, if necessary, to prevent Nanking from interfering with this essentially "Chinese" movement. It was then reported, under date of November 18, and from Tokyo, that an autonomous government would be established within the week. These reports of an autonomous régime to be established, to include five provinces (Hopei, Chahar, Suiyuan, Shansi, and Shantung) and 95 million people, continued to be made during November without the step actually being taken. The necessary popular interest failed to express itself, and, even under strong pressure, the officials failed in most cases to appreciate the advantages of a severance of their connections with Nanking. The Nanking government, on its side, sought to take the initiative out of Japan's hands by sending new officials to North China and by itself organizing different arrangements of a semi-autonomist character in the hope of retaining the loyalty of the North, while avoiding giving serious offense to Japan.

The only affirmative result of these moves and counter-moves was the creation, in December, 1935, of an autonomous area in eastern Hopei province, the governing organ being the East Hopei Autonomous Council. This régime, after its establishment, was completely dominated by the Japanese military authorities at Tientsin and Peip'ing. A second semi-autonomous régime, calling itself the Hopei-Chahar Political Council, not quite so transparently a Japanese-controlled body, also came into being.

---

[8] The complete text of the statement may be found in *Documents on International Affairs*, 1937, London, 1939, pp. 632–638.

This resulted from the policy of the Nanking government, in meeting the crisis, of itself organizing a North China régime, within the limited area where Japan could take direct action, which (1) would be sufficiently unobjectionable to the Japanese military so that its establishment would not be opposed; but which (2) would be essentially Chinese and as responsive to the direction of Nanking as circumstances permitted. Its creation was evidence of two things: (1) the determination of Chiang Kai-shek to temporize as long as possible, and (2) the lack of direct authority of the Nanking government in the area north of the Yellow River, entirely aside from the position of the Japanese. The new régime was somewhat comparable in position and powers to that functioning in the south as the Southwest Political Council. It differed from the latter, in the circumstances of its creation, in that it was an adaptation to Japanese policy rather than an evolution exclusively within the framework of domestic politics. As an adaptation, however, it represented adjustment to the pressures of northern Chinese opinion, expressed from intellectual and student quarters, hostile to the extension of Japanese control in North China, as well as to those of the Japanese military.

The Japanese Army-promoted autonomy movement for the five northern Chinese provinces thus failed of attaining its objectives since all of the area involved except the districts strictly within the demilitarized zone was not completely dissociated from the direction of Nanking. The Japanese were apparently not prepared to push their demands for control of North China to the point where they would have to be enforced. During the period of maneuvering, since the central Chinese government had indicated a readiness to negotiate on the basis of the Hirota Three Points, and also because of the stiffening of the Chinese attitude on account of the pressures of anti-Japanese elements, the Japanese government disavowed responsibility for the autonomy movement. This was done by making it apparent that its inspiration was from the Kwantung Army leadership, and especially from the initiative of Major-General Doihara, rather than from Tokyo. This virtual disavowal of responsibility, evidential of a continuing dualism in the Japanese government, made less effective the Japanese pressure which could be brought to bear locally in the north, outside of the Tientsin area. It thus made it possible for the northern Chinese provincial officialdom to transfer the responsibility for finding a basis of settlement to Nanking.

Clear indications were given in the first months of 1936, however, that the interest of Japan in North China remained and that pressure might, consequently, be expected to continue on the Chinese authorities. For two principal reasons, more hesitancy had to be shown in this movement into North China than had been exhibited by the Army in Manchuria. The first was that the advance contemplated was into China proper, the maintenance of the integrity of which was a matter of much more direct concern to Chinese officialdom and to the articulate classes of China. The second was that the movement was into a region of larger and more clearly established foreign (non-Japanese) interests, and also into one where more difficulty would be found in reconciling treaty obligations with the expansionist program. Thus it was necessary to test out more carefully the possibility of both Chinese and foreign resistance. Nevertheless the attempt at an advance of position to the Yellow River, at least, and possibly to the Yangtze, had its logical justification or explanation as a part of the Japanese program.

Under Army direction the exploitation of Manchuria had been found not to give the returns which had been anticipated. Part of the development, on the economic side, had been competitive with the economic life of Japan rather than strictly complementary or supplementary to it. Furthermore, the attempt to establish self-sufficiency through the formation of a Japanese-Manchukuoan economic bloc had not been successful. Thus an economic interest came to be expressed in the resources of North China. It was argued, for example, that the proper exploitation of the North China cotton areas would free Japan from her dependence on the United States and India for this raw material essential to her textile industry, and that the iron and coal reserves of Inner Mongolia and North China would be even more valuable than those of Manchuria. In addition the Japanese became more and more aware of the industrial problem as one which would have to be solved in terms of markets as well as raw materials. Thus a major emphasis began to be placed on the market possibilities of North China, more extensive than those of Manchuria, which could be developed as a "controlled" outlet for the industrial production of Japan. Underlying the movement into North China, in other words, was a double economic motivation, leading to the view that it, even more than Manchuria, must be regarded as Japan's economic life-line.

Another explanation of the "inevitable" attempt to establish control of North China was political and strategic. The position in Manchuria, it was argued, was insecure as long as there was an unfriendly government in control of the area immediately to the south. It has been pointed out that the problem of restoring and maintaining order in Manchuria had been made much more difficult of solution because of the attitude of the Chinese, who could use North China as a base of propaganda and disturbance. Consequently it was even argued seriously by the Japanese spokesmen that Chinese resistance and lack of coöperativeness forced them to act in North China so as to secure their position north of the Great Wall. Thus the two of Hirota's Three Points had a North China-in-relation-to-Manchuria context. The more chauvinistic elements in the Army, to be sure, did not feel under any need to explain or justify what to them was essentially a program of territorial expansion which was proper and necessary because it would result in the enlargement and the strengthening of Japan. To justify the sacrifices which expansion entailed, however, and thus to maintain the necessary popular support and approval, and also to avoid Western opposition and thus lessen the resistance which would have to be overcome, explanation and justification in terms of the national interest had to be made.

5. THE EFFECTS OF JAPAN'S DOMINANCE IN NORTH CHINA

The most serious immediate consequence to China of the establishment of the East Hopei Autonomous Council was an increase in smuggling into North China. The impotence of the Chinese authority in the Tientsin region after the signature of the Tangku Armistice made it possible for smugglers to introduce goods into the country without payment of the custom charges. It was comparatively easy to bring goods into Hopei province by sea from the Manchurian ports, or overland through the northern passes controlled by the Japanese or the Hopei-Chahar Military Council. The Chinese had been left without any force to police the region. The customs officials, under international supervision, trying to break up the sea traffic were not permitted by the Japanese to use force against the smugglers, the explanation offered being an oral agreement made at the time of the Tangku Truce. China, however, denied that such an agreement had been made. And the areas entered were ones where only officials satisfactory to Japan had been permitted to remain. Thus there was no power in China capable of preventing the northern provinces, as far south as the Yangtze River, from being flooded with Japanese goods, entering without payment of the tariff charges. This meant an important loss of revenue to the Nanking government, and it could only result in driving competitive foreign goods completely out of the North China markets. Consequently protests began to be addressed to the Japanese government by China, and also by England and the United States. The latter objected on the ground that the principle of the Open Door was at stake.

These protests may have had something to do with the development of the movement toward autonomy since the smuggling had become so pronounced and open by August, 1935, and it then met with such protests, that Tokyo could not avoid an investigation into the situation. Whether or not there was this relationship, it can only be concluded that the failure to discourage smuggling represented a form of pressure on China almost as effective in its weakening effects as military action.

At any rate, after the establishment of the East Hopei régime the situation was changed, without any real improvement from the standpoint of the Chinese, the Americans, or the British. The autonomous Council established its own customs charges at 25 per cent of the national tariff. This may have justified the conclusion that the trade was no longer to be classed as smuggling. Nevertheless it facilitated the in-flow of Japanese goods, without the Nanking government regaining any of the revenue lost from the customs, and without the non-Japanese foreign traders regaining equality of commercial opportunity. After this action had been taken, the Japanese used the smuggling as the justification for an attempt to bring all Chinese duties on Japanese goods down to the level established in the Autonomous Area.

Closely related to this smuggling activity, from the standpoint of methods employed as well as from that of legality, was the trade in narcotic drugs. Reference has been made in previous chapters to the initial successes of the Chinese in bringing opium cultivation under control and to the virtual breakdown of control of production, distribution, and consumption during the period of military rule of the provinces. Reference has also been made to the increase in importation of manufactured drugs such as cocaine and heroin during and immediately after World War I. This was connected with the maintenance of foreign post offices in China. After the Washington Conference, and especially during the years after the institution of the National government in China, the earlier movement toward control both of production and of use of opium and its derivatives was resumed in China with support and approval from the Western world. After Japan established control of Manchuria and of Jehol, however, a reverse movement set in. One of the apparent reasons for the occupation of the latter province was the desire to profit from its already extensive opium production. In 1933 an opium monopoly was instituted for Manchuria and Jehol which was characterized before the League's Advisory Committee as "the largest single venture ever undertaken in the illicit traffic in narcotics." From the areas under Japanese control, China began to be flooded again with narcotic drugs, the traffic being largely in cocaine and heroin, and the agents being mainly Koreans, who, as Japanese subjects, were liable to trial and punishment, if apprehended, by the Japanese consular courts, which subjected them to penalties "so light as to constitute no detriment whatever. The drugs, mostly heroin and cocaine, are reported to have been obtained from Japan, Formosa or Dairen. A new source is Tientsin, where numerous Japanese-owned factories producing heroin have been discovered. . . . Aside from the Chinese trafficker, there is overwhelming evidence that the Japanese national is the most sinister character in the illicit drug trade north and south of the Great Wall. . . . The drug traffic in the demilitarized zone and in the Tientsin-Peip'ing area was facilitated by the establishment of a Japanese-supported régime in East Hopei which made possible immense smuggling operations of Japanese goods during the spring and summer of 1936." [9] Thus Japan, which had found it entirely possible as well as desirable to enforce a prohibition of the use of narcotics on its own nationals in Japan and elsewhere, lent itself to, even if it did not itself promote, the spread of the use of narcotics by the Chinese in those areas of China into which it had penetrated.

Beyond the move to break down in fact the customs barrier between Japan and Manchukuo, on the one side, and North China, on the other, and at least not to discourage its nationals from violating the Chinese laws against the importation and the distribution of narcotic drugs, the Japanese policy began to be directed toward the linking of the currency of North China to that of Manchukuo and thus to that of Japan. The transformation of the region north of the Yellow River into an economic dependency of Japan, consequently, was being vigorously promoted during the period from the collapse of the autonomy movement to the time of outbreak of war between Japan and China in the summer of 1937. It was constantly accompanied by the threats of military action which continued to be made after the failure of the autonomy campaign to realize its full objectives.

6. CHINESE POLITICS: 1933–1936

Attention was diverted from the north to the south of China in the early summer of 1936. To understand this development, and also to relate domestic developments to the outbreak of the war, it is necessary at this point to review the internal political situation in China as it changed between 1933 and 1936.

In 1933, the point to which the review of internal political developments was carried in chapter XX, the Nanking government was confronted with several groups challenging its authority. One of these was the semi-independent, or autonomous, government exercising power in Kwangtung and Kwangsi provinces. This government, in Kwangtung, represented elements of the left-wing of the Kuomintang which were non-communistic but which were opposed to the rightist tendencies of Chiang Kai-shek. It regarded itself as the legitimate exponent of the ideas of Sun Yat-sen. These elements acted in alliance with the Kwangsi generals who controlled Kwangsi province, and in Kwangtung itself they were dependent on the support of Chen Chi-tang, the local military commander. But, as an autonomous political régime, the organ of government was the Southwest Political Council. The important members of this government, however,

[9] W. W. WILLOUGHBY, *Japan's Case Examined*, p. 50, quoting F. T. MERRILL, *The Opium Menace in the Far East*, Foreign Policy Association, March, 1937.

were also members of the Central Executive Committee of the Kuomintang, and they intermittently participated in its deliberations and in the
direction of the activities of the Nanking government. The existing Kuomintang Central Executive Committee (the Fourth) had held its first
plenary session at the end of 1931. At that time, to resolve the conflicts
within the party which made the operation of orderly government more
difficult, a standing committee of three members of the Central Political
Council (made up of the Central Executive and Central Supervisory Committees of the party) was instituted. The three, constituting a theoretically
governing triumvirate, were Chiang Kai-shek, Wang Ching-wei, and Hu
Han-min. The last remained rather consistently aloof from Nanking during the following year, but Wang Ching-wei alternated, with some regu-
larity, participation in the government with resignation and opposition.
Under those circumstances, consequently, although it was autonomous,
the Canton régime did not reject the authority of Nanking but rather
periodically objected to the power exercised there by Chiang Kai-shek. Its
leaders sought, through withdrawal, to bring pressure to bear to maintain
a balance of relationship of their own with other factions within the Kuomintang. The tactics employed, and the relationships which existed, were
thus somewhat similar to those of Canton and Peking during the years
from 1918 to 1925.

A second group which did not accept the authority of Nanking was the
Communist Party, which the Lytton Commission in 1932 described "as an
actual rival of the national government." It challenged the authority of
Nanking in a much more direct and fundamental way than did the Canton
government, which was more or less in and out of alliance wih the National
government. The Communists assertedly exercised authority in 1932 over
an area of around 330,000 square miles of territory (over one-sixth of China
proper). The population of the territory under their authority was some
90 million. Thus the Communist Party represented a formidable obstacle
to the attainment of unity under the National government.

As has already been pointed out, it was the existence of communism
which Chiang Kai-shek used as the excuse for not attempting resistance to
Japan either in Manchuria or at the time of the Shanghai incident. Attempts were already being made to dislodge the Chinese Soviets from the
areas under their control when the movement in Manchuria began, and
they were continued after that time. It may, in fact, be said that a common
antipathy to communism served to give Chiang and the Japanese a basis
of understanding sufficient partially to overcome the barrier presented in
the Japanese policy of expansion. The former, at any rate, took the position
that the Communists were the immediately important obstacle to China's
development and he refused to divert his energies or his forces into what

may at the same time have appeared to be a hopeless struggle against Japan.

The four military campaigns that had been directed against the Communists by 1933 had failed, as already indicated, to dislodge them from Kiangsi province, where the Soviet government had been established. In fact, at the end of 1933, it appeared that Fukien province might also come under Soviet control in consequence of a revolt there on the part of the 19th Route Army, [10] which was supported by the Kiangsi Soviet. This alliance failed to accomplish its purpose of detaching the province from the control of the central government, however, and thereafter the government campaign began to attain a measure of success. This revolt occurred at a time when the forces of Chiang were making their sixth drive to eliminate the so-called "red menace" from Kiangsi. After it had been put down, the campaign was carried through to a partially successful conclusion. Success was attained by the end of 1934, however, because of the employment of a different method than that of direct military action. The new method indicated also a general change in the technique of the unification movement, and was especially important for that reason. Nanking had apparently concluded that the best way to secure its power was to proceed gradually, consolidating its position in one small area after another, rather than to spread out its authority more thinly so that it could be readily challenged over a wider territory; and to employ political methods simultaneously with military pressure. Some of these methods were revivals of those employed at the time of the revivification of the Kuomintang as a political force.

The methods employed included: "(1) the organization of the Blue Shirts, a terrorist society of Fascist pattern for the suppression of any radical deviations from Nanking policy and for carrying out certain political projects; (2) political education in government armies; (3) organization of detachments of landlords in the affected areas to supplement the work of the military proper; (4) broad economic and social reforms designed to eliminate the main causes of the Communist movement; (5) the 'New Life Movement' designed to tighten the moral temper of the people and to instil into modern Chinese, and especially the youth, pride in the classical, cultural heritage. The implications of these items are far-reaching. They mean strict suppression of all radical activity, including teaching and literature, in the areas controlled by Nanking. They mean a return to faith in Confucianism and in the ancient heritage of the country—a forceable return if need be." [11]

It is quite obvious that these methods could be, as they were, made of

[10] The force which, under Tsai Ting-kai, had resisted Japan at Shanghai in 1932. He was still its commander.

[11] *Far Eastern Survey*, vol. 4, No. 16, p. 124.

general application to strengthen the position of General Chiang outside of, as well as within, the areas recovered from the Communists. In relation to the latter, they were applied to each area regained, with a view to holding the position after the armies had moved on. That had been the weakness of the military method, used by itself. As soon as the armies moved on the Communists returned, and with the approval of the people.

These were essentially follow-up methods, except for the Blue Shirt activities and the education of the armies. They were made possible of application by the effectiveness of economic combined with military pressures. An economic blockade of the Communist areas was instituted. Motor roads were constructed to facilitate troop movements. And the economic enterprises built up by the Soviet government and its supporters were destroyed by bombing from the air. Troop movement itself was slow, with each advance consolidated before the next one was undertaken, in contrast with the method employed in previous campaigns of making rapid and deep thrusts into enemy territory.

Thus, by the end of 1934, the Communists had been forced to evacuate their strongholds in Kiangsi, and they were prevented from moving into immediately neighboring territory. They were not, however, eliminated. It was here that the government's policy and method failed. The Communists were not able to cope with the forces thrown against them by Chiang Kai-shek. But they were able to break through the blockading forces to the west, partly because the latter were made up of provincial troops less well-equipped, trained, and officered than Chiang's own army, and partly because of a breakdown of coöperation between Nanking and the government at Canton. The result was that by a series of remarkable maneuvers and marches the Red Armies were withdrawn in part to the Kweichow-Szechuan-Hunan border regions, and in part to an already existing Communist center at the point of contact of Szechuan, Shensi, and Kansu provinces. The net effect, then, of the government's victory was not to eliminate the Red Armies but to bring them from the Nanking area into the northwest, where readier contact could be established with Soviet Russia. There also they would produce some embarrassment for Japan, with whose newly asserted sphere of influence they thus had a more direct contact. This latter relationship was especially important because the Communist leaders had changed their emphasis from that of spreading communism to the proclamation of the need to subordinate all other considerations to defense of the country against Japan. Thus, when the situation began to develop in North China in 1935 as a result of the renewal of the Japanese advance, a new factor had been introduced into the political equation of the north. The proclamation by the Communists of anti-Japanism as the slogan for unification, together with the proximity of their base in the northwest to the area which Japan sought to control, gave a new significance to the Japanese hostility to communism. It had a direct bearing on the third of Hirota's points, the advancing of which as a basis for negotiation was shortly followed by the signature of the German-Japanese Anti-Comintern Pact. But this avowed hostility to communism also made it more difficult for Japan to object to the movement of Chiang Kai-shek's troops northward toward the demilitarized zone for the purpose of suppression of communism. Thus, although the Communists had, by the end of 1936, established themselves firmly in the northwest, their presence had the effect of strengthening the position of Chiang Kai-shek in the north, since it gave him an excuse for sending into that area more of his own troops and commanders. The continued "menace" of communism also gave him an excuse for continuing to temporize with Japan while still avoiding complete acceptance of Japan's conditions of settlement of the broader issues raised in the relations of the two countries.

Another advantage that accrued to Chiang and to Nanking from the northwestward movement of communism was the introduction of control from Nanking into Szechuan province. When confronted with the approaching "red menace," at the time of the "long march," the officials there called upon Chiang for financial and military aid. This was granted in return for the establishment of closer relations of dependence on the central government. The same request was made from Yunnan and Kweichow provinces, with the same result. Thus the authority of Nanking was more completely extended over all of the region south of the Yangtze, except for Kwangtung and Kwangsi provinces, and into Szechuan, except for the areas controlled by the Chinese Soviets.

7. ECONOMIC REHABILITATION OF CHINA

The great problem confronting China, aside from that of political unification and that of self-preservation as an entity, was that of economic rehabilitation and modernization. Some progress toward solution of this problem was made during the period under review. That more was not made could be explained on the score of the preoccupation of the government with the struggle to maintain itself and to extend the area of its effective authority, together with the continued diversion of large sums from reconstruction to military purposes.

There were other reasons also for the failure to engage more largely in reconstructive activities. For one thing the revenues of Nanking had been affected first by the loss of Manchuria and Jehol, and then by the inability to collect the customs on goods imported into the northern provinces. The same effect had been felt from the periodic devastation of many of the provinces directly under the control of the National government as a result of flood or drought. This carried with it not merely a loss of revenue but the need to supply funds for relief purposes. Again, China as well as other states had been adversely affected by the depression, the textile industry possibly having been the most seriously affected. Foreign trade fell off in 1934 "by one-third below the 1933 level" for imports, and for exports "by one-eighth, with a fifty per cent reduction in two of the principal staples, raw cotton and silk." [12]

Serious effects were also felt from the silver policy followed by the government of the United States after June, 1934. Both imports and exports fell off rapidly, instead of increasing, as had been predicted, as a result of the rise in the price of silver. Of even more importance, silver, the basis of the Chinese currency, began to be drained out of the country because of the high prices to be realized on it abroad. Appeals to the United States for a change in policy having met with no response, the Chinese government was finally compelled, on November 4, 1935, to abandon the silver standard and set up a managed currency. Silver was nationalized by decree, and the control of the issuance of paper money was given exclusively to three government-controlled institutions, the Central Bank of China, the Bank of China, and the Bank of Communications. The former had been government-controlled from the time of its establishment; the other two had their capitalization increased and were brought under a more complete government control than had previously been the case. And, through their agency, the government assumed complete control of and responsibility for the currency.

While the managed currency system proved more of a success than had been considered by many experts to be possible, its effective establishment and maintenance encountered certain obvious difficulties. One of these was to be found in the inability of the government to control the activities of the foreign banks; to take over their stocks of silver; and to prevent the issuance, as they had in the past, of their own banknotes. A second lay in the lack of confidence which had been engendered among the people in the paper currency, which added to the difficulty of securing control of the stocks of silver in private hands. A third lay in the fact that the policy could not be applied throughout the entire country because of lack of effective control of a number of the provinces by the Nanking government. This was notably true of the north, where Japanese policy interfered with the application of Nanking's currency policy. There the movement was stimulated to break away from China in the matter of currency and tie in to the Manchukuo-Japanese system and, through Japan, into the sterling bloc. Finally, arrangements had to be made for the financing of foreign exchanges.

This latter difficulty, especially, together with the desire to use the cur-

[12] *Survey of International Affairs*, 1934, p. 639.

rency situation to weaken Japan's control of the economic situation, brought about a visit to China of the British expert, Sir Frederick Leith-Ross, who sought to work out arrangements which would tie the Chinese currency to sterling. The plan proposed, however, involved an international loan, to which Japan was opposed, and which did not otherwise prove feasible. Negotiations for a loan were subsequently instituted at Washington. In May, 1936, an agreement was reached under which the United States was to make purchases of silver in gold, the gold proceeds to be utilized for currency stabilization purposes, and to be largely held abroad, in New York, where a branch of the Bank of China was to be established.

In spite of the handicaps of continued civil war, economic depression, currency difficulties, and international pressures, however, there were accomplishments to be credited to the Nanking government's account during 1934 and 1935. These were mainly in the field of communications. New railway construction was undertaken and some old projects carried to completion. Important additions were made to the motor highways of the country. Air lines were established and extended. Radio communications were increased. The fact that activity in the field of communications was intimately related in many instances to the extension of the authority of Nanking by military means may be recognized without detracting from the significance of the improvements made.

The organization of agricultural coöperative societies, a development which was begun before the assumption of power by the Nationalist government, continued. It was stimulated by the enactment of legislation in January, 1934, which legalized the coöperatives. Promotional campaigns, training courses for coöperators and coöperative literature helped to advance the movement. As a result the number of societies had increased by the end of 1934 to 14,649, with a combined membership of 557,521, almost entirely within the territories actually controlled by Nanking. The main function of the coöperatives was the extension of credit facilities in the rural areas. They served the government in this and other ways in the attempt at rehabilitation of the areas regained from Communist control. In this extension of credit they were assisted by the Rural Finance Relief Bureau, formed in 1932, and also by the Four Provinces Agricultural Bank in Hankow, established in 1933. All of this was significant of the desire of the National government to improve the condition of the peasants, but it must be recognized that it was only a beginning which needed to be extended rapidly and broadly if the power of the government was to rest on a foundation of popular support rather than military power. The same thing applied to other features of the reconstruction program, which included flood prevention, reforestation to prevent drought, and scientific study and efforts to improve cotton and raw silk production.

On the industrial side, also, on the basis of private initiative, there was a measure of progress recorded. The government's relation to industrial development was, in large part, represented by its control of the tariff. When autonomy had been regained it was proposed to use the tariff for purposes of protection. This proved to be possible only to a limited extent because of the attitude of Japan, which was able to exert sufficient pressure to bring about tariff revision in 1934, and to prevent the application of the tariff charges in the north by the protection afforded to smugglers and through the actions of the East Hopei Autonomous Council. Thus the tariff came to afford protection against American and British imports, but only to a limited extent, and only in the provinces under Nanking's control, against Japanese manufactures. As has been stated, the actions in the north produced foreign protests to Japan. The Japanese government, however, disclaimed responsibility. At the same time it protested against Chinese curbs put on smuggling, and attempted to use the disregard of tariff regulations as a lever to bring about a further lowering of the tariff.

This renewal of Japanese pressure in 1935 and 1936 had an interesting and possibly unforeseen consequence. It not only caused an adverse popular reaction throughout the north, especially among the students, and renewed popular pressure on Chiang Kai-shek to resist further Japanese expansion at the expense of China by military means, but it also brought about a re-direction of relations between Nanking and Canton.

8. NANKING AND CANTON: 1933–1936

As has been stated, the Nanking government had not been able to exert any effective authority over the two provinces of Kwangtung and Kwangsi. Their relations may be best described as that of unstable alliance. One of the greatest obstacles to amalgamation was the constantly increasing personal authority, within the government and also the party, of Chiang Kai-shek. His supporters were in control of the Central Executive Committee of the party and thus were able to control its agenda and determine its decisions. Through it he could control the Party Congress by determining its composition through manipulation of representation. Thus it was impossible for members of the Canton group in the party to act through party organs to get a real hearing for their point of view as to national policy. For that reason they would not participate in the deliberations of the Central Executive Committee except after negotiations, and under defined conditions. Neither was it possible to secure their agreement to participate in the holding of Party Congresses. These had to be constantly postponed, beginning with the one which should have been held in 1933.

In spite of the failure to hold a Party, or National, Congress of the Kuomintang, however, steps were taken toward the inauguration of constitutional government. A draft constitution was prepared in 1934 and submitted for study to a special committee, preliminary to its consideration by the National Congress which was scheduled for convocation in November, 1935. The Congress was again postponed, but the terms of the constitution were approved by the Central Executive Committee and it was proposed to submit it for adoption to a Congress to be held before the end of 1936. Space prevents a detailed consideration of its provisions. In general it provided for continuation of the Five Power government, with the people given the suffrage to be exercised in the selection of representatives to a People's Congress, which would meet rather infrequently. Beyond the provisions for popular control, the principal change proposed was in the direction of centralization of authority, both territorially and within the central government itself. In effect, it appeared designed to constitutionalize the dictatorship of Chiang Kai-shek. On this basis alone, it was objectionable to the Canton-Kwangsi faction.

The Cantonese leaders had also been most pronounced in their criticism of Chiang for his failure to resist Japan during and after the Manchurian crisis. Thus in September, 1934, a number of southern leaders joined in the signature of a circular telegram, demanding that changes be made in national policies at the Congress which then was scheduled for November and accusing Chiang of having refused to put into effect decisions taken at the Congress in 1931 with reference to resistance to Japan. Not only had there been no attempt at military resistance, but the signature of the Tangku Armistice Agreement, the through-traffic agreement for the Peking-Mukden Railway, the postal arrangements which had been made with Manchukuo, and other concessions to Japan, were considered to be evidences of an unwillingness to carry out Congress directions.

On this issue, it may be noted, there was no agreement at Nanking itself. T. V. Soong had resigned as Finance Minister because of the failure to attempt resistance to Japan, and many others, including such avowed pacifists as the philosopher, Hu Shih, had reached the conclusion that they could not support a government which would not undertake the protection of the country from foreign aggression.

With this feeling existent at Nanking and in the areas under its control, the Cantonese leaders may well have felt that they could strike a successful blow against the growing power of Chiang by making an appeal to the country against the Japanese. If he succumbed to pressure and threw his troops into a struggle against Japan he would inevitably be weakened from the internal military point of view as a result. If he continued to follow his policy of putting internal consolidation ahead of resistance to the foreign foe it might be possible to overthrow him by combining the forces of popular opinion with the armies of Canton and Kwangsi.

Consequently, as the Japanese were renewing their pressure in the late spring of 1936, the southern armies took the field, demanding that Chiang and his generals join with them in an attack on the Japanese in the north. The emphasis in the news thus shifted from North to South China—from Japan to Canton. For a few weeks it appeared that widespread civil war might result, since Chiang made it evident that he would resist a northward move of the southern troops. The southern revolt collapsed, however, without any serious fighting, the result being the extension of the authority of the National government over Kwangtung province. Chiang himself went to Canton to reorganize both the military and the civil government of the province. Nanking officials were put in the directive positions, and financial reforms were immediately instituted which emphasized the reunification of Canton with Nanking. By September an agreement had also been reached with the Kwangsi generals, under which, while more autonomy was left to the province than in the Kwangtung settlement, they were brought into a closer alliance with Chiang Kai-shek and their troops were incorporated into the National Army.

9. CHIANG KAI-SHEK AND THE COMMUNISTS

The Southwestern régime having been disposed of, there remained two major obstacles to the completion of the process of unification. One, of course, was presented in the Japanese position and Japan's policy in the northern and northeastern area. The other was to be found in the consolidation of the Communist position in the Shensi-Kansu border region. The Red Armies had been reunited there, and a Soviet state was in process not only of creation but also of extension in the direction of Shansi and Suiyuan provinces. Chiang had already moved troops against the Communist forces. Chang Hsüeh-liang had been placed in command of the government forces, which were composed in part of the remnants of the old Tungpei (Manchurian) army which had been first driven out of its homeland by the Japanese and then had been withdrawn from North China after its failure to defend Jehol and the passes into the northern plains in 1933. Their past experience and their future interest alike tended to make these troops more responsive to anti-Japanese propaganda than almost any other military force in China. This is an important consideration because their new military duties brought them at the same time back into the area of Japanese activity and into contact with the Red Armies, whose leaders were the most active in carrying on anti-Japanese propaganda.

As early as the end of 1935 Mao Tse-tung, Chu Teh, Chou En-lai, and the other Communist leaders had changed the emphasis in the area under their control as well as in the propaganda carried on during the "Long March" and outside of the sovietized region. They had begun to seek a basis for reunion with the Kuomintang in the formation of a democratic united front against Japan. Thus their new policy conformed to the line then being followed by Communist parties elsewhere. Mao Tse-tung, the Chairman of the Chinese Central Soviet Government, in an interview in 1936, defined the purposes of a democratic union, as seen by the Communists, as being:

(1) to resist the foreign invader, (2) to grant rights to the masses, and (3) to develop the country's economy . . . there must be relief for the peasantry, but . . . "Agrarian revolution is of bourgeois character. It is beneficial to the development of capitalism. We are not opposed to the development of capitalism now in China, but against imperialism. This principle meets the demands of all democratic elements in the country and we support it wholeheartedly." [13]

Specifically, as they came into contact with the government armies sent to bring about their extermination, the Communists asked why they were fighting one another, as Chinese, when their united forces should be directed to the defense of the country against the Japanese. In consequence dissatisfaction grew in the government forces with the policy of the government. That policy seemed to have been subordinating the defense of the country against Japan to the exterminating of Chinese Communists. The result was that the operations against the Red Armies were not carried on with any vigor. In fact, by the end of 1936, not only had the battlefronts been stabilized, but there was also a considerable amount of fraternization between the personnel of the two forces. This had the effect of increasing the dissatisfaction of the leaders of the government troops with their anti-Communist mission.

This growing dissatisfaction was reported to Chiang Kai-shek by Chang Hsüeh-liang when the former flew to Sian, the capital of Shensi province, shortly after he had reorganized the Canton government. Chiang, however, refused either to change his policy, to take the necessary steps to win support for it by justifying it, or to take with sufficient seriousness the report of dissatisfaction. The result was that when he returned to Sian in December, he was subjected to the indignity of being "kidnapped" by his immediate subordinates, who acted, at least in part, under the pressure of their own subordinates. Their avowed purpose, as reflected in the demands they made, was to bring Chiang to a perception of the need for a change in basic policy in the direction of: (1) greater democracy, reversing an apparent trend toward military dictatorship; (2) acceptance of the Communists' proposals for a united front; and (3) early resistance to Japan.

Chiang Kai-shek was seized on December 12. He was released on December 25. Between those two dates the attention not only of China but of the world was focused on the drama being enacted at Sian. Nanking

[13] *Survey of International Affairs*, 1936, p. 885, citing an interview with Edgar Snow.

threatened a direct military and air attack on Sian to bring the rebels to terms and ostensibly to secure the release of the Generalissimo, although it was clear that such action would inevitably result in his death. The indication was that his capture would be used by his opponents in the government of which he was the head to gain control of the government. Thus his life was threatened by his captors and by the policy of those who allegedly were seeking his release. His personal prestige was great enough, however, together with that of his wife, her brother T. V. Soong, and other supporters, so that, when contact had been established with him at Sian, his orders to suspend hostilities until negotiations had been carried to a conclusion or had broken down were obeyed. Thus, although a prisoner, he was able to maintain, for the short time necessary, his dominance at Nanking. The great problem was that of finding a basis of agreement between himself and his captors which would enable them, on their side, to release him without fear of the consequences to themselves, and, on his side, to maintain his prestige as the commander-in-chief and head of the government. The position taken by Chiang at the outset was that there was nothing to negotiate about. Either his captors were his subordinates and should release him and accept the consequences of their insubordination, or they should not consider him as anything but their prisoner. In that case they should kill him, since he could not negotiate with his subordinates and still expect them to act in a disciplined fashion under his command.

Chiang Kai-shek's original stiff attitude of not even being willing to discuss matters with Chang Hsüeh-liang and General Yang Hu-ch'eng, the two principal leaders in the kidnapping, was modified after Madame Chiang arrived at Sian accompanied by T. V. Soong and W. H. Donald, one of his foreign advisers. He was persuaded to listen to Chang and also to give a hearing to Chou En-lai, one of the principal Communist leaders. He steadily refused, however, to give any written commitments with respect to the demands of those who held his person. Consequently his release was finally effected without any formal basis of agreement having been defined. Chang Hsüeh-liang, however, seems to have been persuaded to take that action by a reading of the Generalissimo's diaries. These gave him a new insight into the policies being followed and possibly made him feel that the ends sought would be realized even though Chiang would not formally commit himself. The captors were also persuaded to release him by Communist insistence that killing Chiang, which was the only alternative to his release, would defeat the ends sought since Chiang was the indispensable leader of an anti-Japanese popular front. This latter point of view was reënforced by the popular reception both of the news of the kidnapping and of his subsequent release.

Chiang Kai-shek was returned to Nanking by his captor, Chang Hsüeh-liang, who considered himself to be in custody to the man whom he was releasing. Chang was subsequently tried and punished for his insubordination, although the penalties imposed were apparently more for the record than seriously intended, since they were almost immediately commuted. [14] For the record, also, the eight-point program of the rebels was presented to the Third Plenary Session of the Kuomintang Central Executive Committee, which held that it could not consider it because of the rebellious method of presentation. Similarly, Chiang Kai-shek, assuming responsibility for the episode, tendered his resignation of all of his offices because of his personal inadequacies. This was, of course, not accepted, although he was permitted to retire from active participation in public affairs in order to recover from the physical injuries which he had suffered while attempting to escape capture.

It would be improper to conclude, however, that the Sian episode had only incidental consequences, and that it was in fact terminated with the closing of the official record in the manner just summarized. It quite obviously had the consequence of strengthening the position of Chiang Kai-shek on account of the nation-wide adverse reaction to his detention, which made it impossible for his enemies at Nanking to take advantage of his temporary removal from the leadership. It revealed the solidity of the unification which had been accomplished under his direction, since other subordinate but semi-independent provincial military leaders did not take advantage of his detention to attempt to release themselves from dependence upon the central government. And it established the basis for subsequent "voluntary" agreement between the Communists and the Kuomintang. The former presented their proposals for a change in policy on the part of the Kuomintang and on their own part in a telegram sent to the Central Executive Committee. The Kuomintang, on its side, defined, under four heads, the conditions for reconciliation with the Communists. Negotiations were thereafter carried on, while both sides moved slowly toward the establishment of conditions which would make formal agreement possible. These unavowed negotiations had been carried to the point where an agreement on the conditions for formal end of the civil war, which had in fact been in a state of suspension for some months, was ready for announcement at the time when hostilities with Japan were inaugurated as a result of the Lukouchiao incident of July 7, 1937. Thus the apparent completion of the unification of China was prepared coincidentally with the outbreak of war, and the possibility of its consummation was a prelude to war.

[14] He was, however, not restored then, or thereafter, to office.

10. SINO-JAPANESE RELATIONS: 1936–JULY, 1937

As already indicated, one source of internal dissatisfaction with the Nanking government was its apparent willingness to give way to some extent to Japanese pressure rather than to attempt "national salvation" by resistance even to the ultimate point of war. In other words, while Chiang Kai-shek was attempting to get along with Japan by negotiating settlements of issues which arose or were created, the Chinese were steadily growing more anti-Japanese in sentiment. This was shown in the proclaimed objectives of the southwestern government when it raised the standard of revolt in the summer of 1936. It was also shown in the unwillingness of the Tungpei armies to continue the struggle against the Communists as the anti-Japanese propaganda of the Red Army leaders was brought to their attention. Beyond these indications, there were striking manifestations of the growing anti-Japanese sentiment among the Chinese populace. These occurred at such widely separated places that the feeling must be considered to have been national in character.

The Japanese reply to the expression of anti-Japanese sentiment, considered by Japan to have been deliberately fomented throughout the country, was the augmentation of its naval forces in Chinese waters and the temporary military occupation of the Hongkew district at Shanghai to secure redress for the shooting by Chinese gunmen of three Japanese sailors. At the same time it was demanded that there should be a settlement of all of the points at issue between the two countries, and that this settlement should be made directly by Chiang Kai-shek rather than the Minister of Foreign Affairs, with whom negotiations were then being carried on in connection with earlier questions. Thus Chiang's return to Nanking from Canton was required so that he might assume responsibility for whatever action was taken. He did, following the reëstablishment of control over the southwestern region, have an extended conference with the newly accredited Japanese Ambassador, Shigeru Kawagoe, but thereafter left negotiations in the hands of the Chinese Foreign Minister, Chang Chun, while he was absent from Nanking on tours of inspection.

In the negotiations, spread over some months, the Japanese objective was to secure acceptance of the general principles which had already been defined by them as the basis for the maintenance of friendly relations between China and Japan, and then to settle specific issues within the framework of general principles jointly accepted. The Chinese, however, insisted that the road to general agreement was through adjustment of specific differences. The general principles on which agreement was demanded by Japan involved: the acceptance of responsibility by Nanking for terminating anti-Japanese agitation and preventing its recrudescence; the recognition of Japan's special position in North China, coöperation in the suppression of communism through the brigading of Japanese with Chinese troops wherever the latter were confronted with Communist forces of equal numbers, and also in the areas bordering on Outer Mongolia; the acceptance of advisers in all branches of the Chinese government, including the military establishment as well as the civilian branches of administration; and economic collaboration, including the revision of the Chinese tariff down to the 1928 level. Subsequently these demands were modified somewhat by the Foreign Office.

Possibly an explanation of the "toning down" of the demands as originally presented was to be found in the Chinese reaction to them. Instead of giving way, at least to the extent of allowing negotiation to be restricted to them, the Chinese Foreign Minister formulated a counter-program. This included: Japanese coöperation with China in suppressing Japanese, Korean, and Formosan smugglers on the Chinese coast; abolition of the demilitarized zone set up around Shanghai in the 1932 armistice; annulment of the Tangku Truce and abolition of the demilitarized zone in Hopei; withdrawal of Japanese troops from all positions in Hopei and Chahar provinces; and abolition of Yin Ju-keng's East Hopei Autonomous Régime.

As the negotiations were carried on, the gap between the positions of the two parties tended to be narrowed to the point where agreement seemed to be possible. The ability of the Japanese Army to move independently, however, made agreement at least temporarily impossible, since the Japanese commanders revived direct military pressure in the north by action in support of irregular Manchukuoan-Mongolian forces which had attempted to establish control in Suiyuan province. These forces had met with serious reverses in the fighting with the Chinese, so that Japanese troops had to be sent to their aid. The Chinese military successes made it more difficult for the government to make additional concessions to Japan at Nanking; while the Japanese military intervention with negotiations still going on made it more difficult to accept the Japanese Foreign Office as the authorized agency of negotiation. Thus, for this and other reasons, no agreement had been reached through negotiations when the series of movements in Chinese politics resulting from the Sian kidnapping episode began.

Thereafter a period of quiet came in Sino-Japanese relations. This was partly at least the result of political changes in Japan which brought about the overthrow of the Hirota government at the beginning of 1937. There had been growing dissatisfaction with the inability of the government to reach a settlement with China. The Anti-Comintern Pact signed in November, 1936, had not been received with general favor in Japan, since it had prejudiced relations with England and especially with the Soviet Union, making impossible the conclusion of an agreement on the fisheries question. It was felt that the Hirota government had unduly forwarded the Army move toward the establishment of an anti-parliamentary fascist system in Japan. And there was unrest resulting from the financial burdens entailed by the application of the Army program in Manchuria and also in North China. In spite of all of this the Cabinet reconstruction was controlled by the military leadership, which was able to prevent General Ugaki, a moderate in Army circles, from forming a government. Nevertheless the new Cabinet, when formed under General Hayashi, and with Mr. Naotake Sato as Foreign Minister, was more moderate in its views as to the proper policy to be followed vis-à-vis China than its predecessor. Foreign Minister Sato, in presenting his policy to the Diet, declared his willingness to negotiate with China on the basis of equality, and characterized as premature the formation of economic blocs, such as that with Manchukuo and that proposed with North China. As he later modified his statement of policy, it was formulated essentially as that of economic rather than military diplomacy.

The Sato policy proved to have no long-run significance. It did, however, have the advantage of providing a breathing space during which the evolution of Chinese politics could take place without being affected materially by Japanese pressure. It was possible, however, because of the preoccupation of the military-fascist forces in Japan with the domestic struggle rather than because of general acceptance of it by them as satisfactory. Opposition had begun to become articulate again, with the parties seeking to reëstablish their influence in Japanese politics through expressing and capitalizing the prevalent dissatisfaction with the state of affairs. To meet this the government resorted to dissolution of the Diet, setting the elections for April 30, 1937. The composition of the Diet was changed somewhat as a result of the elections, but not to the advantage of the government. This did not, however, bring about its resignation, which was postponed until May 31, shortly after which a non-party government headed by Prince Konoye was formed as a national government. The Cabinet sought the support of the parties under cover of the supposed liberalism of the Premier. It secured the support of the Army through carrying over into the new Cabinet General Sugiyama as Minister of War and Admiral Yonai as Navy Minister, and of the industrialists through appointments to less important posts. It was this government which was in power, prepared to unify the country through the reinauguration of a strong foreign policy, when the Lukouchiao incident occurred which initiated the undeclared war between China and Japan.

REFERENCES FOR FURTHER STUDY

James M. Bertram, *First Act in China* (1938); the story of the Sian mutiny. T. A. Bisson, *Japan in China* (1938), ch. 2–7; an excellent treatment of developments in China and Japan as they moved toward war. Council on Foreign Relations, *The United States in World Affairs,* annual since 1931. Each contains one or more chapters and appendices, reviewing the Far Eastern situation during the year from the standpoint of the United States. David J. Dallin, *Soviet Russia and the Far East* (1948), ch. 1–8; a penetrating study of Soviet and Communist policies and tactics from 1931 to 1937. John Gunther, *Inside Asia* (1939); especially good on personalities. G. F. Hudson, *The Far East in World Politics,* 2nd ed. (1939). (British Royal) Institute of International Affairs, *Survey of International Affairs, Documents on International Affairs,* 1933–1936. Institute of Pacific Relations, *Far Eastern Survey* (fortnightly), 1934–1937. Owen Lattimore, *The Mongols of Manchuria* (1934); gives historical background as well as a treatment of contemporary relationships. Manchoukuo, *Year Book* (1942); contains much data not elsewhere available. Mitsubishi Economic Research Bureau, *Japanese Trade and Industry, Present and Future* (1936). H. S. Quigley and G. H. Blakeslee, *The Far East, an International Survey* (1935), ch. 2–9. Edgar Snow, *Red Star Over China* (1937); excellent reporting of the Communist movement. Freda Utley, *Japan's Gamble in China* (1938); especially ch. 3. C. F. Wu, *Chinese Government and Politics* (1934). Chitoshi Yanaga, *Japan Since Perry* (1949), ch. 31–34. See also list appended to chapter 24.

CHAPTER XXIV

THE SECOND SINO-JAPANESE WAR

I. THE LUKOUCHIAO INCIDENT

A MINOR incident provoked the Manchurian crisis of 1931. This led to the establishment of Manchukuo. It facilitated a significant change in the balance of economic and political forces in Japan and had important internal consequences for China. The situation resulting from the incident also revealed the fundamental weakness of the existing international order. Similarly, a relatively minor incident at Lukouchiao, a village not far from Peip'ing, inaugurated a series of developments which, in fact even if not by declaration, resulted immediately in war between China and Japan and finally in war between Japan and the Western states. The issues presented in both cases, however, were fundamental rather than incidental, representing the accumulations of historical evolution in the relations of the two states. This evolution has been traced in the preceding chapters. From this point, consequently, it is necessary now to trace the course of the conflict called by the Japanese the China "Affair" or "Incident" and its developing consequences for China, Japan, Southeastern Asia, the Netherlands Indies, the Philippines, and the Western states.

There are contradictory accounts of the incident of July 7, 1937, which precipitated the conflict. The following, however, seem to be the facts. The Japanese, in exercise of their asserted rights under the Boxer Protocol, had maintained a military force for garrison purposes in North China. This force had been substantially increased during and after 1935. The Japanese as well as the other interested governments had assumed the Protocol to be still in force after the transfer of the Chinese capital to Nanking. On that assumption, the Japanese had the right to maintain their troops at certain designated places, but not at Lukouchiao. Their rights in the Tientsin-Peip'ing area, however, had been loosely and expansively construed since 1935 as giving them the right to engage in field maneuvers there. "It was by virtue of this assumed right, wholly unsanctioned by treaty provision, that the Japanese troops were holding maneuvers at Lukouchiao in July, 1936." [1] According to the Japanese version of the incident, Chinese soldiers fired on the Japanese troops during the night of July 7. The Japanese withheld their fire until reinforcements were brought up the next morning, and then only opened fire when, although a joint Sino-Japanese committee [2] had been sent to investigate, the Chinese re-

[1] T. A. BISSON, *Japan in China*, p. 15. Chapter 1 gives a careful review of the circumstances surrounding the incident.

[2] Composed of two Japanese Army officers and three Chinese.

sumed firing. The Chinese version was that the Japanese claimed to have heard firing and, finding one of their men missing, demanded the right to enter the village of Wanping to search for him. They threatened to use force unless the demand was complied with. In spite of the fact that the man turned up, the demand was pressed. The Hopei-Chahar Political Council, [3] theoretically the governing agency in the northern area, sent the joint commission referred to above, at the request of the Japanese, in the hope of preventing the outbreak of hostilities. The Chinese delegates, when they reached the scene, refused to entertain the Japanese demand for the right of entrance to and search of the town. The members of the commission, however, were permitted to enter the town, and negotiations for a settlement continued. While the negotiations were still going on, the Japanese opened fire, which the Chinese returned in self-defense.

Regardless of which account is credited, the fact is that the incident occurred because Japanese troops were in a place where they had no legal right to be, and they were there at a time when, because of the background of relationships in North China between China and Japan, popular Chinese opinion was hostile to the Japanese. Thus the remarkable thing was not that an incident occurred but rather that it had not previously taken place.

Three weeks intervened between the original incident and the outbreak of the real conflagration in North China. This was a period of both confusion and tension. "The disparity in the attitudes assumed by the opponents was marked: irresolution, partial compromise, and difference of opinion on the part of the leading officials of the Hopei-Chahar Political Council; on the side of the Japanese military, unity, determination, and a grim certainty of objective." [4] This objective was the political and economic severance of North China from the remainder of the country, an objective which had been followed steadily, if occasionally deviously, since 1935. If China held firmly to her minimum basis of settlement, as defined by Chiang Kai-shek, no adjustment could be made. This minimum was: no settlement infringing upon the territorial integrity and the sovereign rights of China; no illegal alterations in the status of the Hopei-Chahar Political Council; no agreement to the removal, as a result of outside pressure, of those local officials appointed by the central government, such as the Chairman of the Hopei-Chahar Political Council; no restriction upon the positions now held by the 29th Army.

2. THE OUTBREAK AND THE COURSE OF HOSTILITIES

Despite the apparent irreconcilability of the fundamental positions of China and Japan, negotiations continued until another "incident" oc-

[3] For a discussion of its establishment, see chapter XXIII, sec. 4.
[4] BISSON, op. cit., p. 16.

curred at Langfang on July 26, after which hostilities were resumed. This incident was followed by the presentation of the ultimatum by the Japanese which required the withdrawal of all Chinese troops. Negotiations were terminated when the Chinese General Sung Cheh-yuan, Chairman of the Political Council, refused to comply with the terms of the ultimatum after a compromise offer had been rejected by the Japanese. The Japanese Army thereupon took the field and proceeded to drive the Chinese out of the entire Peip'ing-Tientsin area. While they met with resistance, it was ineffective, largely due to the failure of the Chinese leadership to coördinate command of the troops and to work out in advance plans for military action. This seems to indicate that the Chinese hoped to the very end to find a compromise which, while it might strengthen the Japanese position in North China, would enable the final issue again to be postponed. The Japanese, on the other hand, quite clearly were determined to press matters to a successful conclusion.

If the Nanking government had been willing to accept, although without formal recognition, as in the cases of Manchuria and Jehol, the complete loss of control of the Peip'ing-Tientsin area, or if the Japanese had indicated an intention to content themselves with control of that restricted portion of North China, war might conceivably have been again avoided. Chiang Kai-shek, however, had, during the previous year, so constantly reiterated that China would fight rather than accept a loss of additional territory or of sovereign rights in China proper, and the pressure of opinion on the government demanding resistance was so strong at this time, that the policy and tactics of the years from 1931 to 1937 could no longer be followed. This was especially the case because of the indications which were given of the intention of the Japanese Army not to rest content with the occupation of the Peip'ing-Tientsin area. Troops and supplies were poured into North China in such numbers and amounts that it became clear that the objective was the establishment of control at least over the five provinces north of the Yellow River. This in itself ensured that the Chinese could not compromise on the basis of acceptance of an advance of the Japanese position restricted to the more limited area, even if they had wished to do so.

Meanwhile, at Shanghai there had been incidents which further embittered relations and which led to a concentration of Japanese naval and military forces there, where they confronted the armies of the Chinese central government. After August 9, when shots were exchanged near the Hungjao Airdrome by Chinese and Japanese, events moved steadily toward the crisis, with major hostilities beginning on August 13, 1937. Thus, although fighting had been going on in the north for three weeks, the war between China and Japan really began at Shanghai. Neither party formally declared a state of war to exist. It was called by Japan the "China Incident" for a time and then given the broader title of the "China Affair." For internal as well as international reasons it was apparently felt desirable to minimize its scope and significance. Partly at least because of the American neutrality laws, China accepted the fact of large-scale hostilities without explicit characterization of the resulting situation as one of war in the full international legal sense. From the opening of hostilities at Shanghai, nevertheless, China embarked for the first time in its modern history on military defense of its sovereignty and integrity on a national rather than a regional or local basis.

Between the time when the trouble developed in the north and when the war came to Shanghai the important provincial military leaders came to Nanking to offer their services and reassure Chiang of their loyalty. The Kuomintang-Communist negotiations were rapidly completed; while actually maintaining its separate identity, the Communist-controlled area was formally incorporated into the state as a self-government region, and the Red Armies were given status in the national system as the Eighth Route Army. The Communist leaders and commanders remained in their positions, but they agreed to take and for a time did actually take their direction from Chiang Kai-shek. Theoretically there was subordination of the Communist Party to the National government. Under the circumstances, however, the unity was not that resulting from subordination so much as it was that of alliance for purposes of combined national defense. Certainly, outward unity of command had been attained by the end of August, and the unification of China under the authority of a central government had apparently finally been achieved as a consequence of Japanese pressure. The reality and durability of this unity, however, had to be tested in the fire of a protracted war before they came to be more than tentatively accepted as permanent. Many felt, and this was especially the case with the Japanese, that unity would not endure in the face of military reverses. This serves to explain one aspect of Japanese policy, which was that of establishment of regional governments in the areas which came under their control. These, it was anticipated, would attract the allegiance of the people, including the regional military leaders.

The course of the China-Japan war itself, from the military standpoint, may be briefly summarized. It marked itself out rather definitely into three distinct stages: (1) from the initial outbreak at Shanghai on August 13 to the fall of Nanking on December 15, 1937; (2) from the fall of Nanking to the capture of Canton and Hankow by the Japanese forces in October, 1938; and (3) after the Chinese government's retirement from Hankow to Chungking in Szechuan province.

3. FIRST PHASE OF THE WAR

At Shanghai the Japanese forces faced the armies of the Chinese central government. These proved capable of offering unexpectedly vigorous and effective resistance to the Japanese attack. They were, however, deficient in equipment in comparison with the Japanese so that throughout they fought at a disadvantage. This was especially marked from the standpoint of air power. Although Chiang Kai-shek had been engaged in building up an air force after 1933, there had not been time to attain equality with the Japanese either in size of the force or in the development of a personnel trained for combat purposes. Thus, from the outset, the Japanese had virtually complete command of the air. They used it to engage in extensive bombing operations, at first mainly in the Lower Yangtze region. They sought to destroy such military objectives as air bases, lines of communication, railway terminals, and troop concentrations. There was also, however, extensive and indiscriminate bombing of non-military objectives for the purpose of inducing the terror which it was thought would break the will to resist of the Chinese people, and thus separate them from the government and military forces.

The difficulties of military resistance at Shanghai were enhanced because of the peculiar structure of the city, with its International Settlement and French Concession along the river front. This enabled the Japanese to land their troops with minimum difficulty and gave their naval vessels some protection, since operations had to be carried on by the Chinese so as not to disturb the foreign settlements any more than was absolutely necessary and inevitable under circumstances of war. This consideration, of course, also restricted Japanese operations but did not create such difficulties as to offset the immediate advantages afforded them by the existence of and their participation in the policing of the International Settlement.

It was not until November, 1937, that the Japanese were able to dislodge the Chinese armies from Shanghai. This was finally accomplished not by frontal attack but by flanking operations from the south. A Japanese force was landed at Hangchow Bay on November 5, and it advanced rapidly inland so as to threaten the rear as well as the flank of the Chinese armies, thus compelling them to evacuate Shanghai. This evacuation was effected with some order, preventing the Japanese from turning a retreat into a complete rout, and consequently preventing them from destroying the Chinese armies. The withdrawal was up the Yangtze River to Nanking, where preparations had been made for prolonged defense. Here, however, the Japanese were more quickly successful than they had been at Shanghai. They drove the Chinese out of their capital in less than a month. In the process they shattered Chiang Kai-shek's best forces. This threatened to produce the rout which had been avoided in the withdrawal from Shanghai. The central government offices had, however, been transferred in advance to Hankow and, in some cases, even further up the Yangtze, so that the government itself was able to continue to function. Had the Japanese immediately followed up their victory at Nanking before the Chinese armies could be reconstituted and morale regained, it is quite possible that the events of the next years would have taken a different course. As it was, however, the Japanese forces stopped for the time at Nanking, affording the Chinese the necessary time to recover from the military disaster. Not only did the Japanese commanders give Chiang Kai-shek's armies an opportunity to recover, but at the same time a new incentive to carry on resistance to the end was provided by the behavior of the Japanese troops after Nanking had fallen. Those troops, reputedly highly disciplined, gave themselves over to an orgy of looting and destruction both of life and of property so complete that the world found it hard to credit the foreign eye-witness accounts which subsequently filtered out of Nanking. This, together with the previous and subsequent destruction of life and property in the villages through air raids, stiffened rather than weakened the determination of the Chinese to carry on the war to the bitter end.

Meanwhile the Japanese armies had been carrying on extensive operations in North China, moving southward down the Tientsin-Pukow and the Peking-Hankow [5] railways and westward to Shansi province. In the southward progression they met vigorous resistance from the 29th Route Army, which they had previously dislodged from Peking without much difficulty. By the end of the year, however, they had driven the Chinese forces south to the Yellow River, along the line of the Tientsin-Pukow Railway, where they paused, possibly in the hope that General Han Fu-chu, the Governor of Shantung province, would come to terms with them. To the east, along the Peking-Hankow Railway, the Japanese force moved south of Chêngtingfu, where the Peking-Hankow Railway crosses the east-west railway running from the sea to Taiyüan, the capital of Shansi province. Then, instead of attempting to move further south into Honan province, the attack was directed westward along the railway toward Taiyüan, in support of the force which had been thrown into Shansi from northern Hopei and which had been meeting successful resistance from the former Red Armies, renamed the Eighth Route Army. The convergence of these two forces enabled the Japanese to occupy Taiyüan early in November. This gave them control of southern Shansi in addition to

[5] The name of the former capital was changed back to Peking from Peip'ing about this time. It again became Peip'ing after the war, until made the capital of the Communist "People's Republic."

Hopei and northern Shantung along the railway lines. Beyond this, the Kwantung Army had been able to gain control of Suiyuan province in addition to Chahar, and to establish formally on October 29, 1937, a Federated Autonomous Government of Mongolia. Similarly, on December 14, a provisional government for China was formed at Peking, displacing "Peace Preservation" Commissions which had been earlier constituted for Peking and Tientsin.

Under the auspices of this government, the Japanese military authorities set out to eradicate the anti-Japanese sentiment and activities against which they had been protesting for several years. This was attempted through control of the press and of education. Under the latter head was included revision of textbooks, attachment of Japanese teachers to each school, the requirement of the study of the Japanese language, and vigorous repression of all student activities which might lead to anti-Japanese action.

Thus the first phase of the war ended with the Japanese having virtually attained their original objectives in North China, and with their forces in occupation of the lower Yangtze region. That statement must be qualified, however, to this extent. Actually Japanese control was established only over towns and arteries of communication occupied by their troops. The countryside did not readily accept Japanese political direction. The villages still remained under the control of their own elders and, when organized for the purpose, the peasants gave such support as they could to the guerrilla forces which came to be organized in the area reportedly conquered by Japanese arms. This was particularly true in the north, where, under Communist leadership, the tactics which had earlier been employed so successfully by the Red Armies in the struggle against Chiang Kai-shek were resumed. The Japanese expectation that resistance would cease if they instituted Chinese régimes which the people could accept in preference to that of Chiang Kai-shek was not realized either at this stage or subsequently. Nevertheless an autonomous government had been instituted, and, if the central government of China had been willing to settle on the basis of loss of control of the area north of the Yellow River, from the Japanese point of view hostilities might have been terminated. [6] An expecta-

---

[6] The exact terms of the Japanese were: "(1) Abandonment by China of all anti-Japan and anti-Manchukuo activities and coöperation with Japan for combatting communism; (2) The establishment of certain demilitarized zones; (3) The settlement of Sino-Japanese economic relations; (4) Indemnification for the results of hostilities." Upon inquiry by Ambassador Grew, the Japanese Foreign Minister "said that the demilitarized zones should be created in Inner Mongolia, North China and the district now occupied by Japanese forces south of the Yangtze River between Shanghai and Nanking." The fiction of Chinese sovereignty was to be maintained in these zones. See *Foreign Relations of the United States, Japan, 1931–1941*, I, 434–435, for full text of memorandum by the Ambassador in Japan (Grew) of his conversation with the Japanese Minister of Foreign Affairs (January 10, 1938).

tion of this was part of the explanation of the pause in operations after the capture of Nanking. When, however, it was perceived that defeat of the armies of Chiang Kai-shek did not destroy his prestige nor cause the country to fall apart along regional lines, and when it was seen that gains made could be conserved only by the elimination of Chiang and his government, the Japanese government announced withdrawal of recognition from Chiang and the Kuomintang government. It simultaneously declared a determination to wage the "China incident" struggle until Chiang Kai-shek, as a disturber of the peace of the Far East, had been overthrown.

4. SECOND PHASE OF THE WAR

Thus was inaugurated the second phase of the war, which had many of the characteristics of the first stage. The objective was the new Chinese capital, Hankow, and in the process of its attainment the destruction of the reorganized Chinese armies. To attain this objective, it was necessary to drive the Chinese armies out of the intervening area. Consequently the first objective was made the occupation of Suchow, the junction city of the Tientsin-Pukow and the Lunghai railways. Suchow had been fortified by the Chinese, who, after their recovery from the fall of Nanking, announced their intention to defend it at all costs and virtually challenged the Japanese to attempt to take it. In the spring of 1938 the Japanese armies again took the field, since the capture of Nanking had not been followed by Chinese acceptance of the terms of peace proposed through the German Ambassador at Hankow. The force which had captured Nanking moved north along the Tientsin-Pukow line, having crossed the Yangtze from Nanking, while the northern army followed the same railway south from the Yellow River, where the northern campaign had come to a pause in the fall of 1937. When the Japanese armies crossed the Yellow River, the Governor of Shantung province failed to oppose them with any vigor, and they were enabled to reach the southern part of the province without much difficulty. For his failure Governor Han Fu-chu was cashiered, and the death sentence imposed and executed. After this the resistance of the Chinese forces stiffened. This, coupled with a serious miscalculation of the Chinese strength by the Japanese commanders, enabled the former to inflict a serious defeat on the Japanese at Taierchuang in April, 1938. This victory, the only important one of the war for the Chinese to that time, decidedly strengthened their morale. The Japanese forces were increased, however, and they pushed on to final victory at Suchow in May, but without destroying the Chinese armies. The retirement from Suchow had in it elements of rout, nevertheless, so that a decisive result might have been attained by the Japanese as they followed up the Chinese forces retreating westward along the Lunghai Railway if the dikes of the Yellow River had not been broken at a number of points by flood waters. This made it immediately impossible for the Japanese armies to continue operations in that area.

This compelled them to concentrate on the movement toward Hankow up the Yangtze River. For purposes of this offensive all available troops, including numerous detachments from North China, were brought to the Shanghai-Nanking area. The redistribution of troops, while it enabled the objective at Hankow to be finally attained, made it possible for the guerrilla forces in North China to limit the Japanese occupation strictly to the larger towns and the railway zones, a situation which continued. Even with this concentration of forces it was not until October 25, 1938, that Hankow fell to the Japanese arms. The delay was not entirely due to the resistance of the Chinese armies, although that was substantial. It was also due to the nature of the country to be traversed, taking the Japanese off the line of railways and roads suited to motor transport, and into a region of waterways, lakes, swamps, and flooded rice fields, where the climate was bad and many diseases endemic. To facilitate the advance, furthermore, much work had to be done by the Navy in the way of removing booms and other obstructions to navigation in the Yangtze which the Chinese had placed to prevent a rapid naval-military advance on Hankow. All of this had the effect of slowing down the Japanese advance. After their advance started, however, they reached Hukow, commanding one bank of the narrow passage from Poyang Lake into the Yangtze, in three weeks, and Kiukiang fell by the end of July. From this time, however, their advance was much slower, and it began to appear doubtful whether they would actually attain their ultimate objective. Casualties were heavy for the Japanese as well as the Chinese, although disproportionately great for the latter.

Under these circumstances the Japanese military leaders sought to obscure their lack of success against the Chinese by promoting the view that peace was being sought by the Hankow government, and also by blaming their difficulties increasingly on the foreign aid which, allegedly, was a major factor in enabling the Chinese to maintain themselves. Military supplies had been reaching the Hankow forces mainly from Hongkong and Canton, as places of entry for transport of goods up the Hankow-Canton Railway, the last section of which had just been completed when the war broke out. The Japanese air force consequently had engaged in extensive air bombardments along the line of the railway in the hope of destroying its usefulness. Being unsuccessful in this, Japan finally, in October, 1938, sent a military expedition, supported by naval forces, to Canton, which they occupied on October 21, virtually without resistance from the Chinese. In spite of its primary importance as the one major port of entry for war supplies still remaining in Chinese hands, there had been no real provision made for its defense. This failure may be partially ascribed to a feeling that Canton was protected against the possibility of Japanese attack on account of the British position at Hongkong. This protection existed in fact only so long as the Japanese government felt afraid of the possibility of British action against it. This fear was largely lost when, in connection with the Czechoslovak crisis, the British government entered into the Munich settlement in application of the policy of appeasement. This settlement in Europe, of September 29, 1938, was the direct prelude to the military occupation of Canton by Japan on October 21. Hankow fell four days later, and the second phase of the military struggle between China and Japan came to an end.

5. THE THIRD PHASE

Again, however, the Chinese government retired in good order, this time to Chungking on the upper Yangtze, and the Chinese armies were again evacuated and not destroyed. Thus the second phase of the war ended without bringing about a Chinese capitulation. That there was a measure of war-weariness and pessimism as to the ultimate outcome was shown, however, in a split which occurred in Hankow. Wang Ching-wei sought to institute negotiations looking toward the establishment of peace. He was not able to carry sufficient weight to bring about such a redirection of policy, however, and he had to flee from Hankow, labelled by the government a traitor. Resistance, it was made clear, was to be continued to the bitter end. The Japanese, on their side, before the occupation of Hankow, had indicated that the attainment of that objective would bring their military offensive to an end. Their purpose, thereafter, it was implied, would be to support new Chinese governments in establishing themselves in the coastal area, and to coöperate with them to bring about peace and reconstruction. After the occupation of Hankow, however, the intention was declared of continuing military operations until Chiang Kai-shek and his government, labelled "a mere local régime," had been completely destroyed.[7] Thus both sides anticipated the continuance of the struggle.

During the third phase of the war, China was substantially divided into

[7] Otherwise the Japanese objectives were described in a statement of the Government released on November 3 as being: "the establishment of a new order which will ensure the permanent stability of East Asia. . . . This new order has for its foundation a tripartite relationship of mutual aid and coördination between Japan, Manchukuo and China in political, economic, cultural and other fields. Its object is to secure international justice, to perfect the joint defense against communism, and to create a new culture and realize a close economic cohesion throughout East Asia."

two parts: (1) what came to be called "free" China, which included the provinces west of a line extending roughly from Peking in the north, through Hankow, to Canton in the south; and (2) "occupied China," between that line and the sea. Unoccupied China, however, was itself made up of two distinct and in fact governmentally separate parts, one under the control of the Kuomintang National government at Chungking, and the other under the direction of the Chinese Communist leadership with headquarters at Yenan. Although they were in alliance in the war against Japan, as that war, in its military aspects, assumed the character of a stalemate after 1940, Kuomintang and Communist China again began to face one another as potential enemies. Both were, nevertheless, in effect cut off from access to the Western world except (1) to Russia by caravan and truck in the northwest; (2) through Indo-China, via the French Yunnan Railway, and a motor road from its northern terminus to Chungking; (3) by way of Burma, a motor road between its frontier and Chungking having been rushed to completion and opened to traffic; and (4) by air transport from Hongkong. These were the main avenues of military supply, although considerable importation continued through the few coastal ports not in effective Japanese occupation, and from which there was a possibility of transport to the interior through numerous gaps in the Japanese lines. As time went on an extensive illegal exchange of Chinese for Japanese goods went on between "occupied" and "free" China.

Occupied China, however, as has already been indicated, was not completely within Japan's control or responsive to the direction of the two governments which had been set up, one at Peking and the other at Nanking. Guerrilla forces operated extensively within the occupied area in Central as well as North China, leaving Japan in effective control only of the lines of communication and the principal towns and cities. The foreign residential areas were also for the time beyond the reach of Japanese authority. They afforded centers from which agents of the Chungking and Yenan governments could carry on and direct anti-Japanese activities within the occupied area and also maintain contact with supporting foreign interests.

Under these circumstances the war was protracted as a virtual military stalemate. Having to proceed beyond the railways and other arteries of east-west communication, the Japanese armies were not able to bring about the overthrow of Chiang Kai-shek's government. Occasional limited offensives made some measure of initial progress. Chinese cities, especially the capital, and the vital railways and highways, were constantly bombed from the air. But none of this sufficed to break the deadlock.

The Chinese, on their side, lacked the air power, heavy armament, and modern transport essential to enable them to take the offensive themselves on any large scale. Thus they did not have the power to drive the Japanese armies out of the occupied territory. Consequently the Nationalist armies were concentrated mainly on holding operations over the long front, and on the development of the threat of a major offensive. This helped to tie down large bodies of Japanese troops. Beyond this, effort was directed toward making it impossible for the Japanese to profit economically from their control of the coastal provinces. It was assumed that, unless the Japanese could realize with sufficient rapidity on their venture, the Japanese economy could not stand the strain of continuing operations, or of maintaining solely from Japan's resources the million men which constituted Japan's continental force. With more understanding of its nature, and more experience in its use, the guerrilla type of military activity which this entailed was more successfully undertaken by the Communist armies operating in north and eastern-central China than by forces organized by the Chungking government.

To prevent Japan from gaining economic advantages from her conquest the Chinese, during the first two stages of the war, theoretically followed what they called the "scorched earth" policy. As the armies retired from one position after another, they, together with the people who moved with them as refugees, were supposed to evacuate also machinery and equipment of all kinds, destroying all that had to be left behind which might be of profit to the enemy. This policy, literally applied, also involved the stripping of the countryside of food and other crops. This was designed to compel the Japanese armies to be supported from the home country rather than being able to live off the land occupied. While much equipment was moved or destroyed, frequently the movement or destruction was postponed too long to enable the purpose to be fully accomplished. The owners of either industrial equipment or of crops hesitated to anticipate the necessity of loss of their properties and thus they sometimes prevented the taking of action in time. Nevertheless much was done in application of the "scorched earth" conception.

Subsequent guerrilla operations, during the third stage, were directed toward the same end of lessening the ability of Japan to realize the economic fruits of her victory. In North China, for example, the peasants were persuaded and encouraged to grow food crops rather than the cotton which Japan needed in order that she might be released from the necessity of making extensive foreign (i.e., Indian and American) purchases. Such purchases depleted Japan's foreign exchange, which she needed to conserve in order to pay for imports essential for war purposes. The food crops themselves were, if possible and if necessary to prevent their falling into the hands of the Japanese military, destroyed. This "scorched earth" policy obviously inflicted tremendous hardship on the Chinese who remained, of necessity, in the occupied region. There was always presented a question as to how long the peasant would find the resulting hardship more endurable than the acceptance of the Japanese-dominated governments which were created.

Nevertheless a central feature of the Chinese policy of resistance continued to be the creation of conditions which, it was hoped, would bring about an economic collapse in Japan. This method of resistance, also called that of "trading space for time" was based upon a second important consideration. This was that Japanese activities in the area which they had been successful in occupying would ultimately bring them into conflict with one or several of the major Powers. In other words, it was assumed that if China could protract her resistance long enough the United States, Britain, or the Soviet Union would find it necessary to act in defense of its treaty and trade rights in China. The justification for making and acting on this assumption appears through an examination of international relations in the Far East after 1937. Before undertaking this, however, the non-military effects of the war in and on China and Japan must be considered.

6. JAPAN IN CHINA

The military operations on the continent, as already pointed out, brought Japan into military occupation of the coastal area back to the line roughly extending from Peking through Hankow to Canton. In the attempt to reorganize the life of this area and consolidate the Japanese position therein Japan established a provisional Chinese government responsive to its control and direction at Peking, and subsequently a Reformed Government at Nanking. The initial purpose seemed to be to merge the two, through the extension of the authority of the Nanking government, manipulating it as the alternative government for China to that of Chiang Kai-shek. Movement in that direction, however, was slower than had been contemplated for two principal reasons. The first was the difficulty of reconciling the aims and objectives of factions within the Japanese continental commands. The Kwantung Army was primarily if not exclusively interested in the maintenance of the position won in Manchukuo and in the extension of that position into Inner Mongolia. The North China Command had the five northern provinces as the center of its interest. This could be most effectively safeguarded if control was left with the Peking Provisional Government (established on December 14, 1937), on which it could exert direct authority. The Central China Command, on the other hand, exercised authority in the lower Yangtze valley provinces, and was in the best position to control the "Reformed Government of the Chinese Republic," established on March 28, 1938, and exercising authority from Nanking. If that government were accepted as the government of occupied China, the balance of power, within the Japanese military commands, would be tipped in the direction of the Central China Command. Consequently the other two commands were reluctant to accept Nanking as the center of Chinese authority in opposition to Chiang, except on conditions which would safeguard their dominance in the areas of their primary interest. Thus the establishment of satisfactory and acceptable governmental arrangements necessitated negotiations between the factions in the Japanese military command, carried on both in Tokyo and on the continent. These negotiations resulted first in the establishment of a "United Council of China" on September 22, 1938, which was essentially a liaison committee of members from the rival governments. This was displaced by the establishment of the Wang Ching-wei government on March 30, 1940.

The second difficulty encountered in the constitution of a satisfactory central Chinese government responsive to Japanese direction was that of personnel. The personnel of both the Peking Provisional Government and the Nanking Reformed Government was made up of persons of previous pro-Japanese connections or of relatively little previous importance in Chinese politics. Thus neither government, from the personnel point of view, even if otherwise able to exercise independent authority, could be expected to attract the loyalty either of the people or of officials away from the Chungking government. The problem was that of finding a leading Chinese political figure, in whom the people might have confidence, to head the new government. Early attempts to interest such former leaders as Marshal Wu P'ei-fu failed. The first real opportunity presented itself when Wang Ching-wei, together with some of his followers, left the government after the fall of Hankow in October, 1938, because of Chiang Kai-shek's determination to carry on the war rather than to negotiate a peace settlement. Wang's attitude was denounced as that of a traitor by the National government. This left him with the choice of retirement from politics or an attempt to regain power in association with the Japanese. Not being willing to retire, he attempted the latter, apparently feeling that a satisfactory basis of relationship with Japan could be negotiated.

The negotiations consequently instituted were protracted. Wang realized that any agreement reached, if his government was to have any power to attract support from Chungking, must be based upon at least the nominal independence of China. Any agreement satisfactory to Japan, on the other hand, must ensure that the Chinese government would be sufficiently responsive to Japanese direction so that independence would not interfere with the attainment of the ultimate Japanese objective of dominance, political and economic, of a Japan-Manchukuo-China bloc.

The long-drawn-out negotiations finally resulted in an agreement on the basis of which Japan installed Wang Ching-wei at Nanking on March 30, 1940, as the head of a government competitive with that of Chiang Kai-shek as the government of China.[8] With this government Japan then formally concluded the agreement which was designed to have the effect of transforming Japan's military operations in China from war against China into military support of the recognized government against a domestic enemy. The agreement promised the withdrawal of Japanese troops within two years of the termination of the civil struggle, except from designated areas in North China where they might be maintained for purposes of defense against communism. It also defined the basis for economic "coöperation" in such a fashion as to ensure Japanese supremacy in North China (the original Japanese objective in the war) and a considerable measure of Japanese influence over the rest of China. On the whole, if implemented, the agreement would have left China with nominal independence but in a position of actual dependence on Japan.

While attempting in this fashion to solve the problem of political relations within the occupied area, Japan had been moving toward economic exploitation of her new position. In anticipation of the capture of Hankow in the fall of 1938, a China Affairs Board (or East Asiatic Affairs Board) was established in Tokyo as the central agency, under the Cabinet, for the development and administration of the non-military aspects of continental policy. To an important extent this Board actually drew into its own hands, and from the Cabinet, the control of this area of policy. This was possible because, through its composition, it was more completely under military control than was the Cabinet itself. Its coördinating and supervisory authority extended over all of the continental ventures of Japan. Under it was created the North China Development Company, which was given a virtual monopoly of the fundamental Japanese exploitative activities in the northern provinces of China. The Central China Promotion Company was established to monopolize basic economic activity in the Yangtze provinces. A similar company was planned, but not formally authorized, for South China. A separate agency—created, however, by the Peking government—was the Federal Reserve Bank, which was used in the north to wage war against the Chinese national currency and thus to weaken the financial position of the National government. A similar bank, also with a right of note issue, was established at Nanking after the inauguration of the Wang Ching-wei government.

Under the auspices of these monopoly companies the Japanese moved

[8] This Japanese "puppet" government of China had been recognized July 1, 1941, by Germany, Italy, Spain, Roumania, "Slovakia" and "Croatia." For more detailed treatment of this whole question see HAROLD S. QUIGLEY, *The Far Eastern War, 1937–1941*, ch. 7.

to acquire properties and either to inaugurate new enterprises or to acquire control of established businesses within the occupied area, with a view to integrating its economy with that of Japan-Manchukuo. The movement in this direction was carried further with greater rapidity in North China than elsewhere because (1) there was already a more highly developed position on which to build; (2) North China came within Japanese military occupation at an earlier time than did Central China; and (3) there was less in the way of established Western rights and interests to be considered, and less reason to proceed cautiously to avoid giving undue offense to the Western Powers. The effective exploitation of the entire occupied area, including North China, however, was handicapped by the political activities and the military operations of the guerrilla forces acting under the direction of the Central government. For the references to Japanese political and economic activities within the occupied area must not be understood to mean that Japanese authority extended effectively over the entire area. As previously pointed out, it extended in fact only to the cities and garrisoned towns and along the lines of communication rather than over the countryside. But within reach of the Japanese, even as thus restricted, were the places where economic activity, except the agricultural, centered, and from which it radiated. Thus control of the towns and of communication lines and centers gave initial scope for the extension of Japan's economic control.

The steps taken by Japan to consolidate her economic position in China beyond the formation of the above-mentioned agencies included "the effort to introduce a new currency linked with the yen, tariff revisions by the Japanese-sponsored governments in Peiping and Nanking designed to favor Japanese trade, interference with foreign business and shipping . . . etc." [9] The result was a considerable expansion of trade between Japan and China. This was especially marked on the side of exports from Japan to China, which rose from 190 million yen in 1937 to 343 million yen in 1938. The increase in imports from China was much less marked, totalling from 160 million yen in 1937 to 179 million in 1938. While this left Japan with a favorable balance of trade within the yen bloc sufficiently great to redress the balance which was adverse with the rest of the world, it did not help secure foreign exchange to finance purchases outside the area linked to the yen. Thus for war purposes Japan would have been in a better position if she had been confronted with a constantly increasing adverse balance in her trade relations with China, since, under the circumstances, that would have meant an increasing ability to supply herself with

[9] MIRIAM FARLEY, *Problem of Japanese Trade Expansion,* I. P. R. Inquiry Series, 1939, p. 22.

raw materials from the continent. Part of her expansionist purpose was to create a self-sufficient economic entity in order to release herself from dependence on imports from the outside. To accomplish this purpose it was necessary that China should furnish her raw materials in increasing quantities, as well as a market. The excessive market expansion, however, meant that Japan was forced to import raw materials from outside the bloc in order to manufacture goods to sell in China. The immediate effect of her occupation, consequently, while it meant trade expansion on the continent, was to maintain rather than to lessen her lack of self-sufficiency. She continued to have to import cotton, iron and steel scrap, machines, machine tools, and petroleum products from outside the area of her political control, notably from the United States, in order to maintain her industries and to sustain her war efforts. This might not, however, have continued to be the case in the long run if Japan had had an opportunity, under conditions of peace and stability, fully to attain her objectives and to utilize her opportunities in China.

7. CULTURAL IMPACT OF THE WAR ON "FREE" CHINA

The adverse impact of the war on China, both "occupied" and "free," was tremendous. The war operations themselves involved great destruction of property and loss of life in an ever-widening area. A large part of this, for the civilian population, was due to the Japanese air bombardment, which was directed against towns and cities. In bombing, the Japanese purpose seemed to be to bring about a cessation of Chinese resistance by terrorizing the civilian population. If so, the methods employed, which included rape and pillage as well as attacks from the air, failed. Chinese morale, and with it a determination to continue the war to a decisive end, improved instead of deterioriating during the first years of the war. This is the more noteworthy since the fortunes of war not only necessitated a steady retirement of the Chinese armies and the government into the interior, but also brought about a large-scale shifting of the population. Millions of people were compelled to leave the coastal areas because their homes had been destroyed and the land could not be tilled, or because of their fears of the Japanese, based upon experience as well as reports as to their behavior as occupants. They retired into the interior essentially as refugees within their own country. This, because of the great numbers involved, posed a tremendous problem of readjustment. It also presented a public health problem of magnitude because of the conditions of the migration. Many of these people drifted back to their homes in the occupied area as conditions tended to stabilize in the period of military stalemate. Nevertheless the problems of the refugee, whether in or beyond the occupied area, remained at the end of the war as a direct result of its impact on the country.

Noteworthy among these refugee groups were the students and faculties of the best developed among the colleges and universities of China, and their intellectual derivatives in the arts, sciences, and letters. The new scholar class, as previously indicated, had played a leading role in the early stages of the Kuomintang revolution. The student movement of the 1920's "was particularly significant in that it brought both the new cultural ideas of science and democracy and the new patriotism into a common focus in an anti-imperialist program. More than ever before in modern history the student class assumed responsibility for China's welfare and made an effort through their student organizations to reach the common people in the villages." [10] The fires of patriotism then kindled were fed in the first years of Kuomintang control by means of successes in the treaty-revision movement. But as the Kuomintang program of internal reform and development lost its momentum the scholar class began to divide into three groups. The initially smallest segment of the three began to interest itself in the Communist movement. A second segment, with political rather than economic and social interests, found a comfortable home in the Kuomintang bureaucracy, thus attaining the traditional outlet of Chinese scholarship. The third tended to withdraw from direct political activity, as in 1917–1922, but continued to speak out on public issues. It was from this group that there came scientific research as well as instruction in scientific method; economic research and publication such as issued from the Nan Kai Institute of Economics; social investigations such as those conducted into peasant life and institutions by Dr. Fei Hsiao-tung; a new literature, as exemplified by such social novels as *Rickshaw Boy* by Lau Shaw, and in the poetry and other writings of Kuo Mo-jo; and in the further development of the western-type drama. It was this group, in spite of its withdrawal from direct participation in politics and government, which became more and more critical of authoritarian and repressive tendencies within the Kuomintang and thus the government, but without separating itself from the party as the accepted instrument of government in China.

With these varying degrees of loyalty to the National government, the scholar class, including the students in the colleges and universities, nevertheless remained fundamentally united in opposition to any forces which threatened the independence and integrity of the country. Its greater self-consciousness with respect to the outside world and the pressure which it could bring to bear against China, together with its position in Chinese society, caused it to play a leading role in the development of a spirit of

[10] J. K. FAIRBANK, *The United States and China*, p. 183.

resistance to Japan, following the Manchurian crisis of 1931 and the subsequent attempt by the Japanese to detach North China from the controls of the National government. Thus the National Salvation Movement was begun in 1935 by "professors, students and young intellectuals who were influenced by the student anti-appeasement movement in North China. It had a simple and very clear program. Stop Civil War. Stop appeasement of Japan. Beyond this, however, it developed no ideology or program." [11] Because of patriotic activities of students, especially in the North China institutions, the Japanese marked them and their institutions down as centers of anti-Japanese agitation which must be eliminated as such. Realizing this, some of the colleges moved to new locations in advance of the actual outbreak of hostilities. The students and faculties of others, taking such equipment as they could carry with them, were evacuated from the lower Yangtze area as well as from North China after the outbreak of general hostilities. Individuals, as well as institutions, remaining behind and trying to carry on their activities within the occupied areas, subsequently had to conform to the conditions laid down by the Japanese. This meant that they could carry on at the best only restricted educational and intellectual activities, and at the worst that they might open themselves to the charge of collaboration with the enemy, even though under duress and with the best of intentions.

This mass educational withdrawal into the interior put the intellectual and educational life of China initially on a refugee basis. But the conditions under which it was undertaken and the economic hardships which were entailed even after relocation of Christian universities in combined institutions at Chengtu, and of government colleges and universities at Kunming, immediately caused the patriotic flame to burn more brightly, and was a contributing factor to the maintenance of the national morale. Government, scholars, and people were temporarily brought into a closer and more intimate relationship through shared hardships borne in what was then perceived to be a common cause. It also brought modern ideas into the interior provinces more rapidly and extensively than would otherwise have been possible. But it brought them into areas where traditional China had been longest maintained and under circumstances which left room for doubt as to whether the new would displace the old or succumb to it.

8. EFFECTS OF THE WAR ON THE NATIONAL ECONOMY

Just as the invasion forced educational readjustment, putting new strains on a system which simultaneously had its resources tremendously

[11] P. M. A. LINEBARGER, *The China of Chiang Kai-shek*, p. 175. The Movement is discussed in some detail on pp. 175–180.

decreased, so it also in a somewhat similar fashion compelled a reshaping of the national economy. The forced retirement from the eastern coastal provinces gave new importance to the previously largely neglected south-western provinces which during the war constituted the area of Kuomin-tang control. "Free" China, which had become as a result of the war "interior" China, had to develop an economy capable of supplying the needs of the people, largely on the basis of self-sufficiency, and at the same time capable of sustaining the war effort. The latter required the pro-duction of export commodities to exchange for the necessary imports of war materials as well as machines for industry, trucks for transporta-tion, and airplanes and parts for civil as well as military purposes. Since the industrialized areas of China were those brought under Japanese occu-pation, "free" China virtually had to build from the ground up. Part of the process of construction involved making extended surveys of the resources available, since some of the provinces had been neglected in earlier resource studies. In that, and in actual reconstruction, the govern-ment had to mark out the lines of development and help to finance it. These new tasks put unusual strains on the administrative mechanism and required its adjustment and expansion, particularly at the policy-planning level. To discharge the planning responsibilities three commis-sions were instituted: (1) the Industrial and Mining Readjustment Com-mission, with an initial appropriation of Ch. $10 million; (2) the Agricultural Readjustment Commission, with an appropriation of Ch. $30 million; and (3) the Trade Readjustment Commission, with Ch. $20 mil-lion initially at its disposal. An industrial coöperative movement had also come into being which received some governmental financial support.

The government itself maintained control of the development of basic industries, thus establishing, for war purposes, a measure of state capital-ism. It also had directly to undertake the extension of the transportation system in the interior through the construction of highways and the pro-jection of new railways, and through reorganization which would enable air transport to be extended through the area of "free" China. In this ex-tended governmental activity there was presented an opportunity for per-sonal exploitation by officials which was not altogether disregarded, even in the first years of patriotic fervor. In the last two years of the war, as lethargy replaced enthusiasm and morale deteriorated, official standards of behavior notably declined. But, although both inefficiency and "squeeze" were revealed, in terms of accomplishment it must be recognized that the Chungking officialdom for some time proved reasonably adequate to its new responsibilities.

The work of the Industrial and Mining Readjustment Commission, working with the National Resources Commission, is partially indicated in its title. After 1938 its task was that of organizing the exploitation of the natural resources, other than agricultural, of "free" China. Prior to that, on the industrial side, it had to aid in the evacuation of industrial and factory equipment from war areas. The attempt was made to salvage as much equipment as possible. Thus withdrawal in the face of the Japa-nese armies involved much more than the evacuation of government offices and their records, together with the orderly retirement of troops. Partly because of delay and faulty planning only a portion of the indus-trial equipment could be salvaged and set up for use in the unoccupied provinces, but that portion was of great importance in enabling produc-tion to be developed in interior China. Its reëstablishment had to be planned in relation to the raw materials for its most effective use. And the problem had to be faced of bringing together equipment, either old or new, and trained operatives, evacuated also from the occupied areas.

The industrial coöperatives, inaugurated in July, 1938, well in advance of the fall of Hankow, were designed to build up production for use on the decentralized basis of the village. This was to be done through the formation of producer's coöperatives, which were "to undertake industrial production to satisfy local needs as well as to form an industrial defense system more or less immune from Japan's military attack and economic offensive." [12] Within a year "about 1,300 coöperatives had been established. . . . The variety of types is extensive. They include iron and coal mining, textiles, paper, printing, tobacco, building and building materials, flour and rice milling, pottery and porcelain, dyeing and bleaching, and ma-chine work." [13] From this beginning it was hoped to increase the number of coöperatives to 30,000.

The plan for development of the Chinese industrial coöperatives was originated outside of government circles. As it came to be formally estab-lished, however, it was "a social organization sponsored by the Executive Yuan. Standing somewhere between government and purely private enter-prise, the industrial coöperatives supplemented and were designed to de-velop the facilities—themselves very extensive—which are under full state-capitalist or private control," utilizing "a level of Chinese society hitherto largely unused—the family, guild, village, and volunteer—society devices of the peasantry and townsmen who lived beneath the lowest limits of the scholastic bureaucracy." [14] While the movement had an initially rapid growth in the first war years, it never realized its full possibilities for either war or peacetime purposes because of inadequate financing both by government and from private sources. Fundamentally, its limits were

[12] Lowe Chuan-hua, *Japan's Economic Offensive in China*, p. 94.
[13] E. F. Carlson, *The Chinese Army*, p. 60.
[14] Linebarger, *op. cit.*, p. 224.

set by an increasing emphasis on individual profits both for officialdom and for the still important Chinese businessman. This was a natural result of the swing to the right which showed itself within the Kuomintang during the protracted war stalemate.

On the strictly agricultural side the war presented the problem of increase of production to sustain the armies and the refugee population in addition to the existing agricultural and town inhabitants of the unoccupied provinces. It also presented the problem of readjustment of production to meet the requirements of a war economy largely cut off from its normal trade contacts. The basic problem, again, was that of finance in the form of extension of credits to the peasants to enable improvements to be made in production and to encourage and assist them to change their croppage to meet new needs. This necessitated government action, which was taken under the auspices of the Agricultural Readjustment Commission, which, significantly, was given the largest initial grant of funds for operating purposes. Only in this way could the peasant be given sufficient financial freedom to enable agricultural progress to be made. Thus one effect of the war was to initiate a movement which could have led, as, however, it did not, to the permanent substitution of a satisfactory system of agricultural credits for the old system of usury.

None of the steps taken toward readjustment, however, could do more than ameliorate the consequences of the war for the people of China. In long-run terms, the forced development of the interior provinces under the impact of the war had possibilities of real benefit to China. But the hardships immediately inflicted were extreme. It was impossible to increase industrial and agricultural production to the point where all of the requirements of the people, as well as of the armies, could be met. Nor could government supervision prevent hoarding and speculation in staple commodities. Consequently prices increased constantly, with resulting hardship for the masses and increasing dissatisfaction. It was this which helped to produce the threat of internal division at the beginning of 1941, and to break down official as well as private standards of behavior.

In China, as elsewhere, the terms "right" and "left" have been used as convenient terms to distinguish those who desired to make important changes in the political economy of the country from those who either wanted to maintain with a minimum of change existing conditions or who wanted to restore an earlier status. During and after World War II the Chinese Communist Party was successful in focusing attention on the land question and establishing it as the issue in measuring party attitudes as being "rightist" or "leftist." Its peasant constituency was such that it could advance a "revolutionary" policy of agrarian reform without serious loss of support. In relation to land-tenure changes, as proposed by the Communists, the Kuomintang, which drew support from the landlord and upper-peasant class, became the party of the *status quo,* even though, with respect to other aspects of economic or social change, it had a program of movement from the traditional system. It was not able, in an essentially peasant economy, to focus attention on industrialization as a real alternative in reform to that of agrarian reform.

Consequently it relied for success on its superior military power rather than on the strength of a competitive land reform program which it could not develop and put into effect without alienating important elements within the party. The emphasis on military power, necessitated by the internal struggle as well as by the need to complete and maintain the unification of the country and then to defend it against external aggression, not only absorbed energy and funds but also established within the party in the new officer class a solid core of personal support for Chiang Kai-shek, regardless of the policy issues posed. "With the passage of each year, the proportion of Whampoa (military academy) graduates in the national armies rises. The officers include a high proportion of technically qualified men, whose capabilities and interests are chiefly military. Builders of the new army, they look to the Generalissimo and the Party for dicta on social, economic and political policy." [15] Another element in the Kuomintang, also personally loyal to Chiang Kai-shek, was the so-called C.C. clique, led by Ch'en Li-fu and Ch'en Kuo-fu. The Ch'en brothers were "rightist" in their undeviating hostility to communism. But beyond this their attitude was indicated in the leading role they played in promoting a revival of the Confucian social values. "Ch'en (Li-fu) argues that ancient Chinese culture is the cure for modern China's ills." [16] With westernization as the point of reference, this point of view represented reform looking backward and inward rather than forward and outward. To influence the movement, as well as to serve the Generalissimo, the Ch'en brothers interested themselves in party organization and indoctrination, the one as Minister of Education and the other as the head of the Central Political Institute, the party training school. They sought to develop intra-party discipline in order to maintain the party as an effective instrument of power in the state. Thus they helped to turn into the administrative mechanism those who would exercise authority under direction from above, following faithfully the policy line thus authoritatively set, and without particular concern with the economic or political uses made of party power.

A third element, more reformative and modern, in the sense of an

[15] *Ibid.,* p. 143.
[16] J. K. Fairbank, *op. cit.,* p. 255.

interest in westernization, was to be found in the new commercial, industrial and financial interests which had been in process of development in the cities of the coastal area. Chiang Kai-shek had allied himself with this element at the time of the Communist purge of 1927. It had assisted in financing the government after 1927. From the reform point of view, its interest lay in the development of communications, the extension of banking facilities, and in such other changes as would lay a foundation for industrialization. This idea, rather than that of agrarian reform, gave direction to such development as the circumstances of the decade 1927–1937 permitted. It was its orientation along these lines which made the Kuomintang essentially urban in its outlook and committed it, from the war standpoint, to the attempt to hold cities and lines of communication rather than to conserve its forces for use in guerrilla warfare. This element, it should be noted, was tied in more closely to the landlords than to the peasantry, both from the economic and the class-relationship points of view. It also represented the link between the new China and the Western commercial interests.

With the transfer of the government to Chungking, this modernizing element in the Kuomintang lost its economic basis of strength, since that lay in the cities which came under Japanese control. It remained influential within the bureaucracy, however, to the extent that its services were essential to the organization of the "war-production" of the area of "free" China, and in dealing with the United States and Britain, both in China and abroad. Otherwise, since Szechuan, Yunnan, and other provinces controlled by Kuomintang China had remained largely "traditional" China from the economic, political, and social points of view, the movement southwestward strengthened the position of those around the Generalissimo who had a backward rather than a forward look, and lessened his dependence on the more progressive elements in the party leadership.

The effect of the war had been inevitably to tighten up the party and intra-party controls of an essentially authoritarian system. The repressive activities of censorship and of the secret police were magnified in "free" China to the point where there was little formal freedom of speech and of the press, and consequently no opportunity for effective criticism of public policy or of the activities and behavior of the higher public officials or of individuals protected by them. Much of this tightening was necessary for war purposes. Nevertheless, the net effect of restriction of criticism was to lower public morale, lessen efficiency, and open the way to exploitation of the war for purposes of individual aggrandizement. Even personally honest officials became suspect as "tea-shop" gossip about officialdom was substituted, under these circumstances, for responsible criticism.

The only modification of this situation was that resulting from a continuation of the People's Political Council, established by "order of the Emergency Session of the Kuomintang Party Congress held in Hankow, March 1938." [17] The 200 (increased to 240 in 1940) members of the Council were all appointive. Nevertheless, as a body it was representative of the variety of articulate opinion of the country. Although it was covered up in the formal method of allocation of seats by categories to various groups, it actually gave participation to the opposition parties, including the Communists, through representatives of their own choice. Thus, in a sense, the P.P.C. organized, although not in the European fashion, the "united front" for war purposes. It had the right to advise the government on questions of public policy, and the government, except in emergency cases, was expected to consult it before putting into effect important measures. Thus its role was advisory and consultative and not one of control and direction. Nevertheless, in the five sessions of the first People's Political Council held between 1938 and 1940, and in the sessions of the second Council which held its first session at Chungking in 1941, the opinions of non-Kuomintang China, and of the more critical elements within the party itself, had some opportunity to express themselves and to modify policy.

9. KUOMINTANG-COMMUNIST RELATIONS

The People's Political Council was thus an organizational evidence of the common front of the Kuomintang with the Communist Party, since the latter was given, through it, a small but legal voice in the deliberations of the Chungking government. The controlling elements in the Kuomintang, however, remained suspicious of and antagonistic to the Communists, seeking not only to prevent any extension of their influence but also to restrict their effective participation in the war outside the northwestern area. This attitude not only produced dissension at Chungking but also resulted in local fighting between the Kuomintang and the Communist forces. It was largely the intermediation of the Generalissimo, supported by his then tremendous personal prestige, which enabled these recurrent internal crises to be resolved without the resumption of civil war. He had finally staked his whole political future on carrying through the Japanese war to a successful conclusion. In carrying on the war, especially in its guerrilla phase, the role of the Communists was too important to be summarily eliminated. Furthermore, they represented a link with the Soviet Union, one important external source of supply of armaments. The sup-

[17] On the organization, composition, and significance of the P.P.C. in 1938–1941, see LINEBARGER, *op. cit.*, pp. 69–79.

plies sent in from Russia were sent not to the Communist forces but to the Central government for allocation. Nevertheless it was never entirely clear that the Soviet Union, because of the threat presented to it by Japanese expansionism, would continue to support Chiang Kai-shek if the Chinese government followed a strong internal anti-Communist policy. Thus the anti-Communist tendencies in the Kuomintang were more vigorously repressed when the government was increasingly dependent on Russia as the major external source of supply of war materials than when it had the possibility of imports from the United States and England in important quantities.

Guerrilla warfare strengthened the Communists because they were experienced in organizing and conducting it and thus could supply leadership in training guerrilla forces. Consequently, for a time after the fall of Hankow, their general influence at Chungking increased. They also asked for and received permission to organize guerrilla forces to operate in the Yangtze region south of Nanking. The Fourth Army consequently constituted in that area was Communist. Its operations brought the Communists back into the area from which they had been driven in 1934, thus extending their territorial position, since the Eighth Route Army continued to be based on the northwest Communist area.

In 1941 the antagonism between the Kuomintang and the Communists again flared up. The stronger position taken by the anti-Communist elements possibly resulted from the reopening of the Burma Road by the British, which lessened dependence on Russia as a source of supply, and from the extension of credits to the Chungking government by the United States and Britain. All of this strengthened the position of those in China who preferred an orientation toward the United States and away from the Soviet Union. It may also have been the result of a greater feeling of internal military strength, shown in successful, although limited, operations against the Japanese in South China. It was probably even more due to difficult economic conditions in "free" China. [18]

Whatever the cause, the friction showed itself in a demand of General Ho Ying-chin, Minister of War, in November, 1940, for the withdrawal of the Fourth Army from the south Yangtze area. The Communist leaders, on their side, demanded not only the reconsideration of this order, but action on their earlier request for legalization of their party, release of imprisoned Communists, cessation of action against Communists and their families, and resumption of supplies of ammunition, which, it was charged, had been denied the Communists for 14 months. The issue was so sharply

[18] On the Kuomintang-Communist relationships, and on other areas of political conflict, see EDGAR SNOW, *The Battle for Asia*. Also ANNA LOUISE STRONG, "The Kuomintang-Communist Crisis in China," *Amerasia*, March, 1941.

joined that, at the outset of 1941, it appeared possible that the war effort would be seriously weakened by a renewed outbreak of civil war. This might readily have led to complete collapse of the "united front" and as a result loss of ability to continue resistance to Japan, or the negotiation of a peace with the Wang Ching-wei government on terms embodying substantially the provisions of its agreement with Japan. To avoid this, the Communists made concessions and Chiang was ready to negotiate a new agreement. Consequently the formal split was averted, but relations were essentially those of an armed truce until after the final defeat of Japan. The Kuomintang sought, with some measure of success, to block off the Communist region from the rest of "free" China. With the passage of time, there developed more actual intercourse between occupied China and "free" China than there was between the two parts of the latter.

The above summary of the internal situation as it affected the relations of the Kuomintang with the Communists, up to the end of 1941, points to the conclusion that the political framework of China had been little changed as a result of the impact of the Sino-Japanese war. A new and permanent constitution was still under consideration in the legislative Yuan, and there had been such a movement toward the introduction of democracy as that indicated in the establishment of the People's Political Council. The Kuomintang, however, continued to be the controlling party, and policy decisions were reserved to its organs, especially the Central Executive Committee. War itself, of course, requires a concentration of authority. Thus the war against Japan resulted not only in a maintenance but also in an extension of the concentrated authority of Chiang Kai-shek, modified by the need for balancing the claims of various factions in order to preserve the necessary national unity.

REFERENCES FOR FURTHER STUDY

James Bertram, *Unconquered* (1939); reporting on the war in North China. Evans F. Carlson, *The Chinese Army: Its Organization and Military Efficiency* (1940); a good study. Chiang Kai-shek, *Collected Wartime Messages of Generalissimo Chiang Kai-shek* (1946). Chiang Kai-shek, *Resistance and Reconstruction* (1943); the Generalissimo's exhortations on resistance. China, Ministry of Information, *China Handbook, 1937–1943* (1943); comprehensive survey of major developments in China in six years of war. Must, however, be used with care. Paul H. Clyde, *United States Policy Toward China: Diplomatic and Public Documents* (1940), ch. 46; a careful selection of documents. Foreign Policy Association, *Foreign Policy Reports* (1937–1941); consult index for pertinent reports. Institute of Pacific Relations, *Far Eastern Survey*, vols. 6–10; consult index for pertinent articles. F. C. Jones, *Shanghai and Tientsin* (1940). George W. Keeton, *China, The Far East and the Future of the Pacific* (1949); esp. part II. Lowe Chuan-hua, *Japan's Economic Offensive in China* (1939); worth consulting. Yale Candee Maxon, *Control of Japanese*

Foreign Policy: a Study of Civil-Military Rivalry, 1930–1945 (1957). DAVID N. ROWE, *China Among the Powers* (1945); a good analysis of elements of China's strength and weakness. EDGAR SNOW, *The Battle for Asia* (1941); mature reporting of the internal situation produced in China by the war. GEORGE E. TAYLOR, *The Struggle for North China* (1940); an excellent study based in part on observation. T'IEN CHÜN, *Village in August* (1942); novelized account of guerrilla struggle against Japan in Manchuria. FREDA UTLEY, *Japan's Gamble in China* (1938); esp. ch. 1, 5, 6, 7. W. W. WILLOUGHBY, *Japan's Case Examined* (1940); the case found not to be sustained. QUINCY WRIGHT, *The Existing Legal Situation as It Relates to the Conflict in the Far East* (1939).

Much valuable material can be found in *Amerasia, Asia,* the *Tokyo Gazette* (which published official materials), *Contemporary Japan, Pacific Affairs, Foreign Affairs,* etc.

CHAPTER XXV

INTERNATIONAL RELATIONS: JULY 1937–
DECEMBER 7, 1941

I. THE LEAGUE AND THE SINO-JAPANESE WAR

WHEN the war between China and Japan broke out in July, 1937, the reaction of the Western states was essentially similar to that of 1931–1932. Germany and Italy were, to be sure, ideologically united with Japan in the Anti-Comintern Pact. Both had retired from the League of Nations, thus assuming the same relationship to it and to organized international life as had Japan after 1933. Each, however, and especially Germany, had an interest in avoiding antagonizing China, a country which was important to each from the commercial standpoint. Nevertheless Germany and Italy were responsive to Japanese pressure designed to prevent them from unduly aiding and abetting China. Thus Germany was brought, after initial hesitation, to order the return home of the military mission which had been advising Chiang Kai-shek in the construction of an effective military force, and which continued to advise him in the conduct of the war until some time after the fall of Nanking. Until after the outbreak of war in Europe, however, Germany kept one foot in the Chinese camp by selling military equipment to the Chinese government. The attachment of Germany and Italy to Japan, consequently, and their detachment from the Western powers, while it modified the general position as of 1931, did not fundamentally change it until after 1939.

Continuity with the earlier situation and reaction was both maintained and exhibited through action at Geneva. The earlier formal verdict had been for China and against Japan. This verdict had been reached at Geneva, and supported by Washington. It had not, however, brought about positive action in support of China. The negative action involved in application of the non-recognition policy initiated by the United States had been maintained and applied under the direction of the League's Far Eastern Advisory Committee. After the war broke out in 1937, with League action again invoked by China, the Advisory Committee reported to the Assembly findings favorable to China and a recommendation that the signatories of the Nine Powers Treaty should be requested to consult with a view to finding a solution of the question of Sino-Japanese relations and thus bringing the struggle to an end. These reports were adopted by the Assembly on October 6, 1937. The United States concurred in the findings and recommendation for a conference, much as it had supported the work of the League in 1931–1932.

Before this action had been taken, however, the American Secretary of State had on July 16 circularized a statement of principles which, although put in general terms, was called forth by the developing situation in the Far East and was designed as a warning to Japan. Coincidentally with the presentation of the report of the Far Eastern Advisory Committee on October 5, the American President made his famous Chicago "quarantine" speech. In this address, among other things, he said: "It seems to be unfortunately true that the epidemic of world lawlessness is spreading. . . . War is a contagion, whether it be declared or undeclared. It can engulf states and peoples remote from the original scene of the hostilities. We are determined to keep ourselves out of war, yet we cannot insure ourselves against the disastrous effects of war, and the dangers of involvement. . . . There must be positive endeavors to preserve peace." This seemed to indicate the possibility of positive leadership from the United States at the Conference proposed by the Assembly and which the United States agreed to attend. Adverse domestic reaction to the implications of the President's Chicago speech, however, brought about an immediate softening of its tone and, in spite of these and other words used, created uncertainty as to the actions with which the United States would be willing to associate itself. By the time the Conference convened at Brussels on November 3, it had become clear that it would confine itself to attempts at mediation, seeking to reëstablish peace by direct agreement between China and Japan.

Japan, among the Washington Conference powers, refused to attend the Conference. Of the interested states, not participants in the work of the Washington Conference, one (the Soviet Union) attended the Brussels Conference and sought to bring about vigorous action in restraint of Japan; while the other (Germany) not only failed to attend but attempted an independent mediation as a friend of both parties. In the absence of Japan its point of view was adequately presented and argued by the Italian delegation. Nevertheless, without direct representation from Japan, the exercise of mediatory or conciliatory functions proved impossible. The Conference consequently adjourned on November 24, issuing a declaration of principles and filing a report of its discussions. Thus this attempt to adjust international differences through the method of discussion and voluntary agreement, and in application of accepted international principles, proved to be even less successful than the similar attempt at the time of the first Manchurian crisis.

2. NATIONAL ACTION IN DEFENSE OF FOREIGN INTERESTS

Aside from this attempt at concerted action, the international adjustment to the new situation in the Far East consisted of a series of national reactions in defense of established national interests. Until after the fall of Hankow and the subsequent proclamation of a new order for eastern Asia, the war could be envisaged as exclusively one between China and Japan, without primary significance for the Western Powers. They could, and largely did, conceive of themselves as having mainly a responsibility to their own nationals in China. This could be discharged by seeking to minimize the consequences to them of their presence in a country at war, and by seeking to secure reparation for damage done to property or injury inflicted to persons such as is incidental to but inevitable as a result of the conduct of belligerent operations. The fact that the war was undeclared and waged as an "incident" by Japan gave a broader basis for the making of representations in behalf of injured nationals than would otherwise have existed. Thus, while fighting went on in the lower Yangtze area, where foreign nationals were largely concentrated and where there were the largest foreign property interests, claims of damage to property or injury to person were constant. These were presented through diplomatic channels. The representations made were designed to produce two consequences. One was reparation for damage actually done. The other was the avoidance of future action which would inflict injury on the foreigner and necessitate further demands for reparation. The Japanese response also was along two lines. The military commanders urged foreigners to avoid difficulties by withdrawing from areas of combat, as in the case of the warning issued with respect to the bombardment of Nanking. In the cases of damage done or personal injury inflicted they emphasized foreign responsibility because of the existence of property or the presence of persons in or on the fringes of areas where military actions were being undertaken. In other words, they sought to disclaim responsibility on the plea of military necessity. But, when the representations were vigorously made and the claims sustained after investigation, the Tokyo government usually gave assurances against repetition of actions objected to and on occasion made the reparation demanded. A major difficulty in reaching and maintaining agreement lay in the fact that the assurances were sought at Tokyo from the Foreign Office, while the actions complained of were taken by the military, which was not under the effective control of the government.

Throughout this period, which extended through 1937 and most of 1938, American diplomatic pressure on Japan in support of the interest of nationals was uniformly more effective than was that of Britain. This was especially revealed in the negotiations over the *Panay* incident, when demands for reparation were made because an American naval vessel (the *Panay*) and American merchantmen were attacked by Japanese bombing planes, although they had withdrawn from the area of active hostilities. Immediate apology and full reparation were made, in contrast with the attitude taken over injury inflicted under similar circumstances on British vessels. A number of things help to explain the greater responsiveness of Japan to American than to British pressure. One was the perception of the increasing difficulties of Britain in Europe and of the general tendency in British policy to make concessions in order to avoid difficulties. This was taken as evidence of weakness. Another was the desire to prevent Anglo-American coöperation in defense of common interests. By making appropriate concessions to the Americans it was felt that Washington would continue to follow the road of separate action in defense of particular rather than of common interests. By keeping England and the United States apart, even though it involved concessions to the latter, the former, whose existing material interests were the larger, could be dealt with more drastically. The more concessions made immediately by the state with the larger interests, the more untenable would ultimately become the position of the United States in defense of its lesser material interests. Thus concessions made to serve temporary purposes could subsequently be withdrawn. And finally, and most important of all, if the United States should be pushed beyond the point of diplomatic representations to that of action in defense of its interests, its actions would be much more disastrous to Japan than any which Britain could, under existing circumstances, take. This was on account of the dependence of Japan on imports from the United States of materials essential for war purposes, and on the American market for its exports, essential to finance the necessary imports either from the United States or from other countries.

The distance the Japanese were prepared to go in response to American demands depended upon two considerations. The first was in relation to the nature of the demands. So far as they were related to vested American interests, the Japanese were prepared to go a considerable distance to avoid serious friction. Even in relation to policy centering on the Open Door conception there was a large area within which discussion and agreement could take place until Japan had enlarged her objectives to include the establishment of a "new order in Eastern Asia" to replace the Washington Conference order. After November of 1938, however, the larger policy-positions of the two states were beyond reconciliation. The second consideration in determining the Japanese response to American demands was the conclusion reached, differing from time to time, as to whether the United States would confine itself to diplomatic representation or go beyond that to action in support of its point of view or its demand. American sentiment with respect to war, as embodied in the neutrality legislation enacted during the years from 1935 to 1937, supported the view that the American government, no matter how strongly it talked, would not venture on any course of action which would lead to war. Japanese publicists, both official and unofficial, consequently, consistently expressed the view, which strongly influenced American opinion, that a deliberate modification of trade relations for coercive purposes would lead to war. Whenever there were indications that such action might be taken in spite of the ultimate consequences, or because of a belief that war might not result, the Japanese responsiveness to American diplomatic pressure increased. In spite of evidence of that tendency in Japanese policy, however, because of American sentiment with respect to war the United States did not seriously attempt to implement its views through use of its economic and financial powers during the first three and a half years of the war.

3. INTERNATIONAL RELATIONS: 1939–1941

After the fall of Hankow, in October, 1938, the war in the Far East began to assume almost as much the character of a struggle between the Western powers and Japan as between Japan and China. The occupation of Hankow had been preceded and made readier of accomplishment by the prior occupation of Canton. Fear of complications with Britain, on account of Hongkong, had caused the Japanese to confine their major military efforts to the Yangtze Valley until after the crisis in Europe over Czechoslovakia had reached its peak. The demonstration of German strength and determination, which took Chamberlain to Munich, took Japan to Canton. The Munich Agreement, which, with its antecedents, was read by Japan as evidence of British weakness and lack of determination, was signed on September 29, 1938. Early in October Japanese forces were landed at Bias Bay, and Canton was thereafter occupied. That it was not more adequately defended by the Chinese finds part of its explanation in their feeling that, since its occupation would isolate Hongkong from China, fear of Britain would serve to prevent Japan from moving against it. Once this fear had been removed, as it was in consequence of developments in Europe, an important inhibiting factor in the expression of Japanese policy was at least temporarily removed.

At the same time, however, the United States began to shift from defense of particular interests back to insistence on modification of Japanese policy in the direction of respect for the principle of equality of opportunity. The traditional views of the American government with respect to the Open Door and the integrity of China had not changed but they had not been in the foreground of the diplomatic exchanges after the

Brussels Conference. In the note of October 6, 1938, however, sharp exception was taken to specific Japanese practices, such as the institution of exchange controls and the modification of the customs tariff, in the areas under Japanese occupation, and particularly in North China. These were held to be violative of the Open Door principle. The Japanese reply to this note was not made until November 18. It consisted, in the main, of a rebuttal of the specific American charges. But, in spite of its general disclaimer of intention to discriminate against the rights of American nationals in China, it closed on a note clearly designed to forecast the decisive posing of the issue between the Washington Conference system of relationships and what had been proclaimed as the "new order." The final paragraphs read:

Japan at present is devoting her energy to the establishment of a new order based upon genuine international justice throughout East Asia. . . .

It is the firm conviction of the Japanese Government that in the face of the new situation, fast developing in East Asia, any attempt to apply to the conditions of today and tomorrow inapplicable ideas and principles of the past neither would contribute toward the establishment of a real peace in East Asia nor solve the immediate issues.

Between the time of its receipt of the American note and the sending of its reply the Japanese government had officially proclaimed as its goal the establishment of this "new order." The reference to it in the reply to the United States served to put the Wesern Powers under notice of unilateral abrogation of such elements in the Washington Conference system as were inconsistent with the new policy. The "new order" conception was not then given any precise or detailed content by Japan. The definitions given, however, viewed against the background of action and of evolution of policy, indicated its scope. Its establishment required the replacement of the government of China headed by Chiang Kai-shek with one which would act under the direction of, and thus in "coöperation" with, Tokyo. It involved the liquidation of Western imperialism in China, and ultimately (when it became extended into a "new order for greater East Asia") throughout eastern and southeastern Asia, through the substitution for it of Japanese imperialism, since Japan was to plan, direct, and control "coöperation." Since it contemplated Sino-Japanese coöperation to eliminate communism in the area affected, it was designed to freeze the Russian position in the north, as a minimum, or, as a maximum, to bring about the elimination of Russia from the area east of Lake Baikal. The economic objectives were specifically defined in terms of the creation of a largely self-sufficient economic bloc, initially composed of Japan, Manchukuo, and China. This would inevitably bring about either the "closed door" to non-Japanese trade and investment in the entire area, or access to the continent only through the medium of Japan, and on conditions laid down by it. As thus defined, on the basis of its initial proclamation and its subsequent evolution, Japan would be the sole beneficiary of the "new order," except: (1) as it could be assumed that China would benefit either economically or politically through the establishment of an ultimate Japanese direction of the life of that country; and (2) as other states, because of a demonstration of friendship for Japan, might be given a special position, as against other third parties, within the new framework.

Confronted with this clear challenge to the old order, the United States, in a note of December 31, 1938, reaffirmed its support of the Washington Conference system, and thus of its traditional policies. It did not deny the fact of change, the note stating:

This Government [the American] is well aware that the situation has changed. This Government is also well aware that many of the changes have been brought about by action of Japan. This Government does not admit, however, that there is need or warrant for any one power to take upon itself to prescribe what shall be the terms and conditions of a new order in areas not under its sovereignty and to constitute itself the repository of authority and the agent of destiny in regard thereto. . . .

The Government of the United States has, however, always been prepared, and is now, to give due and ample consideration to any proposals based upon justice and reason which envisage the resolving of problems in a manner duly considerate of the rights and obligations of all parties directly concerned by processes of free negotiation and new commitment by and among all of the parties so concerned. . . . This Government has been and it continues to be willing to discuss such proposals, if and when put forward, with representatives of the other powers, including Japan and China, whose rights are involved, at whatever time and in whatever place may be commonly agreed upon.

Meanwhile, this Government reserves all rights of the United States as they exist and does not give assent to any impairment of those rights.

With this point of view England and France associated themselves. Before its formal exposition the United States, through the Import-Export Bank, on December 15 had established a credit for China of $25 million. In December, also, Britain had granted credits of £450,000 for the purchase of motor trucks, essential for the movement of war supplies along the newly constructed Yunnan-Burma highway. By these and other actions a more positive support of China for the future was indicated.

As Japan found increasing difficulty in resuming the offensive in China, the failure to bring the "China affair" to a rapid and successful conclusion began increasingly to be ascribed to the attitude of the Western Powers. The direct support of Chiang Kai-shek had been limited, but it encouraged continued resistance. Even more, the expression of opinion in the

United States and other Western countries, as well as at Geneva, in support of China encouraged the Chinese to continue the war of resistance. And in the occupied territory the foreign residential areas functioned in support of "free" China and, although administered neutrally, prevented the consolidation of the Japanese position. Even after the fall of Nanking offices of the Chinese government continued to be maintained in the foreign-administered areas at Shanghai, although finally the center of financial operations was shifted to Hongkong. Because the authority neither of Japan nor of the provisional Chinese governments established by Japan was fully accepted in the International Settlement or in the various Concessions, those engaged in anti-Japanese activities, including assassination of Chinese who were known to be coöperating with the Japanese, as well as leading in the organization and direction of guerrilla operations, could use the foreign areas as headquarters and as places of asylum. Funds and other properties of the Chinese government, essential to the maintenance of the exchange value of the Chinese dollar, were kept beyond the Japanese reach in the foreign areas.

Thus there was reason for undertaking an anti-Western offensive as military operations beyond Hankow failed to win a decision. This offensive was the significant development in and after the spring of 1939. The Western diplomatic pressure to bring about a redirection of Japanese policy, brought to bear from October, 1938, through the first months of 1939, was unsuccessful. The objectives included, in addition to the protest of earlier actions and the refusal to accept the "new order," an attempt to bring about the reopening of the Yangtze to trade after the end of formal hostilities in the area between Hankow and Shanghai. Western pressure was followed by Japanese counter-pressure to bring about acceptance by the Western states of the new position as defined by Japan.

The first move in 1939 clearly directed against the Western position was the occupation of the island of Hainan on February 10. Although defended as a move designed to strengthen the blockade against Chinese shipping and to facilitate operations in South China, it was applauded in the Japanese press because it "cut the Hongkong-Singapore line, with the result that Hongkong's existence as a naval base has lost all meaning." This action was protested but not opposed by the French government, which was one of the affected parties because of its earlier non-alienation agreement with China in respect to Hainan, and by the British government since Britain's strategic position was adversely affected. There was similar acquiescence, under protest, in the subsequent assertion of title to the Spratly Islands. Toward the end of February, in consequence of an outburst of terrorism at Shanghai, the Japanese raised questions as to the administration of the International Settlement, and demanded coöperation between Settlement police and the Japanese consular police in the suppression of terrorism. In relation to the latter, a direct agreement was reached with the Settlement authorities on March 4. Subsequently more far-reaching demands were made by Japanese authorities recurrently for enlarged participation in the government and the administration of the Settlement. This represented pressure on the strongest foreign position and the most important center of foreign rights and interests. It consistently met with joint Anglo-American resistance based on the consideration that, regardless of the equities involved, the time was inopportune to undertake any fundamental readjustment in existing arrangements which would involve revision of the Land Regulations.

Meanwhile, in May, the Japanese attack shifted to the International Settlement on Kulangsu Island in the port of Amoy, where the foreign interests affected were relatively unimportant. This action, which involved the sending of a naval force in support of a landing party, was similarly taken ostensibly on account of an alleged failure of the municipal authorities to proceed vigorously against those who had committed acts of terrorism. The attempt to take over control of the International Settlement at Kulangsu was unsuccessful because of the action taken by the United States, Britain, and France in sending equivalent forces in support of the Settlement authorities. The united front presented by the Western Powers at Shanghai and at Kulangsu, on account of the fact that the interests affected were common and could readily be perceived as such, was in large part responsible for their relative success in defending their position.

Possibly with a view to breaking the forming Anglo-American front, although also because of the existing situation at Tientsin, the point of Japanese pressure was thereupon shifted to the British Concession at Tientsin. The active dispute at that place began on April 9, when the Chinese Commissioner of the Customs was assassinated in the British Concession. Demands were made that four individuals suspected by the Japanese of complicity in the assassination, who were held in custody by the British, should be turned over to the Japanese authorities for trial and punishment. The refusal of the Concession authorities to comply with the demand was based on lack of sufficient evidence at hand to support the charges. The failure of the Japanese to get their way led them to serve a virtual ultimatum on the British authorities in June, threatening a blockade of the Concession if the demand was not complied with. The blockade was duly instituted on June 12. It was so rigorously applied that the British Concession was virtually isolated. Blockade measures which were not so rigorous were applied also to the French Concession. Those entering or leaving the British Concession, especially British subjects, were subjected to search under most humiliating conditions. British shipping and trade were interfered with. Food supply within the Concession became more and more restricted. The technique of pressure was strongly reminiscent of that employed by Chinese officials at Canton and in Japan in the pre-treaty period.

Back of the question of rendition of the alleged assassins was the larger question of the uses to which the Concession had lent itself in relation to the struggle between Japan to consolidate its position in North China and China to prevent that consolidation. The foreign position at Tientsin was such that it was difficult to maintain the monopoly position with respect to the trade of North China which Japan sought to establish for herself. The refusal of the foreign banks in the Concession to accept, in place of the Chinese government currency, for foreign exchange purposes, the notes issued by the Federal Reserve Bank established by the Japanese-supported Peking government, strengthened the position of Chungking and correspondingly weakened that of Japan in North China. And the banks in Tientsin held at the disposition of the Chinese National government, and thus kept out of reach of the Japanese, substantial silver stocks. Consequently the underlying issue at Tientsin was the same as at Shanghai, and it reached much deeper than the question of control of terrorism. In relation to the war, the underlying issue was the refusal of the foreign governments completely to acquiesce in the right of Japan, or the Japanese-dominated Chinese governments, to take the steps deemed necessary to eliminate Chiang Kai-shek's authority in the so-called occupied area. In terms of long-run purposes, the issue was the right and ability of Japan to control the conditions of access to China.

The recognition of the existence of these underlying issues helps to make clear the reasons for the entire series of actions directed against the British during the spring and summer of 1939, as well as the seriousness of the negotiations over the Tientsin question which were conducted at Tokyo and which culminated in the signature of the Craigie-Arita Agreement.

Because the emphasis was on British interests and the British position as being under attack, the fact was somewhat obscured that if the attack were successful the interests of other states would be similarly affected. Since the position of all the Western states rested on the same foundations, if the one with the largest interests definitely accepted Japan's terms, it would be difficult if not impossible for the others either separately or collectively to insist on continued respect for their asserted rights. But, because of a differentiation in attitude toward British and other foreigners, the foreign position was not jointly supported except, as at Shanghai, where an international rather than a national Settlement was attacked. Otherwise diplomatic action taken and supported was separate, in defense of the particular interests and in support of the policies of each state even when the separate actions were identical. Thus, for example, since the Americans had no concession at Tientsin, they could be dissociated from the defense of the British Concession. When it was expedient as a method of weakening the position of the British, the Americans and the French could be conciliated and thus made to feel that similar treatment would not be meted out to them.

With Britain's position complicated by its difficulties in Europe, and with internal forces pressing for conciliation of and agreement with the former ally, the British Ambassador in Tokyo finally accepted the formula embodied in the Craigie-Arita Agreement in order to bring about relaxation of the Tientsin blockade, and to define the basis for continued negotiation over the points at issue.

By it,

His Majesty's Government in the United Kingdom fully recognize the actual situation in China, where hostilities on a large scale are in progress, and note that as long that state of affairs continues to exist, the Japanese forces in China have special requirements for the purpose of safeguarding their own security and maintaining public order in the regions under their control, and that they have to suppress or remove any such acts or causes as will obstruct them or benefit their enemy.

His Majesty's Government have no intention of countenancing any acts or measures prejudicial to the attainment of the above-mentioned objects by the Japanese forces and they will take this opportunity to confirm their policy in this respect by making it plain to the British authorities and British nationals in China that they should refrain from such acts and measures. [1]

If this agreement had been implemented in respect either to the immediate issues or with respect to future developments, it would have resulted in a complete Japanese victory at Tientsin and have led to a general weakening of both the foreign and the Chinese position. That it was no more than a temporary diplomatic victory for Japan may be ascribed to the adverse reception accorded to it by British interests in China and elsewhere, but more especially to the notice given by the American government on July 27 of its intention to terminate the American-Japanese Commercial Treaty of 1911. This notice was taken by the Japanese government to mean a possible embargo of trade between the United States and Japan, since, after six months from the time of denunciation, there would be no legal obstacle to such action. The threat caused Japan to be more hesitant in its pressure on the British, while it helped to stiffen the British atttitude in the second stage of the negotiations over the precise questions at issue. Thus the formula agreed upon was not given the broad interpretation and

[1] I. S. FRIEDMAN, *British Relations with China, 1931–1939*, p. 209; citing Parl. Debates, H. of C., vol. 350, col. 994.

application anticipated by Japan even though the initial cause of the controversy at Tientsin was decided essentially on Japanese terms. The alleged assassins were turned over to the local Japanese authorities for trial and punishment; on the ground, however, that additional evidence implicating them had been brought to the attention of the British authorities. Negotiations over the broader economic issues were still going on when the general situation still further changed, with the signature of the German-Soviet Non-Aggression Pact.

4. EFFECTS OF THE ANTI-COMINTERN AGREEMENT

An apparently fixed element in Japanese policy was that embodied in the Anti-Comintern Agreement with Germany and Italy, of hostility to communism and thus to Russia. The Agreement not only attached Japan to the Axis, thus giving her friends in Europe, but presented Russia with a two-front military dilemma and thus gave Japan needed assurance against direct Russian action against her in the Far East. Aside from the United States, Russia was the state thought of by the Japanese as being in a position, if she had a free hand elsewhere, and as having an incentive, effectively to support China and to act decisively against Japan. The Soviet Union had given China a larger measure of direct aid during the course of the war than had any other state. It had further aided China indirectly by immobilizing a large segment of Japan's striking power in Manchukuo, since between a quarter and a half million men, with corresponding equipment, had to be maintained on guard there against a possible Russian attack. The continuing friction, which led to recurrent hostilities (such as those at Changkufeng in the summer of 1938 and on the Mongolian-Manchukuoan frontier in the summer of 1939), constantly underscored this necessity. But in spite of all of this the Russian position remained that of the benevolent neutral rather than that of a participant in support of China.[2]

As part of their pressure on the British, at a time when the latter were negotiating to bring Russia into their European defense system against Germany in the spring and summer of 1939, and also to strengthen themselves vis-à-vis the Russians, the Japanese Army elements which had sponsored the Anti-Comintern Pact sought to transform it into a military alliance between Japan and Germany. In this they were unsuccessful because the Japanese government was not then prepared to commit itself so fully to the Axis in Europe. But the mere fact that an essentially anti-Soviet alliance had been seriously contemplated made the shock of subse-

---

[2] On Russian policy toward China, 1937–1941, see D. DALLIN, *Soviet Russia and the Far East*, pp. 71-76.

quent reversal of the Nazi position with respect to the Soviet Union even more severe than it would otherwise have been.

Thus with uncertainty as to what the abrogation of its commercial treaty with the United States was going to mean in the way of action, and confronted with an apparent reversal of the German attitude toward the Soviet Union, together with the outbreak of war in Europe which immediately followed the signature of the Russian-German Agreement, the Japanese government had to reconsider its position. The government in power, associated with the move toward overt alliance with Germany, resigned. Its successor defined Japan's position as independent with respect to the European war. It instituted negotiations with the United States with a view to preventing the application of an embargo. And it relaxed somewhat its direct pressure on the British, turning its attention in China to the task of bringing the war to an end by establishing a government at Nanking with which it could make peace.

This latter was not accomplished until 1940, when Wang Ching-wei finally agreed upon terms of collaboration with Japan and was consequently officially installed at Nanking as the head of the government. This did not, of course, bring the war to an end, but it did lay the basis for its transformation as rapidly as circumstances permitted into a civil war, with one party supported against the other by Japanese troops.

The negotiations with the United States did not lead to any agreement any more than the installation of the Wang government changed the China war situation. But neither, in spite of the strong words spoken by the American Ambassador, did the termination of the trade treaty, on January 26, 1940, bring about any real adverse modification of the conditions under which trade between the United States and Japan was carried on, even from the standpoint of the supply of essential war materials. The threat of action, however, remained.

When the European war, in the spring of 1940, passed from the passive to the active stage from the standpoint of military operations, Japan was confronted with another new situation. This new situation, growing out of the successive conquests by Germany of Denmark and Norway, Belgium and Holland, and finally France, and the threat, by the end of June, of the destruction of British power, inevitably directed Japan's attention to the possibility of immediately attaining what had previously been thought of only as ultimate objectives. Pressure was quickly applied to the French in Indo-China. This was at first directed toward the acquisition (1) of supervisory rights to ensure that no supplies should reach Chungking through Indo-China, and (2) of air bases from which to operate more readily against the supply route from the Burma frontier. This road had been closed to China by the British during the summer but was subsequently reopened as Britain apparently was compelled to recognize that the protection of her Far Eastern interests against Japan rested with China. The pressure against Indo-China was subsequently directed generally toward bringing the French possessions into what was proclaimed as "a new order for Greater East Asia," and specifically toward giving Japan the right to move troops against China across Indo-China and to use Indo-Chinese airports for war purposes. As Siam (Thailand) also sought extension at the expense of the French colonies, Japan had an instrument at its disposal to lever further concessions from the French than those related to the necessities of the war against China. Having developed a struggle between Thailand and the French colony, the Japanese government asserted the right to mediate, and in the process sought to secure advantages for itself, including base facilities at Saigon as well as territories for Thailand.

Two things prevented the Japanese government from immediately taking full advantage of the new situation in Europe. One was the continued uncertainty of its relations with the Soviet Union. Following the reversal of their own anti-Soviet policy, the Nazis encouraged the Japanese government to seek an agreement with Russia. It was difficult to define the basis of such an agreement without one or the other fundamentally modifying its attitude. It must not be forgotten that they had been engaged in sharp hostilities in the summer of 1939, as in previous years, in the course of which the Russians had shown that they had sufficient military strength to enable them to hold their own against the Japanese army. Under the circumstances, after the signature of the German-Soviet Pact in September, had it not been for the outbreak and the course of the war in Europe an agreement on essentially Russian terms might have had to be contemplated by Japan. But the war served to preoccupy Russia in Europe as effectively as had the earlier threat from anti-Communist Germany. To all intents and purposes it maintained the two-front dilemma for the Soviet authorities. Thus on each side it soon became clear that there was immediately neither more nor less reason for sacrifice of objectives to attain an agreement than there had been before the anti-Comintern front had been broken. After the collapse of France and the anticipated destruction of England, however, a new and important area seemed opened to Japanese expansionism. Vigorous action in southeastern Asia, however, required a lessening of the possibility of friction and hostilities with Russia. Consequently the Japanese government itself was prepared to make readjustments in order to secure an agreement with the Soviet Union. The negotiations looking toward definition of spheres of interest in the north and, on the basis of such definition, the conclusion of a non-aggression pact, were not, however, carried to a successful conclusion until April 13, 1941, when a neutrality pact was signed in Moscow.

The second and equally important obstacle to the expression of a vigorous policy at the expense of the Dutch and British as well as the French lay in an uncertainty, at least, as to the reaction of the United States. On the eve of the occupation of Holland by the Nazis the Japanese Foreign Minister, Arita, made the following statement on April 15, 1940:

> With the South Seas region, especially the Netherlands East Indies, Japan is economically bound by an intimate relationship of mutuality in ministering to one another's need. Similarly other countries of East Asia maintain close economic relations with these regions. That is to say, Japan and all of these countries and regions together are contributing to the prosperity of East Asia through mutual aid and interdependence.
>
> Should the hostilities in Europe be extended to the Netherlands and produce repercussions, as you say, in the Netherlands East Indies, it would not only interfere with the maintenance and furtherance of the above mentioned relations of economic interdependence and of coexistence and of common prosperity, but also give rise to an undesirable situation from the standpoint of the peace and stability in East Asia. In view of these considerations, the Japanese Government cannot but be deeply concerned over any development, accompanying the aggravation of the war in Europe, that may effect the *status quo* of the Netherlands East Indies. [3]

On April 17, Secretary Hull defined the American policy, for reasons set forth, as based upon respect for the maintenance of the *status quo*. [4] This was designed as a warning to Japan.

In May, Holland was invaded and occupied by the Nazis. The fall of France, as previously stated, was followed by Japanese pressure on Indo-China which, while direct, initially was related to the war in China. Subsequently, it was more definitely related to the movement south. With respect to the Netherlands East Indies pressure was also exerted, but at first with a view to the maintenance and the safeguarding of economic relations. The Dutch authorities, while showing a willingness to negotiate, refused to give way to the pressure exerted and made it clear that they intended to maintain the independence, as far as third parties were concerned, of the islands. Specifically, they refused to accept the applicability to them of the Japanese conception of a "Greater East Asia," as that conception was advanced and emphasized by the Japanese Foreign Minister in and after the autumn of 1940.

With the evolution of the war in Europe, American policy swung through an emphasis on western hemisphere defense in anticipation of the overthrow of Britain to armament expansion for purposes of hemisphere defense and also to supply Britain with the arms necessary to en-

---

[3] *Foreign Relations of the United States: Japan,* 1931–1941, II, 281.

[4] For text, Press Release issued by Dept. of State, April 17, 1940, *ibid.,* pp. 281–282.

able it to maintain itself at home and in the empire and, if possible, to win the war. But even at the height of the emphasis on hemisphere defense to repel a possible attack in the Atlantic, the American fleet remained in the Pacific, maintaining the threat of action against Japan in case that country acted to disturb the *status quo* in Malaysia. As the American defense program of armament expansion was inaugurated, furthermore, there began to be imposed more important restrictions on the export of war materials to Japan. Because this was done in relation to the domestic armament program rather than as a measure directed toward the restraint of Japan and expressive of displeasure over the direction of Japanese policy, it did not establish as a certainty American action even of an economic character in implementation of its views. It was, however, a straw in the wind, as was also an enlargement of the financial aid extended to China. The anomaly continued, however, of America supplying Japan with the material essential to the continuation and possible extension of its war effort directed essentially against those whom the United States sought to maintain.

As a method of bringing pressure to bear primarily on the United States and secondarily on Russia, Japan, Germany, and Italy transformed their working political understanding under the Anti-Comintern Pact into a military alliance on September 27, 1940. This had the effect of drawing together the older war in the Far East and the newer one in Europe. It provided, in effect, that if the United States should participate in either war to an extent found by the signatories to extend beyond "short of war" action, the participants in the other war would declare war on the United States. Thus, if the United States should use its fleet in the Pacific to prevent an occupation of the Netherlands Indies by Japan, Germany and Italy would be expected to declare war and wage it in the Atlantic against the United States. Or, if American aid to Britain went beyond the supply position, or threatened to become decisive, Japan would be expected to act against the United States in the Pacific. The signatories, however, were left free to determine, each for itself, what constituted an act of war by the United States which would bring into operation its obligations under the alliance. It was clearly the intention to prevent the United States from taking decisive action in support of England by threatening it with war in the Pacific; or from impeding Japanese progress in the enlarged Far East because of the certainty of America's being thereupon involved in the war with Germany and Italy. Thus its major objective would be realized only if, on account of it, the United States lessened, or did not extend to the full, its support of England and China and, in prospect, of the Netherlands Indies and of Britain in southeastern Asia. This was the case because, if the threat were insufficient to bring about a modification of the direction being taken in American policy and war eventuated, the power situation would not in fact be materially changed since Japan could no more give aid to Germany and Italy in Europe than they could effectively support Japan against the United States in the Far East.

Whether this was recognized clearly in the United States or not, Washington became more and more committed, after the reëlection of President Roosevelt in November, 1940, at least to full economic and financial support of Britain and also China. When Congress convened in January, 1941, a bill was immediately introduced, popularly called the lend-lease bill, which authorized the President to designate countries whose defense was essential to the defense of the United States and to make available to them, on terms and under conditions found to be appropriate by the President, the materials essential to their defense. This bill was introduced and enacted because of the growing popular acceptance of the view that support of Britain and any allies which she had, and of China, was the most effective way of keeping war from the western hemisphere. The lend-lease bill constituted, in effect, an American reply to the Axis military alliance.

In apparent anticipation of the spring offensive of 1941, it became increasingly clear that Germany would like to have Japan extend the sphere of her military operations to include an attack on the British possessions in southeastern Asia concurrently with a German attack on Britain. This Japan was apparently unwilling to undertake without a reasonable assurance either of German success in Europe or of freedom of action vis-à-vis Russia. To survey the situation the Japanese Foreign Minister, Matsuoka, undertook a trip to Europe, ostensibly in response to an invitation to visit Hitler. En route to Berlin, however, and on his way home after visits to Rome and Berlin, Mr. Matsuoka stopped at Moscow.

The impressions of the strength of his allies which the Japanese Foreign Minister received in Europe must have been somewhat contradictory. England had successfully assumed the offensive in North Africa at the time of his preparation to visit Europe. Thereafter came the offensives in East Africa which seemed to put an end to Italian imperial dreams. Greece, drawn into the European war by an Italian attack, not only had repelled that attack but had driven the Italians back of their own frontier in Albania. While Matsuoka was in Europe, the Germans failed to attain success in their diplomatic offensives against Turkey and Yugoslavia. Furthermore, the British consolidated their control of the Mediterranean by a decisive victory over the Italian fleet and demonstrated it by actions against the Italian naval base of Taranto. And Russia, although timidly, took Bulgaria to task for admitting the German armies to its territories and assured Turkey of its benevolent neutrality if the Turks had to defend themselves by arms. In direct reference to Japan, Moscow reports indicated that Japan would have to pay a higher price for an agreement than could have been asked if the British had not been able to maintain themselves against Germany.

But, on the other side, as the Japanese Foreign Minister began his return journey to Tokyo, the European military picture began to change with considerable rapidity. German and Italian armies regained the ground lost in North Africa. The diplomatic defeat in Yugoslavia was avenged by war, that country rapidly coming under German military control. The Greek armies were pushed out of Thrace, and successes were won by the Nazis against the British and Greeks sufficient to throw doubt on the ability of those allies to maintain themselves against the might of the German military machine.

Against this ebb and flow in the fortunes of war in Europe and Africa, Mr. Matsuoka did not lose sight of the major purpose of his trip. The Italian and German setbacks must have impressed him, but the German military successes following the reverses impressed Russia and could not fail to have effect also on Matsuoka. At any rate, before the Japanese Foreign Minister left Moscow on his journey back to Tokyo, he secured a neutrality pact from the Soviet authorities. This pact was signed on April 13, 1941. By it each state agreed to respect the territorial integrity and hold inviolable the territories of the other. This included a Russian pledge with respect to Manchukuo and a Japanese pledge with respect to Outer Mongolia. Thus, although it did not settle specific questions at issue between the two countries, such as frontier demarcation and the fisheries question, it did provide the framework within which settlement might be expected to take place. Of more immediate significance, however, was the provision (Article II) of the pact: "Should one of the contracting parties become the object of hostilities on the part of one or several third Powers, the other contracting party will observe neutrality throughout the duration of the conflict."

This article was designed, from the Japanese standpoint, to free Japan from the prospect of difficulty simultaneously with Russia and the United States. Thus it was the next step in advance from the Axis pact of September, 1940. Since, however, it was not restricted to the Far East, it would have the effect of releasing Japan from her obligation to act against Russia if the Soviet Union should be drawn into the war in its European aspect. In that respect it was in the nature of a retreat from the Axis alliance.

The situation in the Far East, then, had evolved by May, 1941, to the point where Japan had cleared the way, so far as that could be done diplomatically, for action directed against the European possessions in southeastern Asia. The struggle to overthrow Chiang Kai-shek remained on Japan's hands as unfinished business, and with respect to that struggle the Soviet-Japan Pact left the situation unchanged. Moscow remained free, and indicated its intention, to continue its trade in military supplies with the Chungking government. The two major uncertainties in the situation which were presented for judgment at Tokyo were: (1) as to the ability of the British to maintain themselves in Europe and simultaneously to defend themselves successfully in their position in eastern Asia against a Japanese attack, and (2) as to the wisdom of launching an attack on the British and Dutch possessions in the face of the possibility that it would mean war with the United States.

The situation confronting Japan changed, however, between May and July since, after Matsuoka had committed Japan to neutrality in the event that Russia became involved in war with a third party, Germany launched an attack on the Soviet Union (June 21, 1941). This was done without prior notification being given to Japan. Up to that time, the logic of events in Europe had pointed toward redirection of Japan's expansionist objectives from the north to the south. Whether or not to divert attention from the contemplated attack on the Soviet Union, the Nazis themselves, in the spring of 1941, sought to persuade Japan to prepare for an attack on the British possessions in southeast Asia, coördinated with their "decisive" attack on Britain in Europe. The neutrality pact with Russia was designed, from this point of view, to lessen the possibility that Japan would become simultaneously involved in the north and the south, with China remaining unfinished business.

The German attack on the Soviet Union, consequently, produced an initial "confusion and consternation" in Japanese governmental circles. At that time the negotiations with the United States, which were protracted until December 7, 1941, were in mid-course. If successful they would remove the threat of American interference with Japanese activities in the Far East and in southeastern Asia. If German predictions of a quick and decisive victory over Russia in Europe proved correct, Japan might extend and strengthen her position in the north with a minimum application of force, even though she had become further involved in southeast Asia. But if she violated her neutrality pact with the Soviet Union, as requested by the Germans, who now sought to postpone the Japanese action against Britain, which they had been encouraging, and to persuade Japan to open up a Far Eastern front against Russia, before a decision had been reached in Europe, she might assist Germany but weaken herself. On the other hand, if she became too deeply involved in the south she might lose a favorable opportunity to drive Russia out of the Far East.

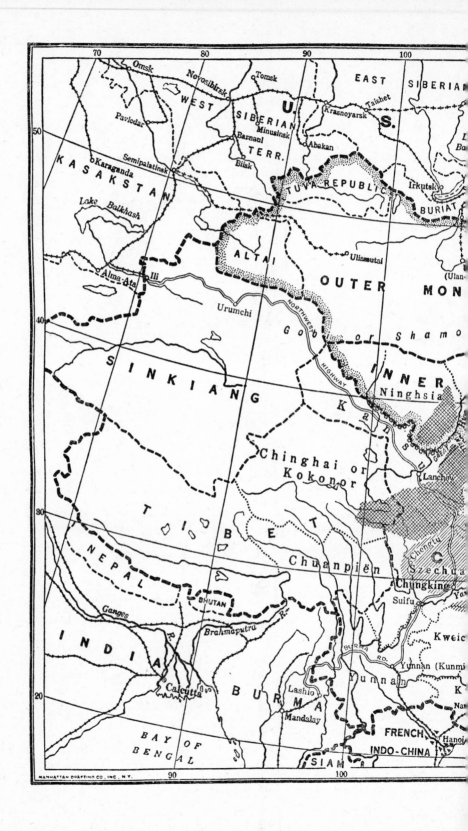

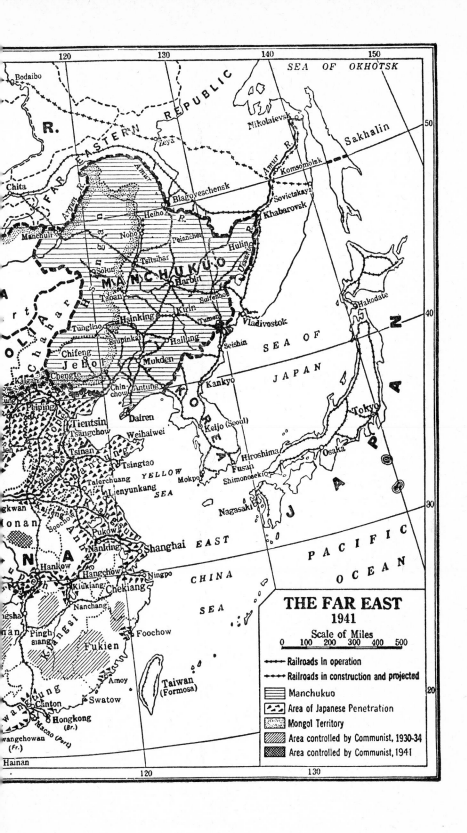

THE FAR EAST
1941

Scale of Miles
0   100   200   300   400   500

•••••• Railroads in operation
•••••• Railroads in construction and projected
▤ Manchukuo
▨ Area of Japanese Penetration
▦ Mongol Territory
▥ Area controlled by Communist, 1930-34
▦ Area controlled by Communist, 1941

The policy that emerged out of the initial confusion was one of "watch-ful waiting" as far as the Soviet-German war was concerned. The pro-Axis orientation of Japanese policy was reaffirmed, but the Russians and Americans were assured that the neutrality pact would, for the time being, be respected, although its author, Matsuoka, was shortly dropped from the Cabinet. The negotiations with the United States were continued in spite of the failure to define any preliminary basis of possible agreement. But the domestic preparations for full war mobilization of the resources of the country were accelerated, and the pressure on Indo-China and the Netherlands Indies was increased rather than relaxed.

5. JAPANESE-AMERICAN NEGOTIATIONS: 1941

By 1941 the United States, in terms of administration policy, had com-mitted itself to the policy of national defense through support of the anti-Axis Powers as the "arsenal of democracy." The passage of the lend-lease bill in March transformed administration policy into national policy. Under its authority China was designated as one of the countries entitled to receive assistance. Consequently it could be anticipated that the limited aid previously given China (represented by an Import-Export Bank loan of $50 million, and a contemplated currency stabilization loan of $50 million), would be materially increased. At the same time "Japan's economy was feeling the pinch of restrictions on exports from the United States and other countries. By the early part of 1941, shipments from the United States to Japan of iron, steel, most important metals, machinery, high quality gasoline and blending agents, and plants and plans for the pro-duction of high quality gasoline had practically ceased." [5] But shipments of petroleum were continued, according to Secretary Hull "lest Japan should use such an embargo as an excuse for taking over the oil produc-tion of the Netherlands East Indies." [6]

Under these circumstances tension between the United States and Japan had increased. It was not lessened as Japan extended her pressure beyond China into southeast Asia and Indonesia. But neither Japan nor the United States was ready to force the issue to the point of war in the Pacific. American opinion, mainly with respect to Europe, had moved beyond insistence on "neutrality" to acceptance of a policy of non-bel-ligerency (a new status which involved all except military, or shooting, participation in war). But time was needed for preparation, from the mili-tary point of view, for war itself. Consequently, when it was unofficially suggested that "the Japanese Government would welcome an opportunity

[5] *Foreign Relations, Japan,* 1931–1941, II, 326.
[6] HULL, *Memoirs,* II, 983.

to alter its political alignments and modify its attitude toward China," [7] the administration, although without great hope of success, indicated its willingness informally to explore the possibility of defining a basis upon which formal negotiations might be instituted.

In the conversations which were instituted after the arrival of Admiral Nomura, the new Japanese Ambassador to the United States, Secretary Hull (April 16) defined four principles as the basis upon which agreement would have to be erected. These were "(1) respect for the territorial integrity and the sovereignty of each and all nations; (2) support of the principle of non-interference in the internal affairs of other countries; (3) support of the principle of equality including equality of commercial opportunity; (4) non-disturbance of the *status quo* in the Pacific except as the *status quo* may be altered by peaceful means." [8] Obviously, any reasonable application of these principles would have required a radical modification of Japan's policy for the future and also an unwinding of the chain of consequences begun as early as 1931.

The Japanese proposals which Secretary Hull had agreed to consider as a basis of negotiations, provided they were founded on these four principles, were presented on May 12, 1941. [9] They were set up under six heads: (1) the concepts of the United States and of Japan respecting international relations and the character of nations; (2) the attitude of both governments toward the European war; (3) the relations of both nations toward the China "affair"; (4) commerce between both nations; (5) economic activity of both nations in the Southwestern Pacific area; (6) the policies of both nations affecting political stabilization in the Pacific area. Disregarding generalities, the Japanese proposed to maintain their obligations of military assistance under the Tripartite Pact, and asked that "the Government of the United States" maintain "that its attitude toward the European war is, and will continue to be, directed by no such aggressive measures as to assist any one nation against another"; that the United States should accept the three principles underlying Japan's China policy, as defined by Prince Konoye and embodied in the agreement made between Japan and the Wang Ching-wei government at Nanking, and "relying upon the policy of the Japanese Government to establish a relationship of neighborly friendship with China (the United States) shall forthwith request the Chiang Kai-shek régime to negotiate peace with Japan"; that restrictions on trade should be lifted and "the United States and Japan shall assure each other to mutually supply such commodities as are, respectively, available or required by either of

[7] *Foreign Relations, Japan,* 1931–1941, II, 328–329.
[8] *Ibid.,* II, 332; also HULL, *op. cit.,* II, 995.
[9] Text of Proposals in *Foreign Relations, Japan,* 1931–1941, II, 420–425.

them"; that "having in view that the Japanese expansion in the direction of the Southwestern Pacific area is declared to be of peaceful nature, American coöperation shall be given in the production and procurement of natural resources (such as oil, rubber, tin, nickel) which Japan needs"; and that the independence of the Philippines should be jointly guaranteed on the basis of its permanent neutrality.

In the ensuing confidential conversations of June and early July the main emphasis was laid upon China, the Americans seeking clarification of the terms of an agreement which would be acceptable to Japan and yet which would provide a basis on which China could be expected to enter upon negotiations looking toward the reëstablishment of peace. The Japanese military moves in Indo-China at the end of July were explained as being "of entirely peaceful character and for self-defense" and necessary because Japanese public opinion had been dangerously aroused because of the successive measures taken by the United States, Great Britain, and the Netherlands East Indies against Japan. In spite of this explanation, however, they strengthened the view that the purpose of the negotiations, as viewed by Japan, was to commit the United States to acceptance of the new status created by Japan by military means, rather than to define an acceptable basis of adjustment between the two governments.

The action taken in response to the Japanese advance into Indo-China was the issuance of an Executive Order (July 26) freezing all Japanese assets in the United States, bringing all financial, import, and export transactions under the control of the American government. Within a few hours Britain and the Dominions followed suit; and the Dutch were to do likewise over the week end.[10] The significant effect of these actions was to institute an Anglo-American-Dutch embargo on the supply of oil and petroleum products to Japan. This was done as much in response to what was known in advance of Japan's future intentions as to the specific action taken at this time. Through Magic (the name given the operation of decoding secret Japanese messages, after the codes had been broken) the highest American officials were from this time on constantly informed as to Japanese plans, as they were transmitted from Tokyo to its responsible official abroad. They could not, however, usually directly act on the basis of this advance knowledge when such action would disclose to the Japanese that their codes had been broken for fear of drying up a valuable source of information. At this time it was learned that "after the occupation of French Indo-China, next on our schedule is the sending of an ultimatum to the Netherlands Indies. In the seizing of Singapore the Navy will play the principal part. As for the Army, in

[10] WALTER MILLIS, *This Is Pearl!*, p. 113.

seizing Singapore it will need only one division, and in seizing the Netherlands Indies, only two." [11]

In spite of information which made it clear that no agreement was possible except on Japan's terms, negotiations were not completely broken off by the United States, since as much time as possible was sought to complete its military preparations. [12] The pressure for continuation of negotiations, however, came from Japan. The urge initially was to secure a relaxation of the economic pressures which, in their intensified form, hurt. To this was joined a desire for time, on the Japanese side, to extend their position into southeast Asia as far as possible "by peaceful means," and to complete their own military preparations. Almost to the end, also, there was apparently the slim hope that the United States would accept Japan's proposals for agreement without substantial modification, so that Japan could attain even her ultimate objectives without war.

Nevertheless from the time of the resignation of the Konoye government, on October 16, and its replacement with the Cabinet headed by General Tojo, the movement was inexorably toward war. The American Ambassador to Japan, Mr. Grew, tried to convince himself, and his government, that this was not necessarily the case [13] but the news received via Magic (which was not transmitted to him) made it difficult for his views to be accepted. On the surface, in spite of the change in government, however, the emphasis was put by Japan on negotiations, to be kept going until the deadline for hostilities had been reached.

Admiral Nomura, not a career diplomat, had been conducting the negotiations for Japan until November. In October, before the change of government in Japan, Foreign Minister Toyoda intimated a desire to send "a diplomat of wide experience to Washington to assist the Ambassador." [14] It was not, however, until November that Saburo Kurusu, former Japanese Ambassador to Germany, entered the negotiations. Shortly thereafter, on November 20, the final Japanese proposals, defining the conditions of a temporary agreement, were presented to the American Secretary of State. The American reply was transmitted on November 26. The American counter-proposals were formulated to keep the negotiations going, if possible, although the information at hand through Magic indicated that a deadline had been set by Japan; that the Japanese proposals were in the nature of an ultimatum, involving acceptance or rejection, without fundamental modification; and that their acceptance without

[11] *Ibid.*, p. 101.

[12] As late as November 27 "General Marshall and Admiral Stark sent a memorandum to the President . . . in which they pleaded for more time. . . . We wanted peace with Japan, but if we could not have peace, then we needed time." HULL, *op. cit.*, II, 1087.

[13] GREW, *Ten Years in Japan*, pp. 459–463.

[14] HULL, *op. cit.*, II, 1034.

serious modification would have involved virtual surrender of its position by the United States. The American note, with its definition of conditions of a *modus vivendi* acceptable to the United States, although apparently thought of as a reasonable counter-proposal, was taken by the Japanese government as a definite rejection of its "ultimatum," since it could only be accepted if Japan was prepared to reorient her Far Eastern policies. Consequently, the "final, the definitive, the irrevocable decision" on war was taken by the Japanese Cabinet when the American reply was received. The conversations at Washington were continued, however, while the Japanese fleet steamed toward Pearl Harbor, where the United States Pacific fleet was concentrated.

REFERENCES FOR FUTURE STUDY

MAX BELOFF, *The Foreign Policy of Soviet Russia, 1929–1941* (1949). T. A. BISSON, *America's Far Eastern Policy* (1945). W. H. CHAMBERLAIN, *Japan Over Asia* (1939); worth consulting. DEPARTMENT OF STATE, *Foreign Relations of the United States, Japan, 1931–1941* (1943), 2 vols. ETHEL B. DIETRICH, *Far Eastern Trade of the United States* (1940); the title indicates its scope. MIRIAM S. FARLEY, *The Problems of Japanese Trade Expansion in the Postwar Situation* (1939); throws light on the effects of the China War on Japanese trade. HERBERT FEIS, *The Road to Pearl Harbor* (1950); one of the best accounts. JOSEPH C. GREW, *Ten Years in Japan* (1944); account of the decade from the diaries of the American Ambassador to Japan. I. S. FRIEDMAN, *British Relations with China, 1931–1939* (1940); a good study of the subject. CORDELL HULL, *Memoirs of Cordell Hull* (1948), 2 vols.; a review of diplomatic developments by the American Secretary of State. FRANK W. IKLE, *German-Japanese Relations: 1936–40* (1957). W. C. JOHNSTONE, *The United States and Japan's New Order* (1941); deals with the effects of the war on American rights, interests, and policy in the Far East. F. C. JONES, *Japan's New Order in East Asia—Its Rise and Fall, 1937–1945* (1954); the best account now available. S. SHEPHARD JONES and DENYS P. MYERS (eds.), *Documents on American Foreign Relations, 1938–1939* (1939), *1939–1940* (1940); annual volumes, with an extensive selection of materials covering the Far East as well as other areas. YALE CANDEE MAXON, *Control of Japanese Foreign Policy; a Study of Civil-Military Rivalry: 1930–1945* (1957). WALTER MILLIS, *This Is Pearl!* (1947); good analysis of American-Japanese relations during 1941. MAMORU SHIGEMITSU, *Japan and Her Destiny* (1958); account of Japanese diplomacy by one of her Foreign Ministers. ROBERT AURA SMITH, *Our Future in Asia* (1940); a sound contemporary study of the American position. SHIGENORI TOGO, *The Cause of Japan* (1956); Japan's Foreign Minister in 1940 presents the Japanese point of view.

CHAPTER XXVI

THE PACIFIC WAR

The attack on Pearl Harbor inaugurated war in the Pacific. At the same time it tied together in a pattern of global war British and Russian resistance to German aggression in Europe and Chinese resistance to Japanese expansion on the Asian continent. It thus was the logical culmination of the series of events which began in Manchuria in 1931. The reciprocal reaction of these events and internal Japanese political and economic developments has been traced up to the outbreak of the war in China in 1937. It now becomes necessary to examine the domestic reaction in Japan to the chain of international events of the years 1937–1941 in order to relate it to the decision on war with the United States, Britain, the British Dominions, and the Netherlands, in addition to China.

I. JAPANESE POLITICS: 1937–1941

The Lukouchiao incident occurred shortly after a new Cabinet had been installed in Tokyo. The Hayashi government, which had been installed in February, 1937, following the overthrow of that headed by Hirota, was replaced on June 4 by one headed by Prince Konoye. Prince Konoye, on the ground of poor health, had declined the premiership at the time when Hirota had been elevated to it from the post of Foreign Minister. But the situation was such a year later that he felt it advisable to disregard that consideration and accept the responsibilities of office. The establishment of the Hayashi government had meant a victory for the Army over the parties and the more conservative capitalists. But Hayashi, even with the support of the newer capitalists who had been profiting from the development of heavy industry, had not been able completely to consolidate the victory. This required either that parliamentary opposition should entirely cease or that the structure of government should be modified so as to make such opposition completely ineffective. The parties, and their capitalist allies, did not attack the fundamental objectives of the government, but they did seek to maintain their parliamentary rights. Thus their attitude was clearly defensive rather than offensive, but it was a defense which at least slowed up the movement toward political reorganization. Impatient of both restraint and slow movement, Hayashi attempted to overcome opposition by securing an Imperial order of dissolution of the Diet. A general election was consequently held at the end of April. This sudden move proved to be a political blunder, since the government went to the country without the support of any organized political group and also without any program which it could ask the voters to support. In the result, the Minseito maintained its position, although with a loss of some seats, and the Seiyukai still had the second position. The two parties, by combination, could poll an absolute majority of the votes in the House of Representatives. In the face of this adverse vote the Hayashi government sought to continue in power. In its attempts to find support it was unsuccessful, and Hayashi finally tendered his resignation on May 31. In the interim, however, his government cleared the ground for future action by establishing a Price Policy Commission, an Education and Culture Commission, and a Cabinet Planning Board.

Although not so described, the Konoye government was essentially national in purpose and character. The Premier was acceptable to the Army leaders, who had sought to put him into office a year earlier. He also had the confidence of the capitalists and the bureaucracy, and was not considered an opponent of the parties. By reputation he fitted the Japanese conception of the liberal without thereby losing in standing with conservatives. Thus his appointment was designed to bring about the political unity which had been lacking since 1931. But, from the standpoint of objectives, it was essentially unity on terms acceptable to the Army. This objective was that of bringing the two-party system of parliamentary politics to an end, and with it the party-capitalist alliance, while extending further Japanese dominance over the continent. But Konoye's purpose was also that of keeping the government in control of the continental movement by keeping ahead of the Army rather than by letting it constantly force the hand of the government as it had done during the years from 1931 to 1937. In doing this the intention does not seem to have been to provoke war with China but to act so vigorously, and with such an appearance of national unity, that China would regard resistance as hopeless.

The major struggle which China's resistance inaugurated, however, naturally increased the already great range of military participation in Japanese politics and government. Thus it promoted and exaggerated existing tendencies. As part of the movement toward unity for war purposes the Army extremists were given representation, along with such moderates as General Ugaki and the leaders of the Seiyukai and Minseito, in a Cabinet Advisory Council which was organized in October, 1937. And, in connection with the extension and tightening of government control over the economic life of the country which finally culminated in the enactment and piecemeal application of the National Mobilization Law, governmental reorganization also was carried along in the direction of increased concentration of authority, with Army dominance in the new organs. A large measure of control in Japan itself, as well as over continental policy, came to be vested in the China Development Board and in a Cabinet inner circle. In both of these bodies the balance of power rested with the Army. [1]

The Konoye government lasted through the first two stages of the war with China, and for a sufficient time after the fall of Hankow for it to block out the lines of general policy for the future. These were formulated as the "new order in Eastern Asia." The creation of the "new order" was proclaimed as the "immutable" objective on November 3, 1938. The specific content of the conception as then formulated was: (1) the replacement of the government of China headed by Chiang Kai-shek with one which would act under the direction of Tokyo and thus one which would "coöperate" with Japan; (2) the liquidation of Western imperialism in China, and ultimately throughout eastern Asia, through the substitution for it of Japanese imperialism; and (3) the freezing of the Russian position in the north, as a minimum, or, as a maximum, the elimination of Russia from the area east of Lake Baikal. The economic objectives of the "new order" were specifically defined in terms of the creation of a self-sufficient economy through the formation of a close Japan-Manchukuo-China closed-door bloc. The creation of this "new order for Eastern Asia" was constantly reaffirmed as the fundamental objective for Japan during the years after its original announcement. [2] Having given birth to this new formulation of policy, the Konoye government, because of internal dissatisfactions, gave way to one headed by Dr. Baron Kiichiro Hiranuma on January 5, 1939. The new Premier was an ultra-nationalist and a person whose earlier activities indicated that he might be expected to carry through vigorously the new continental program of extension of Japanese power, and to consolidate the Army position at home even though he was not a military man. All of these expectations he attempted to realize. Under the direction of his government the attempt was made to resume the offensive in China. When that was unsuccessful, he moved toward the liquidation of Western imperialism through partially implemented attacks on the foreign residential areas in China. At the same time a movement was inaugurated to transform the Anti-Comintern Pact into

[1] In this connection it should also be noted that the wartime Imperial General Headquarters was reëstablished in November, 1937, even though the operations in China were not defined as "war." While the Imperial General Headquarters functions were "the coördination of military and naval activities and liaison between these agencies and other leading organs of the state" (HERMAN BEUKEMA, Contemporary Foreign Governments, p. 283) its reëstablishment, together with the Supreme War Council, strengthened military control of policy.

[2] Although subsequently enlarged, from the standpoint of the area included, into "Greater East Asia," to include southeastern Asia and Indonesia. The economic objective was correspondingly broadened from a Japan-China-Manchukuo bloc into the "Greater East Asia Co-prosperity sphere."

a military alliance. This, however, met with considerable resistance in Japan. Both moves, however, were based upon the view that England and France were sufficiently weak to give way to Japanese pressure in the East coördinated with German-Italian pressure in Europe.

Japanese opinion was terribly shocked when, as one of the important antecedents of the outbreak of war in Europe, Germany and Russia signed a non-aggression pact. This immediately destroyed one of the supports of Japanese policy. The result was the resignation of Baron Hiranuma to clear the way for a possible reorientation of Japanese policy. The resignation of Hiranuma on August 28, 1939, was followed by the reconstruction of the government under the moderate General Nobuyuki Abe, whose declared policy was that of reëstablishing a neutral position for Japan with respect to the European struggle and of improving relations with the United States. American-Japanese relations had been steadily deteriorating owing to the American reaction to Japan's continental policy. This deterioration had led to the denunciation of the American-Japanese commercial treaty of 1911, which was indicated as a step taken to clear the way for the embargoing of trade in war materials between the United States and Japan. The positions of Japan and the United States were so far irreconcilable, however, that Japan could not make sufficient concessions in her continental policy to bring about a lessening of American opposition. The principal concession which it was then proposed to make was the reopening of the Yangtze River to navigation. Even that could not be carried through because of the Army attitude. Thus the Abe government could not maintain itself on the score of accomplishment in that sector of foreign relations. It was overthrown, however, not because of its lack of ability to ameliorate Japan's relations with the United States but on account of domestic dissatisfaction. This was certain to lead to critical discussion and attack when the Diet convened. With a view to forestalling this the Army leaders forced the fall of the government in January, 1940, by the usual method of resignation of the War Minister.

The Abe government was succeeded January 15, 1940, by one headed by Admiral Mitsumasa Yonai. The appointment of one who was thought of as a moderate, friendly to the United States, indicated that the change in government was not due to that aspect of the policy of the Abe government which involved an attempt to improve relations with the United States. The Yonai appointment was a considerable surprise to the Japanese public, however, because it had been forecast that the new premier would be General Shunroku Hata, the retiring War Minister, who was one of the less moderate Army leaders, although the public demand, so far as one was voiced, was for a second Konoye government.

The Yonai government had a tenure of only six months. It survived the criticism in the Diet which had been anticipated. It was able to do so, however, only by forcing the resignation of the parliamentarian, Takao Saito, who had offended the Army because of his criticisms of the failure to end the China war. These criticisms were construed as criticisms of the Army itself. The fall of the Cabinet, however, resulted from criticism from outside Parliament of the Cabinet's failure to take sufficient advantage of the collapse of Holland and France and of the threat to the continued existence of England, in consequence of German victories in Europe, so as rapidly to establish the "new order in Greater Eastern Asia" which had been proclaimed as the Japanese objective.

Preparations for the replacement of the Yonai government were begun in June when Prince Konoye resigned his position as President of the Privy Council (June 24, 1940), announcing as his purpose the formation of a new political organization which would be "a wholly new and idealistic national society."[3] Following this announcement, the established political parties, seeing the handwriting on the wall, all dissolved themselves between July 3 and August 15. With these preliminaries under way, Konoye again became Premier on July 18, 1940. At that time the new party structure had not yet been fully elaborated, nor had the new political and governmental arrangements been fully developed by the end of the year. What was clear, however, was that, on the surface, the movement to "purify" the system through the elimination of the influence of the "corrupt" parties, allied with the capitalists, which had been inaugurated after 1931, had finally attained its objective. The idea of competitive party organization had already been replaced in Konoye's thinking with that of organized "spiritual mobilization." Thus the implications of the move toward organization of the one national party were broader than those presented within the field of party organization.

The new party, called the Imperial Rule Assistance Association (IRAA), came into being on October 12, 1940. Instead of being a political party in either the Western democratic, the fascist, or the communist sense, it actually was designed to be a government-controlled transmission belt to carry government policy downward to the masses and establish widespread support for it. As such it did not meet the requirements when it came to the holding of elections, as was shown in the elections of April, 1942. Neither did it serve to eliminate division, essentially along the lines of the former party alignments, in the Diet. This proved to be the case in spite of the establishment as an IRAA organ of a Diet Bureau of one hundred members, and a Diet Club, designed to provide a "forum of discussion replacing the caucuses of the submerged parties."[4]

[3] HAROLD S. QUIGLEY and JOHN E. TURNER, *The New Japan*, p. 66.
[4] *Ibid.*, p. 71.

Consequently there was shortly (May, 1942) brought into being a complementary agency for purposes more strictly of political action. The new agency was called the Imperial Rule Assistance Political Society (IRAPS). The IRAPS was in effect an organization of the Diet membership, expanding the Diet Bureau of the IRAA, for the purpose of providing an agency for nominating candidates on a non-party basis for election to the Diet. Beyond this it was "designed to thwart efforts to revive the old parties or to create new ones in their image." [5]

The political and spiritual unity behind the government which was sought through the activities of the IRAA and the IRAPS was not maintained as the tide of the war turned against Japan. In the endeavor to reëstablish the national morale, consequently, a new society, the short-lived Political Association of Great Japan (Dai Nippon Seijikai), was created at the instance of the IRAA to replace the IRAPS on March 30, 1945. The IRAA itself went out of existence in June. The new political association existed until after the Japanese surrender, being formally dissolved on September 14, 1945, thus paving the way for the revival, as forecast in occupation policy, of the competitive party system.

Aside from its employment as the agency for tightening the military and bureaucratic control of the government, the Konoye Cabinet (which was reconstructed under his premiership in July, 1941) had the responsibility of attempting to negotiate an acceptance by the United States of Japan's foreign policy objectives. As long as Konoye could hold out a prospect of success in the negotiations instituted in 1941 he had a chance of maintaining some measure of control of the internal situation. This prospect was reduced to a minimum when Japanese assets in the United States and elsewhere were "frozen" in July. Unless the freezing order could be changed, Japan had to move before her resources were too far reduced, or she would ultimately have had to change her policy. It was in apparent reaction to this American action that Konoye suggested, as a last recourse, a personal meeting with the American President. Since this was not arranged, his Cabinet fell and General Hideka Tojo was requested to construct what proved to be a war government, and one which lasted until 1944.

2. ECONOMIC EFFECTS OF THE "CHINA AFFAIR" ON JAPAN: 1937–1941

Just as the effect of the "China affair" was to strengthen already existing political and governmental tendencies in Japan, so its economic effect in many respects was to carry further a movement which antedated the outbreak of the war.

This was notably the case with respect to public finance. The preceding

[5] *Ibid.*, p. 73.

years had witnessed a steady increase in governmental expenditure (from 1,477 million yen in the financial year 1931–1932 to 2,282 million yen in 1936–1937), a constantly increasing proportion of which was devoted to military and naval purposes. Revenue, however, did not show as great an increase. The consequent lack of budgetary balance resulted in an increase in the internally floated national debt from 4,513 million yen in March, 1930, to 9,258 million yen in March, 1937. To this must be added the external debt, which, however, decreased somewhat in the same period. The increase of both expenditure and debt represented mainly the costs of the movement into Manchuria and the attempt to consolidate the military and economic position in Manchukuo.

This type of expenditure (for expansionist purposes) was naturally tremendously increased when real war had to be carried on against China. The budget of the fiscal year 1937 called for expenditures of 5,521 million yen; this was increased to over 8 billion yen in 1938, and to 11,033 million in 1940. [6] This tremendous increase in expenditure brought about large increases in taxes, but a substantial proportion of the war expenses was financed out of domestically floated loans. The public debt of Japan thus increased each year of the China war, rising from the 6,819 million yen of March 31, 1931, to 31,078 million (domestic bonds = 28,611 million yen) as of March 31, 1941. [7] The increasing difficulty found in floating these huge loans resulted in increasing proportions of each issue being held by the Bank of Japan, thus increasing the dangers of inflation.

The sharp rise in taxes, together with the loan subscriptions, meant the devotion of the national income, beyond the maintenance of the population's bare livelihood, to war purposes, defined as including the expenditure on the continent for developmental purposes in addition to that for the support of the military and naval effort. To bring this about the emphasis had to be placed on sacrifice on the part of the people to promote the ends of the state. This was by no means a new emphasis. But the much greater demands made in order to sustain the war effort required an unusual subordination of individual interest to state needs. The willingness of the Japanese to make this subordination helps to account for the failure of many calculations, including the Chinese, as to the duration of the war. The war financing undoubtedly steadily weakened Japan's financial position. Nevertheless it appeared to be as true at the end of 1941 as it had been in 1939 that:

It would be dangerous to conclude that Japan's financial difficulties are so great as to affect dangerously her ability for carrying on the present war. Experience shows that countries far nearer to financial exhaustion than Japan is today have

[6] JEROME B. COHEN, *Japan's Economy in War and Reconstruction*, p. 5.
[7] *Ibid*,

continued to fight with vigor and success. Indeed, it is not clear that financial strain alone can ever affect the issue of a war. But this does not mean that Japan can regard the future with equanimity. Her economic system has undoubtedly been seriously impaired by war-time financial expedients. [8]

But it was not only in the field of public finance that pre-1937 tendencies were shown and exaggerated. The attempt to build up Manchukuo inaugurated an important shift in emphasis in the Japanese industrial economy from light industry, notably textiles, to heavy industry. A heavy industry for export of capital goods to Manchukuo and Korea had to be developed in Japan in order to accomplish the Army purpose of over-seas industrial development. Thus a new emphasis had come to be placed on the metallurgical industries of the country. Since this was necessarily a state-promoted and subsidized development, the private interests participating in and profiting from it attached themselves to the Army leadership, giving Army expansionist plans a greater capitalist support than that leadership had possessed before 1931. Large-scale war effort, coupled with increasing exchange difficulties, inevitably increased this emphasis on the development of the heavy industries. Further expansion, under the impact of war, was accomplished at the expense of the previously dominant export industries. The pre-1937 emphasis had been made at the expense of further expansion of the light export industries but not under circumstances which necessitated their contraction. The post-1937 development, however, necessitated their contraction.

This was the case because of the necessity of restricting imports to materials essential for war purposes, and thus for the heavy (armaments) industries. The Foreign Exchange Control Law, promulgated on March 29, 1933, gave the government powers of regulation which it had begun to exercise in the months before the Lukouchiao incident. These regulations required the permission of the Finance Ministry before foreign exchange could be obtained to pay for imports in excess of 30,000 yen a month. These and similar measures were enacted primarily with a view to protecting the yen. But their effects were also to interfere with the normal functioning of those industries depending on the imports of raw materials. These were, in effect, the major export light industries, and also the heavy industries, including the armaments industries. As war increased the preoccupation with armaments production, a basis began to be laid to ensure the heavy industries priority in the importing of essential raw materials and finished products, since only a limited capacity to finance imports existed. In October, 1937, to provide for the necessary mobilization of exchange, as well as other resources, for war purposes, the Law Concerning

[8] G. C. ALLEN, *Japanese Industry: Its Recent Development and Present Condition*, I.P.R. Inquiry Series, 1939, p. 108. On the general economic as well as financial effects of the decade of preparation for war see COHEN, *op. cit.*, ch. 1.

the Temporary Regulation of Imports and Exports was enacted. This "conferred on the Government the power, not merely of prohibiting or restricting the import and export of certain goods, but also of issuing regulations about the manufacture, distribution and use of goods produced from imported raw materials." [9]

Under this and other measures of similar direction the government controlled imports in the interest of the armaments industry, in the process denying raw materials' imports adequate to the maintenance of the light domestic and export industries at the pre-1937 level, further shifting the internal economic balance. This, it was soon found, placed the state on either or both horns of a dilemma. Exports, beyond the so-called yen bloc (Japan, Manchukuo, and occupied China), were required to help finance essential imports. But to maintain and extend those exports a substantial proportion of the imports needed to be allocated to the non-armaments' export industries. Thus the more exclusive the emphasis which was put on imports for war purposes the more difficult it became to finance those imports. Therefore it became necessary to lessen the emphasis in order to help maintain it. While it proved possible partly to finance necessary war-materials' imports in the first years of the China war through extensive gold shipments, supplemented by the reduced volume of non-armament imports from beyond the yen bloc, this steadily reduced, toward the danger point, the gold reserve. Consequently, it became necessary to find some way at least to maintain the export industries.

This was attempted through the introduction, in August, 1938, of the "link" system, under which exchange was made available for imports of raw materials to manufacture goods for export. The successful operation of this system, which limited manufacture for domestic consumption to raw materials of domestic production, necessitated considerable internal readjustment and a constant enlargement of the area of government control over the domestic economy. The latter was required in any case as it became apparent that the total national strength would have to be applied to make the war effort successful.

Thus, in addition to import controls of various sorts, the "China affair" brought about a constantly increasing government control of the domestic economy to a point which would justify its being described, in form at least, even if the form was not fully put into effect, as "totalitarian." Among the earlier measures directed toward this end may be mentioned the Temporary Capital Adjustment Law of 1937, designed to force the country's savings into the heavy industries; the Act providing for the establishment of a Council for the Control of Iron and Steel, set up in

[9] ALLEN, *op. cit.*, p. 62.

1938; the Cotton Supply and Adjustment Council, created in July, 1938; and the revised Manufacturers' Association Act, of 1937. These and other measures, [10] together with the application of pre-"incident" control measures, some of which went back as far as 1918, helped to prepare the way for the enactment and application of the General Mobilization Law of 1938. This was enacted subject to the understanding that it would not be applied except in the event of war (which, terminologically, had not been inaugurated, since the war in China was still treated as an "incident"). The prolongation and extension of the struggle against the Chinese government, however, led to piecemeal application of the Mobilization Law to the point of its almost total application by the end of 1940. Thus it may be said that one important effect of the China war on Japan was to bring the national economy under "a bewildering variety of government controls . . . added to the already complex 'autonomous' controls and cartel arrangements in all fields of industry. Small business was being squeezed out but big business had not achieved complete control. The government, despite its numerous powers on the statute books, was not a cohesive, unifying directive force in the economic sphere." [11] Government authority itself came to be concentrated finally through the institution of the "one party" system operating under the authority of the state bureaucracy. In effect, this represented a reversion toward the pre-constitutional state of affairs rather than a movement toward a new domestic order.

Not all of Japan's military expenditure, however, had been made for use in the war against China. By means of imports, stockpiles of materials essential for war purposes had been built up to the point where it was asserted that Japan could sustain a major war effort on the basis of accumulated reserves for a maximum period of about two years. [12] Within that period she would have to replace the United States as a source of raw materials in which she was deficient from within the Far Eastern and Pacific area in order to continue on a war basis if she were cut off from the American market either by war or as a result of continued application of the American "freezing" policy. As previously suggested, the conclusion had been reached by November, 1941, that the American policy could not be changed by negotiation. If it could be changed only by a war to be won within the limited period, or at least not lost within that period, further postponements would be hazardous. Consequently, Japan struck, with a view to forcing an early decision.

[10] For analysis of these controls see COHEN, *op. cit.*, pp. 10–33.

[11] *Ibid.*, p. 28.

[12] But "in 1941 we (the United States) mistook Japan's completed preparations for minimum war potential. Japan's stockpiles of raw materials were generally overestimated." *Ibid.*, p. 49.

3. THE PACIFIC WAR: FROM PEARL HARBOR TO MIDWAY

Japan's basic war plan involved seizure of the area of southeast Asia and the islands of the southwest Pacific and the establishment of a strong defensive position which would give her the security which would enable her to consolidate the position won by attack. She expected rapidly to organize the exploitation of the resources of the rich area which would be occupied. "The area to be seized was that within the line which joins the Kuriles, Marshalls (including Wake), Bismarcks, Timor, Java, Sumatra, Malaya and Burma." [13] At the same time, the United States Fleet in Hawaii was to be disposed of as an offensive threat to Japan by an attack on it. These offensive operations, it was anticipated, would create a situation which would make possible a negotiated peace after a relatively short war. The temporary elimination of American striking power in the Pacific, it was thought, would give the Japanese time to complete their conquest and consolidation of Greater East Asia without too significant resistance from the United States. It was considered that it would also enable Japan to establish a defensive barrier to American counter-attack sufficiently formidable to make its penetration too costly for the United States to undertake.

In the first months of the war the Japanese easily realized their original purposes. The attack at Pearl Harbor caught the American defenders by surprise, in spite of the evidence which the American government had of the imminence of the outbreak of war and of the probability of an attack at Pearl Harbor. This permitted infliction of very serious damage to the Pacific fleet which was based there. Hongkong surrendered on December 25, 1941. On February 25, 1942, Singapore surrendered, all of Malaya having previously been overrun by the Japanese. The Philippines held out until the surrender of General Wainwright's forces on Bataan on April 9, and Corregidor on May 6. The Netherlands Indies had been conquered by March, 1942.

The ease with which Japan attained her objectives, as originally set, however, caused the original plan to be enlarged. Time and materials which might have been spent in consolidation within the area were utilized in the conquest of Burma, which was only completed by June, 1942, and in the attempt to extend the defensive perimeter in the Pacific to include: Attu and Kiska, in the Aleutians, thus offering a threat to Alaska; Midway, in the Central Pacific; and the Gilberts and the Solomon Islands in the southwest Pacific.

There were two very serious miscalculations both in the Japanese original and in the revised plans. The first lay in their misreading the effect

[13] U. S. Strategic Bombing Survey (Pacific), *The Campaigns of the Pacific War*, p. 3.

on opinion within the United States of an attack on the American fleet within American waters. Instead of paralyzing the national will and giving greater play to existing American pacifistic and isolationist sentiment, the disaster at Pearl Harbor forged national unity for war purposes and hardened the national determination to make the necessary effort, for reasons of national security, to ensure that Japan should not remain in a

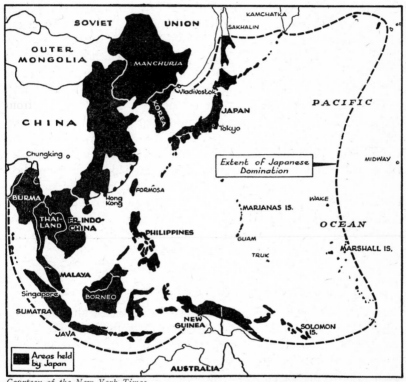

Courtesy of the New York Times

JAPAN'S OUTER LIMITS OF CONQUEST

position to attain her objectives in Greater East Asia. The second was under-estimation of the rapidity with which the United States could translate its resources into ships, planes and guns, and thus bring them to bear for war purposes.

Japan did not possess the reserves of men and material to meet the counter-attack which she deliberately invited. The United States, on the other hand, was just reaching the point in December, 1941, at which her tremendous resources could produce new ships, airplanes, guns, and trained men in all but unlimited numbers. The Japanese onslaught served only to forge our sprawling, confused, uncertain democracy at one blow into the most powerful and best integrated instrument of war which the world has ever seen. [14]

In spite of the losses of the first months of the war, the United States retained sufficient power to turn the Japanese back in the central Pacific in the battle of Midway (June, 1942), after having previously inflicted heavy losses on them in the battle of the Coral Sea (May 7 and 11). This latter action "marked the high tide of Japanese conquest in the Southwest Pacific. Midway climaxed our first half-year of war and marked the opening of a new phase of operations in the Pacific. . . ." [15] Thus Japan not only fell short of attaining her enlarged objectives, but in the attempt expended ships, airplanes and trained manpower, which she could not quickly replace. A further consequence was that she did not develop the defensive strength at the originally set perimeter which had been planned, even though her position appeared very strong.

As a defensive-offensive move, the United States undertook in August, 1942, to clear the Japanese forces out of the Solomon Islands, when "United States Navy and Marine forces seized beachheads on Guadalcanal and Florida Islands and occupied Tulagi." [16] This had been accomplished, after very severe fighting, early in 1943. Together with the successful defense of Port Moresby, in New Guinea, this established a position from which it was possible for the Allied forces to move from the defensive-offensive to the offensive. The Japanese had been contained, and the supply lines to Australia had been made more secure.

4. THE UNITED STATES REGAINS THE INITIATIVE: 1942–1945

This defensive-offensive position had been established with a minimum of ground, air, and naval power. Even before the outbreak of war, American strategic planning, based upon the probability of war against both Germany and Japan, had accepted the necessity of destroying German power prior to that of Japan. [17] After the war broke out, in spite of the fact that the attack was by Japan and in the Pacific, priority in the use of American men and materials was given to the war in Europe. If it had not been for the tremendous expansion of American production, which enabled more materials to be diverted to the Pacific than could have been originally contemplated, offensive operations either in the southwest or the central Pacific could not have been undertaken in the relatively short period of time within which actually the offensive phase of the war in the Pacific was begun.

[14] WALTER MILLIS, *This Is Pearl!*, p. 373.
[15] *War Reports of* GENERAL MARSHALL, GENERAL ARNOLD, ADMIRAL KING, p. 80.
[16] *Ibid.*, p. 81.
[17] ROBERT SHERWOOD, *Roosevelt and Hopkins*, p. 415.

The initiative which had been taken by the American forces by the end of 1942 was never lost. Using island-hopping and by-passing tactics in the southwest Pacific, which left comparatively large Japanese forces "withering on the vine," General MacArthur moved slowly but inexorably back to the Philippines, from which he (together with President Quezon and Vice President Osmeña of the Commonwealth Government) had been evacuated to assume command in the southwest Pacific. Landings were made on Leyte in October, 1944, and Manila had been secured by March, 1945.

Meanwhile, in the central Pacific, the same forward movement had been going on. The Gilberts, the Marshalls, the Carolines, and the Marianas were taken from the Japanese during 1943 and 1944, and, finally, Okinawa and the Ryukyu Islands in April, 1945. This movement gave land bases, supplementing carrier task forces, from which the main Japanese islands could be attacked from the air.

Defense against these converging attacks used up existing Japanese air and naval forces beyond the power of replacement. Strategic bombing of Japan reduced her cities and destroyed her productive power. Her remaining naval power was finally completely destroyed in the battle for control of Leyte Gulf. And, of major importance, submarines had been so effectively employed as virtually to cut Japan off from external sources of supply of necessary raw materials.

Thus even before mid-summer of 1945, it was clear that Japan had lost the war. What was not clear even then, however, was whether her unconditional surrender would take place short of an invasion and military occupation of the home island at a great cost to the Allies. On the assumption that invasion would be necessary, consequently, negotiations were instituted to bring the Soviet Union into the war against Japan. These resulted in the agreements reached at the Yalta Conference on the basis of which Russia prepared to move from neutrality to belligerency. While military preparations for invasion were being made, the first combat atomic bomb was dropped on Hiroshima on August 6, 1945, followed by the second dropped on Nagasaki on August 9. On August 8, Soviet Russia declared war on Japan. On August 10, Japan sued for peace, and the formal surrender agreements were signed on the battleship *Missouri* in Tokyo Bay on September 2, 1945.

5. THE CHINA THEATER

By July, 1942, Japanese arms had driven the Western Powers out of eastern and southeastern Asia, the Philippines, and Indonesia. The Vichy-French colonial government was maintained in Indo-China, to be sure, but it functioned only on terms set by the Japanese and to the extent to which it did not interfere with the attainment of Japan's purposes. Thailand (Siam) was the only technically unoccupied country. Even its government, however, was compelled to respond to Japanese direction and to serve Japan's economic and military purposes. A strong nationalist movement in Thailand, which by a *coup d'état* in 1932 had assumed control of the state, organized the country on a steadily more authoritarian basis. After 1938, partly in response to an internal opposition to the Chinese, partly in admiration of Japan's demonstrated strength and independence of the West, and partly on account of a desire to take advantage of the existing situation to expand, the Thai government oriented itself increasingly toward Japan. When the war broke out, after a token resistance the Japanese were permitted to move troops across the country to facilitate the attack on Burma, and the government steadily found itself increasingly under Japanese direction.

These initial Japanese successes had the effect of cutting China off from contact with the Western world. The soundness of Chiang Kai-shek's view that if the war was continued long enough the United States and Britain would find themselves at war with Japan, and thus China's allies, was demonstrated. The immediate circumstances of the demonstration, however, left China weaker rather than stronger, since even the minimum aid in supplies which she had been receiving overland was cut off. "Except for the thin line of air supply over the 500 miles of the Himalayan Hump between Assam, India, and the Yunnan plateau," isolated but allied China was forced to continue to depend on her own undeveloped resources in order to maintain herself in the war. The airlift over the Hump was one of the war's spectacular achievements. By January, 1944, the monthly tonnage flown into China had been built up to 13,399 tons, and by January, 1945, to 43,896.[18] Even this enlarged tonnage, however, contrasts markedly with the quantities of supplies furnished to the other war theaters from the United States. In any case, China's most critical needs, which "were in trucks and rolling stock, artillery, tanks, and other heavy equipment," could not be flown into the country in any sufficient quantity to enable China to play an offensive role in the war against Japan. It was only in January, 1945, that the land supply route over the Ledo-Burma road was reopened. It was thus only in the last six months of the war that China, as far as military equipment was concerned, began to come into a position of ability to attempt offensive ground operations to clear the Japanese out of the occupied area.

The grand strategy of the global war, as already suggested, gave priority to Europe rather than to the Pacific. The difficulty of building up China

[18] Second Report of the Commanding General of the Army Air Forces, February 27, 1945, *War Reports*, p. 393.

as the base from which to launch the decisive attack against Japan, together with the early successful assumption of the initiative in the Pacific which enabled the war to be carried directly to Japan from Pacific bases, established the role of the China theater in the total war. It was that of immobilizing large bodies of Japanese troops on the continent by holding operations, and of destroying or preventing the diversion of as much of Japan's airpower as possible from the continent. It proved possible to build up General Chennault's Fourteenth Air Force and to supply it sufficiently so that offensive air operations could be undertaken against Japanese installations and Japanese shipping. The Fourteenth Air Force also provided tactical support for the Chinese armies as they attempted to prevent Japanese advances in 1943 and 1944. The war of attrition conducted from bases in China was so far successful that in 1944 the Japanese were compelled to undertake an offensive to reduce these bases. In this they were successful, finally taking and holding Changsha and pushing the area of actual occupation inward so as to include Kweilin and Liuchow, both of which were important air bases. This was accomplished, however, too late for the Japanese to establish satisfactory land communications from Manchuria to Indo-China and the southern region to replace the sea communications which had been cut by submarine and air attack.

In addition to this use of China as a base for operations against Japanese supply lines, the original long-range bombing of the Japanese main islands (except for the Doolittle carrier-based raid) was undertaken from China by the Twentieth Bomber Command. Because of the difficulty of supply and maintenance, however, after Guam and Saipan had been taken from the Japanese the air operations against Japan itself were moved from China to the Marianas.

Without important military successes of their own to feed upon while their allies were successfully carrying the war to the enemy in other theaters, the morale of the Chinese began to decline in and after 1943. The failure to supply their theater, in spite of the difficulties involved, together with the diversion to other theaters of supplies promised them when critical situations developed elsewhere, gave rise to a feeling that China itself was considered relatively unimportant in the total war effort. Had it not been for the conclusion initially reached and constantly insisted upon by Generalissimo Chiang Kai-shek that Japan would be defeated by the superior potential power of the United Nations, a settlement with Japan might have been attempted which would have withdrawn China from the war. The conclusion itself, and the beginning of its verification in 1943 and 1944, kept China in the war. But it also, coupled with what were thought of as evidences of neglect of the China theater, brought about a feeling that the war of resistance would be won for China by the efforts of her allies, making continuance of a major preoccupation with the war effort, in disregard of other considerations, unnecessary. The consequence was deterioration not only of public morale among the people who had been longer at war than anyone else and who were completely war-weary, but also of standards of official conduct. This feeling, furthermore, accentuated the deterioration in Kuomintang-Communist relations which followed the trouble over the Fourth Army. In the last years of the war, coöperation between the two areas against the Japanese enemy was reduced to a minimum. Chiang Kai-shek diverted some of his best troops from operations against the Japanese in order to establish and maintain a blockade between Kuomintang and Communist China. Communist guerrilla operations were designed as much to establish control of local governments against the Kuomintang as to drive out the Japanese. Since recurrent efforts made during the war to bring about an agreement were unsuccessful, the stage was set for the resumption of the civil war at the termination of the war against Japan.

It was the economic situation, however, that both caused and gave evidence of decline of morale in "free" China. The division of the country had disrupted normal internal exchanges; the areas of industrial productivity had been lost to the Japanese; and, finally, outside sources of supply had been cut off. Thus, after 1941, shortages of every kind of commodity, already serious as a result of the developments of 1937–1941, were constantly on the increase. The inevitable result was inflation. This was not controlled by the government in the interest either of the war effort or of the welfare of the individual. Instead, the existing situation caused many officials to use their powers to advance their own private interests. The profits of the trade in goods smuggled, with the connivance of officials on both sides, from occupied into "free" China enriched both traders and officials. It was even more profitable to be able to control the distribution and use of goods flown into China. Even imports made for war purposes under strict government auspices, as well as goods which could be smuggled, began to find their way into private trade channels. Since much of the wealth accumulated by profiteering was illicit, it escaped taxation, and the burden of the war had to be borne, to an increasing extent, by the peasants. But a fair proportion of the taxes collected in kind was retained by the tax-gatherer to cover the costs of collection. Depletion of the food supply as a result of Japanese raids at harvest time, such as those which were made recurrently toward Changsha [19] and thus through China's "rice bowl," added to the scarcity of food

[19] The so-called second and third battles of Changsha were essentially "food requisitioning" operations.

and consequently to the price inflation. Although the critics were unable to suggest what the government could have done which would have effectively controlled the price inflation in the face of the increasing scarcity of food and commodities of all kinds and of its totally inadequate administrative mechanism and financial resources, criticism did, of course, develop. To control the criticism, censorship and police controls were intensified. In this atmosphere, which became one of rumor and gossip since factual reporting was impossible, no stories of corruption in high place, or low, were beyond belief. The fires of disinterested patriotism, which had been kindled by the sacrifices of the war of resistance, and had burned highest during the period of the bombings of defenseless Chungking in 1939–1941, had subsided with the recession of the immediate danger.

By 1944, and before there was any widespread knowledge outside of China of the realities of the internal situation, the country, its people, and its leadership had assumed a symbolic importance because of the length of Chinese resistance to Japanese aggression. It was recognized that the entire world situation would have been quite different if, at any time prior to Pearl Harbor, China had made peace with Japan on terms which would have transformed the country into a Japanese protectorate, so that its man-power and resources could have been developed and applied to realize Japanese purposes. Only in this way, furthermore, could Japan have effectively transformed the war into one of the East against the West. As it was she made effective play on her assumed role of defender of Asia against "Anglo-American imperialism."

To minimize these possibilities, as well as to give China the recognition which her long resistance justified, the United States and Britain finally took the action which put their treaty relations with China on the basis of equality. They announced, on October 9, 1942, their readiness to negotiate immediately for the abolition of extra-territorial rights in China. Treaties were signed on January 11, 1943, between China, on the one side, and the United States and Britain, on the other, abolishing extra-territorial rights and special privileges in China. The conception of equality also gave China a position, never previously conceded, as a Great Power. Thus, when the United Nations organization came into being she was given a permanent seat on the Security Council, with the same right of veto as that possessed by the United States, the Soviet Union, Britain, and France. This, together with her share in the war councils of the United Nations (which, however, fell somewhat short of full equality of participation) added to the prestige of the Chinese government. And, finally, at the Cairo Conference, it was agreed that the war would be waged until Japan had unconditionally surrendered and that the territories taken from China in and after 1894 would be restored to her control.

There was, however, another set of relationships which needs to be examined to make intelligible the situation which developed after 1945. This was primarily within the area of American policy.

"In Anglo-American grand strategy the war against Germany came first. Second came the great 'triphibious' movement across the Pacific toward the Japanese island empire. The China-Burma-India theater was a poor third. Yet in its strategic and political significance this part of the world was of enormous importance." [20] This view as to China's strategic and political significance made it advisable to do whatever was possible and necessary to keep the China front alive. Consequently the American government, shortly after Pearl Harbor, strengthened its military mission and sought to increase its influence in China by sending General Joseph W. Stilwell to the China-Burma-India theater: (1) "To supervise and control all United States defense-aid affairs for China; (2) Under the Generalissimo to command all United States forces in China and such Chinese forces as may be assigned to him; (3) To represent the United States Government on any International War Council in China and act as the Chief of Staff for the Generalissimo; (4) To improve, maintain, and control the Burma road in China." [21]

After he was forced out of Burma by the Japanese, Stilwell's principal preoccupation was with the reconquest of Upper Burma so that land communications with China might be reopened. This he viewed as the essential preliminary to the attainment of his "central military objective," which was to strengthen the Chinese armies and bring their force to bear on the Japanese in Asia." [22] He had finally created the conditions for the attainment of his preliminary objective of reopening land communications by the time of his recall in October, 1944, but only as a result of constant pressure on the Generalissimo and also on the British, with considerable resulting friction with both and also with General Chennault, who had been designated as the ranking American air officer in China at the time of the Stilwell appointment.

The underlying basis of conflict between Stilwell and the Generalissimo was over the role which China should be prepared to play in the Pacific war. The former wanted to utilize American aid so as to bring China's total forces to bear on the Japanese in offensive land operations. To accomplish this, he came to the conclusion that it was necessary to undertake exten-

[20] HENRY L. STIMSON and McGEORGE BUNDY, On Active Service, p. 528. The Stilwell mission to China, as viewed by Secretary Stimson, is discussed pp. 528–541.

[21] United States Relations with China, Dept. of State Pub. 3573, Far Eastern Series 30, 1949, Annex (a), p. 469. This volume is hereafter cited as China White Paper, 1949.

[22] STIMSON, op. cit., p. 532.

sive retraining of the Chinese armies under American military leadership since he had little confidence in the military capabilities of the upper levels of the Chinese command. The attainment of the objective, as he saw it, further required: (1) that the National armies which were withdrawn from military operations against the Japanese to maintain the Kuomintang position against the Communists should be utilized against the Japanese, and (2) that the Communist armies should be similarly utilized and be supported for that purpose, and incorporated in his command. Thus Stilwell's conception of the ultimate role to be played by China went beyond that of holding operations while Japan was brought to surrender by American operations reaching Japan from the central and southwest Pacific. It was also a different role than that envisaged by General Chennault, who saw China as the base for an air offensive directed primarily against Japanese shipping but also against their home islands. With his belief in the possibility of winning a verdict through the use of air power, unsupported by ground forces, which had considerable support in Washington, Chennault argued that a predominant share of the supplies flown into China should be allocated to the use of his air force.

The Generalissimo was much more inclined to accept Chennault's view of strategy than he was Stilwell's since it involved American-Chinese offensive operations without the extensive use of Chinese ground forces. If Anglo-American strategic planning had given a high priority to either C.B.I. or the China theater, and had made good on commitments with respect to supplies or on British support of a Burma offensive, the Stilwell position at Chungking would have been much stronger. But all of the military planning and actions confirmed the view that the war was to be won in any case without the use of China as a primary base for an offensive. The Generalissimo, consequently, was not impelled to put war operations ahead of consideration of domestic politics. Thus he was not willing to weaken his position against the Chinese Communists either by withdrawal of his own troops for use against the Japanese, except in an extreme emergency, or to permit operations by the Communist armies throughout China, even if it had been possible to bring them under American command. In other words, believing correctly that the war would be won in any case, Chiang Kai-shek gave priority in his own thinking to considerations of postwar internal politics.

The American government also thought politically, even though General Stilwell tried to base its actions on war considerations. The Embassy, until his recall, generally supported Stilwell, holding that "we (the American Government) are interested in seeing a prompt solution of a Chinese internal problem which finds the armed forces of China facing one another instead of facing and making war upon Japan." Aside from the military and supply question at issue, consequently, it sought to encourage a political solution of the Communist issue through negotiations between the National government and Yenan. Chiang had committed himself to a political rather than a military solution of the issue at least during the period of the war but he felt that "the United States should tell the Communists to reconcile their differences with and submit to the national government of China." As he informed the Ambassador: "China should receive the entire support and sympathy of the United States Government on the domestic problem of Chinese Communists. . . . In urging that China resolve differences with the Communists," the American government's "attitude is serving only to intensify the recalcitrance of the Communists." [23]

Although General Stilwell was recalled at the insistence of Chiang Kai-shek, the political policy of the United States remained that of supporting a negotiated settlement of the internal problem. The general point of view consistently reported to Washington of declining Nationalist morale and efficiency and of increasing Communist strength [24] caused an emphasis to be put on the necessity of bringing the Communist Party into a coalition government with the Kuomintang as a method of ensuring the integrity and unity of China and also to anticipate a possible assumption of control by the former while the United States was still too exclusively attached to the Kuomintang. As suggested as early as November 15, 1944:

In seeking to determine which faction we should support we must keep in mind these basic considerations: Power in China is on the verge of shifting from Chiang to the Communists. . . . If the Russians enter North China and Manchuria, we obviously cannot hope to win the Communists entirely over to us, but we can through control of supplies and post-war aid expect to exert considerable influence in the direction of Chinese nationalism and independence from Soviet control. [25]

No such choice in favor of the Communists was actually made since Ambassador Hurley, who was appointed after General Stilwell's recall, and, after the war, General Marshall, had to give prior consideration to the Kuomintang, which controlled the government and approach the Communists through the government. Nevertheless the position of the Communist Party was actually strengthened by the American acceptance of it as a contender for power with which Chiang Kai-shek should negotiate with a view to its inclusion in the government. Ambassador Hurley's attempts to bring Yenan and Chungking into agreement on the

[23] *China White Paper*, 1949, pp. 561–562. Ambassador Gauss to Secretary Hull, August 31, 1944.

[24] See Memoranda by Foreign Service Officers in China, 1943–1945, *ibid.*, pp. 564–576.

[25] *Ibid.*, 1949, p. 574.

terms of reconstruction of the government were unsuccessful. They did, however, establish a policy which the United States continued to attempt to put into effect after VJ day.

6. THE GREATER EAST ASIA CO-PROSPERITY SPHERE

It is not possible here to consider in any detail the events of the war in southeast Asia and the southwest Pacific, except as they had continuing consequences. Such consequences were, however, the result of certain aspects of Japanese policy, and these, together with their application, cannot be disregarded.

The war aim of Japan was to create in Greater East Asia a self-sufficient economy—one which could supply its essential needs on a closed-door basis as far as the rest of the world was concerned, and thus one which would be independent of Europe and of the Americas. The achievement of this purpose required that the peoples within the area should be brought to accept the Japanese as liberators, with whom it was to their interest to coöperate politically and under whose direction they would work economically.

The logic of the situation made it easy for the Japanese to assume, temporarily at least, the role of liberators in much of the area. It would have been easier if the recent historical record had been different in Manchuria and in China. Even so, the imposition of Japanese rule in Manchuria and China, and the methods used to disguise as well as to impose it, had not been widely advertised in the southern region, except possibly in the relatively large communities of over-seas Chinese.

The southern region was the colonial area of eastern Asia. It was here that white masters had long ruled the darker-colored natives, exploiting them and their lands' resources primarily in their own interest. The picture was very little changed by reason of the fact that in many cases the instrument of exploitation had been the native ruler, or that the policy of the metropolitan country was in process of relatively slow change in emphasis from that of exploitation toward that of native development. This shift was shown in the increasing, although still small, proportions of the budget devoted to public health and education in the twentieth as contrasted with the nineteenth century, and in the improvement of communications as well as in production methods. But the fact of European rule, to the major benefit of Europeans, remained, and with it the assertion of the superiority of the white man.

The theory of European supremacy had been weakened when Japan had successfully challenged Russia in the war of 1904–1905, and when, after World War I, Japan's status as a Great Power had been accepted. The successes of the Chinese revolution in its nationalist and anti-imperialist phase had the same consequence beyond as well as within China. The humiliations to which individual Westerners had been subjected by the Japanese in China after 1937 (as at Tientsin) had been, in part, designed as a demonstration of the ease with which the Oriental could assert himself against the Occidental. The rapid reduction of such Western bases as Hongkong, Corregidor, and especially Singapore, with the glaring weaknesses shown in their defense, still further lessened Western prestige.

The weakness of the position of the colonial Powers was especially revealed in their unwillingness, or inability, outside of the Philippines, to rally the native peoples to the defense of their countries against the Japanese invader, while at the same time the Western colonial Powers showed themselves unable to defend the colony. This weakness was played up by the Japanese in their portrayal of themselves as liberators. In that role, furthermore, they sought both to enhance their own prestige and to destroy that of the European by their treatment both of prisoners of war and of civilian internees, although the treatment accorded varied with the individuals in charge of the various prisoner-of-war and internment camps.

Having liberated the colonial area from its European masters, the ultimate problem faced by the Japanese was that of disguising their intention to remain as conquerors and exploiters. The immediate problem was that of supply of Japan's war economy.

The first stage of Japanese control was that of direct military rule. Under the circumstances, this was not inconsistent with the role of the liberator, since order had to be restored and defense undertaken. Under cover of military rule, existing stocks of goods were seized and started moving to Japan. This added to Japan's stockpiles of such essential materials as tin, petroleum products, rubber and quinine, without the necessity of finding ways and means of making payment. But supply on this basis was limited to goods already produced and not destroyed by the British, Dutch, and American forces in advance of Japanese military occupation. Further supply depended, in the first place, on the reëstablishment of production. In the second place, it depended on the ability of the Japanese to take over the products of the mines, wells, and fields and move them from the colonial countries to Japan.

Successful allied submarine and air attacks on Japanese shipping, launched with greater rapidity than had been anticipated, reduced and finally virtually eliminated the possibility of Japan's maintaining production even for war purposes from the Greater East Asia storehouse. Even the desperate measures which were taken to replace the shipping lost with the small wooden ships which could be built outside of Japan failed even partially to meet the need. Consequently, in the last year of the war, Japan was forced to meet her needs almost exclusively out of rapidly diminishing domestic stockpiles. The need to conserve oil and gasoline, for example, against the day of attack on the home islands, made it impossible for her to utilize her remaining air and naval forces freely in the defense of her inner perimeter.

These war circumstances made it impossible for Japan to reorganize the economy of Greater East Asia and thus to create the planned "co-prosperity sphere." To a very considerable extent, each country within the sphere was compelled to meet its own needs out of its own resources, and consequently to be organized on a separate rather than an integrated economic basis. Thus Japan was unable to supply goods to the Philippines in exchange for Philippine sugar, chrome ore, tobacco and copra, as the United States had previously done. Burma had its rice but no place to turn to for the goods to exchange for its rice surplus. Japan could not replace Europe and America in Indonesian exchanges. In the attempt to enforce changes in the customary methods of production on an independent country basis, further dislocations were made in the normal economy of the area. Thus "co-poverty" rather than "co-prosperity" resulted in Greater East Asia from the Japanese war of liberation.

After the initial period of undisguised military exploitation and expropriation of resources, the pattern of political rule began to emerge. This pattern, adapted to the different circumstances in each country, was that already woven in Manchuria and occupied China. In the Philippines and Burma, where there were well-developed nationalist movements and an experience in self-government, independent governments were instituted as rapidly as individuals were found who were willing and able to govern along Japanese lines as defined by Japanese advisers. In Malaya direct administration by civilian administrators, working under the Army command, was instituted for the Federated Malay States, into which the Straits Settlements were integrated. A form of self-government was promised in 1943, however, and thereafter advisory councils of Malayans were established, and in 1944 there was some consultation of the ruling Sultans.

In the case of the Netherlands East Indies it was not until the tide of war had so decisively turned against Japan that the Tojo government had been replaced by that headed by Admiral Koiso that the policy of direct military control was modified. It was in September, 1944, that ultimate independence was promised to Indonesia. But the only actual modification of military rule by the conquerors was that made in October, 1943, when an advisory Council, headed by a native nationalist leader, Sukarno, was established.

It was also only under stress of war that Japan's relation to Indo-China was changed. As previously noted, the French officials, after the fall of

France, took their direction from Vichy. This made it possible for Japan to secure such concessions as she needed, including the right to maintain troops in the country, without "liberating" it from European rule. Because of a growing suspicion of her French collaborators, however, Japan took over the colony early in 1945 (March 5). In the months left before the end of the war, the Japanese displaced the French with local nationalist administrators. The theme of liberation and of collaboration under the liberators was played, but, due to the timing, the only beneficiary was the temporarily liberated nationalist movement since the Viet Nam leaders, thus enabled to assume power, had been almost as much opposed to Japanese as to French imperialism.

If Japan had won the war there is little reason to believe that any of the countries of the "co-prosperity sphere" would have been allowed to enjoy the promised independence or self-government, except as their rulers were tolerated by the Japanese because they continued to take their direction from Tokyo. Certainly, even if a theoretical political independence had been conceded, it would not have been allowed to interfere with the realization of Japan's primary purposes, which were economic. This is indicated in the failure to consult the people in the constitution of the new governments in such countries as the Philippines and Burma. Japan selected as collaborators those whom she felt she could trust to act in her behalf, hoping that they could maintain peace and order and revive production with a minimum support of Japanese arms. This, however, was explicable in terms of the war situation, so that nationalists might consider their collaboration as puppets to be justified in the short run to realize long-run purposes. But the history of Japan's relationship to Korea, Manchuria, and China, as giving a clue to what she would do if and as she had the power, could not safely be disregarded by making a distinction between the emergency situation and long-run intentions. Furthermore, the behavior of the Japanese as conquerors in each of the countries occupied was at sharp variance with their professions as liberators. If it had not been for this divergence between profession, or propaganda, and action, a different result might have been achieved when the war entered upon its (for Japan) defensive phase in Burma and the Philippines, as well as in China.

In retrospect, it seems clear that the timing of grants of independence (Burma, August 1, 1943; the Philippines, October 15, 1943), and of rights of advisory participation in government (Indonesia, October 15, 1943; Malaya, 1943, 1944; Indo-China, 1945), was due to the desire to ease the burden of defense by transferring as much of it as possible to those who might be expected to fight for their own liberties with more enthusiasm than for Japan. The return of the Americans, the British, and the Dutch would on this hypothesis be as invaders rather than as liberators from the Japanese. Here again, however, the lateness of the action, but especially the contradictory behavior of the Japanese themselves during the occupation, limited the results from the new policy. The Americans were able to return to the Philippines, supported by an active guerrilla movement, as liberators who had already put the Islands on the road to independence through the Commonwealth régime before the Japanese occupation and grant of independence; and the British and Dutch had the benefit of a reputation as more beneficent masters than the Japanese had shown themselves to be. The return of the British and Dutch to their colonies and the restoration of French control in Indo-China was, however, made much more difficult because of the great increase of nationalist sentiment which Japanese occupation and the Japanese independence and self-government propaganda brought about. The important effects of Japanese policy were felt in the postwar rather than in the war period.

Another part of the Manchukuoan pattern of control introduced into the countries of the southern region was that of what may be called "cultural imperialism." The one-party system of Japan was introduced into the Philippines with the organization of the Kalibapi and into Burma through the Greater Burma Association. Both had the function of developing and organizing support among the people for the puppet governments and thus for Japan. For control purposes the attempt was also made to organize counterparts of the Japanese Neighborhood Associations. But of greater importance for the long run, an emphasis was put on the teaching and study of the Japanese language and of Japanese culture. Selected students, teachers, and journalists were taken to Japan on trips designed not merely to give them a greater first-hand familiarity with conditions there but to impress them favorably with Japanese culture, and to give them a permanent cultural orientation to Japan and thus away from both China and the West.

In the countries of east Asia where there was a system of public education the schools were used not merely for the purpose of instruction in the Japanese language but also for the dissemination of Japanese ideas and values. The vernacular press was utilized in the same way as an instrument of Japanese propaganda throughout the "co-prosperity sphere," as were the other media of mass communication such as the radio, motion pictures, and the stage. Censorship was able to keep out all competitive ideas, except such as could be introduced by means of short-wave radio. State Shinto was introduced as a matter of course as a second center of political-religious influence. In Buddhist countries, such as Burma and Thailand, efforts were made to reactivate Buddhism as a political force, and to ally it with Buddhist Japan. In the Moslem countries, Japan appeared as the protector and fosterer of Mohammedanism. Christianity, of course, because of its Westernism and Europeanism, was not enlisted in the Japanese cultural drive, even though the Christian church in Japan itself had been nationalized after 1926.

There is no way of accurately evaluating the success of the Japanese in their attempt to reorient the thinking and attitudes of the peoples of Greater East Asia. There was certainly a greater impression made in the countries that were completely cut off from access to the non-Japanese world than there was in those, like the Philippines, where at least an underground contact of some proportions continued. There was little success, possibly due to the shortness of time involved, in bringing about either a cultural attachment to Japan or in creating an area consciousness, with Japan at the directive center of the area. Such conferences, for example, as the November, 1943, "Greater East Asia Conference" had some propaganda value but did not serve to bring about any perceptible shift from nationalism on a country basis to regionalism. A great deal of success, however, was attained in the attempt to discredit the West as represented by what was labelled Anglo-American imperialism. It was the participation of China in the war on the side of the United Nations and the failure of India to rise in revolt against Britain which made it difficult for the Japanese to sell the war to Greater East Asia as one of the East in revolt against the West—a racial war. But, as has already been suggested, the chief result of Japan's cultural and political drive was an increase in the number of those wanting independence of outside control; a realization of the possibility of successfully using force against the Westerners to attain nationalist ends; and a greater determination on the part of the nationalist leaders not to return to the *status quo ante* 1941.

REFERENCES FOR FURTHER STUDY

G. C. ALLEN, *Japanese Industry: Its Recent Development and Present Condition* (1939); still worth consulting. ISOSHI ASAHI, *The Economic Strength of Japan* (1939); designed to show the ability of Japan to withstand the economic strains of war. JACK BELDON, *Retreat with Stilwell* (1943); an interesting account of the first phase of the war in Burma. RUTH F. BENEDICT, *The Chrysanthemum and the Sword* (1946); a study of Japan by a leading American anthropologist. T. A. BISSON, *Japan's War Economy* (1945). HUGH BORTON, *Japan Since 1931: Its Political and Social Developments* (1940). HUGH BYAS, *Government by Assassination* (1942); a suggestive treatment of Japanese politics during the 1930's. CLAIRE L. CHENNAULT, *Way of a Fighter* (1949); interesting personalized account of the air war in and from China. Presents Chennault's side of the Stilwell controversy and should be compared with that in *The Stilwell Papers*. JEROME B. COHEN, *Japan's Economy in War and Reconstruction* (1949); the most complete study of the topic. DEPARTMENT OF STATE, Far Eastern Series No. 30, *United States Relations with China* (1949); esp. ch. 3, 4, and annexes. DEPARTMENT OF STATE, *Foreign Relations of the U. S., Japan, 1931–1941* (1943), 2 vols. JOHN F. EMBREE, *The Japanese Nation: A Social Survey* (1945); should be used also for general development of Japan. JOHN F. EMBREE, *The Japanese* (1943); a very useful Smithsonian Institution War Background Study (No. 7 in their series). C. B. FAHS, *Government in Japan: Recent Trends in Its Scope and Operation* (1940). HERBERT FEIS, *The China Tangle* (1953); informed treatment emphasizing American policy. HERBERT FEIS, *The Road to Pearl Harbor* (1950). D. D. GORDON and ROY DANGERFIELD, *The Hidden Weapon: The Study of Economic Warfare* (1947); a careful study of the subject. GREAT BRITAIN, CENTRAL OFFICE OF INFORMATION, *Campaign in Burma* (1946). CORDELL HULL, *Memoirs of Cordell Hull* (1948), 2 vols.; the American Secretary of State's record of the negotiations leading to war and of the war years (in vol. 2, part 5). F. C. JONES, *Japan's New Order in East Asia—Its Rise and Fall, 1937–1945* (1954). F. C. JONES, HUGH BORTON, and B. R. PEARN, *Survey of International Affairs, 1939–1942, The Far East, 1942–1946* (1955). GEORGE W. KEETON, *China, The Far East and the Future* (1949), part III. GEORGE C. MARSHALL, H. H. ARNOLD, and ERNEST KING, *War Reports* (1947); indispensable for military planning and operations. KINOAKI MATSUO, transl. by KILSOO K. HAAN, *How Japan Plans to Win* (1942); interesting preview from Japan. WALTER MILLIS, *This Is Pearl!* (1947); excellent study of the year 1941 in American-Japanese relations. ROBERT E. SHERWOOD, *Roosevelt and Hopkins: An Intimate History* (1948); one of the best books on the political aspects of the war, but mainly concerned with Europe. MAMORU SHIGEMITSU, *Japan and Her Destiny* (1958); account by one who served Japan as Foreign Minister. TOGO SHIGENORI, *The Cause of Japan* (1956); Japan's point of view with respect to the road to war, as presented by the Japanese Foreign Minister in 1940. JOSEPH W. STILWELL, *The Stilwell Papers* (1948); Stilwell's record of his mission to China and its failure. UNITED STATES STRATEGIC BOMBING SURVEY (Pacific), Naval Analysis Division, *Campaigns of the Pacific* (1946); gives data on Japan's strategic plans. UNITED STATES, WAR DEPARTMENT, General Staff, Historical Division, MERRILL's MARAUDERS (1945); operations in Burma. R. S. WARD, *Asia for the Asiatics: The Techniques of Japanese Occupation* (1945); based upon a study of the Hongkong occupation, the book analyzes the techniques used throughout the entire area. W. L. WHITE, *They Were Expendable* (1942); an interesting and vividly written account of an aspect of the operations in the Philippines in their first phase.

CHAPTER XXVII

POSTWAR CHINA

1. POLITICAL IMPLICATIONS OF MILITARY DECISIONS

THE Japanese surrender resulted in the concept of Greater East Asia being replaced by the older one of separation into its component territorial, political, and economic units. Consequently consideration of post-surrender developments will have to be undertaken by countries in the area rather than on an area basis. The nature of the future was, however, somewhat forecast within the area as a whole internationally on the basis of war decisions and war alignments. These need to be considered first of all as creating the general framework within which it was expected that postwar developments in each country would be contained.

At the time when Japan accepted the Potsdam Declaration as the basis for "unconditional" surrender, American power was being focused directly upon Japan. General of the Army Douglas MacArthur had been designated as the Commander-in-Chief of all United States Army Forces in the Pacific, Admiral Nimitz continuing in command of all naval forces. Although mopping-up operations continued in the Philippines, the former Southwest Pacific Command had its energies directed toward planning the invasion of Japan which it had been concluded would be required before surrender could be expected. In China, where the Japanese in 1944 and 1945 launched their only successful offensives, the recall of General Stilwell in the fall of 1944 marked acceptance by the United States government of its inability immediately so to stimulate and redirect the Chinese military effort as to transform China into a major base of operations against Japan. After Stilwell's recall the China-Burma-India theater was divided into the China theater and the Burma-India theater. In the former, General Wedemeyer (General Stilwell's successor) was designated as Chief-of-Staff to Generalissimo Chiang Kai-shek, and as Commander of American forces in the theater. Training of Chinese troops under American guidance continued, as did the bringing in of supplies in enlarged quantities, especially after the reopening of land communications enabled the constantly increased airlift to be supplemented. Stimulated by offensive operations elsewhere, those troops had regained control of the area lost to Japan in their last offensive, putting General Chennault in a position to continue his air offensive and offering the possibility of using Chinese bases on the coast had the Allied offensive strategy against Japan made that advisable. The capitulation of Japan without invasion, however, made it unnecessary for the National government forces to put to the proof their ability, in an offensive coördinated with American operations, to drive the Japanese forces out of occupied China.

The separation of the China-Burma-India theaters had the effect of establishing a primary British responsibility for clearing the Japanese out of southeast Asia. Chinese troops, trained in India and commanded by General Stilwell, with American support had cleared the Japanese out of northern Burma down to Myitkyina, by the end of July, 1944, thus enabling land communications between India and China to be reopened. But after the separation of the two theaters, following the recall of General Stilwell, the reconquest of the remainder of Burma was conducted under British auspices, although with American aid. From Burma it was anticipated that the (British) Southeast Asia Command, instituted as part of the replanning for the concluding phases of the war, would move to clear the Japanese out of Thailand (Siam), Malaya, and the Netherlands East Indies. The liberation of the Philippines and the redirection of the Southwest Pacific Command's effort toward planning and execution of the invasion of Japan lessened the possibility of direct American participation in the elimination of the Japanese from the colonial area, thus enhancing the British role. Whether deliberately or not, this shift of command areas indicated acquiescence on the part of the United States in the determination of future political arrangements by the colonial Powers. Decisions taken on military grounds were to prove to have political consequences here as elsewhere.

2. RUSSIA ENTERS THE PACIFIC WAR

Of even greater political significance were the moves, in anticipation of the necessity of enforcing the surrender of Japan through invasion, to bring the Soviet Union into the Pacific phase of the global war. Although Stalin had indicated earlier an intention to enter the alliance against Japan when the appropriate time came, Russia maintained her neutral status until the eve of Japanese surrender. The force of the Russian argument that more would be lost than gained by her premature entrance into the war against Japan had been recognized during most of the war by the United States and Britain. This argument was that premature action would invite Japanese occupation of the Russian maritime province, as a minimum, and possibly of the entire Russian Far East, since Russian strength in the Far East had been seriously lessened for purposes first of defense against the Nazis and then to mount the offensive which helped to ensure complete victory over Germany. Japan's Kwantung Army, up to the very end of the war, was considered to be capable of either overcoming the available Russian forces or of continuing resistance even after a successful invasion of Japan. The effect on the Kwantung Army of replacement, for purposes of defense of Greater East Asia, of some of its best divisions with poorly trained reservists, and of long-continued garrison duty for the remainder, was not fully appreciated even by the Russians. Consequently there was acceptance of the Soviet view that no excuse, even through limited use of Russian territory for air-base facilities, should be given to the Japanese to regard Russian neutrality as less than perfect. This was even carried to the point of precluding Russian participation in conferences attended by the Chinese. China had to be consulted separately, even if somewhat concurrently, to secure acceptance of the Moscow Declaration, on the basis of which consultations leading to the formulation of the Charter of the United Nations were initiated. At Dumbarton Oaks, although China had been accepted as one of the major Powers, Chinese views on the draft Charter had to be ascertained through discussions separate from those participated in by the Russians with the British and the Americans. There was no Russian representation at the Cairo Conference (the only conference of heads of states in which the Chinese participated). It was subsequently followed by the one with the Russians at Teheran, at which "Marshal Stalin declared that the Soviet Union would enter the war against Japan 'once Germany was finally defeated.' " [1]

It was at the Yalta Conference that the decisions were finally taken on which Russian participation in the Pacific war was based. Conversations had, however, been under way for some months on the nature, extent, and conditions of Russian participation. These were initially confined to the military aspects of the question, including the timing of Russia's entrance, the size of her force and the area within which it would operate, and the supply assistance that would be required for the Soviet forces from the United States. Beyond this, as early as October 15, Stalin had indicated that there would need to be a political agreement, since "The Russians would have to know what they were fighting for; they had certain claims against Japan." [2] It was not, however, until December that Ambassador Harriman secured from Stalin a more detailed statement of what Russia wanted. [3] In reporting this conversation with Stalin to President Roosevelt, Harriman expressed his own view that "if there was no arrangement between the Soviet and Chinese governments before the Soviet Union entered the Pacific war, the Soviet forces would back the Chinese Communists in the North and turn over to them the administration of the Chinese ter-

---

[1] *China White Paper*, 1949, p. 113, note i.

[2] HERBERT FEIS, *The China Tangle* (1953), p. 231. The negotiations preliminary to Yalta are summarized in chapter 22. See also Harriman statement, *Joint* (MacArthur) *Committee Hearings*, part 5, pp. 3329–3342.

[3] Summarized by FEIS, p. 233.

ritories which the Red Army would liberate. . . ." [4] Consequently it is clear that the conditions and some of the hazards of Soviet entrance into the Pacific war had been under consideration for some time before the Yalta Conference of February, 1945.

At the Conference the Soviet government agreed to enter the war against Japan two or three months after the surrender of Germany. It was felt that this interval would give time for the accumulation of supply in the Soviet Far East and for the necessary troop dispositions. In return the Powers agreed to preserve the *status quo* in Outer Mongolia (the Mongolian People's Republic). The Soviet Union was to get back rights which had been taken away from Czarist Russia following the Russo-Japanese war in 1905. Thus the Soviet Union was to recover the southern half of Sakhalin and islands adjacent to it; the commercial port of Dairen was to be internationalized; Port Arthur was to be leased to the Soviet Union as a naval base. Two of the main railway lines across Manchuria would be operated by a joint Soviet-Chinese company, it, however, "being understood that the preëminent interests of the Soviet Union shall be safeguarded." But the conferees agreed that China would retain full sovereignty in Manchuria. [5] In addition to these "former rights of Russia violated by the treacherous attack of Japan in 1904" which were to be restored, the Kuriles were to be handed over to Russia at the end of the war. Churchill and Roosevelt pledged fulfillment of these Russian terms. Since another ally, China, was affected by them, President Roosevelt undertook to follow through with the necessary measures to secure their acceptance by Chiang Kai-shek "on advice from Marshal Stalin." "On advice" meant that Washington would advise China of these terms, but not until Stalin considered the moment appropriate. As an additional safeguard, the agreement stipulated that: "the Heads of the three Great Powers have agreed that these claims of the Soviet Union shall be unquestionably fulfilled after Japan has been defeated."

To further clear the ground for Russia's entrance into the Pacific war, on April 5, 1945, a note was handed to the Japanese Ambassador to Russia, stating: ". . . In accordance with the aforesaid and with Article III of the (Neutrality) pact, which provides for renunciation of the pact in the year before the expiration of the pact's five-year period of effectiveness, the Soviet Government declares to the Japanese Government its wish to renounce the pact of April 13, 1941." Even before this indication of Russian intentions and some months before the first use of the atomic bomb, Japan had approached the Soviet government with a view to securing its

---

[4] *Ibid.*

[5] *Occupation of Japan*, Department of State, Pub. 2671, Far Eastern Series No. 17, p. 2. For text, see *China White Paper*, 1949, pp. 113–114.

mediation in bringing the war to an end. This was then refused, but without the Soviet government informing the Americans or the British of this indication of Japan's growing weakness. As late as July, however, the Japanese were still hopeful that they might use Russia to secure a more favorable peace than one of unconditional surrender.

Movement was rapid from this time until Japanese acceptance of the surrender terms, which were issued on July 26 at Potsdam in the form of a proclamation of acceptable terms for Japanese surrender. It was of the first importance to Russia that an agreement with China should be concluded before she entered the war. Negotiations to that end were begun after some delay, owing to Stalin's desire not to have information of Russian intentions possibly reach Japan via Chungking until the last possible moment. After they were begun in June they had to be pressed so as to be concluded in time to enable Russia to get into the war while it was still underway, with assurance of China's acceptance of her conditions. As a matter of fact the "Treaty of Friendship and Alliance" was only ratified August 14 while the Russian declaration of war on Japan came on August 8. This followed by two days the detonation of the atomic bomb over Hiroshima and was in turn followed on August 10 by Japan's expression of willingness to accept the Potsdam terms of "unconditional" surrender provided that those terms involved no prejudice of "the prerogatives of the Emperor as sovereign ruler." The Allies' attitude toward the Imperial institution had been sufficiently clarified by August 15 so that the acceptance of unconditional surrender could be proclaimed and steps be taken to bring hostilities to an end. The formal signing of the surrender instruments, however, was postponed until September 2. This enabled the Soviet forces to engage in military operations in Manchuria for three weeks. Under the circumstances, which served to lessen the vigor of resistance by the Kwantung Army, this gave the Russians sufficient time to establish control of all of Manchuria as military occupants and to move rapidly into the zone in northern Korea (north of the 38th parallel) allotted to them to receive the surrender of the Japanese forces. Thus with a minimum of effort the Russian position in China and Korea had been strengthened even if compared to that of the time of the Boxer uprising. The rapidity with which the Japanese surrendered after the Russian entrance into the war enabled the claim to be advanced that Soviet intervention was the decisive factor in bringing the war to an end, although the Russians themselves were in possession, at the time of their intervention, of the knowledge that the Japanese were prepared to make peace because of their inability to continue the war. Thus in fact the Soviet Union capitalized on the successful application of American power against Japan.

How ?

The fact that the early Japanese surrender caught the United States, Britain, and China, but not Russia, unprepared for it is indicated in the lack of political preparation for the war's end, except as the assumptions on which planning for the future were based were revealed in the planning for continuation of the war to compel Japan's unconditional surrender. There would seem to have been four of these assumptions. The first was that the *status quo ante* 1941 would be restored in the colonial area, except as, during the war, new policy objectives had been set up by each metropolitan country for its own colonies. The United States had made it clear that it would view with sympathy any moves made by the colonial Powers in the direction of extension of rights of self-government to their colonies, and, for the Philippines, it reiterated its intention to ensure the independence of the Islands. The second was that Japan would not only be defeated by American arms, but that it would also, in consequence, be a major American responsibility to determine and administer policy toward Japan. The third was that China would emerge from the war as a major Far Eastern Power in control of the territories which it had governed at the time of the outbreak of the first Sino-Japanese war. There would, however, be three modifications in this position: (1) Korea would "in due course" become independent of China as well as of other states, and (2) while China, from the standpoint of sovereignty, would include Manchuria, Russia would enjoy with China the use of Port Arthur as a naval base, which would be under Russian military control, although with a Chinese civil administration; Dairen would become an internationalized port open to the commerce of all nations, but with special facilities allocated to the Russians; the former Chinese Eastern and South Manchurian railways would be under joint administration, but with China as the junior partner; and Outer Mongolia would become independent of China. The fourth assumption was that there would be coöperation of the major Powers, based upon mutual trust and confidence, in the Far East and throughout the rest of the world.

This last assumption was expressed in two ways. Specifically, for China, it was thought to be written into the Sino-Russian treaty of 1945 through the provision for Russian assistance in China's reconstruction exclusively through the medium of the National (Kuomintang) government. In general, the idea of Great Power peacetime coöperation was the basis for the organization of the United Nations. Its Charter gave China a permanent seat on the Security Council, with the same right of veto as that of the other major Powers. It also included a Declaration Regarding Non-Self-Governing Territories, setting up international standards for the government of colonies not brought, as ex-enemy territories, under the system of trusteeship. And it included provision for the enforcement of the use of pacific procedures in the settlement of international disputes which could be utilized only on the basis of Great Power agreement.

3. TERMINATION OF JAPAN'S MILITARY OCCUPATION

Of these assumptions the one with respect to China proved no more valid than some of the others. The internal unity, stability, and order which were essential if she was to take the place of Japan as a stabilizing Power in the Far East and as an equal participant with the United States, the Soviet Union, and Britain in the politics of the area did not exist at the time of the Japanese surrender and were not established in the half decade thereafter. Given the conditions existing at the time of the Japanese surrender it can only be concluded that it was hoped that basing action on the assumption would serve to give it ultimate validity. Instead of that hope being realized China rapidly reverted to her prewar status as a "problem" country.

As of VJ day, China was divided into three parts. Kuomintang authority was exerted in the southwestern provinces. The northwestern provinces were controlled by the Chinese Communist Party. And eastern China was still in Japanese occupation. There were, however, numerous Communist enclaves within the Japanese area in North China, and some in central and southeastern China. Through guerrilla operations the Communists had been more successful than the Nationalists in penetrating Japanese-held territory, and thus in extending their influence at the expense both of the Japanese and of the Kuomintang.

The immediate problem, following Japan's acceptance of the surrender terms, was that of taking over control in the occupied area. Responsibility for this was naturally given to the Chinese government, since it involved resumption of control of Chinese territory. An exception was Manchuria, which had been taken over from the Japanese by the Russians subject to an understanding that they would withdraw their troops within three months of the armistice with Japan. The difficulties which arose in occupied China, however, and which created the problem, were not with the Japanese. The Chinese Communists sought the right to receive the Japanese surrender in North China, where they were already established in closer proximity to the Japanese than were Chiang Kai-shek's troops and officials. This right was denied them by the Generalissimo. He, however, lacked the facilities to move his own troops into North China with sufficient rapidity to take over from the Japanese, except as he received assistance from the United States. On the ground that American war responsibilities would not be completely discharged until the Japanese troops in China had been disarmed and repatriated, thus restoring control to Chinese authority, the United States placed its air, land, and naval transport facilities in China (which were greater than those possessed by the Chinese government) at Chiang's disposal to move officials and his troops into the Japanese-held area, in the north as well as the south. This assistance enabled him to forestall the Communists in taking over the major cities and the rail lines of North China, but only at the cost of a threatened resumption of the civil war since it brought his troops into contact with the Communist forces which had already penetrated the countryside. It also brought the United States into a relationship to the internal struggle which was denounced by the Communists as intervention against them on behalf of the National government.

The official American position was that the aid given was a continuation of the common war effort, and any intention to intervene in China's domestic politics was disclaimed. That the assistance given was to and through the recognized government, and that it was limited to assistance enabling it to take over control of territory from the Japanese, was considered to make it not an act of intervention. Nevertheless

The American military authorities and their occupation forces were placed in the unsatisfactory position of finding themselves in between the two contending factions. Civil war broke out. It was attended by loud outcries within the United States from those who sympathized with the Communist faction, demanding the immediate withdrawal of every American soldier from China. It was met with equal virulence on the part of those who sympathized with the National Government, and who believed that Moscow was utilizing the Chinese Communist armies to establish its own immediate control over China and thereby to overthrow the National Government. [6]

Under this double pressure, as soon as the Japanese troops had been substantially repatriated, the United States withdrew most of its troops from China but continued to give non-military aid to China of various sorts, and military assistance in the form of a continuation of a relatively modest military training program, and to sell or lend as surplus some military supplies. The aid (totalling by 1949 in all categories approximately 2 billion dollars) was sufficient to commit the United States to the National government, and thus to arouse continued hostility on the part of the Communists and of other opponents of the Kuomintang régime. It was, however, insufficient so to strengthen the National government as to enable it to maintain itself in North China and Manchuria against the Communists. In effect, the lessening of American support of the Kuomintang government constituted negatively an intervention in favor of the Communists since the measure of superiority of the government forces was the extent of American aid. Whatever course it took after 1945, in other words, the United States was liable to be accused of intervention in China's civil war.

The general objectives of American postwar policy toward China were

[6] SUMNER WELLES, *Where Are We Heading?*, p. 296.

stated by President Truman on December 15, 1945, when he announced the appointment of General Marshall as his Special Representative with the personal rank of Ambassador to China. He declared it to be "the firm belief of the United States Government that a strong, united, and democratic China is of the utmost importance to the success of the United Nations Organization for world peace. . . . The United States recognizes and will continue to recognize the National Government of China and will coöperate with it in international affairs." Thus, as the United States had come to see the political problem, it was one to be solved by broadening the base of the National government and by the substitution of the methods of democracy for those of civil war. The solution consistently seen was that of the replacement of single-party dictatorship by coalition government within the established framework as a means of termination of civil war and moving toward constitutionalism. Practically, this involved basic agreement between Chiang and the Communist leaders on: (1) the extent of Communist participation in a coalition government; and (2) the conditions of transformation of the Nationalist and Communist armies into a national army responding exclusively to the direction of the government of China. In theory these agreements had been made in 1937 in forming the alliance for the "war of resistance" against Japan. In implementation of the alliance, however, the Communists had remained in effective control of their area and their armies. No over-all government for both the Kuomintang and the Communist areas had been created, nor had the Kuomintang and Red armies been amalgamated into a national army.

During the long virtual stalemate in the war against Japan, especially after the Fourth Army incident, as has been noted, relations between the Chungking and Yenan governments deteriorated to the point of virtual non-intercourse between the two areas. This had the effect of lessening the activity and effectiveness of the People's Political Council, in which there had been limited Communist participation in government at Chungking on an advisory basis. It also was a factor militating against the success of the Stilwell mission to China, since Chiang was unwilling to act on General Stilwell's demand that all Chinese troops be utilized against Japan. This would have regularized Communist operations in North and eastern-central China and also weakened the Kuomintang blockade of the Communist area by movement of Chiang's troops to the Japanese fronts.

4. THE HURLEY MISSION

After Stilwell's recall had been forced by the Generalissimo and he and the Ambassador had been replaced by General Albert Wedemeyer and General Patrick Hurley in the early fall of 1944, General Hurley sought to bring about agreement between the Generalissimo and the Communists, having failed, as the President's personal representative, "to promote harmonious relations between Chiang and General Joseph Stilwell and to facilitate the latter's exercise of command over the Chinese armies placed under his direction." His understanding of his mission as Ambassador and of United States policy in China was that he was:

(1) to prevent the collapse of the National Government; (2) to sustain Chiang Kai-shek as President of the Republic and Generalissimo of the Armies; (3) to harmonize relations between the Generalissimo and the American Commander; (4) to promote production of war supplies in China and prevent economic collapse, and (5) to unify all the military forces in China for the purpose of defeating Japan. [On the basis of conversations at Moscow *en route* to Chungking, he felt able to reassure the Generalissimo as to the relations of the Chinese Communist Party with the Soviet Government so that] He now feels that he can reach a settlement with the Communist Party as a Chinese political party without fear of foreign entanglements. . . . Chiang Kai-shek is now convinced that by agreement with the Communist Party of China he can (1) unite the military forces of China against Japan, and (2) avoid civil strife in China. [7]

As a means of instituting direct negotiations between the Kuomintang and the Communists, Ambassador Hurley flew to Yenan on November 7, 1944, where he held direct conferences with Mao Tse-tung. He brought back to Chungking acceptance of a five-point draft agreement "Between the National Government of China, the Kuomintang of China and the Communist Party of China" which, as was later shown, embodied the minimum Communist terms for agreement. The heading itself indicates that the Communists drew a careful distinction between the National Government and the Kuomintang, and their formulated terms indicated, what was also consistently shown in subsequent negotiations, that they were willing to settle on the basis of a coalition government, but only provided that that government had effective authority rather than being subordinated to the ultimate control of the Kuomintang. When that had been accomplished, supported by the legalization of other parties on an equality with the Kuomintang and with the necessary guarantees of freedom for propaganda throughout the entire country for all parties, the Communists would be willing to bring their armies under the control of the National government. This was made clear by General Chou En-lai in comment on the three-point counter-proposals made by the government on November 22. "The one fundamental difficulty with respect to these negotiations, he felt, was the unwillingness of the Kuomintang to forsake one-party rule and accept the proposal for a 'democratic coalition government.'" [8] Subsequently, in commenting on three additional National government pro-

[7] *China White Paper*, 1949, pp. 71–73.
[8] *Ibid.*, p. 77.

posals, General Chou put the Communist position more directly: "the Communist Party would not submit the command of its troops to the Kuomintang Party although it was prepared to turn over command of its troops to the National Government when the one-party rule of the Kuomintang had been abolished and the Government had been reconstituted as a coalition administration representing all parties." [9]

The equally consistently expressed view of the Generalissimo was that embodied in the three-point counter-proposals transmitted to General Chou En-lai on November 22, 1944. Underlying these and other proposals was the view that the National government was making a concession in negotiating with the Communists who were to be viewed as a dissident armed faction rather than as being on a footing of equality, as a government, with itself. It consequently was prepared to promise equal treatment to Communist forces after their reorganization and incorporation into the national army, and "to give recognition to the Chinese Communist Party as a legal party," provided "The Communist Party undertakes to give their full support to the National Government in the prosecution of the war of resistance, and in the post-war reconstruction, and give over control of all their troops to the National Government through the National Military Council. The National Government will designate some high ranking officers from among the Communist forces to membership in the National Military Council." [10] As to the problem of government, the Three-Point Plan reiterated as the "aim of the National Government" the ultimate fulfillment of the three principles program by the pursuit of "policies designed to promote the progress and development of democratic government." Subsequently Chiang extended these proposals to include reorganization of the Executive Yuan to give representation within it to the Communist and other parties, and expressed a willingness to appoint a Communist officer and an American officer to serve with a national army officer "to make recommendations regarding the reorganization, equipment and supplies of Chinese Communist troops, for approval by the Generalissimo" and to appoint "one American Army officer as the immediate commander of Chinese Communist troops for the duration of the war against Japan." [11] Thus it became obvious that, while the Communists would not enter into an agreement short of the ending of single-party Kuomintang control, the Generalissimo would not accept stipulations which would have that effect before decisions had been taken solely by the Kuomintang which would establish the conditions of constitutional government and the ending of the period of tutelage.

[9] *Ibid.*, pp. 79–80.
[10] *Ibid.*, p. 75.
[11] *Ibid.*, p. 79.

Since Ambassador Hurley was committed to the view that American policy was directed toward strengthening the position of the government and of the Generalissimo he could, in the last analysis, only act within limits acceptable to the government. In other words, he could advise the Generalissimo that he "could afford to make political concessions and shorten the period of transition in order to obtain control of the Communist forces," [12] but he could not properly go beyond the tendering of advice. The only way effective pressure could have been put on the Generalissimo to act on American suggestions would have been to condition any and all American aid to China on his acceptance of them. This withdrawal of aid, if he had stood firm, could only have had a weakening effect on the National government and on the position of the Generalissimo. If he had given way to get American aid, the effect would also have been weakening since he would have "succumbed to foreign pressure." But since the Communists were immediately in a sufficiently strong position so that they were not prepared to modify their fundamental demands, and since the Americans were not in a position to apply effective pressure on them in behalf of the government, Ambassador Hurley was actually unable to do more than to get and keep negotiations going, and thus to ensure against the immediate resumption of civil war. [13] This policy of attempting to avert civil war through the negotiation of an agreement between the National government (or the Kuomintang) and the Chinese Communist Party on both political and military issues continued to be followed after the resignation of Ambassador Hurley on November 26, 1945, but with a shift in emphasis away from that of preventing the collapse of the National government and sustaining Chiang Kai-shek as President and Generalissimo to that of reform and reconstruction of the National government.

This shift in emphasis was the result of gradual acceptance of the view, expressed from Chungking in and after 1943, that the National (Kuomintang) government had become "reactionary" and also ineffective, and that "The Chinese Communists have become the most dynamic force in China and are challenging the Kuomintang for control of the country." If civil war broke out, it was argued,

---

[12] *Ibid.*, p. 80. Such a concession was made by Chiang in February, 1945, when he proposed to establish a Political Consultative Conference in which other parties might participate with the Kuomintang in drafting "a constitution to pass control of the National Government to the people and to abolish the one-party rule of the Kuomintang." FEIS, *op. cit.*, p. 222.

[13] As to the strength of the Chinese Communists, the Generalissimo and Ambassador Hurley seem to have concluded that the Communists felt that it rested on their Soviet connection. Disavowed by the U.S.S.R., they would ultimately find it necessary to settle on "moderate" Kuomintang terms. This disavowal Hurley felt had been made by Stalin and Molotov. The Chinese Communist leaders, however, were not convinced of it. Neither, apparently, did they feel that they lacked independent strength.

the Communists would inevitably win . . . because the foreign powers, including the United States, which would support the Government, could not feasibly supply enough aid to compensate for the organic weaknesses of the Government.

In this unhappy dilemma, the United States should attempt to prevent the disaster of civil war through adjustment of the new alignment of power in China by peaceful processes. The desirable means to this end is to encourage the reform and revitalization of the Kuomintang so that it may survive as a significant force in a coalition government. If this fails, we must limit our involvement with the Kuomintang and must commence some coöperation with the Communists, *the force destined to control China,* in an effort to influence them further into an independent position friendly to the United States" [my italics]. [14]

It was the recurrent expression of this point of view, which was contrary to his own, and which sought to develop a different set of policy approaches and emphases than his, that caused General Hurley to hold and express the view that Foreign Service officers sought to sabotage his mission. Thus by the time of the Marshall Mission, the United States was prepared, as the President authorized General Marshall to state frankly to the Generalissimo, to act on the view that "a China disunited and torn by civil strife could not be considered realistically as a proper place for American assistance along the lines enumerated," and that national unity and peace should be brought about by democratizing the government through the broadening of its base "to include other political elements in the country. . . . It is recognized that this would require modification of the one-party 'political tutelage.' " [15] This seemed to involve acceptance by Chiang of the position that had been initially taken by the Communists and that he had first rejected. Subsequently he had proposed convocation under Kuomintang auspices of a Political Consultative Conference to work out arrangements to end the period of tutelage. The Communists had agreed on October 11, 1945, to participate in this Political Consultative Conference.

5. AMERICAN MEDIATION

Thus at the time when General Hurley resigned as Ambassador, the general condition of Kuomintang-Communist relations did not seem too favorable for a non-military solution of China's principal internal political problem. The negotiations had reached a stage of agreement on the general principles set forth in the "Text of the Summary of National Government-Communist Conversations," which had been issued at Chungking on October 11. On the other hand, the Kuomintang-Communist struggle for control of North China and Manchuria had already begun. There had

[14] *China White Paper,* 1949, pp. 64–65.
[15] *Ibid.,* p. 608.

been increasingly frequent and widespread clashes between the armed forces of the government and of the Chinese Communist Party as a result of the refusal of the Communists to recognize orders issued by the National government concerning acceptance of surrender of Japanese and Chinese puppet troops "and of their attempt themselves to accept such surrender, to seize enemy material, and to occupy enemy territory. . . . These clashes spread to other areas as well, to such an extent that competent observers had grave doubts as to the possibility of a peaceful settlement." [16]

It was under these circumstances, then, that the next American attempt to resolve the internal conflict was made when, in December, 1945, General of the Army George C. Marshall was sent by President Truman on an official mission to China. With his great prestige, it was hoped that General Marshall would be able to bring about a military truce and see established a provisional coalition government which could proceed to formulate and supervise the application of fundamental decisions for the creation of a democratic government with authority over all of China. [17]

In anticipation of Marshall's arrival, but also in implementation of the "agreement" of October 11 and as a move toward fulfillment of Chiang's reiterated pledge to move to end the period of tutelage within a year of the end of the war, the Chinese government had taken a step toward the realization of the American objectives with the organization of the People's Consultative Conference (P.C.C.). This step involved resumption of negotiations with the Communists and agreement on their side to participate in the P.C.C.

As it went into the sessions beginning January 10, 1946, and concluding on January 31, the P.C.C. was composed of 9 Kuomintang representatives, 7 from the Communist Party, and 22 representatives of the minor parties [18] and non-party interests. Upon its adjournment the P.C.C. announced agreement on all outstanding issues. One of its published Resolutions provided for the convocation of the National Assembly on May 5 to draft a permanent constitution; establishment of an interim coalition government under a State Council of 40 members, half from the Kuomintang and half from other parties and groups. Chiang was to have a veto over Council discussions, with a three-fifths majority required to override his veto. Another Resolution provided that the *status quo* should be maintained in liberated areas where the Kuomintang and the Communists were contending for administrative control. The *status quo* was to be maintained until

[16] *Ibid.*, pp. 127–130.

[17] On the Marshall Mission, see *China White Paper*, 1949, ch. 5 and Annexes, pp. 61–115.

[18] Democratic League, 2; Young China Party, 5; National Socialist Party, 2; National Salvationists' Association, 2; National Association of Vocational Education, 1; Third Party, 1; non-party representatives, 9. *Survey of International Affairs*, 1939–1946, *The Far East, 1942–1946* (1955), p. 202, note 5.

the National government had been reorganized and the armed forces had been reorganized and reduced in size. A direct agreement was reached between the Kuomintang and the Communist Party on the establishment of a military sub-committee, with General Marshall serving as advisor, to work out the details of military reorganization.

Before the convocation of the P.C.C., General Marshall had been successful in bringing about the truce agreement signed on January 10. This agreement was designed to freeze the existing military position and thus paved the way for the *status quo* agreement referred to above. Troops on both sides were to maintain position. The Communists promised not to interfere with lines of communication and conceded the right of the government to reoccupy Manchuria. Truce teams were sent, where possible, into the field to supervise application of this agreement. These truce teams actually operated to prevent the Nationalist armies, which were then on the offensive, from attaining their objectives and from wiping out large bodies of troops. The truce itself gave the Communists time to reëstablish their position and to assume the offensive.

This truce agreement, however, even if it had been fully implemented in good faith by both sides, did not touch the fundamentals of the problem, although it was an essential preliminary to an attempt to solve it. The political side of the problem had two aspects. The first involved the creation of a provisional government which could act in place of the one-party existing régime. The second involved the establishment of a satisfactory permanent framework of government. Both, from the standpoint of the United States, involved movement toward democracy. The military aspect of the problem was presented in the existence of essentially party armies, which had to be transformed in some fashion into a truly national army, reduced in size from the civil and international war level to that justified in terms of the maintenance of internal order and the fulfillment of China's international obligations. The Kuomintang leadership was insistent on incorporation, in a reduced form, of the Communist armies in the National army (which naturally would be under the control and at the disposition of the National government), in advance of, or at least parallel with, any solution of the political problem, except in terms of general agreement. The Communists were not willing to lose control of their military instrument until a satisfactory political solution had not only been arrived at but actually put into effect. The political solution which they seemed willing to accept was one based upon an acceptance of their position as a minority party, provided there was an implementable guarantee of legality as a party for themselves and other dissident groups as well as the Kuomintang; and freedom of the press, platform, and radio, which would enable them to compete with the Kuomintang in propaganda throughout all of China. Assurance with respect to the carrying out of such an agreement required, from their stand-point, control for the time being of such military force as would compel Kuomintang observance of the agreement, together with coalition govern-ment, on the executive as well as the legislative side, so set up as to give them control in some of the "key" ministries.

Even the prestige of General Marshall was not great enough to break down the barriers to agreement along fundamental lines. His recall, following his appointment as American Secretary of State, had been preceded by a disruption of the negotiations and the resumption, in all but formal declaration, of civil war.

Upon his return to the United States, General Marshall, on January 7, 1947, issued a statement in which he fairly estimated the reasons for the failure of his mission as follows:

> In the first place the greatest obstacle to peace has been the complete, almost overwhelming suspicion with which the Chinese Communist Party and the Kuomintang regard each other.
> On the one hand, the leaders of the Government are strongly opposed to a Communistic form of government. On the other hand, Communists state frankly that they are Marxists and intend to work toward establishing a Com-munistic form of government in China, though first advancing through the medium of a democratic form of government of the American or British type.
> The leaders of the Government are convinced in their minds that the Communist-expressed desire to participate in a government of the type en-dorsed by the Political Consultative Conference last January had for its purpose only a destructive intention. The Communists felt, I believe, that the Govern-ment was insincere in its apparent acceptance of the PCC resolution for the formation of the new government and intended by coercion of military force and the action of secret police to obliterate the Communist Party." [19]

Thus the year (1946) which had begun with a cease-fire and apparent agreement on the method of arriving at a peaceful political solution of the internal problem ended on a note of complete discord. The termination of the Marshall Mission concluded American attempts at mediation between the Kuomintang and the Communists and the endeavor to bring the two parties together in a coalition government.

6. TERMINATION OF "TUTELAGE"

The P.C.C. had set May 5 as the date for convening the National As-sembly. The Communists were, however, unwilling to participate in it unless and until they had an effective voice in determining its composition. This they felt they would have only if, in advance, the powers of govern-ment were transferred to the planned Council of State, agreement on the composition of which had yet to be reached. The assumption made by the

---

[19] *China White Paper,* 1949, p. 686. On the Marshall Mission, see ch. 5, and Annexes, pp. 61–115.

Kuomintang, on the contrary, was that political unification and governmental reorganization would be accomplished under the auspices of the National government, with its composition changed somewhat to meet American specifications with respect to democratization. Broadening the government from its purely Kuomintang base through inclusion of other elements was not thought of, however, as resulting in a loss of Kuomintang control of the movement toward constitutional government. Thus it gave the Communists an opportunity to participate in the work of the National Assembly through representatives of their own choice, and in the Council of State, but only on conditions determined finally by the National government.

Consequently, without any firm agreement with the Communists through prior establishment of a coalition government, after postponement in the hope of reaching an agreement on Communist participation, Chiang Kai-shek announced that the Assembly would be convoked in November, 1946. This would fulfill his promise to introduce constitutional democracy within a year after the cessation of hostilities.

The total membership of the National Assembly was set by the National government at 2,150 delegates. Of these, 950 had been "elected" ten years earlier; 400 members were selected as additional elective members, not replacing the men who had had a ten-year wait but simply joining them; 700 more were arbitrarily assigned to the chief political parties (200 to the Kuomintang, 190 to the Communists, 120 to the Democratic League, 100 to the China Youth Party, and 90 to non-partisan citizens of eminence). The Communists and some of the other groups did not take up their seats and so did not participate in the adoption of the constitution on December 25, 1946. It was, however, promulgated on January 1, 1947, to become effective on December 25, 1947. In the interim, steps were taken looking toward the transfer of power from Kuomintang organs to state organs. Thus the Council of State in April, 1947, became the ruling body. Its membership of 40 was made up of: the 5 Yuan [20] Presidents, *ex officio;* 12 from the Kuomintang; 4 from the China Youth Party; 4 from the Social Democrats; 4 independents. Eleven seats were reserved for the Communists and the Democratic League, but neither was willing to participate in this form of coalition, as it did not actually change the dominant position of Chiang Kai-shek or the Kuomintang. Neither did the Communists come into the Cabinet, constituted on April 23 with non-Kuomintang as well as Kuomintang membership.

Elections were held, under the new constitutional and election laws, for the legislative Yuan in January, 1948; and the National Assembly met at

[20] Each Yuan organized one of the major functions of government, e.g., legislative, executive, judicial, examination, control.

the end of March formally to inaugurate the new system. Its principal task was that of election of the new President and Vice-President. Chiang Kai-shek, as anticipated, was elected to the Presidency for the constitutional term of six years. General Li Tsung-jen, over the expressed opposition of the Generalissimo, was elected, after a sharp contest, as the Vice-President, with a program of reform.

The new constitution postulated extensive rights and duties for the people (Chapter II, Articles 7–24) which could have no practical significance under existing conditions. It provided for a National Assembly to "exercise political power in behalf of the whole body of citizens" (Article 25), whose practical functions, however, were limited to the election of the President and Vice-President, their recall or removal on impeachment by the Control Yuan, and amendment of the constitution or ratification of amendments proposed by the Legislative Yuan (Chapter III, Articles 25–34). It defined the extensive powers of the President and the Vice-President in Chapter IV, Articles 35–52. It provided for the organization and relationships of the executive and legislative branches of the government through the Executive and Legislative Yuan (Chapters V and VI, Articles 53–76), for the Judiciary (Chapter VII, Article 77), and the Examination and Control Yuan (Chapters VIII, IX, Articles 83–106), thus establishing the five-power system of government of Dr. Sun Yat-sen. The territorial distribution of power was made in Chapters X and XI (Articles 107–128). Provision was made in Chapter XII (Articles 129–136) for elections, the recall, the initiative and the referendum, to give expression to Dr. Sun's conception of the democratic process in relation to government. Definitions were made of fundamental national policies in relation to national defense, foreign policy, the national economy, social security, and education and culture in Chapter XIV (Articles 137–169). The concluding chapter provided for the enforcement and amendment of the constitution.

The structure of the constitutional government was erected in 1948, but existing governmental arrangements were actually very little changed. Full-scale civil war had developed by the middle of 1947, following acceptance of the fact that American mediation efforts had failed. Chiang Kai-shek declared the intention of the government to bring the war against the Communists to a victorious conclusion within six months. Initial Kuomintang successes, including the capture of the Communist war capital, Yenan, were followed, however, by serious reverses. Communist military strength steadily increased while that of the Kuomintang declined. The loss of Manchuria to the Communists was accepted when Mukden was ordered evacuated (November, 1948). The destruction of the government armies at Hsüchow in December brought the Communist armies to the Yangtze River.

7. COMMUNIST MILITARY ASCENDANCY

The mounting criticism of President Chiang's political and military failures brought him finally to succumb to the pressure to attempt to bring the military struggle to conclusion through negotiations. Since it was clear that the Communists would not willingly negotiate with him, he retired from the presidency in January, 1948, leaving the conduct of negotiations in the hands of Li Tsung-jen who, as Vice-President, became Acting President.

Negotiations, which were conducted directly and through intermediary groups, failed, however, to produce any agreement. On January 14, 1949, the Communists defined their conditions for peace negotiations. These included the removal from office of Chiang Kai-shek and Li Tsung-jen; a mutual cease-fire order; a new constitution; reorganization of the army and of the political and land systems; confiscation of "bureaucratic capital"; punishment of "war criminals"; the establishment of coalition government without the participation of "reactionaries"; and the abrogation of "traitorous" treaties with foreign powers. These were in effect terms for the unconditional surrender of the Kuomintang so that negotiations could thereafter only be directed toward agreement on their modification or on the conditions of their application. By April 1, the date finally set by the Central Executive Committee (Communist) for the opening of formal peace negotiations, it had been made clear that there would be little modification of these terms, even though the Nationalist Premier, Sun Fo, had announced, on March 3, a Communist agreement to discuss peace terms on a basis of equality with the National government. There was an indication of willingness to restrict the punishment of "war criminals" to the families of Chiang Kai-shek, T. V. Soong, H. H. Kung, and the Ch'en brothers, but the final twenty-four point peace draft submitted to Nanking and rejected on April 19 by the Kuomintang leaders was a demand for surrender rather than a proposal to be negotiated.

There was such a constant apparent deterioration in the National government's military position that there was no real compulsion on the Communists to compromise their demands. All overtures made by the National government for foreign support—even moral support—or to secure mediation failed, so that the Communists had to reckon only with the Kuomintang armies. Their capture of Tientsin and of Peip'ing in mid-January and the failure of the Nationalists' armies to halt them in their move to the Yangtze weakened any bargaining position which the National government might otherwise have established. And the indications that there would be no popular rally in behalf of the Kuomintang, but rather acquiescence in a military verdict against it, established a presumption against the need for a negotiated peace. The only reasons for negotiations, from the Communist side, consequently, were to attempt to create, or to let develop, the conditions for surrender; or to give the necessary time to make their troop dispositions for a military move across the Yangtze. Thus in the April negotiations they called (April 5) upon Acting President Li Tsung-jen to break with Chiang and "American imperialism" and permit an unopposed crossing of the Yangtze, warning him at the same time that they intended to cross regardless of any agreement in the peace negotiations. And they actually launched an attack on the Nationalist bridgeheads north of the Yangtze while negotiations were still under way and before they finally submitted a three-day ultimatum to Li demanding that their armies be allowed to cross the Yangtze and establish ten bridgeheads on the southern side of the river. The rejection of their final surrender ultimatum by the Kuomintang on April 19 was followed by a rapid move on Nanking and Shanghai in the lower Yangtze region, by the occupation of Hankow in central China, and, in October, of Canton.

The failure of the Nationalist commanders to establish a firm line of defense south of the Yangtze or in the northwest caused the British, French, and American Foreign Ministers to release individual but similar press statements on September 17 to the effect that their governments had found no Nationalist groups in China which were worthy of support. This was not only a reaction to the military situation but also expressed a point of view with respect to the Kuomintang and its leadership which the Communists and other non-Kuomintang and anti-Kuomintang elements in China had long been disseminating, and which had been expressed to the American government and public by American officials, correspondents, and publicists since before the end of the war. Secretary of State Acheson's covering letter to the *China White Paper,* released in the summer of 1949, put the seal on official American acceptance of the view of the Kuomintang leadership as corrupt and inefficient, and unworthy of support. But its gradual formulation and expression previously in one form or another was one factor in undermining Kuomintang morale in China and establishing a basis for acceptance among Chinese intellectuals of the view that it had ceased to be a satisfactory instrument of government. Thus the dissemination of the point of view had the ultimate effect of serving to make it one on which it was necessary to base action. The general condemnation of the party leadership made it certain that the government reorganizations attempted after the temporary retirement of Chiang would not enable the Nationalists to gain sufficient domestic or foreign support to make it possible for them to maintain themselves in south China.

The turn of the tide against the Kuomintang, consequently, was due as much to its weakness as to Communist strength. The immediate postwar years had been marked by failure of the Kuomintang to grapple successfully with the problem of reconstruction of the national economy. The National government had been presented with a much more difficult set of problems to solve than those confronting the Communists since it had to restore at least the preëxisting communications system of the country which, in its modern development, fell within its area rather than in the more primitive and undeveloped Communist area. It had to restore the economic life of the urban communities, and reorganize the relationships of town and countryside, a responsibility which did not immediately fall on the Communists since they did not have important cities or towns under their jurisdiction. Only as production was restored and town-country exchanges were facilitated could the increasing inflation and a measure of economic health have been restored. But this was a virtual impossibility as long as the civil war continued. Its responsibilities as the government, as well as the nature of its support, made it necessary for the Kuomintang to employ its military strength to hold the cities and sustain their economic life. To support its position as the National government, Nanking, furthermore, felt impelled to disregard the military advice given it against the attempt to establish control in Manchuria by military means. All of this required it to spread its military force so thin that it was not able to come to grips decisively with the Communist armies and destroy them. With the Nationalist forces committed to holding operations in the cities and along stretched-out supply lines, the Communist armies were able to employ the same guerrilla tactics against them during 1946–1948 that had been used successfully against the Japanese in North China. By disrupting communications they were able not merely to weaken the supply position of the Nationalist armies in Manchuria and in the cities of North China and thus ultimately to force their retirement or capitulation, but they were also able to weaken the national economy through the deliberate prevention of the restoration of the prewar rail network in eastern China. Without normal communications, furthermore, it was impossible for the government to reëstablish the necessary exchanges between town and countryside. And at the same time, responsibility could be attributed to the Kuomintang for its failure to engage in the necessary economic reconstruction. The end product of these military tactics was (1) the depletion of the effective military power of the National government, (2) the consequent increase relative to it of that of the Communist armies and (3) the discrediting of the Kuomintang as an effective agency for national reconstruction.

The National government entered the postwar period with plans for reconstruction which were directed toward laying the foundations for industrialization rather than toward peasant relief and rehabilitation. Execution of the program of industrialization would, in long-run terms, have helped to ameliorate the condition of the peasantry. Successful restoration of the productive and distributive process as of the level of 1936 would have helped to bring the inflation under control and have made life as tolerable as before the war for the peasant. It would not, however, have improved his lot. The Kuomintang failed, consequently, to develop a program of direct action to improve the position of the poorer peasant and the tenant. Regardless of the reasons, its failure here, where it was in direct competition, from the standpoint of a reform program, with the Communists, as well as its inability to revive urban production and town-country exchanges, weakened its appeal and placed its right to govern exclusively on the basis of its initially superior military power. But even that military power rested on a deteriorating rather than an improving internal economic foundation. Reliance was put on American assistance rather than on economic rehabilitation to sustain the military machine.

But the fundamental weakness of the Kuomintang as the governing party came from the widespread and growing feeling that its officialdom was both too corrupt and too inefficient at the top, and that corruption and inefficiency were increasing. The exploitation of position for personal aggrandizement, in terms of either power or enrichment or both, which had shown itself at Chungking reappeared in an even more flagrant form at Nanking. As the inflation mounted, of course, not even the most honest official could meet his family responsibilities from his official income. This might have served to explain the diversion of supplies from their intended public use into the channels of private trade. No explanation, however, served to restore the confidence in government essential if the country was to be held together under it and the war against the Communists carried to a successful conclusion. Those who were thought to be exploiting the country lost their ability to demand from an already tired and disillusioned people new sacrifices for the civil war effort.

Communist successes were, however, the result of their increased strength as well as the weakening power of the Kuomintang. The Party came out of the war with the prestige of its leadership unimpaired. In fact, the view had been widely disseminated that their use of power, where the Communist leaders held it, had been for purposes of social rather than personal advantage. This was shown for example, in the policies followed designed to ameliorate the condition of the peasant. These involved readjustment of land-holdings, mainly at the expense of absentee landlords, and through assistance in bringing into use uncultivated land; and enforced lowering of interest rates and of the proportion of the crop which tenants had to give up in exchange for the right to use land. The program and its execution were such that the Communists came to be somewhat accepted as a party of agrarian reform within the existing system of proprietorship, rather than as one modelling its land policy on that of the Soviet system of collectives at the expense of private holdings. [21]

From the standpoint of government and politics, the Communist Party, although monopolizing the right of party organization, in its area instituted a new "democratic" system in the villages in which it shared administrative responsibility with non-party elements in the community, voluntarily restricting itself to one-third of the seats in councils and in the administration. All decisions, of course, had to fall within the limits of policy set by the party, but ways and means of carrying out that policy could be discussed. As the only organized group with a program defined and agreed upon in advance, Communist Party views could be readily imposed as those accepted by community organs for themselves. But since it did involve some participation in government by non-party members the method of rule served to enlist peasant support of the Red Armies and to emphasize a contrast between the Communist and the Kuomintang régimes. This contrast was also apparent in the superior discipline of the Communist armies. Under orders, they respected peasant property rights to a greater extent than did Kuomintang troops or provincial levies. Supplies were requisitioned, for example, rather than looted. Thus Communist army relations with the peasants in the villages appeared to be planned as those of mutual support while Kuomintang armies appeared, with few exceptions, to be little different from those of the former warlords. Naturally, Communist propaganda played up the "new democracy" and the moderate nature of the agrarian reform program to enlist support both at home and abroad.

The strength which enabled them to take and maintain the offensive in military operations, however, was in large part a result of the situation which developed outside of China proper, especially in Manchuria. On the basis of the Yalta Agreement and the Sino-Russian Pact negotiated in

---

[21] This view of Chinese communism was given to Americans who visited Yenan shortly after VJ day and was subsequently disseminated by them. It was, however, also carried to Chungking by General Hurley from Moscow, where, *en route* to Chungking, he had been given this point of view by Molotov as that of the Russians. "Molotov stressed that it (the Soviet Government) would bear no responsibility for internal affairs or developments in China. Molotov then spoke of the very impoverished conditions of the people in part of China, some of whom called themselves Communists but were related to communism in no way at all. It was merely a way of expressing dissatisfaction with their economic condition and they would forget this political inclination when their economic condition improved. The Soviet government should not be associated with these 'Communist elements' nor could it in any way be blamed for this situation." *China White Paper*, 1949, p. 72. Acceptance of this as the correct view also had the consequence of placing the struggle in China in a civil war context rather than that of an international revolutionary framework at the outset.

fulfillment of its terms, after a plebiscite the independence of (rather than the existing status in) Outer Mongolia from China was accepted. The Russians also strengthened their position in Sinkiang province, where their influence had expanded and contracted during the course of the Sino-Japanese war. And, as already noted, in the final days of the Pacific war the Russians occupied Manchuria. The military evacuation which was to have been effected by December, 1945, was postponed because the presence of "non-governmental troops made it difficult to introduce Chinese (government) troops and administration into Manchuria." Consequently, according to Tass, the Soviet government gave its consent "to postponing the removal of Soviet troops from Manchuria for one month, and this has been acknowledged by the Chinese Government with great satisfaction." [22]

Before the Russian withdrawal had been completed, Soviet agencies had virtually stripped Manchuria of the extensive industrial equipment built up during the period of Japanese ascendancy. The removals were classified by Soviet authorities as war booty which did not need even to be accredited on Japanese reparations account. Thus even if the Chinese National government had been able to reëstablish Chinese control over Manchuria, it would have found itself deprived of what it had looked forward to utilizing as its principal industrial base in undertaking the reconstruction of the Chinese economy; and this by action not of the enemy but of the ally which by treaty had just signified its intention of assisting in the postwar reconstruction of China only through the medium of the National government.

By the time National government forces could be brought into Manchuria the road was blocked by Chinese Communist forces. The Russians, in literal fulfillment of a pledge to the Nationalists, had refused to admit any Chinese Communist Army units, i.e., groups of armed and uniformed men. There was permitted, however, a large-scale movement of unarmed Communist "civilians" into Manchuria from the west and south. "There were instances also of army units, flying Kuomintang banners, which got as far as the cities of southern Manchuria, and the Soviet radio at Khabarovsk announced the arrival of Chinese armies to take over limited areas: soon the Kuomintang banners were furled and the Red Star insignia reappeared." [23] These unarmed Communist forces armed themselves from the accumulations of Japanese arms remaining after the Russians had removed what they needed for their own purposes. Consequently the Kuomintang forces had to fight their way into Manchuria by land routes and were permitted only very restricted rights of entry by

[22] DAVID DALLIN, *op. cit.*, p. 147.
[23] *Ibid.*, p. 249.

way of the ports which the Russians controlled. As the struggle for Manchuria continued, the Communists found arms and equipment replacements available from northern Manchuria and Siberia where the Russians had brought back into use some of the looted arsenal plant facilities. A further source of supply was in the American equipment acquired through the surrender of government troops. From Manchuria, as they solidified their position, they were also able to supply the Communist armies of North China so that the original superiority in arms of the Kuomintang forces, which compelled the Communists to continue their wartime guerrilla tactics, and kept the major cities out of reach of their forces, was replaced by Communist superiority.

In the course of the years after 1945 the originally somewhat obscure relations of the Chinese Communist Party with the Soviet Union were clarified. By 1949 it was no longer possible for it to be accepted as a party of agrarian reform improperly calling itself Communist, and as an instrument of the Chinese national revolution rather than a part of the Communist international movement directed by and utilized as an instrument of the Russian Communist Party. It was this, together with possible continued American assistance to the Kuomintang, which gave international significance to the outcome of China's civil war. Failure in China to perceive the close working relationship between Chinese communism and the Soviet Union enabled the Chinese Communist Party to capitalize on nationalistic feeling by enlarging, through propaganda, awareness of the unconcealed support which was given to the National government by the United States after 1945, and which was successfully characterized as evidence of "American imperialism."

As has been stated, however, by 1949 China north of the Yangtze had been "liberated" from the Kuomintang by the Communist armies, and was labelled as being under the control of the Chinese Communist Party. Some Communist successes had been won, nevertheless, by assimilation of non-Communist (and formerly Kuomintang) commanders and administrators. Thus even in North China administrative authority continued to be exercised in many places by those who had come over to the Communist side by force of circumstance rather than as a result of conversion. This dilution was similar to that which had occurred in the Kuomintang in the course of the rapid unification of the country in the years between 1925 and 1928, when unification was proclaimed. Because of its nature, that unification, consequently, was followed by a continued struggle to maintain and extend effective Kuomintang authority. This had the effect of emphasizing the military at the expense of the civilian apparatus of the party. It also was an important factor as time went on in reducing party enthusiasm for transforming the country along revolutionary lines. The Communists, however, had developed out of experience more skill in propaganda than that possessed by the Kuomintang at the outset of their period of rule, and they had themselves been longer indoctrinated in the Communist articles of faith. This, joined to their recognition of propaganda as an effective instrument of power, put an initial tactical emphasis on thorough indoctrination of new recruits which put them in a stronger position, especially with the intellectuals, than had been established by the Kuomintang at the time of establishment of the Nanking government.

The initial pattern of organization established by the Communist Party was regional. By September, 1949, there had been created or projected for the future six "liberated areas": Northeast China (Manchuria); Northwest China; North China; Central China; East China; and South China. The special administrative districts within these regions, in China proper, were shaped substantially along the older provincial lines as the new pattern began to crystallize. The general scheme of regional government was charted in that of North China, as the first area fully "liberated" from the Kuomintang by the Communist Party. It provided for a large representative assembly, with the principal function of electing the "North China Provisional Government Commission" (initially of 43 Commissioners) which was the "repository of actual governing powers." [24] Thus regional government was so planned as to fix governmental control at the top, with the flow of power downward. The real direction in China proper, however, remained outside formal government in the hands of the Communist Party organization. In Manchuria, although it had been designated one of the six regions, the general pattern initially was modified in the direction of greater autonomy under the control of a Chinese Communist leadership with more intimate immediate contact with the U.S.S.R. than that of the official party headed by Mao Tse-tung.

None of these political and administrative rearrangements within China established a Communist government for China which could demand or expect recognition by the foreign Powers. A movement in that direction was indicated with an announcement by the New China Central News Agency on June 19 of the establishment of the framework of a new People's Consultative Conference designed to establish a "democratic coalition government" for China. This framework was established in a five-day session of a new P.C.C. Preparatory Committee which had been created by the Communist Party and which, although it had non-Communist Party representation as well as that of the Party, accepted in executive sessions the Communist plan for representation in the Chinese People's Political Consultative Conference (C.P.P.C.C.), which was created

[24] A. Doak Barnett to Walter S. Rogers, Institute of Current World Affairs, letter dated Sept. 4, 1949.

as the Communist united front alternative to the Kuomintang's P.C.C.
This representation was designed to exclude from participation "Kuomintang reactionaries," by which was meant any individual or group unacceptable in its point of view to the Communist Party leaders. Thus the
new C.P.P.C.C. was certainly no more representative than had been the
Kuomintang P.C.C. which the Communist leaders had denounced. It
worked in comparative secrecy on a different assignment than that of the

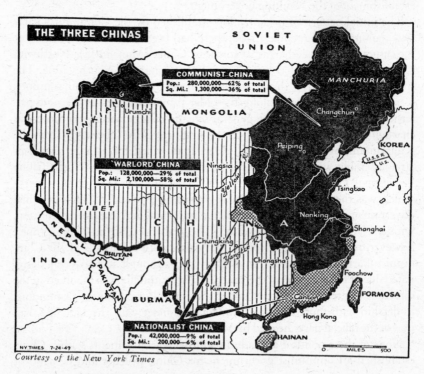

Courtesy of the New York Times

THE SITUATION IN CHINA IN JULY, 1949
("Warlord" China taken over by Communists by March, 1950)

old P.C.C. The task of the latter had been to work out a peaceful solution
of the relations of the Kuomintang and the Chinese Communist Party.
The assignment of the new C.P.P.C.C. was to associate other, but
sympathetic, elements with the Communists in the establishment of a new
central government which could thus present the appearance of coalition
government instead of one-party rule.

The decision taken through the new C.P.P.C.C. was announced on
October 1, although it had been stated on September 18 that "a three day
preliminary meeting of the Political Consultative Conference, just con-

cluded in Peiping, had 'approved in principle' drafts of 'organic' law for the Central People's Government and the Political Consultative Conference," [25] and Mao Tse-tung, on September 21, had proclaimed the "establishment of a new 'People's Republic' of China." The new régime was recognized by the Soviet Union as the government of China on October 2 and shortly thereafter by other states which were accustomed to take their lead in international relations from the U.S.S.R. Concurrently the Soviet Union formally withdrew from all contact with the previously recognized National government at Canton. The latter had already formally lodged an accusation of intervention in the civil war in behalf of the Communists against the Soviet government at the United Nations General Assembly.

While this government structure was being elaborated the Communist armies were continually enlarging the area under their control to the point where, by the end of November, 1949, the Nationalist position was restricted to a portion of Kwangsi province, to Szechuan, where, however, even Chungking was being threatened, to Yunnan, to Hainan Island, and to the island of Formosa, under the personal control of Chiang Kai-shek. Sinkiang province had adhered to the Communist régime before the end of September and the Communist position had, at the same time, been strengthened in Inner Mongolia with the capture of Ninghsia. This extension of the area taken by the Communists from Kuomintang and anti-Communist control continued. By March, 1950, Formosa and the island of Hainan alone remained to the Nationalists, although mopping-up and consolidation operations had to be completed in mainland China by the Communists; and control of Hainan was lost by June.

When the Communists assumed control they had committed themselves, as had the Kuomintang earlier, to the improvement of the lot of the people through a revolutionary program of economic and social change. The way had been paved for change by preceding régimes since the downfall of the Manchus with the proclamation of the Republic in 1911, each of which had contributed something toward breaking the traditional system. The Kuomintang, on the basis of Sunyatsenism, had been instrumental in carrying forward the dissemination of a non-traditional system of economic and social values. But beyond that, it had finally reshaped the treaty relations of China with the West so that they could be conducted on the basis of legal equality; and it had maintained China as an entity against external attack and tendencies toward internal disruption. Thus it had held together a China over which the Communists could establish control. Its preoccupation with national defense and with the maintenance of its own power position within China, however, caused it to fail to

---

[25] New York Times, A. P. Shanghai dispatch, dated September 18.

carry forward its program of internal reform. This failure successfully to move forward along the path of reform Dr. Sun had marked out produced, as stated above, especially among the intellectual class, disillusionment with it as an acceptable instrument of government. Disillusionment with the Kuomintang from this standpoint facilitated the assumption of power by the Communists.

As the National government armies were unable to maintain themselves at the Yangtze, the government was transferred to Formosa (Taiwan), which had been brought back under China's administration at the time of the Japanese surrender. Thereafter, the Kuomintang and also the Communists viewed Formosa as a province of China. It consequently was as the head of the government of China rather than as the government of Formosa that Generalissimo Chiang Kai-shek sought to maintain himself. And it was to complete the establishment of its authority over China that the Central People's Government set up as its objective the overthrow of the National government on Formosa.

The United States, refusing to recognize the Communist régime, maintained relations with the National government on Formosa as the government of China, and initially viewed the possibility of Communist operations against Formosa as in the context of the civil war. Consequently when, in January, 1950, Formosa seemed in imminent danger of overwhelming attack by the Chinese Communists, President Truman proclaimed the intention of the U.S. government not to interfere or to give military assistance to the National government.

All the indications were that if the Communists then, or in the immediately following months, had been able to stage an attack in force against Formosa they would have been successful. The National government's troops, evacuated from the mainland, were not capable then, without American military assistance, of defending the island. What had happened on Hainan, which Chiang had declared would be defended to the end, might readily have happened on Formosa, defended by ill-equipped troops whose morale was low.

The attack, however, was not then launched, and the Korean War significantly changed the situation. The United States proclaimed the neutralization of Formosa for the period of the war and reversed the policy of non-support of the National government, renewing the military assistance which had been cut off and establishing a Military Assistance Advisory Group to work with the National government in transforming its forces from the ill-disciplined horde which had been evacuated from the mainland into a military force capable of defending the island from Communist attack. This had been successfully accomplished by the time of the Korean armistice and the armistice in Indo-China.

The position of defensive strength was further improved when the United States concluded a bilateral defense pact with the National government. The commitment of the United States was restricted to the defense of Formosa and the adjacent Pescadores Islands. It was not a commitment to the general support of the National government, whose objective remained the reëstablishment of power on the mainland and the destruction of the People's Republic. The National government, despite its materially improved military and economic position on Formosa, lacked the resources and the power, without outside assistance, to attain this objective.

REFERENCES FOR FURTHER STUDY

Joseph W. Ballantine, *Formosa: A Problem for United States Foreign Policy* (1952); a careful study. G. W. Barclay, *Colonial Development and Population in Taiwan* (1954). H. Maclear Bate, *Report from Formosa* (1952). John C. Campbell, *United States in World Affairs, 1945–47* (annual thereafter) (1947); both factual and interpretive. Chia-sen Chang, *The Third Force in China* (1952). Chiang Kai-shek, *China's Destiny*, transl. by Wang Chang-hui (1947); first published in China during the war, it has importance as revealing the general outlook of Chiang. Another translation, at the same time, titled *China's Destiny and Chinese Economic Theory*, transl. by Phillip Jaffe, contains additional material and critical notes. Chiang Kai-shek, *Soviet Russia in China: A Summing-Up at Seventy* (1957). Tuan-sheng Chien, *The Government and Politics of China* (1950). China News Service, *Constitution of the Republic of China* (1947); text of the constitution promulgated January 1, 1947. Taylor Cole and J. B. Hallowell (eds.), *Post-War Governments in the Far East* (1947); the three articles on China are well worth consulting. David J. Dallin, *Soviet Russia and the Far East* (1948). Department of State, Far Eastern Series No. 30, *United States Relations with China* (1949); covers the war as well as the postwar period, and contains details on Kuomintang-Communist negotiations as well as on American policy. The annexes give text of documents of the period. Indispensable. John K. Fairbank, *The United States and China* (1948); excellent development of question of what was wrong with Kuomintang, using historical analysis. Herbert Feis, *The China Tangle* (1953). Charles P. Fitzgerald, *Revolution in China* (1952). Harrison Forman, *Changing China* (1948). Randall Gould, *China in the Sun* (1946). Norton S. Grinsberg, *The Economic Resources and Development of Formosa* (1953). Harold R. Isaacs, *No Peace for Asia* (1947); covers rest of area as well as China. The emphasis is on Soviet-U.S. rivalry. George W. Keeton, *China, the Far East and the Future* (1949). Owen Lattimore, *Solution in Asia* (1945). P. M. A. Linebarger, Djiang Chu, and Ardath Burks, *Far Eastern Government and Politics* (rev. ed. 1956). Harley F. MacNair (ed.), *China* (1946); chapters by specialists on a wide variety of cultural, social, economic, and political topics. Robert C. North, *Kuomintang and Communist Elites* (1953). Pan Wei-tung, *The Chinese Constitution: A Study of Forty Years of Constitution-Making* (1946); leads up to the adopting of the new Kuomintang constitution.

GRAHAM PECK, *Two Kinds of Time* (1950). FRED W. RIGGS, *Formosa Under Chinese Nationalist Rule* (1952). L. K. ROSSINGER, *China's Crisis* (1945); analysis of political conditions at end of war. ROBERT AURA SMITH, *The Rebirth of Formosa* (1953). GUNTHER STEIN, *The Challenge of Red China* (1945); early postwar reporting from the Yenan area. ARTHUR H. STEINER, "The United States and the Two Chinas," *Far Eastern Survey*, May, 1953. JOHN LEIGHTON STUART, *Fifty Years in China* (1954). HAROLD M. VINACKE, *The United States and the Far East, 1945–1951* (1952). SUMNER WELLES, *Where Are We Heading?* (1946); ch. 6, The Nationalist Surge in Asia, is worth consulting. THEODORE H. WHITE and ANNALEE JACOBY, *Thunder out of China* (1946); contrasts conditions in Kuomintang and Communist China during and at the end of the war. GERALD F. WINFIELD, *China, the Land and the People* (1948); postwar survey of fundamentals.

CHAPTER XXVIII

THE PEOPLE'S REPUBLIC

I. ESTABLISHMENT OF THE NEW RÉGIME

THE PEOPLE'S GOVERNMENT of the People's Republic of China, proclaimed on October 1, 1949, was established by the Chinese Communist Party (C.C.P.) behind a united front facade (the C.P.P.C.C.). Proposals for an anti-Kuomintang united front were embodied in a May Day slogan in 1948. The cry raised was that "all democratic parties and groups, people's organizations, and social luminaries, speedily convene a political consultative conference, discuss and carry out convoking a people's representative assembly to establish a democratic coalition government." [1]

The C.P.P.C.C. was constituted on the basis of an Organic Law for the C.P.P.C.C., adopted by a preparatory committee established for that purpose and to draft a Common Program and an Organic Law for the Central People's Government. The Organic Law for the C.P.P.C.C. was approved by the Preparatory Committee on September 17, 1949, and the C.P.P.C.C. was convened four days later. Acting as a constituent assembly, the C.P.P.-C.C. then proceeded (September 27) to adopt the Common Program and the Organic Law for the Central People's Government, thus making it possible to proclaim the new régime on October 1.

The C.P.P.C.C. was continued as the organization of the united front, exercising the functions of an "All-China People's Congress" until the establishment of the Congress as "the supreme organ of the state" in 1954. Maintenance of the united front enabled the new government to operate on the theory that it was national and democratic rather than international and class. It was designed as a pre-socialist "new democracy," under which the transition would be effected to a socialist society. As Mao Tse-tung put it in his address "On Coalition Government," delivered to the Seventh Congress of the Chinese Communist Party at Yenan in 1945:

... a new democratic state of a union of democratic classes is different in principle from a Socialist state with a dictatorship of the proletariat. China, throughout the period of her new democratic system, cannot and should not have a system of government of the character of one-class dictatorship of one-party autocracy. We (the Communists) have no reason not to coöperate with

---

[1] As quoted by ALAN B. COLE, "The United Front in the New China," *The Annals of the American Academy of Political and Social Science,* September, 1951, p. 39, from *China Digest,* Vol. 4, No. 1.

non-Communist political parties, social groups, or individuals who are willing to coöperate with the C.P.C. and are not hostile to it. [2]

The participants in the united front were those who were not only willing to coöperate with the Chinese Communist Party but also accepted its leadership and direction. Thus the formulation of policy remained in the hands of the C.C.P. The participating parties (the Revolutionary Committee of the Kuomintang, the China Democratic League, the China Democratic National Construction Association, and others), social groups, and individuals had the function of concurring in policy decisions, of promoting understanding and acceptance of them, and of assisting in their application. Their participation was as instruments of Communist Party rule. [3] They were tolerated, encouraged, and assisted by the C.C.P. as long as they played this role and thus were of service in the establishment and consolidation of the power of the new régime.

2. THE INSTRUMENTALITIES OF RULE

As an instrumentality for "extending ideological and political indoctrination," the Chinese Communist Party had from the beginning sought to establish and maintain youth organizations. The pre-World War II youth organizations had required acceptance of the principles of communism as a qualification for membership. In 1946 the earlier youth organizations began to be replaced experimentally with local organizations open to those who accepted the principles of the "new democracy." These local and regional branches of what was called the New Democratic Youth League had spread widely enough by 1949 so that organization could be established on a national basis. Thus when the new régime was planned, the Communist Party had at its disposal the N.D.Y.L. to rally "the young people of the various classes of the social order" to the support of the new régime. It was initially an auxiliary united front organization having a similar usefulness in broadening support for the Communist Party to that of the non-Communist parties. Having played its role in winning support for the "new democracy" as the "mass organization of progressive youth under the leadership of the Communist Party of China," [4] however, the New Democratic Youth League transformed itself in 1956 into a Communist organization, changing its name to the Communist Youth League, and coming into the same relationship to the C.C.P. as that of the Kom-

---

[2] As quoted in English translation by PETER S. H. TANG, *Communist China Today* (New York, Praeger, 1956), p. 166. Also given, with a somewhat different translation, in CONRAD BRANDT, BENJAMIN SCHWARTZ, and JOHN K. FAIRBANK, *A Documentary History of Chinese Communism* (Cambridge, Harvard University Press, 1952), p. 305. Much of the speech is there published, pp. 295–318.

[3] The position of the non-Communist parties is described in TANG, *op. cit.,* pp. 140–156.

[4] TANG, *op. cit.,* p. 141.

somol to the Soviet Communist Party. By 1955 the Youth League was estimated to have 620,000 branches and 14 million members.

These united front youth and party organizations were further supplemented and extended through the formation of numerous "mass" organizations covering all areas of activity. These included: peasants associations, the All-China Federation of Trade Unions, the All-China Federation of Literary and Art Circles, and the All-China Student's Federation. All of these organizations were controlled by the Chinese Communist Party through Communist leaders who were placed in key positions. They were used for purposes of securing understanding and acceptance of the party line throughout the country.

The government itself, as it was organized under the Organic Law which continued in force until the adoption of a Constitution in 1954, was headed by the Central People's Government Council of 56 members, under the chairmanship of Mao Tse-tung. With a majority of its membership ranking Communist Party members, policy decisions taken by the Party could be established as government policy through formal acceptance by the Government Council. Under the general supervision of the Government Council, the Government Administrative Council carried on the work of government, acting within limits set by the Common Program, adopted and interpreted by the C.P.P.C.C., national laws and decrees, and the decisions and orders of the Government Council.

As the Communists took over the country, it was initially organized territorially on a decentralized basis. Each area, as it was "liberated," was organized into local governments which were integrated on a regional or area basis. An Organic Law of Regional Government Councils was promulgated on December 16, 1949. In its application the country was then organized into seven areas: Northeast (Manchuria); North China; Inner Mongolia; Central China; South China; the Northwest area; and the Southwest. These areas largely conformed to the military-command positions of the Communist armies which "liberated" each from the Kuomintang. To some exent they conformed to natural economic-political or geopolitical subdivisions of the country. They were designed, however, to serve a double purpose. One purpose was to move organization from the local toward the national level. Another was to weaken the natural or historic political and economic connections of provinces which might be exploited against the Communists during the period of consolidation of their power.

The warlord system of the past was rooted in localism and in geopolitical regionalism which had not been completely displaced by the Kuomintang régime during its period of control. Thus the new regionalism seemed designed to nationalize through a further detachment of the people's sentiments and loyalties from their traditional local and provincial bases. [5]

This organization had served its purpose by 1954 and was not provided for in the new constitution then adopted.

3. THE FIRST STAGE OF THE COMMUNIST REVOLUTION

The first stage of the Communist revolution in China, which was viewed as completed by 1954, was considered to be that of "the people's revolution against imperialism, feudalism and bureaucratic capitalism." It was also that of consolidation of the Communist victory over the Kuomintang and the authority over mainland China of the People's Government. Authority had been nationalized and centralized under the firm direction of the Communist Party behind the facade of the united front of "democratic" parties in what Mao Tse-tung called a People's Democratic Dictatorship. In his address on the People's Democratic Dictatorship Mao declared: [6]

Our present task is to strengthen the apparatus of the people's state, which refers mainly to the people's army, people's police, and people's courts, for the defense of the country and the protection of the people's interests; and with this as a condition, to enable China to advance steadily, under the leadership of the working class and the CP, from an agricultural to an industrial country, and from a New Democratic to a Socialist and Communist society, to eliminate classes, and to realize the state of universal fraternity. The army, police, and courts of the state are instruments by which classes oppress classes. To the hostile classes the state is an instrument of oppression. It is violent, and not "benevolent." You are not benevolent. Just so. We decidedly will not exercise benevolence towards the reactionary acts of the reactionaries and reactionary classes. Our benevolence applies only to the people and not to the reactionary acts of the reactionaries and reactionary classes outside the people.

The army, the police, and the courts were effectively used in this period to overcome opposition to Communist Party rule. The party was able to establish its own definitions of the reactionary and of the reactionary classes, changing the definitions to cover identifiable opposition, which then was ruthlessly destroyed if it did not prove susceptible of conversion through the processes of "reëducation," on which almost as much emphasis was placed in the consolidation of the new régime as on the instruments of coercion, although coercion was actually instrumental in reëducation.

The Communist Party lacked the trained personnel in its membership to enable it to accomplish the administrative tasks which it set for itself as the government of China. Its success depended on its ability to attract to its service those with managerial training and experience either in gov-

[5] HAROLD M. VINACKE, *Far Eastern Politics in the Postwar Period* (1956), p. 134.
[6] From *"On the People's Democratic Dictatorship"* (July 1, 1940), as printed in BRANDT, SCHWARTZ, and FAIRBANK, *op. cit.,* pp. 457–465.

ernment or in business. Many with the necessary qualifications initially went along with the Communists because of disillusionment with the Kuomintang government and leadership, to which the Communist régime seemed to offer the only available alternative. But their fundamental assumptions with respect to economic and political society were derived from Western liberal democratic thought and from essentially Confucian premises and not from the doctrines of Marxism-Leninism. And yet it was necessary to ensure, as far as that was possible, their loyalty to the new régime which sought their services. This required reëducation so that they might be brought to an understanding and acceptance of Communist principles and purposes. This involved a double process. The first came to be called "brain-washing." The individual was persuaded, encouraged, or compelled to reach the conclusion that his previous background of ideas, training, and experience had been wrong and to make a public recantation of all views previously held which were inconsistent with the ideology of the new order. At the same time he had to denounce the source of those ideas. Since party propaganda was partly based on hostility to the United States, the public recantation fitted into an existing anti-American emphasis since many Chinese administrators and scholars had received their training in American institutions. Thus renunciation of old ideas involved simultaneous denunciation of the "capitalist-imperialist" United States. In the case of the more prominent intellectuals, their confessions of error were given national publicity through radio broadcasting and publication in papers of national circulation. For the less well-known, as well as in the case of the gentry and rich peasantry, the public meeting was used as the open confessional of past error and proclamation of understanding and acceptance of the new "truth" embodied in Marx-Lenin-Stalinism. Meetings were organized and held constantly at all levels to bring about public dissociation of as many people as possible from traditional beliefs and from the system of ideas and values imported from the non-Communist West. Those of the intellectuals, gentry, and upper capitalist classes who failed to successfully "brain-wash" themselves were liable to treatment as reactionaries, to be purged from the body politic.

Recantation was the negative method of creating loyalty. On the positive side an emphasis was placed on the study, with a view to acceptance, of the new "classics"—the teachings of Marx, Lenin, Stalin, and Mao Tse-tung. Their doctrines became subjects of compulsory study in the schools. For adults a rapid course of intensive indoctrination through lectures, discussion classes, and meetings of all sorts was inaugurated. The new "learning" was capsulized and sloganized and carried to the people by Communist cadres organized and trained for that purpose.

The "mass" or "people's" organizations which were rapidly organized on a national basis by the Communist Party were effective instruments for "reëducation" and thus for the extension of the influence of the party throughout the country much more quickly than would have been possible if the party had had to place sole reliance on the party membership for dissemination of the new doctrines. Party members, organized into cadres for this purpose and placed in positions of leadership in mass organizations, could exercise an influence and control far beyond the numerical strength of the party.

During Yenan days, plays, dances, literature, and the pictorial arts had been successfully employed on a small scale for purposes of political indoctrination. This utilization of the arts and literature as an instrument of politics was continued and enlarged by the party when it attained national power. As in the Soviet Union, so in Communist China the standard for the artist and the writer was set in the service of the Communist Party program. "Our demand, then," Mao Tse-tung said, "is a unity of politics and art, a unity of content and form, and a unity of revolutionary political content and an artistic form of as high a standard as possible."[7]

This meant that art should be expected to express class ideas. Mao rejected as a basis of judgment of art and literature the intrinsic merit of the work itself, viewed solely as art. Consequently it became improper to express and disseminate by any means ideas that were contrary to party doctrine. The choice finally left to the writer or artist was not that between non-use of his talents and their use to serve Communist-defined political and social purposes. The choice was between the latter and the complete loss of status in the new scheme of things.

The emphasis on ideological indoctrination continued until the "new democracy" had been stabilized to the point where the transition toward socialism could begin. By 1957 it was apparently concluded that ideological acceptance had been established to the point where the pressures just described could be relaxed. Mao consequently indicated that the contention of ideas, within the framework, however, of the fundamental principles on which the new order rested, could properly be resumed. His address on "The Correct Handling of Contradictions Among the People," at a closed session of the Supreme State Conference on February 27, covered a great deal of ground, partly in explanation or justification of Marxism as applied in China, but going beyond exposition of past policies into what was generally taken to be the inauguration of a new line of ideological development. The objectives of the People's Democratic Dictatorship had been realized with the establishment of the new régime and the ideological consolidation of its position. The "feudal remnants" had been de-

[7] From speech made at the Forum of Literature and Art at Yenan, May 2 and 23, 1942, from text in BRANDT, SCHWARTZ, and FAIRBANK, op. cit., p. 414.

stroyed, except on Formosa, and the reconstituted body politic had been purged of the old ideas. Thus the contradictions in society resulting from class, which had to be resolved by coercion, no longer existed.

Our democratic centralism means the unity of democracy and centralism and the unity of freedom and discipline. Under this system the people enjoy a wide measure of democracy and freedom, but at the same time they have to keep themselves within the bounds of Socialist discipline. All this is well understood by the people. [8]

The foundations of the Communist state having been firmly laid in China, Mao had apparently come to the conclusion that there was no longer necessity for coercion of the "brain-washing" and forced reëduca tion sort."

While we stand for freedom with leadership and democracy under centralized guidance, in no sense do we mean that coercive measures should be taken to settle ideological matters and questions involving the distinction between right and wrong among the people. . . . We cannot compel people to give up idealism, any more than we can force them to believe in Marxism.

This made necessary the policy embodied in the slogans: "Let a Hundred Flowers Blossom" and "Let a Hundred Schools of Thought Contend." These slogans, said Mao, "were put forward in the light of the specific conditions in China, on the basis of the recognition that various kinds of contradictions still exist in a Socialist society, and in response to the country's urgent need to speed up its economic and cultural development."

"The policy of letting a hundred flowers blossom and a hundred schools of thought contend is designed to promote the flourishing of the arts and the progress of science; it is designed to enable a Socialist culture to thrive in our land."

The same outlook, applied to relations of states within the Communist system, supported the view that there could be rationally different approaches in the application of Marxism—contradictions among Communist states, which, however, were of a different order than those separating Communist from "capitalist-democratic states." These contradictions could be resolved through the democratic method of discussion and negotiation rather than by coercive imposition of one view of the proper method of solution of problems. What was true within a Socialist society was also true among Socialist states.

Contradictions in a Socialist society are fundamentally different from contradictions in old societies, such as capitalist society. Contradictions in capitalist society find expression in acute antagonisms and conflicts, in sharp struggle

[8] All quotations are from the official edited Peking version of Mao's February Speech on Contradictions, as published in the *New York Times*, June 19, 1957.

which cannot be resolved by the capitalist system itself and can only be resolved by Socialist revolution. Contradictions in Socialist society are, on the contrary, not antagonistic and can be resolved one after the other by the Socialist system itself.

On these premises Mao supported the position taken by Poland and moved toward friendly relations with Yugoslavia after Tito and Khrushchev had restored the relations earlier broken when Tito refused to accept Russian domination. The revolt in Hungary, however, he viewed as falling within the category of contradictions between Socialist and capitalist systems that could only be resolved by force. Consequently he gave his approval to Russian military action to suppress the revolt. And as there were indications of a willingness on the part of Poland to withdraw from the Russian Warsaw Pact system and of Yugoslavia to assert independence of judgment in international relations, he sided more and more positively with the U.S.S.R. Since Mao had not joined in the earlier denunciations of Stalin and Stalinism, it was easy for him to support the revival of Stalinism in Russian policy and even to insist on a firmer attitude toward Yugoslav revisionism than would otherwise have been taken by Khrushchev. Thus Mao certainly did not resist, but rather urged, inclusion of a strong denunciation of Titoism in the communique issued at the end of the conference between Mao and Khrushchev, held in Peking August 1–4, 1958. In giving support to Khrushchev on this and other European questions, as well as on the Middle Eastern question, however, the Chinese Communist government was astute enough to use the difficulties faced by the U.S.S.R. in Europe to extract economic and arms concessions as the price of its support of the dominant faction in the Kremlin.

In China the wave of critical discussion of the party and its program which the "hundred blossoms" slogan and the Speech on Contradictions rolled up went beyond the limits viewed as appropriate, being directed against the foundations, as well as the super-structure. It was revealed that many of those earlier converted, especially among the intellectuals, had not been fully purged of their previous beliefs. The relaxation of "thought-control" pressures and the apparent intent not to coerce into conformity, however, served a double purpose. It enabled some accumulated steam to be blown off. But it also identified potential sources of opposition to the new régime. Consequently many critics were either liquidated or divorced from their normal activities and put to work in labor camps or as agricultural laborers, working under party supervision to ensure their good behavior.

The conclusion should not be drawn from what has just been said that no criticism was tolerated within the People's Republic. Self-criticism was not only encouraged but insisted upon. This, however, was in relation to the behavior of the individual as a working member of the new society. This self-criticism was reënforced by encouragement of the members of the group to criticize one another in order to improve performance. Targets were set up and campaigns (such as the 3 anti- and 5 anti-campaigns of 1952, 1953) were waged, under direction from the top, against corruption, inefficiency, bureaucratism, waste, bribery, tax evasion, and other evils. All this, however, was criticism within the framework of dogma and policy, which had to be accepted, and in relation to effectiveness of action in implementation of party decisions.

4. AGRARIAN REFORM

The People's Government obviously had to justify itself in action as well as through the creation of a doctrinal uniformity throughout the country. It had established itself in power in part because it had created the presumption that it would be better able than the Kuomintang to find satisfactory answers to economic problems which had to be solved. Particularly, the Chinese Communist Party had initially posed land reform as the solution of the economic problem in order to win mass support in an agricultural country. As one area after another was "liberated," consequently, violent and exceedingly disorderly local expropriations of land by the landless and poor peasants were undertaken. This initial action was based on the premises established in the Kiangsi Soviet period.

After the establishment of the People's Government, however, partly in order to reëstablish and maintain production, a more moderate national policy was defined in the Agrarian Reform Law of June 30, 1950. As Liu Shao-chi (after Mao, the chief party theoretician) put the purpose of the law: "It is designed to set free the rural productive forces from the shackles of the feudal land ownership system of the landlord class in order to develop agricultural production and thus pave the way for New China's industrialization." [9]

In its terms and in its application the policy formulated in the Agrarian Reform Law represented a move from the Kiangsi Soviet period policy to that followed in the Yenan period. "Private ownership was permitted. The landlords and rich peasants were not liquidated nor were their total holdings redistributed." Landlordism as a "feudal remnant" was, however, no longer tolerated.

The emphasis was shifted from agrarian reform, through such measures as land redistribution and rent and tax adjustments, toward socialization or organization of agricultural production after 1952. As Mr. Tang points out:

[9] Quoted in TANG, *op. cit.,* p. 267.

. . . the agrarian reform served a double purpose. Politically it was a transitional measure paving the way for collectivization, with the greater political reliability offered by the latter. Economically, it was to provide an increase in agricultural production. Both of these purposes were essential to the early socialist industrialization of the country. [10]

While essential in the struggle for power and a necessary step forward in the move toward creation of the Socialist state, the agrarian reform program was based on acceptance of the institution of private property. Indications of an intention to move from this base of private ownership in land and toleration of class distinctions in the countryside as rapidly as circumstances permitted were given in the active promotion of coöperative movements and societies after 1950. By 1953 continued reform under the terms of the Agrarian Reform Law was replaced by a program of large-scale collectivization through state-organized producer coöperatives, developed into collective farms, and the establishment of state farms.

In the development and application of agricultural policy, the Chinese Communist program was derived from that put into effect earlier in the Soviet Union, although the initial emphases were somewhat different and circumstances dictated less drastic and ruthless procedures.

Progress toward socialization of the countryside was, however, more rapid than the Communist leadership itself had apparently anticipated. It was characterized by Mao Tse-tung in 1955 as "the surging tide of socialism in China's countryside." The situation, as described by Mao, was that:

In the second half of 1955 the situation in China has gone through substantial change. By the end of December, 1955, over 60 per cent of the 110 million peasant households—i.e., over 70 million households—have already responded to the call of the CC of the CPC and joined the agricultural producers' coöperatives of the semi-socialist type. . . . This is really an outstanding event. It tells us that in the course of the year 1956 alone, the stage of semi-socialist agricultural coöperation can be in the main achieved. And in the subsequent three or four years—i.e., by 1959 or 1960—the transformation from semi-socialist to full socialist coöperatives can be in the main achieved. [11]

Subsequently it was estimated by the party that 1958 would see achieved "the full socialist stage of collectivization" through the organization of agricultural production in coöperatives.

Not so much progress, however, was made with the establishment of collective and state farms. By 1956 some 29,000 Soviet-type collectives had been organized, mainly in Manchuria. By the end of 1953 it was reported that some 2,340 state farms, 59 of them mechanized, had been established.

[10] *Ibid.*, p. 271.
[11] *Ibid.*, p. 277.

The major drive for the establishment of state farms was not to be undertaken until the period of the second and third Five Year Plans.

In the spring of 1958, however, the government moved to organize agriculture in communes. These were planned as basic units of the Chinese society. By the end of 1958, it was reported that some 500 million peasants had been organized in 24,000 "people's communes," each containing upwards of 20,000 members. The men, and also the women, of the countryside were thus regimented in political and social units organized along essentially military lines for the purpose of increasing agricultural production so as to yield a surplus for state purposes, and also in order to attain the goal of rapid establishment of the Communist state. This undertaking was in advance of the stage of application of Communist theory that had been reached even in the U.S.S.R. and consequently raised questions in the less "advanced" Communist states.

5. INDUSTRIALIZATION AND SOCIALIZATION

Agrarian reform was undertaken in response to a popular demand and was necessary to improve the "people's livelihood." The Communist Party's agricultural program, however, was directed toward the realization of other state purposes than the improvement of the economic position of the peasant as an individual. While the Communist Party came into power in mainland China through the support of the peasantry rather than of urban workers, it had always viewed itself in orthodox Marxist terms as being a proletarian party. Its objective, consequently, was the creation of a proletarian (classless) society and state. Thus the new régime's emphasis actually was on industrialization rather than on the improvement of the lot of the peasantry in an agricultural society. This being the case, as the party approached power and even before the organization and proclamation of the People's Government, the center of gravity of party work had been shifted from the rural areas to the cities. The practical reason for this shift was that the approaching establishment of Communist Party control of mainland China faced the party leaders with the real problem of government. This involved the organization, administration, and development of the entire national economy in place of the least complicated, even though immediately the largest, segment of it. The land problem was only one among a number of economic problems which the new government would have to attempt to solve. Even that problem could not, in fact, be solved by the simple means of land redistribution and tax and rent reform advertised by the Communists as a solution in order to win peasant support. Thus while instituting an agrarian reform program, the new government had initially also to undertake action along lines previously planned by the Kuomintang itself. Action had to be undertaken to stabilize the monetary system and to rehabilitate, reconstruct, and extend the modern communications system, which the Communists themselves had done much to destroy. Conservation work along waterways also was resumed, and plans were made for the development of hydroelectric and other urban projects. Urban industrial production was emphasized as was an increase in agricultural production. The latter was essential as a means of financing the program of industrialization.

All these activities of the government were as necessary and legitimate within the non-Communist framework as in that of communism. Japan, for example, had gone through much the same development in the late nineteenth and early twentieth centuries, the government assisting in that case in the development of a capitalist economy. The ultimate purpose of the Chinese Communist Party in planning industrialization, however, was complete socialization and bureaucratic management of the national economy. It was this purpose rather than the desire to promote the welfare of the people which marked out the lines of development.

At the outset, expediency dictated that a large role be given to private capitalism. By 1952, however, the state had replaced the private capitalist in banking and foreign trade and had a dominant position in heavy industry, with domestic trade, as distinguished from production, and light industry remaining predominantly capitalistic. Propaganda (as in the 5 anti-campaigns of 1952) and regulation were designed to strengthen state controls over privately owned enterprise rather than to nationalize the remaining private sectors of the national economy.

By 1953 the new régime had sufficiently consolidated its power so that more rapid movement could be undertaken toward the ultimate goal. Thus, following the Russian procedure, the first of a series of Five Year Plans was instituted. The program, as forecast in 1953, was based upon the Leninist-Stalinist view, as applied to China, that industry must have a more important place in the national economy than agriculture. Thus a rise in the industrial proportion of the gross national income was planned from the 20 per cent of 1953 to "an additional goal" of 70 per cent. This was estimated to require, first of all, the full development of heavy industry. The program of development, from the point of view of method, had necessarily to be that "exemplified" by the Soviet Union (i.e., the "Socialist method") rather than any "capitalist" method. Following that method it was concluded that "it would be possible to achieve the general goal of industrialization within our generation, the age of Mao Tse-tung." [12]

The period of the first Five Year Plan was 1952–1957. The first half of

[12] See *ibid.*, pp. 291–323, for a discussion of the industrialization program. The quotations are from p. 291. The statement of the principles applied is taken from an editorial of May 22, 1953, in the *People's Daily.*

the period had elapsed, however, before plans had been sufficiently worked out so that a detailed blueprint could be presented to the National People's Congress for formal approval. Production goals, more or less abstractly designed initially, had to be revised to make them conform more closely to the attainable in the light of changing conditions, especially in relation to agricultural productivity, essential for meeting some of the costs of industrialization; and also on account of the state of China's foreign relations. These and other considerations, it was found, militated against setting goals for the increase of plant capacity and industrial productivity in terms of forecast needs. They had to be set (and revised) partly against the current state of productive capacity and skills. In other words, to some extent it was found expedient to set or revise goals in relation to what was being achieved rather than what the leaders felt should be attained. For example, "although the 1953 coal production exceeded the planned target by 9 per cent, the target itself was lowered twice during the year and finally set at 2 per cent less than the output of the previous year." [13]

These revisions of production goals downward were especially marked in the first half of the first period and may be viewed as justified because of the lack of experience of the planners and on account of new problems such as those resulting from the Korean War. After the plan was finally blueprinted for approval, revision of objectives downward while the plan was in process of execution had less theoretical and practical justification. From that point on, criticism could properly be shifted from the planners to those who, in industrial and agricultural production, failed to meet their production quotas. In many respects development fell short of what had been planned. Nevertheless considerable progress was made toward the industrialization of the country in the first decade of Communist control of China. Percentages of increase are, however, somewhat misleading as revealing the extent of progress made, since China started from a very low level of industrial development. The planned percentages show, for example, a 1000 per cent increase in production of locomotives in 1952–1957, and a 5000 per cent increase in production of railway passenger coaches. This, however, meant an increase in the former case from 20 to 200, and in the latter from 6 to 300. Such percentage increases, if realized, were significant in absolute terms but indicated that China had a long way to go to attain industrial strength comparable to that of West Germany, Britain, or Japan. The progress made, however, was very considerable as viewed through, for example, Indian or Indonesian eyes. Because of a similarity of conditions, Asian countries with agricultural economies, seeking a solution for their economic problem through industrialization, began to look to

[13] *Ibid.*, p. 300.

China as a model. To be sure, their leaders had to close their eyes to, or find excuses for, some of the methods used by Communist China, and to substitute a theoretical long-run advantage in relation to the improvement of the condition of the peasantry for the short-run failure of the People's Government actually to improve the "people's livelihood." One thing they could perceive was that China as a state had increased in power vis-à-vis other states and had been successful, as had Japan before it, in liquidating "Western imperialism."

6. THE RECOGNITION QUESTION—FOREIGN RELATIONS

The first state to recognize the People's Republic and to completely terminate relations with the National government was the Soviet Union, followed immediately by the Russian-dominated states of Eastern Europe. The United States not only failed to recognize the new régime after it replaced the National government in control of mainland China, but Washington used its influence against recognition by others and to prevent the transfer of China's seat in the United Nations from the National government's representatives to those of the People's Government. This, together with the Chinese Communist government's intervention in Korea and the consequent designation of the People's Government as an aggressor by the General Assembly of the United Nations, placed the recognition question in the context of the "cold war" after 1950. Before the North Korean aggression, however, seven non-Communist European states and six Asian states had extended recognition, assertedly following a *de facto* policy and thus not expressing approval or disapproval of the new régime. Beyond this, however, India especially expressed opposition to the American policy of non-recognition on the ground that it was interventionist, since it went counter to what the Indian government viewed as the expressed will of the Chinese people as to the nature and form of their own government. This view of American policy was widely disseminated throughout eastern Asia and was a factor in creating suspicion of United States' intentions among the newly independent states.

The Chinese Communists had already characterized the United States as interventionist and thus imperialist because of American support of the National government. The Communists thus sought successfully to capitalize on nationalism, which actually was a stronger force than communism in Chinese politics. The continued virulent anti-American campaigns conducted by the People's Government as expressive of their hostility to "American imperialism" also served to divert attention in China and elsewhere in Asia from consideration of China's relations with the Soviet Union.

7. LEANING-TO-ONE-SIDE POLICY

From the beginning, the Soviet Russian approach to China had been advertised as that of hostility to imperialism, identified with the special rights and privileges possessed by the "capitalist" Western states, including Czarist Russia, in China, as well as with the end-product of imperialism-colonialism in southeastern and southern Asia. By definition, then, capitalism and "bourgeois democracy" became identified with imperialism, and socialism and communism with anti-imperialism. The United States, consequently, as the leading postwar "capitalist" state, was cast inevitably in the role of the "imperialist" enemy, entirely apart from its failure to support the Chinese Communist Party against the National government. It also followed that the leading Communist state—the Soviet Union— would be viewed as the friend of China. This, at any rate, was the conclusion presented by Mao Tse-tung in June, 1949, three months before the proclamation of the People's Republic, in his important "leaning to one side" statement of policy. In his words:

. . . In order to attain victory and consolidate it, we must lean to one side. . . . The Chinese people must lean either to the side of imperialism or to that of Socialism. There can be no exception. There can be no sitting on the fence; there is no third path. Not only in China but throughout the world, one must lean either to imperialism or to Socialism. . . .
Internationally we belong to the side of the anti-imperialist front headed by the Soviet Union.

In application, this point of view led naturally to the signature of the Treaty of Friendship, Alliance and Mutual Assistance on February 14, 1950, which became effective with the exchange of ratifications on September 30, 1950. Although by its terms ostensibly directed against a renewal of Japanese aggression, given the existing circumstances of international politics, this treaty actually was designed to align Communist China with the Soviet Union against the United States. It thus ensured Russia against successful overtures on the part of Communist China to the United States for economic assistance. To further guard against this the two signatories agreed "to develop and consolidate economic and cultural ties between China and the Soviet Union, to render all possible economic assistance and to carry out necessary economic coöperation."

In execution of the latter provision the Soviet Union sent hordes of advisers and technicians into China to assist in the cultural consolidation of the new régime, and to help plan and put into effect the plans for economic development along Communist lines. Direct Soviet military and economic assistance was also given to Communist China, and this was important in increasing China's economic strength and military power.

While not extensive, as measured by need, it was sufficient to enable Chinese Communist leaders to comment favorably on it. Thus Mao Tse-tung and Chou En-lai, in a telegram to Malenkov and Molotov after the death of Stalin, acknowledged "the fraternal aid rendered by the Soviet Union to the Chinese people," characterizing it as "an important factor in the rapid rehabilitation of China's economy and its development along the lines of planned construction." [14]

The commitment of China to the Soviet Union inevitably produced a degree of economic dependence on that country as the only available source of economic assistance on a credit basis. This dependence was expressed in trade as well as aid terms, for, following the definition of China as an aggressor in the Korean War, prohibitions of trade in critical and strategic commodities were applied. This was done because of American insistence. There was constant pressure on the United States from some of its allies, notably Britain and Japan, to relax these trade restrictions after the Korean armistice, but it was not until after 1957 that modification of the items on the embargoed list was begun. The result of the prohibitions was to confine China's trade substantially to the Soviet Union and the states in the Soviet orbit. Exports to China from the West dropped from U.S. $314 million during the first half of 1951 to about $130 million in the second half of that year. In percentages the decline in trade with the West was from 74 per cent in 1950 to about 20 per cent in 1954, a position maintained thereafter. This percentage decline was, according to Communist official reports, of a steadily increasing volume of foreign trade, which enhanced the pressure on the United States of those who sought an opportunity to compete in the China market. It also lent weight to the argument that it was only by giving Communist China access to the markets of the West that China could be detached from the Soviet Union.

Nevertheless, at the end of the first decade of Communist control of China, four-fifths of mainland China's external trade was with the Soviet Union and the so-called "people's democracies" in Eastern Europe. Despite this economic dependence, however, the Soviet Union did not presume to dictate the lines of development for China as if the latter were a Soviet satellite. On the contrary, agreement was reached at the time of conclusion of the Treaty of Friendship on a readjustment of the Russian position in Manchuria along lines favorable to Peking. The readjustments stipulated with respect to Manchurian railways, for example, were made as promised by the end of 1952. Similar readjustments of relationship in Sinkiang province in China's favor had been made by the end of the first decade of life of the People's Republic. In these respects, as well as in the careful behavior of Russian advisers and technicians in China, and in the emphases on the

---

[14] Tang, *op. cit.*, p. 410, citing *Pravda*.

program of cultural exchanges, the Soviet Union indicated acceptance of the Chinese conception of the relationship as that of alliance rather than one of subordination. In the Communist world China accepted Russian leadership as natural and inevitable but asserted for itself a position of "associate" leadership. With respect to the non-Communist world, since the two states reasoned from the same premises they tended to come to similar conclusions. But while this was so, it was also true that in the approach to specific situations there was a division of leadership responsibilities. In Far Eastern situations, increasingly as time went on, the U.S.S.R. played the supporting role to China while China continued to play a generally supporting role to the U.S.S.R. in European and Middle Eastern politics.

Thus it was Peking rather than Moscow which, because of its position and interests, called the tune for that side in the Korean armistice negotiations and in the negotiation of the Indo-Chinese armistice. In the post-armistice attempts to find a political solution for the Korean question at and following the Geneva Conference of 1954, the leading role was played by the Chinese and not by the Russians. On the other hand, China supported the Russian position on the Hungarian question and in relation to other issues involving the freedom of action of the Eastern European Communist states.

The Peking government also naturally took the side of the U.S.S.R. against the United States on general questions arising in international relations, such as that of nuclear and conventional arms limitation, on the need for a summit conference to seek a solution of such questions, and with respect to issues arising in the Middle East. But in these matters, as well as with respect to ideological issues arising within the so-called "Communist camp," the Chinese Communist government did not permit the Russians to act on the assumption that any policy advanced would be automatically endorsed by Peking. That China exercised an influence on the U.S.S.R. was revealed when shifts were made in Russian policy following the August, 1958, conversations of Mao and Khrushchev at Peking. What was shown at that time was a similar relationship to that existing between, for example, Britain and the United States at the time of and following the Suez and Middle East crisis. Beyond this, 1958 revealed the ability of the U.S.S.R. and China to plan the timing of actions undertaken in the European, Middle Eastern, and Far Eastern areas so as to assist one another against a common enemy. Thus when the necessity arose to divert attention from the Eastern European and Middle Eastern areas the Chinese, shortly after the August conference, resumed their offensive against the National government with an artillery barrage directed against the off-shore islands, Quemoy and Matsu, with vigorous Russian propagandistic support. The actual target of both the Russians and the Chinese Communists was, of course, the United States.

Neither state accepted the Japanese peace treaty, which, however, Peking was not asked to sign. Subsequently the Soviet Union "normalized" its relations with Japan while Peking was unable to do so, although a major foreign policy objective of the People's Government was to reëstablish on satisfactory terms economic relations with Japan either with or without formal recognition.

Recognition by Japan was to a large degree dependent upon the attitude of the United States toward the Chinese Communist régime. The unwillingness of the United States to recognize Peking had been strengthened by the Chinese intervention in the Korean War and the acceptance by the United Nations of that intervention as an act of aggression. The Chinese intervention in the Korean War, furthermore, produced commitment, previously avoided, of the United States to the National government on Formosa. These commitments, in turn, made more difficult any change in the American policy of non-recognition of the People's Government. Consequently, a number of questions of relationship in the Far East could only be answered in relation to Korea, to which country we must now turn our attention.

REFERENCES FOR FURTHER STUDY

AMERICAN CONSULATE GENERAL, Hongkong, *Survey of the China Mainland Press,* 1950–; *Current Background Series,* 1950–; *Review of the Hongkong Chinese Press.* HOWARD L. BOORMAN, *Moscow-Peking Axis: Strength and Strains* (1957). CONRAD BRANDT, BENJAMIN SCHWARTZ, and JOHN K. FAIRBANK, *Documentary History of Chinese Communism* (1953); commentary, as well as documents; worth consulting, *especially for pre-1949 period.* JAMES CAMERON, *Mandarin Red* (1955). TIEN-FONG CHENG, *History of Sino-Russian Relations* (1957); a useful study. China Treaties, etc., 1950, *Sino-Soviet Treaty and Agreements,* signed in Moscow on Feb. 14, 1950 (Peking, 1950). BOYD COMPTON, *Mao's China: Party Reform Documents, 1942–49* (Seattle, 1952). ROBERT S. ELEGANT, *China's Red Masters: Political Biographies of the Chinese Communist Leaders* (1951). RONALD HSIA, *Price Control in Communist China* (1953). EDWARD HUNTER, *Brainwashing in Red China* (1951). MALCOLM D. KENNEDY, *A History of Communism in East Asia* (1957). OWEN LATTIMORE, *Pivot of Asia, Sinkiang and the Inner Asian Frontiers of China and Russia* (1950). TIEH-TSENG LI, *Historical Status of Tibet* (1955). SHAW-TONG LIU, *Out of Red China* (1953). MAO TSE-TUNG, *China's New Democracy* (1945); an important exposition. MAO TSE-TUNG, *Selected Works* (New York, 1954). FRANCIS ROBERT MORAES, *Report on Mao's China* (1953). ROBERT C. NORTH, *Moscow and Chinese Communists* (Stanford, 1953). KAVALAM M. PANIKKAR, *In Two Chinas, Memoirs of a Diplomat* (1955). P. S. R. PAYNE, *Mao Tse-tung, Ruler of Red China* (1950). MAX W. PERLEBERG, *Who's Who in Modern China* (1953). FRED W. RIGGS, *The Economics of Red China* (Foreign Policy Association, 1951); *Red China's Fighting Hordes* (1951). W. W. ROSTOW, *The Prospects for Communist China* (1954); a good appraisal. B. Schwartz, *Chinese Communism and the Rise of Mao* (1951); a good ideological study. Agnes Smedley, *The Great Road: The Life and Times of Chu Teh* (1956). Gunther Stein, *The Challenge of Red China* (1945). H. Arthur Steiner (ed.), *Report on China* (American Academy of Political and Social Science, November, 1951); a number of articles are excellent as of the time of writing. Ching-ling (Soong) Sun, *The Struggle for New China* (Peking, 1952). Peter S. H. Tang, *Communist China Today: Domestic and Foreign Policies* (1957); a careful analysis. S. B. Thomas, *Government and Administration in Communist China* (Institute of Pacific Relations, 1953); *Recent Political and Economic Developments in China* (Institute of Pacific Relations, 1950). Richard S. Walker, *China Under Communism: the First Five Years* (1955). Henry Wei, *China and Soviet Russia* (1956); the first half of the book covers the period 1917–1945. Yuan Li-wu, *Economic Survey of Communist China* (1956).

CHAPTER XXIX

THE POSTWAR KOREAN PROBLEM

1. KOREA UNDER JAPAN

THE TRIANGULAR STRUGGLE between China, Russia, and Japan for control of Korea had been resolved decisively in favor of Japan as a consequence of the Russo-Japanese war, which set the stage for the annexation of Korea in 1910. Between 1910 and the outbreak of World War II Japan had exercised its power in its colony with an eye to the interest of the metropolitan country. Korea had been developed economically to serve the interests and meet the needs of Japan and the Japanese with only incidental concern for the interests and needs of the Korean people. The Koreans were exploited economically and kept in a position of political subjection. They were not permitted to secure experience in governmental administration, nor were they permitted participation in the management of the economy of the country. With a view to securing acquiescence in Japanese rule, a policy designed to bring about a loss of the Korean people's cultural identity was also instituted. The Japanese language was substituted for the Korean wherever possible. The Korean literature was suppressed, as were Korean publications. Japanese in Korea were favored, as against Koreans, in the educational system, with the Japanese 2 per cent of the population being given half the funds allotted for elementary education. The emphasis in the schools was directed toward making the Koreans good and loyal subjects of Japan through cultural indoctrination. On the economic side, the policy was enforced of expropriation and sale, mostly to Japanese settlers, of a large part of the public lands which had been of common use to the people. In addition, much of the best privately owned property came into Japanese hands through forced sales, in consequence of which people whose lands had been taken migrated to Manchuria and beyond.

In the 1930's, as military planning for the exploitation of Manchurian resources became possible, Korea began to be developed in relation to the Japanese position in Manchuria, as well as in direct relationship to the developing war economy of Japan itself. Emphasis began to be put on the development of hydroelectric power, on mineral exploitation, and on the creation of plant capacity in Korea itself for the processing of the mineral resources of the country. Thus the northern Korean area south of the Yalu River was given importance in relation to Manchuria as well as assuming a new importance in the Korean economy. This development was accentuated during World War II.

The policies followed by Japan in its Korean colony naturally provoked hostility and resistance, as was revealed in 1919, when the Koreans engaged in widespread passive resistance and at the same time appealed to the Paris Peace Conference for relief. This revolt was ruthlessly suppressed by Japan. Suppression was followed by conciliation in the form of some immediate modifications in the policies being followed, but not to the point of making it possible for a Korean nationalist leadership to maintain itself within the colony. Those who were leaders of the revolt in 1919 enlarged the number of Koreans in exile, furnishing political leadership to those who had emigrated for economic reasons. The emigré Koreans were to be found in numbers in Manchuria and China, in the Russian Far East, and in the United States. Over-seas Koreans were viewed by Japan as its nationals and, as circumstances permitted, utilized as such. Those in exile who sought to exercise leadership in the direction of independence were, of course, severely circumscribed in their contacts with the people in Korea. Thus at the time of the outbreak of World War II, Japan's position in Korea seemed secured against the possibilities of domestic revolt. That war, however, revived and stimulated Korean nationalism by holding out the prospect, if Japan should be defeated, of the reëstablishment of independence. This prospect was described formally as an Allied war objective in the Cairo Declaration of December 1, 1943, subscribed to by Britain, China, and the United States. The objective, as then defined, was accepted subsequently (at the Yalta Conference) by the Soviet Union. It was, however, a commitment to establish a free and independent Korea "in due course" rather than immediately upon the Japanese surrender since, as Secretary of State James F. Byrnes put it, "there was some question whether the (Korean) people were sufficiently trained to assume the responsibilities of government immediately." [1]

By the time of the Japanese surrender, aside from the Koreans themselves, only the United States and the U.S.S.R. were in a position effectively to give meaning to the policy of Korean independence "in due course." They seemed then to be prepared initially to establish a four-power "trustee" supervision of the government of an otherwise independent Korea for such a limited period of time as was required to bring about the orderly creation of a new government, to which complete responsibility could be transferred. But they also agreed on a division of the country into two zones for the military purpose of effecting quickly the surrender of the Japanese forces and the repatriation both of troops and of civilian Japanese. This military decision, apparently taken without agreement to ensure that it would have

[1] JAMES F. BYRNES, *Speaking Frankly* (1947), p. 221.

no political consequences, "provided that Japanese troops north of the 38th parallel should surrender to the Soviet forces and that those south of the 38th parallel should surrender to United States forces." [2] Thus northern Korea came into Russian and southern Korea into American military occupation immediately at the end of the war.

2. TWO ZONES MAINTAINED

Whatever the initial intentions of the two occupying states, this division of Korea was continued for political purposes after the military reasons for its institution had ceased to exist. The Soviet and American commands found it impossible to reach an agreement on the conditions even of local intercourse between the two zones. The broader question was consequently taken up at the Moscow Conference of Foreign Ministers (December, 1945). The agreement then concluded provided for the establishment of a provisional Korean democratic government for the entire country. This provisional government was to be brought into being by a Joint Commission, to be set up on the basis of recommendations made to the Four Powers by the United States and Soviet commands in Korea, "in consultation with Korean democratic parties and social organizations." The Joint Commission and the provisional government, after its institution, were then to submit proposals to the Four Powers, on the basis of which "a Four Power trusteeship agreement for a period of up to five years" would be worked out.

The attempt made in January and February, 1946, in a joint conference of the two commands to agree on the administrative and economic unification of the two zones, through a modification of the barriers which had been erected, proved unsuccessful. Similarly, attempts during 1946 of the Joint Commission which was established in March, 1946, to agree on the conditions of consultation with Korean parties, and on the terms of institution of a provisional government for all of Korea, were a failure. There had been a widespread adverse reaction by all of the Korean parties, except the Communist, to the idea of trusteeship as formulated at Moscow, since the general Korean demand was for independence. The Soviet members of the Joint Commission held that only those parties should be consulted which had shown a willingness to accept fully and freely the Moscow decisions. The American members were not willing to accept this view, which would have restricted consultation to the Communist minority of the Korean people. The same impasse was reached when the Joint Commission resumed its sessions in May, 1947. After the Soviet government had rejected an American proposal of August 26, 1947, which was accepted by Britain and China, that "the four powers adhering to the Moscow Agree-

[2] *Korea, 1945–1948,* Dept. of State, Pub. 3305, Far Eastern Series No. 28, p. 3.

ment meet to consider how that agreement may be speedily carried out," the United States took the question of Korean independence to the United Nations, bringing it before the second regular session of the General Assembly. At that time, through its representatives on the Joint Commission, and subsequently in the General Assembly, the Soviet government proposed the simultaneous withdrawal of the military forces of the occupying powers, thus letting the Koreans organize their own government without outside assistance. This proposal was not acceptable to the United States, which apparently felt that such action would lead to an extension from the northern zone of Communist, and thus Soviet, control over the southern zone. It was also rejected by the General Assembly.

3. THE SOVIET ZONE

The Soviet authorities had moved much more rapidly and effectively than had the Americans to organize their zone.

The Japanese administration, including Korean collaborators, was promptly ousted and in its place was established a newly organized hierarchy of "Peoples' Committees" composed of Korean laborers, farmers and political organizers, with top control exercised by the Russian command. On February 9, 1946, a Provisional Peoples' Committee for North Korea was established as the central governing organ, and the various political parties (Communist, Democratic and Independence) were united in a single New People's Party. An all-Korean "Cabinet" was formed, headed by Kim Il-sung, a well known Korean revolutionist and Communist. No military government administration was established by the Russians, although the Soviet command and the political officers attached to it maintained a close watch over their Korean proteges. [3]

Elections were held in the Soviet zone in November, 1946. These resulted "in a sweeping endorsement of candidates chosen by the single party." Thus the Russians had rapidly created a Korean mechanism of government which, it could be anticipated, would readily respond to their direction, even after the withdrawal of their military forces.

The Russians also quickly dispossessed the Japanese of title to land, distributing their holdings among Koreans. The same policy of redistribution was followed with respect to the larger Korean holdings. Similarly, they sought to revive the industrial production of their area, under Korean rather than Japanese auspices. All of this, as well as the actions taken in the field of government, had the effect of emphasizing Russian occupation as bringing about liberation from the Japanese. It was consequently only as the significance of one-party rule, with a controlled press and a denial of freedom of expression, became evident that the Soviet liberation of their zone seemed to the Korean people less beneficial than the American. This

[3] GEORGE M. McCUNE, "Korea: The First Year of Liberation," *Pacific Affairs*, March, 1947, p. 8.

in turn tended to restore an initial antagonism created by the behavior of the Russian force of a quarter of a million men. There was not only the requisitioning of food and other supplies for this large army but also considerable looting by the troops.

✕ 4. THE AMERICAN ZONE

In the American zone liberation from the Japanese proceeded more slowly than in the Russian, and without the same immediate appearance of transfer of authority to the Koreans themselves on a democratic basis. The Japanese administration was maintained during the first months of liberation, although it was subordinated to the American military command under General John R. Hodge. During January, 1946, authority was transferred to the United States Military Government, under which Koreans came to participate progressively during 1946 in the administrative side of the government. Those upon whom reliance was immediately placed by the Americans were the wealthier Koreans, and especially those who could speak English or Japanese. In this group were included, as time went on, those who, in exile, had professed to speak in the name of the Korean people, and who were brought back from exile in China and the United States to play leading roles in the establishment "in due course" of an independent Korea. While control of policy was retained by Military Government officials, an advisory Council was formed in February, 1946. The method of its constitution, however, gave it such a conservative tone that the leading liberals refused to participate. It was replaced in November by an Interim Legislative Assembly, half of whose members were selected by a system of indirect elections, the other half being appointed by the Military Government.

Before election day, the Communist Party and other leftist elements attacked the election plans and called upon the Korean people to oppose them. South Korea was swept by pre-election strikes, riots, and open rebellion. . . . Leftist elements accused the military government of suppressing all but conservative activity in a reign of terror, while the American command announced that the agitation was a communist plot. A sweeping conservative victory took place at the polls in the midst of this confusion, but even the middle-of-the-road Korean leaders declared the elections to have been fraudulent. [4]

One of the reasons for the confusion was the rapidity with which the way had been opened to the organization of the many political parties which, with freedom of expression and of organization such as the Americans introduced into a country accustomed only to repression, sprang up wholesale around individual leaders. The disorderly and terroristic methods used by the leaders and parties of the right as well as the left were partly the result

---

[4] *Ibid.*, p. 7.

of inexperience with democratic methods and partly a carry-over from past experience under a repressive régime. Under the circumstances, responsibility rested with the Military Government rather than with the Koreans, since it alone had the power to enforce more regular procedures. In any case, the outcome was to associate the anti-Communist and conservative Koreans with government in the southern zone while the reverse was occurring in the north. Internal differences consequently helped to reënforce that division which had been instituted first for military reasons and then maintained because of the growing inability of the Russians and the Americans to agree on the conditions of unification.

5. THE REPUBLIC OF KOREA ESTABLISHED

It was in the face of this division and disagreement that the United States took the Korean question to the United Nations General Assembly. That body, by resolution of November 14, 1947, held that elected representatives of the Korean people should take part in the consideration of the question. To ensure that those representatives should be "in fact duly elected by the Korean people and not mere appointees by military authorities in Korea," a United Nations Temporary Commission on Korea was established "to be present in Korea, with right to travel, observe and consult throughout Korea." The resolution was adopted over the objections of the Soviet Union whose representatives, however, abstained from voting. Because of the Soviet attitude, the Temporary Commission was not admitted to the northern zone in Korea. It was decided, however, to go ahead with the elections in those parts of Korea where the Commission could observe them. Elections were consequently held in the American zone on May 10, 1948. The Commission "Having satisfied itself that the electoral procedures which it recommended had on the whole been correctly applied," in its resolution of June 25 recorded "its opinion that the results of 10 May 1948 are a valid expression of the free will of the electorate in those parts of Korea which were accessible to the Commission and in which the inhabitants constituted approximately two-thirds of the people of all Korea." [5] Those thus elected made up the first Congress of the Republic of Korea, with which the Temporary Commission then carried on consultations with a view to bringing into being a Korean government to which authority could be transferred by the military régimes of the occupying powers. A constitution was adopted on July 12. This constitution provided for a division of the powers of government among: a President, with wide executive powers, in the exercise of which, so far as policy matters were concerned, he had the advice of a Council of State; a National Assembly, to exercise the legisla-

[5] *Year Book of the United Nations*, 1947–48, p. 303. Successive issues of this Year Book summarize accurately developments in their U.N. aspects.

tive power, subject to a suspensive Presidential veto; a Supreme Court, and lower courts to be constituted by law, to exercise the judicial power, and with "jurisdiction to decide finally whether administrative orders and regulations, and dispositions, are consistent with the Constitution and the law"; and executive departments "appointed by the President from among the Ministers. The Prime Minister (appointed by the President with the consent of the National Assembly) shall, under the orders of the President, control and supervise the heads of the departments; he shall take charge of administrative affairs not assigned to any particular department." In addition, the constitution contained a chapter setting forth the rights and duties of citizens, a chapter on economy, one on finance, and one on local autonomous organizations. Provision was made for amendment of the constitution by two-thirds majority of the National Assembly, on proposal of the President or one-third of the members of the Assembly. In addition to its legislative powers, the Assembly, whose members were to serve for four-year terms (except that the first, essentially constituent, National Assembly was to continue for a period of two years before new elections would be held), exercised a measure of power over the President by virtue of its constitutional right to elect the President and Vice-President for four-year terms, and to remove them by impeachment proceedings.

The National Assembly selected Dr. Syngman Rhee as the first President of the Republic and, under his guidance, proceeded to set up the new government. Negotiations were begun in August, 1948, between it and the American military authorities to transfer governmental functions. This was viewed as appropriate since the American authorities, pending consideration by the General Assembly of the United Nations, found the new government "entitled to be regarded as the Government of Korea, envisaged by the General Assembly Resolution of November 14, 1947."

The General Assembly, after consideration of the Report of its Temporary Commission, accepted the Commission's conclusions. Consequently it declared, in the Resolution adopted on December 12, 1948,

that there has been established a lawful government (the Government of the Republic of Korea), having effective control and jurisdiction over that part of Korea where the Temporary Commission was able to observe and consult and in which the great majority of the people of all Korea reside; that this government is based on elections which were a valid expression of the free will of the electorate of that part of Korea and which were observed by the Temporary Mixed Commission; *and that this is the only such Government in Korea.* [6]

Following this action, the United States, China, the Philippines, Britain, and other countries following American leadership in the United Nations,

[6] General Assembly, *Official Records*, 4th Session, Supplement No. 9, U.N. Doc. A1936, p. 3. My italics.

extended *de jure* recognition to the new government as that of the Republic of Korea. [7]

Since the overtures made to the Koreans in the Soviet zone to elect representatives to the National Assembly and thus actually unite the peninsula under the one government were rejected, the country continued to be divided. The new constitution, however, was designed to prevent the perpetuation of this division, since it described the territories of the Democratic Republic as the Korean peninsula and its accessory islands. [8] The actual authority of the government of the Republic, nevertheless, extended only over upwards of 20 million of the total population of about 30 million, and over an area of 37,055 square miles, in contrast with the 48,191 square miles of the Russian zone.

6. NORTH KOREA

In their zone the Russians had devolved authority by 1948 on a "Peoples' " government unified under the control of a Korean Communist Party, which in turn took its direction from the Russians. The authority of this régime was supported by an army with an estimated strength, as of 1947, of 120,000 to 150,000 men, [9] trained, equipped, and indoctrinated by the Russians. This force was sufficient to impose the decisions of the North Korean government on the people in the northern zone. It was also estimated to be strong enough to deal single-handed with the Republic of Korea, if the latter were left to its own resources, since the organized military power of the Republic was represented by a constabulary force of some 26,000 men in 1947. Thus, as measured by a military yardstick, North Korea, without the assistance of the U.S.S.R., was stronger than the Republic of Korea, without the military support of the United States. If the two parts of the country were left to their own devices in seeking unification, which all Koreans desired, it could be more readily imposed from the north than from the south. Consequently the U.S.S.R. could propose the evacuation of all foreign troops from Korea without fear of loss of its own influence in Korea, as an alternative to the American proposal to leave the solution to the United Nations. Simultaneous evacuation, as of 1947, was unacceptable to the United States because it would change the power situation in Korea in favor of the Russians. Nevertheless, without agreement, the Soviet government announced on September 20, 1948, that its troops would all be withdrawn from Korea by January 1, 1949. The United States followed suit six months later, except for personnel left to operate the airport in Seoul and for a

[7] The Soviet group of states, however, continued to support the northern régime after this time.

[8] Furthermore, a proportionate number of seats in the Assembly (100) was set aside to be filled whenever "free" elections should be held in the northern zone.

[9] Some estimates of the size of the North Korean army ran as high as 500,000 men.

Military Advisory Group, with an authorized strength of 500 officers and men, which was established for the purpose of training a Korean constabulary and army. This undertaking had been carried to the point where, by June, 1950, it was asserted that the South Korean army had the capability of defense of the Republic against attack from the north, although without sufficient power to enable the country to be unified from the south by military means. If this were the case, it could be assumed that unification would not take place except as a result of negotiation and that that would be confined to agreement on conditions of application of the United Nations formula of supervised elections. Unless the negotiations were so confined, even assuming relative equality of defensive capacity, the advantage in negotiation would tend to rest with the North Korean régime, since it was organized as a single-party régime facing no effective domestic opposition. The South Korean régime and the parties supporting it had to face serious opposition and probable differences of opinion as to the conditions of political and economic unification. These political differences, which could be exploited in their own interest by the Communists in direct negotiation, had prevented the development of a complete concensus in support of the new Republican government. Thus its authority had, by 1950, not been as completely consolidated in the south as had that of the "Peoples'" government in the north.

The Korean Republic, furthermore, had not yet become a going concern economically. The southern area, in the years from 1945 to 1950, had received some $376 million from the United States for civilian relief and an additional $120 million of Economic Coöperation Administration (E.C.A.) aid. The latter had been used to increase coal production necessary for industrial development as well as for fuel purposes; to finance power projects; and to increase agricultural productivity. Much, however, remained to be done before the Republic would be in a sound economic position. And further internal development was dependent on continuing foreign economic assistance.

The internal political conflicts growing out of personal rivalries for power, however, lessened enthusiasm in the United States for the régime which it had sponsored. Consequently the Congress of the United States first rejected the administration's proposal of a second installment of E.C.A. aid for Korea, and then approved an aid bill of $60 million, 30 million less than had been requested. Thus as the United States terminated its military occupation in Korea, it began to show a reluctance to continue to discharge economic responsibilities.

In some respects the American reactions to the situation in Korea were a reflection of the reaction to the failure of the Kuomintang government to maintain itself against the Communists in China. At any rate, in the general reorientation of policy put under way in 1949, the outer perimeter of American military defense was defined on January 12, 1950, in terms apparently excluding Korea. The new Republic, consequently, seemed to be left to find its own security in the event of an attempt by the North Korea government to extend its authority southward by military means, except as the South Koreans were able to rely on United Nations action to maintain peace and security and to prevent aggression. The United Nations, however, had not yet shown its willingness nor demonstrated its ability to act to maintain peace and security.

7. THE KOREAN WAR

During 1948 and 1949 there had been recurrent incidents in the form of attack and counter-attack across the parallel separating North from South Korea. These probing operations revealed the North Korean troops to be well-trained and well-equipped. "Their direction and equipment were mainly derived from the Soviet Union, and Soviet officers were reported in 1948 and 1949, to be in control down into the lowest echelons." [10] These border pressures were intensified in the spring of 1950. Fearing attack the South Korean government requested further American military assistance. Because of the verbal bellicosity of the Syngman Rhee government, it was apparently felt in Washington that that government was actually seeking to augment its own power so as to enable it to overcome mounting internal opposition and even possibly itself to undertake unification by military means. As it turned out, of course, this view was incorrect. The feared attack in force across the 38th parallel was actually launched on June 25, 1950.

The first phase of the war, in which the defensive capabilities of South Korea were tested, revealed clearly the soundness of the conclusion stated above that the North Koreans possessed a decisive military superiority over South Korea. By June 30, although given initial American air and naval support, South Korean resistance was collapsing. At this point President Truman authorized the use of American ground forces in Korea, and the air force was authorized to bomb North Korean targets. These actions were undertaken in implementation of the Security Council Resolution of June 25.

When, on the evening of June 24, the American Ambassador at Seoul reported the invasion of South Korea, the United States immediately took the question to the United Nations, requesting a meeting of the Security Council the next day. At this meeting a "cease-fire" resolution proposed by

[10] SHANNON McCUNE, "Korea," in L. K. ROSSINGER and Associates, *The State of Asia* (1951), p. 151.

the United States was adopted by a vote of 9–0, with the U.S.S.R.[11] absent and Yugoslavia abstaining. Under this Resolution the North Korean authorities were called upon (1) to cease hostilities immediately and (2) to withdraw their armed forces to the 38th parallel. The United Nations Commission on Korea was requested to observe the withdrawal and to keep the Security Council informed on the execution of this Resolution. And, at the same time, the Security Council called upon members of the United Nations "to render every assistance to the United Nations in the execution of this resolution and to refrain from giving assistance to the North Korean authorities."[12] Instead of retiring to the parallel in compliance with this Resolution, the North Koreans extended operations with a view to presenting the United States and the United Nations with the accomplished fact of unification of Korea under the authority of the northern government.

A third Resolution of the Security Council, adopted on July 7, with the Soviet Union still absent, instituted the United Nations Command in Korea and requested the United States to designate a commander-in-chief for the United Nations force. President Truman immediately designated General of the Army Douglas MacArthur as Commanding General of the United Nations forces in Korea, leaving him concurrently Supreme Commander for the Allied Powers in Japan and Commander-in-chief of United States Forces in the Far East.

In the fulfillment of its obligations as a member of the United Nations, consequently, the United States found itself, by its own decision, and as the result of its own initiatives, back in the position in relation to Korea from which it had asserted its intention to withdraw at the end of 1949. While such states as Britain, Canada, the Philippines, and Turkey contributed to the United Nations force in Korea, the main forces, as well as the command, came from the United States until after the reorganization, reëquipment, and expansion of the Republic of Korea (ROK) military forces was accomplished under American direction and with American assistance. It was the United States which also assumed the largest share of the burden of non-military economic assistance. Thus it became somewhat difficult for the United States to distinguish between the war as its own affair, and the war as a United Nations operation, from the point of view of determination of purposes and objectives as well as the appropriate means of realizing them.

[11] The U.S.S.R. had refused to participate in the sessions of the Security Council because of the continued filling of China's seat by the delegate appointed by the National government rather than by a Chinese Communist government representative. Russian participation was resumed only in August.

[12] From *United States Policy in the Korean Crisis*, Dept. of State, Office of Public Affairs (1950), Pub. 3922, Far Eastern Series No. 34.

The Soviet Union had not accepted the original United Nations decisions as to the method of establishing unity. Relationships were such that the conclusion is warranted that there was a Russian responsibility for the refusal of the North Korean régime to permit the holding of U.N. supervised elections in North Korea. Those relationships, in the absence of evidence to the contrary, support the conclusion that the North Korean attack across the 38th parallel, if not instigated by the Soviet Union, was not disapproved by it. And, as was made clear officially subsequently, if the Soviet Union had attended the June and July meetings of the Security Council its representative would not have concurred in the resolutions proposed by the United States, and consequently no decisions could have been taken. No further decisions, in fact, were taken by the Security Council after the Soviet Union resumed its seat in August. By that time the Russians had taken the position, on the merits, that "the events taking place in Korea were provoked by an attack by forces of the South Korean authorities on border regions of North Korea." Therefore the North Korean attack was defensive and could not properly be viewed as an act of aggression. As to the Security Council resolutions, the Russians held them to be invalid because passed without concurring votes of the Soviet Union and China, since in the latter case, the National government representative, Dr. Tingfu F. Tsiang, had "no legal right to represent China." Thus the view of the Soviet Union was that "the said resolution(s) of the Security Council on the Korean question has no legal force." The Soviet Union consequently viewed itself as "legally free to give such assistance to North Korea as it saw fit." [13]

On this question of legality, the position taken by the United States was that abstention from attendance at Security Council meetings was in itself a violation of the Charter. In any case its legal effect was similar to that of abstention in the voting. This had occurred in the past and had not been construed by the Russians themselves as a non-concurring vote and thus a veto.

This American view prevailed among the members of the United Nations, except for the members of the Soviet bloc, and action was planned and executed within the framework of the resolutions of June 27 and July 7. Since, however, the resumption of his seat by the Soviet representative made it certain that there would be no further action taken by the Security Council, the problem was transferred from that organ to the General Assembly when it convened on September 19.

By that time the military position had begun to be reversed. With the

[13] These views were expressed and elaborated in notes to the United States and to the Secretary-General of the U.N. For texts, see *U.S. Policy in the Korean Crisis,* Doc. 44; U.N. Doc. S/1517, 1596.

apparent possibility of a victory over the North Korean forces, consequently, the General Assembly, in its Resolution of October 7, 1950, extended the objective from that of repelling aggression to that of accomplishment of the original purpose of establishment of a unified Korean state. Thus it recommended:

(A) That all appropriate steps be taken to ensure conditions of stability throughout Korea.

(B) That all constituent acts be taken, including the holding of elections, under the auspices of the United Nations, for the establishment of a unified, independent and democratic government in the sovereign state of Korea.

(C) That all sections and representative bodies of the population of Korea, South and North, be invited to cooperate with the organs of the United Nations in the restoration of peace, in the holding of elections and in the establishment of a unified government. . . .

(D) That United Nations forces should not remain in Korea otherwise than so far as necessary for achieving the objectives specified at (A) and (B) above;

(E) That all measures be taken to accomplish the economic rehabilitation of Korea. [14]

This formulation was a restatement of the objectives of the United States, consistently advanced after 1947. It had been then accepted, except by the Soviet Union and its affiliates, as United Nations policy. The objective had not been attained by the time of its reaffirmation by the General Assembly because military means would have had to be employed to attain the ends sought. The way had been apparently opened to the use of military means for purposes of unification because of prior use of force by the North Koreans and the development of sufficient counter-force not merely to repel aggression but to dispossess the aggressor régime from control of its territories.

This General Assembly Resolution, then, was taken to be an authorization for the United Nations Command in Korea to enlarge the area of military operations to the northern frontier of Korea at the Yalu River if that proved necessary to attain the objectives set forth in the October 7 Resolution. At the time of its adoption South Korean forces had already crossed the 38th parallel. Other United Nations forces had been halted below the parallel, pending an answer to General MacArthur's demand for the surrender of the North Korean forces. Following the communication of the terms of the October 7 Resolution, United States forces crossed the parallel. There was then reason to believe that the United Nations forces had the ability to crush North Korean resistance in the northern part of the peninsula.

At this point decisions were taken as if there had not earlier been created,

[14] See U.N. Doc. A/1435, for full text.

under United Nations auspices, and recognized by the United States, the Republic of Korea, but rather only a South Korean régime. The United Nations Interim Committee on Korea, with the support of the United States, took the position that the government of the Republic of Korea could not extend its civil authority north of the parallel in the wake of its advancing armies. Its plan to extend its administrative and governmental authority beyond the parallel consequently could not be put into effect. Civil authority as well as the military command was to be exercised by the United Nations through the Unified Command. Since this position was supported by the United States it had to be accepted, albeit reluctantly and under pressure, by the South Korean government.

8. THE CHINESE INTERVENTION

Political action in the field, at the United Nations, and in Washington was conditioned by the military situation. This situation began to change as the United Nations forces moved north toward the Yalu River. Chinese "volunteers" in increasing numbers were identified in the ranks of the North Korean armies. In a special report from General MacArthur of November 4, attention was called to the "continued employment of Chinese Communist forces in Korea and the hostile attitude assumed by such forces. . . ." By November 24, when a United Nations offensive designed to drive the enemy forces beyond the Yalu was launched, it was known that there were at least 48,000 Chinese troops on the Korean side of the frontier. It was also known that there were heavy concentrations of Chinese Communist troops along the Yalu in Manchuria. The known facts raised a serious question as to the intentions of Communist China with respect to the Korean War.

The internal situation in China had made it impossible for that country to play the active part in shaping postwar international policy toward Korea that China's position would have justified. As of mid-summer, 1950, when the North Korean attack was launched, the principal concern of the Peking government was the consolidation of its authority throughout China and the elimination of the National government from the area remaining under its control. Peking was, consequently, in the spring of 1950, apparently concentrating its forces opposite Formosa (Taiwan) for purposes of invasion of the island. At this time the defense of Formosa was accepted as the sole responsibility of the National government, since the United States was not only uncommitted to its defense but had indicated that the military resources of the National government would not be supplemented by American military forces. As put by President Truman in January, 1950, [15]

[15] White House Press Release, January 5, 1950.

The United States has no predatory designs on Formosa or on any other Chinese territory. . . . Nor does it have any intention of utilizing its armed forces to interfere in the present situation. The United States will not pursue a course which will lead to involvement in the civil conflict in China.

Similarly, the United States will not provide military aid or advice to Chinese forces on Formosa. . . . The United States Government proposes to continue under existing legislative authority the present ECA program of economic assistance.

The North Korean attack on South Korea produced a double reaction from Washington. United States policy in relation to the war situation in Korea, as set forth above, was developed and applied through the United Nations. At the same time, with a view to the confinement of hostilities to Korea, the United States unilaterally declared the neutralization of Formosa for the period of military operations in Korea. The National government was requested to refrain from engaging in air and sea operations directed against the mainland, and the Communists were debarred from invasion of Formosa. The Seventh Fleet was ordered to enforce this request and prohibition. This in effect reversed the policy defined at the beginning of 1950 since it committed the United States itself (*a*) to action to prevent invasion and (*b*) to the support of the National government in the maintenance of its position on Formosa. Whereas, in application of the earlier policy, military aid to the National government beyond that already given under authorization of the China Aid Act of 1948 and the Mutual Defense Assistance Act of 1949 had been suspended, following a review of policy by the Joint Chiefs-of-Staff in July 1950 military aid began to be resumed. A Military Assistance Advisory Group

was constituted and entered upon its duties early in 1951. Under its advice and with assistance in the form of equipment from the United States, the National Government made steady progress in transforming its forces on Formosa from the ill-disciplined horde evacuated from the mainland into a military force capable of defending the island from Communist attack. The odds which had been strongly in favor of Communist success if an invasion had been attempted in (the spring of) 1950 had been reversed by 1953 when it could be reasonably concluded that the Nationalists were capable of a successful defense of Formosa. In this reversal the shift in American policy brought about by the North Korean attack on the Republic of Korea played a large part. [15]

This American interdiction of Communist attack on Formosa also brought about a redeployment of the Chinese Communist armies from opposite Formosa to Manchuria, making them available for use there, as it proved, for purposes of intervention in Korea. This possibility had been suggested by India when it abstained from voting on the October 7

[15] HAROLD M. VINACKE, *Far Eastern Politics* (1956), pp. 233–234.

Resolution of the General Assembly. [16] Furthermore Chou En-lai, Premier and Foreign Minister of the People's Government of China, had warned over the radio that "China will not stand idly by and see North Korea invaded."

The attempt was made to avoid Chinese intervention by reassurances such as that given in a proposed Security Council resolution of November 10 (sponsored by Cuba, Ecuador, France, Norway, the United Kingdom, and the United States, but vetoed by the U.S.S.R.), which affirmed that it is the policy of the United Nations to hold the Chinese frontier with Korea inviolate and fully to protect legitimate Chinese and Korean interests in the frontier zone. [17]

With this reassurance it seems to have been concluded that the Peking régime would be willing to negotiate a settlement designed to safeguard the legitimate interests of China in North Korea rather than hazard participation in the war beyond that represented by the presence of Chinese "volunteer" troops in the North Korean armies. This view seemed to be confirmed when a delegation from Peking appeared at Lake Success in response to an invitation to the Chinese People's Government, ostensibly to take part in a general discussion of the Korean question, "including United States aggression" in Asia. It proved to be the case, however, that the delegation came not to negotiate but to denounce the United States and to reiterate the Chinese position that peace could only come as a result of the end of American "aggression" through withdrawal of its forces from Korea.

Meanwhile the United Nations offensive, launched November 24, had been contained by the Chinese armies which had been moved across the Yalu into Korea, and by the end of the month the United Nations forces had been driven back to the 38th parallel. After a short pause at the parallel during which the Chinese forces were further increased and strengthened, the Chinese Communist armies in their turn, in January, 1951, launched a major offensive south of the parallel. After initial successes this Chinese offensive was soon contained, and the United Nations undertook limited counter-offensives which, by April, 1951, again brought its forces to and beyond the 38th parallel.

At the point of Communist China's intervention in the Korean War there was a reversion, on the United Nations side, to the original "cease-fire" objective. The initiative directed toward this end was taken by a newly formed Asian-Arab bloc which concerted its action under the leadership of India. At the end of November this bloc advanced proposals which the

[16] At this time India warned the General Assembly, apparently on the basis of its reports from Peking, that the authorization of troop movements north of the parallel might draw Communist China into the struggle.

[17] Text of the Resolution in U.N. Doc. S/1894.

United States accepted, but which the Chinese government, after an apparent initial acceptance, finally rejected as a basis for the negotiation of a settlement. These proposals involved: (1) the ordering of an immediate "cessation of all acts of armed force in Korea"; (2) the establishment of a "demilitarized area across Korea of approximately twenty miles in depth with the southern limit following generally the line of the 38th parallel"; (3) supervision of the cease-fire by a United Nations commission to ensure withdrawal of forces along lines indicated and to ensure against reënforcement designed to change the military situation; (4) exchange of "prisoners of war" on a one-for-one basis, pending final settlement of the Korean question. On the latter issue, the American position was stated to be that of "our clear understanding and also that of the twelve Asian sponsors, that once a cease-fire arrangement has been achieved, the negotiations for a settlement shall be proceeded with at once." [18]

From this time, as the tide of war ebbed and flowed, attempts were made at the United Nations to find a political solution to the problems posed by the Chinese intervention in Korea. While there was consistently shown by the United States—possibly because of its United Nations commitments and connections—a willingness to negotiate, following a cease-fire, the Chinese, and the Russians in support of them, showed an unwillingness to even discuss proposals for a cease-fire except as there was prior acceptance of their terms of settlement of other Far Eastern political issues as well as that posed by the situation in Korea.

The American willingness to negotiate a cease-fire after the Chinese intervention was due to the fear that a military victory in Korea might lead to the general war which Washington had steadily sought to avoid. This was viewed as a real possibility if, to bring the Korean War to a decisive conclusion, military operations had to be undertaken against China in Manchuria or China proper. The United States did finally persuade the General Assembly (February 1, 1951) to adopt a resolution finding Communist China to be guilty of aggression as a result of its intervention in Korea. But it was apparent throughout that there would be strong opposition to any actions which would enlarge the theater of military operations beyond Korea. This attitude of opposition was shown, for example, as there began to be requests from Tokyo for authority to bomb Chinese bases in Manchuria.

9. THE ARMISTICE NEGOTIATIONS

As increasing military pressure was applied to the Chinese forces in Korea, along with some economic pressures in the late winter and early spring of 1951, the Communist attitude toward negotiations began to

[18] Summary from Report of the Group on Cease-Fire. U.N. Doc. A/C 1/643.

change. The Russians proposed in the Security Council the institution of negotiations (*a*) to bring about a cease-fire and (*b*) to determine the conditions of armistice in the Korean War. The purpose, as now seems clear, was, through the institution of negotiations, to slow down the limited United Nations offensive then under way, and if possible to secure the time necessary to reëstablish at least a firm defensive position in Korea. Thus the purpose was essentially a war purpose rather than that of seeking a settlement by political means. General MacArthur had already (March 23) declared himself ready to discuss armistice terms with the Chinese Commander. This offer was rejected by the Chinese Communists on March 29. On June 24, however, the Soviet Foreign Minister said that the U.S.S.R. felt that a cease-fire could be negotiated. Thereupon the new United Nations Commander-in-Chief, General Ridgway, [19] by radio, invited the Chinese and North Korean Commanders to discuss the conditions of armistice. Delegations from the two sides met at Kaesong [20] on July 8, where discussions were held until an agreement had been reached, July 26, on a five point agenda for further discussions. The site of the truce talks was subsequently (October 24) shifted from Kaesong to Panmunjom where the negotiations were intermittently carried on from 1951 through much of 1953 without any substantial agreement being reached on the terms and conditions of armistice. During this period the war itself was continued but without the United Nations forces, which during this time had the power to do so, carrying operations much beyond the 38th parallel.

The principal obstacles to agreement revealed in the Panmunjom discussions were differences over (1) the method of considering the political questions at issue; (2) the rights of the two sides to take actions, after an armistice agreement, which would affect the military *status quo* in the event of resumption of hostilities; and (3) the question of repatriation of prisoners of war. It was because of disagreement on the prisoner-of-war question that negotiations had been finally suspended in October, 1952.

Following the death of Stalin the Soviet government proposed resumption of the negotiations. A change in the attitude of the Soviet government from that shown in negotiations on the prisoner-of-war question within the U.N. enabled the negotiators at Panmunjom to conclude an agreement on April 11, 1953, providing for repatriation of sick and wounded prisoners of war "in accordance with provisions of article 109 of the Geneva Convention relative to prisoners of war." On June 8 an agreement on the conditions of exchange of other prisoners of war was concluded on lines earlier pro-

[19] General MacArthur had been relieved of his commands and recalled to the United States on April 11 because of differences of opinion on policy and on his functions between the General and the administration in Washington.

[20] For a detailed treatment of the armistice negotiations, see WILLIAM H. VATCHER, JR., *Panmunjom* (Praeger, 1958).

posed by the Indian delegation when the conditions of termination of the Korean War were brought under consideration in the General Assembly. The Indian proposals had previously been rejected by the Soviet Union after China had taken the position that they were unacceptable to it. The difference over the prisoner-of-war issue was whether or not prisoners on either side should be compulsorily repatriated if they did not desire repatriation. The American position had been defined by President Truman when he said (May 7, 1952): "We will not buy an armistice by turning over human beings for slaughter or slavery." The Chinese and Russian position was that repatriation was required under the terms of the Geneva Convention, which they insisted should be followed in this respect although they had failed to observe its terms in other respects.

The agreement of June 8 provided that

Within two months after the armistice agreement becomes effective, both sides shall, without offering any hindrance, directly repatriate and hand over in groups all of those prisoners in its custody who insist on repatriation to the side to which they belonged at the time of capture. . . .

Both sides agree to hand over all those remaining prisoners of war who are not directly repatriated to the United Nations Repatriation Commission for disposition. [21]

The Korean government did not wait for the conclusion of an armistice agreement or the setting up of the proposed repatriation machinery but proceeded unilaterally to release North Korean prisoners of war in its custody without repatriating them. This caused the Communists to raise a question of good faith in the execution of agreements, and also one of the willingness and ability of the United Nations Command to exercise control over the actions of the Korean government. It was only after reassurances were given on these questions that the Communists were willing to resume negotiations looking toward an armistice.

The above-mentioned action of the Korean government pointed up one of the continuing anomalies in the Korean situation. The United States and the United Nations had come to the assistance of the government which had been accepted as the Government of the Republic and the "sole" government in the entire peninsula. And yet, from the time of the North Korean attack, the government of the Republic was subordinated to the American government and the United Nations Command as if it were a ward of the supporting states, some of whom were not in sympathy with it. Even in the United States any attempt on the part of the South Korean government, even within its own territory south of the parallel, to act as if it were what it had been officially recognized as being—the government

[21] For text see *American Journal of International Law*, Supplement, Documents, pp. 180–186.

of an independent state—was viewed as unwarranted and presumptuous.

These attitudes were shown throughout the Panmunjom negotiations themselves. Whereas the Chinese spoke almost invariably through the North Korean members of their delegation, it was invariably the American who, instead of a representative of the South Korean government, not only headed the delegation but spoke for it. Thus the United States negotiated with the unrecognized North Koreans instead of the latter facing their real opposite numbers, the South Koreans. If the Chinese had seen fit to displace the North Koreans as the spokesmen for their side it might have been more appropriate for the United States to make the direct confrontation. As it was, however, even the outward appearance of the subordination of the Korean government was maintained, it being apparently put in a position, with respect to a war fought on Korean territory and with respect to the future disposition of authority in Korea, of inability to participate effectively in the determination of the attitude of its United Nations allies with respect to the solution of the Korean question or the termination of the war.

The attitude of President Syngman Rhee throughout was one of determination not to accept any settlement which would preclude or make impossible of early attainment the objective of unification of Korea under his government. Thus he was willing to have the armistice negotiations resumed only if it were understood that a time limit of three months would be set within which they would be satisfactorily concluded, the war to be resumed if no satisfactory agreement had been reached within that period. To him the indefinite protraction of negotiations served no useful purpose. Satisfactory armistice terms, in President Rhee's view, would provide for the immediate withdrawal of all United Nations and Chinese forces, with, however, the United States guaranteeing Korean security. Since the North Korean armies had been virtually destroyed in earlier military operations, ROK's augmented and battle-hardened forces would be able to extend the authority of the Republic over the northern zone if left uncontrolled by the presence of the United Nations forces.

The Eisenhower administration, which succeeded that of President Truman in 1952, was firmly committed to ending hostilities in Korea through the conclusion of an armistice that at least would prevent extension of Communist control below the 38th parallel. Conclusion of an armistice was thus its primary and immediate objective, to which unification of Korea was made distinctly secondary. But, for an armistice to be effective, it would have to be accepted and implemented, no matter how reluctantly, by Korea as well as the United States. Thus the United States, to attain its objective, had to overcome, by persuasion, the reluctance of President Rhee, to agree to the armistice provisions which were acceptable to the United

States. As a result of discussions between President Rhee and Assistant Secretary of State Robertson, it was agreed on June 25 that the two governments would collaborate in the carrying on of armistice negotiations without further obstruction on the part of the South Korean government, and Secretary of State Dulles stated that Rhee had given the United States written assurances that he would not obstruct implementation of the armistice agreement. Nevertheless on July 24, three days before the signature of the agreement, the Korean President raised objections to some of its provisions, including the time limit stipulated for the holding of a conference to consider the political issues involved. At the same time he made it clear that South Korea reserved the right to resume hostilities if the proposed political conference failed to reach a satisfactory agreement on the Korean question.

The armistice agreement was signed on July 27, 1953, by the several parties involved, except for the South Korean representative. It remained in force from that date in spite of dissatisfaction with the execution of some of its provisions, especially in connection with post-armistice supervision of application of its military provisions designed to maintain the power *status quo* in the two zones as of the time of signature of the armistice. The Neutral Nations' Supervisory Committee failed to behave neutrally or to give adequate supervision, especially in the north.

10. THE GENEVA POLITICAL CONFERENCE

The recommendation in the armistice agreement for the holding of a political conference brought the Korean question back into the United Nations for consideration of the composition and terms of reference of such a conference. This also involved agreement between the United Nations and Communist China and the U.S.S.R. As defined in the discussions, the United States' position was that the two belligerent sides should take part in an across-the-table discussion while the other side, and the so-called neutralist states, wanted a round-table discussion in which non-belligerent states might participate without alignment on one side or the other.

These discussions produced no agreement on the questions at issue. However, at a conference held at Berlin in January and February of 1954, the Foreign Ministers of the United States, Britain, France, and the U.S.S.R., "considering that the establishment, by peaceful means, of a united and independent Korea would be an important factor in reducing international tension and restoring peace in other parts of Asia," decided to invite representatives of the Chinese People's Republic, the Republic of Korea, the People's Democratic Republic of Korea, "and other countries whose armed forces participated in the hostilities in Korea" to meet with representatives of the four sponsoring states at Geneva on April 26, 1954, to seek a solution of the Korean question. Since, by this time, there was a struggle, similar to that begun with the invasion of South Korea four years earlier, going on in Indo-China, the purpose of the conference was extended to include Indo-China.

The Geneva Conference, in its turn, failed to produce an agreed solution of the Korean problem viewed as that of unification. The breakdown came over the question of the method of unification through the holding of supervised elections. South Korea took the position that all that was necessary was to complete the implementation of the original United Nations resolution through holding United Nations supervised elections in North Korea, so that the seats in the Parliament which had been reserved since 1947 for representatives from North Korea could be filled. The Communist proposal for holding of elections in South Korea as well was viewed as unnecessary since such elections had just been held there, as prescribed by the terms of the constitution of the Republic. The Communist proposal was held to be unacceptable in any case because it rejected outside supervision. Instead of United Nations supervision the Communists proposed joint supervision by the North and South Korean governments. This would, of course, give status as an accepted government to the North Korean régime, putting it on a footing of equality with the government of the Republic, which had been accepted by the non-Communist members of the United Nations as the sole recognized government in the peninsula.

The Rhee government was persuaded to agree to a compromise viewed as equitable by the United States. This provided for the holding of United Nations supervised elections throughout the entire country, instead of only in the north. Since, however, the Communist side refused to accept this compromise because of unwillingness to accept United Nations supervision, and to withdraw Chinese troops from Korea unless all United Nations troops were simultaneously withdrawn, the Geneva Conference was unable to find an acceptable solution to the Korean problem. The Rhee government continued to be able to exercise authority only within the territorial limits defined in the armistice agreement. It was unable to get support or approval from the United States to undertake a resumption of the war to bring about unification by military means, although President Rhee did announce, on August 15, 1955, that his government no longer recognized the restraining force of the armistice. Rhee had earlier, on the occasion of his visit to the United States after the Geneva Conference (July, 1954), made clear his view that the armistice should be ended and Korea unified by force. Secretary of State Dulles made it equally clear that the United States would not support a policy of military unification, although it continued to favor creation of a "unified, democratic and independent Korea." This objective was also reiterated from time to time at the United Nations when the topic of Korea would be reached on the agenda of the General Assembly.

The 1955 denunciation of the armistice produced no adverse reactions since it occurred after repeated complaints of truce violations in North Korea, with respect to which the Neutral Nations' Supervisory Commission could give no satisfaction. The unwillingness or inability of the Commission to function in North Korea led Syngman Rhee to demand withdrawal of its personnel from South Korea, where it had been permitted to function, by August 13. This was followed by the August 15 announcement with respect to the armistice itself. That the Rhee complaint with respect to the Commission was not without merit was indicated in the grounds assigned by the United Nations Command for its "provisional" suspension within its jurisdiction on May 31, 1956, of the functions of the Neutral Nations' Supervisory Commission.

II. INTERNAL DEVELOPMENTS

As suggested above, some of the difficulties confronting the Korean government grew out of its relationship with the United States, which seemed not to have full confidence in the state and government that the United States had been largely instrumental in bringing into being. From the start, the Korean Republic had been largely dominated by Syngman Rhee, who was elected as President by the Assembly in August, 1948. He was reëlected President (this time, following an amendment of the constitution) by direct popular vote on August 5, 1952. He was subsequently (1956) reëlected for a third term, polling 5,046,437 votes as contrasted to the 2,163,808 votes cast for the opposing candidate. Thus Dr. Rhee headed the government of the Republic from the time of its establishment. This record of reëlection, however, does not warrant the conclusion that the Korean government operated completely harmoniously under the direction of the President. He was initially elected by an Assembly which, under the new constitution, would choose his successor. The membership of the Assembly was divided into numerous parties whose leaders had different points of view and conflicting interests. The Parliamentary interest as a whole, furthermore, was opposed to the effective concentration of too great power in the hands of the President. Broad executive powers were vested in the President, but constitutionally they were to be exercised through the medium of a Prime Minister and other Ministers appointed by and responsible to the President. Until the actual lines of authority were firmly established in action, there was certain to be a struggle for power.

The first years of the new Republic were in fact marked by internal controversy. This was increased rather than lessened by the attempt made by the President to establish himself in a position of personal power and by the attempts of members of his Cabinet to enlarge their own personal followings both in and out of the Assembly.

It was, however, in the relations of the President and the Assembly that the edges of controversy were sharpest, since the struggle for supremacy was institutional as well as personal. The Assembly elected the President and had to confirm appointments to the Cabinet. This gave it the right constitutionally to pass judgment on the use made of power by the President, at least in the selection of his successor and in giving or withholding approval of his nominees in the filling of vacancies as they occurred. As the time for election of a President in 1952 approached, and as it appeared that the President might not be able readily to secure reëlection by the Assembly, he sought to change the method of election to that of direct vote of the people. He consequently employed his full powers of persuasion and coercion to bring about an amendment of the constitution so as to provide for direct election of the President and the Vice-President. It was thus by direct election rather than on account of Parliamentary support that he was enabled to succeed himself in 1952 and again in 1956.

In accomplishing his purpose, both in obtaining the amendment of the constitution and in securing reëlection, President Rhee used a variety of means of pressure as well as persuasion, not confining his actions within the strict bounds of legality nor of the democratic methodology. Aside from that, however, he was able to extend the limits of his authority as chief executive because of the division of the membership of the Assembly into numerous parties, and thus the fragmentation of the opposition.

At the time of establishment of the Republic, political life was organized on a multi-party basis. By the time of the 1956 elections essentially a two-party system had assumed form so that the Liberal Party under Syngman Rhee faced an opposition party formed out of the combination of the Democratic Party, organized in 1955, and the Progressive Party established shortly before the elections. President Rhee's very impressive majority in the election for the presidency may be explained in large part by the death during the campaign of Mr. Shin Ik Hi, the Democratic Party candidate. In spite of vigorous support given him in the campaign, Rhee's running mate was defeated by 200,000 votes by the Democratic Party's candidate for the Vice-Presidency. The Liberal Party, however, retained its majority in the Assembly. Consequently it may properly be concluded that the election results in 1956 constituted personal triumphs for President Rhee and for the Democratic Party's Vice-Presidential candidate rather than a decisive party victory for either the Liberals or the Democrats. From the point of view of politics, otherwise, it indicated a consolidation of forces within a majority and minority party framework, and thus some reduction of the play of personal politics. At any rate the 1956 election was rated a

success by the United Nations Commission for the Unification and Rehabilitation of Korea, which noted that 94.4 per cent of the registered voters
went to the polls. The Commission's conclusion was "that the election
represented another example of the encouraging progress of representative
government in the Republic of Korea."

The Assembly elections held in May, 1958, indicated further consolidation of the move toward a two-party system. As reported immediately
following the voting, [22] while the Liberals remained in the majority with
119 seats, the Democrats increased their representation from 46 in the previous Assembly of 203, to 72 in the new Assembly, which had in addition
21 members elected as independents and 1 representative of the Unification Party. This increase in the representation of the Democratic Party to
more than one-third of the Assembly was significant because it gave the
party the power to block constitutional amendments. The Liberals wanted
to amend the constitution to provide for Assembly election of a successor
in the event of the death of Syngman Rhee, [23] to replace the existing constitutional provision for succession of the Vice-President. The question of
change would not have been raised if the Liberal candidate had been
elected Vice-President in 1956, since he was President Rhee's choice as his
own successor if Rhee did not outlive his term of office.

During this first decade of the life of the Republic the Rhee government
faced economic problems impossible of solution by its own means. The
continued hope of unification retarded the origination of economic plans
based on the territories within the control of the republican government.
This was understandable under the circumstances, since certainly the problem of economic reconstruction would have been much easier to solve if
the resources of the northern and southern zones could have been integrated for use. As it was, more than half the territories of the Republic,
about 80 per cent of its mineral resources, the developed water-power sites,
and the heavy industry, were outside the area of control of the government of the Republic, both before and after the armistice. What it had
within its control was some 70 per cent of the agricultural land and, as
time went on, close to three-fourths of the total population of the peninsula. Even without the added burden and distractions of the war, the
Republic as constituted would have had to rely on assistance from the outside to maintain itself and reconstruct its economy.

For the purpose of assisting Korea, the United Nations established the
Korean Reconstruction Agency in December, 1950. Since its work was
expected to include all of Korea, the Agency program was not intended to
be inaugurated until six months after a truce. Actually it began its work in

[22] *New York Times*, May 4, 1958.
[23] The President was, in 1958, 83 years old.

South Korea alone, and before the truce had been concluded, under an authorization in June, 1952. Its first program included expenditures of about $7 million for school classrooms, $11 million worth of grain to combat food shortages, and $8.5 million worth of fertilizer to increase farm production. After the armistice a full-scale long-term program was undertaken, directed toward industrial production, the restoration of the fishing industry, and the improvement of agriculture through irrigation projects. Altogether the Agency, which finished its work in June, 1958, in six years spent $140 millions on some 4,800 projects in South Korea. The largest contribution to this total expenditure was made by the United States ($92,960,000). Other contributors included: Britain, $28,000,000; Canada, $7,392,00; Australia, $3,612,000; Italy, $2,016,000; Norway, $1,708,000; and the Netherlands, $1,036,000. The other thirty participants contributed the balance.

Beyond this, the United States extended direct aid to Korea, both before and after the armistice, for economic reconstruction as well as for military purposes. This was essential in view of the fact that the Republic was able to meet only an estimated (1955) 57 per cent of its minimum needs from its own resources. This left, by a conservative American estimate, a deficit in 1955 after the payment on all accounts, by the United States, of $700 million in aid payments. Nevertheless Korea made progress in the execution of an ambitious reconstruction program launched in 1955 and aimed in the direction of self-sufficiency, a difficult goal to reach as long as the peninsula remained divided. The launching of this program was significant as an attempt on the part of the Rhee government to assert its independence in planning the economic reconstruction of the country while as largely dependent as it continued to be on American assistance. This assertion of independence led to recurrent differences with the United States on such questions as the exchange rate and whether or not consumers goods should be imported from Japan.

The latter issue was part of the larger question of relations between the Republic of Korea and Japan. Just released from exploitation as a Japanese colony, the Korean government showed a natural reluctance to engage in any relations with Japan except on its own terms. Shortly after the establishment of the Republic, for example, it proclaimed a "Rhee line" which substantially enlarged the accepted area of marginal waters. This was a direct attack on the Japanese fishing industry. The action was probably suggested by the drawing of the "MacArthur Line" which was designed to prevent the revival of the Japanese high-seas fishing industry. Whatever the reason, however, the attempt to prevent the Japanese from fishing on the high seas in the Korean off-shore area resulted in charges and counter-charges of misbehavior. These and other disputes had prevented agreement on the conditions of establishment of normal diplomatic relations between Japan and Korea during the first decade of existence of the Republic.

REFERENCES FOR FURTHER STUDY

Bureau of Internal Relations, *Indian Press Digests,* vol. 3, *Indian Proposals for a Korean Truce* (Berkeley, March, 1954). Kyong-jo Chong, *Korea Tomorrow, Land of the Morning Calm* (1956). Major General William F. Dean, *General Dean's Story,* as told to William L. Worden (1954). Department of State, Pub. 2933, Far Eastern Series No. 8, *Korea's Independence* (with Annex of Documents to 1948); Pub. 3305, Far Eastern Series No. 28, *Korea, 1945–1948* (with 32 selected documents); *United States Policy in the Korean Crisis* (1950). John Dille, *Substitute for Victory* (1954). Miriam Farley, "The Korean Crisis in the United Nations," in L. K. Rossinger and Associates, *The State of Asia* (1951). Leland M. Goodrich, *Korea: Collective Measures Against Aggression* (1953). Leland M. Goodrich, *Korea: A Study of U.S. Policy in the United Nations* (1956). Andrew J. Grajdanzov, *Modern Korea* (1944). Great Britain, Foreign Office, *Korea, 1953,* no. 2; Special Report of the Unified Command on the Korean Armistice Agreement Signed at Panmunjom on July 27, 1953 (1953). Ely Jacques Kahn, *The Peculiar War: Impressions of a Reporter in Korea* (1952). *Keesing's Contemporary Archives,* vols. 7, 8, 9 (London, 1943–1958); good summaries of documents, well indexed for references. Korean Affairs Institute, *Voice of Korea* (Washington 1946–1958), vol. 5, no. 112, Aug. 14, 1948; contains the text of the Constitution of the Republic. *Korean-American Relations: Documents Pertaining to the Far Eastern Diplomacy of the United States* (Berkeley, 1951). Shannon McCune, "Korea," in L. K. Rossinger and Associates, *The State of Asia* (1951). George M. McCune and Arthur L. Grey, Jr., *Korea Today* (1950); well worth consulting. E. Grant Meade, *American Military Government in Korea* (1951). Robert T. Oliver, *Why War Came to Korea* (1950). Robert T. Oliver (ed.), *Korea's Fight for Freedom* (Korean Pacific Press), vol. I, 1951, vol. II, 1952. Robert T. Oliver (ed.), *Korean Report, 1948–52; Review of Governmental Procedures During Two Years of Peace and Two of War* (1952). Republic of Korea, Office of Public Information, *The Republic of Korea: Its Constitution and Government Organization Law.* John M. Riley, Jr., *The Reds Take a City: the Communist Occupation of Seoul* (1951). Donald G. Tewksbury, *Source Materials on Korea Politics and Ideologies,* vol. II of the series, Source Books on Far Eastern Political Ideologies (1950). United Nations, Department of Public Information, *Korea and the United Nations* (1950). United States Senate, 82nd Cong., 1st Session, 5 vols., Military Situation in the Far East: *Hearings before the Committee on Armed Services and the Committee on Foreign Relations* (1951). William H. Vatcher, Jr., *Panmunjom* (1958); a detailed account of the negotiations. Harold M. Vinacke, *The United States and the Far East, 1945–1951* (Stanford, 1952). John N. Washburn, "Russia Looks at Northern Korea," *Pacific Affairs,* vol. 20, no. 22.

CHAPTER XXX

POST-SURRENDER JAPAN

Loss of the Pacific war brought Japan back territorially to its original status. The Kuriles and southern Sakhalin were taken by Russia. Korea, to become "independent in due course," was divided between the U.S.S.R. and the United States for occupation purposes. Formosa had been reclaimed by China. The islands of the Pacific, which had been mandated to Japan after World War I, had been transferred to the United States as a strategic trusteeship under the United Nations. The loss of the war had thus reduced Japan to the four original islands (Honshu, Shikoku, Kyushu, Hokkaido) making up the Japanese state at the time of the Restoration, together with the smaller adjacent islands. But on the home islands there were living, by 1958, over 90 million Japanese, as against the 30 millions of 1867. This was a result of the natural increase of population over the century, together with the repatriation of Japanese from the lost territories of the Empire and from the Greater East Asia Co-prosperity sphere. This meant that a serious problem of livelihood was presented to the Japanese people. This problem could be solved only through the reëstablishment of the foreign trade through which raw materials could be imported to be processed for sale on the world market. But Japan's expansionist policy, ending in the disasters of the war, had created the conditions and the attitudes which prevented an automatic move along this line toward a solution of the problem. The immediate incentives for the victors were in the opposite direction. And, by means of occupation, following "unconditional" surrender, they were in control of the destinies of Japan.

I. OCCUPATION POLICY AND ORGANIZATION

The surrender terms were laid down in the Potsdam Declaration of July 26, 1945, accepted by Japan with the understanding that Allied policy did not involve rejection of the Imperial family as an instrument of rule. Occupation policy was defined first by the United States in the paper "United States Initial Post-Surrender Policy for Japan" which was approved by the President on September 6, 1945. This established the lines of policy for occupation authorities until its substantial reaffirmation by the Far Eastern Commission in the policy decision of June 19, 1947, as the "Basic Post-Surrender Policy for Japan." The purposes of the occupation, as thus defined, were (1) to bring about the complete demobilization and repatriation of Japan's military, naval, and air forces, and thus its disarmament, together with the demilitarization of the country and the punishment of those found guilty of war crimes; (2) to encourage its democratization; and (3) to destroy the existing economic basis of Japanese military strength and not permit it to revive, but to permit the revival of Japanese economic life so as to enable the peaceful requirements of the people and the nation to be met. [1]

The instruments of surrender were signed by General MacArthur as the Supreme Commander of the Allied Powers and by "representatives of the United Nations which had fought in the Pacific" on the Battleship *Missouri* on September 2, 1945. On September 6, General MacArthur was designated as the Supreme Commander for the Allied Powers for the occupation of Japan. Thus it became his responsibility to act so as to realize the purposes initially set forth as American policy objectives. An American character was given to the occupation by reason of the fact that the force initially occupying Japan was American, as well as by the designation of an American as the Supreme Allied Commander, and in consequence of the initial formulation by the United States government of Allied objectives. Before surrender, however, "the United States suggested that there be created an international body to help formulate future policy in Japan and to assist in planning the organization which would be required to make sure that the Japanese fulfilled their obligations." [2] British as well as Soviet objections to the purely advisory commission which the United States had in mind led finally to the creation, on the basis of agreements reached at the Moscow Conference of Foreign Ministers (on December 27, 1945), of the Far Eastern Commission (F.E.C.), with a membership of representatives of eleven, shortly increased to thirteen, states, to sit in Washington, and of an Allied Council for Japan, of representatives of the four major Pacific Powers (the U.S.S.R., China, Britain and the Commonwealths, and the United States), to sit in Tokyo. This organization modified, but did not fundamentally change the American character of the occupation. The real authority continued in the hands of SCAP (Supreme Command Allied Powers).

This Allied authority was erected over, but not in displacement of the Japanese government. The latter was continued as the instrument through which, under SCAP guidance and direction, the purposes of the occupation were to be realized. Anticipating this situation, the pre-surrender government established a Central Liaison Office through which contact between the Japanese government and the occupation authorities could be channeled. Acceptance of this channel of communication meant in

[1] The text of the U. S. Initial Post-Surrender Policy for Japan, together with other relevant documents from the Cairo Conference to mid-1946, is in Dept. of State, *Occupation of Japan: Policy and Progress,* Far Eastern Series No. 17.
[2] *Ibid.,* p. 7.

effect that occupation views, directives, and orders filtered to the Japanese government through an agency which represented a carry-over of traditional Japan into the new order the creation of which SCAP was instructed to "encourage." There was this same carry-over through the Cabinet itself, since the personnel of the successive post-surrender governments was drawn largely from the prewar bureaucracy or party leadership. This had to be anticipated and accepted, in the absence of an internal revolution.

An important exception to the above statement should, however, be noted. The implementation of one element of American and Allied policy made it difficult, if not impossible, for the military leadership of prewar days to be drawn upon for purposes of government. This was also true with respect to those elements of Japanese society held to have responsibility, with the military, for the development of the expansionist and war policies followed by Japan in the decade from 1931 to 1941. An International Tribunal was set up in Tokyo to carry out the provision of the Potsdam Proclamation that "stern justice shall be meted out to all war criminals, including those who have visited cruelties upon our prisoners" and also including those who had formulated aggressive war policies. The Emperor was exempted from trial as a war criminal, since it had been decided to utilize him in the effectuation of Allied policy. But among those tried and punished were: the Premier at the outset of the Pacific War, General Hideki Tojo; Marquis Koichi Kido, Lord Keeper of the Privy Seal; former Foreign Minister Yosuke Matsuoka; and Kiichiro Hiranuma, ex-President of the Privy Council. These trials were extended over the years 1946–1948, the sentences finally imposed being executed in December of 1948. The war-crimes trials were supplemented by "purges," designed to take from directive positions in government first, and subsequently in industry, those who had had any important relationship to the formulation of Japan's war policies. To carry out SCAP directives, the Japanese government issued the first set of purge ordinances January 4, 1946. A year later, by ordinances of January 4 and 14, 1947, the scope of the purge was substantially widened. Thus, even though in their application the purge ordinances were somewhat manipulated for purposes of domestic politics, and although the machinery set up for examination of those coming under the ordinances operated in the direction of leniency, many of the experienced political and industrial leaders of prewar days were made immediately ineligible for post-surrender leadership except by indirection.[3]

[3] "By mid-1947 some 2,200 persons, all outstanding wartime business leaders, had been purged under this program." JEROME COHEN, *Japan's Economy in War and Reconstruction*, p. 432. This was in addition to a larger number of political purgees, but measured against the million and a half who came under the ordinance, it is a small number.

2. DEMILITARIZATION AND DISARMAMENT

On the side of the military, SCAP proceeded vigorously to carry out the policy of demobilization and repatriation of the Japanese armed forces, and that of disarmament. This activity included, for purposes of demilitarization, the formal elimination of the General Staff organizations; prohibition of the para-military organizations into which it was feared that the military might readily retire, and from which they might emerge to reëstablish their position after the termination of the occupation; and the elimination of the War and Marine Departments from the structure of government. In effect, the latter were temporarily continued as civilian demobilization boards until that task had been accomplished. These changes, in themselves, would have had the effect of solving, by elimination, the perplexing prewar political problem of military manipulation of domestic and foreign policy through the right of access to the Emperor which the Chiefs of Staff and the Ministers of War and Marine possessed. In the new constitution, provision was made against the revival of militarism through the renunciation both of war and of force as a means of settling international disputes. In order to accomplish this aim "land, sea and air forces, as well as other military potential, will never be maintained." [4] This, together with the elimination from the constitution of all references to a separate military prerogative of the Emperor, was designed to perpetuate the immediate solution of the problem of military control of policy.

3. DEMOCRATIZATION

Beyond this, a number of steps were taken in the direction of reform which, in total, were intended to result in the democratization of Japan. One of these steps was the substitution of a new constitution for the Meiji Constitution of 1889. Aside from the changes noted above, the constitution which became effective on May 3, 1947, substituted for the principle of Imperial supremacy, on which the Meiji Constitution was founded, that of the supremacy of the Diet as "the highest organ of state power" and "the sole law-making organ of the State." (Art. 41.) Under it the Emperor became "the symbol of the State and of the unity of the people, deriving his position from the will of the people with whom resides sovereign power." (Art 1.) Chapters IV, V, and VII provided for the parliamentary system of government, with a purely civilian Cabinet responsible ultimately to the House of Representatives, and with the Diet having the financial-control powers which it had been granted only in restricted form under the Meiji Constitution. Even Imperial Household

[4] Constitution of 1947, Ch. II.

affairs were brought under Diet control, by provision of law. The Privy Council was done away with, and an elective House of Councillors was substituted for the House of Peers of the Meiji Constitution. The House of Councillors was given what was in effect a suspensive veto in legislation and in this and other ways subordinated to the House of Representatives. An independent judiciary was constitutionally established, and the electorate was given the power of recall, although not of appointment, of judges. Following the American precedent, the Supreme Court, as the court of last resort, was given specifically the "power to determine the constitutionality of any law, order, regulation or official act." (Art 81.) And, in the thirty-one articles of Chapter III of the new Constitution, detailed provision was made, substantially along the lines of American evolution, for the protection of the individual against the improper exercise of state powers. In this bill of rights, it should be noted, the emphasis was placed upon the individual rather than the group or the institution in the attempt to institute a reversal of the traditional point of emphasis in such Asian countries as Japan.

Closely connected with constitutional reform was the change made in the relationship of State, or Shrine, Shinto to the temporal order. The first step in this direction was taken with the issuance of an Imperial Rescript, probably in anticipation of SCAP guidance, on January 1, 1946, in which the Emperor formally divested the Imperial Institution of its divine, or spiritual, origin and attributes and placed his right to rule on the basis of leadership of the nation. SCAP itself directed the abolition of State Shinto, placing responsibility for the voluntary maintenance of shrines on the people. At the same time, sect Shinto was denied the financial support of the state. These actions put the Imperial Institution on an exclusively temporal foundation, thus making it more nearly possible to deal with it on a constitutional and democratic basis. They did not, however, displace the Emperor from his symbolic position as head of the state, and as one to whom his people were attached by inherited ties of personal allegiance. This symbolic position was, as previously noted, written into the constitution.

These and other changes to be considered were made by conservative Japanese governments under, or in anticipation of, direction or guidance from SCAP which, in the first eighteen months of the occupation, went beyond the negative action of forcing removal of impediments to democracy represented by such things as the prewar "thought control" laws, and beyond mere "encouragement" of democratic tendencies. The character of the governments through which SCAP had to act, and whose authority it upheld, gave assurance against the institution of any really radical reform by the Japanese themselves. Thus SCAP, under American and Far Eastern

Commission directives, blocked out the program of reform itself in terms of its judgment as to how democratization might be accomplished, and sought the implementation of its reform program through Japanese some of whose inclinations and interests were against reform.

Since the Meiji Constitution had provided for an elective House of Representatives, elections were not a postwar innovation in Japan. The initial effect of occupation policy, consequently, was to enable life to be reconstructed along prewar lines. Thus elections were held in the spring of 1946, before the creation of the new constitutional order. The second postwar elections—the first under the new constitution—were held in the spring of 1947. Elections were again held in 1949. Since the new constitution gave the franchise to women, in this and subsequent elections the electorate was based upon the principle of universal suffrage. In all the elections held during the period of the occupation, as well as after the conclusion of a peace treaty in 1952, the tendency shown was essentially conservative, the conservative Liberal-Democratic Party securing an absolute majority in the House of Representatives in the 1949 elections.

The occupation emphasis on democratization resulted in the revival of party activity immediately after the surrender. The destruction of the older parties, attempted in and after 1940, through consolidation into the Imperial Rule Assistance Association and the Imperial Rule Assistance Political Society, had not been complete, nor had sufficient time elapsed to eliminate prewar political associations and relationships. Thus the revival of parties took place along lines which reproduced the Seiyukai and the Minseito under the misleading new names of Liberal and Progressive parties, with a leadership of party politicians and bureaucratic politicians carried over from prewar days. A third party, the Social Democratic Party, under the leadership of Katayama, a prewar labor lawyer and politician, competed with the Liberals (who by 1949 had become the Liberal-Democratic Party) and the Progressives (shortly calling themselves the Democratic Party) for control of the Diet. The Social Democrats themselves were divided into a right wing, similar in purposes to the Liberals and Democrats, and a left wing which inclined toward positions taken by the Communists.

The first post-surrender elections, held under the auspices of an inadequately reconstructed government and before it was possible to solidify and organize any new democratic tendencies, gave a Diet majority to the conservative Liberal and Progressive parties, and led to the installation of a Cabinet headed by Yoshida Shigeru, who succeeded to the Liberal party leadership when, shortly after the elections, its first President, Hatoyama, was purged under SCAP orders. This government continued until after the elections of 1947. These elections gave a party composition in the House of Representatives of: 143 Social Democrats; 133 Liberals; and 126 Democrats, with the remainder of the 466 members classified as independents or distributed among minor parties. On this basis, the House designated Katayama (Social Democratic leader) as Premier. His Cabinet was based upon a coalition of the Social Democratic, the Democratic, and the People's Coöperative parties. The failure or inability of the Katayama government to develop and carry vigorously into effect a program of economic readjustment produced sufficient dissatisfaction with it so that it resigned (February, 1948) and was replaced by a Cabinet headed by the Democratic party leader, Ashida Hitoshi. Scandals involving his government, leading finally to Ashida's indictment for perjury, brought about its overthrow (October, 1948) and his replacement as Premier by Yoshida, even though at the time the first Yoshida government was being investigated on the charge of improper use of and accounting for party funds. Even under these circumstances, the elections of January, 1949, gave the Liberals (renamed the Liberal-Democrats) an absolute majority in the Diet.

The scandals involving the rightist parties were the consequence of the methods used by the parties in financing their activities. In the prewar politics of Japan close working relations had been maintained between the industrial and financial capitalists and the political parties. In return for financial support, the parties served as intermediaries between the bureaucracy and government, on the one side, and the managers of the Japanese economy (landlords and Zaibatsu) on the other. Since this older relationship had been disturbed, although not completely displaced, by the economic reforms instituted under SCAP direction, without, however, elimination of the parties' need for large sums for election and other purposes, the parties had established working relations with contractors and others who wanted to undertake and profit from the rebuilding of Japan. It was the open revelation of this relationship which constituted the "scandals." The success in the 1949 elections of the parties which had most effectively exploited this relationship, however, indicated that the system was one generally accepted, whether or not approved.

Another approach to democratization was represented by the program of decentralization. This was designed to lessen control of prefectural and local government by the bureaucracy operating through the Home Ministry. Because of its control of the police and its wide power of appointment and direction of prefectural and local officials the Home Ministry had been a most important agency of authoritarian and bureaucratic rule. Steps had been taken to reorganize the system of police administration on a decentralized basis before the abolition of the Home Ministry at the end of 1947 when its other functions had been eliminated or absorbed by other ministries. This had in effect been forecast in the provisions with respect to local self-government in the new constitution, which established the "principle of local autonomy" for the enactment of regulations by law for the organization and operation of "local public entities." Article 93 of the constitution provided for elective local assemblies and for the selection of officials by "direct popular vote within their several communities." The strength of the tradition centering on the bureaucracy and its allies in the conservative parties' local machines, however, was revealed in the striking tendency of the local electorates to return to office as prefectural governor or mayor those who had previously held office by appointment from Tokyo. Thus at the local as well as the national level, three and a half years of "democratization" had resulted in a reorganization of the political institutional life of Japan so as to make possible the expression of new ideas and forces, but no new political leadership of any real effectiveness had appeared to displace the prewar bureaucrat and politician. If election results are taken as the criterion, the people were content to follow along lines marked out by such of the older leadership as had not been purged under SCAP direction. Even purged leaders continued to exert considerable influence by indirect means.

4. ECONOMIC AND EDUCATIONAL REFORMS

Probably of greater long-run significance than the governmental and political changes instituted by SCAP were those which were economic and educational in their direction. The educational reforms were directed toward a change in emphasis and content in instruction in the schools. They included the introduction of new subjects of instruction and a revision of text materials used for instructional purposes. To change the emphasis the attempt was made to decentralize the system so that there might be a greater possibility of using education for the purpose of development of the individual rather than to promote the ends of the state. Since the organization and methods introduced were American rather than a reorganization of the traditional Japanese, teacher training had to be undertaken. And, if education is put in a broader context than that of formal school instruction, the freeing of the press and the radio from the "thought controls" that had been developed before the war, and extended during its course, was an important part of the relationship of the educational program to the ultimate democratization of Japan.

Similarly, although it had a much more complex motivation, the program of economic change had "democratization" overtones. The revival and great expansion of labor organization from the prewar peak of less than half a million members to the new peak of around six million was one indication of this. The local unions which came into being with rapidity after the old laws were repealed came to be organized nationally along American lines into two major organizations, a Japanese Federation of Labor and a Congress of Industrial Unions. SCAP policy originally encouraged this organization since the conception of union activities initially was along the lines developed in the American labor movement of utilization of organization to improve the economic position of labor. The policy began to change, however, when political significance was perceived in a general strike which was threatened at the end of 1946 and the beginning of 1947. SCAP intervened to prevent such a general strike with alleged political rather than strictly economic purposes, after having tolerated strikes on a fairly wide scale during the first year of the occupation. By 1948 a general shift in policy from reform to revival of the Japanese economy made SCAP less tolerant of strikes with strictly economic objectives since they had inevitably a bad effect on production. The fact that the strike threats in 1948 came largely from organizations of public employees gave a political tinge, in any case, to strikes for wage increases which the inflation justified, except as the government, without pressure, acted to keep wages adjusted to living costs. The fact that the railways, and other utilities, and many of the industries were or had become, partly as a result of occupation policy, government-controlled enterprises, established this dilemma of political as well as economic motivation for both organized workers and SCAP—one not clearly perceived at the time when labor organization was attempted as a projection into Japan of American conceptions. Communist leadership in some of the unions served to create a presumption, furthermore, that strikes with which they were connected had political purposes.

These conceptions of labor organization divorced from political activity and objectives not only created a dilemma because of economic conditions and relationships in post-surrender Japan, but they also made it difficult for any new leadership developed through the unions immediately to play an important part in politics, and thus in the development of public policy. The fact, however, that labor was given the right of organization and that advantage was immediately taken of that right brought into being a new force to be reckoned with, perhaps even more in the future than in the immediate situation.

The labor reforms, viewed in relation to the total problem of demilitarization and democratization, were designed to help produce a balance in the control of the Japanese economy which was lacking in prewar days. Then the control rested in the hands of the great industrial-financial combinations which had close relations with the government. Without other changes, their power might have been modified, within a democratic political system, through the development of strong labor organization.

But initial SCAP policy with respect to these combinations went beyond this type of neutralization of their monopoly of economic-political power. Many of these (Zaibatsu) combines were linked directly with militarism and the so-called militarists. Consequently "SCAP's directives ordering the Japanese Government to stop the manufacture of arms, munitions, and aviation struck at the Zaibatsu specifically as well as war industry generally." [5] Beyond this, on November 6, 1945, a directive was issued ordering the break-up of all the great economic combines. The method had already been tentatively suggested by the Zaibatsu itself, in anticipation of SCAP action. A Holding Company Liquidation Commission was created to take over the assets of the Zaibatsu holding companies for administration pending their resale to investors, so as to give a wider distribution of industrial power. This move, essentially one against monopoly, was subsequently extended beyond the holding company type of financial control of industry into an attempt to break the economic system down into its component, essentially small, but specialized, production units on the basis of the independence of each. Thus the movement against the Zaibatsu (which was fundamentally a pyramiding system of holding companies organized on a family basis) was extended into a movement to bring about industrial as well as financial deconcentration of control. In an attempt to avoid manipulation within this reform program, as well as to remove from directive positions those who had been associated with Japan's war program, the purge was extended in 1947 to include those who had been managing the Japanese economy, even though they had not held government office.

The immediate effect of these economic reforms was to lessen production and thus to put a brake on Japan's economic recovery even to the level of 1930–1934, which was established by the Far Eastern Commission as the ceiling for industrial production. By September, 1948, for example, over-all industrial production had reached only about 58 per cent of the 1930–1934 level. Consequently when, after mid-summer of 1947, the emphasis in occupation policy began to be put on economic recovery the current of economic reform began to flow much less swiftly, if not to be reversed. Reforms which had been directed, but which remained in the paper stage, from the standpoint of Japanese execution, were suspended as SCAP's pressure on the government was relaxed and the emphasis in its "guidance" was shifted.

5. THE LAND REFORM PROGRAM

Another area of economic reform affected agriculture. In prewar industrialized Japan approximately 50 per cent of the population continued

[5] *Occupation of Japan: Policy and Progress*, p. 42.

in agricultural pursuits. By 1949 this proportion had been reduced to about 46 per cent. With the land available, this proportion of the population could not produce sufficient food for the total population. Consequently Japan was a food-importing country, and this food had to be paid for out of exports. But agriculture by itself was not able to produce an adequate livelihood for even the agricultural population. Thus the peasant families came to depend for part of their livelihood on subsidiary occupations such as the production of raw silk, the maintenance of a household industry, and fishing. This supplied a link between agrarian and industrial Japan. But in spite of this the livelihood of the peasant families was not adequate. Debts increased, and as a result many peasant families lost their land, remaining on it, however, as tenants. The share-cropping tenant system, which was the modern counterpart of the economic relationships of the older feudalism, was of such a nature that there was virtually no chance of a tenant regaining title to the land as a result of successful cultivation in good years, coupled with saving. [6]

In postwar Japan, the peasant initially enjoyed an unusual prosperity as compared with other classes in Japanese society. In spite of government controls, he was able to capitalize on the scarcity of food, owing to the cutting-off of prewar external sources of supplementary supply, and on the scarcity of goods of all sorts. The town had go to the country, on terms set by the latter, for the essentials of living. The peasant consequently profited by the reversal of the usual conditions of exchange either: (1) by retaining for his own use a larger proportion of his production; or (2) by exchanging it (frequently on the black market) more advantageously for goods; or (3) by accumulating currency savings which, in spite of inflation, had the value to him of enabling him to benefit from the land redistribution program which represented the occupation's move in the direction of reform of the agricultural life of Japan.

The Land Reform Act of 1946 was directed especially against the existing system of absentee landlordism. Approximately 2 million *chō* (a *chō*, or *chobu*, is 2.45 acres) of land was affected by the act, of which the government had secured for redistribution over a million and a half *chō* by the end of the first quarter of 1948. The program was to be completed within two years. SCAP reported total land sales under the program of 1,320,113 *chō* by the end of July, 1948. In 1947 the program of redistribution was extended to include pasture as well as agricultural land. "By June, 1952, the government had acquired nearly 2 million *chobu* of cultivated land

---

[6] "Throughout the modern era, and especially during periods of agricultural depression, the proportion of the arable land held on tenancies increased. By 1936 this proportion amounted to 46 per cent of the total arable area. . . . It is estimated that before the war the tenant paid on an average about two-fifths of the value of his products to the landlord in rent." G. C. ALLEN, *Japan's Economic Recovery* (1958), pp. 51–52.

and 450,000 *chobu* of pasturage and had resold most of this to the former tenants." [7]

Application of the Reform Act brought about dispossession of all absentee landlords. Other owners of tenanted land were permitted to retain only 1 *chō* of cultivable land in Honshu, Shikoku, and Kyushu, and only 4 *chō* in Hokkaido, "while the holdings of owner-occupiers were limited to an average of 3 *chobu* in the three main islands and 12 in Hokkaido." [8]

This was one of the occupation reforms of probable permanence and real political and social, as well as economic, significance. It was accomplished in such a short period of time because of coöperation of the Japanese themselves and through their detailed administration. As Professor Allen points out, "the reform, though proceeding from the edict of a conqueror, will be difficult to reverse, for the new peasantry is a political force of great influence," [9] taking the place in that respect of the formerly influential landlord class.

The changes made in tenure under the Land Reform Act were significant but in themselves would not either increase production or solve the problem of economic recovery in the agricultural sector of the national economy. For that purpose additional measures were necessary. Thus the main developments which marked a difference between prewar and postwar agricultural life in Japan have been summarized as follows:

(1) a 20 per cent increase in the size of the agricultural population; (2) a conversion of tenants to peasant proprietors, without their incurring any substantial financial liability for this change in tenure; (3) the improvement in the economic position of the working farmer in spite of the increase in the agricultural population, partly through the Land Reform, partly through higher agricultural prices, and partly through new opportunities for non-agricultural employment which have offset the loss of income brought about by the decline in silk raising; (4) the diversification of agriculture through the development of livestock, fruit, and vegetable farming; (5) an increased application of chemical fertilizers and of materials for the control of pests and diseases; (6) a greater use of machinery, although the structure of Japanese agriculture still prevents the efficient use of many types of agricultural machines; and (7) the destruction of the landlord class and the reduction of many of its members to the status of working farmers. [10]

[7] *Ibid.*, p. 57.

[8] *Ibid.*

[9] *Ibid.*, p. 58. From the occupation and the conservative Japanese point of view (apart from SCAP's reformative interest) ". . . the Land Reform was politically expedient, since it helped to damp down revolutionary sentiment among the peasants and to remove a source of unrest that might have shaken the stability of the Japanese government and so weakened the American strategic position in the Far East. Yet it is ironical that the dispossession of a rural middle class should have been undertaken at the behest of the government of a country that asserts so vigorously the rights of private property."

[10] *Ibid.*, pp. 64–65.

While these contrasts with the prewar situation existed, it still had to be recognized, for example, that land-holdings in Japan remained small; that a wide gap continued to exist between farm and urban incomes; that there remained under-employment among the agricultural population; and that there continued to be agricultural overpopulation, which meant a continued movement from the rural areas to the cities.

6. EXTERNAL ASPECTS OF THE ECONOMIC PROBLEM

The economic reforms of the occupation were designed to weaken the position within Japan of the groups held to be responsible for the development and application of the policy of expansion by war and aggression. Economic recovery was not initially assumed as a responsibility of SCAP. Consequently, reforms which at least would have the short-term consequence of retarding industrial recovery even to the 1930–1934 level and thus of maintaining a seriously weakened Japan were pressed on the Japanese government during the first year and a half of the occupation. As an occupied enemy country, furthermore, the necessary steps to reopen normal exchanges between Japan and other countries were not instituted. This meant that there was not promoted, in this early period, an inflow of raw materials to be processed for sale either at home or abroad. At the same time, the reluctance of the Zaibatsu and government elements to accept the implications of the reform program in relation to the distribution of power within Japan caused them to hold back in production as a method of bringing about a redirection of occupation policy. Available stocks, turned over to the old industrial management by the government between the time of acceptance of the need to surrender and the institution of occupation, for example, were funneled into the black market rather than made available for the revival of industry. Inefficient use of existing plant capacity served to scale down that initially ear-marked for removal on reparations account. Rice collections for distribution through the rationing system regularly fell below even low estimates, partly because of the lack of availability of goods needed by the peasants except as they could be secured through black market exchanges, and partly because of the failure of the government to institute an effective system of collections.

All of this, coupled with currency inflation, developed a picture of a steadily deteriorating economy which could not sustain the livelihood of the increased Japanese population, except as SCAP arranged imports of foodstuffs and other necessary commodities from the United States or took such steps as seemed necessary to assist in the revival of Japan's international trade. This was one factor in bringing about a shift in emphasis in SCAP policy from reform, at the temporary cost of weakening Japan, to economic revival. Another factor was the steady deterioration of relationships between the United States and the Soviet Union, coupled with an equally steady deterioration of the position within China of the Kuomintang-dominated National government. The threat of control of China by the Chinese Communist Party, which was the obverse of the anticipated emergence out of the war of a China unified under National government auspices, tended to shift the base in American policy in the Far East vis-à-vis the Soviet Union from China, the war ally, to Japan, the ex-enemy. The circumstances of Far Eastern and international politics, in other words, as they changed during the years 1945–1950, shifted American interest, and with it SCAP policy, from that of weakening to that of strengthening Japan.

This shift in American emphasis from reform to rehabilitation and recovery for Japan was viewed with some alarm by those Far Eastern countries which had found themselves threatened by Japan's economic as well as by her military imperialism. Soviet disapproval of the tendencies in occupation policy was also expressed, both in and out of the Far Eastern Commission. But the effective control of policy, except with respect to the conditions of a peace treaty with Japan, rested with the United States.

The United States itself initiated moves toward a peace settlement, on the basis of which the occupation could be terminated, in the summer of 1947, following a press conference characterization of the occupation by General MacArthur as having virtually attained Allied objectives except in relation to economic recovery. That, he held, could not readily be achieved under the conditions of occupation. The American proposals for a conference among the Allies to work out the conditions of a permanent peace settlement were unacceptable to the Soviet Union and, because of Soviet objections, to the National government of China. The latter attempted to secure agreement on compromise proposals without success. Consequently, SCAP and the Far Eastern Commission remained in control, but with the change in approach to the problem which has been suggested.

The change of policy emphasis away from that of weakening Japan was shown in the movement with respect to the payment of reparations through a transfer of production facilities from Japan to China, the Philippines, and other countries with claims against Japan. [11] Plant and tool production facilities originally ear-marked for removal on the basis of the findings of the Pauley Commission were not only not removed from Japan but much of it was gradually brought back into use on the ground that specific plants were needed in production in order to meet requirements in production set by SCAP. Reports made by subsequent investiga-

[11] The shift in American policy as shown in relation to the reparation problem is traced by COHEN, op. cit., pp. 419–427.

tors of Japan's own requirements were the basis for modification downward of the conclusions of the Pauley Report. In consequence, by August, 1948, SCAP reports showed a shipment out of Japan to advance transfer claimants of only some 18,000 machine tools, of a weight of under 60,000 metric tons.

At the beginning of 1948, the United States representative on the Far Eastern Commission, on the basis of a review of developments, made it clear that the United States had come to the conclusion that more direct and energetic measures should be taken by SCAP to bring about the industrial recovery of Japan since that had not been accomplished by the Japanese themselves. [12] To that end steps had been taken in the second half of 1947 looking toward the reinstitution of foreign trade, with an increasing measure of private participation. Previously imports and exports had been handled entirely on a governmental basis through SCAP. In 1946 this had meant a United States expenditure of $187 million to finance necessary imports to meet the food deficiency. This type of aid was necessarily continued, and in addition import of raw cotton was begun through arrangements with the Commodity Credit Corporation. Under SCAP controls, imports of necessary raw materials increased in value in 1947 over 1946 by upward of $200 million. A parallel, but smaller, increase in the value of exports occurred. Industrial revival depended, however, on a much greater increase in the volume of imports of industrial raw materials than that possible under existing arrangements. Ultimately this importation would have to be financed out of exports. Thus industrial recovery required the reopening of markets to Japanese production. The opening of Japan gradually to private foreign trade represented a move in both directions. This was also true of such trade arrangements, essentially of a barter nature, made under SCAP auspices, as those concluded in 1948, between Japan and Pakistan, and Japan and Australia. These and other actions, such as the promotion of arrangements for a revolving fund, established from a commercial loan, to be used to finance necessary imports, represented the positive aspects of the changed policy designed to re-create Japan's peace economy, with production to be brought to the level of 1930–1934 (subsequently changed to 1932–1936). At that level, it was expected that the Japanese people would at least be self-supporting. It should be noted, however, that as of 1932–1936, Japan was economically the most powerful Far Eastern state, and that she had been able to exercise, by economic means, considerable influence beyond her own territories in eastern and southeastern Asia and the Pacific area.

It was recognition of this fact which produced dissatisfaction, previously

[12] The initially defined policy had been that of non-responsibility for economic recovery. That had been expressly devolved on the Japanese.

referred to, with the new American economic policy among some of the Far Eastern states. And yet it was clear that a way would have to be found to fit Japan into the regional and world economy if the livelihood of the people was to be sustained without continued American support. In the 1930–1934 period Japan obtained 24 per cent of her imports from the U.S. and 53 per cent from Asia (excluding Australia), and shipped 23 per cent of her exports to the U.S., 60 per cent to Asia. In 1947 Japan obtained 92 per cent of her imports from the U.S. and only 6 per cent from Asia, while she shipped only 12 per cent of her exports to the U.S. and 66 per cent to Asia. Obviously something approximating the im-port-export balance of the prewar period in the relations of Japan with Asia would have to be developed if the abnormalities of the postwar period were to be reduced.

One difficulty of accomplishing this lay in the natural fears of the Philippines and other Asian and Pacific countries, as has just been sug-gested. Another developed with the success of the Communists in China. That country had been an important source of raw materials' imports for Japan's industry as well as her principal Asian market. Whether or not agreements on trade could be worked out between Communist China and a Japan under American control remained in doubt at the end of 1949. With the United States in control of Japan, incentives of international communism, of which Chinese communism was a part, were away from action designed to strengthen Japan, just as the tactics of Japanese Com-munists were directed internally toward making economic recovery more difficult. This was on the assumption that the United States viewed Japan as a possible ally in its struggle against the Soviet Union. It was also doubtful whether the United States, under these circumstances, would approve of agreements which might have the effect, through trade, of drawing Japan into the Soviet orbit *via* China. The alternative to agreement was the de-velopment of trade on a *de facto* basis, with all of the uncertainties which that might involve, together with the development of a planned approach to a system of exchanges with the non-Communist countries in the area, and with the plan implemented financially by the United States.

Such an approach required the assumption of responsibility by the United States for either the security against Japan of the other Far Eastern countries, or the assumption of responsibility for the security of a dis-armed but economically recovered Japan. What part of this responsibility would have to be assumed could not, however, be determined in the absence of a peace treaty. Such a treaty was forecast for 1950, the intima-tion being that it would be concluded in the absence of the signature of the Soviet Union and Communist China, if that proved to be necessary.

The negative aspect of the change in American policy was shown in the growing insistence that union labor activity must be restricted where it might lead to lessened production, and thus support of an increased measure of government control of the industrial process. It was also shown in the relaxation of the pressure on the Japanese to carry through the deconcentration program in industrial organization, and in an acquiescence in the view that the purge of industrial managers should not be carried to the point of a lessened industrial efficiency. In other words, in general the emphasis on economic recovery at least to the point of self-support shifted interest from pressing forward the aspects of the reform program which might have a retarding effect on industrial revival. However, it should be noted that, in one respect at least, it was arguable that no change of policy was involved. As the shift in emphasis began to appear SCAP reported that the reform program had been carried through, as far as Allied objectives were concerned, since demobilization and disarmament had been completed and the institutions of democracy had been erected. This left the responsibility of permitting the Japanese to restore their means of livelihood, under safeguards against a revival of militarism and of a war rather than a peacetime economy. This would be a sole Japanese responsibility after the resumption of their independence following the conclusion of a peace treaty. In the absence of a treaty a measure of responsibility for the revival of economic activity had to be assumed by SCAP.

7. JAPAN AND THE KOREAN WAR

At the time of the outbreak of war in Korea in 1950, Japan was thus still an occupied country, completely dependent on the occupying powers for its security. Its military and para-military organizations had been broken up and, by Chapter II of the new constitution, military organization was apparently permanently prohibited.[13] As, however, the international climate began to change, and especially after the Chinese Communists displaced the Kuomintang in control of mainland China, SCAP began to interpret this provision of the new Japanese constitution in relative rather than absolute terms. Thus General MacArthur in his January, 1950, annual "message" to the Japanese people made clear his view that Japan had not renounced the right to arm for purposes of national self-defense. This view was extended by the head of the Government Section of SCAP to include the right of alliance for defensive purposes. The Yoshida government im-

---

[13] This chapter reads: "Article 9. Aspiring sincerely to an international peace based on justice and order, the Japanese people forever renounce war as a sovereign right of the nation and the threat or use of force as a means of settling international disputes.

"In order to accomplish the aims of the preceding paragraph, *land, sea, and air forces, as well as other war potential, will never be maintained. The right of belligerency of the state will not be recognized.*" My italics.

mediately associated itself with this interpretation of the constitution. Since the Socialist opposition parties dissented, the question of rearmament and its nature and extent became and continued after the peace treaty to be an issue in Japanese politics. From the international point of view, dissent to rearmament for defensive purposes was registered by the U.S.S.R. and China. Other Far Eastern and Pacific area states showed themselves to be at most only lukewarm to the idea.

The outbreak of the Korean War resulted in stronger pressures on Japan from the United States to speed up the reëstablishment of its military forces. This was necessary because the United States had immediately to transfer most of its ground forces from Japan to Korea, thus giving responsibility for the maintenance of internal order in, and defense of, Japan to the Japanese government, while at the same time using Japan as a base for United Nations operations in Korea. A move in the direction of rearmament was made, consequently, with the SCAP authorization of a National Police Reserve of 75,000 men to be used to replace the occupation forces sent to Korea. No Japanese troops, however, were recruited for use in Korea itself, although the South Korean government was permitted to recruit Koreans residing in Japan for its own forces.

Beyond this, Japan offered non-military aid to the United Nations forces. This led to the placing of special procurement orders by the United Nations Command which in 1950 had a total value of $149 million. This was in addition to $361 million in foreign aid. American economic aid went down to $164 million in 1951 and then ceased, while special procurement totals went up to $592 million in 1951, $824 million in 1952, $809 million in 1953. They declined to $596 million in 1954, following the Korean armistice. [14]

These special procurement orders, necessitated by the exigencies of the Korean War, greatly stimulated Japan's industrial recovery, which depended upon Japan's ability to finance the imports necessary to keep her machines running and to modernize and expand her plant capacity. After the Korean armistice, Japan continued to receive large dollar payments for the "special procurement" necessary to maintain the American military establishment in Japan agreed upon for security purposes. Thus by 1957 Japan had completed her economic recovery.

Her gross national product (in real terms) was 44 per cent higher than in the middle 1930's and income per head over 10 per cent higher. For several years her international accounts had shown a favorable balance and she had accumulated substantial foreign-exchange reserves. She had carried through the reëquipment of her major industries and productivity had risen well above the prewar level and was rapidly increasing. [15]

[14] Figures from ALLEN, op. cit., table 23.
[15] Ibid., p. 21.

8. THE ECONOMIC RECOVERY PROBLEM

And yet a major preoccupation of Japanese governments continued to be with the economic problem. Industrial recovery had been stimulated and facilitated by American aid and American procurement in Japan. But it had also been made possible, and it had to be maintained, by reëstablishing over-seas markets for the products of Japan's industries. Japanese goods again began to be sold in the American domestic market as well as being purchased by the United States military services and personnel for use in Japan. This began to produce pressures from American manufacturers to restrict imports of Japanese textiles and other competitive products. When Japan was admitted to GATT in 1955, furthermore, several of the member countries invoked the Article in the Agreement which enabled them to discriminate against Japanese imports by quantitative means. By means of direct barter agreements Japan was enabled, with SCAP approval, to work out exchanges of goods with some of the Latin American countries, with Pakistan and India, and with some of the Middle Eastern countries. Special efforts were made, especially by the Kishi government, to get around the barriers to trade with the countries of southern and southeast Asia, Indonesia, and the Philippines which nationalism, as well as Japan's activities in those countries as a military occupant during the war, had erected.

The major prewar market and source of raw materials' supply for Japan had been China, including Manchuria. Together with Japan's Far Eastern colonies (Formosa and Korea), China supplied 36 per cent of Japan's imports and took 39 per cent of her exports, as against 25 per cent of the imports from and 17 per cent of her exports to the United States. The natural tendency in independent Japan's policy, consequently, was to reëstablish the trade with China which would materially help to release Japan from undue economic dependence on the United States developed under postwar circumstances. The establishment of the Communist régime in China; the nature of its relationship with the Soviet Union (and also the Japanese Communist Party); and Communist China's intervention in the Korean War—all militated against the reopening of mutually beneficial trade relations between Japan and Communist China, at least until a basis of accommodation between the United States and the U.S.S.R. and China had been found. This economic side of the problem facing Japan was thus an aspect of the total problem of postwar power relationships in the Far East.

9. PEACE MAKING, 1947–1949

In 1947 both SCAP and Washington, in that order, had reached the conclusion that the purposes of the occupation had been substantially realized and that the conditions of peace between Japan and the Allies should be defined in a peace treaty. As stated above, it had proved to be impossible to reach an agreement between the United States and the U.S.S.R. even on the method of negotiation. Consequently it was not possible to proceed until the United States, faced with growing dissatisfaction with the occupation in Japan and with an increasing pressure of opinion at home to rid itself of the burden of the occupation, made up its mind to end the state of war, whether or not the Soviet Union concurred. A draft treaty was prepared in the U.S. Department of State, and bilateral negotiations were undertaken by Mr. John Foster Dulles, a Republican appointed by the Truman administration for this purpose. This had the effect of avoiding making policy toward Japan a political issue in the United States. From the outset the Soviet Union was invited to participate in the negotiations. No agreement, however, was reached with it. Some modifications were made in the American draft as a result of Mr. Dulles' negotiations with Australia, New Zealand, Britain, Burma, France, and other states. A final Anglo-American draft, thus negotiated, was used as the basis for comment and signature at the Conference convened at San Francisco on September 5, 1951. Forty-nine states signed the Treaty, although all of its terms did not meet with the full approval of all of the signatories. The Philippine delegation, for example, recorded its dissatisfaction with the provisions made for reparations, leaving the way open to future direct negotiations with Japan on the subject. Burma, India, and Yugoslavia declined the invitation to attend the Conference and thus failed to sign the Treaty. The U.S.S.R., Czechoslovakia, and Poland attended the Conference but refused to sign the Treaty. With the Japanese signature, nevertheless, the war in the Pacific was formally ended for all of the belligerents except China, Burma, and the U.S.S.R. India had not been constituted as a state until after 1945, and thus had not been a belligerent in the war except as a part of the British imperial state, so it had not been specially consulted in the prior negotiations among the belligerents. China was not represented at the Conference since the United States continued to recognize the National government while such other states as Britain, India, and the U.S.S.R. had extended recognition to the Communist régime as the government of China. The failure to provide for representation of Communist China was among the reasons why India refused to attend the Conference.

Japan was the only signatory state which had ratified the Treaty by the end of 1951. Consequently it only came into force in 1952, following ratification by the United States and other states which had signed it.

American ratification was delayed until Japan had also accepted the terms of a separate security treaty under which the United States could, after the termination of the occupation, maintain bases and military personnel in Japan. This necessitated the conclusion, February 28, 1952, of an Administrative Agreement which provided for, and defined the limits of, American jurisdiction over all United States and attached civilian personnel in Japan. It also provided for a joint committee to negotiate agreements for facilities and areas to be used by the United States, and for an annual Japanese contribution of $155 million toward garrisoning costs. Thus the conclusion of peace did not result in a complete withdrawal of the United States from a military position within Japan. As a result, the continued presence in Japan of American military personnel, even on agreed conditions and for purposes of security and defense, produced frictions growing out of individual behavior, as in the Girard case, on which the oil of diplomacy had to be used. Beyond this, these security arrangements had the same effect as the economic situation, of restricting the freedom of the Japanese government in exercising judgment especially in the field of foreign policy. It inevitably brought about the alignment of Japan with the United States and its allies against Communist China and the U.S.S.R. In this respect it confined Japanese policy within the limits within which conservative Japanese governments would perhaps have preferred to confine it, as far as general alignment in international politics was concerned.

This alignment determined the choice for Japan as between the Peking and Formosa régimes. Consequently a separate treaty was concluded between Japan and the National government of China. Under the circumstances this presented a special difficulty in determining the extent of territorial application of the terms of the Treaty. The National government sought through the Treaty Japanese recognition of its claim to be the government of all of China. The Japanese sought to restrict the operation of the Treaty to Formosa. The compromise reached and embodied in the Treaty of April 28, 1952, made it applicable to Formosa, the Pescadores Islands, and territories which might subsequently come under the control of the National government. The Japanese government thereafter defined its policy as that of non-recognition of the Chinese Communist government, the chief of the Asia Bureau of the Foreign Office stating that "the treaty with the Nationalist Government applies to all of China. There no longer is a state of war that calls for any further treaty with China."

In this way Japan would seem to have closed a possible gap in the San Francisco Treaty. That treaty provided for a divesting of Japan's title to Formosa, as well as other parts of the pre-1945 Japanese Empire, without formally transferring title from Japan to China. In making this separate peace with the National government, which was ruling Formosa as a province of China, Japan may be viewed as accepting the transfer of its former colony to China.

India also concluded a separate treaty "of perpetual peace and amity" with Japan (June 6, 1952), as did Burma at about the same time. With the ratification of the San Francisco Treaty by the Philippine government, after a settlement of the reparations question in 1956, Japan consequently found itself officially at peace with all states except those in the orbit of the U.S.S.R.

Over the same period in which it had been engaged in reëstablishing its relations with other states, Japan had been seeking reintegration into the organized international community. Moves in this direction had been undertaken, with the encouragement of SCAP before the conclusion of the Peace Treaty. Thus Japan became interested in UNESCO activities before 1950, was admitted to the International Labour Organization, sent observers to GATT meetings and was finally admitted to membership, and participated increasingly directly in numerous international technical conferences. The final step in this direction—membership in the United Nations—could not be taken until December, 1957, because of the state of Japan's relations with the U.S.S.R.

One of the sources of friction between Japan and the U.S.S.R. during the period of the occupation had been the refusal of the Russians to repatriate Japanese prisoners of war. Repatriation was pushed by SCAP, as well as by Japan, and was a perennial topic on the agenda of the so-called Control Council. The Soviet Union took no action to meet Japanese and SCAP criticism until 1949 when, on May 20, the Soviet repatriation authority announced that all remaining prisoners of war held in the U.S.S.R. would be repatriated to Japan by November. The first group of 2000, arriving June 27, engaged in pro-Communist demonstrations upon their arrival, showing themselves to have been heavily indoctrinated while held in Soviet prison camps. Altogether it was reported that some 95,000 had been repatriated by December 15. The Russians claimed that this disposed of the issue, since the 10,000 they admitted still holding were being held for trial as war criminals. The Japanese, however, denied the Russian claim, holding that some 60,000 were still unaccounted for, on the assumption that 150,000 had died in captivity. In spite of this difference the action taken by the Soviet authorities lessened the friction resulting from the repatriation issue.

Another aspect of the problem of relationship with the U.S.S.R. involved the Japanese Communist Party and its activities. Rigorously suppressed before and during the war, it was enabled to resume activities as SCAP, in fulfillment of its mission, required the repeal of "the dangerous thoughts" laws and released from prison and permitted the return to Japan of Communist Party leaders. By 1949, the party, although its membership was not large (around 100,000), had been able to poll some 3 million votes and increase its Diet representation from 4 to 35. It had also been successful in establishing a position of leadership in the newly created labor organizations. The growth in strength of the Communist Party consequently became a matter of such concern to the government that the third Yoshida Cabinet, constituted after the 1949 elections, pledged itself to a determined fight against the Communists. The limits to the action that might be undertaken were set by SCAP which, while not unsympathetic to the anti-Communist program, initially made clear its determination to uphold the new constitutional régime of civil liberties. The Japanese government therefore moved to fulfill its pledge by the creation of a Diet "Un-Japanese Activities Committee." This committee subsequently (October 26, 1949) charged that the Communist Party planned revolution by promoting labor violence and acts of terrorism. This was denied by the party leaders, but some evidence to support the charge was secured by a police raid on party headquarters.

The charge, whether well- or ill-founded, introduced the political struggle into the area of labor relations. SCAP had been tolerant of strikes when they had had an economic motivation but by 1949 had begun to view with disapproval labor agitation which used political means even where, as was true in pre-independence Japan, that was necessary to attain purely economic ends. The charge against the Communists thus helped to move SCAP to approval of government action directed against the Japanese Communist Party.

Ill-advised actions of the Communist Party in other directions further strengthened the position of the government in moving against it. For example, in the spring of 1950, while the repatriation issue was still being pressed, Mr. Tokuda, one of the principal Communist leaders, was reported to have indicated a lack of desire on the part of the Communist Party to have any prisoners repatriated except those fully indoctrinated with Communist principles, who would consequently serve Communist purposes after repatriation. He was further reported to have told a Diet Committee investigating communism that the Soviet and not the Japanese figures on repatriation should be accepted. This fitted into the pattern of outside direction of party activities indicated by a Cominform criticism in January, 1950, of the failure of Sanzo Nosaka, then head of the party in Japan, to lead the party into active operations against the American occupation.

All these developments moved SCAP policy further toward approval of action directed against the Communist Party by the Japanese government. The government, however, preferred to be moved by SCAP rather than to initiate drastic action itself, even with SCAP approval. Consequently it was on the orders of SCAP that the Japanese government barred the twenty-four members of the Communist Party Central Committee from holding public office; suspended publication of the principal Communist paper (*Akahata*) as a foreign subversive instrument, subsequently banning all Communist publications; and issued warrants for the arrest of nine of the principal Communist leaders. These actions drove the Japanese Communist Party underground and at least temporarily eliminated it as a factor in Japanese politics, as was revealed in the failure of the party to hold any of its seats in the Diet in the 1952 elections. Its national status was not improved by the failure of the U.S.S.R. to make peace with Japan in and after 1951.

10. POST-INDEPENDENCE POLITICS

As Japan approached independence an inescapable question was that of the permanence of changes made under the direction or guidance of the occupation authorities. After 1947 and before the actual termination of the occupation, more and more internal freedom of action was permitted the Japanese government. It could, of course, undertake change only with the acquiescence of SCAP until 1952. But, within that limit, indications were given of the nature of the changes which the Japanese would make if and as they had the power to order their own affairs freely.

One aspect of SCAP reform policy had from the start been accepted and applied by Japanese officialdom with great reluctance. This was the policy of making ineligible for public office or for top managerial positions in industry those who had been associated with the development of Japan's expansionist policy. This applied especially to those who came under the "purge" ordinances, although there was also considerable feeling with respect to some (although not all) of those who had been found guilty and imprisoned as "war criminals." Consequently as rapidly as circumstances permitted, the Japanese began to "unpurge" those who had actually been purged and to seek release of war criminals.

A test case among the "purgees" was that of Ichiro Hatoyama, who had been the leader of the Liberal Party and the probable Prime Minister at the time when SCAP made him ineligible to hold office. Hatoyama thereupon prevailed upon Yoshida Shigeru, "a career diplomat without party experience," to accept the leadership of the Juyuto (Liberal) Party. Yoshida was thus enabled to form his first government in May, 1946. Hatoyama thought of himself as being, and for some years was, the head of the party who exercised power through Yoshida as his deputy. By 1950, however, Yoshida had become a seasoned politician and in his later premierships felt himself released from obligation to Hatoyama. Thus when the latter was "depurged" in 1952, it was in application of a general policy toward which Japan had been moving rather than because Yoshida wanted a special dispensation for him so that he could return to power. Hatoyama's return to political life, consequently, had the initial effect of splitting the Liberals into three groups. The elections held in October, 1952, gave the Liberal Party a majority vote in the House of Representatives, with a membership of 240, but it was divided as to leadership between Yoshida (105) and Hatoyama (69), with 66 members uncommitted to either.

Another prewar political leader, Mamoru Shigemitsu, who had been released from prison after serving his term as a war criminal, reëntered political life at the same time as Hatoyama. He became the leader of a reorganization of political elements which took the name of the Progressive Party. The Progressives returned 85 members to the Diet in the 1952 elections.

With the fourth Yoshida government, organized after the 1952 elections, dependent on a divided majority party, its control of the Diet was uncertain, and it shortly encountered a no-confidence vote which necessitated new elections in 1953. In this election the Hatoyama faction campaigned separately from the Liberals and consequently had its representation reduced from 69 to 35. The Yoshida Liberals secured 199 seats, while the Progressives seated 76, the Right-wing Socialists 66, the Left-wing Socialists 72, and the Communists 1. These figures indicate that the Liberal losses, largely in the Hatoyama following, were to the Socialists, both the Right-wing and the Left-wing. This result strengthened the Yoshida position through a composition of his differences with Hatoyama and through the establishment of a better working relationship with the Progressives. Similarity of views and interests, however, drew the Progressives closer to Hatoyama than to Yoshida. Nevertheless the election results enabled Yoshida to form his fifth government, which lasted until the end of 1954. By that time (November 24), the conservative opponents of Premier Yoshida had formed a new party—the Japan Democratic Party. It was made up of Progressives, Japan liberals (who had splintered off in 1953 from the Liberal Party), anti-Yoshida defectors from the Liberal Party, and a few independents. The Democratic Party controlled 121 seats in the House of Representatives, as against 185 Liberals. This brought it to the position where, with the support of the Right-wing Socialists, it could put through a vote of no-confidence in the government.

To avoid the formal overthrow of his Cabinet, which would have had to be followed by new elections, Yoshida resigned, and was succeeded as Premier by Hatoyama, with Shigemitsu designated as Foreign Minister. Right-wing Socialist votes were required, however, to secure a favorable majority for the new government. This support was secured as a result of a pledge by Hatoyama to hold new elections early in 1955. Consequently this first Hatoyama Cabinet had essentially only caretaker functions.

In fulfillment of his pledge to the Socialists, Hatoyama dissolved the Diet on January 24, 1955, and elections were held at the end of February. The elections resulted in a House composed of: 185 Democrats; 112 Liberals; 89 Left-wing Socialists; 67 Right-wing Socialists; 4 Farmer-Labor members; and 2 Communists. The voting showed a slight swing to the left, which was also revealed in elections held in April for the 2,611 seats in Japan's 46 prefectural assemblies. The Diet election results also revealed the fact that, by combination of the two factions, the Socialists could become the second strongest Diet group, with almost as many votes as the Democrats. The results also made Hatoyama dependent on support either from the Liberals or the Right-wing Socialists for a majority in the Diet. The country remained strongly conservative since the two conservative parties polled 64 per cent of the total popular vote. But that would not prevent loss of conservative control of the government if division continued between the two conservative parties. Factional separation also prevented the Socialists from exercising as much influence as their total Diet strength should have given them. Thus an incentive to seek a basis of union existed both on the right and on the left.

The first moves toward union were undertaken by the two wings of the Socialist Party. An agreement to merge was finally reached on October 14, 1955. This merger was followed by that of the Democrats and Liberals, the new party calling itself Liberal-Democratic. These two mergers moved Japan into the pattern of two major parties competing in elections, with the majority party in the Diet constituting the government. Thus in the elections held in November, 1955, which were necessitated by the unstable Parliamentary situation, the Liberal-Democratic Party secured 299 seats and the Socialists 154. Hatoyama thus had a secure position as Premier, a position which he held until he resigned in December, 1956. He was succeeded by Ishibashi Tanzan, who remained in office for a year, when ill health compelled him to resign in favor of his principal competitor for leadership within the Liberal-Democratic Party, Kishi Nobusuke, who still held the premiership at the end of 1958, the Liberal-Democrats having retained their decisive majority position in the elections of May, 1958.

The above account of post-independence politics emphasizes the personal factor in Japan's party life. It should not, however, be concluded that this was the only operative factor in producing intra-party and inter-party divisions affecting the rise and fall of governments. Numerous charges and counter-charges with respect to the improper receipt and use of funds, both public and private, continued to be made with political intent and consequences. Unquestionably there was the factor of corruption in Japanese politics, with the majority or plurality party, because of its control of public office, usually the best target because most vulnerable.

But there was real difference of opinion over questions of public policy, especially as the occupation drew to a close. The Hatoyama following, for example, was critical of the working relationship with the United States maintained by Yoshida, feeling that a greater independence should be asserted. There was a desire on the part of the more nationalist conservatives to amend the new constitution so as to eliminate what they viewed as the more definitely American-imposed features. Constitution revision or amendment, however, required a two-thirds vote in both the House of Representatives and the House of Councillors, as well as popular referendum. The strength of the Socialist Party prevented the initiation of amendments. The Socialists, as well as some conservatives, were opposed to the proposed constitutional changes fearing lest the result would be curtailment of civil liberties and a reversion to the prewar "dangerous thoughts" control under centralized police administration. For the same reason there was opposition to legislative proposals designed to replace the local government system introduced by SCAP with more centralized control of education, police, and civil service. There was opposition to (as well as support for) the reëstablishment of a military defense force lest it revive prewar military controls of important areas of policy. Some who saw the necessity for rearmament wanted to proceed more slowly and cautiously than others, and especially deprecated any action which seemed to be based on American views of need, rather than those independently arrived at by the Japanese government and based upon Japanese interest.

Hatoyama and Shigemitsu, when they reëntered politics and returned to power, took the initiative in seeking to reëstablish relations with the U.S.S.R. and Communist China, something which Yoshida had not undertaken in the years between 1952 and 1955. Thus in December, 1954, the newly designated Foreign Minister in the Hatoyama caretaker Cabinet, Shigemitsu, stated as the policy of the new government the exploration of all available means,

to restore close and cordial relations with our friends in Asia. . . . We are therefore willing to restore normal relations with Russia and China on mutually acceptable terms without prejudice, however, to our basic collaboration with the free nations. As for trade with the Soviet Union and China, we do not necessarily expect much from it at the present juncture, but, all the same, we shall welcome opportunities of expanding the volume which is now rather small.

Early in 1955 Hatoyama followed this statement with an expression of his own view that Japan should take the initiative in calling upon Russia and China to end the state of war. The Russians, in response, indicated their readiness to enter upon negotiations, which were subsequently undertaken at London in June, 1955. The negotiations continued without result during 1955. They were recessed in September to enable the Russian negotiator to attend the United Nations General Assembly meeting in New York. At that meeting the Soviet veto was used to prevent Japan from becoming a member of the United Nations. This action, viewed as taken to enable the U.S.S.R. to put pressure on Japan in the peace negotiations, aroused considerable feeling in Japan. Nevertheless Japan resumed negotiations in January, 1956. By March, agreement had been reached on the less important issues. But neither side was willing to modify its position on the territories in dispute. The Japanese sought the return of south Sakhalin, the southern Kuriles, and Hobomai Islands and Shikotan, off Hokkaido. The Russians indicated a willingness to consider the return of Hobomai Islands and Shikotan, to which they had actually no justified claim except that of war occupation. They refused to consider the restoration of Sakhalin and the Kuriles, however, since they had been promised to Russia in the Yalta agreements. With neither government willing to give way to the other, consequently, negotiations were broken off on March 20.

Thereupon the Soviet government began to apply pressure by restricting Japanese fishing off the Kamchatka coast. This issue then had to be resolved before further attempts could be made to conclude the peace negotiations. A ten-year fishing convention and a three-year air-sea rescue treaty were concluded on May 12, and negotiation concerning the terms of a peace treaty was resumed, Shigemitsu going to Moscow for that purpose. His negotiations with the Soviet Foreign Minister led to no agreement, and negotiations were again suspended—this time to enable the two Foreign Ministers to attend the London Conference on the Suez question.

By this time it had become apparent that Japan would either have to (1) accept the loss of Sakhalin and the Kuriles in order to conclude a definitive peace treaty; (2) look forward to protracted negotiations, with no probable solution in sight; (3) give up negotiation and thus tacitly acquiesce in the postwar status of neither hostility nor peace; or (4) seek a method of restoring relations without concluding a formal peace treaty.

Since Hatoyama was determined not to leave office until this, the major undertaking which he had instituted, had been brought to some sort of at least relatively successful conclusion, in spite of objections on the score of his health he went to Moscow, having found through correspondence that the Kremlin was prepared to settle five major questions: (1) restoration of diplomatic relations; (2) exchange of Ambassadors; (3) fisheries; (4) United Nations membership; and (5) repatriation of Japanese still detained in Russia. Consequently, at Moscow, Hatoyama was able to secure agreement on the terms of a Japanese-Soviet Joint Declaration on the normalization of relations and a protocol on trade. These were signed on October 19, and were ratified by Japan in time for the latter to be admitted to the United Nations in December, 1956. The territorial question was thus left to future decision, although Russia at this time agreed to transfer the Hobomai Islands and Shikotan to Japan, but only after the conclusion of a peace treaty.

While it was possible for the Japanese government to institute negotiations looking toward a peace treaty with the U.S.S.R., this could not be attempted with respect to Communist China since Japan was committed, both by declaration and by circumstance, to deal with China through the National government. In the case of Communist China, furthermore, the incentives were clearly economic rather than political. Consequently the Hatoyama government and its successors tolerated, and within limits encouraged, Japanese to enter into private trade-exchange agreements with Communist China. This enabled trade to be developed, although within limits set by the post-Korean war restrictions and prohibitions on trade required by the United States. In any event, however, the Japanese traders, since they were dealing with state agencies, found themselves in a disadvantageous bargaining position, especially when China began to seek through trade agreements to shape Japan's governmental policy.

Under the circumstances, therefore, the Japanese government put more emphasis on the reëstablishment of friendly relations with the countries of south and southeastern Asia than with Communist China. This was especially evident after Mr. Kishi became Premier and leader of the Liberal-Democratic Party. Thus, before visiting the United States in June, 1957, Prime Minister Kishi went on a "good will" trip to Pakistan, India, Burma, Ceylon, Thailand, and Taiwan. Later in the year he made a similar visit to the Asian countries not included in his first itinerary, and to Australia, New Zealand, and the Philippines. These Asian tours realized the purpose of laying the groundwork for closer and more friendly relations with Japan throughout non-Communist Asia.

On this foundation Japan began to inaugurate a more positive foreign policy, beginning to play a leading role in international relations. This was shown in the controversy over the further testing of nuclear weapons. In this controversy Japan not only coöperated with but began to exercise leadership of the so-called neutralist Asian states. A further step in the direction of leadership was taken with the election of Japan, on October 1, 1957, to a seat on the Security Council of the United Nations.

Thus within this short period after the termination of the occupation, Japan had again become an important factor in the equation of Far Eastern politics.

REFERENCES FOR FURTHER STUDY

EDWARD A. ACKERMAN, *Japan's Natural Resources and Their Relation to Japan's Economic Future* (1953). G. C. ALLEN, *Japan's Economic Recovery* (1958); the best brief analysis of the problem. ASHIDO HITOSHI, "The Rule of Japan Today," *World Affairs Interpreter* (Spring, 1954). W. MACMAHON BALL, *Japan, Enemy or Ally?* (1949); by the Dominion member of the Control Council. T. A. BISSON, *Prospects for Democracy in Japan* (1949); *Zaibatsu Dissolution in Japan.* HUGH BORTON, *Japan's Modern Century* (1955). HUGH BORTON (ed.), *Japan* (1950). JEROME B. COHEN, *Japan's Economy in War and Peace* (1949). DEPARTMENT OF STATE, *The Place of Foreign Trade in the Japanese Economy* (1946), 2 vols. R. C. L. DEVERALL, *Red Star Over Japan* (1952). WALTER C. EELLS, *Literature of Japanese Education, 1945–1954* (1955). MIRIAM S. FARLEY, *Aspects of Japan's Labor Problems* (1950). R. A. FEAREY, *Occupation of Japan: Second Phase, 1948–50* (1950). SHERWOOD M. FINE, *Japan's Postwar Industrial Recovery* (1953). NOBUTAKA IKE, *Japanese Politics, an Introductory Survey* (1957). P. M. A. LINEBARGER, DJIANG CHU, ARDATH BURKS, *Far Eastern Government and Politics* (1956). HAROLD S. QUIGLEY and JOHN E. TURNER, *The New Japan* (1956); detailed treatment of the governmental system. EDWIN O. REISCHAUER, *Japan, Past and Present* (1953); good historical summary as well as treatment of the occupation period. EDWIN O. REISCHAUER, *Japan and America Today* (1953). SIR GEORGE SANSOME, *The Western World and Japan, a Study in the Interaction of European and Asiatic Cultures* (1950). Supreme Commander for the Allied Powers, Government Section, Report, *Political Reorientation of Japan, September, 1945–September, 1948* (1949), 2 vols. RODGER SWEARINGEN and PAUL F. LANGER, *Red Flag in Japan* (1952). ROBERT B. TEXTOR, *Failure in Japan* (1951). HARRY EMERSON WILDES, *Typhoon in Tokyo* (1954). CHITOSHI YANAGA, *Japanese People and Politics* (1956).

CHAPTER XXXI

SOUTHEASTERN ASIA

1. NATIONALISM IN THE AREA

IT HAS already been pointed out that the developments of the war made it impossible for the Japanese effectively to implant and organize the conception of regionalism in Greater East Asia. The net effect, consequently, of the Japanese occupation of the European colonies in Southeastern Asia and the Southwest Pacific, and of the Philippines, was to deepen and widen the channels of nationalism and anti-colonialism. These channels had already begun to be cut before the war, especially in the Philippines, where the movement toward independence was well under way, and in Burma, where British policy had initiated a movement toward Dominion status. The effect of Japanese policy and actions in some respects was thus to ensure that movements already begun would be continued, with the rate of movement not necessarily under the control of the metropolitan country.

While this was not fully appreciated during the war, the colonial powers, nevertheless, in varying degree, had indicated some awareness of the fact that the *status quo ante* 1941 would have to be modified toward self-government, autonomy, or independence. Formal commitments as to change, however, were avoided, apparently for two principal reasons: (1) on the ground that no precise commitment could wisely be made in the absence of fairly exact knowledge of the situation which would actually exist at the end of the war; and (2) on the assumption that the colonial power would be welcomed back into its colony because of a general acceptance of the beneficence of its rule in contrast with that of the Japanese, and that, consequently, it would have freedom to determine the nature and the rate of modification of prewar relationships. Exceptions to this were the commitment of the United States to meet, or possibly advance, if war circumstances permitted, the schedule set up for Philippine independence, and a broad statement by Queen Wilhelmina (December 7, 1942) committing the Netherlands to the establishment of a new form of relationship to the Netherlands Indies. Nevertheless even these exceptions assumed that the power of decision rested exclusively with the colonial power, substantially unmodified by local circumstances resulting from the applications of Japanese policy which strengthened local nationalism and gave it the means of expression. The validity of the assumptions made can, however, best be determined by an examination of postwar developments in each colony.

2. INDO-CHINA

Indo-China was the only colonial territory from which the Japanese did not immediately displace completely the authority of the colonial power. Upon the fall of France, Governor Decoux accepted the authority of the Vichy government and attempted to maintain the French position by adapting his position to Japanese demands, In this, however, he was in effect carrying out agreements made directly between the Vichy government, under German pressure, and the Japanese government. The initial agreement, of August 30, 1940, "not only gave Japan right of passage through French Indo-China and the use of bases in the colony, but recognized the predominant interest of Japan in the Far East in both the economic and the political domain." [1] From this position in Tongking, established apparently to facilitate operations against the Chungking government, the Japanese moved forward in Indo-China to the point where, by the outbreak of the Pacific war, the entire colony was under their influence and their military position was such that they could launch their southward drive on the British and Dutch colonies from southern Indo-Chinese bases. A striking indication of the strength of their political position was given when, as "mediators" between Thailand and Indo-China, they were able to compel acceptance of an award which transferred four provinces of Cambodia and Laos from Indo-China to Thailand. This settled a war undertaken by Thailand (Siam), with Japanese encouragement, to regain territory earlier lost to the French.

This collaboration of the French authorities with the Japanese, while it enabled the fiction of French rule to be maintained until shortly before VJ day, had the effect of lowering French prestige in their colony as much as the ease of Japanese conquest of Singapore did British prestige. The fact that a European colonial régime actually took its direction from Tokyo, even to the point of acquiescing in the military occupation of the colony, pointed up the new, even if temporary, relations of the East and the West. Its significance was not obscured by the fact that anti-Vichy Frenchmen were assisted by a native underground in reaching Chungking, nor by the fact that an underground anti-Japanese movement of some proportions developed in Indo-China.

Indo-chinese Nationalism

This underground movement represented in effect the direction given by the war to the Indo-Chinese nationalist movement. It was consequently

[1] CORDELL HULL, *Memoirs,* vol. I, pp. 903–904.

directed ag inst colonialism itself rather than being exclusively an anti-Japanese and anti-Vichy movement. This nationalism had its initial growth as a reaction against the early French policy of assimilation. It expressed itself particularly in Annam and Tongking. It was stimulated by the Japanese victory over Russia in 1904–1905, by the use of Annamites by France both as laborers and as soldiers in World War I, and by the development and course of the Nationalist revolution in China. The intellectuals who furnished it leadership were educated in the French liberal tradition. "Though France naturally never wanted an indigenous nationalist movement to destroy her sovereignty, French institutions were so impregnated with the liberal ideas of 1789 that they unconsciously fostered patriotism and a love of political liberty in subject peoples," [2] who had an opportunity to become acquainted with them through education. But Annamite traditionalism, which was Chinese in its origin, was strong enough to bring France to modify her attempts at direct rule, and to replace it by indirect government through native institutions in Annam and Tongking. Thus the conception of cultural independence was maintained in the face of the new intellectual orientation of the Annamite intellectuals toward French political ideals. The fact that those ideals were strongly at variance with the practice of colonial government made the intellectuals nationalists rather than supporters of the French régime and of assimilation.

That the nationalist movement before World War II had not developed more strength was due to a number of considerations. One important reason for its lack of strength lay in the lack of homogeneity of the peoples of Indo-China. The Annamites, the most vigorous single element, comprising 16 million of the total of 23 million people of Indo-China, occupied only 11 per cent (285,000 square miles) of the available land of the country.

Moreover the land that they occupy is laid out in a uniquely strange pattern. It extends from the Tonkin delta in the north to the southern tip of Cochin China, a distance of 750 miles. At its northern extremity it embraces 5,800 square miles and at its southern extremity, some 20,000 square miles, but between these two termini it is extremely narrow. In some parts of Annam the territory that is truly Annamite is only a few kilometers wide, and consists of coastal fishing villages some distance behind which lie, first, former lagoons, now filled in and occupied by villages and rice fields, and then mountains which the Annamites have not approached and in which, at a short distance, the first Moi hamlets appear. In some sections Annamite territory is only a narrow corridor; elsewhere, as in certain mountain passes, no Annamites at all are to be found. [3]

[2] EMERSON, MILLS, and THOMPSON, *Government and Nationalism in Southeast Asia*, p. 198.
[3] PIERRE GOUROU, "For a French Indo-Chinese Federation," *Pacific Affairs*, vol. XX, no. 1, p. 24.

The Annamites, moving south from Tongking, thus occupied the coastal plains but not the hinterland, as far south as Cochin China. But administratively even this area was broken up. French authority was first established in Cochin China, which was erected into a colony and brought much more under French cultural and political influence than were the protectorates of Annam and Tongking. And the other two protectorates, which completed French Indo-China, Cambodia and Laos, were non-Annamite in population and more affected by Indian than by Chinese culture. Both of these protectorates had looked to France for support against Thai encroachments, as well as against the further expansion of Annamite influence. Thus Annamite nationalism had not penetrated Cambodia or Laos, and it was less firmly rooted in the colony, Cochin China, than in either Annam or Tongking. Furthermore, before the war, it was divided into several parties with somewhat different aims. One (the Pham-Puynhau Tongking Party) "did not aim at separation from France, and struggled only to obtain constitutional reforms. There was also the revolutionary party of the young Annamites, which united nationalists and Communists until 1928, when the latter broke away. In addition, there was the nationalist Annamite party, terrorists in close alliance with Cantonese groups. . . . Finally and most important, there was the Annamite party headed by Nguyen-Ai-Quoc, which was well organized and also relied on Canton and Moscow." [4]

None of these parties had mass support, except in times of economic distress. "The Annamite masses are, of course, not affected by ideological considerations, but the hardness of their lives makes them susceptible to any propaganda leading toward a change in which they would have nothing to lose and everything to gain." [5] But in terms of economic contrasts, the position of the Chinese (numbering some 400,000) made them almost as much of a target, especially in Cochin China and Cambodia, where about 85 per cent of them were found, as the French themselves. Their position as economic middlemen, and as political intermediaries between the ruling Europeans and the native peasants and workers, identified them as supporters of the rulers and lessened the possibility of development of close relationship between Annamite nationalism and that of China itself.

When defeat was accepted as a certainty by Japan, the Japanese withdrew their support from Admiral Decoux (March 9, 1945) and gave it to a puppet government headed by the Emperor of Annam, Bao Dai. This government's authority, however, was immediately disputed by the nation-

[4] Joseph Handler, "Indo-China: Eighty Years of French Rule," *Annals of the American Academy of Political and Social Science,* vol. CCXXVI, pp. 135–136.

[5] Emerson, Mills, and Thompson, *op. cit.,* p. 204.

alists who had been waging underground resistance against both Japan and the Vichy-controlled colonial régime. Organized as the "Viet Minh, or Viet Nam Independence League" under the leadership of Ho Chi Minh, "veteran nationalist leader and Communist," [6] the nationalists took over from the Japanese-sponsored government immediately upon the capitulation of Japan in August, 1945. Bao Dai abdicated on August 25, and a Declaration of Independence of the Republic of Viet Nam was issued by the nationalists on September 2.

French Postwar Policy

France, however, had no intention of withdrawing from Indo-China. Faced with the possibility that the United States might propose a trusteeship to replace the prewar colonial régime, and also faced with the reaction to Vichy policies, the French government, during the period between the overthrow of Decoux by Japan and the Japanese capitulation, drafted plans for a new colonial régime. As drafted, and as accepted in the new French Constitution, the French Empire was to be transformed into a Union of the metropolitan countries and the colonies. Within the Union, Indo-China was to be transformed into a federation of the four protectorates and the colony of Cochin China.

Neither race, religion nor national origin would bar Indo-Chinese from any federal office in the Federation, the higher echelons of which had hitherto been all-French, while many of the lower ranks had been inadequately manned by a "white proletariat" that also came from France. A dual citizenship of the Indo-Chinese Federation and the French Union would open jobs to Indo-Chinese throughout the empire. Although foreign affairs and defense were to remain a French preserve, the Federation would have its own armed forces which would be open equally to Indo-Chinese and to nationalists from elsewhere in the Union. On every front the Indo-Chinese were to receive encouragement to develop socially, culturally and economically. . . . Hitherto linked economically to France, to the detriment of its more natural ties with the Far East, the country was to develop closer relations with China and other non-French territories. For the first time under France, Indo-China was to enjoy freedom of thought, press, religion and assembly. [7]

Since this program fell far short of independence, or even, actually, of autonomy, its implementation required that France should have reasonably firm control of the situation at the end of the war. The possibility of control was, however, initially reduced by the transfer by Japan of authority to Indo-Chinese governments. It was still further lessened on account of the fact that sufficient time elapsed between the Japanese surrender and the arrival of Allied forces to take over from the Japanese

[6] HAROLD ISAACS, New Cycle in Asia, p. 156.
[7] ELLEN J. HAMMER, "Blueprinting a New Indo-China," Pacific Affairs, vol. XXI, no. 3, pp. 252–253.

forces to enable the proclaimed Viet Nam Republic to establish itself in Tongking, Annam, and Cochin China. The Allied forces which initially arrived to receive the Japanese surrender were British in the south and Chinese in the north, not French. The British at Saigon released French troops from internment, armed them, and transferred control of the city to the French. In the process the Viet Nam régime was forcibly driven from Saigon. "This touched off a bloody guerrilla war, first in Saigon itself and then spreading to the Saigon delta and the whole of Cochin China. British, French, and Japanese troops were employed against the Viet Minh guerrillas. After the coup, the French offered to negotiate with the Viet Minh on the basis of the French government Declaration of March 23, 1945, but this was rejected as being wholly inadequate to meet Vietnamese demands for independence." [8] Full French control had, however, been established in Saigon by the end of 1945, when the British forces were withdrawn since the Japanese had been disarmed and the British mission had thus been completed. This was possible because of the arrival of well-equipped French troops in sufficient strength to support French authority.

A somewhat different situation developed north of the 16th parallel, where the Chinese had the function of receiving the Japanese surrender. There the Viet Nam government was not impeded by the Chinese in the exercise of its functions, including the holding of elections and the establishment of a parliament. The Chinese used their position to persuade the French to agree to a revision of the conditions of relationship between Indo-China and China. In the agreement signed February 28, 1946, Chinese nationals were promised a continuation of the "rights, privileges, and exemptions which they traditionally possessed in Indo-China"; most-favored-nation treatment for Chinese nationals with respect to "the right to travel, reside, conduct commercial, industrial, and mining enterprises, to acquire and possess real property; equality of taxation with Indo-Chinese nationals; and the same treatment as French nationals" in matters of legal procedure and administration of justice. It was further agreed that a special zone, under Chinese customs control, with the necessary facilities, should be established at Haiphong for the service of imports into and exports from China, and that "commercial exchanges between China and Indo-China shall be regulated by a commercial agreement on the basis of most-favored-nation treatment." And, finally, provision was made for a restoration to China of the Indo-China-Yunnan Railway. Following the conclusion of this agreement, the Chinese troops were withdrawn from their zone of military occupation, leaving to the French the remaining problem of adjustment of their relations with the Viet Nam Republic.

[8] ISAACS, op. cit., pp. 156–157.

France and Viet Nam

To pave the way for peaceful entry of French troops into the northern part of Indo-China to replace the Chinese, an agreement was made between France and Viet Nam on March 6, 1946. By this Hanoi agreement France recognized "the Republic of Viet Nam as a Free State, having its government, its Parliament, its army, and its finances, and forming part of the Indo-Chinese Federation and the French Union." [9] The territorial extent of Viet Nam (whether it would include Cochin China) was to be determined by referendum. It was further stipulated that, a favorable atmosphere having been created, negotiations would be instituted to "deal particularly with the diplomatic relations between Viet Nam and foreign states, the future status of Indo-China, and economic and cultural interests." On the basis of this agreement French troops were able to reënter Tongking without opposition. During the period of negotiations, consequently, France was in effective control of Hanoi in the north and of Saigon in the south of the territories claimed by the Republic, and thus had ports of entry from which, as her military establishment was augmented, she could, if necessary, move to extend her control into the hinterland.

It was quickly revealed that the Agreement of March 6 did not carry the same meaning to the French and to the Vietnamese leadership. The fundamental points at issue were defined at conferences at Dalat, in the spring, and at Fontainebleau, in the summer of 1946. One of these concerned the nature of relationships between Viet Nam, on the one side, and Cambodia and Laos on the other. The Viet Nam conception was limited to "federation" of three independent states, with federation in turn construed to mean limited coördination of economic policies, such as customs arrangements and currency. Federation meant to the French, on the other hand, close coördination of policy through the French High Commissioner, who would not only represent France, and the conception of the French Union, but also the Indo-Chinese federation, of which he would be the President. In spite of this fundamental disagreement, however, a *modus vivendi* was signed at Fontainebleau on September 14, 1946. This provided for "one legal currency throughout Indo-China. A mixed commission including representatives of the different states in the Federation was to study the creation of an issuing agency to replace the Bank of Indo-China, and would also coördinate customs and foreign trade. There was also to be an Indo-Chinese customs union, and no internal customs barrier. . . . Another committee was to study the reëstablishment and improvement of communications between Viet Nam and other coun-

[9] Text of the Agreement in *ibid.,* p. 169.

tries in the Indo-Chinese Federation and the French Union. And in response to Vietnamese insistence on their own diplomatic representation abroad, a Franco-Vietnamese commission was to arrange for Vietnamese consular representatives in neighboring countries and for Vietnamese relations with foreign consulates." [10]

The other fundamental difference between Viet Nam and France was over the question of inclusion of Cochin China in Viet Nam, and thus over the frontiers of the republic. In spite of the provision in the March Agreement for a referendum on the question, France set up an autonomous government in Cochin China which could be expected to respond to French direction. Since they had already effectively resumed control of Cambodia and Laos, three of the five prewar parts of Indo-China could then be "federated" under the High Commissioner. These actions made it possible for the French to act in military support of an Annamite government of Cochin China presented as an alternative to that of the Viet Minh, headed by Ho Chi Minh, who was not only a nationalist but also a Communist in his ideology.

The net effect of these differences was the continuation of civil war, with actions on both sides enabling each to accuse the other of bad faith. Viet Nam did not have sufficient military power to dislodge the French from the cities and the coastal area within its claimed territory, nor to force the French to accept its conception of a federation which would be close to independence. It did have the power, however, in spite of augmentation of the French forces in the country, to prevent the restoration of peace and the establishment of French authority throughout Annam and Tongking. There was little enthusiasm for the French-controlled Cochin China government which the French presented as the alternative to that of Viet Nam.

The Bao Dai "Provisional" Central Government of Viet Nam, which asserted authority over the prewar protectorates of Annam and Tongking and the colony of Cochin China, was supported, after its institution, by France as an "associated" state, in the conflict with the Democratic Republic of Viet Nam, which was controlled by the Viet Minh party, and which was popularly referred to as Viet Minh. This Bao Dai government, during 1948 and 1949, negotiated the conditions of Viet Nam's relationship as an "associated" state with France. The general principles of relationship were embodied in the "Agreement of the Bay of Along" (June 6, 1948). Agreements reached by Bao Dai in Paris on March 8, 1949, known as the "Agreements of the Elysée," while generally confirming the stipulations of the Bay of Along Agreement, extended it somewhat and gave it greater precision. Thus by 1950, upon acceptance of these agreements by the French

[10] HAMMER, *op. cit.*, pp. 256–257.

Parliament (February 2), the conception of an Indo-China federation within the earlier formulation of the French Union had been replaced for Indo-China by that of "independent" states (Viet Nam, Cambodia, and Laos) associated with one another and each in separate association with France. This was designed to make it appear that the internal issue did not involve independence. It did have the effect of focusing attention on the Communist, as distinguished from the nationalist, aspects of the Viet Minh and thus of bringing the struggle in Indo-China out of the context of a purely colonial war into that of the larger international conflict. This was facilitated by the victory at about the same time of the Chinese Communists over the National government in mainland China and by the intervention of Communist China in the Korean War. The Communist victory in China brought the Viet Minh into territorial contact with a Communist-controlled state which could assist it against the non- or anti-Communist Viet Nam state. This new situation was crystallized by the recognition by Peking and Moscow of the Ho Chi Minh government, thus legitimatizing assistance to it, and by recognition of the Viet Nam "associated" state by the United States and other Western states. India, Indonesia, and other Asian "neutralist" states, however, refused to recognize the Bao Dai régime because they viewed it as being actually confined within the framework of colonialism and thus not truly independent.

The United States and the Conflict in Indo-China

One important reason why France had not been able to find a solution for the Indo-China question after 1946 was doubt as to actual French purposes and intentions. It was, however, increasingly evident that French resources were not great enough simultaneously to cope with the rebellion in Indo-China and with the problem of domestic reconstruction. The latter was being carried forward with American assistance and, until after 1950, the United States, which was unwilling to support colonialism against nationalism in Indo-China, increasingly objected to the use of American supplies in France to replace French military and economic resources which were transferred to Indo-China to put down the revolt there. After 1950, however, Washington began to view the war in Indo-China as one front in the general struggle against the Soviet Union. The United States, consequently, took a different view of aid to France, translated into assistance to the French in Indo-China. By the time of the armistice negotiations in Korea, the war in Indo-China, with Ho Chi Minh supported by the China which had intervened in the Korea War, was associated in American thinking with the war in Korea to the point where the new (Eisenhower) administration in Washington could declare, in effect, that no solution in Korea would be acceptable which did not carry with it assurance against Chinese Communist support of the Viet Minh. In these terms the United States was prepared, as it had not been previously, to give direct assistance both to France and to the Associated States of Indo-China to prevent successful Chinese intervention in that area.

By abruptly revealing the danger of aggression in Asia and the expansionist character of Asian Communism, the Korean war contributed to speeding American decisions. On June 27 President Truman announced that economic and military aid would be extended to Indo-China in order to enable it to resist aggression. Programs for the provision of arms and supplies were drawn up in the course of Franco-American conversations. The most delicate matter requiring a decision had to do with whether the direct beneficiaries of American aid should be the French army and administration in Indo-China or the still embryonic Vietnamese army. Although Vietnamese nationalist circles were most anxious to receive American aid directly, practical considerations of efficiency finally led to the adoption of a compromise solution: economic aid was given directly to the Associated states through the intermediary of an ECA mission, while military aid would be distributed through the agency of the experienced General Staff of the French army in Indo-China, assisted by an American military mission. [11]

As it proved, this decision was taken too late. The stabilization of the military solution in Korea during the armistice negotiations enabled the Chinese to increase their assistance to the Viet Minh régime sufficiently to enable the latter to enlarge the scope and area of its military operations. Armies were moved into Laos and Cambodia in support of the guerrillas previously operating there, and pressure against the French in Viet Nam was increased. This pressure prevented the French from carrying out their plans for transferring defense responsibilities to Viet Nam because there was no opportunity afforded to recruit, officer, equip, and train Vietnamese armies. Thus France could maintain itself and the Associated States against Viet Minh only by increasing its own military effort. This it was prepared to do only if given assurances of full support by the United States. These assurances were not given.

The Geneva Armistice

Under these circumstances the French insisted that the question of an armistice in Viet Nam should be placed on the agenda of the Geneva Conference of 1954, called initially to seek a solution of the Korean problem. The negotiations at Geneva resulted in an Agreement by which Viet Nam was partitioned at approximately the 17th parallel. The territory to the north, including the Red River delta, Hanoi, and the port of Haiphong came under the authority of the Viet Minh government. The part of Viet Nam south of the demarcation line was left under the control of the

[11] PHILIPPE DEVILLERS, *Asian Nationalism and the West,* W. L. Holland, ed. (New York, Macmillan, 1953), p. 244.

French-supported Viet Nam government. The governments of Laos and Cambodia were left undisturbed, but with the two states neutralized and their armed forces limited to those necessary for self-defense.

This partition, like that of Korea earlier, was designed as a temporary solution of a military problem. Consequently it was agreed that elections would be held throughout Viet Nam within two years. These elections were to be held under supervision of the neutral committee agreed upon for supervision of the armistice. The committee was composed of Poland, India, and Canada, each member having a veto on decisions. This meant, in effect, that the committee was not in a position effectively to discharge its responsibilities. The states which signed these Armistice Agreements guaranteed their application. The United States refused to sign the Agreements, but Washington accepted them in principle and agreed not to undertake military action to upset them.

The Agreements represented a substantial victory for Communist China. The cessation of hostilities put the Viet Minh, and through it China, in a position to employ the methods of conquest—propaganda, infiltration, and subversion—at which they were most adept, not merely in South Viet Nam but also in Cambodia and Laos. The United States, in its attempt to contain communism, was forced to define a new line of defense.

Up to this time the United States had backed away from proposals for other than bilateral defense commitments in the Far Eastern area. In order to secure acceptance of its proposals for a peace treaty with Japan, Washington had concluded separate security agreements with Australia and New Zealand, the Philippines, and Japan. The United States was also committed to the defense of South Korea. As the situation in Indo-China deterioriated, however, the attitude changed, and following the Geneva Conference the United States urged that a conference be held with a view to concerting methods of defense against a further extension of Communist power in Southeast Asia. The American proposals for such a conference were rejected by India, Ceylon, Burma, and Indonesia. Consequently the only Asian states represented at the Conference convened in Baguio, the summer capital of the Philippines, were Pakistan, Thailand, and the Philippine Republic. They, with the United States, Britain, France, Australia, and New Zealand were the signatories of the Manila Treaty, which established the Southeast Asia Treaty Organization (SEATO). The Pact established no binding obligations for joint military action and had no formal organization, except for a secretariat established at Bangkok, beyond a Consultative Council made up of the Ministers to Thailand of the signatory states. Annual meetings of the Foreign Ministers were held each year after 1955, also for consultative purposes.

Since Viet Nam, Laos, and Cambodia were, by definition, outside the sphere of direct military support of SEATO, the new collective defense system, as such, had little significance for those countries. What did affect development in South Viet Nam was American military, economic, and technical assistance, which totaled some $250 million a year in the years 1955–1958. This was essential to the establishment of the authority of the government and for the solution of pressing economic problems of rehabilitation and reconstruction. Similar aid was extended to Laos and Cambodia.

The Diem Régime in South Viet Nam

Bao Dai continued as Chief of State in Viet Nam until 1955, exercising his power from France. On the eve of the Geneva Conference, and in the midst of a steadily deteriorating situation, Bao Dai appointed (June 16, 1954) Ngo Dinh Diem as Premier, complying with Diem's demand that as Premier he be given full powers to govern. It was Diem, a strong nationalist with the apparent confidence of all the non-Communist elements in the country, who faced the difficulties growing out of long-continued civil war and the partition of the country. Under the Armistice Agreements, which he had not signed, his government was denied authority in North Viet Nam and was confronted with the requirement that elections should be held throughout the country in 1956.

The holding of elections which would be really "free" posed the same type of problem in Indo-China as in the Korea of 1947. Northern Viet Nam was unified under the control of a monolithic, authoritarian party, the Communist Party of Ho Chi Minh. If that party should be able to determine the conditions of voting, certainly the outcome in the north would be readily predictable. The southern parties would not be permitted to compete north of the 17th parallel whereas the Communist Party could effectively compete south of it. Thus the probability was that the elections would result in Viet Minh control of the entire country. This probability was certainly an important consideration in causing Premier Diem to avoid, as far as possible, application of the provision for elections in the Geneva Agreements, to which in any case he did not feel at all bound since they had not been accepted by his government. At first he had to proceed cautiously, and on the basis of principle, because of the intermittent pressures of the states which had guaranteed the fulfillment of the terms of the Armistice Agreements. By 1957 when, in July, the Vice-President of the Democratic Republic of Viet Nam (the northern régime) proposed discussions between north and south to consider unifying Viet Nam by free elections, the Diem government felt strong enough to ignore the proposal. Agreement on the conditions of unification seemed no nearer at the end of 1958 for Viet Nam than for Korea.

By that time, however, political stability in the south had been established by the Diem government comparable to that existing in 1954 in the north. When he first assumed the premiership, Diem confronted serious armed factional opposition in South Viet Nam, as well as conflict with the northern government. His difficulties were enhanced by the possibility of appeal from his decisions to Bao Dai, the Chief of State, who continued to exercise influence from France and with at least some measure of French support. To counter this the Diem government was given American support in the form of pressure on Bao Dai to order the Chief of Staff, a leading dissident, to come to France, thus removing him from the local scene. Diem was also strengthened by the American decision to send aid direct to Viet Nam rather than channeling it through France. With American support, furthermore, Diem was able to establish his authority over the sects which, each with its own army, attempted to dispute the authority of the government in different parts of the country. Having thus disposed of the local opposition, Diem took steps to eliminate the absentee influence of Bao Dai. On June 16, 1955, under his persuasion, the "Council of the Imperial Family" dismissed the Emperor from his position as Chief of State. Thereupon Diem assumed office as President of a Republic. This change not only affected Bao Dai but also completed the process of ending the colonial régime in Indo-China, since Cambodia and Laos as well as Viet Nam increasingly established direct relations with the United States and other states, with their governments exercising authority internally independent of France as well as one another.

3. THAILAND (SIAM)

In spite of the fact that it alone of the countries of Southeast Asia had been able to maintain its independence, Siam was placed among the countries of the colonial area from the standpoint of geographic location, having French Indo-China as a neighbor to the west and north, British Burma in the east and northeast, and British Malaya to the south. In this buffer position between French and British territory was to be found a large part of the explanation of the maintenance of its independence, preserved somewhat precariously historically by playing off the British against the French. While maintaining its independence Siam did lose some of its Malay provinces to Britain and provinces bordering Cambodia and Laos to France. Much of this territory was temporarily regained during the period of Japanese ascendancy only to be lost again as a consequence of Japanese defeat. Thus Siam in its modern form as an independent state included some 200,000 square miles of territory. It thus "makes up less than a third of the Indo-Chinese peninsula and contains only one of its five major waterways, the Menam, though with her neighbors she shares two others, the Mekong and the Salwin. The country's four main rivers, the Meping, Mewong, Meyom, and Menam, form a network that offers easy communication between the upland and the sea." [12]

The total population of the country is about 16 million. "Of this number slightly more than 13 million are Thai or regard themselves as Thai, whatever their origin. About 1,600,000 are Chinese or Sino-Thai whose primary loyalty is to China. . . . Between 300,000 and 400,000 Malays live in the extreme south below Satul on the west coast and Songkhla on the east coast." [13]

Another consideration in the maintenance of the independence of Siam was the policy followed by its rulers. Its original orientation toward China was changed with the revelation of China's weakness vis-à-vis the West. The Asiatic-type monarchy was changed into an "enlightened despotism," and serious attempts at westernization of the country were made. The rule was sufficiently enlightened at any rate to prevent the development of internal conditions such as frequently invite foreign intervention. "By decorous and diplomatic statesmanship Thailand progressively cast off the shackles of a semi-colonial status and transformed an Asiatic feudality into a modern, and in many ways model, state—with official friendship for all and little malice toward any but the Chinese within her frontiers. Only with the revolution of 1932 has there appeared a more aggressive, supernationalist policy." [14]

Thai Nationalism

The revolution, or coup d'état, of 1932 was an expression of the desire of an essentially Western-trained intelligentsia to exercise a more decisive influence within the state. Since its creation was the result of the "enlightened" policy followed by the rulers, it may be said that their reforms created the instrument which was to overthrow them. [15] Assumption of control in 1932 was followed by the introduction of a constitutional system of government which was originally pointed toward democracy of the English type. Internal conflicts within the group in control, however, led quickly to the elimination of the liberal and radical elements in the government and control by military elements. This military coup in 1933 was followed by the abdication of King Prajadhipok in 1935, in favor of a minor, Ananda Mahidol, who was being educated in Switzerland. Concurrently, freedom of speech and the press were limited, and authoritarian rather than democratic tendencies were clearly predominant

[12] VIRGINIA THOMPSON, *Thailand: The New Siam*, 1941, p. 3.

[13] K. P. LANDON, "Thailand," *Annals of the American Academy of Political and Social Science*, vol. CCXXVI, p. 112.

[14] THOMPSON, *op. cit.*, p. 211.

[15] EMERSON, MILLS, and THOMPSON, *op. cit.*, p. 118,

by 1938. This did not mean, however, that a static internal policy of an illiberal sort was followed. Reform continued to be promoted from above after 1932, just as it had been during the period of the absolute monarchy. There was substantial progress made in education, with a trebling of appropriations in the three-year period following the fiscal year 1933–1934, and with literacy rising to 30 per cent of the population. Similar progress was made in the field of public health. Communications were extended, particularly with the construction of motor roads. "In agriculture, the government has emphasized coöperative societies and irrigation projects. The land and labor policy of the government has aimed at improvement of the peasant farmer class, the development of a diversified agriculture, and the creation of a Thai middle class." [16]

reforms

The entire internal program of development was nationalistic in the sense that it was designed to strengthen the state, and so to put it in a position to maintain its independence. But a new expression of nationalism marked the attempt to create a Thai middle class. The large numbers of Chinese were the dominant commercial element in the country. The Thai interested themselves in agriculture, in government, and in the professions, so the Chinese had come to fill an economic vacuum rather than to displace the Thai from commerce and from tin and rubber production. Performing a necessary function, they were viewed with tolerance as long as the control which they had over the economic life of the country was not fully perceived. It was only in 1911 that they were classed with other foreigners from the standpoint of payment of the capitation tax.

The tax produced a strike among the Chinese, which brought the economic life of the country to a standstill. This for the first time made the Siamese aware of the extent to which the Chinese controlled the trade of the country, and from this time onwards, not only did the Siamese seek to encourage their own people to enter increasingly into trade, industry and commerce, but they also sought by legislation to limit the flow of Chinese immigrants, to assimilate those Chinese who were already in the country, and to place obstacles in the way of further development of trade and industry. [17]

The natural inclinations of the Thai limited the scope and the success of this anti-Chinese movement until after 1932. In the following decade, however, it was accentuated, in application of the view of Luang Pradist Manudharm "that the poverty of the Thai peasant is directly traceable to the absence of a Thai commercial class. . . . Luang Pradist believed that the forcible ejection of aliens from commerce would create a vacuum

---

[16] LANDON, *op. cit.*, p. 115. The statements in this paragraph are based largely on this article.

[17] GEORGE W. KEETON, *China, the Far East and the Future*, pp. 315–316.

that would suck Thai automatically into the business world." [18] It was, however, only after 1939, when the military authoritarian government had consolidated its control of the country, that a vigorous program of exclusion of Chinese from the economic life of Thailand was put into effect, although the issue had been of importance before then in the development of nationalist support behind the government.

Japan in Thailand

The new, essentially intolerant nationalism of the 1930's coincided with an orientation of the foreign policy of Siam toward Japan as the new strong power in the Far East. The failure of the Western states, through the League, to restrain Japan in Manchuria in 1931–1932 threw Siam back on her historic policy of either playing one power against another, if the situation was one of balance, or of conciliation of the predominant power. The government of Siam evaluated the situation as establishing Japanese predominance. Consequently it abstained when the vote on censure of Japan was taken at Geneva in 1932. Thereafter its ties with Japan were steadily drawn closer. In relation to the internal program, the new relationship with Japan made it possible for Japanese to begin to replace Chinese in commerce and industry, thus paving the way for the more vigorous anti-Chinese policy followed after 1938 since under the terms of the commercial treaty of May, 1938, "Japanese were placed in Siam on the same footing as Siamese from the standpoint of leasing or owning houses, factories, warehouses, cemeteries and charitable institutions." [19] Thus, instead of Thai being sucked into the vacuum in trade and industry created by the attempted elimination of the Chinese, the vacuum was partially filled by Japanese traders and by Japanese goods.

In foreign affairs a new treaty of friendship with Japan was signed in June, 1940, and ratified in December. This coincided with Japan's move into Indo-China, following the defeat of France in Europe, and with the demand by Siam (renamed Thailand in 1939) for the retrocession of four provinces lost to France at the end of the nineteenth century. The people involved were Thai as well as some Cambodians, and it has been suggested that the change of name to Thailand indicated a desire to extend the territories of the state to include all Thai. [20] However that may be, the weak spot in 1940 was Indo-China, and the new relationship with Japan gave Thailand the support of the then strongest Far Eastern Power in presenting her demands at a time when Japan was beginning to move southward ostensibly to strengthen her position against China but, as it

18 LANDON, op. cit., p. 115.
19 KEETON, op. cit., p. 317.
20 EMERSON, MILLS, and THOMPSON, op. cit., pp. 219–220.

developed, also to pave the way for the operations undertaken after December 7, 1941.

In her new role as predominant Power in the Far East, Japan offered her services as mediator between Siam and French Indo-China and compelled a settlement which gave the former the part of the territory in dispute in which she was most interested. This friendly mediation further strengthened the tie between Japan and Thailand while at the same time underscoring Japan's new position in Indo-China. This position of dominance in Indo-China, of course, brought Japanese power, and the ability to exercise it, to the borders of Thailand and thus paved the way for enforcement, if necessary, of the demand made on December 8, 1941, for the right to move Japanese troops across Thailand for an invasion of Malaya. This demand was debated by the Thai government for some five hours, during which time a token resistance was made to the Japanese. The demands were then accepted and thereafter Thailand (December 21, 1941) signed a treaty of alliance with Japan. Shortly thereafter war was declared on Britain and the United States. The latter did not respond by finding itself in a state of war but maintained relations throughout with those Thai officials, especially the Minister in Washington, who refused to concur in the decision of the government, which they held to have acted under Japanese duress.

For the period of the war, Thailand was a Japanese puppet state under the direction of one of its prewar military leaders, Luang Pibul Songgram. The leader of the People's Party, Luang Pradit, remained in office as a member of the government, although he had stood against acceptance of the Japanese demands and refused to vote for the declaration of war. Under his leadership an internal resistance movement was organized which was of considerable service to the wartime United Nations in military operations and internal sabotage toward the end of the war. Thus Thailand and the Philippines were the two Far Eastern countries subjugated by Japan which had governments-in-exile and developed important internal resistance movements.

Postwar Thailand

When the war ended with the Japanese surrender Britain, which had been at war with Thailand (the older name Siam had been resumed until 1949 when the state again officially took the name Thailand), received the Japanese surrender since that area of operations had been brought within the Southeast Asia Command. There had been no prior agreement between the United States, Britain, and China concerning the treatment of Siam at the end of the war, and Britain, when the Japanese were eliminated, presented "the Siamese authorities with a series of far-reaching demands. The British insisted that the whole of Siam's civil administration be placed under British authority, that all Siamese exports be regulated solely by the British government, and in general and until such time as Siam might eventually be received into the membership of the United Nations, that Siam become a British protectorate ... these demands not only were vigorously objected to by the leaders of the Siamese people but they were also vigorously denounced by the Chinese government and less openly but equally condemned by the Government of the United States." [21] As a consequence of this reaction the British position was quickly modified, and the treaty was negotiated (January 1, 1946) with the new government of Siam headed by Luang Pradit by which "Siam restored British rights and territories as they existed on 7th December, 1941, and undertook to pay compensation for losses or damage sustained by British subjects." [22] This meant that the Malayan provinces transferred to Siam by Japan during the war were restored to British control. The treaty also guaranteed Britain the air rights possessed before the war and reëstablished the obligation on Siam's part not to consent to the cutting of a canal across the Kra Isthmus except with British approval. The British, on their side, together with India, sponsored the admission of Siam to the United Nations. This took place without opposition on April 28, 1947. Thus the war ended with a revival of the pre-1932 British predominance in Siam, but with Siam's sovereignty secured.

The end of the war also brought about a revival and amendment of the 1932 constitution. The limited monarchy was restored under King Ananda Mahidol (who was, however, assassinated on June 9, 1946, being succeeded by Phumiphon Adundet who remained in Switzerland until 1950 to continue his studies). A bicameral assembly was instituted in place of the unicameral legislature. The entire membership of the lower house was made elective, instead of half being appointive, and, under the provisions of a new constitution, both houses were made elective. Thus the democratic impulses of the revolution of 1932 expressed themselves constitutionally in 1946.

These political moves, however, did not release Siam from the consequences of the instability and disorganization that the war had brought to the world. In Siam, as elsewhere, there were acute shortages of food and other essential consumer goods during the immediate post-surrender period. To solve the economic problem the government attempted to put into effect plans for control of the national economy. The situation even called for the rationing of rice "in a land that is and has been traditionally one of the world's major rice-producing areas. This decision

[21] SUMNER WELLES, *Where Are We Heading?*, p. 309.
[22] KEETON, op. cit., p. 320.

coincided with the conclusion of a tripartite agreement with Great Britain and the United States to apportion and restrict domestic consumption of rice to facilitate export . . . at a fixed rate of $80 per ton." [23] Neither this nor the other measures taken prevented a serious deterioration of the economic situation.

Songgram's Return to Power

This economic situation, together with dissatisfaction with the behavior of the political groups in power, paved the way for a successful coup d'état in November, 1947. This was engineered by the wartime collaborationist leader, Field Marshal Luang Phibul Songgram, who had rehabilitated himself sufficiently by the end of 1946 to be able to resume active political life. While the coup was engineered by Phibul, its immediate consequence was to return governing power to the conservative civilian leaders (it was viewed as expedient for the military leaders to remain in the background until there was a greater assurance of foreign acquiescence in control by those who had been tainted by collaboration with the Japanese). The new government, consequently, was headed by Khuang Aphaiwong, known as a democratic leader and one who had previously served as Premier.

To meet expressions of popular discontent, the new government promulgated a revised constitution, which was designed to reëstablish the position of the Crown as it existed in 1932 under the then existing constitution. New elections were also promised and were duly held in January, 1948. Since the elections gave the civilian rather than the military elements in the governing coalition a majority, Phibul then faced the choice of waiting to resume power legally after the next elections or of overthrowing the government again by the method of the coup d'état. He chose the latter, displacing the Aphaiwong government on April 8, 1948, with one headed by himself. He was able to maintain his position as the dominant influence in and on the government until 1957, when he was deposed by the same method he had initially selected to attain power. This was possible because of a split on questions of both foreign and internal policy between the three leading military figures. There was also growing popular indignation over the way in which the government manipulated elections. Following the "bloodless revolution" executed by Field Marshal Sarit Thanarat, one of the governing triumvirate, the other two (Phibul and General Phao, the chief of police) left the country and General Sarit ruled through Nai Pote Sarasin who was temporarily designated Prime Minister. After new elections, held in 1957, Thanon Kithikacharon became Prime Minister, General Sarit continuing to remain in the background.

Improvement in economic conditions, partly as a result of American aid,

[23] *New International Yearbook*, 1948, p. 445.

during the decade of Phibul's rule, helped to make Thailand one of the few orderly and stable and relatively prosperous countries in the area. Beginning with the 1946–1947 harvests, rice production reached and sometimes surpassed the prewar level, making possible export surpluses. The postwar demand for rubber and tin, for stockpiling by the United States as well as for current consumption, stimulated production of those commodities. The foreign demand for Thailand's staple exports enabled the country to maintain fairly consistently a favorable foreign trade balance. The restoration of production, furthermore, enabled the government to support increased expenditure out of current income.

Thailand and the Chinese

In the politics of the area, as well as in international relations in general, Thailand generally aligned itself on the same side as the United States. This was only partly because of American economic assistance in the development of the country and of the establishment of a direct trading relationship. The export of rubber and tin from Thai ports directly to the United States, rather than into the channels of world trade through Singapore, certainly had the effect of increasing American influence over the economic life of the country, with a corresponding decrease of that of Britain. But relations with China after the establishment of the Communist Party in power on the mainland had considerable effect in shaping Thailand's foreign policies.

From the start, the Communist People's Government sought to enlist the large Chinese population of Thailand in its behalf as a means of bringing pressure to bear on the government of Thailand. Communist China's actions in late 1949 and early 1950, to be sure, could equally be viewed as a reaction to Thai nationalist actions, which adversely affected and were primarily directed against the large Chinese minority in the country. Nevertheless the indications were that the government of Thailand was aware of the fact that an increasingly strong China might be tempted to seize upon the Thai government's treatment of the Chinese minority as an excuse for intervention in Thai affairs. Thus the presence of these Chinese, coupled with threats of Communist Chinese action in their support, caused Premier Phibul to follow an anti-Communist policy similar to that of the United States after 1949, although he was unwilling to associate himself with proposals from the Philippines, Formosa, and Korea for an anti-Communist Asian alliance until the United States led in its creation in the form of SEATO.

The North Korean attack on South Korea, followed by the Chinese intervention in the Korean War, had the double consequence of immediately relaxing Chinese pressure on Thailand and of further aligning

Thailand with the United States against China, since Thailand sent troops to Korea. These troops, as a component of the United Nations force, fought in Korea against Chinese as well as North Koreans. It was, however, Communist China's direct and indirect pressures in the south which re-shaped Thailand's foreign policy and caused the government to join SEATO. The terms of the Indo-China armistice, coupled with the then weakness of South Viet Nam, threatened to establish the Viet Minh, under China's influence, on or at least much closer to the borders of Thailand. Commitment to the United States' side in the "cold war" was not a large price to pay, under the circumstances, for commitment of the United States to give military assistance in amounts sufficient to enable Thailand to main-tain itself against its neighbors, so long as they were only indirectly assisted by China. Thus it was able to maintain and even strengthen its position vis-à-vis Cambodia, in the face of recurrent border incidents. Its alignment with the United States, furthermore, facilitated the establish-ment of more cordial relations with the Philippines, Laos, and Nationalist China, while not precluding improvement of relations with such generally neutralist states as Burma, which itself had a problem of border relations because of its not completely stabilized frontier in the north. Thus Thailand supported Burma in its attempt to secure the repatriation of Nationalist Chinese troops, who had come to rest on the Burma side of the frontier when driven out of China by the Communists. Subsequently Thailand gave such support as it could to Burma when the Nationalist troops were re-placed by Chinese Communist troops who were not seeking asylum but readjustment of the frontier along lines favorable to China. Coöperative police relations with Malaya were also established to assist in the suppres-sion of Communist guerrilla activity on both sides of the border.

Thus in a period of relative internal stability, external conditions neces-sitated constant concern with and activity in foreign relations. The new role of Thailand in international, and especially in United Nations, affairs was recognized with the elevation of Foreign Minister Narathip (Prince Wan) to the presidency of the General Assembly in 1956, as well as in the active role assigned to the country in SEATO affairs.

4. BURMA

"Burma, wedged between India on the west and China and Thailand on the east," has a land area of 261,789 square miles and a population of 20 million people. [24] About 66 per cent of the total population was Burman, the remainder being the "frontier" peoples, the Shans, Karens, Kachins, Chins, Nagas, and others, together with a foreign population made up of

[24] 1957 United Nations estimate.

over 1 million Indians, less than 200,000 Chinese, 19,000 Anglo-Burmans, and upwards of 11,000 Europeans. Some 80 per cent of the people were Buddhist, including all the Burmans; the Indian population was Hindu; 4 per cent were Moslem; and slightly more than 2 per cent were Christian.

The entire country had been brought within the British Empire by 1886. It was made administratively a part of India in 1897, remaining an Indian province until 1937. During this period the principal change made in government was the application to Burma in 1923 of the Montagu-Chelmsford reforms. Up to that time no attempt had been made to associate the Burman with the processes of government, the Burma Council in 1922 containing "only two elected members, who represented dominant European interests." [25] This meant that Burma was developed fairly typically as an exploitation colony along lines considered advantageous to the metropolitan country. Its agricultural production was mainly rice, with 70 per cent of the total cropped area being in paddy. Of the total prewar production of 6 million tons, approximately half was exported, principally to India, which was also the principal market for the most important non-agricultural commodity, petroleum, of which there was an annual production in the decade 1929–1939 of 250 million gallons. These as well as such other forms of production as that of teak (also primarily an export industry) were administered so as to give

a fat return to the fortunate shareholders, with a margin for new capital equipment foreshadowing still larger profits. All this was wholly the product of about a hundred years of British rule, based on law and individual freedom: freedom for everyone to make money within the limit of laws intended to protect the liberties of property and person. Not without reason those connected with the development of Burma under British rule could look on their handiwork with honest pride. [26]

The Burman, however, had not been connected with this development, except as a cultivator. The period of development had brought him into debt to the Indian money-lender, with the result that by 1938, 25 per cent of the ricelands in the thirteen principal rice-growing districts had passed into Chettyar hands. (The Chettyars were the hereditary banking caste of Hindus from the Madras Presidency.) Like the Thai and the Annamite, the Burman was not attracted into industry and commerce, nor did he find himself adapted to the new capitalistic type of agriculture. But, whereas in other countries of Southeast Asia the industrious and businesslike Chinese supplemented the European in playing the role of capitalist, thereby ultimately incurring the hostility of the native peoples, in Burma it was the Indian who played that role and whose unpopularity supplied

[25] EMERSON, MILLS, and THOMPSON, op. cit., p. 159.

[26] J. S. FURNIVALL, "Twilight in Burma: Reconquest and Crisis," Pacific Affairs, vol. XXII, no. 1, pp. 3–4.

one of the pillars of the nationalism which began to express itself after the first World War.[27] The first result was, as previously stated, the beginnings of the association of Burmans with the processes of government through the introduction of the Indian scheme of dyarchy. Of greater importance was the decision taken on separation in 1935. This reflected public opinion, as well as financial and administrative difficulties resulting from Burma's status as a province of India. Under the Government of Burma Act (1935) which went into effect in 1937, a bicameral largely elective legislature was set up which "controlled all of the administration of Burma except defense, foreign affairs, ecclesiastical affairs (relating solely to the maintenance of fewer than a dozen Anglican chaplains), the excluded areas, and monetary policy. The last related to actual coinage and the external debt, and not to the budget."[28] These important exceptions were powers reserved to the Governor who also had extensive emergency powers.

Burmese Nationalism

In spite of the reservations, the Act put the Burmans a fairly long step ahead of the Indians in the move toward self-government and ultimate Dominion status. In so doing, of course, it increased the desire and demand for complete self-control, and, in the legislature and Council of Ministers, provided agencies for the expression of the desire. All of this, however, was in advance of the preparation of an essentially naive and provincial people to assume and effectively discharge responsibility for their own affairs. Prior to 1923 their only association with government had been below the level of management. "In the routine of general administration Burmans were indispensable, and here many found a subordinate place as clerks, magistrates and judges." The educational system, in a country which had had a tradition of education when the British first arrived, had been directed by the British toward "training men for the employment market" in subordinate and mainly clerical capacities.

As there was no employment for Burmans as engineers and doctors, the scientific branches of education were neglected. In 1936–1937, according to the last prewar quinquennial report on education, only seven Burmans obtained a degree in natural science, four others in medicine and two in engineering. Similarly, as there was no opening for Burmans in industry and commerce, the study of

[27] "Though some observers trace the nationalist movement back to 1905, it may be said generally that the Burmans showed no interest in politics until the World War. The great Hindu-Muslim and caste problems of India did not affect Burma, and the Congress movement found barren soil there." EMERSON, MILLS, and THOMPSON, *op. cit.,* p. 160.

[28] JOHN L. CHRISTIAN, "Burma," *Annals of the American Academy of Political and Social Science,* vol. CCXXVI, p. 122.

economics was neglected. The new educational system did practically nothing to give Burmans an insight into the working of the modern world. From about 1920, on an average some half-dozen men were sent annually to England for various special studies, but most of them were absorbed into government service. . . . Apart from officials and lawyers, there were probably not more than a couple of dozen Burmans, if so many, who knew anything of the world outside Burma.

"And if Burmans knew little of the outer world, they knew perhaps even less of modern Burma," since there was not laid in education the basis for appreciation of the internal problems which the modern economic order brings in its wake. After World War I "the people were allowed to criticise the government, but they had no material for informed criticism," [29] although they had sufficient right of participation in it to begin the process of bringing into being a professional political leadership which, especially after 1937, had some experience with the operations of government.

With the elections of 1936 for the new House of Representatives it was revealed that the basis of democratic government would have to be party coalition, with the parties essentially personal groupings within the general framework of nationalism. "Multiplicity of parties has been the rule, and every Burmese Cabinet formed under the constitution since 1937 has been a coalition. All Burmese politicians claimed to be nationalists, but there was no uniformity of program or method. When the first legislature of 132 members was elected it was said to contain 132 parties." The resulting situation led the Governor from the outset to use his special powers of intervention. It also led to the conclusion, as of 1942, that "There is no reason to suppose that the Burmese politicians . . . could form any stable and competent government without some measure of outside assistance during a period of transition." [30] This conclusion shaped the thinking about the future of the exiled government of Burma established at Simla for the period of the war.

Effects of the War in Burma

The war itself introduced some important changes in the situation which were not fully appreciated by the British at the outset. In the first place, the circumstances and the rapidity of the Japanese conquest of Burma so lessened British prestige that, in spite of Japanese conduct, it was impossible for them to reclaim the position of 1937–1941. And in the second place, by the end of the war a new leadership had emerged which had gained experience and assurance and a feeling of power through organization and operation of an anti-Japanese movement within Burma.

[29] FURNIVALL, op. cit., p. 6.
[30] CHRISTIAN, op. cit., pp. 121–122.

The Japanese invasion had been assisted by anti-British extremist elements in the Thakin party who had previously been pressing for complete independence. They formed a relatively small (about 4,000) Burma Independence Army which set up "Free Burma Administrations" in the wake of the Japanese armies. "These, however, acted in such a violent and high-handed way that the Japanese soon suppressed them and governed the country under military rule." [31] This Japanese military administration outwardly transferred governing power on August 1, 1942, to the Burma Executive, headed by Dr. Ba Maw "a former Premier who at the time of the invasion was interned after serving a sentence for sedition." [32] In spite of the formal grant of independence a year later, it was made ever more apparent that the collaborationist government actually enjoyed little freedom of action and that, under its auspices, Burma was being utilized to serve Japanese purposes. As elsewhere, Japanese propaganda, which had met with considerable success before the invasion, was sufficiently contradicted by Japanese behavior to lose its effectiveness. Consequently, even many of those Burmans who had participated in the invasion went into the anti-Japanese opposition which was organized under the name of the Anti-Fascist Peoples Freedom League (AFPFL).

The Anti-Fascist Peoples Freedom League was quite unlike any Burmese political organization the British had experienced. It was new and different. The Japanese had scarcely overrun Burma before Aung San and the rest of the "Thirty Heroes" who had helped them were organizing to drive them out. A number of groups seem to have been at work, but the most successful were the People's Revolutionary Front, the Communists, and the Burma Defense Army commanded by Major General Aung San. By August 1944 these revolutionary groups had united to form the AFPFL. [33]

The fact that the AFPFL had an army as one of its component groups meant that the British, on their return, were faced for the first time by a political group which had a measure of organized power behind it.

[When the British returned] There was a vast difference between the land to which they returned and that from which they had been driven three years earlier. Then it had been rich in things that measure the material wealth of a nation. . . . Now after little more than three years, they came back to find their work in ruins. During those three years the country had been twice invaded; British and Japanese armies had fought stubbornly throughout the length and breadth of Burma, and each in turn had scorched the earth to cover its retreat. The mines, oil fields and plantations had been deliberately wrecked, and the management and technicians, wholly foreign, and most of the labour, very largely foreign, had fled to India. Agriculture had been unprofitable and

---

[31] Statement of Policy by H. M. Government, May 1945. *Cmd. 6635.*

[32] *Ibid.*

[33] Clarence Hendershot, "Burma Compromise," *Far Eastern Survey,* vol. XVI, no. 12, p. 134.

rice, of which formerly more than three million tons had been exported annually, was worth so little that it was fed to pigs. . . . The productive capacity of the country had fallen by about two-thirds. . . . The moral damage was even more lamentable than the material damage. For three years the youth of Burma, which should have been learning in the towns and villages how to live as citizens, had been apprenticed to the more exciting and less laborious art of guerrilla warfare, without even the benefit of military discipline. [34]

Postwar Government

British plans for meeting the requirements of the postwar situation in Burma were announced in May, 1945, concurrently with the reoccupation of Rangoon. They had been prepared by the Government of Burma in India (the Simla government) and were embodied in the White Paper of the above date. Broadly stated, the plan involved the restoration of substantially the prewar status as quickly as possible. At first there was to be direct rule by the Governor, assisted as rapidly as possible by non-official Burmans. Elections were to be held and the government recon-stituted, if possible within a three-year period, on the basis of the 1935 Act. It was then planned that the parties in Burma should agree on a constitution, after which negotiations would be instituted designed to establish Dominion status for the country. On the economic side, the Simla government had prepared a number of projects designed both to stimulate production and to facilitate a return to the "normalities of competitive business as soon as possible."

The British army was welcomed by the Burmans when the country was liberated from the Japanese. "No one has accused the Burmans of not coöperating fully and effectively against the Japanese from the time of their rising against the latter in March, 1945 until the fighting was concluded well after VJ day." [35] The initial attitudes were, however, soon changed. During the period of military government, administration was in the hands of a Civil Affairs Service (Burma) composed exclusively of returned British residents and "official" Burmans who had been in exile during the three-year period of the Japanese occupation. This disregarded the authority exercised and the services rendered by those Burmans who had not left the country, especially the leaders of the AFPFL. The result-ing situation was not materially improved when, upon the return of the Governor, Sir Dorman-Smith, it was realized that, under the terms of the White Paper, he was required to exercise exclusive powers for an in-determinate period, and that only after the restoration of the status of 1937 could the future position of Burma be brought under consideration. The principal source of opposition to the government was the leader-

[34] Furnivall, *op. cit.*, pp. 3–4.
[35] Hendershot, *op. cit.*, p. 133.

ship of the AFPFL which refused to coöperate with the British on the terms defined by them. "The strength of the AFPFL lay first in their unity and public support, second in their capacity for obstructing the government, and finally in their military strength." [36] The demonstrations of its ability to maintain its unity and direct the activity of its supporters, especially against the threat presented by returned Burmese politicians who were anxious to regain their prewar position of power, made it expedient for the new Governor, Sir Hubert Rance, to constitute an Executive Council of eleven members, six from the AFPFL and five from other parties, in August, 1946. The negotiations which thereafter were instituted resulted in a conference in London between the British Government and a delegation (headed by Aung San, leader of the AFPFL) from the Executive Council of the Governor of Burma. This conference was preceded by a statement by the British Prime Minister on December 20, 1946, that Burma would be granted Commonwealth status or independence, as it desired, "by the quickest and most convenient way possible." Thus the conference really had as its purpose the working out of arrangements away from the policy defined in the 1945 White Paper and toward the nationalist goal of independence. The conclusions reached in January, 1947, were for the convocation of an elective constituent assembly instead of a legislature under the 1935 Act. Until it had met and established a permanent framework of government, a transitional government was to be instituted, with an interim legislative council, as provided by the 1935 Act, of 180 members nominated by the Government from those elected to the Constituent Assembly; an interim government, made up of the Executive Council of the Governor; and a High Commissioner for Burma to represent the Burmese government in London. The British government was to support an application of Burma for membership in the United Nations as soon as possible, and to request of other governments an exchange of representatives with Burma, as desired by that country. The problem of relationship with the frontier areas was to be considered by a committee to be constituted, which committee, it may be noted here, proposed federation of those areas with Burma.

This agreement did not meet the extreme demands of the Burmese nationalists for immediate and unqualified independence. It was held by Aung San, however, to be a sufficiently long step forward to warrant its acceptance, and he was able to carry the country with him over the opposition of the Communist leaders and of leaders of some non-Communist elements. [37] Consequently elections were held in April, with the AFPFL

[36] *Ibid.*, p. 134.
[37] Dr. Ba Maw, for example, refused to sign the agreement as one of the Burmese representatives at London.

securing an overwhelming majority of the seats. The new constitution was adopted on September 24, 1947, and by the Treaty with Britain of October 17, in force from January, 1948, the independence of Burma was recognized.

The constitution of the new state provided it with a President, elected for a five-year term by secret vote of the combined Chambers of the Parliament; a Cabinet, responsible to a majority in the Chamber of Deputies, which, with the President, exercised the executive power; a bicameral legislature, with the upper House a Chamber of Nationalities in which "indigenous minorities control 72 of the 125 seats," an elective Chamber of Deputies, the strongest organ of government; and an independent Supreme Court.

After the elections, and before the completion of the new constitution, the political situation was changed by the assassination July 19, 1947, of Aung San and six other members of the Executive Council by agents of opposition groups led by U Saw. "The objective was apparently to spread confusion preparatory to the overthrow of the government." [38] As indicated in the adoption of the constitution and the proclamation of independence, the action did not attain the desired result, although it did remove some of the ablest and most experienced of the AFPFL leaders. Thakin Nu, in succession to Aung San, as Premier held both the government and the party to the agreed course.

The establishment of independence removed the central issue on which the unity of Burma's political leaders had been based. Consequently the new government was certain sooner or later to encounter opposition. One source of opposition had been revealed late in 1945 and had expressed itself at the All-Burma National Congress of 1946, when the Communist Party began to put itself in the position which led to the expulsion of the Burma Communist Party from the AFPFL in November, 1946. Before this, internal division in the Communist ranks had led to a split and to the formation of the Communist Party of Burma as an opposition group both to the Burma Communist Party and the AFPFL. Since the Government Party's program was one of socialism in the economic reconstruction of the country, it was almost inevitable that a rightist opposition should also develop. And a third source of difficulty came to be presented, after the adoption of the constitution, in the attitude of the Karen people, whose representatives had accepted federation but who did not seem prepared fully to accept the consequences of that decision, and who also were prepared to oppose any Communist influence in the government.

[38] JOHN F. CADY, *The Development of Self-Rule and Independence in Burma, Malaya and the Philippines*, Part I, Burma, p. 19.

Postwar Politics

In its first years the new government had to develop the power to exercise its authority against the Communists who sought to displace it, and against anti-Communist minorities alike. This was a major problem in a country with an established tradition of violence, and one in which the impoverishment of the masses gave them an incentive to lawlessness.

By the end of 1950, although the Karens and the Communists continued to defy the authority of the government, its position had been substantially strengthened. The larger rebel groups had been broken up and scattered in smaller groups throughout the country. Thus the rebels had been weakened but not completely eradicated. These smaller groups were hard to locate and eliminate. They continued to ravage the teak forests, some of the best rice lands in the Irrawady Delta, and the tin mines and rubber plantations in Tenassirim.

By 1952 the government was sufficiently in control of the situation so that the period of transition, during which the Constituent Assembly had exercised the legislative power, could be terminated and elections, as provided for in the constitution, be held. These elections, extending from the fall of 1951 to February, 1952, gave the AFPFL a strong majority (about 80 per cent of the 235 seats) in the Chamber of Deputies and thus renewed that party's mandate. The elections of April, 1956, continued the AFPFL majority, although the National United Front (Communist) gained seats in the Chamber and became the leading opposition party. With this AFPFL majority U Nu, the first Prime Minister after independence, continued in that office until his resignation in 1956. He did not therewith give up power, however, since he named his successor and the new Cabinet members. U Nu resumed the premiership in March, 1957, but resigned again in September, 1958, designating General Ne Win as Premier.

The general lines of internal policy followed by the U Nu government during this first decade of independence may be described as those of moderate socialism. Communications were nationalized, as was the basic understructure of the national economy. Compensation was made, however, to the original owners, mainly British and Indian interests. Both Britain and India acquiesced in the application of this policy, viewing it as appropriate under the circumstances. Britain, as a matter of fact, assisted financially in its execution. Assistance, under the Colombo Plan, and from the United Nations and the United States, thus enabled the government to maintain itself, to execute some of its plans, and to bring about such recovery as the initially disturbed internal conditions permitted. The British withdrawal, together with the conditions of foreign financing, had the effect of bringing Burma into international relations uncomplicated by the question of imperialism or even that of colonialism.

Foreign Relations

Nevertheless Burma was unwilling to align itself, as did Thailand, with the United States and Britain. In general it may be said that its foreign policy was oriented largely along the lines of Indian neutralism, although without acceptance of Indian leadership in Asian affairs because of fear of possible Indian imperialism. Thus Burma took part in the Colombo Conference of 1954, which took the initiative in calling the Bandung Conference of Asian and African states of April, 1955. Previously Burma had recognized the Central People's Government of the People's Republic of China (December, 1949), and representatives were exchanged with Peking in June, 1950. The government of Burma, like that of India, refused to sign the Japanese Peace Treaty, among the grounds assigned being the continued presence on Japanese soil of foreign (i.e., American) troops. A separate treaty with Japan was signed, however, on November 5, 1954, Japan having agreed to make reparations payments of some $250 million in materials and technical aid. And Burma refused an invitation to attend the Baguio (Manila) Conference and to join SEATO.

On the other hand Burma coöperated, short of military participation, in the United Nations attempt to prevent aggression in Korea and in the embargoing of trade in strategic materials with China. For a time, furthermore, it tolerated the presence within its territories of Chinese Nationalist refugees and of Nationalist troops driven across the frontier. As these troops began to overassert themselves, however, the tolerance came to an end and a demand was made in the United Nations for their evacuation. A three-nation military committee made up of representatives of Thailand, the United States, and Nationalist China undertook the supervision of the evacuation of these troops in 1953 and ended its work in 1954, having removed from Burma all of the guerrillas who could be persuaded to leave. About 6,000 anti-Communist Chinese seem to have remained. Their presence led to continuing demands for United Nations action in 1954. The question fell into abeyance, however, in 1956 when Communist Chinese troops were found on the Burma side of the frontier. This Chinese move was designed to bring about a redefinition of the frontier in China's favor. Negotiations to bring about the withdrawal of the Communist troops were carried on during 1956 and 1957, when agreement was reached on the conditions for redrawing the frontier.

The most serious problem confronting the government, however, was that of finding ways and means of disposing advantageously of the country's rice surplus as it approached the prewar level. The economy of the country had long been dominated by rice, which was grown on more than 10 million of the 17 million cultivated acres. Under postwar conditions the government found it difficult in 1951 to dispose of the surplus at the high prices set on the world market. The problem of profitable disposal in the normal markets thereafter began to be complicated by increased production elsewhere, thus lowering the price, and by the policy followed by the United States of relieving distress in some Asian countries through selling its own agricultural surplus below the market prices. Consequently Burma found it necessary to deal more and more with Communist bloc countries on a direct barter basis. Thus in 1955 the Soviet Union agreed to buy 200,000 tons of rice and to supply industrial equipment in return. Similar agreements were made with Communist China, Poland, Hungary, East Germany, Czechoslovakia, and Rumania. By these agreements Burma committed on fixed terms its major foreign trade asset to the Communist countries and soon found itself unable to finance necessary purchases from the sterling and dollar area countries. A rise in the price of rice on the world market, furthermore, meant that Burma was committed to the exchange of its rice surplus at lower values than would otherwise have been possible. And the failure of the Communist countries to meet Burma's requirements, especially for consumers' goods in exchange for rice, produced considerable dissatisfaction with the earlier barter arrangements.

Consequently in 1957 the economic problem was approached by a partial return to trade with non-Communist countries. To enable this to be done a loan of $40 million was accepted from the United States and a similar loan was made by India. Credits were also extended to Burma by the World Bank and on the part of a number of interested countries. A four-year plan was substituted for the previously announced overly ambitious eight-year plan. In this planning, provision was made for the return to private interests of some of the government enterprises.

5. MALAYA

British Malaya projects as a peninsula southward from Thailand and Burma toward what in prewar days was known as the Netherlands East Indies (Indonesia). Thus it is the link between the latter and the continental territories of Southeast Asia. The geographical orientation is strengthened by the cultural, since the Malay peoples in both Malaya and Indonesia are predominantly Moslem.

In the prolonged period of British rule before the Japanese occupation, a pattern of both direct and indirect rule had been evolved, the former for the Crown colony (the Straits Settlements) and the latter for the five Unfederated Malay States and, to a lesser extent, for the four Federated States. "The five independent states retained their predominantly Malay structure of government although their rulers were required to take the advice of British Advisers on all matters except Malay religion and religious customs." [39] The same qualified autonomy existed in each of the Federated States on state matters, defined to include "education, forests, some aspects of public health, agriculture and Islamic law." [40] On other questions the High Commissioner, consulting with the Federal Council, had jurisdiction. The same individual represented British authority as Governor of the colony and as High Commissioner in the "protected" states, but in the former the machinery of government was similar to that in other Crown colonies, while in the latter authority was exercised under the High Commissioner through the Resident adviser in each of the states. He, in turn, had his advice translated into policy through the Malay structure working downward from the Sultan.

Prewar and War Developments

One of the peculiarities of the situation which developed in Malaya, giving some of its direction to political development under British auspices, was the racial composition of the peninsula. The Malays, "the only permanent population that look upon the country as their native land, apart from a small though increasing minority of Chinese and Indians," constituted at the end of 1937 only 42.4 per cent of the total population of Malaya, with the Chinese having 41.3 and Indians 14.8 of the total. [41] The Chinese were a decisive numerical majority in the Straits Settlements. It was only in the Unfederated States that Malay predominance was beyond question.

In the economy of the country the Malay found his place as a rice grower and in other agricultural pursuits as a small peasant proprietor, and as a fisherman. Plantation production of rubber; industry, including the mining and smelting of tin; and commerce were financed and managed by Europeans or Chinese, with some Indian and a slight Japanese participation, the latter controlling the iron mines. Thus, apart from the British, the Chinese had assumed the strongest economic position in Malaya.

If, under these circumstances, there had been a strong nationalistic sentiment developed among the Malays before the war, it would probably have taken an anti-Chinese direction because of their greater numbers and their closer relationship to the people. The British, in spite of their predominant economic influence, were looked upon by the Malays (and also the Chinese and Indians) in fact as well as in name as "protectors"

---

[39] PATRICIA BARNETT, *The Development of Self-Rule and Independence in Burma, Malaya and the Philippines*, p. 53.

[40] *Ibid.*

[41] RICHARD WINSTED, "Malaya," *Annals of the American Academy of Political and Social Science*, vol. CCXXVI, p. 97.

of one from the other. But it took the war to bring into being anything like a vigorous nationalism. The Malay was essentially unpolitical in the Western sense, and the Chinese and Indians, before 1941, even though Malayan-born, developed their political interests and affiliations in relation to China or India rather than the country of their domicile. This, with the Chinese, resulted in some anti-British sentiment at times of Sino-British tension in China, but without changing their non-political role in Malaya or causing them any the less to look to Britain for the fair and full protection of their interests.

The colony and protected states were financially self-supporting except for the outlays made necessary for Imperial defense. And even for that purpose, for which the colony of the Straits Settlements was expected to bear a share of the cost, the states made voluntary contributions. The conception of the problem of defense was based upon the probability of attack from the sea so that expenditure was concentrated upon the building of the great naval base at Singapore and on air bases, with only a small military establishment. It was this, incidentally, which accounted for the ease with which the peninsula was overrun by the Japanese.

Release from the burden of defense made it possible for income to be devoted to the development of public services. Communications facilities were developed, including hard-surfaced roads and a railway line, 1,188 miles long, running from Singapore to Bangkok in Siam. The Public Health and Sanitation services were highly developed. Elementary education, free for the Malays in the vernacular schools, and limited secondary and college education, were provided for out of the public funds. An excellent medical school was maintained and Raffles College was established in 1928 but "A diploma from Raffles College was inacceptable for graduate work in English universities although Raffles trained teachers for the Malayan schools." [42] A few selected students were sent each year to England for their higher education. The revenue to support these services and the civil service was derived, in the Straits Settlements, from duties on tobacco, liquor, and petroleum; from an opium monopoly; and from fees for services of various sorts. Customs and excise taxes were a principal source of revenue in the Unfederated States. And the Federated States had an additional major source of revenue from an export tax on tin as well as that on rubber, from which also the Unfederated States derived considerable revenue. Thus it was possible to provide services from revenue which was not extracted directly from the Malay peasant or the smaller producers. This helps somewhat to explain the greater acceptance of British rule as beneficent than in some of her other colonies, although it should be added that in Malaya, as in many other areas,

[42] BARNETT, op. cit., p. 66.

British rule was synonymous with the introduction of the rule of law and of its impartial administration.

Just as Burma and the Philippines, as staple-crop exporting countries, found the measure of their prosperity in terms of external conditions, Malaya was dependent on the outside world as a market mainly for its tin and rubber. In both of these industries the major investment interest was British. "In the tin industry, while the bulk of the Western capital was British, the capital came also from several European countries, notably France, and from the United States. The bulk of the Asiatic capital invested in tin has been Chinese, but the mining of iron ore was solely in Japanese hands." The rubber estates were 75 per cent European-owned, 16 per cent Chinese, 4 per cent Indian, and 5 per cent Japanese and other Asians. "This excludes 1,250,000 (almost the European-owned acreage) in the possession of smallholders, principally Malay but also Chinese and Indian." [43] The main market for tin and rubber was the United States, but, in spite of the free-trade policy followed for Malaya until the inauguration of Imperial preference, the main source of imports, until cheaper Japanese-made goods began to invade the market in the 1930's, was Britain. Some of the restrictions on free trade introduced in the decade before the war were designed to restrict Japanese imports.

The war, for Malaya as for other southeastern Asian countries, had important consequences. One of these consequences was, of course, that represented by economic disruption and destruction. The fighting itself, coupled with some application of the "scorched earth" policy and with some guerrilla warfare after the Japanese occupation, accounts for much of the destruction. But the inability of Japan to replace the United States, Britain, and Europe in general, as a market for tin and rubber and her inability to maintain necessary imports into Malaya for a period of four years had not only a disrupting but a deteriorating effect on the economy of the country. Thus the end of the war saw Britain faced with a problem of economic reconstruction of some considerable proportions. And the restoration of production in Malaya was of importance to the rest of the world because of its nature.

The cultural program of the Japanese also had postwar implications, as did native resistance to it. The conditions of the occupation had the consequence of developing political self-consciousness among the Malays especially, and of increasing their political maturity. The local barriers to the development of a Malay nationalism, represented by the existence of nine states and a colony, were at least somewhat weakened by the common resistance, on an essentially centralized basis, to Japanese military rule. The Japanese attempts, toward the end of their occupancy, to in-

[43] WINSTED, op. cit., p. 104.

troduce or extend some of the institutions of self-rule also had an effect in developing political self-consciousness. Thus even in Malaya the British did not have, as it proved, complete freedom of decision in planning the postwar political reconstruction of the country.

Malayan Union and Federation

"The British reëntered Malaya early in September 1945 with the military force they had intended to use to oust the Japanese had the Japanese surrender not already occurred. Contact was made with the underground army and civil government was transferred to British Military Administration (BMA) authority." [44] The country was to continue under military administration until plans which had been matured for a change in the system of administration could be put into effect. The general plan, as announced in October, 1945, was to establish a Malayan Union comprising the nine "protected" states and all of the former Crown colony except Singapore, which was to remain a colony. There was to be a common Malay citizenship within the Union. Thus the plan was designed to break down the separatism of the Malay states rather than to destroy the Malay structure of government within the states. British authority was to be represented by a Governor for the Union, and a different individual serving as the Governor of the Colony of Singapore. Both Governors were to have fairly wide powers of legislation and appointment. But, within limits, the plan extended the institutions of self-government, lessening official control of the legislative councils which were to be constituted and establishing a Council of Sultans to advise the Governor on matters which he submitted to it and to enact legislation on religious questions, as recommended by Malay advisory councils.

The preliminary step to the institution of the Union was the revision of the prewar treaties between Britain and the several Sultans on which the protectorates rested. But within the short time it took to secure agreement of the Sultans, considerable opposition to the Union plan developed in Malaya. Among the Malays a "United Malays National Organization" was formed for purposes of opposition. The grounds of opposition were: (1) the inconsistency of the new treaties with Malay custom and tradition, and (2) that the integrity and independence of the Malay race would be undermined by the conditions of Union, especially those providing for Malayan Union citizenship.

After discussion, the British plan for Union was modified along lines proposed by a Malay-British Working Committee. Federation was substituted for Union. More rigid qualifications for citizenship were accepted; a High Commissioner was to represent British authority in place of a

[44] Barnett, *op. cit.*, p. 69.

Governor for the Federation; and the authority of the Council of Sultans, the federal legislative council, and state executive and legislative bodies was increased. The new plan required renegotiation of the treaties with the Sultans.

This plan was supported by the United Malays National Organization which had led the opposition to the plan for the Union, its views, as well as those of the Sultans, having been taken into account by the British. The opposition to the new so-called constitutional proposals was led by a newly formed organization called the Pan-Malayan Council of Joint Action, an amalgamation of Chinese, Indian, and Eurasian groups. Another opposition group—the Malay Nationalist Party—dropped out of the Council of Joint Action after its initial meeting but formed a Malay Council of Joint Action which followed a parallel program. The opposition demanded "a united Malaya, including Singapore, responsible self-government through a fully elected central legislature for the whole of Malaya, and equal citizenship rights for all permanent residents of Malaya." [45]

The two major areas of conflict were over: (1) the issue of citizenship, and (2) the amount of self-government to be instituted. The question of complete union, including Singapore, was to a considerable extent tied in with these two. The issue of citizenship obviously grew out of the major political interest of the Indians in India, especially as independence for India became a reality, and of the Chinese in the politics of China rather than in Malaya. Regardless of the place of birth, both groups felt that their primary allegiance was to the "home" country, and they tended to reproduce the party organizations and affiliations of India and China in Malaya. Thus the Indians, in August of 1946, formed the Malayan Indian Congress, and Chinese divided into a Kuomintang and a Communist organization. What each group preferred was a dual citizenship. Neither wanted to accept as its sole allegiance that of a Malay state. Each wanted local security and neither attempted to play a political role in Malaya until the protection of its interests required local political action.

Self-rule was a demand growing naturally out of war experiences and out of the general climate of opinion at the end of the war. It was a demand, in Malaya, however, of a liberal minority rather than of a majority of the Malays, represented in the United Malays National Organization which supported the position of the Sultans and advocated Federation under Britain rather than self-government, whether or not coupled with independence. The opposition Malay Nationalist Party, on the other hand, "is dominated by liberal Malays from the professional, student and labor groups who have a strong Indonesian orientation.

[45] *Ibid.*, p. 73.

Its program aims at an independent Malaya, composed of both the Malayan Union and Singapore, which would coöperate with Indonesia. The Party is anti-British and anti-Sultan." [46] It also advocated greater local self-government but with safeguards for Malay control.

The postwar plan of government for Malaya, in spite of continued opposition remained that of federation, with a slow pace in the development of self-government, along the lines accepted in 1947, until after 1953. The promotion of labor organization after the war, the increase in the organs for free expression of opinion, and the maintenance of opposition as well as majority parties, all, however, indicated that the problem of government had been complicated for the colonial Power and also for the ruling class, as compared with the essentially apolitical atmosphere of the peninsula in the days before 1941. The nature and tempo of developments, after apparent stability had been reached in 1948, changed, however, under the impact of new political and economic conditions in the non-Malayan as well as in the Malayan world. Malayan rubber production began to be restored, but it had to regain its position in a market in which it had to face the new competition with synthetics. And, in addition to the problem of normal economic readjustment, there was the complication of the problem of restoring order and maintaining production which resulted from the tactics involved in the spread of communism in eastern Asia. In a politically stable world and Far Eastern environment, at least the prewar measure of prosperity could have been rapidly restored in Malaya and with it general acceptance of the newly established postwar scheme of Malayan organization.

Communism in Malaya

It was this element of world political stability, however, which was lacking. The existence of a Communist opposition in Malaya, as well as in the other countries of the area, assured that disturbance would accompany attempts at political and economic reconstruction. The tactics in Malaya were more those of terrorism and of economic sabotage than of organized revolt on a mass basis because of the nature of the internal situation. But this merely changed the problem of establishment and maintenance of public order. The stimulus to "Communist" action was applied from the outside, largely through the medium of those affiliated with the Chinese Communist Party, and it became more positive as Kuomintang resistance within China weakened and the Communist armies moved south. This brought the struggle within the limits of the covert conflict between the United States and the Soviet Union and caused the United States, which also, directly and in relation to the Marshall Plan, had an interest in the restoration of Malayan production, to author-

[46] *Ibid., p. 73.*

ize the sale of arms to the Malayan government for use against the rebels. The soil to be cultivated by Communists in Malaya was poorer than in other countries, from the point of view of a possible seizure of power, but their activities were sufficient to retard economic reconstruction and to add this to other areas of conflict.

The Communists in Malaya were able to maintain themselves against the British forces thrown against them for some time because their bases were in jungle country difficult of access and because they were able, following Mao Tse-tung's dictum, to swim as fish in the sea of the people. Fear of the consequences of non-support was, of course, one reason for this covert support. The growth of nationalistic feeling was another. In terms of the latter consideration, consequently, Communist terrorism was part of the pressure on Britain to make ever-larger concessions to nationalism itself, since the problem could most readily be solved if there was complete local coöperation with the augmented forces operating against the Communists.

The Communist threat was sufficiently grave by 1952 to cause the British government to send General Sir Gerald Templer to Malaya as High Commissioner, his predecessor having been assassinated in October, 1951. Under the new High Commissioner a vigorous campaign against the terrorists was waged with some success but not to the point of their eradication. The terrorists, according to General Templer, had, by 1954 when he retired, withdrawn into the jungle to avoid attack and surrenders had become more difficult to obtain. The Communists' main objectives were: (1) to establish bases for their higher command; (2) to strengthen control of villages and towns on the jungle fringes so that they could get supplies; and (3) to penetrate political parties and trade unions and to build underground organizations in the towns. [47]

The Advance to Self-Government

By this time British policy toward Malaya had been moved in the direction of the establishment of self-government. General Templer, when appointed, had been instructed to "go on with the work of building up a Malayan nation and to give the peoples of Malaya an increasing responsibility for the management of their own affairs." [48] The further this went the more possible it became for the Federation government to develop its own approach to the Communist problem in Malaya. The policy followed was similar to the Magsaysay policy in the Philippines. Thus in 1955

[47] From General Templer's farewell press conference, as summarized in *Chronology of International Events* (London, Royal Institute of International Affairs), vol. 10, no. 11, p. 354.
[48] From *A Monthly Survey of Commonwealth and Colonial Affairs,* issued by the Conservative Research Department in conjunction with the Conservatives Overseas Bureau, no. 18, p. 1.

amnesty was offered to Communist rebels, with an assurance that all giving up Communist activities would be assisted in regaining their normal positions in society and that any who wished to go to China would be permitted to do so. There were, however, very few surrenders. Consequently military operations were resumed, following the breakdown of truce talks. The choice continued to be offered of the olive branch or the sword during 1956 and 1957, with sufficient success so that by the end of 1958 the ten-year struggle against the Communists in the jungle appeared to be nearing an end. Of importance in attaining this result was the fact that by 1958 the olive branch was being extended and also the sword wielded by a Malayan Commonwealth government, materially assisted, to be sure, by Britain, but not as a colonial ruler.

In the Federation which in 1948 superseded the Malayan Union established in 1946, the federal administration included a High Commissioner appointed by the British Crown, an Executive Council, and a Federal Legislative Council, the latter non-elective and designed to give representation to official and communal interests rather than to the people except as organized in occupational or nationality groups. This division into separate communities gave a large measure of control of the powers of government to the High Commissioner and the Executive Council.

The Malays were divided politically into the United Malays National Organization and the Nationalist Party. The former initially supported the policy of federation under the British, as pointed out above, and the position of the Sultans, rather than that of popular self-government, whether or not coupled with independence. An important reason for this was fear of the Chinese minority which remained in the Federation, even with the exclusion from it of Singapore. The opposition Nationalist Party, on the other hand, initially aimed at an independent Malaya—composed of the Malay States, the Settlements, and Singapore—which would coöperate with Moslem Indonesia. Because of its objectives the Nationalist Party was anti-British as well as anti-Sultan, the latter because the party advocated greater local self-government, although with safeguards to ensure Malay control.

The Chinese and Indians tended to reproduce in Malaya the party organizations and affiliations of India and China, although becoming more and more assertive in Malayan affairs. Thus the Indians, in August, 1946, formed the Malayan Indian Congress and the Chinese, as well as being organized in the Malayan Chinese Association, were initially divided between Kuomintang and Communist organizations. Neither group for some time was willing to confine its allegiance to a Malay state. Each wanted local security, however, and neither attempted to play a political role in Malaya until the protection of its interests against the new Malay nationalism necessitated local political action. In bringing this about, the association of Chinese with Communist terrorism also played a significant part.

The discharge of the accepted obligation "to give the peoples of Malaya an increasing responsibility for the management of their own affairs" was held to require the establishment of some system of elections. The problem of elections brought together the questions of citizenship and of self-government. The first question especially served at the outset to separate the Malay, Chinese, and Indian communities. During the negotiations the British dealt mainly with the two organizations, one of Malays and the other of Chinese, which sought development within the existing framework rather than independence or any other fundamental change in the system of federation. These two conservative organizations—the United Malayan National Organization (UMNO) and the Malayan Chinese Association (MCA)—sent a joint delegation to London early in 1954 to raise such questions with the Colonial Secretary as the right of native officials to stand for election to the Legislative Council and the right to vote of designated categories of non-citizens, and an increase to three-fifths of the total membership of the Council of its elected members. While some concessions were made by the British, the demand for three-fifths elective members of the Legislative Council, as against a balance of elected and nominated members which had earlier been proposed, was rejected. This led to a decision by the UMNO and the MCA to withhold coöperation in government by withdrawing "all of their members from all administrative councils on which they serve, from the federal executive down to town council levels."

Despite this threat of non-coöperation the British authorities decided to go ahead with the holding of elections in Singapore as well as in the Federation. Since the holding of elections would be a positive step toward the self-government all parties were now demanding, the Malays National Organization and the Malayan Chinese Association decided to participate in the elections and for that purpose formed an alliance, into which the Malayan Indian Congress also entered. The Alliance slogan in the campaign was that of complete independence at the end of the four-year term of the new Legislative Council.

The Alliance was successful in capturing 51 of the 52 elective seats in the 98-member Legislative Council in the Federal elections held in July, 1955. As a consequence its leader, the head of the UMNO, Tengku Abdul Rahman, became the Chief Minister in the government as reconstituted, with 6 Malay, 3 Chinese, 1 Indian, and 4 European members. This represented a real move toward self-government, attaining the limits set and earlier agreed upon in the constitution. The objectives of the Alliance had, however, been set in advance of those limits. This was indicated in its campaign platform and in post-election statements.

Commonwealth Status Achieved

Tengku Abdul Rahman consequently immediately began to press for constitutional revision, especially with respect to the High Commissioner's veto powers. In the light of the overwhelming victory of the Alliance in the elections, he was able to say: "Today, with support enjoyed by no other government in the world, the alliance represented people. If the High Commissioner vetoed Bills passed in the Council, the alliance would not be working for the people and might as well walk out." Coupled with the pressure which he was able to bring to bear because of his domestic support as Chief Minister, Rahman was able to utilize the problem of Communist terrorism in demanding immediate self-government by insisting that the British government must realize that "unless it gives self-government it is inviting Communism and we have had enough of that during the past seven years." This was because the Communists had been exploiting successfully in Asia the issue of colonialism.

In the new situation produced by the elections the British, consequently, were moved to further concessions. As a result of conferences held in London in January, 1956, it was agreed that full self-government and independence within the Commonwealth would be proclaimed, if possible by August, 1957. Immediately after the London Conference a commission (the Reid Commission) [49] was constituted to draft a constitution for an independent Malaya.

The Reid Commission presented its report on February 20, 1957, including a draft of a constitution. In July the Malayan Legislative Council and also the British Parliament approved the proposed constitution. And at midnight on August 31, Merdeka (independence) was proclaimed and Malaya became an independent member of the Commonwealth. The country was accepted as a member of the United Nations on September 17; acquired membership in the International Bank and the International Monetary Fund on September 26; and became a member of GATT, under sponsorship of the United Kingdom, on October 24. The close working relationship with Britain that was viewed as desirable was provided by the terms of a treaty of defense and mutual assistance which was signed at the capital, Kuala Lumpur on October 13. Thus, by the end of the year 1957, the new state had entered fully upon the international scene.

[49] "The members were the Right Honorable Lord Reid and Sir Ivor Jennings from Britain, Sir William McKell from Australia, Mr. B. Malik from India, and Mr. Justice Abdul Hamid from Pakistan. A Canadian was also appointed but withdrew for reasons of health and was not replaced." *Far Eastern Survey*, October, 1957, note 11, p. 147. Thus the Commission was essentially Commonwealth in composition.

The new constitution, for a federal state, made provision for a Head of State, elected for a five-year term by the rulers of the states from among their own number. On September 2, Sir Abdul Rahman officially became Head of State. The constitutional decision was naturally for the establishment of the parliamentary type of government. Thus the constitution provided for a legislature of two Houses: a Senate of 16 members, appointed by the Head of State to represent sectional or minority interests, together with 2 members elected by the Legislative Assemblies of the separate states; and a House of Representatives, originally of 104 (later 100) members elected by constituencies on the territorial basis. The government was, of course, constituted on the basis of majority support in the House of Representatives. Until new elections could be held the existing Legislative Council was to serve in place of the House of Representatives. This meant that Tengku Abdul Rahman (not a relative of the newly elected Head of State) continued as Prime Minister and would be able to remain in power as long as the major parties remained in alliance. As one writer said: [50]

Some observers believe that the continued existence of the Alliance is precarious now that independence has been achieved. Yet, the Alliance has already survived the public debate on the constitution, and independence was not its only *raison d'être*. Of equal or great importance was the need for the propertied Chinese to have political connections in order to protect their economic interests and also the need of the Malays to have financial assistance. This justification is still valid, although the need of the Malays is now less while that of the Chinese is greater. If the Alliance does stand, its member parties may lose such popular support as they possess to parties willing to exploit communal issues. The UMNO may have to choose between its Chinese allies and the continued support of the Malay community. As elections cannot be held until 1959, any early disintegration of the Alliance government will probably be averted, but should the Alliance split apart, no strong parties exist which can fill the void. Politics will not take definite shape until political leaders come to grips with the issues.

REFERENCES FOR FURTHER STUDY

GEORGE CYRIL ALLEN, *Western Enterprises in Indonesia and Malaya* (1957). SIDNEY D. BAILEY, *Parliamentary Government in Southeast Asia* (1952). W. MACMAHON BALL, *Nationalism and Communism in East Asia* (1952). VERNON BARTLETT, *Report from Malaya* (1954). JOHN F. CADY, "Burma," in JOHN F. CADY, PATRICIA BARNETT, and SHIRLEY JENKINS, *Development of Self-Rule and Independence in Burma, Malaya and the Philippines* (1948). COMMITTEE ON FOREIGN RELATIONS, U. S. SENATE, *Indo-China* (1953). F. S. V. DENNISON, *Public Administration in Burma, a Study of Development During the British Connection* (1953). PHILIPPE DEVILLERS, *Vietnam and France* (1950). WILLARD

[50] J. NORMAN PARMER, "Constitutional Change in Malaya's Plural Society," *Far Eastern Survey*, vol. 26, no. 10 (October, 1957), p. 151.

H. Elsbree, *Japan's Role in Southeast Asian Nationalist Movements, 1940–1945* (1953). Rupert Emerson, Lennox A. Mills, and Virginia Thompson, *Government and Nationalism in South East Asia* (1942). John S. Furnivall, *Colonial Policy and Practice: A Comparative Study of Burma and the Netherlands* (1948). Ellen Hammer, "Indo-China," in L. K. Rossinger and Associates, *The State of Asia* (1951). W. L. Holland (ed.), *Asian Nationalism and the West* (1953). James C. Ingram, *Economic Change in Thailand Since 1850* (1955). Harold Isaacs, *New Cycle in Asia* (1947). S. W. Jones, *Public Administration in Malaya* (1953). Phyllis M. Kaberoy, *British Colonial Policy in Southeast Asia and the Development of Self-government in Malaya* (1944). Enid Lakeman, *Report on Malaya* (1952). Kenneth P. Landon, *Siam in Transition* (1940), *The Chinese in Thailand* (1941). Kenneth P. Landon, "Siam," in Lennox A. Mills and Others, *The World of Southeast Asia* (1949). Bruno Lasker, *Books on Southeast Asia: A Selected Bibliography* (1956). Bruno Lasker, *Human Bondage in Southeast Asia* (1950). Maung Maung, *Burma in the Family of Nations* (1956). Thakin Nu, *From Peace to Stability* (1951). K. M. Panikkar, *The Future of South-East Asia, an Indian View* (1943). Victor W. Purcell, *The Chinese in Southeast Asia* (1951). Lucian W. Pye, *Guerrilla Communism in Malaya, Its Social and Political Meaning* (1956). David R. Rees and Others, *Three Reports on the Malayan Problem* (1949). G. William Skinner, *Chinese Society in Thailand* (1957). Virginia Thompson, *The Minority Problem in Southeast Asia* (1955). Frank N. Trager, *Burma's Role in the United Nations, 1948–1955* (1956). Amry Vandenbosch and Richard R. Butwell, *Southeast Asia Among the World Powers* (1957). Herold J. Wiens, *China's March toward the Tropics* (1954). Maurice Zinkin, *Development for Free Asia* (1956).

CHAPTER XXXII

THE PHILIPPINES AND INDONESIA

I. THE PHILIPPINES

In comparison with Burma, the Japanese occupation found the Philippines considerably further along the road to complete self-government and independence. Under the terms of the Commonwealth Act, Philippine independence was to be proclaimed in 1946 rather than to be achieved at an indeterminate time in the future. Consequently debate over its readiness for independence did not have to be undertaken as a complicating factor in the establishment of government after liberation, as was the case in Burma. With its independence dated, furthermore, the establishment of a constitution and a suitable framework of government had been speeded up, as had also the assumption of governmental and administrative responsibility at all levels by Filipinos. Thus, whereas in 1941 it was proper to conclude that there were not enough Burmans available with sufficient training and experience successfully to operate the government of an independent state, the same conclusion was not warranted for the Philippines. The American policy of Filipinization of the government of the Islands, despite all of its shifts in consistent application after 1905, had developed a much larger and more competent governing class for the Philippines than British policy had produced in Burma. In this respect the contrast was not in the difference in time between the enactment and application of the Commonweath Act for the Philippines and the Government of Burma Act, of 1935 and 1941, but the difference in experience in government between at least 1916 and 1941 for the Philippines and 1937 and 1941 for Burma.

The Philippine Constitutional System

Under the Commonwealth constitution adopted in 1935, as amended in 1940, and as restored with the liberation of the Philippines, the government was of the presidential type. The President and Vice-President were directly elected for a four-year term, with immediate reëlection restricted to one additional term. The two Houses of the legislature were also constituted by direct election. The Senate was composed of 24 members elected at large for six-year terms, one-third being elected each two years. The membership of the House of Representatives was constitutionally fixed at "not more than 120 members," apportioned among the provinces on the basis of population. Given a status independent of the legislature, the Executive had greater constitutional powers in relation to the definition of public policy than even the American President, since he had an item as well as a general veto and could have his views defended in the legislature through the personal appearance in either House of the appointive heads of the several departments of government. On the other hand, the constitutional provision for a Commission on Appointments, made up of twelve members elected from the Senate and twelve from the House, which had to approve all appointments to important offices, including that of head of an executive department, carried with it the possibility of enhancement of legislative influence in the event of a struggle for power between leaders in the legislature and the President.

This constitutional system of self-government was in full and, on the whole, satisfactory operation at the time of the Japanese invasion of the Islands. The political class, under the strong leadership of the elected President, Manuel Quezon, the Vice-President, Sergio Osmeña, Senator Manuel Roxas, and others, had been united, after an initial split, in the overwhelmingly predominant Nacionalista Party. Since the President was generally accepted as the leader of the party which controlled the government, there was substantial Executive direction in the development of policy and its enactment into law by the legislature.

When it became apparent that formal military resistance to Japan could not be sustained successfully in the Islands, President Quezon and Vice-President Osmeña were evacuated, as was General MacArthur; and what was in the nature of a "government-in-exile" was established in Washington.[1] Through General MacArthur's Headquarters established in Brisbane, it maintained such contact as was possible with the guerrilla movement which came into being in the Philippines after the cessation of formal military resistance. In this way the continuity of Commonwealth constitutional government was maintained during the period of the Japanese occupation, even though the war situation made necessary some constitutionally irregular actions. Furthermore, President Roosevelt not only reiterated the pledge of independence within the period set in the Commonwealth Act but proclaimed a willingness to advance the date if war circumstances permitted. Congress, by Joint Resolution of June 29, 1944, "pledged complete independence and authorized the President to proclaim it prior to July 4, 1946."[2]

[1] President Quezon's government-in-exile signed the United Nations Declaration, sat on the Pacific War Council, and was represented at the wartime United Nations conferences held at Hot Springs, Bretton Woods, and San Francisco. JOHN CAMPBELL, *The United States in World Affairs*, 1945–1947, p. 306.

[2] *Ibid.*, p. 307.

Liberation of the Islands

By the time of liberation President Quezon had died in exile and had been succeeded as President by Vice President Osmeña. It was the latter, consequently, to whom the powers of government were transferred by the Americans on February 27, 1945. No military government was formally instituted even for interim purposes, Osmeña and the Commonwealth authorities with him having begun to exercise civil authority in the liberated provinces shortly after the landings at Leyte.

While American military government was not instituted in the Philippines, it was nevertheless true that the American military had a fairly decisive influence over government almost to the time of independence, since the Commonwealth authorities were almost completely dependent on the Americans, and the Americans on the military, for all of the facilities essential to government. Either in the course of military operations or as a result of deliberate destruction by the Japanese much of the inter-island shipping and the land transportation facilities had been destroyed. Planes, motor transport of all kinds, and ships, where available, were American military equipment usable by the Commonwealth authorities only as put at their disposal at the discretion of General MacArthur's Headquarters. Such telephone, telegraph, and radio facilities as existed were American and military. Materials and technicians for the restoration of utilities, public and private buildings, newspapers and radio, docks and wharves, roads and bridges were similarly immediately available to the Commonwealth government only through release to them by the American military authorities. Beyond this immediate and local dependency of the Commonwealth government on the American authorities, there was the larger long-run dependence on the United States for assistance in rehabilitation and reconstruction of the national economy. As it appeared to the Filipino, the destruction of the war had been visited upon him and his country because the government had been loyal to the United States rather than because of the pursuit by the Philippine government of policies which had embroiled the country with Japan. Public statements had led him to believe that this view was accepted in the United States and that the American government accepted the obligation to compensate for the damage resulting from the war and to restore the Philippine economy. With this was inevitably tied up the question of definition of economic relations between the United States and the Philippines after July 4, 1946, when the Commonwealth was to be terminated and the Republic established. The power of decision in all these fundamentally important questions lay with the American Congress, and the undertaking of the needed reconstruction and rehabilitation work was necessarily delayed until, after some months of discussion, Congress enacted the Philippine Reha-

bilitation Act of 1946 and the Philippine Trade Act of 1946.[3] The two
were tied together through a provision in the latter that no payments in
excess of $500 (for war damages) under the terms of the former should
be made until after completion of an executive agreement by which the
Philippine government would accept the stipulations of the Trade Act.

Economic Relation to the United States

The major problem posed at the time of enactment of the Commonwealth law came from the virtually complete economic dependence of
the Islands on the United States. As succinctly put by Paul V. McNutt,
testifying before a Congressional Committee on February 15, 1946:

> In the Philippines the national economy was geared before the war entirely
> and completely to export trade. And 95 per cent of that export trade was with
> the United States. Except for rice and fish, which are locally consumed, 98 per
> cent of all other production in the Philippines, amounting to $266,000,000 in
> 1941, is produced for export. . . . And I might and should say here and now
> that we, the United States, managed it that way. We are responsible for the sole
> dependency of the Philippines on the American market. Our businessmen
> and our statesmen in the past years allowed the Philippines to become a complete
> economic dependency of the United States to a greater degree than any single
> state of the Union is economically dependent on the rest of the United States.[4]

The Commonwealth Act made provision for a gradual readjustment
of the conditions of Philippine access to the American market with a
view to lessening the economic shock at the end of the ten-year period
when independence would be attained. The war situation went further
than had American planning in severing completely, for a four-year
period, all economic exchanges between the Philippines and the United
States. This gave an opportunity to assist financially in the reconstruction
of the economy so as to begin and carry forward the diversification of
production which would have made the Philippines as nearly as possible
economically independent. Such reconstruction would have been slower
as a method of restoration of economic activities and processes than the
attempt to restore established and customary production for prewar
markets, but its attempt would have been more consistent with the declared purpose of establishing an actually independent state.

For a variety of reasons, however, the Trade Act was apparently constructed on the assumption that the relationships of 1941 should first be
reëstablished so that they could then be gradually modified. "The Philippine Trade Act of 1946 is based on the principle of a prolonged period

---

[3] The necessity of enacting this legislation was a consideration in President Truman's
decision not to advance the date of independence.

[4] Quoted by SHIRLEY JENKINS, *The Development of Self-Rule and Independence in Burma,
Malaya and the Philippines*, Part III, The Philippines, pp. 97–98.

of free and preferential trade, and perpetuates the economic dependence of the Philippine Republic on the United States. The Act established exclusive preferential treatment for the United States in such extreme terms that the amendment of the Constitution of the Philippines was required, despite the protection of American rights afforded by the Constitution." [5] This amendment of the Philippine Constitution was made necessary by the stipulation in the Trade Act that American citizens should be put on a footing of equality with Philippine citizens so far as acquisition of title to land and engaging in exploitative and industrial activity were concerned. This gave the American an economic position in the Republic that he had not been conceded when the Philippines were a dependency of the United States.

Beyond these economic definitions of relationship, since the United States assumed responsibility for the future defense of the Islands against external aggression it asked for bases in the Islands. After protracted negotiations agreement was reached on the number and location of bases which was satisfactory to the United States and to the Philippine government, although there was criticism of some of the provisions of these agreements. [6] The base agreement was approved by the Philippine Congress on March 26, 1947. It should also be noted, in connection with these security arrangements, that the United States Congress by Act of June 26, 1946, authorized the President

to provide military assistance to the Philippine Republic "in establishing and maintaining national security, and to form a basis for participation by that government in such defensive military operations as the future may require." The consequent military assistance agreement was signed on March 21, 1947, by the United States Ambassador and President Roxas. For the Philippine Army, over $38 millions had been set aside for 1948, well over half of this sum to be spent on the Military Police. [7]

The Problem of Collaboration

While the conditions of reconstruction and of independence were being defined in Washington, political activity was rapidly resumed in Manila. To restore the constitutional machinery of government required the reconstitution of the legislature. This presented the complication that a large proportion of the members of both Houses had collaborated with the Japanese. American policy, as stated by President Roosevelt in signing two resolutions dealing with the Philippines on June 29, 1944, was that "Those

[5] *Ibid.*, p. 98.

[6] "An agreement was finally signed on March 14, 1948, leasing a number of bases for a 99-year period. The principal base would be at Fort Stotsenberg, near but not in Manila. Ten other army bases and four naval operating areas were specified." CAMPBELL, *op. cit.*, p. 310.

[7] JENKINS, *op. cit.*, p. 96.

who have collaborated with the enemy must be removed from authority and influence over the political and economic life of the country." The first apparent breach in this policy came when General MacArthur separated Manuel Roxas from captured members of the collaborationist government and declared him "liberated" and thus freed without undergoing even the usual clearance procedure.[8] This enabled Roxas to resume his participation in politics and government as the President of the Senate. Its reconstitution, together with the House of Representatives, without the prior holding of new elections, meant that legislation on which action against collaborators would be based would have to be enacted by a legislature many of whose members, except as they were held covered by legislative immunity, were liable to action because they had held positions under the Japanese-sponsored "independent" government. Under these circumstances it was virtually impossible for President Osmeña to respond quickly and decisively to the initial pressures from Washington to proceed against those charged with collaboration, even though this was raised as the primary issue in Philippine politics during the year prior to, as well as immediately after, the establishment of the Republic.

The issue of collaboration in the Philippines, as elsewhere, was one complicated by the question of motive and thus had in it subjective as well as objective considerations. At the one extreme were those who had merely carried on their normal administrative activities as a method of earning a livelihood and of holding the local communities together. Their assistance to the Japanese was passive rather than active. At the other extreme were those who had actively assisted the Japanese in organizing the puppet government and in shaping policy along the lines set in Tokyo. Some of these men had seized the opportunity presented by the Japanese invasion and occupation for personal aggrandizement. Others, it could be subjectively argued, had been initially forced into collaboration. Still others, as nationalists and patriots, had accepted Japanese promises and had served Japan as a means of ensuring the early independence of the country; or they had used collaboration as a cover for their anti-Japanese leadership.

Roxas was apparently put in one of these latter categories by the Americans themselves, but without the categories having been clearly established and proclaimed. His position as President of the Senate, coupled with his unclarified status as a collaborator, put him in a position of leadership, with tacit American support, against the government in its

---

[8] Laurel, Aquino, Osias, and Vargas (the leaders in the Japanese puppet government) were evacuated to Japan and returned to the Philippines by the American occupation authorities to stand trial by the People's Court. Laurel was released on bail, ostensibly to prepare his defense. He used the freedom to campaign for political rehabilitation and power.

attempt to establish machinery for dealing with collaboration in the simplified terms of black and white. A bill was finally enacted establishing People's Courts to try those in custody.

Few prominent collaborators have been tried. As 1947 wore on, the People's Court trying the cases was finding it more and more difficult to secure the necessary witnesses, and many of those appearing seemed no longer anxious to testify. Laurel and his puppet associates were still at liberty, appearing at public functions, making addresses, and enjoying a surprising amount of public support. Their trials have been repeatedly postponed, and they appear confident of their eventual acquittal. [9]

Under the circumstances collaboration could have been best dealt with decisively by the Americans during the immediate post-liberation period when their influence was dominant. It could then have been dealt with for what it actually was—action against the United States. Turning the problem back to the Philippine government and then pressing that government, although ever less strongly, to act decisively, merely had the effect of embarrassing the restored government and making it more difficult for it to maintain itself against the opposition which quickly arose.

The Hukbalihaps

One area of disturbance was in central Luzon where the Hukbalihap (People's Army against the Japanese) movement had its principal center. This movement, while anti-Japanese, had strong overtones of social and economic reform. During the war it had operated equally, as a guerrilla movement, against the Japanese, and against the landlords, who, as a class, collaborated with the Japanese and organized "peace preservation" corps to maintain their own and Japan's position against the guerrillas. Because of a fear that their reforms would be lost and that they would not only lose their influence but possibly also their lives, the Huks refused to surrender their arms upon the liberation of the Islands. Consequently their forces were not incorporated in the Philippine Army. Thus they immediately lost some of their standing as anti-Japanese guerrillas and much of their respectability in the eyes of the Americans. Nevertheless their leaders were among the most insistent that the government bring collaborators to trial and punishment. This subjected the Osmeña government to a double pressure, from the left represented by the Hukbalihaps and the right led by Senator Roxas.

Provision was made by the United States Congress in December, 1945, and by the Philippine Congress in January, 1946, for the holding of the first elections since 1941 so that the Republic, after its inauguration on

[9] JENKINS, op. cit., p. 89. Laurel, it may be noted here, was a candidate for the presidency in the 1949 elections. He ran second but polled a substantial vote.

July 4, 1946, might have a government which did not represent a holdover from prewar days. The collaborationist issue, as well as personal rivalry, had split the old Nacionalista Party into two wings, one headed by the incumbent President, Osmeña, which retained the party name, and the other by Senator Roxas, calling itself the Liberal Party. Since the attempts which were made to bring Osmeña and Roxas together proved unsuccessful it was inevitable that they should compete in the 1946 elections for the presidency. It was almost equally inevitable that a large part of the old party leadership should follow Roxas into his new Liberal Party since they had stayed in the Philippines during the war and were consequently in need of Roxas' protection against the possible charge of collaboration.

Osmeña, consequently, had to combine his own following from the Nacionalista Party with an alliance of the Huks and similar groups, called the Democratic Alliance, in order to make a respectable showing. He was unable to wage a very aggressive campaign because of lack of both resources and facilities. Roxas was supported by the wealthy elements in the Islands as well as, tacitly, by the Americans. More vigorous and less handicapped by scruples than Osmeña, Roxas was able to emphasize in his campaign the failure, even though it was explainable, of the government to bring about a more rapid reconstruction, as well as some of its less excusable mistakes, and to leave the impression that American assistance would be given more readily to a government which he headed than Osmeña had been able to secure. Thus he secured election with 54 per cent of the total popular vote, and his party gained 13 of the 24 seats in the Senate and 58 seats to the opposition's 40 in the House of Representatives.

The Osmeña government, during its short tenure at the end of the Commonwealth period, had of necessity followed a policy of compromise and conciliation toward oppositional elements. Thus it had accepted the Huks' demand for a more liberal division of the crops between landlord and tenant, although not accepting their full program in this respect nor in connection with land redistribution. The attempts made to bring distinguished guerrilla leaders into high governmental position, partly of course to ensure their political support, had had to be compromised because of the control of the legislative Commission on Appointments by Senator Roxas. Competition for the favors of the United States had led to compromises on independence and aid conditions.

President Roxas, on the other hand, while extremely conciliatory toward the United States, immediately indicated an intention to rule with the strong hand of a Quezon. His first move was to prevent the seating of some of the opposition candidates in the legislature who had been certified by the Electoral Commission as having been elected. All but four of the eleven whose election was challenged were, however, finally seated after almost a year of delay. In this action, in the handling of the question of revision of the Constitution to give Americans parity with Filipinos, and in the seating in the House of Representatives of a Spanish-born citizen, the Roxas administration showed a desire to bend the Constitution to serve its own purposes.

The policy followed toward the Hukbalihap Party was also a strong one of forcible suppression, with, however, ultimately an attempt at conciliation marked by some double-dealing on both sides. A primary need, unquestionably, was the restoration and the maintenance of public order. But some of the instruments used, such as the landlord-organized Civilian Guards, were certainly questionable. Some of the terroristic activities they engaged in were more in the nature of feudal vengeance than of attempts to support the public order, and they gave color to the charge that the state was actually using its power against one private interest in support of another. And of course terrorism gave rise to reprisals in kind, regardless of which side initiated it. At the beginning the administration recognized that there was a real question of social and economic policy at issue in which there was much right on the side of opposition when, in conference with peasant leaders, President Roxas agreed to check Military Police atrocities, and to sign a new crop-sharing agreement on a 70-30 basis—a measure which was later passed but which was not complied with in many instances. But in spite of this agreement, although partly because of its lack of effective execution, sanguinary fighting continued, with the emphasis put more and more on forcible suppression by all available means until, after the assassination of President Roxas, adjustment was again, although unsuccessfully, attempted by his successor, Elpidio Quirino.

From the beginning the Huk leaders' charge that their opponents were ex-collaborators with the Japanese was countered by their movement being labeled Communist. This label was justified in terms of the Communist affiliation of Louis Taruc, Castro Alejandrino, and Jesus Lava, who became the leaders of the Huks. "The peasants themselves, of course, knew little of Marxism. . . . They were simply men sick of exploitation and injustice, and they did not care what outsiders called their leaders." [10] Both charges tended to divert attention from the real and pressing issue of reform of the conditions of land tenure and use. As the Communist label came to be generally accepted, especially outside of the Philippines, with the justification that some of the Huk leaders were professed Communists and others were socialists, suppression, without the removal of the causes of

[10] DAVID BERNSTEIN, *The Philippine Story*, p. 254.

the movement which gave it justification after the end of the war, came to be viewed as sound public policy. Nevertheless President Quirino tried negotiation of a settlement as well as forcible suppression. An amnesty agreement was negotiated which enabled Louis Taruc to take the seat in the House of Representatives to which he had been elected. After a short time, however, he was again back among his followers who had not been persuaded that they could safely give up their arms in exchange for amnesty. The end of this period of agreement brought about resumption of the fighting.

Postwar Elections

Another aspect of postwar politics was revealed in the election campaign of 1949 when José P. Laurel proved to be the leading opposition candidate. He made his appeal on strictly nationalist grounds, repudiating the extreme leftist elements in the Osmeña coalition of 1946. The strongest charge against him—that of heading the Japanese puppet government— he disposed of by taking the position that: "This question was resolved most decisively by the people themselves in the election of the late President Manuel Roxas, whose subsequent proclamation of amnesty confirmed the popular will." His positive position, besides a declared hostility to communism, involved Philippine coöperation with the United Nations "as long as that body existed" and the improvement of relations with the United States. Dr. Laurel said he meant by this the revising of the Philippine Trade Act of 1946 and adjusting some of its inequalities working against the Philippines.

" 'I believe,' he said, 'there is enough local capital here to develop this country without further immediate assistance from the United States. But our people lack faith in the present Government and hesitate to invest their money.' " [11] That lack of faith Laurel attributed to the government's corruption, incompetence, and extravagance.

Quirino, on his side, had built toward the campaign by assuming an initiative in the field of foreign affairs through sponsorship of a Pacific Pact through which a common front of the Pacific and Far Eastern countries against communism would be formed. This aligned his government with the policies of the United States, an orientation which was emphasized on the occasion of a trip which he took to the United States.

The campaign and the election held on November 8 were marked by considerable disorder and violence. The result was the election of Quirino to the presidency, with Liberal Party control of the legislature. Laurel, however, polled a large vote, the size of which was a measure both of the extent of his personal comeback as a factor in Philippine politics and the

[11] Interview on October 14, 1949, reported in the *New York Times*.

persuasiveness of the issues on which he campaigned. Indeed, he might well have been elected had it not been for the use made by Quirino and his supporters of the powers of the presidential office.

Neither the political nor the economic condition of the country was good at the time when President Quirino succeeded himself. The principal threat to the government continued to be presented by the Huk rebellion. In 1950 the "Huks seemed to be everywhere; their strength was estimated at 40,000 fully armed members, with about 2,500,000 reserves. They made attacks on the outskirts of Manila and the capital itself seemed in danger." [12]

At this point the President appointed Ramon Magsaysay, a young Congressman of his party, as Secretary of Defense and made him responsible for operations against the Huks. Magsaysay reorganized and strengthened the army, which he then used in place of the constabulary against the Huks. Guerrilla tactics were developed for penetration of areas under Huk control. Rewards were offered for the capture, or information leading to the capture, of the principal Huk leaders. Thus the war was carried to the enemy. On the other hand, amnesty and resettlement, as well as protection, were promised to those, other than the leaders, who surrendered. Furthermore Magsaysay insisted that promises made and accepted in good faith should be kept. These tactics, which continued to be employed, yielded results. By 1958 the only Huk leader still at large was Jesus Lava, and most of his followers had surrendered.

One of the reasons why Magsaysay was successful against the Huks was the reputation which he established for honesty in the administration of the army and the Defense Department. This was generally viewed as a new development, which seemed to give hope of a movement away from the situation widely accepted as existing at the time of the 1949 elections. The political condition then revealed was one of such widespread corruption, coercion, violence, and disorder as to make people cynical over the possibility of developing a healthy democracy in the country. The current running in 1949, however, was shifted by the time of the 1951 elections. The new army under Magsaysay was given the responsibility for policing the elections. Organizations of citizens interested in honest elections came into being to develop an interest among the voters. In consequence the elections of 1951 were not open to the charges made in 1949. The opposition (Nacionalista) party captured all nine of the Senate seats which had to be filled and elected 26 provincial governors, as against the Quirino Liberal Party's 20.

As the time for presidential elections approached, Magsaysay began to be talked about as a desirable presidential candidate of his party in place

[12] AMRY VANDENBOSCH and RICHARD A. BUTWELL, *Southeast Asia Among the World Powers* (1957), p. 89.

of Quirino, who desired reëlection and whose control of the Liberals was such as to enable him to secure renomination. This being the case, the Nationalists interested in nominating someone with a good chance of being elected, approached Magsaysay. Under the circumstances he tendered his resignation as Secretary of Defense, thus making himself available as the Nationalist Party candidate. The Liberals renominated Quirino over the opposition of General Romolo, who had served his country as its representative at the United Nations and as Foreign Minister. Romolo thereupon seceded from the Liberal Party, taking his supporters with him and forming a new party, the Democratic Party, which nominated Romolo for the presidency. To avoid splitting the anti-Quirino vote, however, Romolo withdrew his candidacy, the Democrats entering into a coalition with the Nationalists in support of the latter's candidates, Magsaysay for the presidency, and Garcia for the vice-presidency.

Since both Magsaysay and Romolo had explained their withdrawal of support from Quirino on the grounds of corruption and lack of effectiveness of his administration, corruption in government became the principal issue in the campaign.

The elections were held on November 10, 1953. The result was a triumph for Magsaysay and victory for the Nationalist party. It is properly put in this way because Magsaysay ran well ahead of his ticket. Nevertheless the coalition won an impressive victory, winning the eight Senate seats to be filled and gaining control of the House of Representatives. In the new Senate there were 12 Nationalists, 6 Democrats, 1 Citizens Party member, and only 4 Liberals. The former large Liberal majority in the House was reduced to about one-third of the total membership of the House.

Additional significance, beyond that of party change, was given to the election by the campaign methods employed by Magsaysay and his supporters, who sought to establish direct contact with the people in the villages, instead of reaching them indirectly through contact with provincial and local party leaders. This direct contact Magsaysay as President sought to maintain, inviting everybody in the land, regardless of economic and social status, to bring his complaints directly to the President.

The new President, inaugurated on December 30, 1953, remained in power until the nation was shocked by the news of his death in an airplane accident in 1957. He was succeeded in office by the Vice-President, Carlos Garcia, who pledged himself to continue the Magsaysay policies.

President Garcia, as the Nationalist Party candidate, won the presidency in his own right in the elections held on November 12, 1957. His position seemed to be strong as he entered upon his new term since he had safe party control of both houses of the Congress, and since Senator Claro Recto, who had unsuccessfully disputed the party leadership with Magsaysay, had left the party to make an independent campaign for the presidency. With the presidency Garcia fell heir to the country's economic difficulties. These difficulties had also been inherited by President Magsaysay from his predecessors.

The Economic Problem

Financial and economic conditions under the Quirino administration had seriously deteriorated. In the early postwar years the new Republic had, with limited American aid in the form of a $70 million loan from the Reconstruction Finance Corporation, attained reasonable financial stability. As reconstruction got under way, both internal and foreign trade revived, and with trade some measure of prosperity. Thus the short-run purposes of the Trade Bill, supplemented by payments for war damages, began to be realized. It soon became apparent, however, that such revival and reconstruction as had occurred had been made possible largely because of American governmental assistance, together with some American private investment, rather than because of sound planning and effective execution of plans based upon development and use of the resources of the Philippines. This was recognized, at least in the United States, as deterioration became apparent. Consequently, when President Quirino appealed to the United States for aid, President Truman sent a mission, headed by Daniel W. Bell, to Manila in 1950 to make a study of conditions. The Mission found, among other things, that

while production in general has been restored to almost the prewar level, little of fundamental importance was done to increase productive efficiency and to diversify the economy . . . almost nothing was done to open new lands for the increased population, to improve the methods of cultivation, or to better the position of workers and tenants. While the standard of living of the mass of the people has not reached the prewar level the profits of businessmen and the incomes of large land owners have risen very considerably. [13]

An agreement for the implementation of the recommendations of the Mission was signed on November 14, 1950. Legislation, however, was required before the proposed reforms, such as the reform of the tax structure, could be undertaken. Against opposition the President was able to bring about an adjustment of personal income tax schedules and corporation and excise taxes. The government also placed a 17 per cent levy on foreign exchange and secured the enactment of a minimum wage law for agricultural workers. Following the Mission's recommendation, also, the United States promised financial aid to the Philippines to the amount of some $250

[13] For the complete report, with recommendations, see *Report to the President of the United States by the Economic Survey Mission to the Philippines* (DEPT. OF STATE, Pub. 4010, Far Eastern Series No. 38).

million "chiefly on a project basis and subject to supervision in order to ensure the effective use of funds."

The reforms instituted at this time and the projects executed did not solve the economic problem. Consequently, after his inauguration President Magsaysay undertook to institute further reforms, announcing a five-year development program involving expenditures of $5,000 million. In order to support the program and other increased government expenditures, improved tax collection methods were designed and savings were attempted by such means as the cancellation of the costly international operations of Philippine Air Lines. But the government also had to contemplate further foreign aid if its plans were to be executed. This was subsequently received in the form of Export-Import Bank credits and International Cooperation Administration assistance loans as well as in continuation of direct aid on a project basis. And it was hoped to get a large enough amount in reparations from Japan materially to assist in financing the planned development.

It was, however, not until 1956 that an agreement was reached with Japan. This agreement provided a reparations total of $550 million, mostly in capital goods, but with $30 million in services and $20 million in consumer goods, to be paid in installments. Reparations payments during the first year were limited to materials needed for rural development.

The Magsaysay program also called for land reform. This, as in other Asian countries, was primarily directed against tenancy. The law enacted provided for expropriation of landed estates. After the enactment of the law the government passed out land titles at the rate of some 50,000 a year. Since compensation had to be made for expropriated lands, the land reform program further complicated the problem of finance which was inherited by President Garcia. But fundamentally he faced the economic problem his predecessors had failed to solve—that of too great expenditures on imported luxuries and not enough increase in production to meet the needs of the domestic market and to pay for imports.

Foreign Relations

After its independence had been established the Philippine Republic played an active role in international relations and in Far Eastern politics. The precedents had been set before independence. President Quezon had been one of the signers of the United Nations Declaration of June 10, 1942. He, and after his death Osmeña, had served during the war on the Pacific War Council. The Commonwealth government had signed both the UNRRA and the Bretton Woods Agreements, had taken part in the drafting of the United Nations Charter at San Francisco, the Philippines becoming one of the charter members of the United Nations. General

Romolo, as its chief delegate at San Francisco, was active in the attempt made by the smaller states to restrict the Great Power veto. He also sought to make the provisions of the articles on non-self-governing territories as broad as possible. "Romolo's attitude at San Francisco established the pattern of Philippine foreign policy. While in some matters the island republic follows American policy rather closely, it is quite independent in others." [14]

The active role played by the Philippines in the United Nations after its establishment was recognized with the election of General Romolo as President of the Assembly in 1949, in the election of the Philippines to the Trusteeship Council for the period 1948–1950, and the election to a term, split with Yugoslavia, on the Security Council.

Within the United Nations, as well as occasionally outside it, as at the Bandung Conference, the Philippine government attempted to serve as a bridge between the Asian-African countries and the West. This was difficult because of the unequivocal stand of the Philippines with the United States on many questions and because of the emphasis placed by the Filipino on his Western rather than his Asian background.

The neutralist Asian states viewed Philippine foreign policy as resulting from the dependence of the Republic on the United States. The test, given the circumstances of the times, has been policy with respect to China. Here the United States and the Philippines did see eye to eye, but not necessarily because of dependence of one on the other.

Activities of the relatively small but important Chinese minority in the Philippines had long been of concern to the Filipino and to the government, since Chinese controlled a large share of the retail trade. This concern was increased when the Chinese Communist Party gained control over mainland China, since at that very time the Huk movement, with its Communist leadership, was offering major and military opposition to the government. Support of the Huks by the Chinese Communists would aggravate the difficulties of the government, as would also support of the Chinese in the Islands, against whom the government was impelled to act for economic reasons. Choosing what it viewed as the lesser of the two evils, the Philippine government consequently sided with Nationalist against Communist China. In doing so it, of course, found itself, after 1950, on the same side as the United States.

It was as a member of the United Nations, as well as because of its relations with the United States, that the Philippines sent a military contingent to participate in the Korean War, and generally supported the United States on issues growing out of that struggle.

Manila proceeded independently and in advance of American policy in the attempt to establish a regional Asian collective defense system

[14] VANDENBOSCH and BUTWELL, *op. cit.*, p. 93.

when it called a conference which met at Baguio in May, 1950, but which yielded no results. Thus the Philippine government needed no urging from the United States to associate itself with SEATO.

The Philippines also acted independently in withholding ratification of the Japan peace treaty until it had been able to negotiate a satisfactory agreement on the reparations question.

Nevertheless the country was tied into a relationship with the United States which necessitated that the government move in international relations in the same general direction as the United States. The people and government had not been altogether satisfied with some of the commitments demanded by the United States and had sought, with partial success, to bring about their revision. On such issues, there had been intermittent friction in the direct Philippine-United States relationship, with the Philippine government pressing its point of view beyond what would be viewed as tolerable if it were true, as sometimes charged, that the Philippines stood in the relationship of a satellite to the United States. Fundamentally the not too friendly attitude shown to the Philippines by some of its neighbors, especially Indonesia, resulted from local issues rather than because of the friendly relations of the United States and the Philippines. The charge of subordination to the United States frequently was the excuse rather than the reason for conflict of views.

2. THE REPUBLIC OF INDONESIA

What has come to be called Indonesia (formerly the Netherlands East Indies) is an archipelago extending from Malaya to New Guinea. The chain of islands stretching through 55 degrees of longitude on both sides of the equator extends better than 3200 miles from its western to its eastern limits. These islands supply a remarkably large share of the world output of such tropical products as cane sugar, rubber, tea, coffee, quinine, palm oil, cocoanut products, sisal, kapok, and in the mineral field, oil, tin, and bauxite. Thus Indonesia is one of the world's richest regions.

Of the estimated (1940) 70,000,000 inhabitants of the islands an overwhelming majority were Indonesians who were, however, divided into a large number of ethnic groups. At the last census year (1930) 59,138,000 of the total population of 60,809,000 were Indonesian.

Of the nonindigenous peoples the Chinese are the most numerous, with a total of 1,233,000 in 1930. The Europeans numbered 223,000, inclusive of Eurasians or Indo-Europeans as they are commonly called in the Indies. Arabs, with 70,000 souls, constituted the third largest nonindigenous group. The Europeans, and the Chinese and Arabs to a lesser degree, play a role in the Indies' society far greater than their numerical strength. There were also about 30,000 British Indians in the Indies in 1930. [15]

[15] AMRY VANDENBOSCH, "The Netherlands Indies," *Annals of the American Academy of Political and Social Science*, vol. CCXXVI, p. 86.

The population of Indonesia was heavily concentrated in the islands of Java and Madura which, with an area of only "51,000 square miles, had a population of 41,719,524, or over two-thirds of the total population of the country. The average density per square mile now probably exceeds 900."[16] This contrasts with a density of 2 per square mile of Dutch New Guinea. From the standpoint of religion, Indonesia was overwhelmingly Moslem, Christians numbered over two million, while the million and a half Balinese were Hindu.

In governing their colony the Dutch ruled indirectly as far as possible, maintaining local institutions and especially local (adat) law and customs. Nevertheless, after the Dutch East Indies Company was displaced by the Netherlands Government in 1798 the paramountcy of Dutch authority was kept clearly evident through a centralized and bureaucratic structure. The Governors of the provinces were subordinated to the Governor General who was, in turn, subordinated to the government of Holland. This excessive centralization when "the Governor General at Batavia had minutely controlled the whole government of the Empire, and he in turn had been under the strict supervision of the Government of Holland"[17] began to be modified in the 1920's. More autonomy was given to the colonial government, and the Volksraad (People's Council) created in 1918 gradually assumed more power. "Until 1927 it (the Volksraad) had only advisory powers, but in that year it was given co-legislative powers, which in practice meant that legislative measures normally required the approval of both the Volksraad and the Governor General."[18] Of the 60 members of the Volksraad 30 were Indonesians, of whom 20 were elected, 25 were Europeans, and the remainder were selected by or from among the non-indigenous Asians. Thus the body did not necessarily reflect at all accurately the point of view of the majority of the people.

Development of Indonesian Nationalism

Concurrently with this loosening of centralization in the governmental system and, with it, its earlier counterpart in the form of what was called the "ethical" policy of paying more attention to the social and economic interests and needs of the people, there came the prewar development of Indonesian nationalism. The first nationalist society, Boedi Oetomo (Glorious Endeavor), held its first Congress in 1908. Its purpose was economic and educational improvement of the position of the people.[19] It was fol-

[16] Ibid., p. 86.

[17] LENNOX A. MILLS, in Government and Nationalism in Southeast Asia, Part II, The Governments of Southeast Asia, p. 97.

[18] VANDENBOSCH, op. cit., p. 91.

[19] VIRGINIA THOMPSON, in Government and Nationalism in Southeast Asia, Part III, Nationalism, pp. 184–185.

lowed, and eclipsed, by the Sarikat Islam, first motivated by a desire to effect economic independence from the Chinese. This group held its first Congress in 1913. It grew considerably in the years between 1912 and 1915. Its activities came to be somewhat coördinated with those of the trade unions which came into being during and after the period of the first World War. The more radical members were expelled from the party in 1923, and they went into the Indonesian Communist Party. An attempted Communist insurrection in 1927 was violently suppressed. Thereafter the repressive policy of the government was directed more vigorously against all nationalists, many of whom had the label of Communist attached to them to justify their suppression or exile. An Indonesian Nationalist Party, led by Sukarno, was formed in 1927, but there was not brought into being before World War II, even among the class of intellectuals, one united nationalist organization of a disciplined sort, comparable to the Congress Party of India or the Kuomintang of China, comprehending in its membership all with nationalist aspirations. And, in addition to its disunity, it must be recognized that Indonesian nationalism was not a mass movement, from the standpoint of membership. Political awareness was largely confined to a small but growing class of intellectuals, many of whom were removed in feeling and understanding from the masses. Nevertheless there had been sufficient growth of nationalism to disturb the Dutch and cause them to proceed with some vigor against those who showed political inclinations or who did not formally agree to coöperate, by which was meant accepting the Dutch policy of gradual introduction of self-government, with the pace set by Holland. Numerous Indonesians, where qualified by training, did show their willingness to coöperate by entering the bureaucracy in its lower ranges.

One of the retarding factors in the growth of a competent and experienced Indonesian political leadership was to be found in the lack of emphasis, in Dutch policy, on education. Approximately 93 per cent of the adult Indonesians were illiterate, and only about 400,000 could read Dutch. Those who secured an education in the islands were not encouraged to go abroad even to Holland for advanced studies. But from this small student group came the ideas and much of the initiative which resulted in the prewar nascent nationalist movement. Its ideas were drawn largely from foreign sources, which also provided a basis for ideological division.

Effects of the War on Indonesia

The invasion of the Netherlands by Germany does not seem to have seriously disturbed conditions in Indonesia.

In so far as there was greater interest and concern for the seventy million brown subjects, it was expressed by a strengthened police force, an increase in political arrests, and further restriction of freedom of action. And finally, it was felt that the educated Indonesians could be mollified by pretending to pay attention to their political aspirations. The Visman Commission held hearings to ascertain the political views of the outstanding members of the Indonesian community, but this was the only liberalizing consequence of the occupation of Holland as far as Indonesia was concerned. . . . Experiments (in defense arrangements) with nationalists, who might later be a source of disturbance, were considered unnecessary. The government (in Indonesia) maintained its supercilious attitude right up to the Japanese invasion. [20]

This was, of course, the conclusion of a nationalist leader. The Dutch were more impressed with the purposes of the Visman Commission, and saw a larger change of policy being made.

Since Japan immediately utilized the new conditions in Europe to apply pressure on the Netherlands Indies government for economic concessions, Dutch repression of nationalists may have been due not so much to complacence as to fear and to a possibly short-sighted but real suspicion of the motives of nationalist leaders who declared themselves to be anti-fascist and therefore willing to coöperate in the defense of Indonesia.

However that may be, the Dutch attitude changed with some rapidity after December, 1941. But by that time anti-Dutch feeling among the masses and part of the native leadership had grown "stronger and stronger. This was naturally reflected in the nationalist movement and in its leadership, part of which expressed sympathy for the Axis openly."

"Essentially, the popularity of Japan increased as one aspect of the growing anti-Dutch animus and as a projection of frustrated desire for freedom. . . . The idea grew that the liberation of Indonesia would begin with the expulsion of the Dutch by the Japanese." [21]

However, disillusionment with the Japanese as liberators was quite rapid in Indonesia. As elsewhere in Southeast Asia, the Japanese conquerors moved to Japan, without exchange, as much of everything already produced as possible, and proved unsuccessful in reëstablishing production, in the exports' fields, on a reoriented (to Japan) exchange basis. Thus the years of Japan's rule were years of increasing economic deterioration and impoverishment. And, until Japan's eventual defeat was in sight, military rule was not ameliorated by moves toward greater self-government, or even as much as had been introduced by the Dutch; nor by a proclamation of independence as the goal of Japanese policy. The program of cultural assimilation to Japan, attempted in Indonesia as elsewhere, had little effect

[20] Soetan Sjahrir, *Out of Exile*, p. 218.
[21] *Ibid.*, p. 219.

in modifying the anti-Japanese feeling which soon replaced that expressed in welcoming the Japanese as liberators.

Postwar Dutch Policy

What was known of the adverse effects of and reaction to Japanese rule led the Dutch, until the end of the war, to base their postwar plans on the assumption that they would be able freely to establish the terms and timing of future political development. In this they made the same mistake as the British did with respect to Burma. In neither case did anti-Japanese sentiment and action indicate sentiment in favor of colonialism even if modified in the direction of self-rule and pointed toward an ultimate complete autonomy or even independence. And in Indonesia, as in Burma, the effect of the period of Japanese occupation, and resistance to it, in maturing politically the nationalist leadership was not appreciated.

Dutch postwar policy was announced by Queen Wilhelmina on December 6, 1942. It envisaged at the end of the war a "Conference of the Netherlands Realm" at which there would be "joint consultation about the structure of the Kingdom and its parts in order to adapt it to the changed circumstances." "Ultimately the Queen envisioned 'a commonwealth in which the Netherlands, Indonesia, Surinam, and Curaçao will participate with complete self-reliance and freedom of conduct for each part regarding its internal affairs, but with readiness to render mutual assistance.'" [22] More significance was attached to this declaration in the anti-Axis Western world than in the Indies where it was, under the circumstances, not widely publicized. It represented a move which would have met the desires and demands of prewar Indonesian nationalism. And it might have had greater effect in any case if the general lines of application of the policy, from the Dutch point of view, had been amplified and given greater precision by the end of the war.

In any case, however, the march of events at the end of the war presented the Dutch with a new situation and one which seriously modified their control of postwar developments. In and after 1943, the Japanese began to move to associate Indonesian leaders with the government of the country in an advisory capacity. And, on the eve of the Japanese surrender, those who collaborated with the Japanese, apparently in agreement with the leaders of the internal resistance movement, [23] proclaimed the independence of the country and established the Indonesian Republic, with a constitution and an organized government. This government was supported by forces equipped with Japanese arms seized and turned over

[22] H. ARTHUR STEINER, Post-War Government of The Netherlands East Indies, in "Post-War Government and Politics of the Far East," *Journal of Politics*, vol. IX, no. 4, p. 631.

[23] SJAHRIR, *op. cit.*, pp. 253–264.

to it after the surrender. By the time, in late September, that British forces of the Southeast Asia Command, of which war theater Indonesia had become a part, arrived to receive the Japanese surrender, it had been able to establish and consolidate its authority in Java, Madura, and Sumatra. Thus it had to be reckoned with by the British as well as the Dutch. [24]

For purposes of reoccupation, the Dutch had organized the Netherlands Indies Civil Administration which worked into the Indies from the east as successive islands were recaptured from the Japanese by the forces under General MacArthur.

After the collapse of Japan, NICA established civil government in all of the islands of the Indies accessible to the forces of the Southeast Asia Command, which excluded substantially all of Java, Madura, and Sumatra (except for coastal areas in the vicinity of Batavia and Soerabaya, Java, and around Padang and Medan in Sumatra). In these excluded areas, the Indonesian Republic had established its authority before Allied forces arrived at the end of September, 1945. As of July 15, 1946, all of the Indies under the NICA reverted to Dutch control, and in these regions the government of the Netherlands Indies was reconstituted in its prewar form, in accordance with prewar Dutch colonial legislation. [25]

If the Dutch had been authorized to send in forces of their own large enough to receive the Japanese surrender and take over from the Japanese they might have been able to gain control of the situation. But Allied troops arrived (September 29, 1945) only after a period of delay, and the troops were British and under a British commander who initially limited his mission to effecting the Japanese surrender and evacuating Allied prisoners of war and civilian internees, "and resolutely refused to embark on the reconquest of the entire island (Java) against Indonesian resistance." [26] The British attitude expressed a *de facto* recognition of the Indonesian Republic within the territories under its military control. The enforced delay in entrance of Dutch troops in sufficient strength to attempt the reconquest of Republican territory not only made that reconquest more difficult by enabling the Republican government to perfect its organization and equip its forces but it also created the necessity for prior negotiation with it by the Dutch, thereby giving it still further *de facto* standing.

In the immediately resulting situation fighting and negotiation went on simultaneously. Initially negotiation was made difficult by the unwill-

[24] The Dutch Civil Administration was to take over responsibility, according to invasion plans, after the islands were secure. Here, as elsewhere, invasion plans were not substantially reworked for occupation purposes.

[25] STEINER, *op. cit.*, pp. 627–628.

[26] *Ibid.*, p. 628.

ingness of the Dutch to treat with a government headed by collaborators. The Republican constitution concentrated executive power in the hands of the President, and the President and strongest single force in the government and in the islands was Sukarno, who had been a leading collaborator during the occupation. Mohammed Hatta, another nationalist leader and member of the government of the Republic, had also been a collaborator. In both cases, however, it could be argued that their collaboration had been because of their nationalism rather than because of sympathy with the Japanese, that it had been somewhat forced by circumstances, and that both had maintained friendly relations during the occupation with the internal resistance movement. Nevertheless the immediate Dutch refusal on principle to deal with Sukarno had to be surmounted if there was to be a negotiated settlement. A way of avoidance was found by transferring, by tacit agreement, the President's powers to a Cabinet headed by Soetan Sjahrir, with whom the Dutch were prepared to negotiate.

A second initial obstacle to negotiations was presented in the Republic's refusal to go back to the point from which it would be appropriate to follow the procedures set forth in Queen Wilhelmina's speech of December, 1942, on which procedure the Dutch were stubbornly insistent. A new statement of policy by the Netherlands government on February 10, 1946, however, introduced sufficient modification to enable negotiations to be undertaken. A growing spirit of accommodation on both sides made possible a truce in November, 1946. This was accompanied by Dutch acceptance of Sukarno, which removed the first-mentioned obstacle to negotiation. "The government declared that it no longer considers it conducive to fruitful negotiations to maintain the distinction between Sjahrir, who could be included in the discussions, and Sukarno, who could not. Since the Republic is in fact a political reality at the moment, the Government accepts its organization as it is. Efforts to realize a practical agreement must take precedence over preference for certain persons." Thus the way was finally cleared for the negotiation and ratification (March 25, 1947) of the Linggadjati Agreement setting forth the principles "which were to guide the two governments in subsequent efforts to achieve a completely effective settlement of all outstanding differences." [27] The Republic was recognized to have *de facto* authority over Java, Madura, and Sumatra, and it was agreed that Dutch and Allied forces would be gradually withdrawn from the occupied portions of these islands so that the Republic would have them completely under its control by January 1, 1949. A United States of Indonesia, composed of three Republics (Indonesia, Borneo, and the Great East), was to

[27] *Ibid.*, p. 635.

be set up. A Union was then to be formed of the Kingdom of the Netherlands and the United States of Indonesia, the latter to be sponsored by the Dutch for membership in the United Nations. On the important economic side, it was agreed that "the government of the Republic of Indonesia recognizes the claims of all non-Indonesians to the restoration of their rights and the restitution of their goods as far as they are exercised or to be found in the territory over which it exercises *de facto* authority." [28]

The necessary steps to make the Linggadjati Agreement effective were not taken. Consequently, when proposals which they contained for dealing with the immediate situation, and which the United States, for example, held constituted a "reasonable basis for negotiation," in July, 1947, were met with unacceptable counterproposals, the Dutch resorted to military action, described as "a police measure of a strictly limited sort." These operations were sufficiently extensive to compress the territory controlled by the Republic into a small district along the southern coast of Java in the neighborhood of Jakarta, the capital of the Republic.

At this point, the Indonesian question was brought before the (United Nations) Security Council by India and Australia. "Responding to the urgency of the appeals, the Security Council began its deliberations on July 31, and within forty-eight hours it had adopted the first cease-fire resolution of its career." [29] Although accepted by both sides the first cease-fire resolution produced no significant diminution of the fighting. A consular commission was consequently set up (August 25) to report on observance of the resolution and concurrently a tender was made of good offices. This was accepted and a Committee of Good Offices was established made up of Belgium (selected by the Netherlands), Australia (selected by the Republic), and the United States (designated by the other two).

By January 17, 1948, the Good Offices Committee had brought the two parties to an acceptance of the Renville Agreement "containing a detailed program for a truce and the principles for a future political settlement." The Committee, however, was continued by the Security Council to observe the application of the Agreement and "to keep a special eye on political developments in Western Java and Madura—both areas in which Dutch separatist efforts were under attack by the Republic." [30]

The Renville Truce failed to outlast the year (1948). The attempts of the Good Offices Committee to promote a political agreement on the basis of the principles laid down in the Renville Agreement were unsuccessful. These principles "envisaged a future federated United States of Indonesia, which would become incorporated with the Kingdom of the

[28] *Ibid.*, p. 637.
[29] RUPERT EMERSON, "The Indonesian Case," *World Politics,* vol. I, no. 1, p. 70.
[30] *Ibid.*, p. 71.

Netherlands in an over-all Netherlands-Indonesian Union." [31] This was, in effect, a revival of the Linggadjati formula. But it was additionally agreed that sovereignty should remain with the Kingdom of the Netherlands until, "after a stated interval, the Kingdom of the Netherlands transfers its sovereignty to the United States of Indonesia" or "conferred appropriate rights, duties, and responsibilities on a provisional federal government of the territories of the future United States of Indonesia" in which "provisional federal Government created prior to the ratification of the constitution of the future United States of Indonesia, all states will be offered fair representation."

The Dutch interpreted the above to mean that the final right of decision as to the constitution and powers of a provisional government, prior to the establishment of the United States of Indonesia, rested with them. Both sides recognized that "the nature of this provisional Government was the crucial point." [32] This interpretation the Republic's Government was unwilling to accept since "they thought that the Dutch Government really aimed at the restoration of the old colonial system. . . . For the Republicans, the separation of *de jure* and *de facto* sovereignty meant that they would not surrender their practical attributes of independence to a provisional Government completely under Netherlands authority, but only to a United States of Indonesia." [33]

The ensuing negotiations held under the auspices of the Good Offices Committee were consequently participated in by mutually suspicious and distrustful parties. They extended over much of 1948 without resulting in agreement. While they were going on the Dutch proceeded to organize the territories under their control with a view to the establishment by themselves of a provisional government. This did not facilitate the conclusion of an agreement. Neither did the deterioration of economic conditions in the territory under the Republic while economic progress was being made in the Dutch-controlled portions of the archipelago since the deterioration was blamed by the Republic on blockade conditions established and maintained by the Dutch. The difficulty of agreement was further increased by charges by each side of violation by the other of the Truce itself.

During this period, in August, internal difficulties within the Republic were brought to a head with a Communist attempt to seize power. This brought about unity for the time being sufficient for promptly putting down the revolt. Most of the Communist leaders were captured and resistance became spasmodic and confined to mountainous districts. The

[31] E. A. R., "Indonesia: Political and Economic Realities," *The World Today*, February, 1949, p. 53.
[32] *Ibid.*, p. 54.
[33] *Ibid.*, p. 55.

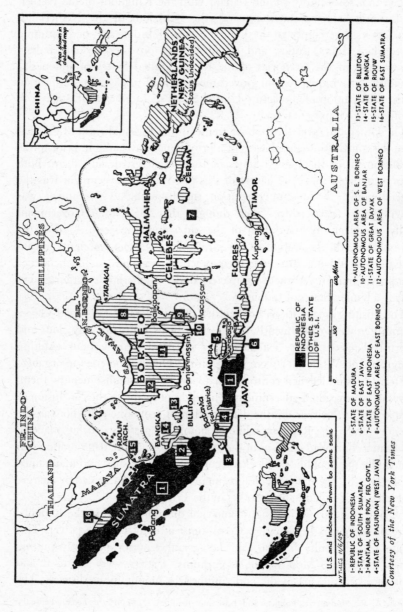

INDONESIA UNDER THE HAGUE AGREEMENT

revolt was symptomatic of the general dissatisfaction with the progress of negotiations.

In December, after failure to agree on a new plan submitted by the United States member of the Committee, the Dutch presented what was essentially an ultimatum to the effect that "a continuation of negotiations would be useless unless the Republican Government bound itself to accept immediately the Netherlands point of view on the basic issues between the parties, including the implementation of the truce." [34] The truce was terminated on December 18, 1948, and the Dutch again resorted to "police" action to resolve the situation. Republican territory was rapidly overrun and the leading members of the government of the Republic were captured.

The Security Council was immediately appealed to for action, and the Dutch, although consistently denying that it had jurisdiction in what they held to be a domestic matter, were again forced to defend their action in an international forum. After protracted discussion the Dutch accepted, under international pressure, the necessity for negotiating rather than imposing a settlement, and, as the *sine qua non* of negotiation, the release of the captured members of the Republican Government. Again, on August 3, 1949, the two entered into truce arrangements to go into effect August 10, "but both sides made clear that only an armed truce existed for the present." [35] This agreement also provided for a round-table conference to be held in Holland to determine the final conditions of relationship.

The Hague Round-Table Conference

The Round-Table Conference was convened at The Hague in August and continued in session until an agreement was finally reached and signed on November 2. The issues that protracted the discussions were: (1) over financial arrangements; (2) the character of the permanent organs of the union to be established between the Netherlands and Indonesia; (3) the status of the Crown as head of the union; and (4) the territories to be included in the United States of Indonesia (i.e., whether or not New Guinea should be included). [36]

The Dutch, in relation to finance, initially asked for veto powers over monetary and some trade policies of the new Republic as long as it was in debt to Holland. This request was, however, withdrawn by October 3. There was, in addition, the question of the amount of the external and internal debt which should be assumed by the new state, the Dutch advancing the figure of 6,100 million guilders which Indonesian figuring

[34] *Ibid.*, p. 62.

[35] *New York Times*, August 4, 1949.

[36] The details of the Conference are taken mainly from the *New York Times* reports by SYDNEY GRUSON.

reduced by some 3 billion guilders on the score of non-obligation with respect to that portion of the debt contracted and used for military and semi-military purposes. A compromise was finally reached which provided "that Indonesia would take over debts of 4,300,000,000 guilders . . . composed of the entire internal debt of the old Netherlands East Indies Government of 3,000,000,000 guilders and its external obligations of 1,300,000,000 guilders." [37]

The other issues were debated to the conclusions embodied in the Hague Statute of Union of November 2, 1949. This established a coöperative union of the two parties "on the basis of voluntariness and equal status with equal rights." (Art. 1, Sec. 1.) It was further stipulated that: "The Union does not prejudice the status of each of the two partners as an independent and sovereign state." (Art. 1, Sec. 2.) The defined purposes of the union were to promote coöperation in the fields of foreign affairs and finance, and also "as regards matters of an economic and cultural nature." (Art. 2. Separate agreements were attached to the Statute on foreign affairs, financial and economic relations, and cultural relations.) A third general article provided that the partners should "base their form of government on democracy"; that they should "aim at an independent judiciary"; and that they should "recognize the fundamental human rights and freedoms enumerated in the appendix to this statute."

The Statute set forth an agreement on Her Majesty Queen Juliana, Princess of Orange Nassau, and her successors, as the head of the Union. Under the Queen, Ministers from the two partners, duly designated for that purpose, were to meet in conference twice a year, and regular contact was to be established between the respective Parliaments of the two partners, their representatives to meet for the first time within eight months of the establishment of the Provisional Parliament of the Republic of the United States of Indonesia. These conference organs were to be served by a secretariat, with each party appointing a Secretary General, "each of whom takes charge of the secretariat by early rotation." (Art. 11.)

The Statute provided for a Court of Arbitration, of three members from each partner, to "take cognizance of legal disputes arising out of the Union Statute, out of any agreement between the partners or out of joint regulations, and brought before the Court by one of the partners against the other or jointly by both partners." Decisions were to be by majority vote, with the President of the International Court of Justice, or another agreed-on international authority, empowered to appoint a person of another nationality to serve as an extraordinary member of the Union Court. Other provisions of the Statute dealt with citizenship and the rights of the citizen of the one partner in the other state; the establishment of

[37] *New York Times* dispatch dated October 24.

High Commissioners, with ambassadorial status; the sharing of expenses, and other matters of detail. It was also agreed before the Round-Table adjourned to postpone decision on the question of New Guinea for a year.

Ratification of the decisions of the Round-Table gave a working basis for gradual solution of the Indonesian problem along lines closer to the positions taken initially by the Republic than by the Dutch. On this basis sovereignty was transferred by the Netherlands to the United States of Indonesia on December 27, 1949.

The federal union of Indonesian states shortly collapsed without trial "under hostile attacks, chiefly in the form of organized popular demonstrations. The federal system was not given a decent legal or constitutional burial; it was just abandoned." [38] The United States of Indonesia was replaced by the unitary Republic of Indonesia on August 15, 1950, by which date a merger of the other states with the Java Republic had been accomplished and an agreement had been reached between the federal government and the several state governments.

The union between Indonesia and the Netherlands had little more life in it than did the United States of Indonesia, even before it was formally brought to an end in 1955. An agreement was concluded in 1954 to terminate the union. It was, however, not ratified by the Indonesian parliament because it did not include modifications of the economic and financial agreements signed at the 1949 Round-Table Conference. Negotiations were resumed in December, 1955, but since no agreement satisfactory to it was reached the Indonesian government denounced the Union agreement and the financial and economic agreements of 1949. In August, 1956, furthermore, Indonesia repudiated its debts, estimated at The Hague at $170 million, to the Netherlands.

The Republic of Indonesia comprised all the territory formerly known as the Netherlands East Indies except for Western New Guinea (called by Indonesia West Irian). The latter remained under Dutch administration pending the conclusion of the agreement on its disposition which was supposed to have been, but was not, reached within a year after the signature of The Hague Round-Table agreements. The question of West Irian thereafter remained as a principal issue affecting adversely the relations of the Netherlands and Indonesia. The Dutch, as they were confronted with unilateral decisions from the other side, became less and less willing to make concessions with respect to West Irian. The Indonesian government, on its side, made determined efforts to bring about what President Sukarno called the "restoration" of West Irian to Indonesia, trying to win support in the United Nations for its claim by defining the issue as one of colonialism.

[38] VANDENBOSCH and BUTWELL, *op. cit.*, p. 35.

Foreign Policy

In general international relations, the new state followed a policy of neutralism similar to that of India. As with India, the determinant in alignments in specific situations was the question of colonialism, identified from the past with the West rather than with communism. Like other newly independent states, Indonesia was overly sensitive to actions or relationships which carried even a slight suggestion of outside control.

Indonesia's principal initiative in the field of foreign affairs was that of being host at the Bandung Conference of 1955, following which it participated in other conferences of Asian-African states and aligned itself with that bloc in the United Nations. Following the policy of neutralism, the Indonesian government refused to join SEATO. It signed but refused to ratify the Japan peace treaty. It refused to accept American economic or military assistance carrying any sort of commitment to support or strengthen the West in the "cold war." And it came into increasingly friendly relations with Communist China when, as a by-product of the Bandung Conference, it proved possible to negotiate a treaty defining the conditions of retention or loss of Chinese nationality on the part of Chinese residing in Indonesia.

Internal Politics

The constitutional machinery of the unitary Republic of Indonesia was relatively simple. The central organ of government was a single-chambered parliament whose members, until elections were held, were appointed by the political parties "under a system of proportional representation established by a presidential committee." The parliament selected Sukarno as the President and titular head of the state, a position which he continued to hold during the first decade of life of the Republic. The first Vice-President (Hatta) was appointed by the President upon recommendation of the House of Representatives. Hatta served as Vice-President until 1956 when he resigned, thus dissociating himself from any connection with Sukarno's plan for a "guided" democracy. Governing power, under the constitution, was vested in a Cabinet, composed under the direction of the President but responsible to the parliament. In constituting a government the President had an influence which came close to being determinative. He could invite one or more party leaders to form a Cabinet, and through them determine the composition of the Cabinet—subject to the approval of the parliament.

The postwar governments, consequently, were constituted on the basis of interparty agreements, and, in the absence of single-party majorities in the House, were made up as party coalitions, although invariably including Ministers without party affiliations. The Natsir Cabinet (September 6,

1950, to March 20, 1951), for example, had as Deputy Prime Minister a non-party man, and non-party Ministers of Internal Affairs, Defense, Communications and Transport, and Education and Culture, but with coalition party support in the parliament. The Cabinet announced on July 31, 1953, from the point of view of party composition, had, in addition to the Prime Minister, 3 members from the Nationalist Party; 3 from the Greater Indonesia Party; and 13 from as many splinter parties, representing points of view from left to moderate right. Actually governments, within limits, were constituted from among a group of essentially professional politicians who made up the new governing class. As one writer characterized Indonesian politics: [89]

. . . in spite of its facade of Western style organization and verbose statements of party principles (Indonesian politics) is carried on in an atmosphere often resembling that of a large, quarrelsome and neurotic family group. . . . Leaving aside imposing claims of party membership, Indonesian political life is a kind of poker game played by a few thousand people all of whom have known each other much too long and too well.

Thus governments were made, unmade, and remade partly in terms of personal relations which affected party relationships.

In the years before elections were held, governments were constructed around one or both of the two most important parties—the Nationalist Party and the Masjumi. The former derived its importance from its early leadership by Sukarno and Hatta (a leadership which Sukarno had no hesitancy in recalling from time to time), and from the role it played against the Dutch. The Masjumi was the leading Moslem party with a nation-wide following. How large the popular following of any of the parties was could only be determined if and as elections were held, as they were finally in 1955.

A total of 37,785,299 votes were reported as cast in the elections. Six parties received more than a million votes each, the remainder being polled by some twenty-eight other political groups or individuals, who campaigned on a national basis, and forty-four others who restricted their efforts to local areas. Twenty-eight parties and individuals won seats, twelve winning only one seat. The Nationalist Party polled 22.3 per cent of the vote cast for parliament and won 57 seats; the Masjumi secured the same number of seats while getting only 20.9 per cent of the vote; the Moslem Teachers' Party (an orthodox Moslem party) had 18.4 per cent of the vote, seating 45 members, thus taking third place among the parties; the Communist Party secured 39 seats, with 16.4 per cent of the total vote; the Moslem Association had 2.9 per cent of the vote and won 8 seats, as did also the

[89] R. C. Bone, "The Future of Indonesian Political Parties," *Far Eastern Survey*, vol. 23, no. 2 (February, 1954), pp. 17–28.

Christian Party with 2.6 per cent. These party positions were substantially maintained in voting later in the year for members of the Constituent Assembly which was to draft a permanent constitution for the country. Thus no party came even close to having a majority in the 257-member parliament, and governments continued to be based on inter-party coalition.

There were two surprises in these elections. One was the strength shown by the Moslem Teachers' Party in competition with the Masjumi for the vote of the Moslem community. The other was the size of the Communist vote. The elections unexpectedly brought the Moslem Teachers' Party into a position of real power which it was difficult for it to use effectively since it had neither an experienced nor a strong leadership.

As to the Communist Party, its success may be explained by the care with which its leaders, after its initial period of anti-Republican activity, cultivated the appearance of being national in its interests rather than being part of an international system directed from Moscow or Peking. It had given its support to the government personally sponsored by President Sukarno and headed by his friend Ali Sastroamidjojo, which was in office for the two-year period just before the elections. This Cabinet was "markedly leftist. Among the new ministers was Iwa Kusuma Sumantri, who had spent some time in Moscow and was imprisoned in 1946 for participation in the attempted Communist coup of that year. He was given the sensitive post of minister of defense." [40] This association with the Nationalists was a very useful cover for the cultivation of support for the Communist Party in the country. The relationship was not really anomalous since at the time the anti-Dutch program which the Nationalists followed, partly, at least, to divert attention from internal difficulties, fitted into the strategy and tactics of international communism.

This Nationalist-Communist collaboration complicated the problem of constructing a government after the elections, since the Moslem parties refused to participate in any government with Communists. The Nationalists, however, were reluctant to give up or seriously jeopardize their alliance with their strongest supporter.

Going against Sukarno's view that the Communists should be included in a coalition Cabinet, Ali Sastroamidjojo formed his second government in 1956 with the parliamentary support of his Nationalist Party, the Masjumi, the Moslem Teachers', and five smaller groups. The coalition controlled a total of 189 votes in the 257-member parliament. Faced by opposition threatening civil war, the Sastroamidjojo government resigned in 1957. Since a government commanding the necessary parliamentary support could not be formed, President Sukarno formed an extra-parliamentarian government headed by Djuanda as Premier.

[40] VANDENBOSCH and BUTWELL, op. cit., p. 42.

Beginning with the constitution of the first Sastroamidjojo Cabinet, Sukarno had exercised an increasingly direct influence over the government but without any real assumption of responsibility. Possibly because of the reception given him on visits to the United States and the Soviet Union, Sukarno took an ever larger view of his position as the head of the state, with powers above those of the government. Thus remarks made on the occasion of a repeat visit to Moscow, Prague, Belgrade, and Peking to the effect that military pacts do "not promote the efforts to reduce international tensions," necessitated a Cabinet statement that Indonesia has "not deviated from its independent foreign policy." Upon his return home in 1956 Sukarno further declared that the creation of political parties after 1945 had been a great mistake and he asked the Constituent Assembly to seek "a unitary republic and prevent the growth of capitalism." "We cannot," he said, "copy the liberal democracy of the West; nor can we import the concept of dictatorship from another range of ideas. . . . For the time being our democracy must be a guided democracy. . . ." The idea apparently was that the guidance proposed should be given by Sukarno himself through the members of a National Council representing a cross section of Indonesian society whom he would designate, and over whom he would preside. The Council would advise a Cabinet containing representatives of all the parties, including the Communists.

It was in connection with this proposal that Mohammed Hatta, a leader second only to Sukarno in public esteem, broke with the President, but refused to reënter active political life as an office holder. The dissent to the proposed solution on the part of all but the Nationalist and Communist parties and some minor groups led to open revolt in 1957, which was not put down until 1958.

The revolt was not caused solely by President Sukarno's proposal to replace the parliamentary democracy with a guided democracy. That proposal, if made before the elections and under different circumstances, might have been accepted as based upon past experience. The idea of democracy itself, and certainly of parliamentary democracy, was an importation rather than a part of the traditional system, at least above the village level. The traditional system was authoritarian. Native authoritarianism was strengthened rather than weakened by colonial rule, except as provision began to be made by the Dutch for more general education, by means of which new conceptions of the role and responsibilities to the people of the government were introduced into the country. These conceptions had not, however, been sufficiently widely disseminated by 1945 to change the authoritarian relationship of leaders to people. To this must be added the fact that the Indonesian parties and their leaders, until the Japanese occupation, had always acted mainly in opposition, opposing what was proposed by the Dutch because they proposed it, regardless of the nature of the proposal. They had never had the opportunity, until almost the end of the war, to oppose responsibly through presentation of courses of action alternative to those of the governing officials. Consequently the force of traditional ways and prior experience tended to take the opposition parties into the channel of negative criticism and to cause the leaders in the government to concern themselves primarily with the maintenance and extension of their own power.

The government of the Republic had the responsibility for maintaining order and reëstablishing the productive life of the country. It had not been successful in extending its authority completely over the entire archipelago as it might have done gradually within the original federal framework which was displaced because of the Dutch influence in organization of state life, especially in the outer islands. There had been

unrest, banditry, lawlessness, and large-scale resistance against the government in many areas of Indonesia. This is a problem with which every government since 1950 has promised to deal drastically, but conditions improve slowly, if at all. There is stealing, murder, the burning of villages. This extraordinary phenomenon is the product of the Japanese invasion and occupation, guerrilla activities against the Dutch, extreme poverty, political discontent, and religious fanaticism. [41]

These conditions gave importance to the army and its leadership, and made it a separate factor in the struggle for power. In this respect, as well as in others, Indonesia had to undergo the same experiences as many other countries moving from colonialism through war to independence. Governments on occasion also fell because of military dissatisfaction or dissent of officers adversely affected by governmental decisions. Thus the revolt of 1957–1958 was inspired by one of the "Colonels," as well as by the anti-Communist Party leaders.

Of even greater importance was the lack of adequately trained personnel, for civil administration as well as in the military. Sound planning was required if order and productivity were to be reëstablished. There were able men in positions of leadership in the government. But the most soundly conceived plans could only yield results if the plans were put into effective operation. In this respect, the conditions of administration of policy rather than the policy itself, to which they might have no alternative to propose, gave a lever for the opposition parties to use against the government. This served to determine the outcome of the struggle between parties and between leaders in the parties. The successful execution of both the short-run and the long-run plans of the government depended upon trained and experienced administrators. Dutch colonial policy had not been, until

[41] *Ibid.*, p. 49.

shortly before the war, expressly directed toward the development of a civil service staffed, except in the lower ranges, with Indonesians. There did, however, exist a body of Dutch-trained administrators. Many of these, especially the Dutch and the Indo-Europeans, aligned themselves against the early Republic in the struggle for independence. From the dominant nationalist point of view this tended to disqualify them for service in the new state, although The Hague agreements stipulated that they should be retained for a two-year period. Many of them viewed this term as sort of a terminal leave and not as an opportunity to establish their loyalty and competence with a view to future service. This reduced substantially the number of available officials, experienced from the Dutch period, to carry out the policies of the Republic. However, there were others who had gained experience of one sort or another during the Japanese occupation. The total available, nevertheless, did not meet the need for trained and experienced civil servants. This forced the use of relatively untrained and inexperienced people in the public services, with a decline in efficiency of administration. Those who had even minimum qualifications were indispensable. Because they viewed themselves as indispensable the civil servants tended to set their own standards of performance. Consequently, after the stimulus supplied by enthusiasm for the cause of independence began to diminish, following its attainment, corruption, laziness, and irresponsibility among public officials posed a serious problem for successive governments.

The effect of lack of experience in government and in governmental administration was paralleled in the management of the economic life of the country. Under the Dutch, the Indies government engaged in a wide range of economic activities. These were taken over by the new government. For their management, also, trained personnel was necessary and, given the nationalist attitude toward the Dutch, lacking. Nevertheless national recovery was dependent upon their revival. Economic solvency was also dependent upon important Western-operated industries such as rubber and petroleum, which accounted in value for over half the total exports.

Labor troubles, hostility toward foreign capital, large-scale thievery and brigandage, illegal occupation of concession lands by peasant squatters, heavy taxes, and exchange restrictions make it difficult for Western enterprises to carry on profitably. . . . Some of the large Dutch companies are transferring their operations to other countries, notably Ethiopia. This is a serious matter for Indonesia, for the Western enterprises are the earners of foreign exchange and a rich source of public revenue. Until Indonesian capital and enterprise can fill this role, the economic outlook will remain gloomy and the government's fiscal situation precarious. [42]

[42] *Ibid.*, p. 52.

This side of the picture was darkened rather than lightened as the Nationalist governments, enthusiastically supported by their Communist Party ally, sought to divert attention from domestic ills by the further stimulation of anti-Dutch sentiment and by action directed against Dutch enterprise and holdings.

The economic problem was also complicated by the demographic situation presented by the concentration of two-thirds of the population (of an estimated 85 million) on Java, constituting one-eleventh of the land area of the country. The Dutch began to try to find a solution to this problem as early as 1905 by encouraging Javanese to move to the Outer Islands. Resettlement was costly and proceeded slowly. The policy was resumed by the Indonesian government in 1950 when 27 families (45 persons) were removed. The numbers resettled each year increased materially, 7,846 families, including 27,643 persons, being resettled in 1954. Government plans called for resettlement of some 2 million persons during a six-year period at a cost of over 4,000 million rupiahs. At the current rate of population increase in Java, however, resettlement could not do more than keep the state of overpopulation of Java at the level of that time. In any event, resettlement does not get at the roots of the problem, which is one of productivity.

Economic deterioration after independence, coupled with marked lowering of standards both of behavior and of performance in government and administration, stimulated unrest and finally brought the country to large-scale revolt in 1957. These conditions were exploited by the Communists as a means of increasing their political following in the country. To this end they cultivated Sukarno and the Nationalists, supporting them vociferously in more and more extreme courses of action. This association caused the revolt to take on more of the character of an anti-Communist movement than would otherwise have been the case. As a result, as the revolting forces were slowly overcome by military operations, the government gave some indications of an intention to conciliate the forces of opposition by moving away from its overly intimate association with the Indonesian Communist Party.

REFERENCES FOR FURTHER STUDY

HERNANDO D. ABAYA, *Betrayal in the Philippines* (1946). JOSE M. ARUEGO, *Philippine Government in Action* (1952). MUHAMMAD ABDUL AZIZ, *Japan's Colonialism and Indonesia* (1955). DAVID BERNSTEIN, *The Philippine Story* (1947). JULIUS A. BOEKE, *Economics and Economic Policy of Dual Societies as Exemplified by Indonesia* (1953). MARGUERITA H. BRO, *Indonesia, Land of Challenge* (1954). JOHN A. CADY, PATRICIA A. BARNETT, and SHIRLEY JENKINS, *The Development of Self-Rule in Burma, Malaya and the Philippines* (1948). J. FOSTER COLLINS, *The United Nations and Indonesia*, International Conciliation, No. 459. RUPERT EMERSON, LENNOX A. MILLS, and VIRGINIA THOMPSON, *Government and Nationalism in South East Asia* (1942). *Far Eastern Survey;* consult index for titles of informed articles. JOHN S. FURNIVALL, *Colonial Policy and Practice* (1948). PIETER S. GERBRANDY, *Indonesia* (1950). G. A. GRUNDER and W. E. KIVIZEY, *The Philippines and the United States* (1951). W. L. HOLLAND (ed.), *Asian Nationalism and the West* (1953). SHIRLEY JENKINS, *American Economic Policy toward the Philippines* (1954). GEORGE McT. KAHIN, *Nationalism and Revolution in Indonesia* (1953). GEORGE McT. KAHIN, *Asian-African Conference, Bandung, Indonesia* (1956). RUPERT G. MARTIN, *Philippine Constitutional Law* (1952). Library of Congress, *Southeast Asia, An Annotated Bibliography of Selected Reference Sources* (1954). PAUL LIETZ, *Calendar of Philippine Documents* (1956). ARTHUR S. PIER, *American Apostles to the Philippines* (1950). CATHERINE PORTER, *Crisis in the Philippines* (1942). MANUEL QUEZON, *The Good Fight* (1946). JOHN H. ROMANI, *The Office of the Philippine President* (1954). SOETAN SJAHRIR, *Out of Exile* (1949); interesting personal account by leader of Indonesian Socialist party. ROBERT AURA SMITH, *Philippine Freedom, 1946–58* (1958). HAROLD W. SUNDSTROM, *Indonesia, Its People and Politics* (1957). AMRY VANDENBOSCH, *The Dutch East Indies: Its Government, Problems, and Politics* (1942). AMRY VANDENBOSCH and RICHARD R. BUTWELL, *Southeast Asia Among the World Powers* (1957). RAYMOND WESTERLING, *Challenge to Terror* (1952). CHARLES WOLF, SR., *The Indonesian Story, the Birth, Growth and Structure of the Indonesian Republic* (1948).

APPENDIX

CONVERSION TABLES

<table>
<tr><td>CHINA</td><td>JAPAN</td></tr>
</table>

MEASURES

CHINA	JAPAN
1 *li* = 0.36 mile.	1 *ri* = 2.44 miles. 1 *chō* = 2.45 acres. 1 *koku* = 4.96 bushels. The metric system was adopted in 1921.

WEIGHTS

CHINA	JAPAN
1 *picul* (100 catties) = 133⅓ pounds. A chest of opium weighs 70 pounds.	1 *kin* = 1.32 pounds. 1 *kwan* = 8.26 pounds. The metric system was adopted in 1921.

MONEY

CHINA	JAPAN
1 *tael* = 1 ounce of silver; the value in foreign trade varies according to the price of silver, which was $0.54 in 1910, $1.34 in 1920, $0.38 in 1930, and $0.64 in 1935. A *tael* is not a minted coin. The currency adopted in 1932 is the *yuan* (100 *fen*), which contains ¾ of an ounce of silver. A "managed" currency was established at the end of 1935.	1 *yen* (100 *sen*)=$0.84 at par; the value on June 21, 1938, was 28.86 cents. Value established April, 1949 at 360 *yen* to the dollar for foreign trade purposes.

RAILROAD GAUGES

CHINA	JAPAN
Chinese railroads have the gauges of the countries building them: Great Britain, Japan, and United States: 56 inches. France: 1 meter. Russia: 60 inches.	Japan uses the 56-inch gauge.

CHINESE PLACE NAMES

Many Chinese place names are compounded of geographical features, cardinal points, colors, and numbers. The following table will be helpful in locating Chinese place names:

shan	mountain	*ti*	earth
shen	pass	*shang*	up
ling	range of mountains	*shia* (*hsia*)	down
hai	sea	*su*	from
wan	bay or bend	*chung*	central
hu	lake	*peh* (*pei*)	north
ho	shallow river	*tung*	east
kiang	deep river	*nan*	south
chwan (*chuan*)	small river	*si* (*hsi*)	west
tao	island	*hwang*	yellow
king	capital	*hung*	red
fu	suffix denoting provincial city	*hei*	black
chow	suffix denoting department city	*pai*	white
hsien	district	*e*	one
shien	county	*erh*	two
kuo	country	*san*	three
tien	heaven	*sze*	four
		wu	five

EXAMPLES

Shantung	East Mountain	Hwang-ho	Yellow River
Shensi	West of the Pass	Szechuan	Four Rivers
Hunan	South of the Lake	Nanking	Southern Capital
Pei-ho	North River (a shallow river)		

PRONUNCIATION OF JAPANESE WORDS [1]

While dialects in Japan are much less important than in China, they do exist, so the Government has selected the Tōkyō dialect as standard Japanese.

In general Japanese words are much less accented than in English. That is to say, most Japanese words have an almost level pitch throughout. If a syllable is accented, it is usually indicated by a slightly higher pitch.

CONSONANTS

The Japanese words, as romanized in this text, contain no L, Q, V, or X and the letter C occurs only in combination with H, which resembles the ch in "church." The consonants are pronounced as in English, with the exception that F is a true labial as in German. G in the Tōkyō dialect has a nasalized sound as in "sing." R is the hardest sound in Japanese to imitate as it resembles a sound between the English R and L. Y is pronounced as in English, except when followed by the vowel e, when it is practically silent as in the name "Iyeyasu."

VOWELS

Vowels are sounded as in Spanish and Italian and are usually short. The vowels o and u may be long, in which case vocalization should be longer. However, this is not indicated in the romanization used in this text. In general, the vowels are pronounced as follows:

a as in "father"
e as in "men"
i as in "machine"
o as in "potato"
u as in "push"

DIPHTHONGS

The diphthongs ae, ai, oi, and ui are not, strictly speaking, true diphthongs but are composed of two separate vowels with the stress and higher pitch falling on the first vowel, thus the diphthongs ae and ai are pronounced much alike in many cases.

[1] Statement prepared by Hugh Borton, Professor of Japanese, Columbia University.

PRONUNCIATION OF CHINESE WORDS [1]

Names of Chinese persons and places, since they are written originally in Chinese characters, can be reproduced in western books only by writing their sound. This is called *transliteration* or *romanization*.

Chinese characters are of course pronounced in different ways in different parts of the Far East; but the Peking dialect (also called Mandarin or *kuan-hua*) is generally taken as the standard. Unfortunately its sounds do not always have exact equivalents in English, and so it is necessary to indicate them by a conventionalized system, in which the English letters do not necessarily have their normal English sound but stand for certain Chinese sounds. The system of romanization commonly used is called the Wade system.

To pronounce the Wade symbols as though they were English words would be to create a new and outlandish spoken language, meaningless both to Chinese and to non-Chinese. It would also be confusing because there would often be two possibilities: e.g. *tao* could be "tah-o" or "tay-o" (whereas it should be "dow"). Therefore in pronouncing the Wade system the attempt must be made to approximate the Chinese sound, rather than invent our own.

Pronunciation in the Peking dialect according to the Wade sytem:

VOWELS: (as in Italian)

a	as in "father"	ê	like the *u* in "under"
e	as in "Edward"	ih	like the *e* in "her" (no real equiv-
i	as in "machine"		alent in English)
o	like "aw" in "saw" (but often like	ü	like the French *u* or German *ü*
	the *u* in "cut")	ǔ	is practically unpronounced
u	as in "lunar"		

CONSONANTS: The apostrophe following a consonant indicates aspiration; and the lack of the apostrophe indicates the lack of aspiration,—which sounds to our ears very much like voicing. Therefore:

(UNASPIRATED)	(ASPIRATED)
ch is sounded like the *j* in "jam"	ch' as in "chin"
k like the *g* in "gun"	k' as in "kin"
p like the *b* in "bat"	p' as in "pun"
t like the *d* in "doll"	t' as in "tap"
ts and tz are sounded like *dz*	ts' and tz' like the *ts* of "Patsy"
j between French *j* and English *r*.	

Most of the other consonants are similar to those in English.

Warning: there are other systems of romanization used in other western languages; in newspapers and popular books the diacritical marks ′ ^ ¨ ˇ are commonly omitted; as a result there are many irregularities to be met with, chiefly due to the dropping of the apostrophe; also k or k' are often substituted for ch or ch' before i.

[1] Slightly modified from a statement prepared by J. K. Fairbank, Department of History. Harvard.

INDEX

Abdul Rahman, 798, 799, 800

Abdul Rahman, Sir, Head of State, Malaya, 800

Abe, Premier, 627

Acheson, Secretary of State, 671

Adams, John Quincy, 42, 434

Administrative Boards, China, 20

Adundet, Phumiphon, 776

Africa, 417

Aglen, Sir Francis, 434

Agrarian reform, China, 595

Agrarian Reform Law, China, 691, 692

Agricultural Adjustment Commission, China, 593

Agricultural coöperatives, 692

Agriculture, China, 38; changes in, 258–263

Aigun, 196; treaty of, 53, 394

Ainu peoples, 77

Akahata, 752

Alaska, 3, 422, 634

Aleutian Islands, 422, 634

Alexander III, Emperor, 149

Alexandrino, Castro, leader of Huks, 810

Alexandrovsk, 394

Alexievsk, 401

"All-China People's Congress," 683

Allen, Professor G. C. (quoted), 740

Alliance (UNMNO and MCA), 798, 799

Allied Council for Japan, 630

Allied Objectives in Japan, 745

Allied offensive strategy, 651

Allied Powers, 372, 380, 399, 400, 402; Siberian operations of, 401

Allies, 377, 379, 380, 382, 390

Altar of Heaven, 241

American aid to China, 659, 662, 663, 671

American capital, 196–200

American economic policy toward Japan, 743, 744

American empire, 480

American government, 196, 200, 417; and Russian entry into war, 653; policies of, 50, 90; proposals of, 91, 200

American interests, 49, 50, 153–155, 194, 195, 415

American investments in China, 477, 478; in Japan, 479

American-Japanese Administrative Agreement, 749

American-Japanese Commercial Treaty, 610

American-Japanese Security Treaty, 748–749

American leadership, China, 376, 377, 381

American mediation in Kuomintang-Communist struggle, 663–665

American Military Government, Korea, 706–707

American missionaries in Korea, 352

American note, Dec. 31, 1938, 606

American objectives, 664

American policy and actions (1937–1938), 602, 641; economic, toward Japan, 745, 746; toward Korea, 751

American postwar policy toward China, 659, 662

American power, 476, 477

American pressure, diplomatic, on Japan, 602

American procurement in Japan, 746, 747

American representative at Peking, 55, 95, 141

American sailors, Korea, 125

American ships, 89

American silver policy, 559

American trade and traders: in China, 33, 34, 47, 154, 156, 189, 478–479; in Japan, 93, 359, 479

American training of Chinese troops, 651, 652

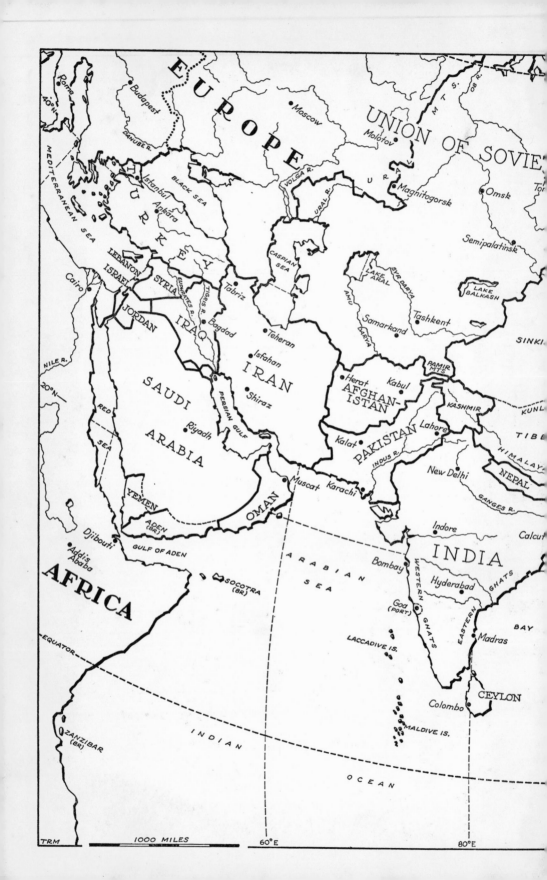